# HANDBOOK OF CHILDREN AND THE MEDIA

# HANDBOOK OF CHILDREN AND THE MEDIA

DOROTHY G. SINGER
JEROME L. SINGER
EDITORS

Sage Publications, Inc.
*International Educational and Professional Publisher*
Thousand Oaks ■ London ■ New Delhi

---

*For information:*

Sage Publications, Inc.
2455 Teller Road
Thousand Oaks, California 91320
E-mail: order@sagepub.com

Sage Publications Ltd.
6 Bonhill Street
London EC2A 4PU
United Kingdom

Sage Publications India Pvt. Ltd.
M-32 Market
Greater Kailash I
New Delhi 110 048 India

Printed in the United States of America

*Library of Congress Cataloging-in-Publication Data*

Main entry under title:

Library of Congress Cataloging-in-Publication Data

Singer, Dorothy G.
Handbook of children and the media / By Dorothy G. Singer, Jerome L. Singer.
p. cm.
ISBN 0-7619-1954-6 (cloth: alk. paper)
1. Television and children—United States. 2. Mass media and children—United States. 3. Video games—Psychological aspects. I. Singer, Jerome L. II. Title.
HQ784.T4 S533 2000
302.23′45′083—dc21 00-009006

01 02 03 04 05 06 07 7 6 5 4 3 2

---

*Acquiring Editor:* Jim Brace-Thompson
*Editorial Assistant:* Anna Howland
*Production Editor:* Diane Foster
*Production Assistant:* Victoria Chen
*Typesetter/Designer:* Marion Warren
*Indexer:* Juniee Oneida
*Cover Designer:* Michelle Lee

# Contents

## COGNITIVE FUNCTIONS AND SCHOOL-READINESS SKILLS



## SOME HAZARDS OF TELEVISION VIEWING: FEARS, AGGRESSION, AND SEXUAL ATTITUDES

# Introduction: Why a Handbook on Children and the Media?

DOROTHY G. SINGER
JEROME L. SINGER

## The Emergence of Mediated Learning in Children's Lives

How do growing children and early adolescents form their impressions, attitudes, action potentials, and, more generally, their imagination of a world beyond the one they can directly experience in their immediate surroundings and family life? Until less than 200 years ago, the vast majority of the world's children and adults depended on the immediate experiences of their senses in a setting limited to the people of tribe and family, the livestock, wild animals, and physical characteristics of a narrow milieu. How could they learn, for example, that there were other tribes or nations, people of different colors or customs, perhaps just over the hills or up the river or across the vast forbidding sea? They heard stories from the family elders or clan wise men. For many human cultures, priests of various religions who had access to ancient, sacred writings could tell tales as part of worship rituals of how the world began, of deities and demons, or of a unique but often invisible God. Temple statuary and, for some religions, painted representations that could be viewed in sacred places on occasional visits during feasts or holy days may have strongly impressed children in ancient Greece or Rome, in India and China, or in medieval and Renaissance Europe.

News of important changes was long delayed. Often, people depended on passing traders, marauding bands, or the very occasional traveling theatrical performers who might appear at an annual festival. A consequence of poor communication affected the financial world. Less than 200 years ago, for example, in the London stock market, prices plummeted in the absence of news about the outcome of the battle of Waterloo being fought by England and Prussia against France just a few hundred miles away across the English Channel. Those few bankers who had a faster signaling and courier boat system learned of the defeat of Napoleon before most of England did. They were vastly enriched because they could buy up shares at the lowest prices. What a contrast with the instantaneous news we receive electronically today! Not only adults are affected nowadays by the rapidity of news dissemination. Children all over the United States, while watching television, directly witnessed the murder of President Kennedy's assassin, Lee Harvey Oswald, in Texas and the explosion of the Challenger space shuttle in Florida. The recent television broadcasts of the fireworks displays and other celebrations of the incoming year 2000 beginning in the Fiji Islands and moving hour by hour around the world created an exciting experience of a "global village" for at least one day.

One might argue that, with the emergence perhaps 6,000 years ago of written language, adults and children might then have had access to learning about the world through reading. The profound impact of reading on modern civilization, especially after the technology of printing was developed 500 years ago at Mainz in Western Europe, is well documented. Until the nineteenth century, however, the vast majority of children even in America and Western Europe were not educated to read (Murray, 1998). Only the sons (and some daughters) of the aristocracy or upper middle classes had the opportunity to learn about history, philosophy, geography, legends, science, and the cultures of other nations or continents, and thus to create for themselves a far-ranging world of the imagination beyond immediate experience.

Consider how world literature and poetry have been enriched because an upwardly mobile glove maker from Stratford, England, sent his son Will to grammar school to learn to read in English and also to acquire "small Latin and less Greek." Such an education outside the aristocracy was so rare that even today there are those who still regard Shakespeare's name as really a "cover" for the actual poetic creations of "well-born" nobility like Lord Bacon or the Earl of Oxford.

This handbook is not, however, a treatise on the tremendous impact of reading on human imagination. Even before the vast world increase in literacy that emerged in the twentieth century in Japan, Russia, and, most recently, China, new sources of information became available to hundreds of millions of children with the scientific development of radio and cinema in the first decades of that same century. Motion pictures spread so rapidly after 1910 that, by the mid-1920s, the silent-film comic character of Charlie Chaplin was known to children on all continents. Phonograph records so proliferated during this same period that children (and adults) began to envision new worlds and cultures from the Italian opera arias sung by Enrico Caruso and the Scottish humor and tunes of Sir Harry Lauder. By the late 1920s, with the further distribution of these sound reproduction processes via radio, a whole new musical form entered human consciousness: the jazz music of African Americans such as Louis Armstrong and its offshoots into "popular" music and "big band swing" promoted by Paul Whiteman, Benny Goodman, and the primarily New York City–based "Tin Pan Alley" lyricists and composers such as Irving Berlin, Jerome Kern, George and Ira Gershwin, Larry Hart, Oscar Hammerstein, Richard Rodgers, and Cole Porter.

Radio in the early 1930s also brought directly into millions of homes the voices of political leaders. During the Great Depression, families from all walks of life gathered together in American homes to listen to the firm and mellifluent voice of President Franklin D. Roosevelt. Millions in Germany during the same period listened and, alas, were inspired by the strident, hate-filled shouting of Chancellor Adolf Hitler.

For children and many adults, radio also brought into the home on a daily basis storytelling, which opened new vistas for the imagination. Children in the United States listened to serial episodes of Tarzan in a largely mythical Africa, the Lone Ranger in a nearly mythical U.S. West, Chandu the Magician with world-ranging episodes, and "Buck Rogers in the twenty-fifth century!" By this time, low-cost talking movies in theaters outside the home were tremendously popular, and these two media became rich sources of incidental education, along with so-called pulp books, magazines, and comic strips in newspapers and book forms.

Books, magazines, and comics required at least moderate literacy and intellectual effort. Radio storytelling demanded some imaginative stretching by the listener. The movies, however, portrayed for children in an almost directly experiential manner a vast outside world ranging from American cowboy adventures in Western mountain ranges to dramatic confrontations between British colonial troops and Hindu or Afghan "native rebels." Sometimes these conflicts were even resolved without bloodshed by the delightful intervention of the dimpled child actress Shirley Temple. Even the more "realistic," contemporary-setting films of the depression era often displayed wealthy urban apartments or salons in which actors such as Norma Shearer, Myrna Loy, William Powell, Melvyn Douglas, or Katharine Hepburn appareled in tuxedos or high-fashion dresses engaged in witty exchanges. And, of course, there were the ultra-sophisticated music and dance films of beautifully groomed Fred Astaire and Ginger Rogers. In effect, films created for child and adolescent viewers an immediate experience of a virtual reality that became at once central to the fantasy lives of the young. The fantasies were so powerful, indeed, that the "stars" of these films have become celebrated almost beyond the glory of the ancient Greco-Roman gods.

## The Impact of Television and the Computer

Consider then the next electronic advance—the television set that entered the homes of millions by the mid-1950s. For millennia before, young children from their earliest ages learned directly from observing or modeling parents, relatives, older siblings, or peers, but there was now a new member of the family that portrayed actions and far-flung settings to them daily for hours at a time. Can there be any real doubt that just in the past half century the television medium has radically altered human experience? It has ushered in an electronic age incorporating all the features stemming from twentieth-century electricity, moving pictures, music reproduction, radio news, music, sports, and storytelling. What impact does the near omnipresence of this medium of entertainment and information have on the cognitive, emotional, social, and behavioral responses of children? These are questions that have stimulated extensive ongoing research. The findings of such studies must take us beyond the accumulation of personal anecdotes to a body of more systematic evidence.

The reader may also ask, however, about the great acceleration of information and electronic media in just the past two decades. We have video games in arcades and in millions of homes. Personal computers have introduced the Internet and World Wide Web into homes and schools. Vast new commercial, entertainment, and informational opportunities beckon from these newest electronic sources of input for children and adolescents. A huge merger has occurred between Time-Warner Communications, which controls the largest sources of *content* (films, videos, music reproduction, key print materials), and America Online, which controls *Internet delivery systems.* Suddenly, at the moment we move into the twenty-first century, almost imponderable new forms of delivery of entertainment, information, and education to children and youth may be in the offing.

The *Handbook of Children and the Media* therefore represents an effort to review, through the contributions of research experts, the past and potential future impact of the electronic media on growing children in America and to some extent all over the world. This volume places greatest emphasis on the television medium as it has developed over the past 50 years. There is good reason for this emphasis. Our most recent research evidence still makes it clear that youth between the ages of 2 and 18 spend, on average, almost 3 hours daily watching television; almost another hour listening to recorded music; nearly an hour with computer games or other computer usage; 39 minutes with radio; and just 44 minutes of reading. The number of television-viewing hours increases between ages 8 and 18 (Associated Press, 1999;[1] see Chapters 1-4). Clearly, television still dominates the attention of our youth, and we must understand its impact, the hazards, and also the constructive educational potential of such heavy viewing of this medium.

There has been a great deal of popular attention on the cognitive, social, and even physiological dangers of television viewing from early childhood to adolescence. Much of this concern has been based on speculation rather than on carefully assembled scientific research data. We, ourselves, as confirmed book lovers, have wondered about the risks of growing up in this picture-centered media world. Our guesses, however, are just useful as suggestions for systematic research. There are no true experts who can pontificate on the hazards or values of television without recourse to the great body of accumulated research evidence. No single research in a given area is usually definitive, of course. What we try to provide in this volume are the issues raised by the electronic media and what methods have been used to gather data that can address these issues. The contributors are themselves experienced investigators who point out the limitations and advantages of particular research methods. Our hope is that a critical reading of these chapters can dispel media myths, dubious generalizations about television hazards, or unsupported and hasty judgments. Readers may not find ultimate truths in these chapters, but we believe they will be guided into a more careful and deliberate examination of how our growing children and grandchildren use, enjoy, learn from, and are advantaged or disadvantaged from regular exposure to television and other electronic media.

## Developmental Processes in Children and Adolescents

Our expectation is that this handbook will appeal to a wide-ranging audience: child development researchers, educators, parents or other child caregivers, journalists, state or federal government policy makers or legislators, child advocates, graduate and undergraduate students, and even those younger students who often write or e-mail us with questions for their school reports. We can hardly expect that anyone will read this book through at one sitting like a Tony Hillerman or John Grisham novel. We have tried, therefore, to attain some unity and focus for all the chapters by asking our authors to keep in mind basic principles of child development and socialization. Even our more policy-oriented or industry-related chapters examine such issues as they bear on the *age-specific cognitive, emotional, motivational,* or *social processes* of childhood and adolescence.

In our own 30 years of research on children's television viewing, we have been dismayed to find that this area of investigation has not been integrated into the basic field of child study. Authors of developmental psychology textbooks often completely ignored the fact that children were spending more hours watching TV programs than talking to their parents, playing, exploring their physical environment, or mastering reading. On the other hand, many researchers of television sought to answer specific questions about the physical or social hazards of regular viewing without putting their findings into the context of the basic cognitive or emotional capacities of children at different age levels. Unfortunately, producers and writers of children's TV shows often seemed oblivious to the great differences between children ages 3 to 5, 7 to 11, and 13 to 15 in attending to, comprehending, and imitating or emotionally responding to not only the content of programming but also the formal features or conventions of the medium (see, e.g., Chapters 5, 6, 8, 9, and 10).

The goal in this handbook, therefore, is to integrate the usage and effects of electronic media exposure on children and adolescents with the basic behavioral research on child development. When do particular skills of attention and concentration develop? How do children learn to understand language and to imitate the words they hear, not only from parents but also from television characters? Our own research over many years—and, of course, the earlier studies and theories of Jean Piaget (1962), Kurt Lewin (1935), Sigmund Freud (1908/1962), and L. S. Vygotsky (1978)—has emphasized how children, usually through symbolic, pretend, or make-believe play, gradually develop a capacity for imaginative thought. Such symbolic play can have enormous adaptive potential (Singer & Singer, 1990). To what extent can television programming, either through its content or its format, influence children's developing imagination? We sought some answers to such questions in the 1970s (Singer & Singer, 1981), but much more study is needed (see Chapters 4, 6, and 9).

A continuing preoccupation of child development research has been the origins and modification of aggressive behavior in children. For the first 60 years of the twentieth century, conceptions such as Freud's (1923/1962) theory of a fundamental aggressive drive or instinct predominated. The critical analyses and careful research on social learning of Albert Bandura (1971a, 1971b) and literally scores of psychophysiological and behavioral empirical studies beginning in the 1960s have pointed much more to aggression as a learned response (Singer, 1971). To the extent that a great deal of aggressive behavior in childhood and adolescence reflects observation, modeling, and imitation of the aggression of parents, siblings, and peers, can we ignore the impact on children of their exposure through television and films or, more recently, to computer games and arcade video games that involve vast amounts of violent actions? (See Chapters 10, 11, and 13.) What are the contingencies of age, cognitive capacity, type of program content, or reality or fantasy depiction that might moderate possible influences on children of the high frequency of vicarious violence that makes up so much of the content of television or of video and computer games?

These few examples should make clear that the great accumulation of research on children and the media can contribute to our understanding of child development more generally and also that principles of developmental psychology can help us interpret the social impact of these media. We urge our readers to keep these issues in mind in examining each chapter.

## The Organization of This Volume

Let us next turn to how we have organized the sections and chapters of this book as a guide to the interests of specific readers. Part 1 is structured to examine the fundamental research knowledge about the possible ways in which the popular media serve (for better or worse) as incidental or planned educators and socializers of children. In the early 1980s, we both participated in the preparation of a large National Institute of Mental Health report on television and behavior (Pearl, Bouthilet, & Lazar, 1982). Perhaps the single major conclusion that emerged from that massive review was that children learn from television even though they watch predominantly for their own entertainment. What they learn, however, is a key question that Part 1 addresses, drawing on more than 40 years of research.

Part 1 begins with four chapters that discuss in up-to-date fashion an area that was one of the earliest studied in media research: How do children use these technologies, and what needs seem gratified by their availability? These chapters set forth the historical background for electronic media use. Although reading itself is not featured in this handbook, we do include a chapter dealing with popular literature such as "pulp fiction" and comic books as a context against which most television viewing or use of videotapes can be set. These four chapters are critical foundations of basic information on how, when, where, how often, and at what ages children or adolescents watch television or engage themselves with videotapes or computers. Researchers or journalists who wish to begin a study or write an article with reference to the above questions will find the most current, carefully researched data in this section.

We turn next to the most frequently asked questions about the impact of media usage, their influence on cognitive functions such as attention, comprehension, imagination, and language. We also include chapters on social behaviors such as alertness or vigilance, fearfulness, and aggression and sexuality. We next address health, including drug usage and eating patterns. The chapters in this section also explore the constructive potential of television viewing in promoting school readiness for very young children or prosocial behaviors such as civility, sharing, and cooperation. Next we consider the fact that most of the television industry in the United States (and, increasingly, around the world) relies on commercials for income. What is the impact of the deluge of such messages on children? We also look more broadly on identity formation, stereotyping, multicultural awareness or tolerance, family life, and ethics or morality.

Parts 2 and 3 of this volume turn to the broader social impact of the media environment: the media industry and formal educational and policy considerations. In these sections, we provide the latest available information and the accumulated research on commercial and public broadcasting approaches to children. We also examine the newest technologies. These chapters are concerned with issues of advocacy for quality programming, parental control, applications of research for producers of programming, and specific school uses of television. They also address the government's role of oversight and regulation of the airwaves, which truly belong to all of us and are only leased to private groups. The economic structure of the television industry is also examined. Finally, the chapters address questions of "what needs to be done" to ensure privacy, parental control, quality programming, and how we can foster media literacy and intelligent and discriminating viewing in children and youth.

We believe that educators, child advocates, policy makers, parents, and journalists will find the second and third parts of this volume especially helpful. Even though innovations in technology occur rapidly, the basic questions on child-media interactions are features of this book, along with an emphasis on how we can investigate the issues in a systematic, reasonably scientific fashion. Our authors are largely science trained, and we have asked them to draw as much as possible on formal research. At the same time, we have asked them to avoid the use of technical jargon and statistical or mathematical content. The extensive bibliographies of each chapter are a valuable resource for researchers who wish to pursue the full technical details of particular investigations summarized here. We believe that the broad readership we expect for a book on children and the popular media will find the subject matter and presentations of this volume engaging, challenging, and deeply informative.

## Note

1. This report sponsored by the Kaiser Family Foundation is described in detail in various chapters of the handbook.

## References

Associated Press. (1999, November 18). Study says tube, not Net, rules playtime.

Bandura, A. (Ed.). (1971a). *Psychological modeling*. New York: Alaine-Atherton.

Bandura, A. (1971b). *Social learning theory*. New York: General Learning Press.

Freud, S. (1962). Creative writers and daydreaming. In J. Strachey (Ed.), *The standard edition of the complete psychological works of Sigmund Freud* (Vol. 9, pp. 141-154). London: Hogarth Press. (Original work published 1908).

Freud, S. (1962). The ego and the id. In J. Strachey (Ed.), *The standard edition of the complete psychological works of Sigmund Freud* (Vol. 19, pp. 3-66). London: Hogarth Press. (Original work published 1923)

Lewin, K. (1935). *A dynamic theory of personality.* New York: McGraw-Hill.

Murray, G. S. (1998). *American children's literature and the construction of childhood.* New York: Twayne/Macmillan.

Pearl, D., Bouthilet, L., & Lazar, J. (Eds.). (1982). *Television and behavior: Ten years of scientific progress and implications for the eighties* (Vols. 1-2). Washington, DC: National Institute of Mental Health.

Piaget, J. (1962). *Play, dreams, and imitation in childhood.* New York: Norton.

Singer, D. G., & Singer, J. L. (1990). *The house of make-believe: Children's play and the developing imagination.* Cambridge, MA: Harvard University Press.

Singer, J. L. (Ed.). (1971). *The control of aggression and violence: Cognitive and physiological factors.* New York: Academic Press.

Singer, J. L., & Singer, D. G. (1981). *Television, imagination, and aggression: A study of preschoolers.* Hillsdale, NJ: Lawrence Erlbaum.

Vygotsky, L. S. (1978). *Mind in society.* Cambridge, MA: Harvard University Press.

# Acknowledgments

We wish to thank the following people for their assistance in preparing this book: Alexandra Diaz-Almaral, Cathleen Otero, Lisa Pagliaro, and Sharon Plaskon.

Our special thank you to our Sage editor Jim Brace-Thompson, who initiated this undertaking and who guided and encouraged us throughout the process.

*Dorothy G. Singer*
*Jerome L. Singer*
Yale University

# PART I

## The Popular Media as Educators and Socializers of Growing Children

### Preliminary Comments From the Editors

We begin this handbook with the most extensively researched areas in the study of children and the media. What does it mean for children's development to be growing up in a milieu in which popular reading literature and especially electronic sources of input compete daily with what children can learn from parents, family, or teachers, the "live" people around them? In the sections that follow, we examine efforts to answer many of the questions that scholars, educators, parents, and policy makers have asked about the influences of the media on children's enjoyment, time distribution, their attention and understanding, their development of imagination, and language. Can watching television lead to constructive influences such as improved school readiness or universally agreed-upon values of cooperation, sharing, and common civility? Are there special features of television and related media that may yield socially undesirable influences on children such as fostering excessive fears, unwarranted aggression, problems of identity, problems in family interaction, excessive materialism, sexual doubts, or confusions? What impact does television viewing have on health habits such as substance abuse or eating patterns, on social attitudes and prejudices, on excessive materialism and even fundamental morality?

#### Children's Uses and Gratifications

We begin by examining in four chapters one of the classic areas for studying the new media: the ways in which children use and enjoy these extrafamilial sources of input. Chapter 1 by Haejung Paik provides a scholarly historical overview of the historical emergence of film, television, and the Internet as developments of the twentieth century that have become pervasive sources of input for children and youth. Chapter 2 by Roger Desmond sets these electronic media against a background of the reading of popular literature, a phenomenon that influenced mainly more educated middle-class children in the late nineteenth century but spread widely to all children in the past century. To what extent does reading comics or "pop" magazines and books intersect and interact with moviegoing and watching television? Chapter 3 by George Comstock and Erica Scharrer draws us more deeply into the ways in which our youth actually watch and devote time to the electronic media, particularly television. This chapter lays out in systematic detail the major research methods and studies that have examined the principal variables of concern, the modes of the viewing experience, the time spent viewing, and the contingent circumstances such as family settings, children's ages, household attributes, and situational factors. Although each individual reader may have personal anecdotal experiences about how, when, and where one viewed TV, this chapter provides the clear research evidence on the normative national uses of the medium.

Chapter 4 by Kaveri Subrahmanyam, Robert Kraut, Patricia Greenfield, and Elisheva Gross carries us beyond popular reading, movies, and television into the burst of new electronic media that marked the last decade of the previous century and that points toward the forms of entertainment of the next century: video games and the computer. What are the special psychological and sociological features of video games and the increasingly varied uses of the Internet? This chapter provides what we now know from research but also points to the many new questions we shall have to ask and seek to answer in the coming decades.

In the next section of the first part of our handbook, we present the rich research literature on the possible significance for the growing child of the extensive exposure to electronic media, especially television, detailed in our beginning chapters. Proving a direct influence of television viewing on children's information-processing capacities, overt behavior, and personality or societal attitudes is no easy task. The chapters in this section detail how difficult it is to show cause-and-effect relationships, but they also exemplify a host of imaginative research methods that have been employed to close in cumulatively on answers to these questions.

## Cognitive Functions and School-Readiness Skills

Chapter 5 by David Bickham, John Wright, and Aletha Huston addresses one of the most frequent and often controversial concerns about television viewing in preschool children. To what extent does the format of American television—characterized as it is by rapid pacing, frequent interruptions either for commercial messages or for changes of subject matter, and shifts in loudness or interpolations of music—have a significant impact on children's attention spans and their ability to comprehend and later to retrieve program information? This is a matter of special concern when we consider whether programs designed especially for children can have an educational value. In the 1970s, as commercial networks and local stations largely abandoned children's programming, leaving that field to the Public Broadcasting System, two models of formatting emerged. These were exemplified by *Sesame Street,* which adopted a variation of the faster-paced, lively, short episode and fast-talking pattern of commercial programming, and *Mister Rogers' Neighborhood,* which emphasized a slow-talking adult host and relatively longer episodes with a pacing more like that of a parent directly addressing a preschool child. These two programs had different goals (cognitive teaching vs. social and personal development) and therefore could not be directly compared. Still, some critics felt that the faster-paced *Sesame Street* style was (a) ineffective in yielding school-readiness learning and "in-depth" processing and (b) potentially training children for anticipating a "jazzy," short-sequenced mode of presentation from their first-grade teachers.

Over the last quarter of a century, these issues have been addressed in research described in Chapter 5. We have also witnessed changes in *Sesame Street* and related programming toward somewhat longer sequences and toward the use of more adult-mediated teaching. The implications for learning from *Sesame Street* are documented in this chapter. The emergence of the *Barney & Friends* series for preschoolers, which seeks to strike a balance between mediation of new information and longer episodes and a livelier, music-rich format, reflects an important new step toward integrating the possible presentation modes. Our own research (in a series of 10 studies) has shown that each half-hour episode of the *Barney* series contains almost 100 mediated teaching instances (as rated by panels of developmentally trained judges), that preschoolers and toddlers actually seem to grasp these same examples, and that (especially if there is adult follow-up) children do improve in vocabulary, general information, and civility after viewing 10 episodes in day care settings (Singer & Singer, 1998). Chapter 5 lays out the critical issues in this area and reviews how one can even investigate longer-term constructive effects on school-readiness skills for preschoolers under various viewing conditions.

In Chapter 6 by Patti Valkenburg, one finds an up-to-date review of how television viewing may be playing a role in the development of young children's creativity and imagination. One might at first surmise that, just as reading exposed children to far-flung lands and myths, legends, or scientific knowledge and clearly fostered imagery and fantasy, the vividness and daily "easy availability" of television might also stir up creative thought processes. Valkenburg examines what research tells us about the contingent circumstances that may foster or inhibit the emergence of the inner dimension of experience in the television viewing of youngsters. Similarly, in Chapter 7, Letitia Naigles and Lara Mayeux, language development specialists, consider whether television viewing can foster or impede the regularly viewing child's vocabulary and grammatical usage. We know from our earlier chapters that very young children are watching, on average, 3 hours of television daily and are exposed to a great range of words and usages far beyond what they might encounter in contacts with parents, siblings, or peers. What are the potential constructive or even negative consequences of viewing on word learning and effective communication?

We continue this section of the potential "good news" about television as a constructive learning tool with Chapter 8 by Dorina Miron, Jennings Bryant, and Dolf Zillmann. These authors address very critical questions about the extent to which emotional arousal, liveliness, humor, and excitement can spur effective learning from television or can simply lead to enjoyment of what was watched at the moment with little subsequent recall of the content. Our older readers may remember that there was once a popular TV show called *Laugh-In* in which sight gags and word play filled the screen at such a rapid pace that we would be laughing throughout the program. Despite the pleasurable experience (which made us want to see the show next week), only rarely could we reconstruct more than a minute portion of the actual jokes in a given episode. Clearly, if television for children is to serve some educational function, some balance must be found between sheer liveliness and effective information processing. Chapter 8 examines this issue in a theoretical and research-data-derived practical fashion.

This section on the constructive teaching potential of television viewing concludes with Chapter 9, by Marie-Louise Mares and Emory Woodard, in which the so-called prosocial contributions of television are considered. What parents or educators would deny that we would hope to see children encouraged to be more helpful to others, to show cooperation, courtesy, and civility, and a reduction in unwarranted aggression? Chapter 9 reviews the results of the cumulative research from television viewing and other media use in this vital area of child development. What has been done, and what more can be done?

## Some Hazards of Television Viewing: Fears, Aggression, and Sexual Attitudes

We turn in this next group of chapters to the "bad news" about television-viewing for children. The stark reality, well-documented by many years of content analyses conducted by the Annenberg School for Communication at the University of Pennsylvania under the leadership of its former dean, George Gerbner (Gerbner, Gross, Morgan, & Signorielli, 1994), is that commercial television programming in news content and entertainment shows is replete with instances of violence. The epidemiological studies of Brandon Centerwall (1989, 1994) strongly suggest that, as television was introduced in the United States and Canada, there was within a few years a sharp increase in the rate of homicides among adults. In South Africa, which resisted the influx of television, the homicide rates for white adults, which were closely comparable to those of the North American countries before the spread of television there, remained level. When, however, television was introduced into South Africa, the same increases in homicide rates a few years later emerged. These suggestive results must be taken seriously for their implications regarding the exposure of millions of young children and adults to incidents of televised violence.

Chapter 10 by Joanne Cantor addresses the impact of the heavy exposure of violence that child viewers experience at home on their fears and their experiences of possible dangers in their daily lives. Chapter 11 by Brad Bushman and L. Rowell Huesmann takes us beyond emotions and attitudes to the realm of overt behaviors. To what extent can we formulate psychological theories to explain how television viewing can influence children to engage in overt aggressive behavior or other antisocial acts? And by what methods can we test these theories either in the laboratory or in field studies of children based on their home viewing of violent program content? This seminal chapter addresses not only American research findings but also those from several European countries and Israel. The authors also consider factors that might mitigate these negative influences of television viewing.

Chapter 12 by Jo Groebel further elaborates on the issues raised by Bushman and Huesmann and not only casts them in a broader European perspective but also presents findings from a worldwide UNESCO-sponsored study of television use in countries from each continent regarding the extent of violent programming and potential child influence. He presents a sobering set of findings on the possible worldwide mutually reinforcing impacts of violent television content, television viewing by children, and overt aggression. Although no historically knowledgeable person would attribute human violence primarily to the influence of films or television, even a modest enhancement of aggressive behaviors in some proportion of the millions of viewing children can no longer be ignored. When we began our research on television 30 years ago, we were concerned primarily with its role in children's imaginative development. We were dismayed to find again and again that the most striking findings for that medium were the associations with aggressive behavior (Singer & Singer, 1980, 1986).

Another area of concern for parents and educators, as well as for those officials confronting public health and social policy issues, is children's sexual attitudes. What are the implications of the very considerable exposure of child viewers to relatively explicit sexual material in film and even more pervasively on television? Chapter 13 by Neil Malamuth and Emily Impett examines what we know about this issue from actual research study. The theoretical and data-based concerns that children may be prematurely aroused, that they may adopt potentially self-defeating or socially risky attitudes are considered here. Although certain religious groups may be offended by almost any sexual exposure or sexual references, the emphasis in this chapter is on identifying evidence of potential harm to children and the creation of public health problems. This approach is extended further in Chapter 14 by Ed Donnerstein and Stacy Smith. Donnerstein and Smith examine the impact of sexual portrayals on television and the Internet. Currently, there is an increase of explicit sexual scenes on television. The staid and proper Public Broadcasting System's airing of *Madame Bovary* in February 2000 offered viewers some highly charged sex scenes that the host felt needed a warning before the program began. If a young person is exploring the

Internet, he or she can easily find a chat room that may be titillating but inappropriate for young viewers. As the authors indicate, there is a need for further careful research concerning the effects of sexual material on the Internet on young people.

## Personality, Social Attitudes, and Health

We move in these next chapters to a consideration of how moderate to heavy viewing of television may be influencing children in their personal development and gender role awareness and in their orientation toward family, the social groups around them, and their substance use or eating behavior. Chapter 15 by Nina Huntemann and Michael Morgan examines the subtle features of a sense of identity, the experience of "who am I?" and "what are my personal qualities?" What features of television content can be shown to influence how young viewers may form a sense of self? Chapter 16 by Robert Kubey and Barna William Donovan carries the theme of self a step further to "self in family." The authors consider the research evidence on how television is watched in the family context (using the important experience sampling method) and then examine what the content of family programming presents to the viewer. As with most of our chapters, suggestions for amelioration of the more negative effects of viewing are discussed. Chapter 17 by Nancy Signorielli moves into the role of gender stereotyping and how television content represents boys and girls and men and women for the child viewer. Her review points up important "effects" as well as "content" research approaches. It also contains constructive suggestions for further research as well as for more educationally sound representations of the sexes.

Chapter 18 by Gordon Berry and Joy Keiko Asamen further points up the risks for children of narrowly focused cultural stereotyping based on the available current television programming. The authors review how cultural stereotype research is carried out and summarize available effect data. They also point toward ways in which television and the emerging computer-based media can lead children toward a richer awareness of the range of human cultural, physical, and social variations.

A feature of most television in the United States and increasingly worldwide that is so pervasive that its message may actually be overlooked is the commercial basis of the medium. Chapter 19 by Dale Kunkel musters a huge panoply of evidence to demonstrate that one of the most powerful of television's socializing influences is that it exposes viewers to thousands of commercials and to a continuous stream of temptations that may create excessive materialism and also the conflicts of aspirations for possessions beyond their own or their families' capacities for achievement. The vulnerability of the young lies in the fact that they (a) may not be capable of clearly separating externally generated commercial messages from their own desires and (b) may not yet be capable, as most adults are, of building up some defense structures or cynicism about advertising appeals. What responsibilities do the industry, parents, or policy makers have in the face of the data reported?

Still another area of television's and other media's appeal lies in children's attraction to popular music. What messages are conveyed in music, on audiotapes and compact discs, and on television in the powerful images of MTV and its variants? The authors of Chapter 20, Donald Roberts and Peter Christenson, examine the scientific literature in this field. For example, they raise the question "Is there a heavy metal syndrome?" and review the available research literature correlating preferences for such music with reckless driving or drug abuse. That watching MTV can be influential at least in changing recreational preferences has recently been demonstrated with the report on the CBS *60 Minutes* program about the tiny Shangri-La monarchy of Bhutan in the Himalayan Mountains. This country allowed television use only in the last year of the twentieth century. A government leader somewhat ruefully reports that children and youth, hitherto seemingly happily conforming to Buddhist ritual and recreation, have now taken to dancing and imitating American MTV!

Our next two chapters review the available literature on how television viewing may be directly influencing children's health habits. A very powerful and disquieting Chapter 21 by Victor Strasburger reviews in detail the methods of study and the findings bearing linkages between television viewing and substance abuse, drinking, or smoking in children and youth. Chapter 22 by Katherine Battle Horgen, Molly Choate, and Kelly Brownell carries this thrust further into an examination particularly of how television commercials create trends toward unhealthy eating habits.

Our Part I concludes with Chapter 23 by Lawrence Rosenkoetter, which takes up the question often raised by politicians and religious groups: Is television damaging the morality of our youth? Alas, the data here are skimpy, but Rosenkoetter brings together what work has been done and points the way toward further needed research.

In summary, Part I provides a pervasive and careful review of the positive and negative influences of television on children and youth. The reader will see that most children watch a great deal of television and that research demonstrates a variety of ways in which their cognitive, social, and health habits reflect that pervasive, intrusive new "member of the family."

## References

Centerwall, B. S. (1989). Exposure to television as a cause of violence. *Public Communication and Behavior, 2,* 1-57.

Centerwall, B. S. (1994). Television and the development of the superego: Pathway to violence. In C. Chiland, J. G. Young, & D. Kaplan (Eds.), *Children and violence: The child in the family* (Monograph series of the International Association for Child and Adolescent Psychiatry and Allied Professions, (pp. 178-197). Northvale, NJ: Jason Aronson, XIII.

Gerbner, G., Gross, L., Morgan, M., & Signorielli, N. (1994). Growing up with television: The cultivation perspective. In J. Bryant & D. Zillmann (Eds.), *Media effects: Advances in theory and research* (pp. 17-42). Hillsdale, NJ: Lawrence Erlbaum.

Singer, D. G., & Singer, J. L. (1980). Television-viewing and aggressive behavior in preschool children: A field study. *Forensic Psychology and Psychiatry, Annals of the New York Academy of Science, 347,* 289-303.

Singer, J. L., & Singer, D. G. (1986). Family experiences and television-viewing as predictors of children's imagination, restlessness, and aggression. *Journal of Social Issues, 42*(3), 107-124.

Singer, J. L., & Singer, D. G. (1998). *Barney & Friends* as entertainment and education: Evaluating the quality and effectiveness of a television series for preschool children. In J. K. Asamen & G. Berry (Eds.), *Research paradigms in the study of television and social behavior* (pp. 305-367). Thousand Oaks, CA: Sage.

CHAPTER 1

# The History of Children's Use of Electronic Media

HAEJUNG PAIK
University of Oklahoma

For every new communication medium that has appeared and spread widely, people have expressed concerns regarding the effects of the medium, especially on children and young adolescents. In the 1920s and 1930s, when motion pictures matured into a major mass medium and moviegoing became a national pastime for family entertainment, questions were raised and charges were made about the possible harmful effects on children. This led to the Payne Fund studies, a scientific assessment of the effects of movie viewing on children and youth in the late 1920s. Next came radio; a special committee was established in the 1930s to study the effects of radio programs on children's emotions, learning, and social adjustment (Gruenberg, 1933). When television sets diffused rapidly into American households, the same concerns resulted in a series of studies in the late 1950s (Schramm, Lyle, & Parker, 1961); a report by the President's Commission on the Causes and Prevention of Violence, a media task force, in the late 1960s (Baker & Ball, 1969); and a federal inquiry in the 1970s (Surgeon General's Scientific Advisory Committee, 1972) and 1980s (Pearl, Bouthilet, & Lazar, 1982). More recently, with the increase in the purchase of video games and in response to the amount of time children and young adolescents spend on the Internet, the same concerns are driving studies on the social impacts of such interactive communication media (Turow, 1999).

Before one can begin to understand the role that each medium plays in children's and early adolescents' lives, it is important to know what each medium is and how it is used. To that end, some of the basic questions that must be considered are as follows: When was the medium invented? How did the medium distribute across society? And what happened to other existing media when the new medium was first introduced? As for how each medium is used, the questions include who watches, how much, when, what programs, why, how, and with whom?

In this chapter, some basic facts are presented about the history and children's use of electronic media—movies, radio, television (including cable television), and interactive media (e.g., computers, video games, educational software, and the Internet)—in the United States. (Audio recorders, videocassette recorders, compact discs, and so on are discussed in later chapters.) Each medium will be considered in a chronological order—when it was first invented or when it became mass communication. Although this strategy is simple and conventional, it must be followed with the understanding that each successive new medium does not replace the previous communication media. For example, in today's "new media environment," many "old" media coexist with "new" media. As such, the discussion will also involve how each new medium has affected the role played by the existing media. Furthermore, given the richness of the history and use of each medium, it is simply impossible to do justice to any of the examined media in the limited space of a single chapter. Therefore, the interested reader is simply referred to the later chapters in this book for a more thorough consideration of each medium and of the various issues surrounding them.

## Movies

### *Early Development*

It is reasonable to state that film was the first mass medium that appeared on the social scene. Although in its early years there was little about the film technology that could be considered electronic, it is fair to classify the current design as one of the electronic media. Several major discoveries and technological innovations from 1824 to 1896 led to the development of the cinema. They included a better understanding of the human perceptual system and of the persistence of vision and the development of photography, which in turn led to the invention of the motion picture camera and projection techniques.

At first, cinemas were simply pictures that appeared to move, such as horse races, various versions of Niagara Falls, and fire engines racing down a street. It was in 1903 that Edwin S. Porter, in his film *The Great Train Robbery,* introduced the two elements of story and editing, and it was not until 1915 when D. W. Griffith used sophisticated shooting of scenes and editing in his film *Birth of a Nation* that cinema techniques showed maturity. By the time of World War I, film became widely accepted as a means of family entertainment, and in the mid-1920s, continued technical improvements were made to keep up with the competition from radio. By the end of the decade, almost all films were "talkies," making them even more attractive.

In 1926, the average weekly movie attendance was 60 million, and in 1929 it reached 95 million (see Figure 1.1). Attendance (and profits) began falling in the depression years only to climb back up to 85 million in 1936, holding relatively steady throughout World War II. During the 1940s, going to a movie was just as much a part of American life as watching television is today. The dramatic change came in 1947, and movie attendance plummeted to its lowest level in 1971. Although attendance has been slowly creeping up, the increase has been insignificant in comparison with the gigantic drop preceding it.

The two significant drops noted in Figure 1.1 are associated with numerous factors. However, the dates of these drops—1930 and 1946—coincide with the dates at which radio and television, respectively, made their pronounced appearance on the media scene. It is interesting that the first drop in movie attendance was quickly reversed in just a few years, while the second drop (mostly due to television) has been a great deal slower in its recovery, increasing only moderately over a period of some three decades.

### *Children and the Movies*

Following the introduction of sound technology, the notion of the cinemas for children began to crystallize. However, many talking

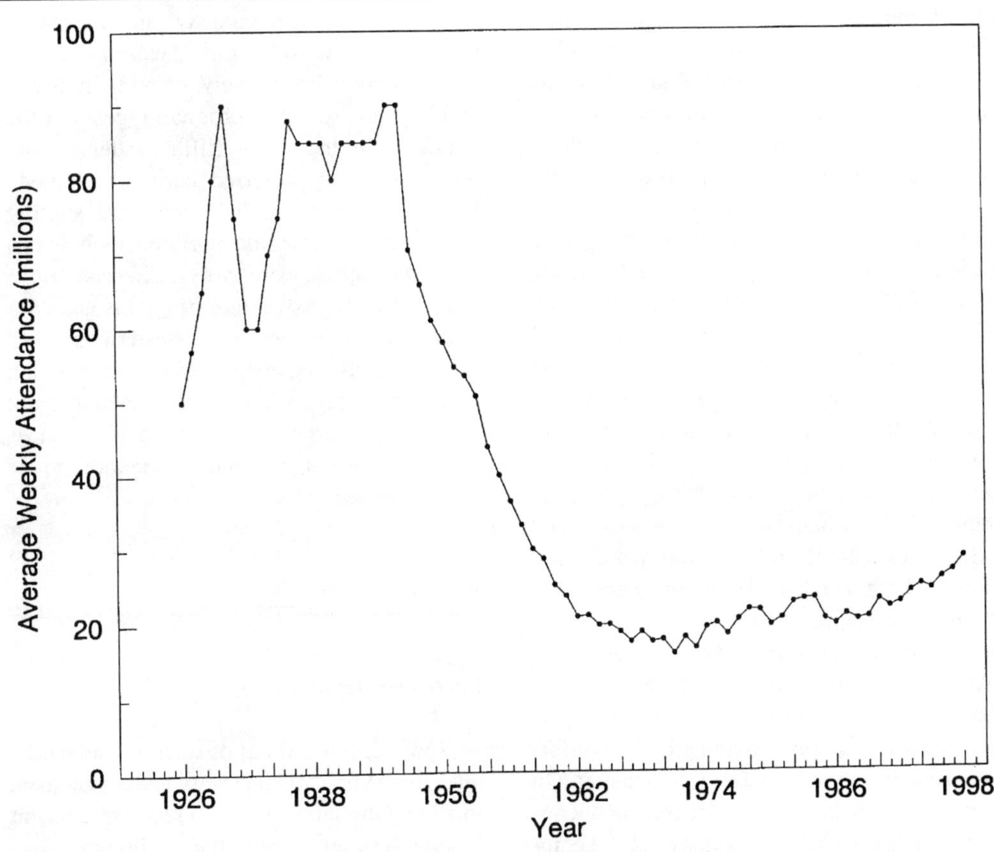


**Figure 1.1.** Movie Attendance, 1926-1998
SOURCE: *Film Facts* (1980, Facts on File) and *1987, 1998 U.S. Economic Review* (Motion Picture Association).

pictures were seen as too mature for children in terms of language and theme. Thus, the practice of separate viewing for children on selected or recommended films began, usually on Saturday mornings or early afternoons. This was initiated by a sense of social responsibility, in conjunction with commercial reasons (Bazalgette & Staples, 1995). Even though through these matinee screenings the movie theaters were able to get an audience at a time when they would otherwise be idle, the industry soon learned that producing films for children was unprofitable. Instead, the industry exerted its efforts in developing a new genre, the family film, attracting both adults and children. In 1937, Walt Disney released *Snow White and the Seven Dwarfs,* the first animated feature-length film in color and with music, which appealed to large audiences of all age groups and social classes. Besides animated features, films such as *Little Miss Marker* (1934), *The Wizard of Oz* (1939), and *Lassie Come Home* (1943) attracted a wide range of family audiences.

In 1929, the average child was attending 1.6 movies per week (Cressey, 1934), but that number differs widely considering age and gender. In particular, adolescents attended movies more frequently than younger children. Dale (1935) indicated that early-elementary-school-age children attended the movies roughly two times a month (or 0.5 times a week), whereas high school and mid- and upper-elementary-school students attended once a week. This is consistent with Charters's (1933) study in which older children 8 to 19 years old were found to attend movies more than twice as frequently as younger children 5 to 8 years old. Furthermore, these studies found that boys attended movies more than girls did.

The attendance patterns have changed in more recent times. The data for Table 1.1 are from *The Kids Study,* by Simmons Market Research (1995), based on 2,118 children 6 to 14 years old. Unlike earlier data, Table 1.1 shows that girls are more frequent moviegoers than boys. As for age dependence, the results depend on the frequency of moviegoing itself. In general, 9- to 11-year-olds go to movies more frequently than both younger (ages 6-8) and older (ages 12-14) children; this pattern applies to both genders. However, among the frequent moviegoers (i.e., two or more times in the last 30 days or five or more times in the last 90 days), attendance increases with age for both boys and girls. The attendance pattern becomes further convoluted when different program types are taken into account. (In order to keep the chapter focused and contained, other variables such as race, socioeconomic status, family background, and so forth will not be considered.)

### *Program Preferences*

According to a study by Witty, Garfield, and Brink (1941), in the early days, teenagers favored comedy and mystery-type films. Girls also favored love stories, whereas boys showed a stronger liking for westerns and newsreels. Older children liked educational features and newsreels more than younger children did. A decade later, Lyness (1951) reported similar findings. Lyness examined whether preferences for particular movie types depended on gender and age. He studied 5th-, 7th-, 9th-, and 11th-grade boys and girls. Results showed a gender difference in favored program types but a more stable preference across different age groups. Overall, boys liked western, war, comedy, and adventure program types, while girls favored a somewhat different list, namely, comedy, musical, and love and romance program types. For the youngest in the study (fifth graders), both boys and girls preferred cartoons, comedy features, and westerns. However, starting from grade 7, program preferences between boys and girls were very different. Boys started favoring adventure programs and continued to favor war and western movies, whereas girls began to prefer musicals and love and romance movies. Interestingly, but perhaps not surprising, program preferences did not change significantly when radio made its appearance.

## Radio

### *Early Development*

Radio developed out of scientific advances made in the field of electricity and magnetism. In 1897, Guglielmo Marconi received a patent for wireless telegraphy, the beginning of radio. In 1919, Marconi sold its American subsidiary to General Electric, which became Radio Corporation of America. In 1920, KDKA in Pittsburgh went on the air, hoping to sell radio receivers. After a slow start, sales of radios reached about a half million in 1924. Soon advertisers realized that, unlike movies, radio offered them direct access to the homes of the listeners, and it could be used to promote products. Stations began selling airtime, and radio broadcasting became a revenue-producing business (Barnoux, 1967). To increase their profitability, groups of stations began working together, sharing the costs of a program and broadcasting the same show on several member stations. This arrangement between stations became known as a network and persisted into the television era. In the 1930s and 1940s, radio flourished, and entire families could be found sitting by their radios, enjoying their favorite shows and news.

**TABLE 1.1** Demographic Breakdown of Children, Who Went to Movies Within the Last 90 Days

| | *% Went to Movies in Last 90 Days* | *% Went to Movies 5+ Times in Last 90 Days* | *% Went to Movies in Last 30 Days* | *% Went to Movies 2+ Times in Last 30 Days* |
|---|---|---|---|---|
| Kids 6-14 | 69.5 | 24.7 | 57.6 | 37.1 |
| Boys 6-14 | 66.1 | 21.8 | 55.5 | 34.2 |
| Girls 6-14 | 73.1 | 27.8 | 59.8 | 40.1 |
| Kids 6-8 | 65.9 | 20.1 | 52.0 | 30.3 |
| Kids 9-11 | 75.2 | 25.9 | 60.6 | 36.8 |
| Kids 12-14 | 67.7 | 29.2 | 60.2 | 44.1 |
| Boys 6-8 | 60.8 | 19.1 | 48.3 | 28.9 |
| Boys 9-11 | 72.1 | 22.1 | 58.1 | 30.7 |
| Boys 12-14 | 65.8 | 25.1 | 60.1 | 42.7 |
| Girls 6-8 | 71.4 | 22.1 | 56.0 | 31.6 |
| Girls 9-11 | 78.5 | 29.9 | 63.2 | 43.2 |
| Girls 12-14 | 69.7 | 31.6 | 60.2 | 45.6 |

SOURCE: Simmons Market Research (1995). Used with permission.
NOTE: Sample size = 2,118.

The growth of radio ownership is shown in Figure 1.2. It shows that, by 1930, 46% of American households had a radio, and 10 years later that number had grown to more than 80%. By 1970, radio ownership had already reached 98%, nearly the current ownership rate (99%). Of course, one may question the appropriateness of radio ownership as a measure of radio's popularity, for it is entirely possible that a great many radios simply sat unused, collecting dust. However, as seen from Figure 1.2, the increase in ownership is matched by a comparable increase in the number of radio stations; presumably, this reflects a growing market meeting the demands of the public. As such, it is reasonable to state that radio's popularity has been steadily rising since the time of its inception. It is then interesting to contrast the steady growth of radio's popularity with the complex and tumultuous pattern of movies' popularity (Figure 1.1); evidently, the popularity of radio has been mostly unaffected by the forces that affected movies.

### *Radio and Children*

Radio programs for children have changed from being an integral part of everyday life to a relatively small segment within the children's entertainment media. Early radio programmers recognized the popularity of children's programs by designating a specific time, usually 5:00 to 6:00 P.M., for "children's hour." The popularity of these programs brought an increase in the number of programs designed for children. For instance, in the New York City area, programs for children increased from 3 in 1928 to 52 by 1934 (Eisenberg, 1936; Jersild, 1939).

In the mid-1930s, children 9 to 12 years old listened to radio approximately 2 to 3 hours a day (DeBoer, 1937; Jersild, 1939). Lyness (1952) surveyed third-, fifth-, seventh-, ninth-, and eleventh-grade students in 1950 who lived in cities that had newspapers, radio stations, and movie theaters (but no television yet). All the children, except third-grade boys, named radio as their most frequently engaged in

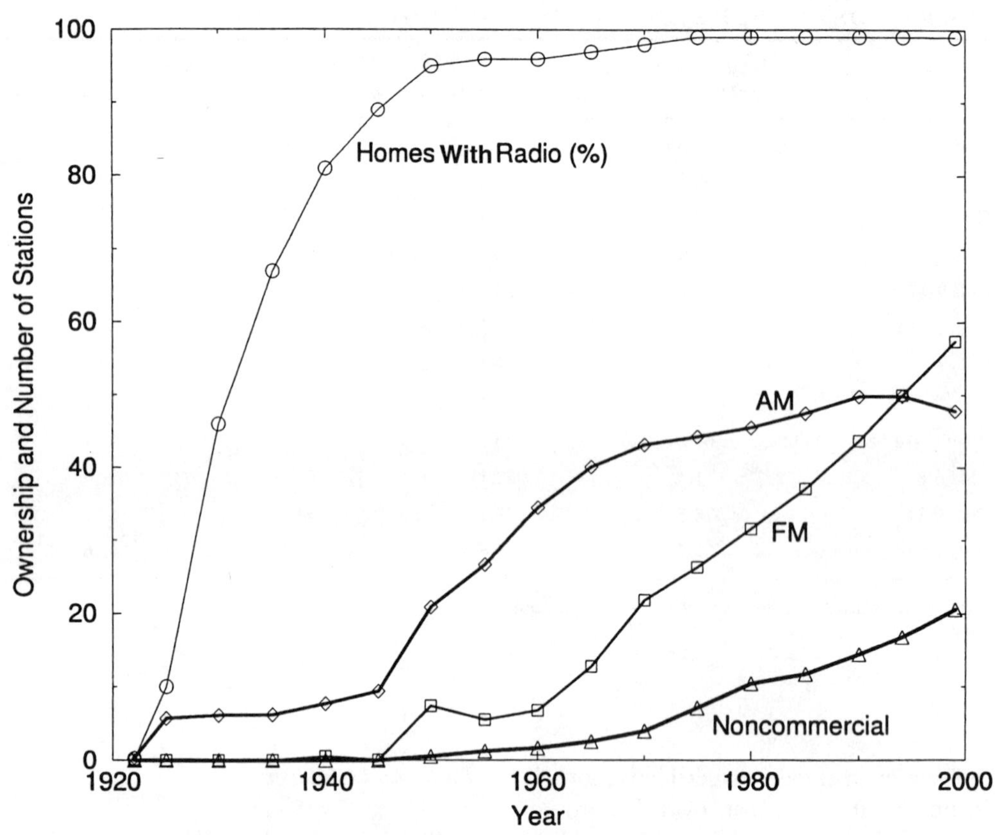


**Figure 1.2.** Growth of Radio, 1922-1999

SOURCE: Radio Advertising Bureau, Mass Media Bureau, and Federal Communications Commission.

NOTE: Ownership is in percentages, and the number of stations is in hundreds.

activity at home in the evening. Overall, for girls time spent listening to radio increased with age, while for boys it decreased after the peak around fifth or seventh grade.

Even when television became the main mass medium, the amount of time that children and young adolescents spent listening to radio was very similar to earlier radio days. Confirming radio's consistent listenership, Lyle and Hoffman (1972) report that, even when television was the most favored medium, among their subjects, half of the first graders and 80% of the sixth graders reported listening to radio on the preceding day. Furthermore, 24% of tenth graders reported listening 5 hours or more a day. This study shows that, regardless of television's dominance, at least children were still enjoying radio. Brown, Childers, Bauman, and Koch (1990) confirmed Lyle and Hoffman's results (listening to 5 hours of radio daily) from 2,056 children 12 to 14 years old. Furthermore, they found that, with increasing age, more time was spent with radio and less with television.

Such a heavy use of radio among adolescents exists even in present times, and it has been explained by many as providing teenagers with acceptable social cues; as giving them something of interest to discuss with their friends (Brown, Eicher, & Petrie, 1986); as an important source for socialization (Adoni, 1979; Mendelsohn, 1964); and even as a way of rebellion against parental norms and a search for identification with peers rather than with adults (Golinko, 1984). Regardless of the explanations, it appears that television did not significantly affect (and has not affected) the time children and adolescents spent with radio.

### *Program Preferences*

In 1937, Clark (1939) obtained data from children 9 to 18 years old on their radio-listening patterns. The study showed that whether children listened to a program was largely determined by the broadcast time of the show. Programs aired at evening hours during weekdays were the most frequently mentioned programs. Regarding the programs aired in those hours, girls 15 to 18 listened more to romantic and historical dramatizations than boys of the same age; boys listened more than girls to dance, popular, and novelty programs. With the increase of age, both boys and girls showed less interest in and greater dislike for children's programs. It was clear, then, that, within a given broadcast time, age and gender influence the degree of preference for certain types of content.

Another study by Lyness (1951) also showed a slight gender and age difference in program choice. The two most preferred program types were comedy and mystery plays for both boys and girls of all ages (except for fifth-grade boys, whose first choice was western shows). The gender difference appeared at the third most preferred program type: Girls preferred drama and music, while boys enjoyed adventure shows and sports. The age difference within each gender was also at the level of the third most preferred program type: For girls, fifth through ninth graders enjoyed drama, while eleventh graders preferred music. For boys, the third most preferred program type was adventure shows for fifth graders; sports for seventh and ninth graders; and music for the eleventh graders.

By the early 1950s, as television was becoming a major threat to radio, radio lost much of its drama and comedy programming to television. This led the radio programmers to shift their emphasis to music programs, with a few features, a little news, and commercials. These programming changes were well received by children. Christenson and DeBenedittis (1986) asked first through fifth graders why they liked to listen to radio. More than 83% gave a response that referred to the musical content of the medium, and only 25% referred to seeking information. In their study, no significant gender or age difference in gratification was found.

More recently, in 1993, Arbitron conducted a special diary pilot study to measure radio-listening habits among 2- to 11-year-olds and adults in their households (Patchen, Burgess, & Cralley, 1994). It was found that, in addition to children's programs, children listened to other programs such as news/talk, country or album rock, and even oldies. The study speculates that some of these programs are not the child's choice but that of their parents. In fact, these were programs heard in the car while driving. The finding is similar to what Clark (1939) had found earlier: Program choices are often not determined by any program or listener attribute but, rather, by the time (and location) of listening.

As for gender differences in contemporary times, Wells and Hakanen (1991) found a gender difference in gratification. They found that female teenagers made greater use of music for mood management (mood enhancing or tranquilizing) than their male counterparts. For males, the most highly rated function of radio was to get excited. This is very similar to the findings of Larson, Kubey, and Colletti (1989), who found that males listen to music that excites them, while females prefer ballads and love songs. The authors speculated that such needs (getting excited) are leading teenage boys to turn away from radio to other alternative sources for defiant rock music. If true, that would imply that teenage girls use radio more than teenage boys do; in fact, that implication has been confirmed by many, including Carroll and colleagues (1993).

## Television

### *Early Development*

When television was first developed in the 1920s and 1930s, the film and radio industries looked on it as more of a novelty than a threat. Close to 3 years after radio broadcasting became a reality in 1920, a primitive version of an all-electronic television system was available. In 1928, telecasting began on an experimental basis, without commercials or an audience. This was followed by its first major public demonstration at the 1939 World's Fair and the first commercial telecasting in 1941. In 1934, Congress passed the Communications Act, empowering the Federal Communications Commission (FCC) with regulatory licensing responsibilities. All broadcasters were (and are) required to maintain an FCC license, and the granting of the license was based on frequency availability and the public's interest.

Television might have gotten off to a faster start were it not for the depression, the growth of the film industry, and World War II. During the war, the FCC placed a freeze on the formation of new television stations, and most efforts were redirected away from television to other war-related technologies. However, at the end of the war, the technologies developed during the war were applied to the television industry. At that point, it was becoming evident that television would constitute a serious threat to movies and radio (Barnoux, 1990).

The structure of early television was modeled after that of radio. It had three television network systems—the National Broadcasting Company (NBC), the Columbia Broadcasting System (CBS), and the American Broadcasting Company (ABC)—and a spectrum that covered comedies, quiz shows, soap operas, suspense programs, variety shows, and westerns. The similarity resulted mostly from the migration of the early developers of television programming (i.e., technicians, writers, directors, actors, musicians, and singers) from the world of radio (Whetmore, 1981).

The "golden age" of television, the 1950s, was a period marked by tremendous growth and innovation. With the end of the FCC's freeze and the cost of TV sets dropping to the point where most moderately affluent families could afford one, television ownership increased exponentially (see Figure 1.3). During this period, television broadcast began at 7:00 A.M. and continued till past midnight. The early morning programs consisted of news summaries and feature stories aimed at families preparing to go to work. Programs from 9:00 A.M. to 5:30 P.M. were directed at housewives and featured game shows, household hints, light interviews, romantic dramatic series, variety shows, and discussions of family and community problems. Following that was the children's hour. From 6:30 to 8:00 P.M., programs were designed to appeal to both adults and children; they included news, sports, and puppet and musical shows. From 8:00 to 11:00 P.M., the programs included drama, variety shows, talent and quiz competitions, and sports events. The closing hours started at 11:00 P.M. with news, followed by feature films and a goodnight chat (UNESCO, 1953). This format has changed little into the present day.

### *Children and Television*

A detailed breakdown of the daily viewing audience in the autumn of 1951 shows that children were watching television throughout the day, and their choices were not limited to children's programs (just as in radio). About 30% of the children under age 16 were watching television at 9:00 A.M., reaching maximum at 5:00 P.M., and falling to less than 8% around 10:00 P.M. (UNESCO, 1953). Children watching adult programs were also

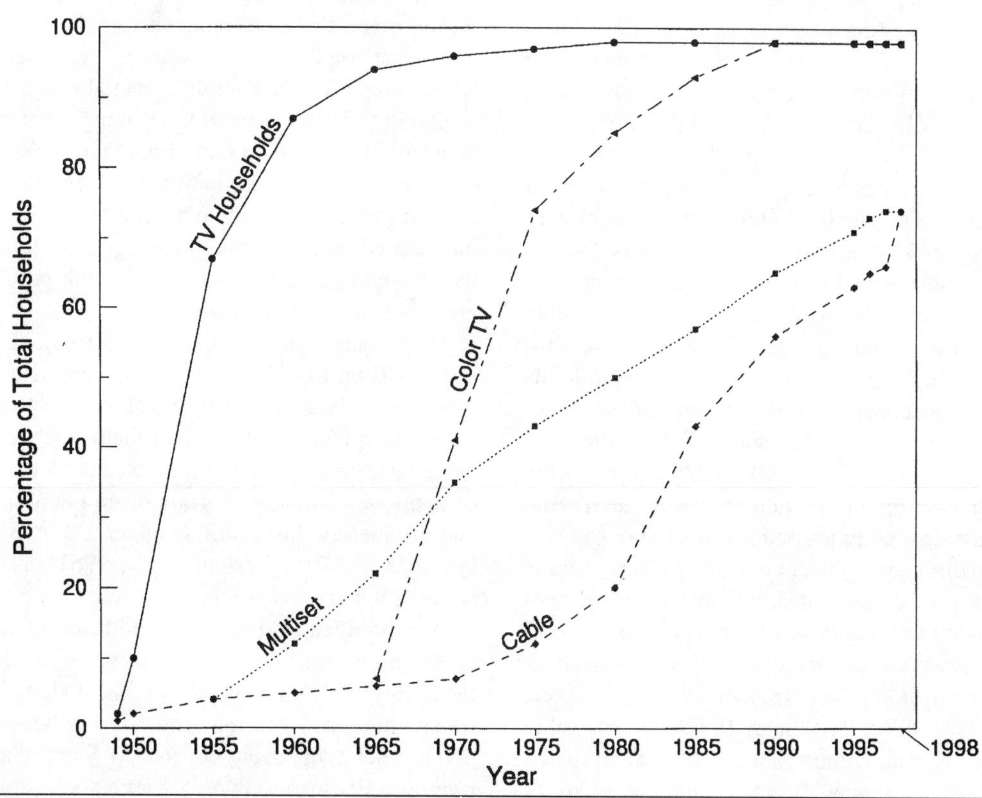


**Figure 1.3.** Growth of TV Ownership: Total, Multiset, Color, and Cable
SOURCE: *1986: The Television Audience* (A.C. Nielsen Company) and *1998 Report on Television* (Nielsen Media Research). Used with permission.

found by Schramm et al. (1961). Their results showed that sixth-grade children were already spending 80% of their viewing time on programs that were intended for adult viewers; even in first grade, nearly 40% of the viewing time was devoted to adult programs. Of course, heavy exposure to television did not begin at first grade.

Children were (and are) exposed to television as early as 6 to 12 months old, and these children responded to television for an average of 1 to 2 hours a day (Hollenbeck & Slaby, 1979). Studies report that about one fourth of 2-year-olds and two thirds of 4-year-olds spend 2 to 4 hours a day watching television (Comstock & Paik, 1991; Friedrich & Stein, 1973; Roberts & Bachen, 1981; Singer & Singer, 1981). As recently as 1998, it was found that young children as early as age 2 watch more than 3 hours daily (Nielsen Media Research, 1998).

As children grow, regular television viewing increases during the preschool years (with a slight decrease when children are going to school), rises up to early adolescence, and finally decreases during teenage years (Comstock, Chaffee, Katzman, McCombs, & Roberts, 1978; Johnstone, 1974; Larson & Kubey, 1985; Rubin, 1977; Schramm et al., 1961). For example, Rubin (1977) found that television viewing declined sharply as adolescents moved through the high school years. The peak in viewing was reached at age 9, and from 9 to 17, the time teenagers spent with television declined.

Such a decrease in television consumption has been explained by the development status of adolescents, which is the product of chronological, biological, or cognitive growth (Wartella, Alexander, & Lemish, 1979). The general notion for development and media use is that development creates both needs and resources for differential use of mass media by children and adolescents. Developmental status influences media choice, degree of media use, and the media content. For teenagers who would like to identify with their peers, the images television portrays are remote from them since television aims for the largest possible audience, making many adolescents grow increasingly distant from the mainstream focus of this appeal and start looking for other media, such as radio (Larson & Kubey, 1985).

And what about gender differences in the viewing time of contemporary children? The answer is complex and controversial, and will be discussed in later chapters. Briefly, there is some evidence that gender differences in television viewing typically appear around 4 or 5 years of age and increase with age (Bianchi & Robinson, 1997; Carpenter, Huston, & Spera, 1989; Singer & Singer, 1981). On the other hand, data from Nielsen Media Research show no gender difference for ages 2 to 11 (Condry, 1989). Huston, Wright, Marquis, and Green (1999), from their 3-year longitudinal study, also find no significant gender difference in children 2 to 4. The studies by Mauldin and Meeks (1991) and Timmer, Eccles, and O'Brien (1985), however, show that, for 3- to 11-year-olds, boys watched more television than girls did, but only on weekends. These diverse findings simply support the initial response; any gender difference is apt to depend on numerous other factors.

### *Program Preferences*

What people state as their preference and what they actually watch can be very different. As a result, there is always a danger of misinterpreting the relationship between preference and actual consumption. Especially when it comes to children's television use, often preferences are influenced by the opinions of others such as family members or peers. Furthermore, there are other factors that dictate what one actually watches, such as whether a preferred program is available, time availability, or broadcast time. Rosengren and Windahl (1989) have pointed out that preferences are more an expression of the individual and the stage of development attained rather than a predictor for actual viewing. With this understanding, the following deals with preferences in television viewing.

Program preferences appear very early, almost as soon as children begin to view television. Preschool children generally prefer the shows designed specifically for them, such as those involving animals, animated characters, or puppets, all in story form with full action, and frequently involving laughter (Lyle & Hoffman, 1972; Schramm et al., 1961). As children mature, program preferences become more diversified, and they begin to favor adult programs as well. In fact, as early as 1951 (Maccoby, 1951), it was known that at all age levels children watch television during hours that are not exclusively devoted to children's programs, indicating that they are exposed to a variety of adult programs. Naturally, as children shift their program preferences toward more adult programming, program preferences become more diverse. A more recent study by Adler and his colleagues (1980), based on an analysis of Nielsen data for 1973, confirms that only 3 of the top 15 shows favored by children were Saturday morning offerings; the remainder were prime-time shows aimed at adults. In short, children's content preferences increasingly approximate adult patterns.

The question then arises as to why children prefer adult programs. As Wartella et al. (1979) explained, it may well be that, in general, television viewing happens in a family context, and it is easy to imagine that other family members' norms and preferences can influence a child's preferences. There are few programs offered for 9- to 11-year-old children, and that may be why children are tuning to adult programs. From the child developmental perspective, early adolescence is when children strive to orient themselves to the adult world, and adults' programs, more than children's, satisfy such needs. Watching adult television programs adds to one's status in peer group relationships.

Finally, program preference is determined to a large degree by motivation and reasons for viewing. Schramm et al. (1961) listed three reasons why children watch television: (a) the passive pleasure of being entertained and living a fantasy; (b) the information that they frequently gain from television even without necessarily seeking information; and (c) television's social utility function, according to which television provides a subject of conversation or a reason to be with other people. They noted that television offers different gratifications to different children but suggested that stimulating fantasy seeking and fantasy behavior is the primary role of television for children. Thus, much of the incidental learning may be a by-product of fantasizing.

Later, Greenberg (1974) surveyed children 9, 12, and 15 years old to investigate their motivation for watching television. Nine-year-olds showed that learning and relaxation were significant motivations for watching television. As for 12- and 15-year-olds, the use of television for passing time and as a habit emerged strongly and was associated with watching all kinds of television content. In short, there are (at least) six different reasons for viewing television (Rubin, 1977): to learn, to pass time or as a habit, for companionship, to forget, for arousal, and for relaxation. It appears that younger children identify with these reasons more strongly than do older ones, but viewing as a pastime or as a habit is the predominant reason for viewing television across the age groups.

### *Viewing Context*

Whether children watch television with family members, siblings, peers, or alone is a significant component of the viewing experience. In the 1940s and early 1950s, television was purchased as a single unit and was placed in the living room. Television brought families together and made family members spend more time at home with one another. However, despite being together in one room, families conversed less than they had before television, and when they did talk to each other, frequently it was in regard to the disagreement over program choices (McDonagh, 1950; Stewart, 1952).

Since the 1950s, there has been a steady increase in the number of homes with more than one television set. According to Nielsen Media Research, in 1998, 74% of U.S. households had more than one television set (see Figure 1.3). With multiple television sets, there have been concerns that television viewing will be a more isolated and private experience. For example, in modern days, parents are being excluded from the viewing experience. Lawrence and Wozniak (1989) surveyed about 150 children 6 to 17 years old and found that entire family viewing is infrequent, and as much as two thirds of their viewing time is with siblings. When they do watch with parents, it is mostly with the father. Another study of more than 300 children ages 3 to 5 shows that coviewing declines with age, and the majority of children's programs are watched without parents (St. Peters, Fitch, Huston, Wright, & Eakins, 1991).

One may wonder why children's isolated viewing should be of concern. There are numerous responses, but one important reason for concern is the possibility that television can become a distraction from other activities, a source of exposure to antisocial behavior, and also void of any prosocial value. Indeed, when children watch television with siblings, the programs they watch are more entertainment and comedy oriented, and very early they abandon watching more informative programs. However, children tend to view informative programs, and for longer periods, when an adult is present (Wright, St. Peters, & Huston, 1990). Though it may be true that fantasizing or arousal alone can have an educational by-product, it is unlikely that information gained in such fashion can be of any long-lasting value.

### Cable Television

Television-related technologies such as cable television have changed the way people use television in American households. Cable television began in late 1948 as a service to households in mountainous or geographically remote areas where reception of over-the-air television signals was poor. However, the cable industry soon realized that additional programming choices could be offered by importing signals from distant stations into markets that were served by only one or two local stations.

It is interesting that, contrary to common belief, when television became a mass medium, the percentage of the American households using over-the-air television was comparable to that subscribing to cable television (see Figure 1.3). The major difference in the emergence of the two media in the early years was the exponential growth of the former as compared to the steady linear growth of the latter. Still, the gradual increase in cable television subscription was sufficient to bring the broadcast industry's attention to its potential competition. This led to the FCC's placing restrictions on cable-delivered programming, from 1966 to 1972, to protect the broadcast industry in the public's interest.

In 1972, the restrictive policies on cable began to relax. This brought the launch of the nation's first pay-TV network, Home Box Office (HBO), in 1975. HBO, using satellite interconnections, brought into the home Hollywood films, made-for-television movies, and special entertainment programming not formerly available to television audiences. This was the beginning of a national satellite distribution system that brought a pronounced growth of services to subscribers. In addition to three television networks, cable television has carried 24-hour channels dedicated to news, sports, music, children, and more.

### Cable and Children

Families with cable services have better reception of network broadcast programs and have access to a wide range of programs targeting more narrowly defined audiences, including children. Indeed, the number of networks with children's programming has increased from four networks (ABC, CBS, NBC, and Public Broadcasting Service [PBS]) to seven (the four networks plus Fox, United Paramount Network [UPN], and Warner Brothers [WB]). Plus, there are now children's cable television channels (Nickelodeon, the Disney Channel, and Cartoon Network) and family-oriented networks that carry some children's programming (Turner Broadcasting System [TBS], USA Network, the Discovery Channel, Turner Network Television [TNT], Music Television [MTV], Arts and Entertainment Channel [A&E], and the Family Channel).

Given the expanded content available on cable television, the question of what children watch arises again. Over a period of three Saturdays, Heeter (1988) surveyed 153 households with cable, 40 of which had children under 18. The share of viewing time to different types of channels revealed that the households with children watched more network programming (61% of viewing time on average) compared with the other households (36%). Network programming during the sample period (8:00 A.M. to noon) was made up exclusively of shows targeted to children. As expected, other households watched more nonnetwork off-air channels. However, channels available only over cable attracted one third of the viewing time of households with children, indicating that children watched those channels despite the fact that there were children's programs on network channels. Interestingly, households without children that watched television on Saturday mornings watched for as much time as households with children.

When Heeter conducted the study, Nickelodeon, for example, drew only 2% of the viewing share. However, more recently, television broadcast networks have begun losing Saturday morning viewers to programs offered on children's cable channels. A survey reports that, in the 1996-1997 season, children 2 to 11 watched an average of 211 hours of basic cable programming, while they watched only 48 hours of broadcast television (Petrozzello, 1998). This shift from broadcast to cable is partially because more programs and time are allocated to children's programs on basic cable than they are on broadcast television.

Given the proliferation of children's shows on cable and the rarity of family viewing, in conjunction with the finding that isolated children tend to view mostly entertainment and comedy shows, the same concerns arise as in the early days of television. In other words, it is possible that the increase of children's shows on cable does not imply a higher quality of viewing. For example, it has been found that children with cable watch more cartoons than children without cable do (simply because cable offers cartoons on weekdays and weekends, whereas most broadcast stations have cartoons only on weekends; Huston & Wright, 1996). As a result, children with cable view fewer child-informative programs.

## Computer-Based Media

The introduction of television into American households marked a transition that allowed for an entirely new experience in the world of mass media. Today, yet another novel transition is taking place, namely the introduction of computer-based technologies into homes. The major and significant difference between these novel media and other mass media is the high level of interaction and active involvement that is called for. The impressive growth of these media is a testament to their popularity, and it is the interactive element with which the old media must compete.

The effects of these interactive media on society have been a topic of active research because of the possibility of adverse or beneficial consequences. And, naturally, the effects on children and adolescents have been of particular concern. Ever since their appearance, computers have been enthusiastically used by children and adolescents. Given the rapid pace at which children are adopting and using computers, and considering the possible educational or social effects that possibly may be more effective than television, it behooves researchers to examine this new relationship. Research in this area, however, is still in its infancy, and so little can be said with great certainty. As a result, much of the following discussion is based on only one source, the Current Population Survey results conducted by the U.S. Census Bureau (1999). A more in-depth discussion will ensue in later chapters of this book.

According to that Census study, 36.6% of American households had computers in 1997. The data also show that personal computer penetration for households with children (ages 6-17) was 51%, while the same number for households with no children was 31%. This implies that the presence of a child in a household is a strong predictor of computer ownership. What is equally interesting is that, with a substantial increase in computer use for all segments of the population, far more children have been using computers than adults (74.4% vs. 47.1%; see Figure 1.4).

When the householder's attributes are considered, the educational background of the householder emerges as a strong predictor of computer ownership; 15% of the children in households where the householder had less than a high school education had a computer, compared with 80% of the children in households where the householder had a bachelor's degree or higher (U.S. Census Bureau, 1999). It is likely that parents purchase computers with their children's education in mind. In fact, data suggest that home computers are used mostly for running educational software. Table 1.2 indicates the home computer uses of children 3 to 17. It shows that, for the entire age range, for both genders, and all income levels, the highest-ranking purpose for using computers is education.

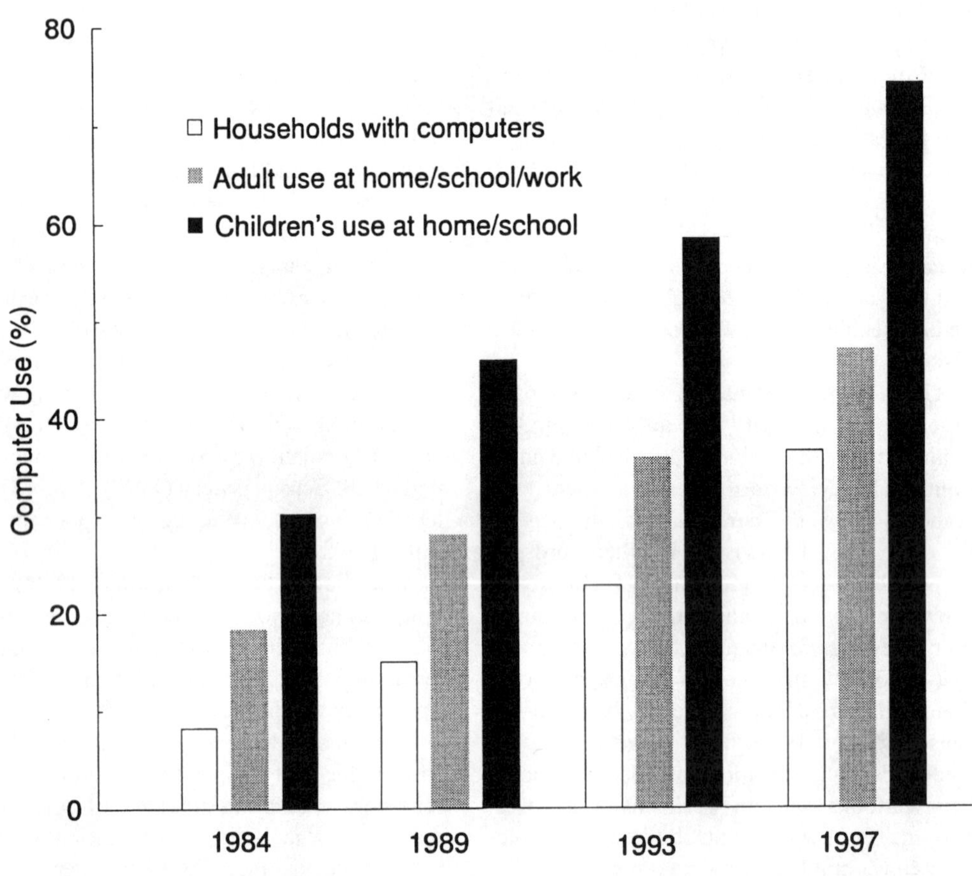


**Figure 1.4.** Computer Presence in the Home, and Use Anywhere, by Year
SOURCE: U.S. Census Bureau Current Population Survey (October 1984, 1989, 1993, 1997).

### *Educational Software*

Educational programs for children have been one of the primary categories in the personal computer market since the technology became available. Such early spread of educational software is promising since it shows that the use of personal computers goes beyond the entertainment function of commercial television, expanding the educational opportunities for children.

The software market has been producing "edutainment" (education + entertainment) programs for children. Typical programs for 6- to 9-month-old infants involve shapes, colors, animal sounds, and nursery rhymes. For toddlers, programs teach numbers and vocabulary while developing computer mouse skills. Some of these programs are spin-offs of television and cable programs for children 12 to 18 months (e.g., *Play With the Teletubbies* from PBS and the British Broadcasting Company [BBC] and *Blue's Clues* from Nickelodeon). According to the numbers in Table 1.2, the edutainment movement has been extremely successful in securing the children's market.

Although at first teenagers posed a difficult challenge, the software industry was soon able to capture that segment of the market as

**TABLE 1.2** Purpose of Computer Use at Home, by Children 3 to 17 Years

| | *Total Number of Children* | *% Word Processing* | *% E-mail* | *% Games* | *% Graphics/ Design* | *% School Assignments* | *% Education Programs* | *% Learning the Computer* | *% Internet* | *% Log-in School* | *% Other Reasons* |
|---|---|---|---|---|---|---|---|---|---|---|---|
| Total using computer at home | 24,550 | 38.9 | 14.7 | 83.0 | 18.0 | 56.2 | 93.3 | 24.6 | 19.9 | 1.7 | 2.0 |
| Age | | | | | | | | | | | |
| 3-5 years | 2,947 | 4.2 | 0.8 | 87.1 | 9.8 | 4.7 | 95.3 | 28.3 | 2.0 | 0.4 | 1.3 |
| 6-11 years | 15,815 | 36.6 | 13.4 | 87.0 | 18.6 | 57.3 | 93.0 | 26.6 | 19.0 | 1.4 | 2.0 |
| 12-17 years | 5,787 | 62.7 | 25.4 | 70.1 | 20.3 | 79.5 | 93.2 | 17.1 | 31.6 | 3.1 | 2.5 |
| Gender | | | | | | | | | | | |
| Male | 12,635 | 36.0 | 14.4 | 86.5 | 17.2 | 55.4 | 93.7 | 24.4 | 20.5 | 1.9 | 1.8 |
| Female | 11,915 | 42.0 | 15.0 | 79.4 | 18.8 | 57.1 | 92.9 | 24.7 | 19.3 | 1.4 | 2.3 |
| Family Income | | | | | | | | | | | |
| Under $25,000 | 2,708 | 30.6 | 8.8 | 80.7 | 14.2 | 49.8 | 88.5 | 25.2 | 11.4 | 0.9 | 3.0 |
| $25,000-$49,999 | 7,090 | 33.7 | 11.3 | 83.6 | 17.8 | 53.8 | 91.3 | 24.2 | 15.2 | 1.8 | 2.0 |
| $50,000-$74,999 | 6,290 | 41.4 | 15.8 | 83.6 | 18.7 | 57.5 | 95.5 | 23.9 | 22.2 | 1.7 | 2.0 |
| $75,000+ | 6,737 | 45.7 | 20.3 | 83.9 | 19.4 | 60.0 | 96.1 | 26.2 | 26.5 | 1.8 | 1.7 |
| Not reported | 1,725 | 37.4 | 12.0 | 78.9 | 16.4 | 56.9 | 90.3 | 21.4 | 18.8 | 1.8 | 2.1 |

SOURCE: U.S. Census Bureau Current Population Survey (October 1997).

well. In 1993, about 30% of children ages 3 to 17 were using computers for educational programs (U.S. Census Bureau, 1995); the same number in 1997 was more than 90%. In fact, in 1997, the most frequent use of home computers for teenagers was for educational programs (U.S. Census Bureau, 1999). There has been a tremendous increase in the use of educational software among children and adolescents. The growth is mostly the result of a wider variety of edutainment packages with much-improved graphics and story lines (Pete, 1996). That accomplishment is even more impressive with the realization that closely competing with educational purposes is the use of home computers for simply playing games (Table 1.2).

### *Video Games*

The first interactive video games originated in 1962. In the 1970s, computers were mostly mainframe computers and, thus, inaccessible to most people. During that time, video games were played in video arcades. Then, in 1972, microcomputer games were introduced alongside arcade systems, and by the 1980s, even home computers were thought of as game computers. In the mid-1980s, video game popularity surged until the overload of similar games led to a decline in interest and sales. But in the late 1980s, the Nintendo system was introduced—a computer solely for games—and the video game industry regained its popularity. In the 1990s, with the growth of CD technology, CD-ROM games led the market with much-improved graphics and realism.

As with other media, the question of who plays, and how much, is a complex one. The answer depends on numerous other variables. Some simple trends, however, are known. For instance, regarding age and gender, it is known (see Table 1.2) that 87% of younger children and 70% of adolescents are playing games on computers, and slightly more boys (87%) are playing games than girls (79%). As for how much, in the 1980s, around the time when video games first became popular, studies reported a wide range of times spent on video games. Selnow (1984) found that heavy players spent 4.5 hours per week playing games at arcades, while light players were spending under 30 minutes per week. (Interestingly, he also found that heavy users of arcade video games were also heavy television viewers.) More recently, Funk (1993), in his survey of 900 fourth through eighth graders, found a playing time that ranges from no time to more than 10 hours per week. One explanation for the wide variation in time use is that initial heavy playing of video games occurs when a system is new to a home, and within a few weeks video game playing normalizes to much lighter play periods (Creasey & Myers, 1986).

Game preferences, too, have been investigated. Funk (1993) surveyed 357 seventh and eighth graders and found that the most popular game category was fantasy violence (32%), followed by sports (29%), general entertainment (20%), human violence (17%), and educational games (2%). The same study also found significant gender differences in game habits and in self-perceptions. In particular, boys spent more time playing video games and favored more violent games. As for girls, those who played more games were likely to show signs of low self-esteem. In a more recent analysis of video game preferences, the same authors (Buchman & Funk, 1996) analyzed 900 children in fourth through ninth grade and revealed that the highest- and the lowest-ranking program preferences found in the earlier study (i.e., fantasy violence and educational games, respectively) maintained the same ranks. However, the rates were alarmingly different: Whereas 32% of the earlier sample had shown preference for fantasy violence, that rate had increased to 50% in the later sample. In the older age groups in the later sample, girls expressed a stronger preference for fantasy (cartoon) violence, while boys were more likely to choose games containing human violence.

Although it is highly likely that video games are here to stay, given their short history it is difficult to anticipate their future consequences.

### *The Internet*

The idea of the Internet dates back to the 1950s, but the current design can be traced to 1969 when the Defense Department computer network allowed military contractors and universities doing military research to exchange information with each other in an electronic fashion. However, the birth of the Internet as a public domain entity had to await the development of the personal computer by International Business Machines (IBM) in 1975—and the price reductions necessary for mass affordability in the early 1980s. Finally, in 1987, the basic structure of the Internet was formed when the National Science Foundation created a network giving researchers access to five supercomputing centers that were connected to hundreds of other networks operated by educational institutions, government agencies, and research organizations (Cozic, 1997; Hudson, 1997). Today, supercomputers play no role in driving the Internet, for it is almost entirely based on thousands of "smaller" and even desktop computers.

Since the late 1980s, the Internet has been growing rapidly, expanding by 50% every year in the 1990s. The growth has been encouraged by ordinary computer users' interest in the World Wide Web (WWW) and other Internet features (Dizard, 2000). The WWW (also known as the Web), one of many Internet-based communication systems, was originally conceived and developed to meet the need for instantaneous information exchange between large high-energy physics collaborations working in different universities and institutes all over the world. That development has been attributed mostly to Tim Berners-Lee and Robert Cailiau, computer scientists at the European Laboratory for Particle Physics (CERN), who developed the first Web client (a browser-editor) and the first Web server, along with most of the communications software, defining URLs, HTTP, and HTML (European Laboratory for Particle Physics, 1998). From there, the Web spread rapidly to other fields and grew to its present impressive size.

A 1998 survey by the NEC Research Institute estimated that the Web contained 320 million publicly indexable pages of information and entertainment (Lawrence & Giles, 1998). Just a year later that number had increased to 800 million, a 250% increase in the number of web pages (Lawrence & Giles, 1999). For Internet consumers, the challenge is finding the desired websites, particularly since no search engine has indexed more than 16% of the Web.

Even 16% of 800 million pages amounts to a great deal of information, and the power of the Internet lies in allowing ordinary users, including children, to access this vast amount of information. The 1997 Census data indicate that nearly 20% of children used home computers to access the Internet, and more recent research suggests that children and teenagers are the two largest growing sectors on the Internet (Jupiter Communications, 1999). According to statistics from Jupiter Communications, approximately 8.6 million kids (5-12 years old) and 8.4 million teenagers (13-18 years old) were on-line in 1998. By 2002, it is projected that these numbers will increase to 21.9 million children (a 155% increase) and 16.6 million teens (almost a 100% increase; Kirchner, 1999).

The uses of the Internet and the various reasons for children's use of it are just as varied as those of other media. The 1997 Census data suggest that the most frequent purpose of Internet use by children and adolescents was to find government, business, health, or educational information (76%); followed by e-mail (57.5%); chat rooms (32%); seeking news, weather, and sports information (28%); newsgroups (5%); and taking courses (3%). When boys and girls are compared, they tend to use the Internet for similar purposes. However, there are two differences. Boys use the Internet more than girls for gathering information on news, weather, and sports (35.4% vs. 19.7%), while girls use the Internet more than boys for e-mail (61.6% vs. 54.4%).

The Internet is truly in its infancy, and if anything has been learned from the history and evolution of other media, it is that during times of transition, when a new medium is introduced, little can be said with certainty. Currently, the Internet appears to have disturbed the partial equilibrium that previous media had been enjoying, and, as a result, the media world appears to be somewhat chaotic. Although only time will tell of the future of the Internet and other media, the policy decisions that are made now, during this time of turmoil, are apt to affect that future.

## Concluding Remarks

The history and evolution of media resemble that of species in nature: The introduction of a new medium (species) typically changes the uses and interactions among the existing media. This is not surprising given that the system consisting of media and ecological systems are both based on very similar principles (e.g., the survival of the fittest). By the same token, the two systems display some generally common features in their evolution. For example, the evolution of ecological systems is marked by what has been termed punctuated equilibrium (Eldridge, 1985; Gould, 1984); rather than in a steady and gradual fashion, changes occur in short-time frames separated by long periods of relative quiescence. This is, in fact, how media have evolved as well. Following the introduction of movies over a short span of time, they enjoyed their golden age, accompanied by relatively little change, until radio came along. The evolution of radio, television, and interactive media has followed the same general pattern.

To illustrate that idea in a bit more detail, consider television. In its early days, television substantially affected activities. Some of the changes were impressive, if not socially significant (e.g., bedtime being postponed about 13 minutes; Schramm et al., 1961). Other more significant changes included less engagement in activities such as reading, visiting with friends, driving for pleasure, participation in sport activities, radio listening, movie attendance, and conversational interaction (McDonagh, 1950). However, in more recent times, even the proliferation of media content distribution channels (i.e., multiple television sets, cable television, and VCRs) has changed our behavior only slightly. Viewers tend to watch similar programs, or even reruns of the same programs, broadcast over the air (Barwise & Ehrenberg, 1988). The viewing behavior follows the same sort of punctuated pattern in that there are times when it is erratic, followed by times of consistent and predictable behavior. The new channels have, therefore, not revolutionized viewing choices or viewing behavior.

Of course, in a punctuated history of media, it is still possible to identify some of the underlying processes. To survive radio's challenge, the motion picture industry was forced to move to sound and later to color films. More direct and compelling challenges to movies came from television. Television provided the same entertainment function that movies provided but with the added convenience of delivering programs directly to homes. To survive this threat, the movie industry had to cooperate with television by providing materials for broadcasting. As for radio, it had to reinvent itself to survive the television challenge. Radio was forced to move from being a staple at the center of the living room to becoming portable and physically going to where television could not. The television industry, in an effort to survive with multimedia, introduced high-definition television, a breakthrough toward the computerization of home television sets. This digital technology is expected to provide multimedia Internet services for the television networks and local stations. Radio, too, has taken the step toward digital broadcasting in what is referred to as digital audio broadcasting.

The Internet offers an environment in which all of these media can coexist. With high-speed Internet connections provided by either telephone wire, a cable television line, or a satellite link, new entertainment options such as movies-on-demand, radio, television, and "live" on-line games against many players scattered around the globe have become reality. One question that arises is the one that has been visited every time a new medium has emerged: namely, that of the effect on children. For example, the interactive and distributed (less centralized) nature of the Internet makes it difficult to monitor children's use of the Internet. The notion of monitoring children's usage patterns of media is not new, but what is new is the significantly larger amount of information to be monitored. And what exacerbated the problem is that almost all of that information is available to children and free of charge. Of course, the Internet can serve both prosocial and antisocial functions, but it is disconcerting that only 6% of the Internet contains educational content. That number is more meaningful when it is compared with the 1.5% of the Internet containing pornographic material (Lawrence & Giles, 1999). Given that 800 million web pages exist, that fraction amounts to 12 million pornographic pages—clearly unsuitable for children.

The discussion of interactive media in this chapter is incomplete because the jury is still out on that topic, and that of the other media is incomplete because there is simply too much to discuss in the span of a single chapter. The primary aim has been to provide only a historical perspective, from the early days to contemporary times, within which the role of children in each medium can be examined in greater detail. The latter task, however, is relinquished to the following chapters.

## References


Adler, R. P., Lesser, G. S., Meringoff, L. K., Robertson, T. S., Rossiter, J. R., & Ward, S. (1980). *The effects of television advertising on children: Review and recommendations.* Lexington, MA: Lexington Books.

Adoni, H. (1979). The functions of mass media in the political socialization of adolescents. *Communication Research, 6,* 84-106.

Baker, R. K., & Ball, S. J. (1969). *Mass media and violence: Staff report to the National Commission on the causes and prevention of violence* (Vol. 9). Washington, DC: U.S. Government Printing Office.

Barnoux, E. (1967). *A tower in Babel: History of broadcasting in the United States.* New York: Oxford University Press.

Barnoux, E. (1990). *Tube of plenty.* New York: Oxford University Press.

Barwise, T. P., & Ehrenberg, A. S. C. (1988). *Television and its audience.* Newbury Park, CA: Sage.

Bazalgette, C., & Staples, T. (1995). Unshrinking the kids: Children's cinema and the family film. In C. Bazalgette & D. Buckingham (Eds.), *In front of the children: Screen entertainment and young audiences* (pp. 92-108). London: British Film Institute.

Bianchi, S. M., & Robinson, J. (1997). What did you do today? Children's use of time, family composition, and acquisition of social capital. *Journal of Marriage and the Family, 59,* 332-344.

Brown, J. D., Childers, K. W., Bauman, K. E., & Koch, G. G. (1990). The influence of mew media and family structure on young adolescents' television and radio use. *Communication Research, 17,* 65-82.

Brown, R. B., Eicher, S. A., & Petrie, S. (1986). The importance of peer group ("crowd") affiliation in adolescence. *Journal of Adolescence, 9,* 73-96.

Buchman, D. D., & Funk, J. B. (1996). Video and computer games in the '90s: Children's time commitment and game preference. *Children Today, 24,* 12-16.

Carpenter, C. J., Huston, A. C., & Spera, L. (1989). Children's use of time in their everyday activities during middle childhood. In M. Bloch & A. Pellegrini (Eds.), *The ecological context of children's play* (pp. 165-190). Norwood, NJ: Ablex.

Carroll, R. L., Silbergleid, M. I., Beachum, C. J., Perry, S. D., Pluscht, P. J., & Pescatore, M. J. (1993). Meanings of radio to teenagers in a niche-programming era. *Journal of Broadcasting & Electronic Media, 37,* 159-176.

Charters, W. W. (1933). *Motion pictures and youth: A summary.* New York: Macmillan.

Christenson, P. G., & DeBenedittis, P. (1986). "Eavesdropping" on the FM band: Children's use of radio. *Journal of Communication, 36*(2), 27-38.

Clark, W. R. (1939). Radio listening activities of children. *Journal of Experimental Education, 8,* 44-48.

Comstock, G., Chaffee, S., Katzman, N., McCombs, M., & Roberts, D. (1978). *Television and human behavior.* New York: Columbia University Press.

Comstock, G., & Paik, H. (1991). *Television and the American child.* San Diego, CA: Academic Press.

Condry, J. (1989). *The psychology of television.* Hillsdale, NJ: Lawrence Erlbaum.

Cozic, C. (1997). *The future of the Internet.* San Diego, CA: Greenhaven Press.

Creasey, G. L., & Myers, B. J. (1986). Video games and children: Effects on leisure activities, schoolwork, and peer involvement. *Merrill-Palmer Quarterly, 32,* 251-262.

Cressey, P. (1934). The motion picture as informal education. *Journal of Educational Sociology, 7,* 504-515.

Dale, E. (1935). *Children's attendance at motion pictures.* New York: Macmillan.

DeBoer, J. J. (1937). The determination of children's interests in radio drama. *Journal of Applied Psychology, 21,* 456-463.

Dizard, W. P. (2000). *Old media, new media: Mass communications in the information age* (3rd ed.). Reading, MA: Addison-Wesley.

Eisenberg, A. (1936). *Children and radio programs.* New York: Columbia University Press.

Eldridge, N. (1985). *Time frames: The rethinking of Darwinian evolution and the theory of punctuated equilibria.* New York: Simon & Schuster.

European Laboratory for Particle Physics. (1998). *A CERN invention you are familiar with: The World Wide Web* [On-line]. [Retrieved June 1999]. Available: www.cern.ch/Public/ACHIEVEMENTS/web.html

Friedrich, L., & Stein, A. H. (1973). Aggressive and prosocial television programs and the natural behavior of preschool children. *Monographs of the Society for Research in Child Development, 38*(4, Serial No. 151).

Funk, J. (1993). Reevaluating the impact of video games. *Clinical Pediatrics, 32,* 86-90.

Golinko, B. E. (1984). Adolescences: Common pathways through life. *Adolescence, 19,* 749-751.

Gould, S. J. (1984). Toward the vindication of punctuational change. In W. A. Berggren & J. A. Van Couvering (Eds.), *Catastrophes and earth history: The new uniformitarianism* (pp. 9-34). Princeton, NJ: Princeton University Press.

Greenberg, B. S. (1974). Gratifications of television viewing and their correlates for British children. In J. G. Blumler & E. Katz (Eds.), *The uses of mass communications: Current perspectives on gratifications research* (pp. 71-92). Beverly Hills, CA: Sage.

Gruenberg, S. M. (1933). Programs for children. In L. Tyson (Ed.), *Radio and education* (pp. 171-195). Chicago: University of Chicago Press.

Heeter, C. (1988). Watching Saturday morning television. In C. Heeter & B. S. Greenberg (Eds.), *Cableviewing* (pp. 89-96). Norwood, NJ: Ablex.

Hollenbeck, A. R., & Slaby, R. G. (1979). Infant visual and vocal responses to television. *Child Development, 50,* 41-45.

Hudson, D. (1997). *Rewired: A brief (and opinionated) Net history.* Indianapolis, IN: Macmillan Technical.

Huston, A. C., & Wright, J. C. (1996). Television and socialization of young children. In T. M. MacBeth (Ed.), *Tuning in to young viewers: Social science perspectives on television* (pp. 37-60). Thousand Oaks, CA: Sage.

Huston, A. C., Wright, J. C., Marquis, J., & Green, S. B. (1999). How young children spend their time: Television and other activities. *Developmental Psychology, 35,* 912-925.

Jersild, A. T. (1939). Radio and motion pictures. In G. M. Wipple (Ed.), *The thirty-eighth yearbook of the National Society for Study of Education* (pp. 153-160). Bloomington, IL: Public School Publishing.

Johnstone, J. W. C. (1974). Social integration and mass media use among adolescents: A case study. In J. G. Blumler & E. Katz (Eds.), *The uses of mass communications: Current perspectives on gratifications research* (pp. 35-47). Beverly Hills, CA: Sage.

Jupiter Communications. (1999, June). *Kids and teens spend $1.3 billion online in 2002* [On-line]. [Retrieved June 1999]. Available: http://jup.com/jupiter/press/releases/1999

Kirchner, J. (1999, August). The Web's hip-hop future. *PC Magazine,* p. 28.

Larson, R., & Kubey, R. (1985). Television and music: Contrasting media in adolescent life. In M. Gurevitch & M. R. Levy (Eds.), *Mass communication review yearbook* (Vol. 5, pp. 395-413). Beverly Hills, CA: Sage.

Larson, R., Kubey, R., & Colletti, J. (1989). Changing channels: Early adolescent media choices and shifting investments in family and friends. *Journal of Youth and Adolescence, 18,* 583-599.

Lawrence, F. C., & Wozniak, P. H. (1989). Children's television viewing with family members. *Psychological Reports, 65,* 396-400.

Lawrence, S., & Giles, L. (1998). Searching the World Wide Web. *Science, 280,* 98-100.

Lawrence, S., & Giles, L. (1999). Accessibility and distribution of information on the Web. *Nature, 400,* 107-109.

Lyle, J., & Hoffman, H. R. (1972). Children's use of television and other media. In E. A. Rubinstein, G. A. Comstock, & J. P. Murray (Eds.), *Television and social behavior: Vol. 4. Television in day-to-day life: Patterns of use* (pp. 129-256). Washington, DC: U.S. Government Printing Office.

Lyness, P. (1951). Patterns in the mass communications tastes of the young audience. *Journal of Educational Psychology, 42*(8), 449-467.

Lyness, P. (1952). The place of the media in the lives of boys and girls. *Journalism Quarterly, 29,* 43-54.

Maccoby, E. (1951). Television: Its impact on school children. *Public Opinion Quarterly, 15,* 421-444.

Mauldin, T., & Meeks, C. B. (1991). Mother's employment status, family income, and children's time allocation. *Home Economics Research Journal, 19,* 271-281.

McDonagh, E. C. (1950). Television and the family. *Sociology and Social Research, 35*(2), 113-122.

Mendelsohn, H. (1964). Listening to radio. In L. A. Dexter & D. M. White (Eds.), *People, society, and mass communications* (pp. 239-249). New York: Free Press.

Nielsen Media Research. (1998). *1998 report on television.* New York: Author.

Patchen, R. H., Burgess, B. B., & Cralley, M. D. (1994). *The Arbitron family radio listening pilot study: Summary of sample performance, respondent reinterview, and ratings results.* New York: Arbitron.

Pearl, D., Bouthilet, L., & Lazar, J. (Eds.). (1982). *Television and behavior: Ten years of scientific progress and implications for the eighties: Vol. 1. Summary report.* Washington, DC: U.S. Government Printing Office.

Pete, H. (1996, September 16). Software become more teen-friendly. *Discount Store News, 35,* 21-23.

Petrozzello, D. (1998, January 5). Kids crave cable. *Broadcasting & Cable, 128,* 18.

Roberts, D. F., & Bachen, C. M. (1981). Mass communication effects. *Annual Review of Psychology, 32,* 307-356.

Rosengren, K. E., & Windahl, S. (1989). *Media matter: TV use in childhood and adolescence.* Norwood, NJ: Ablex.

Rubin, A. M. (1977). Television usage, attitudes, and viewing behavior of children and adolescents. *Journal of Broadcasting, 21,* 355-369.

Schramm, W., Lyle, J., & Parker, E. B. (1961). *Television in the lives of our children.* Stanford, CA: Stanford University Press.

Selnow, G. W. (1984). Playing video games: The electronic friend. *Journal of Communication, 34*(2), 148-156.

Simmons Market Research. (1995). *The kids study.* New York: Author.

Singer, J. L., & Singer, D. G. (1981). *Television, imagination, and aggression: A study of preschoolers.* Hillsdale, NJ: Lawrence Erlbaum.

Stewart, R. F. (1952). *The social impact of television on Atlanta households.* Atlanta: Emory University, Division of Journalism.

St. Peters, M., Fitch, J., Huston, A. C., Wright, J. C., & Eakins, D. J. (1991). Television and families: What do young children watch with their parents? *Child Development, 62,* 1409-1423.

Surgeon General's Scientific Advisory Committee on Television and Social Behavior. (1972). *Television and growing up: The impact of televised violence* [Report to the surgeon general, U.S. Public Health Service]. Washington, DC: U.S. Government Printing Office.

Timmer, S. G., Eccles, J., & O'Brien, K. (1985). How children use time. In F. G. Juster & F. P. Stafford (Eds.), *Time, goods, and well-being* (pp. 353-382). Ann Arbor: University of Michigan Institute for Social Research.

Turow, J. (1999). *The Internet and the family: The view from parents, the view from the press* (Report Series). Philadelphia: University of Pennsylvania, Annenberg Public Policy Center.

UNESCO. (1953). *Television: A world survey.* Paris: Author.

U.S. Census Bureau. (1995). *Current Population Reports (CPR): Computer use in the United States: October 1993* [On-line]. [Retrieved June 1999]. Available: www.census.gov/population

U.S. Census Bureau. (1999). *Current Population Reports (CPR): Computer use in the United States: October 1997* [On-line]. [Retrieved June 1999]. Available: www.census.gov/population

Wartella, E., Alexander, A., & Lemish, D. (1979). The mass media environment of children. *American Behavioral Scientist, 23,* 33-52.

Wells, A., & Hakanen, E. A. (1991). The emotional use of popular music by adolescents. *Journalism Quarterly, 68,* 445-454.

Whetmore, E. J. (1981). *The magic medium: An introduction to radio in America.* Belmont, CA: Wadsworth.

Witty, P., Garfield, S., & Brink, W. (1941). Interests of high school students in motion pictures and radio. *Journal of Educational Psychology, 32*(3), 176-184.

Wright, J. C., St. Peters, M., & Huston, A. C. (1990). Family television use and its relation to children's cognitive skills and social behavior. In J. Bryant (Ed.), *Television and the American family* (pp. 227-251). Hillsdale, NJ: Lawrence Erlbaum.

# CHAPTER 2

# Free Reading

## Implications for Child Development

ROGER DESMOND
University of Hartford

My early memories of childhood reading are among the most vivid in my repertoire. Indeed, I can recall my first flash of literacy. It came at the age of 4 while "reading" a Superman comic. By sounding out consonants and vowels alongside the colorful pictures, I read—with awareness—the words "Look! It's a giant hand!" A flood of sensations overcame me—I could read! I remember eagerly, if haltingly, devouring the comic book and moving on to more challenging material.

I know that one of the books that quickly followed was a richly illustrated volume titled *A Child's Garden of Verses,* by Robert Louis Stevenson. I recall the pastel colors of the illustrations (drawn by, as I recently discovered, the noted American illustrator Jessie Willcox Smith), with images of starfishes on beaches, the moon and stars, and, of course, flower and vegetable gardens. Upon concentration, I recall some of the poems, including "My Garden Sings of Many Things" and "My Shadow." I also have intense memories of Anna Sewell's *Black Beauty,* the original talking horse. It seems clear to me that the *Francis the Talking Mule* films had to have been inspired by that book, as was the TV show *Mr. Ed.* The next books I remember were from *The Adventures of Tom Swift* series; in retrospect, I am certain that they were re-editions of books my father read. Tom was a boy who had adult-like adventures as an explorer and inventor. Who wouldn't prefer his life?

This reading, done in the first three elementary school grades, was purely hedonic; there was no purpose at all, except to absolutely lose myself in the unfolding fantasies of story. This is not to say that these stories had no effects on my early experiences in school, on my view of others, and on fantasy play. I was simply unaware of any outcomes except the immediate and total pleasure I felt when I started to examine a new book. The examination of the influences of reading on child development is the purpose of this chapter. The inspiration, however, comes from these poignant vignettes from my own early years as a reader.

I have chosen the term *free reading* in the title of this chapter after educator Stephen

Krashen's (1993) definition: when children choose their own reading for the purpose of pleasure rather than to produce a book report or to answer specific questions. The thrust of this chapter is on the consequences of pleasure reading on a child's emotional, social, and cognitive development, but some research on the impact of reading on school achievement will also be reviewed. Issues related to the teaching of reading will not be the focus of this chapter, embroiled in the politics of language education as they are presently and also because of their inseparability from more basic lines of linguistic research.

During more than two decades of teaching university courses, I have arrived at the conclusion that the element that most differentiates me from my undergraduates is that I am a book person and they are not. In a recent class of 70 college sophomores, I found 9 who openly admitted that they had read no books for pleasure in their entire lives! Deprived of the joy I experienced as a young reader, it is no wonder that their academic work is not their first priority; to get through school, they have to read!

## Beginning to Read

Children beginning to read must have a number of cognitive subsystems in place, including phonological awareness, memory, the ability to coordinate perception with small motor movement, and a number of other skills. Awareness of the operation of symbols is also necessary. Most children recognize that the golden arches stand for McDonald's by age 3, but this does not mean that they can decode more complex symbols (Snow, Burns, & Griffin, 1998). They must learn how symbols work; that numbers, for example, can be represented by their Arabic symbols or spelled alphabetically, and, above all, that letters *stand for* sounds that can be combined.

Metacognition is also involved in the beginning stages of reading. Children need to grasp that language itself must be thought about and considered from several perspectives. Playing games with sounds, rhyming, and discovering onomatopoeia are all aspects of metacognition that help launch a young reader. Research has demonstrated that, initially, children are trapped by an inability to separate words from their referents; that is, that the word *road* is *not* a long word and that *driveway* is not a short one (Chaney, 1992). The basis for this metalinguistic development is all of the aspects of language inherent in oral language acquisition, including vocabulary development, word recognition, and the resolution of issues such as synonymy and ambiguity.

Research has always indicated rapid vocabulary growth in the first 5 years of life, but more recent work has shown that the exposure to new words alters and refines the semantic representations of words already in the child's vocabulary and the relationships among them (Landauer & Dumais, 1997). Vocabulary growth is more than simply a catalog of words that a child can define.

In careful observations by Katherine Nelson and her colleagues, symbolic play was observed to be important in increasing toddlers' abilities to combine words into sentences (Singer & Singer, 1990, p. 131). Scripted play, built around themes (e.g., "washing clothes," "baking," "working at McDonald's"), produced longer and more complex sentences than did short interjections or brief emotional displays (e.g., "I'm not your friend, then"). Presumably, these more sophisticated expressions produced in play will lead to increased vocabulary, a precursor to sophisticated reading. Scripted, "let's pretend" kinds of play involve descriptions of roles that must be mastered, actions that should be taken, and metaphorical uses of people and objects. This dimension of play will not only draw on elements of stories that children have read but also have the potential to stimulate interest in new stories for play material.

The actual beginning of complete or "adult-like" reading is probably when the child goes beyond asking about the pictures in a book and asks or comments about the meaning of the written text on the page. As Snow et al. (1998) suggest, early reading is a place where children can begin to escape from the immediacy of a situation, being able to speculate about what might be, the past, and issues beyond the immediate environment. These skills will serve them well in both read-alone and school environments, where decontextualized language is a necessity.

What else is required to become a good reader? Apart from sheer vocabulary, lexical-orthographic knowledge, more related to knowledge of spelling than to phonological awareness, is also necessary for reading. This lexical knowledge helps to elicit automaticity in the operation and is acquired through experience, primarily through reading (Stanovich, West, Cunningham, Cipielewski, & Siddiqui, 1996). Phonology and lexical knowledge are separate but overlapping processes, one reinforcing the other as a database for reading begins to accumulate.

A growing body of research suggests that the more children's classroom literacy experience resembles their home experience, the better readers they will become. Children who are dependent on school for their literacy experience begin their reading careers with a deficit. Prior to age 5, readers who have been read to will use language and intonation similar to that used in "real" reading, look at pictures in story-relevant sequences, and insist that adults who are reading silently are not reading. They will frequently examine pages without reading them, instead citing passages that they remember from read-aloud sessions (Sulzby & Kaderavek, 1996). Summarizing work done comparing skilled with less-skilled readers, Snow et al. (1998) conclude,

> Briefly put, we can say that children need simultaneous access to some knowledge of letter-sound relationships, some sight vocabulary, and some comprehension strategies. In each case, "some" indicates that exhaustive knowledge of these aspects is not needed to get the child reading conventionally; rather, each child seems to need varying amounts of knowledge to get started, but then he or she needs to build up the kind of inclusive and automatic knowledge that will let the fact that reading is being done fade into the background while the reasons for reading are fulfilled. (p. 57)

## How Much Do Children Read?

Reading frequency among contemporary young children is sobering, especially from the perspective of a person with a background of extensive reading. A longitudinal study of 25,000 eighth graders (U.S. Department of Education, 1990) found that students watch 21.2 hours of TV per week but read only 1.9 hours outside of school reading, including textbooks! In a related study (Anderson, Fielding, & Wilson, 1988), 90% of a sample of fifth graders spent less than 1% of their leisure time reading, in contrast to 33% of their time watching TV. A recent survey of middle school students revealed that only 27% read for pleasure each day; the same sample reported more than 3 hours of TV viewing per day (Campbell, 1998). Campbell also reports data indicating that approximately 50% read only one book in the past year. One time-use investigation revealed that children below age 12 spend an average of 8 minutes per day reading and an average of 2.3 hours per day watching TV (Timmer, Eccles, & O'Brien, 1985). Data from a recent survey of more than 3,000 children and adolescents are somewhat more encouraging; respondents from ages 2 to 14 reported an average of 45 minutes of reading per day, with 25 minutes devoted to books, 16 minutes to magazines, and 4 minutes to newspapers. Since these data are based on self-reports, the amounts may be slightly exaggerated in favor of higher reading amounts (Roberts, Ulla, Rideout, & Brodie, 1999).

Historical data for comparison with modern children are difficult to come by. Much anecdotal evidence suggests that, earlier in the twentieth century, children read much more than they do today, but there is also evidence that parents and, especially, educators were not as concerned about the value of free reading as they are today, hence less survey data are available (Teale, 1995). In terms of gender differences, we know that, by age 7, girls outperform boys on virtually every measure of reading achievement that exists, and since reading skill is directly related to experience, it is reasonable to suggest that girls read more than boys (Bond, 1991; Dwyer, 1974). It is clear that girls have a much more positive attitude toward reading than boys do, and they like what they read more intensely than their male counterparts (Davies & Brember, 1993).

## Consequences of Poor Reading Skills

Children who do not read often do not read well, and children who do not read well frequently develop into adults who not only miss out on the joys of reading but also suffer in the workplace. A recent survey funded by Coors Brewing Company found that 90% of a sample of Fortune 1000 chief executives identified poor reading as a workplace problem (Downey, 1995). Respondents suggested that many problem readers had devised a variety of workplace strategies to hide the deficit. Robert Fowler, chief executive officer of Hampden Papers, a paper manufacturer in Holyoke, Massachusetts, states, "There used to be a time when we had plenty of jobs for people who were functionally illiterate, but today our machines are very complex" (as cited in Downey, 1995, p. 22). His is one organization that offers workplace reading instruction. Frequent results of this deficiency include accidents, misinterpreted orders, customer complaints, and ghostwritten forms and reports.

Poor readers also suffer in the health care system. Marwick (1997) documents longer hospital stays and higher incidences of illness for poor readers than for minimally literate patients, primarily because they are unable to follow directions for therapy and medication. Beyond these specific areas, Edwards (1979) presents evidence that the cultural disadvantages that accrue from the lack of stimulation offered by reading can result in adults who are generally less socially connected and satisfied at the end of their lives than are capable readers.

Every survey of American education finds a sharp decline in reading ability over the past 20 years. The Scholastic Aptitude Test (SAT) verbal decline of about 60 points, or 12%, over the past 20-plus years is by now axiomatic (Itzkoff, 1993). All but the top two or three colleges and universities have been affected. Professorial anecdotal evidence, witnessed in remedial courses in writing and reading skills, confirms what Charles Murray and Richard Herrnstein and others have reported: The decline at the top of our achievement levels, compared with the days of American world dominance in education, is a reality (Herrnstein & Murray, 1991). Although some critics who seek reform argue for higher salaries for teachers, an end to social promotion, and even focusing the entire first 3 years of school on language arts, it is clear that there is a need for immediate intervention. If children are not reading by the third or fourth grade, their days in school become more like time-serving.

## What Are Children Reading?

In the summer of 1999, two books by the same author topped the U.S. Newswire "bestsellers" list for children under 12. They were *Harry Potter and the Sorcerer's Stone* and *Harry Potter and the Sorcerer's Secrets* by the British author J. K. Rowling. Bookstores were flooded with inquiries and orders for a third book several weeks prior to its publication. The content of these books reveals something known to children's librarians, teachers, and concerned parents: While fads and gimmicks come and go in children's literature, certain timeless themes recur in books that are popular with children. In the case of the Rowling books, the themes are the power of magic and its ability to transform the life of a young orphan. Harry Potter is an 11-year-old English boy who was orphaned when his "good witch" parents saved him from an evil witch. The action surrounds Harry's dual life among the "muggles" (ordinary human beings, including his cruel foster parents) and his teachers at the Hogwarts School of Witchcraft, and his progress toward initiation as a sorcerer/magician.

Analysis of children's Internet comments suggests that the majority of them want to go to Hogwarts when they reach boarding school age and that they "finished the book faster than any they have read." The books are absorbing and invite projection; children live in Harry's world when they read these books. The stories also provide multifaceted characters. There is mischief in the best of them and seductiveness in the most evil. Harry is even prompted to wonder about his own culpability in the sudden disappearance of some of the school's black-hearted magicians.

Other "top 10" books in recent years include a 10-year-old Theodore Geisel (Dr. Seuss) book *Oh, the Places You'll Go!* This is vintage Dr. Seuss, with a lead character who rhymes his way across a story that essentially serves up the image of life as a difficult journey but one in which there is much fun to be had. Comments on the book to the Barnes and Noble (1999) Internet home page indicate that some readers are giving the book as a high school or college graduation gift, which is either an indication of the universal appeal of Dr. Seuss or the lack of success of these institutions in their attempts to introduce more sophisticated literature!

For the 2- to 7-year-old reader, Bill Martin's *Brown Bear, Brown Bear, What Do You See?* is still in the top 10 in sales after 30 years. A book that, thanks to illustrator Eric Carle, vividly depicts a number of baby animals being looked at by their mothers is a formula for popularity. Animals and their lives are another predictor of juvenile popularity. Somewhat anomalous is *Westlandia* by Paul Fleischman, a book about an outcast boy named Wesley who hates football and pizza and suffers for his nonconformity at the hands of his classmates. Over the summer, Wesley creates a civilization in his backyard, which is nourished, housed, clothed, and fed by a mysterious plant that grew from seeds he planted. In the end, Wesley's classmates abandon their criticisms and join his plant civilization. Although this book also centers on a magical theme, the illustrations and text are more grounded in 1990s school reality than is the majority of the other popular books for this age group. A series of investigations illustrates the value of imaginary playmates for the development of imagination, creativity, and general happiness, which may help explain the popularity of this book (Singer & Singer, 1990, p. 104).

A recent study of sixth graders' reading preferences found that their favorite reading materials are not often found in school (Worthy, Moorman, & Turner, 1999). Surveys of what they liked to read showed that the most preferred materials were scary stories and books, comics, magazines about popular culture, and books and magazines about sports. Secondary preferences included books about animals, drawing books, and, for boys, books about cars. Few other gender, income, or reading ability differences were found. The most frequent source for books and magazines was bookstores, rather than school libraries. Schools ranked last in sources for reading material, even among low-income students. As children mature into junior high school years, both boys and girls begin to read mysteries, and girls become increasingly attracted to preadolescent romance novels (Kincade & Kleine, 1993).

## Illustration

Books for children are not pure text. The illustrations are a world apart from adult print-heavy volumes, which typically feature only large oceans of print. Children's illustrations guide the reading of the text and provide imagery for imagination, and sometimes illustration-only cloth books are the child's first introduction to stories in book form. In any serious competition in children's literature, there are usually separate categories for illustration. In books such as Maurice Sendak's *Where the Wild Things Are,* illustrations are the raison d'être for the story, rather than an adjunct to the text.

In a recent scholarly treatise on children's literature, the author focuses on an analysis of illustrations more than on the stories themselves (Spitz, 1999). Spitz argues that "A book that's very beautiful gives a child her first experience with color, with shape, with line" (p. 21). Spitz's reading of *Ferdinand the Bull,* for example, shows the delicate bull's resistance to pressures from his mother and from a matador to be aggressive, but the final illustration shows a small black silhouette of the bull facing away from the reader. Children, she argues, do not subordinate the picture to the words of the story, so they will "see" that the world can be very tough for a shy, gentle child. It is quite possible that one reason for the success of World Wide Web children's book vendors such as *amazon.com* is that they use a medium that allows a potential buyer to preview significant illustrations.

## Magazines

Magazines are very much a part of the reading diet of young and preadolescent readers. Magazines are the second most frequent object of reading time, second only to books; children ages 2 to 14 report an average of 16 minutes per day reading magazines (Roberts et al., 1999). For children ages 4 to 8, *Humpty-Dumpty* has been popular for nearly 50 years. It consists of stories, games, and puzzles that appeal to young children, and it enjoys a favorable reputation among educators. *Ladybug,* for 2- to 6-year-olds, is more focused on stories for children, less on games and puzzles. Slightly more education-oriented and intended for the next age group of 7 to 12 is *Jack and Jill,* another long-running favorite. Scouting magazine *Boy's Life,* for the past 87 years an automatic benefit of membership in the Boy Scouts of America, still offers features on camping and wildlife but, with a nod to the electronic age, contains articles on computers and video games as well.

When the target age of readers approaches the preteen years, approximately age 12, gender differences in magazine preferences begin to emerge (Kantrowitz & Wingert, 1999). In terms of number of subscribers, the top five magazines for boys are *Gamepro, Nintendo Power, Electronic Gaming Monthly, Sports Illustrated for Kids,* and *Sport.* For girls, the best-sellers are *Teen Beat, Super Teen, Teen, All About You,* and *Twist.* It is safe to say that, in the category of boys' magazines, there is a utilitarian dimension to free reading. All of the first three titles are designed to make the reader a better electronic game player, and the last two offer advice in sports. The best-selling girls' magazines are even more homogeneous in that they offer articles about teenage celebrities, makeup, and dating tips and advice from the perspective of popular psychology.

## Comics

The comic form—pictures accompanying stories—has been around nearly as long as print. Although the Hearst Corporation's *Yellow Kid* in the latter decade of the nineteenth century is often credited with being the first color comic, the basic form was in place for centuries before the tabloid. Children have always been drawn to fanciful art and accompanying stories, as in the Superman example in the introduction. Twentieth-century comics brought the superheroes: first Superman, then Batman, Plastic Man, and Spiderman, followed by scores of others. One of the most popular comics in history, for a time coming out weekly, was Captain Marvel—definitely a superhero.

What is the attraction to superheroes? They are powerful and able to help others. Since ancient times, children have been drawn to tales of superhuman figures such as Jason, Hercules, Samson, and Gilgamesh. Children have always been attracted to modern literary characters who are able to defeat enemies and who are in possession of weapons and/or superpowers. In the Diamond Comics Distributors Top 10, a reliable indicator of comic popularity as evidenced by retail sales, Marvel Comics' *X-MEN* appears four times. One of the most popular, *Wolverine,* is a part-wolf humanoid who was originally discovered as a feral child. Among his superpowers are retractable claws, healing power, enhanced senses, and immunity to poison. X-MEN travel through time, in water or in space, and confront formidable foes who also have superpowers. Second only to *X-MEN* in popularity is Todd McFarlane's *Spawn.* Spawn represents another dimension of superhero, a dead man who has been allowed to return to the realm of the living to achieve victory over both living and "undead" villains, including the Mafia! It is tempting to speculate that this series was inspired by the growing preoccupation with supernatural themes in film and television.

## Syndicated Comic Strips

Spawn exhibits many of the qualities of vampires but is essentially a superhero who is out to help people, but he is also "dark" and cynical. He is as culturally removed from comics such as *Archie* or *Peanuts* as he is from any of the Disney characters or comic books inspired by syndicated "strip" comics.

Why the trend toward sinister aspects of superheroes and away from playful animals? Bill Watterson, the now-retired creator of *Calvin and Hobbes,* argues that the newspaper comics of his youth have deteriorated into shadows of their former selves, primarily because of the syndicates who own them (Watterson, 1989). Syndicates demand ownership of the characters, including the right to license them for toys and adjunct products. Consequently, only strips with licensing potential survive, limiting the possibilities for many old, previously popular strips. When a comic creator dies, the strip usually continues, often written by a staff of resident artists who have little investment in the original product. Since syndicates exist to maximize profit, the comic panels have shrunk in size, to the point where good graphic art is impossible to achieve, and dialogue suffers as well. The smaller each panel, the more individual strips can be accommodated in one- or two-page comic sections. As Watterson (1989) states,

> At current sizes, there is no room for real dialogue, no room to show action, no room to show exotic worlds or foreign lands, no room to tell a decent story. Consequently, today's comics pages are filled with cartoon characters who sit in blank backgrounds spouting silly puns. Conversation in a comic strip is a thing of the past. (p. 1)

Although many children still seek "the funnies," newspaper circulation and readership are drastically down from previous decades, particularly for children and adolescents, so it is not surprising that comic strips have suffered. In past decades, many comic books emanated from popular strips, but the future of both in the electronic age is, at best, uncertain.

## Manga and Anime

In the assessment of popular children's entertainment forms, it is impossible to ignore the influence of manga, contemporary Japanese comics, and anime, the animated versions of manga stories. Millions of children and adults are avid consumers of comics; many manga comics are for adults only. The contemporary *Pokemon* series is an example of manga and anime that have been embraced by American children, with much marketing of toys and accessories. The 1970s *Speed Racer* cartoon was originally a Japanese anime, as were the enormously popular 1980s *Transformers* cartoons, animations, and toys. The major difference between Japanese and American comics is that manga portray a more complex and realistic view of life (Izawa, 1995). In manga, the death of a major character is frequently portrayed, whereas in American comics the topic is typically avoided.

Manga often portray adults at work, using high-tech computers and communication technologies, an area of life that is nearly invisible in American comics. The people—generally not superheroes—who populate manga work, go to school, and interact with their parents. Characters also have a "secret life" where friends and robots help them to defeat foes. Foes are not necessarily depicted as the embodiment of evil; enemies of manga characters have complex motives, pursuing rational goals. Unlike American superheroes, manga characters make errors and learn from their mistakes; they grow morally and intellectually as stories develop. Izawa (1995) believes that the "everydayness" of manga may be a liberating factor in readers' identification with characters and events. Finally, unlike American superhero comics, manga stories deliberately end. They are designed to finish with a character getting married, going off to college, or even dying. Grounded in familiar reality, the adventures progress and build a kind of bridge to the fantasy world as they develop. It is possible that, as in my own experience as a new reader, comic book reading can open the door to other genres.

## Mythic Dimensions of Reading

Reading has traditionally introduced children to the realm of myth. Every culture has myths that serve to entertain and to instruct; the heroic stories of any culture convey the norms and values of a people by illustrating their highest and lowest aspirations through the activities of heroes and villains. Just as characters like Hestia, in the Greek myths, embodied the characteristics of home and hearth, classical children's characters also celebrate key values and goals to seek. Certainly, the twentieth-century hero Tom Swift represented innovation and intelligence, along with the courage to employ his inventions to positive goals. Frontier stories of Davy Crockett and Daniel Boone reflect the strong individualism of the pioneer.

It is because of the power of myths that feminists have sought to discover female heroes who present strong, intelligent responses to human problems. The Nancy Drew stories that served as summer reading for many baby boomers featured an intelligent female hero, but one who still lived and worked in a man's world. Judy Blume's books, including *Hello, God, It's Me, Margaret,* were a departure radical enough to get them excluded from many school and public libraries. Blume's books, while still maintaining the innocence of preadolescents, also portrayed girls as sexual beings. In this manner, myths show a young reader who and what is valued in a society, and when conflicting subcultures emerge, myths may be a source of deep concern to those who hold power.

Can other children's media such as comics and TV programs serve mythic functions? Joseph Campbell (1949) observed that there are some key fixed elements of mythic stories. Mythic heroes must respond to a *call to adventure* and *cross thresholds,* often overcoming a *guardian.* With the help of *assistants,* they overcome a series of *tests* leading to the *supreme ordeal* to achieve a reward. They then make a return journey and a *reemergence* in their now peaceful everyday world.

In a comic series like *Superman,* there are signs of this mythic pattern. Most of the stories begin with a call to action; Superman reads a newspaper headline announcing the theft of uranium, for example. Superman is often tested—"that's kryptonite, not uranium!" Helpers may come in the form of his colleagues Lois Lane and Jimmy at the *Daily Planet* newspaper—"Lois, see what you can find out about these thugs!" Guardians (Lex Luthor's henchmen) are confronted. The supreme ordeal is confronted: "I will put on a lead suit, which will let me get past the kryptonite and into their lair!" Where the mythic pattern may break down is here, at the reemergence stage. As Joel Grineau (1997) points out, in comics, "there is rarely that last return home, the final loss of powers, and restoration of the world to its former, better condition. Why? The first axiom in comics is that characters rarely stay dead or retired" (p. 2). Unlike the Japanese manga comics, it is bad form to terminate the ongoing adventures of an American hero.

The *Superman* story has biblical elements as well. Like Moses, the young Superboy is discovered and raised by parents who are not biologically his, after traveling a great distance (in Superboy's case, in a starship from his home planet). The hero is discovered to have superpowers that must be used for leading people to a safe and good place.

Although the reader often sees Superman as drab reporter Clark Kent in his restored everyday world, the comic cannot make a story out of such a humdrum life. But within any one comic, a critical mass of mythic elements seems to be present. A typical story concludes with the elements of reemergence and restoration, at least until the next issue. Children's books can also certainly qualify as mythic, especially those that, like the Harry Potter books, offer a story of triumph over adversity. Many popular children's books are simply good narratives, with no mythical dimension at all.

Animated television characters, even those based on books, operate in only a partial realm of myth. Though there are obstacles to overcome, the most typical mythic elements present are *tests* or action-packed events, few of which lead up to the conquest of a dark force and a return to the everyday world.

## Benefits of Reading Aloud

Clearly, there are aesthetic benefits of reading aloud. Cries of "read to me!" begin with most children as soon as they can pronounce the words. In graduate school, one of the female members of a study group in which I was enrolled had a 4-year-old son who often wanted to extend his bedtime. The child would say, "Please, Mom, read to me for a while—nobody reads as good as you!" The strategy was particularly effective since "mom" had previously been a voice instructor and took particular pride in her oratory skills.

A reasonably large body of research reveals the effectiveness of reading aloud in helping children to become effective readers on their own. Children who are frequently read to before first grade will then "read" their favorite books by themselves by engaging in oral-language-like and written-language-like routines (Teale, 1995). For most children at this age, emergent reading routines include attending to pictures and occasionally to salient print, such as that found in illustrations or labels. A few begin to attend to the print in the main body of the text, and a few make the transition into conventional reading with their favorite books. Another investigation in this tradition found that first graders who were read to from children's trade books outperformed controls on a number of measures of reading comprehension (Feitelson, Kita, & Goldstein, 1986). In a review of research on play, the authors cite a number of renowned scholars and authors, including Goethe, E. B. Browning, G. B. Shaw, and many others, who reported vivid memories of their parents reading to them and the impact of these read-aloud experiences on their literary accomplishments (Singer & Singer, 1990).

Trelease's (1995) review of reading research reveals that, in a number of investigations, early readers were read to as young children. The U.S. Department of Education study (1985) "Becoming a Nation of Readers," a review of more than 10,000 research findings, states that "the single most important activity for building the knowledge required for eventual success is reading aloud to children" (p. 247).

Not every investigation has found positive results of reading aloud, especially if the reader is a teacher (Meyer, Stahl, Waldrop, &

Linn, 1994). This study was a longitudinal investigation of two large cohorts of kindergarten to second-grade students that found that, among kindergarten students, there was a *negative* relationship between reading aloud by kindergarten teachers and students' reading achievement, and no relationship for first graders. This was explained in terms of a displacement effect; teachers who read the most *spent the least amount of time teaching activities positively correlated with reading.* For parents, no relationship between reading aloud and reading achievement in their children was found, but there was a positive association between time spent engaging with print and reading achievement.

How do American children measure up as readers in comparison with children of other nations? A 32-nation reading evaluation of 9-year-olds found that the top four nations were Finland, the United States, Sweden, and France (Eley, 1992). By age 14, however, the U.S. rank dropped to eighth. This suggests that American readers begin reading at very high levels but drop off in preadolescence. Even though Finnish children begin reading instruction later than their U.S. counterparts (at age 7), by age 9, Finns are superior readers. Obviously, since reading is a cumulative skill, American readers are not continuing as readers as they approach junior high school age. Trelease (1995) suggests that a major and crucial difference between Scandinavian and American children is that Scandinavian teachers spend more time reading to students than do American teachers, and periods of silent sustained reading in school are much longer for Scandinavian and European children.

A group of Boston physicians has found an innovative method of encouraging lower-income children to read (Rimer, 1997). When children (ages 6 months to 5 years) go to a clinic for treatment or a check-up, they are given an age-appropriate book. The efforts of the clinic have become a national organization called Reach Out and Read. Funded by foundations and individuals, the organization can provide a 5-year-old with a library of 10 books for under $30. Pediatricians encourage reading aloud by "prescribing" books for their patients. Reading aloud, whether in or out of school, is arguably the most effective activity for increasing reading ability in children.

## Methods of Reading Aloud

Calkins (1997) is a strong advocate of reading aloud. She discusses a number of techniques for introducing reading for pleasure to children. Among her recommendations are to make books in the home unavoidable, to supply a variety of books in varying degrees of difficulty, to invite the child to scan pictures for meaning and story-related information, and to have children write about the books they are reading.

The Family Literacy Foundation (1999), a San Diego–based read-aloud advocacy group, points out vast class differences in reading aloud frequency: "Although a typical middle class child arrives at kindergarten with about 1,000 hours of being read to, his or her low-income neighbor averages just 25 hours." It cites research from a 1994 Carnegie Corporation survey that found that only 50% of infants and toddlers are read to on a regular basis. One of its primary activities to combat these deficiencies is to sponsor programs in which high school students, retired people, and military personnel read aloud to children during after-school hours.

In a volume designed for parents who want to initiate read-aloud activities, two child-reading experts advocate beginning early (Cullinan & Bagert, 1996). Four months of age is not too early, state the authors, and when using "baby" or cloth books, it is best to capitalize on the infant's fascination with sounds. Parents should exaggerate animal and onomatopoetic sounds and, whenever possible, point to illustrations in the book. As the child matures into prekindergarten years, they recommend that parents point to letter combinations that make sounds in books that are read aloud and invite children to speculate on characters' motives for their behavior in stories. After children begin the first few grades, the authors suggest exercises that combine reading with writing, inviting children to read aloud letters to friends and relatives and to make up stories and read them aloud to parents.

## Reading and Play

Children begin dramatic play as soon as they can communicate. Research suggests that children between 2 and 3 spend 10 to 20% of their time in dramatic play, also known as pretend, fantasy, or make-believe play (Haight & Miller, 1993; Miller & Garvey, 1984). Much of this play is book related if it reflects the meanings implicit in books and/or illustrations or when books and reading are part of the play content. Play is like reading in that children perceive that the symbol and referent are arbitrarily associated; a cardboard box, for example, can become a truck, a train, or a boat. They will ultimately need to do the same thing with language—using a variety of symbols to perceive or elicit different meanings in novel contexts. There is evidence that reading ability can be more effectively predicted by children's use of metalanguage—the use of words such as *say, talk,* or *write* during play—than by more conventional indicators (Pellegrini & Galda, 1993). In addition to the cognitive advantages of reading aloud, several investigations indicate that children who are read to before bedtime and whose television watching is controlled are less aggressive and more imaginative than children who do not receive these parental benefits (Singer & Singer, 1990, p. 161).

In an investigation of preschool children who were read to frequently, Rowe (1998) systematically observed a number of instances in which children spontaneously incorporated story content into their play. Two and 3-year-olds played out portions of books that were of interest to them. Rarely did they incorporate entire stories into play sequences. Children were not, however, perfectly loyal to the story texts; they frequently invented dialogue or activities that were based on content from the stories that had been read to them. They would sometimes use books while playing, examining an illustration of a dinosaur, then *becoming* a dinosaur, making imagined reptilian noises as they did so. They also played at reading, sitting stuffed animals on their laps and pretending to read them a story.

The relationships among reading and play observed in this and in other research underline the importance of reading aloud. At the age when children begin to express likes and dislikes of read-aloud stories, they gain material that they can incorporate into social play. The value of reading will be increased beyond its own intrinsic attraction by the extent to which it has play utility, and the joy that comes from being read to will increase. If reading does not become a source for play, it is possible that other media such as television will occupy the role that reading might.

## Reading and Electronic Media: The Case of Television

Critics of television viewing have long suspected that TV viewing is negatively associated with reading (Winn, 1985; Wolfe, Mendes, & Factor, 1984). Early investigations, when television was new, indicated little or no relationship between the two activities. Contemporary critics point out the fallacy of inferring the behavior of modern children from early correlational research (Koolstra & van der Voort, 1996). In the classic study on the role of media in children's lives (which found minimal effects of television viewing on reading), children's reading patterns were set before television was integrated into the culture (Schramm, Lyle, & Parker, 1961). When children's television is removed or decreased, reading increases, so it is tempting to extend the conclusion to a TV-detracts-from-reading hypothesis (Gadberry, 1980). One investigation of students in grades 3 to 5 found a relationship between TV viewing and reading: Time spent reading was inversely correlated with the viewing of aggressive TV programs, and the number of books read was inversely correlated with viewing of game shows (Zuckerman, Singer, & Singer, 1980). The authors interpret their results as evidence for television's displacing some of the exciting and amusing aspects of books.

In more recent research, there is accumulating evidence for the decline of reading ability as a function of TV viewing. In the only published meta-analysis (23 studies, 274 correlations), television viewing was negatively correlated with reading ability and other dimensions of academic achievement, and the magnitude of the correlation rises sharply after 20 hours per week of viewing (Walberg & Haertel, 1992). A review of more than three decades of research also found a consistent negative relationship and concludes that viewing more than 3 hours per day may be the critical peak in the decline of reading ability (Reinking & Wu, 1990). In a longitudinal study of parent-child communication and its implications for media use, preschool children who were heavy viewers of television were less capable readers than lighter viewers by first grade (Desmond, Singer, Singer, Calam, & Colimore, 1985). Gaddy (1986) argues that if television viewing displaces as little as 15 minutes of homework per day, its ultimate impact would be tremendous.

Television may influence the kind of reading that children prefer, not merely the amount. Morgan (1980) found that young adolescents who are heavy viewers of television prefer reading that resembles television content (i.e., stories about love and romance, stories with teenage themes, and articles about film and TV personalities). Lighter viewers predominantly chose fiction and poetry for free reading, and they selected more overall categories of reading than did their heavy-viewing counterparts.

But why the concern? There are voices in the debate over media effects who argue that academics see the decline of reading as one of the apocalyptic horsemen. In terms of media comparisons, there is evidence that children more easily understand information conveyed by television than by print (Bentjes & van der Voort, 1991; Meringoff, 1980). The advantages of reading, however, appear to go beyond mere ease of story comprehension. Reading has positive effects on oral and written expression (Koolstra & van der Voort, 1996), reading ability (Stanovich et al., 1996), and creative imagination (Greenfield & Beagles-Roos, 1988). In a society that values oral and written expression, the accumulating evidence for the negative impact of television on young readers continues to be taken seriously by educators, researchers, and child advocates. Computer use and use of the Internet depend heavily on reading and related skills of sequential processing.

Citing research that demonstrated a negative relationship between TV viewing and comic reading, Koolstra and van der Voort (1996) conducted a panel study of two cohorts of 8- and 10-year-olds to determine the effect of specific television diets on children's book reading. Among their findings were (a) a negative, unidirectional (from TV viewing to reading) association between earlier TV and later book reading; (b) that the amount of variance in reading accounted for by TV viewing across 3 years ranged from 8 to 18%; and (c) that the negative effect of TV viewing was cumulative, increasing up to age 13. In terms of establishing the reasons for the TV-to-reading decline, the investigators found that *attitudes toward reading* were negatively affected by TV viewing, and these negative attitudes led to decreased book reading over time. Second, they found *a deterioration of the ability to concentrate* on book reading as a function of TV viewing. Taken together, these results suggest that the effect of television viewing on these aspects of reading, while not immense, is still large enough to be of concern and that the negative effects of TV accumulate across the early years of school into the preteen years. "As a result of years of pleasant experiences with television, children might come to regard the medium as an easy and attractive source of entertainment that provides more direct satisfaction than books" (Koolstra & van der Voort, 1996, p. 28).

## Complementarity of Reading and Television

Even though there are strengths and weaknesses of each medium, it is difficult to avoid labeling book reading as superior to TV viewing, because the strengths of reading appear to be consonant with academic achievement, a gateway to career and personal success. Few or no studies have been conducted to investigate the impact of reading on TV viewing; no public outcries are heard urging parents to reduce their children's reading. As Neuman (1997) points out, research that compares media is, in a sense, set up to reveal only limitations of media. As she suggests, there are synergistic effects from reading and viewing that may serve to multiply the positive outcomes of each medium. She cites research and anecdotes illustrating that watching a TV version of a popular children's story can elicit questions about characters, the narrative, and even a desire to return to the printed story. Educators have long observed that the presentation of a story on television causes curiosity about and demand for a book. A famous anecdote from the 1970s program *Happy Days* suggested that after Fonzie, an admired character, was seen visiting a library, a sudden increase in library card applications followed.

It is obvious that few children only read or only watch TV. Many 5-year-olds will begin to point out inconsistencies between the video and published versions of a story with which they are familiar. Stories such as *Care Bears, Winnie-the-Pooh, The Cat in the Hat,* and *Arthur* exist in video or TV, books, and CD-ROMs. Most reader-viewers are aware of these cross-media forms and consume them in several formats (a term for cross-medium storytelling is *intertextuality*). It may be that the discussion of the differences among versions is a first important step toward media literacy for the young child. Who should lead these discussions? Parents are clearly the key variable in the media synergy equation. Research has revealed that parents can lead children away from mindless TV viewing and toward more thoughtful concentration on the informative aspects of the medium (Desmond et al., 1985). Parents can purchase videos or obtain them from libraries after reading the stories to their children and act as gatekeepers for a child's synergistic narrative. Conversely, parents can discourage reading by using TV—even educationally whole programming—as a baby-sitter while they are otherwise engaged.

A study of how to increase media literacy in first and second graders included a series of illustrated picture books to heighten children's attention to informative aspects of television (Desmond, 1997). Children in experimental and control groups were given a series of books that discussed topics such as the use of special effects, the need to verify information presented on TV, the exaggerated claims of advertising, and related topics. Experimental groups differed from controls in that experimental groups' books featured illustrations of the actual class of young readers, along with their real first names, in order to offer close attention and rereading of the "customized" books. It was found that the "customized" books about television could increase several aspects of children's comprehension of television, including increased awareness of advertising appeals and how television is produced. The future will bring many more opportunities for intertextuality in bringing stories to children.

## Reading and Computers

Now that the majority of children under 12 have at least occasional access to computers at home or in school, CD-ROMs, the World Wide Web, and on-line chat groups for every interest are a source of reading and information about reading for children and parents. Home pages on the Web exist for children's authors, bookstores with reader-authored reviews, and individual books. Magazines for children on the Web such as *Together On Line* are rich sources for parents and children to learn about and discuss new books. They can also consult pages for nearly every reading and literacy organization in the world with just the click of a mouse on a browser. Computers as a reading resource grow more valuable daily, as universal access moves from dream to reality. Although there is a concern on the part of child advocates regarding video games or obscenity on the Internet that is reminiscent of the criticisms about TV, there are few outcries regarding the threat of computers displacing reading. Most parents and educators are convinced that computer use by children is a positive force in their education and development. But just as there is light and more serious reading, there are certainly different ways to use a computer.

As theorists of digital communication suggest, there are some important differences between printed and electronic texts (Reinking, Labbo, & McKenna, 1997). Primary among these is interactivity. Electronic texts are malleable and fluid; they are not firm and fixed in the manner of printed books and magazines. Although there has always been a kind of *interaction* between readers and texts, the term is more metaphorical with respect to reading. When a reader *interacts* with a text, the term is usually used to mean that the reader brings his or her own experiences and ideas to the material, fantasizing, for example, that he or she is having the adventures of the protagonist. Electronic texts, in contrast, can be monitored to reflect the rate at which they are being read and the order of elements in their organization, and readers can even modify fonts and spacing at will.

It is self-evident that print is hierarchical; readers must follow texts in a presentational order to be able to grasp meaning. Marshall McLuhan (1964) was famous for his free-wheeling discussions of the concept of print linearity. He suggested that following linear texts forced us to perceive the world of events as having beginnings, middles, and ends. Some computer texts can be and are readable in a linear mode, as in the case of newspaper home pages that provide breaking news stories that are updated every few hours. The structure of these "pages" invites the kind of grazing that typifies news reading. Several booksellers are beginning to market electronic books that are simply small handheld computers that can store pages and present texts in the same manner as books do. In a paperless future, readers will simply download books from sellers' sites for a small fee. But the computer's most radical departure from print is represented in *hypertext,* or the nonlinear method of linking separate but related segments of texts connected by links. Nodes of several lines or paragraphs, indicated by underlined or blue-colored words, are instantly accessible by a reader, allowing for a great deal of freedom and individuality in following the author's thoughts.

If this chapter was incorporated with hypertext, you could click a mouse and be linked to the "Reading Is Fundamental" home page in the earlier discussion of reading aloud, have access to a list of children's book recommendations by age, or go immediately to the reference section to answer a question about a source I have used. Research is needed to determine the most effective methods for using hypertexts, but it is clear from my observation that children immediately understand how to navigate hypertexts and that they are willing to use them. Early summaries of research demonstrate a growing effectiveness of hypertexts in school environments, especially in children's applications of concepts from reading (Reinking et al., 1997).

The benefits of hypertext technology are not limited to words. Broderbund Software markets a series of CDs based on Marc Brown's *Arthur* series for young readers that uses hypertext-like object programming to link text, sound, and illustrated image to help young readers. When nearly any object in Arthur's environment is clicked on, the object emits a characteristic sound and the name of the object is highlighted in the text. The actual text is still the center of the experience, but readers are invited to interact with the objects in the stories. Multimedia "books" for children are enormously popular and represent a growth industry for software designers.

Although the Internet, multimedia, word processing, e-mail, and other technologies show promise for increasing the horizons of young readers, computers are present in 62% of U.S. households with children ages 6 to 12 but only 42% are connected to the Internet. This presence is positively correlated with parents' income (Rublin, 1999). These data also reveal that, as of 1998, only 45% of schools had at least one Internet connection. A more recent survey reinforces the gap; while 50% of school-age children in high-income areas use a computer every day, only 29% of lower-income children do so (Roberts et al., 1999). If these emerging technologies are to facilitate reading by children, they must soon be in the hands of families of all income levels.

## Conclusion

I began this chapter with a personal anecdote about my early reading experiences. How can those of us who are entrusted with child raising increase the opportunities for more children to find the joy that I found in the act of reading and begin a lifetime of literacy? It is clear that a parent cannot begin reading aloud too early. Even though a 6-month-old infant may not visibly respond to a parent's story reading, he or she will eventually come to perceive it as unshared time that is centered on the child. Cloth and plastic books with colorful illustrations should be freely available to children at the earliest possible age.

When the child begins to explore the magic of television, a wise parent will purchase, rent, or check out videotaped stories of quality, and one of the most reliable indicators of quality are those tapes that are based on classic children's books and stories. This will allow parents to introduce discussions about the differences between media and to invite their child to create visual scenarios for books that are not available in film or video. It is important for parents to set examples for children by being readers themselves. Children will follow the lead of parents who have home libraries, magazines, and newspapers.

Parents should try to make frequent visits to libraries and bookstores and make sure that their children obtain library cards as early as possible. Most children's librarians are happy to know their clients on a personal basis and can make computer, video, and book recommendations. When children are old enough to make their own book selections, parents should suggest a range of challenging versus "just for fun" material. In the television age, there is a tendency for children to select "television-like books" that are the nutritional equivalent of fast food. As might be expected, many of these books are based on TV programs.

Perhaps the most pressing problem for both parents and the research community is the determination of the place and importance of reading in the spectrum of leisure time activities, especially in light of all the emerging options in electronic media. It is clear that young readers will be spending more time in front of electronic screens in the future than they do now, but what will be the outcomes of this change? One avenue of inquiry that is suggested by the preceding discussion is the area of intervention. Will reading texts from an electronic screen, complete with multimedia accompaniments, continue to provide the same kinds of mental imagery associated with free reading in a quiet place? If not, how can computer use and game playing facilitate reading to provide for some "text time" in the leisure spectrum? There is a current wave of research activity regarding computers in the classroom, but few investigations have begun to examine the implications of new media on the child's relationship with print. The citizen of the future will need to be print literate, knowledgeable about math and science, and media and computer literate as well. There is every reason to believe that all of these activities can be synergistic, with traditional and new media presenting a cornucopia of child-enriching possibilities.

## References


Anderson, R., Fielding, L., & Wilson, P. (1988). Growth in reading and how children spend their time outside of school. *Reading Research Quarterly, 4,* 285-303.

Barnes and Noble. (1999). *Home page: Kids' comments* [On-line]. [Retrieved August 2, 1999]. Available: www.metashopper.com/mps/books/barnesandnoble.htm

Bentjes, J., & van der Voort, T. (1991). Children's written accounts of televised and printed stories. *Educational Technology Research and Development, 39,* 15-26.

Bond, L. (1991). Attainment at primary schools: An analysis of variations between schools. *British Educational Research Journal, 17,* 203-217.

Calkins, L. (1997). *Raising lifelong learners: A parent's guide.* Reading, MA: Addison-Wesley.

Campbell, J. (1949). *Hero with a thousand faces.* Princeton, NJ: Princeton University Press.

Campbell, R. (1998). *Media and culture: An introduction to mass communication.* New York: St. Martin's.

Chaney, C. (1992). Language development, metalinguistic skills, and print awareness in 3-year-old children. *Applied Psycholinguistics, 13,* 485-514.

Cullinan, C., & Bagert, B. (1996). *Helping your child learn to read.* Washington, DC: U.S. Department of Education.

Davies, J., & Brember, I. (1993). Comics or stories? Differences in reading habits and attitudes of girls and boys in years 2, 4, and 6. *Gender and Education, 5,* 305-321.

Desmond, R. J. (1997). Media literacy in the home: Acquisition vs. deficit models. In R. Kubey (Ed.), Media literacy in the information age (pp. 323-345). New Brunswick, NJ: Transaction Publishing.

Desmond, R. J., Singer, J. L., Singer, D. G., Calam, R., & Colimore, K. (1985). Family mediation patterns: Young children's use and grasp of the medium. *Human Communication Research, 11,* 461-480.

Downey, K. (1995, September 12). Illiteracy slows American output. *Detroit News,* pp. 17, 22.

Dwyer, C. A. (1974). Influences of children's sex role standards on reading achievement. *Journal of Educational Psychology, 66,* 811-816.

Edwards, J. R. (1979). *Language and disadvantage.* New York: Elsevier.

Eley, W. B. (1992). *How in the world do students read?* Hamburg, Germany: International Association for the Evaluation of Educational Achievement.

Family Literacy Foundation. (1999). Home page. [Retrieved July 17, 1999].
Available: www.read2kids. org/about.htm

Feitelson, D., Kita, B., & Goldstein, C. (1986). Effects of listening to series stories of first graders' comprehension and use of language. *Research in the Teaching of English, 20,* 339-356.

Gadberry, S. (1980). Effects of restricting first grader's TV viewing on leisure time use. *Journal of Applied Developmental Psychology, 1,* 45-57.

Gaddy, G. D. (1986). Television's impact on high school achievement. *Public Opinion Quarterly, 50,* 340-349.

Greenfield, P. M., & Beagles-Roos, J. (1988). Radio vs. television: Their cognitive impact on children of different socioeconomic and ethnic groups. *Journal of Communication, 38*(2), 71-92.

Grineau, J. (1997). Comic books and the mythic pattern. *Comic Book Conundrum* [On-line]. [Retrieved August 15, 1999]. Available: www.sideroad.com

Haight, W., & Miller, P. (1993). *Pretending at home: Early development in a sociopolitical context.* Albany: State University of New York Press.

Herrnstein, R., & Murray, C. (1991). What's really behind the SAT score decline? *Public Interest, 100,* 32-56.

Itzkoff, S. W. (1993). America's educational decline: The deeper realities. *Mankind Quarterly, 34,* 65-85.

Izawa, E. (1995). *What are manga and anime?* [On-line]. [Retrieved June 5, 1999].
Available: www. rei@mit.edu

Kantrowitz, B., & Wingert, P. (1999, November 18). The truth about "tweens." *Newsweek,* pp. 63-67.

Kincade, K., & Kleine, P. (1993). Methodological issues in the assessment of children's reading interests. *Journal of Instructional Psychology, 20*(3), 224-241.

Koolstra, C., & van der Voort, T. (1996). Longitudinal effects of television on children's leisure time reading. *Human Communication Research, 23,* 4-36.

Krashen, S. (1993). *The power of reading: Insights from the research.* Englewood, CO: Public Libraries Unlimited.

Landauer, T. K., & Dumais, S. (1997). A solution to Plato's problem: The latent semantic analysis theory of acquisition, induction, and representation of knowledge. *Psychological Review, 104,* 211-240.

Marwick, C. (1997). Rising care costs due to patients' lack of literacy. *Journal of the American Medical Association, 278*(12), 971-973.

McLuhan, M. (1964). *Understanding media: The extensions of man.* Cambridge: MIT Press.

Meringoff, L. K. (1980). Influence of the medium on children's story comprehension. *Journal of Educational Psychology, 72,* 240-249.

Meyer, L., Stahl, S. A., Waldrop, J., & Linn, R. (1994). Effects of reading storybooks aloud to children. *Journal of Educational Research, 88,* 69-85.

Miller, P., & Garvey, C. (1984). Mother-baby role play. In I. Bretherton (Ed.), *Symbolic play: The development of social understanding* (pp. 101-130). New York: Academic Press.

Morgan, M. (1980). Television and reading: Does more equal better? *Journal of Communication, 30*(3), 159-165.

Neuman, S. (1997). Television as a learning environment: A theory of synergy. In J. Flood, S. Brice-Heath, & D. Lapp (Eds.), *Handbook of research on teaching literacy through the communicative and visual arts* (pp. 15-23). New York: Simon & Schuster.

Pellegrini, A. D., & Galda, L. (1993). Ten years after: A reexamination of symbolic play and literacy research. *Reading Research Quarterly, 28,* 162-175.

Reinking, D., Labbo, L., & McKenna, M. (1997). Navigating the landscape of literacy: Current theory and research in computer-based reading and writing. In J. Flood, S. Brice-Heath, & D. Lapp (Eds.), *Handbook of research on teaching literacy through the communicative and visual arts* (pp. 77-95). New York: Simon & Schuster.

Reinking, D., & Wu, J. (1990). Reexamining the research on television and reading. *Reading Research Quarterly, 29,* 30-43.

Rimer, S. (1997, December 25). Health clinic's one RX for all: Books. *New York Times,* p. 27.

Roberts, D. F., Ulla, G. F., Rideout, V. J., & Brodie, M. (1999). *Kids and media at the new millennium.* Menlo Park, CA: Kaiser Family Foundation.

Rowe, D. W. (1998). The literate potentials of book-related play. *Reading Research Quarterly, 33,* 10-36.

Rublin, L. R. (1999, November 8). Tuning out: Who wins, loses as kids spend more time on P.C.'s? *Barron's,* pp. 37-42.

Schramm, W., Lyle, J., & Parker, E. (1961). *Television in the lives of our children.* Stanford, CA: Stanford University Press.

Singer, D. G., & Singer, J. L. (1990). *The house of make-believe: Children's play and the developing imagination.* Cambridge, MA: Harvard University Press.

Snow, C., Burns, M., & Griffin, C. (Eds.). (1998). *Preventing reading difficulties in young children.* Washington, DC: National Research Council.

Spitz, E. H. (1999). *Inside picture books.* New Haven, CT: Yale University Press.

Stanovich, K. E., West, R. F., Cunningham, A. E., Cipielewski, J., & Siddiqui, S. (1996). The role of inadequate print exposure as a determinant of reading comprehension. In C. Cornoldi & J. Oakhill (Eds.), *Problems in reading comprehension disabilities* (pp. 15-32). Hillsdale, NJ: Lawrence Erlbaum.

Sulzby, E., & Kaderavek, J. (1996). Parent-child language during storybook reading and toy play contexts: Case studies of normally developing and specific language impaired (SLI) children. In *National reading conference yearbook 37* (pp. 95-106). Washington, DC: National Research Council.

Teale, W. H. (1995). Young children and reading: Trends across the twentieth century. *Journal of Education, 177*(3), 95-128.

Timmer, S., Eccles, J., & O'Brien, K. (1985). How children use time. In F. Juster & E. Stafford (Eds.), *Time, goods, and well being* (pp. 353-369). Ann Arbor: University of Michigan Press.

Trelease, J. (1995). *The read-aloud handbook.* New York: Penguin.

U.S. Department of Education. (1985). *Becoming a nation of readers: A compendium of research on reading and academic achievement.* Washington, DC: Author.

U.S. Department of Education. (1990). *A profile of the American eighth grader: National education longitudinal study of 1988.* Washington, DC: Author.

Walberg, H., & Haertel, G. (1992). Educational psychology's first century. *Journal of Educational Psychology, 84,* 6-20.

Watterson, B. (1989, October 27). *The cheapening of the comics.* Speech at the Festival of Comics, Ohio State University.

Winn, M. (1985). *The plug-in drug: Television, children, and the family.* New York: Viking Penguin.

Wolfe, D., Mendes, M., & Factor, D. (1984). A parent-administered program to reduce children's television viewing. *Journal of Applied Behavior Analysis, 17,* 267-272.

Worthy, J., Moorman, M., & Turner, M. (1999). What Johnny likes to read is hard to find in school. *Reading Research Quarterly, 34*(1), 2-13.

Zuckerman, D., Singer, D. G., & Singer, J. L. (1980). Television viewing by children and related classroom behavior. *Journal of Communication, 30*(1), 166-174.

CHAPTER 3

# The Use of Television and Other Film-Related Media

GEORGE COMSTOCK
Syracuse University

ERICA SCHARRER
University of Massachusetts/Amherst

Television has for many years accounted for a substantial proportion of the time expenditures of children, and its prominence in their lives, reflected in increased household use of television and diminishing differences in children's viewing associated with socioeconomic status (Comstock & Scharrer, 1999; Nielsen Media Research, 1998), has increased. This implies, for most children, an extensive consumption of undemanding entertainment, including many portrayals of conflict and violence, which therefore may have serious consequences represented by effects on affect, cognitions, and behavior. There may be a loss as well of the benefits of foregone opportunities. Our present task is to examine the behavior of children in their use of television and other film-related media, by which we mean the videocassette recorder (VCR) and movies seen in theaters or through in-home playback.

There are very good reasons to give attention to children's use of television and other film-related media. These media certainly provide many moments of piqued interest and enjoyment for children, as they do for teenagers and adults. In this respect, they are merely one of the pleasures afforded by modern life. However, it would be a mistake to think of them as limited to such outcomes. There is ample evidence that, for some children, either the amount viewed or what is viewed may have adverse consequences (Comstock & Scharrer, 1999). Television and other film-related media have been implicated in the displacement of time that might be spent acquiring the basic scholastic skills of reading, mathematics, and writing (Comstock & Scharrer, 1999; Neuman, 1991; Van Evra, 1998; Williams, 1986; see also Chapter 5); in the encouragement of attitudes and practices that delimit concentration while reading and promote a preference for undemanding pictures and texts, such as comic books (Koolstra & van der Voort, 1996); in affecting mood and behavior by contributing to fearfulness, physiologically measured excitation, hyperactivity, and reduced impulse control and attention span (Cantor, 1994a, 1994b; Singer, Singer, Desmond, Hirsch, & Nicol, 1988; see also Chapters 8 and 10); in shaping daydreaming, play, and imaginative processes (Valkenburg & van der Voort, 1994; Valkenburg, Voojis, van der Voort, & Wiegman, 1992; see also Chapter 6); and in the facilitation of aggressive and antisocial behavior (Comstock & Scharrer, 1999; National Television Violence Study, 1996, 1997, 1998; see also Chapters 11 and 12).

The use of these media has also been associated with prosocial outcomes. They can contribute importantly through educational programming to children's scholastic achievement, as exemplified by gains in knowledge of letters and numbers attributable to the viewing of *Sesame Street* (Cook et al., 1975). They can be a part of child-rearing practices that lead to slightly enhanced performance years later in high school (Comstock & Scharrer, 1999; Wright & Huston, 1995; Zill, Davies, & Daly, 1994). By the examples they may give of positive forms of behavior, they can facilitate generosity, tolerance, cooperation, and other modes of behaving that promote constructive social interaction (see Chapters 9, 15, 18, and 23).

The exposure of children to specific content, as Hamilton (1998) points out in his economic analysis of the marketplace for television violence, is to a significant degree the product of what economists call "externalities," or unintended consequences, and the balancing of costs and benefits by television executives and parents. Executives may attract children to unsuitable programs by scheduling them to maximize the adult audience. They also may schedule educational programs at times when the available audience of children is not at its peak because other programs are more profitable in those time slots. Parents may not supervise viewing to an optimum degree because of the inconvenience, or costs, of determining which programs might be harmful or beneficial and of exerting authority. Thus, both executives and parents often act in their narrow, short-term interests rather than acting in terms of longer-range benefits to children and society.

We conceive of the study of media audiences as very broad (Comstock & Scharrer, 1999), including orientation toward a medium; motivations for its use; content selection; various household and situational variables; the regularities that mark audience flow through the day, week, and season; and data on the amount of media use and the demographic variables that predict the amount of use. We attempt to describe children's use of television and other film-related media in the same terms. This has led us to undertake an extensive search for data on these various factors, including such sources as *Communication Abstracts, Dissertation Abstracts International, Psychological Abstracts,* and *Sociological Abstracts,* over the past decade and the bibliographies of studies we obtained. For our statistics on average amounts of use, we rely on the large national samples of Robinson and Godbey (1997) and Nielsen Media Research (1998). These provide reliable and valid estimates of national consumption within the limitations of their modes of measurement. Our data on other questions are less satisfactory because the samples are typically small to moderate in size and, though certainly representative of large numbers of children, they cannot be said to statistically reflect a distinctly identifiable larger population. As a result, much of the time we must confine ourselves to estimates of the direction of a relationship rather than its magnitude.

## Principal Variables

The principal variables that play a role in children's use of television and other film-related media can be divided into four categories: societal and structural factors, household characteristics, child attributes, and situational influences.

### *Societal and Structural Factors*

Societal and structural factors determine the number of channels available, their content, the costs of obtaining access to them, and thus the options open to the young viewer. These factors include governmental and regulatory policies that shape the way the media operate, the economics of program production and distribution that influence what will be offered, and the state of technology that determines what can be received or viewed in the home.

### *Household Characteristics*

Household characteristics play an enormous role in children's use of television and other film-related media. These characteristics include socioeconomic status, which is one of the major predictors of television use at all ages; the norms specifying the degree to which television is central to household life and leisure, including the ubiquity of television use; and the available resources, including the number of television sets, other media, and alternate leisure opportunities.

### *Child Attributes*

Child attributes affect how much is viewed, what is viewed, and, importantly, the how—the attentional manner—of consuming television and other film-related media. The principal variables are age, mental ability, and an outcome affected by both, comprehension, which figures in the shift from a child to an adult mode of viewing.

### *Situational Influences*

Situational influences include transient but repetitive factors that are not firmly rooted in the practices of the household. These include the presence of others (e.g., parents, peers, and siblings) while the child is viewing; clock- and calendar-based influences such as hour of the day, day of the week, and season; and states of mind such as anger and loneliness.

## The Viewing Experience

Television viewing is such an everyday activity that it is easy to overlook its uniqueness among mass media consumption. Every mode of how people attend to the medium is encompassed—"browse, momentarily ignore, assemble into a mosaic of contrasting bits, passingly follow, attentively consume" (Comstock & Scharrer, 1999, p. 61)—with the most striking feature being the large amounts of time in which most viewers are indifferent. The combining of varying degrees of cognitive involvement with waxing and waning physical attentiveness in a context of social conventions and competing activities requires, in our view, an examination of the viewing process as prerequisite to looking at data on time spent viewing and its correlates. This is because hours and minutes spent with television only take on meaning and can only be meaningfully interpreted with knowledge of what constitutes "viewing." We cover four topics: the purposes and motives of viewing; the role in viewing of three typical modes of response; the adoption of these adult-like viewing patterns as children learn to use television; and our explication and operationalization of the concept of viewing.

### *Purposes and Motives*

The two orientations that seemingly describe both the viewing behavior at a given moment and an individual's typical disposition toward the medium so well among teenagers and adults (Comstock & Scharrer, 1999) at first seem embarrassingly obtuse when applied to children. *Instrumental viewing* surely connotes too much in the way of pragmatic motive and denotes too much in the way of use of the medium for information to describe the behavior of children; *ritualistic viewing* would seem to belie the enthusiasm that children bring to their favorite programs and their characters. However, the data convince us that these distinctions can be usefully applied to children, although it is only through changes that occur during childhood that children, as a group, come to parallel the viewing behavior of teenagers and adults.

The distinguishing element is the degree to which the specific content of a program is responsible for viewing (Comstock & Scharrer, 1999; Rubin, 1983, 1984). The first priority in ritualistic viewing is exposure to television, with gratifications maximized by choosing the most pleasing of available options. Thus, programs universally are of some importance but at a subordinate level in ritualistic viewing. Correlates of regular ritualistic viewing are greater overall viewing and a preference for undemanding, entertaining content. Correlates of regular instrumental viewing are lesser overall viewing and a preference for programs that ignite a particular interest. Instrumental viewing, then, represents greater selectivity. Most viewing is ritualistic; our estimate, based on various measures of comparative indifference toward the specific program being viewed (Comstock & Scharrer, 1999), is that about four fifths of viewing is ritualistic.

This accounts for the large amounts of time that have been recorded as devoted to television viewing among all age groups. The devoted concentration called forth by highly interesting fare could only support a few hours of viewing a week. Ritualistic viewing is often characterized by monitoring, in which audience members attend only enough to follow the narrative and use cues in the audio track to determine when to redirect attention to the screen. It is this behavior, then, that underlies the financial foundation of much of the medium, the huge audiences that advertisers seek to reach.

The three major motives that operate within these two orientations for viewing at all ages are (a) diversion and an escape from comparatively less attractive options; (b) surveillance on behalf of social comparison, by which an individual evaluates the merits of his or her personal attributes; and (c) awareness. We define the latter term not solely regarding what is transpiring in the world but primarily in terms of what is occurring on television, the medium that consumes most of the time people allocate to the mass media, and the way that medium covers those events.

In our view, escape in its various guises is primary. Our rationale is the frequency with which stress in a variety of forms predicts greater viewing among both children and those older (Anderson, Collins, Schmitt, & Jacobvitz, 1996; Canary & Spitzberg, 1993; Kubey & Csikszentmihalyi, 1990; Maccoby, 1954; Potts & Sanchez, 1994), as well as by the dominance of pleasure and relaxation when adults cite reasons for viewing (Albarran & Umphrey, 1993; Bower, 1985). The other two are nevertheless important. This is evident from the frequency with which viewers have been found to pay more attention to personages on the screen like themselves, whether the link is race (Comstock, 1991a), age (Harwood, 1997), or gender (Maccoby & Wilson, 1957; Maccoby, Wilson, & Burton, 1958; Sprafkin & Liebert, 1978). It is also apparent from the frequency with which learning is cited as a motive by adults when news viewing alone apparently is not what is meant (Albarran & Umphrey, 1993; Bower, 1985) and the frequency with which the presentational elements—visual imagery, a compelling construction of the spoken and the seen—figure in the quality ascribed to the viewing experience by audience members (Levy, 1978; Neuman, 1982).

### *Three Modes of Response*

The predominance of ritualistic viewing is exemplified by three modes of response to the medium that come to typify viewing as children mature, are characteristic of the viewing of teenagers and adults, and are surprisingly frequent throughout childhood. We emphasize that these modes of response are not universal. There are exceptions to each, typically in the form of the time spent at all ages with favorite programs that seem particularly salient to viewers. Nevertheless, they are the dominant motifs that characterize the bulk of attending to television. They are the *primacy* given to the medium, *low involvement,* and *monitoring.*

*Primacy*

The primacy of the medium is one of the most consistently and clearly documented phenomena of television audience behavior. Although the popularity of specific programs is crucial to the success of the channels on which the programs appear, the audience at a given time, for the most part, is not assembled because of a particular offering but to enjoy what the medium in general has to offer. The primacy, in particular, is represented by the well-known two-step decision process by which programs to be viewed are chosen, by the weak predictability of what will be viewed by the programs preferred by the individual, and by the governing role of time available in whether or not television will be viewed.

The initial step is typically whether or not to view television (Barwise, Ehrenberg, & Goodhardt, 1982; Comstock, Chaffee, Katzman, McCombs, & Roberts, 1978). The second step is to select the most satisfying among the possible options for the person or persons making that decision. The role of specific programs in determining who will view at a given time is comparatively minor.

Preferences for types of programming are surprisingly weak predictors of what people will view. Some programs are certainly more often viewed by those younger or older or by males or females. The particular popularity of talk shows and situation comedies featuring outspoken heroines among young female adults 18 to 34 is an example (Hamilton, 1998). However, when Frank and Greenberg (1980) divided a representative sample of persons 13 years and older into 14 segments based on their interests, they, not surprisingly, found that these viewing segments, which varied widely by age and sex, differed greatly in their seeming preferences for different kinds of television programming. However, a startlingly meager less than 10% of the variation in viewing across 19 categories of programming was statistically predictable from the data on interests and demographics. How can this be?

The answer is that viewing is largely (but not wholly) governed by time available (Comstock, 1991b). Viewing by those older and younger, by females and males, and by children varies across the time of day, the day of the week, and the season depending on the availability of the members of the demographic category to become part of the television audience (Comstock & Scharrer, 1999; Webster & Phalen, 1997). People almost always choose the same option when viewing at a particular time, but substantially more than half the time they fail to see the forthcoming episode of something they have viewed—news, talk, situation comedy, action adventure—because some obligation or preferred activity takes them out of the vicinity of the operating television set (Barwise et al., 1982). When researchers with the United Nations Educational, Scientific, and Cultural Organization (UNESCO) surveyed time use in cities around the globe, including cities in the United States, Eastern and Western Europe, and South America, an extraordinary pattern emerged in regard to television use (von Feilitzen & Carlsson, 1999). Despite the enormous differences that existed in the quality, type, amount, and variety of programming available, the set owners worldwide were very much alike in the amount of time spent with television, a finding consistent with past research (Comstock, 1991b; Robinson & Converse, 1972; Robinson & Godbey, 1997).

These varied data make it clear that the medium of television, and not specific programs, is primary most of the time in assembling an audience. One exception is the rare program that seemingly has no equivalent—that is, not one of a largely fungible genre. A second exception is major events, such as the Super Bowl and other sports spectaculars, unlikely to be matched in interest by other programs (Barwise & Ehrenberg, 1988). Thus, it is programming that conforms to the availability of demographic segments to become part of the audience, with the popularity of specific programs governing the division of the available audience, as exemplified by the role of children on Saturday mornings and, to a lesser extent, weekday afternoons. Children tend to be otherwise unoccupied and therefore available for viewing at these times, inspiring television executives to tailor programs offered during these parts of the day to child audiences. Similar "targeting" of audience segments occurs in other parts of the day, such as the scheduling of soap operas on weekday afternoons to appeal to nonworking women.

### *Low Involvement*

Viewers most of the time are only passively involved in what they view. When large, representative national samples were asked why they viewed the night before, few mentioned a specific program. A majority cited the rewards of viewing television (a further reason to think of the medium as having primacy over individual programs in the assembly of an audience), and not many thought what they had seen was particularly rewarding, pleasurable, memorable, or exciting (Bower, 1985; LoSciuto, 1972). More than one third did not actively choose what they had viewed but watched whatever came on next or a program chosen by someone else (LoSciuto, 1972). In a detailed study of the viewing behavior of two dozen families, between about one half and two thirds of adults said they did not give full attention to programs they considered as having viewed (Hopkins & Mullis, 1985); the higher figure was recorded for women because of their more frequent involvement in household tasks (Robinson & Godbey, 1997). Time-lapse photography (Allen, 1965) and videotaping of viewers (Anderson, Lorch, Field, Collins, & Nathan, 1986; Bechtel, Achelpohl, & Akers, 1972) confirm that attention is typically erratic, with viewers giving no attention to the screen about 40% of the time. People treasure the medium, and many viewers have favorite programs they particularly enjoy, but as these data attest, much of the time they are not deeply engaged in attending to what is on the screen (Barwise & Ehrenberg, 1988).

Low levels of involvement should not be surprising for an activity that consumes almost two dozen hours a week for the average person (Comstock & Scharrer, 1999). Such a large allocation of time does not, in most households, permit its investment in intense concentration. Thus, the huge audiences that constitute the economic foundation of those sectors of the medium deriving much of their income from advertising are in equilibrium with the modest cognitive demands of most programming. It is no accident that those channels that somewhat more often venture into more demanding programming are those least dependent on advertising—cable, particularly premium cable, and public television. Low involvement with television leaves viewers in a state of vague pleasure within which advertisers may effectively court them.

### *Monitoring*

Although, in deference to the felicity of expression and common usage, we use the term *viewing* to refer to attending to television (except when we wish to emphasize the nature of the activity), the more apt term is *monitoring.* The various indexes that point to low levels of involvement in the typical viewing of most programs lead to the conclusion that most of the time viewers pay only sufficient attention to comprehend the unfolding narrative and take in depictions, portrayals, events, and exchanges of particular interest. This phenomenon has been examined primarily among young children, whose attention to the screen varies as a function of the audio and visual cues offered by the medium and the degree to which others in the vicinity are attending to the screen (Anderson & Lorch, 1983; Bryant, Zillmann, & Brown, 1983; Collins, 1981;

Huston & Wright, 1989; Krull, 1983; Lorch, Anderson, & Levin, 1979).

In effect, the viewer, disinclined to invest viewing with much in the way of concentration, seeks signs that will attest to an enhanced likelihood that one or another gratification will be satisfied or that an immediately forthcoming element will be important to understanding what is taking place. This same phenomenon characterizes adult viewing. On average, attention to the screen is at its lowest for content that is either episodic or redundant, or stereotypic and conventionalized. The former types of content, such as news, sports, and commercials, do not require prior attention to one item for future comprehension of another. The latter type, such as soap operas, contain elements that, even if unattended to, can be readily inferred. Attention is at its highest for extended narratives that may present the unexpected (i.e., comprehension as well as various gratifications will rest on attention), such as movies and miniseries (Bechtel et al., 1972).

Television viewing, unlike attending to the screen at a movie theater, conforms to the principle of minimal expended effort. Viewers most of the time adopt a strategy of attending closely only when reward or necessity dictates such an expenditure of effort, and the process involved makes the term *monitoring* more accurate than *viewing* in describing what takes place.

### *Learning to Use Television*

Children literally grow into these patterns of behavior. They learn to use the medium, and by the age of 12, when amount of viewing will peak, their behavior in response to television will be the same as that of adults.

Viewing on a regular basis in a household with television usually begins between the ages of 2½ and 3, with an average estimated in one study of about 1.5 hours per day (Huston et al., 1983); giving attention to the screen, however, has been recorded as early as 6 months of age (Hollenbeck & Slaby, 1979). Viewing then quickly increases, with estimates by the same group of investigators (Huston, Wright, Rice, Kerkman, & St. Peters, 1990) rising to 2.75 hours for those between the ages of 3 and 6, then declining about a half-hour between the ages of 5½ and 7, when activities associated with beginning school temporarily limit available time. As most data indicate, viewing increases again until about age 12 (see Figure 3.1).

Obviously, at the earliest of these ages, the following of a narrative would not be one of the satisfactions of viewing. However, if what is seen performed on the screen is within their physical capability, children as young as 12 and 24 months of age are able to internalize what they see, imitate it on request, and retain this capability for as long as 24 hours after the initial exposure (Meltzoff, 1988). Thus, comprehension of what is represented physically on the screen begins quite early.

Preferences develop very early (see Table 3.1). About four fifths of the 3-year-olds in the Los Angeles area sample of 160 children ages 3, 4, and 5 named a favorite program when asked to do so by Lyle and Hoffman (1972b); by age 5, almost everyone did. Gender and age are major predictors. Both preschool boys and girls are attracted to appealing animal characters, as exemplified by *Sesame Street.* Girls will watch superhero programming in which they have only token representation, as attested to by the child audience for Saturday morning programming (Comstock, 1991a). Gender exerts an influence even among very young children, with twice as many girls as boys (39% vs. 19%) among those ages 3, 4, and 5 naming a family cartoon (*The Flintstones*) as a favorite and three times as many boys as girls (17% vs. 5%) naming a violent cartoon as a favorite.

Age differences are pronounced. In the data Lyle and Hoffman (1972a) obtained from about 1,600 Los Angeles area first-, sixth-, and tenth-grade students, about half of those in the first grade named a situation comedy and about a fourth named a cartoon as favorite. By the sixth grade, only one in 20 named a cartoon; situation comedies remained the

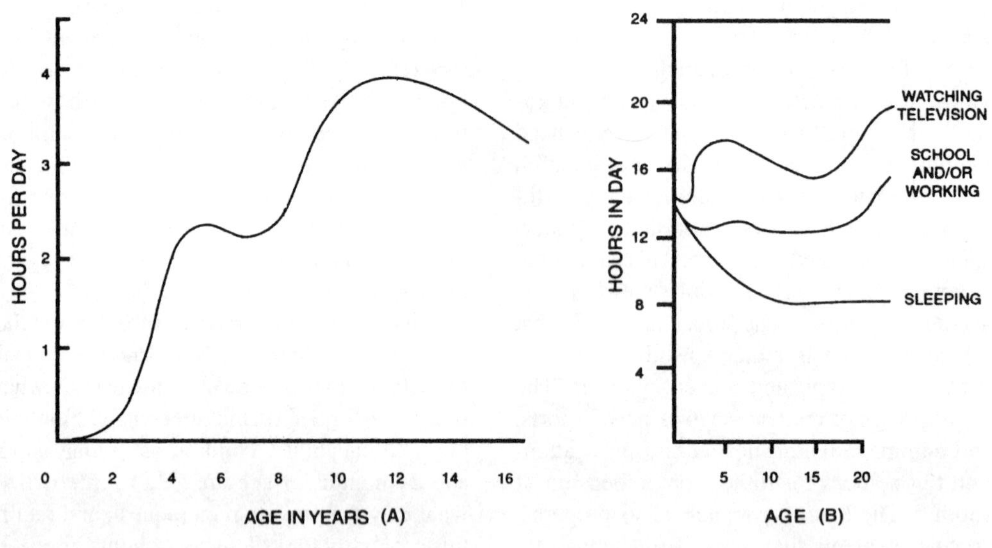


**Figure 3.1.** Television Viewing by Age
SOURCE: (A) Comstock, Chaffee, Katzman, McCombs, and Roberts (1978). Copyright © by Columbia University Press. Reprinted with permission. (B) Condry (1989). Copyright © by Lawrence Erlbaum. Reprinted with permission.

most popular but to a somewhat reduced degree; and all varieties of adult formats were increasing in favoritism. By the tenth grade, the most popular formats were action adventures; dramas; and music, variety, and talk shows (this category now partly replaced by MTV and other music channels).

The viewing of *Sesame Street* and other educational programs designed specifically to appeal to the very young increases between the ages of 3 and 4 and then begins to decline precipitously (Huston et al., 1990). The early gender and age shifts observed by Lyle and Hoffman (1972a, 1972b) represent enduring phenomena because television essentially has not changed in what it makes available to young viewers. Thus, about 20 years later, Huston and colleagues (1990) observed the same patterns in their Topeka sample of more than 300 children 3 to 5 and 5 to 7 years old.

Two concepts proposed by von Feilitzen and Linne (1975) help explain these patterns: *similarity* and *wishful identification.* Similarity refers to the preference for characters like oneself and is very evident among children in the greater attention and greater favoritism they give to portrayals of those of the same gender, age, or race (Comstock, 1991a; Harwood, 1997; Lyle & Hoffman, 1972a; Maccoby & Wilson, 1957; Maccoby et al., 1958; Sprafkin & Liebert, 1978). Wishful identification refers to a preference for characters the young viewer would like to resemble, and it increases with age. Thus, children increasingly come to view programs portraying those who are older, more powerful, and higher in status, while when very young they will prefer programs portraying those who are somewhat dependent on others, as they are, such as cute animals (Comstock, 1991a).

What increasingly becomes the case is the adoption of patterns that characterize teenage and adult viewing, but what is surprising is the occurrence of some of these patterns in the earliest years of viewing. The motive of surveillance, or using television as a source for evaluating oneself, apparently begins very early, as evidenced by very young viewers' preference for those on the screen who have something in common with them. The gratification derived from awareness about the medium similarly would seem to be satisfied by the shifting choices of favorite programs, which also begins among the very young.

**TABLE 3.1** Child and Teenage Viewing Preferences, by Type of Program

| | *Percentage Named as Favorites* | | | | | |
|---|---|---|---|---|---|---|
| | *Preschool Age* | | | *Grade* | | |
| | *3* | *4* | *5* | *1st* | *6th* | *10th* |
| Sitcom | — | 4 | 12 | 22 | 17 | 9 |
| Family sitcom | 5 | 2 | 6 | 25 | 23 | 9 |
| Flintstones | 11 | 29 | 36 | — | — | — |
| Mickey Mouse | 3 | 4 | 12 | — | — | — |
| General cartoon | 8 | 16 | 6 | 24 | 5 | 1 |
| Violent cartoon | 3 | 15 | 12 | — | — | — |
| Bozo, etc. | 8 | 2 | — | — | — | — |
| *Sesame Street* | 30 | 13 | 12 | — | — | — |
| Mister Rogers | 3 | 2 | 6 | — | — | — |
| Don't understand the question | 19 | 4 | 3 | — | — | — |

SOURCE: Lyle and Hoffman (1972a, 1972b).
NOTE: Percentages are rounded to the nearest whole number.

Escape is omnipresent, and the central role of simple pleasure in attending to the images on a television screen is manifest in an oddity of the behavioral science laboratory. Television imagery or its withdrawal can be used to shape the behavior of young children (as could any pleasurable or noxious stimulus) and thus is inherently rewarding (Baer, 1962).

Children are reputed to be tremendous fans of favored programs and their characters, and we have no reason to doubt the accuracy of parental anecdotes, newspaper articles, or the testimony of the shelves and stacks in stores of toys and paraphernalia representing a television program. This devotion is reflected in the greater attention preschool children give to the screen when watching a cartoon compared with a situation comedy (Argenta, Stoneman, & Brody, 1986) and the attention that young children give to children's programming in general (Bechtel et al., 1972). In these instances, they are undeniably instrumental viewers.

However, their viewing of other content and at other times, which will constitute a majority of the viewing of all children, is clearly more ritualistic in nature, and their increasing adoption of a less involved stance toward viewing is quite apparent when the frequency of viewing favorite programs is examined (see Figure 3.2). It increases up to about the age of 9; children are exercising their preferences (which by then would place situation comedies in the forefront, with cartoons dwindling in favor and general audience formats other than situation comedies showing small gains). Then the viewing of favorites declines; children begin to conform to the constraints of the time available to view favorites, as their overall viewing at this point in

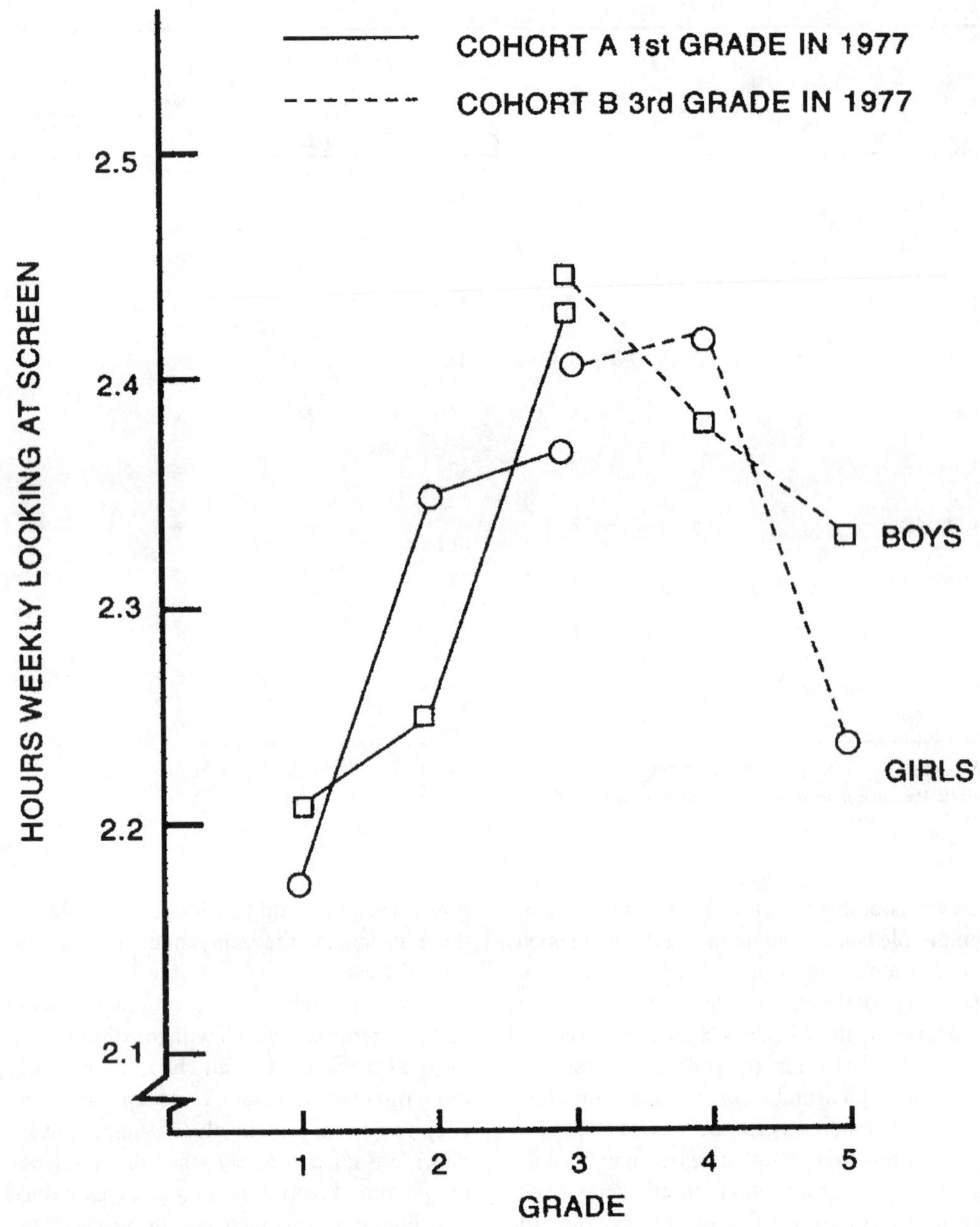


**Figure 3.2.** Change in Frequency of Television Viewing From Grades 1 to 5: Favorite Programs
SOURCE: Eron, Huesmann, Brice, and Mermelstein (1983). Copyright © 1983 by the American Psychological Association. Reprinted with permission.

the life span, on average, is increasing (see Figure 3.1). Children are beginning to resemble adults in their truncated exercise of preferences, an exercise that for both adults and children is only slightly enhanced by the VCR, because only modest amounts of regular recording and replay occur in most households (Comstock & Scharrer, 1999; Lin, 1990, 1993).

Attention to the screen in general typically also will have been rising during these earlier years (see Figure 3.3), because the shifts toward general audience programming on the part of children increasingly require greater attention if they are to understand what is taking place and derive some gratification from following the narrative (D. R. Anderson et al., 1986). Then, at about the same age that time constraints begin to delimit the viewing of favorite programs, attention to the screen begins to decline. Children now have had sufficient experience with television and have attained sufficient cognitive capacity to possess enough knowledge about what is being portrayed so that they can fill in gaps, and have developed sufficient cognitive capability. They are well into the "concrete operational" stage, in the vocabulary of Piaget (Piaget & Inhelder, 1969), so they are able to comprehend most of what is on television about as well as most adults do (Comstock, 1991a), and, consequently, less attention to the screen is required to follow a narrative. They are now monitoring the medium much of the time. Nevertheless, as a careful examination of the data (Figure 3.3) makes clear, young teenagers give more attention to the screen than young children do to satisfy their motive to monitor the general audience programming to which they are now more often attending with comprehension.

By the time young persons are at the midpoint of their teenage years, they will have adopted the adult pattern of viewing in which most television use is ritualistic. The medium will have primacy over specific content, involvement will be comparatively low, and monitoring will describe better the sporadic attention that is typically given to the screen when viewing. However, some programs some of the time will command enough attention and a few viewers will be selective of content in which they are highly interested enough of the time that, for those times and those few viewers, television use is instrumental.

### *Viewing*

We believe that the definition and operationalization of the concept of viewing requires adherence to the way people actually behave when in the vicinity of an operating television set and open to some influence on their attention to the screen of the audio and visual cues it presents. Because monitoring is so often descriptive of what is taking place, we believe our answers must accommodate the considerable lack of immediate attention to the screen. Clancey (1994), in this very vein, has proposed that presence in the room should be sufficient to be counted as a viewer.

We expand this only slightly to include absences that by their brevity are consistent with monitoring. We offer the definition formulated by the first author and his colleagues (Comstock et al., 1978): "a discontinuous, often interrupted, and frequently nonexclusive activity for which a measure in hours and minutes serves only as the outer boundary of possible attention" (pp. 146-147). We operationalize—that is, would measure—these hours and minutes in terms of the time individuals report using the medium, with use divided into three levels: *primary, secondary,* and *tertiary* (Comstock & Scharrer, 1999; Robinson & Godbey, 1997). The first consists of television recorded as a sole activity or foremost activity; it accounts in the average household for slightly more than two thirds of use. The second covers television when it is recorded as specifically secondary to some other activity; this accounts for about one fifth of use. The third includes television that is subordinate to other activities but a set in the vicinity is nevertheless operating (and thus subject to monitoring); this accounts for the remaining approximately 10% of use. These data establish television as an activity that ranks high in the priorities of time allocation despite the irregularities and inconsistencies of attention. They also make it clear that *the majority of use from the perspective of the viewer constitutes the most important activity under way at the time.*

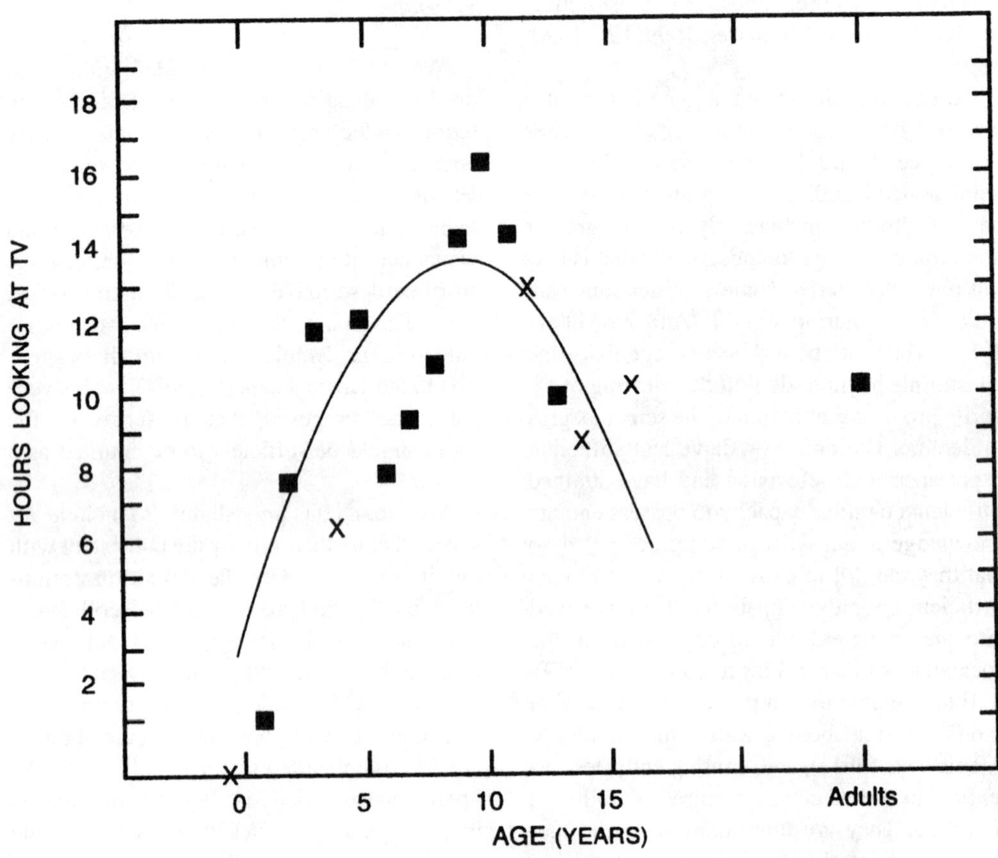


**Figure 3.3.** Weekly Attention to the Screen as a Function of Age
SOURCE: Anderson, Lorch, Field, Collins, and Nathan (1986).

## Viewing Behavior of the Child Audience

We begin our examination of the amount of use of television and other film-related media with a critique of the measurement of viewing. We then turn to the context of other activities within which viewing occurs; the viewing patterns that emerge in connection with our principal variables; developmental processes as they relate to children's television use; changes that have taken place since the introduction of the medium five decades ago; and cross-cultural patterns. The focus will be on television, including VCR use, because motion picture theater attendance is not, in the case of children, a significant factor in media consumption. We will give movie watching some attention in regard to developmental factors (because movie watching and theater attendance increase as children grow older) and changes since the introduction of the medium (because access to movies on the part of the young has increased greatly).

### *Measurement*

Many different sources of data on television viewing exist, and some are less accurate and precise than others. The two principal issues are the validity of the measurement techniques and the representativeness of the sample. Our procedure is to use whatever source best fits our measurement and sample criteria for the question at hand, while sometimes also drawing on sources of lesser quality because their data provide useful and interesting statistics.

We prefer *diary data* that can be recorded post hoc by parents to data produced by Nielsen Media Research's "people meter" that require real-time entry on a remote-control-like device. The latter underestimates the viewing of children (Comstock & Scharrer, 1999), whose real-time behavior may be ignored by adults and who are likely themselves to ignore the task of entry. We obviously also prefer representative national samples. Whenever possible, we draw on the time-use diary data of Robinson and Godbey (1997), who not only have larger representative national samples than Nielsen but require that the total of estimates for all activities conform to a 24-hour day (minimizing the likelihood of misestimates) and, in the case of television, include viewing as a primary, secondary, and tertiary activity (thereby ensuring that all television use is recorded).

Unfortunately, on many points, data from representative national samples are not available. In these cases, we can only offer relationships between variables and not precise estimates of numerical differences that would hold broadly.

### *Other Activities*

Our summary of the data on the context of viewing covers two topics. The first is the standing of television compared with other activities. The second is the relationship between greater amounts of viewing and engaging in voluntary activities such as social interaction, play, lessons, hobbies, and excursions.

#### *Television Compared*

Among the population in general across the life span in the many different societies where time use has been examined, *television invariably ranks third behind sleep,* which is typically first, *and work or school* (Condry, 1989; Robinson & Godbey, 1997). The pattern is only slightly different among children.

The diary data meticulously collected from about 400 children and teenagers between the ages of 3 and 17 (see Table 3.2) by Timmer, Eccles, and O'Brien (1985) indicate that, *at the earliest ages (3-5), television takes up only about half of the time of free play,* which ranks second only to sleep at this age, and *begins to rival play* only among those slightly older (6-8). After this point, television is consistently third on weekdays, and on weekends, when there is no school, it ranks second. The prominence of television after age 9 is consistent with the data collected somewhat differently from fifth graders by Long and Henderson (1973) more than a decade earlier, attesting to a great stability in the allocation of time by children when options also remain stable.

#### *Greater Amounts of Viewing*

Options did not remain stable when television was introduced in the late 1940s. As a result, there was a substantial reallocation of time for everyone, with greater amounts of time spent with mass media overall, principally accounted for by television. There was somewhat less time spent with a wide variety of other activities, including the use of other mass media (Himmelweit, Oppenheim, & Vince, 1958; Murray & Kippax, 1978; Robinson & Converse, 1972; Schramm, Lyle, & Parker, 1961). Similarly, longitudinal data drawn from nearly 2,000 South African seventh to twelfth graders before and after the introduction of television there in 1976 show radio listening and movie attendance most often displaced—though only modestly—and particularly when the medium of television was novel (Mutz, Roberts, & van Vuuren, 1993).

With one important exception, there is very little evidence that greater amounts of television viewing have a detrimental effect on children's engaging in other activities.

**TABLE 3.2** Time Spent by Children and Teenagers in Primary Activities (Mean Hours: Minutes)

| | *Weekdays* | | | | | *Weekend Days* | | | | | |
|---|---|---|---|---|---|---|---|---|---|---|---|
| *Activities* | *3-5[a]* | *6-8* | *9-11* | *12-14* | *15-17* | *3-5* | *6-8* | *9-11* | *12-14* | *15-17* | *Significant Effects* |
| Market work[b] | — | 0:14 | 0:08 | 0:14 | 0:28 | — | 0:04 | 0:10 | 0:29 | 0:48 | |
| Personal care | 0:41 | 0:49 | 0:40 | 0:56 | 1:00 | 0:47 | 0:45 | 0:44 | 1:00 | 0:51 | A, S, A × S (F > M) |
| Household work | 0:14 | 0:15 | 0:18 | 0:27 | 0:34 | 0:17 | 0:27 | 0:51 | 1:12 | 1:00 | A, S, A × S (F > M) |
| Eating | 1:22 | 1:21 | 1:13 | 1:09 | 1:07 | 1:21 | 1:20 | 1:18 | 1:08 | 1:05 | A |
| Sleeping | 10:30 | 9:55 | 9:08 | 7:53 | 8:19 | 10:34 | 10:41 | 9:56 | 10:04 | 9:22 | A |
| School | 2:17 | 4:52 | 5:15 | 5:44 | 5:14 | — | — | — | — | — | |
| Studying | 0:02 | 0:08 | 0:29 | 0:33 | 0:33 | 0:01 | 0:02 | 0:12 | 0:15 | 0:30 | A |
| Church | 0:04 | 0:09 | 0:09 | 0:09 | 0:03 | 0:55 | 0:56 | 0:53 | 0:32 | 0:37 | A |
| Visiting | 0:14 | 0:15 | 0:10 | 0:21 | 0:20 | 0:10 | 0:08 | 0:13 | 0:22 | 0:56 | A (Weekend only) |
| Sports | 0:05 | 0:24 | 0:21 | 0:40 | 0:46 | 0:03 | 0:30 | 0:42 | 0:51 | 0:37 | A, S (M > F) |
| Outdoor activities | 0:04 | 0:09 | 0:06 | 0:07 | 0:11 | 0:06 | 0:23 | 0:39 | 0:25 | 0:26 | |
| Hobbies | 0:00 | 0:02 | 0:02 | 0:04 | 0:06 | 0:01 | 0:05 | 0:03 | 0:06 | 0:03 | |
| Art activities | 0:05 | 0:04 | 0:03 | 0:03 | 0:12 | 0:04 | 0:04 | 0:04 | 0:07 | 0:10 | |
| Other passive leisure | 0:09 | 0:01 | 0:02 | 0:06 | 0:04 | 0:06 | 0:01 | 0:07 | 0:10 | 0:18 | A |
| Playing | 3:38 | 1:51 | 1:05 | 0:31 | 0:14 | 4:27 | 3:00 | 1:32 | 0:35 | 0:21 | A, S (M > F) |
| TV | 1:51 | 1:39 | 2:26 | 2:22 | 1:48 | 2:02 | 2:16 | 3:05 | 2:49 | 2:37 | A, S, A × S (M > F) |
| Reading | 0:05 | 0:05 | 0:09 | 0:10 | 0:12 | 0:04 | 0:09 | 0:10 | 0:10 | 0:18 | A |
| Being read to | 0:02 | 0:02 | 0:00 | 0:00 | 0:00 | 0:03 | 0:02 | 0:00 | 0:00 | 0:00 | A |

SOURCE: Timmer, Eccles, and O'Brien (1985). 

NOTES: A = age effect, significant at $p < .05$ for both weekday and weekend activities unless otherwise specified; S = sex effect, significant at $p < .05$; F > M = females spend more time than males; M > F = males spend more time than females; A × S = age by sex interaction, significant at $p < .05$.

a. Age in years.

b. Market work = obligations outside the home.

Whether the activity in question is socializing with peers, play, lessons, hobbies, or excursions, the relationship with viewing repeatedly has been found to be null or only very modestly inverse with the latter, usually attributable to those who view very little or a very great deal (Lyle & Hoffman, 1972a; Medrich, Roizen, Rubin, & Buckley, 1982; Neuman, 1991; Robinson, 1990). Our interpretation is that children do not typically give up activities that are enjoyable and interesting for television and that viewing is the reciprocal of the availability of such options. The modest inverse relationships principally represent either particularly strong preferences for alternatives among a few (who view very little) or the unavailability of much in the way of alternatives among another few (who view a great deal). *The exception is reading,* for which television can serve as a less demanding, more accessible sedentary substitute (Comstock & Scharrer, 1999; Mutz et al., 1993; Williams, 1986).

### *Viewing Patterns*

Our best estimate of the average amount of viewing by children (ages 2-11) is 3 hours and 7 minutes a day, or 21 hours and 49 minutes a week (see Figure 3.4). This is based on the estimates of total adult viewing by Robinson and Godbey (1997), adjusted for the slightly lower rates of television viewing by children (Comstock & Scharrer, 1999). It is highly consistent with (and in our view, confirmed by) the weekly estimates of 24 hours and 4 minutes obtained by questionnaire from about 275,000 sixth graders, an age when viewing would be above average, as part of the California Assessment Program (Comstock, 1991a). It also closely matches the estimate of 14 hours and 24 minutes obtained for primary viewing only in the diaries of Timmer and colleagues (1985); this would leave about a third of television use unaccounted for that would be explained by secondary and tertiary viewing. Finally, it fits with the substantially higher estimates offered in the mid-1970s by the diaries of the A. C. Nielsen Company. Their sponsorship may lead to samples that overrepresent those who view more than the average, and their diaries have not had the restraining influence of demanding that time recorded viewing must conform to time spent otherwise over a 24-hour day (Robinson & Godbey, 1997). However, the amount of viewing is also importantly influenced by our principal variables.

There is a moderate degree of stability in the amount of television that children view. For example, Tangney and Feshbach (1988) in a sample of 400 elementary school children found correlations of .67 and .65 between adjacent years and .54 between the first and third year in hours spent with television. Some stability would be expected, because for many children the principal variables that influence viewing would not change. What the data attest, then, is that, in fact, there is considerable change in the obligations, alternatives, and preferences for other activities that govern the time available on which television depends.

#### *Societal and Structural Factors*

What is available does not much influence how much children view, but it has an important effect on what they view and the allocation of viewing time between educational and cultural fare and the kinds of entertainment consumed. Time allocated to television by everyone has been very similar across societies and sites despite considerable variation in the number of available channels, hours of operation, diversity, and emphases of programming (Comstock et al., 1978; Robinson & Godbey, 1997). For example, when a single government-sponsored channel was introduced to a remote British Columbia community, viewing patterns in terms of amount quickly came to resemble those of a similar community with access to five channels—two Canadian and three American networks (Williams, 1986).

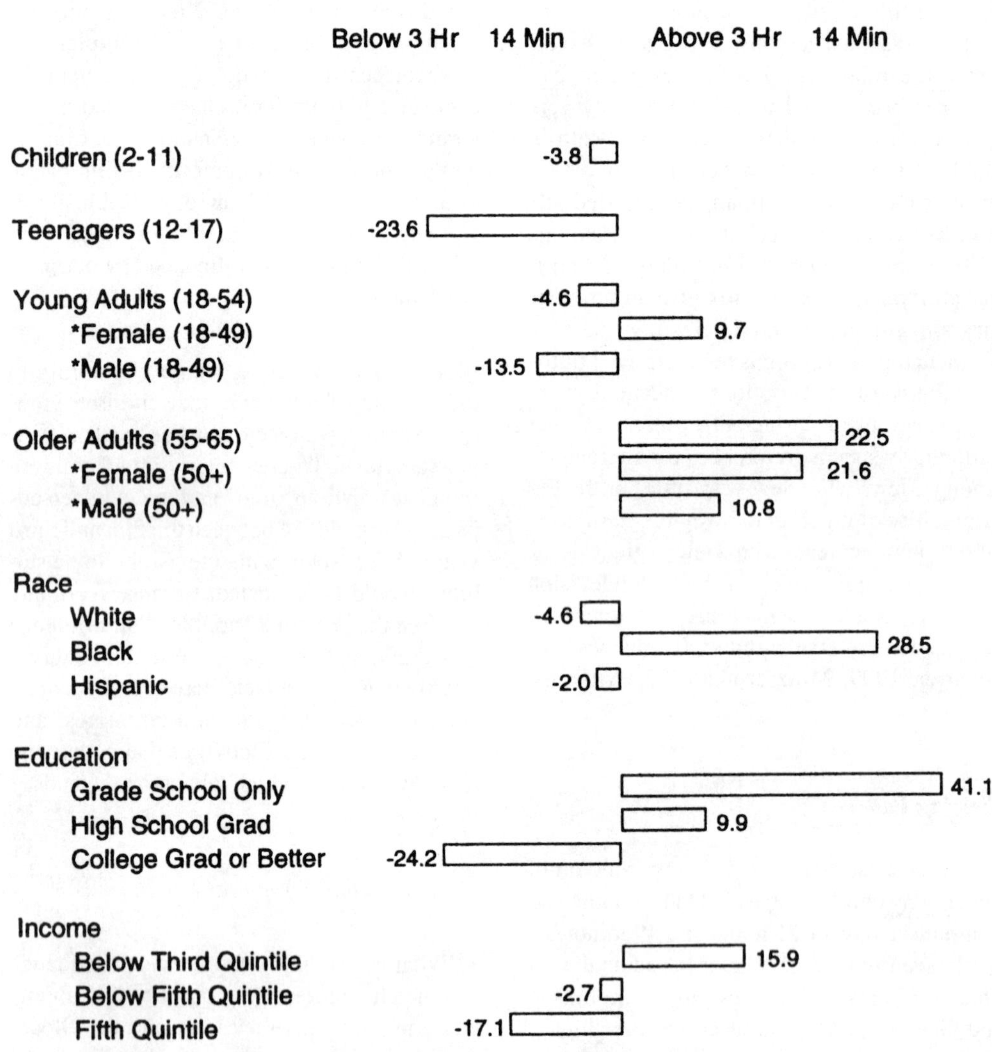


**Figure 3.4.** Amount of Total Viewing, by Demographics

SOURCE: Adapted from Robinson and Godbey (1997). Partial copyright © 1997 by The Pennsylvania State University Press and partial copyright © 1998 by Columbia University Press. Adapted with permission.

However, the degree to which a national television system resembles that of the United States, with its comparative lack of a prescriptive paternalism in regard to how the public should be served and its reliance on advertising for support, is an important determinant of the availability of educational and cultural programming that children will view. It also predicts the availability of light entertainment and provocative (and often salacious) talk shows and the degree to which violence serves as a principal vehicle (Hamilton, 1998). Similarly, while readiness to adopt new technology increases access to television and other film-related media, meaningful diversity is suppressed by the competition that makes entertainment the most effective means to attract audiences of interest to advertisers. The result is that there may not be much in the way of educational and cultural fare for children to view as they grow older (Hamilton, 1998; Huston et al., 1990). Thus, societies that impose more demanding standards of public service are likely to offer more options to children viewing television that might have some constructive influence (see Chapters 19 and 33).

Governmental and regulatory practices also influence what is available. Thus, in the 1990s, the demands in the United States made by Congress and the Federal Communications Commission (FCC) for more educational and cultural programming as a condition of retaining a broadcast license led at first merely to the relabeling of entertainment programming but then, when these bodies signaled this was not sufficient, to the production of much new programming that would more clearly meet these requirements.

### *Household Attributes*

The three principal household variables that influence the amount of television use by children are socioeconomic status, race, and norms about television use. However, resources available and parent communication practices also make a difference.

Viewing is inversely associated with socioeconomic status, with education a more powerful predictor than income, and is greater in black and to a lesser degree in Hispanic than in white households (Anderson, Mead, & Sullivan, 1986; Blosser, 1988; Comstock, 1991a; Comstock et al., 1978; Comstock & Scharrer, 1999; Medrich et al., 1982). Norms favoring heavy use of television (e.g., the absence of rules specifying when viewing is inappropriate) are associated with greater viewing by children in households that otherwise are apparently comparable (Comstock & Scharrer, 1999; Medrich et al., 1982), and only half of parents say they "often" impose rules about how much, when, and what programs may be viewed (Bower, 1985). These three variables, of course, are correlated, with norms favoring the medium—which elsewhere we have called "household centrality of television" (Comstock & Scharrer, 1999)—and households lower in socioeconomic status more frequent among black households, but each also independently accounts for a substantial difference when households are otherwise alike. On the whole, children in the data we judge to be most reliable and valid have viewed only slightly less than adults and a great deal more than teenagers (see Figure 3.4).

The governing role of time availability obviously imposes a ceiling on the effects of greater centrality of television, but they are nevertheless substantial in both the short and long run. Our estimate from the sample of 750 sixth-grade children examined by Medrich and colleagues (1982) is that a pervasive, unrestricted use of television in the household led to about 20% more television use by children (Comstock, 1991a). These are circumstances that apparently apply to a majority of children, because we conservatively combined those registering as moderate and high in centrality to contrast with those registering as low, which resulted in about 80% of the sample falling into the group that comparatively had a lack of household rules and constant television use. Similarly, Rosengren and Windahl (1989) found in Scandinavia that the amount of viewing of a sample of 11- and 13-year-olds was directly correlated with the amount of parental use. This parental endorsement has long-range implications because the amount of viewing by teenagers is predicted by earlier amounts of parental viewing (Rosengren & Windahl, 1989), and the amount of viewing by young adults is predicted by the amount of parental viewing when they were growing up (Kenny, 1985).

Resources available in the household make a contribution. Multisets, available in three fourths of households, mean that children more often will view alone or with other children and will choose their own programming. A national survey of nearly 3,000 households found that about one third of those with children under 12 and about one half with teens had television sets located in the child's bedroom (Sherman, 1996). *Interestingly, higher levels of parental education were associated with fewer sets in children's bedrooms.* In our view, this is a further reflection of the central role of the values associated with greater education in media use. The financial resources often associated with higher education levels that would make a set for a child's room affordable were less important than the greater concern and prescription regarding viewing also accompanying higher levels of parental education.

VCRs, available in 85% of households, mean that children will view more movies, with easier access to those with restricted labels, accounting on the average for about 15% of total viewing (Kubey & Larson, 1990; Sims, 1989). Younger children watch more rented or owned videos than older children do, with one randomly drawn national sample finding that 4-year-olds spend nearly 1.5 hours per day watching videos, compared with 40 minutes for 15- to 17-year-olds (Mares, 1998). Younger children also engage in more repeat viewing of videos and more often coview with parents (Mares, 1998). However, in a substantial number of VCR-owning households with children—perhaps as many as a third—no VCR use will occur during the typical week (Wartella, Heintz, Aidman, & Mazzarella, 1990), and VCR use tends to provide the same gratifications for children as television viewing does (Cohen, Levy, & Golden, 1988). The remarkable amount of VCR use by the very young indicates that many parents cannot find suitable programming on broadcast and cable channels.

The absence of use in many households with children indicates that there is wide variation in the use of this resource (and possibly with the satisfaction with available programming), and the type of satisfaction derived from what these young persons view is the same regardless of source. Higher socioeconomic status implies greater opportunities for children to engage in activities more satisfying than television, which may partly account for the lower levels of viewing. In contrast, higher centrality of television implies the availability of fewer non-television-related media, which would decrease the likelihood that the few children who might take an interest in those media would use them.

Parental communication practices also affect a child's media use. Lack of interaction with parents in the home as a result of the out-of-home employment of mothers or the absence of fathers is associated with more time spent viewing among adolescents (Brown, Childers, Bauman, & Koch, 1990). An emphasis on communication and discussion rather than prescription and the exercise of power in the disciplinary practices of parents is associated with greater viewing of programs portraying constructive behavior (Abelman, 1985); the providing by parents of supplementary information and evaluation in connection with programs (e.g., geographical, historical, or scientific facts; moral implications; the make-believe aspects of stories; Messaris & Kerr, 1983); and improved comprehension of programs on the part of the child (Singer et al., 1988).

Encouraging the expression of opinions and the exchange of ideas in the household increases as a child grows older (Meadowcroft, 1986), presumably because many parents believe this is a province for the more mature. Such encouragement is associated with children with less total television viewing, greater print use, and greater instrumental use of the medium, with the latter two exemplified by higher levels of news consumption (Chaffee & McLeod, 1972; Chaffee, McLeod, & Atkin, 1971). *When the emphasis is on maintaining social harmony without an accompanying emphasis on expression and opinion, total viewing is greater, entertainment viewing is higher, and news consumption is lower.* When expression and opinion are emphasized jointly with social harmony, the heightened total and entertainment viewing vanishes, and news consumption is enhanced even more. In our view, these data overall identify the communication atmosphere established by parents as a key factor in the development of constructive, instrumental use of the media in which entertainment is somewhat diminished but of course—for most young viewers—remains predominant.

### *Child Variables*

The four major child variables that affect viewing are age, mental ability, comprehension, and innate affinity for viewing, with the first by far the most important. The amount of viewing increases during the elementary school years, reaching a peak at about the age of 12 (see Figure 3.1). Then it declines as the greater obligations, opportunities, and time outside the household during the teenage years suppress the amount of time spent in the vicinity of an operating set.

Mental ability among children is inversely associated with television use (Gortmaker, Salter, Walker, & Dietz, 1990), but only very modestly so (Lyle & Hoffman, 1972a), and these differences have been declining with time (Comstock & Scharrer, 1999). The explanations are that particularly bright children often make use of all available media (Schramm et al., 1961) and norms favoring greater consumption of television have become more widespread (Comstock & Scharrer, 1999).

Comprehension plays little role in how much is viewed in total, as is clear from the many hours spent viewing by those too young to fully understand all that is taking place. However, as we have observed, it plays a large role in the degree of attention actually given the screen and therefore in the amount of viewing as a primary activity (see Figure 3.3). Attention rises as children need to pay closer attention to understand the narrative, then declines as greater knowledge about subject matter and the conventions of the medium make close attention less necessary for understanding.

Children also differ in the degree to which television use is innately gratifying. Plomin, Corley, DeFries, and Fulker (1990), using the widely recognized methodology for separating genetic from environmental influences among a sample of 220 children ages 3, 4, and 5 in the well-known Colorado Adoption Project (Plomin & DeFries, 1985), found that amount of viewing was a product of both heredity and environment. Our tentative interpretation is that television is inherently pleasurable, which would help explain why set use is so similar across societies, and that the degree of innate gratification has a basis in the degree of pleasure derived from alpha waves, or holistic, nonverbal, affective right-brain processing (Comstock & Scharrer, 1999; Krugman, 1971; Rothschild, Thorson, Reeves, Hirsch, & Goldstein, 1986).

### *Situational Influences*

We divide situational influences into three categories: the presence of others, temporal factors, and mental states. The first covers the role of parents and other children; the second, the hour of day, day of the week, and season; and the third, emotions such as anger and loneliness, as well as the desire to relax or be entertained.

The attention to the screen, and thus viewing as a primary activity, will vary with the attention given by others in the room, parents and other children (Anderson, Lorch, Smith, Bradford, & Levin, 1981). Parents and other children also will increase viewing by a child in general in the short run by turning on a set and thereby placing the child in the role of a viewer.

Temporal influences are quite marked (Comstock & Scharrer, 1999; Nielsen Media Research, 1998; Robinson & Godbey, 1997; Webster & Phalen, 1997). There is a day cycle in which children's viewing rises in the afternoon and continues through prime time, with a peak at about 8:30 P.M. for those younger (2-5) and at shortly before 9 P.M. for those older (6-11). The younger children view at a greater rate in the early morning and early afternoon. There is also a week cycle, with children's viewing at its highest on Fridays and Saturdays, when they don't have school the next day; this is in contrast to young adults, whose viewing is at a minimum because of competing social and entertainment options. There is also seasonal variation, with children's viewing somewhat higher during the summer when school is out.

Children cite television as a favored activity to relax, to be entertained, and to fend off loneliness (Lyle & Hoffman, 1972a). It is ranked much lower as an antidote for anger or hurt feelings. There is little variation in self-reported gratifications by gender or age.

### *Developmental Processes*

If we take the initial hours of viewing before the age of 3 and the peak levels reached at about the age of 12, the process from attending to imagery with very limited meaning to viewing as an adult covers about 9 years. How much children view is primarily a function of the time they have available without obligations or preferred alternatives. What they view with comprehension and interest changes as they grow up. Cartoons and cartoon-like storytelling swiftly give way to situation comedies. Attention rises as more is needed for comprehension; the medium becomes more central, as does ritualistic viewing, as the opportunity to view favorite programs decreases.

Household characteristics and child attributes affect changes in the amount of viewing and in the division between ritualistic and instrumental use as children mature. Households lower in socioeconomic status and households higher in television centrality will have greater viewing by children and less instrumental use as specific content takes a decidedly subsidiary place to the pleasures of monitoring the most satisfactory of available options. Early instrumental use as exemplified by viewing children's educational programs (of which the best known has been *Sesame Street*), which often will have been the product of thoughtful parental guidance, will lead to less total viewing and greater instrumental viewing when the child becomes a teenager (Rosengren & Windahl, 1989); this is another example of the important role of household characteristics in the media behavior of young people and why the environment established by parents has long-range consequences for their children. Foremost among child attributes is mental ability with those more cognitively capable making comparatively greater use of print as they grow older.

Comprehension is also an important factor. Up to about 6 years of age, greater attention to the screen—which, in our view, represents involvement—is largely confined to cartoons and other children's programs (Bechtel et al., 1972). Then it increases for television in general as the narratives of more programs for general audiences that require greater attention for understanding are given attention up to about the age of 10; it then begins to decline as children have begun to achieve an adult understanding of the medium (D. R. Anderson et al., 1986). This peak essentially coincides with the ages of 7 to 9, when children move from Piaget's preoperational to his concrete operational stage and become more able to understand subtleties of plot and character and place comparatively greater emphasis on meaning and verbal elements than appearances and action. However, much of television in terms of interpreting its narratives becomes understandable before this transition period (Wolf, 1987), which explains why the curve representing attention to the screen presented by D. R. Anderson and colleagues (1986) rises stoutly beginning at age 5. Similarly, children's viewing of favorite programs will peak and decline as there is reduced opportunity, as with teenagers and adults, to view their favorites; at the same time, the amount of viewing in a less attentive way—what we have called monitoring—will continue to increase up until about the age of 12 (Comstock, 1991a).

The national television system influences how much of this experience is likely to be entertainment or to have some cultural or educational value. Programming of the latter sort is more prevalent when reliance on advertiser support is less and the triumvirate of non-paternalism, competition, and entertainment that characterizes American television is restrained (Comstock, 1991b).

Movies played a very minor role in the lives of children with television before widespread adoption of the VCR. For example, Lyle and Hoffman (1972a), in their survey of 1,600 first, sixth, and tenth graders found that, even by the sixth grade, the average amount of time allocated per week to watching movies (other than those shown on broadcast television) was less than 20 minutes, and only 15% had seen a movie at a theater during the past week. We estimate that the VCR increased this figure by almost tenfold (Comstock, 1991a). The developmental significance is that the VCR gives children access to movies, which are more emotionally and psychologically involving than much of television is; are repeatedly viewed, especially among the very young; and may, for older children, include vehicles with restricted labels.

### *Changes*

The pervasive major change in television and other film-related media is the enormous growth in the variety of programming that has become available through large increases in the number of stations: new broadcast networks (including Fox, WB, and UPN), cable systems with premium movie channels, and pay-per-view, in addition to a wide range of broadcast and cable offerings. The VCR, with its choice of recording for playback what is already on television or viewing prerecorded videotapes of films made for theater release or specialized content, also expands viewing choices.

The major significance of greater choice does not lie in the amount of viewing. Amount of viewing is governed largely by the time available for viewing (but not wholly, because very specialized content not fungible with most programs may draw a few viewers who otherwise would not be viewing television at that time, a phenomenon readily visible among adults with major sporting events). The significance lies instead in the degree to which children may view adult content or concentrate their viewing if they wish on one type of content. For example, on one end of the spectrum, they may choose violence and films with restricted labels. On the other, they may select educational videos spawned by successful children's television shows such as *Barney & Friends, Arthur,* and *Blue's Clues.* The foregone opportunities when a national television system does not encourage or require educational and cultural offerings remain. Even at present in the United States, however, the amount of programming in which children can take an honest interest as well as derive some pleasure and an enriching experience is vast compared with past decades.

### *Cross-Cultural Comparisons*

Von Feilitzen (1999) collates worldwide Nielsen people meter data on television viewing by children and teenagers in 10 countries.[1] Groebel (1999) summarizes a survey of the access and use of major media among more than 5,000 12-year-olds in 23 countries.[2] Livingstone, Holden, and Bovill (1999) present the results of a comprehensive survey of media access and use by more than 15,000 children and teenagers in 11 European countries[3] and Israel.

Precise comparisons, as with many of the sets of data on U.S. children, are not possible because of variations in methods and, even when the method is the same, uncertainties over the comparability and representativeness of samples. However, broad patterns are readily discernible.

The most indelible impression is the degree to which television use by children is much the same in all countries. In developed countries, access (households with television) approaches 100%, and amount of viewing (which in this case excluded most secondary and tertiary use) is about 2 hours or more per day. Even in less developed regions, access registers at more than 80%. Time spent with television by children throughout the world is quite similar. Among the 10 countries in the von Feilitzen data (when averaged for children of all ages), the range in the amount of use was less than 1.5 hours per day. Estimates were lowest for South Korea, at 104 minutes, and highest for Argentina, at 191 minutes per day. Television can be fairly described at this point in time as the universal medium.

The second most noticeable pattern is the frequency of differences in access to and use of media other than broadcast and cable television. This is made particularly clear by the 12-country data collected by Livingstone and colleagues in which the measurement of access and use was quite comprehensive. VCR use varies from 16 minutes per day in Germany to 47 minutes per day in Italy among all children. Using the Internet varies from about 4 minutes per day in the Netherlands to about 30 minutes per day in Israel among users only. The amount of time spent reading books differs from a low of 14 minutes in Flanders to a high of 35 minutes per day in Finland among all users.

As Livingstone and colleagues point out, some differences reflect marketing and technological developments (e.g., a great variety of cable offerings that would suppress rental video viewing). Others may reflect differences in cultural and social structure that affect the norms, tastes, and preferences of young people and, presumably, their parents. Some, certainly, can be seen as deficits from the perspective of developing scholastic skills or enjoying a wider or deeper cultural experience.

## Future Research

Our paradigm for describing children's use of television and other film-related media ascribes differences in how much and what is viewed to four sets of principal variables: *societal and structural factors, household characteristics, child attributes,* and *situational influences.* These translate, roughly, into options, norms and practices, individual differences, and transient experience. The first three form the fundamental triangle of influences that determine what the role of the media will be in the life of the individual growing up. What questions, then, do they lead us to ask?

The pioneering surveys of major and comprehensive media use across societies by Groebel (1999) and Livingstone, Holden, and Bovill (1999) exemplify a major priority for future research—examining the changes taking place rapidly now in media beyond the ubiquitous television that still consumes so much of the time of young persons. However, access to and use of media become meaningful only in the context of the two other major questions that must be addressed. The first of these is the experience represented by media use, which may be thought of as the joint product of the content and the responses evoked by that content. The second escalates sharply the degree of concern and interest evoked by the media use of young persons because it asks about the implications of this joint product for emotional, mental, physical, and behavioral well-being as children grow up.

We propose a bold but eminently practical challenge—practical in the sense of serving concretely the interests of parents and their children—to examine the experiences while growing up that seemingly contribute to constructive use of the media during adulthood. Surely, there are regularities in the use of media while growing up that have long-term implications. Our priorities ask for a balance between ritualistic and instrumental use of television, the use of other media (including books, magazines, newspapers, and the Internet) in addition to television, and the placement of media use within a larger framework of the arts, cultural activities, sports, and hobbies and personal interests.

We anticipate that there will be a propitious fit between our fundamental triangle and these outcomes—ones from which we can learn, at the societal and structural, household, and individual levels, about what we might do to achieve our goal. The media are too prominent now in the lives of children not to insist that they and we transcend them.

## Notes

1. Argentina, Australia, Chile, the Czech Republic, Lebanon, the Philippines, South Africa, South Korea, Spain, and the United States.

2. Angola, Argentina, Armenia, Brazil, Canada, Costa Rica, Croatia, Egypt, Fiji, Germany, India, Japan, Mauritius, the Netherlands, Peru, the Philippines, Qatar, South Africa, Spain, Tadjikistan, Togo, Trinidad and Tobago, and the Ukraine.

3. Denmark, Finland, Flanders/Belgium, France, Germany, Italy, the Netherlands, Spain, Sweden, Switzerland, and the United Kingdom.

## References


Abelman, R. (1985). Styles of parental disciplinary practices as a mediator of children's learning from prosocial television portrayals. *Child Study Journal, 17,* 46-57.

Albarran, A. B., & Umphrey, D. (1993). An examination of television motivations and program preferences by Hispanics, blacks, and whites. *Journal of Broadcasting and Electronic Media, 37*(1), 95-103.

Allen, C. L. (1965). Photographing the TV audience. *Journal of Advertising Research, 5,* 208.

Anderson, B., Mead, N., & Sullivan, S. (1986). *Television: What do national assessment tests tell us?* Princeton, NJ: Educational Testing Service.

Anderson, D. R., Collins, P. A., Schmitt, K. L., & Jacobvitz, R. S. (1996). Stressful life events and television viewing. *Communication Research, 23*(3), 243-260.

Anderson, D. R., & Lorch, E. P. (1983). Looking at television: Action or reaction? In J. Bryant & D. R. Anderson (Eds.), *Children's understanding of television: Research on attention and comprehension* (pp. 1-34). New York: Academic Press.

Anderson, D. R., Lorch, E. P., Field, D. E., Collins, P. A., & Nathan, J. G. (1986). Television viewing at home: Age trends in visual attention and time with TV. *Child Development, 57,* 1024-1033.

Anderson, D. R., Lorch, E. P., Smith, R., Bradford, R., & Levin, S. R. (1981). Effects of peer presence on preschool children's television-viewing behavior. *Developmental Psychology, 17*(4), 446-453.

Argenta, D. M., Stoneman, Z., & Brody, G. H. (1986). The effects of three different television programs on young children's peer interactions and toy play. *Journal of Applied Developmental Psychology, 7*(4), 355-371.

Baer, D. M. (1962). Laboratory control of thumbsucking by withdrawal and representation of reinforcement. *Journal of the Experimental Analysis of Behavior, 5,* 525-528.

Barwise, T. P., & Ehrenberg, A. S. C. (1988). *Television and its audience.* Newbury Park, CA: Sage.

Barwise, T. P., Ehrenberg, A. S. C., & Goodhardt, G. J. (1982). Glued to the box? Patterns of TV repeat viewing. *Journal of Communication, 32*(4), 22-29.

Bechtel, R. B., Achelpohl, C., & Akers, R. (1972). Correlates between observed behavior and questionnaire responses on television viewing. In E. A. Rubinstein, G. A. Comstock, & J. P. Murray (Eds.), *Television and social behavior: Vol. 4. Television in day-to-day life: Patterns of use.* Washington, DC: U.S. Government Printing Office.

Blosser, B. J. (1988). Ethnic differences in children's media use. *Journal of Broadcasting and Electronic Media, 32*(4), 453-470.

Bower, R. (1985). *The changing television audience in America.* New York: Columbia University Press.

Brown, J. D., Childers, K. W., Bauman, K. E., & Koch, G. G. (1990). The influence of new media and family structure on young adolescents' television and radio use. *Communication Research, 17*(1), 65-82.

Bryant, J., Zillmann, D., & Brown, D. (1983). Entertainment features in children's educational television: Effects on attention and information acquisition. In J. Bryant & D. R. Anderson (Eds.), *Children's understanding of television: Research on attention and comprehension* (pp. 221-240). New York: Academic Press.

Canary, D. J., & Spitzberg, B. H. (1993). Loneliness and media gratification. *Communication Research, 20*(6), 800-821.

Cantor, J. (1994a). Confronting children's fright responses to mass media. In D. Zillmann, J. Bryant, & A. C. Huston (Eds.), *Media, children, and the family: Social scientific, psychodynamic, and clinical perspectives* (pp. 139-150). Hillsdale, NJ: Lawrence Erlbaum.

Cantor, J. (1994b). Fright reactions to mass media. In J. Bryant & D. Zillmann (Eds.), *Media effects: Advances in theory and research* (pp. 213-246). Hillsdale, NJ: Lawrence Erlbaum.

Chaffee, S. H., & McLeod, J. M. (1972). Adolescent television use in the family context. In G. A. Comstock & E. A. Rubinstein (Eds.), *Television and social behavior: Vol. 3. Television and adolescent aggressiveness* (pp. 149-172). Washington, DC: U.S. Government Printing Office.

Chaffee, S. H., McLeod, J. M., & Atkin, C. K. (1971). Parental influences on adolescent media use. *American Behavioral Scientist, 14,* 323-340.

Clancey, M. (1994). The television audience examined. *Journal of Advertising Research, 34*(4), 1-10.

Cohen, A. A., Levy, M. R., & Golden, K. (1988). Children's uses and gratifications of home VCRs: Evolution or revolution? *Communication Research, 15*(6), 772-780.

Collins, W. A. (1981). Recent advances in research on cognitive processing of television viewing. *Journal of Broadcasting, 25*(4), 327-334.

Comstock, G. (1991a). *Television and the American child.* San Diego, CA: Academic Press.

Comstock, G. (1991b). *Television in America* (2nd ed.). Newbury Park, CA: Sage.

Comstock, G., Chaffee, S., Katzman, N., McCombs, M., & Roberts, D. (1978). *Television and human behavior.* New York: Columbia University Press.

Comstock, G., & Scharrer, E. (1999). *Television: What's on, who's watching, and what it means.* San Diego, CA: Academic Press.

Condry, J. (1989). *The psychology of television.* Hillsdale, NJ: Lawrence Erlbaum.

Cook, T. D., Appleton, H., Conner, R. F., Shaffer, A., Tamkin, G., & Weber, S. J. (1975). *"Sesame Street" revisited.* New York: Russell Sage.

Eron, L. D., Huesmann, L. R., Brice, P., & Mermelstein, R. (1983). Age trends in the development of aggression, sex typing, and related television habits. *Developmental Psychology, 19*(1), 71-77.

Frank, R. E., & Greenberg, M. G. (1980). *The public's use of television.* Newbury Park, CA: Sage.

Gortmaker, S. L., Salter, C. A., Walker, D. K., & Dietz, W. H. (1990). The impact of television viewing on mental aptitude and achievement: A longitudinal study. *Public Opinion Quarterly, 54*(4), 594-604.

Groebel, J. (1999). Media access and media use among 12-year-olds in the world. In C. von Feilitzen & U. Carlsson (Eds.), *Children and media: Image, education, participation* (pp. 61-67). Göteborg, Sweden: Göteborg University, UNESCO International Clearinghouse on Children and Violence on the Screen.

Hamilton, J. T. (1998). *Channeling violence.* Princeton, NJ: Princeton University Press.

Harwood, J. (1997). Viewing age: Lifespan identity and television viewing choices. *Journal of Broadcasting and Electronic Media, 41*(2), 203-213.

Himmelweit, H. T., Oppenheim, A. N., & Vince, P. (1958). *Television and the child.* London: Oxford University Press.

Hollenbeck, A., & Slaby, R. (1979). Infant visual and vocal responses to television. *Child Development, 50,* 41-45.

Hopkins, N. M., & Mullis, A. K. (1985). Family perceptions of television viewing habits. *Family Relations, 34*(2), 177-181.

Huston, A., & Wright, J. C. (1989). The forms of television and the child viewer. In G. Comstock (Ed.), *Public communication and behavior* (Vol. 2, pp. 103-159). New York: Academic Press.

Huston, A., Wright, J. C., Rice, M. L., Kerkman, D., Siegle, J., & Bremer, M. (1983, April). *Family environment and television use by preschool children.* Paper presented at the biennial meeting of the Society for Research in Child Development, Detroit, MI.

Huston, A., Wright, J. C., Rice, M. L., Kerkman, D., & St. Peters, M. (1990). Development of television viewing patterns in early childhood: A longitudinal investigation. *Developmental Psychology, 26*(3), 409-420.

Kenny, J. F. (1985). *The family as a mediator of television use and the cultivation phenomenon among college students.* Unpublished doctoral dissertation, Syracuse University, Syracuse, NY.

Koolstra, C. M., & van der Voort, T. H. A. (1996). Longitudinal effects of television on children's leisure-time reading: A test of three explanatory models. *Human Communication Research, 23*(1), 4-35.

Krugman, H. E. (1971). Brain wave measures of media involvement. *Journal of Advertising Research, 11*(1), 3-9.

Krull, R. (1983). Children learning to watch television. In J. Bryant & D. R. Anderson (Eds.), *Children's understanding of television: Research on attention and comprehension* (pp. 103-123). New York: Academic Press.

Kubey, R. W., & Csikszentmihalyi, M. (1990). *Television and the quality of life: How viewing shapes everyday experience.* Hillsdale, NJ: Lawrence Erlbaum.

Kubey, R. W., & Larson, R. (1990). The use and experience of the new video media among children and young adolescents. *Communication Research, 17*(1), 107-130.

Levy, M. R. (1978). The audience experience with television news. *Journalism Monographs, 55,* 1-29.

Lin, C. A. (1990). Audience activity and VCR use. In J. R. Dobrow (Ed.), *Social and cultural aspects of VCR use* (pp. 75-92). Hillsdale, NJ: Lawrence Erlbaum.

Lin, C. A. (1993). Exploring the role of VCR use in the emerging home entertainment culture. *Journalism Quarterly, 70*(4), 833-842.

Livingstone, S., Holden, K. J., & Bovill, M. (1999). Children's changing media environment: Overview of a European comparative study. In C. von Feilitzen & U. Carlsson (Eds.), *Children and media: Image, education, participation* (pp. 61-67). Göteborg, Sweden: Göteborg University, UNESCO International Clearinghouse on Children and Violence on the Screen.

Long, B. H., & Henderson, E. H. (1973). Children's use of time: Some personal and social correlates. *Elementary School Journal, 73,* 193-199.

Lorch, E. P., Anderson, D. R., & Levin, S. R. (1979). The relationship of visual attention to children's comprehension of television. *Child Development, 50,* 722-727.

LoSciuto, L. A. (1972). A national inventory of television viewing behavior. In E. A. Rubinstein, G. A. Comstock, & J. P. Murray (Eds.), *Television and social behavior: Vol. 4. Television in day-to-day life: Patterns of use* (pp. 33-86). Washington, DC: U.S. Government Printing Office.

Lyle, J., & Hoffman, H. R. (1972a). Children's use of television and other media. In E. A. Rubinstein, G. A. Comstock, & J. P. Murray (Eds.), *Television and social behavior: Vol. 4. Television in day-to-day life: Patterns of use* (pp. 129-256). Washington, DC: U.S. Government Printing Office.

Lyle, J., & Hoffman, H. R. (1972b). Explorations in patterns of television viewing by preschool-age children. In E. A. Rubinstein, G. A. Comstock, & J. P. Murray (Eds.), *Television and social behavior: Vol. 4. Television in day-to-day life: Patterns of use* (pp. 257-273). Washington, DC: U.S. Government Printing Office.

Maccoby, E. E. (1954). Why do children watch television? *Public Opinion Quarterly, 18*(3), 239-244.

Maccoby, E. E., & Wilson, W. C. (1957). Identification and observational learning from films. *Journal of Abnormal and Social Psychology, 55,* 76-87.

Maccoby, E. E., Wilson, W. C., & Burton, R. V. (1958). Differential movie-viewing behavior of male and female viewers. *Journal of Personality, 26,* 259-267.

Mares, M. L. (1998). Children's use of VCRs. *Annals of the American Academy of Political and Social Science, 557,* 120-132.

Meadowcroft, J. M. (1986). Family communication patterns and political development: The child's role. *Communication Research, 13*(4), 603-624.

Medrich, E. A., Roizen, J., Rubin, V., & Buckley, S. (1982). *The serious business of growing up: A study of children's lives outside of school.* Los Angeles: University of California Press.

Meltzoff, A. N. (1988). Imitation of televised models by infants. *Child Development, 59,* 1221-1229.

Messaris, P., & Kerr, D. (1983). Mothers' comments about TV: Relation to family communication patterns. *Communication Research, 10,* 175-194.

Murray, J. P., & Kippax, S. (1978). Children's social behavior in three towns with differing television experience. *Journal of Communication, 28*(4), 19-29.

Mutz, D. C., Roberts, D. F., & van Vuuren, D. P. (1993). Reconsidering the displacement hypothesis: Television's influence on children's time use. *Communication Research, 20*(1), 51-75.

National Television Violence Study. (1996). *National Television Violence Study: Scientific papers, 1994-95.* Studio City, CA: Mediascope.

National Television Violence Study. (1997). *National Television Violence Study* (Vol. 2). Santa Barbara: University of California, Center for Communication and Social Policy.

National Television Violence Study. (1998). *National Television Violence Study* (Vol. 3). Santa Barbara: University of California, Center for Communication and Social Policy.

Neuman, S. B. (1991). *Literacy in the television age.* Norwood, NJ: Ablex.

Neuman, W. R. (1982). Television and American culture: The mass medium and the pluralistic audience. *Public Opinion Quarterly, 46*(4), 471-487.

Nielsen Media Research. (1998). *1998 report on television.* New York: Author.

Piaget, J., & Inhelder, B. (1969). *The psychology of the child.* New York: Basic Books.

Plomin, R., Corley, R., DeFries, J. C., & Fulker, D. W. (1990). Individual differences in television viewing in early childhood: Nature as well as nurture. *Psychological Science, 6*(1), 371-377.

Plomin, R., & DeFries, J. C. (1985). *Origins of individual differences in infancy: The Colorado Adoption Project.* New York: Academic Press.

Potts, R., & Sanchez, D. (1994). Television viewing and depression: No news is good news. *Journal of Broadcasting and Electronic Media, 38*(1), 79-90.

Robinson, J. P. (1990). Television's effects on families' use of time. In J. Bryant (Ed.), *Television and the American family* (pp. 195-210). Hillsdale, NJ: Lawrence Erlbaum.

Robinson, J. P., & Converse, P. E. (1972). The impact of television on mass media usages: A cross-national comparison. In A. Szalai (Ed.), *The use of time: Daily activities of urban and suburban populations in twelve countries* (pp. 197-212). The Hague, The Netherlands: Mouton.

Robinson, J. P., & Godbey, G. (1997). *Time for life: The surprising ways Americans use their time.* University Park: Pennsylvania State University Press.

Rosengren, K. E., & Windahl, S. (1989). *Media matter: TV use in childhood and adolescence.* Norwood, NJ: Ablex.

Rothschild, N., Thorson, E., Reeves, B., Hirsch, J. E., & Goldstein, R. (1986). EEG activity and the processing of television commercials. *Communication Research, 13*(2), 182-220.

Rubin, A. M. (1983). Television uses and gratifications: The interaction of viewing patterns and motivations. *Journal of Broadcasting, 27*(1), 37-51.

Rubin, A. M. (1984). Ritualized and instrumental television viewing. *Journal of Communication, 34*(3), 67-77.

Schramm, W., Lyle, J., & Parker, E. B. (1961). *Television in the lives of our children.* Stanford, CA: Stanford University Press.

Sherman, S. (1996). A set of one's own: TV sets in children's bedrooms. *Journal of Advertising Research, 36*(6), RC9-13.

Sims, J. B. (1989). VCR viewing patterns: An electronic and passive investigation. *Journal of Advertising Research, 29*(2), 11-17.

Singer, J. L., Singer, D. G., Desmond, R., Hirsch, R., & Nicol, A. (1988). Family mediation and children's cognition, aggression, and comprehension of television: A longitudinal study. *Journal of Applied Developmental Psychology, 9*(3), 329-347.

Sprafkin, J. N., & Liebert, R. M. (1978). Sex-typing and children's preferences. In G. Tuchman, A. K. Daniels, & J. Benet (Eds.), *Hearth and home: Images of women in the mass media* (pp. 288-339). New York: Oxford University Press.

Tangney, J. P., & Feshbach, S. (1988). Children's television-viewing frequency: Individual differences and demographic correlates. *Personality and Social Psychology Bulletin, 14*(1), 145-158.

Timmer, S. G., Eccles, J., & O'Brien, K. (1985). How children use time. In F. T. Juster & F. P. Stafford (Eds.), *Time, goods, and well-being* (pp. 353-382). Ann Arbor: University of Michigan, Institute for Social Research.

Valkenburg, P. M., & van der Voort, T. H. A. (1994). Influence of TV on daydreaming and creative imagination: A review of research. *Psychological Bulletin, 116*(2), 316-339.

Valkenburg, P. M., Voojis, M. W., van der Voort, T. H. A., & Wiegman, O. (1992). The influence of television on children's fantasy styles: A secondary analysis. *Imagination, Cognition, and Personality, 12,* 55-67.

Van Evra, J. (1998). *Television and child development* (2nd ed.). Mahwah, NJ: Lawrence Erlbaum.

von Feilitzen, C. (1999). Children's amount of TV viewing: Statistics from 10 countries. In C. von Feilitzen & U. Carlsson (Eds.), *Children and media: Image, education, participation* (pp. 61-67). Göteborg, Sweden: Göteborg University, UNESCO International Clearinghouse on Children and Violence on the Screen.

von Feilitzen, C., & Carlsson, U. (1999). *Children and media: Image, education, participation.* Göteborg, Sweden: Göteborg University, UNESCO International Clearinghouse on Children and Violence on the Screen.

von Feilitzen, C., & Linne, O. (1975). Identifying with television characters. *Journal of Communication, 25*(4), 51-55.

Wartella, E., Heintz, K. E., Aidman, A. J., & Mazzarella, S. R. (1990). Television and beyond: Children's video media in one community. *Communication Research, 17*(1), 45-64.

Webster, J. G., & Phalen, P. F. (1997). *The mass audience: Rediscovering the dominant model.* Mahwah, NJ: Lawrence Erlbaum.

Williams, T. M. (Ed.). (1986). *The impact of television: A natural experiment in three communities.* New York: Praeger.

Wolf, M. A. (1987). How children negotiate television. In T. R. Lindlof (Ed.), *Natural audiences: Qualitative research of media uses and effects* (pp. 58-94). Norwood, NJ: Ablex.

Wright, J. C., & Huston, A. C. (1995). *Effects of educational TV viewing of lower income preschoolers on academic skills, school readiness, and school adjustment one to three years later* [Technical report]. Lawrence: University of Kansas.

Zill, N., Davies, E., & Daly, M. (1994). *Viewing of* Sesame Street *by preschool children in the United States and its relationship to school readiness* [Report prepared for Children's Television Workshop]. Rockville, MD: Westat.

CHAPTER 4

# New Forms of Electronic Media

## The Impact of Interactive Games and the Internet on Cognition, Socialization, and Behavior

KAVERI SUBRAHMANYAM
California State University, Los Angeles

ROBERT KRAUT
Carnegie Mellon University

PATRICIA GREENFIELD
University of California, Los Angeles

ELISHEVA GROSS
University of California, Los Angeles

Over the past few years, U.S. households have added home computers, electronic games, and the Internet to the other technologies—the telephone, radio, TV, and stereo system—that consume children's time. In 1998, 43% of adult Americans owned a personal computer (PC), up from 36% in 1995 (Pew Research Center for People and the Press, 1998). Moreover, PC ownership is higher among households with children than those without, and this rate too is growing. For example, in 1994, 39% of American households with children had personal computers; by 1999, this had jumped to more than 60% for married couples with children (Roberts, Foehr, Rideout, & Brodie, 1999; Turow, 1999; see Figure 4.1). Indeed, computers have replaced television as the favorite medium of children and adolescents (both boys and girls) from 8 to 18 years of age (Roberts et al., 1999).

What, then, is the impact of computer use outside of school on child and adolescent development? During the early 1990s, game playing was the dominant use of computers among children 3 to 17 years of age (U.S. Census Bureau, 1993). The introduction of the Internet, however, has dramatically changed the picture. Recent data suggest that 75% of households with computers currently have Internet access, and the dominant use of the Internet is for electronic mail (Shih & Venkatesh, 1999). Recent surveys (Turow, 1999) suggest that, although games are the most frequent on-line activity among 8- to 12-year-olds, schoolwork has surpassed games as the most frequent on-line activity for teens ages 13 to 17.

But electronic games are not limited to personal computers. Games are also played on other popular computerized platforms such as Nintendo or Sega game systems. In 1999, it was reported that 67% of households with children had such a computer game system (Stanger & Gridina, 1999). For the first time in 1999, video games are even expected to outperform the domestic box office of movies ("Vita Stats," 1999). Electronic games seem to have an especially important place in the lives of boys. In a study of the self-reported leisure-time activities of 2,200 third- and fourth-grade children, the activities most often reported by boys were computer game playing on any platform (33%); in contrast, the activity most often reported by girls was doing homework (39%), with only 9.7% reporting computer game playing (Harrell, Gansky, Bradley, & McMurray, 1997). Although games were clearly the most frequent computerized activity for children, the Internet is the most rapidly growing one; 36.6% of all households with children had Internet services in 1999 (Turow, 1999).

In this chapter, we focus on the impact of the most frequent use of computers—games—and the most rapidly growing and recent use of computers—the Internet (not even mentioned in the 1990 census). Note that games are a category of content and the Internet is a delivery system or medium of communication. An important quality of modern information technology, however, is the complex relationship between content, delivery system, and platform. Thus, electronic games can be played through many different computerized platforms and delivery systems, including stand-alone game sets, arcade consoles, and personal computers, while the Internet can basically deliver anything. Even within the personal computer, games can be delivered through stand-alone pieces of software or through the Internet. Not only can games be downloaded from the Internet, but they can also be played interactively with other live players over the Internet.

## Demographics

The presence of a home computer is closely related to the income and ethnicity of families. By the end of 1998, 88% of American adults with family incomes greater than $75,000 reported owning a personal computer, compared with 47% of those with incomes between $30,000 and $50,000, and only 19% with family incomes less than $20,000. In homes with children from 2 to 18, 78% of white respondents reported a family computer, whereas only 55% of African American and 48% of Hispanic respondents did so (Roberts et al., 1999). On-line access is also strongly correlated with income: 12% of families with annual incomes under $30,000 subscribe to the Internet, compared with 61.1% of families with annual incomes over $75,000 (Stanger, 1998). In addition to replicating this economic gradient of Internet access, Roberts et al. (1999) also found that the

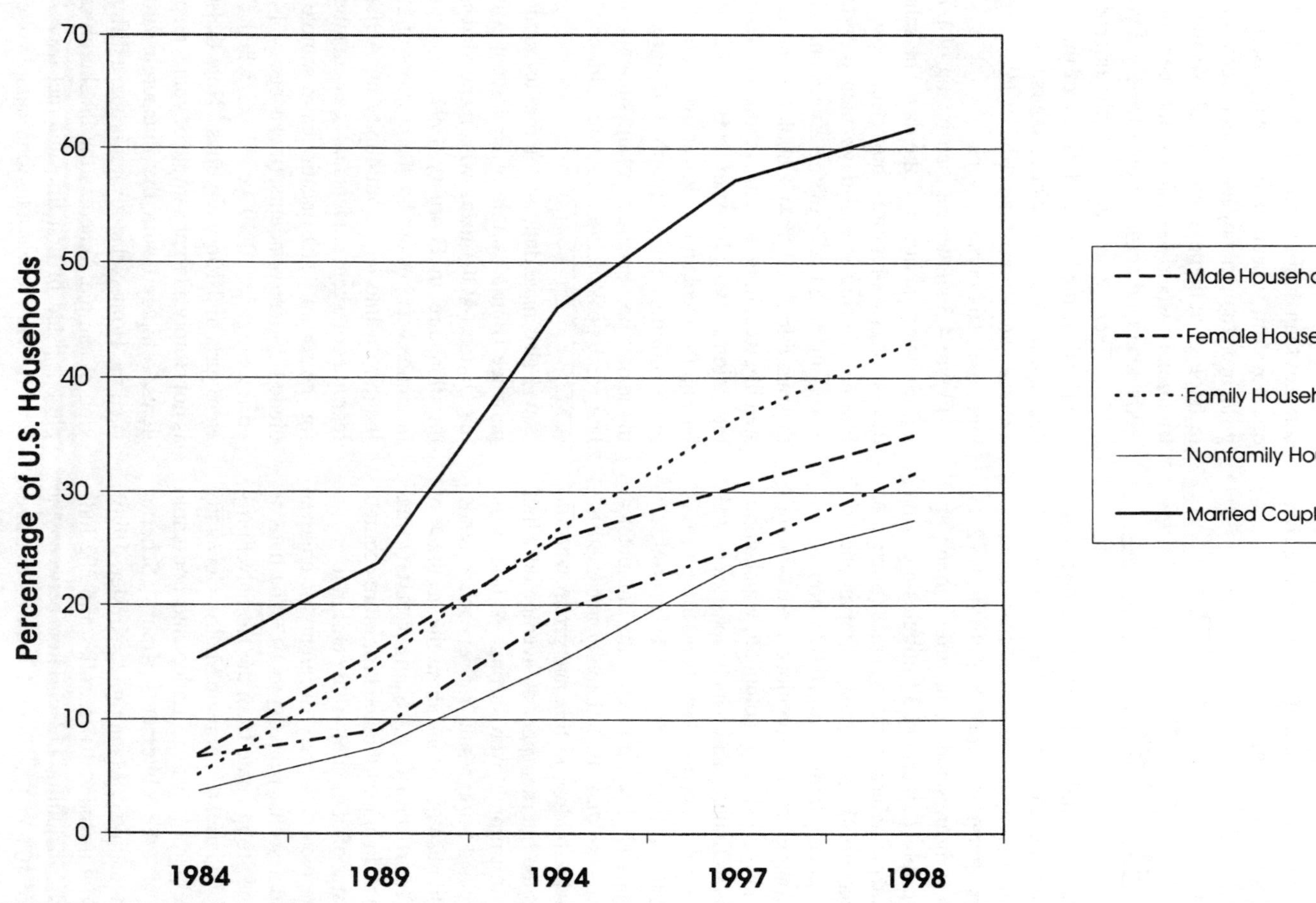


**Figure 4.1.** Percentage of U.S. Households With Personal Computers
SOURCE: Data from the National Telecommunications and Information Administration, *Falling Through the Net: Defining the Digital Divide* (U.S. Department of Commerce, July 1999).

average daily computer use among children and adolescents increased as a function of parental education. Interestingly, stand-alone video game platforms do not vary systematically with income and race (Roberts et al., 1999), supporting the notion that they may be the most democratic means for diffusing computer literacy (Greenfield, 1994).

## Time on Computers

We start by examining research on the amount of time children spend on computers and the time such computer use takes from other activities. Parents report that children (2-17 years) in homes with computers spend approximately 1 hour and 37 minutes a day on computers, including video games (Stanger & Gridina, 1999). In contrast, using an analysis of PC meter data[1] from 10,076 households with computers in September 1996—including who was using the computer, which applications were used, and which websites or web pages were viewed—Coffey and Stipp (1997) reported that half of the 2- to 11-year-olds in these households did not use the computer at all, and less than 10% actually accessed the Internet. Children in this age group who did access the Internet spent on average only half an hour a month Web surfing. Although the Coffey and Stipp results reflect earlier trends, they do raise questions about the accuracy of self-report data (e.g., Stanger & Gridina, 1999) and suggest the need for more accurate estimates of computer use by children.

The picture is very different for children and adolescents from 10 to 19.[2] The data on this age group come from the HomeNet project, a field trial at Carnegie Mellon University whose purpose was to understand household use of the Internet (Kraut, Scherlis, Mukhopadhyay, Manning, & Kiesler, 1996). The trial included 107 families and 302 individuals, including 113 children between the ages of 10 and 19.[3] Table 4.1 shows averages for various measures of Internet use, broken down by generation and gender. In these data, respondents logged onto the Internet personally, and metrics were collected from machine records.

First, and most important, teenagers are much heavier users of the Internet and all its services than their parents are. Among teenagers, boys are substantially heavier users than girls, even though they had equal access to the technology at home. Figure 4.2 shows the distribution of weekly use across the teens in the study, averaged across approximately 2 years of data. Teens who were using the Internet at all (100% of the boys and 81.6% of the girls) during a week used it about 3 hours a week on average, and more than 10% were using it more than 16 hours per week.

Figure 4.3 shows the distribution of Internet use over the hours of the day. The school day strongly structures how teens use the Internet. During school days, their use starts to rise in the middle of the afternoon, when they are dismissed from school, and increases steadily, reaching a peak in the prime-time television viewing hours of 8:00 to 10:00 P.M. Use on the weekends is lower overall because more activities compete with it; it starts later in the day, because many of the students sleep late, and peaks closer to midnight or 1:00 A.M.

We also have data on Internet use and experience from a sample of adolescent America Online (AOL) users who responded to a questionnaire in February 1997. The questionnaire was put out by the creators of Plug In! (an on-line teen community on AOL) to recruit adolescent leaders and "cast members" for the forum.[4] The questionnaire sample included 290 respondents (mean age = 14.89 years; range = 10-19 years), of which 184 were girls and 106 were boys.[5] Note that this is not simply a larger sample of young respondents compared with the Pittsburgh sample (i.e., the HomeNet study); it is also a different kind of sample. Whereas the Pittsburgh sample consisted of first-time Internet users, the Plug In! sample was a national sample of children and adolescents who not only had com-

**TABLE 4.1** Metrics of Internet Use, by Generation and Gender

| *Weekly Usage Measure* | *Teenage Boys* | *Teenage Girls* | *Adult Men* | *Adult Women* |
|---|---|---|---|---|
| Percentage active per week | 58.00 | 44.00 | 37.00 | 35.00 |
| Number of Internet sessions | 5.30 | 2.93 | 1.41 | 1.45 |
| Hours on-line | 4.00 | 1.51 | 0.82 | 0.57 |
| Session length in minutes | 37.98 | 30.83 | 33.54 | 28.13 |
| Hours on e-mail | 1.70 | 0.84 | 0.25 | 0.22 |
| Unique websites visited | 11.17 | 3.89 | 4.34 | 1.93 |
| Mail messages sent | 3.79 | 2.51 | 0.32 | 0.49 |
| Mail messages received | 3.40 | 1.95 | 0.22 | 0.28 |
| Newsgroup messages sent | 0.36 | 0.14 | 0.01 | 0.00 |
| Newsgroup messages read | 4.55 | 2.59 | 0.39 | 0.17 |
| Listserv subscribed to | 0.20 | 0.28 | 0.08 | 0.06 |
| Listserv messages sent | 0.03 | 0.01 | 0.00 | 0.00 |
| Percentage using a MUD or IRC | 38.00 | 25.00 | 0.00 | 0.00 |
| N (windsorized) | 31.00 | 44.00 | 67.00 | 88.00 |
| N (all) | 43.00 | 67.00 | 92.00 | 116.00 |

puters and Internet access at home but were sufficiently "plugged in" to want to become site leaders. (Although this study uses self-report data, we focus on age and gender comparisons within the data set; therefore, any self-report biases should be similar across the comparison groups.)

An analysis of variance on the mean weekly use of Plug In! as a function of gender revealed that there was greater use among boys (mean = 18.9 hours) compared with girls (mean = 13.9 hours) [$F(1, 251) = 6.71$, $p = .01$]. However, when age (preteens = 10-12; teens = 13-15; and older teens = 16-19) was taken into account, there were no reliable differences in mean weekly use [$F(2, 285) = .642$, $p > .05$]. Figure 4.4 shows the distribution of the mean weekly use among preteen, teen, and older teen boys and girls. Although not significant, the means present an interesting trend: Among the boys, the greatest use was by the older teens (mean = 19.84 hours), whereas, among the girls, the greatest use was by the preteens (mean = 20.85 hours).

Prior experience with the Internet (in months) was similarly analyzed by an analysis of variance with age and gender as between subjects factors; again, no reliable effects were obtained. Figure 4.5 shows the distribution of prior experience as a function of age and gender. Examination of means suggests that, although boys had more prior experience with the Internet than girls among the older teens (mean = 13.05 months and 9.68 months, respectively), the gender gap was not present among the teens (mean = 11.92 months for the boys and 11.23 months for the girls) and, in fact, showed a reversal among the preteens, with the girls (mean = 6.29) having more prior experience than the boys (mean = 3.60 months). It is possible that this trend reflects a historical change, with girls now getting socialized with the Internet at an earlier age, compared with earlier times. We

*(text continued on page 82)*

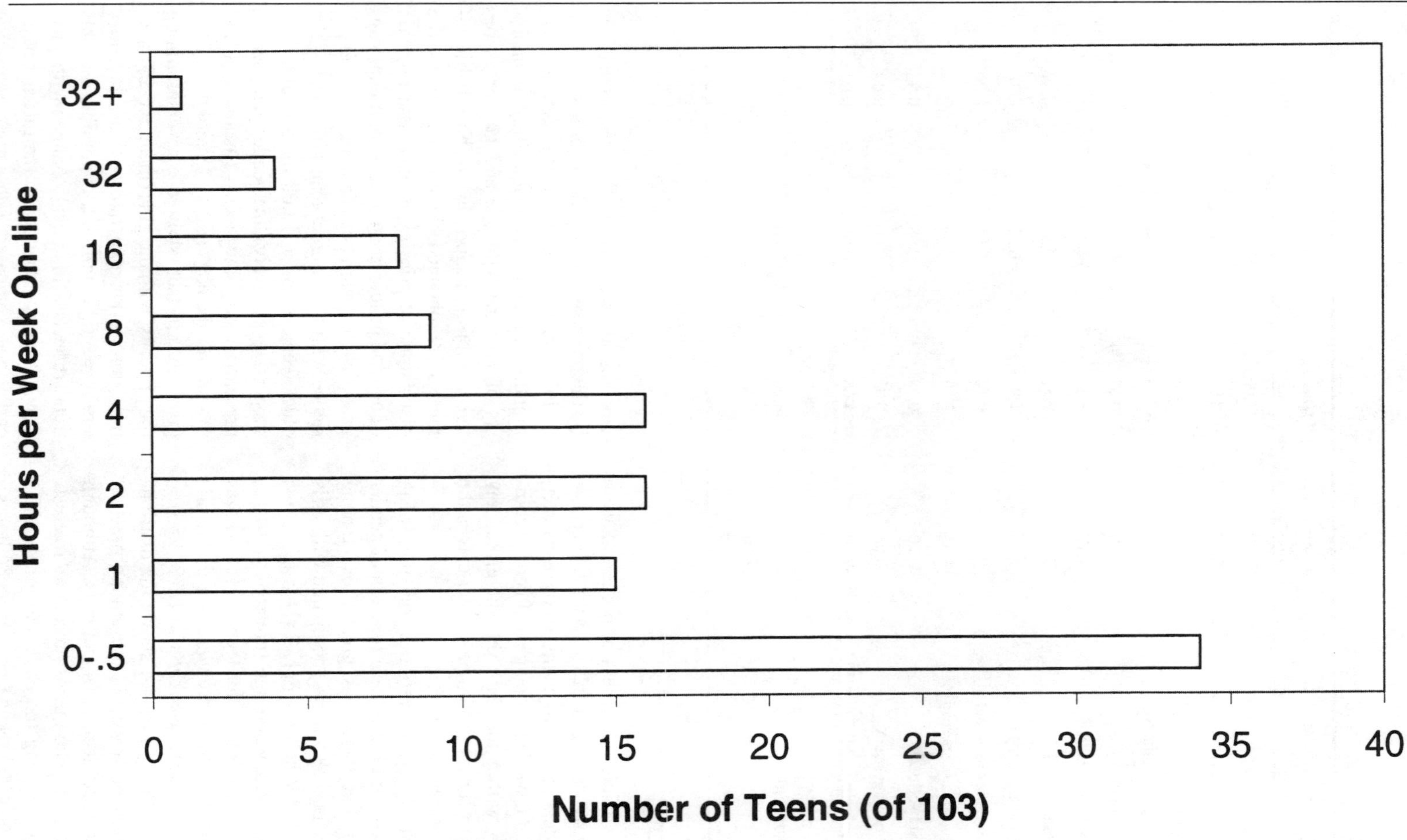


**Figure 4.2.** Distribution of Weekly Internet Use Among Teens
SOURCE: HomeNet Study (1996).

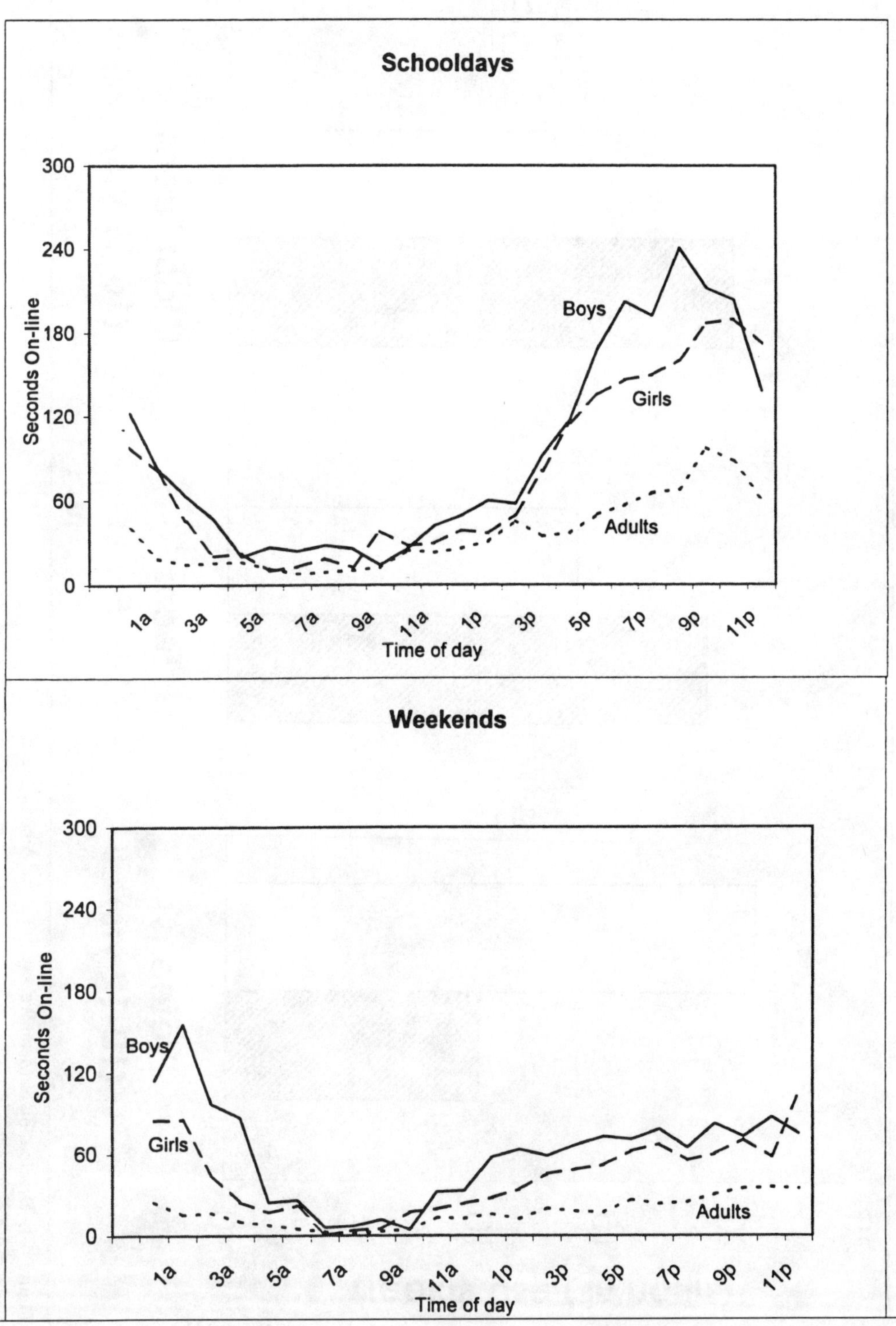


**Figure 4.3.** Distribution of Internet Use, by Time of Day and Type of Day
SOURCE: HomeNet Study (1996).

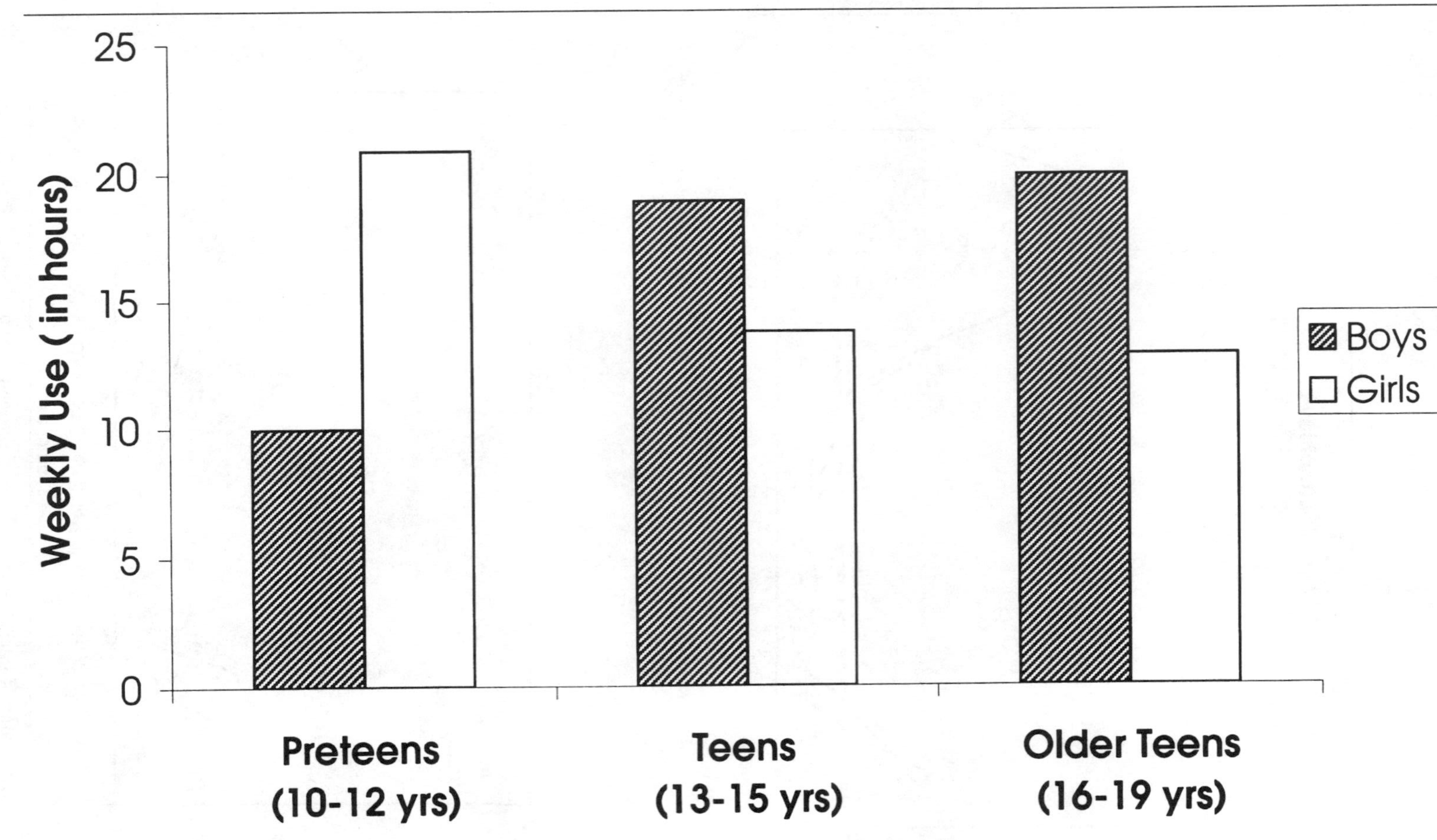


**Figure 4.4.** Distribution of Mean Weekly AOL Use Among Teens
SOURCE: AOL Study (1997).

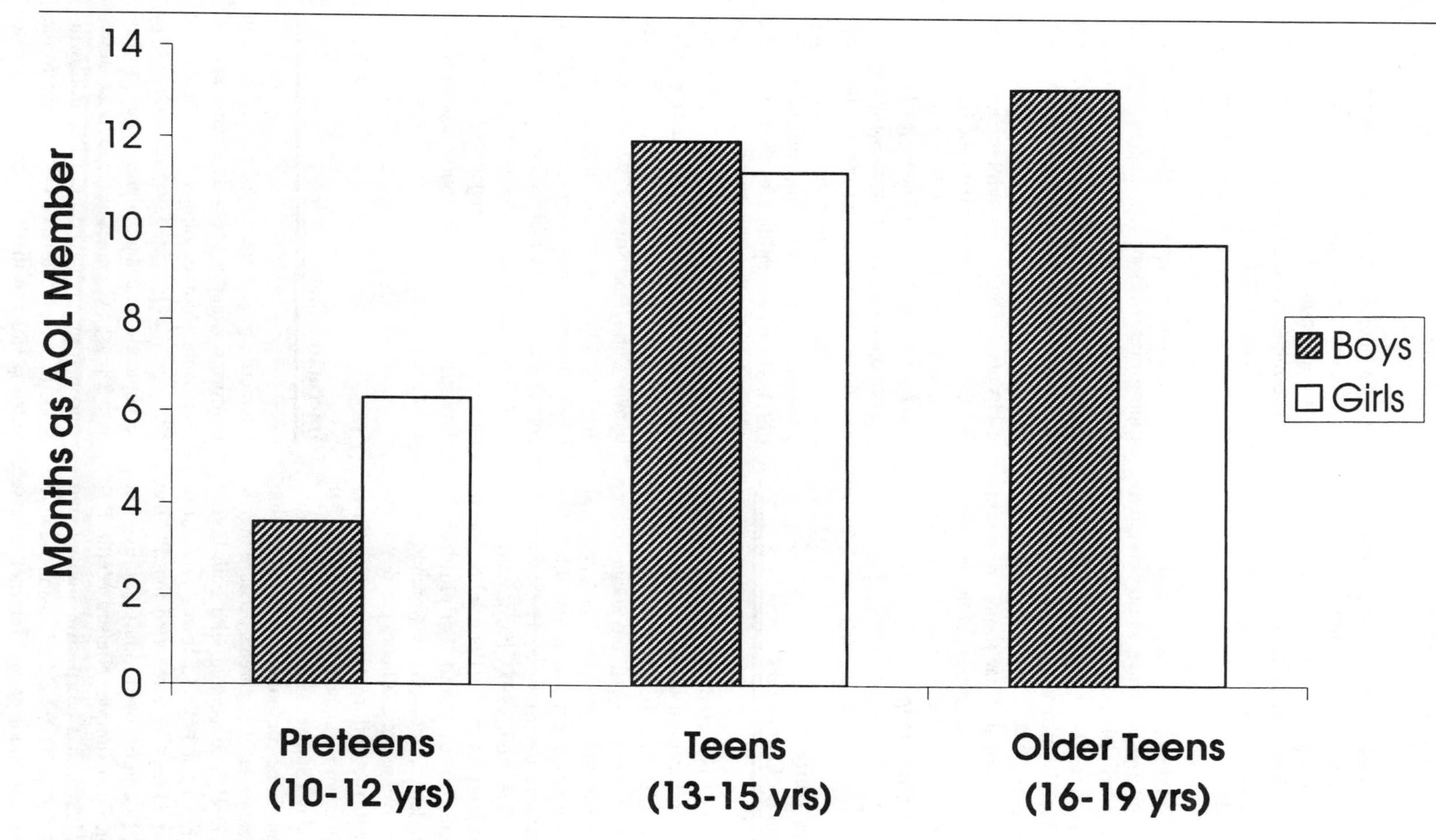


**Figure 4.5.** Distribution of Prior Experience With AOL
SOURCE: AOL Study (1997).

also speculate that the highly social nature of AOL appeals to preteen girls more than to preteen boys, who lag behind their female peers in social development. In addition, girls are generally more social than boys (Grusec & Lytton, 1988).

On the basis of a national survey, Roberts et al. (1999) present a developmental picture of various Internet activities among children and adolescents. Dividing their sample into three age groups—2-7, 8-13, and 14-18—they found a steadily increasing amount of time spent in each succeeding age group on websites and e-mail. Chat rooms were not used at all in the youngest age group but were used equally (and about as much as e-mail) in the two older age groups.

## Activities That Get Displaced by Computers

The evidence is mixed as to whether time spent by children on computers displaces other activities that they engage in such as television viewing, sports, and social activities. There is some evidence that personal computer users might watch less television than nonusers do (Stanger, 1998; Suzuki, Hashimoto, & Ishii, 1997). For instance, the Annenberg report of the 1998 Television in the Home Survey found that children in households with computers watched television an average of 2.3 hours per day, compared with the children in homes without computers, who watched an average of 2.9 hours a day (Stanger, 1998). However, this finding might be confounded with the income and education level of parents because higher income level is associated with both higher ownership of a PC and lower television watching. Others have reported that PC use does not compete with adults' television viewing. For example, Nielsen Media Research (1998), in a prospective study, found little change in household television viewing after the household gained Internet access. Most of the differences in television viewing between households using the Internet and those not using it existed before the households went on-line.

The impact of computers on other activities is varied. According to the Annenberg report (Stanger, 1998), children from homes with computers spend less time watching videotapes and more time doing schoolwork and reading magazines or newspapers compared with children in homes without computers. Interestingly, having a home computer did not affect the time spent playing console-based video games and reading books. Again, these results are difficult to interpret because of the unreliability of self-report data and because of the preexisting differences between families who have computers and those who do not.

A complicating factor in assessing the relationship between computer use and other activities is the increasing systemic relationship between the content of various media (Kinder, 1991). This is exemplified by the trend in the children's software market for tie-ins between games and television characters and shows (e.g., the show *Sabrina, the Teenage Witch* and the computer game *Sabrina, the Teenage Witch*). Coffey and Stipp (1997) even suggest that cross-listings might actually increase television watching among samples of PC users. The concern is that eventually the time spent on electronic media (television, PCs, and the Internet) will negatively affect the time spent on organized sports and other social activities.

## Interactive Games

Interactive games are played on two types of platforms: stand-alone video game and PC platforms. Video games include arcade games, games for game systems such as Sega or Nintendo, and stand-alone games or interactive toys; PC games include those downloaded from or played on a PC. Following Roberts et al. (1999), we will call the former *video games* and the latter *computer games;* we will use the term *interactive games* to cover both types of platforms. We will also consider stand-alone interactive toys as a genre of video games. Incidentally, the stand-alone video game platforms are more popular with children and adolescents than are games played on a computer (Roberts et al., 1999).

Although games are, as we have seen, the most popular use of the computer in most age groups, the actual time spent playing video games may be less than what people have feared. For example, among the heaviest users (boys from 8 to 18 years of age), only 21% of a national sample reported playing games more than 1 hour per day on a stand-alone platform, and only 6% reported playing more than 1 hour per day on the computer (Roberts et al., 1999). These researchers, however, did find a significant negative correlation between video game playing and feelings of contentment and adjustment: The lowest average adjustment scores were received by children and adolescents who reported spending the most time on video games. We cannot know to what extent game playing was a constructive outlet for relatively maladjusted young people versus to what extent it was a causal factor in the maladjustment.

In terms of content, Roberts et al. (1999) found the action adventure genre to dominate accounts of the prior day's video game play in all age groups (2-18 years) and across ethnic groups (white, black, Hispanic). African American youngsters were more than three times as likely as white and Hispanic respondents to report playing classic, gambling, and puzzle-logic games. Again, these researchers confirmed the well-known gender differences. They found almost no girls between ages 2 and 7 playing video games but a substantial number of boys. Between 8 and 18 years of age, boys were more than three times as likely to report playing video games than girls were, and this difference was even bigger for simulation games.

The content situation is quite different for computer games because of two additional important genres found in computer but not video games: education and arts and crafts. In their report for the Kaiser Family Foundation, Roberts et al. (1999) summarize their findings in this way:

> In general, computer game selection looks quite different from video game selection. Among those children who play computer games, educational games dominate the early years; classic and gambling games moving to the fore in the later years, at least in part because of their greater availability—these are the games that come pre-loaded on most new computers. Action and sports games are highly popular among older kids, but never dominate computer game selections the way they do video game selections. (p. 51)

### *Interactive Games and the Development of Cognitive Skills*

The most popular interactive games, the action games, have design features (they are spatial, iconic, dynamic, and have things going on simultaneously in different locations) that may lead to the development of particular information-processing skills. Because the features are common to computer applications of all kinds, the suite of skills that the games develop constitutes a foundational computer literacy. We now summarize the experimental evidence for the role of interactive games in developing cognitive skills.

Subrahmanyam and Greenfield (1994) found that practice on a computer game (*Marble Madness*) reliably improved spatial performance (e.g., anticipating targets, extrapolating spatial paths) compared with practice on a computerized word game. Similarly, Okagaki and Frensch (1994) reported that practice on the computer game *Tetris* (a game that requires the rapid rotation and placement of seven different-shaped blocks, shown in Figure 4.6) significantly improved undergraduate students' mental rotation time and spatial visualization time on computerized spatial performance tests such as those shown in Figure 4.7.

**Figure 4.6.** Example of a Tetris Shape and the Wall Opening Into Which It Has to Be Placed
SOURCE: Okagaki and Frensch (1994).

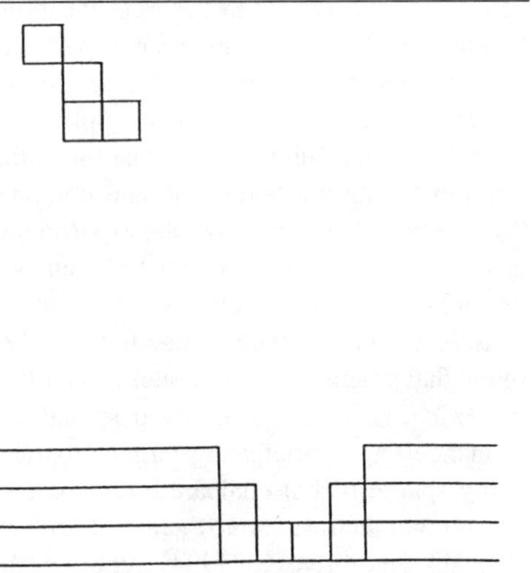

**Figure 4.7.** Example of the Computerized Spatial Visualization Task in Which Subjects Had to Decide Whether or Not a Non-Tetris Shape Would Fit in the Wall Opening at the Bottom of the Screen
SOURCE: Okagaki & Frensch (1994).

Another skill embodied in interactive games is that of iconic or analog representation—in other words, games privilege images over words. In a cross-cultural study carried out in Rome and Los Angeles, Greenfield, Camaioni, and others (1994) found that participants who played *Concentration* on the computer became more iconic and less symbolic in their communication about the animated computer simulation in software called *Rocky's Boot* compared with those who played the same game on a board.

Another study explored the role of interactive games in developing strategies for keeping track of events at multiple locations on a screen. In a task where an icon could appear at either of two locations (but with unequal probabilities), the researchers found that expert video game players had faster response times than novices at both high- and low-probability positions of the icon. Furthermore, they found that 5 hours of playing an action arcade video game, *Robotron,* improved strategies for keeping track of events at multiple locations, but only for the low-probability target position (Greenfield, deWinstanley, Kilpatrick, & Kaye, 1994).

Most of the research on the impact of interactive games on cognitive processing has assessed short-term transfer effects, and little is known about the cumulative impact of electronic games. Recently, Greenfield (1998) suggested that the proliferation of computer games and the corresponding development of iconic representational skills may have a causal role in the recent dramatic increases in nonverbal or performance IQ scores that have occurred in the period of years when modern computer technology was developing and becoming widespread (Flynn, 1994).

Most of the published research on the cognitive impact of game playing has been done with the older generation of arcade games and game systems. Despite advances in interactive technology and the capabilities of current computer games, we believe that the fundamental nature of computer games has remained unchanged. The need for divided attention, spatial imagery, and iconic representation continue to be features of the current generation of games. On the basis of previous research, we would predict no changes in the nature of the effects of computer game playing that stem from structural features of the medium, although the strength of visual effects could change with increasing sophistication of the graphics. Regardless, we need research on the effects of the newer generation of software (both games and nongames such as coloring, creative writing, etc.) and on the effects of multiparty games that are now possible on the Internet.

## *Computer Games and Social Development*

### *Aggression in Computer Games and Its Impact on Children*

Next we address issues surrounding the aggressive content of computer games and their impact on children's behavior. These questions are especially relevant in the context of violent incidents such as the massacre at Columbine High School in Littleton, Colorado, on April 20, 1999, in which children killed children. The Columbine case has highlighted the role of video games because the shooters, Eric Harris and Dylan Klebold, were later described as being "obsessed with violent video games." Harris and Klebold's favorite game was *Doom,* and a customized version of *Doom* was even found on Harris's Internet site. He had gone as far as modifying the game to resemble the subsequent attack on Columbine High. Given such incidents, the violent content of computer games is a major concern among many parents, educators, and policy makers. In this section, we will review the limited research on the links between computer games, access to the Internet, and violent behavior.

Although home education games encourage prosocial behaviors (e.g., when players cooperate or share, they are often rewarded), most commercially available entertainment software involves aggression and competition. Violence is an integral part of computer games today (Provenzo, 1991), but this was not always the case. The first game, *Pong,* was nonaggressive. Aggression started in the second generation with *Breakout,* which involved destruction but no human aggression. *Pac-Man* started animate but nonhuman aggression. The next generation of games such as *The Empire Strikes Back* involved human aggression. Human aggression took on a more fantastic form with *Super Mario Brothers.* It became more personal, with hand-to-hand combat, in games such as *Mortal Kombat.* Violence continues to reign in the current generation of action games, which include titles such as *Doom, Duke Nukem, Mace, Hexen II,* and *Mortal Kombat 2.* Using a content analysis of popular Nintendo and Sega Genesis computer games, Dietz (1998) reports that nearly 80% of the games have aggression or violence as a game objective. Even more troubling is the finding that half of the favorite choices of children were games with violent themes (Funk, 1993). Given the amount of violence in the games, the amount of time children spend playing these games, and their liking for violent games, an important question is whether they have a deleterious impact on children.

One concern is that playing an aggressive or violent interactive game can increase children's aggressive behavior in other situations. Based on the evidence that watching violent TV shows increases children's aggression (Eron, Huesmann, Lefkowitz, & Walder, 1996; Friedrich-Cofer & Huston, 1986), it is possible to assume that the same holds true for interactive games. A review of experimental studies suggests that playing a violent game, even for brief periods of time, can generate short-term transfer effects such as increased aggression in children's free play (Cooper & Mackie, 1986; Irwin & Gross, 1995; Schutte, Malouff, Post-Gorden, & Rodasta, 1988; Silvern & Williamson, 1987), increased aggressive or hostile responses to ambiguous, open-ended questions (Kirsh, 1998), and increased aggressive ideation (Graybill, Kirsch, & Esselman, 1985).

Research on the relationship between the amount of interactive game playing (as measured through self-reports) and aggressive behavior is more ambiguous. For instance, Fling et al. (1992) report that the amount of interactive game play (as measured by questionnaires) was positively correlated with self-reported aggression as well as teachers' ratings of aggression among sixth through twelfth graders. When van Schie and Wiegman (1997), however, had participants (10-14 years) record their out-of-school activities on a daily basis for a week, there was no relationship between the amount of interactive game playing and peer nominations of aggressive behavior. Furthermore, they suggest that the critical variable might be children's preference for aggressive interactive games; those who liked aggressive electronic games were rated as more aggressive by their peers (Wiegman & van Schie, 1998).

Another question is whether exposure to violence and aggression in interactive games will have an anesthetizing effect and desensitize children to violence. Although such desensitization effects have been shown with television (Rule & Ferguson, 1986), this issue needs to be explored with electronic games. One clear problem is the ignorance of parents. Although an electronic game rating system has been in place since September 1994, parents seem unaware of even the most popular violent titles. For example, in a survey of more than 500 parents, it was found that less than 5% of them had ever heard of *Duke Nukem,* a violent electronic game rated M (mature), whereas 80% of junior high students said they were familiar with it (Oldberg, 1998). Also of concern is the growing trend of marketing violence to children. *Duke Nukem* action figures are now found in toy stores, and a number of violent games are advertised through rebellious advertisements in game magazines popular among young boys (Oldberg, 1998).

### *Interactive Games and Their Impact on Prosocial Behavior and Friendships*

Another area of interest is the impact of playing aggressive electronic games on children's prosocial behavior. The limited research on this question suggests that preference for and playing aggressive electronic games lead to less prosocial behavior, such as donating money or helping someone (Chambers & Ascione, 1987; Wiegman & van Schie, 1998).

Another concern is that, because of the solitary nature of most game playing, children will form "electronic friendships" with the machine instead of friendships with their peers. The research suggests that, for the average player, this might not be so, and "boys who play computer games often are more likely to see friends outside school" (Colwell, Grady, & Rhaiti, 1995, p. 201). In addition, no differences have been found in the sociability (Rutkowska & Carlton, 1994) and social interactions (Phillips, Rolls, Rouse, & Griffiths, 1995) of players versus nonplayers. Less is known about the long-term effect of excessive electronic game playing among the 7 to 9% of children who have been identified as playing interactive games for at least 30 hours a week (Griffiths & Hunt, 1995). We agree with Griffiths's (1997) speculation that any activity that is engaged in for a disproportionate amount of time at the expense of other leisure activities must have negative consequences on social and educational development.

The impact of interactive games on family dynamics is another area of interest. In an early study, Mitchell (1985) interviewed 20 families with new home game sets and found that interactive games brought together members of the family for shared play and interaction. We need more research on whether this is still the case given that computers and game sets have become more routine and numerous in U.S. homes, to making sharing less necessary.

A related issue is the fact that children and teens are often more sophisticated than their parents are in their knowledge and ability to navigate computers. In a CNN/USA Today/NSF poll of teenage children between 13 and 17 (*U.S. Teens and Technology,* 1997), 62% said that they could operate electronic equipment or computer software without any help, and 54% reported that they or a sibling were responsible for programming the VCR. Anecdotal observations confirm that children are often more knowledgeable than their parents about computers. Research is needed to assess the impact that such role reversals have on family dynamics and interactions.

### *Gender Issues in Interactive Games*

One issue that has consistently stood out is the gender imbalance in the playing of electronic games. The core audience for game systems such as Nintendo or Sega has always been boys between the ages of 8 and 14; indeed, boys are five times more likely than girls to own a Genesis or Super Nintendo game system (Elmer-Dewitt, 1993). Boys have also been found to spend more time playing interactive games than girls have. In a recent survey of seventh- and eighth-grade students, Funk (1993) reported that 67% of the girls spent an average of 2 hours per week playing electronic games, whereas 90% of the boys spent an average of 4.2 hours per week. This trend continues with the new generation of home games. In a questionnaire study of 11- to 16-year-olds, boys reported playing more often than girls, and they also reported playing for significantly longer periods of time at a given sitting (Griffiths & Hunt, 1995). It is important to keep in mind that, although boys clearly spend more time playing compared with girls, research has found that females are just as likely to be players as males (*U.S. Teens and Technology,* 1997; van Schie & Wiegman, 1997). The gender difference in game playing also spills over to the schools; girls lag behind boys in the school use of computers, and computers are even perceived to belong more to boys than to girls (Cassell & Jenkins, 1998, p. 12).

It was initially believed that girls were turned off by electronic games because of the lack of female protagonists and the violent nature of the games (Malone, 1981). The early efforts of the software industry to create nonviolent games with female protagonists have largely been a failure (Subrahmanyam & Greenfield, 1998). Although one recent "girl software," *Barbie Fashion Designer,* has been very successful, other girl games such as *Let's Talk About Me, Rockett,* and *Barbie Print and Play* have not been as successful. The Barbie character certainly has importance in itself: A number of Barbie games have become bestsellers among girls.

We have recently suggested that the success of *Barbie Fashion Designer* did not stem from the mere presence of Barbie and the lack of aggression but stemmed instead from the fact that it contained features that fit in with girls' play and their tastes in reading and literature in general (Subrahmanyam & Greenfield, 1998; Tizard, Philips, & Plewis, 1976). We proposed that, by helping girls create outfits for Barbie, the computer became a creative tool for girls' pretend play, which tends to be based more on reality and real-life models than that of boys' pretend play. Unlike most games in which the electronic fantasy is primary, the electronic medium became a tool to design a product, which could then be used in play with Barbie dolls. Our analysis suggests that girls like nonaggressive tool software that allows them to enhance popular play themes with realistic familiar characters. One such theme, important in *Barbie Fashion Designer,* is nurturance.

#### *Tamagotchi and Simlife: Issues of Gender, Mental Simulation, and Social Development*

The theme of nurturance is taken to new levels with the *Tamagotchi,* a gender-neutral game that is somewhat more popular with girls. Beyond gender issues, however, the *Tamagotchi* represents another important trend in child-computer interaction, the simulation of artificial life and the interaction between artificial characters and real children (Richard, 1998; Turkle, 1995). This type of electronic game represents a new level in the integration of computers into the social world of children.

The *Tamagotchi* is a small interactive game toy created in Japan that represents a virtual animal. Its game structure is as follows: Each *Tamagotchi*'s owner must take care of it in order to prevent it from "dying." The *Tamagotchi* communicates with its owner by beeps (to attract his or her attention) and by icons (to indicate its immediate needs for food, sleep, or play). The *Tamagotchi* is an artificial life simulation put within the reach of children (Richard, 1998). The goal of the player is to keep the *Tamagotchi* alive as long as possible; to avoid its death, children must take the *Tamagotchi* with them wherever they go. Apparently, *Tamagotchis* stimulate the same emotions as real, live animals and people do. Virtual Internet "cemeteries" for *Tamagotchis* cannot be distinguished from Internet "cemeteries" for real animals and people; the same language is used in both cases (Richard, 1998). Indeed, Richard observed a girl in a restaurant burst into tears; the reason for her sudden emotion turned out to be the death of her *Tamagotchi.* It seems, therefore, that these electronic toys can lead to attachment responses on the part of their owners.

The *Tamagotchi* phenomenon extends Turkle's (1984) observation that people attribute minds to computers. But the *Tamagotchi* leads to a further step; children treat *Tamagotchis* as if they were alive. The *Tamagotchi* phenomenon represents the first major popular success in artificial or virtual life at the child level. But there are other important small-scale successes as well. For example, the game of *Simlife* is an exploration of the emerging field of artificial life (Turkle, 1995, 1997); it is a simulation of evolutionary processes. Turkle's interviews make it clear that children and even adolescents have difficulty in understanding the boundaries between real and artificial life. This may be a factor in the kinds of reactions to *Tamagotchi* death described above.

This phenomenon of integrating simulated life into real life in the domain of electronic games is being reinforced on the Internet, where robot-like programs "run around" multi-user dungeons (MUDs) interacting with "real" characters operated by real people but sometimes indistinguishable from them (Turkle, 1995). *Tamagotchi* and *Simlife* phenomena, therefore, provide a link to important Internet issues that will be developed later in this chapter.

At the same time, *Tamagotchis,* like other interactive games and software, have specific cognitive requirements: The *Tamagotchi* screen presents an iconic code whose meanings and functions must be mastered by the child; thus, it contributes to cognitive socialization to the world of computers. The *Tamagotchi* beeps also socialize the child to respond to the types of messages "wired" adults handle, as with beepers, cell phones, and voice mail (Richard, 1998). Sometimes parents use *Tamagotchis* as training to take care of a real animal.

The actual psychological effects of *Tamagotchis* have not been studied in a systematic fashion. Nonetheless, the popularity of simulation or "virtual life" has continued with the advent of the very popular Furby, which is an electronic toy with fur, eyes, ears, a 200-word vocabulary, and a limited ability to interact with its environment. Clearly, systematic research regarding the child development impact of such robotic games is needed. What is certain at this point is that the *Tamagotchi* represented a new stage in the integration of electronic information in the daily life of children.

### *Closing the Gender Gap?*

The success with girls of *Barbie Fashion Designer* and the *Tamagotchi* is an indication that the gender gap in the out-of-school use of computers might be narrowing. In the *U.S. Teens and Technology* (1997) national survey of teenagers between 13 and 17 years, it was found that, despite differences in game playing, teenage boys and girls report equal levels of usage and express equal levels of confidence in their computer skills. Although boys were more likely than girls to report playing electronic games on a daily basis, this difference did not transfer to computer use, where the same number of boys and girls reported daily use of the computer. Overall, boys reported slightly more time on computers in the past week compared with girls (4.7 vs. 4.1 hours). This difference is due to a small number of boys who report using the computer for more than 20 hours per week. Despite these gains, girls still lag behind boys in the number of higher-level computer science courses they take in high school (AAUW, 1999). Overall, the research suggests that, although girls lag behind boys in some areas of computer use, there are other areas in which they are similar to boys and are even catching up. As we will see, the Internet provides certain activities that strongly contribute to a more equal gender balance in computer use.

## Children, Adolescents, and the Internet

> "I really want to move to Antarctica—I'd want my cat and Internet access and I'd be happy."
> (16-year-old HomeNet participant, 1995)

### *Use of the Internet and Computers by Parents and Their Children*

In this section, we describe how the Internet and computers were used by the HomeNet teenagers in Pittsburgh, Pennsylvania, from 1995 to 1998 and how their lives changed as a result of this use. Starting in 1995, Kraut and colleagues (1996) provided families with computers and connections and carefully documented how they used on-line services such as electronic mail, computerized bulletin boards, on-line chat groups, and the World Wide Web. Data from detailed auditing of their Internet use, quantitative surveys, and interviews with family members provide a rich picture of how this sample was using the Internet and its impact over time. The developmental analysis consisted of comparing the younger generation of children and adolescents (10-19 years) with their parents.

Figure 4.8 shows the purposes for which the sample reported using the Internet, averaged over three time periods between 1995 and 1998. In this figure, a "0" indicates that the Internet was never used for a particular purpose in the preceding 6 months, a "1" indicates that it was used occasionally for that purpose, and a "2" indicates that it was used frequently. The dominant use of the Internet was hedonic—for pleasure rather than for instrumental purposes. This finding was confirmed on a national level by Roberts et al. (1999), who found, for example, that the most frequently visited Internet sites fell in the entertainment category. In the Pittsburgh sample, teens were more likely than adults to report using the Internet for social purposes—communicating with friends, visiting MUDs and chat rooms, getting personal help, and joining groups.[6] In addition, they were more likely to use the Internet for listening to music, playing games, and downloading software and less likely than the adults (especially the men) to view sexual materials.

Like the adults, the teens used the Internet to some extent for instrumental purposes, which in their case meant doing schoolwork and finding educational material rather than using it as part of paid employment. Indeed, the largest single use of the computer in the 10- to 18-year-old group was for schoolwork.[7] Curiously, in contrast to their parents, young people in Pittsburgh were less likely to use the Internet to get product information and to purchase products, presumably because teens are lighter consumers overall than adults, and they were much less likely to have the credit cards necessary for on-line purchasing.

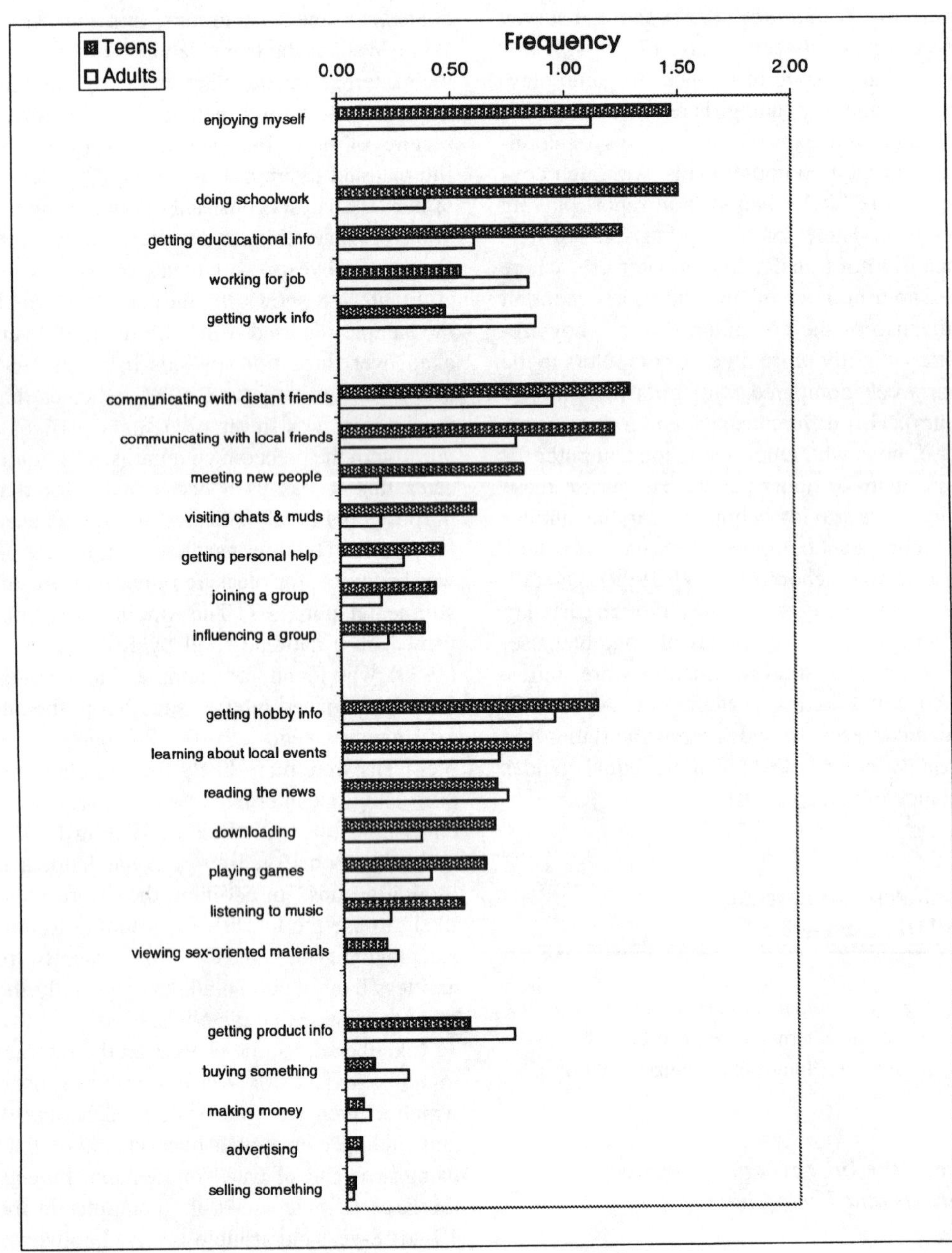


**Figure 4.8.** Teens' Self-Reported Purposes for Using the Internet
SOURCE: HomeNet Study (1996).

### Educational Uses

Many parents buy home computers and subscribe to Internet access to provide educational opportunities for their children. This is consistent with the finding that, in 1994, 45% of U.S. households with children had computers compared with only 30% of households without children (Times Mirror Center for the People and the Press, 1994). According to the interviews, these parents often have a nonspecific goal of preparing their children for the information-age future. Although they anticipate that they are providing an educational resource, once they actually see how their children use computers, they start to see costs along with the benefits. For example, they see their children, as they describe it, "wasting time" on computer games, electronic communication, and browsing the Internet. In fact, a more recent national survey found no relationship between reported daily exposure to computers and school grades (Roberts et al., 1999). The researchers found a significant negative relationship between computer and print exposure; print exposure was the only medium that had a significant positive relationship to school grades.

Nevertheless, most of the HomeNet parents considered time wasted on the computer preferable to time wasted on TV. The interactive nature of on-line services, the possibilities for communication, the use for schoolwork, and, we suspect, the favorable treatment that the Internet gets in advertising and the popular press all contribute to this favorable attitude toward computing. One grandfather, for example, described the benefits that his live-in grandchildren get from computing:

> It's taking them away from TV actually, which they had a problem with. With TV, they would be glued to the screen, especially the seven year old, she was almost mesmerized. You couldn't even communicate with her, she would just sit there with that blank stare on her face and just watch, I still don't believe that she had a clue as to what was going on. It was just emotion. So now she's onto the computer and she stays away from the [TV]. So it's helped keeping them away from the TV.

Teens frequently used both their home computers and the Internet for their schoolwork. Among the teenagers in the HomeNet sample, stand-alone educational applications, such as *KidWorks* or *Thinkin' Things,* were used much less frequently than word processing software, stand-alone games, electronic mail software, and Internet browsers. The most common of the education uses was simple word processing for school assignments. At home, as in the office, the computer has replaced the typewriter. In addition, students use the World Wide Web to find information for various class reports. One student, for example, was able to find information on Pittsburgh's role in the Underground Railroad for a black history month assignment, and one seventh grader included a disputed photograph of the Loch Ness monster he found online to illustrate his report. Students in clubs (e.g., the school newspaper) sometimes used Internet communication to coordinate meetings or to distribute shared materials (e.g., assignments or stories), but this was far less common than using the computer for writing, printing, and research.

Parents in the HomeNet study appreciated the new educational resources that the Internet provided their children but, at the same time, worried about erosion of standards and about the credibility of on-line information. One mother marveled at the wealth of information that her middle school son was able to uncover but also worried that the sheer abundance of the information was devaluing research and critical thought. Others worried about the balanced nature of the information. Another mother was concerned about her 13-year-old son's use of the Internet as a research tool for a paper on the McCarthy era; she felt that it was important for him to read books from the library to get a more balanced set of views, less fraught with ideological problems (Kraut et al., 1996).

### *Interpersonal Communication Versus Information*

For the teenagers in the HomeNet sample, communication with others was a major use of the Internet. Interpersonal communications via electronic mail were more important to them than information acquisition via the Web. When teens described why they used the computer and the Internet in the past 6 months, keeping up with both their local and distant friends was a very important reason, after their schoolwork (see Figure 4.8). It is important to note that, although communication was particularly appealing to girls, it was also the most important use of the Internet for boys.

In addition to being more popular, use of the Internet for interpersonal communication was also more sustaining. Both Web use and e-mail use dropped over the first 2 years that members of the sample were on-line, but the drop in Web use was steeper. In addition, in contrast to people for whom the World Wide Web was their dominant Internet application, people who used e-mail more heavily than they used the Web were more likely to still be using the Internet after their first year. All of these observations suggest that electronic mail was the Internet application that kept people coming back to the Internet. Although these conclusions were based on data from both the teenagers and adults in the sample, in this regard, teenagers and adults treated the Internet similarly.

A closer look at on-line communication shows that the majority of on-line social relationships had their roots outside of the Internet and, for this sample of Internet neophytes, existed prior to their access to the Internet. When keeping up with their close friends and family members, what sociologists term *strong ties* (Granovetter, 1973), electronic mail supplemented the telephone and face-to-face visits but rarely replaced these older communication modes.

Teens would hurry home from school to have e-mail conversations with the friends they had just left. Students frequently corresponded with their parents by e-mail when they went off to college, and one teenager created a distribution list so that all of his high school chums could easily keep in touch as they dispersed around the country. When another student went off to college, she kept up with at least some of her high school friends by electronic mail alone for up to a year. Many of these keep-in-touch communications were small talk—gossip and news of the day, with a here-and-now flavor. These communications existed for the pleasure they brought rather than for their instrumental benefits.

However, in contrast to earlier telecommunications technologies for interpersonal communication, the Internet contains several popular communications applications that encourage strangers to communicate with each other. These include *Usenet newsgroups,* which are topically oriented electronic bulletin boards; *listservs,* which are topically oriented distribution lists for electronic mail; *MUDs* and their variants, which are synchronous communication systems organized around role-playing games; and *chats,* which are more topically oriented, synchronous communication systems. The important similarity among these services is that they provide public spaces on the Internet where people gather, meet each other, communicate or observe others communicating, and occasionally form new relationships. When HomeNet participants were asked how they used the Internet in the prior 6 months, those who participated more in Usenet newsgroups, MUDs, and chats were more likely to report using the Internet for meeting new people.

Teenagers were disproportionately heavier users of MUDs and chats than adults, even after accounting for teenagers' greater use of the Internet overall. This may be because teenagers are in a stage of life when they are sampling personal relationships. Indeed, Roberts et al. (1999) found that, whereas 8- to 13-year-olds most often visited chat rooms that dealt with entertainment topics, 14- to 18-year-olds most frequently visited chat rooms devoted to discussion of relationships and lifestyles. Therefore, it is not surprising that teenagers reported using the Internet to meet new people relatively more than adults did, again after accounting for teenagers' greater use of the Internet overall.

Using an extensive set of clinical interviews, Turkle (1995) discussed other kinds of identity issues brought about by MUDs. People create multiple characters as they role play in different or even the same MUD. Turkle writes about Doug, a Midwestern college junior who plays four different characters (e.g., a seductive woman, a macho cowboy, a rabbit, and a furry animal) distributed across three different MUDs. He talks about turning on different parts of his mind when moving from window to window (Turkle, 1995, p. 13). In addition to raising questions concerning a movement toward multiple identities as a function of participation in MUDs, Doug's experience also illustrates the increasing importance of simulated worlds, a notion introduced by the *Tamagotchi,* and the declining importance of the real world (Turkle, 1995, 1997). There is every indication that socialization by the Internet to form multiple identities and to relate more and more to a simulated social world is reaching an increasingly young audience. Turkle (1995), for example, reports that, although most MUD players are in their teens or 20s, "it is no longer unusual to find MUDs where 8- and 9-year-olds 'play' such grade-school icons as Barbie or the Mighty Morphin Power Rangers" (p. 11). We as yet know little about whether we should appreciate the adaptive value of alter egos or worry about the maladaptive nature of fragmented or multiple personalities.

The Pittsburgh study indicated that young people frequented MUDs and chat rooms for the express purpose of interacting with strangers. In contrast, adults made more of their new on-line relationships through Usenet groups and listservs; they often used these services to get information about hobbies or work and met people as a side effect of these more nonsocial motivations. Typically, the new relationships remain in the electronic domain. People who meet new partners on-line have conversations with them both in the original newsgroup or chat where they first met and by private electronic mail. Less frequently did people (in the Pittsburgh study) whose relationship started on-line meet in the flesh. Meetings occurred if the friend one met on-line lived locally.

It is important, however, to note that this use of the Internet can be a dangerous one. For example, two teenage girls told a journalist that they had invited males they knew only from the Internet to their homes when their parents were not there. In the case of one of the girls, a man appeared at the door who was much older than she expected (Lauren Greenfield, personal communication, May 1999). It is clear that parents generally do not monitor the type of Internet interactions that would lead to such incidents. In a national sample of seventh through twelfth graders, 61% reported that they were "mainly alone" when they visited chat rooms (Roberts et al., 1999).

Although the new relationships of the subjects in the Pittsburgh sample typically remained in the electronic domain, data from people who were independently on-line suggest slightly different trends (McKenna, 1999; McKenna & Bargh, 1998). McKenna (1999) surveyed a large nationwide sample of people (333 females and 234 males from 13 to 70 years old; mean age = 32) who were already on-line (respondents' experience on the Internet ranged from 1 month to 443 months, with a mean of 34 months) and had posted to one of 20 Usenet newsgroups randomly selected for the study. She reports that

> 63% of all respondents had spoken to someone they met via the Internet on the telephone, 56% had exchanged pictures of themselves, 54% had written a letter through the post, and 54% had met with their Internet friend in a face-to-face situation. (p. 3)

While on-line relationships do exist, are they typically "weaker" than comparable relationships people report having off-line? According to Parks and Roberts's (1997) data, people describe their on-line relationships as existing for a shorter time, involving less time spent together, having less breadth, and being less likely to endure than their real-world relationships. However, the strength of relationships created on-line might be related to an individual's self-identity. On the basis of her study of the Usenet participants, McKenna (1999) suggests that "the socially anxious and lonely not only find new friends on the Internet, but they also integrate these friends into their 'real' world" (p. 4). Although McKenna's sample includes 13- to 19-year-olds, she does not report specifically on age-related differences. Even so, given the widely divergent implications of these data and the HomeNet findings, the differences and interactions between on- and off-line relationships demand further study.

### *Social and Psychological Effects of Internet Use*

Despite these findings that the Internet is a social technology used for communication with individuals and groups, other analyses of the HomeNet data demonstrate that use of the Internet is associated with declines in social involvement and the psychological well-being that goes along with it. The data come from an analysis of 169 individuals from 93 households during their first 2 or 3 years on-line. (The 2-year results are reported in Kraut et al., 1996.) They measured the number of minutes that members of the panel reported talking to other household members; the number of people they reported keeping up with, both in Pittsburgh and nationally; and their levels of daily-life stress, depression, and social support. Results show that these variables measured before respondents got their Internet connections did not predict how much they subsequently used the Internet. On the other hand, the greater use of the Internet during their first 12 to 24 months with Internet access was associated with small but statistically significant declines in social involvement (as measured by communication within the family and the size of people's local social networks) and with increases in loneliness (the psychological state associated with lack of social involvement). Greater use of the Internet was also associated with increases in depression. Because initial social involvement and psychological well-being were generally not associated with subsequent use of the Internet, these findings imply that the direction of causation is more likely to run from use of the Internet to declines in social involvement and psychological well-being rather than the reverse.

The statistical interactions of Internet use with age showed that increases in Internet use were associated with larger increases in loneliness and larger declines in social support for teenagers than for adults. There were no statistical interactions between Internet use and age for family communication, depression, or size of social circle.

There are at least two plausible and theoretically interesting mechanisms for these changes, but we have little evidence from our current research to establish which, if either, is correct. The first is that the time people devote to using the Internet substitutes for the time that they had previously spent engaged in social activities. This interpretation is consistent with the finding that people who use the Internet more spend less time talking to other household members. The second explanation is that, by using the Internet, people are substituting a poorer quality social relationship for a better one—that is, substituting weak ties for strong ones (Granovetter, 1973; Krackhardt, 1994). We observed that many of the on-line relationships in our sample, and especially the new ones, represented relatively weak ties with strangers, acquaintances, or nonintimate kin. Research shows that these types of social contact typically provide less social support and less consequential social support than more intimate ties do (Krackhardt, 1994; Wellman et al., 1996).

During respondents' second or third year on-line, use of the Internet did not have the same effects that it had initially. That is, during respondents' first year or two, the more hours they were using the Internet per week, the more their psychological and social well-being declined. During the next 12 months, further use of the Internet was associated with smaller declines in psychological and social well-being or even improvements. (These results are based on one sample that was tested before Internet access and after Years 2 and 3; a second sample was tested before Internet access and after Years 1 and 2.) Initially, hours on-line were associated with increases in loneliness but, subsequently, were associated with declines in loneliness.

There are three competing explanations for these diminished effects or even reversals. First, as with many learning processes, early exposure may have larger consequences than later exposure. Because the initial exposure is completely novel, it generates greater adaptation on the part of users than does later exposure. Second, as the novelty of the Internet wears off, people may be using it more wisely later in their experience than they did early on. Third, over time, the Internet as a technology and set of resources is also changing. To take but one example, during 1995-1996, when respondents were using the Internet for the first time, MUDs and Internet Relay Chat were the two most popular services that could be used to communicate with other people in real time. Because these services connected anyone who logged in to a common site, they increased the likelihood that users would communicate with a stranger. In 1997-1998, in contrast, America Online's Instant Messenger and ICQ were the popular real-time communication services. Both of these services allow users to identify a list of people and to be notified when these people go on-line. These "buddy lists," as they are known, increase the likelihood that people will communicate with known others. Similarly, the growth in the proportion of the population on-line between 1995 and 1998 means that people have more opportunities to communicate with people who are meaningful to them. Their close friends and relatives were more likely to have an Internet account in 1998 than in 1995. Distinguishing between these alternative explanations will require additional research.

## Integrating Internet Use and Interactive Games: The Fifth Dimension

For about 15 years, Michael Cole has been experimenting with the use of electronic communication and games with children in both classroom and after-school settings (Cole, 1996). The after-school programs have been titled "the Fifth Dimension" and are described as follows:

> The Fifth Dimension is a distributed literacy consortium comprised of after-school programs located in Boys and Girls Clubs, YM & YWCAs, recreation centers, and public schools across America, Mexico, Australia, Denmark, and Russia. . . . To an outsider, the Fifth Dimension appears as if children actively engage in computer games and other playful activities. But much more is happening. The Fifth Dimension is an activity system that mixes the leading activities of play, education, peer interaction, and affiliation. . . . About 75% of the activities utilize educational software and computer games. Included are telecommunications activities for searching the Internet, tools for computer-mediated and video-mediated conferencing, and MUSE and MUD activities. The remaining activities are non-electronic and include board games and arts and crafts. The software represents the curricular content of the Fifth Dimension. Subject matter includes social development, communications, reading, writing, math, geography, social studies, health, technology, language, and problem solving. . . . According to the rules of the Fifth Dimension (enshrined in a constitution agreed upon by each child), children make progress . . . by mastering tasks set for them in each game or activity. (Blanton, Moorman, Hayes, & Warner, n.d.)

As can be seen in this description, the electronic games and Internet activities are based in a total social and cognitive environment that includes a ladder of challenges. The Fifth

Dimension programs are permanent; they are staffed by students (working as volunteers or for credit) at local colleges and universities. Elementary school children can participate in the program on a long-term basis. Effects of the total environment are impressive, although we cannot separate out effects of individual components such as particular Internet activities or games. The effects, in well-controlled studies, include advances in reading and mathematics (Blanton et al., n.d.), computer knowledge, following directions, grammar, and school achievement tests (*Summary of Cognitive Evaluation Studies,* n.d.). Perhaps the most important message of the Fifth Dimension, vis-à-vis interactive games and the Internet, is that the maximum positive impact of these computer activities and tools will come about when they are embedded in a total environment that is both constructive and socially mediated.

## Conclusion

In conclusion, the proliferation of computers and on-line access in households with children has raised questions about the extent of computer use by children and the impact of such use on their activities and development. Examination of available research suggests a paucity of accurate estimates (those not based on self-report data) of the actual time spent on computers by children. It appears that children in homes with computers spend less time watching television and more time reading than children in homes without computers do. Because of the growing trend in tie-ins between different media, it is expected that eventually the time spent on all electronic media could negatively affect the time spent on reading, sports, socializing, and other activities.

Research suggests that computer use has changed the balance of cognitive skills from the verbal to the visual. Electronic games provide the training wheels for computer literacy. From the cognitive perspective, they prepare children and adolescents for the increasingly visual domains of science and technology. At the same time, electronic games, computers, and, more recently, the Internet have also changed the balance between real and simulated worlds, with the real world sometimes becoming merely a relatively boring window on the computer screen (Turkle, 1995).

One of the greatest concerns about computer games and the Internet is their increasingly violent content. The limited research on this topic has measured short-term effects and, in general, suggests that playing aggressive games increases and even provides dangerous tools for aggressive behavior in children. The recently instituted ratings system of software by the Entertainment Software Ratings Board is a step in the right direction. Increasing parental awareness of these ratings is critical to controlling children's access to such violent media; otherwise, they may just be used by children to find the most violent and sexually explicit games. In the domain of social development and social relationships, Internet use seems to have augmented trends toward multiple identities, as well as relationships with strangers and even robots. The Fifth Dimension holds promise that, when embedded in an environment that provides structure, guidance, and positive social affiliations, electronic games and the Internet can have important positive outcomes for child development.

## Notes

1. Note that the PC meter data is collected automatically by the computer, which keeps track of usage information.

2. This picture of an increase with age on the Internet is supported by the developmental data of Roberts et al. (1999), who found that, in their national sample, the time on computers showed a many-fold increase between the 2- to 7-year-old group and the 8- to 18-year-old group.

3. The HomeNet study did not collect data from children younger than 10, even though they were in the trial.

4. One of us, Elisheva Gross, was a cocreator of Plug In!

5. A total of 440 questionnaires were submitted, but 157 were blank or had incomplete information. A great number of those incomplete or even blank questionnaires were a result of our young users' unfamiliarity with the technology. For example, it is all too easy to click "send" without pasting in your completed questionnaire. Also, respondents were required to copy and paste the questions into an e-mail; many found this difficult and simply wrote asking to be in the cast.

6. These comparisons control for the greater number of hours per week that teens are on-line compared with adults.

7. The national sample of Roberts et al. (1999) confirms this basic picture but also reveals a developmental trend: Schoolwork is second to gaming in the computer use of 8- to 13-year-olds but rises to the number-one activity in the 14- to 18-year-olds. (Note, though, that Roberts et al. include not only the Internet but all uses of the computer for schoolwork in this finding.)

## References

AAUW. (1999). *Closing the gender gap: How schools still fail our girls.* Washington, DC: Author.

Blanton, W. E., Moorman, G. B., Hayes, B. A., & Warner, M. L. (n.d.). *Effects of participation in the Fifth Dimension on far transfer* [On-line]. [Retrieved December 1999].
Available: www.ced.appstate.edu/projects/5dClhse/pubs/tech/effects.html

Cassell, J., & Jenkins, H. (1998). Chess for girls? Feminism and computer games. In J. Cassell & H. Jenkins (Eds.), *From Barbie to Mortal Combat: Gender and computer games.* Cambridge: MIT Press.

Chambers, J. H., & Ascione, F. R. (1987). The effects of prosocial and aggressive videogames on children's donating and helping. *Journal of Genetic Psychology, 148,* 499-505.

Coffey, S., & Stipp, H. (1997). The interactions between computer and television usage. *Journal of Advertising Research, 37,* 61-67.

Cole, M. (1996). *Cultural psychology: A once and future discipline.* Cambridge, MA: Harvard University Press.

Colwell, J., Grady, C., & Rhaiti, S. (1995). Computer games, self esteem, and gratification of needs in adolescents. *Journal of Community and Applied Social Psychology, 5,* 195-206.

Cooper, J., & Mackie, D. (1986). Video games and aggression in children. *Journal of Applied Social Psychology, 16,* 726-744.

Dietz, T. L. (1998). An examination of violence and gender role portrayals in video games: Implications for gender socialization and aggressive behavior. *Sex Roles, 38,* 425-442.

Elmer-Dewitt, P. (1993, September 27). The amazing video game boom. *Time,* pp. 66-73.

Eron, L. D., Huesmann, L. R., Lefkowitz, M. M., & Walder, L. O. (1996). Does television violence cause aggression? In D. F. Greenberg (Ed.), *Criminal careers* (Vol. 2, pp. 311-321). Aldershot, UK: Dartmouth Publishing.

Fling, S., Smith, L., Rodriguez, T., Thornton, D., Atkins, E., & Nixon, K. (1992). Videogames, aggression, and self-esteem: A survey. *Social Behavior & Personality, 20,* 39-45.

Flynn, J. R. (1994). IQ gains over time. In R. J. Sternberg (Ed.), *Encyclopaedia of human intelligence* (pp. 617-623). New York: Macmillan.

Friedrich-Cofer, L., & Huston, A. H. (1986). Television violence and aggression: The debate continues. *Psychological Bulletin, 100,* 364-371.

Funk, J. (1993). Reevaluating the impact of video games. *Clinical Pediatrics, 2,* 86-89.

Granovetter, M. (1973). The strength of weak ties. *American Journal of Sociology, 73,* 1361-1380.

Graybill, D., Kirsch, J. R., & Esselman, E. D. (1985). Effects of playing violent versus nonviolent video games on the aggressive ideation of aggressive and nonaggressive children. *Child Study Journal, 15,* 199-205.

Greenfield, P. M. (1994). Video games as cultural artifacts. *Journal of Applied Developmental Psychology, 15,* 3-12. (Reprinted in *Interacting with video,* pp. 85-94, by P. M. Greenfield & R. R. Cocking, Eds., 1996, Norwood, NJ: Ablex)

Greenfield, P. M. (1998). The cultural evolution of IQ. In U. Neisser (Ed.), *The rising curve: Long-term gains in IQ and related measures.* Washington, DC: American Psychological Association.

Greenfield, P. M., Camaioni, L., Ercolani, P., Weiss, L., Lauber, B. A., & Perucchini, P. (1994). Cognitive socialization by computer games in two cultures: Inductive discovery or mastery of an iconic code? *Journal of Applied Developmental Psychology, 15* [Special issue: Effects of interactive entertainment technologies on development], 59-85. (Reprinted in *Interacting with video,* pp. 141-168, by P. M. Greenfield & R. R. Cocking, Eds., 1996, Norwood, NJ: Ablex)

Greenfield, P. M., deWinstanley, P., Kilpatrick, H., & Kaye, D. (1994). Action video games and informal education: Effects on strategies for dividing visual attention. *Journal of Applied Developmental Psychology, 15* [Special issue: Effects of interactive entertainment technologies on development], 105-123. (Reprinted in *Interacting with video,* pp. 187-205, by P. M. Greenfield & R. R. Cocking, Eds., 1996, Norwood, NJ: Ablex)

Griffiths, M. (1997). Friendship and social development in children and adolescents: The impact of electronic technology. *Educational and Child Psychology, 14,* 25-37.

Griffiths, M. D., & Hunt, N. (1995). Computer game playing in adolescence: Prevalence and demographic indicators. *Journal of Community & Applied Social Psychology, 5,* 189-193.

Grusec, J. E., & Lytton, H. (1988). *Social development.* New York: Springer-Verlag.

Harrell, J. S., Gansky, S. A., Bradley, C. B., & McMurray, R. G. (1997). Leisure time activities of elementary school children. *Nursing Research, 46,* 246-253.

Irwin, A. R., & Gross, A. M. (1995). Cognitive tempo, violent video games, and aggressive behavior in young boys. *Journal of Family Violence, 10,* 337-350.

Kinder, M. (1991). *Playing with power in movies, television, and video games: From* Muppet Babies *to* Teenage Mutant Ninja Turtles. Berkeley and Los Angeles: University of California Press.

Kirsh, S. J. (1998). Seeing the world through Mortal Kombat-colored glasses: Violent video games and the development of a short-term hostile attribution bias. *Childhood: A Global Journal of Child Research, 5,* 177-184.

Krackhardt, D. (1994). The strength of strong ties: The importance of *Philos* in organizations. In N. Nohria & R. Eccles (Eds.), *Networks and organizations: Structure, form, and action.* Boston: Harvard Business School Press.

Kraut, R., Scherlis, W., Mukhopadhyay, T., Manning, J., & Kiesler, S. (1996). The HomeNet field trial of residential Internet services. *Communications of the ACM, 39,* 55-63.

Malone, T. W. (1981). Toward a theory of intrinsically motivating instruction. *Cognitive Science, 5,* 333-370.

McKenna, K. Y. A. (1999). *Can you see the real me? Formation and development of interpersonal relationships on the Internet.* Manuscript in preparation, New York University.

McKenna, K. Y. A., & Bargh, J. A. (1998). Coming out in the age of the Internet: Identity "demarginalization" from virtual group participation. *Journal of Personality and Social Psychology, 75,* 681-694.

Mitchell, E. (1985). The dynamics of family interaction around home video games. *Marriage & Family Review, 8* [Special issue: Personal computers and the family], 121-135.

Nielsen Media Research. (1998). *Television viewing in Internet households* [On-line]. Available: www.nielsenmedia.com/reports.html/reportontv. html

Okagaki, L., & Frensch, P. A. (1994). Effects of video game playing on measures of spatial performance: Gender effects in late adolescence. *Journal of Applied Developmental Psychology, 15* [Special issue: Effects of interactive entertainment technologies on development], 33-58.

Oldberg, C. (1998, December 15). Children and violent video games: A warning. *New York Times,* p. A16.

Parks, M. R., & Roberts, L. D. (1997, February). *Making MOOsic: The development of personal relationships on-line and a comparison to their office counterparts.* Paper presented at the annual meeting of the Western Speech Association, Monterey, CA.

Pew Research Center for People and the Press. (1998). *Online newcomers more middle-brow, less work-oriented.* Washington, DC: Author. Available: www.people-press.org/tech98sum.htm

Phillips, C. A., Rolls, S., Rouse, A., & Griffiths, M. (1995). Home video game playing in schoolchildren: A study of incidence and patterns of play. *Journal of Adolescence, 18,* 687-691.

Provenzo, E. F., Jr. (1991). *Video kids: Making sense of Nintendo.* Cambridge, MA: Harvard University Press.

Richard, B. (1998). *Digitaler grossangriff auf die seelen junger menschen (spiegel): Die sorge um ein virtuelles wesen (tamagotchi)* [Digital assault on the souls of young people: The concern about virtual beings/entities]. Paper presented at the conference Self-Socialization, Child Culture, and Media, University of Bielefeld, Germany.

Roberts, D. F., Foehr, U. G., Rideout, V. J., & Brodie, M. (1999, November). *Kids and media at the new millennium: A comprehensive national analysis of children's media use.* Menlo Park, CA: Kaiser Family Foundation.

Rule, B. G., & Ferguson, T. J. (1986). The effects of media violence on attitudes, emotions, and cognitions. *Journal of Social Issues, 42,* 29-50.

Rutkowska, J. C., & Carlton, T. (1994). *Computer games in 12-13-year-olds' activities and social networks.* Paper presented at the annual conference of the British Psychological Society.

Schutte, N. S., Malouff, J. M., Post-Gorden, J. C., & Rodasta, A. L. (1988). Effects of playing videogames on children's aggressive and other behaviors. *Journal of Applied Social Psychology, 18,* 454-460.

Shih, C.-F., & Venkatesh, A. (1999). *Intra-household diffusion of new technologies: Conceptual foundation and illustrative example* (Working Paper). Irvine: University of California, Irvine, Center for Research on Information Technology and Organizations.

Silvern, S. B., & Williamson, P. A. (1987). The effects of video game play on young children's aggression, fantasy, and prosocial behavior. *Journal of Applied Developmental Psychology, 8,* 453-462.

Stanger, J. D. (1998). *Television in the home 1998: The third annual national survey of parents and children.* Philadelphia: University of Pennsylvania, Annenberg Public Policy Center.

Stanger, J. D., & Gridina, N. (1999, June 29). *Media in the home: The fourth annual survey of parents and children.* Philadelphia: University of Pennsylvania, Annenberg Public Policy Center.

Subrahmanyam, K., & Greenfield, P. M. (1994). Effect of video game practice on spatial skills in girls and boys. *Journal of Applied Developmental Psychology, 15* [Special issue: Effects of interactive entertainment technologies on development], 13-32. (Reprinted in *Interacting with video,* pp. 95-114, by P. M. Greenfield & R. R. Cocking, Eds., 1996, Norwood, NJ: Ablex)

Subrahmanyam, K., & Greenfield, P. M. (1998). Computer games for girls: What makes them play? In J. Cassell & H. Jenkins (Eds.), *From Barbie to Mortal Combat: Gender and computer games.* Cambridge: MIT Press.

*Summary of cognitive evaluation studies* [On-line]. (n.d.). Available: www.ced.appstate.edu/projects/5dClhse/pubs/tech/studies/studies/html

Suzuki, H., Hashimoto, Y., & Ishii, K. (1997). Measuring information behavior: A time budget survey in Japan. *Social Indicators Research, 42,* 151-169.

Times Mirror Center for the People and the Press. (1994, May). *The role of technology in American life* [Fact sheet]. Washington, DC: Children's Partnership.

Tizard, B., Philips, J., & Plewis, I. (1976). Play in preschool centers: Play measures and their relationship to age, sex, and I.Q. *Journal of Child Psychology and Psychiatry and Allied Disciplines, 17,* 252-264.

Turkle, S. (1984). *The second self: Computers and the human spirit.* New York: Simon & Schuster.

Turkle, S. (1995). *Life on the screen: Identity in the age of the Internet.* New York: Simon & Schuster.

Turkle, S. (1997). Constructions and reconstructions of self in virtual reality: Playing in the MUDs. In S. Kiesler (Ed.), *Culture of the Internet* (pp. 143-155). Mahwah, NJ: Lawrence Erlbaum.

Turow, J. (1999, May 4). *The Internet and the family: The view from the parents, the view from the press.* Philadelphia: University of Pennsylvania, Annenberg Public Policy Center.

U.S. Census Bureau. (1993, October). *Current Population Survey* [On-line]. [Retrieved March 1999]. Available: www.census.gov/population/socdemo/computer/compwork.txt

*U.S. teens and technology* [On-line]. (1997). [Retrieved March 8, 1999].
Available: www.nsf.gov/od/lpa/nstw/teenov.html

van Schie, E. G. M., & Wiegman, O. (1997). Children and videogames: Leisure activities, aggression, social integration, and school performance. *Journal of Applied Social Psychology, 27,* 1175-1194.

Vita stats. (1999, August 30). *Newsweek,* p. 10.

Wellman, B., Salaff, J., Dimitrova, D., Garton, L., Gulia, M., & Haythornthwaite, C. (1996). Computer networks as social networks: Collaborative work, telework, and virtual community. *Annual Review of Sociology, 22,* 213-238.

Wiegman, O., & van Schie, E. G. M. (1998). Video game playing and its relations with aggressive and prosocial behavior. *British Journal of Social Psychology, 37,* 367-378.

CHAPTER 5

# Attention, Comprehension, and the Educational Influences of Television

DAVID S. BICKHAM
JOHN C. WRIGHT
ALETHA C. HUSTON
The University of Texas at Austin

Imagine, for a moment, that we enter a room where a young child is watching television. The child's eyes are fixed on the screen. Her face is almost expressionless, and the flashing of the screen is reflected in her unblinking eyes. We judge that she is entranced, engulfed, possibly even addicted. Is this an accurate observation of what is happening (or not happening) in the mind of the child? Questionable. Is it one that many parents and teachers believe is typical? Definitely.

It is a prevalent assumption in the United States that the physical inactivity common in television watching implies mental and cognitive inactivity. This belief has become so ingrained in our perceptions of the television experience that it has infiltrated our everyday language: Children are said to have become "couch potatoes" and to "veg out" in front of the television. Inherent in this assumption of passivity is an attribution concerning television's power over the young viewer. The bright lights, loud sounds, and quick movements of the television's images are thought to seize and hold captive the child's attention. The viewer is said to be a passive recipient of television and its messages. She is unable to look away, and the viewing act itself interferes with and inhibits any critical thought processes.

Stemming from these assumptions are policies of educators and beliefs of parents about television's alleged inability to teach. Many assume that television, *as a medium,* interferes with active processing and therefore believe that it is not conducive to learning, school achievement, or school readiness. Teachers rarely incorporate television into their curriculum or encourage targeted viewing as an at-home activity.

Let us step back for a moment to question the hypothetical viewing scene described above and the assumptions surrounding it. It is the purpose of this chapter to challenge and correct this popular conception of the medium that occupies more of the American child's waking hours than any other category of time use. What is it that we need to know before we can understand the subtleties of the event we are witnessing? Are the images overpowering to the child, or does she play an active role in her own attention? How do the types of content and styles of production influence the child's attention? Can she play a part in altering these effects? How do the child's goals, experiences, and stage of cognitive development shape the viewing experience and help determine its long-term effects on her?

And what about the potential for learning? Is it possible to have attractive and well-made educational television that uses the enticing qualities of the medium to teach children and prepare them for school and a life of learning? Or do the essential properties of the medium itself make this impossible? Is the best television diet for children well-designed, well-produced educational television, or is it no television at all?

It is the goal of this chapter to question the simple condemnation of the medium itself and all the assumptions that accompany that view. By presenting research evidence portraying the child as an active viewer, busily mastering important content from various sources, we hope to invoke a new image: a picture of a child capable of using the medium to make her own attentional decisions; a child who actively decides what is worth watching and how to get the most out of it; and a child who gradually learns how to use television, and later other media, to better understand and master her world and to choose among the various life goals and options it offers her. Such a picture will do more than dispel hasty and superficial judgments about media per se. It will focus the attention of those who raise and educate children on the medium's ability, when well designed and produced, to have positive, lasting effects on its young viewers.

In the first part of the chapter, we therefore focus on the active-passive dimension with regard to children's attention to and processing of television. In the second part of the chapter, we turn to the related issue of children's learning from television. What are the positive potentials for learning from TV? Can an early start with educational television lead to a continuing high level of academic motivation and achievement (and, yes, even creativity and imagination) throughout the school years? We present research evidence to support our view that children make their own viewing and processing decisions; that they can learn both important facts and critical skills from television; and that the learning strategies and attitudes they pick up from the best of TV for young children positively facilitate school achievement and cognitive development for years to come.

Finally, we hope to show that, because commercial entertainment television made for general audiences also has negative effects on the same children who benefit from its educational and inspirational potentials, the most important belief to correct is the myth that the medium itself has either positive or negative effects. We believe the data indicate that, after the child's initial experience, the medium itself matters hardly at all. It is its content that has lasting, cumulative impact.

## Children's Attention and Comprehension

### *Visual and Auditory Attention*

The standard measure of attention in most laboratory studies is visual fixation on the television screen (Anderson, Alwitt, Lorch, & Levin, 1979). This technique has a number of important advantages over other indexes of exposure. The frequency and duration of looking at TV can be coded quite reliably, with agreement between independent observers typically reaching 90% or higher (Alwitt, Anderson, Lorch, & Levin, 1980; Anderson,

Field, Collins, Lorch, & Nathan, 1985; Calvert, Huston, Watkins, & Wright, 1982). The method corresponds to the everyday definition of attention to television, and it allows for further analysis of which events on the screen coincide with the child's moment-to-moment attention (Anderson & Field, 1983).

A number of physical features of visual and auditory stimuli are known to elicit attention to them and together constitute the properties that make stimuli perceptually salient. These "automatic" attention-eliciting characteristics were listed by Berlyne (1960). They include intensity, contrast, change, movement, novelty, and incongruity. To this list we must add stimuli whose content has important learned meanings, such as sirens, the sensation of momentary weightlessness, and symbols such as the dollar sign or the swastika.

Auditory attention is surely an important factor, because the audio portion of a television program often provides the viewer with information that contextualizes and elaborates the visual content (Anderson & Field, 1983; Lorch, Anderson, & Levin, 1979). Therefore, a child who monitors only the soundtrack may score almost as well on a measure of program comprehension as would an audiovisual viewer of the same information.

Accordingly, Rolandelli, Wright, Huston, and Eakins (1991) constructed a validity bridge from visual to auditory attention in the following way: First, they showed that an alternate measure of visual attention was highly correlated with visual fixation data on the same children. The technique was to degrade electronically the quality of the visual signal by gradually adding visual noise ("salt and pepper" pattern) to the image on-screen, having previously informed the child that TV reception was intermittent and that the child could restore perfect clarity at any time by pressing a large, easy lever. The elapsed time from the beginning of each scheduled degrade to the moment when the child restored clarity with the lever was defined as an inverse measure of attention: The more attentive and interested the child, the earlier in the gradual degrade he or she noticed and restored the clarity of image. This measure was highly correlated with the traditional measure of visual fixation of the screen.

The researchers then arranged similar progressive degradations of the clarity of the audio channel and recorded the moment in each audio degrade into static noise when the child restored audio quality with the lever. They found that auditory attention predicted auditory comprehension (recall of verbal soundtrack), while visual attention predicted visual comprehension (recall of actions and images). When both were degraded simultaneously, speed of restoration was an even better predictor of overall comprehension and recall than either audio or video alone. It appears that looking and listening make separate and sometimes identifiable contributions to understanding, while perceptions of comprehensibility and interest strongly contribute to the decision to attend.

### *Processing Television Content*

If attention is a prerequisite for learning, then producers of educational programs need to concentrate as much on capturing ears and eyeballs as on teaching the content. This assumption has guided much of the research on attention and comprehension, and many researchers have found results supporting a relationship between attention to television and later recall of its messages (Field & Anderson, 1985; Zillmann, Williams, Bryant, Boynton, & Wolf, 1980; Zuckerman, Ziegler, & Stevenson, 1978). The assumed causal relationship from attention to comprehension, however, has also been repeatedly challenged. Lorch et al. (1979), for example, analyzed the relationship between children's visual attention to television and their ability to score high on a test of comprehension of the program's central content. Participants viewed an episode of *Sesame Street* in a viewing room either with toys or without toys. The treatment (availability of toys) succeeded in producing a difference in the amount of attention the two groups paid to the screen: The participants in the nontoy condition spent about twice as much time looking at the television as those in the toy condition did.

The two groups did not, however, differ in their level of comprehension. Visual attention and comprehension were related, but not in a way that implied that more attention simply led to greater comprehension. Those segments of the programs that children comprehended better, they attended to more. It appeared that the children's initial estimate of the probable level of comprehensibility of the segment guided their attention. The authors concluded that cues from the auditory track informed the children of the presence of comprehensible content, which in turn led to the participants' full visual attention. In a context of mostly adult-oriented TV, the children's programs can be identified by their look and sound as the ones most promising for comprehension, and so they receive the most concentrated visual and auditory attention.

### *Formal Features and the "Syntax of Television"*

The content of messages on television is conveyed by the use of various production techniques and conventions that have their own syntactic structure. That is, the formal features of television serve as syntactic markers, while the content constitutes the semantic part of the message. For example, the use of a "lap dissolve" between scenes almost always indicates a change in time or place within the story. Other formal features have been used so often in specific contexts that they have come to communicate semantic information. Scary music, for example, helps the viewer anticipate a scary scene. Because the two are regularly juxtaposed in movies and TV programs, they come to be associated by the child.

Still other features encode program genre (detective/police story, quiz show, situation comedy, news, soap opera, children's cartoon, etc.), context, and characters. Obviously, with viewing experience, children come to know the signs that can be used to identify such attributes as well as the likely intended audience, both of which contribute to the decision to attend or not. The age of the intended audience tells how comprehensible the program story will be (or how much mental effort will be required to process and understand it), while the genre can tell a child who does not know the particulars of the series whether or not it is the kind of show he or she usually likes to watch.

#### *Passive Model*

This model sees control of attention and processing lying mostly in the television program's form and content, and it is more applicable to young children than to older ones. Building on the known reactivity of everyone to stimuli of higher physical salience, as described above, this model predicts that children's attention and processing will be governed primarily by the glitz of the production (i.e., the rapidity of movement and change, and the intensity and salience of both auditory and visual stimuli). This model gives the child little or no credit for working actively to process the message, and critics argue that programs that attract and hold young children's attention by the use of glitz and fast pacing do not elicit or permit the desired thorough processing of the content (Singer, 1980). In the reactive model, therefore, most children's television is seen as inhibiting the careful processing necessary to glean from each scene its most critical content, in order to consider reflectively its meaning. Thoughtful, permanent learning is seen as unlikely from the viewing of programs designed mostly to hold young eyeballs by the use of physically and temporally salient stimuli. Yet that is how most programs for young children are made.

Regardless of the level of active cognition behind the attending, there are certain features of television that embody Berlyne's attention-getting attributes. These include, in addition to perceptually salient features, program switch points such as commercials and station breaks (Anderson & Levin, 1976;

Duck, Gregson, Jones, Noble, & Noy, 1988; Huston & Wright, 1997; Huston et al., 1981). Other features appear in the passive viewer model to suppress attention. Children look away from the television when features such as adult dialogue and adult male speech, animals in the wild, and speech referring to the not here and not now are presented (Anderson & Levin, 1976; Calvert et al., 1982). The alleged effects of perceptual salience on attention are well-known among producers, as evidenced by the high levels of rapid action, rapid tempo, variability, animation, music, and noise in Saturday morning commercial programs (Huston et al., 1981). Perceptual salience is also used in the production of advertisements (Greer, Potts, Wright, & Huston, 1982) in the belief that such features will enhance attention to television commercials. Assuming a relationship between attention and comprehension, perceptual salience could also affect what children understand about a television message. Children allegedly can more easily learn the material that is linked with perceptually salient and attention-enticing features because that is what passive viewers are preprogrammed to attend to.

### *Active Model*

The active model does not reject all of the assumptions on which the passive model is based. Its adherents accept the idea that certain forms and content are prepotent in eliciting attention in infancy and that such features thereby offer some basic supports for active processing that should be taken advantage of in designing positive and constructive children's programs.

The role of the child viewer in the active theory, however, is one in which the child is cognitively involved in the television experience (Anderson & Lorch, 1983). The child's attending is not determined by the images on the screen but by her own agendas and goals (Huston & Wright, 1989). Instead of capturing her attention, formal features are used by the viewer to make her own attentional decisions and viewing choices. In this model, formal features influence comprehension by guiding attention selectively to content that is interesting to and comprehensible by the viewer (Calvert et al., 1982).

If one credits the child with actively trying to make sense of TV, then one's focus is drawn to features other than perceptual salience as determinants of attention. This model credits the child with making continuous decisions about attention based on partial information. That information may include perceived comprehensibility, the interest value of the content area with which the program appears to deal (by title or preview or past experience with the series or genre), the presence of formal features (or characters, or settings) that serve as signals about the intended audience (i.e., for children rather than for adults), or other indicators that the program (or its next scene) will be worth investing in with processing effort and attention in order to understand and remember. In short, the active model views children as working deliberately to solve problems of decoding, interpreting, and, thus, understanding the content. It credits them with using knowledge about the medium and its formal features to do so. The distinction between early passive reactivity and later active control of inputs corresponds to what Wright and Vlietstra (1975) called the distinction between exploration and search.

The feature-marker or stimulus-sampling model of formal features, a theory assuming the active role of the viewer, posits that features supply experienced viewers with information essential to the processing of the content (Hawkins, Yong-Ho, & Pingree, 1991; Huston & Wright, 1983; Lorch et al., 1979). As children spend more and more of their life viewing television, they begin to learn the common production uses of formal features. They acquire the ability to effectively recognize and predict content when viewing specific production techniques. Certain features are linked with content they find appealing, and therefore they increase their attention to them. Other features indicate unappealing or incomprehensible content, and accordingly they reduce their attention in the presence of such features. They play an active role in the viewing experience by using the information provided to them as a guide to regulate their attention. This attention is assumed, in turn, to directly influence their comprehension of content.

Evidence for the feature-marker model comes from observations of children attending selectively to those features that generally carry hints that the program contains child-oriented, and therefore comprehensible, information. Women's voices, child dialogue, nonhuman voices, animation, and music are all features that commonly relay content relevant to children. Male voices and adult dialogue, on the other hand, are associated with information relevant to adults and often incomprehensible to children. Implicit in this theory is the importance of auditory features of a program. Children can monitor the soundtrack and attend to the screen only when types of voices, sounds, or music imply the presence of child-oriented material. This theory allows for an effective, goal-driven division of attention in which the child determines where to direct her attention to fulfill her needs and not waste her energy on uninteresting or incomprehensible content (Campbell, Wright, & Huston, 1987).

To illustrate the ability of young children to control their own attention and processing, Field and Anderson (1985) instructed half of their subjects to view a program and remember as much as they could for a test following the viewing. The other subjects were told only to watch the program for enjoyment. If formal features completely controlled children's attention, then these two groups would attend to the same moments and for the same amount of time. If, however, children's attention was goal oriented and actively controlled by the child, then the group receiving the instructions should attend at a higher rate. Five-year-olds receiving the instructions attended more when the essential information was conveyed visually. When such information was available through the soundtrack, however, there were no differences in attending between the two groups. The goal-oriented children apparently recognized the lack of importance in visual attending when auditory attending was sufficient. This allowed them to invest only the attention necessary to experience the decodable and meaningful messages of the program.

Anderson and his colleagues (e.g., Anderson & Lorch, 1983; Anderson, Lorch, Field, & Sanders, 1981; Lorch et al., 1979) pioneered the theory that children's perceptions of the comprehensibility of a message determine their attention to it. As discussed above, Lorch and colleagues (1979) found that 5-year-olds who attended twice as much to an episode of *Sesame Street* could not recall any more of its content. In an attempt to further measure and understand children's attention, Anderson and his colleagues (1981) edited segments of *Sesame Street* to create bits with varying levels of apparent comprehensibility. Three types of program manipulation were tested. Some segments were edited so that the characters were speaking Greek instead of English. Others were changed to backward speech, and in others the bits of content were sequentially rearranged into a random order.

In general, the results suggest that a child's perceptions of the probable comprehensibility of the bit dictated the amount of attention it received. In all situations, subjects paid attention to the bits for a higher percentage of time when they were unaltered. Greek and backward speech were instantly known to be entirely incomprehensible, and they held attention the least. The random segments were not so manifestly incomprehensible, and the subjects paid correspondingly more attention to them. They worked harder to make sense of scrambled segments because they appeared to be comprehensible and, indeed, retained at least some of their original meaning.

Other research supports this theory by presenting evidence suggesting children's understanding of some of the more complex meanings of formal features. Producers commonly use the technique of *montage* to inform viewers of changes in location, the passing of time, and other meaningful contextual information (Anderson & Field, 1983). This form requires the viewer to make inferences by using cues of setting change without actually seeing any transitions through change on-screen. A scene of a taxi driving by on a busy New York street followed by a closer image of three people in the back of a car implies that the inside of the taxi is now being shown. To comprehend the central content of the story, children must use an understanding of montage as a guide to active inference making. Anderson and Field (1983) tested 4- and 7-year-olds' ability to comprehend and reconstruct information implied by montage. Particular types of implied content were more difficult for children to draw inferences from; time changes were the most difficult, and implied character action the least difficult. The authors conclude that, given that both age groups were successful at using and comprehending montage (the 7-year-olds more than the 4-year-olds), children attend to montage because of their active ability to draw useful information from its implications. Their data on comprehension backed up this interpretation.

Formal features may signal to children that relevant, interesting material is being presented. If, however, the children are not attending to the screen when the feature is being presented, then they can make no decision about the content. By taking periodic samples of the features and content of television, children can direct the bulk of their attention elsewhere when the television's offering is of little interest. Huston and Wright (1983) present a feature-sampling model that explains children's processes of decision making about when to attend. The authors tie the activity to transitional moments in programming. At the onset of any given transition, itself marked by a known formal feature, child viewers are either visually oriented toward the screen or focusing their visual attention elsewhere. If they are viewing the screen, the children use a commercial break, a scene change, or a bit change as the moment to reevaluate their previous viewing decision (Huston & Wright, 1989).

Auditory information provides children who are *not* looking with information that a transition is occurring. They can then sample the new content and reassess their allocation of attention. If the content is not sufficiently enticing to the potential viewer, the sampling does not stop altogether; other program features and contextual features of the viewing environment will lead to further monitoring of program content. Exceptionally salient auditory events such as screams, sirens, and explosions can elicit further samples of content. Also, a reduction in an event competing with television for attention (e.g., a playmate's leaving to go home) can lead to more sampling and subsequently reexamined attentional decisions. Much like the other theories assuming an active role of the viewer, the feature-sampling model illustrates how a child comes to use formal features as an aid in making informed decisions concerning the allocation of attentional energy and effort.

Research has yielded support for the active viewer model. The early studies found that changes in scene, character, and bit led to recruitment of attention in those not watching at the moment of change. Conversely, those viewing at the moment of change promptly looked away (Anderson et al., 1979; Calvert et al., 1982; Huston & Wright, 1989; Wright et al., 1984).

One final point about this model is that it is important to realize that the children are not aware of the activity and decision-making process described. The children being illustrated by this model are aware of what they are watching and know whether or not it meets their current abilities and desires. Bored or confused children are aware of their source of boredom or confusion. The decisions they make are mostly automated and are not motivated by thoughts like "this adult man who is speaking will probably say something that either I do not understand or am not interested in." Attentional decisions are made in the amount of time it takes to press the "channel up" button on a remote control.

### *Resolution of the Active and Passive Models*

At first glance, the active and reactive models appear diametrically opposed. Children are either controlled by the medium or use it deliberately to allocate their attention. Theories such as the feature-sampling model, however, illustrate how the two can be smoothly integrated to complement each other. At different points in the viewing process, formal features serve different purposes in attention and cognition. Similarly, at different points in a viewer's development, features may play different roles. It takes time and experience, for example, for children to learn the connections between form and content. Children under 6 do not recognize instant replay as a repetition of the same event but instead believe that the event actually occurred twice (Rice, Huston, & Wright, 1986). Young children also have difficulty recognizing the difference between advertising and program content. Even the separators used on Saturday morning cartoons do little to aid in distinguishing the content of programs from commercial ads (Palmer & McDowell, 1979).

Implied in the results and theory above is the notion that the feature-sampling model deals not only with viewers' attention but also with their cognitive processing and motivational judgments. Salient features and segment transitions may attract attention through their audiovisual properties, but, in the active models, they merely set the occasion for viewers to decide to continue to invest attention if the program matches their current abilities and needs but otherwise not to make the attentional investment. As sampling occurs, the viewer gains information from the features observed. Animation, character voices, and production style can notify the viewer of content type, age of intended audience, and other program-specific information. The viewer, now more knowledgeable about the show's content, can consider specific cognitive and motivational questions: Is this a program I recognize? Is it a program for people like me? Can I understand it? Does it meet my current viewing goals? Will it be fun to watch? Positive answers to these questions lead to further attention. This attention, however, is constantly reevaluated: Am I understanding this? How much mental energy is required to continue to understand? Is this memorable enough to merit my investment of energy? Transitions in the program elicit a requestioning of the current attentional state based on the cognitive and motivational goals of the child viewer (Huston & Wright, 1989).

Children use different methods of seeking information as they develop. In any particular initially novel setting, they progress from exploring their environment, where interesting stimuli can capture their attention, to searching systematically for the specific knowledge they desire or need at any given moment. In the realm of television, formal features guide this transformation. Infants, knowing little about the connection between form and content, explore their television environment, attending automatically whenever perceptually salient events occur. Their attention is guided mainly by the features and not by the informative utility of the information presented or its relevance to their current processing. Toddlers between 1 and 2 years of age, on the other hand, attend when features mark information interesting to them or relevant to their current goals. They have come to recognize the consistencies among instances of televised events. To these curious and engaged children, the signaling qualities of formal features are useful in providing information about the programs that they are viewing. In other words, this theory predicts that infants, like anyone in a totally novel environment, are more reactive, whereas preschool and older children are familiar with most television contexts and are therefore more cognitively active. This does not mean that older children completely stop attending to salient stimuli or that they never passively surf the channels available, only that they become better at ignoring those features that do not contain pertinent or interesting information. It also does not mean that children as young as 2 are cognitively inactive.

The developmental processes hypothesized by the exploration-search model have met with moderate support. As mentioned above, many researchers have found that salient features can attract attention (e.g., Alwitt et al., 1980; Anderson et al., 1979). When age differences were found in relation to attention to perceptually salient features, they were small and occurred mostly in specific situations (Calvert et al., 1982; Wartella & Ettema, 1974).

In one study, younger children attended slightly more to high-pace rather than low-pace magazine-format programs; no difference was found in the older children, who responded most to continuity of plot (Wright et al., 1984). This early dependence on perceptual salience is a good example of exploration in younger children. They may be attending to any given content because of its salience, and older children may attend to the same content when feature markers indicate that it contains important information. Younger children do have difficulty in discriminating central from incidental information. That difficulty is reduced when relevant content is deliberately marked by salient features (Calvert et al., 1982; Campbell et al., 1987). This finding adds credence to the argument that a developmental shift occurs between a very early dependence of attention on stimulus salience (passive exploration), on the one hand, and the quest for markers to help decode content messages (active search) on the other.

### *Revisiting the Relationship Between Attention and Comprehension*

In combining the active and reactive models of attention, the developmental theory presented by Wright et al. (1984) also indicates a shift in the relationship between comprehension and attention. The attention of a very young, inexperienced viewer is organized around salient formal features. This process leads to the comprehension of the material highlighted by such features: Attention leads to comprehension. Slightly older, slightly more experienced viewers, on the other hand, control their attention and allocate it to the television screen when something interesting and comprehensible is happening. Here, anticipated comprehension and relevance, the products of active analysis, control attention.

Other studies have independently confirmed both Anderson's comprehensibility hypothesis and the feature-signal model of Wright and Huston. Pingree (1986) confirmed that children attend poorly to language-altered bits but equally well to random segments and normal segments. The children were also asked if they found the random segments difficult to understand. The oldest children in the study, 6½-year-olds, reported more difficulty in comprehension of the reordered bits. The author concludes that, because children were paying equal amounts of attention to segments they perceived as having different levels of comprehensibility, other aspects of viewing may be equally important predictors of attention.

Novelty of the stimulus may be one force guiding children's attention. At a microlevel, Hawkins and colleagues (1991) analyzed attention at 3-second intervals to evaluate the attention-comprehension relationship. Attention to language-altered segments dropped off almost immediately. Normal and random segments held attention longer and at a more stable rate. Contrary to Anderson et al. (1981), attention to random bits was higher than to unaltered segments. The older children, according to the authors, recognized these segments as being difficult but judged them to be potentially comprehensible; they invested higher levels of attention in them accordingly. By doing so, they made them more familiar and more comprehensible, thus enhancing their interest level when seen again later.

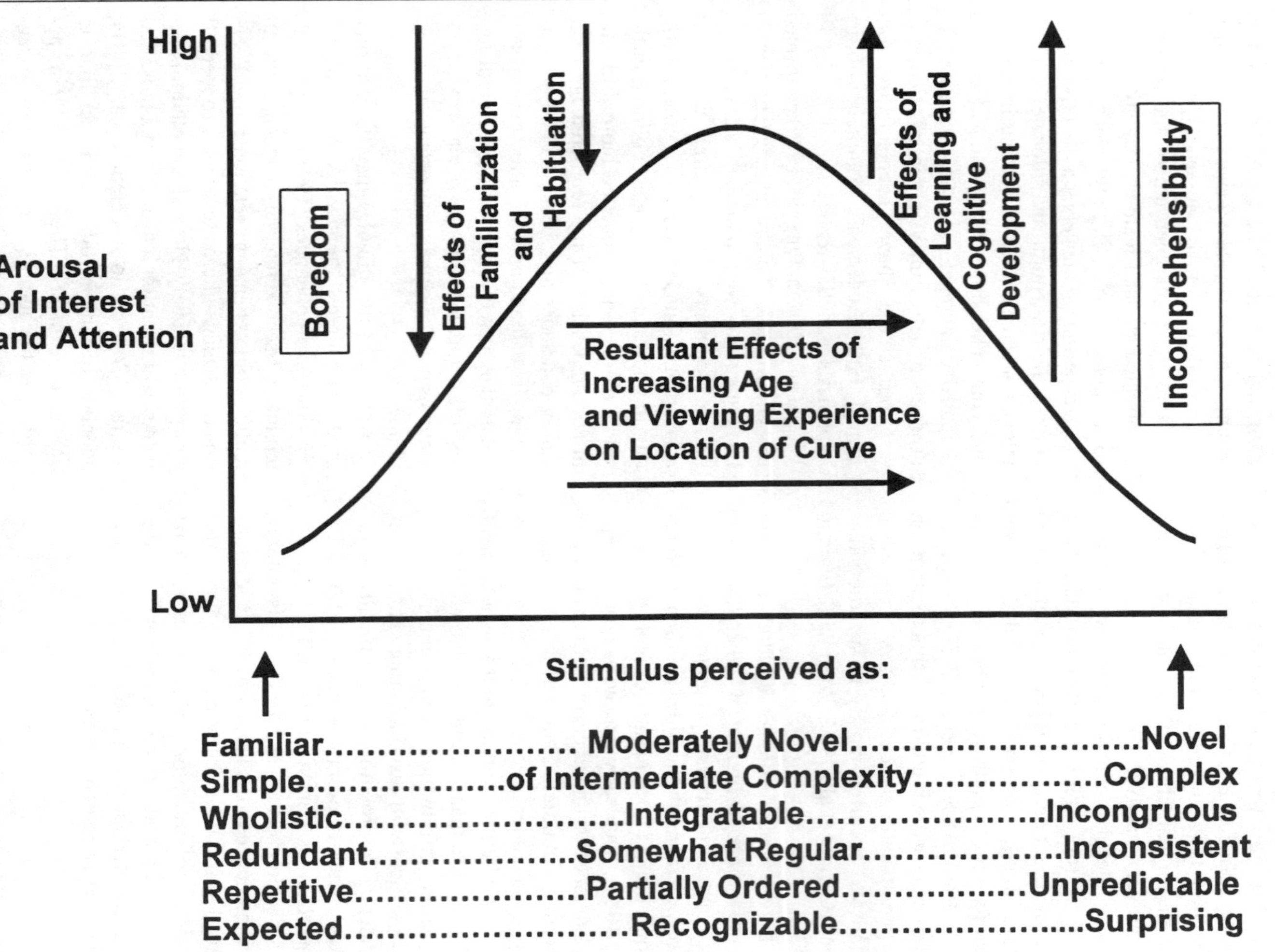


**Figure 5.1.** The Traveling Lens Model

## The Traveling Lens Model

A more comprehensive model incorporates the attention and comprehension findings along with the well-explored phenomena of attentional habituation and attentional inertia. It is called the traveling lens model (Rice, Huston, & Wright, 1982). The model's key features are shown in Figure 5.1.

An inverted U function, the lens from which the model gets its name, serves as a graphical explanation of the theory. The x-axis can denote any variable that indicates changing levels of the ease of comprehension of the stimulus. Examples include familiarity versus novelty, simplicity versus complexity, redundancy versus inconsistency, and repetition versus unpredictability. The y-axis is the level of arousal of interest and the level of attention of the child. The peak of the curve therefore denotes where the stimuli are that receive maximum time and attention from the child. The stimuli are, in this example, television moments, bits, segments, episodes, or series. Moderate levels of comprehensibility characterize a peak in interest. Information falling to the left of the peak is overly familiar or boring; the farther to the right of the peak, the more nearly incomprehensible the material. Thus, the two tails fail to arouse interest or receive attention for opposite reasons: One (the left) is too well-known already to be challenging, and the other (the right) is too complex and difficult to be readily understood. Between the middle and the right tail of the curve, attention to and interest in rather difficult but not totally incomprehensible events begin to occur, but they require greater mental effort than the most preferred intermediate-level stimuli, as found by Hawkins et al. (1991).

Although the lens predicts attention to content at any given moment in time, its movement over time from left to right in the stimulus array is its dynamic aspect. As a child watches more television, his or her familiarity with the stimuli increases. On the left side (increasing boredom), the same repetition that is initially responsible for familiarity eventually inhibits interest through the process of habituation of attention over repeated exposures. Habituation is therefore a reduction in attention as a part of the "been there, done that" reaction. The same process of familiarization, however, has the opposite effect on attention and interest on the right side, or leading edge of the lens. Here, although exposure is limited at first, as familiarity slowly grows, perceived comprehensibility is enhanced, and truly difficult materials become challenging and then interesting. As the elevation of interest is suppressed on the left and raised on the right, the whole lens moves to the right with respect to the ordered array of stimuli. As a result of both cognitive development and experience with the medium over time, a child's allocation of attention shifts toward increasingly complex material. The child's ability to comprehend drives his or her attention. Much like a wave, the medium in which the lens exists does not move or change; rather, it is characteristics within the individual child that cause the progressive shift of the lens. Though attention on the leading edge of the lens is at first sporadic, accidental, and ineffective, over time looking there increases, not only because the rest (on the left) is boring but because occasional or even unintended looking at the mostly incomprehensible gets a boost from another phenomenon of attention: attentional inertia (Anderson et al., 1979).

Attentional inertia is the well-documented phenomenon in which looks are most vulnerable to ending in their earliest moments. Conversely, the longer they continue, the lower the probability of their ending in the next moment, say, 5 seconds. The more time a look has lasted and the more attention one has invested in it, the stronger the forces that sustain its continuance and the weaker the impulse to look away (Anderson, Choi, & Lorch, 1987). Inertial properties offset the tendency of habituation to keep one exclusively interested in what is moderately nifty, novel, fleeting, and incongruous. It can be experienced when one is "surfing" the TV channels with a remote control and finds something moderately interesting to look at for a while. But often the material turns out to be difficult to make sense of, coming in, as one did, in the middle of a story. Nevertheless, the longer one looks, the more invested one becomes in making sense of the story and finding out how it all turns out. Its appeal remains high even though one's conscious reflective reaction would be that this material is not worth watching. Eventually, of course, the look ends, often because external events break the cycle and one looks away.

The lens moves not because the stimuli themselves are changing but only because items on one side are rising to a peak while those on the other side are continuously declining in interest value. The result is a wavelike migration of interest and attention toward the yet-to-be-mastered stimuli found at the relatively more complex and difficult end of the gradient.

## Educational Television Relies on Active Processing

Let us return for a moment to the viewing experience described at the beginning of this chapter. Our perspective of what the child is experiencing and what she will take away from the experience will be very different when we begin to focus on what she is watching. Suddenly, we realize that she is attending to a well-produced program designed to teach children her age developmentally significant material. In other words, she is watching an educational program. Concerns about the power of the medium over the child have been addressed, and now with the introduction of educational content, the viewing experience can be seen to have a potential positive impact on the viewer's readiness for school and her academic achievement when she gets there. Let us next consider the evidence on such deliberate manipulations of the traveling lens.

One production technique used by many program designers, including the Children's Television Workshop, is the incorporation of attention-holding, salient features into such programs as *Sesame Street.* Although this technique has been criticized as creating a television environment that is too fast paced to allow for deep processing (Singer, 1980), it can be done so that it aids in teaching messages to children. A program designed in this manner can contain humor, puppets, children's and women's voices, or any of the previously described salient features that draw attention. Capturing and holding attention is necessary, but not sufficient, to teach a message, especially when the audience of younger children is unable to separate the central messages from the incidental ones. By using salient features selectively to highlight central content, producers can guide children toward a fuller understanding and better recall of the message (Calvert et al., 1982). In *Sesame Street,* for example, counting becomes a song, and the numbers may change colors, move, dance, or, in some cases, even talk. The features draw attention to and aid in the child's recall and recognition of the numbers. The pace with which the alphabet is recited can be slowed so that viewers at home actively "prompt" the character's recitation, thereby rehearsing what is to be learned.

Informed use of formal features can enhance the educational television experience in ways beyond recognition of central content. When the process of attentional inertia is considered, the potential for teaching that stems from capturing and maintaining attention becomes clear. The use of salient features and production techniques seen by children as conveying comprehensible material gains initial attention, and attentional inertia maintains that attention. Producers cognizant of these facts can insert into a well-designed, attention-holding program bits of information slightly more complicated than the majority of the program's content. Because attentional inertia will maintain attention through these less readily comprehensible segments, children viewing the program will be exposed to material they might have otherwise ignored (Anderson & Field, 1983). Complex, inconsistent, and unpredictable material begins to become more familiar. The child's lens of attention moves to the right.

Layering, as this technique has become known, is based on Vygotsky's notion that there is for every concept and for every child a "zone of proximal development" (ZPD)—that is, a level of difficulty between the hardest already mastered and the best a child can do with supporting prompting help (Vygotsky, 1978). In a layered program, children are offered content that is not immediately familiar and accessible but is moderately novel and challenging. To be effective, layering must offer one level of content that falls on the edge of each child's ability to understand. When multiple levels of complexity of the same material are deliberately provided, not only does the program hold interest for a wider range of ages and abilities but repeated viewing of familiar segments can advance the child's comprehension to successively deeper layers of the same presentation without losing attention.

*Preplays* can serve to attune the child to what additional or new levels of meaning can be mined from a familiar or apparently "easy" segment. Recapitulations *after* the presentation may be helpful for rehearsing and remembering what was learned, but preplays serve better to control the level and success of initial processing attempts (Calvert, Huston, & Wright, 1987; Kelly & Spear, 1991; Neuman, Burden, & Holden, 1990).

Repetition, another simple technique designed to deepen processing, is beginning to be used by today's producers. In *Teletubbies,* a program designed for 1- and 2-year-olds, immediately after a short video the characters chant for it to be played "again, again." It is then repeated in its entirety without change, and yet audience interest is maintained. A Nickelodeon program, *Blue's Clues,* using a slightly different technique, rebroadcasts the same episode every day for a 5-day period, and research indicates that the audience for that episode grows each day (Crawley, Anderson, Wilder, Williams, & Santomero, in press). With such techniques, children are exposed to previously incomprehensible material, allowing the attentional lens to travel into new domains of difficulty without producing failure or discouragement for the child.

## Positive and Long-Term Effects of Educational Television

Our perception of the television experience described at the beginning of the chapter has changed dramatically. We now understand that the viewer not only actively participates in the viewing process but may attend to a program designed to hold her attention and elicit her highest potential of cognitive processing. Will she take with her information that will educate and prepare her for school, or will the effects of her attention to an educational program quickly dissipate? To find an answer, we turn to long-term studies of the cumulative effects of viewing different kinds of programming on subsequent achievement in school.

Consider one exemplary program as representative of the best research-based use of the techniques described above for producing optimal attention and processing of educational content. Since the show's inception, the designers of *Sesame Street* have used child development experts as consultants in the creation of their programs. A curriculum carefully designed to prepare children for school was adopted, and production techniques designed to maximize visual attention were employed. Early in its now 30-year-old life, researchers began to assess *Sesame Street's ability to educate. The first studies found that children encouraged to watch Sesame Street* scored higher than a control group on tests of skills that the program was designed to teach (Ball & Bogatz, 1970; Bogatz & Ball, 1971). The methods of these studies, however, were seen by some as flawed. Researchers reanalyzing the data argued that the parents' involvement in the child's viewing choices accounted for at least part of the observed effects of *Sesame Street* (Cook et al., 1975).

### *The Early Window Project*

With the overwhelming success of *Sesame Street,* it is virtually impossible to compare American children who have watched the program with those who have not—all kids watch it. In a sample of 2- and 4-year-olds drawn in the early 1990s, 80% of the educational television viewing reported was of *Sesame Street* (Wright & Huston, 1995). To examine the effects of watching *Sesame Street,* methods other than comparing watchers and nonwatchers must be used.

In a study called "the Early Window Project," the Center for Research on the Influences of Television on Children (CRITC) undertook a 3-year longitudinal investigation of the effects of educational television viewing from age 2 to 5 and from 4 to 7 in relatively low-income families (Huston, Wright, Marquis, & Green, 1999; Wright & Huston, 1995; Wright et al., in press). By including children who in the course of the study would enter school for the first time, the investigators were able to examine the association of viewing patterns with academic skills, school readiness, and school adjustment, measured 1 to 3 years later.

From 1990 to 1994, four waves of data collection occurred. At each wave, each child's academic and language skills were assessed, and the Home Observational Measure of the Environment (HOME), a measure of how supportive the home environment is for education and cognitive development, was administered. Approximately every other month throughout the 3 years between waves of data collection, parents were asked to complete a 24-hour time-use diary for their children, including titles of all television programs they viewed. In the office visits at each wave of data collection, the children were interviewed, completed a battery of tests of school readiness and achievement in reading and math, and were videotaped as they watched a TV program with their parent.

It may not be surprising that the researchers found positive relationships between watching educational TV and tests of achievement and school readiness (Wright et al., in press). Because it is likely that parents who encourage the watching of educational children's programs such as *Sesame Street* also encourage other activities that lead to school readiness, statistical controls were put in place for parents' education and income. To level the playing field on the basis of initial differences in ability, individual differences in the children's vocabulary test scores at the beginning of the study were also statistically controlled. The HOME score and the primary language spoken in the house were also controlled because they were correlated with both the viewing of educational TV and measured school readiness.

Overall, viewing *Sesame Street* and similar programs at ages 2 and 3 predicted higher scores at age 5 on measures of language, math, and school readiness. Viewing at age 4 and beyond, however, did not significantly affect later scores. Apparently, there is a window of opportunity where educational television can have its longest, most powerful effects. During this time, however, viewing general audience (adult) entertainment programs and, to a lesser extent, commercial cartoons was found to be detrimental to children's academic future. Viewing such entertainment programming at early ages predicted lower levels of school readiness at age 5.

Not only did the educational TV viewers do better on standardized tests, but they were rated by their first school teachers as more ready to learn, in terms of attitude and preacademic skills, than were their peers who did not watch such programs (Huston et al., 1999; Wright & Huston, 1995; Wright et al., in press).

Young children who habitually view developmentally appropriate educational television programs are prepared to learn much more than is offered on *Sesame Street.* They have learned basic concepts, and the language needed to apply them, that they can build on. These children also discover that learning is fun. They eagerly anticipate going to "real school." When it is time for them to enter school, they are more prepared for and excited about learning. Small differences in a child's approach to school at this early stage have the potential to diverge into different tracks, leading to quite distinct outcomes in terms of later school achievement. They can initiate a trajectory leading to an increased level of academic success that may continue well beyond elementary school.

### *Long-Term Effects: The Recontact Project*

The finding that early viewing of educational programs such as *Sesame Street* enhances the scholastic potentials of a 5-year-old may be easily accepted, but what is learned from early television that could still influence that child in his or her adolescence? *Sesame Street* does not teach information that is taught and tested in high school courses, so how could watching it at a young age help children's academic performance in high school? Is it not more likely that early educational viewing effects simply fade away by the time children enter third or fourth grade?

To answer that question, a follow-up study was undertaken in the early 1990s to recontact 15- to 19-year-old young people who had participated in one of two projects 10 to 14 years earlier when they were 5 years old. Daniel Anderson at the University of Massachusetts, Amherst, had studied 334 children from the Springfield, Massachusetts, area in the early 1980s, while Wright and Huston had studied 326 children living in Topeka, Kansas, at age 5, one or two years later. Because both studies had used many of the same measures on their separate preschool samples (e.g., the Peabody Picture Vocabulary Test [PPVT]) and the same measure of TV viewing (i.e., family diaries of all TV use in the household), the authors pooled their samples for the recontact study and attempted to locate and interview the participants from their earlier studies.

Among those relocated, 570 teenage youth, with parental consent, agreed to participate, a response rate of 87%. The surveyed samples were comparable in their parent education and family income to those not found or not consenting to participate, with the exception that there were fewer children living with a single parent in the group that was found and participated. The new sample consisted of adolescents ranging in age from 15.0 to 19.3 years (Anderson, Huston, Smith, Linebarger, & Wright, in press).

The results showed both positive relationships of preschool educational program viewing and negative relationships of general audience entertainment viewing to transcript grades in English, science, and math. These associations were in the same direction for boys and girls, but much stronger for boys than for girls. A boy who watched 5 hours of educational programming per week at age 5 had a grade point average approximately .35 higher than if he had never watched the program. A girl, having watched the same amount of such programs, could only expect about a .10 increase in her high school GPA associated with that early viewing. Conversely, the negative relationship between commercial entertainment viewing and achievement was stronger for girls than it was for boys. The gender differences seem puzzling until one considers the different developmental trajectories for the two sexes.

Early viewing may set distinctive positive or negative trajectories for both sexes, but when the developmental trajectory typical for one sex is in the *same general direction* as the effect of one kind of preschool viewing, then that effect is minimized. That was the case involving general audience noneducational programming for boys and most educational programming for girls. Conversely, when the direction of the early viewing's effects ran *counter* to the typical developmental course for that sex, then the effect size was maximized. This was the case when preschool boys watched educational and prosocial programs and when girls watched violent cartoons and general audience programs.

Put another way, we need to take account of different baselines of school readiness for each gender. Girls, at age 5, are generally considered more prepared for the structured learning environment of formal schooling than boys are. The experience meshes well with how girls are raised: Success in school depends on self-control, inhibition of impulses, and the ability to follow directions. Young boys, as most kindergarten teachers will attest, are not as prepared for school as girls are. Their verbal skills are somewhat lower, and they are more restless and likely to "act out." The boost in school readiness provided by educational programs may, therefore, instill in boys a much-needed and self-perpetuating self-control and desire to learn. On the other hand, such viewing diets may not contribute as much to girls' school readiness above and beyond their already high baseline.

The negative effects of some entertainment programs beg for a similar interpretation. Violent programs may not affect boys' success in school for two reasons: (a) Because most boys watch this genre, for any given individual, viewing violent cartoons does not make him atypical for his gender, and (b) boys' baselines of aggression and activity, two areas influenced by violent and general audience programs, are already high. The reverse, therefore, is true for girls: (a) Watching violent cartoons sets a girl apart from her peers, and (b) small increases in a girl's aggressive baseline could more readily and visibly affect her behavior at school and in classes.

Preschool educational viewing was also associated positively with creativity for both sexes (Anderson et al., in press). Scores of creativity were based on a fluency-of-recategorization procedure, sometimes called the "unusual uses test," which was administered as a timed task during the phone interviews of teenagers. Children who watched more educational television, and especially *Mister Rogers,* scored higher on the test for creativity. The control variables used in these regressions included parents' education, birth order, and, in some analyses, the child's preschool PPVT score (cf. Singer & Singer, 1981).

As in the Early Window study of school readiness, the long-term effects obtained demand a latent mediating variable to complete the explanation. The authors proposed that a positive attitude toward school, an enjoyment of learning, the experience of early academic success, and related latent variables would account for the continuity between early viewing and high school achievement. That is, although viewing *Sesame Street* does not teach a youngster the specific knowledge necessary to excel in high school, it may help increase the skills and attitudes required to achieve such knowledge. Research to confirm or correct that interpretation is needed.

Just as the bottom line in the first part of this chapter was that viewing is an active process involving perceiving, learning, thinking about, and encoding the content, so it is the conclusion of the second part that it is not the medium that has effects but the processing of its content. Television in the United States today is not a homogeneous and monolithic entity, and one may well doubt that it ever was. When educational or violent messages are presented in children's favorite medium at an early age, they have long-lasting effects. Analogous findings may be seen in the work of Huesmann and his colleagues (Huesmann & Miller, 1994), who have shown that violence viewing at age 8 is a better predictor of aggressive behavior at age 28, and even 38, than is adult violence viewing. A case for the primacy of early experience with media can clearly be made.

## Looking Ahead

Television, through its form and its content, is capable of drawing children into its programming, teaching them age-specific messages, and affecting their lives long after its screen has been permanently redirected to adult fare. Over the past 40 years, television has developed from the newborn member of the media family, full of novelty and potential, into the grandfather of media. A new generation of media is now beginning its conquest of the communications world. The new forms, including many forms of the Internet, thrive on interactivity and live interpersonal communication. The question, then, is what can we expect of these new media in terms of attention and comprehension by young users? Are models borrowed from television research sufficient to explain how children will interact with the new media? Or will new theoretical models be needed?

While comprehensibility of new media may affect their use, will children be able, as they are with television, to use the new media's forms to judge quickly the intended level of difficulty? This inference is more problematic. Currently, most websites use bright colors, graphics, movement, and animation to maintain attention. These features, while signifying child content on television, provide little information for the Internet user. Apart from the use of specific, well-known characters and blatantly child-oriented images, it may be difficult for children to determine the intended audience of a specific site. As the Internet ages, however, it is likely that this will change. Faster connections will allow for more consistent use of audio, which is likely to become essential in a child's attentional decisions regarding the Internet. Sites on the Web being developed specifically for girls and the burgeoning array of choices for children will likely take on common characteristics to inform their young audiences of the child relevance of the material they offer.

The effects of the content of television are often dependent on the role a caregiver plays in the viewing experience. Frightening material can become less frightening (Cantor, 1996) and educational material more enlightening when coviewing caregivers respond appropriately to television programs (Singer & Singer, 1998). But what is the role of the parent in terms of new media? Will the interactive and programmable quality of new technologies act as surrogate parents during a child's media use? The current software to filter websites, monitor chat and MUD (multi-user domain) rooms, and advise parents about games is not yet well enough developed to substitute for parental guidance. But technology is advancing quickly. Recent research suggests that computerized dolls that communicate with both the television and the child can help create a more interactive, engaging viewing experience (Strommen & Alexander, 1999). Although it is certain that caregivers will remain an important component of the media experience, a formal redefinition of their role should be undertaken by researchers.

Will CD-ROM computer games and platform video games for young children, and perhaps e-mail and Web surfing, be the next popular media to be linked to distinctive developmental trajectories? We hazard a guess that it will be the software—that is, the programmatic content of new media—rather than their particular forms and formats that will determine their long-term effects on the development of children. One thing is clear: What you do most and earliest with media, and the level and type of content you choose to do it with, has a lot to do with your subsequent development as a person.

Contrary to Marshall McLuhan's famous dictum, the *medium* is not the lasting message, the *message* is the message, and much depends on how a young child selects and processes those messages, whereas much less depends on the medium through which he or she chooses to do so.

The research reviewed in this chapter brings good news for parents in that opportunity can be maximized and risk factors minimized by choosing for their children's earliest diets only the very best of programming made to serve the informational and educational needs of children. We owe them no less.

## References

Alwitt, L. F., Anderson, D. R., Lorch, E. P., & Levin, S. R. (1980). Preschool children's visual attention to attributes of television. *Human Communication Research, 7*(1), 52-67.

Anderson, D. R., Alwitt, L. F., Lorch, E. P., & Levin, S. R. (1979). Watching children watch television. In G. Hale & M. Lewis (Eds.), *Attention and cognitive development.* New York: Plenum.

Anderson, D. R., Choi, H. P., & Lorch, E. P. (1987). Attentional inertia reduces distractability during young children's TV viewing. *Child Development, 58,* 798-806.

Anderson, D. R., & Field, D. E. (1983). Children's attention to television: Implications for production. In M. Meyer (Ed.), *Children and the formal features of television* (pp. 56-96). Munich, Germany: Saur.

Anderson, D. R., Field, D. E., Collins, P. A., Lorch, E. P., & Nathan, J. G. (1985). Estimates of young children's time with television: A methodological comparison of parent reports with time-lapse video home observation. *Child Development, 56,* 1345-1357.

Anderson, D. R., Huston, A. C., Smith, K. L., Linebarger, D. L., & Wright, J. C. (in press). Adolescent outcomes associated with early childhood television viewing: The Recontact Study. *Monographs of the Society for Research in Child Development.*

Anderson, D. R., & Levin, S. R. (1976). Young children's attention to "Sesame Street." *Child Development, 47,* 806-811.

Anderson, D. R., & Lorch, E. P. (1983). Looking at television action or reaction? In J. Bryant & D. R. Anderson (Eds.), *Children's understanding of television: Research on attention and comprehension* (pp. 1-33). New York: Academic Press.

Anderson, D. R., Lorch, E. P., Field, D. E., & Sanders, J. (1981). The effects of TV program comprehensibility on preschool children's visual attention to television. *Child Development, 52,* 151-157.

Ball, S., & Bogatz, G. A. (1970). *The first year of* Sesame Street: *An evaluation.* Princeton, NJ: Educational Testing Service.

Berlyne, D. E. (1960). *Conflict, arousal, and curiosity.* New York: McGraw-Hill.

Bogatz, G. A., & Ball, S. (1971). *The second year of* Sesame Street: *A continuing evaluation.* Princeton, NJ: Educational Testing Service.

Calvert, S. L., Huston, A. C., Watkins, B. A., & Wright, J. C. (1982). The relation between selective attention to television forms and children's comprehension of content. *Child Development, 53,* 601-610.

Calvert, S. L., Huston, A. C., & Wright, J. C. (1987). Effects of television preplay formats on children's attention and story comprehension. *Journal of Applied Developmental Psychology, 8,* 329-342.

Campbell, T. A., Wright, J. C., & Huston, A. C. (1987). Form cues and content difficulty as determinants of children's cognitive processing of televised educational messages. *Journal of Experimental Child Psychology, 43,* 311-327.

Cantor, J. (1996). Television and children's fear. In T. MacBeth (Ed.), *Tuning in to young viewers: Social science perspectives on television.* Thousand Oaks, CA: Sage.

Cook, T. D., Appleton, H., Conner, R. F., Shaffer, A., Tamkin, G., & Weber, S. J. (1975). *"Sesame Street" revisited.* New York: Russell Sage.

Crawley, A. M., Anderson, D. R., Wilder, A., Williams, M., & Santomero, A. (in press). Effects of repeated exposures to a single episode of the television program *Blue's Clues* on the viewing behaviors and comprehension of preschool children. *Journal of Educational Psychology.*

Duck, J. M., Gregson, R. A., Jones, E. B., Noble, G., & Noy, M. (1988). Children's visual attention to "Playschool": A time series analysis. *Australian Journal of Psychology, 40,* 413-421.

Field, D. E., & Anderson, D. R. (1985). Instruction and modality effects on children's television attention and comprehension. *Journal of Educational Psychology, 77*(1), 91-100.

Greer, D., Potts, R., Wright, J. C., & Huston, A. C. (1982). The effects of television commercial form and commercial placement on children's social behavior and attention. *Child Development, 53,* 611-619.

Hawkins, P. R., Yong-Ho, K., & Pingree, S. (1991). The ups and downs of attention to television. *Communication Research, 18*(1), 53-76.

Huesmann, L. R., & Miller, L. S. (1994). Long-term effects of repeated exposure to media violence in childhood. In L. R. Huesmann (Ed.), *Aggressive behavior: Current perspectives* (pp. 153-186). New York: Plenum.

Huston, A. C., & Wright, J. C. (1983). Children's processing of television: The informative functions of formal features. In J. Bryant & D. R. Anderson (Eds.), *Children's understanding of television: Research on attention and comprehension* (pp. 37-68). New York: Academic Press.

Huston, A. C., & Wright, J. C. (1989). The forms of television and the child viewer. In G. Comstock (Ed.), *Public communication and behavior* (Vol. 2, pp. 103-158). San Diego, CA: Academic Press.

Huston, A. C., & Wright, J. C. (1997). Mass media and children's development. In W. Damon (Series Ed.) & I. E. Sigel & K. A. Renninger (Vol. Eds.), *Handbook of child psychology: Vol. 4. Child psychology in practice* (4th ed., pp. 999-1058). New York: John Wiley.

Huston, A. C., Wright, J. C., Marquis, J., & Green, S. (1999). How young children spend their time: Television and other activities. *Developmental Psychology, 35,* 912-925.

Huston, A. C., Wright, J. C., Wartella, E., Rice, M. L., Watkins, B. A., Campbell, T., & Potts, R. (1981). Communicating more than content: Formal features of children's television programs. *Journal of Communication, 31*(3), 32-48.

Kelly, A. E., & Spear, P. S. (1991). Intraprogram synopses for children's comprehension of television content. *Journal of Experimental Child Psychology, 52,* 87-98.

Lorch, E. P., Anderson, D. R., & Levin, S. R. (1979). The relationship of visual attention to children's comprehension of television. *Child Development, 50,* 722-727.

Neuman, S. B., Burden, D., & Holden, E. (1990). Enhancing children's comprehension of a televised story through previewing. *Journal of Educational Research, 83*(5), 258-265.

Palmer, E. L., & McDowell, C. N. (1979). Program/commercial separators in children's television programming. *Journal of Communication Research, 29,* 197-201.

Pingree, S. (1986). Children's activity and television comprehensibility. *Communication Research, 13,* 239-256.

Rice, M. L., Huston, A. C., & Wright, J. C. (1982). The forms and codes of television: Effects of children's attention, comprehension, and social behavior. In D. Pearl, L. Bouthilet, & J. Lazar (Eds.), *Television and behavior: Ten years of scientific progress and implications for the eighties.* Washington, DC: U.S. Government Printing Office.

Rice, M. L., Huston, A. C., & Wright, J. C. (1986). Replays as repetitions: Young children's interpretation of television forms. *Journal of Applied Developmental Psychology, 7,* 61-76.

Rolandelli, D. R., Wright, J. C., Huston, A. C., & Eakins, D. (1991). Children's auditory and visual processing of narrated and nonnarrated television programming. *Journal of Experimental Child Psychology, 51,* 90-122.

Singer, J. L. (1980). The power and limits of television: A cognitive-affective analysis. In P. Tannenbaum (Ed.), *The entertainment function of television.* Hillsdale, NJ: Lawrence Erlbaum.

Singer, J. L., & Singer, D. G. (1981). *Television, imagination, and aggression: A study of preschoolers.* Hillsdale, NJ: Lawrence Erlbaum.

Singer, J. L., & Singer, D. G. (1998). *Barney & Friends* as entertainment and education: Evaluating the quality and effectiveness of a television series for preschool children. In J. Asamen & G. Berry (Eds.), *Research paradigms in the study of television and social behavior* (pp. 305-367). Thousand Oaks, CA: Sage.

Strommen, E., & Alexander, K. (1999, April). *Learning from television with interactive toy characters as viewing companions.* Paper presented at the biennial meeting of the Society for Research in Child Development, Albuquerque, NM.

Vygotsky, L. (1978). *Mind in society.* Cambridge, MA: Harvard University Press.

Wartella, E., & Ettema, J. S. (1974). A cognitive developmental study of children's attention to television commercials. *Communication Research, 1,* 69-88.

Wright, J. C., & Huston, A. C. (1995). *Effects of educational TV viewing of lower income preschoolers on academic skills, school readiness, and school adjustment one to three years later.* New York: Children's Television Workshop.

Wright, J. C., Huston, A. C., Murphy, K. C., St. Peters, M., Pion, M., Scantlin, R. M., & Kotler, J. A. (in press). The relations of early television viewing to school readiness and vocabulary of children from low income families: The Early Window Project. In S. Fisch & R. Truglio (Eds.), *"G" is for growing: Thirty years of research on* Sesame Street. Mahwah, NJ: Lawrence Erlbaum.

Wright, J. C., Huston, A. C., Ross, R. P., Calvert, S. L., Rolandelli, D., Weeks, L. A., Raeissi, P., & Potts, R. (1984). Pace and continuity of television programs: Effects on children's attention and comprehension. *Developmental Psychology, 20,* 653-666.

Wright, J. C., & Vlietstra, A. G. (1975). The development of selective attention: From perceptual exploration to logical search. In H. W. Reese (Ed.), *Advances in child development and behavior* (Vol. 10, pp. 195-239). New York: Academic Press.

Zillmann, D., Williams, B. R., Bryant, J., Boynton, K. R., & Wolf, M. A. (1980). Acquisition of information from educational television programs as a function of differently paced humorous inserts. *Journal of Educational Psychology, 72,* 170-180.

Zuckerman, P., Ziegler, M., & Stevenson, H. W. (1978). Children's viewing of television and recognition memory of commercials. *Child Development, 49,* 96-104.

# CHAPTER 6

# Television and the Child's Developing Imagination

PATTI M. VALKENBURG
Amsterdam School of Communications Research, University of Amsterdam

Over the past decades, a variety of studies have investigated environmental and developmental influences on creative achievement. One of the most clear-cut findings obtained in these studies is that individuals who make creative contributions as adults tend to come from families in which a favorable background for the development of intellectual abilities is provided (see Mumford & Gustafson, 1988, for a review). If environmental forces in childhood can affect later creative achievement, one might also expect that cumulative exposure to television, beginning in infancy, is a socializing factor with a great potential to influence children's developing imagination.

The question of whether and how television viewing affects children's imagination has been debated since the medium became part of everyday life, and there is still no consensus on this issue. On the one hand, television viewing is believed to produce a passive intellect and to reduce imaginative capacities. On the other hand, there has been enthusiasm about educational television viewing fostering children's creative thinking skills (see Valkenburg, 1999a; Valkenburg & van der Voort, 1994; van der Voort & Valkenburg, 1994, for reviews). If television does have a positive or negative impact on children's imagination, it is especially important to understand the nature of this impact. In this chapter, I review the available research evidence on television's effects on children's imagination. I also present the different stimulation and reduction hypotheses that have been proposed in the literature and discuss the validity of each of these hypotheses.

## The Development of Imagination in Childhood

Before reviewing the effects literature, it is necessary to define the different aspects of children's imagination that have been identified in the literature. Most publications on television's influence on imagination are characterized by fuzziness and a lack of precise definitions of the concept of *imagination.* There are many closely related concepts in use, such as *fantasy, daydreaming, imaginativeness, imaginative play, creative imagination,* and *creativity.* These terms are sometimes used as synonyms, and sometimes they refer to different phenomena. In my view, it is better to ignore the terms and definitions used in studies of television's influence on imagination and focus instead on the way in which imagination has been operationalized. Then it becomes clear that the research refers to three related but clearly distinguishable imaginal processes: (a) *imaginative play,* (b) *daydreaming,* and (c) *creativity.*

*Imaginative play* (fantasy play, pretend play) can be defined as play in which children transcend the constraints of reality by acting "as if" (van der Voort & Valkenburg, 1994). In imaginative play, children pretend that they are someone else, that an object represents something else, or that the participants are in a different place and time (James & McCain, 1982). Imaginative play can make an important contribution to the cognitive and social development of the child (Piaget, 1972; Singer & Singer, 1990). Children who exhibit a great deal of imagination in their play are better able to concentrate, develop greater empathic ability, and are better able to consider a subject from different angles (Singer & Singer, 1990). They are happier, more self-assured, and more flexible in unfamiliar situations (Singer & Singer, 1990). Moreover, there are indications that a high level of imaginative play in childhood is positively related to creativity in adulthood (Dansky, 1980; Fisher, 1992). It has been suggested that the "as if" nature of imaginative play helps the child in breaking free of established associations or meanings and thereby encourages children's creativity in the long term (Sutton-Smith, 1966).

Children's imaginative play is influenced by environmental and developmental factors. The first manifestations of imaginative play appear at about 12 or 13 months of age (see Fein, 1981, for a review). A child closes his or her eyes pretending to sleep without actually doing so or pretends to drink out of an empty cup. Between 20 and 26 months, children's imaginative play becomes increasingly independent of the immediate reality. An inanimate object (a stick or sponge) might be treated as if it were animate, and a great many objects might be used as cups, telephones, or beds (Fein, 1981).

By age 3, children's fantasy play becomes more social. Children progressively begin to play together with their playmates. In addition, their fantasy play develops from loose fragments into play based on elaborated plots. The development of imaginative play reaches its peak between ages 5 and 7 (Fein, 1981). In this period, children start to distinguish between fantasy and reality and recognize that other children can have different perspectives (thoughts, feelings, and motives) than they themselves have (Selman, 1980). This is the period in which they seem to delight in the most elaborated forms of social imaginative play.

From the age of 7, however, public imaginative play progressively declines. By this time, school achievement starts to gain prominence in the child's life, and open utterances of imaginative play are often discouraged by parents and teachers. It has been suggested that this emphasis on conventional behavior is the reason why children's internal processes, in the form of fantasizing and daydreaming, start to blossom (Singer & Singer, 1990).

*Daydreaming* (or fantasizing) refers to mental processes such as musing, mind wandering, internal monologue, and being lost in thought. Daydreaming is a state of consciousness characterized by a shift of attention. Instead of focusing on external stimulation or on a physical or mental task, the child's attention turns to thoughts and images that are based in memory (Singer, 1975).

Finally, *creativity* (or creative imagination) is defined as the capacity to generate many different novel or unusual ideas. Creativity seems to start around 5 or 6 years of age (see Mumford & Gustafson, 1988, for a review). Some researchers believe that younger children cannot be creative because they are unable to differentiate outer stimuli from the internal experience of the stimuli (Piaget, 1972; Smith & Carlsson, 1985). Many preschool children, for instance, believe that dreams are real entities that occur outside their body. It is not until around 9 years of age that they recognize that dreams are the products of thoughts (Piaget, 1929). This could explain why *divergent thinking tests* (tests that require creative thinking in response to open-ended problems) have been shown to be useless instruments with kindergarten children (Runco, 1992).

Daydreaming and creativity overlap to some extent. Both types of imagination require the generation of ideas, and, in both activities, associative thinking plays a role. However, there are also important differences between the two activities. First, daydreaming is an inner activity, which most people treat as extremely private (Klinger, 1990); creativity, on the other hand, demands communication (Knowles, 1985) and is often overtly observable in its products. Second, through daydreams, children can give free rein to their ideas and wishes in a process that is free from evaluation. Creativity, by contrast, is often subject to evaluation (Pickard, 1990), and the product of creativity has to meet one or more specified requirements.

Studies on the influence of television on the three types of imagination have addressed quite different research questions. Research on television's influence on imaginative play and creativity has usually focused on the question of whether television has a positive or negative effect on the quality or quantity of children's imaginative play or creative products. Studies on television's effect on daydreaming have primarily investigated whether viewers who frequently watch certain types of television content tend to fantasize more frequently about themes that correspond to that content. Specifically, they have showed that children who watch a great deal of television violence more often have aggressive and heroic daydreams. Because the research on television's impact on daydreaming differs so much from that on television's impact on imaginative play and creativity, I will limit my review in this chapter to the latter two types of imagination. Readers interested in media effects on daydreaming should refer to Valkenburg and van der Voort (1994).

## The Impact of Television on Children's Imaginative Play and Creativity

Researchers have advanced contradictory opinions about the influence of television on imaginative play and creativity. Some authors believe that television encourages play and creativity. I refer to this view as the stimulation hypothesis. Many others, however, argue that television hinders imaginative play and creativity, a position I call the reduction hypothesis.

### *Stimulation Hypothesis: The Potential of Educational Programs*

According to the stimulation hypothesis, television enriches the store of ideas from which children can draw when engaged in imaginative play or creative tasks. Adherents of the stimulation hypothesis argue that television characters and events are picked up, transformed, and incorporated in children's play and products of creativity and that, as a result, the quality or quantity of their play and creative products is improved.

There is indeed evidence to suggest that children use television content in their imaginative play (e.g., James & McCain, 1982) and creative products (e.g., Vibbert & Meringoff, 1981). However, the fact that children incorporate television content in their play and creative products does not necessarily mean that their television-related play or creative products are more imaginative. There is as yet no empirical evidence that the quality or quantity of imaginative play and creative products is improved through television viewing in general. None of the studies that have been conducted have demonstrated that, overall, television viewing is positively related to imaginative play (Shmukler, 1981; D. G. Singer & Singer, 1976; Singer & Singer, 1981; Singer, Singer, & Rapaczynski, 1984a) or creativity (Childs, 1979; Furu, 1971; Peterson, Peterson, & Caroll, 1987; Singer et al., 1984a; Wade, 1971; Zuckerman, Singer, & Singer, 1980). There is little indication, therefore, that overall television viewing stimulates children's imaginative play or creativity.

Even though a stimulating effect does not appear to be true of TV viewing in general, it has been suggested that educational viewing might stimulate children's imagination (Schmitt et al., 1997). There is some experimental evidence that a children's program specifically designed to stimulate children's imagination can promote imaginative play (J. L. Singer & Singer, 1976), although other studies suggest that these increases are limited to children originally low in imagination (Tower, Singer, Singer, & Biggs, 1979) and to play contexts with play materials related to the program seen (Friedrich-Cofer, Huston-Stein, McBride Kipnis, Susman, & Clewett, 1979).

In the case of creativity, the effects of educational viewing have been studied in only one correlational study (Schmitt et al., 1997). The results suggested that viewing educational programs would lead, over time, to an increase in children's creativity. Although promising, the available research evidence is as yet too limited to justify decisive conclusions on the beneficial effects of educational programming on children's imaginative play and creativity. Future research should pay closer attention to the differential effects of various types of television content on children's imaginative play and creativity. It is possible that children's imaginative play and creativity benefit from educational programs meant to foster imagination.

### *Reduction Hypotheses: Does Television Stifle Children's Creative Capacities?*

The majority of studies suggest that television in general and television violence in particular have a reductive effect on imaginative play and creativity (Valkenburg & van der Voort, 1994; van der Voort & Valkenburg, 1994). In the case of imaginative play, each of the different types of research that has been conducted provides indications that television viewing and imaginative play are negatively related. First, most quasi-experimental studies carried out in the early years of television indicate that the introduction of television resulted in a loss of playtime (Maccoby, 1951; Schramm, Lyle, & Parker, 1961). Second, the correlational studies showed that children who watch a great deal of violence engage less frequently in imaginative play (Shmukler, 1981; D. G. Singer & Singer, 1976; Singer et al., 1984a). Finally, a series of experimental studies indicated that programs with a high level of violence hinder imaginative play (Huston-Stein, Fox, Greer, Watkins, & Whitaker, 1981; Noble, 1970, 1973).

In the case of creativity, the overall results are in the same direction. First, a quasi-experimental study carried out in the introductory stage of television showed that television's arrival resulted, over time, in a decrease in creativity (Harrison & Williams, 1986). Second, the majority of the correlational studies showed that, overall, television viewing is negatively related to creativity (Childs, 1979; Furu, 1971; Peterson et al., 1987; Singer et al., 1984a; Wade, 1971; Zuckerman et al., 1980). Finally, most experiments that established the short-term effects of exposure to films suggest that television leads to less creativity than do radio or written texts (Greenfield & Beagles-Roos, 1988; Greenfield, Farrar, & Beagles-Roos, 1986; Kerns, 1981; Meline,

1976; Valkenburg & Beentjes, 1997; Vibbert & Meringoff, 1981).

The available research evidence explains why the reduction hypothesis has a larger following than the stimulation hypothesis. To date, six types of reduction hypotheses have been proposed in the literature: namely, the displacement hypothesis, passivity hypothesis, rapid-pacing hypothesis, visualization hypothesis, arousal hypothesis, and anxiety hypothesis. Four hypotheses pertain to the impact of television on both imaginative play and creativity; the other two hypotheses have been proposed for only imaginative play (the anxiety hypothesis) or only creativity (the visualization hypothesis). In each of the hypotheses, the reductive effect of television is attributed to a special property of television. The first four reduction hypotheses attribute the reductive effect to some structural characteristic of television such as its visual nature or its rapid pace. The other two hypotheses attribute television's negative influence on imaginative play and creativity to a specific type of program—namely, action-oriented and violent programs.

### *Displacement Hypothesis*

In this hypothesis, the reductive effect of television on imaginative play and creativity is a result of the popularity of the medium. It is argued that children spend a considerable portion of their free time watching television, at the expense of other leisure activities. In the case of imaginative play, the displacement hypothesis assumes that television viewing takes up time that could otherwise be spent on imaginative play (e.g., Singer & Singer, 1990). In the case of creativity, it is argued that television viewing occurs at the expense of other leisure activities such as reading or listening to the radio, which are thought to stimulate creativity more than television viewing does. In other words, in the case of creativity, television's reductive effect is not the result of television viewing itself but the fact that television viewing displaces the time for other, more beneficial activities.

The displacement hypothesis was tested during the introductory stage of television, when households with and without television could still be compared (Maccoby, 1951; Murray & Kippax, 1978; Schramm et al., 1961). Although none of the studies investigated the effect of the arrival of television on the time devoted to imaginative play, they did investigate the consequences for playtime in general. Two of the three studies found that television watching occurred at the expense of playtime in general (Maccoby, 1951; Schramm et al., 1961). Since, on average, approximately one third of general play is spent on imaginative play (Fein, 1981), it is likely that television had a reductive effect on imaginative play as well.

In the case of creativity, the displacement hypothesis argues that television viewing takes time from other activities that are thought to be more beneficial for creativity than television viewing is, with the result that creativity is hindered. There is, indeed, evidence to suggest that the arrival of television resulted in a displacement of other media such as the cinema, comic books, and radio (see Anderson & Collins, 1988, for a review). It is, however, still unknown whether this displacement of verbal media leads to a reduction in creativity. A study that was conducted during the introductory stage of television in Canada (Harrison & Williams, 1986) demonstrated that the arrival of television resulted in a decrease in children's imagination, but the study did not check whether this reductive effect was caused by a diminished use of radio and books by children.

### *Passivity Hypothesis*

Adherents of the passivity hypothesis see television as an "easy" medium, requiring little mental effort (Salomon, 1984). With a minimum of mental effort, the child viewer consumes fantasies produced by others. According to the passivity hypothesis, this leads to a passive "let you entertain me" attitude that undermines children's willingness to use their own imagination in play and creative products (Harrison & Williams, 1986; Singer et al., 1984a).

The passivity hypothesis has never been tested, for either imaginative play or creativity. Although it is unknown whether the mechanisms proposed by the passivity hypothesis are responsible for a reduction effect on imaginative play and/or creativity, it is possible to examine whether the existing research gives reason to believe that these mechanisms occur at all. The passivity hypothesis first assumes that the processing of television information requires little mental effort and that this low level of mental effort leads to a tendency to expend little mental effort in other domains. It also assumes that children's willingness to put effort in play and creative thinking is undermined because they consume fantasies produced by others.

Despite popular stereotypes of children just sitting and staring at the screen, there is evidence that the child viewer is cognitively far from passive. Even very young children actively screen television offerings for attractiveness and understandability and make an effort to interpret television images in their own terms (Collins, 1982). This does not necessarily imply that the amount of mental effort children invest in processing television programs is large. There is evidence that, for older elementary school children, television viewing requires less mental effort than reading does (Salomon, 1984). However, because both the content and formal features of television are more difficult for younger children to comprehend, younger children may invest more mental effort in watching than older children do (Field & Anderson, 1985).

There is some evidence, then, that television viewing requires relatively little mental effort. However, it has never been investigated whether this leads to a general tendency to expend little mental effort, including a diminished tendency to invest mental effort in imaginative play or creative activities. Of course, child viewers consume fantasies produced by others, but there is little reason to assume that this leads to reductions in fantasy play or creativity. Children who read a story, listen to a radio story, or watch a play also consume fantasies produced by others. But nobody has ever argued that print stories or theater hinder children's imaginative play or creativity. Therefore, there is little reason to assume that television's reductive effect on imaginative play and creativity is caused by a television-induced passive "let you entertain me" attitude.

### *Rapid-Pacing Hypothesis*

The rapid-pacing hypothesis attributes television's reductive effect on imaginative play and creativity to the rapid pace of television programs. According to this hypothesis, the viewer is confronted with images that must be instantaneously processed because scenes are presented in rapid succession. Viewers are thus allowed little time to process the information at their own rate or to reflect on program content. The hypothesis argues that rapidly paced television programs encourage cognitive overload, impulsive thinking, hyperactivity, and a nonreflective style of thinking (Anderson, Levin, & Lorch, 1977). Because both imaginative play and creative tasks require children to fix their attention for a longer period, the quality or quantity of imaginative play and creative products could be impaired.

Of course, rapidly paced programs leave children less room for reflection on program content than slowly paced programs do. However, there have been no indications that a rapid program pace per se leads to cognitive overload, impulsive thinking, or shortened attention spans. Anderson et al. (1977) found no immediate effect of rapidly paced television on perseverance in puzzle solving and impulsive thinking. Zillmann (1982) suggests that fast-paced programs may even foster the child's attention. Zillmann and colleagues observed that the fast-paced interspersion of attention-catching stimuli in educational programs, compared with the slow-paced interspersion of the same materials, resulted in superior information acquisition.

Because there is no evidence of ill effects of fast-paced programs on children's attention spans and cognitive style, it is not likely that children's imaginative play and creativity will be hindered by program pace as such. It is no surprise, therefore, that several experimental studies reported that program pace did not affect children's imaginative play (Anderson et al., 1977; Greer, Potts, Wright, & Huston, 1982; Tower et al., 1979). It should be noted, however, that these experiments used only benign, nonviolent programs. It is very well possible that the combination of a rapid pace and violence, which is common in many action-adventure children's programs, does lead to hyperactivity, impulsive thinking, and reduced attention spans. The rapid-pacing hypothesis has never been tested with these types of programs, not for imaginative play or for creativity.

### *Visualization Hypothesis*

The visualization hypothesis has only been proposed and tested in regard to creativity and not in regard to imaginative play. This hypothesis attributes the reductive effect of television on creativity to the medium's visual nature. Television, unlike radio and print, presents viewers with ready-made visual images and leaves them little room to form their own images. When engaged in creative thinking, viewers find it hard to dissociate themselves from the images supplied by television, so they have difficulty generating novel ideas (Greenfield & Beagles-Roos, 1988; Meline, 1976; Valkenburg & Beentjes, 1997).

Seven experimental studies have been designed to test the visualization hypothesis. In all of these *media-comparison experiments,* children were presented with either a story or a problem. The stories or problems were presented in either television (audiovisual), radio (audio), or print (written text) format. The text of the story or problem was usually kept the same, whereas the presentation modality was varied. After the presentation of the stories and problems, children were given a creative task. They were asked, for instance, to find a solution to a problem, to make a drawing, or to complete a story that was ended just prior to the end.

Six experiments were carried out in the United States (Greenfield & Beagles-Roos, 1988; Greenfield et al., 1986; Kerns, 1981; Meline, 1976; Runco & Pezdek, 1984; Vibbert & Meringoff, 1981), and one was conducted in the Netherlands (Valkenburg & Beentjes, 1997). In sum, with the exception of one study (Runco & Pezdek, 1984), all of the media-comparison studies showed that verbally presented information evoked more novel ideas than did television information. According to the authors, the television presentations led to fewer novel ideas than did the radio and print presentations because children in the video condition had difficulty dissociating themselves from the television images during creative thinking.

However, the results of the media experiments can also be explained in a different way. According to a rival hypothesis, verbal presentations, such as radio and print, might elicit more novel responses than television presentations not because verbal presentations are more stimulating for creativity but because they are *remembered less well.* The faulty-memory hypothesis disputes that the superior production of novel ideas after a verbal presentation should be attributed to creativity. According to this hypothesis, the novel ideas produced by children after radio listening are not creative responses but merely inventions to fill in holes in a faulty memory.

A part of the faulty-memory hypothesis is that radio information is remembered less well than television information. This assumption is supported by experimental evidence; several studies have shown that children remember radio information less well than television information (e.g., Beagles-Roos & Gat, 1983). However, to date, none of the media-comparison experiments has investigated whether the relatively poor recall of radio information is responsible for the incorporation of more novel ideas in children's creative products.

A recent experiment was specifically designed to test the faulty-memory hypothesis (Valkenburg & Beentjes, 1997). Children in two age groups were assigned to think up an ending for an incomplete television or radio story. An extra radio condition was included in which children were exposed twice to the same radio story in order to stimulate their recall of the radio story. Because there is ample evidence that repetitive stimulus presentation improves recall, the authors expected that the double presentation of a radio story would stimulate children's recall. Therefore, the faulty-memory hypothesis was tested by examining whether a double presentation of a radio story would result in fewer novel ideas than a single presentation. In addition, the faulty-memory hypothesis would predict that a double-story presentation would result in a superior quality of novel ideas because of a lower number of irrelevant fabrications. To test these predictions, the number of novel ideas in children's story completions was counted. In addition, independent judges assessed the quality of the story completions.

As expected, it was found that the double presentation of the radio story improved children's story recall. However, the faulty-memory hypothesis did not receive support: In comparison with a single radio presentation, double presentation of a radio story did not lead to fewer novel ideas or to stories of a lower quality. Because the faulty-memory hypothesis was not supported, the visualization hypothesis is as yet still the only plausible explanation for differences in novel ideas following radio presentations. The majority of the media-comparison experiments suggest that verbal information is more stimulating to creativity than is television information, although it should be recognized that the effect sizes of the differences in favor of radio have usually been small.

## The Effects of Television Violence on Imagination

### *The Arousal Hypothesis*

Like the rapid-pacing hypothesis, this hypothesis assumes that television promotes hyperactive and impulsive behavior. However, the hyperactivity is not seen as a result of the rapid pace of television programs but is attributed to the arousing quality of action-oriented and violent programs. This arousing quality is assumed to foster a physically active and impulsive behavior orientation in children, which in turn disturbs the sequential thought and planning necessary for organizing plots of make-believe games and creative tasks (Singer et al., 1984a).

Although television viewing appears to be generally associated with relaxation, violent programs can produce intense arousal in children (Zillmann, 1991). In addition, there is evidence that the frequency with which children watch violent and/or action-oriented programs is positively related to restlessness in a waiting room (Singer, Singer, & Rapaczynski, 1984b) and impulsivity at school (Anderson & McGuire, 1978). Finally, it has been demonstrated that watching violent programs may diminish children's tolerance of delay and persistence in free play (Friedrich & Stein, 1973).

Because research does indicate that violent programs can induce an impulsive behavior orientation, it is no surprise that many television-imagination effect studies have demonstrated that watching violent programs can adversely affect children's imaginative play (Huston-Stein et al., 1981; Noble, 1970, 1973; Shmukler, 1981; D. G. Singer & Singer, 1976; Singer & Singer, 1981; Singer et al., 1984a) and creativity (Singer et al., 1984a; Zuckerman et al., 1980). However, even though these studies established that violent programs can hinder children's imaginative play and creativity, they failed to investigate whether it was the arousal provoked by television violence that was responsible for the reductions in imaginative play and creativity. In other words, although there is convincing evidence that violent programs can foster a physically and cognitively impulsive behavior orientation, it has not been directly investigated whether a heightened level of arousal was responsible for the observed reductions in imaginative play and creativity.

### *Anxiety Hypothesis*

The anxiety hypothesis provides a plausible rival explanation for the reductive effect of television violence on children's imagination. This hypothesis also argues that violent programs hinder children's imaginative play, but the reduction effect is not attributed to the arousal that violent programs produce but to the fright reactions they generate. The anxiety hypothesis assumes that the television-induced fright leads to regression in behavior, which is expressed in a reduction in the quantity or quality of imaginative play (Noble, 1970, 1973).

Although the anxiety hypothesis has only been advanced with regard to television's influence on imaginative play, in my view it also provides a plausible explanation for reductive effects of violent programs on creativity. First, there is ample evidence that violent programs can induce intense fright reactions in children (Cantor, 1998). Second, there are indications that high levels of anxiety can disrupt fantasy play (see Fein, 1981, for a review) and creativity (e.g., Smith & Carlsson, 1985). What remains to be proved, however, is whether television-induced fright is responsible for the reductive effects on imaginative play and creativity.

In summary, there is evidence that television violence has a negative effect on children's imaginative play and creativity and that the causal mechanisms proposed by the arousal and anxiety hypotheses actually operate. However, what remains to be proved is whether it is arousal or anxiety that is responsible for television-induced decreases in imaginative play and creativity. In fact, it is possible that both the arousal and the anxiety hypotheses are valid reduction hypotheses. It is widely recognized that different types of media violence evoke different reactions in different viewers (Paik & Comstock, 1994). It could be that an arousing children's program such as *The Mighty Morphin Power Rangers* may affect imaginative play and creativity through arousal, whereas frightening movies such as *It, The Excorcist,* or *Friday the Thirteenth,* which have been shown to disturb many young viewers (Cantor, 1998; Valkenburg, Cantor, & Peeters, 2000), may reduce children's imaginativeness through fright.

## The Effects of Video and Computer Games: Some Preliminary Thoughts

A relatively new concern among parents and educators is the effect of video and computer games on children's imagination. Advocates usually view the games as a benign activity with great potential to promote children's problem-solving skills. Opponents are concerned that the games hinder children's creativity, because, for instance, the child player must follow preset rules to succeed (Funk, 1993).

Very little research has examined the effects of video and computer games on children's imaginative play and creativity. The only experiment that has as yet focused on this research question compared imaginative play after a 6-minute aggressive cartoon (*Road Runner*) and an aggressive video game (*Space Invaders*) of the same length (Silvern & Williamson, 1987). No significant effect of a violent video game on children's imaginative play was found. However, this finding should be interpreted with caution because of the very low number of children in each experimental condition ($n = 7$) and the subsequent lack of power of the statistical tests (see Cohen, 1988, for a discussion).

Some of the concerns about the effects of video and computer games on the child's imagination are similar to the concerns raised about television. This is understandable because computer games have a number of characteristics that have been used to explain television's reductive effects on imagination, such as their potential to displace other leisure activities, their rapid pace, and their potential to induce arousal or fright in children. However, there are also some obvious differences between television and computer games that disqualify some reduction hypotheses advanced about television's impact on imagination. For example, unlike television, computer games require active control and a high level of involvement and interactivity; playing computer games is certainly not a passive activity (Denot-Ledunois, Vardon, Perruchet, & Gallego, 1998). As a result, few people would argue that computer games impair children's creativity because they lead to a passive "let you entertain me" attitude.

Although there is very little empirical evidence of the positive or negative effects of video and computer games on imaginative play and creativity, I can give some preliminary thoughts about the potential effects of the games on children's imagination, which may inspire future researchers interested in this research question. I will discuss which mechanisms that were proposed in existing hypotheses on television's influence on imagination and creativity may also hold for video and computer games.

### *Stimulation Hypothesis*

As discussed earlier, there is little evidence that, overall, television stimulates children's imaginative play and creativity, but special programs designed to foster imagination have the potential to encourage imaginative play and creativity. Many educational computer games, in particular the so-called *adventures* or *fantasy role-playing games,* are designed to foster imagination, and this is exactly what many game producers tell parents in their product information. To my knowledge, no academic research has tested whether such computer games actually do what their producers claim. It is possible that educational computer games designed to foster imagination have a potential to encourage children's creative capacities.

### *Displacement Hypothesis*

Video and computer games are rapidly gaining prominence as a preferred leisure activity, and thus, as with television viewing, they have a potential to displace other activities, such as imaginative play and reading. There is some correlational evidence that video game use is negatively related to the reading time of boys (Lin & Lepper, 1987); however, this study cannot rule out the reverse explanation that boys who do not read frequently are more interested in video games. A study by Creasey and Myers (1986), in which computer game users were compared with nonusers, demonstrated that a newly introduced video game computer in the home mainly displaced television viewing and movie attendance. The introduction of the video game computer had no significant reductive effect on reading for pleasure, radio listening, peer interactions, or homework. The study also found that the displacement effects were short lasting. Early decreases in television viewing, for example, started to disappear after several weeks.

A variant of the displacement hypothesis proposes that computer games impair children's imagination because they are played according to preset rules. It is argued that children, who predominantly play rule-based games, do not get sufficient practice in "divergent" and "as if" experiences and that, as a result, their development of imaginal skills is impaired. Although it is important that children get the opportunity to practice divergent thinking skills, it is wrong to suppose that all video and computer games have preset rules (Valkenburg, 1999b). In some adventure and fantasy role-play games, children are given the opportunity to give free rein to their fantasies and ideas. They can draw, compose music, and create stories, and although nobody would recommend that parents replace all real-life drawings and stories with computer-generated ones, there is little reason to assume that these computer games hinder children's creativity through a lack of practice in divergent thinking tasks.

### *Rapid-Pacing Hypothesis*

Like television, computer games use a high tempo, which qualify them for the rapid-pacing hypothesis. As discussed earlier, in the case of television, there is little indication that children's imagination is hindered through the rapid pace of television because there is no evidence that a rapid pace per se leads to impulsivity and a nonreflective style of thinking. Therefore, there is also little reason to assume that the rapid pace of computer games will impair children's imagination.

### *Arousal and Anxiety Hypotheses*

Finally, many computer games are at least as violent in nature as certain television programs (e.g., Provenzo, 1991) and therefore have a similar potential to induce arousal and fright in children. To tease out which causal mechanisms are responsible for a potential negative effect on children's imaginative play and creativity, research into the effects of violent computer games should include measures of arousal and fright and compare arousing/frightening with arousing/nonfrightening computer games.

## Concluding Comments and Suggestions for Further Research

Research on the impact of television on children's imagination originated in the 1950s (Himmelweit, Oppenheim, & Vince, 1958; Maccoby, 1951), developed in the 1970s, flourished in the 1980s, and waned in the early 1990s. With the exception of the works of Dorothy and Jerome Singer, the study of the relationship between television and imagination is characterized by an ephemeral research interest. Researchers contributed with at most one or two studies, after which they disappeared again. This could be the reason why empirical research in this field has usually not been guided by explicit theoretical models. Most studies have examined the relationship between television viewing and imagination as an input-output measure without attempting to explore the mechanisms that might be responsible for television's reductive or stimulating effect. Therefore, the existing research does not allow us to single out which of the hypotheses discussed in this chapter is the most plausible. Future research should derive from more sophisticated theoretical models and should pay closer attention to the question of *how* television or computer games may affect imaginative play and creativity.

Further research should also determine whether the content of television or computer games moderates the relationship between television viewing and imagination. As argued earlier, most previous research in this field has treated television viewing as a one-dimensional construct. However, including total viewing time as an independent variable only makes sense if the displacement hypothesis is tested. Tests of all other hypotheses demand a differentiation in types of content, at least in terms of violent and educational content.

Finally, new research should pay more attention to child characteristics. A basic assumption in modern theories of media effects is that children are active and motivated explorers of what they see on television (Valkenburg & Cantor, 2000). Another assumption is that any effect of television on children is enhanced, channeled, or mitigated by what the child viewer makes of it. To understand media effects on children, then, it is crucial to gain insight into the different antecedents of children's selective exposure to media (e.g., Valkenburg & Janssen, 1999). In the literature to date, too few attempts have been undertaken to explore the dynamic elements of child variables in the television-imagination relationship. There is a strong need for more elaborated theoretical models in which child factors (e.g., developmental level, intelligence) and different environmental agents (e.g., media exposure, family influences) all operate as interacting determinants of children's developing creativity.

## References

Anderson, C., & McGuire, T. (1978). The effect of TV viewing on the educational performance of elementary school children. *Alberta Journal of Educational Research, 24,* 156-163.

Anderson, D. R., & Collins, P. A. (1988). *The impact on children's education: Television's influence on cognitive development* (Working Paper No. 2). Washington, DC: Office of Educational Research and Improvement. (ERIC Document Reproduction Service No. ED 295 271).

Anderson, D. R., Levin, S. R., & Lorch, P. E. (1977). The effects of TV program pacing on the behavior of preschool children. *AV Communication Review, 25,* 159-166.

Beagles-Roos, J., & Gat, I. (1983). Specific impact of radio and television on children's story comprehension. *Journal of Educational Psychology, 75,* 128-137.

Cantor, J. (1998). *"Mommy, I'm scared": How TV and movies frighten children and what we can do to protect them.* San Diego, CA: Harcourt Brace.

Childs, J. H. (1979). Television viewing, achievement, IQ, and creativity. *Dissertation Abstracts International, 39,* 6531A.

Cohen, J. (1988). *Statistical power analysis for the behavioral sciences* (2nd ed.). Hillsdale, NJ: Lawrence Erlbaum.

Collins, W. A. (1982). Cognitive processing in television viewing. In D. Pearl, L. Bouthilet, & J. Lazar (Eds.), *Television and behavior: Ten years of scientific progress and implications for the eighties* (DHHS Publication No. ADM 82-1196, pp. 9-23). Washington, DC: U.S. Government Printing Office.

Creasey, G. L., & Myers, B. J. (1986). Video games and children: Effects on leisure activities, schoolwork, and peer involvement. *Merrill-Palmer Quarterly, 32,* 251-262.

Dansky, J. L. (1980). Make-believe: A mediator of the relationship between play and associative fluency. *Child Development, 51,* 576-579.

Denot-Ledunois, S., Vardon, G., Perruchet, P., & Gallego, J. (1998). The effect of attentional load on the breathing pattern in children. *International Journal of Psychophysiology, 29*(1), 13-21.

Fein, G. G. (1981). Pretend play in childhood: An integrative review. *Child Development, 52,* 1095-1118.

Field, D., & Anderson, D. (1985). Instruction and modality effects on children's television attention and comprehension. *Journal of Educational Psychology, 77,* 91-100.

Fisher, E. P. (1992). The impact of play on development: A meta analysis. *Play and Culture, 5,* 159-181.

Friedrich, L. K., & Stein, A. H. (1973). Aggressive and prosocial television programs and the natural behavior of preschool children. *Monographs of the Society for Research in Child Development, 38*(4, Serial No. 151), 1-64.

Friedrich-Cofer, L. K., Huston-Stein, A., McBride Kipnis, D., Susman, E. J., & Clewett, A. S. (1979). Environmental enhancement of prosocial television content: Effects on interpersonal behavior, imaginative play, and self-regulation in a natural setting. *Developmental Psychology, 15,* 637-646.

Funk, J. B. (1993). Video games. *Adolescent Medicine: State of the Art Reviews, 4,* 589-598.

Furu, T. (1971). *The function of television for children and adolescents.* Tokyo: Monumenta Nipponica, Sophia University.

Greenfield, P. M., & Beagles-Roos, J. (1988). Radio vs. television: Their cognitive impact on children of different socioeconomic and ethnic groups. *Journal of Communication, 38*(2), 71-92.

Greenfield, P. M., Farrar, D., & Beagles-Roos, J. (1986). Is the medium the message? An experimental comparison of the effects of radio and television on imagination. *Journal of Applied Developmental Psychology, 7,* 201-218.

Greer, D., Potts, R., Wright, J. C., & Huston, A. C. (1982). The effects of television commercial form and commercial placement on children's social behavior and attention. *Child Development, 53,* 611-619.

Harrison, L. F., & Williams, T. M. (1986). Television and cognitive development. In T. M. Williams (Ed.), *The impact of television: A natural experiment in three communities* (pp. 87-142). New York: Academic Press.

Himmelweit, H., Oppenheim, A. N., & Vince, P. (1958). *Television and the child: An empirical study of the effects of television on the young.* London: Oxford University Press.

Huston-Stein, A., Fox, S., Greer, D., Watkins, B. A., & Whitaker, J. (1981). The effects of action and violence on children's social behavior. *Journal of Genetic Psychology, 138,* 183-191.

James, N. C., & McCain, T. A. (1982). Television games preschool children play: Patterns, themes, and uses. *Journal of Broadcasting, 26,* 783-800.

Kerns, T. Y. (1981). Television: A bisensory bombardment that stifles children's creativity. *Phi Delta Kappan, 62,* 456-457.

Klinger, E. (1990). *Daydreaming: Using waking fantasy and imagery for self-knowledge and creativity.* Los Angeles: Tarcher.

Knowles, R. T. (1985). Fantasy and imagination. *Studies in Formative Spirituality, 6,* 53-63.

Lin, S., & Lepper, M. (1987). Correlates of children's usage of videogames and computers. *Journal of Applied Social Psychology, 17,* 72-93.

Maccoby, E. E. (1951). Television: Its impact on school children. *Public Opinion Quarterly, 15,* 421-444.

Meline, C. W. (1976). Does the medium matter? *Journal of Communication, 26*(3), 81-89.

Mumford, M. D., & Gustafson, S. (1988). Creativity syndrome: Integration, application, and innovation. *Psychological Bulletin, 103,* 27-43.

Murray, J. P., & Kippax, S. (1978). Children's social behavior in three towns with differing television experience. *Journal of Communication, 28*(1), 19-29.

Noble, G. (1970). Film-mediated aggressive and creative play. *British Journal of Social & Clinical Psychology, 9,* 1-7.

Noble, G. (1973). Effects of different forms of filmed aggression on children's constructive and destructive play. *Journal of Personality and Social Psychology, 26,* 54-59.

Paik, H., & Comstock, G. (1994). The effects of television violence on antisocial behavior: A meta analysis. *Communication Research, 21,* 516-546.

Peterson, C. C., Peterson, J. L., & Caroll, J. (1987). Television viewing and imaginative problem solving during preadolescence. *Journal of Genetic Psychology, 147,* 61-67.

Piaget, J. (1929). *The child's conception of the world.* London: Routledge & Kegan Paul.

Piaget, J. (1972). *Play, dreams, and imitation in childhood.* London: Routledge & Kegan Paul.

Pickard, E. (1990). Toward a theory of creative potential. *Journal of Creative Behavior, 24,* 1-9.

Provenzo, E. F. (1991). *Video kids: Making sense of Nintendo.* Cambridge, MA: Harvard University Press.

Runco, M. A. (1992). Review: Children's divergent thinking and creative ideation. *Developmental Review, 12,* 233-264.

Runco, M. A., & Pezdek, K. (1984). The effect of television and radio on children's creativity. *Human Communication Research, 11,* 109-120.

Salomon, G. (1984). Television is "easy" and print is "tough": The differential investment of mental effort as a function of perceptions and attributions. *Journal of Educational Psychology, 76,* 647-658.

Schmitt, K. L., Linebarger, D., Collins, P. A., Wright, J. C., Anderson, D. R., Huston, A. C., & McElroy, E. (1997, April). *Effects of preschool television viewing on adolescent creative thinking and behavior.* Poster presented at the biennial meeting of the Society for Research in Child Development, Washington, DC.

Schramm, W., Lyle, J., & Parker, E. (1961). *Television in the lives of our children.* Stanford, CA: Stanford University Press.

Selman, R. L. (1980). *The growth of interpersonal understanding.* New York: Academic Press.

Shmukler, D. (1981). A descriptive analysis of television viewing in South African preschoolers and its relationship to their spontaneous play. *South-African Journal of Psychology, 11,* 106-109.

Silvern, S. B., & Williamson, P. A. (1987). The effects of video game play on young children's aggression, fantasy, and prosocial behavior. *Journal of Applied Developmental Psychology, 8,* 453-462.

Singer, D. G., & Singer, J. L. (1976). Family television viewing habits and the spontaneous play of preschool children. *American Journal of Orthopsychiatry, 46,* 496-502.

Singer, D. G., & Singer, J. L. (1990). *The house of make-believe.* Cambridge, MA: Harvard University Press.

Singer, J. L. (1975). *The inner world of daydreaming.* New York: Harper & Row.

Singer, J. L., & Singer, D. G. (1976). Can TV stimulate imaginative play? *Journal of Communication, 26*(3), 74-80.

Singer, J. L., & Singer, D. G. (1981). *Television, imagination, and aggression: A study of preschoolers.* Hillsdale, NJ: Lawrence Erlbaum.

Singer, J. L., Singer, D. G., & Rapaczynski, W. S. (1984a). Children's imagination as predicted by family patterns and television viewing: A longitudinal study. *Genetic Psychology Monographs, 110,* 43-69.

Singer, J. L., Singer, D. G., & Rapaczynski, W. S. (1984b). Family patterns and television viewing as predictors of children's beliefs and aggression. *Journal of Communication, 34*(2), 73-89.

Smith, G., & Carlsson, I. (1985). Creativity in middle and late school years. *International Journal of Behavioral Development, 8,* 329-343.

Sutton-Smith, B. (1966). Piaget on play: A critique. *Psychological Review, 73,* 104-110.

Tower, R. B., Singer, D. G., Singer, J. L., & Biggs, A. (1979). Differential effects of television programming on preschoolers' cognition, imagination, and social play. *American Journal of Orthopsychiatry, 49,* 265-281.

Valkenburg, P. M. (1999a). Television and creativity. In M. Runco & S. Pritzker (Eds.), *Encyclopedia of creativity* (Vol. 1). New York: Academic Press.

Valkenburg, P. M. (1999b). *Vierkante ogen: Opgroeien met TV en PC* [Square eyes: Growing up with TV and PC]. Amsterdam: Rainbow Pocket Books.

Valkenburg, P. M., & Beentjes, J. W. J. (1997). Children's creative imagination in response to radio and television stories. *Journal of Communication, 47*(2), 21-38.

Valkenburg, P. M., & Cantor, J. (1999). Children's likes and dislikes in entertainment. In D. Zillmann & P. Vorderer (Eds.), *Entertainment: The psychology of its appeal* (pp. 135-152). Hillsdale, NJ: Lawrence Erlbaum.

Valkenburg, P. M., Cantor, J., & Peeters, A. (2000). Fright reactions to television: A child survey. *Communication Research,* 82-99.

Valkenburg, P. M., & Janssen, S. J. (1999). What do children value in entertainment programs? A cross-cultural investigation. *Journal of Communication, 49,* 3-21.

Valkenburg, P. M., & van der Voort, T. (1994). Influence of TV on daydreaming and creative imagination: A review of research. *Psychological Bulletin, 116,* 316-339.

van der Voort, T. H. A., & Valkenburg, P. M. (1994). Television's impact on fantasy play: A review of research. *Developmental Review, 14,* 27-51.

Vibbert, M. M., & Meringoff, L. K. (1981). *Children's production and application of story imagery: A cross-medium investigation* (Technical Report No. 23). Cambridge, MA: Project Zero, Harvard University. (ERIC Document Reproduction Service No. ED 210 682).

Wade, S. E. (1971). Adolescents, creativity, and media: An exploratory study. *American Behavioral Scientist, 14,* 341-351.

Zillmann, D. (1982). Television viewing and arousal. In D. Pearl, L. Bouthilet, & J. Lazar (Eds.), *Television and behavior: Ten years of scientific progress and implications for the eighties: Vol. 2. Technical reviews* (DHHS Publication No. ADM 82-1196, pp. 53-67). Washington, DC: U.S. Government Printing Office.

Zillmann, D. (1991). Television viewing and psychological arousal. In J. Bryant & D. Zillmann (Eds.), *Responding to the screen: Reception and reaction processes* (pp. 103-133). Hillsdale, NJ: Lawrence Erlbaum.

Zuckerman, D. M., Singer, D. G., & Singer, J. L. (1980). Television viewing, children's reading, and related classroom behavior. *Journal of Communication, 30*(1), 166-174.

CHAPTER 7

# Television as Incidental Language Teacher

LETITIA R. NAIGLES
LARA MAYEUX
University of Connecticut

*There once was a girl from St. Kitt*
*Who watched some TV for a bit.*
*She learned verbs and nouns*
*Such as "running" and "hounds"*
*But her grammar was changed not a whit.*

*Can* children learn languages from the electronic media? Writers of popular fiction and screenplays evidently think so, creating characters who readily acquire new languages by watching TV or movies in those languages (e.g., Rainer Hartheim in *The Thorn Birds* [McCullough, 1977], Isabel in *Le Divorce* [Johnson, 1997], and Madison the mermaid in the 1984 movie *Splash*). And yet, if language learning were this straightforward in the real world, would not second-language classrooms simply show TV programs and films all the time and let those dull grammar drills and vocabulary tests fall by the wayside? The short answer is one that language acquisition researchers have known for years: Language is best learned through conversations carried out between interacting people, one of whom is the language learner himself or herself (Clark & Clark, 1977). And to the extent that television viewing differs from this scenario in that children are passive nonparticipants as television programs progress before their eyes and ears, it is extremely unlikely that any

AUTHORS' NOTE: The preparation of this chapter was aided by a Large Faculty Research Grant from the Research Foundation of the University of Connecticut. Address correspondence to Letitia R. Naigles, Department of Psychology, 406 Babbidge Road, U-20, University of Connecticut, Storrs, CT 06269-1020, (860) 486-4942.

language is being acquired from such viewing. Some have gone as far as fearing that television viewing *displaces* critically needed conversational interaction (Winn, 1985).

The problem with this short answer is that, as many parents and child development researchers know, young children frequently *are* active participants as they watch television—and those studied rarely watch alone. Lemish and Rice (1986) observed the behavior of 1- and 2-year-olds during home television viewing and found that at least half of the sample frequently or occasionally called attention to or labeled objects on the screen for their coviewing parents. Moreover, many of the children older than 20 months of age asked questions about what was being shown on the screen and repeated some or all of what they had just heard. Singer and Singer (1998) report that preschoolers, too, can be extremely attentive while viewing an engaging television program, frequently laughing at the appropriate points and repeating parts of the ongoing dialogue. The possibility remains that children *can* acquire at least some aspects of language through their viewing of television; the purpose of our chapter is to survey the available evidence to see what children actually *do*.

As we shall see, the question of whether children learn language from television input does not yield a simple answer. In particular, the answer seems to vary by the type of language being assessed; thus, we will address the influences of television on grammatical development and lexical development separately. Moreover, the answer seems to vary by the type of television being viewed; we will primarily focus on the effects of educational television programs. And, finally, the answer may vary depending on the age or developmental level of the children; thus, it will be important to keep in mind the extent to which there is a match between the properties of language assessed and the ages of the children being studied. Because most research concerns the influences of TV on *first*-language acquisition, most relevant children are under 5 years of age.

## Does TV Viewing Influence Grammatical Development? Probably *Not*

To fully evaluate the extent to which television viewing might influence grammatical development, it is necessary to understand both the child's task in acquiring the grammar of his or her native language and how natural language input (i.e., language arising within social interactions in which the child is a participant) may facilitate children's acquisition of grammar. We will briefly discuss these topics before assessing the extent to which television input includes language-relevant facilitatory properties and, finally, the available evidence directly relating children's television viewing and their grammatical development.

### *The Child's Task in Grammatical Acquisition*

Learning a language is all about discovering the relationships between various *forms*—words, phrases, sentences, and discourse—and various *meanings*—objects, categories, events, propositions, and social interactions (Gleitman & Wanner, 1984). Moreover, the forms and meanings themselves must be discovered as well. None of these discoveries can be thought of as easy or straightforward.

First, natural human speech does not include spaces between words, commas between phrases, or periods at the ends of sentences. A more accurate visual depiction of running speech (say, ordering at a restaurant) might be *illhavethebowloftomatosoupwithacupofcoffeeandshellhavethehotdogbutwithoutmustardandsomechocolatemilk.* To discover such forms as phrases and sentences, infants must perform some *segmentation* of the continuous stream of sound they hear. Moreover, children must also determine their language's canonical *word order.* For example, sentences typically proceed in subject(S)-verb(V)-object(O) order in English,

Gregory gave a book to Beverly,

but in SOV order in Japanese (from Clancy, 1985, p. 374),

Taroo ga Hanako ni hon o age–ta

Taroo SUBJ[1] Hanako IO book DO give–PAST.

And adjectives precede their nouns in English,

The pink dress,

but follow them in French,

La robe rose,

The dress pink.

The functions and arrangements of the *grammatical* words must also be discovered. For example, children must learn that *a* and *the* both precede nouns but the former indicates nonspecific nouns (*a cat*) whereas the latter indicates specific ones (*the cat*), and the modals, or "helping verbs," *can, will, may, have, do,* and *be* typically follow the subjects in statements but precede them in questions:

She can walk now.

Can she walk now?

They must learn that all main verbs receive tense, but some verbs in subordinate clauses do not:

Beverly likes (tensed) the mall.

Beverly likes to go (untensed) to the mall.

And as if that were not enough, children must also arrive at an adult-like understanding of the relevant objects, events, and relations—the meanings—to which these forms refer. That is, children must conceive of the referring event of *she can walk now* as *young female reveals ability to walk* and not *young female only stumbles occasionally* or *young female makes mom and dad happy* to learn the appropriate meaning for that sentence.[2]

### *How Natural Language Input Facilitates Grammatical Development*

Especially in developed cultures, adults (and older children) typically speak differently to young children than they do to other adults. This *child-directed speech* (CDS) has several properties that are considered to be helpful for children's grammatical development. For example, CDS has a distinctive *prosody,* which is relatively slow and melodic, with dramatic but regular pitch changes throughout utterances, lengthening of the final syllable of the utterance, and longer pauses between clauses and sentences (Fernald et al., 1989; Gleitman, Gleitman, Landau, & Wanner, 1987):

Loook at the BIRD, baaaaaby. [pause] Seee the biiiird?

These properties could help the child segment the sound stream by highlighting the beginnings and ends of clauses and sentences within longer utterances (Morgan & Demuth, 1996). Moreover, CDS is heavily weighted toward questions (both yes-no questions such as *Do you want some milk?* and *wh-* questions such as *Where did you put that ball?*) and repetitions that minimally change their own or the child's speech:

Child: I want milk.

Adult: You want more chocolate milk or white milk?

or

Adult: Shall we go to the park?

Child: Yes!

Adult: Let's walk to the park with the new swings, OK?

In one of the most robust findings in the language acquisition literature, mothers' frequent use of yes-no questions consistently predicts their children's subsequent frequent use of modal verbs (Hoff-Ginsberg, 1985, 1986; Newport, Gleitman, & Gleitman, 1977). It is easy to see why: In yes-no questions (but not *wh-* questions), modals occupy the first position in the sentence, which is usually highly stressed (e.g., pronounced loudly) and so more salient to the child. The frequency of adult repetitions, too, seems to positively predict the speed with which children's utterances grow in length and complexity (Hoff-Ginsberg, 1986).

Other properties of CDS, rather than highlighting the form of the utterance, seem to help target its meaning. For example, mothers may choose to talk about that which their children are interested in or looking at, so the utterance may be more easily mapped onto an event or proposition. In general, children and mothers frequently *jointly construct* their social interactions so that each more easily understands the other's intentions and thus are more likely to understand the other's language. Thus, hearing "Do you want some water?" while climbing the stairs for one's nap might be considered to be confusing to a child; however, if the child routinely asks for water at just this point in the nap-taking routine, then the utterance may accurately reflect the child's current thinking (for more discussion, see Clark & Grossman, 1998; Clark, 1996; Tomasello, 1990; Tomasello, in press).

### *Does TV Include Such Facilitative Properties?*

Mabel Rice and her colleagues (Rice, 1984; Rice & Haight, 1986) have performed detailed analyses of the language used in several educational TV programs such as *Mister Rogers' Neighborhood, Sesame Street,* and *Electric Company.* Overall, these programs manifested several of the relevant properties of CDS. That is, characters' utterances included many repetitions and yes-no questions and were predominantly "event casts," or descriptions, of ongoing events visible on the screen. Unfortunately, the melody and prosodic stress of the utterances were not assessed; however, the overall rate of speech (averaging 111.5 words/minute) did compare favorably with the rate of speech found in naturalistic mother-child storytelling situations. The researchers also uncovered some differences between the programs. For example, *Mister Rogers* included the most yes-no questions, and *Sesame Street* scored highest on *wh-* questions. All three shows rated equally high on the amount of speech whose meaning was immediately represented in the context.

Given the properties discussed above, the most obvious drawback to television input for language development is that the language of television is *not* constructed jointly with the child viewer. For instance, consider a hypothetical situation in which the TV screen is showing Mr. Rogers building a wooden chair and Mr. Rogers himself is describing what he is doing as he builds. If the child viewer is not focusing on that aspect of the scene but is instead wondering (for example) why Mr. Rogers isn't wearing his sweater or where King Friday or Owl is, or how the wood shavings could be used for a bird's nest, then the child will not be able to make the form-meaning pairings based on Mr. Rogers's speech that are so critical for learning language. The question becomes, then, How frequently might this be the case? Can we find any evidence that children who watch TV have learned something about grammar and that children who watch more TV are progressing more rapidly in their grammatical development?

### *Does TV Influence Grammatical Development?*

There have been two ways to study the potential influence of TV on grammatical development. One way involves children who receive only TV input in a given language and asks how much they learn about the grammar of that language. Only two published reports have taken this route, and one (Snow et al., 1976) only cites a personal communication to the effect that Dutch children who watch German TV do not achieve "appreciable control of German nor understand what the programs are about" (p. 2). To be sure, it is possible that the German programs watched by these youngsters did not include the CDS properties found in the American programs analyzed by Rice.

Sachs, Bard, and Johnson (1981) carried out a more detailed analysis of the speech of a 3-year-old hearing boy of deaf parents whose only exposure to English, until he began preschool at age 3, came from the family's TV. About the time he began preschool, a sample of his spontaneous speech was recorded and analyzed. Although the child did produce English words in multiword utterances, his word order did not conform to English SVO order (e.g., "I want that make," "my mommy in house apple," and "off my mittens"). Moreover, some grammatical morphemes were entirely missing (the copula "to be," conjunctions) while others (modals, plural *-s*, past *-ed*, and articles *a* and *the*) appeared only about 30% of the time in their obligatory contexts (compared with 71% of the time from normally developing children producing utterances of the same length). Overall, the picture is of idiosyncratic combinations of English words, uninformed by conventional English sentence structure. Clearly, this boy had *not* acquired English grammar from his television viewing, although, once again, we do not know what programs he watched or the extent to which they included relevant properties of CDS.

It is obviously unethical for researchers to deliberately deprive children of natural linguistic interaction to investigate the extent to which they can learn a language from television input alone. Thus, the more recent studies relating television viewing and grammatical development have been correlational in nature. These ask the question, Do children who watch more TV display more sophisticated grammar or faster grammatical development? The data, thus far, are mixed. Selnow and Bettinghaus (1982) collected spontaneous language samples from 3- to 5-year-olds and asked their parents to keep a weeklong diary of which television programs the children watched. The language samples were scored for their syntactic complexity (e.g., longer utterances and correct uses of grammatical morphemes yielded higher scores), and the diaries were coded for the number of hours of TV watched, both overall and by program type (e.g., educational, family drama, sports). Few correlations were obtained, and the only one that approached significance was *negative:* The more television viewed, the *lower* the child's language score.

In a study we have just completed (Mayeux & Naigles, 2000), we collected standardized language comprehension data (the Test of Auditory Comprehension of Language-3 [TACL-3]; Carrow-Woolfolk, 1999) from sixty 3- and 4-year-old children, as well as information from their parents concerning how much television—and educational television—they watch per week. We obtained only one statistically significant correlation between these two measures; namely, that the amount of television (not just educational television) watched per week correlates *negatively* (and statistically reliably) with children's scores on the grammatical morphemes subsection of the TACL-3. These findings implicate the kind of displacement theory mentioned in the introduction, that children who watch television are missing out on natural linguistic input. However, Singer and Singer (1981) found modest *positive* correlations between the amount of *educational television* preschool-age children watched over a 2-week period and their uses of imperative sentences (commands) and exclamations in spontaneous speech.

There is a problem concerning the interpretation of such correlational studies. First, given that the TV and language data were collected at the same point in each child's development, it is not clear which is the causal factor and which the effect (see also Rice, 1983). That is, the amount of television viewing could have caused the slightly lower (in ours or Selnow and Bettinghaus's study) or slightly higher (in Singer and Singer's study) language scores. However, it is just as likely that children who have lower overall grammatical scores but produce more commands and exclamations like to watch more television. That is, is the child's language level driving the television watching, or is the television watching driving the child's language level?

### *Summary*

Overall, there seems to be little indication that children are gleaning much about their grammar specifically from television viewing. The child studied by Sachs et al. (1981) displayed fairly aberrant grammatical development during the period when he was only exposed to television input (subsequently, after entering preschool and speech therapy, his language developed to near-normal conditions). The children studied by us (Mayeux & Naigles, 2000), by Selnow and Bettinghaus (1982), and by Singer and Singer (1981) showed only slightly negative (Mayeux & Naigles; Selnow & Bettinghaus) or slightly positive (Singer & Singer) correlations between their television viewing and grammatical development. From these studies, then, it seems unlikely that children learn much about grammar specifically from television input. In the face of Rice's findings that the *language* of television is similar to that of CDS, this conclusion supports the notion that grammatical development requires a socially based construction of meaning that is carried out jointly by children and their caregivers in order to proceed (Clark & Clark, 1977; Tomasello, 1990).

Given the paucity of the available studies, though, we would like to suggest some qualifiers to the above conclusion, as well as some possible directions for future research. First, we are not sure it makes sense to expect that some moderate amount of television viewing should influence overall grammatical development. This hypothesis makes the assumption that sheer amount of linguistic input always makes a difference—that more linguistic input (via television) or less linguistic input (which is carried by social interaction) should have a direct effect on children's grammatical development. Researchers in language acquisition have been trying for years to find stable frequency-based predictors of children's grammatical development in their mothers' speech, with only mild success (see Gleitman, Newport, & Gleitman, 1984; Hoff-Ginsberg & Shatz, 1982). As mentioned earlier, only maternal yes-no questions and repetitions have consistently yielded positive effects.

Erika Hoff-Ginsberg has recently demonstrated that differences in the sheer amount of speech children hear do not seem to influence their early grammatical development. She compared mother-child dyads from upper-middle-class homes with those from working-class homes and found that higher socioeconomic status (SES) mothers produced more and longer utterances to their children than lower SES mothers (Hoff-Ginsberg, 1991). However, the children's growth in utterance length (i.e., more words, more grammatical morphemes) in the two groups was indistinguishable, at least into their third year (Hoff-Ginsberg, 1998). The idea is that there is some threshold of input that children must receive to acquire their grammar, but variation above that threshold has little effect (e.g., Pinker, 1994). Likewise, variation in television input and/or in natural linguistic input because of moderate TV viewing might be expected to have little effect because the children's natural linguistic input is already above threshold.

We also do not think that definitive studies have been conducted showing that children *cannot* learn anything about grammar from television input. This is because the studies conducted to date either have looked at television input too generally or have targeted inappropriate aspects of children's grammar as the dependent variable. Sachs et al.'s (1981) case study indicates that children cannot acquire all aspects of grammar solely from television input, but might children be able to acquire some aspects of grammar from some specific types of television input? For example, recall the robust finding that maternal use of yes-no questions predicts toddlers' subsequent use of modals. And recall that some television programs (i.e., *Mister Rogers*) were found by Rice and Haight (1986) to include more yes-no questions than others (i.e., *Sesame Street*). One testable prediction might be that toddlers who are heavy watchers of *Mister Rogers* show more frequent use of modals than do toddlers who are heavy watchers of *Sesame Street.* Of course, the degree to which the primary caregivers of the children in the two groups used yes-no questions would need to be held constant to eliminate a potentially confounding factor. And notice that we have restricted the age level of this prediction to toddlers, because the original finding with mother-child dyads held most strongly for children of this age level.

Indeed, our final point relates to the importance of choosing the appropriate "match" between the age of the child subjects and the linguistic variable of interest. The correlational studies have generally included children who are preschool age (3-5 years), but the measures have not generally included the aspects of grammar that children of this age are acquiring. That is, English-learning preschoolers are in the process of mastering the passive voice, complex multiclause sentences, negation, and anaphora, whereas the measures investigated by most researchers[3]—word order, general sentence complexity, modals, and imperatives—are typically acquired by children between the ages of 2 and 3. Perhaps a future investigation of television's influence on preschool children's grammatical development might compare the development of, say, the passive voice in two groups of children. One group would view one set of television shows that included many passive sentences (e.g., *The People's Court*) and the other group would view a different set of television shows that were similar in many respects to the first set but did not include any passives. All other things being equal (and natural input would need to be assessed to demonstrate this), an advantage in passive use in the first group after viewing could be attributed to the shows. Until such studies are conducted, though, our conclusion must be that television input has little influence on children's grammatical development.

## Does Television Viewing Influence Lexical Development? Probably *Yes*

The plan of this section is identical to that of the previous one. First, we briefly summarize the child's task in learning words, then we discuss how natural language input facilitates this task. Next, we consider the extent to which television input includes similar properties, and, finally, we will be in a position to assess the observed relationships between children's television viewing and their lexical development.

The child's task of learning the meanings of words bears considerable—although not complete—resemblance to his or her task of learning grammar. For example, the challenge of segmenting the sound stream is the same, except that here, the child must distinguish individual *words* in addition to phrases and sentences. Thus, the restaurant order mentioned above *(illhavethebowloftomatosoupwith acupof coffeeandshellhavethehotdogbutwithoutmustard andsomechocolatemilk)* must be segmented so that *the, bowl, of, tomato,* and *soup* are all recognized as distinct lexical items. Furthermore, meanings must be mapped onto these words, and here the child faces Quine's (1960) problem of translation and induction. Namely, the child's visual-spatial world is so rich in supporting *possible* meanings that any given word's meaning is vastly underdetermined. Notice first that the visual-spatial context of the above restaurant order does not even include any of the referents of the words!

Moreover, even if a parent says "here comes my bowl of soup" when the order is brought, there are a plethora of possible referents for, say, *bowl: bowl, soup, red* (the color of the soup), *plastic* (the substance of the bowl), *round* (the shape of the bowl), *hot* (the temperature of the soup), *spoon, tray* (other salient objects), *place-in-front* (a salient action), and so on. Somehow, the child must determine which meaning is the correct one.

A third issue for lexical development (we present here just a sketch; for more in-depth discussions, see Gleitman & Gleitman, 1997; Woodward & Markman, 1998) involves establishing the relations *between* word meanings. That is, it is not enough to know that *soup* refers to *soup;* children must also come to know, for example, that *soup* is a kind of *food* and that *chicken noodle* is a kind of *soup.* Noun meanings often stand in *taxonomic* or hierarchical relations to each other, going from the most general relation (*food, animal, vehicle*) to the most specific (*chicken noodle, cocker spaniel, cable car;* see Keil, 1979; Rosch, Simpson, & Miller, 1976; Waxman & Kosowski, 1990). Verb meanings relate to each other on other dimensions, such as *causality* (distinguishing *come* and *go* from *bring* and *take*), *directionality* (*come* vs. *go* or *enter* vs. *exit*), *manner* (*run* vs. *walk* or *speak* vs. *sing*), and *certainty* (*think* and *guess* vs. *know;* see Levin, 1993; Talmy, 1985; Urmson, 1963). Thus, it is not enough to know what "walking" or "thinking" *is;* children must also come to learn how each action or process "fits" in the organization of other actions and processes.

### *How Natural Language Input Facilitates Lexical Development*

Certainly, the child does not face the task of learning words with only a continuous stream of speech, on the one hand, and an incredibly rich visual-spatial world, on the other. The prosodic qualities of CDS, especially the dramatic pitch excursions and regular patterns of emphasis, serve to highlight some syllables in an utterance over others. In languages such as English, those highlighted (or stressed) syllables most often correspond to the content words of the utterance (e.g., "LOOK, the DOG is RUNning!"; see Fernald & Mazzie, 1991). Thus, the task of segmenting the sound stream into words for which meanings must be sought is made easier by the melody and emphasis naturally used in the speech of adults to children.

The task of determining the meanings of words can be facilitated by specific types of adult-child interaction and input. For example, when adults label objects for young children, they typically only do so after having established *joint attention* to a given object with the child. That is, the adult makes sure that the child is looking at the same place that the adult is looking. In a clever series of studies, Dare Baldwin (1993a, 1993b) has shown that children 18 months of age and older can exploit this joint attention (and, indeed, can establish it themselves) to figure out to which of several novel objects a single novel word refers (see also Hollich, Hirsh-Pasek, & Golinkoff, 1998). Joint attention may not be deterministic enough to learn verb meanings, though, because a given action or event can be viewed from any number of perspectives (e.g., *throwing* a ball can also be seen as *catching* and *flying through the air;* see Gleitman, 1990). Luckily, adults provide more clues by placing the verbs in sentences: "She is X-ing the ball" could refer to *throw* or *catch* but not to *fly,* whereas "The ball is X-ing" can refer to *fly* but not to *throw* or *catch.* Naigles and Hoff-Ginsberg (1998) analyzed the speech of mothers to their toddlers, and the speech of the toddlers themselves 10 weeks later, and found that those verbs that the mothers used in more diverse sentences were the same verbs that the toddlers were subsequently able to use more frequently (see also Gillette, Gleitman, Gleitman, & Lederer, in press; Landau & Gleitman, 1985). Thus, the task of learning the meanings of words is made easier by the social interactions that adults and children engage in and by the specific sentence frames with which verbs are used.

### *Does TV Include Such Facilitative Properties?*

We turn again to the analyses Mabel Rice and her colleagues performed on the language used in educational television programs (Rice, 1984; Rice & Haight, 1986). As far as prosody goes, the utterances spoken on children's educational television appear to be similar to those of CDS. For example, Rice reported that many new or novel words in programs such as *Sesame Street* and *Electric Company* were prosodically stressed (i.e., spoken more loudly than the rest of the words in the sentence). Thus, children viewing these shows might easily distinguish these words from the rest of the speech stream.

Rice also suggested that two aspects of educational television programs might facilitate the child's determination of word meanings. First, Rice and Haight (1986) found that approximately 60% of the utterances of *Mister Rogers* and *Sesame Street* referred to objects or events that were immediately present on the screen (see also Anderson, Lorch, Collins, Field, & Nathan, 1986). Thus, for a majority of the time, children need not look far to find possible referents for unfamiliar words. Second, Rice (1984) pointed out that the visuals of television can provide additional clues because of the camera's ability to zoom in on, or switch over to, a specific aspect of an object or event that is being talked about. If the speech on the program concerned *soup,* for example, the television screen could display just the soup part of a bowl of soup (zooming in past the bowl), eliminating *bowl* and *plastic* as possible referents. Moreover, if the speech on the program was about *red,* the television screen could display cut after cut of objects that differed on every dimension except their *redness.* Rice reported that the 6.5-minute segment of *Mister Rogers* that she analyzed included 29 cuts, suggesting that the producers of the program were taking advantage of this formal television feature.

Although sentence frame information was not analyzed explicitly, Rice and Haight (1986) reported that both *Sesame Street* and *Mister Rogers* included numerous utterance repetitions. To the extent that these included full sentences and were not always exact repetitions, they might be considered to provide information about verbs and their meanings. In sum, it appears that the language and visuals of children's educational television provide at least some of the characteristics of CDS that have been shown to facilitate "natural" lexical development. We next turn to evidence that children actually can learn about word meanings from watching TV.

### *Does TV Influence Lexical Development?*

We have divided this subsection into two parts. The first part presents evidence that children can learn something about the meanings of words from watching specialized videos that were designed with word learning in mind. These laboratory-based studies serve to demonstrate that the medium "works," that children pay enough attention to the language and visuals of television to demonstrate some short-term word acquisition. The second part considers the evidence that children can learn about the meanings of words from watching standard broadcast television programs either at home or in day care settings. These "naturalistic" studies provide support for the claim that, over time, children accrue a considerable amount of information about the meanings of words from watching television.

Naigles and her colleagues (Koenig & Naigles, 1996; Naigles, 1990, 1998; Naigles & Kako, 1993) used a video paradigm to investigate whether toddlers could learn the meanings of novel verbs by exploiting the sentence frames the verbs were presented in. On a typical "program," two novel actions would be presented simultaneously, one of which was causative (e.g., a duck pushing a rabbit over) and one of which was noncausative (e.g., the duck and rabbit bending their arms in unison). The audio, presented over a centrally placed speaker, introduced a novel verb in either a transitive sentence ("the duck is blicking the bunny") or an intransitive sentence ("the duck and the bunny are blicking"). After several presentations, the two actions were separated and children were asked to "find blicking." Throughout, their eye movements were tracked, and the findings were that the children who had heard the verb in the transitive frame preferred to watch the causative action when asked for "blicking," whereas the children who had heard the verb in the intransitive frame preferred to watch the noncausative action. For our purposes, this study (and the others like it) demonstrates that very young children can link actions and verbs when the actions are presented as dynamic videos and the verbs are presented in simultaneous voice-overs. These studies have not tested children's production or comprehension of the verbs outside of the video context, however.

Rice and her colleagues (Rice, 1990; Rice, Buhr, & Oetting, 1992; Rice, Oetting, Marquis, Bode, & Pae, 1994; Rice & Woodsmall, 1988) have conducted several studies in which preschool-age children were shown animated programs 6 minutes long with voice-over narration containing 20 low-frequency words (e.g., *grammophone*). The words were heard when the referent objects, attributes, or actions were shown on the screen. Each word was heard at least three times on a given program. Paired control children watched the same programs but heard voice-over narration that included the high-frequency synonyms of the target words (e.g., *record player*). Prior to watching the program, all children were given a pretest consisting of each (low-frequency) target word accompanied by four still clips from the program. Only one of the clips accurately depicted the target word, and the children were scored for the number of correct clips they chose. After viewing the program twice within the space of a week, all children were tested on the target words again. The question was, Did the children improve from the pretest to the posttest? The findings were generally positive: Children who heard the low-frequency words improved significantly more than children who heard the high-frequency words. Five-year-olds, with an average gain of 4.8 words, improved more than 3-year-olds, who averaged a gain of 1.5 words. Follow-up studies established that 5-year-olds with specific language impairment also showed significant gains in their posttest comprehension scores if they viewed the video with the low-frequency words; however, they required upwards of 10 presentations of each word to demonstrate such gain. Normally developing preschoolers maintained their higher word comprehension scores for 1 to 3 days after the posttest was administered.

Taken together, these laboratory-based studies demonstrate that young children can begin to learn the meanings of words by viewing their referents on video in seminatural contexts while coincidentally hearing the words themselves. The studies of Rice and her colleagues further show that the meaning that is learned can be accessed in a somewhat different context (isolated still clips) and that three to five repetitions are sufficient for the word-meaning link to be retained for at least a couple of days. The next question is, Do children use these abilities when they are watching television at home or in day care?

A longitudinal study by Rice and her colleagues (Rice, Huston, Truglio, & Wright, 1990) assessed children's vocabulary growth over a 2.5-year span via the Peabody Picture Vocabulary Test (PPVT). The children were either 3 or 5 years of age at the beginning of the study. Their parents recorded the amount of the children's television viewing in semiannual weeklong diaries, yielding four or five diaries per child over the 2.5-year span. Rice et al. wondered if the amount of viewing of *Sesame Street* (the only program that appeared in every child's diary) predicted the children's degree of vocabulary growth over the 2.5-year span.

The most compelling finding for our purposes was the *positive* correlation between the younger children's final PPVT score (i.e., at the end of the study) and the amount of *Sesame Street* they watched during both the first year of the study (Diaries 1 and 2) and the second year of the study (Diaries 4 and 5). That is, those children who watched more hours of *Sesame Street* showed greater gains in vocabulary between the ages of 3 and 5 years than the children who watched fewer hours did. And it is important to note that this positive correlation held even after such vocabulary-influencing variables as parental education, number of siblings, and initial PPVT scores were partialled out, so this finding does not just hold for children whose parents are more educated, who have more siblings, and/or who started out with higher PPVT scores. The direction of causality of this correlation is clear: that greater *Sesame Street* watching leads to higher subsequent PPVT scores, not that higher PPVT scores lead to greater *Sesame Street* viewing. Rice et al. note with interest that there were no significant effects with the older cohort, who were 5 years old at the beginning of the study. They suggest that the language of *Sesame Street* holds no more new words for this age group (it is, after all, targeted to preschoolers), so additional viewing serves no vocabulary-enhancing function.

This study is one of the most convincing that television viewing positively influences young children's lexical development. Our main concern is that the link between the television viewing and the words learned is indirect rather than direct. That is, Rice et al. (1990) were unable to draw any direct links between specific words that were both used frequently on *Sesame Street* and acquired by the children over the 2.5-year span. Thus, we cannot be sure that (or whether or how much) those specific words that each child gained during the 2.5 years were gleaned from watching *Sesame Street.* The next two studies tried to make this link more explicit, investigating some effects of viewing *Barney & Friends.*

Singer and Singer (1998) investigated the extent to which preschoolers could learn about unfamiliar nouns by watching 10 preselected episodes of *Barney & Friends.* The nouns chosen were usually involved in the central themes of a given episode (e.g., *pirate* and *map* for an episode about hunting for buried treasure) and were repeated frequently throughout that episode, but they might not appear in any of the other nine episodes. In their procedure, children were first asked to define each of the 10 target nouns; these pretest definitions were accepted without comment and scored for correctness and completeness. Then one group of children watched the 10 episodes over the course of 2 to 3 weeks, one episode per school day. The episodes were shown at the children's day care centers, so the children viewed *ensemble.* The other group of children engaged in their usual day care activities (in separate rooms from the viewers). At the end of the 2 to 3 weeks, all children were given the vocabulary test again.

Singer and Singer found that the *Barney* watchers showed significant gains in their vocabulary test scores from pre- to posttest, while the non-*Barney* watchers' scores remained stable. The television watchers appeared to have gained enough knowledge about at least some of the words (with an average gain of two words) to produce more correct or complete definitions after viewing the episodes. The nonwatchers learned nothing about the words from their usual activities. Lest the reader wonder if, perhaps, any children had seen any of these episodes at home, we note that the Singers used episodes that had been produced only recently and had not yet been released for broadcast. Moreover, the changes in vocabulary scores did not correlate with the children's reported home viewing of television, which is as expected when one considers the specialized nature of these words.

Singer and Singer were unable to investigate whether children could also learn about unfamiliar *verbs* from *Barney & Friends* because so few low-frequency verbs were used in the episodes. However, in a collaborative effort, Naigles and colleagues (1995a, 1995b; Naigles, in press) investigated the extent to which preschool-age children could learn more about *familiar* verbs from viewing *Barney & Friends.* The design was similar to the above study: Two groups of children were pretested on two tasks involving verb knowledge; then one group watched the 10 episodes while the other group engaged in their usual day care activities; and then both groups were posttested on the same two tasks. The tasks involved two different aspects of complex verb knowledge. First, we investigated the children's understanding that *think* and *guess* convey less *certainty* than *know* by presenting two puppets who disagree on where a hidden object is. One puppet says he "thinks" or "guesses" the object is located in one box, whereas the other puppet says he "knows" the object is located in the other box. The child's task was to select the hiding place; no reinforcement was given. Three-year-olds typically perform at chance levels, whereas 4- and 5-year-olds typically select the correct box better than 60% of the time (Moore, Bryant, & Furrow, 1989).

Second, we investigated the understanding that verbs such as *bring, take, push,* and *put must* be causative, involving both an agent (the bringer, taker, pusher, or put-er) and a patient (the thing brought, taken, pushed, or put). We asked children to act out (with toys) sentences in which the target verbs were presented, either with an overt patient (e.g., "The zebra takes the chicken") or without one (e.g., "The zebra takes"). The ability to repair the latter types of sentences has been shown to be fragile in 3- and 4-year-olds but robust in 5-year-olds (Hochberg, 1986; Naigles, Fowler, & Helm, 1992; Naigles, Gleitman, & Gleitman, 1993). All of the target verbs appeared in the 10 episodes of *Barney & Friends,* although some appeared more frequently than others.

Overall, the children who viewed the *Barney* episodes performed significantly differently at posttest, both from the nonwatchers and from their own pretest scores. Interestingly, it was not the case that viewing *Barney* always led to improved scores. That is, the viewers did demonstrate *increased* understanding of the agent-patient nature of the four action verbs in that they repaired more of the ungrammatical sentences ("The zebra takes") in the posttest than they had in the pretest and more than their nonwatching peers did. In contrast, the viewing children simultaneously demonstrated *decreased* understanding of the certainty distinction between *think* and *guess,* and *know:* More of their scores worsened, while more of the nonwatchers' scores improved! Such split findings can only be plausible if they can be tied to specifics of the input of the 10 episodes: What did *Barney & Friends* include that could have facilitated learning about the agent-patient nature of the four action verbs while minimizing the certainty distinction between the three mental verbs?

As it turned out, these 10 episodes of *Barney* were replete with uses of *think* and *guess* that actually conveyed *certainty* rather than *uncertainty.* For example, one character might say, "I think it's time to go home," indicating by his immediate departure that he was utterly certain that playtime was over. These are entirely acceptable uses of *think* and *guess* (and their common use in television and by polite middle-class mothers may be part of the reason why this distinction is not acquired until children are close to 5 years of age); however, they do not serve to illuminate the adult meaning of *uncertainty* (as would, for example, the utterance "I *think* the other horse was under here, but I'm not sure"). The children who watched the episodes evidently picked up the *certainty* senses that were conveyed, reinforcing their lingering notion that the target verbs did not differ on the certainty dimension. The facilitating effect of *Barney* on the children's understanding of the agent-patient verbs seems to be more subtle and can be traced to the highly frequent uses of the *noncausative counterparts* of the target verbs in the 10 episodes. For example, the more the children heard *come* and *go* being used in agent-only sentences in *Barney & Friends* (e.g., "She's coming over to my house today"), the more they may have realized that *bring* and *take* could not appear in similar sentences (e.g., "The zebra is taking next to the giraffe") and, hence, the more they repaired these anomalous sentences (see Naigles et al., 1995b, for a complete discussion; see also Bowerman, 1983; Clark, 1987, 1993).

### *Summary*

Taken together, these studies provide strong evidence that children can learn about words and their meanings from television programs. Moreover, the evidence supports the influence of television at two different stages in the process of learning words. The laboratory studies and the *Barney* study conducted by the Singers demonstrated that young children can *begin* to learn about a word from television input. That is, because these studies all showed significant gains in unfamiliar (or novel) word understanding after viewing, they indicate that children can gain some knowledge about a word that is *first* heard on TV. The longitudinal study by Rice et al. (1990) and the *Barney* studies conducted by Naigles, the Singers, and their colleagues demonstrate further that children can *extend, enhance,* or *restrict* the meanings of words they have already heard via the input of television.

Given these compelling findings, what remains to be done? One important question at this point concerns whether children can acquire vocabulary from television programs that are *not* specifically designed for them. For example, do children who watch numerous televised sporting events, cooking shows, or science shows pick up the specialized vocabulary of these activities (e.g., *bunt* and *offside* for sports, *meringue* and *flambé for cooking, microscopic* and *plume* for science)? If so, at what ages? Such a study has the potential to tell child language researchers just how important specific aspects of CDS are for word learning. And it might also reveal the limitations of the television medium for vocabulary instruction. Of course, a major concern with this type of study involves *the extent to which the vocabulary of the television programs is repeated or otherwise emphasized by adults or peers in the child's life, especially if this occurs while viewing.* That is, if children do acquire some of the vocabulary of television programs, is this because they gleaned their information solely from the TV or also from the language of the coviewing adult? Some of the studies reviewed above included additional groups to address this question; thus, we next revisit some old studies (and introduce one new one) with this issue in mind.

## How Does Adult Mediation Influence Language Development via Television?

Young children may watch television entirely by themselves (St. Peters, Fitch, Huston, Wright, & Eakins, 1988) or with an adult or older child present who is frequently also watching the television program and so available for consultation, conversation, and outright labeling (Lemish & Rice, 1986). The obvious question is, To what extent does the language input of such conversations and consultations account for the observed findings that children learn about the meanings of words from television programs? For example, imagine a situation in which a 3-year-old and her mother are watching a *Sesame Street* scene in which Bert and Ernie are talking about a game of soccer they had played. Flashbacks of the game are also shown; it seems that Ernie made several goals, but at one point he kicked the ball yet missed the goal. In all likelihood, the screen shows the ball bounding past the goal while Ernie is heard voicing his dismay (or perhaps Bert his chagrin), but nonetheless *miss* is a difficult concept to abstract from the relevant event. The child picks up on the word *miss* and repeats it: "missed the goal?" So the mother elaborates: "'Miss the goal' means that Ernie wanted to kick the ball into the goal, and he tried to kick the ball into the goal, but he did not succeed. The ball did not go into the goal, so he *missed* the goal."

How much of the child's acquisition of the meaning of *miss* can be attributed to viewing the television program and how much to the mother's elaboration? If the mother had gone on to give her own example of *missing,* which manifestation would be most important in the child's subsequent representation? These are questions for which we have no definitive answers now; however, three studies have tried to address the adult mediation issue by assessing vocabulary growth under varying viewing conditions.

The strongest findings of adult mediation come from Singer and Singer's (1998) study of noun learning via the *Barney* episodes. In addition to the *Barney* watchers and nonwatchers, a third group was included; these children watched the 10 *Barney* episodes and participated in 30-minute lessons about the episodes. Each lesson was held immediately after the episode was shown and was led by the children's preschool teacher. Outlines of lesson plans were provided for each teacher; however, each was free to "use their own judgement and knowledge" (Singer & Singer, 1998, pp. 330-331) for the actual lesson. The unfamiliar words in each episode, a subset of which formed the basis for the vocabulary test, were included in each lesson plan, and these were mentioned during the lessons themselves.

During the testing phase, Singer and Singer found that the children in this third *Barney*-and-teaching group outperformed both of the other groups on the vocabulary test. That is, although the *Barney*-only group significantly improved from pre- to posttest, and the nonwatching group did not, the *Barney*-and-teaching group improved considerably more than the *Barney*-only group did.[4] In sum, when adult mediation is presented in a formal teaching mode, it clearly enhances the lessons available from television. It is important to remember, though, that the findings for those children who did not receive any lessons after viewing the *Barney* episodes were also positive, indicating that they had acquired some aspects of word meaning simply from watching the program.

The other two studies of adult mediation are more closely concerned with adult *coviewing*—that is, the possible effects of adult input during the actual viewing of the television programs. This is closer to the "natural" situation for most young children. Arraf (1990) attempted to investigate this by asking parents who were keeping a diary of their child's television viewing about their own degree of involvement and interaction with the child in television-related contexts. For example, parents who maintained that they always or almost always watched and discussed television programs with their child were rated more highly on parent-child television interaction (PCTVI) than parents who rarely or never watched or discussed programs with their child. The diaries also included information about who actually watched television with the child during the target week; however, these data were not included in the reported analyses. At about the same time that the diaries were being kept, the children were administered a standardized language (primarily vocabulary) assessment at their preschool.

Arraf's results indicated that the parents who were more involved in their child's television viewing had children whose language scores were higher. Unfortunately, these findings suffer from the same issues as those from the earlier onetime correlational studies; namely, which variable is the cause and which the effect? Do higher language scores (i.e., children who talk more) yield more television-involved parents (i.e., parents who talk more), or vice versa? Moreover, both language scores and PCTVI scores correlated highly with child IQ, and no analyses were reported that partialled out IQ before investigating the effect of the PCTVI variable. It is therefore possible that the correlation of child language score and PCTVI is attributable to the well-known fact that children with higher IQs have parents who are more involved in their children's upbringing. These findings are not sound enough to draw conclusions from.

The most direct data about adult coviewing come from the aforementioned longitudinal study of vocabulary development by Rice et al. (1990). Their viewing diaries included information concerning which television-watching sessions were coviewed with an adult and which were experienced by the child alone. When Rice et al. considered these two types of sessions separately, they found that the "solo" sessions predicted subsequent increases on the PPVT but the "coviewing" sessions did not (with other relevant variables partialled out). That is, viewing *without* an adult at ages 3 to 3½ positively predicted vocabulary at age 5, but viewing *with* an adult at the same ages yielded no significant relations to later vocabulary (Rice et al., 1990, p. 426). At the very least, then, the child's growth in vocabulary that was related to television viewing cannot be attributed to the program-related adult commentary during the viewing.

Taken together, the three available studies provide little evidence that the observed influences of television on vocabulary development in preschool-age children can be explained away as the linguistic influences of adult coviewers. Arraf's (1990) PCTVI index did correlate positively with child vocabulary level; however, this index included more parental behaviors than coviewing and was potentially confounded with child IQ. Rice et al.'s (1990) comparison of the effects of children's viewing television "solo" versus viewing with an adult yielded more positive predictions for the former types of sessions than for the latter. And Singer and Singer (1998) obtained significant vocabulary gains in preschoolers after they watched *Barney* in the company of peers, as well as after they watched *Barney* with peers and then experienced a relevant lesson. What's missing, of course, is an assessment of the type of situation with which we began: namely, when a child is viewing a television program that includes many unfamiliar words and/or concepts. *This may be just the situation in which adult coviewing* is *facilitative of vocabulary growth, because the adult can provide explicit definitions, explain potential confusions, and include additional exemplars.* However, the data available thus far suggest that, *when the language of television is pitched at the level of the child who is viewing,* adult coviewing is not necessary for word acquisition to occur.

## Conclusions

Can children learn language from watching television? Our review of the literature suggests that there are two answers to this question: yes and no. The answer is yes if the type of language concerns *word learning* or *vocabulary acquisition* and if the television program falls into the category of "educational" TV. That is, the most compelling findings come from the domain of lexical development, in which children either learned something about new words or extended their understandings of familiar words, typically from watching programs such as *Sesame Street* or *Barney & Friends* (e.g., Naigles et al., 1995a, 1995b; Rice et al., 1990; Singer & Singer, 1998). In contrast, if the language domain in question is *grammar,* then the answer seems to be no. Far fewer studies have been performed, but the overall gist is clear: Television input does not provide any facilitation of grammatical development. The possible reasons for this lack of influence are numerous. For example, perhaps the child does not have enough of a participatory role while viewing, so he or she is unable to fully understand the subtleties and nuances of the grammatical forms in the linguistic input (Clark & Clark, 1977). Or perhaps grammatical development is so robust that a few extra hours of television input per week do little to change its course (e.g., Hoff-Ginsberg, 1998; Pinker, 1994). Or perhaps television viewing can facilitate some aspects of grammatical development in the same ways that maternal input is facilitative, but these ways are subtle and have yet to be fully investigated.

The case study reported by Sachs et al. (1981), though, provides a lower bound to these possibilities: If a child's entire linguistic database consists only of television input, he or she may succeed in picking up a few words; however, the child's vocabulary will be limited and his or her *combinations* of words are unlikely to resemble those of the target language. Thus, even though the above review suggests that television input can facilitate some aspects of lexical development, and even if future television research is able to demonstrate some facilitative effects on grammatical development, there is *nothing* to suggest that television input could ever replace natural language input for child language learners. If the environmental influences on child language acquisition were thought of as a four-course dinner, then the place of television input is as one of the options on the dessert plate.

## Notes

1. SUBJ indicates the "subject marker," IO the "indirect object marker," and DO the "direct object marker."

2. This is only a brief sketch of the child's task in learning a language. For more complete descriptions, please see Hoff-Ginsberg (1997) and Pinker (1994).

3. In our study, we found no significant correlation between the amount of television viewing the children engaged in and their performance on the "complex structure" subsection of the TACL-3, which included comprehension of interrogatives, negatives, the passive voice, embedded sentences, and conjoined sentences.

4. Unfortunately, there were no reliable findings from a fourth teaching-only group who heard the lessons but did not watch the *Barney* episodes; it is interpreted that the lessons alone were not as effective as *Barney* plus lessons.

## References


Anderson, D., Lorch, E., Collins, P., Field, D., & Nathan, J. (1986). Television viewing at home: Age trends in visual attention and time with TV. *Child Development, 57,* 1024-1033.

Arraf, S. (1990). *An analysis of the effects of television viewing patterns, IQ, SES, and gender on receptive and expressive language development of preschool children.* Unpublished doctoral dissertation, Wayne State University, Detroit, MI.

Baldwin, D. (1993a). Early referential understanding: Infants' ability to recognize referential acts for what they are. *Developmental Psychology, 29,* 832-843.

Baldwin, D. (1993b). Infants' ability to consult the speaker for clues to word reference. *Journal of Child Language, 20,* 395-418.

Bowerman, M. (1983). Evaluating competing linguistic models with language acquisition data: Implications of developmental errors. *Quaderni de Semantica, 3,* 5-66.

Carrow-Woolfolk, E. (1999). *Test for Auditory Comprehension of Language* (3rd ed.). Austin, TX: PRO-ED.

Clancy, P. (1985). The acquisition of Japanese. In D. Slobin (Ed.), *The cross-linguistic study of language acquisition: Vol. 1. The data* (pp. 373-524). Hillsdale, NJ: Lawrence Erlbaum.

Clark, E. (1987). The principle of contrast. In B. MacWhinney (Ed.), *Mechanisms of language acquisition* (pp. 3-20). Hillsdale, NJ: Lawrence Erlbaum.

Clark, E. (1993). *The lexicon in acquisition.* Cambridge, UK: Cambridge University Press.

Clark, E., & Grossman, J. (1998). Pragmatic directions and children's word learning. *Journal of Child Language, 25,* 1-18.

Clark, H. (1996). *Using language.* Cambridge, UK: Cambridge University Press.

Clark, H., & Clark, E. (1977). *Psychology and language.* New York: Harcourt Brace Jovanovich.

Fernald, A., & Mazzie, C. (1991). Prosody and focus in speech to infants and adults. *Developmental Psychology, 27,* 209-221.

Fernald, A., Taeschner, T., Dunn, J., Papousek, M., deBoysson-Bardies, P., & Fukui, I. (1989). A cross-linguistic study of prosodic modifications in mothers' and fathers' speech to preverbal infants. *Journal of Child Language, 16,* 477-501.

Gillette, J., Gleitman, H., Gleitman, L., & Lederer, A. (in press). Human simulation of vocabulary learning. *Cognition.*

Gleitman, L. (1990). The structural sources of verb meanings. *Language Acquisition: A Journal of Developmental Linguistics, 1,* 3-55.

Gleitman, L., & Gleitman, H. (1997). What is a language made of? *Lingua, 100,* 29-67.

Gleitman, L., Gleitman, H., Landau, B., & Wanner, E. (1987). Where learning begins: Initial representations for language learning. In F. Newmeyer (Ed.), *The Cambridge Linguistic Survey* (Vol. 3). Cambridge, UK: Cambridge University Press.

Gleitman, L., Newport, E., & Gleitman, H. (1984). The current status of the motherese hypothesis. *Journal of Child Language, 11,* 43-79.

Gleitman, L., & Wanner, E. (1984). Current issues in language learning. In M. Bornstein & M. Lamb (Eds.), *Developmental psychology: An advanced textbook: Vol. 2. Perceptual, cognitive, and linguistic development.* Hillsdale, NJ: Lawrence Erlbaum.

Hochberg, J. (1986). Children's judgments of transitivity errors. *Journal of Child Language, 13,* 317-334.

Hoff-Ginsberg, E. (1985). Some contributions of mothers' speech to their children's syntactic growth. *Journal of Child Language, 12,* 367-385.

Hoff-Ginsberg, E. (1986). Function and structure in maternal speech: Their relation to the child's development of syntax. *Developmental Psychology, 22,* 155-163.

Hoff-Ginsberg, E. (1991). Mother-child conversation in different social classes and communicative settings. *Child Development, 62,* 782-796.

Hoff-Ginsberg, E. (1997). *Language development.* Pacific Grove, CA: Brooks-Cole.

Hoff-Ginsberg, E. (1998). The relation of birth order and socioeconomic status to children's language experience and language development. *Applied Psycholinguistics, 19,* 603-629.

Hoff-Ginsberg, E., & Shatz, M. (1982). Linguistic input and the child's acquisition of language. *Psychological Bulletin, 92,* 3-26.

Hollich, G., Hirsh-Pasek, K., & Golinkoff, R. (1998). Introducing the 3-D intermodal preferential looking paradigm: A new method to answer an age-old question. In C. Rovee-Collier, L. Lipsitt, & H. Hayne (Eds.), *Advances in infancy research* (Vol. 12, pp. 355-374). Stamford, CT: Ablex.

Johnson, D. (1997). *Le divorce.* New York: Plume.

Keil, F. (1979). *Semantic and conceptual development.* Cambridge, MA: Harvard University Press.

Koenig, P., & Naigles, L. (1996). *One-word speakers interpret a novel word as an action.* Poster presented at the International Conference on Infancy Studies, Providence, RI.

Landau, B., & Gleitman, L. (1985). *Language and experience: Evidence from the blind child.* Cambridge, MA: Harvard University Press.

Lemish, D., & Rice, M. (1986). Television as a talking picture book: A prop for language acquisition. *Journal of Child Language, 13,* 251-274.

Levin, B. (1993). *English vocabulary classes and alternations.* Chicago: University of Chicago Press.

Mayeux, L., & Naigles, L. (2000). *Linguistic and social influences on children's developing understanding of mental states.* Manuscript in preparation, University of Connecticut.

McCullough, C. (1977). *The thorn birds.* London: Harper & Row.

Moore, C., Bryant, D., & Furrow, D. (1989). Mental terms and the development of certainty. *Child Development, 60,* 167-171.

Morgan, J., & Demuth, K. (1996). *Signal to syntax: Bootstrapping from speech to grammar in early acquisition.* Mahwah, NJ: Lawrence Erlbaum.

Naigles, L. (1990). Children use syntax to learn verb meanings. *Journal of Child Language, 17,* 357-374.

Naigles, L. (1998). Developmental changes in the use of structure in verb learning: Evidence from preferential looking. In C. Rovee-Collier, L. Lipsitt, & H. Hayne (Eds.), *Advances in infancy research* (Vol. 12, pp. 298-318). Stamford, CT: Ablex.

Naigles, L. (in press). Manipulating the input: Studies in mental verb acquisition. In B. Landau, J. Sabini, E. Newport, & J. Jonides (Eds.), *Essays in honor of Henry and Lila Gleitman.* Cambridge: MIT Press.

Naigles, L., Fowler, A., & Helm, A. (1992). Developmental shifts in the construction of verb meanings. *Cognitive Development, 7,* 403-427.

Naigles, L., Gleitman, H., & Gleitman, L. (1993). Children acquire word meaning components from syntactic evidence. In E. Dromi (Ed.), *Language and cognition: A developmental perspective.* Norwood, NJ: Ablex.

Naigles, L., & Hoff-Ginsberg, E. (1998). Why are some verbs learned before other verbs? Effects of input frequency and structure on children's early verb use. *Journal of Child Language, 25,* 95-120.

Naigles, L., & Kako, E. (1993). First contact in verb acquisition: Defining a role for syntax. *Child Development, 64,* 1665-1687.

Naigles, L., Singer, D., Singer, J., Jean-Louis, B., Sells, D., & Rosen, C. (1995a). *Barney says, "come, go, think, know": Television reveals a role for input in later language acquisition.* Hartford: Connecticut Public Broadcasting.

Naigles, L., Singer, D., Singer, J., Jean-Louis, B., Sells, D., & Rosen, C. (1995b, June). *Watching "Barney" affects preschoolers' use of mental state verbs.* Paper presented at the annual meeting of the American Psychological Society, New York City.

Newport, E., Gleitman, H., & Gleitman, L. (1977). Mother, I'd rather do it myself: Some effects and non-effects of maternal speech style. In C. Snow & C. Ferguson (Eds.), *Talking to children: Language input and acquisition* (pp. 109-150). Cambridge, UK: Cambridge University Press.

Pinker, S. (1994). *The language instinct.* New York: William Morrow.

Quine, W. V. O. (1960). *Word and object.* Cambridge, MA: Harvard University Press.

Rice, M. (1983). The role of television in language acquisition. *Developmental Review, 3,* 211-224.

Rice, M. (1984). The words of children's television. *Journal of Broadcasting, 28,* 445-461.

Rice, M. (1990). Preschoolers' QUIL: Quick incidental learning of words. In G. Conti-Ransden & C. Snow (Eds.), *Children's language* (Vol. 7). Hillsdale, NJ: Lawrence Erlbaum.

Rice, M., Buhr, J., & Oetting, J. B. (1992). Specific language-impaired children's quick incidental learning of words: The effect of a pause. *Journal of Speech and Hearing Research, 35,* 1040-1048.

Rice, M., & Haight, P. (1986). "Motherese" of "Mr. Rogers": A description of the dialogue of educational television programs. *Journal of Speech and Hearing Disorders, 51,* 282-287.

Rice, M., Huston, A., Truglio, R., & Wright, J. (1990). Words from "Sesame Street": Learning vocabulary while viewing. *Developmental Psychology, 26,* 421-428.

Rice, M., Oetting, J. B., Marquis, J., Bode, J., & Pae, S. (1994). Frequency of input effects on word comprehension of children with specific language impairment. *Journal of Speech and Hearing Research, 37,* 106-122.

Rice, M., & Woodsmall, L. (1988). Lessons from television: Children's word learning when viewing. *Child Development, 59,* 420-429.

Rosch, E., Simpson, C., & Miller, S. (1976). Structural bases of typicality effects. *Journal of Experimental Psychology: Human Perception and Performance, 4,* 491-502.

Sachs, J., Bard, B., & Johnson, M. (1981). Language learning with restricted input: Case studies of two hearing children of deaf parents. *Applied Psycholinguistics, 2,* 33-54.

Selnow, G. W., & Bettinghaus, E. (1982). Television exposure and language development. *Journal of Broadcasting, 26,* 469-479.

Singer, J., & Singer, D. (1981). *Television, imagination, and aggression: A study of preschoolers.* Hillsdale, NJ: Lawrence Erlbaum.

Singer, J., & Singer, D. (1998). *Barney & Friends* as entertainment and education: Evaluating the quality and effectiveness of a television series for preschool children. In J. Asamen & G. Berry (Eds.), *Research paradigms, television, and social behavior* (pp. 305-367). Thousand Oaks, CA: Sage.

Snow, C. E., Arlman-Rupp, A., Hassing, Y., Jobse, J., Joosten, J., & Vorster, J. (1976). Mothers' speech in three social classes. *Journal of Psycholinguistic Research, 5,* 1-20.

St. Peters, M., Fitch, M., Huston, A., Wright, J., & Eakins, D. (1988). *Television and families: What do young children watch with their families?* Paper presented at the Southwest Society for Research in Development, New Orleans.

Talmy, L. (1985). Lexicalization patterns: Semantic structure in lexical forms. In T. Shopen (Ed.), *Language typology and syntactic description* (Vol. 3). New York: Cambridge University Press.

Tomasello, M. (1990). The social bases of language acquisition. *Social Development, 1,* 67-87.

Tomasello, M. (in press). Perceiving intentions and learning words in the second year of life. In M. Bowerman & S. Levinson (Eds.), *Language acquisition and conceptual development.* Cambridge, UK: Cambridge University Press.

Urmson, J. (1963). Parenthetical verbs. In C. Caton (Ed.), *Philosophy and ordinary language* (pp. 220-246). Urbana: University of Illinois Press.

Waxman, S., & Kosowski, T. (1990). Nouns mark category relations: Toddlers' and preschoolers' word-learning biases. *Child Development, 61,* 1461-1473.

Winn, M. (1985). *The plug-in drug.* New York: Penguin.

Woodward, A., & Markman, E. (1998). Early word learning. In W. Damon, D. Kuhn, & R. Siegler (Eds.), *Handbook of child psychology: Vol. 2. Cognition, perception, and language.* New York: John Wiley.

CHAPTER **8**

# Creating Vigilance for Better Learning From Television

DORINA MIRON
JENNINGS BRYANT
DOLF ZILLMANN
College of Communication and Information Sciences, University of Alabama

This chapter examines the relationships between attention, especially vigilance, and children's learning from television programming. The first two sections discuss concepts. The third section presents theories of attentional processes that address learning from television. Section four elaborates on factors that affect learning from television. Throughout the chapter, we reflect on possibilities for producers to enhance the attention-getting power of educational programs.

## Vigilance and Learning

Cognitive psychologists seem to agree that learning is the process by which relatively permanent changes occur in behavioral potential (or probability) as a result of experience. In this chapter, we examine learning that occurs from watching television. Bandura's social learning (1977) and social cognitive (1994) theories, which address vicarious learning, posit that four processes—attention, retention, motor reproduction, and motivation—mediate learning. Our discussion will focus on the role of attention in learning from television.

Whereas learning typically refers to the process of adaptation of behavior, memory is considered the product of the change, the relatively permanent record of the experience that underlies learning (Anderson, 1995; Mowrer & Klein, 1989). In this chapter, retention will be the typical measure of learning.

When we speak of attention as a factor in learning, we usually refer to vigilance, that is, sustained attention, defined as a steady state of alertness and wakefulness (Weinberg & Harper, 1993). This includes the ability of observers to maintain the focus of their attention and to remain alert to stimuli for prolonged periods of time (Davies & Parasuraman, 1982; Parasuraman, Warm, & Dember, 1987; Warm, 1984, 1993; Warm, Dember, & Hancock, 1996; Weinberg & Emslie, 1991).

## Vigilance and Attention

The way an organism responds to various stimuli depends on which areas of the brain are activated by the respective stimuli and to what level. One role of attention is to modulate this process of selective activation.

Neuroscientists distinguish three major attention functions: orienting or stimulus foveation, focusing or signal/target detection, and vigilance or maintenance of a state of alertness (Posner & Petersen, 1990). Vigilance in the most restricted sense is maintenance of a state of alertness associated with expectation of a target (Deese, 1955). In television, program designers, through strategic sequential presentation of stimuli, can create such expectations. Viewers experience vigilance as alertness to the stimuli they expect.

The role of vigilance in a strict sense is to allow fast selection of a response based on a lower quality of information, which results in a higher rate of response errors. Vigilance thus defined does not affect the build-up of information in the sensory or memory systems, but it does affect the rate of response (Posner & Petersen, 1990).

## Vigilance and Information Processing

Researchers have looked at the effects of television on information processing from two broad perspectives: arousal systems and cognitive processes. We will discuss theories proposed from each perspective.

### *Arousal Systems*

Traditionally, arousal is discussed in connection with vigilance as a way to account for attentional decrement resulting from excessively low levels of stimulation. Causes of understimulation may be stimulus simplicity or repetition, and the effect is a decrease in responsiveness to external stimulation, leading to a decline in the efficiency of signal detection (Warm et al., 1996). Mackworth (1970a, 1970b) proposed a habituation theory to account for a decrement in short-term vigilance.

Zillmann (1982) promoted the complementary view of arousal as an incremental process. He pointed out that

> in behavior theory (e.g., J. S. Brown, 1961; Hull, 1943, 1952; Spence, 1956), in activation theory (e.g., Duffy, 1962; Lindsley, 1951, 1957), and in emotion theory (Schachter, 1964; Zillmann, 1978), arousal has been conceived of as a unitary force that energizes or intensifies behavior that receives direction by independent means. (p. 53)

Routtenberg (1968, 1971) distinguished two arousal systems with distinct anatomical structures and functions. The cortical system, or reticular activating system, was found to produce cortical arousal and serve attention, perception, and response preparation. The limbic system was found to be responsible for basic vegetative processes, including affective and emotional reactions (independent of hedonic valence). The most common index of cortical arousal is alpha wave blocking, and frequently used measures of limbic (autonomic) arousal are heart rate, skin temperature, and skin conductance (Zillmann, 1982). According to Routtenberg's model, the vigilance function is performed by the cortical system and is distinct from emotional arousal. From the perspective of educational television, the problem is how to choose stimuli to trigger the appropriate kind of arousal and attentional processes to optimize the learning of different kinds of information, ranging from language and science to art and self-defense. The choice is not simple, because, although the two types of arousal are distinct, they are closely related in a functional way.

Both the orienting response and the defensive response produce cortical arousal, which serves attention, but they also tend to produce limbic/autonomic arousal, which serves to maintain the cortical arousal.

Research on diminished cortical and limbic arousal as an effect of exposure to television focused on the "zombie viewer" type (Lesser, 1972, 1974, 1977). This label was used to describe children's alleged passive-mindless-hypnotic-addictive viewing of television and reflected both popular and expert concerns about children's learning from educational television. The spark that enflamed criticism was an experiment by Krugman (1971), who examined a single research participant who viewed only three TV commercials. The researcher claimed to have found dominant alpha activity during viewing (indicating low cortical arousal). Mulholland (1974) found that the alpha state experienced by children while viewing was episodic, not dominant. Mulholland ventured to hypothesize that, by watching television, children learn how to operate at a low level of attention, which can be considered a valuable strategic skill.

In an attempt to provide a definitive answer to the question of whether television has a hypnotizing effect on viewers or makes them more passive, Miller (1985) conducted six experiments on a total of 56 research participants, mostly college students. He concluded that, "with respect to our brainwave patterns, television viewing appears to be nothing special" (p. 514). According to Miller's data, television viewing is predominantly a beta brainwave pattern that indicates a more active than inactive viewer; beta activity tends to increase rather than decrease over half-hour and hour viewing times (and, conversely, alpha tends to decrease), indicating that television tends to activate viewers rather than make them passive; and television viewing is not primarily a right-brain activity (involving pattern rather than sequential processing of visual rather than verbal information), and neither hemisphere tends to dominate during television viewing. In conclusion, the zombie-viewer line of research initiated in the 1970s was theoretically closed by Miller's findings in the mid-1980s. Nevertheless, residual smoke from the hot flames persists in the form of speculation that television "may be subtly yet profoundly changing the structure of consciousness" (Miller, 1985, p. 508).

Another theoretical issue of pragmatic relevance for educational television is the optimal level of arousal. Researchers tend to agree that, because arousal underlies and energizes attention, its relationship with learning has the same inverted-U pattern as the relationship between attention and learning or attention and performance (Yerkes & Dodson, 1908). Very low and very high levels of arousal are accordingly expected to result in poor learning, and moderate levels are believed to enhance attention and learning. High arousal narrows attention, reduces fine discriminations (Kahneman, 1973), reduces cue utilization (Easterbrook, 1959), and, in case of divided attention, increases the attentional bias in favor of the primary task (Eysenck, 1982).

The control or manipulation of viewer arousal in educational television is difficult because of the considerable freedom of choice children have when deciding when and what to watch and for how long. This discretion raises problems of the dynamics of arousal over the short and long term. For instance, within a short time range, the excitation transfer theory (Zillmann, 1971) predicts that residues from a preceding affective reaction combine with excitation produced by subsequent affective stimulation and result in a cumulative (i.e., disproportionate) affective reaction to the subsequent stimulus. Adding complexity, the law of initial values predicts that the magnitude of an excitatory reaction decreases as the level of initial arousal increases (Sternbach, 1966; Wilder, 1957). In television viewing, this means that the same stimulus (program) will elicit stronger arousal in unaroused or normally aroused viewers than in already highly aroused viewers. A ceiling effect for television viewing may be reached and maintained. As far as long-term effects are concerned, arousal reactions to repeated stimuli of a certain kind tend to habituate and decrease in intensity (Zillmann, 1982).

Two major lessons can be derived from these considerations for educational television strategies. The general lesson is that excessive reliance on arousing stimuli to enhance attention may sometimes result in comparatively high levels of arousal in the short run and/or unexpectedly low arousal in the long run. Both phenomena diminish attention and jeopardize learning. An additional lesson concerns the tendency to make children's programs too simple, with a lowest-denominator audience standard in mind. What happens in such situations "might be termed the paradox of automation: Although automation is designed to reduce the workload of operators, it may place them at a functional disadvantage through understimulation" (Warm et al., 1996, p. 185). The implication of this observation for educational television is that an effort to make information too easy to process may have the undesirable effects of understimulation, low arousal, and, consequently, poor vigilance and retention. That is why the appropriate/moderate level of difficulty should be a crucial concern for producers of educational programs for children.

### *Cognitive Strategies*

The cognitive processes associated with sustained attention are also important. Huston and Wright (1983) proposed a sampling model of attention, according to which viewers make sequential decisions to continue or discontinue (or resume) watching based on programming cues and learned associations with cognitive and affective expectations of television content. A sequence of decisions involves a progress in terms of depth and detail of cue analysis, and a continued and increasingly elaborate processing is conducive to deeper involvement with the content. The model predicts that incomprehensible content will cease to be attended.

#### *Attentional Inertia*

Paradoxically, this strategic sampling approach is facilitated by an opposite nonstrategic phenomenon called attentional inertia (Anderson, Alwitt, Lorch, & Levin, 1979; Anderson, Choi, & Lorch, 1987; Anderson & Lorch, 1983), which is a lag in reacting to changes in television content: The more attention viewers have been paying to the program, the more likely they are to continue to do so. Automatic short-term vigilance persistence helps the viewer extend processing to apparently incomprehensible elements of television content, trying to make sense of them, and thus promotes learning. Distractibility lowers significantly (i.e., inertia becomes manifest) after a child has maintained attention to television for 15 seconds or longer (Anderson et al., 1987).

Thorson, Reeves, and Schleuder (1985) proposed a more elaborate model of attention decisions that includes two types of judgments: one based on the continuous assessment of immediately incoming stimuli—in Omanson's (1982) terms, on-line processing—and another based on judgments about "chunks" (i.e., meaningful clusters of information items)—in Omanson's terms, off-line processing. According to Hawkins, Kim, and Pingree (1991), the first type would involve mostly heuristic decisions based on formal features, whereas the second type would involve schematic decisions that take more time and more television content. If we consider attentional inertia within the framework of Thorson et al.'s (1985) model, we may expect the automatic short-term processing lag to expand with age and knowledge by incorporating discrete incomprehensible content elements into meaningful chunks and by deriving expectations about subsequent content based on chunks rather than isolated elements. Research results seem to support this hypothesis, showing that older children are capable of more sustained attention and tend to extend effort longer to understand incomprehensible content (Hawkins et al., 1991). The discussion of the importance of schema knowledge for children's attention will be resumed in the next section in connection with programming features that elicit attention.

### *Does Comprehension Drive Attention?*

Thorson et al.'s (1985) two-tier model of attention and Omanson's (1982) distinction between on-line (data-driven) and off-line (schema-driven) processing are conciliating products of a dispute that pushes for a trend reversal in television processing theory. The initiator of the dispute was D. R. Anderson, who, in the early 1980s, proposed a cognitive involvement model, arguing that attention to television is attracted and maintained by "cognitive involvement and active comprehension of content" rather than by "salient noncontent features" (Anderson, Lorch, Field, Collins, & Nathan, 1986, p. 1025). Anderson emphasized the progressive nature of cognitive processing and the contingency of the attention/involvement level on understanding.

Supporters of the data-driven processing challenged Anderson's "understanding and looking hypothesis" (Verbeke, 1988, p. 67), arguing that there is no understanding without looking. They claimed that visual attention is a prerequisite for understanding and perceived Anderson's model as a claim that understanding is an antecedent of attention.

This chicken-and-egg dispute needs to be put into context. If we think of the role of arousal as an energizer of cognitive processes (Zillmann, 1982) and admit the need for adjusting the level of arousal to meet current cognitive needs, then Anderson's level of "understanding" provides this feedback. On the other hand, as proposed by Chaiken (1980), the heuristic, schema-based processing tends to be preferred to systematic processing because it saves mental effort. The use of schemata facilitates understanding, which decreases the need for arousal as energizer of the understanding (sense-making) process and thus reduces attention to material that is easy to understand. This framework is not incompatible with Verbeke's (1988) thesis that viewers, while paying attention to television, work their way through the material, trying to make sense of it by "locating a sequence of causally or purposefully connected events or states" (p. 73); this locating process involves the use of both TV content knowledge and world knowledge. What Anderson's theory did was to transcend the bit-by-bit processing view that posited attention as a condition for understanding in order to be able to account for sustained attention. His higher-level, process-in-progress approach simply added the feedback loop from understanding to attention. Efforts to disprove Anderson's cognitive involvement model failed, and a "concession" was made that "how much a child is watching is . . . a reflection of an attention managing style" (Verbeke, 1988, p. 89). But this, again, is not incompatible with the situated version of Anderson's model, in which schema-based understanding of TV content is only one component of motivation to watch (i.e., the feedback for sustained attention), in competition with alternative attractions (Anderson, 1983).

### *Viewing Styles*

So far, we have examined roles of attention captured by models proposed to explain television processing. We will now refer to viewing styles as patterns of behavior involving choices that in some way or another affect attention to and learning from television. The viewing style topic bloomed in television literature in the early 1980s when Bryant, Zillmann, and Brown (1983) revisited Lesser's (1972, 1974) classification of children's styles as zombie (passive), dual-attention (sharing attention with other activities, monitoring the television flow for personally relevant content), and modeling (actively relating/responding to TV content). That classification reflected three levels of attention: a minimal/base level; an intermediate level of vigilance in the restricted sense of alertness to personally relevant cues coming from various sources; and a high level of attention associated with relatively strong arousal, enhanced cognitive processing, and participative action.

At the same time, Anderson and Lorch (1983) discussed different perceptions that theorists (and the public at large) entertained about television viewing, reflected in two types of theories that concern the processing of television. One type assumed reactive viewers whose attention was automatically captured by salient features of the television material, whose processing and comprehension of the material was limited (under a limited-capacity assumption) by frequent reorienting to new stimuli, and whose learning was imperfect or incomplete, leading to "considerable recognition . . . without efficient retrieval" (Singer, 1980, p. 38). The other type of theories assumed active viewers who distributed their attention between television and other events in their environment and among various elements of the program. Under the active viewing model, children would be able to gauge their mental effort depending on how much they wanted to understand and retain from the program. Children's decisions about what to process from the television fare, and how deeply, would be determined by their expectations about the program based on their prior knowledge of television and of the world.

An interesting angle on active viewing was introduced by Salomon's (1981, 1983a, 1983b, 1984) theory of differential investment of mental effort. According to Salomon, learners' perceptions about media messages included perceived self-efficacy in handling them. The perceived difficulty of a message could be associated with the medium (print generally being considered harder than television), the format of the message, or the specific information conveyed by the message. The viewers' perceptions of self-efficacy determined the amount of invested mental effort (AIME), which affected learning. Salomon (1984) found that self-efficacy correlated positively with AIME in print and negatively in television. The theory implies an inherent disadvantage of television in eliciting mental effort (which can include attention). The perception of realism, found by Salomon (1984) to contribute to the impression of easiness, is enhanced in television by film footage and live performances. On the other hand, animation, largely used in children's television, involves message simplification. And the easier a TV message is perceived, the less focused attention it will get.

It is hoped that the discussion of attention in relation to processing strategies has sensitized designers of educational programs to a couple of issues that have practical relevance. First, relying on attentional inertia to help children process and understand new or difficult items of information is risky, especially with young children, whose attention span is smaller because of lower schematization of knowledge, which results in poorer anticipation. Extensive schematization of content intended to expand the attention span and facilitate understanding triggers more schematic processing and reduces the depth of understanding. On the other hand, the build-up of cognitive involvement cannot be controlled through program qualities because of the situatedness of TV viewing that involves competition for children's attention. The use of form-related stimuli to create and maintain arousal as a component of or condition for attention may focus young children's attention away from what is intended to be central content. Last but not least, given the intermittent nature of focused attention and the fragmentariness of viewing because of children's high distractibility, educational content needs to be sequentially organized in small fragments with a high level of independence, in which new items are nested in a "framework" repeated in each fragment to ensure comprehension even without watching preceding fragments. The framework repetition requires formal variation to avoid being perceived as a

Lorch, 1983; Anderson, Lorch, Field, & Sanders, 1981) involvement model of attention, because slower action allows for deeper processing and thus facilitates involvement and sustained attention. Further research is needed to clarify (a) whether boys are more susceptible than girls to formal high-action cues and therefore more likely to be distracted from central processing, and (b) whether boys' and girls' attention is differently affected by programming rich in orienting cues (eliciting stronger cortical arousal) and by emotional programming (eliciting stronger limbic arousal).

Another gender-related peculiarity is the fact that boys' attention to the audio and video tracks of television is less dissociated than girls' is (Rolandelli, Wright, & Huston, 1982). Girls appear to use single modality cues more readily than boys do (Rolandelli et al., 1982), but they tend to orient more to the audio track (Halpern, 1986) and have better memory for auditory information than boys do (Rolandelli, 1985). Girls tend to listen without looking more often but still retain the same amount of information from the program. An explanation that may account for these observations is that, during preschool and early school years, girls' verbal development is, on the average, slightly more advanced than boys' (Halpern, 1986).

These findings relative to gender as a factor of attention to and learning from television indicate that boys and girls might profit differentially from information presented in the two modalities (Alvarez et al., 1988). To the extent that producers of educational programs produce programs designed more for one gender than the other, this information may be useful for choosing the predominant modality for conveying the most important information.

### *Intelligence*

A legitimate question raised by Swanson and Cooney (1989) is whether individual differences in sustained attention relate to primary mental abilities. Research findings are inconsistent; some studies found evidence that intelligence does affect vigilance, whereas others found no significant correlations (Swanson & Cooney, 1989).

The limited-resource model posits relatively stable interpersonal differences in attentional resources across task situations, directly correlated with IQ levels. The arousal model of attention assumes that increased time on tasks leads to a decrement in arousal levels as a function of IQ. Empirical findings show low positive correlations between attentional capacity and IQ. Carter and Swanson (1995) claimed that the findings do not provide enough support either for a direct relationship between intelligence and attention or for a relationship mediated by arousal. Swanson (1989) proposed an alternative model in which the correlation between IQ and vigilance is mediated by central processing capacity, which involves the use of attention strategies.

### *Temperament and Personality*

An individual's temperament includes behavioral features that are relatively stable over time. Such features discussed in the literature as relevant to attentional processes are attention span, persistence, and inhibitory control.

The attention span refers to how long an activity is being pursued. Persistence refers to the continuation of an activity in the face of obstacles (Silverman & Gaines, 1996; Thomas, Chess, & Birch, 1968) and the ability to work on dull, tiring, or boring tasks (Buss & Plomin, 1975). Inhibitory control is the capacity to delay responding to an attractive stimulus. Performance on all three measures improves with age (Ruff, 1990; Vaughn, Kopp, & Krakow, 1984), but the three features appear to be relatively independent (e.g., Silverman & Gaines, 1996).

Interpersonal differences in inhibitory control emerge as early as 24 months of age and develop throughout childhood and adolescence (Golden, Montare, & Bridger, 1977; Ippolito, 1993; Levy, 1980; Luria, 1959;

known schema and being disregarded (possibly, together with embedded new items).

## Factors Involved in Vigilance

An attempt will be made in this section to cover major factors of attention to and learning from television. We will discuss variables related to viewers, programming features, and situation factors.

### *Viewer-Related Factors*

The amount of attention a child pays to television at any particular moment depends on factors that vary in their stability over time. The viewer's gender, for instance, influences attentional patterns and is a fixed characteristic of the person. At the other extreme, age is inexorably changing. The attentional factors situated between these extremes can be assessed in terms of degree of stability, degree of controllability, and relevance to producers of educational programming.

#### *Gender*

Great consistency across a large number of studies indicates that boys' visual attention to television is greater than girls' (Alvarez, Huston, Wright, & Kerkman, 1988; Anderson et al., 1987; Field & Anderson, 1985; Greer, Potts, Wright, & Huston, 1982; Potts, Huston, & Wright, 1986; Rolandelli, Wright, & Huston, 1985; Wright, Calvert, Huston-Stein, & Watkins, 1980; Wright et al., 1984). The finding holds when appealing distractors are provided (Anderson et al., 1987; Wright et al., 1984). But gender differences in visual attention are not typically associated with differences in comprehension, and males' greater visual attention does not typically lead to greater recall of content (Alvarez et al., 1988).

Rather inconsistent findings about th ferential impact of programming conta action and violence on children's atte maintained controversies in media effect erature. Feminist critics of television bla television for its male bias, the arguments ing that the majority of main characters male, and male characters engage in mos the interesting activities (Sternglantz Serbin, 1974; Williams, Baron, Philli Travis, & Jackson, 1986). Moreover, ma programs (e.g., cartoons, action-adventure ries) have plots, content themes, and beha iors that are masculine sex-typed (Signoriel Gross, & Morgan, 1982). A popular hypoth sis among researchers and theorists is that th formal features of television—such as anima tion, rapid action, sound effects, and frequen cuts—might appeal to boys more than to girl because those features are associated with masculine sex-typed content (Welch, Huston-Stein, Wright, & Plehal, 1979) and carry masculine connotations even when used with neutral content (Huston, Greer, Wright, Welch, & Ross, 1984).

Although violence is a frequent ingredient of action programming that increases arousal and attention, some authors claim that action and the formal features associated with it are actually more critical than violent content per se for maintaining young children's attention (Huston-Stein, Fox, Greer, Watkins, & Whitaker, 1981; Potts et al., 1986). The fac that differences in attention to high and lov action were found to be greater for live tha for animated shows (Potts et al., 1986) sug gests as a general explanation the orienting re actions elicited by action programming, whic may be stronger with males under a hypothe sis of gender specialization for environment surveillance and danger detection (because either the genetic development of the specie or different gender socialization). Such a hy pothesis has some support in findings th girls' attention is higher under low-action tha under high-action conditions (Alvarez et a 1988). But this finding might also be e plained through Anderson's (Anderson

Silverman & Ippolito, 1995; Silverman & Ragusa, 1990). Persistence is a costs-rewards trade-off and develops as a component of strategic attention, through exercise that may be emphasized by educators both at home and at school. Given the limited opportunity for children to interact with television on specific tasks, the role of the medium in educating or promoting persistence and inhibitory control is small.

As far as the attention span is concerned, fears were repeatedly expressed that the fragmentariness and fast pace of children's programming are undermining the development of their attention span, triggering item-by-item processing with emphasis on formal features rather than processing of meaningful chunks. What critics would like to see is programming with more structure and continuity that presents information at a slower pace, leaving children time for more elaborate cognitive processing. Such programming would facilitate the exercise of sequential-task vigilance that focuses more on content cues. This correction is suggested as a means of counterbalancing the almost exclusive exercise of alertness to simultaneous stimuli imposed by programming loaded with formal attention getters, which may increase arousal and elicit orienting response but take processing resources away from central content.

Depending on their typical alertness, people can be classified as more or less vigilant (Type A vs. Type B). Type A personalities involve hypervigilance (Price, 1982), superior inhibitory control, and persistence. Type A persons focus on tasks (Jennings, 1983) and tend to ignore external peripheral stimuli and to suppress internal cues that might interfere with their performance (Carver, Coleman, & Glass, 1976; Strube, Turner, Patrick, & Perrillo, 1983; Weidner & Matthews, 1978). Although most studies addressed Type A personality as an antecedent of coronary heart disease and were conducted on middle-aged males, research by Matthews (1978, 1980) showed that children as young as kindergarten age can be successfully classified as Type A or Type B. According to Price (1982), Type A behavior is to a large extent "learned very early in life" (p. 48) from models provided by family, school, and mass media. Educators push children to "hurry up," "try harder," "be number one," be competitive. On the other hand, the media emphasize suspense (anticipatory reactions) as well as success through fast, opportunistic, and aggressive action.

Using Bandura's (1971) theory that consistent models enhance social learning, we can assume that each generation will exhibit stronger Type A behavior than the preceding one. As observed by Price (1982), extreme Type A behavior may hinder rather than facilitate children's success because "hypervigilance can lead to a chronic inability to concentrate, due in large part to racing thoughts and intrusive worries" (p. 123). In addition, Type A responses to situations are faster at the cost of being more schematic—that is, nonspecific and therefore less adequate. Another problem seems to be gender stereotyping, particularly through exemplification in the media, with males being pushed harder than females toward Type A behavior. Added to the boys' higher rate of Type A behavior resulting from their higher level of androgens (male hormones), stereotyped modeling enhances boys' arousability and risks of schematic and aggressive reactions to stimuli. Television producers should be aware that the overuse of suspense to heighten arousal and maintain attention tends to create in the audience chronic hypervigilance that jeopardizes learning from television.

A personality distinction that involves vigilance ability is between extroverts and introverts, who differ in their excitation-inhibition balance. Introverts were hypothesized to have a higher level of basal/tonic/habitual cortical arousal (Eysenck, 1983; Parasuraman, 1985) or higher arousability (Eysenck, 1982, 1988, 1989). Higher arousal helps introverts sustain their attention better, which makes them more efficient learners. In a study by Checcino (1997) on seventh graders, introversion did not appear to affect grade point averages (GPAs) directly, but it correlated negatively with self-concept. These two variables, together with gender, accounted for 15% of the GPA variance. Girls were found to have lower self-concept and higher GPAs. Since gender and extroversion or introversion appear to affect learning in general, research is warranted on the impact of these factors on children's learning from television.

*Age*

The Piagetian operational theory of intelligence (Piaget, 1947/1973) outlined four stages of cognitive development. The sensorimotor intelligence (ages 0 to approximately 2 years) was described as nonreflective intelligence in action. During the preoperational stage (2 to 6 or 7 years), children develop representational skills and intuitive regulation closely modeled on perceptual data. Concrete logical operations develop during the early school years (ages 6-7 to 11-12), and formal operations with abstractions begin at the age of 11 or 12. In Piagetian terms, cognitive activity consists of assimilation of new information to existing knowledge and accommodation (restructuring/change) of existing knowledge to coherently include new information.

Gibson and Rader's (1979) theory of attention development similarly posited a progress with age from focusing on perceptual features for the purpose of object differentiation to focusing on conceptual features for the purpose of identifying utility, which derives from functionality, which in turn involves causal relationships.

If we consider television viewing within this theoretical framework, preschool children can be expected to pay most attention to salient formal features of programming and to process sensory material primarily in terms of differentiations, with more assimilation (addition to previous knowledge) than accommodation (changes in the stored knowledge). The video track is likely to elicit attention through such elements as colors, shapes, contrasts, and change, and the audio track through music, noises, or different voices. Even in the late preschool years, children attend to and comprehend visual information more than verbal information (e.g., Bellack, 1984; Ward & Wackman, 1973).

Vigilance improves with age. The ability to develop an expectation for an event and attend to the place of occurrence in its absence was observed in 5-month-old infants (Ruff, Capozzoli, Dubiner, & Parrinello, 1990), and a dramatic rise in visual attention to television was found between ages 12 and 23 months (Carew, 1980). Ruff, Capozzoli, and Weissberg (1998) argued that attention during television viewing changes most in the period from 30 to 42 months. According to Anderson et al. (1986), visual attention increases sharply in the years from 1 to 5 and then slowly through later childhood. After age 3, they say, individual differences become more prominent than age differences.

If we were to single out the most important benefit of growing up in terms of attention, that would be the development of attentional strategies, which is driven by two factors. On the one hand, television is a dual-modality medium that requires parallel processing. The efficiency of learning from television depends on the development of skills and strategies for distributing attentional resources between the two channels that convey information simultaneously. On the other hand, television competes for children's attention with all sorts of visual and auditory distractions and attractions from the environment. Thus, children are constantly making choices what to attend to. According to Anderson, Field, Collins, Lorch, and Nathan (1985), children spend about a third of their time with TV not looking at television. Allen (1965) found that children 1 to 10 years old averaged 52.0% visual attention to TV, and those 11 to 19 averaged 68.8% (whereas adults averaged 63.5%). This situation poses the problem of children's effective monitoring of the television program while they are engaged in parallel activities.

Monitoring skills and strategies develop with age (Baer, 1997) and are made possible by neurological changes (Thatcher, 1994) that make the right-hemisphere vigilance system more available (Posner & Petersen, 1990; Ruff & Rothbart, 1996). According to Pingree

(1986), children as young as 3 monitor the television audio track even when they are looking elsewhere and can shift their attention back to the screen when an auditory cue suggests that something significant is occurring. Baer (1997; Baer & Lorch, 1990) found that children ages 7 to 10 tended to look at television when it was most necessary to do so to build a coherent story representation, and they recalled auditory information most when it was story relevant. Field and Anderson (1985) found that the correlation between learning from the auditory channel and learning from the visual channel diminished with age (between 5 and 9 years), which indicated increasingly independent processing in the two channels.

As children grow older and improve their monitoring of television, they appear to deploy their attention more sparingly and to target it more and more as a function of personal relevance of the television material. The use of the audio track seems to specialize with age for monitoring lower-interest programming, which is processed schematically. Cues of personal relevance shift attention from the auditory channel used for monitoring to the video track and switch processing from schematic to central. Relevance cues gain more weight with age and overpower the sensory features of the television material as attention getters.

### *Schema Development*

Under Chaiken's (1980) heuristic-systematic processing model, by default, individuals use heuristics to minimize cognitive effort. In the case of television viewing, especially under heavy cognitive load (due to program complexity at the formal and/or semantic levels), the use of schemata facilitates the selection and processing of information. When children are engaged in parallel activities, one of which is television watching, schemata are crucial filters for monitoring (minimally processing) the information related to secondary activities. Such monitoring makes possible a flexible allocation of attention among activities depending on comparative levels of salience at each particular moment.

The most useful schemata for processing television content are generally believed to be the story schemata, defined as "memory structures which consist of clusters of knowledge about stories and how they are typically structured and the ability to use this knowledge in processing stories" (Meadowcroft, 1985, p. 7). Children with a good grasp of story schemata exhibit reduced processing effort, increased memory of central story content, increased efficiency in the deployment of cognitive resources, and greater flexibility of capacity allocation to program content (Meadowcroft, 1985).

Variance in knowledge of story grammar was found mostly among very young children from about 2 to 5 years of age (e.g., Applebee, 1977). Story schemata appear to be well mastered after age 7 (at the Piagetian stage of concrete operations). Preschoolers at the preoperational stage of development (ages 2 to 6-7 years) are able to use story schemata only when the content is simply structured and causal linkages are clearly stated (Mandler & Johnson, 1977). This means that the use of schemata stored in long-term memory depends on the schematization level of the material to be processed. This interaction will be discussed in connection with programming features relevant to vigilance.

Another type of schemata useful for processing television content is that related to television practices, formats, and techniques. As persistently suggested and demonstrated by Dorothy and Jerome Singer (e.g., Singer, Singer, & Zuckerman, 1981; Singer, Zuckerman, & Singer, 1980), educating children about television-related schemata benefits comprehension of programming. In addition, once children habituate to television techniques, their attention to visual and sound effects may diminish, leaving more processing capacity available for content.

Both story schemata and television-related schemata function as frameworks for encoding, storage, and retrieval processes. Their relevance to our discussion of vigilance comes from the fact that they influence both what television material is attended to and the amount of effort allocated for that material. An immature selection style is characterized by the allocation of attention to stimuli with highly salient features, such as movement, and shows little evidence of habituation (e.g., Fishbein, 1976; Gibson & Rader, 1979). Mature attention styles are more flexible and are guided by the individual's knowledge and goals. Development is assumed to be in the direction of increased control, flexibility, and efficiency of attention deployment (i.e., less attentional effort for comprehending and learning). Skills associated with the execution of mature selection styles develop throughout childhood, with a dramatic progress between 6 and 8 years (e.g., Brown & French, 1976; Collins, Wellman, Keniston, & Westby, 1978; Dent & Thorndyke, 1979).

As far as children's strategic behavior is concerned, educators may help by promoting metacognition, that is, "awareness of what skills, strategies, and resources are needed to perform a task effectively and the ability to use self-regulatory mechanisms to ensure successful completion of the task" (Schindler, 1986). According to Flavell (1979; Flavell & Wellman, 1977), three categories of metacognitive knowledge may help children become better learners: knowledge about their own enduring characteristics, especially their potential to engage in certain tasks; knowledge about the purposes, scopes, and requirements of the task; and knowledge of strategies relevant to the task. If we consider vigilance during television watching from a metacognitive perspective, a child's attentional self-regulation would involve awareness of his or her ability to sustain attention to television, assessment of how much attention is needed to understand a program (and eventually to learn from it), and the use of skills and strategies for maintaining attention.

A metacognitive-training question is how to enhance these three categories of knowledge in early childhood. Within the Piagetian framework, operations with abstractions such as "attention" are unlikely before school age. Instructions such as "Pay attention" must be made more specific (e.g., "Look there") in order to get young children to act on them. Most frequently in early childhood, attention to television is simply elicited and automatically sustained by the flow of stimuli in conjunction with children's comprehension of content and format. Young viewers pay attention to television until they get distracted by other stimuli. Deliberate, conscious self-monitorization of attention is unlikely because self-perception in parallel with stimulus perception would be too complex for young children's cognitive capacity. On the other hand, children's television typically is a recreational medium. Its content is neither hard nor compelling enough to require self-monitorization and strategic resource deployment. Consequently, attention allocation is spontaneously made.

The main trigger of preschoolers' attention to television is stimulus salience (due to formal features and personal relevance). Stimuli guide and sustain attention. But two more factors are also involved: broad assessments of medium difficulty and program difficulty. According to Salomon (1983b, 1984), cumulative watching of television results in an overall perception of how "hard" or "easy" television is when compared with other media, as well as particular perceptions about how difficult the programs they watch are. These perceptions gauge the allocation of attentional and processing resources. Hard versus easy assessments are also a component of program preferences. A *hard* label is bad to the extent that it reduces chances that a child attends to a program. But if expected gains exceed expected processing costs and the child chooses to attend, the same label becomes good because it causes more cognitive resources to be allocated during watching, which results in better understanding and learning.

Once perception of difficulty was acknowledged as a significant factor of attention to television, educators were called on to enhance children's metacognition by teaching them story schemata and television conventions and techniques. That required more participation and effort from parents and teachers. The task involved directing children's attention to story patterns and television practices and tricks and providing explanations. The goal was to initially increase vigilance to schemata, gradually habituate children to conventions, and ultimately enable them to use those schemata for more efficient processing of the television fare. This kind of metacognitive support is easy for educators, who can provide on-line commentary and eventually recapitulate or rehearse the new information at the end of the viewing session and/or link new information items from session to session.

What has not been addressed so far as an educational objective is children's metacognition in terms of awareness of personal ability to follow and understand television programming. The reason may be that facilitating this kind of metacognition is more difficult. It would involve more structuring of children's experience with television by manipulating the level of program difficulty as well as the type and level of distraction. The participative role of educators from this perspective would be to coach children for assessing what they have understood and what they have missed and why. Repeated exposure with increased attention (mandated/directed vigilance and/or decreased distraction) would help children become aware of the benefits of sustained attention and the attentional strategies that are available. This kind of metacognitive support requires much more effort from educators, who are supposed to choose videotapes or tape television programs and organize viewing sessions around teaching objectives (e.g., understanding how much external distractors obstruct comprehension and memory or how much focusing attention and repeating the exposure help comprehension).

In light of these metacognitive considerations, future research may address such questions as the following: Do children start to benefit from the two types of metacognitive support (i.e., enrichment of story and television schemata and assessment of own processing ability) at different ages? Do the two types of support affect children's attention to and learning from educational programs differently?

### *Programming-Related Factors*

Many concerns have been expressed about the limitations imposed by television as a medium on the processing of its content. For example, McLuhan (1964, 1978) claimed that the low resolution of the TV picture required a constant reflexive perceptual closure response on the part of the viewer, which accounted for the paradoxical passive involvement of TV viewers. Salomon (1983a, 1983b, 1984) proposed that television is perceived as easier to process than other media and consequently is processed more superficially, with the effect of poorer learning.

As technology advances toward higher fidelity of image and sound, thus reducing the sensory gap between real life and television content, concerns shift away from the peculiarities of television as a carrier technology and focus on the real(istic)-unreal(istic) distinction at the level of programming. This has become a critical issue because the blurring line between reality and fantasy on television may cause children to develop a distorted image of reality. On the other hand, the interest in medium effects migrated from television (one-way) communication to computer-mediated communication, which is interactive (e.g., e-mail, bulletin boards). So, current television-effects research is mostly devoted to programming-effects and research on effects of programming features is proliferating.

From a vigilance perspective, both formal features and content features of television programming can be discussed as facilitators or inhibitors of attention. Traditionally, emphasis on form and exploitation of attention-getting production techniques was criticized for diverting children's attention away from content and jeopardizing the educational potential of television.

*Formal Features of Programming*

The potential of formal features to affect vigilance is related to humans' orienting response to changes and unusualness in the environment. According to Berlyne (1960), such properties as intensity, contrast, change, movement, novelty, and incongruity make stimuli perceptually salient, that is, alerting.

In a situation of low-vigilance television watching, associated with low interest in content, systematic manipulation at the formal level may help increase nonspecific alertness and thus improve program processing. But the effectiveness of this strategy is theoretically related to processing capacity—that is, it depends on the density and number of simultaneous manipulations. Under low interest in content, the orienting response prevails over the semantic processing of content, and if the viewer is bombarded with peripheral stimuli, their processing may take up most or all cognitive resources, worsening instead of improving attention to content.

Under high interest in the program, the orienting responses triggered by formal-feature manipulations compete for resources with the ongoing semantic processing. Strong formal stimuli may diminish or disrupt the processing of content. Theoretically, as long as peripheral stimulation through formal features does not push a child anywhere close to the upper limit of his or her processing capacity, it can be expected to increase arousal and thus benefit the processing of content. This is likely to happen at medium levels of intensity and density of formal stimuli.

The possibilities of manipulating visual and auditory material have been inflated by progress in film production technology, and combinations of such manipulations are now practically infinite. Contrast and atypicality can apply to visuals in terms of luminosity, color, shape, contour sharpness, and movement and to voices, noises, and music in terms of sound volume and quality. Another attention-arresting possibility is that of atypicality in pairing visuals with auditory signals, such as having a mailbox talk when opened or flowers produce music when moved by the wind.

An essential element of change is pace, or scene change, which automatically triggers the orienting response. Research confirms that pace tends to enhance attention, but only for younger children, who are more perceptually oriented and therefore more attentive to salient formal features than to reflective features of content (Campbell, Wright, & Huston, 1987; Greer et al., 1982; Huston & Wright, 1983; Huston et al., 1981; Huston-Stein & Wright, 1979; Wright & Huston, 1981). Moreover, pace improves younger children's vigilance only to less schematically organized magazine programs (Wright et al., 1984). Some studies failed to find a consistent influence of pace on attention (e.g., Anderson & Levin, 1976), probably because scene change is often associated with other salient formal features such as fades, dissolves, zooms, or pans, or by auditory features such as music, sound effects, or speech (Wright et al., 1984), all of which have confounding effects.

When high pace is coupled with high density of salient formal features, young children's attentional capacity is overburdened and semantic processing of content is reduced, particularly under conditions of poor schematization of content. Singer (1980) suggested that sensory bombardment may leave young viewers with no time to think about what they are being presented and thus undermines rehearsal and storage of information. Research conducted by Singer and Singer (1998) on children's learning from *Barney & Friends* accounted for the educational effectiveness of the program in terms of clear explanation of procedures and attitudes being taught "at a pace children can grasp" (pp. 363-364). The researchers suggested that "we need a new type of aesthetic in video cinematography . . . geared to the cognitive level of the viewing audience" (p. 364).

As children get older, they attend increasingly to reflective features (Calvert, Huston, Watkins, & Wright, 1982; Wartella & Ettema, 1974). Also, habituation to formal manipulations in television makes them orient less to visual and auditory effects, and knowledge schematization helps them to use their processing capacity more efficiently and strategically. Consequently, older children's attention to and learning from television are less likely to be impaired by manipulation of formal-feature salience.

The notion that fast-paced programming is detrimental to vigilance was challenged by Zillmann (1982; Zillmann, Williams, Bryant, Boynton, & Wolf, 1980), who argued that the "rapid fire" presentation in educational television tends to produce cortical arousal and therefore should be expected to create alertness at least for short periods of time, especially in children with little motivation to pay close attention and learn from exposition.

The two positions may be reconciled by considering the likelihood of beneficial effects (through arousal) of moderately fast-paced programming and the pernicious effects (due to limited processing capacity) of exceedingly fast-paced programming. Consequently, producers may consider testing programs in order to reach the optimal pace. For entertainment, arousal benefits of rapid-fire presentation may prevail, but for educational purposes, information load should be the primary concern.

### *Content Features of Programming*

The effects of content-related factors on attention to and learning from television are much more complicated and are often compounded by formal-feature variability, either spontaneous or manipulated. From a content perspective, vigilance can be regarded as alertness, primarily to stimuli that carry threat information and secondarily to those carrying opportunity information. Cues of enjoyment may be considered opportunity indicators. A third possibility is vigilance driven by the individual's long-term, transitory, or momentary interests. Stimuli belonging to the three categories may simultaneously come from television and children's viewing environments. They compete for children's attention with other stimuli that have no meaning but still elicit orienting responses as mere change phenomena. In addition, alternatively or simultaneously, children's attention may be inwardly directed to physiological information and/or their own thoughts. Cases of exclusive attention to television content are rare.

We limit our discussion in this chapter to three major issues. One is the role of emotionally negative and positive information in the orienting response. Another issue is arousal as a factor of vigilance to content cues and of learning. The third aspect is content difficulty as a factor of attention and learning.

*Emotionally Negative and Positive Content.* Attention to television content is most likely to be automatically engaged by threatening content. Children's programming that contains threatening material belongs to the dangerous-action and fear-appeal categories. Occasionally, news, history, and science programs also include threatening stimuli and cause automatic deployment of attention.

According to the Pollyanna principle (Matlin & Stang, 1978), people tend to view desirable events as common, frequent, and typical, and undesirable events as uncommon, infrequent, and atypical. Consequently, the information value of undesirable traits is higher (Pratto & John, 1991). Shoemaker (1996) interpreted this statistical bias as an outcome of natural selection for survival. She argued that humans are "hardwired" for bad news, they scan the environment for danger more than for opportunities, and they allocate cognitive resources preferentially to negative information. The outcome of this asymmetry in information processing is a higher accessibility of negative information stored in long-term memory, regardless of stimulus base rate (Pratto & John, 1991). This phenomenon indicates a close association between attention, judgment, and memory during automatic, non-goal-directed information-processing purposes. From this theoretical perspective, the claims that television watching tends to be a mindless activity (e.g., Mander, 1978; Winn, 1977) appear to be misguided.

The potential of children's programming to attract automatic attention increases with the amount of "negative" information related to threats and dangers. The strength of negative stimuli as vigilance triggers depends directly on the intensity of their perceptual features and inversely on their base rate. The problems with the intensity of negative stimuli frequently presented on television are viewer habituation and desensitization, which reduce children's capacity to react to real-life dangers. Producers of educational programming may exploit the natural advantage of threat or fear-based messages in eliciting vigilance and use them to stimulate deployment of cognitive resources to subsequently presented methods for dealing with critical or dangerous situations, thus facilitating learning. But producers must keep in mind that the more threat and danger are shown on television in general, the less effective each instance will be in eliciting arousal and attention. This is one more example of the classical tragedy of the commons, in which individual users of a common good (in this case, the arousing potential of fear stimuli) make excessive use of that good and deplete the resource.

In the psychology literature devoted to coping behavior, vigilance is often used to designate an "intensified intake and processing of threatening information" (Khrone, Hock, & Kohlmann, 1992, p. 73). In this sense, it is opposed to cognitive avoidance, which means turning away from threat-related cues. According to Khrone's (1978) model of attention allocation in threatening situations, the first phase involves attention for the purpose of identifying threat-related cues, and, in the second phase, attention is directed toward or away from such stimuli. The direction is dictated, respectively, by either intolerance of uncertainty and the need to learn more about the danger or intolerance of emotional (somatic) arousal and the need to block processing of threatening information. These theoretical possibilities indicate that vigilance to programming, including negative stimuli, depends on producers' ability to enhance uncertainty and the need for information without exceeding a bearable level of arousal. Their target needs to be curiosity rather than extreme emotionality.

The role of emotionally positive stimuli as attention getters is also important. According to the feature/signal hypothesis (Huston & Wright, 1983), children learn quite early the regular and consistent associations between formal features and content. That knowledge makes their choices more dependent on formal features than educators would like. We must admit that learning is work and what children are after is enjoyment, not effort. Stimulating curiosity, the spontaneous need to know, is probably the best way to promote learning from television. But cues of newness and direct relevance to children may not suffice to elicit attention when competing with enjoyment cues. Therefore, producers of educational programs understandably favor enjoyment cues over curiosity enticers. But an exaggeration in this direction, especially in the absence of curiosity-eliciting stimuli, conveys the wrong message that the program is pure entertainment, and, according to Salomon's (1981, 1983a, 1983b, 1984) theory of mental effort, children will pay superficial attention to it and will learn less than from nonentertaining material.

Research until the 1980s examined a large diversity of program features that convey the promise of enjoyment. Experiments were not concerned with the systematicity of the stimuli being tested as much as with their common function and strength as attention getters and cues for children. This explains why formal and content features were often thrown in together (e.g., animation, second-person address, character-voice narration, and sprightly music; Campbell et al., 1987). But research became increasingly sophisticated in terms of stimuli comparison and classification and goals. The pragmatic interest in effects began to be replaced by a theoretical interest in explaining the development of cues as stable associations between formal features and content. A study by Ruff and colleagues (1990) found that infants as young as 5 months repeatedly exposed to puppet events came to have expectations in connection with salient formal features such as variety of puppets, volume and animation of sound, light brightness, and degree of movement, and they began to attend to the place of occurrence at times of nonoccurrence. This phenomenon indicates that the development of interest, presumably based on increased arousal and enjoyment associated with the puppet events, motivated the infants to be vigilant.

In addition to formal features promising enjoyment (e.g., lively music, cheerful voices), the content itself may enhance vigilance through semantically entertaining features such as humor. Research by Zillmann et al. (1980) with preschoolers and first graders showed that, although initial attention to nonhumorous and humorous programs did not differ, humor prevented vigilance decrement associated with nonhumorous material and produced superior information acquisition. Zillmann and Bryant (1983) found that nonvivid humor facilitated attention and learning only minimally with younger children but considerably with older children. On the other hand, vivid humor had strong facilitatory effects with all children. Extremely funny humor, however, may engage and preoccupy children to a degree that nullifies the positive effect of increased vigilance (Schramm, 1972; Zillmann & Bryant, 1983). More sophisticated forms of humor such as irony, which contains distortions and contradictions that are not readily recognizable, tend to be counterproductive for learning (Cantor & Reilly, 1979; McGhee, 1979) because they produce confusion. Comprehension and enjoyment of distorting humor become possible only at the formal operational level of cognitive development—that is, in early adolescence (Helmers, 1965; McGhee, 1979). Producers of educational programming need to consider not only age appropriateness of various forms of humor but also complexity and intensity that may challenge viewers' processing capacity and jeopardize learning.

*Arousing Content.* The arousal model of vigilance (Davies & Parasuraman, 1982; Dember & Warm, 1979; Frankmann & Adams, 1962; Loeb & Alluisi, 1984; Parasuraman, 1984) predicts attention decrement through habituation (Mackworth, 1968, 1969) caused by repetitive, monotonous stimuli presented at a slow pace. According to Posner (1978), stimulus repetition creates pathway inhibition; that is, it decreases responsiveness to that stimulus and reduces the ability of the stimulus to elicit central processing. This implies that low vigilance is associated with peripheral, nonsystematic processing, which is consistently claimed to be a major problem for children's learning from television.

To be able to sustain central processing, television programming needs to be semantically salient or interesting. As already mentioned, this can be achieved through information that is novel and relevant to child viewers and is delivered at a conformably fast pace. Also as mentioned earlier, neural responsiveness can be maintained through quantitative and qualitative changes in the pattern of stimulation (Sharpless & Jasper, 1956). In semantic terms, this involves a wide range of themes and frequent thematic change. Diversity and sustained pace enhance arousal but at the same time increase program complexity. This raises the question of how much material can be retained and how well.

In his review of the relationship between arousal and retention, Anderson (1995) mentioned Levonian's (1972) findings that arousal diminished encoding but enhanced memory of information encoded in a high arousal state. A comprehensive body of research in the 1960s and early 1970s (Kleinsmith & Kaplan, 1963, 1964; Levonian, 1967, 1968, 1972) indicated that a low level of arousal—like that observed during much of children's television watching—is conducive to poor short-term memory but good long-term memory, whereas high arousal serves short-term memory better (Crane, Dieker, & Brown, 1970). One implication of these findings is that little arousing educational television helps children acquire a larger amount of information that they hold in their memory for a longer time. Another implication is that information retained from highly arousing programming may be less complete but is more accessible in short-term memory. So, producers who consider using arousing contexts are faced with a trade-off between the quantity and the quality of the information that can be retained. They also need to take into account a serious risk associated with the use of fear and violence as means of enhancing arousal and attention: Children are likely to forget the contingent circumstances and to recall and rehearse only the fear and/or aggression. Over time, television that arouses through violence may build up an inventory of negative feelings and aggressive behavior schemata, which may vitiate the psychological and social climate of a whole generation of viewers. Such harmful overall side effects may outweigh any positive main effects in terms of curriculum learning.

*Perceived Difficulty of Content.* The most intricate aspect of vigilance is its relationship to content difficulty. Research findings support the hypothesis of a curvilinear relationship between content difficulty and attention, with attention being greatest at intermediate levels of difficulty (Anderson & Lorch, 1983; Campbell et al., 1987; Rice, Huston, & Wright, 1982). Very easy and familiar content tends to receive low attention because it has become redundant and predictable, therefore useless and unexciting. Vigilance decrement in this case is accountable for through low arousal. Very difficult content also tends to depress attention because the child is poorly equipped with the schemata or other cognitive structures needed for processing the material. Vigilance decrement in this case can be accounted for through low comprehension. At moderate levels of difficulty, attention and learning (comprehension and recall) are highest (Campbell et al., 1987) because novelty arouses interest and prior knowledge provides the framework for assimilating the new information.

Programming difficulty has been operationalized in terms of objective features of the television material (e.g., information quantity/density, pace, order/structure/schematization) or viewers' subjective evaluations of the material (e.g., predictability, discriminability/salience, comprehensibility). We focus our discussion on the latter category, with incidental references to the objective factors.

Vigilance described as expectation of certain stimuli involves the notion of predictability. Higher levels of uncertainty about the occurrence and schedule of critical signals result in lower vigilance (Lanzetta, 1986) and a more conservative response performance (Baddley & Colquhoun, 1969; Colquhoun, 1961). The expectancy theory predicates expectations about the temporal distribution of critical signals on their previous occurrence (Baker, 1963; Deese, 1955). In programming terms, a relatively stable pattern of occurrence of the stimuli to be attended can be expected to improve alertness to them.

Vigilance can also be regarded as a discrimination exercise in which critical signals occur against and have to be distinguished from a background of regularly occurring neutral events. The distinction is made along certain specified dimensions (Lanzetta, 1986). Vigilance can be enhanced by increasing the discriminability of critical signals (Adams, 1956; Thurmond, Binford, & Loeb, 1970; Warm, Loeb, & Alluisi, 1970; Wiener, 1964). In the case of television programming, that can be achieved by increasing contrasts between the stimuli of interest and the neutral material. Another possibility would be to educate viewers about distinctive features that are not salient enough, which may happen more often at the level of meaning than at the level of form. The formal features that pose problems for children's attentional response, comprehension, and learning are probably the make-believe artifacts used in television. The more educated the children are about such features, the more adequately they deploy their attention.

According to Lanzetta (1986), vigilance may involve comparative judgment—that is, simultaneous discrimination among co-occurring stimuli (e.g., identifying the needed tool among other tools in a tool box)—or absolute judgment—that is, successive discrimination between currently perceived stimuli and information present in memory (e.g., thinking what tool would be appropriate for a specific task and who might have it and be willing to lend it). Most viewing situations involve vigilance to several stimuli and simultaneous use of both types of judgments. This may raise demands on cognitive resources to critical levels and may thus entail vigilance decrement (Davies & Parasuraman, 1982; Parasuraman, 1979). Producers should be aware of this danger and keep the density of simultaneous stimuli low, especially when the learning task requires absolute judgment.

One challenge to discrimination is high similarity between target and background stimuli. According to Posner (1978), such situations involve processing of both types of stimuli in more or less the same pathways, and that jeopardizes the ability to react to the target. For example, it is harder to distinguish a turquoise pencil from blue or green pencils than from red or yellow ones.

Another threat to discriminability is the repetition of background neutral events, which habituates the nonspecific alpha block and thus increases neural noise (Mackworth, 1968, 1969). Vigilance capacity is unnecessarily dispersed between target and background stimuli, and the response to the target becomes less effective. For instance, if the purpose of a program is to teach turquoise and the color samples presented to children to choose from repeat purple more often than turquoise, the viewers tend to forget about turquoise and develop vigilance for purple. This phenomenon can be aggravated by a high rate (fast pace) of background events (Metzger, Warm, & Senter, 1974) that some authors believe to be a prepotent psychophysical factor in sustained attention (Bowers, 1983; Dember & Warm, 1979; Mackworth, 1968, 1969; Warm & Berch, 1984; Warm & Jerison, 1984). In our example, the faster the succession of color samples that include purple more often than turquoise, the faster the extinction of vigilance for turquoise and the emergence of vigilance for purple.

As a general conclusion to discriminability, attentional capacity can be concentrated on central elements of programming by reducing the density and pace of noncentral stimuli, as well as reducing their similarity to central stimuli. If we want to teach turquoise, we must show it together with few and sharply contrasting colors, in a slow to moderately paced succession of color samples in which turquoise is consistently repeated and the other colors are never or rarely repeated.

A third subjective factor of content difficulty is comprehensibility. According to the cognitive involvement model (Anderson et al., 1981; Lorch, Anderson, & Levin, 1979), perceived comprehensibility of the content facilitates attention. Wright et al. (1984) found that comprehensibility predicts attention more than attention predicts comprehensibility. This means that content comprehension is more critical to attention than vigilance is to comprehension and learning.

Comprehensibility as a function of knowledge, which develops with age, poses different vigilance problems for different age groups. Older children have more knowledge that they can use as a framework for processing new information, so they understand novel things faster and better. Younger children are more dependent on formal features of content, and their vigilance depends to a large extent on sensory feature recognizability.

Comprehensibility as a function of content may involve a wide range of variables. First, if we try to convey a large amount of information at the same time, alertness to myriad targets will result in missing many of them and/or attending little to any one of them. Reduced processing of each information item will diminish comprehension. So, if better learning is the ultimate goal, simultaneously presenting fewer things should be more effective. Second, redundancy between the video and the audio tracks, order, coherence, and schematization of content make a program look more comprehensible, reduce cognitive costs, and eliminate the waste of cognitive resources. Structure injected into programs guides attention and facilitates processing. For example, stories were found to receive more attention than magazine programs (which have less structured information), and attention and comprehension were found to covary with one another more in animated (structured) than in live (less structured) shows (Wright et al., 1984). But, on the other hand, too complex structures may require too much effort for grasping components and their links, which diminishes resources available for schema instantiation (i.e., matching the incoming information to known schemata). For example, if we see three children running after a soccer ball, we immediately assume they are playing soccer. But if we see 6 children swimming in a pool toward a floating ball while 10 others are standing on the pool border, we are not sure whether the swimmers are trying to rescue the ball for the 10 children who are waiting or the 6 are playing polo while the 10 are watching. We need to keep monitoring the scene, collect more information, and analyze details such as children's clothing and attitudes before we can decide.

The effectiveness of content schematization in enhancing comprehensibility depends on the viewers' level of schema development. Wright et al. (1984) noticed that the covariance between attention and comprehension was highest with older children (who have stronger schema skills) exposed to animated (structured) programming.

An experiment conducted by Meadowcroft (1985) on children ages 5 to 8 examined the independent and combined effects of these two factors on attention and learning. She found that, in general, children with more developed schemata allocated less attention (had higher efficiency) than children with poor schema development. All children allocated more capacity to central content than to incidental content. Children with more developed schemata paid more attention to central content when the material presented to them was structured as a story (the attention to incidental content was not different between story and nonstory). Children with poor schema development allocated more attention to nonstructured material and were less efficient in processing the story (structured material). In the case of children with poor schema development, the levels of attention to central and incidental content were not affected by the presence or absence of a story schema.

Meadowcroft's results indicate that the patterns of relations among variables are complex and often paradoxical (e.g., comprehensibility may engage viewers and sustain their attention, but it may also decrease the need for attending to the material). And the more variables are examined in combination, the worse the theoretical confusion. For example, the influence of pace on vigilance can be expected under an arousal hypothesis to benefit attention deployment and under a comprehensibility hypothesis to burden children's processing and reduce attention (Wright et al., 1984). Opposite predictions and inconsistent empirical data that support both hypotheses threaten to void the theories of explanatory power. More systematic research is needed to overcome the dilemmas and explicate nonlinear relationships. As we have already suggested, in the case of pace, the arousal hypothesis may be more applicable up to a certain event rate, beyond which the limited-capacity model governs the process. It is possible that, within a certain pace range, both arousal and limited-capacity effects occur and cancel each other. That may explain complaints in literature that findings about pace effects are inconclusive (e.g., Anderson & Levin, 1976; Wright et al., 1984).

The pace issue is not trivial for producers in the context of recent findings that private television has fast-paced shorter events (Hooper & Chang, 1998). Visual overload caused by high event rates alters the way visual information is being processed. Visual search becomes slow and serial (Posner & Petersen, 1990), and comprehension relies more on schematic/automatic processing. If the educational goal of a program is to get children to think about, understand, and connect new things to previous knowledge, then information overload is bad. If the goal is to rehearse information and promote automation in the use of existing information, then a higher informational load paired with content schematization will serve the purpose. On the other hand, if we consider a televised message as incorporating educational information and form information, then children with developed/schematized knowledge of television and story conventions will make less effort to understand form and will have more cognitive resources available for processing educational content.

Although very serious, the problem of pace is not insoluble. A study by Tamborini and Zillmann (1985) addressed Singer and Singer's (1979) concern that pace reduces thinking and tested three methods suggested by the critics for improving format to counteract negative pace effects: curiosity-arousing questions, personalized communication style (direct address and eye contact), and pauses for thinking. The first two methods involve use of schemata that have an engaging effect. The third method is expected to eliminate the pace-related time crunch responsible for diminished thinking. Experimental results showed significant main effects of personalized communication style on attention, total learning, and verbal learning; a significant main effect of thinking time on visual learning; and a tendency of personalized style to interact with thinking time as predictors of total and visual learning. Questions without a personalized style were not found effective in eliciting attention. A surprising finding was that questions delivered using a personalized style increased eyes-off-screen. This phenomenon was interpreted as a sign of deeper thinking manifested as an attention shift from perception (vigilance) inward to thinking.

Tamborini and Zillmann's (1985) experiment once again emphasized the complex nature of the relationship between pacing and schematization as factors of vigilance. We may conclude the discussion of program-related factors of attention to and learning from television with Wright et al.'s (1984) observation that

> neither comprehensibility nor salience alone determine the nature and extent of processing. Rather, it appears that they are determined instead by a combination of schematic knowledge and strategic decision making at key points in the response to the level of processing demanded or supported by the program's format and structure. (p. 665)

### *Situational Factors*

The least apparent and frequently ignored situational variable that affects vigilance is the time of the day. The circadian rhythm has been found to influence the level of arousal. As arousal increases from morning toward evening, cognitive efficiency should be expected to increase too. Nevertheless, research findings seem to converge on a decrease of vigilance (response speed and accuracy) in the second part of the day. In general, vigilance performance was found to be best in the morning (Coyle, 1992; Dunne, Roche, & Hartley, 1990; Mathur, 1991; Rana, Rishi, & Sinha, 1996) and worst in the afternoon (Rana et al., 1996). But circadian variability of vigilance is high. One reason is that humans may be "morning types" (more vigilant in the first part of the day) or "evening types" (Akerstedt & Froberg, 1976; Horne & Ostberg, 1977). Also, an interaction between sex and time of the day as vigilance factors was documented on certain types of tasks (Baker, 1987; Christie & McBreauty, 1979; Rana et al., 1996). Girls were found to be more accurate (made fewer omission errors) than boys in the morning and early afternoon but not in the evening (Rana et al., 1996).

Variation in vigilance during the day affects memory and learning not only quantitatively but also qualitatively. Findings by

Folkard, Monk, Bradbury, and Rosenthal (1977) showed that retention of information depended on the variation of arousal levels related to time of day, as follows: Short-term memory (immediate recall) was better for information acquired in the morning (9:00 A.M.) at a time of relatively low arousal, whereas long-term memory (recall 1 week later) was better for information acquired in the afternoon (3:00 P.M.) at a time of relatively higher arousal.

These findings indicate to programmers and producers that, in general, educational material is bound to receive more attention in the morning. Matinal viewing may benefit children more in terms of instrumental knowledge for short-term use, whereas evening viewing may serve long-term memory objectives better.

If we consider stimulus type as a situational factor of vigilance, then real life, where all senses can be engaged, is a stronger attention getter than television, which uses only the visual and the auditory modalities. This, together with the opportunity for action in real life, makes the environment more engaging than the world of television. The attractiveness of television can be expected to depend on its complementarity to real life. TV presentations of realities beyond children's reach, fiction, and high levels of excitement and enjoyment can capture children's attention and retain it for a while. But young children are hyperactive, and the very limited opportunity for action and interaction that television provides dooms it to intermittent attendance, which is often a secondary activity.

The educators' question is how to integrate the pockets of TV watching in a child's life and use the medium more effectively as an educational tool. The traditional approach is to have children coview with peers and/or adults for the purpose of discussion, which makes possible the rehearsal of knowledge and its expansion by pooling and sharing coviewers' knowledge. This method helps children learn that knowledge develops through additions and changes of perspective.

Another possible approach is to create activity and interactivity situations based on the program. For example, "how to" or "let's do" tasks can be proposed to children, prompting them to use the knowledge provided by the program. The immediate applicability of knowledge made available on television is likely to enhance children's attention to and retention from the program.

If we transfer the notion of difficulty from television content to the viewing situation, the TV flow of information meanders between center and periphery in the children's attentional field. When the child is more alert to television than to other elements in the environment, nontelevision stimuli function as distractors and introduce noise that diminishes and can eventually reorient or divert attention to more compelling sources. Making television "competitive" through a high density of salient and arousing stimuli increases the risk of cognitive overload and poor attendance to educational content. A more effective strategy may be a sparing, intermittent use of salient cues to hook back viewers who have defected.

For children who watch in solitude, the situation may be understimulating, and monotonous programming may depress arousal and vigilance to levels that are insufficient to ensure systematic processing of central information. Actions in the program to counteract vigilance decrement, as, for instance, taking a pen to draw something, or having a drink, or looking up a rare and intriguing word in a dictionary, may suggest frequent simple actions in the immediate environment. For young children, lively songs to sing along with and dance to may be arousing.

From a vigilance perspective, children's learning from television seems to be, ultimately, a function of producers' ability to go beyond program design and construct viewing-acting-learning situations. Such an integrative approach will require more complex research to beat the barrier between children's real world and the virtual world of television. The emphasis in educational television research will probably shift from stimuli processing toward interaction and motivation.

## References


Adams, J. A. (1956). Vigilance in the detection of low-intensity visual stimuli. *Journal of Experimental Psychology, 52,* 204-208.

Akerstedt, T., & Froberg, J. E. (1976). Interindividual differences in circadian patterns of catecholamine excretion, body temperature, performance, and subjective arousal. *Biological Psychology, 4,* 277-292.

Allen, C. (1965). Photographing the TV audience. *Journal of Advertising Research, 14,* 2-8.

Alvarez, M. M., Huston, A. C., Wright, J. C., & Kerkman, D. D. (1988). Gender differences in visual attention to television form and content. *Journal of Applied Developmental Psychology, 9,* 459-475.

Anderson, D. R. (1983). *Young children's television viewing: The problem of cognitive continuity* (Working Paper). University of Massachusetts, Department of Psychology.

Anderson, D. R., Alwitt, L., Lorch, E., & Levin, S. (1979). Watching children watch television. In G. Hale & M. Lewis (Eds.), *Attention and cognitive development* (pp. 331-361). New York: Plenum.

Anderson, D. R., Choi, H. P., & Lorch, E. P. (1987). Attentional inertia reduces distractibility during young children's TV viewing. *Child Development, 58,* 798-806.

Anderson, D. R., Field, D., Collins, P., Lorch, E., & Nathan, J. (1985). Estimates with young children's time with television: A methodological comparison of parent reports with time-lapse video home observation. *Child Development, 56,* 1345-1357.

Anderson, D. R., & Levin, S. R. (1976). Young children's attention to "Sesame Street." *Child Development, 47,* 806-811.

Anderson, D. R., & Lorch, E. P. (1983). Looking at television: Action or reaction? In J. Bryant & D. R. Anderson (Eds.), *Children's understanding of television: Research on attention and comprehension* (pp. 1-34). New York: Academic Press.

Anderson, D. R., Lorch, E. P., Field, D. E., Collins, P. A., & Nathan, J. G. (1986). Television viewing at home: Age trends in visual attention and time with TV. *Child Development, 57,* 1024-1033.

Anderson, D. R., Lorch, E. P., Field, D. E., & Sanders, J. (1981). The effects of TV program comprehensibility on preschool children's visual attention to television. *Child Development, 52,* 151-157.

Anderson, J. R. (1995). *Learning and memory: An integrated approach.* New York: John Wiley.

Applebee, A. N. (1977). A sense of story. *Theory Into Practice, 16,* 342-347.

Baddley, A. D., & Colquhoun, W. P. (1969). Signal probability and vigilance: A reappraisal of the "signal-rate" effect. *British Journal of Psychology, 60,* 169-178.

Baer, S. A. (1997). Strategies of children's attention to and comprehension of television (Doctoral dissertation, University of Kentucky, 1996). *Dissertation Abstracts International, 57*(11-B), 7243.

Baer, S. A., & Lorch, E. P. (1990). *Effects of importance on children's visual attention to television.* Paper presented at the biennial meeting of the Southeastern Conference on Human Development, Richmond, VA.

Baker, C. H. (1963). Signal duration as a factor in vigilance tasks. *Science, 141,* 1196-1197.

Baker, M. A. (1987). *Sex differences in human performance.* New York: John Wiley.

Bandura, A. (Ed.). (1971). *Psychological modeling: Conflicting theories.* Chicago: Aldine-Atherton.

Bandura, A. (1977). *Social learning theory.* Englewood Cliffs, NJ: Prentice Hall.

Bandura, A. (1994). Social cognitive theory of mass communication. In J. Bryant & D. Zillmann (Eds.), *Media effects: Advances in theory and research* (pp. 61-90). Hillsdale, NJ: Lawrence Erlbaum.

Bellack, D. R. (1984). An investigation of developmental differences in attention and comprehension of television (Doctoral dissertation, University of Kentucky, 1983). *Dissertation Abstracts International, 44*(7-B), 2263.

Berlyne, D. E. (1960). *Conflict, arousal, and curiosity.* New York: McGraw-Hill.

Bowers, J. C. (1983). *Stimulus homogeneity and the event rate effect in sustained attention.* Unpublished doctoral dissertation, University of Cincinnati, OH.

Brown, A. L., & French, L. A. (1976). Construction and regeneration of logical sequences using causes or consequences as the point of departure. *Child Development, 47,* 930-940.

Brown, J. S. (1961). *The motivation of behavior.* New York: McGraw-Hill.

Bryant, J., Zillmann, D., & Brown, D. (1983). Entertainment features in children's educational television: Effects on attention and information acquisition. In J. Bryant & D. R. Anderson (Eds.), *Children's understanding of television: Research on attention and comprehension* (pp. 221-240). New York: Academic Press.

Buss, A. H., & Plomin, R. (1975). *A temperament theory of personality development.* New York: John Wiley.

Calvert, S. L., Huston, A. C., Watkins, B. A., & Wright, J. C. (1982). The effects of selective attention to television forms on children's comprehension of content. *Child Development, 53,* 601-610.

Campbell, T. A., Wright, J. C., & Huston, A. C. (1987). Form cues and content difficulty as determinants of children's cognitive processing of televised educational messages. *Journal of Experimental Child Psychology, 43,* 311-327.

Cantor, J., & Reilly, S. (1979, August). *Jocular language style and relevant humor in educational messages.* Paper presented at the Second International Conference on Humor, Los Angeles.

Carew, J. (1980). Experience and the development of intelligence in young children at home and in day care. *Monographs of the Society for Research in Child Development, 45*(6-7, Serial No. 187).

Carter, J. D., & Swanson, H. L. (1995). The relationship between intelligence and vigilance in children at risk. *Journal of Abnormal Child Psychology, 23,* 201-220.

Carver, C. S., Coleman, A. E., & Glass, D. C. (1976). The coronary-prone behavior pattern and the suppression of fatigue on a treadmill test. *Journal of Personality and Social Psychology, 33,* 460-466.

Chaiken, S. (1980). Heuristic versus systematic processing and the use of source versus message cues in persuasion. *Journal of Personality and Social Psychology, 39,* 752-766.

Checcino, D. J. (1997). Relationships among personality type, self-concept, grade point average, and gender of seventh graders (Doctoral dissertation, George Mason University, 1996). *Dissertation Abstracts International, 57*(8-A), 3401.

Christie, M. J., & McBreauty, E. M. T. (1979). Psychophysiological investigations of post lunch style in male and female subjects. *Ergonomics, 22,* 307-323.

Collins, W. A., Wellman, H., Keniston, A. H., & Westby, S. D. (1978). Age-related aspects of comprehension and inference from a televised dramatic narrative. *Child Development, 49,* 389-399.

Colquhoun, W. P. (1961). The effect of "unwanted" signals on performance in a vigilance task. *Ergonomics, 4,* 42-51.

Coyle, K. (1992). Circadian variation in cognitive functioning (Doctoral dissertation, University of Wales College of Cardiff, 1989). *Dissertation Abstracts International, 51,* 1914.

Crane, L. D., Dieker, R. J., & Brown, C. T. (1970). The psychological response to the communication modes: Reading, listening, speaking, and evaluating. *Journal of Communication, 20,* 231-240.

Davies, D. R., & Parasuraman, R. (1982). *The psychology of vigilance.* London: Academic Press.

Deese, J. (1955). Some problems in the theory of vigilance. *Psychological Review, 62,* 359-368.

Dember, W. N., & Warm, J. S. (1979). *Psychology of perception* (2nd ed.). New York: Holt, Rinehart & Winston.

Dent, C., & Thorndyke, P. W. (1979). *The use of schemata in children's comprehension and recall of narrative texts.* Santa Monica, CA: RAND.

Duffy, E. (1962). *Activation and behavior.* New York: John Wiley.

Dunne, M. P., Roche, F., & Hartley, L. R. (1990). Effects of time of day on immediate recall and sustained retrieval from semantic memory. *Journal of General Psychology, 117,* 403-410.

Easterbrook, J. A. (1959). The effect of emotion on cue utilization and the organization of behavior. *Psychological Review, 66,* 183-201.

Eysenck, H. J. (1983). Is there a paradigm in personality research? *Journal of Research in Personality, 17,* 369-397.

Eysenck, M. W. (1982). *Attention and arousal.* Berlin: Springer.

Eysenck, M. W. (1988). Individual differences, arousal, and monotonous work. In J. P. Leonard (Ed.), *Vigilance: Methods, models, and regulation* (pp. 111-118). Frankfurt, Germany: Peter Lang.

Eysenck, M. W. (1989). Individual differences in vigilance performance. In A. Coblentz (Ed.), *Vigilance and performance in automatized systems* (pp. 31-40). Dordrecht, The Netherlands: Kluwer.

Field, D. E., & Anderson, D. R. (1985). Instruction and modality effects on children's television attention and comprehension. *Journal of Educational Psychology, 77,* 91-100.

Fishbein, H. D. (1976). *Evolution, development, and children's learning.* Pacific Palisades, CA: Goodyear.

Flavell, J. H. (1979). Metacognition and cognitive monitoring: A new era of cognitive-developmental inquiry. *American Psychologist, 34,* 906-911.

Flavell, J. H., & Wellman, H. M. (1977). Metamemory. In R. V. Kailand & J. W. Hagan (Eds.), *Perspectives on the development of memory and cognition* (pp. 3-33). Hillsdale, NJ: Lawrence Erlbaum.

Folkard, S., Monk, T. H., Bradbury, R., & Rosenthal, J. (1977). Time of day effects in schoolchildren's immediate and delayed recall of meaningful material. *British Journal of Psychology, 68,* 45-50.

Frankmann, J. P., & Adams, J. A. (1962). Theories of vigilance. *Psychological Bulletin, 59,* 257-272.

Gibson, E. J., & Rader, N. (1979). The perceiver as performer. In G. A. Hale & M. Lewis (Eds.), *Attention and cognitive development* (pp. 1-21). New York: Plenum.

Golden, M., Montare, A., & Bridger, W. (1977). Verbal control of delay behavior in two-year-old boys as a function of social class. *Child Development, 48,* 1107-1111.

Greer, D., Potts, R., Wright, J. C., & Huston, A. C. (1982). The effects of television commercial form and commercial placement on children's social behavior and attention. *Child Development, 53,* 611-619.

Halpern, D. F. (1986). *Sex differences in cognitive abilities.* Hillsdale, NJ: Lawrence Erlbaum.

Hawkins, R. P., Kim, J. H., & Pingree, S. (1991). The ups and downs of attention to television. *Communication Research, 18,* 53-76.

Helmers, H. (1965). *Sprache und Humor des Kindes* [Children's speech and humor]. Stuttgart, Germany: Ernst Klett.

Hooper, M. -L., & Chang, P. (1998). Comparison of demands of sustained attentional events between public and private children's television programs. *Perceptual and Motor Skills, 86,* 431-434.

Horne, J. A., & Ostberg, O. (1977). Individual differences in human circadian rhythms. *Biological Psychology, 5,* 179-190.

Hull, C. L. (1943). *Principles of behavior: An introduction to behavior theory.* New York: Appleton-Century-Crofts.

Hull, C. L. (1952). *A behavior system: An introduction to behavior theory concerning the individual organism.* New York: John Wiley.

Huston, A. C., Greer, D., Wright, J. C., Welch, R., & Ross, R. (1984). Children's comprehension of televised formal features with masculine and feminine connotations. *Developmental Psychology, 20,* 707-716.

Huston, A. C., & Wright, J. C. (1983). Children's processing of television: The informative function of formal features. In J. Bryant & D. R. Anderson (Eds.), *Children's understanding of television: Research on attention and comprehension* (pp. 35-68). New York: Academic Press.

Huston, A. C., Wright, J. C., Wartella, E., Rice, M. L., Watkins, B. A., Campbell, T., & Potts, R. (1981). Communicating more than content: Formal features in children's television programs. *Journal of Communication, 31*(3), 32-48.

Huston-Stein, A., Fox, S., Greer, D., Watkins, B. A., & Whitaker, J. (1981). The effects of TV action and violence on children's social behavior. *Journal of Genetic Psychology, 138,* 183-191.

Huston-Stein, A., & Wright, J. C. (1979). Children and television: Effects of the medium, its content, and its form. *Journal of Research and Development in Education, 13,* 20-31.

Ippolito, M. F. (1993). *Standards as a correlate of delay of gratification in 24-month-old children.* Unpublished master's thesis, Bowling Green State University, Bowling Green, OH.

Jennings, J. R. (1983). Attention and coronary heart disease. In D. S. Krantz, A. Baum, & J. E. Singer (Eds.), *Handbook of psychology and health* (Vol. 3, pp. 85-124). Hillsdale, NJ: Lawrence Erlbaum.

Kahneman, D. (1973). *Attention and effort.* Englewood Cliffs, NJ: Prentice Hall.

Khrone, H. W. (1978). Individual differences in coping with stress and anxiety. In C. D. Spielberger & I. G. Sarason (Eds.), *Stress and anxiety* (Vol. 5, pp. 233-260). Washington, DC: Hemisphere.

Khrone, H. W., Hock, M., & Kohlmann, C.-W. (1992). Coping dispositions, uncertainty, and emotional arousal. In K. T. Strongman (Ed.), *International review of studies on emotion* (Vol. 2, pp. 73-95). Chichester, UK: Wiley.

Kleinsmith, L. J., & Kaplan, S. (1963). Paired-associate learning as a function of arousal and interpolated activity. *Journal of Experimental Psychology, 65,* 190-193.

Kleinsmith, L. J., & Kaplan, S. (1964). Interaction of arousal and recall interval in nonsense syllable paired-associate learning. *Journal of Experimental Psychology, 67*(2), 124-126.

Krugman, H. D. (1971). Brainwave measures of media involvement. *Journal of Advertising Research, 11,* 3-9.

Lanzetta, T. M. (1986). Effects of stimulus heterogeneity and information processing load on the event rate function in sustained attention (Doctoral dissertation, University of Cincinnati, 1985). *Dissertation Abstracts International, 46*(10-B), 3623.

Lesser, G. S. (1972). Learning, teaching, and television production for children: The experience of *Sesame Street. Harvard Educational Review, 42,* 231-272.

Lesser, G. S. (1974). *Children and television: Lessons from* Sesame Street. New York: Random House.

Lesser, G. S. (1977). *Television and the preschool child.* New York: Academic Press.

Levonian, E. (1967). Retention of information in relation to arousal during continuously presented material. *American Educational Research Journal, 4*(2), 103-116.

Levonian, E. (1968). Short-term retention in relation to arousal. *Psychophysiology, 4,* 284-293.

Levonian, E. (1972). Retention over time in relation to arousal during learning: An explanation of discrepant results. *Acta Psychologica, 36,* 290-321.

Levy, F. (1980). The development of sustained attention (vigilance) and inhibition in children: Some normative data. *Journal of Child Psychology and Psychiatry, 21,* 77-84.

Lindsley, D. B. (1951). Emotion. In S. S. Stevens (Ed.), *Handbook of experimental psychology* (pp. 473-516). New York: John Wiley.

Lindsley, D. B. (1957). Psychophysiology and motivation. In M. R. Jones (Ed.), *Nebraska Symposium on Motivation* (pp. 44-105). Lincoln: University of Nebraska Press.

Loeb, M., & Alluisi, E. A. (1984). Theories of vigilance. In J. S. Warm (Ed.), *Sustained attention in human performance* (pp. 179-200). Chichester, UK: Wiley.

Lorch, E. P., Anderson, D. R., & Levin, S. R. (1979). The relationship of visual attention to children's comprehension of television. *Child Development, 50,* 722-727.

Luria, A. R. (1959). Experimental study of the higher nervous activity of the abnormal child. *Journal of Mental Deficiency Research, 3,* 1-22.

Mackworth, J. F. (1968). Vigilance, arousal, and habituation. *Psychological Review, 75,* 308-322.

Mackworth, J. F. (1969). *Vigilance and habituation.* Baltimore, MD: Penguin.

Mackworth, J. F. (1970a). *Vigilance and attention: A signal detection approach.* New York: Penguin.

Mackworth, J. F. (1970b). *Vigilance and habituation: A neuropsychological approach.* Baltimore, MD: Penguin.

Mander, J. (1978). *Four arguments for the elimination of television.* New York: Quill.

Mandler, J., & Johnson, N. (1977). Remembrance of things parsed: Story structure and recall. *Cognitive Psychology, 9,* 111-151.

Mathur, K. (1991). TOD dependent performance efficiency in student nurses. *Journal of Human Ergology, 20,* 67-75.

Matlin, M., & Stang, D. (1978). *The Pollyanna principle.* Cambridge, MA: Schenkman.

Matthews, K. A. (1978). Assessment and developmental antecedents of Pattern A behavior in children. In T. M. Dembrowski, S. M. Weiss, J. L. Shields, S. G. Haynes, & M. Feinleib (Eds.), *Coronary-prone behavior.* New York: Springer.

Matthews, K. A. (1980). Measurement of Type A behavior pattern in children: Assessment of children's competitiveness, impatience-anger, and aggression. *Child Development, 51,* 466-475.

McGhee, P. E. (1979). *Humor: Its origin and development.* San Francisco: Freeman.

McLuhan, M. (1964). *Understanding media: The extensions of man.* New York: McGraw-Hill.

McLuhan, M. (1978, April 3). A last look at the tube. *New York Times Magazine,* p. 45.

Meadowcroft, J. M. (1985). *Children's attention to television: The influence of story schema development on allocation of cognitive capacity and memory.* Unpublished doctoral dissertation, University of Wisconsin, Madison.

Metzger, K. R., Warm, J. S., & Senter, R. J. (1974). Effects of background event rate and artificial signals on vigilance performance. *Perceptual and Motor Skills, 38,* 1175-1181.

Miller, W. (1985). A view from the inside: Brainwaves and television viewing. *Journalism Quarterly, 62,* 508-514.

Mowrer, R. R., & Klein, S. B. (1989). Traditional learning theory and the transition to contemporary learning theory. In S. B. Klein & R. R. Mowrer (Eds.), *Contemporary learning theories: Pavlovian conditioning and the status of traditional learning theory* (pp. 3-17). Hillsdale, NJ: Lawrence Erlbaum.

Mulholland, T. (1974). Training visual attention. *Academic Therapy, 10,* 5-17.

Omanson, R. (1982). An analysis of narratives. *Discourse Processes, 2,* 195-224.

Parasuraman, R. (1979). Memory load and event rate control sensitivity decrements in sustained attention. *Science, 205,* 924-927.

Parasuraman, R. (1984). The psychology of sustained attention. In J. S. Warm (Ed.), *Sustained attention in human performance* (pp. 61-101). Chichester, UK: Wiley.

Parasuraman, R. (1985). Sustained attention: A multifactorial approach. In M. I. Posner & O. S. M. Marin (Eds.), *Attention and human performance* (Vol. 11, pp. 493-511). Hillsdale, NJ: Lawrence Erlbaum.

Parasuraman, R., Warm, J. S., & Dember, W. N. (1987). Vigilance: Taxonomy and utility. In L. S. Mark, J. S. Warm, & R. L. Huston (Eds.), *Ergonomics and human factors: Recent research* (pp. 11-32). New York: Springer.

Piaget, J. (1973). *The psychology of intelligence.* Totowa, NJ: Littlefield & Adams. (Original work published 1947)

Pingree, S. (1986). Children's activity and television comprehensibility. *Communication Research, 13,* 239-256.

Posner, M. I. (1978). *Chronometric explorations of the mind.* Hillsdale, NJ: Lawrence Erlbaum.

Posner, M. I., & Petersen, S. E. (1990). The attention system of the human brain. *Annual Review of Neuroscience, 13,* 25-42.

Potts, R., Huston, A. C., & Wright, J. C. (1986). The effects of television form and violent content on boys' attention and social behavior. *Journal of Experimental Child Psychology, 41,* 1-17.

Pratto, F., & John, O. P. (1991). Automatic vigilance: The attention-grabbing power of negative social information. *Journal of Personality and Social Psychology, 61,* 380-391.

Price, V. A. (1982). *Type A behavior pattern: A model for research and practice.* New York: Academic Press.

Rana, N., Rishi, P., & Sinha, S. P. (1996). Vigilance performance in children in relation to time of the day. *Psychological Studies, 41*(1-2), 10-15.

Rice, M. L., Huston, A. C., & Wright, J. C. (1982). The forms of television: Effects on children's attention, comprehension, and social behavior. In D. Pearl, L. Bouthilet, & J. Lazar (Eds.), *Television and behavior: Ten years of scientific progress and implications for the eighties* (pp. 24-38). Washington, DC: U.S. Government Printing Office.

Rolandelli, D. R. (1985). *Young children's auditory and visual processing of narrated and nonnarrated television programming.* Unpublished doctoral dissertation, University of Kansas, Lawrence.

Rolandelli, D. R., Wright, J. C., & Huston, A. C. (1982, April). *Auditory attention to television: A new methodology.* Paper presented at the biennial meeting of the Southwestern Society for Research in Human Development, Galveston, TX.

Rolandelli, D. R., Wright, J. C., & Huston, A. C. (1985, May). *Children's auditory and visual processing of narrated and nonnarrated television programming.*

Paper presented at the annual meeting of the International Communication Association, Honolulu, HI.

Routtenberg, A. (1968). The two-arousal hypothesis: Reticular formation and limbic system. *Psychological Review, 75,* 51-80.

Routtenberg, A. (1971). Stimulus processing and response execution: A neurobehavioral theory. *Psychology and Behavior, 6,* 589-596.

Ruff, H. A. (1990). Individual differences in sustained attention during infancy. In J. Colombo & J. Fagen (Eds.), *Individual differences in infancy: Reliability, stability, and prediction* (pp. 247-270). Hillsdale, NJ: Lawrence Erlbaum.

Ruff, H. A., Capozzoli, M., Dubiner, K., & Parrinello, R. (1990). A measure of vigilance in infancy. *Infant Behavior and Development, 13,* 1-20.

Ruff, H. A., Capozzoli, M., & Weissberg, R. (1998). Age, individuality, and context as factors in sustained visual attention during preschool years. *Developmental Psychology, 34,* 454-464.

Ruff, H. A., & Rothbart, M. K. (1996). *Attention in early development: Themes and variations.* New York: Oxford University Press.

Salomon, G. (1981). Introducing AIME: The assessment of children's mental involvement with television. In H. Kelly & H. Gardner (Eds.), *Viewing children through television* (pp. 89-102). San Francisco: Jossey-Bass.

Salomon, G. (1983a). The differential investment of mental effort in learning from different sources. *Educational Psychologist, 18*(1), 42-50.

Salomon, G. (1983b). Television watching and mental effort: A social psychological view. In J. Bryant & D. Anderson (Eds.), *Children's understanding of television: Research on attention and comprehension* (pp. 181-198). New York: Academic Press.

Salomon, G. (1984). Television is "easy" and print is "tough": The differential investment of mental effort in learning as a function of perceptions and attributions. *Journal of Educational Psychology, 76,* 647-658.

Schachter, S. (1964). The interaction of cognitive and physiological determinants of emotional state. In L. Berkowitz (Ed.), *Advances in experimental social psychology* (Vol. 1, pp. 49-80). New York: Academic Press.

Schindler, R. A. (1986). Hyperactive and non-hyperactive children's knowledge and use of factors affecting attention (Doctoral dissertation, Texas A&M University, 1985). *Dissertation Abstracts International, 47*(1-A), 132.

Schramm, W. (1972). What the research says. In W. Schramm (Ed.), *Quality in instructional television.* Honolulu: University Press of Hawaii.

Sharpless, S., & Jasper, H. H. (1956). Habituation of the arousal reaction. *Brain, 79,* 655-680.

Shoemaker, P. J. (1996). Hardwired for news: Using biological and cultural evolution to explain the surveillance function. *Journal of Communication, 46*(3), 32-48.

Signorielli, N., Gross, L., & Morgan, M. (1982). Violence in television programs: Ten years later. In D. Pearl, L. Bouthilet, & J. Lazar (Eds.), *Television and behavior: Ten years of scientific progress and implications for the eighties* (Vol. 2, pp. 158-173). Washington, DC: U.S. Government Printing Office.

Silverman, I. W., & Gaines, M. (1996). Using standard situations to measure attention span and persistence in toddler-aged children: Some cautions. *Journal of Genetic Psychology, 157,* 397-410.

Silverman, I. W., & Ippolito, M. F. (1995). Maternal antecedents of delay ability in young children. *Journal of Applied Developmental Psychology, 16,* 569-591.

Silverman, I. W., & Ragusa, D. M. (1990). Child and maternal correlates of impulse control in 24-month-old children. *Genetic, Social, and General Psychology Monographs, 116,* 435-473.

Singer, D. G., Singer, J. L., & Zuckerman, D. M. (1981). *Teaching television: How to use TV to your child's advantage.* New York: Dial Press.

Singer, D. G., Zuckerman, D. M., & Singer, J. L. (1980). Helping elementary children learn about TV. *Journal of Communication, 30*(3), 84-93.

Singer, J. L. (1980). The power and limitations of television: A cognitive-affective analysis. In P. Tannenbaum (Ed.), *The entertainment functions of television* (pp. 31-65). Hillsdale, NJ: Lawrence Erlbaum.

Singer, J. L., & Singer, D. G. (1979, March). Come back, Mister Rogers, come back. *Psychology Today,* pp. 56, 59-60.

Singer, J. L., & Singer, D. G. (1998). *Barney & Friends* as entertainment and education: Evaluating the quality and effectiveness of a television series for preschool children. In J. K. Asamen & G. L. Berry (Eds.), *Research paradigms, television, and social behavior* (pp. 305-367). Thousand Oaks, CA: Sage.

Spence, K. W. (1956). *Behavior theory and conditioning.* New Haven, CT: Yale University Press.

Sternbach, R. A. (1966). *Principles of psychophysiology: An introductory text and readings.* New York: Academic Press.

Sternglantz, S. H., & Serbin, L. A. (1974). Sex role stereotyping in children's television programs. *Developmental Psychology, 10,* 710-715.

Strube, M., Turner, C., Patrick, S., & Perrillo, R. (1983). Type A and Type B attentional responses to aesthetic stimuli: Effects on mood and performance. *Journal of Personality and Social Psychology, 45,* 1369-1379.

Swanson, H. L. (1989). The effects of central processing strategies on learning disabled, mildly retarded, average, and gifted children's elaborative encoding abilities. *Journal of Experimental Child Psychology, 47,* 370-397.

Swanson, H. L., & Cooney, J. B. (1989). Relationship between intelligence and vigilance in children. *Journal of School Psychology, 27,* 141-153.

Tamborini, R., & Zillmann, D. (1985). Effects of questions, personalized communication style, and pauses for reflection in children's educational programs. *Journal of Educational Research, 79*(1), 19-26.

Thatcher, R. W. (1994). Cyclic cortical reorganization: Origins of human cognitive development. In G. Dawson & K. W. Fischer (Eds.), *Human behavior and the developing brain* (pp. 232-266). New York: Guilford.

Thomas, A., Chess, S. S., & Birch, H. G. (1968). *Temperament and behavior disorders in children.* New York: New York University Press.

Thorson, E., Reeves, B., & Schleuder, J. (1985). Message complexity and attention to television. *Communication Research, 12,* 427-454.

Thurmond, J. B., Binford, J. R., & Loeb, M. (1970). Effects of signal-to-noise variability over repeated sessions in an auditory vigilance task. *Perception and Psychophysics, 7,* 100-102.

Vaughn, B. E., Kopp, C. B., & Krakow, J. B. (1984). The emergence and consolidation of self-control from eighteen to thirty months of age: Normative trends and individual differences. *Child Development, 55,* 990-1004.

Verbeke, W. (1988). Preschool children's visual attention and understanding behavior towards a visual narrative. *Communication & Cognition, 21,* 67-94.

Ward, S., & Wackman, D. B. (1973). Children's information processing of television advertising. In P. Clark (Ed.), *New models for mass communication research* (Vol. 2, pp. 119-146). Beverly Hills, CA: Sage.

Warm, J. S. (1984). An introduction to vigilance. In J. S. Warm (Ed.), *Sustained attention in human performance* (pp. 1-14). Chichester, UK: Wiley.

Warm, J. S. (1993). Vigilance and target detection. In B. M. Huey & C. D. Wickens (Eds.), *Workload transition: Implications for individual and team performance* (pp. 139-170). Washington, DC: National Research Council, National Academy Press.

Warm, J. S., & Berch, D. B. (1984). Sustained attention in the mentally retarded: The vigilance paradigm. In N. R. Ellis & N. W. Bray (Eds.), *International review of research in mental retardation* (Vol. 13, pp. 1-41). New York: Academic Press.

Warm, J. S., Dember, W. N., & Hancock, P. A. (1996). Vigilance and workload in automatic systems. In R. Parasuraman & M. Mouloua (Eds.), *Automation and human performance: Theory and applications* (pp. 183-200). Mahwah, NJ: Lawrence Erlbaum.

Warm, J. S., & Jerison, H. J. (1984). The psychophysics of vigilance. In J. S. Warm (Ed.), *Sustained attention in human performance* (pp. 15-60). New York: John Wiley.

Warm, J. S., Loeb, M., & Alluisi, E. A. (1970). Variations in watchkeeping performance as a function of the rate and duration of visual signals. *Perception and Psychophysics, 7,* 97-99.

Wartella, E., & Ettema, J. S. (1974). A cognitive developmental study of children's attention to television commercials. *Communication Research, 1,* 69-88.

Weidner, G., & Matthews, K. A. (1978). Reported physical symptoms elicited by unpredictable events and the Type A coronary prone behavior pattern. *Journal of Personality and Social Psychology, 36,* 1213-1220.

Weinberg, W. A., & Emslie, G. J. (1991). Attention deficit hyperactivity disorder: The differential diagnosis. *Journal of Child Neurology, 6* (Suppl.), S23-S36.

Weinberg, W. A., & Harper, C. R. (1993). Vigilance and its disorders. *Neurologic Clinics, 11,* 59-78.

Welch, R. L., Huston-Stein, A., Wright, J. C., & Plehal, R. (1979). Subtle sex-role cues in children's commercials. *Journal of Communication, 29*(3), 202-209.

Wiener, E. L. (1964). Transfer of training in monitoring: Signal amplitude. *Perceptual and Motor Skills, 18,* 104.

Wilder, J. (1957). The law of initial values in neurology and psychiatry: Facts and problems. *Journal of Nervous and Mental Disease, 125,* 73-86.

Williams, T. M., Baron, D., Phillips, S., Travis, L., & Jackson, D. (1986, August). *The portrayal of sex roles on Canadian and U.S. television.* Paper presented to the Working Group on Sex Roles at the Conference of the International Association for Mass Communication Research, New Delhi, India.

Winn, M. (1977). *The plug-in drug.* New York: Viking.

Wright, J. C., Calvert, S. L., Huston-Stein, A., & Watkins, B. A. (1980, May). *Children's selective attention to television forms: Effects of salient and informative production features as functions of age and viewing experience.* Paper presented at the meeting of the International Communication Association, Acapulco, Mexico.

Wright, J. C., & Huston, A. C. (1981). The forms of television: Nature and development of television literacy in children. In H. Gardner & H. Kelly (Eds.), *Viewing children through television* (pp. 73-88). San Francisco: Jossey-Bass.

Wright, J. C., Huston, A. C., Ross, R. P., Calvert, S. L., Rolandelli, D., Weeks, L. A., Raeissi, P., & Potts, R. (1984). Pace and continuity of television programs: Effects on children's attention and comprehension. *Developmental Psychology, 20,* 653-666.

Yerkes, R. M., & Dodson, J. D. (1908). The relation of strength of stimulus to rapidity of habit formation. *Journal of Comparative and Neurological Psychology, 18,* 459-482.

Zillmann, D. (1971). Excitation transfer in communication-mediated aggressive behavior. *Journal of Experimental Social Psychology, 7,* 419-434.

Zillmann, D. (1978). Attribution and misattribution of excitatory reactions. In J. H. Harvey, W. J. Ickes, & R. F. Kidds (Eds.), *New directions in attribution research* (Vol. 2, pp. 335-368). Hillsdale, NJ: Lawrence Erlbaum.

Zillmann, D. (1982). Television viewing and arousal. In D. Pearl, L. Bouthilet, & J. Lazar (Eds.), *Television and behavior: Ten years of scientific progress and implications for the eighties* (Vol. 2, pp. 53-67). Washington, DC: U.S. Government Printing Office.

Zillmann, D., & Bryant, J. (1983). Uses and effects of humor in educational ventures. In P. E. McGhee & J. H. Goldstein (Eds.), *Handbook of humor research: Vol. 2. Applied studies* (pp. 173-193). New York: Springer-Verlag.

Zillmann, D., Williams, B. R., Bryant, J., Boynton, K. R., & Wolf, M. A. (1980). Acquisition of information from educational television programs as a function of differently paced humorous inserts. *Journal of Educational Psychology, 72,* 170-180.

CHAPTER 9

# Prosocial Effects on Children's Social Interactions

MARIE-LOUISE MARES
EMORY H. WOODARD
University of Pennsylvania

## Prosocial Effects of Television

Over the years, public and scholarly attention has focused on the accumulation of evidence that television contributes to violence and hostility. The possibility that television viewing may also foster friendly, prosocial interactions has received less attention. The aim of this chapter is to discuss the weight of evidence that viewing can have positive effects on children's social encounters and to review the conditions under which such effects are strongest.

As we have argued elsewhere (Mares & Woodard, in press), there is no inherent reason why television viewing should have only negative effects. After all, most negative effects of viewing are explained by two basic mechanisms. One is that we learn by observation how to do things and whether it is appropriate to do them. The second is that we have emotional responses while watching television that affect our responses to similar real-world events. As Rushton (1979) pointed out, both of these mechanisms are relevant to the viewing of prosocial material as well. In fact, Rushton suggested that prosocial content could potentially have *stronger* effects on viewers than antisocial content because prosocial behaviors are more in accord with established social norms. Individuals who respond with aggression to friendly overtures or to requests for help are less likely to be rewarded by other members of society than are those who respond more positively. Are negative effects really much stronger and more dominating than positive effects? Meta-analyses give us some crude answers.

## Comparing Prosocial and Antisocial Effects: Meta-Analyses

Meta-analyses involve averaging statistical information across studies on a particular topic in order to estimate the overall strength of an effect. What does a prosocial effect size mean? In experiments, the effect size is often the difference between a control group and a group exposed to prosocial content, or between a group that sees some negative content and a group that sees some positive content. In surveys, the effect size is often the correlation between how much prosocial television content children watch and how positively they behave. It can be thought of as the difference between heavy and light viewers of prosocial television content.

Hearold (1986) analyzed 230 studies on television and social behavior published prior to 1978 and compared positive and negative outcomes of viewing. Her estimate of the average strength of antisocial effects combined a variety of outcomes such as aggression, criminal behavior, and stereotyping. Her estimate of the average prosocial effect size included a wide range of positive outcomes, including friendly interactions, imagination, buying books, library use, safety activism, and "conversation activism." Hearold concluded that positive effects of viewing were twice as strong and more enduring than antisocial effects, both in the laboratory and in more natural conditions. This appeared to support Rushton's (1979) strong prosocial effects hypothesis.

Two more recent meta-analyses suggest that positive and negative effects may be roughly equivalent in strength, at least if they are more narrowly defined. Paik and Comstock (1994) provided a partial update of Hearold's estimates of antisocial effects, limiting their analysis to studies of the effects of television violence on viewer aggression or criminal activity. They reported an overall negative effect of violent television content that was approximately double the antisocial effect found by Hearold. Whereas she had reported very weak antisocial effects (roughly equivalent to a Pearson correlation of .15), they reported a correlation of .32.

Inspired by Paik and Comstock, we updated Hearold's estimates of prosocial outcomes, including a number of studies published after Hearold's cut-off date of 1978 (Mares & Woodard, in press). Our definition of prosocial outcomes was restricted to studies measuring the effects of prosocial content on children's social interactions (i.e., we did not include outcomes such as borrowing books from the library). Studies were included if they were published in journals, contained sufficient statistical information to calculate effect sizes, and measured one of four outcomes. A total of 34 studies were included, with 108 comparisons, and a total sample of 5,473 children (see the appendix at the end of this chapter). The first outcome examined was a broad variable labeled "positive interaction," used to capture measures such as "friendly play" or "peaceful conflict resolution." Studies that simply gave a measure of "prosocial behavior" were coded in this category. The second category was aggression: Would prosocial depictions reduce aggressive behavior among children? Although it was possible to think of this as the other end of the "positive interaction" continuum (and simply reverse the sign for effects of prosocial content on aggression), we decided to treat this as a separate though related variable. Both physical and verbal aggression were included. The third category was altruism, which included sharing, donating, offering help, and comforting. The final outcome was stereotype reduction—the effects of counterstereotypical portrayals of gender and ethnicity on attitudes, beliefs, and behaviors. Although this last variable is often treated as a separate topic and not included in the prosocial literature, we argued that stereotypes have implications for social interactions. Messages that reduce social stereotypes should result in more positive encounters between groups, which was the overall focus of the meta-analysis.

Our final estimate of the effect of prosocial content was virtually the same as Hearold's: Prosocial content had a weak to moderate effect (roughly equivalent to a Pearson correlation of .27). Effects were strongest for studies of altruism, largely because such studies were more likely to model behaviors identical to the observed outcome, whereas efforts to promote other prosocial behaviors were less likely to have identical treatments and tasks. Effect sizes for positive interaction, aggression reduction, and stereotype reduction were remarkably similar to one another. Overall, then, our best guess at this point is that the effects of violent content and of prosocial content are reasonably close in magnitude, though violent content may be somewhat more powerful.

## But What *Is* Prosocial?

One of the most common objections to meta-analyses is that they average statistical information for too many different outcomes that are not really a single variable. This is not an insurmountable objection. One can provide effect-size estimates for subsets of measures and groups (e.g., altruism among preschool girls vs. altruism among preschool boys). The larger question is what should we mean by "prosocial" content and effects?

Our definition of prosocial outcomes is clearly narrower than Hearold's (1986) definition. We considered friendly interaction, aggression reduction, altruism, and stereotype reduction as the boundaries both for our meta-analysis and for this chapter. This leaves out a host of other, very positive outcomes. The most obvious one is learning. We did not examine content if the only goal was to teach children specific educational content (e.g., language and number skills, science, and mathematics). We also did not consider content that was intended to provide children with educational tools, such as reasoning and logic. Our focus was on the potential for fostering social interactions that are nonviolent and positive in tone (see Mares & Woodard, in press, for further discussion of definitional issues).

### *Legislative Attempts to Define Prosocial Programming*

Above is our pragmatic solution to the need for definitions. But, for producers and regulators, the boundaries are often more problematic. Kunkel (1991, 1998) has outlined the history of struggles between producers, advocacy groups such as Action for Children's Television, and regulators over what should constitute prosocial and educational programming and how many hours per week should be required. We do not attempt to duplicate Kunkel's expert recounting of these epic battles. However, it is worth noting that, prior to the 1990 Children's Television Act, there were no real attempts on the part of regulators to say what should count as prosocial or educational programming, let alone to regulate how much of it there should be on television or what time it should be shown.

In the 1990 Children's Television Act, policy makers stated that programs would meet requirements for children's educational or informational content if they "further the positive development of the child in any respect, including the child's cognitive/intellectual or emotional/social needs" (Federal Communications Commission [FCC], 1991, p. 2114). It was left to the broadcaster to determine what this would mean and when the programming should be aired.

Kunkel and Canepa (1994) conducted a content analysis of license renewal claims submitted to the FCC in 1992, examining the types of programs that were claimed to meet these new requirements. They found that major stations aired about 4 hours per week of educational or prosocial programming. A number of programs, such as *Beakman's World* and *CBS Storybreak,* were legitimate efforts to fulfill the educational programming obligation. Others, such as *GI Joe, Teenage Mutant Ninja Turtles,* and the *Jetsons,* were more problematic. In addition, several programs that were originally aired in prime time, such as *Full House* and *Life Goes On,* were recategorized as content specifically designed for children.

To clarify apparent confusion in the industry and increase compliance with the law, the FCC enacted a processing guideline known as the "3-hour rule" that went into effect in 1997. Under the 3-hour rule, broadcasters who wish to have their license renewals expedited are required to air a minimum of 3 hours a week of educational and informational (E/I) television that meets the "cognitive/intellectual or social/emotional" needs of children. The E/I programs must be specifically designed for children ages 16 and under and must air between the hours of 7:00 A.M. and 10:00 P.M. Broadcasters are required to place an on-air symbol at the beginning of E/I programs to indicate to the public that they are educational, and they must provide this information to listing services such as the local newspaper and *TV Guide.*

### *How Much Prosocial Content Is There on Television?*

Early content analyses conducted during the 1970s found considerable variability in the frequency of various types of prosocial behavior. Liebert and Poulos (1975) analyzed broadcasting programming for 1974 and reported that, although there were an average of 11 altruistic acts and 6 sympathetic behaviors per hour of programming, resistance to temptation and control of aggressive impulses occurred less than once per hour (see also Poulos, Harvey, & Liebert, 1976). Liebert and Sprafkin (1988) concluded that children watching during the 1970s (when a number of the studies discussed in this chapter were conducted) were exposed to a fair number of prosocial interpersonal behaviors but few instances of self-control behaviors.

Early content analyses also indicated that prosocial acts often appeared in the context of aggression. Greenberg, Atkin, Edison, and Korzenny (1980) analyzed the favorite programs of a sample of fourth, sixth, and eighth graders. They found that these programs contained an average of 42.2 acts of antisocial behavior and 44.2 acts of prosocial behavior in an average hour. The prosocial behavior included displays of altruism, empathy, and discussion of feelings. Liss and Reinhardt (1980) analyzed prosocial cartoons (those with moral messages apparent to the adult researchers) and standard cartoons. They found that both types of cartoons contained equal amounts of aggression.

More recently, the Annenberg Public Policy Center has conducted annual content analyses of all children's programs aired over the course of a composite week in Philadelphia, a large urban media market. Woodard (1999) examined the frequency with which programs contained social lessons about how to live with oneself (e.g., intrapersonal skills such as understanding emotions, self-esteem, and overcoming fears) and how to live with others (interpersonal skills such as acceptance of diversity, altruism, and cooperation).

In the1998/1999 sample, 50% of all children's shows contained at least one social lesson. These were mostly concentrated in programming for preschool children; 77% of preschool children's programming contained a social lesson. PBS programming for children contained the most social lessons (72% of programs), followed by premium cable channels such as the Disney Channel and HBO (59% of children's programs). PBS also had the most programs with traditionally academic lessons (89% of programs).

Schmitt (1999) reported that, of the subset of children's programs designated as meeting the "educational and/or informational needs of children," 75% of those offered by the commercial broadcast networks were prosocial in nature, when *prosocial* was also broadly defined as "learning to live with oneself and others." That is, broadcasters appeared to be meeting the 3-hour rule by focusing on general prosocial messages rather than conveying traditionally academic information on topics such as reading, writing, and arithmetic.

### *How Much Prosocial Content Do Children See?*

Out of the top 20 shows most watched by children between the ages of 2 and 17, according to Nielsen ratings, only four contained social lessons in the episodes analyzed: *Boy Meets World, Disney's One Saturday Morning, 7th Heaven,* and *Hey Arnold!* (Woodard, 1999). Of those four, only two contained prosocial lessons as we have defined them in this chapter: *Disney's One Saturday Morning* and *7th Heaven.* Of these two, only *Disney's One Saturday Morning* was designed explicitly for children. The example of *7th Heaven,* a prime-time program produced for a general audience yet extremely popular among children, highlights the need to investigate the possibility of prosocial effects from programming that was never originally intended for young audiences. While it is clear that it is worth examining what happens when children watch *Sesame Street* or *Barney,* if these programs are actually watched by fewer children than seemingly adult content is, we should also focus on the effects of that adult content.

## Investigating Prosocial Effects

Research strategies for investigating television effects have evolved over the years, and this is seen in research on prosocial effects as clearly as in other areas. Early studies of prosocial effects were often simple one-shot tests of modeling. As we mentioned earlier in our discussion of strong effect sizes in studies of altruism, these simple tests of modeling generally found quite strong positive effects. The two other main types of research, field experiments and surveys, have generally found weaker effects (Mares & Woodard, in press), suggesting that prosocial effects are, not surprisingly, weaker in situations in which prosocial messages compete with other activities and interests. In this section, we give examples of each type of research, simultaneously providing examples of each of the four categories of prosocial behavior. This section is definitely *not* a comprehensive list of studies of prosocial effects. We refer readers to earlier literature reviews such as Rushton (1982) and to the reference section of our meta-analysis (in the Appendix) for more extensive lists. The purpose here is to illustrate the types of strategies that have been used to investigate prosocial outcomes. Readers will note that the majority of studies cited here were published in the 1970s and 1980s. Few studies of prosocial effects were conducted in the 1990s, despite the fact that many questions remain about how best to achieve prosocial outcomes of viewing. Although some more recent studies have examined prosocial programs such as *Sesame Street* or *Mister Rogers' Neighborhood,* they have typically measured cognitive outcomes rather than variables related to social interaction (e.g., Rice, Huston, Truglio, & Wright, 1990).

### *One-Shot Exposures*

In a well-known study of altruism, Poulos, Rubinstein, and Liebert (1975) randomly assigned 30 first-grade children to one of three viewing conditions: a prosocial episode of *Lassie* in which Jeff risked his life to save a puppy; a neutral episode of *Lassie;* or a neutral episode of *The Brady Bunch.* After viewing the episode, the children were told how to play a "game" in which they could accrue points by pressing a button. The more points they earned, the larger the prize they would win. At the same time, they were asked to listen to puppies in a distant kennel and to push a help button if the puppies seemed distressed. As children played the game, the recorded puppy sounds grew increasingly loud and intense. The researchers compared the average number of seconds children spent pushing the help button (and thereby sacrificing points in the game) in each of the conditions. Children who saw the prosocial episode pushed the help button nearly twice as long as children in the other two conditions.

Collins and Getz (1976) studied the effects of prosocial versus aggressive messages on children's cooperative play by assigning 60 children ages 9, 13, and 16 to one of two versions of an episode of *The Mod Squad.* The conflict in the episode centered on a police captain who, while acting as legal guardian for a young boy, was framed on a bribery charge. In the aggressive version, the police captain refused to cooperate with investigators, single-handedly engaging in physical combat with the villain who framed him. In the prosocial version, the children saw three scenes in which the investigators gathered clues, engaged in nonviolent negotiation, and collaborated on a constructive solution to the problem.

After watching the episode, children were asked to "help us on another project" involving the "help-hurt" machine. They were told that the light on the gray response box in front of them would flash whenever their partner in the project made an error on a hearing test. The child could then push one of two buttons: a green "help" button that would help the other by eliminating a distracting background noise or a red "hurt" button that would make the distracting sound louder. The longer they pushed the button, the stronger the effect on the volume of the distracting sound. Children who had seen the prosocial version spent more time pushing the help button and less time pushing the hurt button than did those who had seen the aggressive version of *The Mod Squad.*

Finally, in a study of stereotype reduction, Pingree (1978) showed 227 children in third and eighth grade commercials featuring women in either traditional or nontraditional roles. One third of the children were told that those they would see were real people who actually did the things portrayed, one third were told that they would see actors who did not do such things in real life, and the final third were given no instructions. She found that stereotyping was reduced in the nontraditional condition, particularly when children were told that these were real people. However, among eighth-grade boys, there appeared to be something of a contrary reaction; stereotyping was significantly higher in the nontraditional condition than in the traditional condition.

### *Repeated Exposure/Field Experiments*

Some of the major investigations involving repeated exposure to real television content in relatively uncontrolled environments have involved *Sesame Street, Mister Rogers' Neighborhood,* and *Barney.* These studies are discussed later in this chapter in sections devoted specifically to these three shows. In general, field experiments have often looked at the effect of using a particular prosocial program as part of the school or preschool experience. As such, children generally watch whole episodes every week for a number of weeks and are then evaluated, often by observation over several days or weeks rather than by performance on a single task.

Ahammer and Murray (1979) studied the effectiveness of different strategies for teaching altruism. They assigned 97 children ages 4 and 5 to one of six conditions. In the prosocial television condition, children watched 20 half-hour episodes over 4 weeks. The episodes, chosen from programs such as *Lassie, I Love Lucy,* and *Gilligan's Island,* had been previously scored by the researchers as high in prosocial themes such as sympathy, resisting temptation, and control of aggressive impulses. In three other training conditions, children did not watch television. Instead, they were trained in activities such as role playing and recognition of facial expression. An additional group of children watched neutral television programming (i.e., low in both prosocial and aggressive content) instead of receiving any training, and a final group simply carried out their usual classroom activities. The prosocial television was significantly less successful than the three teacher training conditions in promoting altruism (measured by sharing raisins, helping another child with a game, and performance on the "cooperation/competition table"). When the researchers compared the prosocial TV condition with the neutral TV condition, there was a significant positive effect for boys on one of the three measures, but no significant effects for girls.

Elias (1983) examined whether videos could be used as one component of treatment for boys with serious emotional and educational disturbances. The 10 videos, shown twice a week for 5 weeks, portrayed realistic scenarios of common problematic situations such as teasing and bullying, dealing with peer pressure, learning how to express feelings, and coping with new social situations. After watching each video, the boys were encouraged to discuss what they had seen and how they felt about it. The boys were measured on a variety of behavioral and emotional outcomes related to interactions, both for 3 months before and 2 months after the video series. Compared with control children who did not see the videos, experimental participants were rated by their counselors as less emotionally detached, less isolated, having improved in their ability to delay gratification, and having decreased in overall personality problems. These effects were still evident 2 months after the intervention.

In a study of stereotype reduction, O'Bryant and Corder-Bolz (1978) showed 67 children 5 to 10 years old nine half-hour cartoons over a month. Embedded in each cartoon were commercials for a fruit juice drink. In the traditional condition, the commercials featured a female telephone operator, fashion model, file clerk, and manicurist. In the nontraditional condition, the commercials featured a female pharmacist, welder, butcher, and laborer. Over the course of the month, children saw many repetitions of the commercials. Comparisons between pre- and posttest scores on tests of occupational stereotyping found that children exposed to the nontraditional commercials were significantly more likely to say that a traditionally male job was also appropriate for a woman. Moreover, girls in the nontraditional condition gave higher ratings to traditionally male jobs when asked how much they would like to have that job in the future. Boys' ratings of future interest in traditionally male jobs were lower in the experimental condition—apparently, seeing a woman in those roles was a deterrent. This effect is consistent with Pingree's (1978) findings of a "backlash" among boys and underlines the point that seemingly prosocial content can have unintended effects on subgroups.

Finally, in one of the largest and most impressive studies of stereotype reduction, Johnston and Ettema (1982) examined the effectiveness of *Freestyle.* Their field experiment involved more than 7,000 fourth- through sixth-grade children in seven sites across the United States. Classrooms were randomly assigned to watch 26 episodes of *Freestyle,* a public television program designed to reduce stereotypes about gender roles. Children were assigned to watch the program in school and engage in teacher-led discussions about the material, watch it at school without any such discussions, or watch it at home. The students completed extensive questionnaires before seeing any episodes and then after the exposure period. Compared with a control group, there were significant positive changes in perceptions of personal ability and interest in various types of jobs, and reductions in stereotypes about gender roles in employment. These effects were strongest when the program was viewed in the classroom and accompanied by teacher-led discussions. Much smaller effects were observed among students who simply watched the program in school or at home. This is a pattern that will reappear in other studies discussed later in this chapter: Strong positive effects are most likely to occur when viewing is combined with follow-up discussions or activities.

### *Correlational Studies*

These studies generally answer the following question: How much effect can we observe when children simply self-select to watch prosocial programming at home? That is, these studies examine the effects of everyday viewing rather than special interventions. The results of correlational studies are more descriptive of general audiences than the types of studies discussed above are, but, as in all correlational studies, the question whether prosocial programming *causes* prosocial outcomes is plagued by issues of causal direction and spuriousness. Perhaps children who are already tolerant, friendly, caring people are attracted to prosocial programming. In addition, prosocial behavior and prosocial viewing may both be influenced by third variables such as parental style, gender, and so forth. Overall, once these possible third variables are statistically controlled, most correlational studies find very weak effects of prosocial viewing (Mares & Woodard, in press).

Sprafkin and Rubinstein (1979) studied 500 children ages 7, 8, and 9 in middle-class communities. The children reported how often they watched each of 55 television series regularly broadcast at the time of the study. These programs had been previously analyzed by the researchers for frequency of prosocial and antisocial acts so that each child received a measure of prosocial and antisocial exposure, as well as overall television viewing. Two weeks later, the children filled out the prosocial behavior measure, in which they listed which children in the classroom "help others, share things with others, try to make other people feel good, do nice things" (p. 270). Teachers also filled out the prosocial behavior measure for each child. Thus, each child received a prosocial behavior score based on the number of peer and teacher nominations.

The strongest predictors of prosocial behavior in the study were background variables. Children who were high academic achievers or whose parents were well educated received more nominations. Girls were also rated as more prosocial than boys. Compared with these effects, television viewing was only weakly related to prosocial behavior, but the pattern was fairly clear. Total television viewing was negatively related to prosocial behavior: Heavy viewers received fewer nominations. However, prosocial television viewing was positively related to prosocial outcomes: Children who watched more prosocial programming received more nominations, even after controlling for background variables. Still, readers are reminded that this was a very weak effect. The partial correlation between prosocial viewing and behavior was .12, which translates into very minimal differences between heavy and light viewers of prosocial content.

Singer, Singer, and Sherrod (1979) studied 141 preschool children's television viewing habits (as reported by parents) and their behavior during free play. Overall, television viewing was positively related to aggression, *except* for viewing of educational programming such as *Sesame Street, Zoom,* and *Mister Rogers' Neighborhood.* Viewing of these educational programs was, in fact, positively correlated with prosocial interactions and cooperative behavior with peers during free play. The results also indicated that girls and children with higher intelligence scores were more likely to watch educational programs and to be more prosocial and cooperative. As we mentioned before, it is very difficult in correlational studies to untangle the causal paths between groups of variables.

In a study involving 466 second- and third-grade children in the Netherlands over a period of 3 years, children were measured three times on a number of variables, including exposure to prosocial television content and levels of prosocial behavior (Wiegman, Kuttschreuter, & Baarda, 1992). As in Sprafkin and Rubinstein's (1979) report, prosocial and antisocial exposure was measured by the frequency of viewing specific programs, and prosocial behavior was assessed by peer nominations. Wiegman and his colleagues found no relationship between prosocial viewing and prosocial behavior, despite the considerable power granted by such a large sample size. If anything, the relationship tended to be very weakly negative rather than positive. Wiegman et al. noted that watching prosocial content was very highly correlated (i.e., $r = .90$) with watching antisocial content; children who saw the most prosocial content were simply heavy television viewers and thus were exposed to numerous antisocial models as well.

Most recently, Rosenkoetter (1999) conducted a series of studies on the relationship between watching adult situation comedies and prosocial behavior. Undergraduates rated a list of 30 adult situation comedies on a five-point scale (*not prosocial* to *definitely prosocial*). This list was then used to assess prosocial exposure among first and third graders by measuring the frequency with which they watched each program. The children's prosocial behavior was assessed by mothers' reports about the frequency with which their child shared, helped others, and so on. In one study, Rosenkoetter found a significant positive relationship between prosocial situation comedy viewing and prosocial behavior, but only among first graders. This correlation was quite strong (.57), but, in the absence of any control variables apart from gender, the result must be interpreted with some caution. In another study reported in the same paper, Rosenkoetter found a small, marginally significant correlation between viewing prosocial adult situation comedies and mothers' reports, but only among children who were able to identify the moral lesson in a sample episode of *Full House.* There was no relationship between prosocial viewing and behavior among the children who did not perform well on this task.

Rosenwasser, Lingenfelter, and Harrington (1989) investigated whether children's knowledge of three television programs featuring relatively nontraditional gender roles (*The Cosby Show, Growing Pains,* and *Who's the Boss?*) was correlated with less stereotyped perceptions of gender roles. They asked 114 kindergarten and second-grade children a series of questions about the three programs (e.g., Who's the smallest girl?) as a way of approximating their exposure to, interest in, and comprehension of the programs. In addition, they measured the children's gender role perceptions (e.g., Who should be a doctor? Who can run fastest? Who should play with dolls?). They found some weak correlations between knowledge of nontraditional shows and nontraditional attitudes, but only 4 out of 25 correlations were significant, so this level is barely above chance.

Finally, Abelman (1985) investigated the interaction between the amount of prosocial television viewed and parents' styles of disciplining their child: Would prosocial content have stronger effects in some types of families than in others? He surveyed mothers of fourth- and fifth-grade children about their disciplinary styles (inductive techniques such as reasoning, explanation, and appeals to the child's pride vs. sensitizing techniques such as physical punishment and deprivation of privileges or objects). Children were asked about the frequency with which they watched 29 prime-time programs. These were then content analyzed for frequency of prosocial and antisocial acts. The children also answered questions about their probable behavior in social situations (e.g., how they would cope with bullies). Their answers were coded to form a "prosocial disposition" score. Abelman found a moderate overall correlation (without controls for background variables) between children's prosocial exposure and their prosocial predispositions of .42. However, this relationship was strongly dependent on parenting style: Children whose parents used inductive techniques showed a stronger relationship (.48) than children whose parents used sensitizing techniques (.14).

## Three Major Examples of Prosocial Programming

There have been a number of outstanding programs over the years designed to foster intellectual activity, tolerance, friendliness, and so on. Some examples of such programming produced by PBS include *Big Blue Marble, Electric Company,* and *3-2-1 Contact* and more recent shows such as *Arthur* and *Barney & Friends.* More recently, Nickelodeon and Disney have produced programming designed to meet the social and emotional needs of children, including *Blue's Clues, The Journey of Allen Strange,* and *Omba Mokomba.* Of these programs, three have received the most attention (both positive and negative) and the highest ratings over the years. In this section, we discuss some of the research on the prosocial effects of these three programs.

### *Sesame Street*

Numerous articles and books have been written about the conception and early years of *Sesame Street.* In its original conception, the program emphasized certain cognitive skills that would provide the basis for school curriculum, such as knowledge of letters and numbers. Later, the mission of the program expanded to include broad prosocial messages about cooperation and positive interactions. Despite early controversies that *Sesame Street* may have actually widened the educational gap between those of lower and higher socioeconomic status (e.g., Cook et al., 1975), considerable research has demonstrated the effectiveness of the program in teaching children material related to language, reading, and mathematics (Rice et al., 1990; Zill, Davies, & Daly, 1994).

Of most interest to us here is the research on the effects of *Sesame Street* on children's social interactions. The evidence, overall, suggests that, to the extent that positive effects occur, they appear with repeated long-term exposure rather than with onetime viewing of a single episode.

Silverman and Sprafkin (1980) used *Sesame Street* to test two different strategies for showing children how to get along with each other. One strategy involved showing conflicts that were resolved in a positive manner. The other simply involved showing prosocial situations devoid of all conflict. Both approaches were being used on *Sesame Street* at the time and had not been evaluated. In two studies reported in the same paper, children ages 3 to 7 watched approximately 16 minutes of *Sesame Street* featuring either conflicts and their resolutions or prosocial-only interactions. Control groups saw material with no social lessons. Pairs of children then played a marble game designed to measure cooperation: They could maximize the number of marbles they both got by taking turns, or they could ruin each other's chances by pulling simultaneously. Silverman and Sprafkin found that the prosocial-only conditions had virtually no effect on cooperation measured by the marble game; scores were equivalent to those in the control group. The conflict-resolution strategy seemed to backfire: Children who saw the conflict tended to cooperate *less* than those in the control group.

Bankart and Anderson (1979) also studied children's aggression levels during free play and reported that four episodes of *Sesame Street* shown over a 4-day period significantly reduced boys' and girls' aggression. Four episodes of *The Little Rascals* had no such effect.

Gorn, Goldberg, and Kanungo (1976) assessed the effects of *Sesame Street* on children's tolerance for playmates of different ethnic and racial backgrounds. They assigned 205 white English Canadian children 3½ to 5½ years old to watch 12 minutes of *Sesame Street* programming with multicultural inserts or without the inserts. The children were then shown two sets of four photos taken from the inserts. One set contained white children, and the other showed children described rather ambiguously by the researchers as Oriental and Indian. The child then chose which of the photographed children should be brought to the nursery school the next day. The control group that did not see the inserts showed a marked preference for playing with the white children rather than the nonwhite children (67% vs. 33%). This was reversed among children who saw the multiracial inserts; 71% preferred nonwhites and 29% preferred whites. However, in one of very few prosocial projects involving delayed testing, Goldberg and Gorn (1979) expanded their earlier study and found that children tested a day after viewing the multicultural inserts were no longer significantly more willing to play with nonwhite playmates than those who had not seen the inserts.

Early studies of *Sesame Street* confirmed that the message of tolerance in *Sesame Street* took time to extract. Ball and Bogatz (1979) conducted longitudinal studies of children exposed to *Sesame Street* and reported that children's attitudes toward members of other races were unaffected after a year of viewing but had become significantly more tolerant after 2 years.

### *Mister Rogers' Neighborhood*

The differences in production techniques used in *Sesame Street* and *Mister Rogers' Neighborhood* are profound, particularly in terms of the speed at which content is presented, the number of cuts and edits, and the use of animation. In addition, as previously noted, the primary goal of *Sesame Street* was the development of cognitive skills, with an additional component of prosocial learning. Social and affective messages are the primary focus of *Mister Rogers' Neighborhood.* Tower, Singer, Singer, and Biggs (1979) compared the effects of the two programs on a variety of outcomes, including children's expressions of positive affect and their interactions and cooperation with peers and adults. Fifty-eight preschool children were exposed to daily episodes of *Sesame Street, Mister Rogers' Neighborhood,* or neutral films. Their free-play behaviors were observed in the week before and the week after the 2-week experimental period. Tower et al. found small positive changes as a result of viewing both programs compared with the control group. However, the effects seemed to vary depending on the IQ of the children. Although there were no significant differences in effects of viewing among children with high intelligence scores, average-IQ children who watched *Mister Rogers' Neighborhood* became more cooperative with adults, while average-IQ children who watched *Sesame Street* became less cooperative. The researchers suggested that the rapid pace of *Sesame Street* might have made it more difficult for average-IQ children to extract prosocial messages.

Friedrich and Stein conducted a series of studies on prosocial effects using *Mister Rogers' Neighborhood.* In the first study (Friedrich & Stein, 1973), 93 preschool children watched television or films 12 times over a 4-week period. The prosocial group watched *Mister Rogers' Neighborhood;* the aggressive group watched *Batman* and *Superman;* and the control group watched neutral films (e.g., about farms and animals). Observers rated the children's aggressive and prosocial behavior during free play for 3 weeks before the experimental period, during the 4-week experimental period, and then for 2 weeks afterward. Children who watched *Mister Rogers' Neighborhood* showed several positive changes. They persisted longer on tasks, were more likely to obey rules, and were more likely to delay gratification without protest. In addition, children from families with lower socioeconomic status also showed an increase in prosocial playground interactions (e.g., more cooperation and friendliness). These effects continued, though they tapered off somewhat, over the 2-week postviewing period. Children from higher socioeconomic backgrounds had initially been more prosocial, and they did not change significantly after seeing *Mister Rogers' Neighborhood.* Despite the positive effects of watching *Mister Rogers* as part of the preschool day, Friedrich and Stein found no correlation between the frequency of watching *Mister Rogers* at home and children's baseline measures of prosocial behavior.

In a second study, Friedrich and Stein (1975) focused on investigating whether children could generalize the lessons from *Mister Rogers* to their own lives and whether the effects of the program would be stronger if viewing was accompanied by training in skills related to prosocial behavior. They assigned 73 kindergarten children to watch four episodes of *Mister Rogers* and receive differing types of training: verbal labeling (children were taught to describe how characters had felt and behaved) and role playing (children used hand puppets to reenact scenes from the episodes). Over the next few days, the children were tested for their memory of the content and their willingness to help. Helping related to the program was assessed by observing whether the child helped a puppet from the program during a reenactment of one of the scenes. More generalized helping was measured by observing how children responded when shown a torn collage that had been made and accidentally damaged by another child. Friedrich and Stein found slightly higher helping behaviors among the children who had watched *Mister Rogers* than among those in the control group. For boys, the role-playing training appeared to strengthen the effects of the program, and verbal labeling actually was associated with some decreases in helping.

In their third project, Friedrich-Cofer, Huston-Stein, Kipnis, Susman, and Clewett (1979) focused on the effects of *Mister Rogers* on "urban poor children" (p. 637). They had 141 children in urban Head Start programs watch 20 episodes over a period of 8 weeks. Comparisons were made between children who watched *Mister Rogers* at the Head Start Center without any additional prosocial materials; those who watched it and also had access to prosocial books, games, and so on; and those who watched it, had access to the prosocial materials, and also had follow-up activities such as verbal labeling and role playing. A control group simply saw neutral films. Friedrich-Cofer et al. found that *Mister Rogers' Neighborhood* alone produced relatively few behavioral changes. Those who watched the program and had access to the prosocial materials became more active overall; they had more positive interactions but more aggressive interactions as well. The most successful group, in terms of prosocial behavior, was the one made up of children who watched the program and also received training in role playing and verbal labeling. That group showed significant increases in positive social interactions without any increases in aggression.

In all three of these studies, then, *Mister Rogers* did have some positive effects, but the effects were much stronger when viewing was accompanied by activities designed to explicitly teach the types of behaviors modeled in the program. Similarly, Singer and Singer (1983) reported that children who saw short television segments in the context of lessons emphasizing prosocial themes and activities were more likely to show increases in prosocial behaviors than were those who saw the segments without the additional training.

### *Barney & Friends*

This program was initially produced for television in 1993, and, in part because it is so much younger than *Sesame Street* or *Mister Rogers' Neighborhood,* there is much less research on its effects. As is generally well known, Barney is a purple dinosaur who comes to the aid of a sprightly set of multicultural children. The program features simple story lines focusing on one or two cognitive tasks such as color recognition, but it is most notable for the absence of conflict, the emphasis on cooperation, and the expression of positive affect.

Singer and Singer (1998) conducted a series of studies evaluating the effectiveness of *Barney & Friends.* In the first study, 121 preschool children, largely from white, middle-class families, were assigned to one of four groups. The first group watched 10 episodes of *Barney* over 2 weeks, with each episode followed by a lesson designed to expand on the message of the episode. The second group watched the 10 episodes without the follow-up lessons. The third group received the lessons without watching the program, and the fourth group simply followed the usual day care routine. Children were pre- and post-tested on their knowledge of the material presented in the programs, including lessons from Barney about good manners. The pattern of results was very consistent. Children showed the strongest gains when viewing was combined with follow-up lessons, moderate gains from viewing without the lessons, and negligible gains just from the lessons. Average scores for knowledge of manners were approximately 10 out of a possible 12 for the viewing-plus-training group, 5 for the viewing group, and 3 for the control group.

In a second study reported in the same paper, the Singers investigated whether the same strong positive effects would be observed in populations that were not middle class. They chose five diverse regions of the United States and selected day care centers with children of low socioeconomic status and greater ethnic and racial diversity. Within each day care, children were assigned to one of three groups: *Barney & Friends* with follow-up lessons, *Barney & Friends* without the lessons, or a control group that received no special treatment. In this study, the pattern of results was somewhat different. The viewing-plus-lessons group performed significantly better on most measures of learning from the program, but there were no consistent significant effects of watching the program without the lessons. Moreover, there were no effects of either viewing condition on measures related to good manners and civility. When the researchers investigated the lack of effects on knowledge of manners, they noted that the second study did not use a particular episode emphasizing good manners that had been used in the first study. Although the program as a whole features exemplars of cooperation and courtesy, the children in these populations did not appear to extract those messages successfully.

*Barney & Friends* overtly emphasizes positive affect and positive interaction. Happy children hug and sway on-screen, singing the "I Love You, You Love Me" song. Do children who watch this program actually become any more loving and caring? That they enjoy watching is evidenced by both the high ratings and the extraordinary amount of merchandise sold. Whether they also imitate the happy, friendly interactions modeled on the television screen remains a fascinating research question that clearly merits more work.

## Lessons From the Research: When Are Prosocial Effects Strongest?

### *What Types of Content Are Most Effective?*

Despite all the research that has been done, questions remain about how best to design prosocial content. The conclusions that emerged from our meta-analysis are discussed here, but we also point out the areas where further research is needed.

First, the more specific the model, the more effective it appears to be. That is, studies in which children were shown the exact set of steps for positive behavior, typically immediately before they were given an opportunity to imitate the model, generally reported the highest effect sizes. In the prosocial literature, these were typically studies of altruistic behavior in which children donated tokens or candy, having just seen the model donating the same thing. Thus, although the violence literature suggests that children are quite capable of generalizing from one specific form of violence (e.g., hitting someone with a hammer) to another (e.g., punching someone in the playground), specificity may be more important for prosocial outcomes. That said, there are no systematic comparisons between highly specific modeling and more "general kindness" or "goodness" themes even though such a study would be relatively easy to perform.

The second conclusion is that the combination of aggression and a prosocial theme is particularly pernicious. That is, showing violence and mayhem in the cause of social justice or followed by a rapid conclusion in which the villains are punished for their aggression may be more deleterious to children's prosocial interactions than showing violence unadulterated by any prosocial theme. How did we reach this conclusion? Not only is it specifically illustrated in Silverman and Sprafkin's (1980) study discussed in the section on *Sesame Street,* but it was also evident from the results of our meta-analysis. When we compared children who watched aggressive content with children who watched prosocial content, we found an average effect size ($r$) of .26. One way to conceive of this effect size is to think of it as the difference between the average scores of the aggression groups and the prosocial groups. When we compared children who watched prosocial content with those who watched aggressive-prosocial content, the effect size ($r$) was .39. That is, children who watch aggressive-prosocial content are even further away from the prosocial groups than those who watch unadulterated aggression. This is highly problematic given evidence that children are typically exposed to both types of content rather than one or the other (Liss & Reinhardt, 1980; Wiegman, Kuttschreuter, & Baarda, 1992).

There are many questions that remain unanswered about how to design effective prosocial messages. Does it make a difference if the prosocial outcome is rewarded? Paik and Comstock (1994) reported that reward made no difference for modeling of violent content. Is the same thing true if one wants to encourage children to act in positive ways that may involve some sacrifice on their part? Does the type of reward (extrinsic vs. intrinsic) affect children's responses? How realistic does the reward have to be for the effects to endure? If, as we shall see in the discussion of altruism in a popular children's book, helping behavior is rewarded by receiving an extremely rare and valuable present, what are the implications for children's helping when they do not receive such gifts as rewards?

Are prosocial effects short-lived? Is it critical to present prosocial content just before children are given the chance to imitate it? Unfortunately, of the 108 effect sizes that we were able to examine, 103 were measured with less than a day's delay. Although we found no significant effects of the length of delay between exposure and measurement, there is no clear answer to this question. Similarly, there are no clear answers to the questions of whether live models are more effective than animated models or whether humor is an effective tool in prosocial content.

### *Which Groups Are More Strongly Affected?*

We examined age, gender, ethnicity, and socioeconomic status to see if some groups are more strongly affected by prosocial messages than others and to see how group effects for prosocial content differed from those found for violent content.

Effect sizes for prosocial content differed by age group. The effect size increased sharply from ages 3 to 7, peaked at 7, and then appeared to decline almost as sharply between 7 and 12. From 12 years old and on, the effect of prosocial content continued to decline but at a much slower rate. The stronger effects on younger children are consistent with Paik and Comstock's (1994) findings that the youngest children were most strongly affected by violent content, possibly reflecting a relative lack of skepticism or critical viewing skills. In the case of prosocial outcomes, age differences may also reflect the types of programming available to children of different ages. There may be more effective prosocial content available to younger children than to older children. In an analysis of the quality of programming available to children, Woodard (1999) found that high-quality programs were more likely to be preschool programs. Of all the preschool programs, 73% were high quality, compared with 28% and 29% of elementary-age and teenage programs, respectively, in the 1998-1999 television season. The distribution of quality programs for children of different ages was quite similar to the distribution found in the 1997-1998 season, when 85% of the preschool programs were high quality, 21% of the elementary-age shows were high quality, and 28% of the teen programs were high quality (Jordan, 1998). In fact, the prevalence of high-quality programming for preschoolers is a trend seen throughout the Annenberg Public Policy Center's analyses of children's television (Jordan, 1996; Jordan & Woodard, 1997).

Effect sizes for prosocial content also differed by the socioeconomic status of the children in the studies. Prosocial television had almost twice as much effect on children from middle- to upper-class settings as it did on children from lower-class settings, though there are notable exceptions, such as the study of *Mister Rogers' Neighborhood* by Friedrich and Stein (1973). Maybe the happy worlds of prosocial programming resonate most strongly with those members of the audience who inhabit worlds of relative affluence. It may also be the case that parents with more education and money are more likely to coview with their child and to buy supplementary materials related to the programs.

There were no gender differences in prosocial outcomes (surprising given strong gender differences in violence effects). There were also no differences by ethnicity. However, we would suggest that research is needed to examine the effects of having same-race or same-ethnicity models for prosocial outcomes versus the effects of showing other groups modeling the desired behavior.

### *The Importance of Adult Mediation*

One of the more consistent findings is that prosocial effects are much stronger and persistent when adults actively elaborate on television content. The work by Friedrich and her colleagues, as well as the research by the Singers, makes it clear once again that using television merely as a baby-sitter is to deprive children, even if viewing consists of prosocial lessons. As Abelman (1991) has illustrated, successful mediation can be as simple as labeling and commenting on prosocial acts as they appear on the screen.

## An Unexplored Area: Prosocial Effects of Other Media

Research has focused on the role of television in prosocial behavior, and for that reason, we devoted most of our chapter to this topic. However, it is of both theoretical and practical interest to know what role other media may have. We have found no research on this area, but there are certain obvious differences between media that may impinge on prosocial effects. We highlight some of these differences below in the hope of provoking further research on this topic.

### *Books*

As a teaching tool for prosocial themes, books have some characteristics that are worth considering. First, it is probably easier to find a book related to a specific concern (e.g., my child does not interact well, hits others, is a tease, lies, etc.) than it is to find a relevant television episode or even a video. Not only is there a plethora of manuals for anxious parents on how to redirect children's behavior toward more prosocial outcomes, but there are numerous books aimed at children themselves designed to teach positive behaviors or prepare them for morally challenging situations.

Reading such books is probably less accidental and more likely to require parental interaction than is exposure to a prosocial television program. Having bought or borrowed such a book, parents may be more likely to sit and read the book with the child and may even use it as a starting point for discussion. Television programs with prosocial themes make convenient, guilt-free baby-sitters. Books with prosocial themes, on the other hand, require some effort on somebody's part in order to enter the house or classroom and, at least for young children, require a literate person to read the message out loud before exposure can occur.

The flip side of this observation is that the audience for prosocial messages in a book may be smaller and is almost certain to be less diverse than the audience for a television program. Accidental exposure to a positive program may be the only media source of prosocial messages for a child whose parents do not buy or borrow books. Children whose parents or teachers read *The Berenstain Bears and the Truth* are probably privileged to begin with in having adults who are sufficiently involved and concerned to make the effort.

Finally, books afford the possibility for repeated exposure to a message. Such repetition is available for television content only if a program is videotaped. Given children's fondness for repetition (see Mares, 1998), it is possible that they will happily read the same prosocial story several times (thereby reinforcing the message), but they are typically unable to see a particular prosocial television episode repeatedly.

### *Children's Computer Software*

Probably the most striking comparison between computer software and other media considered in this chapter is the price of admission. Children's computer access remains segregated by parental income. A 1999 national survey by the Annenberg Public Policy Center (Stanger & Gridina, 1999) examined computer ownership among households with children between the ages of 2 and 17. It found that 41% of households with annual incomes below $30,000 had computers, whereas 94% of households with incomes above $75,000 had computers. It is true that some schools and libraries offer children computer access, but school use of computers fluctuates with the financial status of the district and the training of the teachers. Only a minority of day care and after-school providers are likely to invest in a fleet of computers for individual use rather than a sole television set that can entertain a group of children.

In addition, prosocial software is expensive. Many prosocially themed books cost less than $5. Prosocial software typically costs more than $20. Given that software typically cannot be played with before purchasing and cannot be returned after opening, parents make a considerable leap of faith and show substantial investment in their child's social outcomes when they buy a CD-ROM purporting to teach their children life skills. Libraries, a potential source of free access, typically carry a much smaller collection of software than of books. Computers also require more specialized knowledge for use than other media considered here do (particularly television). Although such knowledge may be more fun or more intuitive for children to acquire than the knowledge required to read is, computer skills are still less widely and less systematically taught in school than reading. In short, then, children who form the audience for prosocial computer games are likely to be a small, rather privileged group.

Apart from these considerations, how effective are computer games at fostering friendly interactions? There has been little research to date. More recently, computer games have been the focus of attention as a powerful tool for teaching children how to kill one another, both by providing them with the skills needed to aim and fire and by desensitizing them to realistic images of blood and suffering (Emerson, 1999; Tilley, 1999). The same features of computer games that have been implicated in teaching violence should potentially be relevant to prosocial interactions as well. Given appropriately designed games, children can rehearse their behavior in realistic social situations. Their behavior has consequences within the confines of the game, and the game can be played repeatedly so that choices can be revised.

### *Children's Websites*

At least three features of the Internet make it a promising medium for conveying prosocial content. First, it is much easier for small, prosocial groups to reach an audience. A prime-time television program can cost as much as $13 million per episode (Higgins, 1998), whereas a website can be designed and hosted for free save for the cost of using a personal computer to access the service providers (Beizer, 1999). Related to the affordability of the Internet is the ability to target narrow audiences. Without the need to attract a mass audience, Web content providers can provide a customized experience for their users. Finally, interactivity is a prominent feature of many websites. For instance, children communicate directly with content providers, favorite characters, and even each other in cyberspace, presenting extraordinary opportunities to rein force and extend the positive message of the website.

Despite the relative ease of providing prosocial content on-line, a question remains about just how many children can actually get to that content. Only 41% of families with children between the ages of 2 and 17 have access to the Internet. Only 15% of families with children between the ages of 2 and 17 and household incomes of less than $30,000 per year have access to the Internet (Stanger & Gridina, 1999).

How likely is it that children encounter prosocial content designed for them on the

World Wide Web? Media Metrix (1999), an Internet and digital media measurement service, lists the top 500 websites that attract the largest number of visitors over the course of 1 month. We consulted the July 1999 list and found that only 10 of the sites contained content for children, only 2 of which contained prosocial material. Both sites were created by Nickelodeon, and the primary focus of each was to promote Nickelodeon's cable programming. It was only by following a series of links from the preschool home page that young children would reach a prosocial game (based on the program *Blue's Clues*) that involved figuring out how to comfort a crying infant. For older children, there was a link to the "Big Help," which provided detailed information about how to organize, promote, and run a volunteer project in their neighborhood. Thus, despite the apparent possibilities of the World Wide Web, it appears to be a medium that is underused at the moment for prosocial purposes.

As we noted in the conclusion to our meta-analysis, research on violence continues apace. Research on prosocial effects has largely languished since the 1970s. This would be justified only if it were clear that prosocial effects seldom occur and should be considered a lost cause or if research had already answered all the important questions about how to design effective prosocial messages. We hope that we have shown in this chapter that neither of these is true. Many important questions remain, but there is considerable reason for optimism.

# Appendix

## List of Effects

| *Author*[a] | *Year* | *N*[b] | *Age*[c] | *Design* | *Effect Size*[d] |
|---|---|---|---|---|---|
| Abelman | 1985 | 286 | 120 | Correlational | 0.4200 * |
| Ahammer | 1979 | 30 | 58 | Experimental | –0.0770 * |
| Ahammer | 1979 | 24 | 53 | Experimental | 0.2520 * |
| Bankart | 1979 | 22 | 54 | Quasi-Experimental | 0.9500 * |
| Baran | 1979 | 81 | 96 | Experimental | 0.3170 * |
| Baran | 1979 | 81 | 96 | Experimental | 0.3170 * |
| Baran | 1979 | 81 | 96 | Experimental | 0.4310 * |
| Bryan | 1970 | 72 | 108 | Experimental | 0.2170 |
| Collins | 1976 | 54 | 158 | Experimental | 0.4760 * |
| Collins | 1976 | 54 | 158 | Experimental | 0.3050 * |
| Collins | 1976 | 54 | 158 | Experimental | 0.4650 * |
| Collins | 1976 | 54 | 158 | Experimental | 0.3990 * |
| Davidson | 1979 | 36 | 66 | Experimental | 0.7090 * |
| Davidson | 1979 | 36 | 66 | Experimental | 0.6330 * |
| Drabman | 1977 | 40 | 60 | Experimental | 0.3980 * |
| Drabman | 1977 | 40 | 60 | Experimental | 0.3380 * |
| Durkin | 1984 | 99 | 150 | Experimental | 0.1860 |

| *Author*[a] | *Year* | *N*[b] | *Age*[c] | *Design* | *Effect Size*[d] |
|---|---|---|---|---|---|
| Durkin | 1984 | 99 | 150 | Experimental | –0.1170 |
| Durkin | 1984 | 99 | 150 | Experimental | –0.0190 |
| Durkin | 1984 | 99 | 150 | Experimental | –0.1690 |
| Durkin | 1984 | 99 | 150 | Experimental | 0.1200 |
| Durkin | 1984 | 99 | 150 | Experimental | -0.1370 |
| Durkin | 1984 | 99 | 150 | Experimental | 0.2070 |
| Durkin | 1984 | 99 | 150 | Experimental | 0.1730 |
| Elias | 1983 | 109 | 132 | Experimental | 0.2920 * |
| Elliott | 1970 | 48 | 72 | Experimental | 0.7550 * |
| Elliott | 1970 | 48 | 72 | Experimental | 0.7550 * |
| Elliott | 1970 | 48 | 72 | Experimental | 0.8570 * |
| Forge | 1987 | 40 | 50 | Experimental | 0.4020 * |
| Friedrich-Cofer | 1979 | 141 | 50 | Experimental | 0.0000 |
| Friedrich-Cofer | 1979 | 141 | 50 | Experimental | 0.2880 * |
| Friedrich-Cofer | 1979 | 141 | 50 | Experimental | 0.2310 * |
| Friedrich-Cofer | 1979 | 141 | 50 | Experimental | –0.0620 |
| Friedrich-Cofer | 1979 | 141 | 50 | Experimental | 0.3980 * |
| Friedrich-Cofer | 1979 | 141 | 50 | Experimental | –0.1600 |
| Friedrich-Cofer | 1979 | 141 | 50 | Experimental | 0.2490 * |
| Friedrich-Cofer | 1979 | 141 | 50 | Experimental | –0.2990 * |
| Friedrich-Cofer | 1979 | 141 | 50 | Experimental | –0.1360 * |
| Geller | 1978 | 24 | 57 | Experimental | 0.5670 * |
| Goldberg | 1979 | 167 | 48 | Experimental | 0.2260 * |
| Goldberg | 1979 | 167 | 48 | Experimental | 0.0000 * |
| Gorn | 1976 | 205 | 54 | Experimental | 0.2390* |
| Houser | 1978 | 156 | 88 | Experimental | 0.6630 * |
| Houser | 1978 | 156 | 88 | Experimental | 0.7040 * |
| Keller | 1974 | 19 | 46 | Experimental | 0.4900 * |
| Keller | 1974 | 19 | 46 | Experimental | 0.3240 * |
| Liss | 1980 | 60 | 67 | Experimental | 0.9611 * |
| Liss | 1980 | 60 | 67 | Experimental | 0.9753 * |
| Liss | 1980 | 60 | 67 | Experimental | 0.9765 * |
| Liss | 1980 | 120 | 91 | Experimental | 0.2693 * |
| Liss | 1980 | 120 | 91 | Experimental | 0.1049 * |
| McArthur | 1976 | 20 | 49 | Experimental | 0.4630 * |
| McArthur | 1976 | 20 | 49 | Experimental | 0.4670 * |
| O'Bryant | 1978 | 67 | 87 | Experimental | 0.2160 * |
| O'Bryant | 1978 | 67 | 87 | Experimental | 0.4060 * |
| O'Bryant | 1978 | 67 | 87 | Experimental | 0.3830 * |
| O'Bryant | 1978 | 67 | 87 | Experimental | –0.1020 * |

| *Author*[a] | *Year* | *N*[b] | *Age*[c] | *Design* | *Effect Size*[d] |
|---|---|---|---|---|---|
| O'Connor | 1969 | 13 | 42 | Experimental | 0.6300 * |
| O'Connor | 1972 | 31 | 42 | Experimental | 0.6010 * |
| Pingree | 1978 | 227 | 132 | Experimental | –0.2760 |
| Pingree | 1978 | 227 | 132 | Experimental | –0.0610 |
| Pingree | 1978 | 227 | 132 | Experimental | 0.2780 * |
| Rao | 1987 | 16 | 56 | Experimental | 0.5620 * |
| Rao | 1987 | 16 | 56 | Experimental | 0.4850 * |
| Rao | 1987 | 16 | 56 | Experimental | 0.4830 * |
| Rosenwasser | 1989 | 114 | 66 | Correlational | –0.0250 |
| Rosenwasser | 1989 | 114 | 66 | Correlational | –0.0400 |
| Rosenwasser | 1989 | 114 | 90 | Correlational | 0.4750 * |
| Rosenwasser | 1989 | 114 | 90 | Correlational | 0.1650 |
| Rosenwasser | 1989 | 114 | 66 | Correlational | 0.2300 * |
| Rosenwasser | 1989 | 114 | 66 | Correlational | 0.0650 |
| Rosenwasser | 1989 | 114 | 90 | Correlational | –0.0200 |
| Rosenwasser | 1989 | 114 | 90 | Correlational | 0.3150 * |
| Rosenwasser | 1989 | 114 | 66 | Correlational | 0.0100 |
| Rosenwasser | 1989 | 114 | 66 | Correlational | 0.2530 * |
| Rosenwasser | 1989 | 114 | 90 | Correlational | 0.3950 * |
| Rosenwasser | 1989 | 114 | 90 | Correlational | 0.1050 |
| Rushton | 1975 | 72 | 108 | Experimental | 0.2870 * |
| Rushton | 1975 | 72 | 108 | Experimental | 0.1970 * |
| Silverman | 1980 | 90 | 60 | Experimental | 0.1070 * |
| Silverman | 1980 | 90 | 60 | Experimental | 0.4350 * |
| Silverman | 1980 | 90 | 60 | Experimental | –0.3520 * |
| Silverman | 1980 | 24 | 36 | Experimental | –0.5090 * |
| Silverman | 1980 | 24 | 36 | Experimental | –0.4790 * |
| Silverman | 1980 | 24 | 36 | Experimental | 0.3670 * |
| Silverman | 1980 | 24 | 36 | Experimental | 0.5880 * |
| Sprafkin | 1975 | 30 | 78 | Experimental | 0.8560 * |
| Sprafkin | 1975 | 30 | 78 | Experimental | 0.1360 |
| Sprafkin | 1979 | 393 | 102 | Correlational | 0.0800 |
| Teachman | 1981 | 120 | 108 | Experimental | 0.1450 * |
| Teachman | 1981 | 120 | 108 | Experimental | –0.0080 |
| Teachman | 1981 | 120 | 108 | Experimental | 0.4270 * |
| Teachman | 1981 | 120 | 108 | Experimental | 0.0850 |
| Toeplitz-Winiewska | 1977 | 152 | 200 | Experimental | –0.2490 * |
| Toeplitz-Winiewska | 1977 | 152 | 200 | Experimental | 0.1440* |
| Toeplitz-Winiewska | 1977 | 152 | 200 | Experimental | –0.3300 * |
| Toeplitz-Winiewska | 1977 | 152 | 202 | Experimental | 0.2300 * |

| Author[a] | Year | N[b] | Age[c] | Design | Effect Size[d] |
|---|---|---|---|---|---|
| Toeplitz-Winiewska | 1977 | 152 | 202 | Experimental | 0.0200 |
| Toeplitz-Winiewska | 1977 | 152 | 202 | Experimental | 0.2800 * |
| Tower | 1979 | 58 | 50 | Experimental | 0.0440 |
| Tower | 1979 | 58 | 50 | Experimental | 0.2000 * |
| Tower | 1979 | 58 | 50 | Experimental | 0.1290 * |
| Tower | 1979 | 58 | 50 | Experimental | 0.2510 * |
| Tower | 1979 | 58 | 50 | Experimental | 0.2900 * |
| Tower | 1979 | 58 | 50 | Experimental | 0.3160 * |
| Tower | 1979 | 58 | 50 | Experimental | 0.4190 * |
| Tower | 1979 | 58 | 50 | Experimental | 0.3870 * |
| Zimmerman | 1975 | 37 | 132 | Experimental | 0.3080 * |

a. The first author is listed here; see the Meta-Analysis References for complete citations.
b. Total number of subjects in the referenced study.
c. The average age of subjects in months.
d. An asterisk denotes that the effect size was significant at the .05 level.

## Studies Referenced in Meta-Analysis


Abelman, R. (1985). Styles of parental disciplinary practices as a mediator of children's learning from prosocial television portrayals. *Child Study Journal, 15,* 131-145.

Ahammer, I. M., & Murray, J. P. (1979). Kindness in the kindergarten: The relative influence of role-playing and prosocial television in facilitating altruism. *International Journal of Behavioral Development, 2,* 133-157.

Bankart, C. P., & Anderson, C. C. (1979). Short-term effects of prosocial television viewing on play of preschool boys and girls. *Psychological Reports, 44,* 935-941.

Baran, S. J., Chase, L. J., & Courtright, J. A. (1979). Television drama as a facilitator of prosocial behavior: "The Waltons." *Journal of Broadcasting, 23,* 277-284.

Bryan, J. H., & Walbek, N. H. (1970). The impact of words and deeds concerning altruism upon children. *Child Development, 41,* 747-757.

Collins, W. A., & Getz, S. K. (1976). Children's social responses following modeled reactions to provocation: Prosocial effects of a television drama. *Journal of Personality, 44*(3), 488-500.

Davidson, E. S., Yasuna, A., & Tower, A. (1979). The effects of television cartoons on sex-role stereotyping in young girls. *Child Development, 50,* 597-600.

Drabman, R. S., & Thomas, M. H. (1977). Children's imitation of aggressive and prosocial behavior when viewing alone and in pairs. *Journal of Communication, 27*(3), 199-205.

Durkin, K., & Hutchins, G. (1984). Challenging traditional sex-role stereotypes in careers education broadcasts: The reactions of young secondary school pupils. *Journal of Educational Television, 10,* 25-33.

Elias, M. J. (1983). Improving coping skills of emotionally disturbed boys through television-based social problem solving. *American Journal of Orthopsychiatry, 53,* 61-72.

Elliott, R., & Vasta, R. (1970). The modeling of sharing: Effects associated with vicarious reinforcement, symbolization, age, and generalization. *Journal of Experimental Child Psychology, 10,* 8-15.

Forge, L. S., & Phemister, S. (1987). The effect of prosocial cartoons on preschool children. *Child Study Journal, 17,* 83-87.

Friedrich-Cofer, L. K., Huston-Stein, A., Kipnis, D. M., Susman, E. J., & Clewett, A. S. (1979). Environmental enhancement of prosocial television content: Effect on interpersonal behavior, imaginative play, and self-regulation in a natural setting. *Developmental Psychology, 15,* 637-646.

Geller, M. I., & Scheirer, C. J. (1978). The effect of filmed modeling on cooperative play in disadvantaged preschoolers. *Journal of Abnormal Child Psychology, 6,* 71-87.

Goldberg, M. E., & Gorn, G. J. (1979). Television's impact on preferences of non-white playmates: Canadian "Sesame Street" inserts. *Journal of Broadcasting, 23,* 27-32.

Gorn, G. J., Goldberg, M. E., & Kanungo, R. N. (1976). The role of educational television in changing the intergroup attitudes of children. *Child Development, 42,* 277-280.

Houser, B. B. (1978). An examination of the use of audiovisual media in reducing prejudice. *Psychology in the Schools, 15*(1), 116-122.

Keller, M. F., & Carlson, P. M. (1974). The use of symbolic modeling to promote social skills in preschool children with low levels of social responsiveness. *Child Development, 45,* 912-919.

Liss, M. B., & Reinhardt, L. C. (1980). Aggression on prosocial television programs. *Psychological Reports, 46,* 1065-1066.

McArthur, L. Z., & Eisen, S. V. (1976). Television and sex-role stereotyping. *Journal of Applied Social Psychology, 6*(4), 329-351.

O'Bryant, S. L., & Corder-Bolz, C. R. (1978). The effects of television on children's stereotyping of women's work roles. *Journal of Vocational Behavior, 12,* 233-244.

O'Connor, R. D. (1969). Modification of social withdrawal through symbolic modeling. *Journal of Applied Behavior Analysis, 2,* 15-22.

O'Connor, R. D. (1972). Relative efficacy of modeling, shaping, and the combined procedures for modification of social withdrawal. *Journal of Abnormal Psychology, 79*(3), 327-334.

Pingree, S. (1978). The effects of nonsexist television commercials and perceptions of reality on children's attitudes about women. *Psychology of Women Quarterly, 2,* 262-277.

Rao, N., Moely, B. E., & Lockman, J. J. (1987). Increasing participation in preschool social isolates. *Journal of Clinical Child Psychology, 16*(3), 178-183.

Rosenwasser, S. M., Lingenfelter, M., & Harrington, A. F. (1989). Nontraditional gender role portrayals on television and children's gender role perceptions. *Journal of Applied Developmental Psychology, 10,* 97-105.

Rushton, J. P., & Owen, D. (1975). Immediate and delayed effects of TV modelling and preaching on children's generosity. *British Journal of Social and Clinical Psychology, 14,* 309-310.

Silverman, L. T., & Sprafkin, J. N. (1980). The effects of *Sesame Street's prosocial spots on cooperative play between young children. Journal of Broadcasting, 24,* 135-147.

Sprafkin, J. N., Liebert, R. M., & Poulos, R. W. (1975). Effects of a prosocial televised example on children's helping. *Journal of Experimental Child Psychology, 20,* 119-126.

Sprafkin, J. N., & Rubinstein, E. A. (1979). Children's television viewing habits and prosocial behavior: A field correlational study. *Journal of Broadcasting, 23*(3), 265-276.

Teachman, G., & Orme, M. (1981). Effects of aggressive and prosocial film material on altruistic behavior of children. *Psychological Reports, 48,* 699-702.

Toeplitz-Winiewska, M. (1977). Influence of various models on aggressive behavior in individuals with different socialization experience. *Polish Psychological Bulletin, 8*(4), 215-222.

Tower, R. B., Singer, D. G., Singer, J. L., & Biggs, A. (1979). Differential effects of television programming on preschoolers' cognition, imagination, and social play. *American Journal of Orthopsychiatry, 49,* 265-281.

Zimmerman, B. J., & Brody, G. H. (1975). Race and modeling influences on the play pattern of boys. *Journal of Educational Psychology, 67*(5), 591-598.

## References


Abelman, R. (1985). Styles of parental disciplinary practices as a mediator of children's learning from prosocial television portrayals. *Child Study Journal, 15,* 131-145.

Abelman, R. (1991). TV literacy III: Gifted and learning disabled children: Amplifying prosocial learning through curriculum intervention. *Journal of Research and Development in Education, 24,* 51-60.

Ahammer, I. M., & Murray, J. P. (1979). Kindness in the kindergarten: The relative influence of role-playing and prosocial television in facilitating altruism. *International Journal of Behavioral Development, 2,* 133-157.

Ball, S., & Bogatz, G. A. (1979). *The second year of* Sesame Street: *A continuing evaluation.* Princeton, NJ: Educational Testing Service.

Bankart, C. P., & Anderson, C. C. (1979). Short-term effects of prosocial television viewing on play of preschool boys and girls. *Psychological Reports, 44,* 935-941.

Beizer, D. (1999, March 22). A website of your own. *PC Magazine Online.* [Retrieved September 26, 1999]. Available: www.zdnet.com/pcmag/stories/reviews/0,6755,392606,00.html

Collins, W. A., & Getz, S. K. (1976). Children's social responses following modeled reactions to provocation: Prosocial effects of a television drama. *Journal of Personality, 44,* 488-500.

Cook, T. D., Appleton, H., Conner, R. F., Shaffer, A., Tamkin, G., & Weber, S. J. (1975). Sesame Street *revisited.* New York: Russell Sage.

Elias, M. J. (1983). Improving coping skills of emotionally disturbed boys through television-based social problem solving. *American Journal of Orthopsychiatry, 53,* 61-72.

Emerson, B. (1999, July 20). Bigger, badder, bloodier: It must be a computer game. *San Diego Union-Tribune,* Computer Link, p. 17.

Federal Communications Commission. (1991). Policies and rules concerning children's television programming: Memorandum opinion and order. *Federal Communications Commission Record, 6,* 2111-2127.

Friedrich, L., & Stein, A. H. (1973). Aggressive and prosocial television programs and the natural behavior of preschool children. *Monographs of the Society for Research in Child Development, 38*(4, Serial No. 151).

Friedrich, L., & Stein, A. H. (1975). Prosocial television and young children: The effects of verbal labeling and role playing on learning and behavior. *Child Development, 46,* 27-38.

Friedrich-Cofer, L. K., Huston-Stein, A., Kipnis, D. M., Susman, E. J., & Clewett, A. S. (1979). Environmental enhancement of prosocial television content: Effect on interpersonal behavior, imaginative play, and self-regulation in a natural setting. *Developmental Psychology, 15,* 637-646.

Goldberg, M. E., & Gorn, G. J. (1979). Television's impact on preferences of non-white playmates: Canadian "Sesame Street" inserts. *Journal of Broadcasting, 23,* 27-32.

Gorn, G. J., Goldberg, M. E., & Kanungo, R. N. (1976). The role of educational television in changing the intergroup attitudes of children. *Child Development, 42,* 277-280.

Greenberg, B. S., Atkin, C. K., Edison, N. G., & Korzenny, F. (1980). Antisocial and prosocial behaviors on television. In B. S. Greenberg (Ed.), *Life on television: Content analysis of U.S. TV drama.* Norwood, NJ: Ablex.

Hearold, S. (1986). A synthesis of 1043 effects of television on social behavior. In G. Comstock (Ed.), *Public communication and behavior* (Vol. 1, pp. 65-133). New York: Academic Press.

Higgins, J. M. (1998, January 16). "ER" may get more spots, lose Clooney. *Broadcasting & Cable,* p. 17.

Johnston, J., & Ettema, J. S. (1982). *Positive images: Breaking stereotypes with children's television.* Beverly Hills, CA: Sage.

Jordan, A. B. (1996). *The state of children's television: An examination of quantity, quality, and industry beliefs* (Report No. 2). Philadelphia: University of Pennsylvania, Annenberg Public Policy Center.

Jordan, A. B. (1998). *The 1998 state of children's television report: Programming for children over broadcast and cable television* (Report No. 23). Philadelphia: University of Pennsylvania, Annenberg Public Policy Center.

Jordan, A. B., & Woodard, E. H. (1997). *The 1997 state of children's television report: Programming for children over broadcast and cable television* (Report No. 14). Philadelphia: University of Pennsylvania, Annenberg Public Policy Center.

Kunkel, D. (1991). Crafting media policy: The genesis and implications of the Children's Television Act of 1990. *American Behavioral Scientist, 35,* 181-202.

Kunkel, D. (1998). Policy battles over defining children's educational television. *Annals of the American Academy of Political and Social Science, 557,* 39-53.

Kunkel, D., & Canepa, J. (1994). Broadcasters' license renewal claims regarding children's educational programming. *Journal of Broadcasting and Electronic Media, 38,* 397-416.

Liebert, R. M., & Poulos, R. W. (1975). Television and personality development: The socializing effects of an entertainment medium. In A. Davids (Ed.), *Child personality and psychopathology: Vol. 2. Current topics* (pp. 61-97). New York: John Wiley.

Liebert, R. M., & Sprafkin, J. (1988). *The early window: Effects of television on children and youth.* New York: Pergamon.

Liss, M. B., & Reinhardt, L. C. (1980). Aggression on prosocial television programs. *Psychological Reports, 46,* 1065-1066.

Mares, M. L. (1998). Children's use of VCRs. *Annals of the American Academy of Political and Social Science, 557,* 120-132.

Mares, M. L., & Woodard, E. H. (in press). Positive effects of television on children's social interactions: A meta-analysis. In R. Carveth & J. Bryant (Eds.), *Meta-analyses of media effects.* Hillsdale, NJ: Lawrence Erlbaum.

Media Metrix. (1999). *Media Metrix top 500* [On-line]. [Retrieved September 6, 1999]. Available: www.mediametrix.com/Top500/Top500.html

O'Bryant, S. L., & Corder-Bolz, C. R. (1978). The effects of television on children's stereotyping of women's work roles. *Journal of Vocational Behavior, 12,* 233-244.

Paik, H., & Comstock, G. (1994). The effects of television violence on antisocial behavior: A meta-analysis. *Communication Research, 21,* 516-546.

Pingree, S. (1978). The effects of nonsexist television commercials and perceptions of reality on children's attitudes about women. *Psychology of Women Quarterly, 2,* 262-277.

Poulos, R. W., Harvey, S. E., & Liebert, R. M. (1976). Saturday morning television: A profile of the 1974-75 children's season. *Psychological Reports, 39,* 1047-1057.

Poulos, R. W., Rubinstein, E. A., & Liebert, R. M. (1975). Positive social learning. *Journal of Communication, 25,* 90-97.

Rice, M. L., Huston, A. C., Truglio, R., & Wright, J. C. (1990). Words from *Sesame Street:* Learning vocabulary while viewing. *Developmental Psychology, 26,* 421-428.

Rosenkoetter, L. I. (1999). The television situation comedy and children's prosocial behavior. *Journal of Applied Social Psychology, 29,* 979-993.

Rosenwasser, S. M., Lingenfelter, M., & Harrington, A. F. (1989). Nontraditional gender role portrayals on television and children's gender role perceptions. *Journal of Applied Developmental Psychology, 10,* 97-105.

Rushton, J. P. (1979). Effects of prosocial television and film material on the behavior of viewers. In L. Berkowitz (Ed.), *Advances in experimental social psychology* (pp. 321-351). New York: Academic Press.

Rushton, J. P. (1982). Altruism and society: A social learning perspective. *Ethics, 92,* 425-446.

Schmitt, K. L. (1999). *The three hour rule: Is it living up to expectations?* (Report No. 30). Philadelphia: University of Pennsylvania, Annenberg Public Policy Center.

Silverman, L. T., & Sprafkin, J. N. (1980). The effects of *Sesame Street's* prosocial spots on cooperative play between young children. *Journal of Broadcasting, 24,* 135-147.

Singer, J. L., & Singer, D. G. (1983). Implications of childhood television viewing for cognition, imagination, and emotion. In J. Bryant & D. R. Anderson (Eds.), *Children's understanding of television* (pp. 265-295). New York: Academic Press.

Singer, J. L., & Singer, D. G. (1998). *Barney & Friends* as entertainment and education. In J. K. Asamen & G. Berry (Eds.), *Research paradigms, television, and social behavior* (pp. 305-367). Thousand Oaks, CA: Sage.

Singer, J. L., Singer, D. G., & Sherrod, L. R. (1979). *Prosocial programs in the context of children's total pattern of TV viewing.* Paper presented at the biennial meeting of the Society for Research in Child Development, San Francisco.

Sprafkin, J. N., & Rubinstein, E. A. (1979). Children's television viewing habits and prosocial behavior: A field correlational study. *Journal of Broadcasting, 23,* 265-276.

Stanger, J., & Gridina, N. (1999). *Media in the home 1999: The fourth annual survey of parents and children* (Survey Series No. 5). Philadelphia: University of Pennsylvania, Annenberg Public Policy Center.

Tilley, S. (1999, September 15). Learning to kill? Videogames called "murder simulators." *Toronto Sun,* p. C6.

Tower, R. B., Singer, D. G., Singer, J. L., & Biggs, A. (1979). Differential effects of television programming on preschoolers' cognition, imagination, and social play. *American Journal of Orthopsychiatry, 49,* 265-281.

Wiegman, O., Kuttschreuter, M., & Baarda, B. (1992). A longitudinal study of the effects of television viewing on aggressive and prosocial behaviors. *British Journal of Social Psychology, 31,* 147-164.

Woodard, E. H. (1999). *The 1999 state of children's television report: Programming for children over broadcast and cable television* (Report No. 28). Philadelphia: University of Pennsylvania, Annenberg Public Policy Center.

Zill, N., Davies, E., & Daly, M. (1994). *Viewing of* Sesame Street *by preschool children in the United States and its relationship to school readiness.* Rockville, MD: Westat.

CHAPTER **10**

# The Media and Children's Fears, Anxieties, and Perceptions of Danger

JOANNE CANTOR
University of Wisconsin-Madison

Television and movies provide a multitude of images that have the capacity to worry, frighten, or even traumatize children. Moreover, the intensity and variety of these images have greatly expanded over the last decade. This recent trend may be attributable to an increasingly desensitized adult population who patronize movies that continue to escalate in their levels of violence and the vividness of their special effects (Federman, 1998; Fiore, 1999). It may also be a function of the wide adoption of cable television, which has spawned competition among all channels for the attention of the consumer. Furthermore, the growing prevalence of television news shows and the increasing display of video footage of catastrophic and sensational events proliferate the worrisome images even more (Klite, Bardwell, & Salzman, 1997).

Although the impact of media violence on children's aggressive behavior has been at the center of research debates and public attention for decades, the impact of images of violence, danger, death, and destruction on children's perceptions, worries, and fears has received much less attention.

## The Impact of Habitual Viewing Practices on Perceptions, Fears, and Anxieties

One way in which the impact of media on children's perceptions and worries has been studied is by the "cultivation" paradigm (e.g., Gerbner, Gross, Morgan, & Signorielli, 1994), in which a child's amount of television viewing is related to his or her perceptions of how dangerous the world is. One of the assumptions underlying this body of work is that the most important features of the television landscape pervade all forms of programming. Accordingly, predictions about a child's view of the world are made on the basis of how much television a child watches, independent of his or her particular choice of shows. The research of Gerbner and his associates has shown, for example, that heavy television viewers perceive the chances of being involved in violence as greater than light viewers do. They are also more prone to believe that others cannot be trusted (e.g., Gerbner, Gross, Morgan, & Signorielli, 1980).

Although cultivation analysis has been criticized for the assumption that television content is rather homogeneous (Hawkins & Pingree, 1981), recent surveys have documented the association between heavy television viewing, independent of program choice, and negative emotional consequences. A survey of more than 2,000 third through eighth graders in Ohio public schools revealed that, as the number of hours of television viewing per day increased, so did the prevalence of symptoms of psychological trauma such as anxiety, depression, and posttraumatic stress (Singer, Slovak, Frierson, & York, 1998). Similarly, a survey of the parents of almost 500 public school children in kindergarten through fourth grade in Rhode Island revealed that the amount of children's television viewing (especially television viewing at bedtime) and having a television in their own bedroom were significantly related to sleep disturbances (Owens et al., 1999). Although these survey data cannot rule out the alternative explanation that children experiencing trauma or sleep difficulties are more likely to turn to television for distraction, they are consistent with the conclusion that exposure to frightening and disturbing images on television contributes to a child's level of stress and anxiety. Indeed, 9% of the parents in the study by Owens et al. (1999) reported that their child experienced TV-induced nightmares at least once a week.

## Effects of Exposure to Individual Programs and Movies

The fright-producing impact of media depictions has most often been studied in terms of the immediate emotional impact of specific programs and movies, and the study of children's fright reactions to media fare goes back long before the introduction of television. For example, as early as the 1930s, Blumer (1933) reported that 93% of the children he questioned said they had been frightened or horrified by a motion picture. More recently, about 75% of the respondents in two separate samples of preschool and elementary school children said that they had been scared by something they had seen on television or in a movie (Wilson, Hoffner, & Cantor, 1987). Cantor and Nathanson (1996) reported that 43% of a random sample of parents of elementary school children in Madison, Wisconsin, said that their child had experienced enduring fright as a function of exposure to television. In the first random national survey of its kind in the United States, Gentile and Walsh (1999) reported that 62% of parents with children between the ages of 2 and 17 said that their child had become scared that something they saw in a TV program or movie might happen to them. Finally, in a random national survey of 7- to 12-year-old children in the Netherlands, 31% of the respondents reported having been frightened by television during the preceding year (Valkenburg, Cantor, & Peeters, 2000).

An experimental study explored the impact of witnessing scary media events on the subsequent behavioral choices of children in kindergarten through fifth grade (Cantor & Omdahl, 1991). In this experiment, exposure to dramatized depictions of a deadly house fire or a drowning increased children's self-reports of worry about similar events in their own lives. More important, these fictional depictions affected the children's preferences for normal, everyday activities that were related to the tragedies they had just witnessed: Children who had seen a movie depicting a drowning expressed less willingness to go canoeing than other children did; those who had seen the program about a house fire were less eager to build a fire in a fireplace. Although the duration of such effects was not measured, the effects were undoubtedly short-lived, especially because debriefings were employed and safety guidelines were taught so that no child would experience long-term distress (Cantor & Omdahl, 1999).

There is growing evidence, in fact, that the fear induced by mass media exposure is often intense and long-lasting, with sometimes debilitating effects (Cantor, 1998). In a study designed to assess the severity of enduring fright reactions to mass media, Johnson (1980) asked a random sample of adults whether they had ever seen a motion picture that had disturbed them "a great deal." Forty percent replied in the affirmative, and the median length of the reported disturbance was 3 full days. Respondents also reported on the type, intensity, and duration of symptoms such as nervousness, depression, fear of specific things, and recurring thoughts and images. On the basis of these reports, Johnson judged that 48% of these respondents (19% of the total sample) had experienced, for at least 2 days, a "significant stress reaction" as the result of watching a movie. Johnson argued that

> it is one thing to walk away from a frightening or disturbing event with mild residue of the images and quite another thing to ruminate about it, feel anxious or depressed for days, and/or to avoid anything that might create the same unpleasant experience. (p. 786)

On the basis of his data, he concluded that such reactions were more prevalent and more severe than had previously been assumed.

Recent retrospective studies of adults' detailed memories of having been frightened by a television show or movie provide more evidence of the severity and duration of media-induced fear (Harrison & Cantor, 1999; Hoekstra, Harris, & Helmick, 1999). In these studies, involving samples of undergraduates from three universities, the presence of vivid memories of enduring media-induced fear was nearly universal. All of the participants in the Hoekstra et al. (1999) research reported such an incident. In the Harrison and Cantor (1999) study, 90% reported an intense fear reaction to something in the media, despite the fact that the respondents could receive full extra credit for participating in the study if they simply said "no" (meaning "I never had such an experience") and thereby would avoid writing a paper and filling out a three-page questionnaire.

As for the effects reported, both studies revealed a variety of intense reactions. In Hoekstra et al.'s (1999) study, 61% reported a generalized fear or free-floating anxiety after viewing; 46% reported what they called "wild imagination" ("monsters under the bed" or "someone sneaking up on you"); 29% reported a specific fear (e.g., sharks, power tools, spiders); and more than 20% reported a variety of sleep disturbances, including fear of sleeping alone, nightmares, insomnia, or needing to sleep with the lights on. Of the students reporting fright reactions in Harrison and Cantor's (1999) study, 52% reported disturbances in eating or sleeping, 22% reported mental preoccupation with the disturbing material, and 35% reported subsequently avoiding or dreading the situation depicted in the program or movie. Moreover, one third of those who reported having been frightened said that the fear effects had lasted more than a year. Indeed, more than one fourth of the respondents said that the emotional impact of the program or movie (viewed an average of 6 years earlier) was still with them at the time of reporting!

The most extreme reactions reported in the literature come from psychiatric case studies in which acute and disabling anxiety states enduring several days to several weeks or more (some necessitating hospitalization) are said to have been precipitated by the viewing of horror movies such as *The Exorcist, Invasion of the Body Snatchers,* and *Ghostwatch* (Buzzuto, 1975; Mathai, 1983; Simons & Silveira, 1994). Most of the patients in the cases reported had not had previously diagnosed psychiatric problems, but the viewing of the film was seen as occurring in conjunction with other stressors in the patients' lives.

## Limited Evidence for Catharsis or Anxiety Reduction

Given the prevalence of intense anxiety reactions to scary media images, the question naturally arises as to why horror films, violent fare, and other frightening images are so popular. A variety of theories have been advanced to account for the enduring popularity of frightening media (see Goldstein, 1998, for a variety of viewpoints on the attractions of violence). Prominent among the theories is the notion of sensation seeking (Zuckerman, 1979), which contends that risk taking helps individuals seek their optimal level of arousal. Apter (1992) argues that individuals can experience excitement rather than anxiety when confronting danger when the event is experienced through a "protective frame." He further argues that our modern society, which has reduced most day-to-day threats to an individual's safety, makes it more necessary than ever to seek safe ways to experience excitement.

There have been some arguments, particularly in the psychoanalytic literature, that scary images in the media reduce rather than increase anxieties by allowing children to confront their real fears in a safe context. Bettelheim (1975) is most frequently associated with this argument, although his claims were related to violent fairy tales that are presented orally rather than to mass media presentations that involve moving images. In any event, no systematic evidence for this therapeutic effect of fairy tales has been presented (Cantor, 1998).

There are some limited circumstances, however, when a frightening media depiction might be effective in alleviating anxiety. This anxiety-reducing effect appears to occur only when the story induces no more than a mild level of fear and when the outcome of the story reveals that the danger can be effectively counteracted (Bryant, Carveth, & Brown, 1981; see also Cantor & Nathanson, 1997).

Instances in which frightening media depictions reduce anxiety seem to be the exception rather than the rule, especially when children are concerned. As detailed above, many studies demonstrate that enduring emotional disturbances occur in a substantial proportion of children and that these responses are often intense and disruptive to a child's well-being.

## Developmental Differences and Media-Induced Fear

A large body of research has examined two major developmental issues in fright reactions to media: (a) the types of mass media stimuli and events that frighten children at different ages, and (b) the strategies for preventing or reducing unwanted fear reactions that are most effective for different-aged children (Cantor, 1994). Experiments and surveys have been conducted to test expectations based on theories and findings in cognitive development research. The experiments have had the advantage of testing rigorously controlled variations in program content and viewing conditions, using a combination of self-reports, physiological responses, the coding of facial expressions of emotion, and behavioral measures. For ethical reasons, only small excerpts from relatively mild stimuli are used in experiments. In contrast, the surveys have investigated the responses of children who were exposed to a particular mass media offering in their natural environment, without any researcher intervention. Although less tightly controlled, the surveys permit the study of responses to much more intensely frightening media fare.

### *Developmental Differences in the Media Stimuli That Produce Fright*

One might expect that, as children get older, they become less and less susceptible to all media-produced emotional disturbances. However, this is not the case. As children mature cognitively, some things become less likely to disturb them, whereas other things become potentially more upsetting. This generalization is consistent with developmental differences in children's fears in general. According to a variety of studies using diverse methodologies, children from approximately 3 to 8 years of age are frightened primarily by animals; the dark; supernatural beings such as ghosts, monsters, and witches; and anything that looks strange or moves suddenly. The fears of 9- to 12-year-olds are more often related to personal injury and physical destruction and the injury and death of family members. Adolescents continue to fear personal injury and physical destruction; in addition, school fears and social fears arise at this age, as do fears regarding political, economic, and global issues (see Cantor, Wilson, & Hoffner, 1986, for a review).

#### *Perceptual Dependence*

The findings regarding the media stimuli that frighten children at different ages are consistent with observed changes in children's fears in general. This section summarizes broad generalizations and supportive findings. The first generalization about fright-provoking stimuli is that the relative importance of the immediately perceptible components of a fear-inducing media stimulus decreases as a child's age increases. Research on cognitive development indicates that, in general, very young children react to stimuli predominantly in terms of their perceptible characteristics and that, with increasing maturity, they respond more and more to the conceptual aspects of stimuli (see Flavell, 1963; Melkman, Tversky, & Baratz, 1981). Research findings support the generalization that preschool children (approximately 3-5 years old) are more likely to be frightened by something that *looks* scary but is actually harmless than by something that looks attractive but is actually harmful; for older elementary school children (approximately 9-11), appearance carries much less weight relative to the behavior or destructive potential of a character, animal, or object.

One set of data that supports this generalization comes from a survey conducted in 1981 (Cantor & Sparks, 1984) asking parents to name the programs and films that had frightened their children the most. In this survey, parents of preschool children most often mentioned offerings with grotesque-looking, unreal characters, such as the television series *The Incredible Hulk* and the feature film *The Wizard of Oz;* parents of older elementary school children more often mentioned programs or movies (e.g., *The Amityville Horror*) that involved threats without a strong visual component and that required a good deal of imagination to comprehend. Sparks (1986) replicated this study using children's self-reports rather than parents' observations and obtained similar findings. Both surveys included controls for possible differences in exposure patterns in the different age groups.

A second investigation that supports this generalization was a laboratory study involving an episode of *The Incredible Hulk* (Sparks & Cantor, 1986). In the 1981 survey of parents, this program had spontaneously been mentioned by 40% of the parents of preschoolers as a show that had scared their child (Cantor & Sparks, 1984). The laboratory study concluded that preschool children's unexpectedly intense reactions to this program were partially from their overresponse to the visual image of the Hulk character. When participants were shown a shortened episode of the program and were asked how they had felt during different scenes, preschool children reported the most fear after the attractive, mild-mannered hero was transformed into the monstrous-looking Hulk. Older elementary school children, in contrast, reported the least fear at this time, because they understood that the Hulk was really the benevolent hero in another physical form and that he was using his superhuman powers to rescue a character who was in danger.

Another study (Hoffner & Cantor, 1985) tested the effect of appearance more directly by creating four versions of a story in which a major character was either attractive and grandmotherly looking or ugly and grotesque. The character's appearance was factorially varied with her behavior; she was depicted as behaving either kindly or cruelly. In judging how nice or mean the character was and in predicting what she would do in the subsequent scene, preschool children were more influenced than older children (6-7 and 9-10 years) by the character's looks and less influenced than older children by her kind or cruel behavior. As the age of the child increased, the character's looks became less important and her behavior carried increasing weight. A follow-up experiment revealed that all age groups engaged in physical-appearance stereotyping in the absence of information about the character's behavior.

Harrison and Cantor's (1999) retrospective study of fright responses also provided evidence in support of the diminishing influence of appearance. When descriptions of the program or movie that had frightened respondents were categorized as involving immediately perceptible stimuli (e.g., monstrous-looking characters, eerie noises) or not, the percentage of respondents whose described scene fell into the former category declined as the respondent's age at exposure increased.

### *Fantasy Versus Reality as Fear Inducers*

A second generalization that emerges from research is that, as children mature, they become more responsive to realistic dangers and less responsive to fantastic dangers depicted in the media. The data on trends in children's fears suggest that very young children are more likely than older children and adolescents to fear things that are not real (i.e., their occurrence in the real world is impossible, such as monsters). The development of more "mature" fears seems to presuppose the acquisition of knowledge regarding the objective dangers posed by different situations. One important component of this knowledge includes an understanding of the distinction between reality and fantasy, a competence that develops only gradually throughout childhood (see Flavell, 1963; Kelly, 1981; Morison & Gardner, 1978; Rapaczynski, Singer, & Singer, 1982).

This generalization is supported by Cantor and Sparks's (1984) survey of parents. In general, the tendency to mention fantasy offerings (depicting events that could not possibly occur in the real world) as sources of fear decreased as the child's age increased, and the tendency to mention fictional offerings (depicting events that could possibly occur) increased. Again, Sparks (1986) replicated these findings using children's self-reports. Further support for this generalization comes from a study of children's fright responses to television news (Cantor & Nathanson, 1996). A random survey of parents of children in kindergarten, second, fourth, and sixth grade showed that fear produced by fantasy programs decreased as the child's grade increased, whereas fear induced by news stories increased with age. Valkenburg et al. (2000), in their random survey of Dutch children, also found a decrease in fright responses to fantasy content between the ages of 7 and 12.

### *Responses to Abstract Threats*

The third generalization from research is that, as children mature, they become frightened by media depictions involving increasingly abstract concepts. This generalization is clearly consistent with the general sources of children's fears cited earlier. It is also consistent with theories of cognitive development (e.g., Flavell, 1963), which indicate that the ability to think abstractly emerges relatively late in cognitive development.

Data supporting this generalization come from a survey of children's responses to the television movie *The Day After* (Cantor et al., 1986). Although many people were concerned about young children's reactions to this movie, which depicts the devastation of a Kansas community by a nuclear attack (Schofield & Pavelchak, 1985), developmental considerations led to the prediction that the youngest children would be the least affected by it. In a random telephone survey of parents conducted the night after the broadcast of this movie, children under 12 were reportedly much less disturbed by the film than were teenagers, and parents were the most disturbed. The very youngest children seem to have been the least frightened. The findings seem to be due to the fact that the emotional impact of the film comes from the contemplation of the potential annihilation of the earth as we know it, a concept that is beyond the grasp of the young child. The visual depictions of injury in the movie were quite mild compared with what most children have become used to seeing on television.

A study of children's reactions to television coverage of the war in the Persian Gulf also supports the generalization that, as they mature, children are increasingly responsive to abstract as opposed to concrete aspects of frightening media (Cantor, Mares, & Oliver, 1993). In a random survey of parents of children in public school in Madison, Wisconsin, conducted shortly after the Gulf War, there were no significant differences between first, fourth, seventh, and eleventh graders regarding the prevalence or intensity of negative emotional reactions to television coverage of the war. However, children in different grades were upset by different aspects of the coverage. In their descriptions of the elements that had disturbed their child the most, parents of younger children, but not of adolescents, stressed the visual aspects of the coverage and the direct, concrete consequences of combat (e.g., the missiles exploding). As the child's age increased, the more abstract, conceptual aspects of the coverage (e.g., the possibility of the conflict spreading) were cited by parents as the most disturbing.

In summary, research on the relationship between cognitive development and emotional responses to television can be very helpful in predicting the types of television programs and movies that are more or less likely to frighten children of different ages. In addition to providing empirical tests of the relationship between cognitive development and affective responses, these developmental findings can help parents and other caregivers make more sensible viewing choices for children (Cantor, 1998).

### *Developmental Differences in the Effectiveness of Coping Strategies*

No matter how well intentioned or careful or sensitive parents are to the emotional vulnerabilities of their children, children are likely to be frightened at one time or another by what they see on television. Research in cognitive development has also been used to determine the best ways to help children cope with fear-producing stimuli or to reduce children's fear reactions once they occur (Cantor, 1998).

Developmental differences in children's information-processing abilities yield differences in the effectiveness of strategies to prevent or reduce their media-induced fears (Cantor & Wilson, 1988). The findings of research on coping strategies can be summed up in the following generalization: In general, preschool children benefit more from "noncognitive" than from "cognitive" strategies; both cognitive and noncognitive strategies can be effective for older elementary school children, although this age group tends to prefer cognitive strategies.

*Noncognitive Strategies*

Noncognitive strategies are those that do not involve the processing of verbal information and appear to be relatively automatic. The process of visual desensitization, or gradual exposure to threatening images in a nonthreatening context, is one such strategy that has been shown to be effective for both preschool and older elementary school children. In one experiment, gradual visual exposure to filmed footage of snakes tended to reduce fear reactions to the "snake pit" scene from the action-adventure film *Raiders of the Lost Ark* (Wilson & Cantor, 1987). In a second experiment (Wilson, 1987), exposure to a realistic rubber replica of a tarantula reduced the emotional impact of a scene involving tarantulas in *Kingdom of the Spiders*. In a third experiment (Wilson, 1989a), exposure to a live lizard reduced children's expression of fear while watching a scene involving deadly lizards in *Frogs*. In a fourth experiment (Weiss, Imrich, & Wilson, 1993), exposure to graphic photographs of worms taken from the horror film *Squirm* reduced children's self-reports of fear during a scene from that movie. Finally, fear reactions to the Hulk character in *The Incredible Hulk* were reduced by exposure to footage of Lou Ferrigno, the actor who plays the character, having his makeup applied so that he gradually took on the menacing appearance of the character (Cantor, Sparks, & Hoffner, 1988). None of these experiments revealed developmental differences in the technique's effectiveness.

Other noncognitive strategies involve physical activities such as clinging to an attachment object or having something to eat or drink. Although these techniques are available to viewers of all ages, there is reason to believe that they are more effective for younger than for older children. First, it has been argued that the effectiveness of such techniques is likely to diminish as the infant's tendency to grasp and suck objects for comfort and exploration decreases (Bowlby, 1973). Second, it seems likely that the effectiveness of such techniques is partially attributable to distraction, and distraction techniques should be more effective in younger children, who have greater difficulty allocating cognitive processing to two simultaneous activities (e.g., Manis, Keating, & Morison, 1980).

Children seem to be intuitively aware that physical techniques work better for younger than for older children. In a study of children's *perceptions* of the effectiveness of strategies for coping with media-induced fright, preschool children's evaluations of "holding onto a blanket or a toy" and "getting something to eat or drink" were significantly more positive than were those of older elementary school children (Wilson et al., 1987). Harrison and Cantor's (1999) retrospective study also showed that the percentage of respondents who reported having used a "behavioral" (noncognitive) coping strategy to deal with media-induced fear declined as age at exposure to the frightening fare increased.

Another noncognitive strategy that has been shown to have more appeal and more effectiveness for younger than for older children is covering one's eyes during frightening portions of a presentation. In an experiment by Wilson (1989b), when covering the eyes was suggested as an option, younger children used this strategy more often than older children. Moreover, the suggestion of this option reduced the fear of younger children but actually increased the fear of older children. Wilson noted that the older children recognized the limited effectiveness of covering their eyes (while still being exposed to the audio features of the program) and may have reacted by feeling *less* in control, and therefore more vulnerable, when this strategy was offered to them.

*Cognitive Strategies*

In contrast to noncognitive strategies, cognitive (or "verbal") strategies involve verbal information that is used to cast the threat in a different light. These strategies involve relatively complex cognitive operations, and research consistently finds such strategies to be more effective for older than for younger children.

When dealing with fantasy depictions, the most typical cognitive strategy seems to be to provide an explanation focusing on the unreality of the situation. This strategy should be especially difficult for preschool children, who do not have a full grasp of the implications of the fantasy-reality distinction. In an experiment by Cantor and Wilson (1984), older elementary school children who were told to remember that what they were seeing in *The Wizard of Oz* was not real showed less fear than their classmates who received no instructions. The same instructions did not help preschoolers, however. A more recent study (Wilson & Weiss, 1991) again showed developmental differences in the effectiveness of reality-related strategies.

Children's beliefs about the effectiveness of focusing on the unreality of the stimulus have been shown to be consistent with these experimental findings. In the study of perceptions of fear-reducing techniques, preschool children's ranking of the effectiveness of "tell yourself it's not real" was significantly lower than that of older elementary school children (Wilson et al., 1987). In contrast to both preschool and elementary school children, who apparently view this strategy accurately, parents do not seem to appreciate the inadequacy of this technique for young children. Eighty percent of the parents of both the preschool and elementary school children who participated in another study (Wilson & Cantor, 1987) reported that they employed a "tell them it's not real" coping strategy to reduce their child's media-induced fear.

For media depictions involving realistic threats, the most prevalent cognitive strategy seems to be to provide an explanation that minimizes the perceived severity of the depicted danger. Not only is this type of strategy more effective with older children than with younger children, but in certain situations it has been shown to have a fear-enhancing rather than anxiety-reducing effect with younger children. In the experiment involving the snake-pit scene from *Raiders of the Lost Ark* mentioned earlier (Wilson & Cantor, 1987), a second experimental variation involved the presence or absence of reassuring information about snakes (e.g., the statement that most snakes are not poisonous). Although this information tended to reduce the fear of older elementary school children, kindergarten and first-grade children seem to have only partially understood the information, responding to the word *poisonous* more intensely than to the word *not*. For them, negative emotional reactions were more prevalent if they had heard the supposedly reassuring information than if they had not heard it.

Data also indicate that older children use cognitive coping strategies more frequently than preschool children do. In the survey of reactions to *The Day After* (Cantor et al., 1986), parents' reports that their child had discussed the movie with them after viewing it increased with the age of the child. In a laboratory experiment involving exposure to a scary scene (Hoffner & Cantor, 1990), significantly more 9- to 11-year-olds than 5- to 7-year-olds reported spontaneously employing cognitive coping strategies (thinking about the expected happy outcome or thinking about the fact that what was happening was not real). Finally, Harrison and Cantor's (1999) retrospective study showed that the tendency to employ a cognitive strategy to cope with media-induced fear increased with the respondent's age at the time of the incident.

Studies have also shown that the effectiveness of cognitive strategies for young children can be improved by providing visual demonstrations of verbal explanations (Cantor et al., 1988) and by encouraging repeated rehearsal of simplified, reassuring information (Wilson, 1987). In addition, research has explored some of the specific reasons for young children's inability to profit from verbal explanations such as those involving relative quantifiers (e.g., "some are dangerous, but most are not"; Badzinski, Cantor, & Hoffner, 1989) and probabilistic terms (e.g., "this probably will not happen to you"; Hoffner, Cantor, & Badzinski, 1990). It is clear from these studies that it is an extremely challenging task to "explain away" threats that have induced fear in a child, particularly when there is a strong perceptual component to the threatening stimulus and when the reassurance can only be partial or probabilistic rather than absolute (see Cantor & Hoffner, 1990).

## Gender Issues and Media-Induced Fright

### *Gender Differences in Media-Induced Fear*

There is a common stereotype that girls are more easily frightened than boys (Birnbaum & Croll, 1984; Cantor, Stutman, & Duran, 1996) and, indeed, that females in general are more emotional than males (e.g., Fabes & Martin, 1991; Grossman & Wood, 1993). There is quite a bit of research that would seem to support this contention, although the gender differences may be less strong than they appear at first glance. Moreover, the observed gender differences seem to be partially attributable to socialization pressures on girls to express their fears and on boys to inhibit them.

Peck (1999) conducted a meta-analysis of the studies of media-induced fear that were produced between 1987 and 1996. Her analysis, which included 59 studies that permitted a comparison between males and females, reported a moderate gender-difference effect size (.41), with females exhibiting more fear than males. Females' responses were more intense than those of males for all dependent measures. However, the effect sizes were largest for self-report and behavioral measures (those that are under the most conscious control) and smallest for heart rate and facial expressions. In addition, the effect size for gender differences increased with age.

Peck (1999) also conducted an experiment in which male and female college students were exposed to two scenes from the *Nightmare on Elm Street* series of movies, one featuring a male victim and the other featuring a female victim. She found that women's self-reports of fear were more intense than those of males, especially when the victim was female. However, when the victim was male, certain responses (pulse amplitude and hemispheric asymmetry) suggested that men were experiencing more intense physiological reactions than women.

Although more research is needed to explore the extent of gender differences in media-induced fear and the factors that contribute to them, these findings suggest that the size of the gender difference may be partially a function of social pressures to conform to gender-appropriate behavior.

### *Gender Differences in Coping Strategies*

There is some evidence of gender differences in the coping strategies used to counteract media-induced fear, and these gender differences may also reflect gender role socialization pressures. Hoffner (1995) found that adolescent girls reported using more noncognitive coping strategies than boys did, but there were no gender differences in the use of cognitive strategies. Similarly, Valkenburg et al. (2000) found that, among 7- to 12-year-old Dutch children, girls reported resorting to social support, physical intervention, and escape more often than boys did, but there was no gender difference in the use of cognitive reassurance as a coping strategy.

Both of these findings are consistent with Hoffner's (1995) explanation that, because boys are less willing to show their emotions than girls are, they avoid noncognitive strategies, which are usually apparent to others. In contrast, the two genders employ cognitive strategies with equal frequency because these strategies are less readily observable.

## Implications for Parents and Educators

### *Parental Knowledge and Children's Exposure*

It has been noted that parents often are not aware of the frequency or severity of their children's fright reactions. For example, Cantor and Reilly (1982) found that parents' estimates of the frequency of their children's media-induced fright reactions were significantly lower than their children's self-reports. This finding may be due in part to children's reluctance to admit to their parents that they have been scared in an attempt to appear mature or to avert parental restrictions over their future viewing. Parents also underestimate their children's exposure to scary media. Research suggests that children often experience fright reactions to programs that many parents would not expect to be scary (Cantor, 1998). Nevertheless, there is evidence that children are widely exposed to televised stimuli that were originally intended for adults and that are considered frightening by a large proportion of adult moviegoers. Sparks (1986), for example, reported that almost 50% of the 4- to 10-year-olds he interviewed had seen *Poltergeist* and *Jaws,* and substantial proportions of his sample had seen *Halloween* and *Friday the 13th.* Most of this viewing was done in the home, on cable television.

### *Coviewing and Emotional Responses*

Research has focused on the role that coviewing can play in reducing fright reactions to media. Hoffner and Haefner (1997) asked first- through sixth-grade children to recall a time when they watched a television show with someone who became scared and to describe how (if at all) they had attempted to comfort the frightened coviewer. Almost 40% said that they recalled watching a program with a frightened sibling (indeed, 5% said they remembered watching a program during which their mother had become frightened!). Approximately half of the girls and 30% of the boys said that they had tried to comfort the frightened coviewer. Comforting messages ranged from simple distraction attempts to a discussion and explanation of the coviewer's fear. Even the youngest children adjusted the sensitivity of their comforting strategy based on the intensity of the coviewer's fright response.

How effective are siblings at providing comfort for one another? Wilson and Weiss (1993) studied preschoolers' reactions to a scary television program when viewed with or without an older sibling. More than half of the sibling pairs talked about how scary the program was while watching the movie, and more than a third of the older siblings actively tried to provide comfort by offering reassurance, a hug, or a hand to hold. The older siblings' comforting attempts seem to have worked: Compared with children who watched the scary program alone, preschoolers who viewed with an older sibling were less emotionally aroused and liked the program more.

### *Advice for Parents*

The research presented here suggests that media content can have substantial negative effects on children's emotional well-being and that these effects can sometimes endure for long periods of time. Moreover, unhealthy effects on a child can be physical as well as emotional, such as when children are suddenly reluctant to sleep alone (or to sleep at all) or to engage in everyday activities that remind them of the fear-provoking television show or movie. These findings highlight the importance of taking the child's media exposure seriously and of trying to prevent severe emotional disturbances to the extent possible.

The research leads to a variety of recommendations for parents (Cantor, 1998):

1. The amount of time children spend watching television should be limited.

2. Parents should be especially concerned about children's viewing before bedtime and should not allow children to have a television in their bedroom.
3. Parents should become aware of the content of the television programs and movies their children see, by watching programs and movies beforehand, by acquiring whatever information is available from television and movie ratings, by reading reviews and program descriptions, and by watching programs with their children.
4. Parents should monitor their own television viewing and realize that children may be affected by programming that their parents watch even if they do not seem to be paying attention.
5. Parents should consider various available blocking technologies, such as the V-chip, which is now required in all new televisions with a diagonal screen size of 13 inches or larger.
6. An awareness of the developmental trends in the stimuli that frighten children can help parents make wiser choices about programming that their children may safely view.
7. An understanding of the types of coping strategies for dealing with media-induced fears can help parents reduce their children's fears once they have been aroused.

## Conclusions and Future Directions

The issue of media and children's fears provides a vivid illustration of how powerful a force the media can be to disrupt children's lives. Although parents have recently been given some help in protecting their children—television ratings and the V-chip—there are trends that suggest that the problem may be worsening. In addition to the increasingly sensational nature of television and movie content, computers are taking up more and more of children's time. A national survey (Kaiser Family Foundation, 1999) conducted between November 1998 and April 1999 showed that, on a typical day, 51% of 8- to 18-year-olds use a computer, and these children spend an average of more than an hour and a half a day using them. Although some of this time is spent doing schoolwork, the survey revealed that about half of this computer time is spread between playing games, participating in chat rooms, and surfing the Web. The contents to be found in these activities are very diverse, but they may include such unsavory aspects as explicit pornography, extreme violence, and real strangers seeking to harm children. The Kaiser survey also noted that there is very little parental supervision of children's media use. Therefore, research in this area is sorely needed to explore the contents that are available to children via computer, to investigate how children access and respond to the various contents, and to identify the consequences.

In addition to the spread of computers, the technology by which media content is transmitted is rapidly evolving to permit the display of bigger, more realistic, and more vivid high-definition images. "Virtual reality" systems take this process even further, resulting in experiences that seem astonishingly similar to undergoing a real event. It seems only logical that these advances will make scary images all the more frightening to children.

As media continue to evolve and become more pervasive and more readily accessible, it is expected that the calls for better ways to protect children will expand further. The marketing of violent programming to children has already come under scrutiny by the Federal Trade Commission, and movie theater owners have agreed to check the identification of youngsters who buy tickets for R-rated movies. Although they have been slow to catch on, blocking technologies for television, filtering software for Web browsers, and the labeling of the contents of all forms of programming can be expected to improve as more and more parents become convinced that they are essential to protecting their children.

## References


Apter, M. (1992). *The dangerous edge: The psychology of excitement.* New York: Free Press.

Badzinski, D. M., Cantor, J., & Hoffner, C. (1989). Children's understanding of quantifiers. *Child Study Journal, 19,* 241-258.

Bettelheim, B. (1975). *The uses of enchantment: The meaning and importance of fairy tales.* New York: Vintage Books.

Birnbaum, D. W., & Croll, W. L. (1984). The etiology of children's stereotypes about sex differences in emotionality. *Sex Roles, 10,* 677-691.

Blumer, H. (1933). *Movies and conduct.* New York: Macmillan.

Bowlby, J. (1973). *Separation: Anxiety and anger.* New York: Basic Books.

Bryant, J., Carveth, R. A., & Brown, D. (1981). Television viewing and anxiety: An experimental examination. *Journal of Communication, 31*(1), 106-119.

Buzzuto, J. C. (1975). Cinematic neurosis following *The Exorcist. Journal of Nervous and Mental Disease, 161,* 43-48.

Cantor, J. (1994). Fright reactions to mass media. In J. Bryant & D. Zillmann (Eds.), *Media effects: Advances in theory and research* (pp. 213-245). Hillsdale, NJ: Lawrence Erlbaum.

Cantor, J. (1998). *"Mommy, I'm scared": How TV and movies frighten children and what we can do to protect them.* San Diego, CA: Harcourt Brace.

Cantor, J., & Hoffner, C. (1990). Children's fear reactions to a televised film as a function of perceived immediacy of depicted threat. *Journal of Broadcasting & Electronic Media, 34,* 421-442.

Cantor, J., Mares, M. L., & Oliver, M. B. (1993). Parents' and children's emotional reactions to televised coverage of the Gulf War. In B. Greenberg & W. Gantz (Eds.), *Desert Storm and the mass media* (pp. 325-340). Cresskill, NJ: Hampton Press.

Cantor, J., & Nathanson, A. (1996). Children's fright reactions to television news. *Journal of Communication, 46*(4), 139-152.

Cantor, J., & Nathanson, A. (1997). Predictors of children's interest in violent television programming. *Journal of Broadcasting & Electronic Media, 41,* 155-167.

Cantor, J., & Omdahl, B. (1991). Effects of fictional media depictions of realistic threats on children's emotional responses, expectations, worries, and liking for related activities. *Communication Monographs, 58,* 384-401.

Cantor, J., & Omdahl, B. (1999). Children's acceptance of safety guidelines after exposure to televised dramas depicting accidents. *Western Journal of Communication, 63*(1), 1-15.

Cantor, J., & Reilly, S. (1982). Adolescents' fright reactions to television and films. *Journal of Communication, 32*(1), 87-99.

Cantor, J., & Sparks, G. G. (1984). Children's fear responses to mass media: Testing some Piagetian predictions. *Journal of Communication, 34*(2), 90-103.

Cantor, J., Sparks, G. G., & Hoffner, C. (1988). Calming children's television fears: Mr. Rogers vs. the Incredible Hulk. *Journal of Broadcasting & Electronic Media, 32,* 271-288.

Cantor, J., Stutman, S., & Duran, V. (1996). *What parents want in a television rating system: Results of a national survey.* Chicago: National PTA. Available: www.pta.org/programs/tvrpttoc.htm

Cantor, J., & Wilson, B. J. (1984). Modifying fear responses to mass media in preschool and elementary school children. *Journal of Broadcasting, 28,* 431-443.

Cantor, J., & Wilson, B. J. (1988). Helping children cope with frightening media presentations. *Current Psychology: Research & Reviews, 7,* 58-75.

Cantor, J., Wilson, B. J., & Hoffner, C. (1986). Emotional responses to a televised nuclear holocaust film. *Communication Research, 13,* 257-277.

Fabes, R. A., & Martin, C. L. (1991). Gender and age stereotypes of emotionality. *Personality and Social Psychology Bulletin, 17,* 532-540.

Federman, J. (1998). *Executive summary: National Television Violence Study* (Vol. 3). Santa Barbara: University of California, Santa Barbara, Center for Communication and Social Policy.

Fiore, F. (1999, September 23). Study: Act of TV, film violence every four minutes. *Capital Times* (Madison, WI), p. 10A.

Flavell, J. (1963). *The developmental psychology of Jean Piaget.* New York: Van Nostrand.

Gentile, D. A., & Walsh, D. A. (1999). *MediaQuotient™: National survey of family media habits, knowledge, and attitudes.* Minneapolis, MN: National Institute on Media and the Family.

Gerbner, G., Gross, L., Morgan, M., & Signorielli, N. (1980). The "mainstreaming" of America: Violence profile no. 11. *Journal of Communication, 30*(3), 10-29.

Gerbner, G., Gross, L., Morgan, M., & Signorielli, N. (1994). Growing up with television: The cultivation perspective. In J. Bryant & D. Zillmann (Eds.), *Media effects: Advances in theory and research.* Hillsdale, NJ: Lawrence Erlbaum.

Goldstein, J. (Ed.). (1998). *Why we watch: The attractions of violent entertainment.* New York: Oxford University Press.

Grossman, M., & Wood, W. (1993). Sex differences in the intensity of emotional experience: A social role interpretation. *Journal of Personality and Social Psychology, 65,* 1010-1022.

Harrison, K., & Cantor, J. (1999). Tales from the screen: Enduring fright reactions to scary media. *Media Psychology, 1*(2), 97-116.

Hawkins, R. P., & Pingree, S. (1981). Uniform messages and habitual viewing: Unnecessary assumptions in social reality effects. *Human Communication Research, 7,* 291-301.

Hoekstra, S. J., Harris, R. J., & Helmick, A. L. (1999). Autobiographical memories about the experience of seeing frightening movies in childhood. *Media Psychology, 1*(2), 117-140.

Hoffner, C. (1995). Adolescents' coping with frightening mass media. *Communication Research, 22,* 325-346.

Hoffner, C., & Cantor, J. (1985). Developmental differences in responses to a television character's appearance and behavior. *Developmental Psychology, 21,* 1065-1074.

Hoffner, C., & Cantor, J. (1990). Forewarning of a threat and prior knowledge of outcome: Effects on children's emotional responses to a film sequence. *Human Communication Research, 16,* 323-354.

Hoffner, C., Cantor, J., & Badzinski, D. M. (1990). Children's understanding of adverbs denoting degree of likelihood. *Journal of Child Language, 17,* 217-231.

Hoffner, C., & Haefner, M. J. (1997). Children's comforting of frightened coviewers: Real and hypothetical television-viewing situations. *Communication Research, 24,* 136-152.

Johnson, B. R. (1980). General occurrence of stressful reactions to commercial motion pictures and elements in films subjectively identified as stressors. *Psychological Reports, 47,* 775-786.

Kaiser Family Foundation. (1999, November 17). *Kids & media @ the new millennium.* Menlo Park, CA: Author.

Kelly, H. (1981). Reasoning about realities: Children's evaluations of television and books. In H. Kelly & H. Gardner (Eds.), *Viewing children through television* (pp. 59-71). San Francisco: Jossey-Bass.

Klite, P., Bardwell, R. A., & Salzman, J. (1997). Local TV news: Getting away with murder. *Press/Politics, 2*(2), 102-112.

Manis, F. R., Keating, D. P., & Morison, F. J. (1980). Developmental differences in the allocation of processing capacity. *Journal of Experimental Child Psychology, 29,* 156-169.

Mathai, J. (1983). An acute anxiety state in an adolescent precipitated by viewing a horror movie. *Journal of Adolescence, 6,* 197-200.

Melkman, R., Tversky, B., & Baratz, D. (1981). Developmental trends in the use of perceptual and conceptual attributes in grouping, clustering, and retrieval. *Journal of Experimental Child Psychology, 31,* 470-486.

Morison, P., & Gardner, H. (1978). Dragons and dinosaurs: The child's capacity to differentiate fantasy from reality. *Child Development, 49,* 642-648.

Owens, J., Maxim, R., McGuinn, M., Nobile, C., Msall, M., & Alario, A. (1999). Television-viewing habits and sleep disturbance in school children [Abstract]. *Pediatrics, 104*(3), 552. Available: www.pediatrics.org/cgi/content/full/104/3/c27

Peck, E. Y. (1999). *Gender differences in film-induced fear as a function of type of emotion measure and stimulus content: A meta-analysis and a laboratory study.* Unpublished doctoral dissertation, University of Wisconsin-Madison.

Rapaczynski, W., Singer, D. G., & Singer, J. L. (1982). Teaching television: A curriculum for young children. *Journal of Communication, 32*(2), 46-55.

Schofield, J., & Pavelchak, M. (1985). "The Day After": The impact of a media event. *American Psychologist, 40,* 542-548.

Simons, D., & Silveira, W. R. (1994). Post-traumatic stress disorder in children after television programmes. *British Medical Journal, 308,* 389-390.

Singer, M. I., Slovak, K., Frierson, T., & York, P. (1998). Viewing preferences, symptoms of psychological trauma, and violent behaviors among children who watch television. *Journal of the American Academy of Child and Adolescent Psychiatry, 37*(10), 1041-1048.

Sparks, G. G. (1986). Developmental differences in children's reports of fear induced by the mass media. *Child Study Journal, 16,* 55-66.

Sparks, G. G., & Cantor, J. (1986). Developmental differences in fright responses to a television program depicting a character transformation. *Journal of Broadcasting & Electronic Media, 30,* 309-323.

Valkenburg, P. M., Cantor, J., & Peeters, A. L. (2000). Fright reactions to television: A child survey. *Communication Research, 27,* 82-99.

Weiss, A. J., Imrich, D. J., & Wilson, B. J. (1993). Prior exposure to creatures from a horror film: Live versus photographic representations. *Human Communication Research, 20,* 41-66.

Wilson, B. J. (1987). Reducing children's emotional reactions to mass media through rehearsed explanation and exposure to a replica of a fear object. *Human Communication Research, 14,* 3-26.

Wilson, B. J. (1989a). Desensitizing children's emotional reactions to the mass media. *Communication Research, 16,* 723-745.

Wilson, B. J. (1989b). The effects of two control strategies on children's emotional reactions to a frightening movie scene. *Journal of Broadcasting & Electronic Media, 33,* 397-418.

Wilson, B. J., & Cantor, J. (1987). Reducing children's fear reactions to mass media: Effects of visual exposure and verbal explanation. In M. McLaughlin (Ed.), *Communication Yearbook 10* (pp. 553-573). Beverly Hills, CA: Sage.

Wilson, B. J., Hoffner, C., & Cantor, J. (1987). Children's perceptions of the effectiveness of techniques to reduce fear from mass media. *Journal of Applied Developmental Psychology, 8,* 39-52.

Wilson, B. J., & Weiss, A. J. (1991). The effects of two reality explanations on children's reactions to a frightening movie scene. *Communication Monographs, 58,* 307-326.

Wilson, B. J., & Weiss, A. J. (1993). The effects of sibling coviewing on preschoolers' reactions to a suspenseful movie scene. *Communication Research, 20,* 214-248.

Zuckerman, M. (1979). *Sensation seeking: Beyond the optimal level of arousal.* New York: John Wiley.

CHAPTER 11

# Effects of Televised Violence on Aggression

BRAD J. BUSHMAN
Iowa State University

L. ROWELL HUESMANN
University of Michigan

Any discussion of the relationship between violence in the mass visual media and real-world violence must be prefaced by a brief review of what a century of research has revealed about the causes of violent and aggressive behavior in general. We wish to emphasize three important points at the outset. First, the aggressive behavior studied by researchers in this field is not the same as the assertive behavior that people often admire in so-called aggressive executives. Rather, it is behavior intended to harm another individual. Second, severe aggressive behavior is virtually always caused by multiple factors (cf. Huesmann & Eron, 1986). Any statement that a specific act of violence is "caused" by a single event is an oversimplification. Numerous factors influence the development of aggressive tendencies in children and young adults in the long run and the commission of violent acts in the short run. Biological predispositions can increase or decrease the likelihood of aggression (Raine, Brennen, & Farrington, 1997). A wide range of community, peer, and family characteristics can socialize children to be more or less aggressive (Berkowitz, 1993). And there are situational factors (e.g., frustrations, guns, insults) over which one may have little control that can stimulate aggression or nonaggression in almost anyone. Third, childhood is the time when the foundation for lifelong aggressive or nonaggressive lifestyles is laid. The more aggressive child generally grows up to be the more aggressive adolescent, young adult, and adult (Huesmann, Eron, Lefkowitz, & Walder, 1984).

The theme of this chapter is *not* that media violence is *the* cause of aggression and violence in our society or even that it is the *most* important cause. The theme is that accumulat-

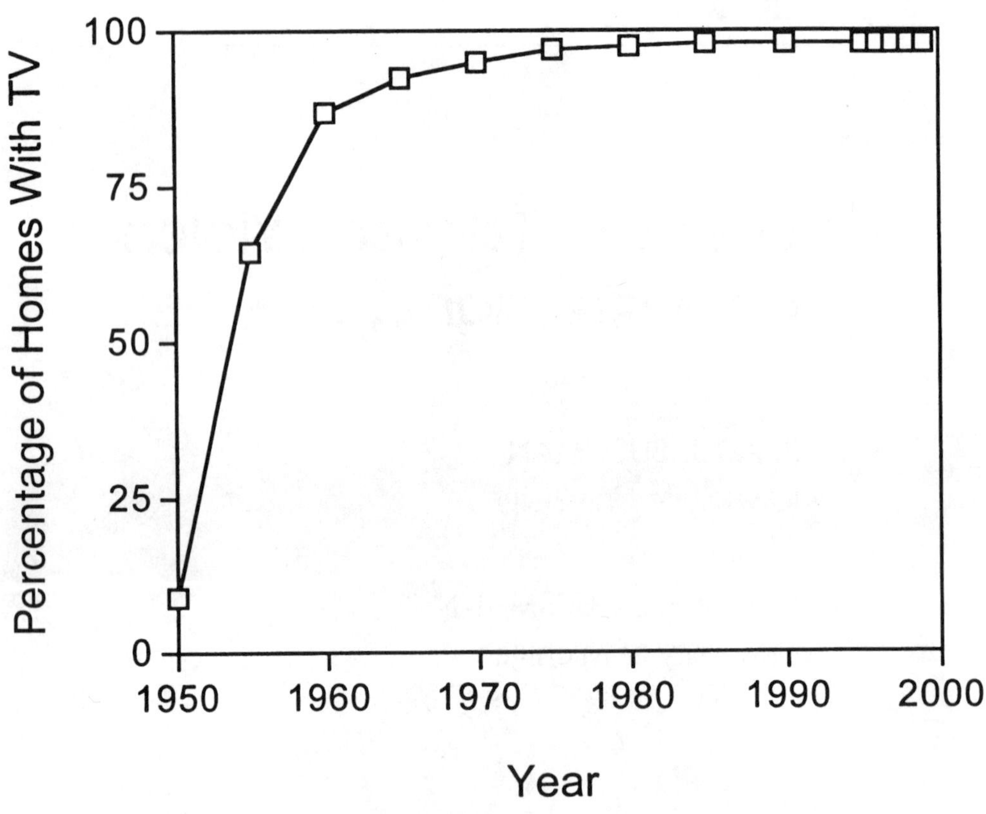


**Figure 11.1.** Percentage of American Households With TV
SOURCE: Data were obtained from Nielsen Media Research (1998).

ing research evidence has revealed that media violence is *one* factor that contributes significantly to aggression and violence in our society.

## How Widespread Is Television Violence?

### *Pervasiveness of Television*

Since its introduction to American society, television has become an integral part of nearly every home. Television was introduced to the United States at the 1939 World's Fair in New York. Two years later, on July 1, 1941, the Federal Communications Commission (FCC) licensed and approved the first commercially available television stations. Because of World War II, however, full-scale television broadcasting was suspended until 1946. In 1950, about 9% of American homes had TV sets. It didn't take long for television ownership to increase. By 1955, it was up to about 65%, and by 1965, it reached about 93%. Since 1985, television ownership has been about 98% (see Figure 11.1).

In addition to the number of households with television, one can also use the number of television sets in use as a measure of television saturation. In the United States, there are 776 television sets in use per 1,000 people (see Table 11.1). It is estimated that there are

**TABLE 11.1** Television Sets in Use per 1,000 People in 1995, by Country

| *Country* | *Televisions* | *Country* | *Televisions* |
|---|---|---|---|
| Pakistan | 22 | Uruguay | 305 |
| Guatemala | 54 | Taiwan | 317 |
| India | 61 | Trinidad and Tobago | 318 |
| Algeria | 71 | Puerto Rico | 322 |
| Paraguay | 73 | South Korea | 323 |
| Honduras | 80 | Portugal | 332 |
| Dominican Republic | 87 | Argentina | 347 |
| Syria | 89 | Singapore | 362 |
| Peru | 100 | Kuwait | 379 |
| South Africa | 101 | Russia | 379 |
| Philippines | 121 | Iceland | 382 |
| Egypt | 126 | Czech Republic | 406 |
| Iran | 140 | Poland | 408 |
| Cyprus | 143 | Italy | 436 |
| Morocco | 145 | Hungary | 441 |
| Indonesia | 147 | Greece | 442 |
| Ecuador | 148 | Iceland | 447 |
| Tunisia | 156 | Switzerland | 461 |
| Panama | 169 | Belgium | 464 |
| Venezuela | 180 | Sweden | 476 |
| Colombia | 188 | Australia | 482 |
| Mexico | 192 | Spain | 490 |
| Cuba | 200 | Netherlands | 495 |
| Romania | 201 | Austria | 497 |
| Costa Rica | 220 | New Zealand | 508 |
| Thailand | 221 | Finland | 519 |
| Malaysia | 231 | Denmark | 536 |
| Turkey | 240 | Germany | 550 |
| China | 250 | Norway | 561 |
| Saudi Arabia | 257 | France | 579 |
| Lebanon | 268 | Luxembourg | 591 |
| Brazil | 278 | United Kingdom | 612 |
| Chile | 280 | Japan | 619 |
| Jamaica | 285 | Canada | 647 |
| Israel | 295 | United States | 776 |

SOURCE: Adapted from the U.S. Census Bureau (1998).

more television sets in the United States today than there are toilets. In other industrial countries, television sets are also common commodities (Table 11.1). Even in some Third World countries, television sets are fairly common.

Not only are there more TV sets today than ever before, but they are also on longer. The average number of hours American households spend viewing TV has increased from 4.5 hours per day in 1950 to 7.25 hours per day in 1998 (see Figure 11.2). By age 65, the average American will have spent the equivalent of 9 years glued to the tube (Nielsen Media Research, 1998). In the United States, children spend more time watching television than they spend at school, and adults spend more time watching television than they spend doing any other activity except sleeping and working (Huston et al., 1992). One telling statistic is that, at 10:00 A.M. on any Saturday morning, more than 60% of American children are watching TV (Comstock & Paik, 1991)!

### *The Extent of Violence in Television Programming*

Surveys indicate that most Americans consider "TV" to be an acronym for "too violent" (e.g., Brower, 1993; Fischer, 1994; *TV Guide,* 1992; Zipperer, 1994). If most Americans say they do not like it, then why is so much violence on television? Television industry leaders answer this question by claiming that their programs merely reflect the violence that already exists in society. For example, Howard Stern, president of the CBS Broadcasting Group, said the TV industry is "merely holding a mirror to American society" (as cited in West, 1993, p. 40). However, few scholars of the subject accept this claim. As film critic Michael Medved (1995) has written,

> If this were true, then why do so few people witness murders in real life but everybody sees them on TV and in the movies. The most violent ghetto is not in South Central L.A. or Southeast Washington D.C.; it's on television. About 350 characters appear each night on prime-time TV, but studies show an average of seven of these people are murdered every night. If this rate applied in reality, then in just 50 days everyone in the United States would be killed and the last left could turn off the TV. (pp. 156-157)

The amount of violence that occurs in television programs far exceeds the amount of violence that occurs in the streets of America. Even in reality-based TV programs, violence is grossly overemphasized. For example, one study compared the frequency of crimes occurring in the real world with the frequency of crimes occurring in the following reality-based police TV programs: *America's Most Wanted, Cops, Top Cops, FBI, The Untold Story,* and *American Detective* (Oliver, 1994). The real-world crime rates were obtained from the Federal Bureau of Investigation (FBI) Uniform Crime Reports. Seven categories of crime are reported annually by the FBI: murder, forcible rape, robbery, aggravated assault, burglary, larceny, and motor vehicle theft. Murder, forcible rape, robbery, and aggravated assault are classified as violent crimes (against people), whereas burglary, larceny, and motor vehicle theft are classified as nonviolent crimes (against property). About 87% of the crimes occurring in the real world are property crimes, whereas only 13% of crimes occurring in reality-based TV programs are property crimes (see Figure 11.3). The largest discrepancy between the real world and the world depicted on television is for murder—the most violent crime of all. Only 0.2% of the crimes reported by the FBI are murders, whereas about 50% of the crimes shown in reality-based TV programs are murders.

Over time, the number of violent acts an individual sees on television can accumulate to staggering numbers, much like the U.S. na-

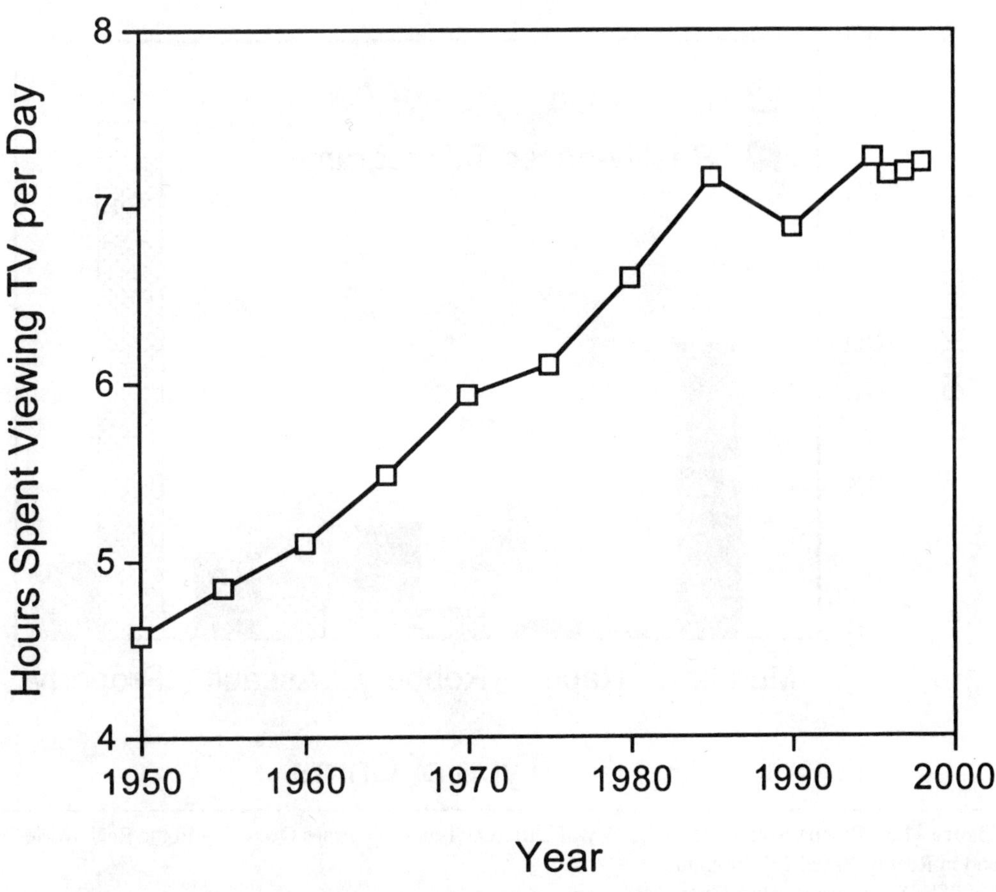


**Figure 11.2.** Time Spent Viewing TV per American Household per Day
SOURCE: Data were obtained from Nielsen Media Research (1998).

tional debt and foreign trade deficit statistics. By the time the average American child graduates from elementary school, he or she will have seen more than 8,000 murders and more than 100,000 other assorted acts of violence (e.g., assaults, rapes) on network television (Huston et al., 1992). The numbers are higher if the child has access to cable television or a videocassette player, as most do. If one looks at the distribution of violent portrayals over time of day and day of the week, the situation looks particularly bad for children. The highest proportion of violence is shown on Saturday mornings and in late afternoons and early evenings when most children are watching TV (Comstock & Paik, 1991).

A recent content analysis reveals how violence is portrayed on television (National Television Violence Study, 1996, 1997, 1998). Researchers sampled more than 8,000 hours of programming on cable and broadcast television between the hours of 6:00 A.M. and 11:00 P.M., 7 days a week, for 3 consecutive years. A content analysis of the programs showed that about 60% contained violence. Less than 4% of the violent programs contained an antiviolence theme.

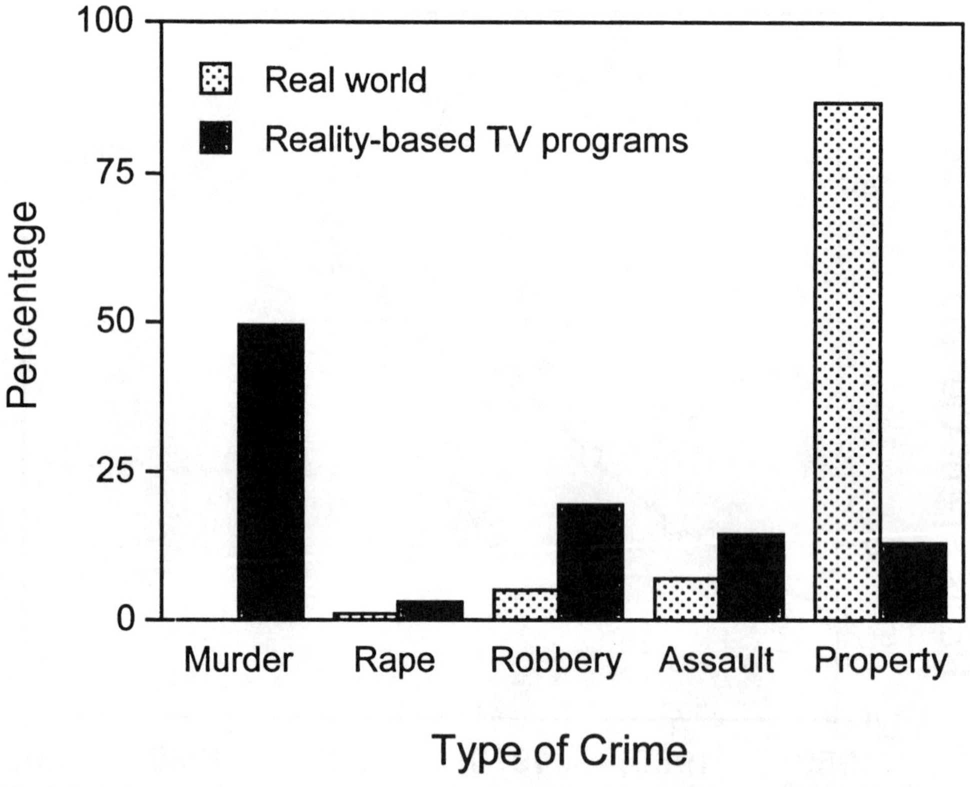


**Figure 11.3.** Comparison of the Frequency of Different Types of Crimes Occurring in the Real World and in Reality-Based TV Programs
SOURCE: Data were obtained from Oliver (1994).

Although violence in the "real" world is seldom glamorous, sanitized, or trivial, violence in TV's "reel" world is often portrayed this way. The following statistics were obtained from the National Television Violence Study (1996, 1997, 1998).

*Violence on Television Is Often Glamorized*

Nearly 40% of the violent acts were perpetrated by "good" characters. Even when the perpetrators of violence were "bad" characters, more than 40% went unpunished. Almost three fourths (73%) of the perpetrators of violence showed no remorse for their actions.

*Violence on Television Is Often Sanitized*

More than half (55%) of the victims of violence show no pain or suffering. More than one third (36%) of the victims experienced unrealistically low levels of harm. Only 15% of the violent programs portrayed the long-term consequences of the violence to the victim's family, friends, and community.

*Violence on Television Is Often Trivialized*

Even though more than half (53%) of the violent scenes on television were lethal, more

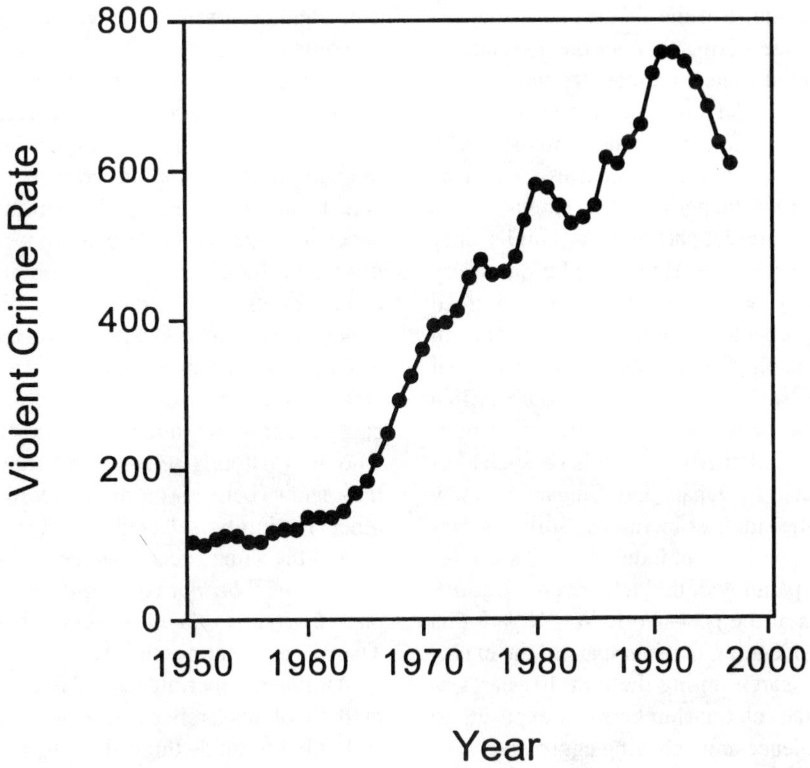


**Figure 11.4.** U.S. Violent Crime Rate per 100,000 Inhabitants

than 40% of the violent scenes were portrayed as humorous.

## The Explosion of Violence in the "Real" World for the Post-TV Generation

Scholars have been investigating television violence as a potential contributor to societal violence almost since the moment television started to become an integral part of children's lives in the 1950s. One of the reasons is that the trend of violence in the industrialized world, and in the United States in particular, has paralleled the increase in television usage during the second half of the twentieth century. As Figure 11.4 shows, the increase in violence in the United States during the second half of the twentieth century has closely paralleled the introduction of the television into the lives of our children. If one compares Figure 11.4 with Figure 11.1, one can see that the substantial increase in violence in the post–World War II period began in 1965, exactly when the first generation of children raised on TV began to reach the prime ages for committing violent crimes.

Of course, such comparisons of demographic trends are not proof of any relationship. Numerous factors influence homicide rates, including simple demographic trends in the population. But the fact remains that the homicide rate during this period skyrocketed in the United States, the country where children were encountering the greatest exposure to media violence of any country in the world. Homicide rates in other countries have risen as well during the period when television has become an integral part of every child's early learning experience. However, the rates vary dramatically across countries, reflecting all the multiple factors that influence violence in a society. Countries with economic and social upheavals such as Russia and South Africa show some of the greatest increases. Countries with rigid societal controls on social behavior such as Japan and Singapore show some of the smallest increases. Still, the general rise in violence in industrialized societies that has paralleled the telecommunications revolution of the post–World War II period is certainly one thing that has sparked the explosion of research during the past 40 years examining the relationship between exposure to media violence and behaving aggressively.

## How Researchers Study the Relationship Between Television Violence and Aggression

All *true experiments,* whether conducted in laboratory or field (i.e., "real" world) settings, share two essential features. The first feature is that the researcher has control over the procedures, manipulating the TV violence variable and holding all other variables constant. All those who participate in the experiment are treated in exactly the same manner—except for the TV program they are exposed to. By exercising control, the researcher attempts to ensure that any differences in aggression observed are produced only by the TV program shown and not by other extraneous variables.

The second feature is that participants are randomly assigned to groups. If there are two TV programs (e.g., violent vs. nonviolent), for example, the researcher flips a coin to determine who gets assigned to what program. Participants do not get to choose the type of TV program they want to watch. Random assignment is the great equalizer. It ensures that the participants in one group are no different from the participants in another group before exposure to the TV program. If there are differences in aggression between groups after exposure to the TV program, these differences cannot be from any preexisting differences between participants. These two features of true experiments allow researchers to test very clearly whether exposure to TV violence causes aggression in the short run. If children who are randomly selected and shown a violent show behave more aggressively than other randomly selected children who are treated the same except for seeing the violent show, *it must be that viewing the show caused the children to behave more aggressively.* There is no other possibility.

Although experimentation is the preferred method of research because it allows cause and effect to be distinguished, there are some problems with true experiments. They do not say much about long-term effects, for example. One can hardly force a sample of children to watch one or another type of TV program for several years. Also, the types of TV programs children are shown and the types of behaviors they are allowed to do in experimental studies are limited by ethical constraints. So true experiments by themselves are not sufficient to determine the real-world importance of how TV violence affects children.

A popular alternative approach to the true experiment has been the *cross-sectional field study.* In a cross-sectional field study, the researcher does not try to control variables or randomly assign participants to groups. Instead, the researcher merely observes people's TV viewing habits and their aggressive behaviors to see if they are correlated. Does the person who watches more violence behave more aggressively? This type of study can be used to investigate whether TV violence viewing over a long period of time is related to more serious forms of aggression (e.g., murder, assault) that cannot be studied in true experiments. If a relationship is found, one cannot conclude from this kind of study alone whether it is because TV viewing is causing children to behave aggressively, because aggressive children like watching violence, or because something else such as low IQ or poverty is stimulating children to both watch more violence and behave more aggressively. One knows from this type of study simply whether viewing violence and behaving aggressively are associated with each other.

*Longitudinal field studies* go one important step beyond cross-sectional field studies. The variables of interest are observed over two or more distinct time periods (e.g., at the beginning of the study and 6 months later or even 20 years later). The longitudinal field studies provide two distinct improvements over cross-sectional field studies. First, one can see if long-term relations differ from short-term relations. Is childhood TV violence viewing associated with behaving aggressively only in childhood, or is it associated with behaving aggressively 20 years later as well? Second, if there are long-term relations, it allows one to test the relative plausibility of competing causal theories about violence viewing causing aggression or aggression causing violence viewing. Is it more plausible that TV violence viewing causes later aggression or that aggression causes later TV violence viewing? Of course, longitudinal field studies are extremely difficult to do, requiring many years and a lot of money to complete.

## How Researchers Combine the Results From Different Studies

The most common error that people make in attempting to interpret the research on media violence and aggression is to focus on only one of the above three types of studies and ignore the others. Substantial research has been completed using all three types of studies: true experiments, cross-sectional field studies, and longitudinal field studies. One must integrate all three bodies of research to gain an accurate picture of what the scientific evidence shows.

In evaluating the results of any study, one needs to attend to both the statistical significance of the effect and the magnitude of the effect. A result is significant if the probability of it occurring simply by chance can be shown to be very small. The effect size of a significant result is a standardized measure of how "big" the result really is. For example, if one is looking at the results of a cross-sectional field study on media-related aggression, one might first ask whether the association discovered is big enough that it could not have occurred by chance. Then one would like to quantify the size of the association on a standardized scale. This would be the effect-size estimate for the study.

Although there are several different effect-size measures, in this chapter we use the correlation coefficient, denoted by *r.* In any study, the computed correlation between watching TV violence and behaving aggressively would indicate the strength of the relationship between those two measures that was found in that study. The absolute value of the correlation indicates the strength and can range from 0 to 1. The sign of the correlation indicates the direction (direct/positive vs. inverse/negative) of the relation.[1] In social science research, virtually no correlations are very close to 1; they tend to lie somewhere between −.75 and +.75. Conventional values can be used to interpret the magnitude of a correlation coefficient. Cohen (1988) has defined a "small" correlation as ± .1, a "medium" correlation as ± .3, and a "large" correlation as ± .5 or greater.

Most general reviews of the research on media violence employ either a narrative approach in discussing key studies or a meta-analytic approach in which effect-size estimates from multiple studies are combined. Whenever possible in this chapter, we use the meta-analytic approach to review and integrate the results from studies of TV-related aggression (for detailed descriptions of meta-analytic procedures, see Cooper & Hedges, 1994; Hunt, 1997; Hunter & Schmidt, 1990; Rosenthal, 1991; Wang & Bushman, 1999). In the meta-analytic review, the reviewer uses statistical procedures to integrate the findings from a collection of studies and describes the results using numerical effect-size estimates. Traditional narrative reviews are more likely than meta-analytic reviews to rely on the subjective judgments, preferences, and biases of the reviewer.

## What the Scientific Data Say About the Relationship Between TV Violence and Aggression

Paik and Comstock (1994) recently conducted a comprehensive meta-analytic review of the effects of TV violence on antisocial behavior. Antisocial behavior was defined as aggressive behavior (e.g., giving another person electric shocks, verbally insulting another person), violent criminal behavior (e.g., homicide, assault), and nonviolent criminal behavior (e.g., burglary, grand theft). The meta-analyses examined the results of 217 different studies of the relationship between exposure to media violence and aggressive behavior. The overall computed effect sizes (correlations) between TV violence and all three types of behavior (aggressive behavior, violent criminal behavior, and nonviolent criminal behavior) were significant (*r*s = .32, .10, and .28, respectively). The overall correlation between TV violence and the combined antisocial behavior measure was .31, a significant and medium-size effect according to Cohen.

### *True Experiments*

It is useful to examine TV violence effects for different types of studies. True experiments provide the best test of the short-term effects of TV violence. The typical paradigm is that randomly selected children are shown either a violent or nonviolent short film and then are observed as they play with each other or with objects such as Bo-Bo dolls. The consistent finding is that children who watch a violent film clip behave more aggressively immediately afterward. Children who view violence behave more aggressively toward persons (Bjorkqvist, 1985; Josephson, 1987) and toward inanimate objects (Bandura, 1977; Bandura, Ross, & Ross, 1961, 1963a, 1963b). The effects occur for all children, boys and girls, black and white, normally aggressive or normally nonaggressive. In the laboratory experiments, the aggressive behaviors tend to be milder (e.g., pushing and shoving in Bjorkqvist's 1985 study), but in the field experiments, they tend to be stronger (e.g., fighting in hockey games in Josephson's 1987 study). Paik and Comstock's (1994) meta-analysis showed that the aggregated correlation between TV violence and antisocial behavior was .40 for the laboratory experiments they reviewed and .30 for the field experiments they reviewed. Both overall effect sizes are significant and are between moderate and large in size. Because these are true experiments, the direction of causality is unambiguous and the conclusion is inescapable. Exposing young viewers to TV violence causes them to behave more aggressively in the short run.

### *Cross-Sectional Field Studies*

It is easier to measure serious violent and nonviolent criminal behavior in nonexperimental studies than it is in true experimental studies. Most of the cross-sectional field studies reviewed by Paik and Comstock (1994) used measures of "real" antisocial behavior. The overall correlation (effect size) that they found for such studies was also significant, though much lower than for experiments, .19. This correlation is small to medium in size, but even a small effect can have substantial social impact when one is dealing with homicide or other serious aggression.

### *Longitudinal Field Studies*

Longitudinal field studies provide the best test of the long-term effects of TV violence, but not many have been completed. Among those longitudinal studies reviewed by Paik and Comstock (1994) in their meta-analysis, the overall correlation (effect size) between TV violence and antisocial behavior was .19. Again, this is a significant effect, and it is small to medium in size. Several of these longitudinal studies have attracted wide attention because of the compelling nature of their results. For example, Eron, Huesmann, Lefkowitz, and Walder (1972) reported that the correlation between a boy's exposure to TV violence at age 8 and his aggression at age 18 was .31, whereas the correlation from age 8 aggression to age 18 exposure to TV violence was about zero. The surgeon general cited these results in justifying his 1972 national warning that "television violence, indeed, does have an adverse effect on certain members of our society" (Steinfeld, 1972, p. 26).

More recently, Huesmann (1986) showed that these same boys' violent criminal behavior at age 30 was predicted by their violence viewing at age 8. A longitudinal study funded by NBC showed weak effect sizes for TV violence viewing predicting aggression over a variety of age ranges and lags, but the effects were in the direction of TV violence viewing increasing aggression in 12 of 15 cases. A cross-national longitudinal study by Huesmann and his colleagues (Huesmann & Eron, 1986) found that exposure to TV violence at age 6 or 8 predicted aggression 2 years later among many boys and girls in the United States, Finland, Poland, and Israel. More recently, Huesmann and Moise (1999) reported significant longitudinal effect sizes for TV violence viewing at age 6 or 8 predicting antisocial and aggressive behavior in American men and women at age 23 (*r*s = .21 and .19, respectively). Moreover, these effects remain significant when early aggression, early intellectual functioning, social class, and other variables are controlled.

Although media violence effects tend to be greater for true experiments than for field studies, the same pattern of results is found in both settings. This is true not only in the domain of aggression (Anderson & Bushman, 1997) but in many other domains as well (Anderson, Lindsay, & Bushman, 1999). The larger effect size found for experiments may be substantially due to the different kind of aggression measures used in experiments compared with field studies. Experiments tend to employ measures that can be more accurately assessed and have less noise in them. It is difficult or impossible to study criminal behaviors using experimental designs. It is also difficult to explain variation in criminal behavior, especially violent criminal behavior. Between the years 1950 and 1998, only about 11% of the crimes recorded by the FBI were violent crimes (U.S. Federal Bureau of Investigation, 1951-1999). These two problems might explain why TV violence effects are larger for experimental designs than for nonexperimental designs and why TV violence explains more of the variation in nonviolent criminal behavior than in violent criminal behavior.

In summary, the scientific data lead to the same inescapable conclusion: TV violence increases aggression. True experiments have shown conclusively that exposing children to violent TV causes them to behave more aggressively immediately afterward. Cross-sectional field studies have shown conclusively that the children who are watching more violence on TV are the same children who are behaving more aggressively. Longitudinal field studies have shown that children who grow up watching a lot of TV violence are likely to behave more aggressively later in childhood, in adolescence, and in young adulthood. This finding holds up even if one controls for differences in initial aggressiveness, intellectual functioning, and social class. The bottom line is that, on average, TV violence is making our children behave more aggressively in childhood, and the aggressive habits they learn from TV in childhood carry over into adolescence and even young adulthood.

## How Large Is the Effect of Television Violence on Aggression?

Some people claim that the effect of televised violence on aggression is so small that the risks to society and its members are negligible. There are several ways to interpret the magnitude of the relationship between TV violence and aggression. One way is to use Cohen's (1988) conventional values for "small," "medium," and "large" effects. Recall that, for the correlation coefficient, these values are ±.1, ±.3, and ±.5, respectively. In the Paik and Comstock (1994) meta-analysis, the overall correlation between TV violence and antisocial behavior is .31, a "medium"-size effect.

Another way to interpret the magnitude of a correlation is by the Binomial Effect Size Display (Rosenthal & Rubin, 1982). It assumes that the base rate for the to-be-predicted behavior is 50%. The Binomial Effect Size Display estimates the percentage of people who should exhibit the behavior if they are above versus below the median (i.e., 50th percentile) on the predictor variable. In this chapter, we are interested in whether exposure to violent media predicts aggressive behavior. The .31 correlation is equivalent to aggressive behavior being exhibited by 65.5% of those above the median in exposure media violence but only by 34.5% of those below the median in exposure media violence. This 31% difference hardly seems like a trivial effect.

A third way to interpret the magnitude of a correlation is to compare it with correlations from other domains. Figure 11.5 compares media violence effects with several other effects (Bushman, Phillips, & Anderson, 2000). All of the effects are significantly different from zero. Note, however, that the second largest effect is for TV violence. Most people would agree that the other effects in Figure 11.5 are so strong that they are obvious. For example, most people would not question the assertion that calcium intake increases bone mass or that wearing a condom decreases the risk of contracting HIV, the virus that causes AIDS. Why, then, do some people still question the assertion that viewing violence increases aggression? Probably the major reason is that people do not understand psychological processes as well as they understand physiological processes.

Perhaps one of the best parallels is the relationship between smoking and lung cancer (Bushman, Phillips, & Anderson, 2000). The correlation between media violence and aggression is only slightly smaller than that between smoking and lung cancer (Figure 11.5). Not everyone who smokes gets lung cancer and not everyone who gets lung cancer is a smoker. Even the tobacco industry agrees that smoking causes lung cancer. Smoking is not the only factor that causes lung cancer, but it is an important factor. Similarly, not everyone who watches violent television becomes aggressive and not everyone who is aggressive watches violent television. Watching violent TV programs is not the only factor that causes aggression, but it is an important factor.

The smoking analogy is useful in other respects. Like a first cigarette, the first violent movie seen can make a person nauseous. Later, however, one relishes more and more. The effects of smoking and viewing violence are cumulative. Smoking one cigarette probably will not cause lung cancer. Likewise, seeing one violent movie probably will not turn a child into a psychopathic killer. But repeated exposure to both cigarettes and violent media can have harmful long-term consequences.

Just because TV violence does not increase aggression noticeably in *everybody* does not mean that it does not increase aggression in *anybody*. Medved (1995) points out that,

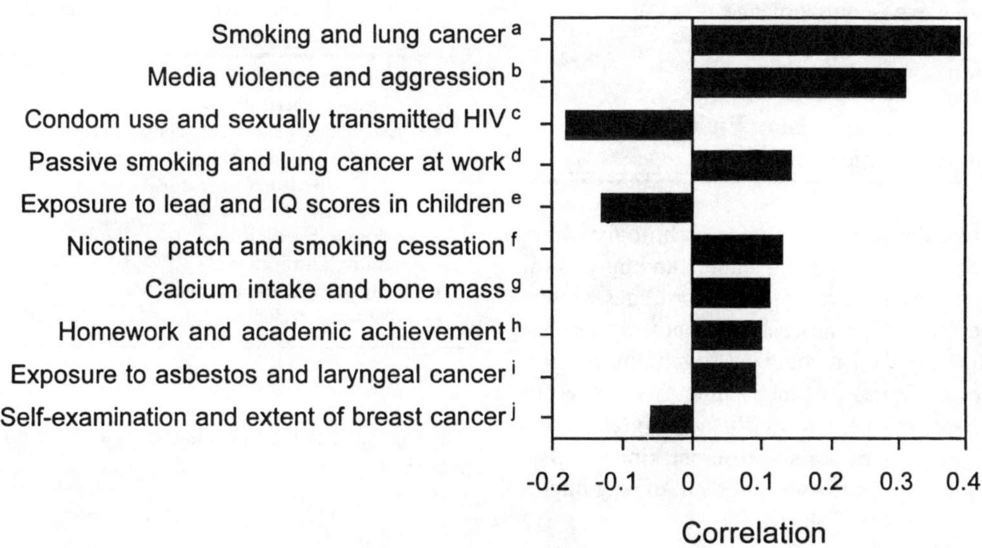


**Figure 11.5.** Comparison of Television Violence Effects With Effects From Other Domains

SOURCE: Data were obtained from Bushman, Phillips, and Anderson (2000).

NOTE: A correlation coefficient can range from –1 (a perfect negative linear relation) to +1 (a perfect positive linear relation), with 0 indicating no linear relation. According to Cohen (1988), a small correlation is ±.1, a medium correlation is ±.3, and a large correlation is ±.5. All of the correlations were significantly different from 0.

a. The effect of smoking tobacco on lung cancer was estimated by pooling the data from Figures 1 and 3 in Wynder and Graham's (1950) classic article. The remaining effects were estimated from meta-analyses.

b. Paik and Comstock (1994).

c. Weller (1993).

d. Wells (1998).

e. Needleman and Gatsonis (1990).

f. Fiore, Smith, Jorenby, and Baker (1994).

g. Welten, Kemper, Post, and van Staveren (1995).

h. Cooper (1989).

i. Smith, Handley, and Wood (1990).

j. Hill, White, Jolley, and Mapperson (1988).

when an ad is shown on TV, no one expects that it will sell the product to everybody. If the ad influences just one in a thousand viewers, it is considered highly successful. Suppose, for example, that violent TV programs make only 1% of the population more aggressive enough that they harm someone. Should society be concerned about a percentage so small? We believe that society should be concerned even if TV violence only stimulates 1% of the population to commit acts of harm they would not otherwise have committed. Suppose that 10 million people watch a violent TV program. If only 1% of the viewers will become so much more aggressive afterward that they harm one person, then the violent TV program will have harmed 100,000 people! Because so many people are exposed to TV violence, the effect on society can be immense even if only a small percentage of viewers are seriously affected by viewing violence. Furthermore, one must not forget that, just as with cigarette smoking, everyone is affected in some way by being exposed to violence.

## Why Does Television Violence Increase Aggression?

Over the past 40 years, psychologists have gained a rather good understanding of how and why media violence stimulates violent behavior. The processes are not mysterious; they are well-recognized psychological processes. It has just taken time to see how the processes operate to influence aggressive behavior. There are six different kinds of psychological processes that seem to play important roles (see Table 11.2).

Before discussing these processes in more detail, let us dispense with one theory that has plagued discussions of the role of media violence for decades, *catharsis theory,* which dates back to Aristotle. This theory posits that watching aggression purges angry feelings and aggressive tendencies or drives. *There is not a shred of convincing scientific data to support this theory.* Certainly, physically aggressive actions can reduce tension in subjects who have been frustrated (Hokanson & Burgess, 1962), but so can physical exertion that is nonaggressive. The more important fact is that there are no convincing data to indicate that watching violent acts reduces tension or the propensity to act aggressively (Doob & Wood, 1972). The one field study often cited as demonstrating a catharsis effect (Feshbach & Singer, 1971) has methodological flaws (Huesmann, Eron, Berkowitz, & Chaffee, 1991) that the authors have recognized. As shown above, the majority of evidence demonstrates that violence viewing and aggression are *positively* related, which contradicts the catharsis hypothesis. Furthermore, studies that have examined the relationship between fantasizing about aggression and aggressive behavior have shown that children who fantasize more behave more aggressively (Huesmann & Eron, 1986; Viemero & Paajanen, 1992). As an explanation of the relationship between aggressive behavior and viewing violence, catharsis theory can be put to rest.

**TABLE 11.2** Psychological Processes Through Which Media Violence Influences Aggressive Behavior

- Observational learning of behaviors and scripts
  - Fantasy rehearsal
- Observational learning of beliefs and attitudes
  - Hostile attributional bias
  - Normative beliefs
  - Cognitive desensitization
- Emotional desensitization
- Cognitive justification
- Cognitive cueing and priming
- Arousal and excitation transfer

### *Observational Learning of Behaviors and Scripts*

Children learn both specific aggressive behaviors and attitudes supporting more complex aggressive behaviors through observational learning. It has become an accepted tenet of developmental theory that, through imitation and vicarious reinforcements, children develop habitual modes of behavior that are resistant to extinction (Bandura, 1977, 1986). But there are additional predictions of vicarious learning theory that have also been confirmed. For instance, it has been shown that the extent to which a child imitates an actor is greatly influenced by the reinforcements an actor receives. If the actor is rewarded for a behavior, the child is more likely to imitate that behavior (Bandura, 1965; Bandura et al., 1963a, 1963b; Walters, Leat, & Meaci, 1963). If the actor is punished for a behavior, the child is less likely to imitate that behavior (Bandura, 1965; Walters & Parke, 1964). On TV, about 75% of violent acts go unpunished (National Television Violence Study, 1996). Other studies have indicated that the persistence of such learned behavior seems to depend on the direct reinforcements the child receives (Bandura, 1965; Hayes, Rincover, & Volosin, 1980). Finally, whether the child identifies with the model (Huesmann & Eron,

1986; Huesmann, Lagerspetz, & Eron, 1984) and whether the model is perceived as possessing valued characteristics also appear to influence whether a child will imitate the model (Bandura et al., 1963b; Hicks, 1965; Neely, Hechel, & Leichtman, 1973; Nicholas, McCarter, & Hechel, 1971). On TV, nearly 40% of the violent acts are perpetrated by characters who possess valued characteristics that would make them attractive role models for viewers (National Television Violence Study, 1996, 1997, 1998).

More recently, Huesmann (1988, 1998) extended the concept of observational learning to argue that children learn what might be called social scripts for complex aggressive behaviors from observing violent dramas in the media (Huesmann, 1982, 1986, 1988; Huesmann & Miller, 1994). Scripts are programs for how to solve social problems. Children may employ these scripts automatically, with little or no thought. Often, a script is suggested by what a child observes, and the child fantasizes about behaving that way. Such cognitive rehearsals of the script make the use of the script even more likely. Fantasizing about the violence one has seen on TV thus becomes an important mediating variable that exacerbates the effects of viewing violence.

### *Observational Learning of Beliefs and Attitudes*

A substantial body of data has accumulated indicating that media violence also changes beliefs and attitudes about violence. It tends to make viewers believe the world is more hostile than it really is; it promotes the acceptability of behaving aggressively; and it desensitizes viewers to thinking about violence.

#### *TV Violence Shapes Schemas About How Hostile the World Is*

Viewing television cultivates a sense of personal risk in the real world (Gerbner & Gross, 1976, 1981).[2] In comparison with light TV viewers, heavy TV viewers are more anxious about becoming victims of violence, are less trusting of others, and are more likely to perceive the world as a dangerous, mean, hostile place. Such hostile attributional biases promote aggressive interactions with others (Crick & Dodge, 1994). If people perceive the world to be a dangerous place, not only are they more likely to carry a weapon to protect themselves, but they are also more likely to misinterpret others' actions as hostile and provocative and to behave aggressively in retaliation.

One of the general themes in social psychology is that people's perceptions of a situation are more important for understanding their behavior than are the objective features of the situation. Consider, for example, the classic study of the 1951 Princeton-Dartmouth football game (Hastorf & Cantril, 1954; also see Loy & Andrews, 1981). The two rival universities played a grudge match in which noses were broken, fists were thrown, and players were ejected. Some time later, students from each school were shown a film of the game and were asked to play the role of a scientist observer, noting each infraction and who committed it. Even though the students from the two universities saw exactly the same game on film, they rated it very differently. For example, the Princeton students "saw" twice as many Dartmouth infractions as the Dartmouth students "saw."

#### *TV Violence Changes Normative Beliefs About Violence*

In the United States and elsewhere, a "culture of violence" is said to exist (e.g., Anderson, 1990; Cohen & Nisbett, 1997; Shirley, 1993; Somers, 1976). Certainly, this is one of the factors that promotes violent behavior. If it is not obvious that violent behavior is wrong, it is more likely to happen. A variety of studies have shown that more aggressive children are less likely to believe that aggression and violence are wrong (Huesmann & Guerra, 1997). From the standpoint of psychological theory, this is not surprising. People (especially children) tend to behave consistently with their beliefs, and if they believe violence is justified when one is sufficiently provoked, they are more likely to behave aggressively. Did the young perpetrators of the Columbine massacre in Littleton, Colorado, believe they were justified in what they were doing because they had been provoked? Quite probably they did. Constant exposure to scenes of heroic characters being provoked and then using violence in retaliation promotes this type of thinking. This is a very important effect of TV violence. Longitudinal studies have shown that early exposure to TV violence in childhood is related to having normative beliefs more accepting of violence even 15 years later in young adulthood (e.g., Huesmann & Moise, 1999).

#### *TV Violence Produces a Cognitive Desensitization to Violence*

One of the factors that inhibits aggressive and violent behaviors in socialized humans is that we are not "used" to it. The more we see violence around us, the more we experience it, or even the more we think about it, the more "used" to it we become. Just as soldiers who have been in the front lines for a long time become inured, at the cognitive level, to the horrors of the death all around them, the children who are constantly observing violence around them or in the mass media become more inured to thinking about violence. Psychologists call this a cognitive desensitization to violence. The problem is that, as children become more "used" to violence, it becomes easier for them to behave aggressively. And repeated exposures to TV violence produce this cognitive desensitization. The more televised violence a child watches, the more accepting the child's attitude toward aggressive behavior becomes (Dominick & Greenberg, 1972; Drabman & Thomas, 1974a, 1974b; Thomas & Drabman, 1975). This cognitive desensitization then makes people's own aggression more acceptable to them.

### *Emotional Desensitization*

We have designated the changes in attitudes brought about by frequent violence viewing as a cognitive desensitization to violence. Similarly, there is some evidence that a real emotional desensitization can occur. In one quasi-experimental field study (Cline, Croft, & Courrier, 1973), boys who regularly watched a heavy diet of television displayed less physiological arousal in response to new scenes of violence than did control subjects. Although these results have apparently been difficult to replicate in the field, Thomas, Horton, Lippincott, and Drabman (1977) found similar short-term effects in laboratory studies of changes in skin conductance in response to violence. It should not be surprising that emotional and physiological responses to scenes of violence produce habituation, as do responses to other stimuli. The problem is that the arousal that is naturally stimulated by observing violent behaviors is unpleasant for most people and therefore inhibits aggressive actions (Halpern, 1975; Winn, 1977). Once this arousal habituates, aggression is no longer inhibited. People, and children in particular, find it easier to think about behaving aggressively and easier to behave aggressively if they do not have unpleasant emotional responses to violence.

### *Cognitive Justification Processes*

The justification process is a psychological phenomenon that explains why people who are aggressive like to watch violent television (Huesmann, 1982). People watch violence because it allows them to justify their own behavior as being normal. Justification involves the observational learning of attitudes, but it operates in the opposite direction from desensitization. A child's own aggressive behaviors normally should elicit guilt in the child, but this guilt is relieved if the child who has behaved aggressively watches violent television. Thus, the child who has behaved aggressively watches violent television shows to justify his or her own aggressiveness. The problem is that the reduction in guilt that viewing violence provides makes continued aggressive and violent behavior by that child even more likely.

### *Cognitive Cueing and Priming*

Whereas the observational learning process explains how exposure to media violence can teach lasting aggressive habits, the cueing and priming processes explain how aggressive habits learned in other venues may be "triggered" by violent media displays. Berkowitz (1984) has proposed that "the aggressive idea suggested by a violent movie can *'prime'* other semantically related thoughts, heightening the chances that viewers will have other aggressive ideas in this period" (p. 411). In addition, thoughts are linked, along the same sort of associative lines, not only to other thoughts but also to emotional reactions and behavioral tendencies (Bower, 1981; Lang, 1979). Thus, viewing TV violence can activate a complex of associations consisting of aggressive ideas, emotions related to violence, and the impetus for aggressive actions. The appearance of a specific stimulus in the child's environment (e.g., a threat or a weapon) may then *cue* aggressive scripts or ideas that are more readily accessible because they have been *primed* by the violence viewing.

This idea of cognitive cueing and priming is useful in explaining why the observation of aggression in the media is often followed by aggressive acts that differ from the observed behavior. Many studies have demonstrated this phenomenon using television violence (Berkowitz, 1970; Berkowitz & Rogers, 1986; Worchel, 1972; Wyer & Hartwick, 1980; Wyer & Srull, 1980) and using music video violence (Hansen & Hansen, 1990). For example, in one study, it was found that subjects who viewed slides of weapons were more willing to severely punish a target than were those subjects who viewed neutral slides (Leyens & Parke, 1975). Presumably, viewing the weapons stimulated other aggressive ideas and emotions that then affected the viewers' subsequent attitudes and behaviors.

Even innocuous objects that have been paired in the past with observed aggression might serve as stimulating cues in the future. One study that demonstrated this effect quite nicely was Josephson's (1987) study of schoolboy hockey players. In this study, the boys were deliberately frustrated and then shown either a violent or nonviolent television program. A walkie-talkie radio was held by the actor in the violent program but not by the actor in the nonviolent program. During a subsequent hockey game, boys were most aggressive if they had previously seen the aggressive film *and the referee in their current game carried a walkie-talkie radio.*

This idea of cueing seems particularly important in reference to the effects of violent music videos. The audio portion of the video may serve as a cue for aggression observed in the video, causing these aggressive acts to be retrieved when the music is heard in the future.

### *Arousal and Excitation Transfer*

Until one becomes desensitized to it, media violence is arousing. Several studies have demonstrated that increasing a subject's general arousal increases the probability of aggressive behavior when this excitation transfers to actual behavior (e.g., Geen & O'Neal, 1969; Zillmann, 1971). Thus, exciting and stimulating scenes in the mass media may make aggressive behavior more likely immediately afterward because of the excitement they create.

These six major processes—four long-term (observational learning of behaviors, observational learning of cognitions, desensitization, and cognitive justification) and two short-term (cueing and priming and excitation transfer)—probably account for most of the impact of TV violence on a viewer's aggressive behavior. The processes may not seem as inevitable as infection by a virus or the start of a cancer by a carcinogen, but they are well-understood psychological processes that operate in humans. The outcome of such processes is highly predictable—an increase in the likelihood that the young viewer of violent TV will behave more aggressively.

## What Kinds of Violence Have the Biggest Effects?

Do all kinds of TV violence have the same effects? Does TV violence affect all people to the same extent? Given the substantial effect sizes that have been found in all the various types of research, these are important questions. Let us first deal with the "what kinds" of violence question.

Recent surveys of television violence have shown that about 75% of violent acts on TV are unpunished and almost 40% are committed by attractive and heroic characters (National Television Violence Study, 1996). Observational learning theory tells us that these are the "best" kinds of violence to show if we want children to imitate the violent scripts they see and adopt attitudes and beliefs condoning violence (Bandura, 1986). Violent acts that are perceived as morally justified and rewarded produce the strongest learning effects (Berkowitz, 1993). Other characteristics of the format of almost any violent presentation increase learning effects compared with many nonviolent presentations. For example, learning does not occur without viewer attention, and the rapid movements, changes in audio levels, and changes in emotions produced by violent scenes are very good at attracting children's attention (Comstock & Paik, 1991).

At the same time, certain viewer characteristics that lead to different interpretations of violent content have been shown to be important in determining how much influence TV violence has on a viewer. Huesmann and Eron (1986) have reported data from several different countries showing that children who perceive TV violence as more realistic and who identify more with the aggressive characters in the violent programs are influenced more by the violence. The children most at risk for behaving aggressively when they become young adults are not only those who watched a steady diet of TV violence but also those who perceived it as realistic and who identified with the aggressive characters (Huesmann & Moise, 1999).

## Who Is Most Affected by Television Violence?

Jack Valenti, president of the Motion Picture Association of America, has said that, when his two children were younger, they watched a lot of violent TV. "They are now adults," Valenti said, "and their integrity is preserved, and their values are intact, and their standards of conduct, I think, are pretty good" (as cited in Medved, 1995, p. 156). As media violence researchers, we have personally heard some version of this argument numerous times. Many people think that, although television violence can harm other people, it will not harm them personally (e.g., Innes & Zeitz, 1988). This optimistic bias is called the "third-person effect." It is robust and pervasive (Davison, 1983). Most often, it is coupled with the implied argument that TV violence only affects a small number of people. In this section, we show that, *although TV violence may affect some types of people more than others, it has an effect on everyone.*

### *Age of Viewer*

In the meta-analysis by Paik and Comstock (1994), an inverse relationship was found between age and the magnitude of the effect of TV violence on aggression and other antisocial behaviors. *The effects of TV violence were greatest for the youngest age group* (see Figure 11.6). This finding is consistent with what is known about the cognitive development of children. During the first years of life, children are developing social scripts and be-

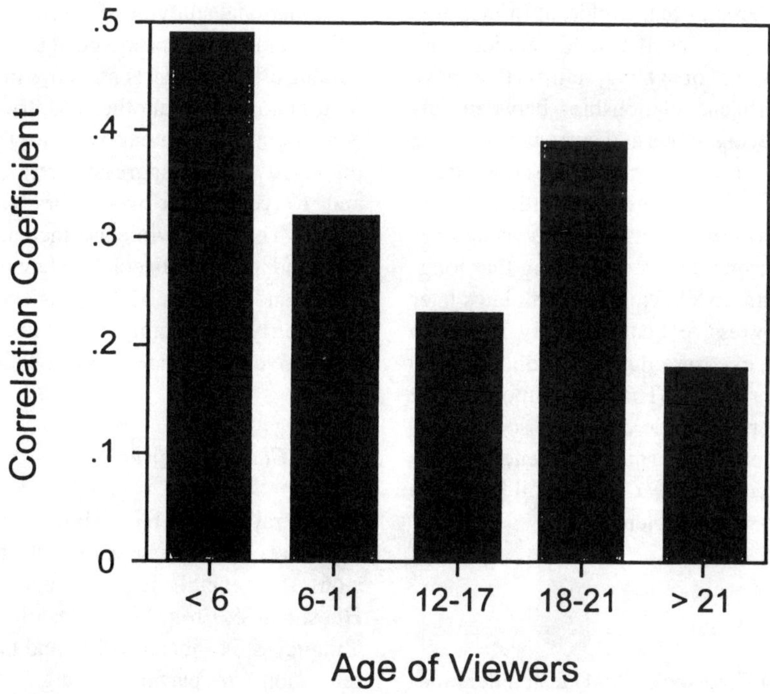


**Figure 11.6.** Effects of TV Violence on Antisocial Behavior for Viewers of Different Ages
SOURCE: Data were obtained from Paik and Comstock (1994).

liefs that will influence behavior throughout their lifetime. As we noted at the beginning of this chapter, there is no better predictor of the chances that an adult will behave aggressively than whether that adult was an aggressive child. Childhood is the cradle of social behavior.

There are also more specific reasons why TV violence should have its biggest effects on young children. Younger children have a more difficult time distinguishing fantasy from reality—everything looks real to them (e.g., Davies, 1997; McKenna & Ossoff, 1998). Young children are more likely to imitate the unrealistic violence of cartoons and fantasy shows than are older children, and they are less likely to perceive crime shows and so on as unrealistic. As discussed earlier, children who think that TV violence is realistic are more influenced by it. Previous research has also shown that TV violence is more likely to increase aggression when the violence is perceived as justified than when it is perceived as unjustified. But younger children have a more difficult time understanding such things as portrayed motives for aggression. Finally, as described above, TV violence is more likely to increase aggression when viewers identify with the aggressive character than when they do not identify with the aggressive character. The age group most susceptible to the influence of television role models is young children (e.g., King & Multon, 1996), who are more likely to identify with violent TV characters and imitate them than are older children or adults.

Early reviews of age effects focused on small differences in responses to experimental manipulations for children of different ages (Dorr & Kovaric, 1980). The more important question is whether adults and older teenagers respond differently than children. In fact, it is difficult to find specific field studies with older teenagers or young adults that have shown significant relationships between current TV viewing habits and current aggressive behavior. Experimental studies do show short-term effects with college-age youth and even some longer-term effects on attitudes and beliefs. The strong consistent finding that long-term exposure to TV violence stimulates later habitual aggressive behavior only seems to hold up for exposure during childhood up to about the early teens. This is an important fact to remember when one considers social solutions to the problem of media violence. We especially need to protect young children from exposure to media violence.

### *Sex of Viewer*

Paik and Comstock (1994) tested the moderating role of viewer sex in their meta-analysis of the effects of TV violence on antisocial behavior. In experimental studies, TV violence had a slightly stronger effect on males than on females (*rs* = .44 and .39, respectively). In nonexperimental studies, TV violence had the same effect on males and females (*rs* = .18 and .19, respectively). Their meta-analysis ignored how these effects may have changed over the past quarter century as female sex roles have changed in most industrialized societies. An examination of a few specific studies suggests that the effect of TV violence on females' behaviors has only become apparent during recent years as more aggressive female models have appeared on TV and as it has become more socially acceptable for females to behave aggressively.

In their longitudinal studies of girls growing up in the 1950s and early 1960s, for example, Eron and Huesmann (Eron et al., 1972; Huesmann, 1986) found no long-term effects of early childhood exposure to TV violence on girls' aggressive behavior at the time, 10 years later, or 22 years later. The significant effects they found were only for boys. In their cross-national study of girls growing up in the 1970s and 1980s, however, they found comparable effects for girls and boys in the United States and in several other countries. For both genders, early high exposure to TV violence predicted greater aggressiveness at the time and 15 years later when they were young adults. Thus, TV violence increases aggressive and other antisocial behaviors in both males and females as long as society treats them fairly comparably and as long as female aggressive models are shown on TV.

### *Social Class of Viewers*

Several studies have shown that children from lower social classes watch more television in general (e.g., Greenberg, 1974; Huesmann & Eron, 1986; Huston et al., 1992; Tangney & Feshbach, 1988) and more violent television in particular (e.g., Chaffee & McLeod, 1972) than do children from middle or upper social classes. It is also well established that children from lower social classes are more at risk to become violent young adults (Huesmann, 1986; Wilson & Herrnstein, 1985). Thus, a plausible conjecture might be that low social class is responsible for the relationship between TV violence viewing and aggression. The data contradict this conjecture. Within every social stratum, viewing TV violence increases the likelihood of behaving aggressively (Eron et al., 1972; Huesmann & Eron, 1986; Huesmann & Moise, 1999). Statistical controls for social class do not remove this effect, and only a few studies have shown a difference in effect sizes for different social strata (e.g., Noble, 1970).

### *Family Environment*

It is not surprising that the family environment can influence the risks associated with viewing TV violence. If parents and older siblings have a heavy diet of TV violence, then

ed to more TV ental behaviors e the influence 989; Tangney &

Obviously, imit the number of hours their child watches TV and restrict the types of programs the child can watch (e.g., programs with a "V" content code), the effects will be reduced. There is evidence that the effects of viewing violence can also be reduced by the parent's coviewing with the child (Tangney & Feshbach, 1988). Unfortunately, studies have shown that children watch TV with their mother less than 10% of the time (Comstock & Paik, 1991). Coviewing allows parents to discuss with their child how unrealistic the scene really was, what motivated characters to use violence, what a better response could have been, how the character might have solved the problem differently, and what the painful consequences of violence are. Parents can also be reassuring if something on TV seems frightening to the child (see Cantor, 1998a, and Chapter 10 for some excellent suggestions for helping a child who has been frightened by media violence).

### *Aggressive Predisposition of Viewers*

There are theoretical reasons for predicting that the people who are most affected by TV violence are those who are characteristically aggressive. For example, the priming and cueing process described above explains how already existing aggressive scripts and beliefs might be activated when someone views TV violence. Bushman (1995, 1996; Bushman & Geen, 1990) recently extended this theory to explain how individual differences in aggressiveness could moderate the effect of viewing TV violence. In comparison to their less aggressive counterparts, individuals who are characteristically aggressive are presumed to have more extensive aggressive associative networks in memory. Because they have more extensive aggressive networks, televised violence should have the strongest effect on aggressive people. The bulk of experimental evidence is consistent with these predictions. Immediately after watching a violent TV program, people who are characteristically aggressive have more aggressive thoughts and ideas, feel more angry inside, and behave more aggressively in comparison to those who are not characteristically aggressive (Bushman, 1995; Bushman & Geen, 1990; Friedrich & Stein, 1973; Josephson, 1987; Russell, 1992).

It is important to understand that this process predicts a less intense effect of media violence on low-aggression children only in the short run. Cueing and priming are not long-term socializing processes. In every longitudinal study that has examined both low- and high-aggression children, there has been evidence of TV violence affecting both types of children (see, for example, Eron et al., 1972; Huesmann, 1986; Huesmann & Eron, 1986; Huesmann & Moise, 1999; Milavsky, Kessler, Stipp, & Rubens, 1982).

One of the reasons why the TV violence effect may be so powerful is that aggression and TV violence viewing seem to feed on each other, at least in the short run. Although little evidence has been reported that more aggressive children turn to watching more violent TV in the long run, more aggressive children do seem to be attracted to viewing violent programs in the short run (e.g., Bushman, 1995; Fenigstein, 1979; Gunter, 1983; O'Neal & Taylor, 1989). This reciprocal relationship between TV violence and aggression can create a vicious cycle. Children are stimulated to behave aggressively by watching TV violence. They behave aggressively. Then they turn back to watching TV violence because it makes them feel better about having behaved aggressively, and the cycle continues. The fact that aggressive behavior usually makes children unpopular, and unpopular children watch more TV, may add to the process.

### *Intellectual Functioning of Viewers*

Theoretically, one could argue that the effects of TV violence on aggression should be either greater for children with higher intellectual ability because they learn better or smaller for children of high intellectual ability because they are better able to perceive the unreality of TV violence. Several studies have shown that children with lower intellectual ability watch more television in general (e.g., Sprafkin & Gadow, 1986) and watch more violent television in particular (e.g., Chaffee & McLeod, 1972; Sprafkin & Gadow, 1986; Stein & Friedrich, 1972; Wiegman, Kuttschreuter, & Baarda, 1986). In addition, it is well established that children with low intellectual ability are more at risk of growing up to behave aggressively and violently (Berkowitz, 1993; Huesmann, Eron, & Yarmel, 1987; Wilson & Herrnstein, 1985). As with social class, one might then ask whether the observed relationship between TV violence viewing and aggressive behavior could simply be the result of low-IQ children watching more TV violence and behaving more aggressively. The answer is no! Most longitudinal studies have shown that the relationship between early exposure to TV violence and later aggressive and violent behavior remains robust even when one controls statistically for differences in intellectual or educational background (Belson, 1978; Eron et al., 1972; Huesmann & Eron, 1986; Huesmann & Moise, 1999; Singer & Singer, 1981). Low intellectual functioning does account for some of the relationship (e.g., Sprafkin, Gadow, & Grayson, 1987; Wiegman et al., 1986), but TV violence clearly affects both smart children and less smart children.

## Effects of Warning Labels, Age-Based Ratings, and Content Codes on Attraction to Televised Violence

Because of political pressure exerted in the last decade, today's violent television programs often contain a warning label (e.g., "This program contains violence. Viewer discretion is advised"), an age-based rating (e.g., "TV-M, Mature Audiences Only. . . . This program may be unsuitable for children under 17"), a content code (e.g., "V," for violence), or some combination of the three. Although warning labels and age-based ratings are directed at parents to permit them to monitor what their children watch on television, viewers of all ages might also use them to select TV programs. In particular, a number of researchers and policy makers have worried that warnings and ratings could make violent TV programs "forbidden fruits" and attract young viewers.

Attorney General Janet Reno has speculated that labels, warnings, and restrictive ratings might do nothing to reduce the amount of violence on television and might even increase the audience for it (Drevitch, 1994). According to Peggy Charren, founder of Action for Children's Television, "If you tell everybody, 'Hey, this program is going to be terribly violent and scare the wits out of you,' you'll get every teenager in America watching it" (as cited in Drevitch, 1994, p. 13). TV executives have been among the forefront of those making this argument. For example, Leslie Moonves, president of CBS entertainment, said, "My 12-year-old son, I'll take him to the video store and I'll say, 'What do you want to get?' He says, 'Anything with an "R" on it.' He does not even care what the movie is" (as cited in Bark, 1997, p. 63). Of course, the arguments of such executives must be read in light of their vested economic interest in violence and fear that ratings will reduce the economic viability of violence. Clearly, they fear that if warning labels and age-based ratings for a given program are considered by the public as a warning of the potentially harmful effects of television violence, then fewer people might watch the program. This would especially be true if the warning comes from an authoritative source and is seen by everyone as a warning about "tainted fruit" rather than simply an attempt to forbid a desirable fruit.

The bulk of the experimental evidence suggests that warning labels and age-based ratings draw viewers to violent programs, but content codes do not have this effect (Bushman, 1997; Bushman & Stack, 1996; Cantor, 1998b; Cantor & Harrison, 1997; Cantor, Harrison, & Nathanson, 1997). In the typical study, subjects are given a set of fictitious titles from which to select a film to view. In one randomly selected group, a film receives one rating; the other group receives a different rating. Labeling a program as violent does not seem to make it more attractive, but labeling a program as "restricted" or for mature audiences does seem to increase its attractiveness to viewers. In particular, age-based restrictive ratings are much more likely to draw young viewers to violent programs than to repel them. Warning labels and age-based ratings increase attraction to violent programs in both male and female viewers ranging in age from 5 to 77 years.

Regarding the source of the warning, Bushman and Stack (1996) found that a warning from the U.S. surgeon general almost doubled the number of people who chose to watch a violent film. However, content codes (e.g., the code "V" for violence) did not show such an effect. Content codes do not appear to increase the attractiveness of a violent program (Bushman, 1997; Bushman & Stack, 1996; Cantor, 1998b; Cantor & Harrison, 1997; Cantor et al., 1997). This finding also applies to both males and females ranging in age from 5 to 77 years.

One of the problems with these experimental studies is that they cannot assess how the protective actions of parents in response to age-based ratings might balance out the attraction they provide for children and actually result in less exposure for children. It is clear from this research, though, that content codes are a much better bet for reducing the amount of TV violence to which our children are exposed.

For the TV industry, age-based ratings and warning labels serve the function of averting censorship policies being imposed by outside groups while not reducing the attractiveness of programming to young viewers. It is somewhat ironic that, even though age-based ratings and warnings can increase the attractiveness of TV programs with violence, the TV industry can claim that it is attempting to be more sensitive to the potentially harmful effects of TV violence.

## Counteracting the Harmful Effects of Television Violence

### *The Role of Parents and Guardians*

Sitting a child in front of a TV set can buy a parent time, a precious commodity to any parent, especially those who are single. However, the TV set is a shoddy baby-sitter, especially when TV content is not monitored. Parents are in the best position to counteract the harmful effects of TV violence on the child. The primary TV exposure a child experiences occurs in the home. TV viewing habits are established early in life and are quite persistent over time. The harmful effects of violent TV are also greatest for young children (e.g., Paik & Comstock, 1994). Thus, parents should take an active role rather than a passive role in counteracting the potentially harmful effects of TV violence.

Training for parents includes informing them of the negative effects TV violence can have on their child and teaching them how to counteract these negative effects. Parents should teach their child how to be a critical TV viewer. Previous research has shown that teaching children critical TV viewing skills can make them less susceptible to the harmful effects of TV violence (e.g., Abelman & Courtright, 1983; Eron, 1982; Singer & Singer, 1983; Watkins, Sprafkin, Gadow, & Sadetsky, 1988). Parents need to watch TV with their children and to discuss the unreality of the violence they see (Tangney & Feshbach, 1988).

### *The Role of the Television Industry*

Some in the TV and film industry claim that viewing violence is therapeutic because it allows individuals to drain their angry and aggressive impulses into harmless channels, producing a cathartic effect. As we pointed out earlier in this chapter, viewing violence is not cathartic. In her review of the relevant literature, Tavris (1988) concluded, "It is time to put a bullet, once and for all, through the heart of the catharsis hypothesis. The belief that observing violence (or 'ventilating it') gets rid of hostilities has virtually never been supported by research" (p. 194).

Others in the TV and film industry claim that violent media have no effect on violence and aggression. Consider the following quotes.

> *If you cut the wires of all TV sets today, there would still be no less violence on the streets in two years.*
>
> Jack Valenti, President of the Motion Picture Association of America

> *No TV set ever killed a kid.*
>
> Lucie Salhany, Chairperson of Fox Broadcasting

> *I don't think there is any correlation between violence on TV and violence in society.*
>
> Jim Burke of Rysher Entertainment

These kinds of opinions seem foolish in light of the scientific data. On the one hand, the TV industry charges hundreds of thousands of dollars for a few minutes of commercial airtime, claiming that TV advertisements can sell anything from canned goods to political candidates. On the other hand, the TV industry asserts that the hours of programming surrounding the few minutes of advertisements have no effect on viewers. This is an absurd contradiction. As former FCC chairman Reed Hundt said, "If a sitcom can sell soap, salsa and cereal, then who could argue that TV violence cannot affect to some degree some viewers, particularly impressionable children?" (as cited in Eggerton, 1994, p. 10).

Historically, violent TV programs have attracted *smaller* audiences than nonviolent programs have (Hamilton, 1998). Violent programs are valued by advertisers, however, because they attract younger viewers (e.g., 18- to 49-year-olds) and because they are slightly less expensive for the networks to purchase (Hamilton, 1998). Violent programming is also more likely to be exported to foreign broadcast markets than other types of programming, perhaps because violence loses less in translation than, for example, situation comedies that rely on some knowledge of the popular culture. According to Gerbner, "Violence travels well in foreign markets. It is a low-cost, high-circulation commodity" (as cited in Jenish, 1992, p. 40). In time, violent media might become America's most exportable commodity, making the United States the "bread-casket for the world" (Hammerman, 1990, p. 79).

It is unlikely that moral appeals from parents and other concerned citizens will influence the TV industry to reduce the amount of violent programming. The bottom line really determines what programs are shown on television. If advertisers refused to sponsor them, violent TV programs would become extinct. Several years ago, a spokesperson for the J. Walter Thompson Company stated, "The more we probe the issue, the more we are convinced that sponsorship of television violence is potentially bad business, as well as a social risk" ("Lousy Frames," 1977, p. 56).

The available research evidence is consistent with this conclusion in ways that TV executives might not realize. Commercial messages actually seem to be less effective if they are embedded in violent programs than if they are embedded in nonviolent programs (Bushman & Phillips, in press). Even if a commercial is interesting, enjoyable, and persuasive, it will not be very effective if the potential buyer cannot remember it. Violent action-adventure programs excite and arouse viewers. Previous research has shown that arousing programs impair attention to, as well as processing and storage of, commercial messages (e.g., Mundorf, Zillmann, & Drew, 1991; Pavelchak, Antil, & Munch, 1988; Singh & Churchill, 1987). But even when violent and nonviolent programs are matched in terms of how exciting and arousing they are, violence impairs memory for commercial messages (Bushman, 1998).

The negative effect of TV violence on memory for commercial messages is at least partly due to the anger induced by the violence. Violent programs make viewers angry, and the more angry viewers are, the less they remember about commercial messages (Bushman, 1998). There are at least two reasons why anger might interfere with memory for commercials. First, the angry mood induced by violent TV programs might activate other aggressive thoughts and memories in viewers that interfere with rehearsal of commercial messages. Second, people who are angry might try to repair their moods, which takes a lot of effort and energy. During the time that advertisers hope viewers are absorbing their commercial messages, viewers may actually be focusing on themselves, trying to calm the anger brought on by what they have just seen on the screen. Thus, sponsoring violent programs might not be a profitable venture for advertisers.

### *The Role of the Government*

The government has been involved in the TV violence debate since the 1950s. In 1972, the surgeon general concluded that TV violence was harmful to children and issued his famous warning about it (Steinfeld, 1972). Only recently has Congress actually acted to do something about the problem. The 1996 Telecommunications Act was passed and signed into law. This act mandated that new television sets be manufactured with a V-chip (short for violence-chip), a silicon sentry that will allow parents to block out TV programs with objectionable content. The act also mandated that TV programs be rated or labeled to provide information that can be read by the V-chip. When the V-chip is activated by a special code inserted by broadcasters into the TV signal, it scrambles the reception of the incoming picture.

One problem with the V-chip is that some parents have difficulty with modern technology. During a Senate Commerce Committee hearing in July 1995, a Zenith television executive who was demonstrating how the V-chip worked struggled for more than 10 minutes and was unable to get the device to work, finally pleading to an aide, "Am I doing something wrong?" (Gray, 1996, p. 30). If this expert on V-chip technology can't make it work, how will the average parent make it work?

A bigger problem concerns the rating system adopted. Within a year of passage of the 1996 Telecommunications Act, the TV industry announced a new age-based rating system referred to as "TV Parental Guidelines." The television rating system is similar to the movie rating system used by the Motion Picture Association of America. Children's programs are designated with one of two ratings: (a) "TV-Y, All Children," or (b) "TV-Y7, Directed to Older Children." Other programs are designated with one of four ratings: (a) "TV-G, General Audience" ("Most parents would find this program suitable for all ages"); (b) "TV-PG, Parental Guidance Suggested" ("Some parents would find this program unsuitable for younger children"); (c) "TV-14, Parents Strongly Cautioned" ("Many parents would find this program unsuitable for children under 14"); and (d) "TV-M, Mature Audiences Only" ("This program may be unsuitable for children under 17"). Some violent TV programs also contain warning labels (e.g., "Due to some violent content, parental discretion is advised"). When applicable, TV programs are designated with one or more content codes. The five content codes are (a) "V" (violence), (b) "FV" (fantasy violence), (c) "S" (sex), (d) "L" (adult language), and (e) "D" (suggestive dialogue).

On the basis of the available empirical evidence, we can expect that these ratings will have a "forbidden fruit" effect on young viewers (see Chapter 34). Parents may try to limit children's exposure to programs rated "mature," but children will try hard to see them too. The better approach would be simply to use content codes rather than warning labels and age-based ratings. Content codes are quite informative (e.g., they allow parents to decide which programs are appropriate for their children), but they do not draw viewers to violent programs. In other words, inform viewers but do not give them unwanted advice about what they should not watch on TV. The vehemence with which the TV industry has attacked content ratings makes one suspect that economic fear of sponsors rejecting violent shows is what has driven the TV industry's objections to content ratings.

## Conclusion

In this chapter, we have reviewed the evidence relating TV violence to aggressive and violent behavior and have concluded that (a) TV violence has a short-term stimulating effect on aggressive behavior for viewers of all ages, and (b) TV violence has a long-term socializing effect that makes lifelong aggressive behavior more likely for children who watch a lot of it while growing up. We have concluded that this effect is not something that happens only to already aggressive children, only to poor children, or only to less intelligent children. Just as cigarette smoking raises the risk of lung cancer in everyone, exposure to a lot of media violence raises aggression in everyone.

Researchers have made substantial progress in understanding the psychological processes involved in how media violence affects children. Children who watch TV violence imitate the aggressive scripts they see; they become more condoning of violence; they start to believe the world is a more hostile place; they become emotionally desensitized to violence; the violence they see justifies to them their own violent acts; the arousal of the violence they see arouses them; and the violence they see cues aggressive ideas for them.

Unfortunately, understanding the process by which media violence may engender aggression in children does not immediately suggest a solution. Still, five points provide us with guidelines.

First, we need to be more concerned about the effects of TV violence on children than about the effects of TV violence on teenagers and adults. Media violence may have short-term effects on adults, but the real long-term effects seem to occur only with children. This makes some societal controls more palatable in a free society.

Second, the violent films and programs that may have the most deleterious effects on children are not always the ones that adults and critics believe are the most violent. The type of violent scene the child is most likely to use as a model for violent behavior is one in which the perpetrator of the violence is rewarded for the violence. Thus, a violent act by someone like "Dirty Harry" that results in a heinous criminal being eliminated and brings glory to Harry is of much more concern than a bloodier murder by a despicable criminal who is brought to justice. Parents need to be educated about these facts.

Third, we need to be aware that media violence can affect any child from any family. It is not, as some have suggested, only the already violence-prone child who is likely to be affected. True, media violence is not likely to turn an otherwise fine child into a violent criminal. But, just as every cigarette one smokes increases a little bit the likelihood of a lung tumor someday, every violent show one watches increases a little bit the likelihood of behaving more aggressively in some situation.

Fourth, broadcasters and film and program makers cannot avoid all responsibility and expect parents, governments, and others to control viewing violence. The argument that people watch it, so we give it to them, is not valid in a modern socially conscious society. It is unrealistic to expect parents to completely control what children watch in a society with multiple TVs in each household, VCRs everywhere, and both parents working.

Finally, we must recognize the economic realities of media violence. Violence sells. Both children and adults are attracted to violent scenes by the action and intense emotions. Many of the most popular shows and popular films for children have contained violence. The income that a film generates is directly affected by how many viewers watch it. Even a 1% increase in viewers can increase profits by millions of dollars; the ability of violence to attract viewers is an important factor. Furthermore, violence is generally less expensive to produce because one can get by with trite, mundane stories that are poorly acted when one has violence to attract viewers (Gerbner & Gross, 1981). On the other hand, successful dramatic stories cost correspondingly more and require better talent.

What is the solution? Better parental control, more government control, training children not to be affected by media violence, electronic chips that cut out violence, and boycotting sponsors of violence may all be needed. Society needs to make decisions based on an appropriate balance between freedom of expression and protection of our children, and it is time for society to take this problem seriously and act. The future of our children and society is too precious for us not to act.

## Notes

1. More precisely, the correlation between exposure to media violence and aggressive behavior represents the extent to which a graph of the two measures is a perfectly straight line. In other words, a correlation measures the "linear" relationship between two measures. A correlation of 0 means that there is no linear relation between the measures. However, the two might still be systematically related in some nonlinear manner.

2. Not all studies have replicated this finding (e.g., Hughes, 1980; Wober & Gunter, 1982).

## References

Abelman, R., & Courtright, J. A. (1983). Television literacy: Amplifying the cognitive level effects of television's prosocial fare through curriculum intervention. *Journal of Research and Development in Education, 17,* 46-57.

Anderson, C. A., & Bushman, B. J. (1997). External validity of "trivial" experiments: The case of laboratory aggression. *Review of General Psychology, 1,* 19-41.

Anderson, C. A., Lindsay, J. J., & Bushman, B. J. (1999). Research in the psychological laboratory: Truth or triviality? *Current Directions in Psychological Science, 8,* 3-9.

Anderson, E. J. (1990). *Streetwise: Race, class, and change in an urban community.* Chicago: University of Chicago Press.

Bandura, A. (1965). Influence of models' reinforcement contingencies on the acquisition of imitative responses. *Journal of Abnormal and Social Psychology, 66,* 575-582.

Bandura, A. (1977). *Social learning theory.* Englewood Cliffs, NJ: Prentice Hall.

Bandura, A. (1986). *Social foundations of thought and action: A social-cognitive theory.* Englewood Cliffs, NJ: Prentice Hall.

Bandura, A., Ross, D., & Ross, S. A. (1961). Transmission of aggression through imitation of aggressive models. *Journal of Abnormal Social Psychology, 63,* 575-582.

Bandura, A., Ross, D., & Ross, S. A. (1963a). Imitation of aggression through imitation of film-mediated aggressive models. *Journal of Abnormal and Social Psychology, 66,* 3-11.

Bandura, A., Ross, D., & Ross, S. A. (1963b). Vicarious reinforcement and initiative learning. *Journal of Abnormal and Social Psychology, 67,* 601-607.

Bark, E. (1997). TV industry rates the ratings after the first month. *New Jersey Star Ledger.*

Belson, W. (1978). *Television violence and the adolescent boy.* Hampshire, UK: Saxon House.

Berkowitz, L. (1970). Aggressive humor as a stimulus to aggressive responses. *Journal of Personality and Social Psychology, 2,* 359-369.

Berkowitz, L. (1984). Some effects of thoughts on antisocial and prosocial influences of media effects: A cognitive-neoassociation analysis. *Psychological Bulletin, 95,* 410-427.

Berkowitz, L. (1993). *Aggression: Its causes, consequences, and control.* New York: McGraw-Hill.

Berkowitz, L., & Rogers, K. H. (1986). A priming effect analysis of media influences. In J. Bryant & D. Zillmann (Eds.), *Perspectives on media effects* (pp. 57-82). Hillsdale, NJ: Lawrence Erlbaum.

Bjorkqvist, K. (1985). *Violent films, anxiety, and aggression.* Helsinki: Finnish Society of Sciences and Letters.

Bower, G. H. (1981). Mood and memory. *American Psychologist, 36,* 129-148.

Brower, A. (1993, November 1). Public enemy no. 1? Most adults are offended by television's sex and violence. *Mediaweek,* p. 18.

Bushman, B. J. (1995). Moderating role of trait aggressiveness in the effects of violent media on aggression. *Journal of Personality and Social Psychology, 69,* 950-960.

Bushman, B. J. (1996). Individual differences in the extent and development of aggressive cognitive-associative networks. *Personality and Social Psychology Bulletin, 22,* 811-819.

Bushman, B. J. (1997, September). *Effects of warning labels on attraction to television violence in viewers of different ages.* Paper presented at the Telecommunication and Policy Research Conference, Alexandria, VA.

Bushman, B. J. (1998). Effects of television violence on memory of commercial messages. *Journal of Experimental Psychology: Applied, 4,* 291-307.

Bushman, B. J., & Geen, R. G. (1990). The role of cognitive-emotional mediators and individual differences in the effects of media violence on aggression. *Journal of Personality and Social Psychology, 58,* 156-163.

Bushman, B. J., & Phillips, C. M. (in press). If the television program bleeds, memory for the advertisement recedes. *Current Directions in Psychological Science.*

Bushman, B. J., Phillips, C. M., & Anderson, C. A. (2000). *Media violence and the American public: Scientific facts versus media misinformation.* Manuscript under review.

Bushman, B. J., & Stack, A. D. (1996). Forbidden fruit versus tainted fruit: Effects of warning labels on attraction to television violence. *Journal of Experimental Psychology: Applied, 2,* 207-226.

Cantor, J. (1998a). *"Mommy, I'm scared": How TV and movies frighten children and what we can do to protect them.* San Diego, CA: Harcourt Brace.

Cantor, J. (1998b). Ratings for program content: The role of research findings. In K. Jamieson (Ed.), *Annals of the American Academy of Political and Social Science, 557* [Special issue], 54-69.

Cantor, J., & Harrison, K. (1997). The relationship between media consumption and eating disorders. *Journal of Communication, 47*(1), 40-67.

Cantor, J., Harrison, K., & Nathanson, A. (1997). Ratings and advisories for television programming: University of Wisconsin, Madison, study. In *National Television Violence Study* (Vol. 2). Newbury Park, CA: Sage.

Chaffee, S. H., & McLeod, J. M. (1972). Adolescent television use in the family context. In G. A. Comstock & E. A. Rubinstein (Eds.), *Television and social behavior: Vol. 3. Television and adolescent aggressiveness* (pp. 149-172). Washington, DC: U.S. Government Printing Office.

Cline, V. B., Croft, R. G., & Courrier, S. (1973). Desensitization of children to television violence. *Journal of Personality and Social Psychology, 27,* 360-365.

Cohen, D., & Nisbett, R. E. (1997). Field experiments examining the culture of honor: The role of institutions in perpetuating norms about violence. *Personality and Social Psychology Bulletin, 23,* 1188-1199.

Cohen, J. (1988). *Statistical power analysis for the behavioral sciences* (2nd ed.). Hillsdale, NJ: Lawrence Erlbaum.

Comstock, G. A., & Paik, H. (1991). The effects of television violence on aggressive behavior: A meta-analysis. In *A preliminary report to the National Research Council on the understanding and control of violent behavior.* Washington, DC: National Research Council.

Cooper, H. (1989). *Homework.* New York: Longman.

Cooper, H., & Hedges, L. V. (Eds.). (1994). *The handbook of research synthesis.* New York: Russell Sage.

Crick, N. R., & Dodge, K. A. (1994). A review and reformulation of social information processing mechanisms in children's adjustment. *Psychological Bulletin, 115,* 74-101.

Davies, M. M. (1997). *Fake, fact, and fantasy: Children's interpretations of television reality.* Mahwah, NJ: Lawrence Erlbaum.

Davison, W. P. (1983). The third-person effect in communication. *Public Opinion Quarterly, 47,* 1-15.

Dominick, J. R., & Greenberg, B. S. (1972). Attitudes toward violence: The interaction of television exposure, family attitudes, and social class. In G. A. Comstock & E. A. Rubinstein (Eds.), *Television and social behavior: Vol. 3. Television and adolescent aggressiveness* (pp. 314-335). Washington, DC: U.S. Government Printing Office.

Doob, A. N., & Wood, L. E. (1972). Catharsis and aggression: Effects of annoyance and retaliation on aggressive behavior. *Journal of Personality & Social Psychology, 22*(2), 156-162.

Dorr, A., & Kovaric, P. (1980). Some of the people some of the time—but which people? Televised violence and its effects. In E. L. Palmer & A. Dorr (Eds.), *Children and the faces of television* (pp. 183-199). New York: Academic Press.

Drabman, R. S., & Thomas, M. H. (1974a). Does media violence increase children's toleration of real-life aggression? *Developmental Psychology, 10,* 418-421.

Drabman, R. S., & Thomas, M. H. (1974b). Exposure to filmed violence and children's tolerance of real life aggression. *Personality & Social Psychology Bulletin, 1*(1), 198-199.

Drevitch, G. (1994, February 11). Murder, she saw. *Scholastic Update,* pp. 12-13.

Eggerton, J. (1994, January 31). Hundt hits television violence. *Broadcasting and Cable,* p. 10.

Eron, L. D. (1982). Parent-child interaction, television violence, and aggression of children. *American Psychologist, 37,* 197-211.

Eron, L. D., Huesmann, L. R., Lefkowitz, M. M., & Walder, L. O. (1972). Does television violence cause aggression? *American Psychologist, 27,* 253-263.

Fenigstein, A. (1979). Does aggression cause a preference for viewing media violence? *Journal of Personality and Social Psychology, 37,* 2307-2317.

Feshbach, S., & Singer, R. D. (1971). *Television and aggression: An experimental field study.* San Francisco: Jossey-Bass.

Fiore, M. C., Smith, S. S., Jorenby, D. E., & Baker, T. B. (1994). The effectiveness of the nicotine patch for smoking cessation. *Journal of the American Medical Association, 271,* 1940-1947.

Fischer, R. L. (1994, July). Is it possible to regulate television violence? *USA Today,* pp. 72-75.

Friedrich, L. K., & Stein, A. H. (1973). Aggressive and prosocial television programs and the natural behavior of preschool children. *Monographs of the Society for Research in Child Development, 38*(4, Serial No. 151, pp. 1-63).

Geen, R. G., & O'Neal, E. C. (1969). Activation of cue-elicited aggression by general arousal. *Journal of Personality and Social Psychology, 11,* 289-292.

Gerbner, G., & Gross, L. (1976). Living with television: The violence profile. *Journal of Communication, 26,* 172-199.

Gerbner, G., & Gross, L. (1981). The violent face of television and its lessons. In E. I. Palmer & A. Dorr (Eds.), *Children and the faces of television: Teaching, violence, selling* (pp. 149-162). New York: Academic Press.

Gray, T. E. (1996, April 15). V-chip: The Betamax of the '90s. *Broadcasting and Cable,* p. 30.

Greenberg, D. F. (1974). British children and televised violence. *Public Opinion Quarterly, 38,* 531-547.

Gunter, B. (1983). Do aggressive people prefer violent television? *Bulletin of the British Psychological Society, 36,* 166-168.

Halpern, W. I. (1975). Turned-on toddlers. *Journal of Communication, 25,* 66-70.

Hamilton, J. T. (1998). *Channeling violence: The economic market for violent television programming.* Princeton, NJ: Princeton University Press.

Hammerman, J. K. (1990, October). Dead men don't smirk. *Esquire,* p. 79.

Hansen, C. H., & Hansen, R. D. (1990). Rock music videos and antisocial behavior. *Basic and Applied Social Psychology, 11,* 357-369.

Hastorf, A., & Cantril, H. (1954). They saw a game: A case study. *Journal of Abnormal and Social Psychology, 49,* 129-134.

Hayes, S. C., Rincover, A., & Volosin, D. (1980). Variables influencing the acquisition and maintenance of aggressive behavior: Modeling versus summary reinforcement. *Journal of Abnormal Psychology, 89,* 254-262.

Hicks, D. J. (1965). Imitation and retention of film-mediated aggressive peer and adult models. *Journal of Personality and Social Psychology, 2,* 97-100.

Hill, D., White, V., Jolley, D., & Mapperson, K. (1988). Self examination of the breast: Is it beneficial? Meta-analysis of studies investigating breast self examination and extent of disease in patients with breast cancer. *British Medical Journal, 297,* 271-275.

Hokanson, J. E., & Burgess, M. (1962). The effects of status, type of frustration, and aggression on vascular processes. *Journal of Abnormal & Social Psychology, 65*(4), 232-237.

Huesmann, L. R. (1982). Information processing models of behavior. In N. Hirschberg & L. Humphreys (Eds.), *Multivariate applications in the social sciences* (pp. 261-288). Hillsdale, NJ: Lawrence Erlbaum.

Huesmann, L. R. (1986). Psychological processes promoting the relation between exposure to media violence and aggressive behavior by the viewer. *Journal of Social Issues, 42*(3), 125-139.

Huesmann, L. R. (1988). An information processing model for the development of aggression. *Aggressive Behavior, 14,* 13-24.

Huesmann, L. R. (1998). The role of social information processing and cognitive schemas in the acquisition and maintenance of habitual aggressive behavior. In R. G. Geen & E. Donnerstein (Eds.), *Human aggression: Theories, research, and implications for policy* (pp. 73-109). New York: Academic Press.

Huesmann, L. R., & Eron, L. (1986). *Television and the aggressive child: A cross-national comparison.* Hillsdale, NJ: Lawrence Erlbaum.

Huesmann, L. R., Eron, L. D., Berkowitz, L., & Chaffee, S. (1991). The effects of television violence on aggression: A reply to a skeptic. In P. Suedfeld & P. Tetlock (Eds.), *Psychology and social policy* (pp. 191-200). New York: Hemisphere.

Huesmann, L. R., Eron, L. D., Lefkowitz, M. M., & Walder, L. O. (1984). The stability of aggression over time and generations. *Developmental Psychology, 20,* 1120-1134.

Huesmann, L. R., Eron, L. D., & Yarmel, P. W. (1987). Intellectual functioning and aggression. *Journal of Personality and Social Psychology, 52,* 232-240.

Huesmann, L. R., & Guerra, N. G. (1997). Normative beliefs about aggression and aggressive behavior. *Journal of Personality and Social Psychology, 72*(2), 408-419.

Huesmann, L. R., Lagerspetz, K., & Eron, L. D. (1984). Intervening variables in the television violence–aggression relation: Evidence from two countries. *Developmental Psychology, 20*(5), 746-775.

Huesmann, L. R., & Miller, L. S. (1994). Long-term effects of repeated exposure to media violence in childhood. In L. R. Huesmann (Ed.), *Aggressive behavior: Current perspectives* (pp. 153-186). New York: Plenum.

Huesmann, L. R., & Moise, J. (1999, September). *The role of cognitions in mediating the effect of childhood exposure to violence on adult aggression: A 15-year comparison of youth in four countries.* Paper presented at the European Conference on Developmental Psychology, Spetses, Greece.

Hughes, M. (1980). The fruits of cultivation analysis: A reexamination of some effects of television watching. *Public Opinion Quarterly, 44,* 287-302.

Hunt, M. (1997). *How science takes stock: The story of meta-analysis.* New York: Russell Sage.

Hunter, J. E., & Schmidt, F. L. (1990). *Methods of meta-analysis: Correcting error and bias in research findings.* Newbury Park, CA: Sage.

Huston, A. C., Donnerstein, E., Fairchild, H., Feshbach, N. D., Katz, P. A., Murray, J. P., Rubinstein, E. A., Wilcox, B. L., & Zuckerman, D. (1992). *Big world, small screen: The role of television in American society.* Lincoln: University of Nebraska Press.

Innes, J. M., & Zeitz, H. (1988). The public's view of the impact of the mass media: A test of the "third person" effect. *European Journal of Social Psychology, 18,* 457-463.

Jenish, D. (1992, December 7). Prime-time violence: Despite high ratings for violent shows, revulsion is growing over bloodshed on TV. *Macleans,* p. 40.

Josephson, W. L. (1987). Television violence and children's aggression: Testing the priming, social script, and disinhibition predictions. *Journal of Personality and Social Psychology, 53,* 882-890.

King, M. M., & Multon, K. D. (1996). The effects of television role models on the career aspirations of African American junior high school students. *Journal of Career Development, 23,* 111-125.

Lang, P. J. (1979). A bio-informational theory of emotional imagery. *Psychophysiology, 16,* 495-512.

Leyens, J. P., & Parke, R. D. (1975). Aggressive slides can induce a weapons effect. *European Journal of Social Psychology, 5,* 229-236.

Lousy frames for beautiful pictures: Are they changing? (1977, May 23). *Advertising Age,* p. 56.

Loy, J. W., & Andrews, D. S. (1981). They also saw a game: A replication of a case study. *Replications in Social Psychology, 1,* 45-59.

McKenna, M. W., & Ossoff, E. P. (1998). Age differences in children's comprehension of a popular television program. *Child Study Journal, 28,* 53-68.

Medved, M. (1995, October). Hollywood's 3 big lies. *Reader's Digest,* pp. 155-159.

Milavsky, J. R., Kessler, R., Stipp, H., & Rubens, W. S. (1982). Television and aggression: Results of a panel study. In D. Pearl, L. Bouthilet, & J. Lazar (Eds.), *Television and behavior: Ten years of scientific progress and implications for the eighties: Vol. 2. Technical reviews.* Washington, DC: U.S. Government Printing Office.

Mundorf, N., Zillmann, D., & Drew, D. (1991). Effects of disturbing televised events on the acquisition of information from subsequently presented commercials. *Journal of Advertising, 20,* 46-53.

National Television Violence Study. (1996). *National Television Violence Study* (Vol. 1). Thousand Oaks, CA: Sage.

National Television Violence Study. (1997). *National Television Violence Study* (Vol. 2). Studio City, CA: Mediascope.

National Television Violence Study. (1998). *National Television Violence Study* (Vol. 3). Santa Barbara: University of California, Santa Barbara, Center for Communication and Social Policy.

Needleman, H. L., & Gatsonis, C. A. (1990). Low-level lead exposure and the IQ of children. *Journal of the American Medical Association, 263,* 673-678.

Neely, J. J., Hechel, R. V., & Leichtman, H. M. (1973). The effect of race of model and response consequences to the model on imitation in children. *Journal of Social Psychology, 89,* 225-231.

Nicholas, K. B., McCarter, R. E., & Hechel, R. V. (1971). Imitation of adult and peer television models by white and Negro children. *Journal of Social Psychology, 85,* 317-318.

Nielsen Media Research. (1998). *Galaxy explorer.* New York: Author.

Noble, G. (1970). Film-mediated aggressive and creative play. *British Journal of Social and Clinical Psychology, 9*(1), 1-7.

Oliver, M. B. (1994). Portrayals of crime, race, and aggression in "reality-based" police shows: A content analysis. *Journal of Broadcasting and Electronic Media, 38,* 179-192.

O'Neal, E. C., & Taylor, S. L. (1989). Status of the provoker, opportunity to retaliate, and interest in video violence. *Aggressive Behavior, 15,* 171-180.

Paik, H., & Comstock, G. (1994). The effects of television violence on antisocial behavior: A meta-analysis. *Communication Research, 21,* 516-546.

Pavelchak, M. A., Antil, J. H., & Munch, J. M. (1988). The Super Bowl: An investigation into the relationship among program context, emotional experience, and ad recall. *Journal of Consumer Research, 15,* 360-367.

Raine, A., Brennen, P., & Farrington, D. (1997). Biosocial basis of violence. In A. Raine, P. Brennen, D. P. Farrington, & S. A. Mednick (Eds.), *Biosocial basis of violence.* New York: Plenum.

Rosenthal, R. (1991). *Meta-analytic procedures for social research* (2nd ed.). Newbury Park, CA: Sage.

Rosenthal, R., & Rubin, D. B. (1982). A simple, general purpose display of magnitude of experimental effect. *Journal of Educational Psychology, 74,* 166-169.

Russell, G. W. (1992). Response of the macho male to viewing a combatant sport. *Journal of Social Behavior and Personality, 7,* 631-638.

Shirley, I. (1993). The culture of violence. *Community Mental Health in New Zealand, 7,* 3-9.

Singer, D. G. (1989). Caution: Television may be hazardous to a child's mental health. *Journal of Developmental and Behavioral Pediatrics, 10,* 259-261.

Singer, J. L., & Singer, D. G. (1981). *Television, imagination, and aggression: A study of preschoolers' play.* Hillsdale, NJ: Lawrence Erlbaum.

Singer, J. L., & Singer, D. G. (1983). Psychologists look at television: Cognitive, developmental, personality, and social policy implications. *American Psychologist, 38,* 826-834.

Singh, S. N., & Churchill, G. A. (1987). Arousal and advertising effectiveness. *Journal of Advertising, 16,* 4-10, 40.

Smith, A. H., Handley, M. A., & Wood, R. (1990). Epidemiological evidence indicates asbestos causes laryngeal cancer. *Journal of Occupational Medicine, 32,* 499-507.

Somers, A. R. (1976). Violence, television, and the health of American youth. *New England Journal of Medicine, 294,* 811-817.

Sprafkin, J., & Gadow, K. D. (1986). Television viewing habits of emotionally disturbed, learning disabled, and mentally retarded children. *Journal of Applied Developmental Psychology, 7,* 45-59.

Sprafkin, J., Gadow, K. D., & Grayson, P. (1987). Effects of viewing aggressive cartoons on the behavior of learning disabled children. *Journal of Child Psychology and Psychiatry and Allied Disciplines, 28,* 387-398.

Stein, A. H., & Friedrich, L. K. (1972). Television content and young children's behavior. In J. P. Murray, E. A. Rubinstein, & G. A. Comstock (Eds.), *Television and social behavior: Vol. 2. Television and social learning* (pp. 202-317). Washington, DC: U.S. Government Printing Office.

Steinfeld, J. (1972). *Statement in hearings before Subcommittee on Communications of Committee on Commerce* (U.S. Senate, Serial No. 92-52, pp. 25-27). Washington, DC: U.S. Government Printing Office.

Tangney, J. P., & Feshbach, S. (1988). Children's television viewing frequency: Individual differences and demographic correlates. *Personality and Social Psychology Bulletin, 14,* 145-158.

Tavris, C. (1988). Beyond cartoon killings: Comments on two overlooked effects of television. In S. Oskamp (Ed.), *Television as a social issue* (pp. 189-197). Newbury Park, CA: Sage.

Thomas, M. H., & Drabman, R. S. (1975). Toleration of real life aggression as a function of exposure to televised violence and age of subject. *Merrill-Palmer Quarterly, 21,* 227-232.

Thomas, M. H., Horton, R. W., Lippincott, E. C., & Drabman, R. S. (1977). Desensitization to portrayals of real life aggression as a function of television violence. *Journal of Personality and Social Psychology, 35,* 450-458.

*TV Guide.* (1992, October 10-16). TV Guide poll: Would you give up TV for a million bucks? *TV Guide, 40,* 10-13, 15, 17.

U.S. Federal Bureau of Investigation. (1951-1999). *Uniform crime reports.* Washington, DC: U.S. Government Printing Office.

Viemero, V., & Paajanen, S. (1992). The role of fantasies and dreams in the TV viewing–aggression relationship. *Aggressive Behavior, 18*(2), 109-116.

Walters, R. H., Leat, M., & Meaci, L. (1963). Inhibition and disinhibition of responses through empathic learning. *Canadian Journal of Psychology, 17,* 235-243.

Walters, R. H., & Parke, R. D. (1964). Influence of response consequences to a social model on resistance to deviation. *Journal of Experimental Child Psychology, 1,* 269-280.

Wang, M. C., & Bushman, B. J. (1999). *Integrating results through meta-analytic review using SAS® software.* Cary, NC: SAS Institute.

Watkins, L. T., Sprafkin, J., Gadow, K. D., & Sadetsky, I. (1988). Effects of a critical viewing skills curriculum on elementary school children's knowledge and attitudes about television. *Journal of Educational Research, 81,* 165-170.

Weller, S. C. (1993). A meta-analysis of condom effectiveness in reducing sexually transmitted HIV. *Social Science and Medicine, 36,* 1635-1644.

Wells, A. J. (1998). Lung cancer from passive smoking at work. *American Journal of Public Health, 88,* 1025-1029.

Welten, D. C., Kemper, H. C. G., Post, G. B., & van Staveren, W. A. (1995). A meta-analysis of the effect of calcium intake on bone mass in young and middle aged females and males. *Journal of Nutrition, 125,* 2802-2813.

West, W. (1993, July 5). TV's bigwigs are a smash at the Capitol Hill comedy club. *Insight on the News,* p. 40.

Wiegman, O., Kuttschreuter, M., & Baarda, B. (1986). *Television viewing related to aggressive and prosocial behaviour.* Enschede, Netherlands: University of Twente.

Wilson, J. Q., & Herrnstein, R. J. (1985). *Crime and human nature.* New York: Simon & Schuster.

Winn, M. (1977). *The plug-in-drug.* New York: Viking.

Wober, M., & Gunter, B. (1982). Television and personal threat: Fact or artifact? A British survey. *British Journal of Social Psychology, 21,* 239-247.

Worchel, S. (1972). The effect of films on the importance of behavioral freedom. *Journal of Personality, 40,* 417-435.

Wyer, R. S., Jr., & Hartwick, J. (1980). The role of information retrieval and conditional inference processes in belief formation and change. In L. Berkowitz (Ed.), *Advances in experimental social psychology* (Vol. 13). New York: Academic Press.

Wyer, R. S., Jr., & Srull, T. K. (1980). The processing of social stimulus information: A conceptual integration. In R. Hastie, T. M. Ostrom, E. B. Ebbesen, R. S. Wyer, D. L. Hamilton, & D. E. Carlston (Eds.),

*Person memory: The cognitive basis of social perception.* Hillsdale, NJ: Lawrence Erlbaum.

Wynder, E. L., & Graham, E. A. (1950). Tobacco smoking as a possible etiological factor in bronchiogenic carcinoma. *Journal of the American Medical Association, 143,* 329-336.

Zillmann, D. (1971). Excitation transfer in communication-mediated aggressive behavior. *Journal of Experimental Social Psychology, 7,* 419-434.+

Zipperer, J. (1994, February 7). Violence foes take aim: Advertisers and affiliates caught in the crossfire. *Christianity Today,* pp. 40-42.

CHAPTER **12**

# Media Violence in Cross-Cultural Perspective

## A Global Study on Children's Media Behavior and Some Educational Implications

JO GROEBEL
European Institute for the Media,
Dusseldorf/Paris

*I want you to put more life into your dying.*

Samuel Goldwyn

### Media Violence at the Turn of the Century

With incidents like the school shooting in Littleton, Colorado, in 1999, the media violence debate has reached yet another peak. The young students who killed their schoolmates had not only extensively watched violent media content but had also actively produced hateful websites and videos "announcing" their action. Children in the twenty-first century are brought up in a media environment in which the idea of communication convergence has become reality. There is a permanent crossover between TV and Internet content, between computer games and telecommunication, between editorial media contributions and merchandising. Although most of this may serve socially constructive structures, increasing information and facilitating communication, it of course can also be applied in negative ways. Violence has always been a particularly successful media market factor: It attracts high attention among male adolescents, its language is universal, and, with the often simple dramaturgy, it can be more easily produced than complex dialogue-based stories. TV was the dominating medium in the life of children during the second half of the twentieth century. It was often blamed for having negative effects on the young, but it undoubtedly also created numerous prosocial consequences with programs such as *Sesame Street* and *Mister Rogers' Neighborhood* in the United States, *Die Sendung mit der Maus* in Germany, and *Villa Klokhuis* in the Netherlands, to name but a few.

The year 2000 faces a different situation. TV may still be around, but in most Western children's lives, it is no longer true that one dominating medium is the nearly "single source" for information and passive entertainment. In the new century, people will grow up in a "digital environment." With Internet TV, with technologies such as replay, with mobile phones connected to the Web, any content is potentially accessible at any given moment in any given situation. In addition, consumers have become "prosumers"; they create and communicate their own media content like the young killers did in Littleton.

However, the media and media effects debate in the twentieth century had predominantly been a Western, and more specifically an American/Anglo-Saxon, issue. There have been incidents all over the world similar to the Littleton one (e.g., in Brazil, in Germany, in Scotland). However, relatively little research has been conducted concerning a really global approach to media violence. In the 1980s, Huesmann and Eron (1986) presented a cross-cultural study with seven countries involved, including Australia, Israel, Poland, and the United States. In the 1990s, a group of researchers started an international analysis on the media environment of European children in the tradition of Hilde Himmelweit's landmark 1958 study on television (Livingstone, 1998). But even these and similar studies concentrated on the more developed parts of the world. A really global approach including a representative sample of all cultures, regions, and developmental states of the world was absent.

Apart from a media policy perspective, such a global study is also significant from a scientific point of view. It could identify:

- The impact of different cultural norms on possible media effects
- The interaction between media violence and *real* violence in the immediate environment of children
- The differences between world regions with a highly developed media landscape and those with only a few basic media available

In this situation, UNESCO (United Nations Educational, Scientific, and Cultural Organization) decided to initiate a project that would analyze the international importance of the issue. In particular, possible cultural differences, as well as the influence of different aggressive experiences in the actual environment (war and crime) and the different media environments for the children, were to be identified. To that end, an intercultural questionnaire study was developed. About 5,000 12-year-old boys and girls from 23 different countries around the world participated in the project. This means that this study is the biggest of its kind ever conducted with respect to the number of subjects and countries included. For at least half of the countries involved in this research study, it was the first time that research of this type had been undertaken.

## The Role of Media Violence in Children's Lives

Children and adolescents have always been interested in arousing, and often even violent, stories and fairy tales (Singer & Singer, 1990). With the arrival of mass media—film and, in particular, television—however, the quantity of aggressive content daily consumed by these age groups has dramatically increased. As real violence, especially among the youth, at the same time, is still growing, it seems plausible to correlate media violence and aggressive behavior. With more recent media developments, video recorders, computer games, and the Internet, one can see a further increase of extremely violent images, which obviously find much attention. Videos present realistic torture scenes and even real murder; computer games enable the user to actively simulate the mutilation of "enemies"; and the Internet, apart from its prosocial possibilities, has become a platform for child pornography, violent cults, and terrorist guidelines. Even with these phenomena, however, it is crucial to realize that the primary causes for aggressive behavior will most likely be found in the family environment, the peer groups, and, in particular, the social and economic conditions in which children are raised (Groebel & Hinde, 1991).

Yet media play a major role in the development of cultural orientations, worldviews, and beliefs, as well as in the global distribution of values and (often stereotyped) images. They not only are mirrors of cultural trends but can also channel them and are themselves major constituents of society. Sometimes they are even direct means of intergroup violence and war propaganda. All in all, it is important to identify their contribution to the propagation of violence, if one considers possibilities of prevention.

With the technical means of automatization and, more recently, of digitization, any media content can potentially become global. Not only does individual news reach nearly any part of the world, but mass entertainment has become an international enterprise. For example, American or Indian movies can be watched in most world regions. Much of what is presented contains violence. In high literature art, as well as in popular culture, violence has always been a major topic of human communication. Whether it is the Gilgamesh, a Shakespearean drama, the Shuihu Zhuan of Luo Guanzhong, Kurosawa's *Ran,* stories of Wole Soyinka, or ordinary detective series, people always seem to be fascinated by aggression. This fascination does not necessarily mean that destructive behavior is innate; however, it draws attention because it is one of the phenomena of human life that cannot be immediately explained and yet demands consideration of how to cope with it if it occurs. Nearly all studies around the world show that men are much more attracted to violence than women are. One can assume that, in a mixture of biological predispositions and gender role socializations, men often experience aggression as rewarding. It fits with their role in society but once may have also served as a motivation to seek adventure when exploring new territory or protecting the family and the group. Without an internal (physiological thrill seeking) and an external (status and mating) reward mechanism, men may have rather fled, leaving their dependents unprotected. But, besides "functional" aggression, humankind has developed "destructive" aggression, mass murder, hedonistic torture, and humiliation, which cannot be explained in terms of survival. It is often these that are widely distributed in the media.

The media themselves differ in their impact. Audiovisual media in particular are more graphic in their depiction of violence than books or newspapers are; they leave less freedom in the individual images that the viewers associate with the stories. As the media become ever more perfect with the introduction of three dimensions (virtual reality) and interactivity (computer games and multimedia), and as they are always accessible and universal (video and the Internet), the representation of violence "merges" increasingly with reality.

Another crucial distinction is that between "context-rich" and "context-free" depictions of violence. Novels or sophisticated movies usually offer a story around the occurrence of violence, what its background is, and what its consequences are. Violence as a pure entertainment product, however, often lacks any embedding in a context that is more than a clichéd image of good and bad.

The final difference between the individual media forms concerns their distribution. A theater play or a novel is nearly always a singular event. The modern mass media, however, create a time and space omnipresence. Even here a distinction between problematic and nonproblematic forms of media violence has to be made. A news program or a TV documentary that presents the cruelty of war and the suffering of its victims in a nonvoyeuristic way is part of an objective investigation or may even serve conflict-reduction purposes. Hate campaigns, on the other hand, or the glorification of violence stresses the "reward" characteristics of extreme aggression. In general, one can roughly distinguish between three different modes of media content (see Table 12.1):

- Purely investigative (typically, news)
- Message oriented (e.g., campaigns and advertisements)
- Entertainment (e.g., movies and shows)

Although often these criteria may not be easy to determine, there are clear examples for each of the different forms. Reality TV or paparazzi activities may have to do with the truth, but they also, in the extreme, influence this very truth through their own behavior (witness the discussion surrounding Princess Diana's death). Through the informal communication patterns on the Internet, as well, rumors have become part of serious news reporting, as the discussion concerning Bill Clinton and Monica Lewinsky has shown. Whether true or not, deviant groups and cults can influence the global information streams more efficiently than ever before. The cases of Serbia and Rwanda, on the other hand, have demonstrated the role that "traditional" mass propaganda (i.e., radio) can still play in genocide.

Finally, many incidents around the world indicate that children often lack the capacity to distinguish between reality and fiction and that they take for granted what they see in entertainment films, thus stimulating their own aggression (Singer & Singer, 1990). If they are permanently exposed to messages that promote the idea that violence is fun or is adequate to solve problems and gain status, then the risk that they learn these attitudes and behavior patterns is very high.

### *Theories and Research Studies*

Many scientific theories and studies have dealt with the problem of media violence since the beginning of the twentieth century. Most of them originate in North America, Australia and New Zealand, or Western Europe. But, increasingly, Asia, Latin America, and Africa are contributing to the scientific debate. The studies cover a broad range of different paradigms: cultural studies, content analyses of media programs, and behavioral research. However, the terms *aggression* and *violence* are exclusively defined here in terms of behavior that leads to harm of another person. For phenomena in which activity and creativity have positive consequences for those involved, other terms are used.

Recently, scientists have overcome their traditional skepticism and have come to some common conclusions. They acknowledge a media effect risk that depends on the message content, the characteristics of the media users and their families, and their social and cultural environments. All in all, children are more at risk of being influenced than adults are. But certain effects, such as habituation, also hold for older age groups. Whereas short-term effects may be described in terms of causal relationships, the long-term impact is more adequately described as an interactive process that involves many different factors and conditions. Yet, since the commercial and the political worlds strongly rely on the influence of images and messages (as seen in the billion-dollar turnover of the advertising industry or the important role of media in politics), it seems naive to exclude media violence from any effects probability.

The most influential theory on this matter is probably the social learning approach by Albert Bandura (1977) and his colleagues. Because much of what people learn happens through observation in their immediate environment, it can be concluded that similar processes work through the media. Many studies have demonstrated that children especially either directly imitate what they see on the screen or integrate the observed behavior patterns into their own repertoire. An extension of this theory considers the role of cognitions. If I see that certain behavior, such as aggression, is successful, I believe that the same will be true in my own life. Groebel and Gleich

**TABLE 12.1** Potentially Problematic and Nonproblematic Forms of Media Content

| *Mode* | *Investigative* | *Message Oriented* | *Entertainment* |
|---|---|---|---|
| Problematic | Voyeurism | Censorship; propaganda | Rewarded violence |
| Nonproblematic | Classical journalism | Antiviolence campaigns | Stories; thrills |

(1993) show in European and U.S. studies that nearly 75% of the aggressive acts depicted on the screen have no negative consequences for the aggressor in the movie or are even rewarded. The script theory, among others, propagated by Huesmann and Eron (1986), assumes the development of complex worldviews ("scripts") through media influence. If I overestimate the probability of violence in real life (e.g., as a result of its frequency on the TV screen), I develop a belief system in which violence is a normal and adequate part of modern society. The role of the personal state of the viewer is stressed in the frustration-aggression hypothesis (see Berkowitz, 1962). Viewers who have been frustrated in their actual environment (e.g., have been punished, insulted, or physically deprived) "read" the media violence as a signal to channel their frustration into aggression. This theory would explain why particular children in social-problem areas are open to media aggression effects.

The contrary tendency has been assumed in the catharsis theory and later the inhibition theory by Seymour Feshbach. As in the Greek tragedy, aggressive moods would be reduced through the observation of similar states with others (substitute coping). Inhibition would occur when the stimulation of one's own aggressive tendencies would lead to learned fear of punishment and thus contribute to its reduction. Although both approaches may still be valid under certain circumstances, they have not been confirmed in the majority of studies, and their original author, Feshbach (1985) now also assumes a negative effects risk.

A lot of the fascination of media violence has to do with physiological arousal. Action scenes, which are usually part of media violence, seize the viewer's attention and create at least a slight "kick," probably more so among males. At the same time, people tend to react more aggressively in a state of arousal. This would again explain why arousing TV scenes would lead to higher aggression among frustrated or angered viewers, as Zillmann (1971) explains in his excitation transfer theory. In this context, it is not the content but the formal features, sound and visual effects, that would be responsible for the result. Among others, Kunkel et al. (1994 -1995), Malamuth (1987), and Linz and Malamuth (1993) have investigated the effect of long-term exposure to extremely violent images. Men in particular get used to frequent bloody scenes; their empathy toward the aggression victim is reduced.

The impact of media violence on anxiety has also been analyzed. Gerbner (1993) and Groebel (Groebel & Hinde, 1991) both have demonstrated in longitudinal studies that the frequent depiction of the world as threatening and dangerous leads to more fearful and cautious attitudes toward the actual environment. If people are already afraid or lack contrary experiences, they develop an anxious worldview and have difficulties distinguishing between reality and fiction.

Cultural studies have discussed the role of the cultural construction of meaning. The decoding and interpretation of an image depend on traditions and conventions. This could explain why an aggressive picture may be "read" differently, for example, in Singapore and in Switzerland, or even by different groups within a national culture. These cultural differences definitely have to be taken into account. Yet the question is whether certain images can also immediately create emotional reactions on a fundamental (not culture-bound) level and to what extent the international mass media have developed a more homogeneous (culture-spanning) visual language. Increasingly, theories from a non-Anglo-Saxon background have offered important contributions to the discussion.

Groebel has formulated the compass theory (Groebel, 1998). Depending on already existing experiences, social control, and the cultural environment, media content offers an orientation, a frame of reference that determines the direction of one's own behavior. Viewers do not necessarily adapt simultaneously to what they have observed, but they measure their own behavior in terms of distance to the perceived media models. If extreme cruelty is "common," for example, just kicking another seems to be innocent by comparison if the cultural environment has not established a working alternative frame of reference (e.g., social control, values).

In general, the impact of media violence depends on several conditions: media content, roughly 10 acts of violence per hour in the average programming (see the recent U.S. National TV Violence Study by Kunkel et al., (1994-1995); media frequency; culture and actual situation; and the characteristics of the viewer and his or her family surrounding. Yet, since the media now are a mass phenomenon, the probability of a problematic combination of these conditions is high. This is demonstrated in many studies. On the basis of scientific evidence, one can conclude that the risk of media violence prevails.

## The UNESCO Study

### *Method and Design*

A study that is to be conducted in different countries and cultures faces several problems. The logistics are difficult; many countries do not have scientific faculties that can run the study there; and the cultures are so different that not only language problems but also differences in the social meanings of terms appear. Therefore, the authors of this project chose a standardized procedure. All logistics were centrally organized by the World Organization of the Scout Movement from their Geneva headquarters. The organization used its international network of National Scout Organizations to conduct the study in the respective countries. However, those who filled in the questionnaires were average children from a representative sample of the respective participating countries. To that end, two officers of the Scout Movement traveled to the countries in the sample (see below) and instructed their local representatives on how to apply the procedure. In addition, the World Scout Organization took care of the translations into the different national languages and the necessary pretests in each country. The advantage of the Scout Movement, apart from its logistics, is its strict political and ideological independence. Thus, no intended or unintended interference based on a certain belief system was to be expected.

Although language and meaning are always culture bound, we chose a questionnaire procedure to analyze the relationship between media preferences and aggression. By applying exactly the same questions all over the world, a maximum comparison was possible. Because we limited the items to descriptive, preference, and behavioral data, excluding evaluations and performance measures, we assume a relatively culture-independent measurement. Of course, systematic differences in preferences are indicators of cultural specifics. That was exactly what we wanted to measure. The reliability and the validity of the data are not reduced through that approach. The regional pretests demonstrated that all children could understand the questionnaire that they had to fill in during classes and that all items were meaningful to them. Of course, without financial and time constraints, an even better pretesting would have been possible. However, the a posteriori analyses confirmed the quality of the work.

The questionnaire itself consisted of a mixture of text questions, with mostly multiple-choice answers, and very simple (again, culture-free) sketches that depicted a number of social situations. The children then had to choose between several options (e.g., an aggressive or a peaceful solution) to a depicted conflict. Several factors were investigated: the children's demographics, their social and family situation, media use and preferences, level of aggression in their environment, their own aggressive tendencies, level of anxiety, and their perception of values and orientations. In total, 60 different variables were included.

The sample for the study consisted of an original core group of 23 different countries around the world, where, depending on country size, between 150 and 600 12-year-old schoolchildren (boys and girls) were to be investigated. The countries were selected to represent different regions and social development structures, cultures, and economic and social circumstances. After finishing the remaining core data, 5,500 international 12-year-olds contributed to the project. The participating countries were Angola, Argentina, Armenia, Brazil, Canada, Costa Rica, Croatia, Egypt, Fiji, Germany, India, Japan, Mauritius, the Netherlands, Peru, the Philippines, Qatar, South Africa, Spain, Tadjikistan, Togo, Trinidad and Tobago, and the Ukraine.

A quota sample was used that considered three criteria in addition to age: gender, rural versus metropolitan environment, and high versus low level of aggression in the students' actual environment.

With the last two, the sample was systematically structured. Gender was assumed to be equally distributed across the schools. In addition, the types of schools were nationally chosen to represent the respective school systems.

The age was fixed at 12 years to standardize possible developmental effects. Many studies have dealt with age differences, and the age of 12 seems to be a period when the interest in media is particularly high but, at the same time, children are still in the process of socialization. At this age, children start to become adolescents and are particularly interested in adult role models and respective media images. Of course, "psychological age" and maturity may differ interculturally, but still fundamental developmental stages are valid across cultures, as many studies have shown. In any case, we decided to standardize the age factor.

The gathering of the data started in late 1996 and finished in early 1998.

### *The Results*

About 350,000 individual pieces of data were obtained and processed (more than 5,000 students with more than 60 variables each). In the first step, simple analyses were applied to get a general overview of the demographics, the global media use, and the state of violence among children around the world. In addition, the first indicators of the correlation between media use and individual aggression were obtained. In this stage, most results are based on frequency and percentage tables, plus a few cross-tabulations.

#### *Demographics*

*Global Statistics.* The participants in the study were 2,788 boys and 2,353 girls; all were 12 years old. Boys (54.2%) were slightly more represented than girls (45%). However, this was intended because we regarded boys as a bigger risk group.

About 80% of the children lived with both parents, 13% lived with only their mother, and 2.5% with only their father. The remainder lived with relatives, in orphanages, or alone. Forty-nine percent lived in a big city, 28% in a small town, 20% in little villages, and the remaining 3% in camps or isolated houses. The majority of children had fathers who worked as employees; 10% did not know their father's profession (because they may have not known him). About 9% of the children already had experienced fleeing a country. Nearly 40% of the mothers around the globe took care of the household as their primary profession. Most children (about 90%) lived in small to medium-size families either alone with their parents or with just one or two brothers or sisters. About one third of the children were rated (by the local scout representatives) as living in an aggressive environment or as facing serious problems. The originally proposed 50% match could not be reached, because several countries seemed to have hardly any such area that could be easily identified.

*Regional Differences.* We concentrated on four regions, not the individual countries: Africa, Asia/Pacific, Europe/Canada, and Latin America. By doing so, we brought together areas that, among themselves, may differ immensely. We "merged" Europe and Canada because we assumed some common cultural roots. This, of course, is also partly true for Europe and Latin America. However, for Latin America, there was a sufficient number of countries to form their own cluster. In any case, this clustering was not more than a first testing of rough cultural differences or overlaps.

Africa had the fewest children in the sample who lived together with both parents (approximately 72%), and Asia had the most (88%). Latin America (75%) and Europe/Canada (83%) were in between. Asia had the most children living in big cities (56%), and Europe/Canada (43%) the least.

Africa had the most refugees (12%), and Latin America the least (4%).

Not all of these numbers may fit with an objective global count, but some regions were not accessible at all. We also could only investigate children who were able to read. Yet, for the purpose of the study, the data seem to be sufficiently valid.

A remarkable difference appeared with respect to the mother's profession. Whereas in Latin America 51% and in Asia 55% of the mothers were reported to take care (exclusively) of the household, the numbers for Europe/Canada were 33% and for Africa, 9.9%. For different reasons, most mothers in these two regions also worked in other positions (i.e., took care of everything or were employed).

All the countries taken together represented the complete United Nations Developmental Program (UNDP) index range.

### *Media Use*

*Global Statistics.* Of the school areas in our sample, 97% could be reached by at least one TV broadcast channel. For most areas, the average was four to nine channels (34%); 8.5% received one; 3% received two; 9% received three; 10% received 10 to 20; and 18% received more than 20 channels. The percentages are minimum values because 17% did not answer this question.

In our global sample, 91% of the children had access to a TV set, primarily at home. Thus, the screen has become a universal medium around the world. Whether it is the favelas, a South Pacific island, or a skyscraper in Asia, television is omnipresent, even if we consider that we did not cover some regions where TV is not available at all. This result justifies the assumption that TV still is the most powerful source of information and entertainment outside face-to-face communication. This is confirmed by further statistics. Radio and books have similar distributions (91%, 92%).

The remaining media follow way behind: newspapers, 85%; tape recorders (e.g., cassettes), 75%; comics, 66%; video recorders, 47%; video games (e.g., Gameboys), 40%; personal computers, 23%; and the Internet, 9%.

The children reported how much time they spend with several favorite activities. They spent an average of 3 hours daily in front of the TV screen. That is at least 50% more time spent with this medium than with any other activity, including homework (2 hours), helping the family (1.6 hours), playing outside (1.5 hours), being with friends (1.4 hours), reading (1.1 hour), listening to the radio (1.1 hour), listening to tapes or CDs (0.9 hours), or using the computer (0.4 hours, for whom it applies). Thus, TV dominates the life of children around the globe.

*Regional Differences.* Europe/Canada have the highest distribution of TV (nearly 99%), and Africa the lowest (83%). Actually, in our study, the distribution of TV may be overrepresented for Africa because we did not consider nonschool groups or areas without any electricity available. Latin America comes a close second after Europe/Canada (97%); Asia has 92%. The order is roughly the same with most other audiovisual media such as videos, personal computers, and games. Radio still plays an important role in Africa, where the percentage is similar to Europe/Canada and Latin America (approximately 90%) and is slightly higher than in Asia (88%).

### *Orientations and Values*

*Global Statistics.* Emotional states, as well as ideals, are important factors that moderate how children cope with their environment and how they evaluate what they observe in the media. Of course, the media themselves can influence these states and norms.

What was the general emotional state of the children? About two thirds reported that they are happy most of the time. About one quarter knew the feeling but do not regularly experience it, and about 2.5% said that they are never happy. There was no difference between boys and girls. Nearly half of the children are anxious most of the time or often, again with no difference between boys and girls. About 17% of the children reported that they would like to live in another country (either for adventure or for escapism reasons). Although the majority of the children are relatively happy, a remarkable number live in a problematic emotional state.

Which kind of people were perceived as role models by the children? They could give a name, which then was ordered along a list of different characteristics. The results again demonstrate the importance of the media. Most children (26%) named an action hero, followed by pop stars and musicians (18.5%). However, there are important gender differences. Of the boys, 30% mentioned an action hero, as compared with 21% of the girls. But for the female group, this character came second after pop stars and musicians (girls, 27%; boys, 12%). Other personalities played a less important role. About 8% named a religious leader, 7% a military leader (boys, 9%; girls, 3.4%), 6% a philosopher or scientist, 5% a journalist, and only 3% a politician. The remaining were personal acquaintances or have other roles. This confirms the global trend: Action heroes and pop stars are the favorite role models among children. Nevertheless, religious beliefs are still widely spread: About 90% of the children reported that they believe in (a) god.

What were the personal values of the children? The favorite wish of 40% was to have a family, either because they live in a functioning parent-child relationship or because they lack it but would like to have it. For 10%, having enough food was the favorite. This may mean that this group regularly experiences food deprivation. For 25% of the boys, the favorite wish was always to be a winner; 19% of the girls said the same.

*Regional Differences.* The emotional states seem to differ somewhat between the world regions. While happiness is more or less equally distributed (with Latin America being a little "happier" than Africa, Europe/Canada, and Asia, respectively), remarkable differences occur when it comes to being anxious. Around 50% of the children in Africa, Latin America, and Asia were (very) often anxious, as compared with about 36% in Europe/Canada. There are also regional differences concerning the favorite heroes: Asia has the highest ranking for action heroes (34%), Africa the lowest (18%), and Latin America and Europe/Canada in between (25% each). This may have to do with the significantly lower saturation of audiovisual media in Africa, but it may also have other cultural reasons.

However, there is a clear correlation between the presence of TV and reporting action heroes as favorites. The favorites in Africa were pop stars or musicians (24%), with Asia the lowest (12%). Africa also had high rankings for religious leaders (18%), as compared with Europe/Canada (2%), Latin America (6%), and Asia (6%). Military leaders scored highest in Asia (9.6%) and lowest in Europe/Canada (2.6%). Journalists scored well in Europe/Canada (10%) and low in Latin America (2%). Politicians ranked lowest in Europe (1%) and highest in Africa (7%). Again, there may be a correlation with the distribution of mass media: The more TV, the higher the rank of mass media personalities and the lower the traditional ones (e.g., politicians and religious leaders). In Europe/ Canada, journalists got 10 times as many votes as politicians. There is a strong correlation between the accessibility of modern media and the predominant values and orientations.

### *Violence and Aggression*

*Global Statistics.* As reported, roughly one third of the children in the sample lived in a high-aggression environment or problematic neighborhood. This ranges from high-crime areas and (refugee) camps to economically poor environments, which, of course, do not have to be aggressive per se. Yet, in these areas, more than twice as many people seem to die by being killed by others than those in the low-problem neighborhoods do (children's reports: 16% vs. 7%). Again, twice as many children there were members of an armed gang (5.2%), as compared with the low-aggression areas (2.6%). They reported more personal enemies (9% vs. 5.9%) and regarded attacking more often as fun than did the children from the low-aggression neighborhoods (8% vs. 4.7%). They also had used weapons against someone more often (7.5% vs. 5.5%). Thus, it comes as no surprise that they were also more anxious (most of the time: 25% vs. 19%) and would like to live in another country (53% vs. 46%). But they also reported happiness similar to the low-aggression group.

However, their worldview was obviously influenced by their experience. Nearly one third of the aggression-environment group believe that most people in the world are evil (compared with slightly more than a fifth of the low-aggression-area group). The pattern is clear and plausible: In high-problem areas, children not only experience more aggressive behavior, they also are emotionally and cognitively affected (e.g., they engage in more hedonistic violence, experience more anxiety, and have a more pessimistic worldview).

*Regional Differences.* Different forms of aggression are evaluated differently in the cultures of the world. We wanted to know whether a physical attack or a verbal insult is perceived as more "damaging." The results confirm the cultural differences. In Europe and Canada, children regarded a physical attack with fists as worse (55.5%) than being called insulting names (44%). In Asia, the opposite was the case. For nearly 70%, verbal insults were worse than physical attacks (29%). Latin America was balanced (50% each), and Africa was similar to Asia (verbal, 60%; physical, 35%).

To classify different forms of aggression, we presented a number of simple sketches that showed a variety of social situations: a verbal conflict, a physical attack, a recorder damaged by another child, a stereo that a child urgently wanted to have, and a group of people hanging around. For each of these situations, the children were asked to say how the involved persons would react and what they themselves would do in a similar situation.

In situations of social conflict, children in Africa reported most frequently that they would regard physical attacks as an adequate reaction: 32% reported that hitting the other as a reaction to a verbal insult was adequate (compared with 15% in Asia, 14% in Latin America, and 16% in Europe/Canada); 9% even reported shooting the other as adequate.

Nearly one third in Africa reported that a group of people hanging around would attack another group as the next action (compared with 28% in Asia, 20% in Europe/Canada, and 19% in Latin America). At the same time, children in Africa experienced having a gun as a powerful feeling more often than children in the other regions did (25%, compared with 18% in Latin America, 18% in Europe/Canada, and 10% in Asia). They also reported that they themselves have a gun (4.5%; Latin America, 3.5%; Asia, 3.3%; Europe/Canada, 2.4%). In general, children in Africa and Asia have twice as often used a weapon against someone (7.1% and 8.3%, respectively) as those in Latin America and Europe/Canada (4.4% and 3.6%, respectively).

All in all, the children's aggressive behavior patterns and perceptions are a mirror of what they experience in their real environment: frustration, aggression, problematic circumstances. However, to what extent do the media contribute to these patterns? To what extent do they channel the already existing aggressive dispositions?

### *Media Violence*

*Global Statistics.* Most studies show that the relationship between media violence and real violence is interactive. Media can contribute to an aggressive culture; people who are already aggressive use the media as further confirmation of their beliefs and attitudes, which, in turn, are reinforced through media content. This interaction is especially true for long-term developments.

At this stage of the study, we can offer some correlations between media and "real" violence. A one-directional effect cannot be assumed on the global level and could also not be empirically tested. The study focuses on the role of the media in the complex system of culture and personal experiences.

To identify the relationship between media and actual experiences for high- and low-aggression environments, we asked the children whether what they saw in the media resembled their own experiences. In all cases, the high-aggression-area group reported a stronger overlap between reality and fiction than the low-aggression-area group did (movies, 46% vs. 40%; TV, 72% vs. 69%; radio, 52% vs. 48%; comics, 26% vs. 22%; all in all, not an extreme but homogeneous trend). Thus, they are more probably confronted with similar aggressive messages in their actual environment and in the media than are children from a less violent neighborhood.

Obviously, media content reinforces the already mentioned belief that most people are evil. Many children are surrounded by an environment in which both "real" and media experiences support the view that violence is natural. The fascination of violence is often related to strong characters who can control their environment, are (in the end) rewarded for their aggression, and can cope with nearly every problem. The message is at least threefold:

- Aggression is a good means to solve conflicts.
- Aggression offers status.
- Aggression can be fun.

The larger-than-life hero, of course, is an old theme of art and literature. It serves both needs, the compensation of one's own deficits and the reference point for one's own behavior. Relatively new, however, is the global uniformity of such heroes through the mass media and their commercial weight. One such media figure is the Terminator character from two movies of the same name, starring Arnold Schwarzenegger. Our results confirm that the Terminator is a cross-cultural hero. About 88% of the world's child population (if our sample is representative) know him. In the comparison between high- and low-aggression areas, it is remarkable that 51% of the children in the high-aggression environment would like to be like him, as compared with 37% in the low-aggression neighborhoods. He seems to represent the characteristics that children think are necessary to cope with difficult situations. Equally successful are heroes like Rambo and, of course, "local" heroes from the respective domestic media markets (e.g., India, Brazil, or Japan). An aggressive media hero is particularly "successful" as a role model in the more violent areas of the world. Some of these heroes have become culture-spanning icons.

Are there any systematic patterns in the aggressive cognitions that link personal motives, actual environment, and media content? We analyzed the correlation between different forms of sensation seeking (the motive to be thrilled through risk and adventure), a relatively stable personality characteristic, on the one hand, and different actual and media environments, on the other. There was no difference in sensation seeking in the high- and low-aggression environments. That is plausible, as this personality characteristic is assumed to be highly genetically determined, thus relatively free of environmental influences. However, when we split up the sample into one group with a comparatively well-developed technological infrastructure and one with a less well-developed one (criterion: distribution of computers, then "median"-split = 50% high/low dichotomy), the picture changed. Twice as many children in the "high technology" group as in the "low technology" group reported a risk-seeking tendency (20% vs. 10%).

*Regional Differences.* In terms of regions, Africa had by far the lowest (7.3%) and Europe/Canada (18.9%) the highest scores, with Asia (18.5%) and Latin America (15.9%) following closely. This may have to do with two aspects. The sensory stimulation is probably higher in high-technology environments; it thus creates a generally higher state of permanent arousal. With a higher availability of media programming, the risk-seeking tendency is modeled into uniform patterns that mirror the content of the media (e.g., the car chase as a movie icon).

To test the latter, we linked the sensation-seeking tendency in an additional analysis with the preference for media content. The picture is clear: Children, and in particular boys, with a risk-seeking tendency have a higher preference for aggressive media content than those who lack this tendency (for boys, 40% vs. 29%). When asked whether they themselves would want to be involved in an aggressive situation, the tendency was even stronger: 47% of those who prefer aggressive media content would also like to be involved themselves in a risky situation (as compared with an average of 19% with other media preferences; range = 15-23%). In the recent analysis, this result comes closest to a direct effects measure: There is a link between the preference for media violence and the need to be involved in aggression oneself.

The overall result can be interpreted as follows: The tendency of sensation seeking is possibly genetically determined, with an extremely strong gender influence (25% of the boys but only 4% of the girls report risk seeking). The level and direction of this tendency, however, is moderated through the environment. When violence is presented as "thrilling" in the daily media environment, this reinforces the "reward characteristics" of the respective behavior. When children actually experience violence in their immediate environment, the hedonistic value of heroism takes the place for its "survival" value (see the action hero results under "Orientations and Values"). Thus, depending on the "real" environment, media violence can serve different functions. Nevertheless, in both cases it confirms the "reward characteristics" of aggressive behavior.

## Conclusions and Recommendations

At this stage, we can summarize the role of the media in the perception and application of aggression as follows: Media violence is universal. It is primarily presented in a rewarding context. Depending on the personality characteristics of the children, and depending on their everyday life experiences, media violence satisfies different needs:

- It "compensates" children's own frustrations and deficits in problem areas.
- It offers "thrills" for children in a less problematic environment.
- For boys, it creates a frame of reference for "attractive role models."

There are many cultural differences, and yet the basic patterns of the media violence implications are similar around the world. Individual movies are not the problem. However, the extent and omnipresence of media violence contribute to the development of a global aggressive culture. The "reward characteristics" of aggression are more systematically promoted than nonaggressive ways of coping with one's life. Therefore, the risk of media violence prevails.

The results demonstrate the omnipresence of TV in all areas of the world. Most children around the globe seem to spend most of their free time with the medium. What they get is a high portion of violent content.

Combined with the real violence that many children experience, the probability is high that aggressive orientations are promoted rather than peaceful ones. But also in lower-aggression areas, violent media content is presented in a rewarding context. Although children cope differently with this content in different cultures, the transcultural commonality of the problem reflects the fact that aggression is interpreted as a good problem solver for a variety of situations.

Children want a functioning social and family environment. Since they often seem to lack these, they seek role models that offer compensation through power and aggression. This explains the universal success of movie characters like the Terminator. Individual preferences for films like this are not the problem. However, when violent content becomes so common a phenomenon that it creates an aggressive media environment, the probability that children will develop a new frame of reference in which problematic predispositions are channeled into destructive attitudes and behaviors increases immensely.

What are possible solutions? Probably more important than the media are the social and economic conditions in which children grow up. However, the media also are active contributors to cultures, beliefs, and orientations. Centralized control and censorship are not efficient and do not meet the criteria for democratic societies. Three major strategies should therefore be considered:

- Public debate and "common ground" talks between politicians, producers, and teachers
- The development of professional codes of conduct and self-discipline for producers
- Innovative forms of media education to create competent and critical media users

With communication systems like the Internet, the media are even more omnipresent and universal. As a consequence, the new digital environment demands at least as much attention and ethical/educational consideration as mass media, culture, and education in the traditional world. The debate should not center on how to get children and adolescents to avoid the media but how to use the media for entertaining and constructive goals.

## References

Bandura, A. (1977). *Social learning theory.* Englewood Cliffs, NJ: Prentice Hall.

Berkowitz, L. (1962). *Aggression: A social psychological analysis.* New York: McGraw-Hill.

Feshbach, S. (1985, September). Media and delinquency. In J. Groebel (Chair), *Scientific aspects of crime prevention.* Symposium conducted at the 7th United Nations Congress on the Prevention of Crime, Milan, Italy.

Gerbner, G. (1993). *Violence in cable-originated television programs: A report to the National Cable Television Association.* Washington, DC: NCTA.

Groebel, J. (Ed.). (1997). *New media developments: Trends in communication* (Vol. 1). Amsterdam: Boom Publishers.

Groebel, J. (1998). *The UNESCO global study on media violence. A joint project of UNESCO, the World Organization of the Scout Movement, and Ultrecht University.* Paris: UNESCO.

Groebel, J., & Gleich, U. (1993). *Gewaltprofil des deutschen Fernsehens* [Violence profile of German television]. Leverkusen, Germany: Landesanstalt fur Rundfunk Nordrhein-Westfalen, Leske & Budrich.

Groebel, J., & Hinde, R. A. (Eds.). (1991). *Aggression and war: Their biological and social bases.* Cambridge, UK: Cambridge University Press.

Huesmann, L. R., & Eron, L. D. (1986). *Television and the aggressive child: A cross-national comparison.* Hillsdale, NJ: Lawrence Erlbaum.

Kunkel, D., Wilson, B. J., Linz, D., Potter, J., Donnerstein, E., Smith, S.L., Blumenthal, E., & Gray, T. (1994-1995). The effects of exposure to media violence. In J. Federman (Ed.), *National Television Violence Study* (pp. I-1 to I-169). Studio City, CA: Mediascope, Inc.

Linz, D., & Malamuth, N. (1993). *Pornography.* Newbury Park, CA: Sage.

Livingstone, S. (1998). *A European study on children's media environment.* London: World Summit on Children's Television.

Malamuth, N. (1987). *Do sexually violent media indirectly contribute to antisocial behavior?* In M. R. Walsh (Ed.), *The psychology of women: Ongoing debates* (pp. 441-459). New Haven, CT: Yale University Press.

Singer, J. L., & Singer, D. G. (1990). *The house of make-believe.* Cambridge, MA: Harvard University Press.

Zillmann, D. (1971). Excitation transfer in communication mediated aggressive behavior. *Journal of Personal Social Psychology, 7,* 419-434.

CHAPTER 13

# Research on Sex in the Media

## What Do We Know About Effects on Children and Adolescents?

NEIL M. MALAMUTH
EMILY A. IMPETT
University of California, Los Angeles

### Overview

Research into the ways that media influence children and adolescents has mainly revolved around two interrelated themes: that media messages, especially those featuring violent or sexual content, often teach objectionable beliefs and behaviors and that young people are particularly vulnerable to such messages (Roberts, 1993). These concerns continue to underlie most of the studies focusing on sexual content despite the emergence of recent interest in other areas of media influence (Singer & Singer, 1998). Some segments of the general public have recently become particularly vocal about their anxiety regarding sexual content in the media, for they have perceived a dramatic increase in the frequency of such content. By way of protest, for example, the Parents Television Council, chaired by celebrity Steve Allen, placed full-page ads in major newspapers seeking to support political and fund-raising campaigns against media "filth and sex" (as well as violence), primarily because of the alleged effects on children (e.g., see the Parents Television Council ad in the *Los Angeles Times* on October 7, 1999, p. E4). One ad claims that there is "massive evidence" to support a wide range of negative effects.

In response to such public concerns, technological and legal mechanisms have been introduced to enable parents to restrict their children's exposure to "objectionable" media. For example, the V-chip is an electronic device that allows parents to filter out programs that contain certain content that they do not want their children to view. Naturally, the success of this system is dependent on the accuracy of the program ratings provided by the television industry. Unfortunately, however, a recent systematic evaluation of these ratings found that a large majority of programs that contain sexual behavior were not appropriately labeled as sexual in nature (Kunkel et al., 1998).

Similarly, the U.S. Supreme Court will soon decide a case involving a challenge to the Playboy Corporation. It is based on a law that requires cable companies producing sexually explicit programs to block "signal bleed." Congress passed the "signal bleed" law as part of the Communications Decency Act of 1996 (Exon, 1996), parts of which have been judged unconstitutional by the Supreme Court (*Reno v. American Civil Liberties Union,* 1997). The purpose of this segment of the law was to protect young people from inadvertent exposure to fleeting images or sounds that might come through to nonsubscribers even though the program is scrambled or largely blocked. In both of these instances, it appears that the currently available technological means of restricting what some people perceive as intrusive sexual content into American homes may not sufficiently change the availability of such content. It is likely that the controversy over this matter will become even more heated in the next few years.

This chapter is designed to examine scientific theory and research regarding the effects of sexual content in the mass media on children's and adolescents' attitudes about sex and their sexual behaviors. Research on sexual media has often been divided into two categories. The first may be referred to as "embedded sexual content." Here the sexual content is embedded within a larger context that includes considerable nonsexual content; the primary purpose is not to sexually arouse the consumer, although this may be one of the varied effects of exposure and a significant contributor to its mass appeal. Such content would be illustrated by a soap opera in which some of the scenes, although typically not a majority, include references to or actual portrayals of sexual interactions. Such embedded sexual content would often be depicted with only opaque or limited explicitness. The second category, which we will refer to as "sexually explicit media," consists of materials that primarily depict nudity and simulated or actual sexual acts (e.g., intercourse, fellatio, etc.) not embedded or interwoven with much nonsexual content. The primary function of such portrayals for consumers is to view nudity or sex, often as a stimulant for sexual arousal. Sometimes the distinction between embedded and explicit sexual content is not so clear. For example, *Playboy* magazine regularly includes considerable nonsexual content (e.g., interviews with jazz artists) as well as nude portrayals, and the Starr Report, an official state document focusing on President Bill Clinton, included much sexually explicit content. Nevertheless, there are still some meaningful distinctions that may be made between these two types of media that will help frame our discussion.

This chapter is primarily focused on research on "embedded sexual content," but we also briefly consider some relevant findings on sexually explicit media. Although in focusing on the first category we primarily consider research in which the participants have been below the age of 18, some of the studies we draw on used young adult participants, typically college students. Because there are sound theoretical and empirical reasons to assume that the effects found with these young adults would also be expected for younger individuals, we include these studies as well.

According to public perceptions, both children and adults believe that the media have become a very central source of information about sex for young people. Louis Harris and Associates (1987) found that 64% of U.S. adults think that television encourages young people to initiate sexual activity. In addition, a study of roughly 1,000 adolescents revealed that television is considered to be their greatest source of pressure to become sexually active (Howard, 1985). According to a Time/CNN poll (Stodghill, 1998), 29% of U.S. teens cited television as their principal source of information about sex, up from 11% in a similar poll conducted in 1986. While 45% mentioned "friends" as their major source, only 7% of teens identified parents, and 3% cited sex education. Of course, such studies seek to disentangle these influences into separate categories, but, in reality, these factors may actually interact in important ways. For example, children may be more influenced by sexual media when they watch television with friends as opposed to alone. The act of viewing enticing sexual images with friends may affect pressures that teens already feel to talk about or engage in various sexual activities in order to fit in and feel normal.

Of course, the public at large may believe that children and adolescents are influenced by sexual portrayals in the media, but scientific research may or may not support such beliefs. Before proceeding to discuss theory and research pertaining to potential influences of mass media containing sexual content, we will first consider the extent to which youth are actually exposed to such content and the nature of the portrayals to which they are exposed.

## Content and Frequency of Exposure to Sexual Content

In this section, we summarize research on the frequency of both media with embedded sexual content and sexually explicit media.

### *Embedded Sexual Content*

Various commentators have recently noted that there has been a dramatic increase in sexual content in the media. For example, *USA Today* noted that "prime time is saturated with sex, and more explicitly so than ever. A look at the TV season that is unfolding this week will leave even jaded viewers stunned of what they see" (Levin, 1999, p. E1). Similarly, a recent cover article in the magazine *Entertainment Weekly* (Jacobs, 1999) bore the headline "Sex on TV: It's Everywhere You Turn, but Just How Far Will It Go?" This article focused on how television programs are engaging in fierce competition to lure teenage audiences by dramatically increasing the sexual content of their programs:

> In this post-Lewinsky world, as networks compete with cable, and cable competes with Internet, and everyone competes with R-rated antics on the big screen, it seems TV has sex on the brain. It's everywhere. Flip to *Ally McBeal* and see the under-the-knee orgasm trick. Check out *Friends,* where Chandler and Monica have all-day nooky sessions. Drink in Howard Stern's CBS shows, where he slathers mayonnaise and bologna on a woman's naked tush. Look at MTV's new series *Undressed,* where, in the first episode, a character snuggles up to a seven-inch vibrator. And sample the WB's *Dawson's Creek, Buffy the Vampire Slayer,* and *Felicity,* where there's more deflowering going on than in a badly managed greenhouse. (pp. 22-23)

Does systematic research support the common perception that sexual images and messages are increasing in frequency? There have not yet been published analyses of the content in the last year or so, when the alleged dramatic increases in sexual content are purported to have been particularly sharp. But even studies analyzing the content of prime-time television, soap operas, and music television in earlier years found what by most standards would be considered large amounts of implicit sexual activity. An average of three sexual acts per hour across all types of television programming was documented by Greenberg (1994). On the basis of an estimate of 1 hour of viewing per evening on weekdays and 2 hours on the weekends (low estimates compared to adolescents' actual viewing averages), Greenberg calculated that a viewer would be exposed to 27 sexual acts per week, or a minimum of 1,400 per year. Studies focusing on sexuality in advertising conducted in the mid-1980s generally reported that sexually oriented appeals were quite prevalent and increased over time (e.g., Soley & Kurzbard, 1986; Soley & Reid, 1988). Reichert (1999) found similar results by assessing images of men and women in magazine ads in 1983 and 1993. The data showed a significant increase in the proportion of sexually oriented appeals over a 10-year period. They reported a 32% increase between 1983 and 1993 in the number of couples engaged in sexually suggestive contact. More specifically, in 1983, 21% of the couples in the ads were shown engaging in sexually suggestive contact; by 1993, more than half (53%) did so. These changes were more substantial in "gendered magazines" such as *Cosmopolitan* and *Esquire* than in general interest magazines such as *Time* or *Newsweek*.

Content analyses of soap operas reveal a similar increase in sexual portrayals, although the frequency estimates vary considerably (Greenberg & Brand, 1993; Greenberg & Busselle, 1996; Lowry & Towles, 1989). In such soap operas, it is primarily unmarried rather than married heterosexuals who have sex and these differences have increased over the years. For example, Greenberg and Busselle (1996) found that the average hourly number of sexual incidents in soap operas increased from 3.7 in 1985 to 5.0 in 1994. Rates of intercourse among married couples stayed the same, whereas rates of unmarried sex increased; the ratio of unmarried to married intercourse increased from 2:1 to 3:1 over the decade. In contrast to what is portrayed in the media world, studies with representative samples have shown that, in the "real world," there are not substantial differences in the frequency of sex as a function of people's marital status (Laumann, Gagnon, Michael, & Michaels, 1994).

In addition to changes in the frequency of sex among unmarried individuals, Greenberg and Busselle's 1996 soap opera analysis indicated that differences across the decade can be accounted for by an increase in date-rape story lines (there were none in 1985) and issues related to pregnancy. The 1994 soap operas depicted considerable amounts of negative consequences of engaging in various sexual acts as well as rejection of sexual overtures. The researchers state that the growing frequency of sexual incidents in recent years can be attributed to increases in "disgust" as well as "lust" themes. They state that viewers are currently "provided with a more balanced presentation of the benefits and the consequences of sexual activity than reported in earlier studies" (p. 160).

Ward (1995) reviewed the 12 prime-time television programs that children and adolescents watched most during the 1992-1993 season. Her study is an intriguing content analysis of the thematic content of discussions about sexuality on television. The results revealed that the most common types of messages about sexuality centered on the male sexual role. The theme that men typically view women as sexual objects and value them based on their physical appearance was particularly common. Fewer messages focused on the female sexual role, but the most common theme was that women are attracted to specific types of men (i.e., physically attractive, wealthy, romantic, or sensitive). Surprisingly, few messages were concerned with women's passivity or the idea that women set limits on men's sexual advances. Another common theme was the presentation of sexual relations as a competition between men and women. In her discussion of the content analysis, Ward points out:

> On the one hand, frank discussions of sexuality on television may seem to be liberal and progressive, a powerful step forward from the days in which the word "pregnant" was unacceptable and married couples slept in separate beds. However, the content of these discussions is still traditional in many respects, especially concerning the importance of physical appearance for women and "scoring" for men. (p. 611)

In another recent study, Grauerholz and King (1997) conducted a content analysis of 48 hours of prime-time television focusing on the portrayal of sexual harassment. According to their definition of such harassment, many instances were portrayed, but none were labeled as harassment. Instead, they were typically portrayed in humorous ways, and victims experienced little harm or difficulty in stopping the harassment.

### *Sexually Explicit Media*

The "pornography industry" was recently described by *Forbes* magazine as a $56 billion global industry that has become much more mainstream in recent years. Some "hard core" Internet pornography companies are now even listed on the Nasdaq stock exchange (Morais, 1999). When writers describe this sexually explicit media industry, they are typically referring to the type of sexually explicit media consumed primarily by male audiences (Malamuth, 1996). This is also our focus here. Indeed, when it comes to obviously sexually explicit media, this is a much larger segment of the media compared with content designed for female audiences. For example, the number of magazines featuring female nudity (e.g., *Playboy, Penthouse, Oui,* etc.) is many times greater than the similar content for females (e.g., *Playgirl*), where a substantial number of the consumers are gay men.

There are many content analyses of sexually explicit media. The findings were summarized by Malamuth (1996). Most commonly, the portrayals are of female nudity and of men having casual sex with numerous, easily accessible young women. Most of the focus is on physical attributes and activities (rather than emotional or relational elements). It should also be noted, however, that there is a very large media industry called "romance novels," which often have a high degree of sexual explicitness as well (Abramson & Pinkerton, 1995). These novels are consumed mostly by females, including many teenage girls, but they generally have very different content than the sexually explicit content primarily consumed by men (summarized above). (As described by Symons, 1979, similar differences in male and female patterning are evident in homosexual sexually explicit media.) Malamuth (1996) analyzed the explanations for these gender differences in some detail.

The data summarized earlier indicate that exposure to various types of embedded sexual content is likely to be very frequent among many youth, but there are also data suggesting that many young people are often exposed to at least some sexually explicit media, even though, by law, much of this material is supposed to be restricted from children. For example, Bryant (1985) conducted a study to obtain normative information on the amount of exposure that children have to various types of R- and X-rated media. The findings indicated that, by age 15, 92% of males and 84% of females had looked at or read *Playboy* or *Playgirl;* by age 18, the proportion rose to 100% of males and 97% of females. The average age of first exposure was reported to be 11 for males and 13 for females. With regard to X-rated films, 92% of 13- to 15-year-olds said they had already seen such a film, with an average reported age at first exposure of 14 years, 8 months. Similar findings were also recently reported by Kahn-Egan (1998). This investigator conducted a study of the ease of accessibility of various types of sexually explicit media, including the Internet, and also surveyed several hundred third through eighth graders about their actual exposure to such media. She found evidence for easy accessibility to such media, including many sites on the Internet that are supposed to be restricted to adults only. In addition, a high percentage of the sample (48%) reported having visited Internet sites with various types of "adult" content. Sexual content was the most popular type of adults' site visited.

## Theorized Influences

In this section, we discuss some general theoretical issues pertaining to media effects. Although these are clearly relevant to the topic of sexual media, they are applicable to many other content areas as well. We will later consider the extent to which research on sexual media can benefit from more systematic guidance by relevant theory.

### *Reality and Fantasy*

One of the most important questions regarding media effects concerns the extent to which people may be immune to influence when they are aware that portrayals are fictional. (Of course, it should be noted that much of the sexual content in the media in recent years, such as the explicit descriptions of President Clinton's interactions with Monica Lewinsky, described nonfictional events.) Much of the content we are focusing on (e.g., soap operas) presumably is recognized as fiction by many observers. In some ways, it might be argued that the distinction between fantasy and reality is somewhat different in the sexual arena than it is in many other areas. For example, when someone is portrayed as having shot another individual in a fictional media episode, the viewer can assume that the person was not actually shot. However, when someone undresses in front of the camera, viewers can reasonably assume that the person has actually consented to be portrayed in the nude (except in rare cases when "body doubles" or computer morphing is used).

The distinction between fantasy and reality is an important one. The perceived realism of fiction affects its impact on judgments and behavior (e.g., Busselle, 1998; Geen, 1975). However, media research has documented reliable effects even when participants are clearly aware that they are viewing or reading fictional portrayals. For instance, Strange and Leung (1999) recently found that both factual and fictional news stories had similar influences on changing participants' judgments about the causes and solutions for societal problems (e.g., education and health care). In addition, the authors found that the greater the extent that the stories (factual or fictional) evoked participants' memories of related experiences, the more likely they were to influence the participants' subsequent judgments.

These data fit in well with recent theorizing and integration of the available scientific literature regarding how people comprehend and validate social information. For example, Wyer and Radvansky (1999) describe a model that views comprehension as a process of constructing "situation models." They note that, in modern societies, a major source of the situation models that people construct is the mass media, particularly television. They further note that an important feature of human information processing is the ability to add "tags" to representations (e.g., situation models) to denote that they are false (e.g., no matter how many times you see Santa Claus on television, you still perceive him as a fictitious character). However, they argue that, because information acquired from television is typically not extensively thought about (also see Silverblatt, 1995), situation models constructed about fictitious people and events via the mass media are unlikely to be tagged as such. These models may therefore be stored in ways similar to models of events that have occurred in real life and often not be subject to source monitoring (Johnson, Hashtroudi, & Lindsay, 1993). Consequently, the models of fictitious events may be retained and used as a basis for inference without discounting (based on the context in which they were formed).

Support for these predictions has been found in various studies in which people estimated the incidence of different situations that were overrepresented on television relative to real life. As expected, the magnitude of their overestimates increased with the amount of television they watched (Shrum & O'Guinn, 1993; Shrum, O'Guinn, Semenik, & Faber, 1991; Shrum, Wyer, & O'Guinn, 1998).

*We speculate that the extent of influence via experiencing an event in the mass media may be related to the fact that, although humans have some ability to "decouple" fiction and reality, our evolutionary environments did not have selection pressure to develop highly attuned mechanisms for such distinctions.* For instance, in some recurring ancestral environments of our species, storytellers probably often told fictional tales. However, it was much easier then to discriminate between such narrative and the "real world" than it is today to distinguish real events from those depicted via the sophisticated technology of current times. Therefore, humans probably did not evolve well-developed mechanisms to be immune to the type of portrayals common in today's mass media. Those motivated to minimize the effects of media exposure (e.g., parents) may have to stimulate considerable "extra" cognitive effort to get "tags" of falsity regularly added to their children's media experiences.

### *Social Learning Theory*

Although it has been argued that sexual portrayals in the media often provide young people with powerful messages concerning how to be sexual, why to have sex, and appropriate sequences of sexual activities (e.g., McCormick, 1987), there is not currently a well-developed theoretical perspective to guide research specifically in this area. However, as Huesmann and Malamuth (1986) noted, social learning theory provides a particularly useful framework for guiding research on media effects in various areas. By summarizing here some of the key points of this theory and related research in areas other than sexual media, we hope to contextualize the existing research and to help develop an agenda for future research.

Although various scholars have contributed to the development of social learning theory (see Hogben & Byrne, 1998), we rely here on the most influential version, that of Albert Bandura (1973, 1977, 1986). A central tenet of this theory is that both children and adults are often influenced by observing other humans, both by direct observations and via the media. With respect to sexual behavior, social learning theory suggests that both what is portrayed in the media and what may be left out (e.g., caring, mutual respect, tenderness) may (a) affect interpretations, perceptions, attitudes, perceived norms, and other cognitive/emotional processes; (b) teach novel modes of sexual behavior; (c) facilitate already learned behaviors perceived as socially acceptable; and/or (d) strengthen or weaken inhibitions concerning previously learned but socially discouraged forms of sexual behavior. Some of the findings reported below support such predictions, but it is clear that there is much more research needed to systematically assess such potential varied influences and the conditions under which they do or do not occur.

Some scholars have criticized social learning theory on the grounds that it is a simplistic "imitative model" that "assumes that people are made of unimprinted wax and stamped with whatever messages role models present" (Bart & Jozsa, 1980, p. 217). We believe that such criticism is largely unwarranted. Social learning theory is not simply a "monkey see, money do" theory. Bandura (1977) has emphasized that learning through modeling others is not simply a matter of copying or mimicking what others do but involves abstracting rules concerning appropriate behavior and the likely consequences of various types of actions. The circumstances and the actual actions that an individual might engage in do not have to be identical to those depicted in the media for modeling to occur via the learning of a symbolic rule or message. It is therefore important in research to consider the specific messages that are communicated (e.g., sex between unmarried individuals is OK) rather than the sexual content per se (although the very inclusion of sexual portrayals may at times communicate messages, such as those regarding the appropriateness of public displays of sexual behavior). Some of the research described below on embedded sexual media supports this general prediction regarding the importance of the message conveyed.

Through observation of others (in the media or in daily life), children gradually build a repertoire of knowledge containing mental models of different types of social situations, possible behavioral responses to those situations, and possible outcomes resulting from different behavioral choices. Thus, the form of behavior, the situations in which the behavior occurs, its appropriateness for certain situations, and the probabilities of various consequences can be learned by children. The organized mental representations of this learned information are called scripts (Huesmann, 1988). Although observing others is a critical component of social learning, it is further strengthened when a child actually enacts what has been learned via observational mechanisms by actual direct experience (enactive learning). But these, of course, are not necessarily mutually exclusive or even independent processes, and observing others engage in a behavior may increase the likelihood that the observer will attempt the behavior and thereby learn via direct experience. Observational learning may be particularly important in some areas of behavior, such as in environments where experimentation with actual sexual behaviors may be strongly frowned on. Moreover, the use of sexual media to stimulate sexual arousal, sometimes accompanied by masturbation and sexual pleasure, may have conditioning effects influencing sexual desires and behaviors (Check & Malamuth, 1986).

Social learning theory places emphasis on the interactive influences of environmental factors (e.g., media exposure) and other mediating and moderating influences. This is encapsulated in the concept of reciprocal determinism, which Bandura (1977) defined as "a continuous reciprocal interaction between personal, behavior and environmental determinants" (p. 194). This concept encompasses bidirectional influences by which individuals' characteristics (e.g., gender, personality, etc.) may affect selecting or attending to certain content in the media and the extent to which such experiences are pleasurable or otherwise influential. In general, this concept points to the need to consider various moderating variables that affect the impact of media exposure. In briefly describing some of the research on sexually explicit media, we consider findings relevant to the concept of reciprocal determinism.

In keeping with the concept of reciprocal determinism, social learning theory emphasizes that the consumer's interpretations and evaluations of media messages strongly mediate the effects of exposure. Therefore, various dimensions powerfully influence what is learned from observing others and how such learning may affect behavior. Some of the dimensions suggested by social learning theory have been verified by various studies on children and adults in a wide variety of content areas. These include the consequences of the behaviors depicted; the extent to which the viewer perceives the depiction to be realistic; the extent to which he or she identifies with the protagonists; and whether the information is distinctive, functional, and salient and not contradicted by direct experience or other more "primary" influences such as strong peer groups or influential family members (Bandura, 1977; Basil & Brown, 1997; Comstock, 1978). In keeping with such research findings, below we describe research showing that dimensions such as familial or parental influence and a person's degree of actively cognitively processing media information both moderate the effects of sexual portrayals in the media.

Age may also be an important moderator of observational learning via the media and other sources. Children as young as 2½ years old acquire much information through symbolic media, including television; very young children (e.g., 2-year-olds), however, may not yet be able to use symbolic representation and may therefore not be similarly influenced (Troseth & DeLoache, 1998). Even after infancy, it is generally the case that, as children age, they are better able to attend to, process, and understand media messages (Emmers-Sommer & Allen, 1999). However, it is generally expected that among youth there is an inverse correlation, though far from perfectly linear, between age and susceptibility to media influences (see Roberts, 1982, 1993). This is expected since young people's behavioral patterns may be less well established, they may be less skillful in analyzing the degree of realism of mediated information (Markham,

Howie, & Hlavacek, 1999), and they may be less confident about their own values or views. Therefore, findings of media influences on young adults may serve as a sound basis for anticipating at least the same degree of effects with younger individuals (Malamuth, 1993). This is important in this area because conducting experimental research in which participants are exposed to various types of sexual stimuli may be more ethically acceptable with young adults than with preadults.

## Research Findings on Effects of Sexual Media

### *Effects of Exposure to "Embedded Sexual Content" on Youth*

In presenting the relevant research findings, we first examine studies that have used correlational data and then research that has randomly assigned participants to various conditions (i.e., experimental methods). Next, we consider both correlational and experimental research that has included some key moderating variables.

#### *Correlational Studies*

Varied studies have extended the research on people's beliefs about the effects of sexual media on children and have actually investigated the association between children's exposure to sexual images and their attitudes and behaviors. One line of research addressed the impact of viewing soap operas on estimates of "real-life" events related to sexuality. Buerkel-Rothfuss and Mayes (1981) surveyed 290 college students and found that exposure to soap operas was related to their perceptions of certain problems in the real world. Even after the researchers controlled for grade point average, year in school, age, gender, and self-concept, they found that soap opera viewers estimated more occurrences of divorce, illegitimate children, and abortions than did nonviewers. This study suggests that higher television watchers tend to believe that what they see on television represents reality.

If viewers tend to believe that media images represent reality, how do they react when their own experiences do not match those portrayed on television? Perhaps exposure to sexual media images generates expectations of immediate sexual gratification that are not matched in "real life." To address this question, Baran (1976b) examined the association between exposure to sexual media and adolescents' satisfaction with their own sexuality. The researcher surveyed 202 high school students and found that the more pleasure teens perceived television characters as having during sexual acts, the less the viewers were satisfied with their own experiences of intercourse. In addition, students who thought that television accurately portrayed sexual behavior were more likely to be dissatisfied with either their first experience of intercourse or their virginity (if sexually inexperienced). Baran (1976a) replicated these findings in a study of 207 college students.

Another line of research focused on the association between exposure to sexual media and adolescents' premarital sexual permissiveness. Premarital sexual permissiveness is often conceptualized and measured with both attitudinal (i.e., the extent to which participants agree with the statement "Young people should not have sex before marriage") and behavioral (i.e., the age when the participant experienced his or her first act of intercourse) components. Some survey research has found that, among young people, the volume of general media consumption is not correlated with sexual permissiveness; however, some measures of exposure to sexually suggestive materials, including Music Television (MTV) and R-rated films in particular, have been found to be associated with premarital sexual permissiveness (Brown & Newcomer, 1991; Strouse & Buerkel-Rothfuss, 1987).

For example, a three-wave longitudinal study of junior high school students (Brown & Newcomer, 1991) found that neither the total amount of television viewing nor the total amount of sexually oriented television viewing related to the likelihood of engaging in heterosexual intercourse earlier or later. Rather, the proportion of sexual programming viewed relative to all types of programming viewed (conceptualized as assessing the extent to which adolescents seek out sexual content when watching television) was significantly related to adolescents' sexual activity status. This relationship held even after the researchers controlled for previous noncoital experiences and perceived influence of friends.

In addition, in a study of 457 college students, Strouse and Buerkel-Rothfuss (1987) found that, among females, MTV consumption was the most powerful predictor of sexual attitudes and expectations about sexuality and love relationships, as well as the number of sexual partners. For males, self-esteem was the most powerful predictor of sexual attitudes and behavior, while MTV consumption was the fourth most important predictor of the number of sexual partners.

A cautionary reminder needs to be mentioned concerning conclusions that can be drawn from such correlational studies. These studies demonstrate associations in "real-world" settings among frequency of using sexual media, various attitudes regarding sexuality, and sexual behaviors. Because they are correlational in nature, however, we cannot draw the conclusion that viewing a higher concentration of sexual content on television leads to changes in attitudes or behavior. Rather, the rival hypothesis that teenagers who are already sexually active and condone various sexual activities actively select sexual television programming cannot be fully discounted. It may well be, as suggested by the concept of reciprocal determinism described above, that both sequences are at work: As adolescents mature, some actively seek or pay more attention to media with greater amounts of sexual content, and there may be corresponding changes in attitudes and modeling of behaviors. In addition, "hidden" third variables such as social desirability in reporting, personality factors, or peer pressures may be responsible for the associations.

### *Experimental Studies*

In contrast, experimental studies (in which participants are randomly assigned to contrasting conditions) provide a basis for reaching causal conclusions. Two such studies found support for the effects of exposure to sex music videos on sexual attitudes. One of these (Calfin, Carroll, & Schmidt, 1993) reported that college students who were exposed to a music video were more likely to exhibit more liberal attitudes toward premarital sex than were those who did not see the video. A study of even younger participants, seventh and ninth graders, found that those who were exposed to less than an hour of MTV were more likely than unexposed adolescents to approve of premarital sex (Greeson & Williams, 1986).

### *Research Using Moderating Variables*

As summarized above, several lines of research reveal an association between exposure to sexual materials and various attitudinal and behavioral changes among youth. Some studies document an association; others employ experimental methods to make stronger causal claims. Obviously, not all people are affected all of the time. An analysis of potential moderating variables may help to further explain why some children and adolescents are so susceptible to television messages while others remain relatively unaffected. We will consider two possible moderators of the impact of music videos in particular on youth: gender and family environment.

Because females are generally the more "reluctant" sex (whether because of social rearing or "biological" factors or both of these influences), Strouse, Buerkel-Rothfuss, and

Long (1995) posited that females might have more latitude than males to change their permissiveness in a "liberal" direction. Indeed, they found a stronger correlation between the amount of exposure to MTV and premarital sexual permissiveness for high school females than for high school males. Similarly, recall the study mentioned previously in which MTV consumption was the most powerful predictor of sexual attitudes and behavior for females but not for males (Strouse & Buerkel-Rothfuss, 1987).

Certain sexual messages may be more influential for females, but the opposite may be true for other types of sexual content. For example, Malamuth and Check (1981) conducted an experiment (i.e., randomly assigning participants to conditions) in a relatively naturalistic setting. This study used R-rated feature-length films (which have been shown on cable without any editing and on network television with minor deletions). Rather than testing the impact of sexual content per se, this study tested the effects of differing messages contained within sexual content (e.g., that sexual aggression against women has positive consequences). Male and female undergraduate students were randomly assigned to one of two exposure conditions. Participants in the experimental condition were given free tickets to view feature-length films (on two different evenings) that included portrayals of women as victims of sexual aggression, suggesting that the aggression was justified and/or had "positive" consequences (e.g., aroused the women sexually). On the same evenings, participants in the control condition were given tickets to other films that did not contain any sexual violence. Participants viewed these films with moviegoers who purchased tickets and were not part of the research. Classmates of the recruited participants who did not see the films were also studied as an "untreated" control group.

Several days after the films were viewed, a "Sexual Attitude Survey" was administered to the entire class. (Participants were not aware of the relationship between this survey—purportedly administered by a polling agency—and the earlier movies some students had seen as part of an ostensibly unrelated study.) Responses were assessed by scales embedded within many irrelevant items intended to disguise the purpose of the survey. Exposure to the films portraying "positive" effects significantly increased the scores of male but not female participants on measures assessing acceptance of the use of aggression against women in sexual and nonsexual interactions.

More recently, Weisz and Earls (1995) successfully implemented a replication of the study by Malamuth and Check (1981). Although they used different participants, films, settings, and some measures, they also found that "viewing sexually aggressive films significantly increased men's but not women's acceptance of cultural stereotypes indicating that women deserve or secretly desire rape" (p. 81).

Another potentially important moderator of media effects is a child's family environment. For example, Singer and Singer (1986) suggested that when parents take an active mediating approach toward television, including regularly critically commenting about program content, children may develop a more discriminating stance toward media content. These children may not be as vulnerable to the more negative media effects and some may even learn constructive approaches by virtue of such parental mediation. A study of thousands of high school students (Peterson, Moore, & Furstenberg, 1991) found support for the role of family environment as a moderator of media effects on adolescents' sexual behavior. The researchers found that, for girls, those who less frequently discussed television with their parents had nearly twice the sexual experience rate of those whose discussions were more frequent, and those who watched television apart from their parents had more than three times the rate of those who watched with their parents. For boys, they found a strong positive correlation between viewing time and sexual experience among those who viewed television apart from their parents (but no such correlation for those boys who watched with their parents). For the boys who watched television without their parents, the sexual experience rate for the heavy viewers was nearly six times that of the lightest viewers. Again, we must point out that this study is purely correlational. Boys and girls were not randomly assigned to groups in which they viewed television shows alone or with their parents. Instead, the children and their parents chose to watch television either separately or together; therefore, we cannot be confident that watching television with parents causes children to have lower sexual experience rates.

In an experimental study of 13- to 14-year-old boys and girls, Bryant and Rockwell (1994) found further evidence for the moderating effects of family environment variables in relation to media impact. We will describe these studies in considerable detail because they are particularly germane to the focus of this chapter since they studied youths and their methodology enables "cause and effect" conclusions. In three separate studies, the researchers reported that exposure to television portrayals of sexual relations between unmarried partners affected teenagers' subsequent moral judgmental values relating to premarital and extramarital sex. The first study in this series differed in two ways from the other two studies. In the first study only, there was a condition in which participants were exposed to media portrayals of sex between married individuals. Here no effects were found on any of the dependent measures. We will return to discuss this aspect of the data later. Also, this first study did not include any moderator variables.

In the second and third of this series of studies, however, the investigators did examine moderating effects. They randomly assigned participants to either (a) watch 15 hours (3 hours a night for 5 consecutive evenings) of television programming containing sexual relations between unmarried partners, (b) watch 15 hours of television programming containing nonsexual relations between adults, or (c) a no treatment control condition in which participants read books or magazines. The researchers sought to determine whether prior exposure to television affects teenagers' subsequent moral judgmental values concerning television segments depicting sexual violations ranging from mild indiscretions (e.g., one actor accusing another of wanting to go to bed with an acquaintance for material gain) to more severe sexual transgressions (e.g., sexual infidelity). They also included dependent measures assessing moral judgments of nonsexual, criminal, and antisocial behaviors. Each participant provided ratings on 10-point scales assessing three dimensions of moral judgment: (a) How bad, morally speaking, is the indiscretion, impropriety, transgression, or crime that was perpetrated? (b) How much has the victim—or victims—been wronged? and (c) How much has the victim—or victims—suffered?

Results of these latter two Bryant and Rockwell (1994) studies indicated that participants who watched television programs depicting sex between unmarried partners indicated that the victim was less wronged and did not judge the sexual impropriety as severely as did the other two groups (there was no effect for victim suffering). Again, because participants were randomly assigned to conditions in this study, we can be relatively certain that the type of television programs viewed actually influenced the participants' subsequent judgments. However, two other variables moderated this effect. The first was "how cognitively active the audience member is in seeking, selecting, receiving, perceiving, processing, and interpreting television's messages" (p. 189). The second variable was the openness of each teen's family communication style. When participants engaged in active viewing and came from families with an open communication style, the effects of exposure to sexual television programming were completely mitigated.

The presentation of this research, however, lacked some information typically provided in research reports (e.g., the details of statistical analyses such as $F$ and $p$ values). Without these details, it is difficult to draw some inferences that may be helpful in assessing the magnitude of the effects reported (although the investigators did indicate that the effects were statistically significant). Furthermore, it is important to note that the effects found were for "sexual acts" only (i.e., extra- or nonmarital sex) and did not occur on any of the measures depicting nonsexual, criminal, or antisocial behavior.

Regardless of this and other limitations, findings from numerous studies illustrate the importance of thinking critically about how other variables may moderate the effects of sexual media on young people's attitudes and behaviors. Taken together, the Peterson et al. study (1991) and the Bryant and Rockwell study (1994) demonstrate that family communication styles may interact with media influences in important ways to shape teens' sexual attitudes and behavior. In keeping with the predictions of social learning theory (see above) and the findings of Malamuth and Check (1981) and Weisz and Earls (1995), the first experiment reported by Bryant and Rockwell (1994) also suggests that it may not be the sexual content per se that has the effect but the particular messages embedded in the content (i.e., because sexual acts between married individuals were not found to have any significant effects but those between unmarried individuals did have effects).

## Research on Sexually Explicit Media With Young Adults

A substantial number of studies have examined the effects of various types of sexually explicit media on adults, particularly focusing on young adults between the ages of 18 and 22. The findings of such studies have been summarized in various reviews (e.g., Linz & Malamuth, 1993; Malamuth, 1993, 1998, 1999) and recent meta-analyses (Allen, D'Alessio, & Brezgel, 1995; Allen, D'Alessio, & Emmers-Sommer, 1999; Allen, Emmers, Gebhardt, & Giery, 1995). Although there are some differences in the findings across studies, taken as a whole, the research provides evidence that, under some conditions, exposure to sexually explicit material can affect fantasies, attitudes, perceptions of norms, and behavior. In particular, however, this literature is important to consider in the context of evaluating the impact of sexual media because it highlights the importance of individual difference variables such as personality characteristics. Although the important role of such individual difference variables has been emphasized in other areas of media research and related investigations (e.g., Aluja-Fabregat & Torrubia-Beltri, 1998; Finn, 1997; Singer & Salovey, 1991), it has not often been examined in the research on embedded sexual media summarized above. From the findings on sexually explicit media, it is clear that the effects are not necessarily the same for all individuals and for all environments, so differing conclusions may be justified when moderating factors are taken into consideration (e.g., Barak, Fisher, Belfry, & Lashambe, 1999; Bogaert, 1993; Ceniti & Malamuth, 1984; Donnerstein, 1984; Donnerstein & Berkowitz, 1981; Frable, Johnson, & Kellman, 1997; Jansma, Linz, Mulac, & Imrich, 1997; Malamuth, 1978, 1981, 1998; Malamuth & Check, 1983; Malamuth, Check, & Briere, 1986; Malamuth & McIlwraith, 1989; McKenzie-Morh & Zanna, 1990; Pryor, LaVite, & Stoller, 1993). These include the cultural milieu, the individual's background, gender, personality characteristics, the particular content of the stimuli (messages conveyed, the consequences of the acts depicted, the degree of sexual explicitness of the material, the degree of arousal generated, etc.), and the current circumstances of the environment in which the person is exposed to the stimuli. This has been demonstrated in both correlational and experimental studies and in studies using various dependent measures, including sexual arousal, fantasies, attitudes, and behavior. Moreover, this line of research suggests that the type of media people select and find gratifying is predictably related to their personalities and other individual difference characteristics and thereby provides support for the social learning concept of reciprocal determinism.

## Conclusions

At the beginning of this chapter, we described a recent newspaper ad asserting that there was "massive evidence" of negative effects of sexual and other media on children. Although this ad lumped together research on sex and research on violence, its primary political focus was on sexual content, vulgarity, and other "filth." Clearly, our comprehensive search of the literature on this topic has not yielded such overwhelming evidence with regard to sexual media. It has, however, yielded sufficient data, we believe, to justify certain conclusions.

1. There is a great deal of sex in the media showing or implying acts such as premarital and extramarital sex. The amount of such content has been steadily increasing in many areas of the media. Children and adolescents are exposed to these media regularly. Although sex is sometimes portrayed in the context of loving relationships, this is often not the case. Varied consequences of such acts are shown, but they are often not negative. There are considerable differences in the way males and females are portrayed, and the themes often correspond to "stereotypical" roles. Sexual overtures that might legally be defined as sexual harassment are often treated in a humorous way without serious consequences.
2. Both young people and adults believe that they are affected by such sexual content. When people are asked about the effects of pornography, they often tend to believe that others are adversely affected but that they personally are far less vulnerable (Gunther, 1995). When asked about what we have labeled "embedded sexual media," however, many young people do rank the media as powerful personal influences.
3. Under some conditions, exposure to sexual content in the media is likely to affect some young people's judgments and attitudes regarding sexual behaviors (e.g., premarital and extramarital sex) and possibly influence their sexual behaviors. We feel justified in reaching this conclusion even though there are only a few studies in this area specifically studying children and adolescents. Some of these present correlational data and some experimental research. There are also data with young adults in this area and a great deal of research in other content areas demonstrating effects that we believe provide a theoretically sound justification for also supporting the conclusion that sexual media are probably both reflecting and contributing to more permissive sexual attitudes and behaviors. With few exceptions in research on sexually explicit media (e.g., Zillmann & Bryant, 1988), there are no data supporting claims of sexual media's impact on a general "moral degeneracy" or a fundamental shift in values such as increasing the desire for instant gratification at the expense of long-term happiness (e.g., see Odone, 1998). Indeed, the research by Bryant and Rockwell (1994) that provided the most convincing evidence to date for actual cause-and-effect relationships of "embedded sexuality" on teenagers' judgments of sexual behavior actually assessed moral judgments in various other areas

(e.g., nonsexual, criminal, or antisocial behavior). It found no such effects. It is important in future research to assess whether repeated exposure over time might have such "spillover" effects or whether the effects are limited only to judgments of sexual behavior.

4. The effects of exposure to sexual media may be moderated by many other factors, including family communication styles, cognitive style, and personality characteristics. When effects occur, their degree and sometimes even their direction are likely to vary as a function of such moderators. To the extent that predictions have been tested, the findings are generally consistent with predictions derived from social learning theory, including support for reciprocally deterministic effects, by which individual difference variables affect the kind of media people seek, and their media exposure in turn affects some of their characteristics.

Although we believe that these conclusions are justified, we might add that evaluating them negatively or positively will probably depend on certain personal values, in contrast to findings in areas such as media violence (in which effects on aggressive behavior will generally be judged similarly by most people). Those individuals who clearly hold what are frequently referred to as "conservative sexual attitudes" (e.g., premarital and extramarital sex are wrong) will probably view these types of effects of sexual mass media very negatively. Those who hold views that are more mixed (e.g., "protected" premarital sex among teenagers is OK but extramarital sex is wrong) may have ambivalent reactions to these conclusions. In contrast, others may see the increase of sexual content in the media, as well as the effects found to date, as a positive step to a generally relaxed approach to sexuality (e.g., Abramson & Pinkerton, 1995) and to stimulating more open discussion with children about sex (e.g., Johnson, 1999).

## Directions for Future Research

An emphasis for additional research is undoubtedly justified in this area, but we hope that future work will be more theory driven and proceed beyond addressing questions that have been focused on to date. The following are some general comments and suggestions to help guide such research.

Although communication researchers often seek to disentangle the influence of the mass media from other factors, implicitly they understand that no influence on human thinking or behavior works in a vacuum. Media influences interact with a variety of other factors, sometimes counteracting them, sometimes reinforcing them, and at other times having little effect. The degree of influence that media have on a person may largely depend on how that exposure interacts with other factors. For example, people raised with little education about sexuality or in families in which discussion of sex was treated as "taboo" may be more susceptible to the influences of media than those reared with considerable education about sex (Malamuth & Billings, 1986). We believe that the study of the effects of mass media in any area, including this one, would ideally be conducted within the larger context of a theoretical model incorporating the complex interactions among several levels of analysis. These would include factors encompassed within the biological, psychological, and sociological levels (Mayer, 1999). This would include the evolved psychological mechanisms of the mind, individual and family developmental histories, cultural environments, personality characteristics, and situational dynamics (see Malamuth & Addison, in press, for an example of such an analysis of media effects on aggression).

In this chapter, we have emphasized the importance of analyzing the messages conveyed in the media. But even any single program may convey a plethora of messages, some of them clearly contradictory. It is therefore necessary to pay considerable attention to the subtleties, the multiple levels, and the complexities of the messages. For example, we recently chose to informally examine the messages conveyed in an episode of one of the leading syndicated morning television shows, the *Maury Povich Show.* It aired (on October 20, 1999) a half-hour program titled "Shocking Teen Sex Secrets Revealed." The first half of the show consisted of scantily clad teenage girls boasting of their highly promiscuous sexual exploits in ways that we believe would be quite tantalizing to many viewers, particularly young males. Interspersed throughout, but particularly in the last third of the show, were adults' (e.g., a mother, a psychologist, and a motivational speaker) critical comments and warnings about venereal diseases. The show ended with a brief portrayal of the young girls' visit to a "sex addicts boot camp," which was portrayed to have successfully changed the attitudes of some of the teenagers. Others continued to be defiant and boastful. *We believe that it would be useful in future research to conduct a multifaceted analysis of the diverse and often conflicting messages in such shows and how they are perceived, understood, and assimilated by viewers of various ages.*

It is also important to examine how mass media influences may occur through indirect mediating processes (e.g., Kelley, Buckingham, & Davies, 1999). For example, Rimal, Flora, and Schooler (1999) have provided considerable supportive evidence that media campaigns designed to change behaviors affecting cardiovascular health (i.e., diet, exercise, and smoking) primarily induce change not by influencing behaviors directly but by changing processes such as information seeking and interpersonal communication that ultimately change behaviors. Similarly, sexual content viewed on television may stimulate discussion among teenagers and their peers. Such discussion can often reinforce media models and messages, but it can support rejection of media messages as well (Durham, 1999).

Finally, an important distinction in social learning theory is between the acquisition of behavioral potential and overt behavioral expression. For example, a child may learn about and develop greater interest in certain sexual behaviors by watching media or may change his or her perceptions of social norms. Although such norms may be strongly related to behaviors (e.g., Fishbein et al., 1995), their influence may not be observed until a later time when placed in a similar situation. Therefore, the learning that has occurred may not necessarily be apparent in any direct modeling behavior until the "right" environmental circumstances are present. Such delayed effects would be best addressed in longitudinal studies.

## References


Abramson, P. R., & Pinkerton, S. D. (1995). *With pleasure: Thoughts on the nature of human sexuality.* New York: Oxford University Press.

Allen, M., D'Alessio, D., & Brezgel, K. (1995). A meta-analysis summarizing the effects of pornography: II. Aggression after exposure. *Human Communication Research, 22,* 258-283.

Allen, M., D'Alessio, D., & Emmers-Sommer, T. (1999). Reactions of criminal sexual offenders to pornography: A meta-analytic summary. In M. Roloff (Ed.), *Communication yearbook 22* (pp. 139-169). Thousand Oaks, CA: Sage.

Allen, M., Emmers, T., Gebhardt, L., & Giery, M. A. (1995). Exposure to pornography and acceptance of rape myths. *Journal of Communication, 45*(1), 5-26.

Aluja-Fabregat, A., & Torrubia-Beltri, R. (1998). Viewing of mass media violence, perception of violence, personality, and academic achievement. *Personality and Individual Differences, 25,* 973-989.

Bandura, A. (1973). *Aggression: A social learning analysis.* Englewood Cliffs, NJ: Prentice Hall.

Bandura, A. (1977). *Social learning theory.* Englewood Cliffs, NJ: Prentice Hall.

Bandura, A. (1986). *Social foundations of thought and action: A social cognitive theory.* Englewood Cliffs, NJ: Prentice Hall.

Barak, A., Fisher, W. A., Belfry, S., & Lashambe, D. R. (1999). Sex, guys, and cyberspace: Effects of Internet pornography and individual differences on men's attitudes toward women. *Journal of Psychology & Human Sexuality, 11,* 63-91.

Baran, S. J. (1976a). How TV and film portrayals affect sexual satisfaction in college students. *Journalism Quarterly, 53,* 468-473.

Baran, S. J. (1976b). Sex on TV and the adolescent self-image. *Journal of Broadcasting, 20,* 61-68.

Bart, P. B., & Jozsa, M. (1980). Dirty books, dirty films, and dirty data. In L. Lederer (Ed.), *Take back the night: Women on pornography* (pp. 204-217). New York: Morrow.

Basil, M. D., & Brown, W. J. (1997). Marketing AIDS prevention: The differential impact of hypothesis versus identification effects. *Journal of Consumer Psychology, 6,* 389-411.

Bogaert, A. (1993). *The sexual media: Role of individual differences.* Unpublished doctoral dissertation, University of Western Ontario, London, Ontario, Canada.

Brown, J. D., & Newcomer, S. F. (1991). Television viewing and adolescents' sexual behavior. *Journal of Homosexuality, 21*(1/2), 77-91.

Bryant, J. (1985). Frequency of exposure, age of initial exposure, and reactions to initial exposure to pornography [Report presented to the Attorney General's Commission on Pornography, Houston, TX]. In D. Zillmann & J. Bryant (Eds.), *Pornography: Research advances and policy considerations.* Hillsdale, NJ: Lawrence Erlbaum.

Bryant, J., & Rockwell, S. C. (1994). Effects of massive exposure to sexually oriented prime-time television programming on adolescents' moral judgment. In D. Zillmann, J. Bryant, & A. C. Huston (Eds.), *Media, children, and the family.* Hillsdale, NJ: Lawrence Erlbaum.

Buerkel-Rothfuss, L. L., & Mayes, S. (1981). Soap opera viewing: The cultivation effect. *Journal of Communication, 31*(3), 108-115.

Busselle, R. W. (1998). Media examples and social reality construction: The role of exemplar accessibility and exemplar realism. *Dissertation Abstracts International Section A: Humanities & Social Sciences, 58*(9-A), 3348.

Calfin, M. S., Carroll, J. L., & Schmidt, J. (1993). Viewing music-video tapes before taking a test of premarital sexual attitudes. *Psychological Reports, 72,* 475-481.

Ceniti, J., & Malamuth, N. (1984). Effects of repeated exposure to sexually violent or sexually nonviolent stimuli on sexual arousal to rape and nonrape depictions. *Behaviour Research and Therapy, 22,* 535-548.

Check, J., & Malamuth, N. (1986). Pornography and sexual aggression: A social learning theory analysis. In M. L. McLaughlin (Ed.), *Communication yearbook 9* (pp. 181-213). Beverly Hills, CA: Sage.

Comstock, G. (1978, March). *Television and social values.* Paper prepared for the National Institute of Mental Health planning project Television as a Teacher, Bethesda, MD.

Donnerstein, E. (1984). Pornography: Its effects on violence against women. In N. M. Malamuth & E. Donnerstein (Eds.), *Pornography and sexual aggression* (pp. 53-81). Orlando, FL: Academic Press.

Donnerstein, E., & Berkowitz, L. (1981). Victim reactions in aggressive erotic films as a factor in violence against women. *Journal of Personality and Social Psychology, 41,* 710-724.

Durham, M. G. (1999). Girls, media, and the negotiation of sexuality: A study of race, class, and gender in adolescent peer groups. *Journalism & Mass Communication Quarterly, 76,* 193-194.

Emmers-Sommer, T. M., & Allen, M. (1999). Surveying the effect of media effects: A meta-analytic summary of the media effects research in *Human Communication Research, 25,* 478-497.

Exon, J. (1996, November). Commentary: The Communications Decency Act. *Federal Communications Law Journal, 49,* 95-97.

Finn, S. (1997). Origins of media exposure: Linking personality traits to TV, radio, print, and film use. *Communication Research, 24*(5), 507-529.

Fishbein, M., Trafimow, D., Middlestadt, S. E., Helquist, M., Francis, C., & Eustace, A. (1995). Using an AIDS KABP survey to identify determinants of condom use among sexually active adults from St. Vincent and the Grenadines. *Journal of Applied Social Psychology, 25,* 1-20.

Frable, D. E. S., Johnson, A. E., & Kellman, H. (1997). Seeing masculine men, sexy women, and gender differences: Exposure to pornography and cognitive constructions of gender. *Journal of Personality, 65,* 311-355.

Geen, R. G. (1975). The meaning of observed violence: Real vs. fictional violence and consequent effects on aggression and emotional arousal. *Journal of Research in Personality, 9,* 270-281.

Grauerholz, E., & King, A. (1997). Prime time sexual harassment. *Violence Against Women, 3,* 129-148.

Greenberg, B. S. (1994). Content trends in media sex. In D. Zillmann, J. Bryant, & A. C. Huston (Eds.), *Media, children, and the family.* Hillsdale, NJ: Lawrence Erlbaum.

Greenberg, B. S., & Brand, J. E. (1993). Television news and advertising in schools: The "Channel One" controversy. *Journal of Communication, 43*(1), 143-151.

Greenberg, B. S., & Busselle, R. W. (1996). Soap operas and sexual activity: A decade later. *Journal of Communication, 46*(4), 153-160.

Greeson, L. E., & Williams, R. A. (1986). Social implications of music videos on youth: An analysis of the content and effects of MTV. *Youth and Society, 18,* 177-189.

Gunther, A. C. (1995). Overrating the X-rating: The third-person perception and support for censorship of pornography. *Journal of Communication, 45,* 27-38.

Harris, L., & Associates. (1987). *Attitudes about television, sex, and contraceptive advertising: A survey of a cross-section of adult Americans.* New York: Planned Parenthood Federation of America.

Hogben, M., & Byrne, D. (1998). Using social learning theory to explain individual differences in human sexuality. *Journal of Sex Research, 35,* 58-71.

Howard, M. (1985). Postponing sexual involvement among adolescents: An alternative approach to the prevention of sexually transmitted diseases. *Journal of Adolescent Health Care, 6,* 271-277.

Huesmann, L. R. (1988). An information processing model for the development of aggression. *Aggressive Behavior, 14,* 13-24.

Huesmann, L. R., & Malamuth, N. M. (1986). Media violence and antisocial behavior: An overview. *Journal of Social Issues, 42,* 1-6.

Jacobs, A. J. (1999, August 6). The XXX files. *Entertainment Weekly,* pp. 20-25.

Jansma, L., Linz, D., Mulac, A., & Imrich, D. (1997). Men's interactions with women after viewing sexually explicit films: Does degradation make a difference? *Communication Monographs, 64,* 1-24.

Johnson, M. K., Hashtroudi, S., & Lindsay, D. S. (1993). Source monitoring. *Psychological Bulletin, 114,* 3-28.

Johnson, T. C. (1999). *Understanding your child's sexual behavior: What's natural and healthy.* Oakland, CA: New Harbinger.

Kahn-Egan, C. N. (1998). *Pandora's boxes: Children's reactions to and understanding of television and Internet rules, ratings, and regulations.* Unpublished doctoral dissertation, Florida State University.

Kelley, P., Buckingham, D., & Davies, H. (1999). Talking dirty: Children, sexual knowledge, and television. *Childhood: A Global Journal of Child Research, 6,* 221-242.

Kunkel, D., Farinola, W. J. M., Cope, K. M., Donnerstein, E., Biely, E., & Zwarun, L. (1998). *Rating the TV ratings: One year out. An assessment of the television industry's use of V-chip ratings* [Report to the Kaiser Family Foundation]. Santa Barbara: University of California, Santa Barbara.

Laumann, E. O., Gagnon, J. H., Michael, R. T., & Michaels, S. (1994). *The social organization of sexuality: Sexual practices in the United States.* Chicago: University of Chicago Press.

Levin, G. (1999, September 24). TV turns on. *USA Today,* pp. E1-E2.

Linz, D., & Malamuth, N. (1993). *Pornography.* Newbury Park, CA: Sage.

Lowry, D. T., & Towles, D. E. (1989). Soap opera portrayals of sex, contraception, and sexually transmitted diseases. *Journal of Communication, 39,* 76-83.

Malamuth, N. (1978, September). *Erotica, aggression, and perceived appropriateness.* Paper presented at the 86th annual convention of the American Psychological Association, Toronto, Canada.

Malamuth, N. (1981). Rape fantasies as a function of exposure to violent-sexual stimuli. *Archives of Sexual Behavior, 10,* 33-47.

Malamuth, N. (1993). Pornography's impact on male adolescents. *Adolescent Medicine: State of the Art Reviews, 4,* 563-576.

Malamuth, N. (1996). Sexually explicit media, gender differences, and evolutionary theory. *Journal of Communication, 46*(3), 8-31.

Malamuth, N. (1998). The confluence model as an organizing framework for research on sexually aggressive men: Risk moderators, imagined aggression, and pornography consumption. In R. Geen & E. Donnerstein (Eds.), *Aggression: Theoretical and empirical reviews* (pp. 229-245). New York: Academic Press.

Malamuth, N. (1999). Pornography. In L. Kurtz (Ed.), *Encyclopedia for violence, peace, and conflict.* New York: Academic Press.

Malamuth, N., & Addison, T. (in press). Integrating social psychological research on aggression within an evolutionary-based framework. In G. Fletcher & P. Clark (Eds.), *Blackwell handbook of social psychology.* Malden, MA: Blackwell.

Malamuth, N., & Billings, V. (1986). The functions and effects of pornography: Sexual communication vs. the feminist models in light of research findings. In J. Bryant & D. Zillmann (Eds.), *Perspectives on media effects* (pp. 83-108). Hillsdale, NJ: Lawrence Erlbaum.

Malamuth, N., & Check, J. (1981). The effects of mass-media exposure on acceptance of violence against women: A field experiment. *Journal of Research in Personality, 15,* 436-446.

Malamuth, N., & Check, J. (1983). Sexual arousal to rape depictions: Individual differences. *Journal of Abnormal Psychology, 92,* 55-67.

Malamuth, N., Check, J., & Briere, J. (1986). Sexual arousal in response to aggression: Ideological, aggressive, and sexual correlates. *Journal of Personality and Social Psychology, 50,* 330-340.

Malamuth, N., & McIlwraith, B. (1989). Fantasies and exposure to sexually explicit magazines. *Communication Research, 15,* 753-771.

Markham, R., Howie, P., & Hlavacek, S. (1999). Reality monitoring in auditory and visual modalities: Developmental trends and effects of cross-modal imagery. *Journal of Experimental Child Psychology, 72,* 51-70.

Mayer, J. D. (1999). A framework for the study of individual differences in personality formations. In J. A. Singer & P. Salovey (Eds.), *At play in the fields of consciousness: Essays in honor of Jerome L. Singer.* Mahwah, NJ: Lawrence Erlbaum.

McCormick, N. B. (1987). Sexual scripts: Social and therapeutic implications. *Sex and Marital Therapy, 2,* 3-27.

McKenzie-Morh, D., & Zanna, M. (1990). Treating women as sexual objects: Looking to the (gender schematic) male who has viewed pornography.

*Personality and Social Psychology Bulletin, 16,* 296-308.

Morais, R. C. (1999, June 14). Porn goes public. *Forbes Magazine,* p. 214.

Odone, C. (1998, December 18). On television, on billboards, in poetry, at dinner parties, and even on the tube—sex is everywhere. *New Statesman, 127,* 17.

Parents Television Council. (1999, October 7). [Advertisement]. *Los Angeles Times,* p. E4.

Peterson, J. L., Moore, K. A., & Furstenberg, F. F. (1991). Television viewing and early initiation of sexual intercourse: Is there a link? *Journal of Homosexuality, 21,* 93-118.

Pryor, J., LaVite, C., & Stoller, L. (1993). Sexual cognition processes in men high in the likelihood of sexual harassment: The person/situation interaction. *Journal of Vocational Behavior, 42,* 68-83.

Reichert, T. (1999). Cheesecake and beefcake: No matter how you slice it, sexual explicitness in advertising continues to increase. *Journalism & Mass Communication Quarterly, 76,* 7-20.

Reno v. American Civil Liberties Union, S. Ct., No. 96-511 (1997).

Rimal, R. N., Flora, J. A., & Schooler, C. (1999). Achieving improvements in overall health orientation: Effects of campaign exposure, information seeking, and health media use. *Communication Research, 26,* 322-348.

Roberts, D. F. (1982). Television and sexual learning in childhood. In U.S. Department of Health and Human Services, *Television and behavior: Ten years of scientific progress and implications for the eighties* (Vol. 2). Washington, DC: U.S. Government Printing Office.

Roberts, D. F. (1993). Adolescents and the mass media: From "Leave It to Beaver" to "Beverly Hills, 90210." *Teachers College Record, 94,* 629-644.

Shrum, I. J., & O'Guinn, T. C. (1993). Processes and effects in the construction of social reality: Construct accessibility as an explanatory variable. *Communication Research, 20,* 436-471.

Shrum, I. J., O'Guinn, T. C., Semenik, R. J., & Faber, R. J. (1991). Process and effects in the construction of normative consumer beliefs: The role of television. *Advances in Consumer Research, 18,* 755-763.

Shrum, I. J., Wyer, R. S., & O'Guinn, T. C. (1998). Cognitive processes underlying the effects of television consumption. *Journal of Consumer Research, 24,* 447-458.

Silverblatt, A. (1995). *Media literacy: Keys to interpreting media messages.* New York: Praeger.

Singer, J. L., & Salovey, P. (1991). Organized knowledge structures and personality: Person schemas, self-schemas, prototypes, and scripts. In M. J. Horowitz (Ed.), *Person schemas and maladaptive interpersonal patterns* (pp. 37-79). Chicago: University of Chicago Press.

Singer, J. L., & Singer, D. G. (1986). Family experiences and television viewing as predictors of children's imagination, restlessness, and aggression. *Journal of Social Issues, 42,* 107-124.

Singer, J. L., & Singer, D. G. (1998). *Barney & Friends* as entertainment and education: Evaluating the quality and effectiveness of a television series for preschool children. In J. K. Asamen & G. L. Berry (Eds.), *Research paradigms, television, and social behavior* (pp. 305-367). Thousand Oaks, CA: Sage.

Soley, L. C., & Kurzbard, G. (1986). Sex in advertising: A comparison of 1964 and 1984 magazine advertisements. *Journal of Advertising, 15,* 46-54.

Soley, L. C., & Reid, L. N. (1988). Taking it off: Are models in magazine ads wearing less? *Journalism Quarterly, 65,* 960-966.

Stodghill, R. (1998, June 15). Where'd you learn that? *Time,* pp. 52-59.

Strange, J. J., & Leung, C. C. (1999). How anecdotal accounts in news and in fiction can influence judgments of a social problem's urgency, causes, and cures. *Personality and Social Psychology Bulletin, 25,* 436-449.

Strouse, J. S., & Buerkel-Rothfuss, N. (1987). Self-reported media exposure and sexual attitudes and behaviors of college students. *Journal of Sex Education and Therapy, 13,* 43-51.

Strouse, J. S., Buerkel-Rothfuss, N., & Long, E. C. J. (1995). Gender and family as moderators of the relationship between music video exposure and adolescent sexual permissiveness. *Adolescence, 30,* 505-521.

Symons, D. (1979). *The evolution of human sexuality.* Oxford, UK: Oxford University Press.

Troseth, G. L., & DeLoache, J. S. (1998). The medium can obscure the message: Young children's understanding of video. *Child Development, 69,* 950-965.

Ward, L. M. (1995). Talking about sex: Common themes about sexuality in the prime-time television programs children and adolescents watch most. *Journal of Youth and Adolescence, 24,* 595-615.

Weisz, M. G., & Earls, C. M. (1995). The effects of exposure to filmed sexual violence on attitudes towards rape. *Journal of Interpersonal Violence, 10,* 71-84.

Wyer, R. S., & Radvansky, G. A. (1999). The comprehension and validation of social information. *Psychological Review, 106,* 89-118.

Zillmann, D., & Bryant, J. (1988). Effects of prolonged consumption of pornography on family values. *Journal of Family Issues, 9,* 518-544.

CHAPTER **14**

# Sex in the Media

## Theory, Influences, and Solutions

ED DONNERSTEIN
University of California, Santa Barbara

STACY SMITH
Michigan State University

The mass media have been shown to have an influence on a broad range of behaviors and attitudes, including aggression, social stereotyping, prosocial behavior, and social attitudes. The area of aggression has been studied extensively, and, as researchers, we now have a strong theoretical base for drawing conclusions about the impact of exposure to violent media (see Chapters 11 and 12). We seem to have less research, however, on sexual content. This does not imply that there is less concern about the potential effects from exposure to sexual content. In fact, it is quite the opposite. In a major Kaiser Family Foundation report, Huston, Wartella, and Donnerstein (1998) noted that, while research in this area was lacking, there were a number of important reasons to be concerned about the potential influence of sexual media content on children and adolescents. First, children watch a great deal of adult programming, and, as content analysis reveals, there has been a steady increase in the nature of sexual portrayals in the mass media. Second, children and adolescents now have access to a much broader range of media content than they did in the past, especially with the advent of new technologies such as the Internet. More important, according to Huston et al. (1998), sex education or other useful sources of sexual information have not been increasing, thus leaving many children with the mass media or peers for their "sexual education."

In this chapter, we will examine what is known about the role of sexual media content on children's and adolescents' behavior and attitudes. We have divided this chapter into six major sections. The first section focuses on the type of sexual content in the mass media. Understanding the prevalence of sexual content will help illustrate the risk that these portrayals may be posing to viewers. In the second section, we examine what the research community has concluded about the effects of exposure to sexual content. We will find that, unlike the media violence issue, there is a lack of research in this area, which makes specific conclusions difficult. In the third section, we examine intervening variables that may ultimately mediate the influence of sexual media content. We believe that it is important for researchers to consider a range of intervening factors as they begin to formulate studies in this area. Next we look at a number of major theoretical positions that should help us understand why sexual media content could potentially influence children's and adolescents' behaviors and attitudes. In the fifth section, we will examine what we know about Internet access. Although our knowledge base in this area is limited, there are a number of concerns with regard to sexual content that need to be addressed. Finally, we will take a look at various solutions that might be considered in mitigating any undesirable effects from exposure to sexual media content.

## Content Analyses: What Types of Sexual Content Exist?

Increasingly, parents, educators, and policy makers are expressing concern about the amount of sexual content on television. Many are arguing that exposure to talk about sex or sexual behavior on television is having a negative effect on society, especially among adolescents. To illustrate, a recent poll of 1,000 adults conducted by *U.S. News & World Report* revealed that 90% of Americans believe that depictions of sex or references to sex contribute to young people having sex (Impoco et al., 1996). Furthermore, 94% indicated that talk about sex or sexual behaviors on TV lead to violence against women, and 84% stated that such portrayals contribute to extramarital affairs.

Given these concerns, it becomes important to document just how much talk about sex, as well as sexual behavior, is on television. Over the last three decades, several content analyses have taken a close look at the amount and nature of sex on TV (for reviews, see Greenberg & Hofschire, 2000; Huston et al., 1998). In this section, we will first provide an overview of the general trends in sexual content across the entire landscape of television programming. Then we will describe the amount and nature of sexual content in day parts (i.e., prime time) and program genres (i.e., soap operas, music videos, and movies) that are popular with child and adolescent viewers.

### *Entire Landscape*

To date, only one study has examined the amount of sexual content across the entire landscape of American television (Kunkel et al., 1999). Funded by the Kaiser Family Foundation, Dale Kunkel and his colleagues at the University of California, Santa Barbara, assessed the relative frequency and nature of sexual depictions on television. The study is funded biennially so that comparisons of the amount and context of sexual messages on television can be compared reliably over time. The results from the first year of the study were released in February 1999. Given its comprehensiveness and rigor, the study's definition, units of analysis, measures, sample, and results are delineated below.

Conceptually, Kunkel et al. (1999) employed a liberal definition of sex. In particular, sex was defined as "any depiction of sexual activity, sexually suggestive behavior, or talk about sexuality or sexual activity" (p. 8). By using this definition, the authors were able to measure not only different types of sexual behaviors but also the amount of firsthand and/or secondhand conversations about sex on television.

Sex was measured at two distinct levels or units of analysis. The first and most microscopic unit was the scene. A scene was simply a sequence or interaction between characters that did not shift in time or place. Several contextual variables were assessed at this level. For example, the type of sexual behavior (e.g., physical flirting, passionate kissing); the type of talk about sex (e.g., comments about own or other's sexual actions or desires, talk about previous sex, talk about sex crimes, talk toward sex); the degree of explicitness (e.g., provocative dress, disrobing, discreet nudity, nudity); the age and relationship of the characters involved in intercourse; and the presence or absence of alcohol and/or drugs were measured at the scene level.

The second unit of analysis was the program. Program-level contextual measures are important because they capture the nature or way in which sex is framed or treated across the entire unfolding narrative. Several variables were created to assess the extent to which a program strongly emphasized the risks and responsibilities associated with engaging in sexual behavior. The presence or absence of three types of themes was coded: sexual patience (i.e., abstaining from or waiting to have sex for moral, emotional, or health-related reasons), sexual precaution (i.e., the use of or talk about preventive measures to reduce the risk of sexually transmitted diseases [STDs]), and sexual risks and/or negative consequences (i.e., unwanted pregnancy, STDs, AIDS).

In terms of the sample, the researchers randomly sampled and taped a composite week of television content. In explication, programs were randomly drawn from October 1997 to March 1998 across 10 channels from early in the morning until late at night (e.g., 7:00 A.M. to 11:00 P.M.). Five channel types were included in the sample: broadcast (ABC, CBS, NBC, Fox), public broadcasting (PBS), independent (KTLA), basic cable (Lifetime, TNT, USA), and premium cable (HBO). All sports and news programming were excluded from the sample, however. Thus, a total of 16 hours of programming content was sampled per day from 10 channels to build a composite week of more than 1,100 shows.[1]

Overall, the findings show that sex is prevalent on American television. A majority of the programs (56%) featured some form of sexual content.[2] Of these shows, an average of 3.2 sexual scenes were shown per hour. However, a great deal of the "sex" on television is verbal in nature. More than half of the shows in the sample (54%) included "talk about sex," whereas less than a quarter (23%) featured "sexual behavior." These findings suggest that the types of images that Americans are concerned about occur quite frequently across the entire landscape of television.

The results also indicate that certain "types" of sexual talk and behavior are more common on television than others. Out of all the scenes that contained "talk about sex" (*N* = 2,067), two thirds featured comments about people's current or future sexual interests. In addition, 15% of the scenes contained discussions about previous intercourse, 9% included conversations about sex-related crimes, 4% featured talk toward sex, and 2% included expert advice or information about sex.

The most prevalent types of sexual behaviors are "precursory" acts, or those actions leading up to intercourse. For example, half of the scenes featured passionate kissing, 26% physical flirting, and 7% intimate touch. Only 15% of the scenes featuring sexual behavior included intercourse, and those intimate acts were more likely to be implied (12%) rather than shown on-screen (3%). Looking more closely at those scenes featuring intercourse-related acts, 73% of the characters were 25 years in age or older, and nearly half of the characters (47%) were *not* in an established or committed relationship with each other. This latter finding is consistent with other studies revealing that most sexual acts or intercourse-related behaviors on television usually occur between characters who are not married (Fernandez-Collado, Greenberg, Korzenny, & Atkin, 1978; Lowry & Towles, 1989a; Sapolsky, 1982). Finally, very few scenes juxtaposed intercourse-related behaviors with alcohol or drug use (15% and 2%, respectively).

Messages of sexual risk and responsibility are extremely rare on television. Less than 10% of all programs (9%) with any sexual content mentioned the risks and/or responsibilities associated with sexual behavior. Furthermore, only 1% of the shows with any sexual content emphasized strongly throughout the plot a theme of sexual patience, precaution, or risk and responsibility. Of those shows portraying sexual intercourse (implied or depicted), 59% depicted the characters experiencing no consequences of such intimate behavior.

In total, several conclusions can be drawn from the Kunkel et al. (1999) investigation. First, sex is commonplace on television, with talk occurring significantly more frequently than actual behavior. Second, the act of sexual intercourse is rarely shown on television. When intercourse is shown, however, it is more likely to be implied rather than depicted on-screen. Third, the characters who are shown engaging in intercourse are mostly adults and oftentimes are not in committed relationships with their sexual partners. Fourth, very few programs featuring sex emphasize the possibly negative outcomes associated with unprotected or unsafe sexual practices.

### *Prime Time*

Because many of the shows that attract the largest child and adolescent audiences are aired during prime time (Stipp, 1993), researchers have focused on quantifying the prevalence of sexual content in programs airing between 8:00 and 11:00 P.M. (Franzblau, Sprafkin, & Rubinstein, 1977; Kunkel, Cope, & Colvin, 1996; Lowry & Shidler, 1993; Lowry & Towles, 1989a; Sapolsky, 1982; Sapolsky & Taberlet, 1991; Ward, 1995). Despite the fact that many of these investigations have used different measures, several consistent patterns have emerged across the studies' findings.

First, the amount of general sexual content in prime time has increased dramatically over time (Kunkel et al., 1996; Sapolsky, 1982). For example, 43% of all shows that aired during the "family hour" in 1976 contained some form of sexual content. Twenty years later, that figure (75%) has almost doubled (Kunkel et al., 1996). Second, talk about sex is much more frequent in prime time than is sexual behavior (Kunkel et al., 1999; Sapolsky, 1982). For example, Sapolsky (1982) found that verbal references to sex occurred twice as frequently in prime time as sexual behaviors did. Third, the physical act of intercourse is rarely portrayed explicitly on prime time (Lowry & Shidler, 1993; Lowry & Towles, 1989a; Sapolsky, 1982). When intercourse does occur, it is more likely to be verbally referred to or implied rather than depicted on-screen.

Fourth, sexual behaviors usually occur between characters who are not married (Fernandez-Collado et al., 1978; Lowry & Towles, 1989a; Sapolsky, 1982). For instance, Lowry and Shidler (1993) found that heterosexual intercourse (verbal, implied, and physical) and erotic touching were more likely to be shown between unmarried characters than married ones. Finally, the possible life-threatening (HIV/AIDS) or life-altering (pregnancy, STDs) consequences of sexual intercourse are seldom discussed or presented (Kunkel et al., 1999; Lowry & Shidler, 1993; Lowry & Towles, 1989a).

### *Soaps*

Teenage females are attracted to soap opera programming, with *All My Children* and *General Hospital* often drawing the largest audiences (Greenberg & Linsangan, 1993; Greenberg, Linsangan, Soderman, Heeter, Lin, Stanley, & Siemicki, 1993; Greenberg, Stanley, Siemicki, Heeter, Soderman, & Linsangan, 1993; Strasburger, 1995). As a result, it is important to examine the frequency and types of messages about sex young adolescents are being exposed to in such programming. In terms of sheer prevalence, soaps are filled with sexual content. For example, Kunkel et al. (1999) recently found that 85% of soap operas on TV featured some form of sexual content, and almost half showed sexual behavior. Similar to other types of shows, the most frequent types of sexual acts in soap operas are depictions involving unmarried couples and long kisses (Greenberg & Busselle, 1996; Greenberg & D'Alessio, 1985; Heintz-Knowles, 1996; Lowry & Towles, 1989b). Behaviors involving prostitution, petting, and homosexuality are depicted infrequently in this genre.

Has the amount and nature of sex in soaps changed appreciably over time? Greenberg and Busselle (1996) attempted to answer this question by comparing the prevalence and context of sexual messages in episodes of the same soaps in 1985 and 1994. The results revealed that the amount of sexual acts per hour increased 35% between these two points in time (3.7 to 5.0 acts per hour). However, it must be noted that some of this increase is attributable to date-rape story lines that were featured in the sample. Intercourse was more likely to be depicted between unmarried people than married couples at a rate of three incidents to one, which was considerably higher than the rate observed in 1985 (two to one). Sexual intercourse was also being shown increasingly more visually between the two points in time. Indeed, a recent content analysis of a month of episodes from 10 soap operas revealed that sexual behaviors were almost three times as likely to be presented visually than verbally (Heintz-Knowles, 1996).

### *Music Videos*

A majority of adolescents in the United States have access to a variety of music video channels such as Black Entertainment Television (BET), Country Music Television (CMT), Music Television (MTV), the Nashville Network (TNN), and Video Hits-One (VH-1; Kaiser Family Foundation, 1999a; Nielsen Media Research, 1998). Research also reveals that many teens seek out such programming, especially on MTV. For example, a recent report from the Annenberg School of Communication (1997) reveals that 53% of 10- to 17-year-olds surveyed reported viewing MTV. Furthermore, Sun and Lull (1986) surveyed 603 ninth through twelfth graders and found that 80% reported viewing MTV, and, of those, the "average" adolescent watched approximately 2 hours of music videos per day. These figures suggest that music videos are a staple in the media diet of most adolescents.

How much sex are young viewers being exposed to in music videos? (See Chapter 20 for very recent findings.) Generally, studies reveal that music videos feature some form of sexual content (Baxter, De Reimer, Landini, Leslie, & Singletary, 1985; Brown & Campbell, 1986; Seidman, 1992; Sherman & Dominick, 1986; Sommers-Flanagan, Sommers-Flanagan, & Davis, 1993; Vincent, Davis, & Boruszkowski, 1987). For example, Baxter et al. (1985) found that 60% of the music videos in their sample featured sexual content (i.e., feelings or impulses). Sherman and Dominick (1986) found that 76% of 166 concept videos analyzed featured some form of sexual content, at a rate of 4.78 sex acts per video. Research also reveals that the context or way in which sexual content is featured in music videos may contribute to negative effects. More than three fourths (81%) of music videos featuring violence also contain sexual content (Sherman & Dominick, 1986), which heightens the risk of desensitization, as will be illustrated in the next section. When compared with men, women are more likely to be shown wearing provocative clothing (Seidman, 1992), engaging in implicitly sexual behavior (Sommers-Flanagan et al., 1993), and being the targets of aggressive, explicit, or implicit sexual acts (Sommers-Flanagan et al., 1993).

### *Movies*

Given the proliferation of cable, satellite, and VCR technology in the United States, young viewers may have unlimited access to exceedingly graphic and explicit sexual content in R- and X-rated films. One content analysis of popular R-rated films found an average of 17.5 sex acts and 9.8 instances of nudity per film (Greenberg, Siemicki, Dorfman,

Heeter, Stanley, Soderman, & Linsangan, 1993). Females were four times more likely to be shown nude than were males. Greenberg, Siemicki et al. (1993) found that, similar to broadcast television, the most frequent type of sexual activity in R-rated films was intercourse among unmarried characters. Of particular concern is adolescents' exposure to films featuring the mixture of sex and violence. Yang and Linz (1990) found that, although infrequent, the juxtaposition of sex and violence is equally common in R-, X-, and XXX-rated films.

### *Summary*

The focus of this section was to review the prevalence and context of sexual messages on television. The literature review revealed that sex is commonplace across the landscape of American television. For most day parts and program genres, talk about sex is more likely to be portrayed than behavior is, and unmarried characters are more likely than married characters to be shown talking about or engaging in intercourse. Problematically, the risks and responsibilities of sexual intimacy are rarely discussed on television. As such, television continues to present a very sanitized and risk-free message about the potentially life-altering consequences of unprotected intercourse in today's society.

## Effects Studies: Does Viewing Sexual Content Have an Impact?

Given the frequency of sexual depictions on television, the next question to ask is whether exposure to such portrayals influences adolescents' thoughts, attitudes, and behaviors. A recent survey conducted by the Kaiser Family Foundation (1999b) reveals that TV may be an important socializing agent about sex. Of the 13- to 15-year-olds interviewed, almost two thirds (61%) stated that their peers learn "a lot" about issues like sex, drugs, and violence from TV, movies, and other entertainment media. In contrast, less than half (44%) stated learning "a lot" about these topics from schools and teachers, and a little more than a third (38%) reported acquiring "a lot" of information from their mothers. These findings suggest that many teenagers may be turning to the mass media because they do not get enough information about sex at home or in school. In the section that follows, we will examine what research reveals about the effects of media portrayals of sex on youth.

### *Experiments*

To date, only a handful of experiments have been conducted on the impact of sexual talk or images on adolescents (Bryant & Rockwell, 1994; Greenberg, Linsangan, & Soderman, 1993; Greenberg, Perry, & Covert, 1983; Greeson & Williams, 1986). A few of these studies have examined adolescents' learning of information from sexual portrayals. For example, Greenberg et al. (1983) examined the impact of two CBS programs designed to educate boys and girls about sexual facts and feelings. Regarding sex, 5th- and 6th-grade children were assigned to either watch or not watch a show about sexual information (e.g., dating, menstruation, reproduction, physical changes, and intercourse). The results revealed that viewers learned significantly more factual information about sex than did nonviewers.

At least one study suggests that children are also learning sexual facts from fictional entertainment fare. Greenberg, Linsangan, and Soderman (1993) exposed ninth and tenth graders either to a variety of scenes about prostitution and sexual activity among married characters or to a variety of scenes about homosexuality and sexual activity among unmarried characters. All of the clips were taken from soap operas, prime-time dramas, or situation comedies. The results revealed that viewers were significantly more likely than nonviewers to learn the meaning of words and phrases commonly used to refer to sexual activity (e.g., "freebie," "shooting blanks," "getting in a family way") in three domains: homosexuality, prostitution, and married intercourse. Together, these findings suggest that adolescents are attending to and acquiring information about sex from both instructional and entertainment formats.

Other experiments have assessed the impact of sexual portrayals on adolescents' attitudes about sex and sexual issues. For instance, Greeson and Williams (1986) examined the effects of exposure to music videos on seventh and tenth graders' attitudes toward premarital sex. These researchers found that adolescents exposed to music videos were significantly more likely to express approval of teenage premarital sex than were adolescents who were not exposed to such content.

Although these effects are rather short-term in nature, at least one study has documented that massive exposure to sexual messages also can influence adolescents' attitudes about sex. Bryant and Rockwell (1994) were interested in the impact of repeated viewing (3 hours per night for 5 consecutive nights) of sexual content on 13- to 14-year-olds' moral judgments. Adolescents were exposed to a steady diet of either (a) content featuring sexual relations between married characters, (b) segments depicting sexual relations between unmarried characters, or (c) content showing nonsexual relations between adults. Three days to a week after exposure, adolescents viewed a series of scenes, some featuring nonsexual transgressions and others depicting sexual indiscretions. After viewing each clip, the teens made a series of moral evaluations about the content of the segments (i.e., How bad was the depicted behavior? How wronged was the victim?). The results revealed that adolescents exposed to the steady diet of sexual relations between unmarried characters rated sexual scenes of impropriety as significantly less bad than did their peers in the other two conditions. These findings were replicated in a subsequent experiment that included a nonviewing control group. As demonstrated in the previous section, these results are particularly problematic given the fact that the majority of sexual portrayals on television involve unmarried characters (Fernandez-Collado et al., 1978; Lowry & Towles, 1989a; Sapolsky, 1982).

Most of the previous studies have relied on showing adolescents either depictions of talk about sex or very inexplicit portrayals of sexual behavior from broadcast television. Given the fact that nearly 75% of all homes in the United States subscribe to cable programming (Kaiser Family Foundation, 1999a; Nielsen Media Research, 1998), many young teens may have access to a variety of R- and even X-rated films featuring erotic or pornographic content. In fact, Buerkel-Rothfuss, Strouse, Pettey, and Shatzer (1993) found that 63% of the high school students surveyed reported most frequently watching R-rated movies. Brown and Bryant (1989) found that 92% of the 13- to 15-year-olds interviewed reported that they had watched an X-rated film (cf. Strasburger, 1995, p. 53).

For obvious ethical reasons, researchers have not examined the impact of exposure to such depictions on youth. However, a series of studies with adults revealed that viewing sexually explicit content featuring violence (i.e., slasher films) can emotionally desensitize viewers (Linz, Donnerstein, & Penrod, 1988). Linz, Donnerstein, and Penrod (1984) exposed men to a series of sexually violent films over the course of 5 days. Immediately after exposure each day, men's perceptions of and emotional reactions to the films were assessed. When compared to their impressions of the first film, the results showed that the men rated the last film as less violent, experienced fewer negative emotional reactions, and perceived the film to be less degrading to women. Heavy exposure to the films also "spilled over" and influenced men's perceptions of violence in other domains. Subjects exposed to the massive diet of slasher films judged the victim of a violent assault and rape to be significantly less injured than did subjects in a nonviewing control condition. These findings reveal that exposure to the juxtaposition of sex and violence may be a particularly lethal combination for adolescent males who are in the process of developing norms and beliefs about the opposite sex and relational intimacy.

In total, three main conclusions can be drawn from the experimental research. First, teenagers are learning facts about sex from television. Whether adolescents are acquiring knowledge about reproductive processes or are learning the meaning of sexual slang, television can be an effective and powerful agent in the sexual socialization of youth. Second, teenagers' attitudes toward coital behavior are influenced by exposure to sexual content on television. Viewing scenes of pre- or extramarital sex may be having a negative effect on young viewers' attitudes and beliefs about early initiation of intercourse. Third, exposure to the mixture of sex and violence may be desensitizing young viewers. Such depictions may also be teaching male adolescents myths about rape and about the victims of sexual assault. Although the experimental evidence is informative, it still does not address the question of whether viewing sex in the media is related to increases in adolescent intercourse. The answer to this question is the focus of the next section of this chapter.

### *Surveys*

Only a couple of studies have examined the relationship between adolescents' viewing of sexual content on television and their sexual behavior. For example, Brown and Newcomer (1991) were interested in whether the amount of exposure to sexual messages on television was associated with the initaition of coital behavior (p. 79). The researchers found a positive relationship between exposure to "sexy" television content and adolescent intercourse. Stated differently, adolescents exposed to a high proportion of "sexy" television shows were significantly more likely to report having had intercourse than were those exposed to a lower proportion of such programming. Because these findings are based on correlational data, the causal direction between these two variables is impossible to ascertain. It is altogether possible that exposure to sex on television leads to increased acceptance of and desire to engage in premarital intercourse. Alternatively, it is also possible that sexually promiscuous teens are seeking out and watching more television with sexual overtones.

One study has attempted to shed light on the direction of causality between these two variables. Using a longitudinal panel design, Peterson, Moore, and Furstenberg (1991) were interested in whether early viewing of a steady diet of television content was related to teens' subsequent initiation of sexual intercourse a few years later. The results showed that no such relationship exists. That is, early exposure to television in general was not associated with increased self-reports of having had sexual intercourse. These findings must be interpreted with caution, however. Peterson et al.'s (1991) exposure measures were based on parents' reports of their child's viewing patterns. Studies show that parents tend to underestimate children's time spent with and reactions to TV (Cantor & Reilly, 1982; Peterson et al., 1991). Also, the researchers' exposure variable included all forms of television content. Thus, we still do not know whether viewing a steady diet of sexual talk or behavior on television contributes to the early initiation of intercourse among teens.

In total, the goal of this section was to review what we know about the impact of exposure to sexual content on adolescents' thoughts, attitudes, and behaviors. The experimental research shows that viewing sexual content can have a considerable influence on adolescents' sexual learning and attitudes toward intercourse. However, we still know little about the relationship between repeated viewing of sexual content and teens' early initiation of coitus. Clearly, experimental, survey, and longitudinal research is needed to help fully understand how television is contributing to young viewers' sexual socialization.

## Intervening Variables: What Are Factors Mediating Effects?

The impact of sexual messages on adolescents may be influenced by several other factors. That is, the type of content viewed, the type of viewer, and the type of viewing environment may independently and interactively influence how adolescents interpret and ultimately respond to media messages featuring sexual content. In the section that follows, we will review several factors that have been found to mediate or moderate the impact of sexual content on youth.

In terms of content factors, not all sexual portrayals may pose the same risk to viewers. That is, some depictions may *increase* the risk of negative effects, whereas others may actually *decrease* such risks. For example, a program may depict the potentially life-altering or life-threatening consequences associated with unprotected intercourse such as unwanted pregnancies, STDs, and HIV/AIDS. Exposure to such horrific repercussions may inform or remind young viewers about the health risks associated with unsafe sex. In fact, research in the TV violence arena reveals that depicting the negative consequences of violent behavior curbs or reduces the risk of aggression in both children and adults (Bandura, 1965; Wilson et al., 1999). Clearly, research is needed on all those contextual features (i.e., humor, character attractiveness rewards, punishments, consequences, explicitness, realism) of sexual portrayals that may increase or decrease the risk of negative effects.

Viewer variables may also moderate the impact of sexual messages on adolescents. The first characteristic is *age* (Kaiser Family Foundation & Children Now, 1996). Younger adolescents have considerably less knowledge about and real-world experience with sexual issues and events. As a result, younger viewers may have difficulty understanding many of the verbal references to sex that often appear on television. Indeed, Silverman-Watkins and Sprafkin (1983) found that younger adolescents (12-year-olds) were significantly less likely to understand televised sexual innuendos than were their older counterparts (14- and 16-year-olds). These findings suggest that scenes involving talk or jokes about sex may have little impact on younger adolescents.

The second characteristic is *gender.* Girls are more attracted to television content that features story lines about romance and interpersonal relationships. Such story lines are likely to contain talk about sex or sexual behavior. As a result, young females may enjoy watching more inexplicit sexual content on television than their male counterparts. In fact, Greenberg, Linsangan, and Soderman (1993) found that adolescent girls reported liking sexual television content from prime-time and afternoon fare significantly more than adolescent boys did. Given their increased liking, young female viewers may be more susceptible to learning and adopting attitudes about sex that are consistent with those presented in such programming (Strouse, Buerkel-Rothfuss, & Long, 1995; Thompson, Walsh-Childers, & Brown, 1993). Young males, on the other hand, may be more influenced by explicit portrayals of sexual content and the mixture of violence and sex (Linz et al., 1984).

The third characteristic is *perceived realism.* Theory posits and research reveals that realistic depictions typically exert a greater influence on viewers than do unrealistic or fantastic ones (Atkin, 1983; Berkowitz & Rogers, 1986; Huesmann, 1988). It should follow that adolescents' perceived realism of TV sex will also moderate the impact of such portrayals. Teens who perceive sexual depictions on TV to be real may develop unrealistic beliefs and expectations about intercourse. Such unrealistic sexual expectations may cause adolescents to be disappointed with their initial coital experience. Indeed, research has found an inverse relationship between perceived realism of characters' sexual prowess or pleasure and students' satisfaction with their initial coital experience (Baran, 1976). However, it must be noted that a positive relationship has also been observed between students' satisfaction with sexual intercourse and perceptions of the reality of TV sex (Baran, 1976). Given these inconsistent results, additional research is needed to clarify how and when perceived realism of sexual portrayals moderates adolescents' beliefs about intercourse.

Environmental variables may also moderate the effect of sexual messages on adolescents. Perhaps one of the most important is the adolescent's *family environment.* Studies show that children who come from homes with little or dissatisfying parental involvement are more at risk for engaging in early coital behavior (Peterson et al., 1991; Strouse et al., 1995). Yet research also shows that parents who openly communicate and actively coview television content with their children can help to inoculate them from the potentially detrimental effects of exposure. For example, Bryant and Rockwell (1994) found that open family communication and active viewing interactively mitigated the negative effects of massive exposure to 15 hours of pre-, extra-, or nonmarital sexual content on teens' moral judgments.

### *Summary*

In total, the aim of this section was to examine the factors that may mediate or moderate the impact of sexual content on youth. As noted above, content factors, individual difference variables, and environmental influences independently and interactively influence how children interpret and ultimately respond to televised depictions of or references about sex. Surely, more research is needed to fully understand what types of children may be most at risk for engaging in early as well as unsafe sexual intercourse.

## What Theories Might Account for the Influence of the Sexual Media?

Although, overall, the research in the area of sexual media content is somewhat sparse, there are a number of theoretical positions that would suggest that exposure to sexual content could be influential on the behavior and attitudes of viewers. As Comstock and Paik (1991) note, the influence of the mass media is more than just time allocation. According to these authors, the mass media can have significant effects on socialization by providing models that may be emulated or by cultivating beliefs about the world that may later serve as the basis for behavior. The modeling effect can best be explained by social learning theory (i.e., Bandura, 1986). This theory holds that modes of response are acquired either through direct experience or indirectly through the observation of models, like those presented in the mass media. Through the observation of mass media models, the observer comes to learn which behaviors are "appropriate"—that is, which behaviors will later be rewarded and which will be punished. Implicit in this approach is the assumption that most human behavior is voluntarily directed toward attaining some anticipated reward.

Many laboratory studies have demonstrated that children acquire novel behaviors by observing models (e.g., Bandura, 1986). This simple and straightforward approach to mass media effects gained wide acceptance among psychologists. Research in the ensuing years has centered on those variables that facilitate the acquisition of responses through observational learning (Comstock & Paik, 1991). One important factor for predicting when a model will be imitated is the viewer's identification with the actor or actress. Research has supported the notion that children (and adults) are most likely to imitate a model they perceive as having valued characteristics, such as attractiveness or hero status (Huesmann, 1998). Interestingly, research on the effects of media violence on children has revealed that both males and females are likely to identify with male rather than female models, and we should expect similar influences with sexual content.

In the last decade, researchers have taken issue with the idea that social learning theory alone gives a full account of the effects of exposure to the mass media. Berkowitz (Berkowitz & Rogers, 1986) points out that, if observational learning refers to the *lasting* acquisition of novel behavior or new knowledge, many media influences cannot be attributed to such learning. Many media effects appear to be transient and are subject to a "time decay."

Berkowitz has offered an alternative explanation for media effects influenced by theorizing in cognitive psychology. Basically, the explanation is as follows: When people witness an event through the mass media, ideas are activated that, for a short period of time, tend to "prime" or evoke other semantically related thoughts (events that are similar to those being depicted). After an idea is activated, there is a greater likelihood that it and associated thought elements will come to mind again. Since individuals are now thinking of the events they have viewed and relating them to their own experiences, there is a higher probability of behaving in a manner similar to that portrayed in the media. This process of thought activation has been termed a "priming effect." Berkowitz suggests, for instance, that aggressive ideas brought on by viewing violence in the mass media can prime other semantically related thoughts, increasing the probability that they will come to mind. For example, if the viewer observes someone on television being insulted and then this person acts aggressively, the observer might remember a time when he or she was insulted, bringing back into memory feelings of anger. Once these additional thoughts have come to mind, they influence aggressive responding in a variety of ways. There is no reason to expect that sexual content would not act accordingly.

Berkowitz's explanation is appealing because it provides a way of unifying several tangents of mass media research by invoking one relatively simple explanation. As we have noted, the observer's identification with media characters influences the extent to which the observer will mimic observed behavior. This current explanation suggests that viewers who identify with certain actors may be vividly imagining themselves as these characters and may be thinking of themselves as carrying out the depicted actions. Identification with characters in the mass media should activate high imagery thoughts, and the subsequent priming of these ideas might influence subsequent behavior. Given the attractiveness of most characters engaged in sexual behavior and the sexual "curiosity" of young viewers, we could imagine that the effects for sexual content could potentially be greater than those for violent media.

Traditional social learning theory has demonstrated that the audience's willingness to imitate someone is greatly influenced by the outcomes experienced by models. It is as if viewers draw a lesson from what they see: "What happens on the screen might also happen to me if I engage in the same behavior." Berkowitz's reformulation suggests that, rather than learning a lesson, observers who witness the consequences of another's actions recall other occasions in which the same outcome occurred. With this outcome now in mind, viewers might overestimate the frequency and probability of the same type of consequence actually occurring to them. Thus, observing desirable consequences for a given behavior may increase viewers' willingness to perform that kind of behavior themselves. As we have seen from the section on content analysis, positive outcomes for sexual behaviors are quite often the norm. From either the modeling or the cognitive theoretical perspective, these behaviors, particularly when performed by models one can identify with, have a high likelihood of being emulated.

Another set of ideas used to account for the impact of the mass media can be grouped under the rubric of "cultivation effects." Initially developed by George Gerbner (Gerbner, Gross, Morgan, & Signorielli, 1994), cultivation theory presumes that extensive exposure to the mass media shapes our perceptions of social reality. Indeed, research has shown that heavy viewers tend to have a perception of social reality that "matches" or reflects the one presented on television. When compared with light viewers of television, heavy viewers tend to see the world as a more crime-ridden and dangerous place and tend to be more fearful of walking alone in their own neighborhoods. Cultivation theory has also been used to explain our perceptions and stereotypes about gender, race, and other conceptions that are often presented in a stereotypic manner on TV. On the basis of these trends, heavy viewers' perceptions, beliefs, and attitudes about sexuality should also be strongly influenced by media portrayals of sex.

### *Summary*

Together, three theories suggest that exposure to sexual depictions in the mass media may have an impact on adolescents. Social learning posits that mass media characters serve as potent role models to learn about sexual issues and events. Priming, on the other hand, provides a cognitive explanation of the short-term impact of sexual images on youth. Cultivation theory focuses on the long-term influence that heavy viewing of sexual content may be having on youngsters' beliefs about social reality.

## The Internet: New Technology and New Access

Unlike traditional media such as TV, radio, and recorded music, the Internet gives children and adolescents access to just about any form of sexual content they can find. For the first time, these individuals will be able (with some work) to have the ability to view almost any form of sexual behavior. Unlike in years past, this can be done in the privacy of their own room with little parental knowledge. A recent Time/CNN survey of teenagers ("Raising Our Kids Online," 1999) reveals some interesting findings on the use of and concerns about the Internet among this age group: (a) 82% use the Internet, (b) 75% believe that the Internet was very or somewhat responsible for the school shooting in Colorado, (c) 44% have seen X-rated content, and (d) 62% say parents know little or nothing about the websites they visit. This same poll shows that, in 1998, 17 million 2- to 18-year-olds were on-line. It is expected that in 5 years this figure will grow to roughly 42 million.

For decades, parents and others have been concerned about the potentially "harmful" influences of exposure to sexual media content. The major difference today, compared with those concerns in the past, is a technology that children and adolescents are often more sophisticated in and knowledgeable about than their parents. Too often we hear of computer-phobic adults who posses little knowledge of this expanding technology. Such resistance to the technology, combined with a limited knowledge base, will make solutions to potential problems like easy access to sexual images even more difficult. Furthermore, when policy and advocacy groups attempt to inform parents about the Internet, we would argue that it does little good to tell them to contact *www.hereforhelp.com* when they are often ignorant about these terms and World Wide Web usages.

### *The Internet: What Is It?*

Very often, we refer to the Internet more generally as the Net. This expanding technology is simply a vast group of computer networks linked around the world. It has a number of various components familiar (at least in terminology) to most of us that have the ability to deliver sexual messages:

1. E-mail for electronic communication, in which phone numbers and photographs can be exchanged
2. Bulletin board systems for posting of information
3. Chat rooms that can be used for real-time posting and conversations (once

again, the ability to exchange personal information such as addresses is readily available)

4. The World Wide Web, which combines visuals, sound, and text together in a manner that allows linkages across many sites that are related to a particular topic (these topics obviously can be those related to sex such as pornography or bestiality)

It is important to note that we take the position that the Web, and other Internet components, are extremely beneficial and educational. As with any new technological advance, Internet will have some "downsides." However, the potential drawbacks of Internet use should not supercede the vast usefulness of Web information as a resoruce for learning.

### *Concerns About the Net*

Of greatest concern is sexual content or exploitation targeting children. Such material ranges from photographs to the Net equivalent of "phone sex," sometimes with a live video connection. Sending of sexual information over e-mail or posting on bulletin boards by those targeting children has been a long-term issue. Adult websites that feature "hard core" sexual depictions are of equal concern.

Highly sophisticated search engines, such as Lycos, will allow the user to type in words and word combinations that will ask the computer to search for almost any sexual content. Even if an adult site is accessed, it is not "officially" blocked to minors unless certain blocking software is implemented (which often is not entirely effective). Most sexually explicit adult sites will merely indicate (a) that the site contains sexually explicit pictures, (b) that it may be offensive to viewers, and (c) that the viewer must be at least 18 years of age, and if not they must exit the site immediately. Needless to say, there are probably a high percentage of sexually curious adolescents, and even children, who will simply click their mouse and indicate they are of age and enter the adult site. Once within one of these sites, the viewer will be able to link into other similar sites offering samples of pictures, text, and video of a "hard core" sexual nature.

In many ways, one has to search for the sexual sites. It is true that search engines exist to help, but the usual Internet user is not going to come in contact with inappropriate content without making a conscious decision to find these sites. However, in recent years it has become known that certain adult sites have used address codes that are quite similar to popular Internet websites, oftentimes leading the user unknowingly into an area he or she did not wish to visit. For example, if children are looking for information about the White House and type *www.whitehouse.com* instead of *www.whitehouse.gov* (not an unlikely mistake), they will find themselves linked to an adult website. While some might consider these typing "errors" intentional on the part of the adult websites, they can be averted with careful monitoring and by bookmarking these well-known educational sites. In addition, as we will discuss below, certain blocking software can reduce the possibility of unwanted or accidental access.

It is important for us to note that there is a strong need for research in this area. Unlike our knowledge of other media systems such as TV, we are only beginning to explore the usage, content, and effects of Internet access among children. The Kaiser Family Foundation report on sexual media content (Huston et al., 1998) called for the start of systematic research into these areas. We believe that this is essential given preliminary surveys on children's use of and access to the Internet and the availability of sexual content.

## Possible Solutions to Mitigate the Harmful Effects of Sexual Content

We take the position that the effects of viewing sexual content in the mass media can be mitigated. In an examination of the psychological research, we find that educational efforts in terms of media literacy/critical viewing and media-initiated programs can be effective. In this section, we would like to note these alternatives to governmental and industry regulations (i.e., the V-chip and TV ratings) as a solution to the problem. Although many of these solutions are currently being applied within the media violence area, they are, we believe, potentially effective for sexual content as well.

### Critical Viewing

Children can be taught "critical viewing skills" by parents and in schools so that they learn to better interpret what they see in the media (e.g., Huston et al., 1998). For example, children can learn to distinguish between fictional portrayals and factual presentations. In addition, children can be taught to recognize ways in which sexual behaviors may be portrayed unrealistically (e.g., when it is portrayed without any negative consequences). Children can also learn to think about alternatives to those portrayed, a strategy that is particularly effective when an adult viewing with the child expresses his or her opinion (see Chapter 38).

In addition, a large number of professional organizations concerned with the well-being of children and families (e.g., the American Academy of Pediatrics, the American Medical Association, and the American Psychological Association) have recommended that professionals take a more active role in reducing the potential impact of media. Research on intervention programs has indicated that we can reduce some of the impact of the media by "empowering" parents in their roles as monitors of children's television viewing. For example, in studies concerned with media violence, parents who view programs with their children and discuss the realities of violence, as well as alternatives to aggressive behaviors in conflict situations, can actually reduce the negative impact (i.e., increased aggressiveness) of media violence (Donnerstein, Slaby, & Eron, 1994). A number of programs are currently being developed by researchers to be used by parents in their interactions with children during the viewing of television (Strasburger, 1993). One would hope that parents and children can have more open and honest discussions of sexuality.

### Media Initiatives

Another educational resource is the mass media themselves. Professionally produced educational movies that are also designed to be entertaining have great potential for informing the public and, under some conditions, might even change attitudes and behaviors. An example is in the area of mass media sexual violence, which research has demonstrated can have an antisocial impact. In September 1990, NBC aired a made-for-TV movie about the trauma and aftermath of acquaintance rape. This program, titled *She Said No,* was featured during prime-time hours and attracted a large audience. *She Said No* also received critical acclaim, winning an award from American Women in Radio and Television for its realistic portrayal of the plight of a rape victim. An evaluation of the effectiveness of this movie was undertaken by Wilson, Linz, Donnerstein, and Stipp (1992). The study measured whether exposure to this movie would decrease acceptance of rape myths and/or increase awareness of date rape as a serious social problem.

The study employed a total of 1,038 adults, randomly selected from four locations in the United States, who were assigned to view or not view *She Said No* over a closed-circuit channel, prior to the network broadcast of the film. Individuals from this representative sample were randomly assigned to view or not view the made-for-TV movie in their own home—a more naturalistic viewing environment than is achieved in most media experiments. The viewers and nonviewers were contacted the next day and asked about acceptance of rape myths and perceptions of rape as a social problem.

The results of this study indicated that the television movie was a useful tool in educating and altering perceptions about date rape. Specifically, exposure to the movie increased awareness of date rape as a social problem across all viewers, independent of gender or age. The movie also had a prosocial effect on older females, who, compared with older women who did not view the movie, were less likely to attribute blame to women in date-rape situations after exposure.

### *The Internet*

In thinking about solutions to children's and adolescents' access to inappropriate Internet content, there are possible considerations in addition to those mentioned above. The first would be government regulation, in which laws are passed restricting the content. The second would be technology itself through blocking software and some form of rating system. Finally, there is parental supervision.

#### *Government Regulation*

In the United States, the First Amendment protects offensive speech from censorship, including sexually explicit materials. In general, the U.S. courts have struck down most content restrictions on books, magazines, and films. There are, of course, exceptions, such as "obscenity," child pornography, and certain types of indecent material depending on the time, place, and manner of the presentation. In 1996, Congress passed a bill to deal specifically with Internet content regulation known as the Communications Decency Act.

The Supreme Court ruled on the Communications Decency Act and, as expected, held it to be unconstitutional and an infringement on freedom of speech. Likewise, other courts have noted that service providers, such as America Online, cannot be held liable for the sending of pornographic materials over the Internet. It is obvious that the courts are well aware that government regulation in this area would be difficult or near impossible given not only the vastness of materials available but also the global scope of the Internet.

#### *Blocking Technology*

One potential solution has been the development of software that is designed to block unwanted sites. This blocking software can block known adult sites, for instance, or any site containing predetermined words such as *sex, gambling,* and other unwanted content. There are a number of these types of software available that perform these and other functions.

It should be remembered that none of these blocking systems is completely effective. The Web changes quite rapidly, and software designed for today may not be entirely appropriate tomorrow. In one recent test of the effectiveness of blocking adult sites ("A Parent's Guide to Cyberspace," 1997), it was found that one program was able to block out 18 of 22 selected sites but another program blocked none. Other programs were able to block about half the adult sites. Furthermore, those blocking e-mail or chat-room communications were often defeated by either transposing letters or renaming the Web browser on the hard disk.

#### *The Role of Parents*

The role of parents in working with their children and becoming familiar with this technology is critical. Parents can monitor their children's access and have discussions about the types of content they have encountered. Children can be taught "critical viewing skills" in their schools and by their parents so that they learn to better interpret what they encounter on television and the Web (e.g., Singer, Singer, Desmond, Hirsch, & Nicol, 1988).

The Internet is a technology that will become more accessible worldwide over the years and will only improve in its capacity to stimulate and enrich our lives. As with any new technology, we need to understand its potential for increasing our children's educational opportunities, while at the same time recognizing its limitations.

## Summary and Conclusions

It would be safe to conclude that the mass media are contributors to a number of antisocial behaviors and health-related problems in children, adolescents, and adults. We discussed in the previous section a number of ways in which media effects can be mitigated. We would like to note that a number of other suggestions might also be effective.

In their report for the National Television Violence Study, Wilson et al. (1998) suggested a number of recommendations for the media industry, policy makers, and parents as a means of confronting the problem of media violence. We would like to suggest some of these recommendations once again but with respect to sexual content. For the media industry, the following can be recommended:

- Produce more programs that show positive sexual content.
- Be creative in showing more sexual content that may have consequences (e.g., STDs) and more depictions that focus on nonrisky sexual behaviors (e.g., the use of condoms).
- Ensure that ratings for sexuality on television and in the movies take into account the context of the portrayals.

In considering those who recommend and make policy in the area of the mass media, the following are offered:

- Continue to monitor the nature and extent of sexuality on television.
- Recognize that context is an essential aspect of media depictions of sex, and rely on scientific evidence to identify the context features that pose the most risk.
- Ensure that television program ratings accurately convey to parents the risks associated with different types of sexual portrayals.

And, finally, for parents, the authors of the National Television Violence Study recommended the following, which we adapt for sexual content:

- Be aware of the potential risks associated with viewing televised portrayals of sex (e.g., learning, cultivation).
- Consider the context of sexual depictions in making viewing decisions for children.
- Consider a child's developmental level when making viewing decisions.

We consider these to be viable and realistic recommendations because they are based on a knowledge base supported by scientific research. We suggest that stronger reliance be placed on educational and media interventions specifically directed to changing beliefs about sexuality. Our ever-increasing knowledge of media effects, attitude formation and change, child development, and human behavior positions researchers as a force in the solution to the problem of exposure to mass media sexual content.

## Notes

1. Kunkel et al.'s sample also included an oversample of prime-time programming. Specifically, these researchers randomly sampled 2 additional weeks of television shows from the broadcast networks (ABC, NBC, CBS, and Fox).

2. All of the analyses exclude children's programming.

## References


A parent's guide to cyberspace. (1997, May). *Consumer Reports,* pp. 44-50.

Annenberg School of Communication. (1997). *Television in the home: The 1997 survey of parents and children, 2.* Philadelphia, PA: Author.

Atkin, C. (1983). Effects of realistic TV violence vs. fictional violence on aggression. *Journalism Quarterly, 60,* 615-621.

Bandura, A. (1965). Influence of models' reinforcement contingencies on the acquisition of imitative responses. *Journal of Personality and Social Psychology, 1,* 589-595.

Bandura, A. (1986). *Social foundations of thought and action: A social cognitive theory.* Englewood Cliffs, NJ: Prentice Hall.

Baran, S. J. (1976). Sex on TV and adolescent sexual-image. *Journal of Broadcasting, 20,* 61-68.

Baxter, R. L., De Riemer, C., Landini, A., Leslie, L., & Singletary, M. W. (1985). A content analysis of music videos. *Journal of Broadcasting and Electronic Media, 29,* 333-340.

Berkowitz, L., & Rogers, K. H. (1986). A priming effect analysis of media influences. In J. Bryant & D. Zillmann (Eds.), *Perspectives on media effects* (pp. 57-82). Hillsdale, NJ: Lawrence Erlbaum.

Brown, D., & Bryant, J. (1989). Uses of pornography. In D. Zillmann & J. Bryant (Eds.), *Pornography: Research advances and policy considerations* (pp. 3-24). Hillsdale, NJ: Lawrence Erlbaum.

Brown, J. D., & Campbell, K. (1986). Race and gender in music videos: The same beat but a different drummer. *Journal of Communication, 36,* 94-106.

Brown, J. D., & Newcomer, S. F. (1991). Television viewing and adolescents' sexual behavior. *Journal of Homosexuality, 21,* 77-91.

Bryant, J., & Rockwell, S. C. (1994). Effects of massive exposure to sexually oriented prime-time television programming on adolescents' moral judgment. In D. Zillmann, J. Bryant, & A. C. Huston (Eds.), *Media, children, and the family: Social scientific, psychodynamic, and clinical perspectives* (pp. 183-196). Hillsdale, NJ: Lawrence Erlbaum.

Buerkel-Rothfuss, N. L., Strouse, J. S., Pettey, G., & Shatzer, M. (1993). Adolescents' and young adults' exposure to sexually oriented and sexually explicit media. In B. S. Greenberg, J. D. Brown, & N. Buerkel-Rothfuss (Eds.), *Media, sex, and the adolescent* (pp. 99-113). Cresskill, NJ: Hampton Press.

Cantor, J., & Reilly, S. (1982). Adolescents' fright reactions to television and films. *Journal of Communication, 32*(1), 87-99.

Comstock, G., & Paik, H. (1991). *Television and the American child.* New York: Academic Press.

Donnerstein, E., Slaby, R. G., & Eron, L. D. (1994). The mass media and youth aggression. In L. D. Eron, J. H. Gentry, & P. Schlegel (Eds.), *Reason to hope: A psychosocial perspective on violence and youth* (pp. 219-250). Washington, DC: American Psychological Association.

Fernandez-Collado, C. F., Greenberg, B. S., Korzenny, F., & Atkin, C. (1978). Sexual intimacy and drug use in TV series. *Journal of Communication, 28,* 30-37.

Franzblau, S., Sprafkin, J. N., & Rubinstein, E. A. (1977). Sex on TV: A content analysis. *Journal of Communication, 27*(2), 164-170.

Gerbner, G., Gross, L., Morgan, M., & Signorielli, N. (1994). Growing up with television: The cultivation perspective. In J. Bryant & D. Zillmann (Eds.), *Media effects* (pp. 17-41). Hillsdale, NJ: Lawrence Erlbaum.

Greenberg, B. S., & Busselle, R. W. (1996). Soap operas and sexual activity: A decade later. *Journal of Communication, 46*(4), 153-161.

Greenberg, B. S., & D'Alessio, D. (1985). Quantity and quality of sex in the soaps. *Journal of Broadcasting and Electronic Media, 29,* 309-321.

Greenberg, B. S., & Linsangan, R. (1993). Gender differences in adolescents' media use, exposure to sexual content, and parental mediation. In B. S. Greenberg, J. D. Brown, & N. Buerkel-Rothfuss (Eds.), *Media, sex, and the adolescent* (pp. 134-144). Cresskill, NJ: Hampton Press.

Greenberg, B. S., Linsangan, R., & Soderman, A. (1993). Adolescents' reactions to television sex. In B. S. Greenberg, J. D. Brown, & N. Buerkel-Rothfuss (Eds.), *Media, sex, and the adolescent* (pp. 196-224). Cresskill, NJ: Hampton Press.

Greenberg, B. S., Linsangan, R., Soderman, A., Heeter, C., Lin, C., Stanley, C., & Siemicki, M. (1993). Adolescents' exposure to television and movie sex. In B. S. Greenberg, J. D. Brown, & N. Buerkel-Rothfuss (Eds.), *Media, sex, and the adolescent* (pp. 61-98). Cresskill, NJ: Hampton Press.

Greenberg, B. S., Perry, K. L., & Covert, A. M. (1983). The body human: Sex education, politics, and television. *Family Relations, 32,* 419-425.

Greenberg, B. S., Siemicki, M., Dorfman, S., Heeter, C., Stanley, C., Soderman, A., & Linsangan, R. (1993). Sex content in R-rated films viewed by adolescents. In B. S. Greenberg, J. D. Brown, & N. Buerkel-Rothfuss (Eds.), *Media, sex, and the adolescent* (pp. 45-58). Cresskill, NJ: Hampton Press.

Greenberg, B. S., Stanley, C., Siemicki, M., Heeter, C., Soderman, A., & Linsangan, R. (1993). Sex content on soaps and prime-time television series most viewed by adolescents. In B. S. Greenberg, J. D. Brown, & N. Buerkel-Rothfuss (Eds.), *Media, sex, and the adolescent* (pp. 29-44). Cresskill, NJ: Hampton Press.

Greenberg, B. S., & Hofschire, L. (2000). Sex on entertainment television. In D. Zillmann & P. Vorderer (Eds.), *Media entertainment: The psychology of its appeal* (pp. 93-112). Hillsdale, NJ: Lawrence Erlbaum.

Greeson, L. E., & Williams, R. A. (1986). Social implications of music videos for youth: An analysis of the content and effects of MTV. *Youth & Society, 18*(2), 177-189.

Heintz-Knowles, K. E. (1996). *Sexual activity on daytime soap operas: A content analysis of five weeks of television programming.* Menlo Park, CA: Kaiser Family Foundation.

Huesmann, L. R. (1988). An information-processing model for the development of aggression. *Aggressive Behavior, 14,* 13-24.

Huesmann, L. R. (1998). The role of social information processing and cognitive schema in the acquisition and maintenance of habitual aggressive behavior. In R. G. Geen & E. Donnerstein (Eds.), *Human aggression* (pp. 73-110). San Diego, CA: Academic Press.

Huston, A. C., Wartella, E., & Donnerstein, E. (1998). *Measuring the effects of sexual content in the media: A report to the Kaiser Family Foundation.* Menlo Park, CA: Kaiser Family Foundation.

Impoco, J., Bennefield, R. M., Pollack, K., Bierck, R., Schmidt, K., & Gregory, S. (1996, April 15). TV's frisky family values. *U.S. News & World Report,* pp. 58-62.

Kaiser Family Foundation. (1999a, November). *Kids and media at the new millennium.* Menlo Park, CA: Author.

Kaiser Family Foundation. (1999b, March). *Kids ready to talk about today's tough issues before their parents are: Sex, AIDS, violence, and drugs/alcohol* [On-line]. Available: www.kff.org/content/archive/1460/kids_cp.html

Kaiser Family Foundation & Children Now. (1996). *The family hour focus groups: Children's responses to sexual content on TV and their parents' reactions.* Menlo Park and Oakland, CA: Authors.

Kunkel, D., Cope, K. M., & Colvin, C. (1996). *Sexual messages on family hour television: Content and context.* Menlo Park and Oakland, CA: Children Now and the Henry J. Kaiser Family Foundation.

Kunkel, D., Cope, K. M., Maynard Farinola, W. J., Biely, E., Rollin, E., & Donnerstein, E. (1999). *Sex on TV.* Menlo Park, CA: Kaiser Family Foundation.

Linz, D., Donnerstein, E., & Penrod, S. (1984). The effects of multiple exposures to filmed violence against women. *Journal of Communication, 34*(3), 130-147.

Linz, D., Donnerstein, E., & Penrod, S. (1988). Effects of long-term exposure to violent and sexually degrading depictions of women. *Journal of Personality and Social Psychology, 55,* 758-768.

Lowry, D. T., & Shidler, J. A. (1993). Prime time TV portrayals of sex, "safe sex," and AIDS: A longitudinal analysis. *Journalism Quarterly, 70*(3), 628-637.

Lowry, D. T., & Towles, D. E. (1989a). Prime time TV portrayals of sex, conception, and venereal disease. *Journalism Quarterly, 66,* 347-352.

Lowry, D. T., & Towles, D. E. (1989b). Soap opera portrayals of sex, contraception, and sexually transmitted diseases. *Journal of Communication, 39*(2), 76-83.

Nielsen Media Research. (1998). *1998 report on television.* New York: Author.

Peterson, J. L., Moore, K. A., & Furstenberg, F. F. (1991). Television viewing and early initiation of sexual intercourse: Is there a link? *Journal of Homosexuality, 21,* 93-118.

Raising our kids online. (1999, May 10). *Time,* p. 42.

Sapolsky, B. (1982). Sexual acts and references on prime time TV: A two year look. *Southern Speech Communication Journal, 47,* 212-226.

Sapolsky, B. S., & Taberlet, J. O. (1991). Sex in prime time television: 1979 vs. 1989. *Journal of Broadcasting and Electronic Media, 35,* 505-516.

Seidman, S. A. (1992). An investigation of sex-role stereotyping in music videos. *Journal of Broadcasting and Electronic Media, 36,* 209-216.

Sherman, B. L., & Dominick, J. R. (1986). Violence and sex in music videos: TV and rock 'n' roll. *Journal of Communication, 36,* 79-93.

Silverman-Watkins, L. T., & Sprafkin, J. N. (1983). Adolescents' comprehension of televised sexual innuendos. *Journal of Applied Developmental Psychology, 4,* 359-369.

Singer, J. L., Singer, D. G., Desmond, R., Hirsch, B., & Nicol, A. (1988). Family mediation and children's cognition, aggression, and comprehension of television: A longitudinal study. *Journal of Applied Developmental Psychology, 9,* 329-347.

Sommers-Flanagan, R., Sommers-Flanagan, J., & Davis, B. (1993). What's happening on music television? A gender role content analysis. *Sex Roles, 28,* 745-753.

Stipp, H. (1993). The challenge to improve television for children: A new perspective. In G. L. Berry & J. K. Asamen (Eds.), *Children and television: Images in a changing sociocultural world* (pp. 296-302). Thousand Oaks, CA: Sage.

Strasburger, V. (1993). Children, adolescents, and the media: Five crucial issues. In V. C. Strasburger & G. A. Comstock (Eds.), *Adolescent medicine: State of the art reviews* (Vol. 4, no. 3). Philadelphia, PA: Hanley & Belfus.

Strasburger, V. (1995). *Adolescents and the media: Medical and psychological impact.* Thousand Oaks, CA: Sage.

Strouse, J. S., Buerkel-Rothfuss, N., & Long, E. C. J. (1995). Gender and family as moderators of the relationship between music video exposure and adolescent sexual permissiveness. *Adolescence, 30*(119), 505-521.

Sun, S. W., & Lull, J. (1986). The adolescent audience for music videos and why they watch. *Journal of Communication, 36,* 115-125.

Thompson, M., Walsh-Childers, K., & Brown, J. D. (1993). The influence of family communication patterns and sexual experience on processing of a movie video. In B. S. Greenberg, J. D. Brown, & N. Buerkel-Rothfuss (Eds.), *Media, sex, and the adolescent* (pp. 248-263). Cresskill, NJ: Hampton Press.

Vincent, R. C., Davis, D. K., & Boruszkowski, L. A. (1987). Sexism on MTV: The portrayal of women in rock videos. *Journalism Quarterly, 64,* 750-755, 941.

Ward, L. M. (1995). Talking about sex: Common themes about sexuality in the prime-time television programs children and adolescents view most. *Journal of Youth and Adolescence, 24,* 595-615.

Wilson, B. J., Kunkel, D., Linz, D., Potter, W. J., Donnerstein, E., Smith, S. L., Blumenthal, E., & Berry, M. (1998). Violence in television programming overall: University of California, Santa Barbara study. In *National Television Violence Study* (Vol. 2, pp. 3-204). Newbury Park, CA: Sage.

Wilson, B. J., Linz, D., Donnerstein, E., & Stipp, H. (1992). The impact of social issue television programming on attitudes toward rape. *Human Communication Research, 19,* 179-208.

Wilson, B. J., Linz, D., Federman, J., Smith, S. L., Paul, B., Nathanson, A., Donnerstein, E., & Lingsweiler, R. (1999). *The choices and consequences evaluation: A study of Court TV's anti-violence curriculum.* Santa Barbara: University of California, Santa Barbara, Center for Communication and Social Policy.

Yang, N., & Linz, D. (1990). Movie ratings and the content of adult videos: The sex-violence ratio. *Journal of Communication, 40*(2), 28-42.

CHAPTER **15**

# Mass Media and Identity Development

NINA HUNTEMANN
MICHAEL MORGAN
University of Massachusetts Amherst

Scholarship on child development and the media is premised on the notion that the availability of mass media, particularly television, marks childhood as a fundamentally different phenomenon today than in previous generations. Especially in industrialized societies, the vast majority of children born since 1960 have grown up in households in which the television is on for many hours a day, every day. Today's children—and most of their parents—have never known a world without TV. The extensive role television plays in the daily lives of children and adolescents is bolstered by other, complementary media such as films and magazines, and its impact is deepened by the explosions of newer technologies (e.g., cable, VCRs, satellites, computer games, and the Internet). All together, the massive flow of popular images, representations, and symbolic models disseminated by the media profoundly shapes what young people think about the world and how they perceive themselves in relation to it.

This chapter explores the role mass media play in the process of identity development and suggests areas for further research. The pervasiveness of the media, and the extent to which their stories permeate family life, peer interaction, and the entire process of growing up, means that young people today have far more vicarious (yet vivid and "realistic") experiences of other people and roles than ever before. The media provide an extraordinary quantity of examples of different types of people behaving in different types of ways in different types of situations. Yet just under the surface of this vast flow of images lie systematic patterns of inclusion and exclusion, of conventions and stereotypes, reflecting ideology and social power.

All this has significant implications for young people struggling to forge a sense of identity. Since its invention about a hundred years ago, "adolescence" has never been an easy period emotionally, socially, or physically; arguably, at the dawn of the twenty-first century, it is more complex and challenging than ever before. To Erikson (1959, 1968), the successful transition from adolescence to adulthood depends on the formation of a coherent sense of identity, which is not an easy task. The popular media offer attractive avenues to ease the difficult and disturbing tensions of this developmental stage—broadly shared definitions of taste, style, values, models of personalities and roles, signposts for identities. The fact that what they provide are *mediated representations* is not in itself especially important in this context; it matters little whether young people perceive such images as true or false, as realistic or fictional. Every exposure to every media model provides a potential guide to behavior or attitude, a potential source of identification, a human exemplar we may use—whether in accordance with the model or explicitly contrary to it, and whether consciously or not—to define and construct our identities.

## What Is Identity?

Before we can consider the media's contribution to identity development, we should first discuss just what we mean by "identity." "Identity" is by no means a new concept, but in recent years it has taken on new levels of social, political, and psychological importance, and complex new layers of meaning. When we use the term *identity* in everyday conversation, the word seems reasonably clear and unambiguous. As with so many concepts, on the other hand, when it's placed under the lens of academic scrutiny, it becomes a slippery, problematic, and even contradictory notion. (Unfortunately, the term is notably absent from Raymond Williams's 1976 book *Keywords,* an exploration of the diverse social and cultural meanings that swirl around such "simple, everyday" words as *behavior, family, critical, individual, personality,* and many others.)

Commonly, we tend to think of "identity" as something that resides somewhere within an individual, some profound and all-encompassing sense of the self that remains relatively fixed and stable once it is attained, recognized, or discovered. One may "discover" one's identity by maturation, deep introspection, and "soul searching." Yet, somewhat paradoxically, identity may be externally and socially defined; one may "adopt" an identity by virtue of identification with a person or group. There is thus a curious tension between the personal and social aspects of identity, because it is partly informed by elements of both personality and social role. Although it is assumed that identity constitutes what makes someone "unique" (every identity is presumably different from every other identity; it is seen as something deep and ineffable and personal), it can be powerfully associated with our membership (or lack of membership) in some group, religion, or nationality. Along these lines, Tajfel (1978) developed an elaborate theoretical framework for studying "social identity" as something distinct from one's "personal identity" based on traits, appearance, and so on (see also Robinson, 1996). Identity therefore requires both individuation and social relatedness (Josselson, 1980).

There are familiar images from fables and myths, as well as examples from everyday life, of being "in search of" one's identity, trying to solve the puzzle of "who I really am." Succeeding in this quest is defined as essential; being "without" an identity or having an "identity crisis" (an allegedly common ailment during adolescence) is an unenviable status. Yet this is by no means easy to resolve. As Ezra Pound put it, "The real meditation is . . . the meditation on one's identity. Ah, voilà une chose!! You try it. You try finding out why you're you and not somebody else. And who in the blazes are you anyhow? Ah, voilà une chose!" (as cited in *Your Ultimate Quotation Center,* 1999).

Identity is coveted and contested; we demand the right to determine our own. When Susan Faludi (1991) argues that feminism "asks that women be free to define themselves—instead of having their identity defined for them, time and again, by their culture and their men" (p. xxiii), she is drawing on a notion of identity as a mechanism of social control. For one group to impose "identity" on another, in effect forcing a group to internalize others' demands for their exploitation, constitutes an extraordinarily powerful form of hegemony. On the other hand, those who resist such domination are often accused of engaging in "identity politics."

Ultimately, "identity"—as a sense of our subjective personhood—is not a fixed, internal phenomenon. Rather, it is a dynamic, shifting, continuous, sociocultural *process.* Identity is fluid, partly situational, and thus constantly under construction, negotiation, and modification. As a process, it is actively constructed as it is expressed—and vice versa.

Thus, identity is multidimensional. It is defined, shaped, and transformed by a vast range of factors: physical, sexual, emotional, religious, racial, ethnic, institutional, familial, and more. At some time or place, it may privilege personal descriptors or qualities: "fat," "funny," "clever," "unartistic," "nervous," "sociable," "athletic," or thousands more. It may be strongly shaped by diverse sociodemographic characteristics (some of which are more straightforward, stable, or changeable than others), including gender, age, class, religion, ethnicity, nationality, or race. It may also overlap with whatever social role we happen to be playing at any given moment—mother, nephew, student, shopper, team member, stamp collector, airline passenger, voter, and so on.

Components of identity reflect and result from social interactions with family, friends, peers, authorities, and others, as well as from mass media images and values. Indeed, since the media influence how people treat us, as clusters of demographic and cultural characteristics, social interactions are in part informed by the shared understandings or stereotypes about people that the media provide. This influence is not, of course, literal or simple. Identity is often defined in opposition, contradiction, or coherence with popular or vivid media stereotypes. The lack of a precise translation, as with many areas of media effects research, makes the task of understanding how mass media influence identity development a complex one.

## Media and Identity

The significance of mass media in the daily lives of children cannot be overstated. For example, television alone occupies 4 hours of a child's day. Every year a child sees 20,000 TV commercials and, over his or her youth, will spend more time watching TV than in school. Although no one image or program or activity will necessarily alter a child's consciousness or directly influence behavior, the quantity and redundancy of mass media images accumulate as part of the overall childhood experience. As Comstock (1993) states,

> The influence of the medium [television] resides not in affecting how people behave but in what they think about. The medium becomes a socio-cultural force not because people are what they see, but because what they see and talk about are important parts of their experience. (p. 118)

This accumulated experience contributes to the cultivation of a child's values, beliefs, dreams, and expectations, which shape the adult identity a child will carry and modify throughout his or her life. The potential contribution of the media to identity development is immense (Swidler, 1986).

Yet the importance of mass media in forming a child's identity is never constant. At a very young age, children gain most of their sense of self from their parents. In fact, children see themselves as an extension of their parents during the first few years of life. Over time, other factors, such as peers and nonfamily authority figures, influence identity development. During adolescence, the presence and direct influence of parents, siblings, and other family members diminishes as teenagers search for independence and autonomy. It is during this time when young adults search for ways to define themselves outside of their parents and family unit (Steinberg & Silverberg, 1986). It also the time when, although television viewing decreases from 4 to 2 hours daily, teenagers listen to popular music 4 hours a day, attend more movies than any other segment of the population, and, for girls, purchase more than 4 million teen magazines a month. Interpretations of media content, and the implications of that content for identity development, vary systematically with age and developmental stage (Granello, 1997).

The research reviewed below provides an overview of childhood identity development in relation to mass media, with a primary focus on adolescents. The reason for this is twofold. First, as stated above, early adolescence marks the beginning of a child's autonomous sense of self. Adolescents' values and beliefs are becoming uniquely their own, separate from, and perhaps even contrary to, the values of their parents. Second, the research methods most often employed to examine the influence of mass media on identity development tend to rely on lengthy, informal conversations with children. It would seem that the nature of this ethnographic research requires a level of self-reflection from the interviewees that is unusual in children under the age of 10 or 11. For these reasons, the body of literature featured below emphasizes teenage identity development in its relationship with the mass media.

### *Multidirectional Patterns*

The media play a reciprocal and multifaceted role in the ongoing process of identity development among young people. Indeed, this is an area in which concerns about media uses, functions, impacts, and reception all intersect in dynamic ways.

Teens are a critical target audience for numerous mass media—radio, television, movies, magazines, and more. Young "hip" characters dominate TV programs and films, in large part because of attempts by producers to attract the lucrative youth market. Young audience members learn many lessons from the portrayals that result from these commercial imperatives, as media figures, celebrities, stars, and characters become icons for emulation. These media models not only provide countless elements of style, outlook, and value that can be incorporated into one's own identity but also define and perpetuate common social categories as well. A viewer, for example, may learn the social definition of what it means to be a young black female or a working-class white male. Moreover, these elements may guide our schemas and expectations in dealing with different types of people, which may then indirectly contribute to others' sense of identity. Young people may accept or reject these representations, but they cannot avoid having to deal with them.

The stories on television and other media demonstrate modes of problem solving, with lessons of what works and what does not, and for whom. These stories illustrate what "popular kids" are like, who is successful and who is not. They offer modes of acting, of engaging in social interaction, and of thinking about oneself in terms of what kind of "self" one chooses to construct. The most urgent and compelling stories of all—those of advertising—promote a sense of self and identity that can only be constructed meaningfully through consumption. Indeed, perhaps the dominant message of commercial media is that the actualization of the self depends entirely on what products we buy. Consumption not only satisfies our deepest desires and solves almost any problem, it is also how we know who we are.

Yet it is not simply that media *affect* young people's identity development through the establishment and glorification of role models and commodities (although the extent of this particular impact should not be underestimated; cf. Shaw, Kleiber, & Caldwell, 1995). It is important to stress that young people also actively *use* media to define themselves, and media can help children and adolescents make sense of their lives as a form of self-socialization. Indeed, Arnett (1995) casts "identity formation" as one of the five dominant uses of media by adolescents (the others being entertainment, high sensation, coping, and youth culture identification).

Moreover, media choices and behaviors "can be a personal expression of adolescent identity development" (Huston, Wartella, & Donnerstein, 1998, p. 11). Media preferences constitute a kind of badge of identity that young people use to define themselves, both to themselves and to others. These preferences and habits signify membership in various taste cultures that unite (and divide) teens in subcultures, distinct from children and adults. These may be oppositional subcultures, as in the case of "media delinquents" (Roe, 1995), or they may be the result of carefully structured and efficient marketing strategies. Either way, media usage itself functions as a commodity, as a signal of group membership, style, and values. Music, for example, is "important to adolescents because it helps define their public self outside the family" (Larson, 1995, p. 543). Similarly, coviewing certain programs can foment group identity (Granello, 1997). Beyond providing a coin of exchange in everyday conversation, the specific media choices children and adolescents make represent an integral aspect of self-definition—both for the self and for others. It is this extremely wide range of ways in which media can affect young people's sense of identity that makes this influence so complex, and so important.

## Methodological Approaches

The first step in understanding how mass media influence the identity development of children is that something needs to be known about the content of the mass media, particularly the images and representations portrayed that may contribute to children's conception of themselves and others. Content analysis represents the overwhelming bulk of this scholarship. This is both a strength and a limitation of existing research. Literally an assessment of the messages of mass media, content analysis studies have included the examination of Saturday morning cartoons (Thompson & Zerbinos, 1995), prime-time television programs (Elasmar, Hasegawa, & Brain, 1999; Ward, 1995), horror films (Cowan & O'Brien, 1990; Weaver, 1991), Sunday comics (Brabant & Mooney, 1999), television commercials (Bretl & Cantor, 1988), children's television advertising (Smith, 1994), teen magazines (Evans, Rutberg, Sather, & Turner, 1991), music videos (Seidman, 1992), soap operas (Greco Larson, 1991), and much more. From these content analyses, a general inventory of the most common images and representations in mass media is developed. This inventory is categorized into themes such as sex roles; the depiction of race, gender, class, and sexuality; and portrayals of work, politics, and citizenship.

To make the connection between the content of mass media and its influence on the identity development of children, researchers move beyond the media text—the collection of television programs, magazines, music lyrics, and so on—to the child audience and ask the question, How do mass media images influence a child's self-concept? Methods employed here include self-administered surveys and media reporting (Larson, 1995), one-on-one interviews (Steele & Brown, 1995), and participant observation (Milkie, 1994). The purpose is to investigate the evasive and complex relationship between childhood and mass media. How is mass media content integrated into children's lived experience—that is, the practices and experiences of their everyday life—and how does that experience in turn shape their understanding of themselves and the world in which they live?

It is a difficult process to parse out the influences of peers, parents, and community from mass media. In a sense, a complete disconnect does not reflect the wedded relationship in which peers, parents, and community are likewise exposed to mass media. Parents, for example, also derive conceptions about the world partly from media and integrate those conceptions into their ideas and practices about parenting as well as into their relationships with their children. To cleanse the research subject of any influence other than mass media is not only impossible but undesirable if we wish to grasp the fullness of identity.

## Gender: Masculinity and Femininity Role Learning

A well-studied area of children's identity development and the media is the analysis of gender role learning. Whether a child is a boy or girl is perhaps the most significant aspect of self that a child develops within the first few years of life. Taking cues from parents, other children and adults, and the media, a child quickly learns what it means to be a girl or a boy and how that difference dictates behavior. As a child will discover at a very young age, transgressing socially constructed gender expectations can invite painful alienation and ridicule. As a result, children observe carefully the particulars about being masculine or feminine. Toward this task, the media provide a constant source of information about gender distinctions and a massive number of normative models of male and female behavior.

Countless content analyses have examined the roles for girls, boys, women, and men portrayed in the media, particularly television programming and advertising. Common findings observe that, despite some progress, men outnumber women two or three to one in prime-time television, and women are younger than men and are typically cast in traditional and stereotyped roles (Signorielli, 1989). Even though the overall number of women on television may have increased over the decades, women's gains are limited mainly to minor roles (Elasmar et al., 1999), and conventional portrayals dominate.

Sex role research finds that children will replicate the role expectations seen in the media when asked about appropriate chores for boys and girls (Signorielli & Lears, 1992). Television can also strengthen the consistency between adolescents' gender-based attitudes about chores and their actual behavior in the family (Morgan, 1987). The medium's contributions to the endorsement and maintenance of traditional gender roles have been observed over time in longitudinal data and in diverse cultural contexts (Morgan, 1982, 1990). Ethnographic work (Milkie, 1994) has shown how teens make meanings from media content in terms of conventional gender roles; boys reproduce gendered meanings by "appropriating scenes . . . that embody traditional male culture, identifying with the models of masculinity available through media content and imputing stereotypical notions of gender to the mass media" (p. 354).

As children mature, television use decreases, but other media, magazines and music in particular, increase in use and significance for the young adult's navigation of gender identity. Duke and Kreshel (1998) found that young adolescent girls used teen magazines to develop their notions of femininity, of what it means to be a woman. Femininity was largely defined in the magazines as based in physical appearance and a girl's success at relationships with other girls and boys. In addition, the magazines provided insights into the needs and wants of boys and how girls could fulfill those desires. Girls negotiate the meanings of femininity offered in the magazines with the expectations and values of their peers. The imprint of teen magazine gender roles is not universally or uniformly accepted, but their representations serve to reproduce dominant gender trajectories that readers must either conform to or deviate from. Thus, they contribute to a cultural context in which girls tend to identify their role as women as determined in part by how they please men and by their ability to look physically appealing.

## Sexuality

Media have potentially vast impacts on the development of children's and adolescents' perceptions of their sexual identities. Young people are immensely curious about the subject of sex—not only its biological and physical aspects but also its emotional and social implications—and parents and schools are inconsistent in providing adequate information. This leaves peers and media as crucial sources almost by default (Brown, Walsh-Childers, & Waszak, 1990; Huston et al., 1998). Television and other media may thus play a key role in the emergence and definitions of sexual perceptions, assumptions, and behaviors (Singletary, Ziegler, Reid, & Milbourne, 1990), especially as they normalize culturally defined modes of gender and sexuality (Williams, 1996).

The bulk of existing research consists of content analyses rather than studies of the media's effects. Research on music videos (Seidman, 1992), soap operas (Greenberg & Busselle, 1996; Olson, 1995), prime-time television (Kunkel, Cope, & Colvin, 1996; Lowry & Shidler, 1993), television advertising (Kuriansky, 1996; Signorielli, McLeod, & Healy, 1994), women's and teen-oriented magazines (Walsh-Childers, 1997), and movies (Greenberg, Brown, & Buerkel-Rothfuss, 1993; Weaver, 1991) has substantiated what casual observation suggests: There has been a steady increase in the representation of sex in the media (implicit and explicit, verbal and visual) from the 1970s through the 1990s.

Inferences about causal direction are highly tenuous, but teenagers who choose to watch sexual content on television are more likely to have had physically intimate relations and/or intercourse (Brown & Newcomer, 1991; Brown, White, & Nikopoulou, 1993; Ward & Rivadeneyra, 1999). Moreover, teenage viewers of music videos are more likely than nonviewers to be accepting of premarital sex (Greeson & Williams, 1987; Strouse, Buerkel-Rothfuss, & Long, 1995). Whatever one's moral position on sex in the media, these tendencies are worrisome given that the consequences of sex, such as pregnancy and sexually transmitted diseases (STDs), are rarely addressed.

One pervasive media lesson is that physical and sexual attractiveness is a critical asset (Ward, 1995). This invites (and even demands) self-image comparisons with the media-defined "ideal" body. These comparisons will be favorable for few teens. The perfect bodies that populate the media—print and electronic, programs and commercials, across all genres—are a key element in marketing strategies that use the body (especially the female body) to attract audiences and sell goods. The images can contribute to feelings of inadequacy, isolation, and self-rejection, especially among young people who feel vulnerable and insecure about the many physical and social changes taking place. They can also contribute to dangerous eating disorders. Girls, especially overweight girls, may be more susceptible to these kinds of consequences. Of course, as in any other area of media effects, such outcomes are neither automatic nor uniform; they depend on a wide variety of personal and social factors (Henderson-King & Henderson-King, 1997).

Content studies reveal not merely a great deal of sexual content but very specific patterns of portrayals. "Sex in the media" largely means heterosexual sex between unmarried partners. This is by far the most frequent type of sexual representation. Accordingly, although the assumption of heterosexuality is a deeply ingrained cultural habit, the media play a major role in perpetuating such an assumption (Herek, 1992). This puts nonheterosexual teens in a situation similar to that of members of certain ethnic minority groups (see below): They are invisible, disempowered, and have no role models to look toward to help structure identity (Gross, 1994).

Few groups in society experience such strong tensions over sexuality as gay and lesbian teens do. In a cultural climate that is still largely hostile to homosexuality, the paucity of positive role models in the media is disturbing. As Kielwasser and Wolf (1994) note, "Gay and lesbian youth are not only excluded from representation on television, they are also never addressed as members of the audience" (p. 66). These authors also point out that, although gay and lesbian adults may "subversively deconstruct" heterosexist media texts, young gay people may not have the developmental skill or world knowledge to do so.

Representations of gay characters on television are increasing (DeCaro, 1999). Following the much-publicized coming out of the title character on the situation comedy *Ellen* in 1998, program producers and advertisers began to be less apprehensive that gay characters would cause viewer outrage and lost profits (Wilke, 1998). Still, the Gay and Lesbian Alliance Against Defamation (GLAAD) notes that the 28 gay, lesbian, or transgender characters appearing in the 1999-2000 TV season (broadcast and cable) represent just 2% of total portrayals, and these characters are mostly cast in minor roles. Mirroring the more general tendencies in the portrayal of women and minorities, these nonheterosexual characters are almost exclusively white and male; lesbians and gay people of color remain largely invisible ("GLAAD Says 1999-2000," 1999). Moreover, Hart (1999) points out that popular shows such as *Beverly Hills, 90210* perpetuate the image of the person with AIDS as a lone gay male dying in a cold hospital room, which ignores the important changes that have taken place in the demographics of the epidemic. Thus, representations relevant to sexual identity are closely interwoven with many other layers of media portrayals, and it is these complex but coherent multidimensional clusters that must be taken into account in trying to understand the media's role in adolescent identity development.

## Race and Ethnicity: Alienation Versus Integration

Racial and ethnic stereotypes persist despite decades of attempts to eradicate them, from the civil rights movement to more recent initiatives to promote multiculturalism. The perseverance of stereotypes is one of the ways in which dominant groups can maintain their position in the hierarchy and impose their will on others (recall the Faludi quote above about women "having their identity defined for them"). One reason they persist is that group members enhance their self-esteem by favorably comparing themselves with relevant others (Harwood, Giles, & Ryan, 1995). The media rarely create these stereotypes; most have deep historical roots. Yet the media play a significant role in repeating, normalizing, and perpetuating many negative images of specific groups, and this can have crucial implications for how minority children view themselves.

One of the most powerful mechanisms of keeping power away from a group is to render its members invisible. In the case of the media, those who are not represented do not exist; invisibility indicates the absence of social power (Gross, 1994). Children and adolescents who do not see characters "like themselves" on television are learning a fundamental lesson about their group's importance in society. Daily, they are being sent a loud and clear message that they do not count for very much in society.

Numerous content analyses of media programming indicate not only that ethnic minorities are greatly underrepresented but also that, when they are present, they are negatively portrayed. Typically, ethnic minorities are associated with crime, violence, alcohol and drug abuse, and unemployment. They are generally not shown in cross-ethnic interactions or relationships unless involved with authority figures and institutions (Huston et al., 1992). Children's programming and commercials are highly segregated. White and nonwhite children rarely play together (Barcus, 1983). On the basis of this near invisibility, unattractive portrayals, and socially segregated programming, Palmer, Taylor Smith, and Strawser (1993) found that minority children who watch more television experience lowered self-concept, feel alienated, and are uninterested in being part of life outside their immediate community. These researchers concluded that "the television tool through which [minorities] sought socialization and integration in the final analysis segregate[d] them" (p. 145).

Similarly, Allen (1993) states that the distorted view of African heritage in the mass media and public education system has "miseducated African-American children to believe they have no African heritage of which they should be proud" (p. 155). Instead, minority children are ashamed and may reject any associations with nonwhite, non-European heritage. For example, Allen found that the "African-American child may feel ambivalent about his or her racial identity and often will prefer characters on television that do not resemble themselves" (p. 170).

Still, minority children and adolescents often prefer to watch programs portraying members of their own ethnic groups (Greenberg & Brand, 1994), just as viewers would rather watch characters of their own age (Harwood, 1997). This attraction to characters with similar social identities is especially pronounced among those who more strongly identify themselves as members of specific social groups, and the desire to bolster social identity may drive viewing choices (Harwood, 1999). Thus, identity development can be especially precarious, and the role of media especially significant, in the case of those minority groups who remain nearly invisible in the world of television, such as Latinos, Asians, and Native Americans. Young people who belong to these and other neglected groups, searching in vain to find programs featuring characters like themselves, have ample opportunity to absorb the message that the majority culture does not value them very highly.

Learning the lesson that "society devalues my ethnicity," whether through media or other means, can have at least three potential (and not necessarily exclusive) outcomes: (a) The child may infer that, if it is undesirable to be a member of that group, minority status implies some personal deficiency, with negative repercussions on personal ethnic identity (i.e., "being a member of that group is bad, so I am bad"); (b) if membership in that ethnic group is undesirable, then denying that membership offers a solution (i.e., "being a member of that group is bad, so I will try to look, act, and think of myself as a nonmember of that group"; of course, this is easier for some minority groups than for others); and (c) the social undercutting of that minority status can *increase* frustration with and rejection of the majority culture, intensifying attachment to the minority culture and making identification with it even stronger (i.e., "the people I know and love are members of that group, so society is wrong and unjust, and my allegiance to that group is stronger"). In other words, resentment may serve paradoxically to raise consciousness, creating a backlash effect in which invisible minorities demand greater rights and representations.

A critical challenge for future research is to determine which of these three is most likely, for whom, and under what circumstances. It is worth noting that the only scenario of these three that positively *strengthens* ethnic identity is the third one, the one that involves rejecting dominant social values. Thus, although television and other popular media often function as social and cultural homogenizers (Morgan, 1986), their role in generating a backlash that foments "identity politics" and increases alienation and fragmentation should not be overlooked. Indeed, this is a plausible but markedly underresearched media effect.

## Class/Work: Occupational Preparation

Work in the media is portrayed in particularly limited ways. Although vastly improved from the 1970s and '80s, the division of labor among men and women is still highly traditional; women typically fill domestic, nurturing occupational roles and men are shown working outside the home in successful positions as doctors, lawyers, and business leaders. Work, overall, is glamorized. Professionals are greatly overrepresented on television, and working-class employees, save for police officers, are underrepresented (Signorielli, 1993, p. 321). In addition, Signorielli found that television characters were rarely depicted actually working, except in law enforcement and medical occupations (p. 325). The overall message about work that the media offer is that work is about status, power, and money but does not require any difficult labor.

How this media portrayal of working life translates into children's expectations about their future in the workforce reveals an interesting contradiction. Signorielli (1993) found that adolescents who were heavy viewers of television aspired to jobs with status but indicated they wanted the work they actually performed to be easy (p. 337). Similarly, Wright et al. (1995) interviewed second and fifth graders about their perceptions of the daily activities of police officers and nurses. Children who watched more television tended to have unrealistic assumptions about the occupational duties of law enforcement and medicine, including inflated salaries and dramatic workdays without negative consequences. Heavy-viewing children also tended to aspire to jobs shown on television (see also Wroblewski & Huston, 1987).

## New Media and Identity

The 1990s saw the explosive introduction of another medium that, like television, promises to alter the experiences of childhood once more: the computer and all its related technology (the Internet, video games, virtual reality simulators, etc.). Children born since the mid-'90s are growing up with computers and, like their parents with television, will never know a world without computer technology.

In the introduction to her book *Life on the Screen,* Sherry Turkle (1995) writes, "Computer screens are the new location for our fantasies, both erotic and intellectual. We are using life on computer screens to become comfortable with new ways of thinking about evolution, relationships, sexuality, politics, and identity" (p. 26). In chat rooms, on web pages, and in on-line games, computers offer us—children and adults—the opportunity to play with our identities in ways never before possible. We can pretend to be someone else, a different gender, age, race, or class; we can hold an exotic occupation, walk if paralyzed, see if blind. It is not simply that we can pretend to be someone else—there's nothing particularly new about that—but that we can bring *others* in on our fantasy who have no direct way of knowing whether the public identity we announce is ours or not. It is a brave—and dangerous—new world of who we are and who we can be, which may intensify or resolve the ongoing tensions between the personal and social dimensions of "identity." How this new technology can influence children's understanding of themselves and the world in which they live is important uncharted territory, just beginning to be explored.

In this new area of research, several scholars have turned toward postmodern theory for understanding the ways in which we experience identity on-line (see Haraway, 1991; Stone, 1995; Turkle, 1995). These authors suggest that cyberspace challenges our reliance on embodied communication and on fixed gender, sexual, class, racial, and other identities and allows us to experience the fluidity and multiplicity of identity construction. This postmodern vision presents computer-mediated communication as a potential catalyst for social transformation because new technologies offer the opportunity to reconstruct society free from the "appropriating, incorporating, totalizing tendencies of Western theories of identity" (Haraway, 1991, p. 158). Although theoretically intriguing, so far postmodern approaches to new media and identity development have proven difficult to investigate empirically.

## Conclusions and Future Research

After half a century of television, we know quite a bit about which stereotypes, conventional models, and dominant roles persist. Updated content analyses should continue to monitor media representations of gender, race, class, occupation, sexuality, age, physical ability, and so forth. Some may consider this "old news," but the continued monitoring of the symbolic environment is essential to understanding media effects.

Despite the extensive research that exists on content patterns, the connection between how different groups are represented in the media and how that translates into self-concept and identity development requires far more theoretical and methodological attention than has been brought to bear to date. There is a tendency in this research to investigate the identity development of nondominant populations—women and girls, people of color, and gay men and lesbians. Although there is a great deal of scholarship on the development of feminine, racial minority, and homosexual identities (in both content analysis and effects research), research on the construction of masculinity, whiteness, and heterosexuality is less prevalent.

There was a time in media effects research when representations of nondominant populations were ignored and the consumption and influence of media among minority children were assumed to be like that of the majority (i.e., white, middle-class boys). Now, with the recognition that children's relationships to media messages vary, we have, perhaps, the opposite situation. Attention to nondominant children can have the effect of "normalizing" dominant identities, suggesting that a tangible "identity" belongs only to those *different* from the assumed majority. Without the comparable investigation of dominant and nondominant audiences and media messages, we cannot understand how boys and girls construct their gender identity *in relationship with* masculine and feminine media representations; how they construct their racial identity from images of both white people and people of color; or understand sexual development as dependent on both straight and gay depictions of sexuality. That being said, it is also critical to recognize that these categories of gender, race, and sexuality oversimplify what are in fact complex continua rather than simple dichotomies.

As we noted at the start of this chapter, identity is an active process, as is the negotiation of symbolic media messages into the everyday life of children and adults. Also, it is vital to recall that the media-identity relationship is not a one-way street; identity also shapes how we respond to media content (Cohen, 1991; Davis & Gandy, 1999; Durkin & Nugent, 1998), setting up complex dynamics that will vary by developmental stage and a vast range of other factors.

Understanding these critical processes will require creative syntheses of the entire spectrum of methodological approaches. Ethnographic methods, such as one-to-one interviews and participant observation, can provide thick descriptions of daily life, allowing for the messy and complex connections between identity and culture. Large-scale survey research can uncover broad patterns of associations between media exposure and beliefs about self and others (e.g., pride in group membership, self-esteem, endorsement of nontraditional roles, etc.) for different groups of children and adolescents. Focus group research can shed light on how young people make sense and meaning out of various types of portrayals and representations. Most important, theoretical work is needed to give us richer and more meaningful conceptualizations of "identity" as a dynamic and complex interplay of personal, social, and cultural influences. From there we may shed a little more light on how children integrate and negotiate symbolic media messages with the various and intertwined daily influences on their conception of who they are in relation to the world in which they live.

## References


Allen, R. L. (1993). Conceptual models of an African-American belief system. In G. L. Berry & J. K. Asamen (Eds.), *Children and television: Images in a changing sociocultural world* (pp. 155-176). Newbury Park, CA: Sage.

Arnett, J. (1995). Adolescents' uses of media for self-socialization. *Journal of Youth and Adolescence, 25,* 519-534.

Barcus, F. E. (1983). *Images of life on children's television.* New York: Praeger.

Brabant, S., & Mooney, L. A. (1999). The social construction of family life in the Sunday comics: Race as a consideration. *Journal of Comparative Family Studies, 30,* 113-114.

Bretl, D. J., & Cantor, J. (1988). The portrayal of men and women in U.S. television commercials: A recent content analysis and trends over 15 years. *Sex Roles, 18,* 595-609.

Brown, J. D., & Newcomer, S. F. (1991). Television viewing and adolescents' sexual behavior. *Journal of Homosexuality, 21,* 77-92.

Brown, J. D., Walsh-Childers, K., & Waszak, C. S. (1990). Television and adolescent sexuality. *Journal of Adolescent Health Care, 11,* 62-70.

Brown, J. D., White, A. B., & Nikopoulou, L. (1993). Disinterest, intrigue, resistance: Early adolescent girls' use of sexual media content. In B. S. Greenberg, J. D. Brown, & N. L. Buerkel-Rothfuss (Eds.), *Media, sex, and the adolescent* (pp. 183-195). Hillsdale, NJ: Lawrence Erlbaum.

Cohen, J. R. (1991). The "relevance" of cultural identity in audiences' interpretations of mass media. *Critical Studies in Mass Communication, 8,* 442-454.

Comstock, G. (1993). The role of television in American life. In G. L. Berry & J. K. Asamen (Eds.), *Children and television: Images in a changing sociocultural world* (pp. 117-131). Newbury Park, CA: Sage.

Cowan, G., & O'Brien, M. (1990). Gender and survival vs. death in slasher films: A content analysis. *Sex Roles, 23,* 187-196.

Davis, J. L., & Gandy, O. (1999). Racial identity and media orientation. *Journal of Black Studies, 29,* 367.

DeCaro, F. (1999, May 1). In with the out crowd. *TV Guide, 47,* 44-47.

Duke, L. L., & Kreshel, P. J. (1998). Negotiating femininity: Girls in early adolescence read teen magazines. *Journal of Communication Inquiry, 22*(1), 48-71.

Durkin, K., & Nugent, B. (1998). Kindergarten children's gender-role expectations for television actors. *Sex Roles, 38,* 387-402.

Elasmar, M., Hasegawa, K., & Brain, M. (1999). The portrayal of women in U.S. prime time television. *Journal of Broadcasting & Electronic Media, 43,* 20-33.

Erikson, E. H. (1959). *Identity and the life cycle.* New York: International Universities Press.

Erikson, E. H. (1968). *Identity: Youth and crisis.* New York: Norton.

Evans, E. D., Rutberg, J., Sather, C., & Turner, C. (1991). Content analysis of contemporary teen magazines for adolescent females. *Youth & Society, 23*(1), 99-120.

Faludi, S. (1991). *Backlash: The undeclared war against women.* New York: Crown.

GLAAD says 1999-2000 primetime TV lineup "barely realistic" [Press release]. (1999, August 23). [Retrieved September 24, 1999]. Available: www.glaad.org/glaad/press/990823.html

Granello, D. H. (1997). Using *Beverly Hills, 90210* to explore developmental issues in female adolescents. *Youth & Society, 29,* 24-54.

Greco Larson, S. (1991). Television's mixed messages: Sexual content on *All My Children. Communication Quarterly, 39*(2), 156-163.

Greenberg, B. S., & Brand, J. E. (1994). Minorities and the mass media: 1970s to 1990s. In J. Bryant & D. Zillmann (Eds.), *Media effects: Advances in theory and research* (pp. 273-314). Hillsdale, NJ: Lawrence Erlbaum.

Greenberg, B. S., Brown, J., & Buerkel-Rothfuss, N. L. (Eds.). (1993). *Media, sex, and the adolescent.* Cresskill, NJ: Hampton Press.

Greenberg, B. S., & Busselle, R. W. (1996). Soap operas and sexual activity: A decade later. *Journal of Communication, 46,* 153-160.

Greeson, L. E., & Williams, R. A. (1987). Social implications of music videos for youth: An analysis of the content and effects of MTV. *Youth & Society, 18,* 177-189.

Gross, L. (1994). What is wrong with this picture? Lesbian women and gay men on television. In R. J. Ringer (Ed.), *Queer words, queer images: Communication and the construction of homosexuality* (pp. 143-156). New York: New York University Press.

Haraway, D. (1991). A cyborg manifesto: Science, technology, and socialist-feminism in the late twentieth century. In D. Haraway, *Simians, cyborgs, and women: The reinvention of nature* (pp. 149-181). New York: Routledge.

Hart, K. P. (1999). Retrograde representation: The lone gay white male dying of AIDS on *Beverly Hills, 90210. Journal of Men's Studies, 7,* 201-213.

Harwood, J. (1997). Viewing age: Lifespan identity and television viewing choices. *Journal of Broadcasting & Electronic Media, 41,* 203-213.

Harwood, J. (1999). Age identification, social identity gratifications, and television viewing. *Journal of Broadcasting & Electronic Media, 43,* 123-133.

Harwood, J., Giles, H., & Ryan, E. B. (1995). Aging, communication, and intergroup theory: Social identity and intergenerational communication. In J. F. Nussbaum & J. Coupland (Eds.), *Handbook of communication and aging research* (pp. 133-159). Hillsdale, NJ: Lawrence Erlbaum.

Henderson-King, E., & Henderson-King, D. (1997). Media effects on women's body esteem: Social and individual difference factors. *Journal of Applied Social Psychology, 27,* 399-417.

Herek, G. M. (1992). The social context of hate crimes: Notes on cultural heterosexism. In G. Herek & K. Berril (Eds.), *Hate crimes: Confronting violence against lesbians and gay men* (pp. 89-104). Newbury Park, CA: Sage.

Huston, A. C., Donnerstein, E., Fairchild, H., Feshbach, N. D., Katz, P. A., Murray, J. P., Rubinstein, E. A.,

Wilcox, B., & Zuckerman, D. (Eds.). (1992). *Big world, small screen: The role of television in American society.* Lincoln: University of Nebraska Press.

Huston, A. C., Wartella, E., & Donnerstein, E. (1998, May). *Measuring the effects of sexual content in the media: A report to the Kaiser Family Foundation.* Menlo Park, CA: Kaiser Family Foundation.

Josselson, R. (1980). Ego development in adolescence. In J. Adelson (Ed.), *Handbook of adolescent psychology* (pp. 140-167). New York: John Wiley.

Kielwasser, A. P., & Wolf, M. A. (1994). Silence, difference, and annihilation: Understanding the impact of mediated heterosexism on high school students. *High School Journal, 77,* 58-79.

Kunkel, D., Cope, K. M., & Colvin, C. (1996). *Sexual messages on family hour television: Content and context.* Oakland, CA: Children Now and the Henry J. Kaiser Family Foundation.

Kuriansky, J. (1996). Sexuality and television advertising: An historical perspective. *SIECUS Report, 24,* 13.

Larson, R. (1995). Secrets in the bedroom: Adolescents' private use of media. *Journal of Youth and Adolescence, 24*(5), 535-550.

Lowry, D. T., & Shidler, J. A. (1993). Prime time TV portrayals of sex, "safe sex," and AIDS: A longitudinal analysis. *Journalism Quarterly, 70,* 628-637.

Milkie, M. A. (1994). Social world approach to cultural studies: Mass media and gender in the adolescent peer group. *Journal of Contemporary Ethnography, 23*(3), 354-380.

Morgan, M. (1982). Television and adolescents' sex-role stereotypes: A longitudinal study. *Journal of Personality and Social Psychology, 43,* 947-955.

Morgan, M. (1986). Television and the erosion of regional diversity. *Journal of Broadcasting & Electronic Media, 30,* 123-139.

Morgan, M. (1987). Television, sex-role attitudes, and sex-role behavior. *Journal of Early Adolescence, 7,* 269-282.

Morgan, M. (1990). International cultivation analysis. In N. Signorielli & M. Morgan (Eds.), *Cultivation analysis: New directions in media effects research* (pp. 225-247). Newbury Park, CA: Sage.

Olson, B. (1995). Sex and soaps: A comparative content analysis of health issues. *Journalism Quarterly, 71,* 840-850.

Palmer, E. L., Taylor Smith, K., & Strawser, K. S. (1993). Rubik's tube: Developing a child's television worldview. In G. L. Berry & J. K. Asamen (Eds.), *Children and television: Images in a changing sociocultural world* (pp. 143-154). Newbury Park, CA: Sage.

Robinson, W. R. (Ed.). (1996). *Social groups and identities: Developing the legacy of Henri Tajfel.* Boston: Butterworth Heinemann.

Roe, K. (1995). Adolescents' use of socially disvalued media: Toward a theory of media delinquency. *Journal of Youth and Adolescence, 25,* 617-629.

Seidman, S. A. (1992). An investigation of sex-role stereotyping in music videos. *Journal of Broadcasting, 36,* 209-216.

Shaw, S. M., Kleiber, D. A., & Caldwell, L. L. (1995). Leisure and identity formation in male and female adolescents: A preliminary examination. *Journal of Leisure Research, 27,* 245-264.

Signorielli, N. (1989). Television and conceptions about sex-roles: Maintaining conventionality and the status quo. *Sex Roles, 21,* 337-356.

Signorielli, N. (1993). Television and adolescents' perceptions about work. *Youth & Society, 24*(3), 314-341.

Signorielli, N., & Lears, M. (1992). Children, television, and conceptions about chores: Attitudes and behaviors. *Sex Roles, 27,* 157-170.

Signorielli, N., McLeod, D., & Healy, E. (1994). Gender stereotypes in MTV commercials: The beat goes on. *Journal of Broadcasting & Electronic Media, 38,* 91-101.

Singletary, M. W., Ziegler, D., Reid, K., & Milbourne, C. (1990, June). *Media use and high school students' perceptions of sexual behavior: A cultivation analysis.* Paper presented at the annual meeting of the International Communication Association, Dublin, Ireland.

Smith, L. J. (1994). A content analysis of gender differences in children's advertising. *Journal of Broadcasting and Electronic Media, 38,* 323-337.

Steele, J. R., & Brown, J. D. (1995). Adolescent room culture: Studying media in the context of everyday life. *Journal of Youth and Adolescence, 24*(5), 551-576.

Steinberg, L., & Silverberg, S. B. (1986). The vicissitudes of autonomy in early adolescence. *Child Development, 57,* 841-851.

Stone, A. R. (1995). *The war of desire and technology at the close of the mechanical age.* Cambridge: MIT Press.

Strouse, J., Buerkel-Rothfuss, N., & Long, E. C. (1995). Gender and family as moderators of the relationship between music video exposure and adolescent sexual permissiveness. *Adolescence, 30,* 505-521.

Swidler, A. (1986). Culture in action: Symbols and strategies. *American Sociological Review, 51,* 273-286.

Tajfel, H. (1978). Social categorization, social identity, and social comparison. In H. Tajfel (Ed.), *Differentiation between social groups: Studies in the social psychology of intergroup relations* (pp. 61-76). London: Academic Press.

Thompson, T. L., & Zerbinos, E. (1995). Gender roles in animated cartoons: Has the picture changed in 20 years? *Sex Roles, 32,* 651-674.

Turkle, S. (1995). *Life on the screen: Identity in the age of the Internet.* New York: Simon & Schuster.

Walsh-Childers, K. (1997). *A content analysis: Sexual health coverage in women's, men's, teen, and other specialty magazines.* Menlo Park, CA: Kaiser Family Foundation.

Ward, M. L. (1995). Talking about sex: Common themes about sexuality in the prime-time television programs children and adolescents view most. *Journal of Youth and Adolescence, 24*(5), 595-615.

Ward, M. L., & Rivadeneyra, R. (1999). Contributions of entertainment television to adolescents' sexual attitudes and expectations: The role of viewing amount versus viewer involvement. *Journal of Sex Research, 36*(3), 237-249.

Weaver, J. B. (1991). Are "slasher" horror films sexually violent? A content analysis. *Journal of Broadcasting and Electronic Media, 35,* 385-392.

Wilke, M. (1998, June 22). "Ellen" legacy: Gay TV roles are more acceptable, but number drops for fall season. *Advertising Age, 69,* 25, 31.

Williams, J. P. (1996). Biology and destiny: The dynamics of gender crossing in *Quantum Leap. Women's Studies in Communication, 19,* 273-290.

Williams, R. (1976). *Keywords: A vocabulary of culture and society.* New York: Oxford University Press.

Wright, J. C., Huston, A. C., Truglio, R., Fitch, M., Smith, E., & Suwatchara, P. (1995). Occupational portrayals on television: Children's role schemata, career aspirations, and perceptions of reality. *Child Development, 66,* 1706-1718.

Wroblewski, R., & Huston, A. C. (1987). Televised occupational stereotypes and their effects on early adolescents: Are they changing? *Journal of Early Adolescence, 7,* 283-297.

*Your ultimate quotation center* [On-line]. (1999). [Retrieved September 17, 1999]. Available: www. cybernation.com/victory/quotations/subjects/quotes_identity.html

CHAPTER **16**

# Media and the Family

ROBERT KUBEY
BARNA WILLIAM DONOVAN
Rutgers University

"If we are forced, at every hour, to watch or listen to horrible events, this constant stream of ghastly impressions will deprive even the most delicate among us of all respect for humanity," writes one well-known critic. "Then shall we simply allow our children to listen to any story anyone happens to make up, and so receive into their minds ideas often the very opposite of those we shall think they ought to have when they are grown up?" writes another.

With the state of the family structure and the welfare of children always at the flash point of political and social discourse, studies of the media are ever more challenged to probe and understand the familial use of mass media products and the impact this behavior has on the structure, function, and mind-set of the family.

As we begin the twenty-first century, the two critics quoted above would seem to be referring to a media environment of confrontational, salacious talk shows, sexually graphic and violent dramas, random and senseless killings in the news media, or a dose of in-your-face professional wrestling. The sources of such criticism might be anyone from Pat Robertson to William Bennett or Tipper Gore. Yet the writers are, respectively, Cicero, writing of the Roman theater in the first century B.C., and Plato, writing in the *Republic* more than 2,300 years ago. The fears have been the same for more than two millennia, and the rhetoric hardly changes.

Recent decades have seen the state of the family as it relates to the media at the center of political debate. The controversy ignited by Dan Quayle's 1992 *Murphy Brown* remarks still resonates today (Morgan & Leggett, 1999). In an age of communication technology explosion, where cable and satellite channels increase the range and amount of content, where high-definition television increases the quality of the televised image, and where the Internet and the World Wide Web massively increase the available sources of information, the impact of the electronic media on the family needs to be studied as much now as ever.

## Media in the Home

Observations in the early 1950s held that the television set froze the natural order of family interaction—talking, joking, arguing, catching up on the disparate experiences of each family member (Bronfenbrenner, 1973; Maccoby, 1951). When the TV is on, there is "more privatization of experience; the family may gather around the set, but they remain isolated in their attention to it" (Maccoby, 1951, pp. 428-429). Frankfurt School scholars argued that the socializing role of the family had been supplanted by the mass media, advertisers, and celebrities (Horkheimer & Adorno, 1972; Marcuse, 1964). Indeed, for scores of critics, the family's role in instilling values and standards of behavior has been usurped by the media industries and their motivation to instill consumerist values.

When Holman and Jacquart (1988) indicated that marriages might stay stronger if spouses were involved in leisure-time activities, thereby increasing interpersonal communication rather than quietly watching TV, the popular press quickly declared that less television was a key to improved marriages and stable families.

But television also brings families together. Television's unifying effect on the family was observed as early as 1949; the medium acted as a catalyst in bridging generational gaps (Riley, Cantwell, & Ruttiger, 1949). Among those who wished to increase contact with the family, television use was actually preferred to the use of other media (Friedson, 1953). Other scholars who have pointed out that greater family solidarity may be achieved via television-induced interaction and conversation include Brody, Stoneman, and Sanders (1980); Faber, Brown, and McLeod (1979); Fine (1952); Foley (1968); Katz and Foulkes (1962); Katz and Gurevitch (1976); Lull (1980); and Lyle (1972).

But the experience of television in the family context has also been shown to be complex beyond the arguments citing mere divisive or unifying effects. As Coffin argued in 1955, television viewing can often do both. Television can be "credited with increasing the family's fund of common experience and shared interests and blamed for decreasing conversation and face-to-face interaction" (p. 634). Indeed, Rosenblatt and Cunningham (1976) suggested that television viewing can also serve as a means to avoiding tense interaction in crowded homes where conflict avoidance through spatial separation is impossible.

At this point, McLeod, Fitzpatrick, Glynn, and Fallis's (1982) call for a broader definition of the positive and negative effects media use may have on families in the National Institute of Mental Health's report still needs to be heeded. As is the case generally in media effects research, data prompting researchers to draw conclusions rarely explain clear cause-and-effect relationships. Illustrating this dilemma is Chaffee and Tims's (1976) study on viewing content determined by companions around the TV set. Junior and senior high school students in the study regularly watched different programs depending on whether they watched with parents or with siblings. The direction of cause and effect was complex at best, meaning that one cannot know without clear study—and even then—if the choice of programming was adapted to one's coviewers or if the children watching TV selected their coviewers for a particular program. In the same way, easy conclusions cannot be reached about whether the atmosphere in a family is fostered by TV use or whether family members use television in ways that accommodate an already existing family orientation or mood. Generally speaking, the direction of causality in such situations is at the very least two-way and mutually reinforcing. One cannot really separate the chicken from the egg, and the assumptions of clean cause-effect relationships are just that, assumptions.

## Time and Experience With Television

Adding a new and significant dimension has been the proliferation of new media technologies and the subsequent increase in the sheer volume of information and entertainment available. Much of the earliest research questioning whether television inhibited family interaction or promoted it was done in households with only one TV set. As television technology improved and became ever more affordable, the households added first one and then another TV set, coupled with radio, CD players, VCRs, and Internet-connected computers, all of them capable of individualized use.

One of the early and notable significant changes in family life that attended the growing ubiquity of a new medium of communication occurred with radio. For much of a decade, the American family gathered around a singular living room radio, but as the sets became less expensive, radios began to occupy space in multiple rooms in the home, permitting family members to break away into different locales.

This trend was repeated even more dramatically over the first 15 years of television's arrival on the national scene. And this time the eventual effect on program content was unmistakable. Once families moved from having a singular living room set where they often watched TV together to having multiple sets in the family room, dens, bedrooms, and kitchens, programmers began developing more niche programming driven by the demographics of age.

The most telling sign was the demise of the family variety show by the mid-1970s. Families in the 1950s and 1960s had religiously gathered together to view CBS's Ed Sullivan program almost every Sunday night with its very intergenerational provision of an older comedian for grandma and grandpa, a middle-aged crooner for the parents, a rock group for the teens, and Topo Gigio, a cute puppet mouse for the children. Some of these performers were designed to appeal to more than one age group (e.g., a circus performer spinning dishes atop tall sticks for the whole family). But with the family members attracted to age-niche programming in different rooms, ratings for the family variety show fell, and it has been a nearly nonexistent form of American television for more than 20 years now. Among the precious few current network programs that a whole family might watch and enjoy together are the funniest home video programs and the new revival of the prime-time high-stakes quiz shows.

According to the 1999 Kaiser Family Foundation report, children's media use now totals an entire full-time workweek, often using several media at the same time. The same research shows that children are exposed to heavy doses of media fare at a very early age. Children between the ages of 2 and 7 are already using media for 3.5 hours each day. A third of them have a TV in their bedroom, 16% have a VCR, and 13% have a video game console in their bedroom. As children grow older, substantially more of them are likely to have electronic media in their bedrooms. Of children 8 years old and older, 65% have a TV in their room and 21% have a computer.

The most noteworthy finding of the Kaiser Family Foundation report, for the purposes of this chapter, is that so much of children's media use is unsupervised; this is especially notable in light of findings dating back more than two decades that watching and talking with children helps them view more actively and intelligently (Singer & Singer, 1976). Almost half of the children in the Kaiser Foundation survey reported having no rules governing their TV watching. Diaries kept by the children in the study revealed that those older than 7 almost never watch TV with their parents. Parents of children between 2 and 7 report that 81% of the time they are doing something else while their children watch television.

These findings take on another character when considered in light of our own studies of media use relying on the experience sampling method (ESM). We examined how people use and experience television at home and with their families, as well as how media use is related to the use of time and experience in non-TV settings.

In ESM research, subjects are given paging devices (beepers) and small booklets of self-report forms. Each time the respondents are randomly signaled—usually six to eight times each day for a week—they fill out a report form telling us where they are, what they are doing, and how they feel on a set of very simple psychological measures. This way behavioral reports are generated as people actually engage in media use, allowing for a comparison between media use and all the other things people do on a daily basis.

One of the things we found that people do when they watch television with others is talk. Talking occurred 21% of the time adults viewed with their family members. When adults were with family members but not watching television, they talked 36% of the time, more than with TV but not as much more as many had thought (Kubey & Csikszentmihalyi, 1990). In other words, the early arguments that television completely froze interaction, that the viewing experience was purely "parallel," were almost certainly an artifact of the very early novelty of the medium when Maccoby made her observation in 1951. But the conclusion still holds that television watching is a less active form of family interaction than is almost anything else a family finds to do together. And the research jury is still out on the potential beneficial effects of parents and children playing video games together.

Partly because they talk a good deal when they view television, respondents' ESM reports show that familial television viewing is a significantly more challenging activity than viewing alone. Respondents also report feeling more cheerful when viewing TV with the family than when viewing alone. However, much larger experiential differences are observed between family time *without* TV and family time *with* TV. Without TV, adult respondents reported time spent with the family as being more challenging and significantly more psychologically and physically activating, but significantly less relaxing than time spent with the family with television.

The dose of individuals' media intake has also been shown to be related to the quality of family life they experience. At home, heavy television viewers are likely to spend more time alone (Kubey, 1994), but they do not report particularly negative experiences with their families. In fact, heavy viewers report feeling significantly more "free" (vs. constrained) during non-TV activities with family members than do light viewers. Furthermore, heavy viewers are no more likely to be "alienated from the family," as measured on Maddi's Alienation Index (Kubey & Csikszentmihalyi, 1990; Maddi, Kobasa, & Hoover, 1979).

ESM research also shows that television is usually experienced passively. Viewing involves little concentration but does elicit feelings of relaxation. Not surprisingly, in the instance of family group viewing, the experience is more sedate when compared with TV-free family activities. For heavy TV viewers, the whole of family life beyond viewing is perceived as being less active.

Marriage and having children generally reorients people from social lives focusing on friends to time spent at home with each other and the children, and television viewing is often a pleasurable homebound experience for families. Time spent watching television is often the compromise activity that families choose and, after a time, almost automatically and habitually do together (Kubey, 1996).

To summarize, there is as much evidence in the research literature to show that television brings family members together as there is that it rends them apart. More time spent viewing is correlated with more time spent with the family. Television, after all, is in many ways a conservative medium attempting to gather and hold the largest audiences possible. As a result, a lot of content, particularly through the first two decades of the medium's history in the United States, is articulated particularly well with conventional family interests and values.

This relationship is particularly telling among children and adolescents (Kubey, 1990). Indeed, one marker of becoming adolescent in contemporary society is a movement *away* from television and many hours spent with the family and *toward* more time spent outside the home with friends and listening to music (Larson, Kubey, & Colletti, 1989). It is interesting to note that adolescents who watch more television report feeling better during time spent with the family and relatively worse with friends, whereas adolescents who listen to more music feel worse with the family and better with friends (Larson & Kubey, 1983).

## Film and Television Content and Family Values

The rise of the mass media has constituted an alteration in the frequency with which certain kinds of messages about what is to be valued in society are communicated. Prior to the rise of the mass media, there were three primary societal institutions charged with the responsibility of socializing the young and moving them toward particular ideals of what they should know about and value on reaching their majority. These three institutions were the church, the family, and the school. The mass media that rose up in the first three decades of the twentieth century constituted a new fourth voice heard by the young. But this fourth institution, unlike the others, is only marginally responsible for formal socialization. Yet it *does* socialize.

The mass media, particularly as they are constituted in the United States, are operated by individuals and corporations who stand to profit by attracting and holding the attention of audiences. Their prime responsibility is to themselves and to stockholders, and only secondly, at best, do they operate in the public interest and to the varying and often minimal requirements of the Federal Communications Commission or Congress.

Although qualitative research on media creators has demonstrated that there are television and film performers and creators who adhere to strict personal standards (Gitlin, 1983), the popular media have also revealed many entertainment personalities who don't see themselves as role models. And although it is the case that many of the messages promulgated on television are conservative, in the mainstream, and supportive of family values, it is also the case that other messages may either directly or indirectly controvert processes and orientations that are critical to sustaining families.

The creation of what is seen, read, and heard in the media, however, must be understood within the context of broader social trends. It is an undeniable fact that TV, film, and radio producers cannot create successful content that does not, in some way, reflect already existing social realities. Arguments of the inherent conservatism of the media state that mass media industries are reluctant to present ideas that truly conflict with too many people's values too much of the time lest audiences turn away and advertising revenue dry up (Gitlin, 1972, 1983). Thus, the racy and violent images that critics regularly excoriate and public opinion polls denounce must appeal to sizable audiences.

From a family perspective, the most notable shifts in the 1950s and 1960s media were the rise of rock 'n' roll—still the art form of choice for adolescents as they begin to rebel and make their break from identifying with the family to the peer group—and youth culture movie stars such as Marlon Brando and James Dean, whose films chronicled youth angst, delinquency, and, notably, significant problems of the family unit.

In 1950s America, the film industry, even in the wake of Senator McCarthy's attacks, no longer needed to churn out only optimistic visions of the American way of life, as they had done in a time of war. Film entertainment began to take on edgier subjects (Schrader, 1986). It could move from teenage Andy Hardy (late 1930s and early 1940s) making his way through the trials of adolescence with the guidance of a benevolent adult to a tormented James Dean in *Rebel Without a Cause* (1955), failed by the family and by adult society.

The film and music sectors of the mass media quickly learned to capitalize on teenage rebellion because it was profitable. Referring to a mix of conservative values and material appealing to more base, antisocial, and hedonistic instincts, Daniel Bell (1976) articulates how the rise in images of sexuality and violence constituted "cultural contradictions of capitalism."

Relative to film and music, television would take longer to change, but when it did, it changed because of similar social and economic forces. While James Dean and Marlon Brando on the big screen made parents nervous in the 1950s, the TV images of that same time were generally so benign that they still make many today nostalgic. Others, however, argue that such images were both *benign and misleading,* at considerable variance with the realities of family life in that decade.

The change of television from an orderly landscape, one of intact nuclear families, to one of shifting, relativistic values and varying and often conflicting points of view has been argued to be a result of the late-twentieth-century shift from a universalist worldview of enlightenment values to the quicksand-like world of postmodernity. As Elkind (1993) writes, "The assumptions that societies, as they become progressively civilized, educated and cultured, also become more humanitarian and less savage is no longer tenable" (p. 601).

In the 1950s, TV showed an ideal world to which, it was incorrectly assumed, everyone aspired. Families were together (almost exclusively white), they loved each other, they lived in safe neighborhoods, and kids could count on adults to help them through the trials and tribulations of adolescence. But not only were those images something very difficult to live up to, they were also often unrealistic and overly sentimental. Television producers increasingly dispel the myths of middle-American perfection, as well as the myth of a singular desirable way of life. In the postmodern television landscape, the chaos of the world is depicted more frequently in the medium's fictional offerings. The once-sacred nuclear family's role as a haven against the threats and disorder of the world is questioned and alternatives are sometimes considered.

Although the image of the family has changed on TV, the industry's reliance on the family in programs and plots and on family viewership and patronage of advertised goods has not. Not all TV genres can easily accommodate families or family themes. Police or action-adventure shows, for example, glorify single males and bachelorhood (Cantor, 1990). In police dramas, single life is preferred, with fewer than one out of five major characters being married (Signorielli, 1991). Living the single life in this genre has the advantage over marriage and domesticity. Single men on television are more effective and powerful, concludes Signorielli (1982). Shows promising story lines of crime fighting and investigation cannot be weighed down by domesticity. This, of course, is a general trend but not an absolute rule. In the 1980s, Don Johnson's *Miami Vice* character was married in a highly publicized sweeps month episode, then his wife was killed off in the following episode. As TV critics remarked, macho sex symbol Johnson couldn't very well drive around Miami with a baby seat in his Ferrari Testarossa.

But, from the earliest days of TV, family-oriented story lines often dominated evening lineups (Gerbner, Gross, Morgan, & Signorielli, 1980; Greenberg, 1982; Head, 1954; Signorielli, 1985; Smythe, 1954). Situation comedies and soap operas are the perfect vehicles to deal with the family, and it is hard to imagine these genres without family life at the center. The major comedy format *is* the family sitcom. Its mise-en-scène is the family home, its main sets the living room and the kitchen. Here, both implicitly and explicitly, the internal world of a family sitcom is one of the most desirable places one could hope to inhabit.

Traditionally, the sitcom world is one in which the most disturbing behaviors of contemporary society, and the rest of the TV world—murder, rape, domestic violence, marital breakup, and child abuse—do not take place, and certainly not directly to the central characters. Although on rare occasions "very special episodes" of such shows do deal with the darker side of life (e.g., *All in the Family*'s Edith Bunker nearly raped or threatened by breast cancer), violence is not a regular staple of the sitcom landscape—indeed, it is nearly nonexistent. In this sense, just as most of us like to think of our own families as safe havens away from the turmoil of the world beyond, so too does the family sitcom serve as an oasis amid the often cruel flotsam and jetsam found elsewhere on the small screen.

Content analyses of general situation comedy and family drama behavior abound, and this is significant because the type of behavior these programs represent may be more readily imitated by viewers given the sheer identifiability of the settings of the shows (Comstock & Strzyzewski, 1990). Abelman (1986) concludes that, although there exists a "relatively equal amount of antisocial and prosocial behavior on television, prosocial fare is not as visually stimulating or identifiable in the context of a program as is antisocial fare" (p. 55). Conflict, after all, is the very nature of conventional drama. Without it, no drama, no entertainment vehicle, exists. However, as writers and TV and film producers have come to learn, antisocial plot resolutions can sometimes be as popular as prosocial resolutions. The vanquishing of a particularly heinous villain or getting the upper hand on a romantic rival in a relationship-oriented drama does not always sell as well if it is done in a cozy, prosocial manner. And television research has long been concerned that individuals may learn of and model undesirable ways to deal with social and familial situations by supplementing their observations of the real world with messages from television (Bandura, 1971; Dail & Way, 1985; Gerbner, Gross, Morgan, & Signorielli, 1980, 1986; Greenberg, Hines, Buerkel-Rothfuss, & Atkin, 1980).

Certainly, compared with police and action shows, characters on situation comedies engage in more prosocial behavior (Greenberg, Atkin, Edison, & Korzenny, 1977). In fact, Cantor (1990) argues that the world of domestic dramas may easily be regarded as a fantasy world, where life and people are better than what is most often encountered in the real world. Certainly, in the early days of the sitcom, parents often gave their children advice and the children often took it (Fisher, 1974). The communicative behaviors among family members are, for the greater part, positive in the family program (Skill & Wallace, 1990).

The family unit that has steadily transformed from the prototypical 1950s "perfect" middle-class nuclear family of *Leave It to Beaver, The Donna Reed Show,* or *Father Knows Best* has been classified by Chesebro (1979) and Steenland (1985) under a number of specific categories encompassing programs from various decades. They identify the childless couples (*The Honeymooners, Mad About You* [for four seasons]); communal families (*Gilligan's Island, The Mary Tyler Moore Show, Friends*); geriatric families (*The Golden Girls*); unmarried men (*Bachelor Father, Diff'rent Strokes, Full House*) and women (*Julia, One Day at a Time, Grace Under Fire*) as parents; aggregate or "blended" families (*The Brady Bunch, Step by Step*); and trial or probationary marriages (*Ned and Stacey*). Although these "familial" arrangements deviate, often radically, from the nuclear family structure—a "hook" selling these shows is the question of "how can they make it work?"—the programs, nevertheless, exist in an idealized world where positive, prosocial behaviors achieve positive results. Indeed, the characters *can* make it "work." Jerry Seinfeld's vigorous insistence that the characters in his program experience "no learning, no growing, no hugging" indicates the "feel good" state of general affairs in the rest of the sitcom world.

Situation comedies are mostly set in middle-class households—after all, the largest sector of the audience must be reached—but the lives of families across the socioeconomic spectrum, from working and middle classes to the upper middle and upper classes, have been depicted within the genre (Cantor, 1990). Working-class comedies have been seen as some form of a feminist ideal, according to Cantor (1990). Classic programs, from *The Life of Riley* and *I Remember Mama* to *All in the Family,* enact a world of diminished male supremacy. The typical blue-collar sitcom family is one ostensibly ruled over by a buffoonish, clueless, yet good-hearted and lovable man (even if he's a bigot, as in the case of *All in the Family*) and a sensible and strong woman. The father figure of the working-class family tries to enjoy his society-granted status as ruler of the family, the king of his castle. But he's often a blowhard and a loudmouth, and the programs suggest that neither he nor the marriage nor the family itself would last long without the levelheaded intelligence and common sense of his wife. The loudmouth, blowhard blue-collar guy of the sitcom, however, is never abusive; he's not an alcoholic or ever unfaithful. In fact, underneath his macho blustering, he has a heart of gold neither his wife and family nor the audience can help but love.

No sitcom is sunnier in disposition than that of the middle-class family (Cantor, 1990). Here, husbands and wives are nearly equal, and their skill at managing the family and raising kids is laudable. Conflict between spouses is rare, although when it happens it is often resolved using affiliative communication techniques (Comstock & Strzyzewski, 1990). And the conflicts are resolved quickly. In the middle-class television sitcom families, fathers do sometimes know best. The roles of women in these sitcoms have expanded: Many of them are professionals, such as Claire Huxtable (Phylicia Rashad) of *The Cosby Show,* Elise Keaton (Meredith Baxter) of *Family Ties,* and Maggie Seaver (Joanna Kerns) of *Growing Pains* in the 1980s.

Although conflicts in family programs nearly doubled over the late 1970s and the late 1980s across the socioeconomic spectrum, again they were almost always successfully resolved using affiliative, prosocial communication techniques (Heintz, 1992). Conflicts children face in latter-day sitcoms are also greater in scope and intensity, more realistic than in the classic perfect-family sitcoms (Larson, 1991)—problems ranging from drugs or alcohol to cheating in school, pressure to have sex, or even problems of violence involving guns, date rape, or child abuse in "very special episodes"—but the solutions are nearly as idealized as the rest of existence in the programs' universe.

Even though the problems and the makeup of the families have changed, becoming more complex or unconventional, these fictional worlds still operate according to internal rules adhering close to the Golden Rule. While television has turned somewhat more ambiguous since the 1970s and the postmodern worldview crisis of the post-Vietnam and post-Watergate era, that segment of the world inside the tube focusing on the family has remained the most desirable still. In medical dramas, by contrast, beloved protagonist doctors make mistakes. In the world of crime and punishment, lawyers like Perry Mason, or his 1980s/1990s reincarnation Matlock, who only defended innocent clients, have given way to *The Practice,* in which the heroic defense lawyers routinely release criminals back to the streets. On critically acclaimed police dramas such as *NYPD Blue, Law and Order,* or *Homicide,* crime often does pay, the guilty are not always punished, the innocent suffer, and justice is denied. In this TV landscape, however, the programs dealing with families are more orderly and idealized. Children, more often than not, are taught, and they believe, that the universe has a just order to it. Honesty is the best policy, good people are eventually rewarded, and family members can reach positive solutions to interpersonal problems.

Throughout the 1990s, another "youth quake" of aggressively spending teens made up a vigorous consumer market, with youth-themed films and TV shows in frantic production. Many of them present a worldview of youth supremacy and adult obsolescence. Lauded by critics, the TV program *Buffy the Vampire Slayer* is an allegory of modern teen life—one replete with violent threats facing teenagers in such traditionally safe environments as the middle-class suburb and high school. All but one of the adult characters are completely oblivious to the dangerous world of the teens, leaving children to survive evil among doltish and useless adults, a vision comparable to Elkind's (1993) postmodern analysis:

> The concept of wise, mentoring adults who impart their knowledge, skills, and values to the innocent, naïve, next generation has also become blurred. . . . These children, from an early age, live independent lives outside the home, and this independence helps to break down the distinction between parents and children. (p. 602)

Of course, this sort of youth-oriented program in which children fend for themselves is not recent. The signature film of this "genre" is *Rebel Without a Cause* (1955), in which James Dean, Natalie Wood, and Sal Mineo, all miserably failed by their inept or absent parents, form their own new nuclear family, right down to settling into an abandoned home with Dean and Wood playing parents to Mineo's child. Twelve years later, *The Graduate* (1967) served up two affluent suburban families, lost and dysfunctional and badly out of touch with the needs and worldviews of their 21-year-old offspring. In the 1980s, a number of highly popular feature films operated on the premise of children having to solve dangerous problems that adults had created but were unable or unwilling to deal with. In *Wargames* (1983), a high school computer hacker saves the world from nuclear annihilation. In *Red Dawn* (1984), actors Charlie Sheen and Lea Thompson form the resistance against foreign invaders. A teenager steals a fighter jet and rescues his father held hostage in a Middle Eastern dictatorship in *Iron Eagle* (1986). The operating formula in youth-oriented entertainment is power and autonomy to children.

## Immediate Gratification and the Family

Although filled with idealized notions of what a family or a marriage should be like, the commercial considerations of the media impress a format of presentation on programming that might well have undesirable effects on its viewers. The immediacy and speed of information, the immediacy of stimuli and gratifications, is one such dubious trait of media programming.

The orientation toward immediate gratification so common to contemporary media and quick solutions to problems is in conflict with many of the basic commitments and slow, gradual processes necessary to sustain the family, a social arrangement that one hopes will endure for at least the 18 odd years that a child lives with his or her parents.

What might this mean for the family? First, a single parent often heads sitcoms. Why? So that the parent can also play out story lines with romantic and sexual possibilities, spicing up the plot and holding viewers' attention. *Bachelor Father* is perhaps the most notable of these from the mid-1950s, followed by a host of others, some just as vapid (e.g., *My Three Sons, The Courtship of Eddie's Father*) and some more socially relevant such as *One Day at a Time*. Even the intact marital unit has become more sexualized and available for sexual hijinks (e.g., *Married . . . With Children*). With ads promising quick solutions and with the propensity to convey information quickly, the commercial electronic media may well contribute to an expectation that we should obtain gratification immediately and that solutions should come easily and quickly.

If people have been conditioned to expect quick and easy solutions, if they are impatient and not prepared to persist and to endure difficult times, complexity, and uncertainty from time to time, then being a husband or wife, and especially a parent, may well be roles that they are not prepared to successfully enact.

Because holding attention is the sine qua non of the commercial media, other things happen as well. Sound bites in television and in radio must be short, and scenes must change rapidly lest the audience grow bored or change the channel (Adatto, 1990; Hallin, 1992).

The advertising that supports the media also suggests to us that we should never feel bad for too long. After all, there is one nostrum or another for almost anything that ails us, and these medications, as often as not, are positioned within the context of one family member helping another quickly gain the fast relief promised. The emphasis in much advertising on products that can make one feel better almost immediately may well be related to some of our culture's problems with drug abuse. And given that drug abuse can seriously disturb a family's life, this may be another way that the form, style, and content of the commercial mass media indirectly contribute to familial problems.

In a review on the effects of television on scholastic performance written for the U.S. Department of Education, one of the few consistent findings cited across many studies was that children who viewed television heavily, especially violent programming, had more difficulties in impulse control, task perseverance, and delay of gratification (Anderson & Collins, 1988; see also Singer & Singer, 1983). That such children grow into adults is unquestionable. Whether these problems are sustained into adulthood is not clear.

In other research, self-labeled television "addicts" scored significantly higher than "nonaddicted" viewers on measures of mind wandering, distractibility, boredom, and unfocused daydreaming (McIlwraith, 1990; Smith, 1986). Whether television itself can be held directly responsible remains unclear. But it seems plausible that some of the people who spend 4 and 5 hours almost every day over decades watching television may be less practiced in directing their own attention, in entertaining themselves, and in maintaining psychological equilibrium when left to their own devices than those who are infrequent viewers (Kubey, 1986). And if self-control is a problem for a parent, there are almost certainly going to be repercussions for the family as a whole.

Commercial pressures in the mass media, along with the general speed of technological development, also result in an emphasis on "the new." Products, programs, fashions—things are better if they are new. Not only is the family not new, but such an orientation may contribute to older extended members of the family, such as grandparents, being more easily deemed obsolete, not "with it," or even useless (Kubey, 1980). Grandparents may not know a lot about the World Wide Web, how to program a VCR, or about CD players or the latest rap group, but they may well be wise about life.

## Competing for Attention

One area of concern rarely, if ever, examined concerns family members who feel that they must compete with the people on television for the attention of other family members. This is not an insignificant problem, yet there is virtually no research that bears on it.

It is undeniably the case that, from time to time, and in some families frequently, people are neglected or ignored by other family members because of television viewing or other media involvement. The image of the father who comes home from work to find that his children can barely greet him with a hello because they are watching a rerun of *Bonanza* is legion in film, and, although fictionalized, such images retain a basis in reality. Our society even has the term *football widow* to describe a woman who feels neglected by her husband because he watches so many football games on television over his 2 days at home with her each fall weekend.

Most problematic of all are cases in which the emotional and physical needs of children are neglected because of a parent's extreme involvement with television. Although very inconclusive, and counterintuitive, one study has indicated that hyperactive and attention deficit disorder children do not watch more television than nonhyperactive children do. Instead, this research found that the parents of ADHD children watch *more* television than do the parents of non-ADHD children (Shanahan & Morgan, 1989). One of the researchers' unusual speculations is the possibility that some children may actually be mimicking television's kinetic nature in an attempt to be as exciting as the tube in order to win parental attention. There may well be more sound interpretations, but this one is especially disturbing even to consider.

The increasing ubiquity of Internet access at home raises another potentially problematic trend, one that remains understudied to date. Much has been written on how home and work are merging, with more workers on flexible time and with communication technologies enabling them to work from home. But what does it do to the processes of family life when Mom or Dad is furiously drafting an important e-mail memo to all the staff at work just 10 feet from where the children are playing in the adjacent room? Speaking from the first author's personal experience, the sense of urgent immediacy of responding to and sending e-mail memos, drafts of coauthored articles, and grant proposals while at home *does* interfere with a more consistent family atmosphere in the home (and my children will attest to this). Yet it seems difficult as a contemporary academic—and this is no doubt true of other occupations as well—to *not* stay in touch with work concerns late into the evening, during weekends, and even over the holidays. When the children 10 feet away come into the study asking for attention, to play, for a drink or a cookie, the hardworking parent is *not* in a family frame of mind.

Of course, well before the arrival of the Internet, parents did work at home via phone, legal pad, and computer, but there is little question that the Internet has added a new and more immediate means of communication into the home, one that was largely absent only 5 years earlier.

Our contemporary communications technologies have changed the way we work and live, right down to *where* and *when* we work. These changes are clearly affecting the ebb and flow of family life, but no research that we have located to date solidly confirms measurable effects. Yet, no doubt, they exist.

Parents are not the only family members hooked up to the newer media technologies of video games, computers, and the Internet. Although children and adolescents still spend proportionately more time with traditional media (56% of their media use time is devoted to TV, movies, and videos; 22% to CDs and the radio; and only 5% each spent on video games and computers), the computer and Internet mystique has a very strong hold on young people (Kaiser Family Foundation, 1999). According to the Kaiser study, if the children surveyed were forced to choose between media, a majority (33%) would pick a computer with Internet access.

## Devaluation of Spouses and Monogamy

Modern-day royalty, especially in the United States, are not necessarily the rich but the beautiful and talented. Never before in the history of the human species has there been such a form of distraction in the home wherein the most beautiful, interesting, and engaging people that a culture can find are presented incessantly in full living color. Television and film—and the increasing World Wide Web—are thick with extremely attractive young adults, as well as intense love scenes, in large part, once again, because of the commercial domination of these media and the goal of attracting and holding audiences.

The question arises whether this constant barrage of attractive opposite-sex celebrities on television brings any new pressures to a marriage, whether men in particular, and women to a somewhat lesser degree, are more likely to feel that they are somehow missing something if their spouse is not as young, as beautiful, or as svelte as the people on television.

There is also constant pressure on women in our culture to compete with the thousands of attractive women who appear on television. (The same phenomenon goes on for men as well, but its effects are likely to be less pervasive if for no other reason than that women have been historically valued for their appearance more than men have been.)

We might also ask whether film and television overromanticize the intensity of love and passion between men and women, thereby making it more likely for some people who have been married or involved for a number of years to feel that the reduced intensity of their own romance and lovemaking pales by comparison. Put another way, does television leave some people thinking to themselves, "Am I missing something"? The possibility arises that some people may be more likely to look outside the marriage for romantic and/or sexual satisfaction to get for themselves that *something* that they are more intensely aware they are missing precisely because of what they see routinely in the media. And it is no accident that, on average, women on TV are roughly 10 years younger than men (Kubey, 1980; Signorielli & Gerbner, 1978).

Although a clear directional cause is not established, evidence does exist that viewers of pornography are more dissatisfied with their spouses (Zillmann & Weaver, 1989). A growing yet still relatively small body of research on pornography and its effects on attitudes toward marriage, sex, relationships, and the general human worth and welfare of others gives cause for concern with the breakneck-paced proliferation of new technologies. After all, many new media technologies are quickly harnessed for the dissemination of pornography. The Internet and World Wide Web's ability to reach into homes and unleash a mass of unregulated images is especially troubling given the Kaiser Family Foundation's (1999) report of how adept even the youngest children are at computer use and how little supervision they experience. And, for more than 15 years now, the videocassette has substantially increased the availability of pornography for home viewing—if not in "your home," then perhaps at the neighbor's house down the street where your children play.

Potential damage to young viewers, as well as to family and marriage-sustaining value systems, is illustrated by research pointing to a coldness and indifference to human worth (especially that of women) after nonusers are exposed to pornography. Here, the Zillmann and Weaver (1989) sexual callousness model suggests how prolonged pornography use could lead to a climate of misogyny, aggressiveness, and violence toward women. Pornography frequently depicts indiscriminately voracious sexual appetites among women and, in certain genres, their "enjoyment" of abuse, rape, and degradation, and this is particularly alarming (Brownmiller, 1984, p. 42). Research demonstrating significant correlations between pornography use and sex crimes (Baron & Strauss, 1984; Court, 1984; Kutchinsky, 1973), the use of pornography by child molesters before and during their attacks (Marshall, 1988), and the ambivalence of pornography users toward the punishment of sex crimes (Weaver, 1987; Zillmann & Weaver, 1989) indicates some of the potential threats such media products pose, even as researchers still cannot perfectly disentangle cause from effect and as theoretical and policy debates continue about how a civilized society should deal with pornography in its midst.

As Zillmann (1994) draws a comparison between the value systems repeated in erotic and pornographic media and family values, he argues that they are inherently antithetical to the value systems needed to sustain a healthy, safe, and nurturing family environment. As we have argued earlier, the family is essentially a relationship founded on long-term commitment. For Zillmann, and for us, it consists of parents' commitments to each other, to the long-term intellectual, moral, and economic well-being of the family unit, and, above all, the commitment to the day-to-day welfare of their children. Long-term commitment, however, is the antithesis of pornography. The scenarios depend on casual meetings between strangers, quick sexual gratification that's approached as the satisfaction of a physical need alone with no emotional investment, then a parting of these strangers apparently never to interact again. Pornography deems promiscuity and transience in relationships as normal and desirable. Physical gratification is valued above all other concerns—such as the emotional, spiritual, or intellectual investment in an interpersonal relationship—and pornography suggests that relationships between people need to last only as long as the physical satisfaction is sustained in ever more novel and exotic ways.

Almost as disturbing as the implication of the devaluation of women is Zillmann's (1994) work indicating an indifference to having children exhibited by both young male and female research subjects exposed to pornography in an experimental setting. The desire to have children—especially girls—was shown to diminish among these research subjects, at least in their self-reports on a questionnaire administered 1 week after the experimental exposure. Evidence of a reduced interest in an enduring family unit is suggested.

## Media Courtship Behavior as Preparation for Marriage and Family

Married couples and families can also be conceived of as audiences, or as members of an audience. Indeed, for many married couples and in many families, the majority of time spent together is as an audience. This is an important fact that, to our knowledge, has never been dealt with in research. A question develops: How critical in courtship and the decision to marry have similar leisure orientations and film and television tastes become?

In contemporary times, an increasing number of people meet their future spouses through shared leisure activities. Consider the period of courtship in which a couple spends a huge percentage of its time together on dates, at movies and concerts, or watching TV. Modern courtship could be increasingly thought of as a testing period for a lifetime of sharing entertainment and being members of an audience together. Presumably, some relationships break down in the early courtship stage partly because the two people's tastes in leisure activities and in film and television vary severely.

Certainly in previous centuries, similar tastes for entertainment had to be of far less import to the nature and experience of courtship, if for no other reason than that so much less time was spent being entertained. Today, in contrast, millions of married couples spend 15 to 20 hours almost every week, week in and week out, over decades, receiving entertainment and information together as audience members. Viewed in this way, there may be extraordinary impacts of the media on family life that are much greater and pervasive than we typically think, impacts that are extraordinarily difficult to observe or measure as they speak to very gradual changes in the ways that the relationships themselves are formed and maintained.

## Avenues for Action

As for what can be done, first, parents need to exercise greater control and become more vigilant with regard to what their children are being exposed to, and for how long. With the new modes of delivery, and the greater diversity of what is now available, especially via cable, the VCR, and the Internet, the challenge to parents is greater than it has ever been, but many parents exercise very little control over what their young children view or are unaware of potential problems that the media pose (Kaiser Family Foundation, 1999; Kubey, 1991). For example, some parents permit—or even encourage—their young children to watch horrific and graphically violent material on TV. Other parents are unaware that their young adolescents are watching hard-core pornography at the neighbor's house or late at night via cable or the Internet.

There is also a role for the government, as well as for political action groups, and for citizens working with one another or alone. There will always be disagreements over the precise effects of different kinds of content and different media on both individuals and families. Because in most cases we cannot predict precisely what the effects might be, many researchers are reluctant to prescribe solutions. But some solutions involve common sense. Children should not be exposed to excessively graphic violence or pornography (Kubey, 1987). We also do not need to wait for definitive social science research findings to set policy in these areas. We should be urging the media industries to more effectively regulate themselves and exercise greater restraint. And we should be urging the government to bring greater pressure on media industries to better serve the public interest. One avenue is for parents and educators to use the Children's Television Act to encourage local TV stations to provide more programs of value to children. And there is a myriad of media public action groups that one can join and participate in.

The Supreme Court decided years ago that commercial speech was different from other forms of speech and did not always deserve the same protections. With media such as videos, television, and radio that are widely available and that enter people's homes, the government retains a limited right to take steps to serve the greater good. Protections vis-à-vis the Internet are harder to settle on, especially as the case law is so new.

Families need to be encouraged to use the media together and, especially, to use the media more critically. To accomplish this, we must encourage media literacy training and critical viewing skills to be taught formally in our school systems (Kubey, 1991; Singer, Zuckerman, & Singer, 1980). Media education is now called for in some form in 48 states (Kubey & Baker, 1999) but is not delivered as widely as it is mandated. Meanwhile, both Canada and Australia now call for media education nationwide, and media education is increasingly developed in England, Scotland, and many European countries.

Media education is important because parents cannot do the job entirely by themselves, and some parents will not do the job regardless. The commercial media industries are also not likely to change the practices that they employ to attract and hold attention, and the FCC or the government is not likely to significantly alter the commercial dominance of the media in our society. What we can do is better prepare children and parents to analyze and think more critically about what they view, read, and listen to, and the family and our society will be better for the effort.

## References


Abelman, R. (1986). Children's awareness of television's prosocial fare: Parental discipline as an antecedent. *Journal of Family Issues, 7,* 51-66.

Adatto, K. (1990). *Sound bite democracy: Network evening news presidential campaign coverage, 1968 and 1988* (Research Paper R-2). Cambridge, MA: Harvard University, Joan Shorenstein Barone Center.

Anderson, D., & Collins, P. (1988). *The impact on children's education: Television's influence on cognitive development.* Washington, DC: U.S. Department of Education.

Bandura, A. (1971). *Social learning theory.* New York: General Learning Press.

Baron, L., & Strauss, M. A. (1984). Sexual stratification, pornography, and rape in the United States. In N. M. Malamuth & E. Donnerstein (Eds.), *Pornography and sexual aggression* (pp. 185-209). Orlando, FL: Academic Press.

Bell, D. (1976). *The cultural contradictions of capitalism.* New York: Basic Books.

Brody, G. H., Stoneman, Z., & Sanders, A. (1980). Effects of television viewing on family interactions: An observational study. *Family Relations, 29,* 216-220.

Bronfenbrenner, U. (1973). In J. Clayre (Ed.), *The impact of broadcasting.* London: Compton Russell.

Brownmiller, S. (1984, November). The place of pornography: Packaging eros for a violent age [Comments to a forum held at the New School for Social Research in New York City moderated by L. H. Lapham]. *Harper's* pp. 31-39, 42-45.

Cantor, M. G. (1990). Prime-time fathers: A study in continuity and change. *Critical Studies in Mass Communication, 7,* 275-285.

Chaffee, S. H., & Tims, A. R. (1976). Interpersonal factors in adolescent television use. *Journal of Social Issues, 32,* 98-115.

Chesebro, J. W. (1979). Communication, values, and popular television series: A four year assessment. In G. Gumpert & R. Cathcart (Eds.), *Inter/media: Interpersonal communication in a media world* (pp. 528-560). New York: Oxford University Press.

Coffin, T. (1955). Television's impact on society. *American Psychologist, 10,* 634.

Comstock, J., & Strzyzewski, K. (1990, Summer). Interpersonal interaction on television: Family conflict and jealousy on primetime. *Journal of Broadcasting and Electronic Media, 34*(3), 263-282.

Court, J. H. (1984). Sex and violence: A ripple effect. In N. M. Malamuth & E. Donnerstein (Eds.), *Pornography and sexual aggression* (pp. 143-172). Orlando, FL: Academic Press.

Dail, P. W., & Way, W. L. (1985). What do parents observe about parenting from prime-time television? *Family Relations, 34,* 491-499.

Elkind, D. (1993, October). Adolescents, parenting, and media in the twenty-first century. *Adolescent Medicine: State of the Art Reviews, 4*(3), 599-606.

Faber, R. J., Brown, J. D., & McLeod, J. M. (1979). Coming of age in the global village: Television and adolescence. In E. Wartella (Ed.), *Children communicating: Media and development of thought, speech, and understanding* (pp. 215-249). Beverly Hills, CA: Sage.

Fine, B. J. (1952). *Television and family life: A survey of two New England communities.* Boston: Boston University, School of Public Relations.

Fisher, C. (1974). Marital and familial roles on television: An exploratory sociological analysis (Doctoral dissertation, Iowa State University, 1974). *Dissertation Abstracts International, 35,* 599A.

Foley, J. M. (1968). *A functional analysis of television viewing.* Unpublished doctoral dissertation, University of Iowa.

Friedson, E. (1953). The relation of the social situation of contact to the media in mass communication. *Public Opinion Quarterly, 17,* 230-238.

Gerbner, G., Gross, L., Morgan, M., & Signorielli, N. (1980). *Media and the family: Images and impact.* Paper presented at the National Research Forum on Family Issues, White House Conference on Families, Washington, DC.

Gerbner, G., Gross, L., Morgan, M., & Signorielli, N. (1986). Living with television: The dynamics of the cultivation process. In J. Bryant & D. Zillmann (Eds.), *Perspectives on media effects.* Hillsdale, NJ: Lawrence Erlbaum.

Gitlin, T. (1972). Sixteen notes on television and the movement. In G. White & C. Newman (Eds.), *Literature in revolution* (pp. 335-366). New York: Holt, Rinehart & Winston.

Gitlin, T. (1983). *Inside prime time.* New York: Pantheon.

Greenberg, B. (1982). Television and role socialization: An overview. In B. Pearl, L. Bouthilet, & J. Lazar (Eds.), *Television and behavior: Ten years of scientific progress and implications for the eighties* (pp. 179-190). Washington, DC: U.S. Government Printing Office.

Greenberg, B., Atkin, C., Edison, N., & Korzenny, F. (1977). *Pro-social and anti-social behaviors on commercial television in 1976-1977* [Report by Michigan State University, Department of Communication]. Washington, DC: U.S. Office of Child Development.

Greenberg, B. S., Hines, M., Buerkel-Rothfuss, N., & Atkin, C. K. (1980). Family role structure and interactions on commercial television. In B. S. Greenberg (Ed.), *Life on television: Content analyses of U.S. TV drama* (pp. 149-160). Norwood, NJ: Ablex.

Hallin, D. C. (1992). Sound bite news: Television coverage of elections, 1968-1988. *Journal of Communication, 42,* 5-24.

Head, S. W. (1954). Content analysis of television drama programs. *Quarterly of Film, Radio, and Television, 9,* 175-194.

Heintz, K. E. (1992, Fall). Children's favorite television families: A descriptive analysis of role interactions. *Journal of Broadcasting and Electronic Media,* pp. 443-451.

Holman, T. B., & Jacquart, M. (1988). Leisure-activity patterns and marital satisfaction: A further test. *Journal of Marriage and the Family, 50,* 69-77.

Horkheimer, M., & Adorno, T. W. (1972). The culture industry: Enlightenment as mass deception. In M. Horkheimer & T. Adorno (Eds.), *The dialectics of enlightenment* (pp. 120-167). New York: Seabury Press.

Kaiser Family Foundation. (1999). *Kids and media at the new millennium: A comprehensive analysis of children's media use.* Menlo Park, CA: Author.

Katz, E., & Foulkes, D. (1962). On the use of the mass media as "escape": Clarification of a concept. *Public Opinion Quarterly, 26,* 377-383.

Katz, E., & Gurevitch, M. (1976). *The secularization of leisure, culture, and communication in Israel.* Cambridge, MA: Harvard University Press.

Kubey, R. (1980). Television and aging: Past, present, and future. *Gerontologist, 20,* 16-35.

Kubey, R. (1986). Television use in everyday life: Coping with unstructured time. *Journal of Communication, 36,* 108-123.

Kubey, R. (1987, June 24). *Testimony on Senate Bill 844, 100th Congress: A television violence antitrust exemption* [Hearing before the Subcommittee on Antitrust, Monopolies, and Business Rights of the Committee on the Judiciary, U.S. Senate, Serial No. J-100-27]. Washington, DC: U.S. Government Printing Office.

Kubey, R. (1990). Television and family harmony among children, adolescents, and adults: Results from the experience sampling method. In J. Bryant (Ed.), *Television and the American family* (pp. 73-88). Hillsdale, NJ: Lawrence Erlbaum.

Kubey, R. (1991, March 6). The case for media education. *Education Week, 10,* 27.

Kubey, R. (1994). Media implications for the quality of family life. In D. Zillmann, J. Bryant, & A. C. Huston (Eds.), *Media, children, and the family: Social scientific, psychodynamic, and clinical perspectives.* Hillsdale, NJ: Lawrence Erlbaum.

Kubey, R. (1996). Television dependence, diagnosis, and prevention: With commentary on video games, pornography, and media education. In T. MacBeth (Ed.), *Tuning in to young viewers: Social science perspectives on television* (pp. 221-260). Newbury Park, CA: Sage.

Kubey, R., & Baker, F. (1999, October 27). Has media literacy found a curricular foothold? *Education Week, 19,* 56.

Kubey, R., & Csikszentmihalyi, M. (1990). *Television and the quality of life: How viewing shapes everyday experience.* Hillsdale, NJ: Lawrence Erlbaum.

Kutchinsky, B. (1973). Eroticism without censorship. *International Journal of Criminology and Penology, 1,* 217-225.

Larson, M. S. (1991, Fall). Sibling interactions in the 1950s versus 1980s sitcoms: A comparison. *Journalism Quarterly, 68*(3), 381-387.

Larson, R., & Kubey, R. (1983). Television and music: Contrasting media in adolescent life. *Youth and Society, 15,* 13-31.

Larson, R., Kubey, R., & Colletti, J. (1989). Changing channels: Early adolescent media choices and shifting investments in family and friends. *Journal of Youth and Adolescence, 18,* 4.

Lull, J. (1980). Family communication patterns and the social uses of television. *Communication Research, 7,* 319-334.

Lyle, J. (1972). Television in daily life: Patterns of use. In E. Rubinstein, G. Comstock, & J. Murray (Eds.), *Television and social behavior: Vol. 4. Television in day-to-day life: Patterns of use* (pp. 1-32). Washington, DC: U.S. Government Printing Office.

Maccoby, E. (1951). Television: Its impact on school children. *Public Opinion Quarterly, 15,* 421-444.

Maddi, S. R., Kobasa, S., & Hoover, M. (1979). An alienation test. *Journal of Humanistic Psychology, 19,* 73-76.

Marcuse, H. (1964). *One dimensional man.* Boston: Beacon.

Marshall, W. L. (1988). The use of sexually explicit stimuli by rapists, child molesters, and nonoffenders. *Journal of Sex Research, 25,* 267-288.

McIlwraith, R. D. (1990, August). *Theories of television addiction.* Talk given to the American Psychological Association, Boston.

McLeod, J. M., Fitzpatrick, M. A., Glynn, C. J., & Fallis, S. (1982). Television and social relations: Family influences and consequences for interpersonal behavior. In D. Pearl, L. Bouthilet, & J. Lazar (Eds.), *Television and behavior: Ten years of scientific progress and implications for the eighties* (Vol. 2, pp. 272-286). Washington, DC: U.S. Government Printing Office.

Morgan, M., & Leggett, S. (1999). Television and family values: Was Dan Quayle right? *Mass Communication & Society,* 2(1/2), 47-63.

Riley, J., Cantwell, R., & Ruttiger, K. (1949). Some observations on the social effects of television. *Public Opinion Quarterly, 13,* 223-224.

Rosenblatt, P., & Cunningham, M. (1976). Television watching and family tensions. *Journal of Marriage and the Family, 31,* 105-111.

Schrader, P. (1986). Notes on film noir. In B. K. Grant (Ed.), *Film genre reader* (pp. 170-182). Austin: The University of Texas Press.

Shanahan, J., & Morgan, M. (1989). Television as a diagnostic indicator in child therapy: An exploratory study. *Child and Adolescent Social Work, 6,* 175-191.

Signorielli, N. (1982). Marital status in television drama: A case of reduced options. *Journal of Broadcasting, 26*(2), 585-597.

Signorielli, N. (1985). *Role portrayal and stereotyping on television: An annotated bibliography of studies relating to women, minorities, aging, sexual behavior, health, and handicaps.* Westport, CT: Greenwood.

Signorielli, N. (1991). Adolescents and ambivalence toward marriage: A cultivation analysis. *Youth and Society, 23*(1), 121-149.

Signorielli, N., & Gerbner, G. (1978). The image of the elderly in prime time television drama. *Generations, 3,* 10-11.

Singer, D. G., & Singer, J. L. (1976). Family television viewing habits and the spontaneous play of preschool children. *American Journal of Orthopsychiatry, 46,* 496-502.

Singer, D. G., Zuckerman, D. M., & Singer, J. L. (1980). Teaching elementary school children television viewing skills: An evaluation. *Journal of Communication, 30,* 84-93.

Singer, J. L., & Singer, D. G. (1983). Implications of childhood television viewing for cognition, imagination, and emotion. In J. Bryant & D. R. Anderson (Eds.), *Children's understanding of television: Research on attention and comprehension* (pp. 269-296). New York: Academic Press.

Skill, T., & Wallace, S. (1990, Summer). Family interactions on primetime television: A descriptive analysis of assertive power interactions. *Journal of Broadcasting & Electronic Media, 34*(3), 243-262.

Smith, R. (1986). Television addiction. In J. Bryant & D. Zillmann (Eds.), *Perspectives on media effects* (pp. 109-128). Hillsdale, NJ: Lawrence Erlbaum.

Smythe, D. W. (1954). Reality as presented by television. *Public Opinion Quarterly, 18,* 143-156.

Steenland, S. (1985). *Prime time kids: An analysis of children and families on television.* Washington, DC: National Commission on Working Women.

Weaver, J. B. (1987). Effects of portrayals of female sexuality and violence against women on perceptions of women (Doctoral dissertation, Indiana University, Bloomington, 1988). *Dissertation Abstracts International, 48*(10), 2482-A.

Zillmann, D. (1994). Erotica and family values. In D. Zillmann, J. Bryant, & A. C. Huston (Eds.), *Media, children, and the family: Social scientific, psychodynamic, and clinical perspectives* (pp. 199-213). Hillsdale, NJ: Lawrence Erlbaum.

Zillmann, D., & Weaver, J. B. (1989). Pornography and men's sexual callousness toward women. In D. Zillmann & J. Bryant (Eds.), *Pornography: Research advances and policy considerations* (pp. 95-125). Hillsdale, NJ: Lawrence Erlbaum.

CHAPTER 17

# Television's Gender Role Images and Contribution to Stereotyping

## Past, Present, Future

NANCY SIGNORIELLI
University of Delaware

Television is the central and most pervasive mass medium in the American culture. Over the years, it has come to play a distinctive and historically unprecedented role as our nation's most common, constant, and vivid learning environment. Americans spend much of their time in the world of television, whether watching broadcast programming, cable, or a movie or time-shifted program on the VCR. In the average home, the set is turned on for about 7 hours each day, and the average person watches more than 3 hours a day (Vivian, 1999). Children, the older generation, and minorities typically watch the most television. Today, however, with the proliferation of cable systems on most college campuses, even college students watch a considerable amount of television. Consequently, as we enter the twenty-first century, very few people escape exposure to television's vivid and recurrent patterns of images, information, and values.

Television is first and foremost the nation's and the world's storyteller—it tells most of the stories to most of the people most of the time. It is the wholesale distributor of images and the mainstream of popular culture. Children are born into homes in which, for the first time in human history, a centralized commercial institution, rather than parents, church, or school, tells most of the stories. The world of television shows and tells us about life—people, places, striving, power, and fate. It shows and tells us how things work and what to do about them. It presents the good and bad, the happy and sad, the successful and the failures, and it tells us who's on the top and who's on the bottom. The characters in television programs do not live or die but are created or destroyed to tell the story. This storytelling function of television is extremely important because these stories teach viewers about the intricacies of the world and its peoples.

Understanding and examining the underlying structure of these stories, and especially the stereotypes that pervade their characterizations, has been the goal of numerous research studies since the 1950s. This line of research has proliferated during the past 50 years, and it is important now to step back and take stock of what we have done, what we have found, and to think about where we should go in the future.

## The Research Question in Perspective

The study of the mass media can be viewed as a three-step process: (a) examining the images people encounter in the media, (b) ascertaining what impact or effects these images may have, and (c) understanding the institutional processes that create these images and ensure their success and/or failure. Although all three steps are interconnected and our understanding of any one necessitates answering questions associated with the other two, it is obvious that, without understanding the nature of the images, we really cannot understand the nature of their effects or what institutional forces may be involved in their shaping or their success. Consequently, a major research question in mass media research asks how different thematic elements and kinds of people are portrayed in the media.

Most American families bought their first television set during the early to mid-1950s. As more and more homes had television sets and more and more people began to watch on a regular basis, scholars began to study this new phenomenon, and the first studies about television content were published (Head, 1954; Smythe, 1954). Moreover, the first congressional hearings about television, focusing particularly on television violence, were convened in 1954. Research on television content and its effects was particularly stimulated by the forces that affected the United States during the late 1960s, notably national turmoil, civil rights, and the women's movement. Two national commissions were appointed to uncover the dynamics of these forces on society. In essence, the agendas of these commissions set the stage for early and ongoing research on media images.

The national turmoil that rocked the country after the assassinations of Martin Luther King Jr. and Bobby Kennedy stimulated concern about violence in society and in the media. The National Commission on the Causes and Prevention of Violence was appointed to examine violence in society, including violence on television (see Baker & Ball, 1969), and commissioned one study to ascertain the amount of violence on television (Gerbner, 1969).

Continued national unrest, as well as concerns about television's impact on Americans, further encouraged researchers to pursue this line of study. Financial assistance was also provided by increased government funding for research about television violence. In 1969, even before the report of the National Commission on the Causes and Prevention of Violence was released, Congress appropriated $1 million and set up the Surgeon General's Scientific Advisory Committee on Television and Social Behavior. This committee funded 23 projects, dealing primarily with violence on television and its effects (Gerbner, 1972; Surgeon General's Scientific Advising Committee, 1972). Although interest in television violence faded somewhat during the 1980s, congressional concern about media violence again increased during the 1990s, culminating in the development of ratings for television programs and the V-chip technology.

Concern with civil rights, during the late 1960s and early 1970s, contributed to the proliferation of studies on minority images. The Kerner Commission, appointed by President Johnson to investigate racial disturbances in many U.S. cities, charged that these disturbances could be traced, in part, to the U.S.

mass media industry's failure to serve and adequately represent minority interests. In short, the Kerner Commission found that the media seemed to encourage racial conflict by presenting black Americans in negative and limited ways, and it suggested that the industry, and its regulating agencies, give priority to improving coverage related to minority groups (Kerner Commission, 1968).

Finally, the events and increased consciousness that marked the late 1960s also led to a "new beginning" for the women's movement, women's issues, and the notion of equality for women. Coupled with this was concern for how women were presented in the media. Scores of studies documenting the underrepresentation and negative images of women on television and in advertising were being undertaken despite the lack of a national commission to provide funding for research. This body of research has continued during the past 50 years, with concern about the media's, particularly television's, influence on gender role stereotypes as high on the research agenda today as it was during the early 1970s.

Research exploring these issues proliferated. Most of the early studies were concerned with determining baseline measures (e.g., how much violence, how many minorities, how many women), particularly in prime-time network dramatic programming, the programs watched by most Americans. Later research examined the representation of women in relation to topics such as age, marital status, and occupation, as well as differences across program genres and delivery systems. This chapter will discuss the theoretical orientations of research on gender stereotypes and summarize the findings of this research, with most emphasis on the studies conducted during the 1990s.

## Theoretical Orientations

Socialization is the way people learn about their culture and acquire its values, beliefs, perspectives, and social norms. It is an ongoing social process; we are socialized and resocialized throughout the life cycle. Traditionally, parents, peers, teachers, and the clergy have had the major responsibility for socialization. Numerous studies have found, however, that, in today's society, the mass media play a very important role in the socialization process (Berry & Mitchell-Kerman, 1982; Roberts & Bachen, 1981; Roberts & Maccoby, 1985). Stereotypes, in particular, play an important part in television's role as an agent of socialization. Stereotypes are conventional or standardized images or conceptions; they are generalizations or assumptions that are often based on misconceptions. Stereotypes typically lack originality—they fall back on commonly known and often one-dimensional elements of portrayal. They appeal to people's emotions rather than their intellect. Television programs with limited time to devote to character development often resort to stereotypes. The concern is that viewers, especially children, who are continually exposed to television's stereotyped roles may develop conceptions and perceptions about people that reflect the stereotypical images they see in the media.

The actual processes of media socialization, however, are different from those used by more traditional agents of socialization. Media socialization does not permit face-to-face social interaction and may lack some of the seductive or coercive powers of traditional agents who have the tools of interpersonal communication at their disposal (Wright, 1986). Nevertheless, the media have their own brand of seductiveness, and much of the socialization through the media may involve observational and/or social learning.

Social or observational learning theory (Bandura & Walters, 1963) examines the role of modeling in a child's social development. It posits that viewers, especially children, imitate the behavior of television characters in much the same way that they learn social and cognitive skills by imitating their parents, siblings, and peers (Lefkowitz & Huesmann, 1980). Bandura's (1986) extension of cognitive processing to social learning theory (social cognitive theory) adds rules and strategies to the traditional why, what, and when of behavior change. Television provides not only specific responses but the strategies and rules viewers may use to copy what they observe (Comstock, 1989). Television's stereotypes are particularly suited to the processes of social cognitive theory because they provide simplistic, often one-dimensional models of behaviors, strategies, and rules that appear regularly in many different genres of programs.

A second theoretical orientation that is relevant to the media's role as an agent of socialization is cultivation theory (Gerbner, Gross, Morgan, & Signorielli, 1994). This theory explores the general hypothesis that the more time viewers spend with television, the more likely their conceptions about the world and its people will reflect what they see on television. Thus, to understand the effects of television on attitudes, beliefs, and behavior, television must be studied as a collective symbolic environment of messages with an underlying pattern or formulaic structure. Because of commercial constraints, television presents a common worldview and common stereotypes through a relatively restrictive set of images and messages that cut across all programs in all delivery systems. The term *cultivation* refers to "the specific independent (though not isolated) contribution that a particular consistent and compelling symbolic stream makes to the complex process of socialization and enculturalization" (Gerbner, 1990, p. 249). Studies conducted in the tradition of cultivation theory continually show that television content has little diversity and has frequently recurring features and thematic elements (Gerbner et al., 1994).

## Images on Television

The world of television drama, with its ongoing schedule changes, gives the illusion of constant change. Yet the hundreds of content analyses (see, for example, Signorielli, 1985) examining media images present a very different picture. In short, when all is said and done, the world of television—its themes, characterizations, and stereotypes—exhibits considerable and remarkable stability.

Certain key aspects of television's portrayals have undergone little overall change in the past 50 years. The underrepresentation of women is one of these elements. In study after study, men have outnumbered women in prime-time dramatic programming (Davis, 1990; Greenberg & Collette, 1997; Selnow, 1990; Signorielli, 1985, 1989, 1993; Signorielli & Bacue, 1999). The earliest studies of network television broadcast during the early 1950s (e.g., Head, 1954; Smythe, 1954) found three men for every one woman. In most of the studies conducted during the 1970s and early 1980s, there was a high degree of consistency in the television world's demography, with men typically outnumbering women by three to one (see Signorielli, 1985). More recent studies put the ratio at two to one (Greenberg & Collette, 1997; Signorielli & Bacue, 1999).

Greenberg and Collette (1997), using *TV Guide* synopses and operating under the assumption that change should occur primarily in new programming, examined the basic demography of each season's new programs. This analysis described, over 27 seasons, the consistent underrepresentation of women among new characters. In addition, most of the new characters were young or middle-aged, and many appeared in more traditional than nontraditional occupations. Olson and Douglas (1997) studied 10 situation comedies broadcast between the 1950s and the 1990s and found that gender roles fluctuated over this 40-year period. Moreover, more recent programs (*Roseanne, Home Improvement*) contained fewer positive characterizations than earlier programs. Although the television character population has continued to move toward greater representation of women, the numbers still favor men. In an analysis of a sample of programming broadcast during 1992 and 1993, even though close to 40% of the characters were women, most of these females were cast in minor rather than major roles (Elasmar, Hasegawa, & Brain, 1999). Moreover, most of the women in major roles were in situation comedies. Women were underrepresented in all genres of prime-time programming in the mid-1990s (Lauzen & Dozier, 1999). Signorielli and Bacue (1999), in an analysis of weeklong samples of prime-time network programming broadcast between 1967 and 1998, isolated a statistically significant linear trend ($F = 89.91$; $df = 1{,}34$; $p < .001$) in the numbers of female characters. The proportion of women increased significantly and steadily between 1967 and 1998—moving from 24% of the characters in 1967 to a high of 43% in 1996 and down to 38% in the spring of 1998.

Cable programs have similar patterns even though cable, because of its numerous channels, has been heralded for its likelihood to provide greater diversity in programming. Gerbner (1993), comparing the demography of network and cable programming, determined that the patterns of underrepresentation in broadcast programming were also prevalent in samples of cable TV. Kubey, Shifflet, Weerakkody, and Ukeiley (1995) discovered that, in an analysis of 1,035 randomly selected 10-second intervals of programming on 32 different cable channels throughout the day, males outnumber females by about 2.5 to 1 across all channels. The male-female distribution is even more lopsided when looking at programming on channels that can be received only by cable (i.e., the nonbroadcast channels). Moreover, the distribution was most skewed in programming seen during the prime-time hours.

In addition to underrepresentation, the world of television has consistently presented stereotyped images of both men and women. A meta-analysis of eight content analyses (Herrett-Skjellum & Allen, 1996) yielded strong evidence of gender-typed stereotypes on television. In particular, studies have consistently shown that women in prime time are likely to be younger than men (Gerbner, Gross, Signorielli, & Morgan, 1980; Vernon, Williams, Phillips, & Wilson, 1990), are cast in traditional and stereotypical roles (Signorielli, 1989), and are more likely to have blond or red/auburn than black or brown hair (Davis, 1990). This is not to say that change has not occurred or that nontraditional women do not appear on television; it is just that these images are not presented consistently. Most of us can easily cite many examples of women on TV who are not stereotyped, and much of the research examining nonstereotyped roles has focused on small and select groups or samples of programs (see, for example, Atkin, 1991; Reep & Dambrot, 1987). Moreover, in more recent programs (e.g., *Ally McBeal*), many of the female characters who break with the stereotypes on one dimension of their portrayal (e.g., their occupation and success in the world of work) fall back on traditional stereotypes when involved in or dealing with a romantic relationship (Signorielli & Kahlenberg, in press).

Signorielli and Bacue (1999), examining more than 30 years of programming, reported considerable consistency in characterizations of the 1990s compared with earlier years. One consistent stereotype is that the women are younger than the men. Television places great value on youth, with the greatest emphasis on the youthfulness of women. The message of the 1990s was still that a woman's value is in her youthfulness. On television, women, on average, tend to be about 4 years younger than the men. Moreover, the proportion of women categorized as young adults was greater during the 1990s than it was in the 1970s and 1980s. Other analyses of programming broadcast in the 1990s also found that most of the female characters were in their 20s and 30s, and very few were categorized as over 50 (Elasmar et al., 1999; Lauzen & Dozier, 1999). Similarly, Signorielli and Bacue (1999) reported that the proportion of older characters on television remained very small. Moreover, they observed a very negative message of aging, particularly for women, which was especially pronounced for characters categorized as 65 or older. On the one hand, 65-year-old men are found in jobs and are more likely to be categorized as middle-aged than elderly. On the other hand, most of the women over 65 are seen as elderly (not middle-aged), and they do not continue to work outside the home. This stereotype has not changed in 30 years of network broadcast programming (see Gerbner et al., 1980).

Along with images of youthfulness, the media, particularly television, present very stereotyped images of women's and men's bodies. Female characters on television typically have thin and almost "perfect" bodies; their weight is judged as average or below average, and very few (fewer than 1 in 10) are even somewhat overweight (Fouts & Burggraf, 1999). Moreover, these characters, particularly those who are quite thin, often receive positive comments about their bodies and how they look. At the same time, the media ideal for male characters, over the years, has become more muscular (Mishkind, Rodin, Silberstein, & Striegel-Moore, 1986).

Another set of stereotypes emerges in occupational portrayals. On television, occupations, although varied, are stereotyped and often gender-typed. In fact, Herrett-Skjellum and Allen's (1996) meta-analysis determined that the most evidence for stereotypes occurs in occupational portrayals. The early studies of prime-time programming found that women's employment possibilities were somewhat limited, with clerical work the most common job (Signorielli, 1984, 1993; Steenland, 1990; Vande-Berg & Streckfuss, 1992).

Today, more women on television are employed outside the home, and their jobs are a little more prestigious than 30 years ago (Signorielli & Bacue, 1999). For example, the percentage of women cast in the professions increased from the 1970s to the 1990s. Whereas in the 1970s women were often depicted in traditional female occupations such as teachers, nurses, secretaries, and clerks, during the 1980s and 1990s fewer women were cast in these jobs and more were found in traditional male jobs or in gender-neutral jobs. Men, on the other hand, appeared most frequently in traditional male occupations, and very few were presented in traditional female jobs. Interestingly, many of the women who could be categorized by occupation held blue-collar jobs (Elasmar et al., 1999).

Similarly, Signorielli and Kahlenberg (in press), in an analysis of network prime-time programs broadcast during the 1990s, reported some improvement in the occupational portrayals of women and people of color. For example, when compared with their male counterparts, females, especially white women, were equally likely to be portrayed as professionals and more likely to be portrayed in white-collar jobs. Nevertheless, more females than males still could not be classified by occupation or were portrayed as not working outside of the home, and fewer females than males were found in the military and law enforcement.

The world of work presents stereotypical portrayals in regard to gender, race, and marital status. Themes of romance and marriage were pervasive on television, especially for women (Signorielli, 1982). When compared with men, more women, especially women of color, were classified by marital status and, in general, were more likely to be portrayed as married or formerly married. During the 1990s, however, women of color were less likely than white women to be married; race was not a predictor of marital status for men.

Even though in the 1990s more and more women were mixing marriage, homemaking, and raising children with careers (women today make up 46.1% of the workforce), the television world has not kept up with societal changes in regard to women's marital status and employment. Single and formerly married female characters still dominate the television women's workforce. Married women are still more likely to be seen as not working or not classified by occupation than as working outside the home. The patterns are somewhat different, though, for white women and women of color. Married women of color are almost equally likely to be portrayed as working than as not working outside the home. In contrast, among the single and formerly married women, white women are more likely than minority women to be portrayed as working outside the home (Signorielli & Kahlenberg, in press).

On the other hand, there are relatively few differences between work and marital status for white men and men of color. Regardless of marital status, men of color are more likely than white men not to be classified as working (Signorielli & Kahlenberg, in press). For married males, themes of romance, home, marriage, and family do not necessarily influence whether they are depicted in the workforce. Overall, television continues to reinforce the stereotype of men as the breadwinners and presents married women with reduced options, for they can rarely successfully combine marriage and employment.

### *The Soaps, Children's Programming, Commercials, and MTV*

Women in the soaps (daytime serial dramas) generally have parity with the men and are sometimes presented as equal (Cassata & Skill, 1983; Katzman, 1972) and often quite positively (Downing, 1974). The overall impression, however, is that the traditional woman has life just a little easier and is seen in a more positive light; she often triumphs, while the liberated or modern woman is punished or has a harder time (Cantor & Pingree, 1983). Minority men and women, on the other hand, tend to be quite underrepresented on the soaps (Cantor & Pingree, 1983).

Women are especially short-changed and underrepresented on children's programs. In cartoons, studies consistently find that men outnumber women by four or five to one (Signorielli, 1984, 1991) and that, once again, women are presented in very stereotypical roles (Levinson, 1975; Streicher, 1974). Gender role portrayals also do not differ in programs that are toy based compared to those that are not toy based (Eaton & Dominick, 1991). Public television programs for children, although better on some dimensions, still fall short in relation to basic demography (Dohrmann, 1975; Matelski, 1985). Men also do not fare well in children's programming; they are more likely to rely on aggression and to receive disapproval (Nolan, Galst, & White, 1977).

Even though female underrepresentation and many stereotypes continued in the cartoons of the 1990s, there have been some changes. Thompson and Zerbinos (1995) found that female cartoon characters of the 1990s were more assertive, intelligent, independent, and more likely to show leadership qualities than the characters of the 1970s and 1980s. Nevertheless, female characters were also more likely than male characters to be portrayed in traditional stereotypes such as being more emotional, romantic, affectionate, and domestic. Male characters also changed during the 1990s; today, male characters are presented as more intelligent, more technical, more aggressive, and as asking and answering more questions but bragging less. Finally, in the cartoons of the 1990s, male characters typically have recognizable jobs, whereas the females are often cast as caregivers.

As with children's programs, commercials are also sex-typed and stereotyped on numerous dimensions (Courtney & Whipple, 1983). Strong links typically are made between attractiveness and the presentation of women (Downs & Harrison, 1985; Lin, 1997); women are also often placed in domestic settings advertising products for the home (Bretl & Cantor, 1988; Craig, 1992a). Older adults, especially older women, are underrepresented in television commercials, although this may vary by the product advertised (Ray & Harwood, 1997). Interestingly, award-winning commercials from the 1980s show women in more diverse occupations and job-related activities than similar commercials from the 1950s (Allan & Coltrane, 1996). Research consistently shows that a woman's voice is rarely used as a voice-over and that men are presented as authoritative, even for products used primarily by women (Allan & Coltrane, 1996; Bretl & Cantor, 1988; Dominick & Rauch, 1972; Lovdal, 1989; O'Donnell & O'Donnell, 1978). Women are much more likely than men to be found in commercials for over-the-counter medications and are typically presented as the experts in home health care (Craig, 1992b). Although men and women are more equally represented (in terms of numbers) in prime-time commercials (Bretl & Cantor, 1988), women are somewhat less represented in award-winning commercials (Allan & Coltrane, 1996) and very underrepresented in commercials aired during children's programs (Doolittle & Pepper, 1975; Riffe, Goldson, Saxton, & Yu, 1989). Sex-typing in children's commercials also exists at the structural level: Male-oriented commercials contain more cuts, loud music, and boisterous activity, while female-oriented commercials contain more fades and dissolves, soft music, and quiet play (Welch, Huston-Stein, Wright, & Plehal, 1979).

In the past 20 years, music videos have become an important television genre for adolescents. Women, however, are very underrepresented in videos (Brown & Campbell, 1986; Caplan, 1985; Gow, 1996), and stereotyped sex roles abound (Vincent, 1990; Vincent, Davis, & Boruszkowski, 1987). Sherman and Dominick (1986) found that women were presented as submissive, passive, physically attractive, and sensual and were often used as decorative objects, particularly in concept videos. Men, on the other hand, were in control of relationships. Other male images in videos include gang members, thugs, and gangsters, while female images include nightclub performers, temptresses, servants, and goddesses (Aufderheide, 1986). Videos in the early 1990s continued to present women so that their physical appearance rather than their musical ability was emphasized (Gow, 1996), and, compared with the men, the women in these videos were more likely to wear sexually revealing clothes (Seidman, 1992). Similarly, the commercials on MTV present the message that a woman's first objective is to look beautiful so that she can attract attention (Signorielli, McLeod, & Healy, 1994).

Country music videos present similar images. Although the country music industry proclaimed 1997 as the Year of the Woman, an analysis of videos on Country Music Television (CMT) aired during January 1997 demonstrated that, while a small number of female artists received the same degree of coverage as male artists, the overall ratio of male to female artists was three to one. These videos contained two dominant images. Women in the videos of female artists were presented as fully equal to the men, although there were one or two instances of very stereotyped behavior. The women in the videos of male artists, on the other hand, were seen in very traditional and stereotyped roles (Andsager & Roe, 1999).

### *Overview*

There has been improvement in the presentation of women on television over the past 50 years. First, the proportion of women has gone from a quarter to more than a third of all characters, a statistically significant, if small, increase (Signorielli & Bacue, 1999). Nevertheless, the number of female characters depends on program genre. Women make up at least half of the characters in situation comedies and soap operas but are practically invisible in action-adventure programs (Steenland, 1990). Second, women's work roles have improved, with more women presented in "typically male" or gender-neutral occupations. Women, however, are also likely to be portrayed as affluent and rarely have problems with child care, harassment, or sex discrimination (Huston et al., 1992). In addition, television's single parents, whether male or female, frequently enjoy live-in domestic help and rarely experience the financial problems most single-parent families face on a daily basis (Moore, 1992).

## The Impact of Stereotyping on Viewers

The description of television images is an important and necessary first step in understanding the role of television in society. Clearly, one cannot assess effects without knowing what people see. Consequently, as awareness of the images of men and women on television and in other media became known, research turned to examining the impact of these images. Viewers, particularly children, are aware of and expect to find stereotyped images on television (Reeves & Greenberg, 1977). Thompson and Zerbinos (1997), for example, discovered that children perceived stereotyped cartoon characters: Boys were active and violent, whereas girls were concerned with appearances and seen more often in domestic settings. Similarly, Wroblewski and Huston's (1987) analysis indicated that children were aware of television's stereotyped occupational images. Moreover, children as young as kindergarten age are aware of television's gender stereotypes and are able to predict whether men or women (or boys or girls) would be found in these activities on television (Durkin & Nugent, 1998). Even though viewers, particularly children, perceive the existence of gender stereotypes on television, the more important question is how these stereotypes influence their attitudes and behaviors. Thus, a particularly important area of investigation is the cultivation of gender role attitudes in both adults and children.

### *Cultivation of Gender Role Images*

The influence of the mass media, especially television, on conceptions relating to gender roles is an important area of investigation. This research differs from research relating to perceptions of gender roles (stereotyping) in programming, "identification" with (wanting to be like) specific characters, and counterstereotyping because it examines how the media may be shaping people's, and especially children's, views of what it means to be a man or a woman. This, in turn, may aid or abet those goals (e.g., occupational, educational, personal) a person may set out to achieve. Clearly, the evidence points to the fact that society's notions of appropriate roles for men and women have changed (Harris & Lucas, 1976; Signorielli, 1989). We still must determine whether the media, notably television, have helped or hindered this process.

Studies of television's impact or effects are generally hampered because it is almost impossible to find control groups who are not exposed to television. Moreover, those who do not watch television tend to be a small but quite eclectic group (Jackson-Beeck, 1977), and television's pervasiveness and the overall similarity of its imagery across all types of programs has resulted in an erosion of regional diversity (Morgan, 1986). Finally, nontraditional or nonsexist portrayals of male and female roles have only recently appeared with some regularity.

The research generally points to the existence of a relationship between television viewing and having more stereotypic conceptions about gender roles. Two meta-analyses have found support for this relationship. Herrett-Skjellum and Allen (1996) examined 19 nonexperimental and 11 experimental studies dealing with television and gender role stereotypes and found an average effects size of .101. Similarly, Morgan and Shanahan (1997), in a meta-analysis of all published studies relating to cultivation theory, found an average effects size of .102 in the analysis of 14 cultivation studies relating to gender roles.

Although the absolute size (.101 and .102) of these effects is small, we cannot automatically discount the findings as meaningless. First, the effect is seen in numerous studies conducted by a large number of different and independent research teams in a wide variety of settings. Second, small effects often are important in the overall picture. For example, a difference of 1 or 2 percentage points (the differential seen in many cultivation studies) may differentiate between winning or losing an election or the success or failure of a television show. Finally, because television is such a ubiquitous medium and accumulated exposure to its messages is important, just about everyone should be affected, in some way, by viewing. In short, then, the cards are stacked against finding evidence of cultivation, and finding even small effects has far-reaching consequences.

Herrett-Skjellum and Allen (1996) found all positive relationships and no age-related patterns, concluding that these studies, particularly those using nonexperimental designs, seem to indicate that television viewing is particularly related to conceptions about occupations. Finally, Hearold's (1986) meta-analysis of 230 studies found that television viewing had a strong effect on role stereotyping. The next two sections of this chapter discuss many of the studies included in these meta-analyses as well as other studies that also provide support for this finding.

### *Nonexperimental Studies*

Beuf (1974), in a study of 3- to 6-year-old children, found that those children who watched more television were more likely to stereotype occupational roles. This research also found that preschool-age boys were unable to say "what they would be when they grew up" if they were a girl, whereas the girls always had a response when asked what job they would have if they were a boy. Gross and Jeffries-Fox (1978), in a panel study of 250 eighth-, ninth-, and tenth-grade children, discovered that television viewing was related to giving sexist responses to questions about the nature of men and women and how they are treated by society. Pingree (1978) found that television commercials influenced children's attitudes about gender role stereotypes. Third- and fifth-grade children who watched more television were more likely to exhibit traditional sex role stereotypes for gender-related qualities (e.g., independence, warmth) and gender-related activities (playing sports or cooking) (Rothschild, 1984). Finally, Katz and Coulter (1986) uncovered more gender stereotyping among children who watched a lot of television compared with children who spent a lot of time reading.

There is additional support for the notion that television viewing contributes to children's perceptions about appropriate male and female behaviors. Freuh and McGhee (1975), in a study of children in kindergarten through sixth grade, found that those who spent more time watching television exhibited greater sex-typing than those who spent less time watching television. Similarly, in another study, heavy viewers had more stereotyped perceptions of gender roles than light viewers did. For male stereotypes, there was an interaction effect indicating that, among light viewers, the perception of male stereotypes declined with age, whereas among heavy viewers male stereotypes remained with increasing age. An interaction was not found for the perception of female stereotypes (McGhee & Freuh, 1980). Studies by Morgan (1982, 1987) and Morgan and Rothschild (1983) also indicate that television cultivates gender role attitudes among adolescents. Morgan and Harr-Mazar (1980) found that television seems to cultivate attitudes about when to form a family and how many children to have. Morgan and Rothschild (1983) also demonstrated that children who watch more television were more likely to endorse traditional divisions of labor between the sexes.

Morgan (1982), in a 3-year panel study of sixth- through eighth-grade children, found that levels of sexism were higher among all boys and lower-class girls and that television cultivates notions such as "women are happiest at home raising children" and "men are born with more ambition than women." Among girls, the amount of television viewing was significantly associated with scores on an index of gender role stereotypes 1 year later, over and above the influence of demographics and earlier scores on this same index; there was no evidence that gender role stereotyping leads to more television viewing. For boys, the patterns were reversed; there was no relationship between viewing and gender role attitudes, but greater sexism was related to more viewing 1 year later. Overall, this study reveals that television viewing is most likely to make a difference among those who are otherwise least likely to hold traditional views of gender roles, a concept cultivation theory refers to as "mainstreaming."

In a second study of 287 adolescents, using measures taken at two points in time, Morgan (1987) determined that television viewing made an independent contribution to adolescents' gender role attitudes over time, but television viewing was not related to some of their specific behaviors in relation to seven specific chores. Signorielli and Lears (1992), in a cross-sectional replication of this analysis with a sample of children in the fourth and fifth grades, also isolated statistically significant relationships between viewing and having gender-typed attitudes toward chores but no relationship between viewing and actually doing gender-stereotyped chores. Moreover, attitudes toward gender-stereotyped chores and actually doing "girl" or "boy" chores were related but gender specific. Children, particularly those who said they watched more television, who had more stereotyped ideas about who should do which chores were more likely to do those chores traditionally associated with their gender.

There is support for the relationship between television viewing and conceptions about male and female roles in two studies analyzing data from the Monitoring the Future Survey fielded in 1985 (Signorielli, 1991, 1993). One of these analyses (Signorielli, 1991) found that high school students' conceptions about marriage reflected the ambivalent presentation of marriage in prime-time network programming. Television viewing was positively related to high school students saying they probably would get married, have children, and stay married to the same person. At the same time, there was a positive relationship between viewing and expressing the opinion that one sees so few good or happy marriages that one could question marriage as a way of life. In another analysis of this data set (Signorielli, 1993), conceptions about work reflected two contradictory views about work that appear on television. Television viewing was related to adolescents (a) wanting to have high-status jobs that would also give them a chance to earn a lot of money and (b) wanting to have jobs that were relatively easy with long vacations and time to do other things in life.

In another study of the potential effects of television's stereotyped occupational portrayals, 5th- and 6th-grade children knew about jobs they typically encountered on television as well as experienced in real life (Wroblewski & Huston, 1987). Occupations on television, however, were seen as more sex-stereotyped than jobs in real life. The children had more negative attitudes about men holding television's typically feminine jobs than men having jobs that women typically hold in real life. The girls in this sample were particularly positive about television's typically masculine jobs.

There are only a few studies examining the relationship between conceptions about gender roles and television viewing among adults. Volgy and Schwartz (1980), in a study of registered voters in a southwestern city, found a positive relationship between viewing entertainment programs and the acceptance of traditional sex roles. Pingree, Starrett, and Hawkins (1979), using a small sample of women in Madison, Wisconsin, reported a positive relationship between viewing daytime serial dramas and supporting traditional family values and family structures. Ross, Anderson, and Wisocki (1982), using a sample of 78 college students and a group of 19 older adults, discovered that the amount of sex role stereotyping in self-descriptions was positively correlated with the amount of viewing of stereotyped television programs.

Finally, an analysis of the National Opinion Research Center's (NORC) general social surveys fielded between 1975 and 1986 provides support for a general hypothesis that those who watch more television will have more sexist views and a mainstreaming hypothesis that certain groups of respondents who espouse very different views when they are light viewers will have more similar outlooks regarding women's role in society as heavy viewers (Signorielli, 1989). This analysis suggests that, even though there was a decrease in the number of respondents who agreed with sexist statements between the 1970s and 1980s, television viewing was related to the maintenance of notions of more limited roles for women in society, particularly in regard to politically oriented issues.

### *Experimental Studies*

Further evidence comes from a number of experiments conducted both in the laboratory and in the field. Children who viewed commercials in which females were cast in typically male occupations were more likely to say that this occupation was appropriate for women (Atkins & Miller, 1975). Another laboratory experiment was designed to determine the effects of exposure to beauty commercials "on the perceived importance of beauty commercial themes in social relations on adolescent female viewers" (Tan, 1979, p. 284). The results revealed that high school girls exposed to beauty commercials rated beauty characteristics significantly more important "to be popular with men" than did girls who saw neutral commercials. Those girls exposed to beauty commercials also rated beauty as personally more important than did those who saw neutral commercials. In addition, Geis, Brown, Walstedt, and Porter (1984) reported that women who viewed traditionally sex-typed commercials, compared with men and women who saw reversed-role commercials, emphasized homemaking rather than achievement themes in an essay imagining what their lives would be like in 10 years.

Finally, one of the very few studies having natural control groups of children who had very little, if any, exposure to television revealed changes in conceptions about gender roles after television became available to the control groups (Williams, 1986). In this study, girls in NOTEL (town without television) and girls in UNITEL (town with very limited television) had weaker gender-typed views than girls in MULTITEL (town with greater television availability). Two years after the introduction of television into NOTEL and an increase of television's availability in UNITEL, the girls in NOTEL had become significantly more sex-typed, and the views of both these girls and the girls in UNITEL were similar to the views of the girls in MULTITEL. Similar results were found for boys in these towns, except for anomalous high scores for the UNITEL boys in the first phase of the study (Kimball, 1986).

## Conclusions and Implications

This review has explored gender role socialization from a communication research perspective. Overall, research examining the presentation of gender roles on television indicates a stable image that, in most cases, is very supportive of the status quo, especially in relation to physical appearance and marriage. Although occupational portrayals have exhibited some change, those women most likely to work outside the home are single or formerly married. Thus, the consistent image is that the woman who is married cannot mix marriage, child rearing, and working outside the home. Moreover, women who do not fit stereotypical molds on one dimension of their characterization, such as their occupation, often revert to very traditional gender role stereotypes regarding their interpersonal relationships with men. These images serve to support the notion that women should not outshine men, particularly those they are married to or have an ongoing romantic relationship with (Institute for Mental Health Initiatives, 1997).

Research on the impact of such images in regard to conceptions about sex roles points to the existence of a relationship between television viewing and having more stereotypic conceptions about gender roles. These relationships exist at all stages of the life cycle. We have found evidence in samples of preschoolers, middle and high school students, college students, and adults. Support has also been found in both experimental and non-experimental settings. In essence, television may be contributing to the maintenance of notions of more limited roles for women in society because the images seen on television typically foster the maintenance of the status quo vis-à-vis men's and women's roles in society.

### *What Must Be Done*

In retrospect, it is quite obvious that research has shown that, although on certain dimensions (e.g., the number of men and women on television) there has been some change in the images of women on television during the past 50 years, there is also a lot of stability in what we see. We have amassed a considerable body of research, and the methodology used to conduct this research has shown steady improvement. We have a broad base of knowledge about images on television. Do we know all we need to know? Do we need to continue to conduct research about these topics?

Some would answer a resounding "yes" to the first question and "no" to the second. I do not agree and think many of my colleagues would support my response. Yes, we do know a lot, and a lot of what we know indicates little overall change in character portrayals from year to year. But that is an important finding and must be monitored. If women continue to expand their roles and presence on television, it should eventually make a difference. In addition, network programming, although still a mainstay of viewing (or, at least, time shifting), no longer has more than the lion's share of the audience, and there is a need to expand our analyses to the increased offerings of cable systems. Network programming itself has changed with the addition and success of new networks, so today there are seven viable broadcast television networks. Most of what we know reflects programming on four of these networks (ABC, CBS, FOX, and NBC). There is, however, considerable need to expand our analyses to programs on the three newer networks (UPN, the WB, and PAX), because these networks appear to cater to both adolescent and minority audiences. Similarly, there is a need to update our knowledge of the images in programming, especially children's programming, on PBS. Finally, we must continue to monitor the effects of the continued conglomerization and globalization of media. For example, the recent acquisition of CBS by Viacom may lead to the demise of UPN, one of the new networks whose programming has targeted minority audiences and, recently, young male viewers (Mifflin, 1999).

We need up-to-date content studies because studies of television effects must be grounded in their findings. The research paradigm noted at the beginning of this chapter gives media research the broad-based perspective it needs. It is only when we have information about the images to which people are exposed that we can start to assess their impact. Finally, there is a considerable need to conduct studies of the institutions that produce these messages and determine their fate. We need to understand why women have not made greater inroads in joining the ranks of those involved in television and film production as writers, directors, and producers. Do women indeed reach and fail to break through the glass ceiling? Do women "jump off" the uppermost rungs of the career ladder because their biological clocks are running out or because they realize that they want to be full participants in their children's lives? Above all, we need to ascertain how to get better representation of women and people of color in the industry that makes pictures and tells the stories. For example, it will be important to continue to monitor the industry's response to the assertion of the NAACP that most of the prime-time programs aired in the fall of 1999 did not adequately represent minority groups (Daley, 1999).

To date, studies of the gender makeup of the television industry seem to indicate that having women involved in television production does make some difference in the types of stories that are produced and the types of characters in these stories. Steenland (1990, 1995), looking at writers, producers, directors, and executives in Hollywood in 1990, found that men's roles were more varied and interesting because programs were typically created and produced by men. She speculated that, because there were few women in these positions, the most women could accomplish was "damage control" (p. 63). Women in the industry, for example, can lower the level of gratuitous violence and reduce the amount of offensive language and/or leering camera angles. In Steenland's (1995) opinion, women in the early 1990s could not really make much of a difference because they did not have the level of control needed for change. Seger (1996) and Lauzen and Dozier (1999), on the other hand, discovered that women working in the industry did make a difference in the types of programs and characterizations. There was a strong relationship between women writers, directors, and producers and their creative works. Women writers, in particular, felt that they should be the voice of women, and they tried to develop characters who were well defined and autonomous (Seger, 1996). Similarly, Lauzen and Dozier (1999) found that programs with women executive directors typically had more female characters than programs in which there were no women in industry roles. Interestingly, they uncovered some support for their hypothesis that female characters who use more powerful language (interrupt others, have the last word, etc.) in programs had women involved behind-the-scenes. Nevertheless, less than one third of the programs in these samples had women in behind-the-scene roles (producers, directors, etc.).

Thus, one of the ways that women's images on television can be improved is by having more women in positions of power—as producers, directors, writers, and so on. Moreover, writers and producers must get the message that there are many different ways that they can improve how they present women on television. Characterizations and character development, for example, should not rely on or resort to stereotypes. Rather, as suggested by the Institute for Mental Health Initiatives (1997), successful female characters on television should do the following:

- Have jobs or be involved in activities that they truly love
- See being a woman as a help rather than a hindrance in their professional work
- Have and seek mentors within the course of the story
- Say what they truly think in a nonconfrontational way
- Look at the humor in situations without becoming the brunt of the joke
- Have faith in and believe in themselves

We know where the deficiencies lie, and we have some idea of how to eliminate them. Continued research can only facilitate this process and prevent us from becoming complacent about what we see on TV. Our research on effects is just beginning to make inroads in understanding the powerful impact of this medium on our lives. It is imperative that we continue this line of research. This research, however, must be driven by specific information on what people see when they watch television, not what we think they see. We have come a long way in the past 50 years. We cannot forget that we still have a long way to go.

## References

Allan, K., & Coltrane, S. (1996). Gender displaying television commercials: A comparative study of television commercials in the 1950's and 1980's. *Sex Roles, 35*(3/4), 185-203.

Andsager, J. L., & Roe, K. (1999). Country music video in country's year of the woman. *Journal of Communication, 49*(1), 69-82.

Atkin, D. (1991). The evolution of television series addressing single women, 1966-1990. *Journal of Broadcasting & Electronic Media, 35*(4), 517-523.

Atkins, C., & Miller, M. (1975). *The effects of television advertising in children: Experimental evidence.* Paper presented to the International Communication Association, Mass Communication Division.

Aufderheide, P. (1986). Music videos: The look of the sound. *Journal of Communication, 36*(1), 57-78.

Baker, R., & Ball, S. (Eds.). (1969). *Violence and the media.* Washington, DC: U.S. Government Printing Office.

Bandura, A. (1986). *Social foundations of thought and action: A social cognitive theory.* Englewood Cliffs, NJ: Prentice Hall.

Bandura, A., & Walters, R. H. (1963). *Social learning and personality development.* New York: Holt, Rinehart & Winston.

Berry, G., & Mitchell-Kerman, C. (Eds.). (1982). *Television and the socialization of the minority child.* New York: Academic Press.

Beuf, A. (1974). Doctor, lawyer, household drudge. *Journal of Communication, 24*(2), 142-154.

Bretl, D. J., & Cantor, J. (1988). The portrayal of men and women in U.S. television commercials: A recent content analysis and trends over 15 years. *Sex Roles, 18*(9-10), 595-609.

Brown, J. D., & Campbell, K. (1986). Race and gender in music videos: The same beat but a different drummer. *Journal of Communication, 36*(1), 94-106.

Cantor, M. G., & Pingree, S. (1983). *The soap opera.* Newbury Park, CA: Sage.

Caplan, R. E. (1985). Violent program content in music video. *Journalism Quarterly, 62*(1), 144-147.

Cassata, M., & Skill, T. (1983). *Life on daytime television: Tuning-in American serial drama.* Norwood, NJ: Ablex.

Comstock, G. (1989). *The evolution of American television.* Newbury Park, CA: Sage.

Courtney, A. E., & Whipple, T. W. (1983). *Sex stereotyping in advertising.* Lexington, MA: Lexington Books.

Craig, R. S. (1992a). The effect of television day part on gender portrayals in television commercials: A content analysis. *Sex Roles, 26*(5-6), 197-211.

Craig, R. S. (1992b). Women as home caregivers: Gender portrayal in OTC drug commercials. *Journal of Drug Education, 22*(4), 303-312.

Daley, D. (1999, July 27). "Clueless" networks scramble to diversify lily-white casts. Wilmington, DE *News Journal,* p. D6.

Davis, D. M. (1990). Portrayals of women in prime-time network television: Some demographic characteristics. *Sex Roles, 23*(5/6), 325-332.

Dohrmann, R. (1975). A gender profile of children's educational TV. *Journal of Communication, 25*(4), 56-65.

Dominick, J. R., & Rauch, G. E. (1972). The image of women in network TV commercials. *Journal of Broadcasting, 16*(3), 259-265.

Doolittle, J., & Pepper, R. (1975). Children's TV ad content: 1974. *Journal of Broadcasting, 19*(2), 131-142.

Downing, M. H. (1974). Heroine of the daytime serial. *Journal of Communication, 24*(2), 130-137.

Downs, A. C., & Harrison, S. K. (1985). Embarrassing age spots or just plain ugly? Physical attractiveness stereotyping as an instrument of sexism on American television commercials. *Sex Roles, 13,* 9-19.

Durkin, K., & Nugent, B. (1998). Kindergarten children's gender-role expectations for television actors. *Sex Roles, 38*(5/6), 387-402.

Eaton, B. C., & Dominick, J. R. (1991). Product-related programming and children's TV: A content analysis. *Journalism Quarterly, 68,* 67-75.

Elasmar, M., Hasegawa, K., & Brain, M. (1999). The portrayal of women in U.S. prime time television. *Journal of Broadcasting & Electronic Media, 43*(1), 20-34.

Fouts, G., & Burggraf, K. (1999). Television situation comedies: Female body images and verbal reinforcements. *Sex Roles, 40*(5/6), 473-481.

Freuh, T., & McGhee, P. (1975). Traditional sex-role development and amount of time spent watching television. *Developmental Psychology, 11,* 109.

Geis, F. L., Brown, V., Walstedt, J. J., & Porter, N. (1984). TV commercials as achievement scripts for women. *Sex Roles, 10*(7/8), 513-525.

Gerbner, G. (1969). Dimensions of violence in television drama. In R. Baker & S. Ball (Eds.), *Violence and the media* (pp. 311-340). Washington, DC: U.S. Government Printing Office.

Gerbner, G. (1972). Violence in television drama: Trends and symbolic functions. In G. A. Comstock & E. A. Rubinstein (Eds.), *Television and social behavior: Vol. 1. Media content and control* (pp. 28-187). Washington, DC: U.S. Government Printing Office.

Gerbner, G. (1990). Epilogue: Advancing in the path of righteousness (maybe). In N. Signorielli & M. Morgan (Eds.), *Cultivation analysis: New directions in media effects research* (pp. 249-262). Newbury Park, CA: Sage.

Gerbner, G. (1993). *Violence in cable-originated television programs.* Philadelphia, PA: Annenberg School for Communication.

Gerbner, G., Gross, L., Morgan, M., & Signorielli, N. (1994). Growing up with television: The cultivation perspective. In J. Bryant & D. Zillmann (Eds.), *Media effects: Advances in theory and research* (pp. 17-41). Hillsdale, NJ: Lawrence Erlbaum.

Gerbner, G., Gross, L., Signorielli, N., & Morgan, M. (1980). Aging with television: Images on television drama and conceptions of social reality. *Journal of Communication, 30*(1), 37-47.

Gow, J. (1996). Reconsidering gender roles on MTV: Depictions in the most popular music videos of the early 1990's. *Communication Reports, 9*(2), 151-161.

Greenberg, B., & Collette, L. (1997). The changing faces on TV: A demographic analysis of network television's new seasons, 1966-1992. *Journal of Broadcasting & Electronic Media, 41,* 1-13.

Gross, L., & Jeffries-Fox, S. (1978). What do you want to be when you grow up, little girl? In G. Tuchman,

A. K. Daniels, & J. Benet (Eds.), *Hearth and home: Images of women in the mass media* (pp. 240-265). New York: Oxford University Press.

Harris, L. H., & Lucas, M. E. (1976). Sex-role stereotyping. *Social Work, 21,* 390-395.

Head, S. (1954). Content analysis of television drama programs. *Quarterly of Film, Radio, and Television, 9,* 175-194.

Hearold, S. (1986). A synthesis of 1043 effects of television on social behavior. In G. Comstock (Ed.), *Public Communication and Behavior* (Vol. 1). Orlando, FL: Academic Press.

Herrett-Skjellum, J., & Allen, M. (1996). Television programming and sex stereotyping: A meta-analysis. In B. R. Burleson (Ed.), *Communication yearbook 19* (pp. 157-185). Thousand Oaks, CA: Sage.

Huston, A. C., Donnerstein, E., Fairchild, H., Feshbach, N. D., Katz, P. A., Murray, J. P., Rubinstein, E. A., Wilcox, B. L., & Zuckerman, D. (1992). *Big world, small screen: The role of television in American society.* Lincoln: University of Nebraska Press.

Institute for Mental Health Initiatives. (1997). Women's work: Will it ever be done? *Dialogue, 5*(1), 1-4.

Jackson-Beeck, M. (1977). The non-viewers: Who are they? *Journal of Communication, 27*(3), 65-72.

Katz, P. A., & Coulter, D. K. (1986). *Progress report: Modification of gender: Stereotyped behavior in children* (Grant No. BNS-8316047). Washington, DC: National Science Foundation.

Katzman, N. (1972). Television soap operas: What's been going on anyway? *Public Opinion Quarterly, 36*(2), 200-212.

Kerner Commission. (1968). *Report of the National Advisory Commission on Civil Disorders.* Washington, DC: U.S. Government Printing Office.

Kimball, M. M. (1986). Television and sex-role attitudes. In T. M. Williams (Ed.), *The impact of television: A natural experiment in three communities.* New York: Academic Press.

Kubey, R., Shifflet, M., Weerakkody, N., & Ukeiley, S. (1995). Demographic diversity on cable: Have the new cable channels made a difference in the representation of gender, race, and age? *Journal of Broadcasting & Electronic Media, 39*(4), 459-471.

Lauzen, M. M., & Dozier, D. M. (1999). Making a difference in prime time: Women on screen and behind the scenes in the 1995-96 television season. *Journal of Broadcasting & Electronic Media, 43*(1), 1-19.

Lefkowitz, M. M., & Huesmann, L. R. (1980). Concomitants of television violence viewing in children. In E. L. Palmer & A. Dorr (Eds.), *Children and the faces of television: Teaching, violence, selling* (pp. 163-181). New York: Academic Press.

Levinson, R. M. (1975). From Olive Oyl to Sweet Polly Purebread: Sex-role stereotypes and televised cartoons. *Journal of Popular Culture, 9*(3), 561-572.

Lin, C. A. (1997). Beefcake versus cheesecake in the 1990s: Sexist portrayals of both genders in television commercials. *Howard Journal of Communications, 8*(3), 237-249.

Lovdal, L. T. (1989). Sex role messages in television commercials: An update. *Sex Roles, 21*(11/12), 715-724.

Matelski, M. G. (1985). Image and influence: Women in public television. *Journalism Quarterly, 62*(1), 147-150.

McGhee, P. E., & Freuh, T. (1980). Television viewing and the learning of sex-role stereotypes. *Sex Roles, 6*(2), 179-188.

Mifflin, L. (1999, September 26). UPN's "Moesha": The nonwhite hit nobody knows. *New York Times,* p. 29.

Mishkind, M. E., Rodin, J., Silberstein, L. R., & Striegel-Moore, R. H. (1986). The embodiment of masculinity. *American Behavioral Scientist, 29,* 545-562.

Moore, M. L. (1992). The family as portrayed on prime-time television, 1947-1990: Structure and characteristics. *Sex Roles, 26,* 41-60.

Morgan, M. (1982). Television and adolescents' sex-role stereotypes: A longitudinal study. *Journal of Personality and Social Psychology, 43,* 947-955.

Morgan, M. (1986). Television and the erosion of regional diversity. *Journal of Broadcasting & Electronic Media, 30*(2), 123-139.

Morgan, M. (1987). Television, sex-role attitudes, and sex-role behavior. *Journal of Early Adolescence, 7*(3), 269-282.

Morgan, M., & Harr-Mazar, H. (1980). Television and adolescents' family life expectations. Unpublished manuscript, Annenberg School of Communications, Philadelphia, PA.

Morgan, M., & Rothschild, N. (1983). Impact of the new television technology: Cable TV, peers, and sex-role cultivation in the electronic environment. *Youth and Society, 15*(1), 33-50.

Morgan, M., & Shanahan, J. (1997). Two decades of cultivation research: An appraisal and meta analysis. In B. R. Burleson (Ed.), *Communication yearbook 20* (pp. 1-46). Thousand Oaks, CA: Sage.

Nolan, J. D., Galst, J. P., & White, M. A. (1977). Sex bias on children's television programs. *Journal of Psychology, 96,* 197-204.

O'Donnell, W. J., & O'Donnell, K. J. (1978). Update: Sex-role messages in TV commercials. *Journal of Communication, 28*(1), 156-158.

Olson, G., & Douglas, W. (1997). The family on television: Evaluation of gender roles in situation comedy. *Sex Roles, 36,* 409-427.

Pingree, S. (1978). The effects of non-sexist television commercials and perceptions of reality on children's attitudes about women. *Psychology of Women Quarterly, 2,* 262-276.

Pingree, S., Starrett, S., & Hawkins, R. (1979). *Soap opera viewers and social reality.* Unpublished manuscript, University of Wisconsin-Madison, Women's Studies Program.

Ray, A., & Harwood, J. (1997). Underrepresented, positively portrayed: Older adults in television commercials. *Journal of Applied Communication Research, 25,* 39-56.

Reep, D. C., & Dambrot, F. H. (1987). Television's professional women: Working with men in the 1980's. *Journalism Quarterly, 64*(2/3), 376-381.

Reeves, B., & Greenberg, B. (1977). Children's perceptions of television characters. *Human Communication Research, 3*(2), 113-127.

Riffe, D., Goldson, H., Saxton, K., & Yu, Y. (1989). Females and minorities in TV ads in 1987 Saturday children's programs. *Journalism Quarterly, 66*(1), 129-136.

Roberts, D. F., & Bachen, C. M. (1981). Mass communication effects. *American Review of Psychology, 32,* 307-356.

Roberts, D. F., & Maccoby, N. (1985). Effects of mass communication. In G. Lindzey & E. Aronson (Eds.), *Handbook of social psychology* (3rd ed.). Reading, MA: Addison-Wesley.

Ross, L., Anderson, D. R., & Wisocki, P. A. (1982). Television viewing and adult sex-role attitudes. *Sex Roles, 8*(6), 589-592.

Rothschild, N. (1984). Small group affiliation as a mediating factor in the cultivation process. In G. Melischek, K. E. Rosengren, & J. Stappers (Eds.), *Cultural indicators: An international symposium.* Vienna, Austria: Osterreichischen Akademie der Wissenschaften.

Seger, L. (1996). *When women call the shots: The developing power and influence of women in television and film.* New York: Henry Holt.

Seidman, S. A. (1992). An investigation of sex-role stereotyping in music videos. *Journal of Broadcasting & Electronic Media, 36,* 209-216.

Selnow, G. W. (1990). Values in prime-time television. *Journal of Communication, 40*(2), 64-74.

Sherman, B. L., & Dominick, J. R. (1986). Violence and sex in music videos: TV and rock 'n' roll. *Journal of Communication, 36*(1), 79-93.

Signorielli, N. (1982). Marital status in television drama: A case of reduced options. *Journal of Broadcasting, 26*(2), 585-597.

Signorielli, N. (1984). The demography of the television world. In G. Melischek, K. E. Rosengren, & J. Stappers (Eds.), *Cultural indicators: An international symposium.* Vienna, Austria: Osterreichischen Akademie der Wissenschaften.

Signorielli, N. (1985). *Role portrayal on television: An annotated bibliography of studies relating to women, minorities, aging, sexual behavior, health, and handicaps.* Westport, CT: Greenwood Press.

Signorielli, N. (1989). Television and conceptions about sex roles: Maintaining conventionality and the status quo. *Sex Roles, 21*(5/6), 341-360.

Signorielli, N. (1991). Adolescents and ambivalence toward marriage: A cultivation analysis. *Youth & Society, 23*(1), 121-149.

Signorielli, N. (1993). Television and adolescents' perceptions about work. *Youth & Society, 24*(3), 314-341.

Signorielli, N., & Bacue, A. (1999). Recognition and respect: A content analysis of prime-time television characters across three decades. *Sex Roles, 40*(7/8), 527-544.

Signorielli, N., & Kahlenberg, S. (In press). *Television's world of work in the nineties. Journal of Broadcasting & Electronic Media.*

Signorielli, N., & Lears, M. (1992). Children, television, and conceptions about chores: Attitudes and behaviors. *Sex Roles, 27,* 157-170.

Signorielli, N., McLeod, D., & Healy, E. (1994). Gender stereotypes in MTV commercials: The beat goes on. *Journal of Broadcasting & Electronic Media, 38*(1), 91-101.

Smythe, D. W. (1954). Reality as presented by television. *Public Opinion Quarterly, 18,* 143-154.

Steenland, S. (1990, November). *What's wrong with this picture? The status of women on screen and behind the camera in entertainment TV.* Washington, DC: National Commission on Working Women of Wider Opportunities for Women.

Steenland, S. (1995). Content analysis of the image of women on television. In C. M. Long (Ed.), *Women and media: Content, careers, and criticism* (pp. 179-189). San Francisco: Wadsworth.

Streicher, H. W. (1974). The girls in the cartoons. *Journal of Communication, 24*(2), 125-129.

Surgeon General's Scientific Advisory Committee on Television and Social Behavior. (1972). *Television and growing up: The impact of televised violence.* Washington, DC: U.S. Government Printing Office.

Tan, A. S. (1979). TV beauty ads and role expectations of adolescent female viewers. *Journalism Quarterly, 56*(2), 283-288.

Thompson, T. L., & Zerbinos, E. (1995). Gender roles in animated cartoons: Has the picture changed in 20 years? *Sex Roles, 32*(9/10), 651-673.

Thompson, T. L., & Zerbinos, E. (1997). Television cartoons: Do children notice it's a boy's world? *Sex Roles, 37*(5/6), 415-432.

Vande-Berg, L., & Streckfuss, D. (1992). Prime-time television's portrayal of women and the world of work: A demographic profile. *Journal of Broadcasting & Electronic Media, 36*(2), 195-208.

Vernon, J. A., Williams, J. A., Jr., Phillips, T., & Wilson, J. (1990). Media stereotyping: A comparison of the way elderly women and men are portrayed on prime-time television. *Journal of Women & Aging, 2*(4), 55-68.

Vincent, R. C. (1990). Clio's consciousness raised? Portrayal of women in rock videos, re-examined. *Journalism Quarterly, 66*(1), 155-161.

Vincent, R. C., Davis, D. K., & Boruszkowski, L. A. (1987). Sexism on MTV: The portrayal of women in rock videos. *Journalism Quarterly, 64*(4), 750-755, 941.

Vivian, J. (1999). *The media of mass communication.* Boston: Allyn & Bacon.

Volgy, T. J., & Schwartz, J. E. (1980). Television entertainment programming and sociopolitical attitudes. *Journalism Quarterly, 57*(1), 150-155.

Welch, R. L., Huston-Stein, A., Wright, J. C., & Plehal, R. (1979). Subtle sex-role cues in children's commercials. *Journal of Communication, 29*(3), 202-209.

Williams, T. M. (1986). *The impact of television: A natural experiment in three communities.* New York: Academic Press.

Wright, C. W. (1986). *Mass communication: A sociological perspective* (3rd ed.). New York: Random House.

Wroblewski, R., & Huston, A. C. (1987). Televised occupational stereotypes and their effects on early adolescents: Are they changing? *Journal of Early Adolescence, 7,* 283-298.

CHAPTER **18**

# Television, Children, and Multicultural Awareness

## Comprehending the Medium in a Complex Multimedia Society

GORDON L. BERRY
University of California, Los Angeles

JOY KEIKO ASAMEN
Graduate School of Education and Psychology, Pepperdine University

### Television and Its Multimedia Relatives in a Changing Multicultural Society

The transformations taking place in society as a result of the rapid advancements in the types of technologies that produce new forms and ways of communicating are not make-believe, *Star Wars*–type cinematic images or creative metaphors to simulate change. We are simply in the world, in general, and the United States, in particular, shaping vast and interlocking multimedia systems that will not only fuel new scientific knowledge but also drive popular culture. Our challenges from the present and emerging technologies that are fueling the advances in new forms of electronic and print media are not based on whether we—the men, women, and children—can cognitively process, interpret, absorb, and handle them. Rather, a part of the challenge turns on whether we, as a people, can exploit these new multimedia and communication reservoirs so that they can be a source of supply for creating informed citizens and the needed elements of social capital for building and maintaining a more just, humane, and civil society. These challenges from a media-rich environment are also coming at a time when American society is going through another social transformation in terms of a shifting demographic landscape that will ultimately define the country's cultural and ethnic makeup.

The nexus involving our emerging technologies and multimedia with the changing multicultural landscape of the country offers both opportunities and challenges. Among the opportunities is the potential for the new technologies to foster a greater understanding and civil dialogue about cultural pluralism that is at the heart of a culturally diverse country. A type of diversity and cultural pluralism described very early by Gordon (1978) is the belief that there is strength in variety, and the United States as a whole benefits from the contributions of different groups of people. In such a country, the present immigration and differential fertility rates virtually ensure that, sometime in the middle of the twenty-first century, the United States will become what is called a "minority-majority" society (Chisman, 1998)—that is, a society in which the various minority groups or groups of color collectively constitute a majority. This demographic future is, according to Chisman, already here in many urban cores, in some suburbs, and in the entire metropolitan areas of a few cities where Hispanics, African Americans, Asians, and other ethnic and racial minorities outnumber white Americans. If present trends continue, the state of California will have minority-majority demographics by the year 2005. This "diversification" of the United States can be seen more dramatically by data showing that the population is increasingly aging, people with disabling or handicapping conditions are seeking more opportunities, and women presently represent one of the growing groups entering the labor force of the future.

The changing demographics of the country toward a new type of multicultural landscape mean that our educational, religious, political, economic, and familial institutions will need to be oriented to reach out and embrace the principles of cultural diversity, cross-cultural understanding, cultural enrichment, and cultural pluralism. The type of cultural pluralism that is called for during this period of change was articulated by the American Association of Colleges of Teacher Education (AACTE, 1973) and reported in the *Journal of Teacher Education.* The AACTE stated,

> To endorse cultural pluralism is to understand and appreciate the differences that exist among the nation's citizens. It is to see these differences as a positive force in the continuing development of a society that professes a wholesome respect for the intrinsic worth of every individual. . . . To accept cultural pluralism is to reject separatism. . . . It is a concept that aims toward a heightened sense of being and of wholeness of the entire society based on the unique strengths of each of its parts. (p. 264)

The model put forth by the AACTE can be interpreted as one that suggests that to believe in its definition of cultural pluralism is to endorse the principle that there is "no one model American." Indeed, a major goal of a culturally pluralistic society would be to strive for unity in diversity (Axelson, 1993). Although, technically, everyone in a pluralistic society is multicultural to some degree, our broad-based focus looks at this complicated issue using as our frame of reference racial/ethnic groups, religious groups, gender/women, social class, the elderly, the disabled/handicapped, and gay and lesbian groups. Recognizing the difficulties inherent in the scope of this multicultural perspective, however, we will tend to focus on the media and women, African Americans, Asian Americans, Hispanic Americans, and Native Americans. We would also include under the multicultural umbrella the emerging immigrant groups and new Americans who are a part of the country and who bring with them their special religions and languages, as well as some established white Americans of the underclass. These are, we would argue, the groups of people who have often been excluded, misrepresented, victimized, and marginalized in our society.

*Multicultural, cross-cultural, cultural diversity,* and *cultural pluralism,* although having some differences in terms of their strict meanings, will be used interchangeably in this chapter. These terms are used with a full recognition that the issues associated with the broad notions of multiculturalism as an ideal or concept are not foreign to our thinking or our history because they involve the ability to recognize, understand, and appreciate the cross-cultural nature of American society. And yet American society is not unique in its concern and struggles over multicultural ideals, principles, and goals. The real issue is to what extent a society is willing to venture to ensure that the traditions, customs, values, and beliefs of a people different from the dominant majority will be recognized (Jackson, 1995). It is the recognition of the cross-cultural mosaic that is at the core of American life and the tremendous power of television and the other media to transmit the meaning of multiculturalism that will be the thrust of the ideas in this chapter. More narrowly, the focus of this chapter is on the potential effects of television and other media on the multicultural awareness and comprehension of the early-age child and adolescent; it will also identify research paradigms that will provide strategies and information for better understanding the psychosocial impact of various media forms on these developing children.

The challenges that arise between an emerging multimedia environment and the dynamic changes in cultural diversity are related, in part, to the ability of the United States to maintain its First Amendment media-related creative freedoms while understanding the role, power, and responsibilities of the new technologies. To understand in the multicultural context of this chapter means to be mindful of the historical and present-day images, cultural representations, and stereotypic hegemonic presentations that have, at times, fairly and unfairly characterized many of the ethnic, gender, religious, class, and social role portrayals in the electronic and print media. To understand from a multimedia perspective is to comprehend the roles that the various media presently play or can play in a democratic society. These media, for the purpose of our discussion, are broadcast television, cable television, radio, recorded music, advertising through these various media, Internet services, websites, direct broadcast satellite services, video and electronic games, and other popular and emerging forms of mass communication. These are the media referred to by Firestone and Garmer (1998) as the ones that supply our cultural icons and stereotypes, suggest consumer demands and wishes, and convey much of the news and information people use on a daily basis. In sum, they both define and reflect the society's culture, values, and traditions.

Clearly, both the challenges and promises of our present and future multimedia environment, along with its technological advances, make it imperative that we understand its tremendous growth in society. Anthony Corrado (1996) notes that, with the development of fiber optics and digital compression, the boundaries between traditionally separate electronic media, such as television, telephone, and computer networks, are breaking down. The result will be an interactive multimedia environment in which the average citizen will have on-demand access to video, audio, text, and data transmissions with the click of a handheld control. These new forms suggest that a fiber the size of a human hair can deliver every issue ever made of the *Wall Street Journal* (Adler, 1997). More than 20 million Americans already have access to the Internet, and that number is expected to grow dramatically over the next 10 years. This point is highlighted by the fact that more than 30% of the households in the United States now own a personal computer, a percentage that is projected to rise to at least 67% by the year 2010 (Corrado, 1996).

All of the emerging technologies that are creating our multimedia environment will continue to have profound psychosocial effects on the multicultural understanding of people in the United States and the world. Of all the various types of media, it is the medium of television that will, in one new form or another, continue to exercise a major influence related to the way we see ourselves and others in a growing culturally diverse country.

Indeed, the entire digital revolution that is coming to television only symbolizes the new wave of power and influence of this medium. By converting from analog to digital transmission of audiovisual signals, write Firestone and Garmer (1998), television broadcasters (telecasters) are transforming the living room; digital television can deliver high-definition pictures and CD-quality audio to create a true home theater. Telecasters, through digital technology, will also be able to target specific messages to different individual receivers and send audio, video, and text simultaneously. Most important, digital broadcasters may eventually enable interactive communication with the audience over the airwaves.

Television in its present form has revolutionized the way the world has been both entertained and informed. We are now at a point in history where this same medium, as a close relative to other forms of media, has served as a type of technological gateway for many of the new and emerging audiovisual advances of tomorrow. Television is, therefore, that connecting link and an electronic springboard in our popular culture that brings together many other forms of media. Dorr (1986), referring to television as a purveyor of information and education in our popular culture, noted that films and books are the inspirations for television programs; theatrical films later appear on television; television personalities and programs are featured in magazines and newspapers; films, video games, and personal computers are advertised on television; and an advertising campaign for a product or service is simultaneously conducted over television, radio, and magazines. It has been these commonalties between television and other media that have caused this chapter to refer to them as "multimedia relatives." Television is, however, a very unique and special medium in its own right in American life and culture. It is unique and special because of its tremendous presence and attractiveness as an entertainment, educational, and informational source for messages, images, and cross-cultural portrayals that teach and cause people to learn. It is unique and special because of the visibility and prestige it bestows on people, places, and things it selects to champion (Berry, 1998).

The ubiquity, uniqueness, and specialness of this medium can be seen in the fact that television sets are now in 99% of all American households. More homes have television sets in them than they do indoor plumbing or telephones. The Annenberg Public Policy Center (1997) reported in a survey of more than 1,000 parents and 300 of their 10- to 17-year-old children the following: (a) Nearly 80% of the households with children have an average of 2.5 working television sets per household; (b) two in five (40.7%) of the children have television sets in their bedrooms; (c) the VCR is the most common media delivery system in the homes with televisions; and (d) only half the households surveyed reported having a subscription to a daily newspaper, but nearly two thirds have video game equipment. Of the nine in-home activities measured after sleeping (8.8 hours), watching television was the most common use of time by children, according to their parents. Children 2 to 17 spend, on average, 2.1 hours in front of the television, more time than is spent doing schoolwork (1.3 hours), reading a book (.99 hours), using the home computer (.87 hours), playing video games such as Sega or Nintendo (.75 hours), or reading a magazine or newspaper (.38 hours). Children also spend an average 1.1 hours per day in front of their sets watching videotapes. The Annenberg study demonstrates the ubiquitous nature and power of television in relation to other media forms.

## Television, Developing Children, and Learning in a Multicultural and Multimedia Society

A variety of publics associated with television and other electronic media express a great many concerns related to their positive and negative impact on young viewers. Most of the concerns have been, of course, about the perceived negative effects on children related to whether the nature of the content of the programs or games had the ability to influence attitudes, values, violent behavior, and learning. Clearly, it is not inconsistent or surprising that the established and emerging media forms would attract so much attention from adults. After all, adults are charged with the socialization of the young, and the medium of television and its emerging multimedia relatives deserve detailed analysis and constructive criticism, the type of constructive criticism and analysis one would give to any social force that intrudes into the socialization process of children and wraps its messages and content around the core of their psychosocial thought. As Firestone and Garmer (1998) suggested, one is hard-pressed to think of any common experience that binds Americans together more than television, with its pervasive reach into both the American home and its psyche.

Television is, by itself, also a natural medium of concern because few, if any, social scientists, broadcasters, educators, parents, and child advocacy groups would deny the ability of its content to teach. The developing child can be uniquely susceptible to the power and presence of the attractive characters and images and the accompanying formal features that serve to highlight television's content. Fact or fiction, real or unreal, television programs create cognitive and affective environments that describe and portray people, places, and things that carry profound general and specific cross-cultural learning experiences for the child and early adolescent who are growing and developing in a media-rich information age.

Television as a part of this information age remains a major player in the sociopsychological attitudinal equation that helps to decide how the young people in U.S. society acquire, process, interpret, and act toward the cross-cultural portrayals and social roles of people that are culturally similar to and different from them. A key set of words in the previous sentence is "helps to decide" because we take the position that the child is not simply an observer when looking at television or merely a passenger on the "information highway" but a cognitively active viewer and participant when engaged in television and related audiovisual media forms.

The information age, with its new forms of media, just as with television, will carry into the future many of their distinctive features that will play a role in the types of learning experiences provided to young viewers. We know from the research, for example, that television has some special and distinctive features that relate to how the content delivers its messages to children. According to Meringoff et al. (1983), this distinctiveness derives, in part, from the following:

1. The medium's particular physical inheritance, that is, its combination of pictures, print, and sound (speech), sound effects, and music.
2. The symbol systems or languages that pictures and sounds make use of to represent content, such as verbal language.
3. The particular rule and conventions in use regarding the treatment of material, such as jump cuts used to indicate changes in time and place.
4. The kinds of programming it makes available. (p. 152)

The distinctiveness of the medium of television and the quantitative and qualitatively special ways in which it might advance gender, multiethnic, and cross-cultural images and portrayals become important because of the cognitive activity generated by the viewer when processing the audiovisual elements of the televised content. That is, children watching television acquire a certain amount of practice and familiarity with the structure and form of the medium that make it continually easier for them to master and process its audiovisual conventions or principles. Thus, the more the viewers participate in the audiovisual environment of television, and with the increase in their age, the greater their ease in learning and processing the content from the medium. When the content being processed is related to cross-cultural themes, researchers are not always clear how children acquire social attitudes, stereotypical beliefs, and prejudices related to race, sex, or gender. Social scientists have known for some time, however, that children learn social, racial, and religious prejudices in the course of observing and being influenced by the existence of patterns in the culture in which they live (Birnbaum & Croll, 1984; Clark, 1963; Katz, 1973). Researchers have, over the years, also become interested in what happens as people learn by watching others. This line of inquiry, pioneered by Albert Bandura and originally called observation learning, has evolved into what is known as social cognitive theory (Bandura, 1986; Eggen & Kauchak, 1997).

Social cognitive theory is important to our discussion of how and what cross-cultural attitudes young viewers acquire from television because central to this concept is the idea that people learn through interacting with and observing each other. The primary mechanism in this process is modeling, and this refers to changes in people that result from observing the actions of others. Indeed, the models that individuals create in their mind from television and various forms of media, the family, and the peer group, as well as educational and religious institutions, help them to process information about people, places, and things they encounter in real life (Murray, 1993). They can even use these models to process information about people and cultural groups with whom they have had little or no contact, except through the various media and other forms of popular culture. Thus, one small part of the complicated cognitive processing matrix relates to a number of stored categories, bits of information, and images that assist the learner in understanding his or her environment. These stored categories and bits of information are referred to as schemas (also called schemata). Although there can be some disagreement among specialists in learning theory as to their meaning, schemas can be seen as complex knowledge structures that represent one's understanding of events and objects (Eggen & Kauchak, 1997). Entman and Rojecki (1998) referred to schemas as mental filing cabinets that allow the individual to group like objects together in the mind.

Schemas can also guide a person's actions. One type of schema is a script. A script is an organized plan of action in a particular situation; it can provide a basis for how a person might or should act in certain situations (Eggen & Kauchak, 1997; Walker, 1996). Scripts as a type of schema, we would argue, also play a part in the way in which individuals perceive the ethnic, gender, social class, and religious social roles of others they experience in their daily activities and the multimedia world.

The concept of social roles naturally comes into play at this point in our discussion of the impact of various media on the multicultural views of the child and developing adolescent. Social role in this context is based on the principle that each individual tends to occupy or is perceived to be in a position in groups to which he or she belongs, and other people tend to behave and agree on certain expectations concerning his or her behavior (Goldenson, 1994). McConnell (1980) suggests that a social role is a more or less stereotyped set of responses that a person makes to related or similar situations. There are, to be sure, general and specific social role attitude consequences that children can acquire from the portrayals of people, places, and things on television. Greenberg and Atkin (1982) see these portrayals as being able to alter cognitions, aspirations, expectations, and beliefs.

Each person brings to a new situation a complex set of plans, private images, and anticipations. These plans or anticipatory schemata are not only specific to situations but involve strategies of search and selection related to the kind of information to be processed (Singer & Singer, 1983). Social role schemas in particular can carry certain expectations for behavior and are one plausible way to account for racial or ethnic stereotyping. Stereotypes have been described as a particular kind of role schema that organizes people's expectations (Fiske & Taylor, 1991; Mancuso, 1997). According to Mancuso (1997), children's comprehension of television content is an active process guided by schemata or learned expectations about what is likely to occur. Through the process of assimilating new information to that already stored in a schema, individuals interpret and make sense of the bits and pieces of new data they encounter, but this mental organizational system can lead to the inaccurate beliefs that underpin prejudiced thinking and unflattering stereotypes stored in schemas (Entman & Rojecki, 1998). Faulty social role understandings and personal beliefs can be especially troublesome for children and developing adolescents who have limited experiences and are in the process of developing a type of worldview about themselves and others.

Robert Entman and Andrew Rojecki (1998) concluded from their research on images of minority groups that the cognitions and emotions that the majority of white Americans develop about people of color arise significantly from mass media. From their study, these researchers provided evidence for the ways in which the images may undermine trust and empathy across racial or ethnic barriers. Among the major elements of the imagery were the following:

- Association of minority group members with negative values and antisocial behavior
- Implications carried by both inclusions and exclusions that minority group members are fundamentally different from white Americans in undesirable ways
- Depictions of minority group members as more homogeneous and less differentiated than members of the dominant group
- Portrayals of minority group members as rarely in intimate or even moderately close and positive relationships with whites (Entman & Rojecki, 1998, p. 82)

Some authorities fear that, if biased media portrayals are frequently presented with the social and psychological power of mass entertainment, they place a burden on the ability of the people to fully understand the meaning associated with living together in a multicultural society (Wilson & Gutierrez, 1995).

It is the world of television today and its vast multimedia spin-offs of tomorrow from which the developing child and adolescent must construct a major part of their positive and negative attitudes about others. The cognitive and affective effects of these various forms and types of media are important in terms of a child's attitude formation toward others, argued Kitano (1980), since their portrayal of racial and ethnic groups may be a person's principal source of information. Using the principle established by Kitano, one can easily hypothesize that, for children living in somewhat sheltered social environments and who are beginning to form personal attitudes about themselves and others, stereotyped media portrayals of ethnic groups and communities with whom they have little contact could increase the probability of the faulty images becoming their reality. Indeed, the possibility of children developing stereotypical ethnic, gender, class, and religious social views is ratcheted upward when the media frequently repeat these faulty portrayals using popular characters and when the values and behaviors in the child's home offer few, if any, competing positive images.

Few people would doubt that the manner in which people are portrayed on television, in videos, over the Internet, and in the other electronic and print media offers a unique challenge in terms of the multicultural views that developing children will be exposed to and embrace. It is important to pause long enough, however, to also consider the sociocultural messages that are being communicated when market forces and other attitudinal factors do not consider the value of a multicultural presence in programs on a pervasive and prestigious medium such as television. A number of social observers were struck, therefore, when in 1999 the major networks announced their fall schedules. Of the 26 new comedies and dramas premiering that fall, none featured a minority in a leading role. Minority characters in supporting roles were sparse, with few African Americans in those roles and Latinos, Asian Americans, Native Americans, and other ethnic groups nonexistent (Lowry, Jensen, & Braxton, 1999). This limited multicultural representation in the schedule of the major media networks was a reality despite the fact that, a number of years before, the U.S. Commission on Civil Rights (1977) wrote about the importance of visibility on this medium in a culturally diverse society. The commission noted the following:

> Television does more than simply entertain or provide news about major events of the day. It confers status on those individuals and groups it selects for placement in the public eye, telling the viewer who and what is important to know about, think about, and have feelings about. (p. 1)

Thus, the commission concluded that those who are made visible through television become worthy of attention and concern; those whom television ignores remain invisible.

Television is the medium that still anoints the people and ideas that it selects to advance on the screen. It is also the springboard for other media in the present and the future because it learned very early how to tell stories, show pictures, select popular characters, and provide sound from a small screen. Clearly, many of the concerns, as well as the positive potential, that researchers and social observers raised about television content can now be directed to one of the greatest communicating vehicles, the computer and its Internet. The Internet was estimated in 1999 to have 2,000 on-line sites that offered games and other content that preached religious and racial hatred aimed at children (Martinez, 1999). If the research data on the Internet and the other emerging media follow that of their cousin television, we can expect that constant negative themes and portrayals of various groups will continue to cultivate faulty attitudes in developing children. Even when people recognize that the material they are viewing is fictional, its messages and images can gradually shape expectations and beliefs about the real world (Huston et al., 1992).

We know that what children learn from the content of television, the computer, and the emerging media depends on an entire range of psychosocial and developmental factors that make up their worldview. Realizing the complicated nature and unanswered issues about child and adolescent learning related to race, ethnicity, class, religion, gender, disabilities, age, and other misrepresented or underrepresented social roles, we have thus far argued that, when they are distorted, inaccurate, or unfair, television and other media can potentially harm children's social development (Geiogamah & Pavel, 1993; Graves, 1993; Hamamoto, 1993; Kovaric, 1993; Makas, 1993; Signorielli, 1993; Subervi-Vélez & Colsant, 1993). We are also aware that there is some evidence that television and other media, with the appropriately crafted content, can assist children toward a better level of cross-cultural understanding. If the evidence falls on both the positive and negative side of this question, then we would now like to offer some research paradigms that might serve to address these questions in the future.

## Research Paradigms for Studying Complex Multimedia Questions in a Multicultural Society

Studying how television and, more recently, other media forms influence the social behavior and worldview of developing children who interact with these media has challenged social scientists since the first television studies some 40 years ago. Although we have, for example, evidence that viewing violent television programming increases the likelihood of a child behaving in an aggressive manner or incorporating into his or her schema that violence is an appropriate way of resolving conflict, we know little about the processes behind these effects (Murray, 1998). The inability to understand the socialization effects of television also applies to how developing children learn about themselves and others (Berry, 1993). Further complicating the scientist's quest for answers to complex multimedia research questions is the host of research paradigms that are available to seek these answers (Asamen, 1998).

For the most part, social scientists divide research methods into two philosophical camps, positivistic/postpositivistic and phenomenological, also known broadly as quantitative and qualitative methods, respectively. The former includes the traditional, more constrained quantitative research paradigms such as experimental and quasi-experimental designs and descriptive models of research that are heavily reliant on obtaining a large, randomly selected subset of the population. The latter methods are rooted in a constructivist perspective. That is, the reality constructed by the participant to explain his or her behavior takes salience over the investigator's hypotheses about the participant's behavior, and understanding the "case" or the "culture" often takes precedence over concern for the generalizability of the findings to the population at large. As is obvious, the overall objective of these two sets of methods is what characteristically distinguishes the positivists from the phenomenologists.

Despite the strengths of experimental designs in studying precise cause-effect relationships, the application of quantitative research paradigms to the study of television introduces some unique challenges. Ward and Greenfield (1998) discuss some of the major issues raised when experimental studies are conducted to further our understanding of media concerns. One concern is the experimental treatment and dependent variables that are used in experiments, which raise questions about the relevance of these findings to the real world. Other concerns relate to "the complexity of television content and viewing experiences" (p. 69) that make re-creating real-life viewing experiences in a laboratory setting impractical. Unlike experimental studies, quasi-experimental studies are conducted in the field or a naturalistic setting (MacBeth, 1998), hence minimizing the threats to external validity cited by Ward and Greenfield. In the execution of both experimental and quasi-experimental studies, issues of internal validity need to be considered, although field studies could pose more challenges in this regard than laboratory-based experimental investigations.

Besides experimental studies, a number of different quantitative research paradigms have been used for the study of children and adolescents and the television-viewing practices, effects, and sample characteristics of viewers. These other methods include surveys, panel studies, cross-sectional studies, quantitative content analyses, model building, and meta-analyses (Palmer, 1998), as well as correlational research (MacBeth, 1998).

In contrast to the constrained, deductive nature of quantitative paradigms, qualitative research paradigms, or what Anderson (1998) refers to as hermeneutic empiricism, emphasize the importance of the social context in which the participants exist as a way of fully appreciating the phenomenon under study. Rather than testing the investigator's hypothesis about the participant's behavior, qualitative investigators focus on generating hypotheses to broaden our perspective about the participant's behavior. Qualitative investigations take into account all variables that can be practically included in the study. In contrast, quantitative studies gather data on an exclusive set of variables that are selected by the investigator regardless of the salience these variables might have to the participants themselves.

Examples of qualitative research paradigms include case studies, ethnography, critical studies, naturalistic inquiry, emancipatory action research, phenomenological research, and life history (Comstock, 1998; Lindlof & Meyer, 1998; Palmer, 1998). As so clearly articulated by Lindlof and Meyer (1998), the qualitative investigator seeks information that helps him or her make sense of social behavior that is rooted in the meaning that is shared among members within a particular cultural context. These methods of inquiry are systematic, although by their very nature they allow for adaptability during the course of the interpretive process.

Investigators tend to lean in the direction of being either predominately positivistic or phenomenological in their preferred research paradigms, depending on their philosophical perspective, education and training, and experiences as investigators. On the other hand, it is not uncommon to find investigators who integrate the two research perspectives, because they are viewed as complementary rather than irreconcilable polar opposites. In other words, the assets that each perspective brings to the investigation only enhance both the scientific validity and the contextual relevance of the study results. Singer and Singer (1998), in relating their evaluation studies of the *Barney & Friends* television series, discuss how they moved between formal quantitative ratings of content and qualitative ratings to investigate the educational potential of these episodes.

Still another research paradigm that is less discussed but worthy of inclusion with the positivistic and phenomenological paradigms is what Mertens (1998) refers to as emancipatory research. The philosophical underpinnings of an emancipatory paradigm are clearly political in nature and argue for the need to conduct studies that take into account the phenomenology of oppressed or marginalized members of society so as to empower these individuals. Studies from this perspective can be conducted using quantitative methods, while being vigilant to the potential of generating biased results; qualitative methods, which are naturals given the phenomenological emphasis; or a combination of quantitative and qualitative methods.

When the desire is to understand what and how developing children learn about themselves and others from media, collaboration among social scientists from diverse research perspectives, we propose, is the most efficacious means of furthering our current understanding. On one hand, there are clearly some generalizations that can be applied to all children, regardless of their ethnicity, gender, religion, social class, and physical condition. It is in this arena that quantitative research paradigms excel. On the other hand, we must also acknowledge that there does not exist a "universal" child; therefore, understanding a child within his or her sociocultural context is also relevant to our understanding of how children process the values and images portrayed on television and its media relatives. The need for conducting studies that result in contextually relevant findings favors the qualitative research paradigms. The integration of knowledge gained from the perspective of positivists and phenomenologists ensures our forward movement in media research.

We propose a schema for achieving the integration of knowledge to which we refer by delineating some philosophical dimensions along which we believe investigators are guided in their inquiry process, whether consciously or unconsciously. These philosophical dimensions include (a) etic and emic, (b) reality and relativity, and (c) objective and relational. These dimensions, if taken as polar opposites, tend to fall along the quantitative-qualitative dichotomy, but we advance the notion that the dichotomy can be dispensed with in favor of "research pluralism." Rather than an "either/or" standpoint, we propose to view research from an "and" perspective. As with cultural pluralism, we believe research pluralism allows us to achieve wholeness by drawing on the strengths of diverse perspectives to arrive at answers to complex multimedia questions that challenge social scientists in a multicultural society.

### *Etic and Emic*

Draguns (1981), in referring to counseling across cultures, refers to the emic-etic dichotomy: knowledge that is unique to a culture (emic) versus knowledge that is universal and cuts across cultures (etic). In research, investigators make a similar decision depending on the favored research paradigm. Quantitative investigators strive for generalizability that favors a more etic-oriented research philosophy, whereas qualitative investigators endeavor to particularize rather than generalize, which is clearly more emic in its orientation. We maintain that etic *and* emic perspectives need to be preserved in conducting multimedia research.

For example, a number of natural experiments have studied the use and effects of television introduced to communities that had either no or limited access to the medium (MacBeth, 1998). These studies, many of which have been conducted internationally, have provided us with insight into the ways that television has affected viewers within diverse cultural contexts over time and in their everyday lives. Lindlof and Meyer (1998) would add that *how* television and other electronic media fit into the everyday life of audiences, using observation data and interviewing and the concomitant analysis-interpretive process, also provides valuable insight. In fact, the changes observed over time and among members of a family in response to their television or VCR use or microcomputer, CD-ROM/DVD player, and Internet access provide a "face" to the experience that cannot be captured relying only on questionnaires, surveys, or other objective means of measuring behavior. This qualitative methodology provides an opportunity to discover what is unique about particular families who have access to media, so the full range of viewers can be considered, and, perhaps, in so doing, empowering the less "typical" families.

When we rely solely on that which is "typical" rather than balance what surfaces as typical against that which is unique, we run the risk of ethnocentric notions guiding decisions and devaluing rather than celebrating multiculturalism. This concern was referred to earlier when discussing the lack of a multicultural presence in the fall 1999 television schedules of the major networks. It would seem that an enlightened investigator who is studying multimedia phenomena and their pervasive influence on our diverse society would have to weigh carefully both etic and emic perspectives in the design of his or her study.

### *Reality and Relativity*

When research paradigms are generically described, we often see the description of "one reality" when characterizing quantitative research, whereas the existence of "multiple realities" is used to describe qualitative research (Denzin & Lincoln, 1994; Mertens, 1998; Taylor & Bogdan, 1984). From the quantitative perspective, the investigator selects the variables to study, proposes a hypothesis regarding the nature of the relationship for the variables selected, designs a study that tests the hypothesized relationship and controls for environmental influences and participant variability that may confound the study results, and moves from data collection to data analysis to interpretation. This description implies that there is a single reality, that of the investigator, that explains what might be observed among study participants. If the investigator has been thoughtful to issues of validity in the design and execution of the investigation and finds statistically significant results, a compelling argument can be made for supporting the investigator's reality.

A qualitative investigator, on the other hand, looks at phenomena holistically by allowing the participants themselves to identify the salient variables, rather than imposing what he or she believes is important on the participants. Furthermore, the investigator is as interested, perhaps even more so, in generating hypotheses as in testing hypotheses and does not want to disturb the natural context in which the participants exist so that what is observed preserves the integrity of the participants' own life experiences. Data collection/analysis/interpretation, as a package, is dialectical, not linear, so until "theoretical saturation" is achieved, the cycle does not come to an end. The presence of participant input is evident throughout the course of this type of investigation. What results moves away from that which is typical to reflect the diverse social constructions that exist in a multicultural society.

A socially responsible multimedia investigator values the contributions of both reality *and* relativity when designing and conducting studies in a multicultural context. The value placed on television, as a medium of entertainment, is a reality, with a vast majority of American households owning television sets, and it is a reality that television influences behavior and attitude formation. A number of quantitative investigations have supported these observations. But how and why the medium is so influential is best studied in relation to the cultural context in which this medium is presented. A good example of this reality-relativity issue is programming for Spanish-English bilingual/bicultural children in the United States that would not be part of the experience of non-Spanish-speaking children. According to Subervi-Vélez and Colsant (1993), these children are not only consumers of English-language programming but may have the additional influences of Spanish-language programming offered in the United States and Spanish-language programming from Mexico and Puerto Rico if they are immigrants to the United States or itinerant U.S. residents. Within such a cultural context, how might television influence the self- and other perceptions of these bicultural/bilingual children? After all, these children do have more access to Latino role models than do Latino children who rely solely on English-language programming or who are non-Spanish speaking. It is also important not to overlook the fact that Latino children represent diverse subcultures within the Spanish-English bilingual/bicultural communities. This additional layer of diversification adds another form of cultural relativity that needs to be considered in understanding the influence of this medium within the broadly defined group referred to as Latino.

### *Objective and Relational*

In quantitative research, the investigator strives for a dispassionate relationship with the study participants. The investigator controls the experimental setting, manipulates the experience of the participants, and defines and measures behavior using objective forms of measurement. Emphasis is placed on the value of impartiality achieved by minimizing contact between the investigator and participants. There is a great deal of wisdom in taking this rigorous approach in the design and execution of research studies. By eliminating counterinterpretations, a stronger case is made for a precise cause-effect relationship. By the investigator's remaining in the background, less criticism may result concerning the unintentional (or intentional) influence that he or she might have exerted over the participants, hence threatening the validity of the study.

In comparison, qualitative investigators embrace the investigator-participant "interactive link" (Mertens, 1998), and the investigator becomes still another aspect of the cultural context inhabited by study participants. It is explicitly acknowledged that an investigator holds some level of influence over the study participants, and this potential influence is factored into the design and execution of the study. With this method of study, investigators can obtain a more profound understanding of the thoughts, beliefs, and feelings of study participants. The relationship that has developed between the investigator and the participant allows the investigator access to information about the participant that might be otherwise off limits if an investigator were to maintain a more objective, aloof demeanor during data collection. This research approach certainly opens the investigator up to criticisms regarding the validity of his or her study. To counter these criticisms, verification or confirmatory procedures (e.g., triangulation of data, multiple sources of evidence) are introduced into the design of qualitative studies to contend with these potential threats.

We hold that a responsible multimedia investigator who is studying phenomena in a multicultural context integrates both objective *and* relational perspectives into the design of his or her research study. The rigor of research paradigms that emphasize objectivity in combination with the richness of research paradigms that are relational in nature allow us to understand what a person might think, believe, and feel as well as why he or she thinks, believes, and feels this way. We know that children learn about themselves and others from television and its electronic kin, but we also want to know how television might be used to encourage children to behave in a prosocial manner or to adopt a worldview that embraces diversity rather than tolerates, fears, or denies its existence.

## Children in a Multicultural and Multimedia Society: Future Perspectives

This chapter began with a series of concepts that argued about the important role television and the emerging media play and will play in a postmodern society in which multiculturalism plays a significant role. An impressive assemblage of electronic and print media has the potential to carry messages and images that can shape the worldview of developing children. Television and its electronic kin of the future can influence children's values and beliefs about the nature of equality, equity, and social justice through what journalists report, what network executives choose to air, what fictional characters and assumptions about human existence writers invent, and the games computer programmers design. These highly attractive communication vehicles set the psychosocial context for the multicultural views many children and adolescents will hold as they grow and develop.

This chapter argues forcibly that television and other media have contributed toward the negative perception of the social contributions made by ethnic minorities, women, religious groups, social and economic groups, and a variety of other cultural groups, especially for those individuals who do not have access to or are unwilling to seek diverse experiences in their lives. These inaccurate representations can become a part of the individual's schema about others and can serve as the basis for faulty beliefs about others, prejudiced thinking, and subtle and not so subtle stereotypes. We also hope that we have successfully balanced our reservations about these media with the important contribution that television and other media forms have made to communicating positive multicultural views and building cultural bridges. We must recognize the benefit that developing and growing children have derived from these electronic tools. To further complicate our understanding of the power and potential of television and other media as purveyors of both positive and negative views, we must be mindful of how a child's development influences his or her learning experience and the acquisition of social role understanding.

Although we still have a number of unanswered questions about how television influences the values and beliefs of developing children, we know even less about the influences exerted by the other emerging electronic media. To further complicate the issue, there exist electronic "concepts" that we have yet to experience. With the ever-changing demographics of our society that parallels the fast pace with which we are being introduced to new forms of technology, social scientists are facing a significant challenge in both the identification of issues and the best approach to seeking resolutions for these issues. We have proposed that socially responsible investigators need to be pluralistic in their research approach to meet the demands of our rapidly changing multicultural and multimedia society.

## References

Adler, R. (1997). *The future of advertising: New approaches to the attention economy.* Washington, DC: Aspen Institute.

American Association of Colleges of Teacher Education. (1973). No model American: A statement on multicultural education. *Journal of Teacher Education, 14,* 264.

Anderson, J. A. (1998). Qualitative approaches to the study of the media: Theory and methods of hermeneutic empiricism. In J. K. Asamen & G. L. Berry

(Eds.), *Research paradigms, television, and social behavior* (pp. 205-236). Thousand Oaks, CA: Sage.

Annenberg Public Policy Center. (1997). *The 1997 survey of parents and children* (No. 2). Philadelphia: University of Pennsylvania, Annenberg Public Policy Center.

Asamen, J. K. (1998). Research paradigms, television, and social behavior: A scientist's contribution to initiating social change. In J. K. Asamen & G. L. Berry (Eds.), *Research paradigms, television, and social behavior* (pp. 413-415). Thousand Oaks, CA: Sage.

Axelson, J. A. (1993). *Counseling and development in a multicultural society.* Pacific Grove, CA: Brooks-Cole.

Bandura, A. (1986). *Social foundations of thought and action: A social cognitive theory.* Upper Saddle River, NJ: Prentice Hall.

Berry, G. L. (1993). Introduction: Television as a worldwide cultural tapestry. In G. L. Berry & J. K. Asamen (Eds.), *Children and television: Images in a changing sociocultural world* (pp. 1-4). Newbury Park, CA: Sage.

Berry, G. L. (1998). Black family life on television and the socialization of the African American child: Images of marginality. *Journal of Comparative Family Studies, 2,* 233-242.

Birnbaum, D. W., & Croll, W. L. (1984). The etiology of children's stereotypes about sex differences in emotionality. *Sex Roles, 10,* 677-691.

Chisman, F. P. (1998). Delivering on diversity: Serving the media needs and interests of minorities in the twenty-first century. In A. K. Garmer (Ed.), *Investing in diversity: Advancing opportunities for minorities and the media* (pp. 1-30). Washington, DC: Aspen Institute.

Clark, K. B. (1963). *Prejudice and your child.* Boston: Beacon Press.

Comstock, G. (1998). Television research: Past problems and present issues. In J. K. Asamen & G. L. Berry (Eds.), *Research paradigms, television, and social behavior* (pp. 11-36). Thousand Oaks, CA: Sage.

Corrado, A. (1996). Electrons in cyberspace: Prospects and problems. In A. Corrado & C. M. Firestone (Eds.), *Electrons in cyberspace: Toward a new era in American politics* (pp. 1-31). Washington, DC: Aspen Institute.

Denzin, N. K., & Lincoln, Y. S. (1994). Introduction: Entering the field of qualitative research. In N. K. Denzin & Y. S. Lincoln (Eds.), *Handbook of qualitative research* (pp. 1-17). Thousand Oaks, CA: Sage.

Dorr, A. (1986). *Television and children: A special medium for a special audience.* Beverly Hills, CA: Sage.

Draguns, J. G. (1981). Counseling across cultures: Common themes and distinct approaches. In P. B. Pedersen, J. F. Draguns, W. J. Lonner, & J. E. Trimble (Eds.), *Counseling across cultures* (Rev. ed., pp. 3-21). Honolulu: University of Hawaii Press.

Eggen, P., & Kauchak, D. (1997). *Educational psychology: Windows on classrooms.* Upper Saddle River, NJ: Prentice Hall.

Entman, R. M., & Rojecki, A. (1998). Minorities in mass media: A status report. In A. K. Garmer (Ed.), *Investing in diversity: Advancing opportunities for minorities and media* (pp. 67-85). Washington, DC: Aspen Institute.

Firestone, C. M., & Garmer, A. K. (Eds.). (1998). Foreword. *Digital broadcasting and the public interest.* Washington, DC: Aspen Institute.

Fiske, S., & Taylor, S. E. (1991). *Social cognition.* Reading, MA: Addison-Wesley.

Geiogamah, H., & Pavel, D. M. (1993). Developing television for American Indian and Alaska Native children in the late 20th century. In G. L. Berry & J. K. Asamen (Eds.), *Children and television: Images in a changing sociocultural world* (pp. 191-204). Newbury Park, CA: Sage.

Goldenson, R. M. (1994). *The encyclopedia of human behavior: Psychology, psychiatry, and mental health.* New York: Doubleday.

Gordon, M. M. (1978). *Human nature, class, and ethnicity.* New York: Oxford University Press.

Graves, S. B. (1993). Television, the portrayal of African Americans, and the development of children's attitudes. In G. L. Berry & J. K. Asamen (Eds.), *Children and television: Images in a changing sociocultural world* (pp. 179-190). Newbury Park, CA: Sage.

Greenberg, B. S., & Atkin, C. K. (1982). Learning about minorities from television: A research agenda. In G. L. Berry & C. M. Kernan (Eds.), *Television and the socialization of the minority child* (pp. 215-243). New York: Academic Press.

Hamamoto, D. Y. (1993). They're so cute when they're young: The Asian-American child on television. In G. L. Berry & J. K. Asamen (Eds.), *Children and television: Images in a changing sociocultural world* (pp. 205-214). Newbury Park, CA: Sage.

Huston, A. C., Donnerstein, E., Fairchild, H., Feshbach, N. D., Katz, P. A., Murray, J. P., Rubinstein, E. A., Wilcox, B., & Zimmerman, D. (1992). *Big world, small screen: The role of television in American society.* Lincoln: University of Nebraska Press.

Jackson, M. L. (1995). Counseling: Historical perspectives. In J. G. Ponterotto, M. Casas, L. A. Suzuki, & C. M. Alexander (Eds.), *Handbook of multicultural counseling* (pp. 3-16). Thousand Oaks, CA: Sage.

Katz, P. A. (1973). Stimulus predifferentiation and modification of children's racial attitudes. *Child Development, 44,* 223-237.

Kitano, H. L. (1980). *Race relations.* Englewood Cliffs, NJ: Prentice Hall.

Kovaric, P. M. (1993). Television, the portrayal of the elderly, and children's attitudes. In G. L. Berry &

J. K. Asamen (Eds.), *Children and television: Images in a changing sociocultural world* (pp. 243-254). Newbury Park, CA: Sage.

Lindlof, T. R., & Meyer, T. P. (1998). Taking the interpretive turn: Qualitative research of television and other electronic media. In J. K. Asamen & G. L. Berry (Eds.), *Research paradigms, television, and social behavior* (pp. 237-268). Thousand Oaks, CA: Sage.

Lowry, B., Jensen, E., & Braxton, G. (1999, July 20). Networks decide diversity doesn't pay. *Los Angeles Times,* pp. A1, A12.

MacBeth, T. M. (1998). Quasi-experimental research on television and behavior: Natural and field experiments. In J. K. Asamen & G. L. Berry (Eds.), *Research paradigms, television, and social behavior* (pp. 109-151). Thousand Oaks, CA: Sage.

Makas, E. (1993). Changing channels: The portrayal of people with disabilities on television. In G. L. Berry & J. K. Asamen (Eds.), *Children and television: Images in a changing sociocultural world* (pp. 255-268). Newbury Park, CA: Sage.

Mancuso, A. (1997). *An examination of television and real life experiences as sources of children's race schemas.* Unpublished doctoral dissertation proposal, University of California, Los Angeles.

Martinez, A. (1999, July 25). Hatred's children. *Los Angeles Times,* pp. B1, B4.

McConnell, J. V. (1980). *Understanding human behavior: An introduction to psychology.* New York: Rinehart & Winston.

Meringoff, L. K., Vibbert, M. M., Chair, C. A., Fernie, D. E., Banker, G. S., & Gardner, H. (1983). How is children's learning from television distinctive? Exploiting the medium methodologically. In J. Bryant & D. Anderson (Eds.), *Children's understanding of television: Research on attention and comprehension* (pp. 151-179). New York: Academic Press.

Mertens, D. M. (1998). *Research methods in education and psychology: Integrating diversity with quantitative and qualitative approaches.* Thousand Oaks, CA: Sage.

Murray, J. P. (1993). The developing child in a multimedia society. In G. L. Berry & J. K. Asamen (Eds.), *Children and television: Images in a changing sociocultural world* (pp. 9-22). Newbury Park, CA: Sage.

Murray, J. P. (1998). Studying television violence: A research agenda for the 21st century. In J. K. Asamen & G. L. Berry (Eds.), *Research paradigms, television, and social behavior* (pp. 369-410). Thousand Oaks, CA: Sage.

Palmer, E. L. (1998). Major paradigms and issues in television research: Field of dreams, world of realities. In J. K. Asamen & G. L. Berry (Eds.), *Research paradigms, television, and social behavior* (pp. 39-65). Thousand Oaks, CA: Sage.

Signorielli, N. (1993). Television, the portrayal of women, and children's attitudes. In G. L. Berry & J. K. Asamen (Eds.), *Children and television: Images in a changing sociocultural world* (pp. 229-242). Newbury Park, CA: Sage.

Singer, J. L., & Singer, D. G. (1983). Implications of childhood television viewing for cognition, imagination, and emotion. In J. B. Bryant & D. R. Anderson (Eds.), *Children's understanding of television: Research on attention and comprehension* (pp. 265-295). New York: Academic Press.

Singer, J. L., & Singer, D. G. (1998). *Barney & Friends* as entertainment and education: Evaluating the quality and effectiveness of a television series for preschool children. In J. K. Asamen & G. L. Berry (Eds.), *Research paradigms, television, and social behavior* (pp. 305-367). Thousand Oaks, CA: Sage.

Subervi-Vélez, F. A., & Colsant, S. (1993). The television worlds of Latino children. In G. L. Berry & J. K. Asamen (Eds.), *Children and television: Images in a changing sociocultural world* (pp. 215-228). Newbury Park, CA: Sage.

Taylor, S. J., & Bogdan, R. (1984). *Introduction to qualitative research methods: The search for meanings* (2nd ed.). New York: John Wiley.

United States Commission on Civil Rights. (1977). *Window dressing on the set: Women and minorities in television.* Washington, DC: U.S. Government Printing Office.

Walker, J. (1996). *The psychology of learning: Principles and processes.* Upper Saddle River, NJ: Prentice Hall.

Ward, L. M., & Greenfield, P. M. (1998). Designing experiments on television and social behavior: Developmental perspectives. In J. K. Asamen & G. L. Berry (Eds.), *Research paradigms, television, and social behavior* (pp. 67-108). Thousand Oaks, CA: Sage.

Wilson, C. C., & Gutierrez, F. (1995). *Race, multiculturalism, and the media: From mass to class communication.* Newbury Park, CA: Sage.

CHAPTER **19**

# Children and Television Advertising

DALE KUNKEL
University of California Santa Barbara

In most countries of the world, television is operated primarily, if not exclusively, as a commercial enterprise (Head, 1985). The economic engine that drives most of this enterprise is advertising (Alexander, Owers, & Carveth, 1993; Owen & Wildman, 1992). Because children begin television viewing at a very young age, they inevitably encounter advertising messages much sooner than they develop the ability to effectively recognize such content as commercial persuasion. Consequently, this topic area is an important site for researchers examining children's developing cognitive abilities and how they influence comprehension of television advertising throughout early childhood.

The evidence in this realm is important not only for scientific purposes, such as understanding the social effects of media advertising on children of different ages, but also for policy decision making. An inherent legal principle holds that advertising must be "fair" and "not deceptive" in order to enjoy protected status under the law (Richards, 1990). Yet the limitations in young children's comprehension of commercial messages often have been argued to raise fundamental questions of fairness (Choate, 1980; Federal Trade Commission, 1978; Kunkel & Roberts, 1991).

This chapter incorporates both of these distinct and important perspectives. First, it reviews and assesses the cumulative body of scientific evidence regarding how children understand television advertising and how they are influenced by it. It then examines the governmental regulations and industry self-regulatory policies that have been devised to protect children in this realm and considers their fit with the relevant empirical evidence. Before engaging these two major perspectives, this review first assesses the extent to which child viewers are likely to encounter advertising messages, as well as the nature of the advertising messages they are most likely to see.

## Children's Exposure to Television Advertising

Children's exposure to television advertising has long been conceptualized as a simple by-product of their time spent watching television. In the late 1970s, a research team funded by the National Science Foundation (NSF) estimated that children viewed an average of about 20,000 commercials per year (Adler et al., 1977). That estimate was based on a formula that multiplied the average number of hours a child viewed during the year (weekly estimate × 52) by the average number of commercials aired per hour on television. That same approach underlies the subsequent estimate that children typically viewed more than 30,000 product commercials per year in the late 1980s (Condry, Bence, & Scheibe, 1988) and more than 40,000 television ads per year in the early 1990s (Kunkel & Gantz, 1992). Indeed, with the growing proliferation of 15-second spots, even these enormous figures may underestimate the true number of commercials viewed by the average child at the dawn of the new millennium (Comstock & Scharrer, 1999).

Although estimates such as these underscore the tremendous volume of commercials most children will encounter, the changing nature of the television environment may now render them inadequate, if not misleading, as estimates of total advertising exposure. This is because a key premise on which the estimates were initially based—that advertising levels were largely consistent across varying program sources—no longer seems to hold true.

For children's programs, the level of commercial advertising found on cable channels appears to be substantially lower than on broadcast channels. For example, the largest study of advertising content in the published literature, which sampled more than 600 hours of children's programs, found that network broadcasters aired the greatest amount of commercials, averaging 10:05 minutes per 1 hour of children's shows (Kunkel & Gantz, 1992). Independent broadcasters followed closely behind at 9:37 per hour, while cable channels such as USA (7:49/hour) and Nickelodeon (6:28/hour) devoted much less time to commercial messages. Furthermore, many program sources do not rely on advertiser support at all and thus present their content without commercial interruption. These include public television, premium cable channels (e.g., HBO), and videocassette sales and rentals, which collectively may account for a substantial proportion of young children's television viewing time.

No published study has yet reported data for the average amount of time children spend watching advertiser-supported channels, and without such a figure, it is problematic to attempt any inferentially derived estimates for total ad exposure. Indeed, many families specifically seek out sources of programming for their children that are commercial-free, such as the many popular PBS children's programs including *Barney & Friends* and *Sesame Street.*

Yet if any growth in non-advertiser-supported television programming has served to reduce the level of children's advertising exposure as compared with past years, another shift in the television environment portends movement in the opposite direction. Since the mid-1980s, policy deregulation has allowed advertisers to promote products directly within the body of "program" content, even in programs specifically designed for children (Kline, 1993; Kunkel, 1988b). These so-called program-length commercials have prospered in the children's television marketplace for many years following their initial legalization in 1984 (Pecora, 1998). The boundary between commercial and noncommercial content has been blurred as never before by media industry practices in the 1990s (Effron, 1999; Thorson & Schumann, 1999).

Considering all these factors, it is virtually impossible to offer a single summary figure that represents the extent to which children encounter advertising on television. On the whole, it is clear that the commercial content targeting youth is greater in recent years than ever before, in part simply because the economic stakes are so high. In the United States alone, children age 14 and under spent $24 billion and influenced $188 billion in family purchases in 1997 (McNeal, 1998).

## The Nature of the Advertising Environment

A substantial amount of children's television viewing, particularly after the preschool years, consists of programs primarily intended for adults (Roberts, Foehr, Rideout, & Brodie, 1999). As a result, much of the advertising content children see is likely to be adult oriented, in terms of both the merchandise featured and the form or style of the commercial message. However, because most adult-oriented advertising features products and appeals of limited salience to youth, children are less likely to attend closely to them (Greer, Potts, Wright, & Huston, 1982) or to pursue "purchase-influence attempts" after viewing adult-oriented ads (Gorn & Florsheim, 1985). Thus, concern about the influence of advertising on children has focused primarily on commercials designed specifically for child audiences (Choate, 1980; Rossiter, 1980). Accordingly, the emphasis here will be specifically on commercials designed primarily for children, for it is these ads that are most likely to attract children's attention and to have the most immediate effects on young viewers.

Throughout the 1970s, Barcus (1971, 1972, 1975a, 1975b, 1978) conducted a series of studies of children's advertising content that provide a rich foundation of knowledge about the commercials aired during that period. In a summary of that body of work, Barcus (1980) observed that more than 80% of all advertising to children falls within four product categories: toys, cereal, candy, and fast food restaurants. The stability of this pattern was confirmed by subsequent research in the early 1990s (Kunkel & Gantz, 1992), which reported data strikingly similar to Barcus's earlier findings. For example, compare the following results from Barcus's largest data set (Barcus, 1977) with those of Kunkel and Gantz (1992) on the distribution of ads by product type: Toys (18%/17%), cereal (25%/31%), candy (29%/32%), and fast food (10%/9%) all held virtually identical market shares over the years. It is apparent that the nature of the products marketed to children in television commercials has remained remarkably stable over time.

Another pattern that has held constant over time is the seasonal variation in product advertising that occurs each year during the pre-Christmas months. During this period, toy commercials gain a much larger share of the market, jumping from their normal rate of about one in every five or six commercials to half or more of all ads in children's programs (Atkin & Heald, 1977; Barcus, 1976; Condry et al., 1988; Kunkel & Gantz, 1994). This increase in toy advertising generally displaces commercials for cereal and candy, which then reemerge after the holidays in their normal volume.

The most common theme or appeal (i.e., persuasive strategy) employed in advertising to children is associating the product with fun and happiness, rather than providing any factual product-related information (Atkin & Heald, 1977; Barcus, 1980; Kunkel & Gantz, 1992). For example, a commercial featuring Ronald McDonald dancing, singing, and smiling in McDonald's restaurants without any mention of the food products available there would be categorized as employing a fun/happiness theme. Barcus (1980) noted that this pattern was common with cereal advertising, which frequently features spokescharacters (e.g., Tony the Tiger, Cap'n Crunch) in an adventure scenario; in contrast, it is impossible to discern the major grain used in the cereal in most cases unless it is included as part of the product name (e.g., corn flakes).

Finally, a common feature of advertising to children is the use of product disclosures and disclaimers such as "batteries not included" or "each part sold separately" (Stern & Harmon, 1984). Studies make clear that young children do not comprehend the intended meaning of the most widely used disclaimers (Liebert, Sprafkin, Liebert, & Rubinstein, 1977; Stern

& Resnik, 1978). Fewer than one in four kindergarten through second-grade children could grasp the meaning of "some assembly required" when shown a commercial, but the use of child-friendly language such as "you have to put it together" more than doubled the proportion of children who understood the qualifying message (Liebert et al., 1977).

The phrase "part of a balanced breakfast" is another frequent disclosure, included in most cereal ads to combat the concern that sugared cereal products hold little nutritional value for children. Atkin and Gibson (1978) found that, consistent with the data on toy disclaimers, fewer than one in three 4- to 7-year-olds had any idea what the term *balanced breakfast* means. Rather than informing young viewers about the importance of a nutritious breakfast, this common disclaimer actually leaves many children with the misimpression that cereal alone is sufficient for a meal (Palmer & McDowell, 1981).

These findings regarding children's interpretation of disclosures and disclaimers in television commercials underscore the importance of examining how children of different ages make sense of advertising messages. In addressing that topic, it is essential to start at the most fundamental level of information-processing tasks that are involved when children view commercials on television. Thus, we now turn to a careful examination of that comprehension process.

## Children's Comprehension of Advertising

At what point do children perceive advertising as a category of message content that is separate and distinct from programs? When do children begin to apply a degree of skepticism to their understanding of advertising claims and appeals? Researchers have clearly devoted greater attention to these and related questions than to any other topic in the realm of children and television advertising, in part because of the importance of such findings for public policy makers who seek to protect children's interests.

Children must acquire two key information-processing skills to achieve "mature" comprehension of advertising messages. First, they must be able to discriminate at a perceptual level commercial from noncommercial content, and, second, they must be able to attribute persuasive intent to advertising and to adjust their interpretation of commercial messages consistent with that knowledge. Each of these capabilities develops over time, largely as a function of cognitive growth and development rather than the accumulation of any particular amount of experience with media content.

### *Program/Commercial Discrimination*

Given the similarities in terms of production conventions and featured characters found in both children's television programs and commercials, it is hardly surprising that very young children experience difficulty distinguishing between these two types of content. Numerous investigations of children's program/commercial discrimination document confusion on the part of a substantial proportion of children below the age of about 4 or 5 years.

Research using direct verbal questioning to measure children's ability to discriminate programs from commercials indicates that children first recognize this difference based on either affective ("commercials are more funny than programs") or perceptual ("commercials are short and programs are long") cues (Blatt, Spencer, & Ward, 1972; Ward, Reale, & Levinson, 1972). These studies report that a majority of children below age 5 exhibit "low awareness of the concept of commercials, frequently explaining them as part of the show" (Ward et al., 1972, p. 486).

Some have argued that young children's limited verbal abilities might be masking their true competence in discriminating programs from commercials when only direct questioning is used to measure such ability (Gunter,

1981; Levin, Petros, & Petrella, 1982). However, techniques that avoid dependence on children's language skills have also been used to explore this issue. For example, Palmer and McDowell (1979) showed kindergarten and first-grade children (approximately 5-7 years old) videotapes of children's shows with commercials included. At predetermined points, the tape was stopped and children were asked whether what they were just watching was "part of the show" or "a commercial." The findings indicate that children correctly identified a commercial about 64% of the time in one program and 55% of the time in the other, both of which are only slightly above chance for a dichotomous measure.

Surprisingly, the Palmer and McDowell (1979) experiments also revealed that the use of program/commercial separation devices (e.g., "We'll be right back after these messages") commonly found in children's programming did not help child viewers to recognize advertising content. This finding has been corroborated by other studies that examined the separation devices typically employed by the major broadcast networks (Butter, Popovich, Stackhouse, & Garner, 1981; Stutts, Vance, & Hudleson, 1981), probably because these separation devices tend to be highly similar in form and style to their adjacent program environment. In contrast, Ballard-Campbell (1983) devised a perceptually distinct separator and found that such a device can indeed be effective in helping young children to identify commercials.

In the Ballard-Campbell (1983) study, a separator introduced a commercial with the words "OK kids, get ready for a commercial. Ready? Here comes a commercial." At the same time, a red stop sign was shown. After the commercial, the children saw a green "go" sign and were told, "The commercial is over. Now let's go back and see the program again." Children who saw the distinct separator performed significantly better at differentiating program/commercial content in the show than did same age children who saw either a typical network separator or no separator at all. Four-year-olds improved to 76% correct discrimination, 6-year-olds to 80%, and 8-year-olds to 91%.

A subsequent investigation (Kunkel, 1988a) found that, even once children can correctly apply the label "a commercial" to advertising, they do not necessarily understand that such content is separate and conceptually distinct from the adjacent program material. Data from this study indicate that, although 91% of 3- to 5-year-olds could correctly apply the term *commercial* to an ad inserted in a program, only 31% recognized that a commercial just viewed was not part of the story in the adjacent program material. It appears that children's initial use of the concept of a commercial does not reflect the understanding that such content is independent and disconnected from the adjacent entertainment program that surrounds it.

To summarize, the evidence is clear that a substantial proportion of young children, likely constituting a majority of those below ages 4 to 5, do not consistently discriminate between television program and commercial content. By about age 5, however, most children have developed the ability to distinguish between these two quite well at a perceptual level. Yet such differentiation is only the first of two critical information-processing tasks that young children must master to achieve mature comprehension of advertising messages.

### *Recognition of Persuasive Intent*

The primary purpose of all television advertising is to influence the attitudes and subsequent behavior of viewers. For adults, the recognition that a given piece of television content is a commercial triggers a cognitive filter or defense mechanism that takes into account factors such as the following: (a) The source of the message has other perspectives and other interests than those of the receiver, (b) the source intends to persuade, (c) persuasive messages are biased, and (d) biased messages demand different interpretive strategies than do unbiased messages (Roberts, 1982).

When these considerations can all be taken into account in a child's processing of advertising messages, then that child can be said to have developed mature comprehension of the advertising process.

Young children, by virtue of their limited cognitive development, typically lack the ability to apply such considerations to their understanding of television advertising. Below the age of approximately 7 or 8 years, children tend toward egocentrism and have difficulty taking the perspective of another person (Flavell, 1977; Kurdek & Rodgon, 1975; Selman, 1971; Shantz, 1975). Certainly, role-taking ability is a progressively developing skill, and even preschoolers ages 3 to 5 can demonstrate some competency in simple role-taking tasks that emphasize highly concrete elements (Urberg & Docherty, 1976). In more abstract situations, the outcome can be very different. One study demonstrated that 6-year-olds were unable to self-promote—that is, to describe themselves favorably to enhance their chances of being selected for a team (Aloise-Young, 1993). Given the complexities involved in appreciating the source's perspective in the advertising process, there is a strong theoretical basis to expect that young children will have difficulty recognizing the persuasive intent underlying television advertising. A substantial body of empirical evidence confirms this expectation.

Typical of studies on this topic, Ward and Wackman (1973) interviewed children ages 5 to 12 to determine their understanding of the purpose of advertising. Rather than conducting their analysis by age, however, these researchers used independent measures to categorize children into three levels of cognitive ability, with the lowest level equivalent to Piaget's preoperational stage of development. Fifty-three percent of the 5- to 6-year-olds and 41% of the 7- to 8-year-olds were categorized as "low" in cognitive level. Low cognitive level was found to be a significant predictor of a low level of understanding of the persuasive intent of commercials. This study concludes that "the low cognitive level children cannot abandon their own perspective and take the perspective of the advertiser when viewing commercials" (Ward & Wackman, 1973, p. 127).

Numerous other studies (Blosser & Roberts, 1985; Donahue, Meyer, & Henke, 1978; Robertson & Rossiter, 1974; Rossiter & Robertson, 1974; Ward, Wackman, & Wartella, 1977) have produced comparable findings that age is positively correlated with an understanding of commercials' persuasive intent, with 7 to 8 years the approximate point that such ability typically develops. Faber, Perloff, and Hawkins (1982) found that, consistent with theoretical expectations, children's skill at role taking was the best predictor for comprehension of advertising's persuasive intent.

As with the measurement of children's program/commercial discrimination, however, some have raised concerns that children may "know more than they can tell" and perform poorly on measures of persuasive-intent recognition primarily because of their limited ability to verbalize such understanding for researchers (Macklin, 1983; Young, 1990). To overcome this potential limitation, one particularly controversial study created a nonverbal technique to measure persuasive-intent attribution (Donahue, Henke, & Donahue, 1980). Children ages 3 to 6 were asked to choose between two pictures (one of a mother and child buying cereal at a supermarket and one of a child watching television) to indicate what the commercial they had just seen wanted them to do. The results indicated that about 80% of the subjects picked the supermarket picture, a finding that the authors interpreted as indicating an understanding of advertising's persuasive intent. However, numerous attempts to replicate these findings have proven unsuccessful (Ballard-Campbell, 1983; Kunkel, 1988a; Macklin, 1985).

Each attempt to replicate this finding used the type of nonverbal measure identical to that employed by the Donahue et al. (1980) study, with the only methodological difference being the addition of one or two more picture alternatives to minimize the possibility of children selecting the correct option by chance. In one case, only 13% of 4-year-olds and 33% of 6-year-olds chose the correct picture (Ballard-Campbell, 1983); in another, 24% of 4- to 5-year-olds and 30% of 7- to 8-year-olds responded correctly (Kunkel, 1988a); and in the third study, 17% of 3- to 5-year-olds selected the correct alternative once across two different chances, though only 3% selected correctly across both trials (Macklin, 1985). The use of other nonverbal measures (e.g., game playing) to assess children's comprehension of commercial intent has yielded essentially the same result: 3- and 4-year-olds evidenced almost no responses that could be classified as persuasive-intent attribution, although a minority of 5-year-olds were successful at demonstrating some "emerging understanding" (Macklin, 1987, p. 238). Thus, the evidence as a whole clearly suggests that most children younger than about age 7 or 8 do not typically recognize that the underlying goal of a commercial is to persuade the viewer.

Furthermore, even if the data reported in studies such as these indicated stronger performance at recognizing that an ad seeks to have the viewer buy its product, such evidence would address only the most rudimentary aspect of persuasive-intent attribution. That is, just because a child understands that an ad seeks to sell a product, it does not necessarily follow that the child will recognize the bias inherent in persuasive messages and therefore view advertising claims and appeals more skeptically. As Roberts (1982) notes, each of these elements represents an increasingly sophisticated level of understanding about the advertising process, all of which are essential to achieve mature comprehension. If there is a shortcoming in research in this area, it is that too many studies limit their measurement of children's comprehension of persuasive intent solely to items that assess whether or not a child recognizes that an ad seeks to sell a product, rather than probing more deeply for the related cognitive capabilities that Roberts posits are equally crucial elements of a child's defense against commercial persuasion.

In sum, the numerous empirical studies in this realm indicate that at least half of the children below age 7 or 8 are generally unable to recognize the persuasive intent of television advertising, even when this skill is measured in only its most rudimentary form (i.e., selling intent). Although the use of nonverbal measurement techniques might suggest that younger children can recognize persuasive intent, both methodological and conceptual weaknesses cast doubt on the validity of such evidence, which renders the findings of statistical meta-analyses in this realm (e.g., Martin, 1997) of limited value. Overall, the weight of the evidence indicates that the ability to recognize persuasive intent is not well developed for most children until at least the age of 7 or 8.

## Children's Attitudes Toward Television Advertising

Research consistently indicates that children's attitudes toward commercials as a genre (as opposed to an individual ad for a given product) are negatively correlated with age; that is, the older a child is, the less likely he or she will hold a positive attitude toward television advertising. This is logical given that older children are more likely to comprehend the persuasive intent of advertising, which provides them with the foundation for recognizing the manipulation inherent in advertising messages. However, the age at which children actually develop a negative attitude toward commercials, if in fact such a perspective evolves during childhood, has not been precisely defined.

In one study typical of findings in this area, the proportion of children indicating that they like *all* commercials declined from 69% in first grade to 56% by third grade to 25% by fifth grade (Robertson & Rossiter, 1974). Other investigations demonstrate that preschool and early grade school children generally like to watch Saturday morning commercials; older elementary-school-age children are less positive but at worst express ambivalent feelings (Atkin, 1975; Rossiter, 1977; Ward & Wackman, 1972).

Children find the music, humor, and attention-getting production conventions that predominate in commercials attractive (Greer et al., 1982; Macklin, 1988; Wartella & Ettema, 1974; Wartella & Hunter, 1983) and hence tend to respond to them quite favorably. Even for older children ages 9 to 11, who generally have developed the ability to recognize persuasive intent in commercials and are therefore more likely to be cynical and suspicious about advertising, positive attitudes toward individual commercials are a common response (Adler et al., 1977; Adler et al., 1980). Taken as a whole, the available evidence indicates that children do not react negatively to television commercials as a genre in nearly the same way that adults do (Barling & Fullager, 1983), although older children tend to hold less positive attitudes toward advertising than younger children do.

## Effects of Television Advertising on Children

One way of conceptualizing the impact of television advertising on children is to distinguish the intended from the unintended effects of exposure. For example, a cereal ad may have the intended effect of generating product purchase requests and increasing product consumption, but it may also contribute to unintended outcomes such as misperceptions about proper nutritional habits and/or parent-child conflict should a child's purchase-influence attempt be rejected by the parent. Comstock and Paik (1991) prefer the terminology of "primary" and "secondary" effects but still rely on the same criterion suggested here—the direct promotion of the advertiser's economic interest—as the basis for conceptualizing the different types of impacts of television commercials on child audiences. Thus, the following sections will examine the effects of television advertising on children from each of these two distinct perspectives.

### *Intended Effects*

Advertisers are interested in outcomes such as viewers' recall for the product, desire for the advertised product, and—depending on the age of the child—either purchase-influence attempts or actual purchase of the product. Although some commercial campaigns certainly are more successful than others, studies have documented the general effectiveness of advertising across all of these areas.

Children's recall of television commercials has been examined from a variety of perspectives. When experiments measure recall of advertisements immediately following viewing, more than half of the children studied tend to remember an ad for products such as toys, cereals, and ice cream even when it is shown just once during a program (Gorn & Goldberg, 1977, 1980; Zuckerman, Ziegler, & Stevenson, 1978). Recall can also be inferred from survey data indicating the source of children's product knowledge. When children are asked where they learned about toys they would like to have, they most often identify television commercials as the source (Caron & Ward, 1975; Donahue, 1975), a finding that is corroborated by parental reports (Barry & Sheikh, 1977; Isler, Popper, & Ward, 1987).

Brand preferences can be manipulated by exposure to a single commercial (Goldberg, Gorn, & Gibson, 1978; Resnik & Stern, 1977), although stronger effects (e.g., increased desire for the advertised product or increased preference for the advertised brand over other competing brands) are more likely to result from repeated exposure to television commercials (Galst & White, 1976; Gorn & Goldberg, 1982; Robertson & Rossiter, 1977). It is interesting to note that, even though children's recall of commercials may decay quickly over time, positive attitudes toward an advertised product can persist a week later even after the ad has been forgotten (Silverman, Jaccard, & Burke, 1988).

Experimental studies that compare children who are shown a particular commercial with those who are not provide some of the most direct evidence of advertising impact. Although it is typical for half or more children in a control group to spontaneously report strong desire for a given toy or cereal (i.e., even without being shown a related commercial), exposure to an ad leads to statistically significant increases in children's desire for the advertised merchandise (Atkin & Gibson, 1978; Stoneman & Brody, 1981).

Certain advertising strategies tend to enhance the effectiveness of advertising appeals to children. For example, advertising for cereal and fast food meals often emphasizes premium offers such as a small toy figure included along with the product. In one study in which researchers unobtrusively observed parents and children shopping at the supermarket, it was found that almost half of the children making product purchase requests in the cereal aisle were influenced by premium offers (Atkin, 1978). Another study found that commercials offering premiums were more persuasive than commercials featuring popular program figures, even when such ads were embedded in programs featuring the same characters (Miller & Busch, 1979), a practice known as host selling.

Characters are nonetheless influential in shaping children's views of advertised products. Experiments presenting virtually identical versions of ads, one with and one without a celebrity endorser, show that popular figures significantly enhance children's liking of the product (Atkin & Block, 1983; Ross et al., 1984). Indeed, when program characters appear in a commercial aired during that character's show, they not only enhance children's liking of the advertised product (Kunkel, 1988a) but also make it more difficult for children to discriminate between program and commercial boundaries (Kunkel, 1988a; Wilson & Weiss, 1992).

From the advertisers' perspective, the ultimate intended effect of airing a commercial is for their product to be subsequently purchased by viewers. Both Atkin (1978) and Galst and White (1976) found that the amount of prior television viewing was a significant predictor of the frequency of children's product purchase requests at the supermarket. In the latter study, three fourths of all parent-child exchanges about products were child demands for merchandise advertised on television. Even cross-cultural research comparing families from Japan, England, and the United States has demonstrated a positive relationship between children's amount of television viewing and their product purchase requests, although notably the level of purchase-influence attempts was greatest in the United States (Robertson, Ward, Gatignon, & Klees, 1989).

Finally, research also makes clear that children's purchase-influence attempts have a relatively high degree of success. Frequent parental yielding to children's purchase requests has been reported in studies that rely on parent self-reports (Frideres, 1973; Ward & Wackman, 1972) as well as unobtrusive observation of behavior in the supermarket (Atkin, 1978; Galst & White, 1976). In sum, although the process may be indirect, television commercials targeted at children are highly effective at accomplishing their intended goal of promoting product sales.

### *Unintended Effects*

Although each ad may have as its primary purpose promoting the sales of its featured product, the cumulative impact from the totality of television advertising to children may exert far broader sociological influence. Some have suggested that one of the long-term effects of children's exposure to commercials is an increase in materialistic attitudes (Goldberg & Gorn, 1978; Moschis & Moore, 1982), though such an assertion is particularly difficult to establish given that relatively few American children grow up without extensive media exposure. In other areas, however, the unintended effects of advertising have been more convincingly demonstrated.

Arguably the most visible of the unintended effects is the influence of television advertising on children's eating habits (Dietz, 1990; Jeffrey, McLellarn, & Fox, 1982). It was established in an earlier section that commercials for candy, snacks, and fast food are mainstays of the advertising presented during children's programs. It has also been well documented that such ads are typically effective in persuading children to like and request the product (Galst & White, 1976; Goldberg et al., 1978; Taras, Sallis, Patterson, Nader, & Nelson, 1989). In a study with particularly strong external validity, Gorn and Goldberg (1982) controlled the advertising shown to 5- to 8-year-old children at a 2-week-long camp. Some children saw commercials for fruit and fruit juice, while others viewed ads for candy and Kool-Aid, a sugar-sweetened drink. As expected, children's actual food and drink choices during the camp were significantly influenced by the ads they viewed.

The broader concern here, of course, is that commercials for candy, snacks, and sugared cereals far outnumber commercials for more healthy or nutritious foods (Atkin & Heald, 1977; Barcus, 1980; Kunkel & Gantz, 1992). One study even suggests that the influence of ads for healthy foods can be overcome when a commercial for snack foods (e.g., Hostess cupcakes) is shown at the same time (Cantor, 1981). The general finding that eating habits formed during childhood often persist throughout life underscores the serious implications of advertising influence in this realm (Jacobson & Maxwell, 1994).

There has been substantial research assessing the influence of commercials for sensitive products not intended for children, including drugs and medicine as well as alcoholic beverages. Although some modest short-term effects have been demonstrated on brand choice, studies do not indicate any long-term impact on children's beliefs or attitudes about medicine use or on their requests to parents for medicine to cure their ills (Almarsdottir & Bush, 1992; Butter, Weikel, Otto, Wright, & Deinzer, 1991; Robertson, Rossiter, & Gleason, 1979; Rossiter & Robertson, 1980).

In contrast, as Comstock and Paik (1991) note, the nature of television advertising for proprietary drugs differs substantially from advertising for alcoholic beverages such as beer products. This factor, along with the symbolic role that alcohol plays as young people make the transition from child to young adult in American society, may help to explain the findings that exposure to alcohol advertising exerts at least a modest degree of influence on young people's alcohol expectancies (Grube, 1993; Grube & Wallack, 1994; Slater et al., 1997), which have in turn been shown to predict drinking behaviors (Goldman, Brown, & Christiansen, 1987; Smith & Goldman, 1995). In summarizing this work, Atkin (1995) notes, "The key question is no longer whether advertising influences drinking, but what degree of impact occurs" (p. 66).

Another important area of unintended effects involves parent-child conflicts that emerge when refusals occur in response to children's purchase-influence attempts (Robertson, 1979). Parents obviously cannot honor all purchase requests triggered by television advertising, particularly given that the average child is likely to see more than 40,000 commercials a year (Kunkel & Gantz, 1992). In one study, Atkin (1975) found that more than half of the children reported becoming angry or arguing when a toy request was denied; in another (Atkin, 1978), he observed high rates of child disappointment and anger in response to the majority of parent refusals for cereal requests at the supermarket. Other studies confirm these patterns (Goldberg & Gorn, 1978; Sheikh & Moleski, 1977). In sum, the frequent purchase requests associated with children's advertising exposure may place strain on parent-child interaction at times, an issue of consequence largely because of the sheer volume of commercials viewed by most children.

## Policies Restricting Television Advertising Directed at Children

Although the unintended effects of commercials raise important social issues, the fundamental policy concern surrounding children and television advertising revolves around the question of fairness. Are young children, who possess only limited capability for evaluating commercial persuasion, fair targets for advertising? Is it fair to allow unlimited advertising during children's programming, or should restrictions be placed on the amount of commercials? Does fairness require special safeguards to limit certain types of advertising strategies directed at children?

The answers to these questions require value judgments that can only be reached as part of the political process of constructing public policy. Interestingly, some of those value judgments have changed over time as regulatory tides have seemed to ebb and flow at different points in television's history. This section provides a brief historical perspective on the most important federal regulatory policies pertaining to children's television advertising.

### *Regulation by the Federal Communications Commission*

The Federal Communications Commission (FCC) has the responsibility of establishing public interest obligations for broadcasters who are licensed by the agency to use the publicly owned airwaves. In the early 1970s, a public interest organization known as Action for Children's Television (ACT) petitioned the FCC to devise policies to protect children who are too young to effectively recognize and defend against televised commercial persuasion (Adler, 1980; Cole & Oettinger, 1978).

The outcome of this petition was the commission's adoption of the first federal policies restricting television advertising to children. More specifically, guidelines were devised in two distinct areas: one involving specific limitations (12 minutes/hour on weekdays and 9.5 minutes/hour on weekends) on the overall amount of advertising allowed during children's programs, and a second establishing that a "clear separation" must be maintained between program and commercial matter (FCC, 1974). In the latter realm, three applications of the separation policy were adopted:

1. *Bumpers.* Program/commercial separation devices, termed *bumpers* by the broadcast industry, were required during all children's shows. These devices are roughly 5-second segments shown before and after commercial breaks that say something such as "And now a word from our sponsor."
2. *Host selling.* Program characters or "hosts" were prohibited from promoting products during commercials embedded in or directly adjacent to their show. For example, a Flintstones cereal commercial would not be allowed during the *Flintstones* cartoon show.
3. *Program-length commercials.* The promotion of products within the body of a program's story or entertainment content was prohibited. Any material that constituted advertising had to be confined to identifiable commercial segments.

These policies remained in full force for a decade but then encountered a major shift in the regulatory philosophy at the FCC. Amid the general tide of governmental deregulation that occurred under the Reagan administration during the 1980s (Horwitz, 1989), the children's advertising policies were significantly relaxed in 1984. All limits on the amount of advertising time were deregulated. The FCC asserted at the time that "marketplace forces can better determine appropriate commercial levels than our own rules" (FCC, 1984, p. 33598) and thus rescinded all restrictions on the amount of commercial content, whether directed to audiences of children or adults.

The FCC's logic was that, if stations exceeded viewers' tolerance for advertising, then the size of the audience would drop, advertising rates would decline, and the broadcaster would be forced by economic considerations to reduce the number of commercials. The key to this formulation is that the viewer must be able to recognize advertising messages and react to them adversely, at least when they appear in large quantity.

Although such a position might be reasonably inferred for audiences of adults, it is at fundamental odds with the scientific evidence documenting young children's limited understanding of television advertising. How could very young children be expected to react negatively to "too much" advertising if they lack the ability to even recognize it as a perceptual category? And even once children develop the ability to discriminate programs from commercials, it is not until age 7 or 8 that they begin to appreciate advertising's persuasive intent, which is the first point at which advertising begins to assume any negative connotations for the viewer. In other words, the FCC's deregulation of its policies limiting children's advertising time essentially flew in the face of the relevant scientific evidence, and this problem formed the basis for a U.S. Court of Appeals ruling in 1987 forcing the agency to reconsider its decision to deregulate (*Action for Children's Television v. FCC*, 1987).

The court's reconsideration order was rendered moot when the Children's Television Act was enacted by Congress in 1990. This law focused primarily on educational programming requirements but also reinstated time restrictions on advertising to children as a statutory requirement for broadcasters. These new commercial limits, which remain in effect today, allow no more than 10.5 minutes per hour on weekends and 12 minutes per hour on weekdays during children's television programs.

Interestingly, the congressionally mandated limits were also extended for the first time to cable television networks. Although cable lacks the public interest obligations of the broadcast industry, and hence there is some question whether the government has legitimate authority to regulate its content in such direct fashion, the industry accepted the regulation willingly. Acceding to the policy helped the industry in its overall relations with Congress (Kunkel, 1991), and this "pill" was relatively painless to swallow because the new regulatory limits were well above the levels of advertising presented on most cable programming for children at the time (Kunkel & Gantz, 1992).

At the same time that the FCC deregulated its commercial time limits in 1984, it also abandoned its restriction on program-length commercials; the bumper and host-selling policies, however, were left untouched, and both remain in effect today. When Congress reinstated the commercial time limits in 1990, it was hesitant to reenact the program-length commercial prohibition because, by that time, children's product-related programming had grown to be a staple of the industry (Kunkel, 1988b). Reinstating a ban might mean driving from the airwaves some of the most popular children's cartoon programs, certainly not an attractive prospect for elected representatives.

Congress finessed the issue by ordering the FCC to reconsider a ban but left it up to the agency to determine how to define a program-length commercial. In the midst of a children's television environment now predominated by product-related programming, and at a time when the commission was still controlled by marketplace proponents, the FCC crafted a predictable solution. It reinstated a prohibition against children's program-length commercials but in so doing devised a new, "improved" definition for the restricted programming. The new definition is "a program associated with a product in which commercials for that product are aired" (FCC, 1991, p. 2117).

A long-standing policy that was never deregulated was the FCC's restriction on host selling. Host selling refers to the use of children's program characters in ads placed adjacent to the program in which they appear. Since 1974, this policy has effectively banned the practices that the FCC now defines as a program-length commercial. Yet in children's television today, the characters are the products; it is difficult to conceive of program-related products that would not involve a popular program character and hence violate the host-selling policy when aired adjacent to the character's show. By redefining a program-length commercial as tantamount to host selling, the FCC has seemingly reinstated a restriction on program-length commercials without actually limiting any ongoing program practices. In fact, under the new definition of program-length commercials, it would be possible for a program to include unlimited product promotions within the body of the show as long as the broadcaster did not present any "traditional" 15- or 30-second ads for the related products at the same time. From this perspective, one can appreciate why the current restriction on program-length commercials has yet to accomplish any reduction in the use of children's programs to promote toys and other products to children.

### *Regulation by the Federal Trade Commission*

The Federal Trade Commission (FTC) shares authority with the FCC for regulating television advertising, although each agency has a somewhat different emphasis. The FCC's primary goal is to ensure that broadcasters perform in the public interest, however the agency chooses to define that term. The FTC, on the other hand, had (at least in the 1970s) the authority to regulate any advertising deemed "unfair" or "deceptive," regardless of its medium of presentation (Lesch, 1983).

In 1978, the FTC shocked the broadcasting and advertising industries by attempting to exercise that authority in unique fashion. It formally proposed a rule that would either ban or severely restrict all television advertising to children (FTC, 1978). The agency's case was quite straightforward. It argued that all advertising directed to children too young to understand a message's persuasive intent was inherently unfair and deceptive. The FTC's proposal was supported by a 300-plus-page review of the relevant scientific research documenting its claim.

The painstaking level of detail the FTC pursued in marshaling its supporting evidence contrasted sharply with a serious miscalculation about the extent of the political opposition to its proposal (Kunkel & Watkins, 1987). The broadcasting and advertising industries were joined by many of America's largest corporate conglomerates in opposing the ban. These businesses owned subsidiaries producing toys, sugared cereals, and numerous other types of child-oriented merchandise. Fearing adverse impacts on their profits, these industries initiated campaigns to influence the public to oppose the ban. A key element of their strategy was the claim of First Amendment protection for the right to provide "information" about products to America's budding consumers.

The FTC's formal rule-making process for implementing the proposed ban moved forward. Open hearings were held. Elaborate briefs assessing the research evidence regarding children's comprehension of advertising were submitted by all sides. On this front, the forces seeking regulation fared reasonably well. Although some inevitable qualifications were lodged, a consensus emerged among researchers that young children were indeed uniquely vulnerable to television's commercial claims and appeals.

At the same time, however, a much different outcome was occurring on other fronts of the political battle. Using their influence with elected officials, the FTC's corporate opponents succeeded in derailing the agency's proposal, employing an innovative strategy. Responding to corporate pressure, Congress rescinded the agency's authority to restrict advertising deemed unfair by enacting legislation ironically titled the FTC Improvements Act of 1980. Besides removing this aspect of the FTC's jurisdiction, the act specifically prohibited any further action to adopt the proposed children's advertising rules. The agency soon issued a final ruling on the case formally implementing the congressional mandate (FTC, 1981), and since then there has been no further effort to resurrect this initiative.

### *Industry Self-Regulation*

The actions of both the FCC and FTC in the 1970s rendered children's television advertising a controversial topic. In the face of public criticism and concern about the issue, both the broadcasting and advertising industries employed self-regulatory efforts to avoid more stringent governmental restrictions (Armstrong, 1984). The self-regulatory Code of the National Association of Broadcasters (NAB), which addressed a wide range of programming practices, was eliminated in 1982 for reasons entirely unrelated to the children's advertising issue (Maddox & Zanot, 1984). That left the advertising industry's self-regulatory framework as the only remaining effort, a situation that is still the case today.

The Children's Advertising Review Unit (CARU), a subsidiary of the National Council of Better Business Bureaus, was first created in 1974. The CARU operation, which is funded by contributions from the advertising industry, relies on the good-faith cooperation of advertisers to accomplish its work. The CARU guidelines are intended to "encourage truthful and accurate advertising sensitive to the special nature of children" (Weisskoff, 1985, p. 12).

Guidelines are established in such areas as product presentations and claims, sales pressure, disclosures and disclaimers, and safety concerns. Within each area, a range of criteria is included indicating practices to be either avoided or required. Some of these standards are fairly specific, such as the requirement that "a product should be demonstrated in a way that can be duplicated by the child for whom the product is intended." Others are more vague and general, such as the admonition that "care should be taken not to exploit a child's imagination" (Children's Advertising Review Unit, 1996).

Although many elements of the guidelines are not amenable to any empirical evaluation of compliance, those that are were examined in an independent study of more than 10,000 commercials directed at children (Kunkel & Gantz, 1993). Overall, just 4% were found to present violations of CARU standards. Among the most common violations were ads that placed greater emphasis on a premium than on the advertised product.

Notwithstanding the finding that some ads (albeit a small proportion) clearly violate CARU standards, there are other perspectives that underscore the limits of self-regulation. At a microlevel, for example, self-regulation does not require that youngsters be able to comprehend the disclosures and disclaimers commonly found in children's advertising; if it did, the evidence is clear that few commercials could claim compliance. But at a macrolevel, self-regulation obviously cannot address fundamental concerns about the legitimacy of all television advertising to children. That concern has been resolved differently in other countries of the world such as Australia, Canada, and England, which do not allow *any* advertising targeting audiences of preschool-age children.

## Conclusion

Children are a special audience, with limited information-processing capabilities that constrain their early understanding of the nature and purpose of television advertising. Because of these limitations, young children are simply more easily persuadable than older children or adults. They are more trusting of advertising claims and appeals and more susceptible to commercial persuasion. This situation has led to actions on the part of both the government and the advertising industry to protect children's interests.

Although most of these measures are clearly of value, they hardly resolve all of the concerns about children's unique vulnerability to television advertising. Of course, parents have an important role to play in this equation in terms of socializing their children's consumer behavior. More recently, media literacy curricula in the schools have been employed to teach children to be "smarter" consumers of television advertising as well as programming. Yet neither of these mediators can accelerate young children's understanding of the advertising process beyond the limits of their cognitive capabilities at certain key points in their development.

Given the huge economic stakes that are now associated with marketing to children, one can certainly expect that the issues in this realm will continue to generate controversy. Indeed, such issues are growing far more complicated in new media environments such as the Internet, which already delivers an astounding amount of marketing messages to children (Montgomery & Pasnik, 1996). The challenge for the future is not only to consider children's vulnerability to commercial persuasion in the television environment but to extend our current base of knowledge by exploring the media environments of the twenty-first century, which no doubt will hold more surprises than anyone can envision today.

## References


Action for Children's Television v. FCC, 821 F. 2d 741 (D.C. Cir. 1987).

Adler, R. (1980). Children's television advertising: History of the issue. In E. Palmer & A. Dorr (Eds.), *Children and the faces of television* (pp. 237-249). New York: Academic Press.

Adler, R., Friedlander, B., Lesser, G., Meringoff, L., Robertson, T., Rossiter, J., & Ward, S. (1977). *Research on the effects of television advertising to children: A review of the literature and recommendations for future research.* Washington, DC: U.S. Government Printing Office.

Adler, R., Lesser, G., Meringoff, L., Robertson, T., Rossiter, J., & Ward, S. (1980). *The effects of television advertising on children: Review and recommendations.* Lexington, MA: Lexington Books.

Alexander, A., Owers, J., & Carveth, R. (1993). *Media economics: Theory and practice.* Hillsdale, NJ: Lawrence Erlbaum.

Almarsdottir, A., & Bush, P. (1992). The influence of drug advertising on children's drug use attitudes and behaviors. *Journal of Drug Issues, 22,* 361-376.

Aloise-Young, P. (1993). The development of self-presentation: Self-promotion in 6 to 10 year-old children. *Social Cognition, 11,* 201-222.

Armstrong, G. (1984). An evaluation of the Children's Advertising Review Unit. *Journal of Public Policy and Marketing, 3,* 38-55.

Atkin, C. (1975). *Effects of television advertising on children: Survey of children's and mothers' responses to television commercials* (Report No. 8). East Lansing: Michigan State University, Department of Communication.

Atkin, C. (1978). Observation of parent-child interaction in supermarket decision-making. *Journal of Marketing, 42,* 41-45.

Atkin, C. (1995). Survey and experimental research on effects of alcohol advertising. In S. Martin (Ed.), *The effects of the mass media on the use and abuse of alcohol* (pp. 39-68). Bethesda, MD: National Institutes of Health.

Atkin, C., & Block, M. (1983). Effectiveness of celebrity endorsers. *Journal of Advertising Research, 23*(1), 57-61.

Atkin, C., & Gibson, W. (1978). *Children's nutrition learning from television advertising.* East Lansing: Michigan State University, Department of Communication.

Atkin, C., & Heald, G. (1977). The content of children's toy and food commercials. *Journal of Communication, 27*(1), 107-114.

Ballard-Campbell, M. (1983). *Children's understanding of television advertising: Behavioral assessment of three developmental skills.* Unpublished doctoral dissertation, University of California, Los Angeles.

Barcus, F. E. (1971). *Saturday children's television: A report of TV programming and advertising on Boston commercial television.* Newtonville, MA: Action for Children's Television.

Barcus, F. E. (1972). *Network programming and advertising in the Saturday children's hours: A June and November comparison.* Newtonville, MA: Action for Children's Television.

Barcus, F. E. (1975a). *Television in the after-school hours.* Newtonville, MA: Action for Children's Television.

Barcus, F. E. (1975b). *Weekend children's television.* Newtonville, MA: Action for Children's Television.

Barcus, F. E. (1976). *Pre-Christmas advertising to children.* Newtonville, MA: Action for Children's Television.

Barcus, F. E. (1977). *Children's television: An analysis of programming and advertising.* New York: Praeger.

Barcus, F. E. (1978). *Commercial children's television on weekends and weekday afternoons.* Newtonville, MA: Action for Children's Television.

Barcus, F. E. (1980). The nature of television advertising to children. In E. Palmer & A. Dorr (Eds.), *Children and the faces of television* (pp. 273-285). New York: Academic Press.

Barling, J., & Fullager, C. (1983). Children's attitudes to television advertising: A factorial perspective. *Journal of Psychology, 113,* 25-30.

Barry, T., & Sheikh, A. (1977). Race as a dimension in children's TV advertising: The need for more research. *Journal of Advertising, 6,* 5-10.

Blatt, J., Spencer, L., & Ward, S. (1972). A cognitive developmental study of children's reactions to television advertising. In G. Comstock & E. Rubinstein (Eds.), *Television and social behavior* (Vol. 4). Washington, DC: U.S. Government Printing Office.

Blosser, B., & Roberts, D. (1985). Age differences in children's perceptions of message intent: Responses to TV news, commercials, educational spots, and public service announcements. *Communication Research, 12,* 455-484.

Butter, E., Popovich, P., Stackhouse, R., & Garner, R. (1981). Discrimination of television programs and commercials by preschool children. *Journal of Advertising Research, 21*(2), 53-56.

Butter, E., Weikel, K., Otto, V., Wright, K., & Deinzer, G. (1991). TV advertising of OTC medicines and its effects on child viewers. *Psychology and Marketing, 8*(2), 117-128.

Cantor, J. (1981). Modifying children's eating habits through television ads: Effects of humorous appeals in a field setting. *Journal of Broadcasting, 25,* 37-47.

Caron, A., & Ward, S. (1975). Gift decisions by kids and parents. *Journal of Advertising, 15*(4), 12-20.

Children's Advertising Review Unit. (1996). *Self regulatory guidelines for children's advertising* [Online]. Available: www.caru.org/caruguid.asp

Choate, R. (1980). The politics of change. In E. Palmer & A. Dorr (Eds.), *Children and the faces of television* (pp. 323-338). New York: Academic Press.

Cole, B., & Oettinger, M. (1978). *Reluctant regulators.* Reading, MA: Addison-Wesley.

Comstock, G., & Paik, H. (1991). *Television and the American child.* New York: Academic Press.

Comstock, G., & Scharrer, E. (1999). *Television: What's on, who's watching, and what it means.* New York: Academic Press.

Condry, J., Bence, P., & Scheibe, C. (1988). Nonprogram content of children's television. *Journal of Broadcasting, 32,* 255-270.

Dietz, W. (1990). You are what you eat—what you eat is what you are. *Journal of Adolescent Health Care, 11*(1), 76-81.

Donahue, T. (1975). Effect of commercials on black children. *Journal of Advertising Research, 15*(6), 41-46.

Donahue, T., Henke, L., & Donahue, W. (1980). Do kids know what TV commercials intend? *Journal of Advertising Research, 20,* 51-57.

Donahue, T., Meyer, T., & Henke, L. (1978). Black and white children: Perceptions of television commercials. *Journal of Marketing, 42,* 34-40.

Effron, E. (1999, February). The big blur: Seeing double. *Brill's Content,* pp. 44-45.

Faber, R., Perloff, R., & Hawkins, R. (1982). Antecedents of children's comprehension of television advertising. *Journal of Broadcasting, 26,* 575-584.

Federal Communications Commission. (1974). Children's television programs: Report and policy statement. *Federal Register, 39,* 39396-39409.

Federal Communications Commission. (1984). Revision of programming and commercialization policies, ascertainment requirements, and program log requirements for commercial television stations. *Federal Register, 49,* 33588-33620.

Federal Communications Commission. (1991). Policies and rules concerning children's television programming: Memorandum opinion and order. *Federal Communications Commission Record, 6,* 2111-2127.

Federal Trade Commission. (1978). *FTC staff report on television advertising to children.* Washington, DC: Author.

Federal Trade Commission. (1981). *In the matter of children's advertising: FTC final staff report and recommendation.* Washington, DC: Author.

Flavell, J. (1977). *Cognitive development.* Englewood Cliffs, NJ: Prentice Hall.

Frideres, J. (1973). Advertising, buying patterns, and children. *Journal of Advertising Research, 13,* 34-36.

Galst, J., & White, M. (1976). The unhealthy persuader: The reinforcing value of television and children's purchase influence attempts at the supermarket. *Child Development, 47,* 1089-1096.

Goldberg, M., & Gorn, G. (1978). Some unintended consequences of TV advertising to children. *Journal of Consumer Research, 5,* 22-29.

Goldberg, M., Gorn, G., & Gibson, W. (1978). TV messages for snacks and breakfast foods: Do they influence children's preferences? *Journal of Consumer Research, 5,* 73-81.

Goldman, M., Brown, S., & Christiansen, B. (1987). Expectancy theory: Thinking about drinking. In H. Blane & K. Leonard (Eds.), *Psychological theories of drinking and alcoholism* (pp. 181-226). New York: Guilford.

Gorn, G., & Florsheim, R. (1985). The effects of commercials for adult products on children. *Journal of Consumer Research, 11,* 962-967.

Gorn, G., & Goldberg, M. (1977). The impact of television advertising on children from low income families. *Journal of Consumer Research, 4,* 86-88.

Gorn, G., & Goldberg, M. (1980). Children's responses to repetitive television commercials. *Journal of Consumer Research, 6,* 421-424.

Gorn, G., & Goldberg, M. (1982). Behavioral evidence of the effects of televised food messages on children. *Journal of Consumer Research, 9,* 200-205.

Greer, D., Potts, R., Wright, J., & Huston, A. (1982). The effects of television commercial form and commercial placement on children's social behavior and attention. *Child Development, 53,* 611-619.

Grube, J. (1993). Alcohol portrayals and alcohol advertising on television: Content and effects on children and adolescents. *Alcohol Health and Research World, 17*(1), 61-66.

Grube, J., & Wallack, L. (1994). Television beer advertising and drinking knowledge, beliefs, and intentions among schoolchildren. *American Journal of Public Health, 94,* 254-259.

Gunter, B. (1981). Measuring children's comprehension of television commercials. *Current Psychological Reviews, 1,* 159-170.

Head, S. (1985). *World broadcasting systems: A comparative analysis.* Belmont, CA: Wadsworth.

Horwitz, R. (1989). *The irony of regulatory reform: The deregulation of American telecommunications.* New York: Oxford University Press.

Isler, L., Popper, E., & Ward, S. (1987). Children's purchase requests and parental responses: Results from a diary study. *Journal of Advertising Research, 27*(5), 28-39.

Jacobson, M., & Maxwell, B. (1994). *What are we feeding our kids?* New York: Workman.

Jeffrey, D., McLellarn, R., & Fox, D. (1982). The development of children's eating habits: The role of television commercials. *Health Education Quarterly, 9,* 174-189.

Kline, S. (1993). *Out of the garden: Toys, TV, and children's culture in the age of marketing.* London: Verso.

Kunkel, D. (1988a). Children and host-selling television commercials. *Communication Research, 15,* 71-92.

Kunkel, D. (1988b). From a raised eyebrow to a turned back: The FCC and children's product-related programming. *Journal of Communication, 38*(4), 90-108.

Kunkel, D. (1991). Crafting media policy: The genesis and implications of the Children's Television Act of 1990. *American Behavioral Scientist, 35,* 181-202.

Kunkel, D., & Gantz, W. (1992). Children's television advertising in the multi-channel environment. *Journal of Communication, 42*(3), 134-152.

Kunkel, D., & Gantz, W. (1993). Assessing compliance with industry self-regulation of television advertising to children. *Journal of Applied Communication Research, 21,* 148-162.

Kunkel, D., & Gantz, W. (1994, July). *Children's television advertising at Christmas time.* Paper presented at the annual conference of the International Communication Association, Sydney, Australia.

Kunkel, D., & Roberts, D. (1991). Young minds and marketplace values: Research and policy issues in children's television advertising. *Journal of Social Issues, 47*(1), 57-72.

Kunkel, D., & Watkins, B. (1987). Evolution of children's television regulatory policy. *Journal of Broadcasting and Electronic Media, 31,* 367-389.

Kurdek, L., & Rodgon, M. (1975). Perceptual, cognitive, and affective perspective taking in kindergarten through sixth-grade children. *Developmental Psychology, 11,* 643-650.

Lesch, W. (1983). The Federal Trade Commission and the control of deceptive advertising. In R. Bostrom (Ed.), *Communication yearbook 7* (pp. 476-499). Beverly Hills, CA: Sage.

Levin, S., Petros, T., & Petrella, F. (1982). Preschoolers' awareness of television advertising. *Child Development, 53,* 933-937.

Liebert, D., Sprafkin, J., Liebert, R., & Rubinstein, E. (1977). Effects of television commercial disclaimers on the product expectations of children. *Journal of Communication, 27*(1), 118-124.

Macklin, M. (1983). Do children understand TV ads? *Journal of Advertising Research, 23*(1), 63-70.

Macklin, M. (1985). Do young children understand the selling intent of commercials? *Journal of Consumer Affairs, 19,* 293-304.

Macklin, M. C. (1987). Preschoolers' understanding of the informational function of television advertising. *Journal of Consumer Research, 14,* 229-239.

Macklin, M. C. (1988). The relationship between music in advertising and children's responses: An experimental investigation. In S. Hecker & D. Stewart (Eds.), *Nonverbal communication in advertising* (pp. 225-243). Lexington, MA: Lexington Books/D. C. Heath.

Maddox, L., & Zanot, E. (1984). Suspension of the NAB code and its effect on the regulation of advertising. *Journalism Quarterly, 61,* 125-130, 156.

Martin, M. C. (1997). Children's understanding of the intent of advertising: A meta-analysis. *Journal of Public Policy & Marketing, 16*(2), 205-216.

McNeal, J. (1998). Tapping the three kids' markets. *American Demographics, 20*(4), 37-41.

Miller, J., & Busch, J. (1979). Host selling vs. premium TV commercials: An experimental evaluation of their influence on children. *Journal of Marketing Research, 16,* 323-332.

Montgomery, K., & Pasnik, S. (1996). *Web of deception.* Washington, DC: Center for Media Education.

Moschis, G., & Moore, R. (1982). A longitudinal study of television advertising effects. *Journal of Consumer Research, 9,* 279-286.

Owen, B., & Wildman, S. (1992). *Video economics.* Cambridge, MA: Harvard University Press.

Palmer, E., & McDowell, C. (1979). Program/commercial separators in children's television programming. *Journal of Communication, 29*(3), 197-201.

Palmer, E., & McDowell, C. (1981). Children's understanding of nutritional information presented in breakfast cereal commercials. *Journal of Broadcasting, 25,* 295-301.

Pecora, N. (1998). *The business of children's entertainment.* New York: Guilford.

Resnik, A., & Stern, B. (1977). Children's television advertising and brand choice: A laboratory experiment. *Journal of Advertising, 6,* 11-17.

Richards, J. (1990). *Deceptive advertising: Behavioral study of a legal concept.* Hillsdale, NJ: Lawrence Erlbaum.

Roberts, D. (1982). Children and commercials: Issues, evidence, interventions. *Prevention in Human Services, 2,* 19-35.

Roberts, D., Foehr, U., Rideout, V., & Brodie, M. (1999). *Kids & media @ the new millennium: A comprehensive national analysis of children's media use.* Menlo Park, CA: Kaiser Family Foundation.

Robertson, T. (1979). Parental mediation of advertising effects. *Journal of Communication, 29*(1), 12-25.

Robertson, T., & Rossiter, J. (1974). Children and commercial persuasion: An attribution theory analysis. *Journal of Consumer Research, 1,* 13-20.

Robertson, T., & Rossiter, J. (1977). Children's responsiveness to commercials. *Journal of Communication, 27*(1), 101-106.

Robertson, T., Rossiter, J., & Gleason, T. (1979). Children's receptivity to proprietary medicine advertising. *Journal of Consumer Research, 6,* 247-255.

Robertson, T., Ward, S., Gatignon, H., & Klees, D. (1989). Advertising and children: A cross cultural study. *Communication Research, 16,* 459-485.

Ross, R., Campbell, T., Wright, J., Huston, A., Rice, M., & Turk, P. (1984). When celebrities talk, children listen: An experimental analysis of children's responses to TV ads with celebrity endorsements. *Journal of Applied Developmental Psychology, 5,* 185-202.

Rossiter, J. (1977). Reliability of a short test measuring children's attitudes toward television commercials. *Journal of Consumer Research, 3,* 179-184.

Rossiter, J. (1980). Children and television advertising: Policy issues, perspectives, and the status of research. In E. Palmer & A. Dorr (Eds.), *Children and the faces of television* (pp. 251-272). New York: Academic Press.

Rossiter, J., & Robertson, T. (1974). Children's television commercials: Testing the defenses. *Journal of Communication, 24*(4), 137-144.

Rossiter, J., & Robertson, T. (1980). Children's dispositions toward proprietary drugs and the role of television drug advertising. *Public Opinion Quarterly, 44,* 316-329.

Selman, R. (1971). Taking another's perspective: Role-taking development in early childhood. *Child Development, 42,* 1721-1734.

Shantz, C. (1975). The development of social cognition. In E. Hetherington (Ed.), *Review of child development research* (Vol. 5). Chicago: University of Chicago Press.

Sheikh, A., & Moleski, M. (1977). Conflict in the family over commercials. *Journal of Communication, 27*(1), 152-157.

Silverman, W., Jaccard, J., & Burke, A. (1988). Children's attitudes toward products and recall of product information over time. *Journal of Experimental Child Psychology, 45,* 365-381.

Slater, M., Rouner, D., Domenech-Rodriguez, M., Beauvais, F., Murphy, K., & Van Leuven, J. (1997). Adolescent responses to TV beer ads and sports content/context: Gender and ethnic differences. *Journalism and Mass Communication Quarterly, 74,* 108-122.

Smith, G., & Goldman, M. (1995). Alcohol expectancy theory and the identification of high risk adolescents. In G. Boyd, J. Howard, & R. Zucker (Eds.), *Alcohol problems among adolescents: Current directions in prevention research.* Hillsdale, NJ: Lawrence Erlbaum.

Stern, B., & Harmon, R. (1984). The incidence and characteristics of disclaimers in children's television advertising. *Journal of Advertising, 13*(2), 12-16.

Stern, B., & Resnik, A. (1978). Children's understanding of a televised commercial disclaimer. In S. Jain (Ed.), *Research frontiers in marketing: Dialogues and directions* (pp. 332-336). Chicago: American Marketing Association.

Stoneman, Z., & Brody, G. (1981). The indirect impact of child-oriented advertisements on mother-child interactions. *Journal of Applied Developmental Psychology, 2,* 369-376.

Stutts, M., Vance, D., & Hudleson, S. (1981). Program-commercial separators in children's television: Do they help a child tell the difference between Bugs Bunny and the Quik Rabbit? *Journal of Advertising, 10,* 16-25, 48.

Taras, H., Sallis, J., Patterson, T., Nader, P., & Nelson, J. (1989). Television's influence on children's diet and physical activity. *Developmental and Behavioral Pediatrics, 10*(4), 176-180.

Thorson, E., & Schumann, D. (1999). Introduction. In E. Thorson & D. Schumann (Eds.), *Advertising and the World Wide Web* (pp. 1-2). Mahwah, NJ: Lawrence Erlbaum.

Urberg, K., & Docherty, E. (1976). Development of role-taking skills in young children. *Developmental Psychology, 12,* 198-203.

Ward, S., Reale, G., & Levinson, D. (1972). Children's perceptions, explanations, and judgments of television advertising: A further exploration. In G.

Comstock & E. Rubinstein (Eds.), *Television and social behavior* (Vol. 4). Washington, DC: U.S. Government Printing Office.

Ward, S., & Wackman, D. (1972). Children's purchase influence attempts and parental yielding. *Journal of Marketing Research, 9,* 316-319.

Ward, S., & Wackman, D. (1973). Children's information processing of television advertising. In P. Clarke (Ed.), *New models for mass communication research.* Beverly Hills, CA: Sage.

Ward, S., Wackman, D., & Wartella, E. (1977). *How children learn to buy: The development of consumer information processing skills.* Beverly Hills, CA: Sage.

Wartella, E., & Ettema, J. (1974). A cognitive developmental study of children's attention to television commercials. *Communication Research, 1,* 69-88.

Wartella, E., & Hunter, L. (1983). Children and the formats of television advertising. In M. Meyer (Ed.), *Children and the formal features of television* (pp. 144-165). Munich, Germany: K. G. Saur.

Weisskoff, R. (1985). Current trends in children's advertising. *Journal of Advertising Research, 25*(1), 12-14.

Wilson, B. J., & Weiss, A. J. (1992). Developmental differences in children's reactions to a toy advertisement linked to a toy-based cartoon. *Journal of Broadcasting & Electronic Media, 36,* 371-394.

Young, B. (1990). *Television advertising and children.* Oxford, UK: Clarendon Press.

Zuckerman, P., Ziegler, M., & Stevenson, H. (1978). Children's viewing of television and recognition memory of commercials. *Child Development, 49,* 96-104.

CHAPTER **20**

# Popular Music in Childhood and Adolescence

DONALD F. ROBERTS
Stanford University

PETER G. CHRISTENSON
Lewis & Clark College

Recently, we asked a sample of junior and senior high school students from Northern California what media they would choose to take with them if they were stranded on a desert isle. They were allowed to select a first, second, and third choice from the following list: TV set, books, video games, computer, newspapers, VCR and videotapes, magazines, radio, and music recordings and the means to play them. Since radio is almost exclusively a music medium among adolescents, radio and recordings were combined into a single "music" category (Roberts & Henriksen, 1990). As Table 20.1 illustrates, music came out well ahead of television (which placed second overall) at all grade levels. More than 80% of the total sample made music one of their first three choices, and music was the first choice for nearly half. By eleventh grade, music was selected first by a margin of two to one.

Given such data, it is interesting to note the overwhelming extent to which concerned adults—critics, parents, and researchers—view television as the center-stage medium in childhood and adolescence. We agree with Keith Roe that, "in terms of both the sheer amount of time devoted to it and the meanings it assumes, it is music, not television, that is the most important medium for adolescents" (Roe, 1987, pp. 215-216), our only suggestion being that one could safely add "and many children" to the end of the phrase. Research indicates that popular music listening reaches parity with television viewing as early as fifth or sixth grade (Christenson, 1994).

The imbalance in the research toward the effects of television is not difficult to explain. Television has pictures and popular music does not (except in music videos, of course), and perhaps this factor logically tilts things

**TABLE 20.1** Which Medium Would Adolescents Take to a Desert Isle?

| | *Seventh Grade* | | *Ninth Grade* | | *Eleventh Grade* | |
|---|---|---|---|---|---|---|
| | *TV* | *Music* | *TV* | *Music* | *TV* | *Music* |
| First choice | 26% | 40% | 29% | 44% | 26% | 52% |
| First two choices | 43% | 66% | 49% | 73% | 43% | 80% |
| First three choices | 57% | 82% | 65% | 86% | 61% | 90% |

NOTE: Figures are rounded to the nearest percentage.

toward TV. In other words, Tennyson may have been right when he observed, "Things seen are mightier than things heard." Television, moreover, is highly "visible" to adults in ways that go beyond its visual portrayals. Much of children's TV viewing takes place in the company of parents, and, even if parents are not present, they often view the same programs their children do or encounter their children's favorite shows while scanning through the channels with the remote control. Popular music is considerably less visible in this sense. Young people's music listening is less likely than TV viewing to occur in the presence of adults, and parents are unlikely to expose themselves incidentally to their children's favorite music (Christenson, 1994). Many adults consider the sound and message of contemporary popular music irritating, irrelevant, or both, and tend to avoid it scrupulously.

At the same time, an awareness of popular music's importance in the socialization process seems to be emerging in both the research community and the public at large. In part, this increased attention results from the extreme, "edgy" nature of the messages and images contained in today's music and music videos. As dramatically different as rap and heavy metal music are, the lyrics and music video imagery associated with these two music genres have in recent years drawn increasingly vocal condemnations from parents, teachers, media commentators, and mainstream cultural authorities for reputed misogyny, sexual explicitness, violence, racism, and glorification of drugs and alcohol.

It was the inflammatory nature of rock lyrics that in 1985 gained a group of concerned parents under the leadership of Tipper Gore an audience with the Senate Commerce Committee on the issue of "porn rock," in the process forcing the music industry to begin placing warning labels on music with explicit lyrics. A decade later, the Senate Juvenile Justice Committee aired a similar set of concerns from a contingent of citizens outraged by "gangsta rap." In 1995, when Senator Robert Dole opened his 1995 presidential campaign by declaring war on Hollywood's "nightmares of depravity," rap music was just as high on his enemy list as movies or TV (Lacayo, 1995). President Clinton delivered a similar salvo in his 1996 State of the Union Address. Even more recently, popular music has been implicated in media accounts of a string of tragic school shootings. Several of the shooters, it seems, have shared an obsession with the music of hard-edged rock performers such as Marilyn Manson. Oversimplified and alarmist as these public discussions have been, they bespeak an awareness of popular music's role in the process of growing up. Fortunately, an increasing number of researchers have come to the same awareness, and their work is the primary focus of this chapter.

## Amount of Listening

As we have noted, most children and adolescents report that popular music is at least as important to them as television, and generally more so (Christenson & Roberts, 1998; Leming, 1987; Newspaper Advertising Bureau, 1980). How much time they actually spend with music, however, is a complicated issue. Some of the research on time expenditure finds more TV viewing than music listening. For example, whereas the Radio Advertising Bureau (1990) reported 2.5 hours of average weekday radio listening among 12- to 17-year-olds, Nielsen Media Research (1989) put average daily television viewing at just over 2.8 hours for the same age group. Other research reports higher amounts for both media but still gives television a slight edge (Brown, Campbell, & Fischer, 1986; Brown, Childers, Bauman, & Koch, 1990).

In our view, however, most studies have a tendency to underestimate young people's popular music listening. Music is often a secondary, background activity appearing in the adolescent's environment without any conscious decision to introduce it. For example, a teenager may be driving to school while chatting with a friend, all the while "listening" to music emanating from a car radio left on by a sibling who used the car the previous evening. Obviously, music's tendency to slip between foreground and background raises questions about what kind of "listening" should be counted as true *exposure.* We believe background listening ought to count, and for those who might disagree we offer this challenge: Simply turn off the "background" music when adolescents are studying, chatting, or doing chores and observe their responses. It should also be noted that music-listening estimates based only on *radio* use (e.g., Brown et al., 1986; Brown et al., 1990; Greenberg, Ku, & Li, 1989; Lyle & Hoffman, 1972) will produce lower figures than those that include questions about CD and tape playback and time spent watching music videos.

Research that looks at *all* listening, whether from radio or other sources and whether background or foreground, finds levels of exposure to music at least as high as TV in late grade school and considerably *higher* in adolescence. For example, Greenberg and his colleagues (1989) asked sixth and tenth graders how much time they had spent the previous day watching television, listening to the radio, and listening to audio recordings. Sixth graders reported 4.1 hours of television viewing and 3.8 hours of music listening (radio and recordings combined). Tenth graders reported 4.9 hours of music versus 3.9 hours of TV. In their study of San Francisco Bay Area high schools, Roberts and Henriksen (1990) had students estimate the amount of time they spent on school days listening to the radio, listening to recordings, and watching music videos, including the time music was on in the background of other activities. As shown in Table 20.2, television consumed anywhere from 2 to 2.5 hours of time each day, depending on age and gender, whereas music occupied from 3 to almost 4 hours per day. Music time exceeded television time by amounts ranging from less than half an hour (for ninth-grade boys) to almost 2 hours (for eleventh-grade girls).

By these estimates, then, preadolescents and adolescents spend somewhere between 3 and 4 hours a day with popular music, compared with 2 to 3 hours per day watching television. Of course, not all groups of youth pay equal attention to popular music. Age makes a big difference. Though many young people begin listening to popular music early in grade school (Christenson, DeBenedittis, & Lindlof, 1985), music consumes much more time in preadolescence and adolescence. Girls listen more than boys do, and substantially more by high school (Greenberg et al., 1989; Roberts & Henriksen, 1990; see Table 20.2), and African American youth listen more than whites (Brown et al., 1990). Despite the considerable attention given to music videos by critics and researchers, it should be noted in passing that music video viewing occupies relatively little time compared with music listening. Most published reports set the average viewing at between 15 and 30 minutes a day (Christenson, 1992a; Kubey & Larson, 1989; Leming, 1987; Wartella, Heintz, Aidman, & Mazzarella, 1990). Interestingly, interest in music videos seems to peak early in adoles-

**TABLE 20.2** Daily Minutes of School Day TV and Music

| | *Ninth Grade* | | *Eleventh Grade* | |
|---|---|---|---|---|
| | *Boys* | *Girls* | *Boys* | *Girls* |
| Television | 154 | 139 | 137 | 115 |
| Radio | 79 | 134 | 87 | 107 |
| Recordings | 77 | 82 | 95 | 91 |
| MTV | 40 | 33 | 23 | 22 |
| "All music"[a] | 179 | 230 | 200 | 227 |

SOURCE: Adapted from Roberts and Henriksen (1990).
a. "All music" data are from a separate question worded to include background listening, not simply the sum of radio, recordings, and MTV.

cence, dropping off into the high school years, even as overall involvement in music continues to rise. The decrease in attention to music videos mirrors the decrease in adolescents' attention to television in general as the academic and social demands of high school take more of their available time.

## Popular Music Uses and Gratifications

In his 1962 essay "Popular Songs and the Facts of Life," S. I. Hayakawa wrote these words about the role of blues music in the African American community of the time:

> I am often reminded by the words of blues songs of Kenneth Burke's famous description of poetry as "equipment for living." In the form in which they developed in Negro communities, the blues are equipment for living humble, laborious, and precarious lives of low social status or no social status at all—nevertheless, they are valid equipment. (p. 161)

Contemporary popular music provides no less valid equipment for living the life of an American adolescent. It is important to keep in mind that, despite the concentration on deviant adolescents and styles in the research and commentary on pop music (Kotarba & Wells, 1987), listening to popular music is properly seen as a natural and generally benign part of growing up in contemporary Western society. At the simplest, most global level, children, adolescents, and adults—all of us, in other words—listen to music because, above all, it gives us *pleasure.* For adolescents, especially, the pleasure is intense and tends to be associated with the most intense, "peak" experiences of life. As Lull (1992) puts it, "Music promotes experiences of the extreme for its makers and listeners, turning the perilous emotional edges, vulnerabilities, triumphs, celebrations, and antagonisms of life into hypnotic, reflective tempos that can be experienced privately or shared with others" (p. 1).

On a more specific level, music can relieve tension; provide escape or distraction from problems; relieve loneliness; fill the time when there is nothing much to do; ease the drudgery of repetitive, menial tasks and chores; fill uncomfortable silence; provide topics of conversation; make parties more lively; teach new vocabulary; articulate political attitudes; and perform many other uses for the listener (Christenson & Roberts, 1998). It is, in other words, an equipment with many uses. For the purposes of this chapter, we will organize them into the following categories: affective uses, social uses, and the uses of lyrics.

### *Affective Uses*

The research on popular music uses and gratifications points to a principle we have labeled "the primacy of affect" (Christenson & Roberts, 1998). That is, for most young people, music use is driven primarily by the motivation to control mood and enhance emotional states. When they want to be in a "certain" mood, when they feel lonely, when they seek distraction from their troubles, music tends to be the medium they choose (Brown, 1976; Christenson et al., 1985; Larson, Kubey, & Colletti, 1989; Lyle & Hoffman, 1972; Roe, 1985).

Most listening, hence most of the use of music for mood management, is *solitary* rather than social. By late grade school, the typical listening situation is alone in the bedroom. Christenson (1994) found that about 40% of third and fourth graders and 70% of fifth and sixth graders said they were usually alone when they listened to music, compared with 1 in 10 who said they were usually with friends (Christenson, 1994). Listening with parents present was rare at both ages. The predominance of solitary listening strengthens in middle and late adolescence, during which perhaps as much as two thirds of all music listening is solitary (Larson & Kubey, 1983).

As it does in so many areas related to popular music use, gender makes a difference in terms of mood management. Consistently, research shows that males are more likely than females to use music as a tool to increase their energy level and seek stimulation—that is, to get "pumped up" or "psyched up." Females, on the other hand, are more likely than males to listen to lift their spirits when they're down or lonely or even to dwell on a somber mood (Arnett, 1991a; Larson et al., 1989; Roe, 1985; Wells, 1990). Larson and his colleagues (1989) write,

> For girls, whose listening tastes are more often directed toward ballads and love songs, music is not elevating, but rather is associated with sadness, depression and sometimes anger. While boys appear to use music to pump themselves up, young adolescent girls' use of music may be driven more by a need to both explore and cope with new concerns and worries that accompany this age period, perhaps especially those surrounding intimate relations that are so often the themes of these songs. (p. 596)

Although it is less common overall, the practice of matching music with negative moods applies to many boys as well. In the same way that girls often listen to sad songs when they are sad, many male heavy metal fans apparently listen to angry music when they are angry. In one study, a typical heavy metal fan said he sought out "full-blown thrashing metal" when he was "mad at the world" (Arnett, 1991a).

### *Social Uses*

Some scholars contend that, important as certain personal affective gratifications are, the social uses and meanings of popular music provide the real key to understanding its niche in the lives of youth (Frith, 1981; Lull, 1987; Roe, 1984, 1985). We propose two divisions within the broad category of social uses: "quasi-social" uses and "socializing" uses. By "quasi-social," we mean listening that occurs alone but still serves goals and needs related to social relationships. Perhaps the classic example of quasi-social use is when music replaces or invokes the presence of absent peers, thus relieving feelings of loneliness. For instance, Gantz and his colleagues report that two thirds of a sample of college respondents said they listened either "somewhat" or "very frequently" to "make me feel less alone when I'm by myself" (Gantz, Gartenberg, Pearson, & Schiller, 1978). This study and others also suggest that the use of music to relieve loneliness—that is, to provide the sense of company when one is alone—is significantly more common for girls than for boys (Larson et al., 1989; Roe, 1984). Solitary music listening may also prepare adolescents for *future* peer interactions and relationships. To a large extent, those who know nothing about pop culture or current music trends are relegated to the periphery of teen culture. Conversely, pop music "experts" tend to have more friends and enjoy enhanced status in the adolescent social structure (Adoni, 1978; Brown & O'Leary, 1971; Dominick, 1974).

### *Socializing Uses*

Obviously, popular music is often directly attached to social occasions. As Lull (1987) points out, such occasions may take various forms. In romantic dyads, music is used to accompany courtship and sexual behavior. In friendships, music often provides both the basis for the initial relationship and the glue that holds it together over time. In larger gatherings, such as parties, dances, or clubs, music reduces inhibitions, attracts attention and approval, provides topics for conversation, and, of course, encourages dancing. Indeed, the best testimony to the importance of music in socializing is the virtual impossibility of envisioning a teen party without music.

Adolescents differ in the extent to which they incorporate popular music into social interactions. Females are somewhat more likely than males to use music in a socializing context (Carroll et al., 1993; Gantz et al., 1978), and, on average, females report more interest in dancing (Roe, 1985; Wells, 1990). African American youth are not only generally more involved with music than white youth but are more involved in dancing and more likely to view the ability to dance well as an important personal attribute (Kuwahara, 1992; Lull, 1992). The use of music in social contexts also varies according to music taste and subcultural membership. An ethnographic study of club behavior revealed quite different patterns of interaction between "metalheads," who engaged in relatively little cross-sex communication of any kind, and the crowd referred to as "yuppies" or "preppies," who were much more likely to engage in boy-girl chatting and dancing.

### *The Uses of Lyrics*

Although children and adolescents usually say it is the "sound" that attracts them to their favorite music, lyrics are mentioned as a primary gratification by a significant number of youth and a secondary gratification by most (Gantz et al., 1978; Roe, 1985). Even Rosenbaum and Prinsky (1987), whose work has been interpreted in the press as evidence of the *unimportance* of lyrics, report that 17% of male adolescents (12-18 years) and nearly 25% of females said they liked their favorite song "because the words express how I feel." Rouner (1990) asked Cleveland area high school students to rank music against several other possible sources of moral and social guidance, including parents, teachers, friends, church leaders, and coworkers. Sixteen percent ranked music in the top three sources of moral guidance, and 24% placed music in the top three for information on social interaction. For better or worse, then, lyrics are often attended to, processed, discussed, memorized, even taken to heart.

Given the controversy surrounding heavy metal and rap lyrics, it is interesting to note that heavy metal and rap fans report much higher levels of interest and attention to lyrics than do teens in general (Arnett, 1991a; Kuwahara, 1992). Two general patterns seem to emerge from the research on attention to lyrics: First, the more *important* music is to an adolescent, the more importance he or she places on lyrics relative to other elements of music gratification, and, second, attention to lyrics is highest among fans of *oppositional* or controversial music, whether it be 1960s protest rock or the heavy metal and rap of today. In other words, the more defiant, alienated, and threatening to the mainstream a music type is, the more closely its words are followed (Christenson & Roberts, 1998).

## Music Preferences

To most adults, all contemporary popular music sounds pretty much the same. If distinctions are made at all, they are typically between "rock" and the two most visible and controversial current pop music genres, heavy metal and rap. A close look at youth culture, however, reveals a boggling variety of popular music genres. *Billboard* magazine currently reports more than 20 different music charts, and the distinctions recognized by *Billboard* by no means exhaust the divisions drawn in contemporary youth culture (Christenson & Roberts, 1998). A current inventory of popular music types might include Top 40, rap, contemporary hits, easy listening, album rock, soft rock, hard rock, classic rock, grunge, alternative, new age, world beat, progressive rock, reggae, protest rock, industrial rock, salsa, house, hip-hop, ska, high life, technopop, synthpop, college rock, alternative rock, death metal, trash metal, and thrash punk, as well as a number of still-popular categories from the past (new wave, punk, surfer music, Motown, psychedelic rock, etc.). Most teenagers could easily add another 10 or 20 entries to the list.

To be sure, not all of these genres are truly distinct (some "types" are really the same thing by a different name, others are very closely related musically and culturally), and others do not really figure very much into teen culture. The key point, however, is that young people do not simply listen to "rock" music but to a certain type of music. The diversity and selectivity of popular music taste matter for two reasons. First, assuming for the moment that music listening may have some impact on adolescents, this impact will depend on the specific type they choose. Three hours a day of death metal is a different thing than three hours a day of soft rock ballads, and the effects of the two ought to be different. Second, distinctions in music preference matter because of their linkage with individual and group identity; they tell us something about who adolescents think they are and how they function in their society. Differences in music preference are not random or idiosyncratic but are related to a variety of social background, peer group, and individual differences.

Of all the demographic and background predictors of music taste, race and ethnicity may be the most powerful (Christenson & Roberts, 1998; Denisoff & Levine, 1972). Entire genres of popular music are linked unambiguously and proudly with their racial and ethnic roots: for example, R&B, soul, and rap with African American culture; salsa with Hispanic culture; and reggae with its Jamaican heritage. Dykers (1992) reports that 70% of a broad sample of black teenagers reported rap as their favorite music type, while only 22% mentioned either pop rock or "Top 10." Very few cited rock, heavy metal, punk, or country. With the exception of the pop/Top 10 category, the preferences of the white youth were distributed much differently: Both rock and heavy metal drew a quarter of the responses, and only 13% mentioned rap (Dykers, 1992).

Gender is as nearly a powerful predictor as race. Two primary gender differences emerge from the research on music preferences. The first and most fundamental musical gender gap is the separation between pop (female) and rock (male) tastes. Whatever the historical era and whatever the population being studied, females exhibit greater attraction to the softer, more romantic, more mainstream forms (e.g., pop, disco, soft rock, Top 40), while males gravitate to the harder-edged rock forms (e.g., heavy metal, hard rock, punk, grunge, psychedelic rock). Second, males are more likely than females to adopt nonmainstream, fringe, or "progressive" music affinities (Christenson & Peterson, 1988; Christenson & Roberts, 1998; Dykers, 1992; Tanner, 1981; Wells, 1990).

The basic gender differences in music taste have proven so robust that it is reasonable to speculate what might explain them. As we noted earlier, females tend to use music in different ways and for different reasons than males do, and these disparities imply different music preferences. Dancing, for example, tends to be more important to girls, so "danceability" becomes a more important criterion of music taste for girls than for boys. In addition, it would seem logical for girls to avoid music with reputations for misogynist or macho-aggressive messages such as hard rock, heavy metal, and rap. More broadly, it is undeniable that girls are expected to be popular, deferent, romantic, nurturant, and to *fit in,* while boys are expected to be independent, aggressive, competitive, and to *stand out.* These conventional social expectations also help to explain boys' preference for powerful, aggressive, defiant, "on-the-edge" forms of music and girls' inclination toward romantic, acceptable, mainstream music.

The research also finds a close connection between music preference and where youth stand in their peer culture. "Music style"—that is, the selection of a certain type of music and a personal style to go with it—is one of the most powerful identifying markers in the school crowd structure. Some groups—"alterna-chicks," "punkers," "metalheads," "rastas," and so on—are labeled *primarily* on the basis of music choice (Christenson & Roberts, 1998). Keith Roe's (1984) examination of Swedish adolescents is particularly informative on the relationship between school variables and music preference. Roe argues that the connection between school orientation and popular music taste arises from the process of academic evaluation. This inevitably creates an "in group" who are popular with other youth and share the dominant values and goals of the school structure and an "out group" of youth who operate on the margin and harbor antischool, antiadult feelings. Roe says it is quite natural to expect the in group to adopt relatively nonthreatening music and the out group to gravitate toward a more defiant cultural form. Indeed, this is exactly what he found: The more successful, pro-school youth tended to prefer classical music, jazz, and mainstream pop, while the kids with lower levels of commitment to school and lower academic achievement tended to be drawn to "disapproved" and "oppositional" music forms such as hard rock and punk. Studies conducted in the United States and Canada find essentially the same pattern. In a 1992 survey of more than 2,800 high school students in the Southeast, only 1 in 10 heavy metal fans expressed certainty that they would attend college, compared with 25% of pop and rock fans (Dykers, 1992). Similarly, Hakanen and Wells (1993) report that adolescents' school grades were strongly related to music taste, more strongly even than to parental education.

## Is There a Heavy Metal Syndrome?

Much of the research on music preferences has focused on heavy metal fans, and the findings do indicate that this group possesses different characteristics than other youth. With regard to school, heavy metal fans report more conflict with teachers and other school authorities and perform less well academically than those whose tastes run more to the mainstream (Christenson & van Nouhuys, 1995; Hakanen & Wells, 1993). They tend to be distant from their families (Martin, Clarke, & Pearce, 1993) and are often at odds with their parents. When relationships with parents are described as satisfactory, it is usually because the parents let the kids go their own way (Arnett, 1991a). At the same time, there is no evidence that heavy metal fans see themselves as socially isolated. They are just as satisfied with the quality of their peer relationships as nonfans are (Arnett, 1991a). If anything, the peer group exerts a more powerful influence on heavy metal fans than on most other adolescents (Gordon, Hakanen, & Wells, 1992).

According to Arnett (1991a, 1991b), hardcore heavy metal fans tend to be driven by a generalized tendency to seek sensation and thrills and a need to engage in a variety of risky behaviors, more or less "to see what it would be like." In accord with his thesis, he reports differences between heavy metal fans and nonfans not only in their expression of sensation-seeking motivations generally but also in their self-reports of specific reckless behaviors, including drunk driving, casual sex, and marijuana and cocaine use. Other research has found a similar connection between risky, reckless attitudes and behavior and the choice of heavy metal music (Martin et al., 1993). Wass and her colleagues (Wass, Miller, & Reditt, 1991) report that youth in juvenile detention were three times as likely as regular high school students to be metal fans (see also Epstein, Pratto, & Skipper, 1990; Tanner, 1981).

The research also suggests a connection between heavy metal and sexual behavior. In one study, 54% of a group of high-school-age heavy metal fans said they had had sex with a casual acquaintance, compared with 23% of nonfans (Arnett, 1991b). Other research shows a correlation between a taste for heavy metal and approval of premarital sex (Yee, Britton, & Thompson, 1988). More relevant to the nature of heavy metal music's treatment of women, Hansen and Hansen (1991a) found that the amount of time college students listened to heavy metal was correlated with a "macho" personality. Specifically, exposure to heavy metal correlated positively with "male hypersexuality" (as indicated by the level of agreement with the idea that "young men need sex even if some coercion of females is required to get it") and negatively with general respect for women. Christenson and van Nouhuys (1995) report a connection between heavy metal and interest in other-sex contact as early as 11 or 12 years.

Concern has also been expressed over the potential impact of heavy metal music's often dismal, depressed view of the world and its depiction of depression and suicide. Arnett (1991a) writes,

> One can hear an echo in (heavy metal themes) of concerns with social issues from the music of the 1960's, but with this difference: the songs of the sixties often lamented the state of the world but promised a brighter future if we would mend our ways; heavy metal songs often lament the state of the world but do not provide even a hint of hope for the future. Hopelessness and cynicism pervade the songs. (p. 93)

Martin and his colleagues' data (1993) from more than 200 Australian high school students showed that those who preferred heavy metal or hard rock music reported feelings of depression, suicidal thoughts, and deliberate infliction of self-harm more frequently than others in the sample. For instance, 20% of the male and more than 60% of the female heavy metal/hard rock fans reported having deliberately tried to kill or hurt themselves in the last 6 months, compared with only 8% and 14%, respectively, of the pop fans.

Do these various findings support the notion of a "heavy metal syndrome," that is, of a constellation of related traits with heavy metal at the focal point? Probably not. If there is a "syndrome" at work here, it is a "troubled youth syndrome," not a heavy metal syndrome. Leaving aside for now the question of whether popular music exercises any influence on adolescents' values and behavior, assuredly the consumption of heavy metal is not what brings together the various "at-risk," "troubled," or "alienated" characteristics with which heavy metal fandom is associated. The best way to phrase the relationship is to say that white adolescents who are troubled or at risk gravitate strongly toward the style of music that provides the most support for their view of the world and meets their particular needs: namely, heavy metal.

The point can be further clarified, perhaps, by juxtaposing these statements: (a) Most heavy metal fans are not particularly troubled or at risk, but (b) those who are troubled or at risk tend overwhelmingly to embrace heavy metal. In other words, whatever percentage one uses to estimate the proportion of heavy metal fans in the total adolescent population, they surely number in the tens of millions. Most of these young people are not on drugs, not in jail, not failing in school, not depressed, perhaps not even particularly at odds with their parents (except maybe when it comes to music). Arguing the other way, however, if we know a youth is white, male, 15 years old, drug involved, and in trouble with the law, then the odds are *very high* indeed that his music of choice will be some form of hard rock or heavy metal.

Our rejection of the idea of a true heavy metal syndrome should not be taken to imply that heavy metal music plays only a peripheral role in the lives of its devotees. Heavy metal fans are an especially committed, devoted audience. Those who love it are highly absorbed in their musical identity, in terms of both listening time (Wass, Miller, & Stevenson, 1989) and a variety of other music-related behavior. Arnett (1991a) reports that high school students describing themselves as "metalheads" spent more than twice as much on albums, concerts, and music equipment as a comparison group of nonmetal fans. They also tended to express very high levels of personal identification with their favorite performers, were more likely to say lyrics are important to them, claimed a deeper understanding of lyrics, and were more likely than other youth to adopt their favorite musicians as role models (Arnett, 1991a; see also Wass et al., 1989). As Arnett points out, heavy metal plays a crucial role in the lives of the alienated and disaffected youth who seek it out; for many such youth, listening to heavy metal is what matters to them most.

## Making Sense of Popular Songs

Most of the criticism aimed at current popular music and music videos stems from the assumption that "content"—that is, the attitudes, values, and behaviors portrayed in lyrics and music video images—may influence how young listeners think and act. Not surprising, it is a concern that emphasizes the negative. It is doubtful whether nearly as much attention would be paid to popular music if children and adolescents were listening to hymns or traditional folk songs. Instead, public anxiety is fueled by trends toward sexual explicitness and by a clear increase in lyric treatments of such topics as violence, misogyny, racism, suicide, Satanism, and substance use (Carey, 1969; Christenson & Roberts, 1998; Fedler, Hall, & Tanzi, 1982; Roberts, Henriksen, & Christenson, 1999). Equally important is the emergence in the early 1980s of music videos, which made it possible for adults to "see" what their children were listening to.

Claims that popular song lyrics pose a danger implicitly assume that young people interpret songs in much the same way that adult critics do. That is, for sexually explicit lyrics to promote teenage sexual activity or for substance use portrayals to encourage experimentation with illicit drugs, young audiences presumably must find sexual or substance-related messages in the songs. Indeed, to be truly "influenced," young people probably need to go a step further and connect such messages to their own lives. The problem with such assumptions, of course, is that several decades of communication research show quite clearly that message interpretation is as much a process of construction as of recognition or discovery. Thus, the sense that young people make of popular songs depends not only on what the lyric brings to them but on what they bring to the lyric.

The research on comprehension of song lyrics and music videos usually takes one of three approaches: (a) It compares young people's understanding of particular songs to some "definitive" interpretation; (b) it compares and contrasts interpretations of the same song given by different groups of young people; or (c) it examines how young people think about and relate popular songs to their own lives. Each approach provides different insights on how children and adolescents make sense of lyrics and music videos. In studies of the first type, the standard for comparison is typically an adult "expert" reading of the text; experts range from songwriters (Denisoff & Levine, 1971) to mass media commentators (Robinson & Hirsch, 1972) to teachers and parents (Leming, 1987) to the judgments of the researchers themselves (Greenfield et al., 1987; Robinson & Hirsch, 1972; Rosenbaum & Prinsky, 1987). Assuming such readings set a valid standard, studies of this type find relatively low levels of lyric comprehension—that is, substantial numbers of youth fail to produce responses matching the researchers' criterion for correctness. For example, Denisoff and Levine (1971) found that only 14% of San Francisco Bay Area college students understood the 1965 protest rock hit "Eve of Destruction" in terms of the songwriter's intent—namely, the threat of nuclear destruction. Another 45% showed partial understanding, and 41% showed none.

When Patricia Greenfield and her colleagues (1987) asked fourth-, eighth-, twelfth-grade, and college students to explain such terms as *hometown jam* and *yellow man* from Bruce Springsteen's "Born in the USA" ("Got in a little hometown jam so they put a rifle in my hand/Sent me off to a foreign land to go and kill the yellow man"), a good deal of misunderstanding emerged, especially among the younger participants. Only 20% of the fourth graders and 60% of the eighth graders correctly identified *hometown jam* as some kind of dilemma the singer encountered in the place where he grew up; only 10% of fourth graders, 30% of eighth graders, and 50% of twelfth graders understood *yellow man* as referring to a North Vietnamese soldier. Most striking, however, is how few listeners of any age understood what the researchers saw as the song's general message of "despair, disillusionment, and resentment." No fourth graders, 30% of eighth graders, 40% of twelfth graders, and just half the college students interpreted the song in these terms. Rather, many seemed to simply take the upbeat title and catchphrase of the refrain at face value.

Of course, if we assume that a particular lyric has just one correct meaning, a great many adults do not get the message either. Ronald Reagan, for example, invoked "Born in the USA" as a patriotic and optimistic view of America during his 1984 presidential campaign, and the New York City affiliate of Planned Parenthood called Madonna's "Papa Don't Preach" a potent message about the "glamour of sex, pregnancy, and childbearing" even as the California chapter of Feminists for Life in America labeled it a positive, pro-life song (cited in Brown & Schulze, 1990). James Leming (1987) attempted to establish the "correct" meaning of various rock lyrics for his study of adolescent comprehension by asking public school children to decide what different songs meant. Although fair consensus emerged for some of the songs (e.g., most interpreted Olivia Newton John's "Physical" as suggesting casual sex), on others, he found substantial levels of disagreement. Half of the group understood "I Want a New Drug" by Huey Lewis and the News as a metaphor for a search for love, but the other half took it literally as a quest for a drug with no side effects.

The point, of course, is that to presume a single, correct meaning for a song ignores the constructive nature of interpretation (not to mention centuries of honest debate over what particular poems, plays, or paintings "mean"). It also runs the risk of overlooking all the information that may be embedded in the nature of young people's "misinterpretations." Right or wrong, the fact that a significant group of young adolescents in Leming's study understood "Physical" as a call to aerobic exercise tells us something. More broadly, it can be argued that the most interesting question is not whether a set of interpretations is correct or incorrect but what explains the variation.

Studies comparing different groups to one another rather than to some objective criterion demonstrate that the variation in interpretation can often be predicted on the basis of differing cognitive abilities, social backgrounds, and personal experiences. Some of the variation seems to be attributable to the developmental progression from concrete to abstract cognitive operations. Greenfield and her colleagues (1987) found that fourth graders' misinterpretations of "Born in the USA" tended to be quite concrete (e.g., a yellow man is "a man who fell in yellow paint"), whereas college students erred at a more abstract level (e.g., "a yellow man is any kind of Communist!"). Similar age differences were found in response to Madonna's plaint from "Like a Virgin": "Made it through the wilderness, somehow I made it through/Didn't know how lost I was until I found you." Many of the youngest listeners interpreted the song as a description of a perilous wilderness trek. High school and college students were more likely to read "rough times" and "emotional loneliness" into the phrase. Similar age differences emerge in the interpretation of music videos. Christenson (1992b) compared 9-/10-year-olds' and 12-year-olds' descriptions of the major theme of Billy Ocean's music video "Get Outta My Dreams, Get Into My Car." Most of the older group made sense of the video in relatively abstract terms, focusing on the male-female relationship (e.g., "it's about a guy who likes a girl and wants to know her better"). The younger children, however, spoke about concrete events and details (e.g., "it's about a guy who wants to take a girl for a ride in his car"). Some simply said it was about a guy and his car.

Robinson and Hirsch (1972) found that, whereas middle-class adolescents interpreted the vocalist of the rock hit "Green Light" as wanting a date with a girl, adolescents from working-class homes said "he wanted the girl to go all the way," thus providing a hint that differential expectations related to social background play a role in the interpretation process. Equally instructive in this regard is the work of Brown and Schulze (1990) on college students' interpretations of music videos. Noting evidence associating race and gender with different sexual norms, attitudes, and behaviors among U.S. adolescents, they reasoned that these differences might play a role in the process of interpreting music videos. The most interesting results from the study came in response to Madonna's controversial "Papa Don't Preach" video, which depicts a young woman struggling to tell her father that she is pregnant. Whereas more than half of the white participants understood the video as being primarily about teen pregnancy, only 40% of African American females and 21% of African American males saw this as the central theme. Rather, the African American participants tended to view the father-daughter relationship as the central issue in the video. Both race and gender affected the likelihood of a participant mentioning the issue of marriage in his or her interpretation of the video: White males were most likely to mention the possibility of marriage in the future (65%) and black males least likely (21%). Interestingly, the direction of the gender difference depended on race: White females were less likely than males to mention marriage, whereas African American females were more likely. Clearly, young people's cultural and personal experiences exert a powerful influence on how they interpret popular music content; it is so powerful, in fact, that "Papa Don't Preach" could be seen as anything from "a commercial for teenage pregnancy" (Goodman, 1986) to a testament to an anthem for female independence. There can be substantial and valid variations in how youth interpret songs.

At the same time, it would be a mistake to characterize interpretations as completely random or idiosyncratic. Even in the study by Brown and Schulze, adolescents from similar backgrounds or with similar experiences agreed on roughly similar interpretations. Christine and Ranald Hansen (1991b) have argued that, although listeners may vary in interpretations of *specific elements in particular lyrics,* a good deal of similarity prevails in perceptions of general themes. They found that even when circumstances made it difficult for college students to agree about specific elements in a particular song's lyrics (e.g., when lyrics were garbled or overpowered by the sound of the instruments in the song), there was still a great deal of consensus on general themes. Students' popular music-related schemas (e.g., for certain music genres) produced high levels of agreement in regard to overall themes on the basis of a few sketchy cues. Taking a specific example from the study, their schema for "heavy metal" music produced agreement on a song's central theme (e.g., suicide) even though there was considerable disagreement as to the meaning, or even the existence, of a particular phrase in the lyrics (e.g., "suicide is slow with liquor").

Thompson and her colleagues (Thompson, Walsh-Childers, & Brown, 1993) distinguish between two kinds of mental structures that may play a role in how listeners make sense of lyrics. "Content-specific" structures refer to personal knowledge (or schemas) related to the particular subject matter of a song. For example, depending on experience, some youths approach a song about male-female relationships with fairly elaborated mental schemas of sexual activity, others with relatively meager conceptualizations. "Generic" structures, on the other hand, relate to how individuals typically deal with new information regardless of topic. Some individuals absorb new information uncritically, while others test, evaluate, and elaborate; some focus on message source, others on message content; some seek cognitive conflict, others avoid it.

Thompson et al. (1993) found that both kinds of mental structures influenced how high school students responded to the "Papa Don't Preach" video. In terms of content-specific structures, girls with more sexual and pregnancy experience and more complex teen pregnancy schemas interpreted the video more personally, making more connections to their own lives than did girls with less experience and less elaborated schemas. Among boys, however, no relationship emerged between content-specific schemas and responses to the video, a gender difference that the authors explain on the basis of the song's focus on a young woman. At the generic level, the findings indicated that both boys and girls processed the video differently depending on their "family communication environment"—that is, whether they came from family backgrounds that stressed the maintenance of interpersonal harmony or from families emphasizing the exploration and testing of new ideas (see Chaffee & McLeod, 1972; Ritchie, 1991). For example, girls from families that emphasized the maintenance of social harmony drew more inferences about the video and made more connections between the video and their own lives than did girls from families that placed little emphasis on social harmony. In other words, both content-specific schema and generic information-processing structures interacted with the content of the video to shape the nature, complexity, and intensity of students' responses.

In sum, we find, first, that variant readings of popular songs are more common than many observers and critics of contemporary popular music assume, and, second, the variance is related in predictable ways to group and individual differences. It seems that when it comes to interpreting popular music, "it is not so much a case of 'you are what you hear' as 'you hear what you are'" (Christenson & Roberts, 1998, p. 179).

## The Effects of Popular Music and Videos

The effects of popular music on youth have been examined in several domains, including social interactions, schoolwork, hearing, and, speculatively at least, mood and emotion (see Christenson & Roberts, 1998). It is fair to say, however, that most of the concern about the effects of contemporary popular music has focused on the attitudinal and behavioral impact of some of its more "extreme" messages. It is not surprising, perhaps, that a generation raised on "When I want you in my arms, all I have to do is dream" (Everly Brothers, 1958) is upset to find its children and grandchildren listening to "Hey, we want some pussy" (2 Live Crew, 1990). Nonetheless, even though a relatively small proportion of popular songs and music videos really push the edge on topics such as sex, violence, racism, misogyny, suicide, and Satanism, those that do contain such messages not only attract a good deal of press but often raise legitimate questions about the role popular music plays in the socialization of youth. The fundamental concern is that kids will adopt beliefs, attitudes, and behaviors articulated in at least some of the songs.

As we have noted, a number of correlational studies report positive associations between exposure to heavy metal music and a variety of troublesome attitudes and behaviors. Drunk driving; casual sex; experimentation with marijuana and cocaine; conflict with parents, school, and legal authorities; anti-establishment attitudes; permissive sexual attitudes; Satanic beliefs; and low levels of trust in others have all been implicated in this regard (Arnett, 1991a, 1991b; Christenson & van Nouhuys, 1995; Gordon et al., 1992; Hansen & Hansen, 1991a; Martin et al., 1993; Wass et al., 1991). None of these studies, however, allow the inference that heavy metal has produced the associated characteristics. With most of the findings, it seems quite likely that the associations may be the result of the operation of a third variable (e.g., social class or family environment) or that the causal arrow runs in the opposite direction. As we have already noted, for example, Roe's (1984) longitudinal data argue that alienation from the school culture precedes rather than follows a taste for "oppositional" music such as heavy metal.

Experimental studies on popular music effects are relatively recent, and most focus on music videos. We have found only two published experimental studies on the effects of music per se. One found no difference in college students' expressions of hostility subsequent to listening to aggressive music (Wanamaker & Reznikoff, 1989). The other found that male undergraduates who heard either sexually violent heavy metal or Christian heavy metal were *both* more likely than those who listened to classical music to express negative attitudes toward women (St. Lawrence & Joyner, 1991). It is interesting to note that this study failed to find a difference between the effects of Christian heavy metal with nonviolent lyrics and heavy metal music containing aggressive lyrics, thus providing some indication that the "sound" may matter at least as much as the verbal message.

Experiments on the effects of music often involve high school or undergraduate college students viewing various types of music videos, then completing immediate postexposure belief and attitude measures. Using this approach, Greeson and Williams (1986) found that seventh and tenth graders who had viewed 30 minutes of music videos with high concentrations of sex, violence, and antiestablishment themes showed higher approval of premarital sex than did similar participants who had viewed 30 minutes of videos randomly taped off the air. Among tenth graders, these videos also reduced disapproval of violence. Peterson and Pfost (1989) showed undergraduate males collections of music videos that varied in both eroticism and violence, resulting in four stimulus types: erotic/violent, erotic/nonviolent, nonerotic/violent, and nonerotic/nonviolent. Of the four types of content, only the violent images had much of an effect: Males who watched violent videos scored higher than other groups on measures of negative affect and "antagonistic orientation toward women."

Unfortunately, the preceding studies all employed designs that were reactive in nature. Participants completed the dependent measures immediately after viewing, and it is difficult to believe that they did not form hypotheses about the intent of the research. Some more recent experiments have incorporated better disguises, typically by engineering situations in which participants hear music under the guise of one kind of activity but respond to dependent measures in the process of a second, quite independent activity. Johnson, Jackson, and Gatto (1995) showed identical groups of 11- through 16-year-old lower-income African American boys either eight violent rap videos or eight nonviolent rap videos, ostensibly as part of a memory test. After completing the "memory study," participants moved on to a second study of "decision-making skills" in which they answered questions about two brief stories. One story described an incident in which a young man physically attacks both his girlfriend and an old male friend of hers after seeing the two exchange a friendly hug and kiss. The second scenario involved an exchange between two old high school friends, one of whom is now working hard attending college, the other of whom drives a BMW and wears nice clothes and jewelry, with no indication of how he can afford such nice things. The results indicated an effect of videos on both approval of violence and academic aspirations. Those who had viewed the violent videos were more likely than those in either the nonviolent video group or the no-video control group to condone the attack against the girl's old friend and to say that they would have done the same thing. Boys who watched either violent or nonviolent rap videos were less likely than those in the control group to want to be like the young man who was attending college or to believe he would ever finish school.

Other studies using this sort of two-phase experimental design have also found that music video content can alter viewers' subsequent assessments of other people and other people's behavior. Viewing "antisocial" rock videos has been shown to increase college students' acceptance of what they presume to be real-life rude and defiant behavior (Hansen & Hansen, 1990). Exposure to music videos displaying highly gender-stereotyped behavior has resulted in significant effects on how students evaluate the subsequent behavior of "real" men and women in realistically staged situations (Hansen & Hansen, 1988). Watching various types of "sexy" music videos has caused students to rate men and women in subsequently viewed nonsexy television commercials as more attractive, sexier, and generally similar to the actors portrayed in the videos (Hansen & Krygowski, 1994).

Zillmann and his colleagues (1995) used an elaborate experimental procedure to examine the effect of politically radical rap music on race-related political attitudes. First, under the impression that their task was to evaluate music videos, white and African American high school students saw one of three sets of music videos: popular rock videos, nonpolitical rap videos, or radical political rap videos. The students later participated in a presumably unrelated study of student politics in which they responded to one of six ostensible candidates for student office. Three of the candidates were white, and three were African American. Within each race, the candidates took one of three political stances: a racially liberal stance, a racially radical stance, or a neutral stance. The videos had no effect on the political attitudes of African American adolescents. White participants, however, were influenced. Exposure to the radical political rap videos dramatically increased white listeners' support for the message of racial harmony advocated by an African American candidate and decreased their acceptance of a conservative white candidate arguing against affirmative action. As the authors note, this finding runs contrary to the frequently voiced claim that radical rap makes white kids more racially defensive.

## Suicides and Shootings

It is a huge leap from the short-term outcomes demonstrated in the research on the effects of popular music to the claims currently being made in public discussion about popular music's role in recent teenage suicides and school shootings. Yet certain facts surrounding these tragic events have led to charges that popular music—indeed, popular culture in general—is at least partially to blame (Christenson & Roberts, 1998; Egan, 1998; Litman & Farberow, 1994; "Rock on Trial," 1988; *Vance v. Judas Priest,* 1990). A few comments on this issue are in order here. It is true that a number of adolescent suicide victims have spent the hours immediately prior to taking their lives immersed in heavy metal. It also turns out that several of the young people involved in recent schoolyard shootings have been avid fans of Marilyn Manson and similar "goth rock" performers. However, the argument that exposure to popular music can operate as a first or primary cause of such drastic behaviors is tenuous. Literally millions of heavy metal and "gangsta rap" fans spend hours with their chosen music genres and never threaten either others or themselves. In all likelihood, they are as contented and well-adjusted as any other segment of youth. Moreover, most professionals concerned with the causes of suicide and violence point to a broad array of conditions unrelated to popular culture (depression, access to guns, substance abuse, "conduct disorders," etc.) that seem to be necessary precursors of such drastic acts. Indeed, these conditions have characterized most or all of the incidents at issue in the recent debate (Berman & Jobes, 1991; Egan, 1998; Levy & Deykin, 1989).

This is not, however, to absolve popular music from a role in at least some suicides and violent incidents. Recall earlier points about the uses of music and about heavy metal fans in particular. First, one of the more important functions of popular music for adolescents is mood management, what we have called "the primacy of affect" (Christenson & Roberts, 1998). Teenagers frequently use music as a tool to maintain or change particular moods, and they quite readily admit that music has direct, profound effects on their emotions. Arnett (1991a), for example, describes a hardcore fan who admitted listening to heavy metal because it put him in the mood to "go and beat the crap out of somebody." Moreover, some of the research on music's impact on mood suggests what might be called an "amplification effect," a strong tendency for music to heighten whatever emotional state a listener brings to a listening situation—including anger and depression (Gordon et al., 1992; Wells, 1990). As we noted in our earlier consideration of a possible "heavy metal syndrome," although it is not legitimate to assume that all fans of extreme music are "troubled," kids who *are* troubled are very likely to be fans of extreme music. In other words, there is substantial evidence that adolescents who are depressed, angry, alienated, experiencing suicidal thoughts, having family problems, abusing drugs or alcohol, having difficulty at school, and so on, constitute a group that is particularly drawn to the sort of angry, nihilist music that celebrates these "troubled" states and traits. These factors, when coupled with the high levels of identification with the music and its performers, seem at the least worrisome.

To immerse oneself in angry, desperate, depressing music seems a poor strategy for coping with anger, despair, and depression. Litman and Farberow (1994) contend that "addictive and antisocial behaviors" are at first adopted as *alternatives* to suicide, but, when they fail, and if conditions worsen, such behaviors may actually function as *contributory causes* of suicide. It seems reasonable to propose that if a preoccupation with heavy metal is carried to an extreme by troubled and at-risk kids, it too may become an addictive, antisocial behavior—a form of "media delinquency" (Roe, 1995)—that is more likely to deepen the problem than alleviate it. For that small minority of kids who are already alienated and disturbed, for whatever reason, extreme music may be another risk factor for violence or suicide.

## Coda

Does this mean that the booming bass and screeching guitars parents hear behind their adolescent offspring's bedroom doors or the green-haired, leathered, and pierced dervish whirling across the music video screen is turning young people into monsters? Generally not. For most kids, most of the time, music is a source of pleasure. They listen not to analyze lyrics and learn about the world, not to sort out emotions and feelings, not to facilitate social interaction, but simply because they like it. To be sure, popular music does teach them things, does help them to sort out emotions and feelings, does facilitate social interaction. It is, as we have noted, the medium that matters most to adolescents, and not least because it addresses issues that are central to them—love, sex, loyalty, independence, friendship, authority—with a directness they often do not get from adults. Although many teenagers will discuss sensitive personal issues with the significant adults in their lives, just as many will avoid such discussions, opting instead for what they perceive as more legitimate sources—other youth, to be sure, but also the culture of youth. For most of today's adolescents, popular music functions not just as equipment for living but as *essential* equipment for living. But most will survive it, just as their parents did.

## References


Adoni, H. (1978). The functions of mass media in the political socialization of adolescents. *Communication Research, 6,* 84-106.

Arnett, J. (1991a). Adolescence and heavy metal music: From the mouths of metalheads. *Youth and Society, 23*(1), 76-98.

Arnett, J. (1991b). Heavy metal music and reckless behavior among adolescents. *Journal of Youth and Adolescence, 20,* 573-592.

Berman, A. L., & Jobes, D. A. (1991). *Adolescent suicide: Assessment and intervention.* Washington, DC: American Psychological Association.

Brown, J. D., Campbell, K., & Fischer, L. (1986). American adolescents and music videos: Why do they watch? *Gazette, 37,* 19-32.

Brown, J. D., Childers, K., Bauman, K., & Koch, G. (1990). The influence of new media and family structure on young adolescents' television and radio use. *Communication Research, 17,* 65-82.

Brown, J. D., & Schulze, L. (1990). The effects of race, gender, and fandom on audience interpretations of Madonna's music videos. *Journal of Communication, 40,* 88-102.

Brown, J. R. (1976). Children's uses of television. In R. Brown (Ed.), *Children and television* (pp. 116-136). Beverly Hills, CA: Sage.

Brown, R., & O'Leary, M. (1971). Pop music in an English secondary school system. *American Behavioral Scientist, 14,* 401-413.

Carey, J. (1969). Changing courtship patterns in the popular song. *American Journal of Sociology, 4,* 720-731.

Carroll, R., Silbergleid, M., Beachum, C., Perry, S., Pluscht, P., & Pescatore, M. (1993). Meanings of radio to teenagers in a niche-programming era. *Journal of Broadcasting and Electronic Media, 37*(2), 159-176.

Chaffee, S. H., & McLeod, J. M. (1972). Adolescent television use in the family context. In G. A. Comstock & E. A. Rubinstein (Eds.), *Television and social behavior: Vol. 3. Television and adolescent aggressiveness* (pp. 149-172). Washington, DC: U.S. Government Printing Office.

Christenson, P. (1992a). The effects of parental advisory labels on adolescent music preferences. *Journal of Communication, 42*(1), 106-113.

Christenson, P. (1992b, Fall). Preadolescent perceptions and interpretations of music videos. *Popular Music and Society, 16*(3), 63-73.

Christenson, P. (1994). Childhood patterns of music use and preferences. *Communication Reports, 7*(2), 136-144.

Christenson, P., DeBenedittis, P., & Lindlof, T. (1985). Children's use of audio media. *Communication Research, 12,* 327-343.

Christenson, P., & Peterson, J. (1988). Genre and gender in the structure of music preferences. *Communication Research, 15*(3), 282-301.

Christenson, P., & Roberts, D. F. (1998). *It's not only rock and roll: Popular music in the lives of adolescents.* Cresskill, NJ: Hampton Press.

Christenson, P., & van Nouhuys, B. (1995, May). *From the fringe to the center: A comparison of heavy metal and rap fandom.* Paper presented at the annual meeting of the International Communication Association, Albuquerque, NM.

Denisoff, R. S., & Levine, M. H. (1971). The popular protest song: The case of "Eve of Destruction." *Public Opinion Quarterly, 35,* 119-124.

Denisoff, R. S., & Levine, M. H. (1972). Youth and popular music: A test of the taste culture hypothesis. *Youth and Society, 4*(4), 237-255.

Dominick, J. (1974). The portable friend: Peer group membership and radio usage. *Journal of Broadcasting, 18*(2), 164-169.

Dykers, C. (1992, May). *Rap and rock as adolescents' cultural capital at school.* Paper presented at the annual meetings of the International Communication Association, Miami, FL.

Egan, T. (1998, June 14). From adolescent angst to shooting up schools. *New York Times,* p. 1.

Epstein, J., Pratto, D., & Skipper, J. (1990). Teenagers, behavioral problems, and preferences for heavy metal and rap music: A case study of a Southern middle school. *Deviant Behavior, 11,* 381-394.

Fedler, F., Hall, J., & Tanzi, L. (1982). Popular songs emphasize sex, de-emphasize romance. *Mass Communication Review, 9,* 10-15.

Frith, S. (1981). *Sound effects: Youth, leisure, and the politics of rock 'n' roll.* New York: Pantheon.

Gantz, W., Gartenberg, H., Pearson, M., & Schiller, S. (1978). Gratifications and expectations associated with popular music among adolescents. *Popular Music and Society, 6*(1), 81-89.

Goodman, E. (1986, September 20). Commercial for teen-age pregnancy. *Washington Post,* p. A-23.

Gordon, T., Hakanen, E., & Wells, A. (1992, May). *Music preferences and the use of music to manage emotional states: Correlates with self-concept among adolescents.* Paper presented at the annual meetings of the International Communication Association, Miami, FL.

Greenberg, B., Ku, L., & Li, H. (1989, June). *Young people and their orientation to the mass media: An international study. Study 2: United States.* East Lansing: Michigan State University, College of Communication Arts.

Greenfield, P. M., Bruzzone, L., Koyamatsu, K., Satuloff, W., Nixon, K., Brodie, M., & Kingsdale, D. (1987). What is rock music doing to the minds of our youth? A first experimental look at the effects of rock music lyrics and music videos. *Journal of Early Adolescence, 7,* 315-329.

Greeson, L., & Williams, R. A. (1986). Social implications of music videos for youth: An analysis of the content and effects of MTV. *Youth and Society, 18,* 177-189.

Hakanen, E., & Wells, A. (1993). Music preference and taste cultures among adolescents. *Popular Music and Society, 17*(1), 55-69.

Hansen, C., & Hansen, R. (1988). How rock music videos can change what is seen when boy meets girl: Priming stereotypic appraisal of social interactions. *Sex Roles, 19,* 287-316.

Hansen, C., & Hansen, R. (1990). The influence of sex and violence on the appeal of rock music videos. *Communication Research, 17,* 212-234.

Hansen, C., & Hansen, R. (1991a). Constructing personality and social reality through music: Individual differences among fans of punk and heavy metal music. *Journal of Broadcasting and Electronic Media, 35,* 335-350.

Hansen, C., & Hansen, R. (1991b). Schematic information processing of heavy metal lyrics. *Communication Research, 18,* 373-411.

Hansen, C. H., & Krygowski, W. (1994). Arousal-augmented priming effects: Rock music videos and sex object schemas. *Communication Research, 21,* 24-47.

Hayakawa, S. I. (1962). *The use and misuse of language.* Greenwich, CT: Fawcett.

Johnson, J. D., Jackson, L. A., & Gatto, L. (1995). Violent attitudes and deferred academic aspirations: Deleterious effects of exposure to rap music. *Basic and Applied Social Psychology, 16*(1/2), 27-41.

Kotarba, J., & Wells, L. (1987). Styles of adolescent participation in an all-ages, rock 'n' roll nightclub: An ethnographic analysis. *Youth and Society, 18*(4), 398-417.

Kubey, R., & Larson, R. (1989). The use and experience of the new video media among children and young adolescents: Television viewing compared to the use of videocassettes, video games, and music videos. *Communication Research, 17,* 107-130.

Kuwahara, Y. (1992). Power to the people, y'all: Rap music, resistance, and black college students. *Humanity and Society, 16*(1), 54-73.

Lacayo, R. (1995, June 12). Violent reaction. *Time,* pp. 25-30.

Larson, R., & Kubey, R. (1983). Television and music: Contrasting media in adolescent life. *Youth and Society, 15*(1), 13-31.

Larson, R., Kubey, R., & Colletti, J. (1989). Changing channels: Early adolescent media choices and shifting investments in family and friends. *Journal of Youth and Adolescence, 18*(6), 583-599.

Leming, J. (1987). Rock music and the socialization of moral values in early adolescence. *Youth and Society, 18,* 363-383.

Levy, C. J., & Deykin, E. Y. (1989). Suicidality, depression, and substance abuse in adolescence. *American Journal of Psychiatry, 146,* 1462-1467.

Litman, R. E., & Farberow, N. L. (1994). Pop-rock music as precipitating cause in youth suicide. *Journal of Forensic Sciences, 39,* 494-499.

Lull, J. (1987). Listeners' communicative uses of popular music. In J. Lull (Ed.), *Popular music and communication* (pp. 140-174). Newbury Park, CA: Sage.

Lull, J. (1992). Popular music and communication: An introduction. In J. Lull (Ed.), *Popular music and communication* (2nd ed., pp. 1-32). Newbury Park, CA: Sage.

Lyle, J., & Hoffman, H. (1972). Children's use of television and other media. In E. Rubinstein, G. Comstock, & J. Murray (Eds.), *Television in day-to-day life: Patterns of use* (pp. 129-256). Washington, DC: U.S. Government Printing Office.

Martin, G., Clarke, M., & Pearce, C. (1993). Adolescent suicide: Music preference as an indicator of vulnerability. *Journal of the Academy of Child and Adolescent Psychiatry, 32*(3), 530-535.

Newspaper Advertising Bureau. (1980). *America's children and the mass media.* New York: Author.

Nielsen Media Research. (1989). *Nielsen newscast.* Northbrook, IL: Author.

Peterson, D. L., & Pfost, K. S. (1989). Influence of rock videos on attitudes of violence against women. *Psychological Reports, 64,* 319-322.

Radio Advertising Bureau. (1990). *1989-90 radio facts.* New York: Author.

Ritchie, L. D. (1991). Family communication patterns: An epistemic analysis and conceptual reinterpretation. *Communication Research, 18,* 548-565.

Roberts, D. F., & Henriksen, L. (1990, June). *Music listening vs. television viewing among older adolescents.* Paper presented at the annual meetings of the International Communication Association, Dublin, Ireland.

Roberts, D. F., Henriksen, L., & Christenson, P. (1999, April). *Substance use in popular movies and music.* Washington, DC: Office of National Drug Control Policy.

Robinson, J. P., & Hirsch, P. M. (1972). Teenage response to rock and roll protest songs. In R. S. Denisoff & R. A. Peterson (Eds.), *The sounds of social change: Studies in popular culture* (pp. 222-231). Chicago: Rand McNally.

Rock on trial. (1988, October 15). *Economist,* p. 38.

Roe, K. (1984, August). *Youth and music in Sweden: Results from a longitudinal study of teenagers' media use.* Paper presented at the meetings of the International Association of Mass Communication Research, Prague, Czech Republic.

Roe, K. (1985). Swedish youth and music: Listening patterns and motivations. *Communication Research, 12*(3), 353-362.

Roe, K. (1987). The school and music in adolescent socialization. In J. Lull (Ed.), *Popular music and communication* (pp. 212-230). Beverly Hills, CA: Sage.

Roe, K. (1995). Adolescents' use of socially disvalued media: Towards a theory of media delinquency. *Journal of Youth and Adolescence, 24,* 617-631.

Rosenbaum, J., & Prinsky, L. (1987). Sex, violence, and rock 'n' roll: Youth's perceptions of popular music. *Popular Music and Society, 11*(2), 79-89.

Rouner, D. (1990). Rock music use as a socializing function. *Popular Music and Society, 14*(1), 97-107.

St. Lawrence, J. S., & Joyner, D. J. (1991). The effects of sexually violent rock music on males' acceptance of violence against women. *Psychology of Women Quarterly, 15,* 49-63.

Tanner, J. (1981). Pop music and peer groups: A study of Canadian high school students' responses to pop music. *Canadian Review of Sociology and Anthropology, 18*(2), 1-13.

Thompson, M., Walsh-Childers, K., & Brown, J. D. (1993). The influence of family communication patterns and sexual experience on processing of a music video. In B. Greenberg, J. D. Brown, & N. L. Buerkel-Rothfuss (Eds.), *Media, sex, and the adolescent* (pp. 248-262). Cresskill, NJ: Hampton Press.

Vance v. Judas Priest, WL 130920 (Nev. Ct. 1990).

Wanamaker, C. E., & Reznikoff, M. (1989). Effects of aggressive and nonaggressive rock songs on projective and structured tests. *Journal of Psychology, 123,* 561-570.

Wartella, E., Heintz, K., Aidman, A., & Mazzarella, S. (1990). Television and beyond: Children's video media in one community. *Communication Research, 17,* 45-64.

Wass, H., Miller, D., & Reditt, C. (1991). Adolescents and destructive themes in rock music: A follow-up. *Omega, 23*(3), 193-206.

Wass, H., Miller, D., & Stevenson, R. (1989). Factors affecting adolescents' behavior and attitudes toward destructive rock lyrics. *Death Studies, 13,* 287-303.

Wells, A. (1990). Popular music: Emotional use and management. *Journal of Popular Culture, 24*(1), 105-117.

Yee, S., Britton, L., & Thompson, W. (1988, April). *The effects of rock music on adolescents' behavior.* Paper presented at the annual meeting of the Western Psychological Association, Burlingame, CA.

Zillmann, D., Aust, C. F., Hoffman, K. D., Love, C. C., Ordman, V. L., Pope, J. T., Seigler, P. D., & Gibson, R. J. (1995). Radical rap: Does it further ethnic division? *Basic and Applied Social Psychology, 16,* 1-25.

CHAPTER **21**

# Children, Adolescents, Drugs, and the Media

VICTOR C. STRASBURGER
University of New Mexico School of Medicine

*Joe Camel is little more than a child molester for the tobacco industry—seductive, predatory, lethal.*

Editorial, *USA Today,* June 2, 1997

*You don't see dead teenagers on the highway because of corn chips.*

Jay Leno, when asked why he does commercials for Doritos corn chips but refuses to do beer commercials. *TV Guide,* June 10, 1989

*Whether we like it or not, alcohol advertising is the single greatest source of alcohol education for Americans.*

Representative Joe Kennedy (D., Mass.), cosponsor of the Kennedy-Thurmond bill to require strict labeling of all advertisements for alcohol products. *American Medical News,* April 20, 1992

The so-called War on Drugs has been waged by the federal government for decades in a variety of locales *except* the media (see Figures 21.1 and 21.2). At the same time that parents and school programs are trying to get children and teenagers to "Just Say No" to drugs, $8 billion worth of cigarette and alcohol advertising is very effectively working to get them to just say yes to smoking and drinking (Strasburger & Donnerstein, 1999). According to two recent content analyses, television programs, movies, and popular music and music videos all contain appreciable content depicting smoking, drinking, or illicit drug

**Figure 21.1.** One Editorial Cartoonist's View of the "War on Drugs"
SOURCE: Copyright © Jim Borgman, *Cincinnati Enquirer.*

use (Gerbner & Ozyegin, 1997; Roberts, Henriksen, & Christenson, 1999). Although there are few data showing that drug advertising or drug content has a direct, cause-and-effect impact on adolescents' drug use, there are numerous correlational studies that speak to the impact of a variety of media on teenagers. Considering all of the studies done to date, there is sufficient evidence to warrant a total ban on cigarette advertising in all media, severe restrictions on alcohol advertising, and major changes in the way that cigarettes, alcohol, and illegal drugs are portrayed in movies.

## Adolescent Drug Use

Illegal drugs certainly take their toll on American society, but two legal drugs—tobacco and alcohol—pose a far greater danger to children and teenagers. Both represent significant "gateway" drugs and are among the earliest drugs used by children or teens. A child who smokes tobacco or drinks alcohol is 65 times more likely to use marijuana, for example, than a child who never smokes or drinks (National Institute on Drug Abuse [NIDA], 1995). And the effect is ongoing: A child who uses marijuana is 100 times more likely to use cocaine compared with abstaining peers (NIDA, 1995). The younger a child begins to use cigarettes, alcohol, or other drugs, the higher the risk of serious health problems and abuse carrying over into adulthood (Belcher & Shinitzky, 1998).

Every year, more than 400,000 Americans die from cigarette use—more than are killed by AIDS, alcohol, automobile accidents, murder, illegal drugs, suicide, and fires combined (Institute of Medicine, 1994). An estimated 3,000 teenagers begin smoking each day, and

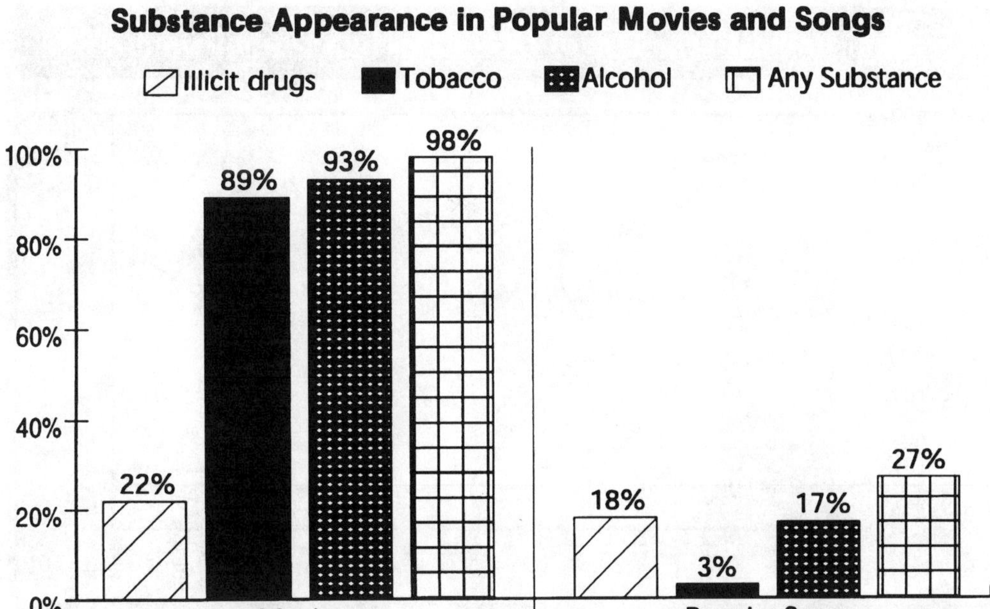


**Figure 21.2.** The most recent and comprehensive content analysis of a variety of popular media found that tobacco, alcohol, and illicit drugs are very prevalent in movies that are popular with children and teens but considerably less prevalent in popular music.
SOURCE: Roberts, Henriksen, and Christenson (1999).

about one third of them will eventually die from a tobacco-related illness (U.S. Department of Health and Human Services, 1994). New evidence concerning early smoking is alarming: Damage to lung cell DNA may occur, producing physiologic changes that may persist despite quitting smoking (Wiencke et al., 1999). Tobacco is the only legal product that, when used as directed, kills.

Increasingly, tobacco is being marketed overseas, particularly in Third World countries, with precipitous increases in smoking rates resulting (Mackay, 1999). The United States is the leading producer of cigarettes, exporting three times as many cigarettes as any other country (MacKenzie, Bartecchi, & Schrier, 1994). If current smoking rates continue, 7 million people in developing countries will die of smoking-related diseases annually. And one fifth of those living in industrialized countries will die of tobacco-related disorders (Peto, Lopez, Boreham, Thun, & Heath, 1992; "Tobacco's Toll," 1992).

Alcohol, too, is a killer, with more than 100,000 deaths annually in the United States attributed to excessive consumption (Doyle, 1996). It is the most commonly abused drug by children ages 12 to 17. Alcohol-related automobile accidents are the number-one cause of death among teenagers, and alcohol consumption typically contributes to homicides, suicides, and drownings—three of the other leading causes of death (Comerci & Schwebel, 2000). Often, older children and preteens experiment with alcohol first before other drugs. Drinking alcohol may contribute

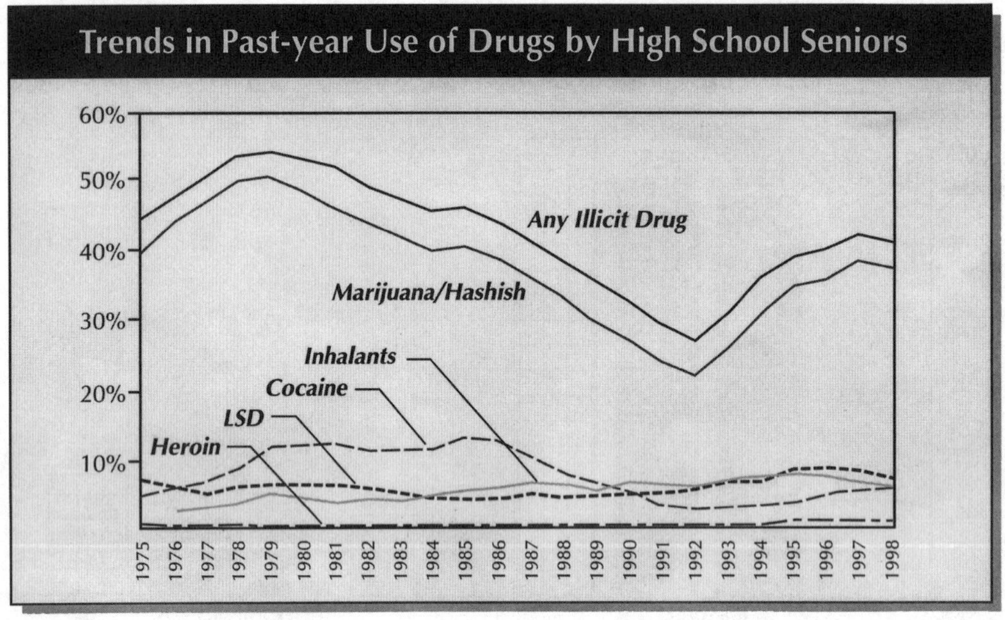


**Figure 21.3.** National Trends in Adolescent Drug Use, 1975-1998
SOURCE: Johnston, O'Malley, and Bachman (1998).

to premature sexual intercourse, lower grades, and experimentation with other drugs. Young people who drink are nearly eight times more likely to use other illicit drugs than those who never drink (American Academy of Pediatrics, 1995).

The best data regarding adolescent drug use come from the Monitoring the Future Study, funded by the National Institute for Drug Abuse and conducted annually since the mid-1970s by the Institute for Social Research at the University of Michigan (see Figure 21.3 and Tables 21.1 and 21.2; Johnston, O'Malley, & Bachman, 1998). These data are unique: Nearly 50,000 students nationwide were surveyed, most recently in 1998, with equal numbers of males and females in the eighth, tenth, and twelfth grades at more than 420 public and private schools. No data are perfect, however. The Monitoring the Future Study fails to capture high school dropouts, who may be using and abusing drugs at higher rates than their school peers. It also depends on self-reports by teenagers. But no other collection of data is as extensive over as long a period of time.

Highlights include the following:

*High levels of smoking among teenagers.* More than one third of American students smoke by the time they complete high school. Two thirds of teenagers have tried smoking, including nearly half of all eighth graders surveyed. Overall, cigarette use has increased by 32% between 1991 and 1997, following a decade of relative stability. Other surveys have found that smoking among college students has risen as well (Wechsler, Rigotti, Gledhill-Hoyt, & Lee, 1998).

*High levels of alcohol use among teenagers.* Although the percentage of "ever-users" decreased to 81% in 1998 from a high of 93% in 1980, 62% of high school seniors report having been drunk at least once, and one third reported having had five or more drinks in a row in the 2 weeks prior to being surveyed.

**TABLE 21.1** Adolescent Drug Use, 1998

| *Drug* | *% Ever Used* | *% Used During Past Year* |
|---|---|---|
| Any illicit drug | 54.1 | 41.4 |
| Any illicit drug other than marijuana | 29.4 | 20.2 |
| Alcohol | 81.4 | 74.3 |
| Ever been drunk | 62.4 | 52.0 |
| Cigarettes | 65.3 | — |
| Marijuana | 49.1 | 37.5 |
| Smokeless tobacco | 26.2 | — |
| Stimulants | 16.4 | 10.1 |
| Inhalants | 15.2 | 6.2 |
| Hallucinogens | 14.1 | 9.0 |
| Other opiates | 9.8 | 6.3 |
| Cocaine | 9.3 | 5.7 |
| Sedatives | 9.2 | 6.0 |
| Steroids | 2.7 | 1.7 |
| Heroin | 2.0 | 1.0 |

SOURCE: Adapted from the Monitoring the Future Study (Johnson et al., 1998, December 18).
$N$ = 15,200 twelfth graders.

- *A leveling off of illicit drug use among teenagers.* Such use peaked at 66% in 1981 and declined to a low of 41% in 1992. Currently, 54% of twelfth graders report having ever used an illicit drug. Nearly 30% have used an illicit drug other than marijuana.
- *A leveling off in marijuana use among teenagers.* Marijuana use peaked in 1979, when 60% of high school seniors reported ever having tried it. Now 49% of seniors have tried marijuana.
- *Marijuana, cocaine, and heroin use bottomed out in the early 1990s but has risen among children and teenagers since then at all grade levels.* This trend is now leveling off and may be in the process of reversing once again.

The United States is not alone in experiencing increasing rates of adolescent drug use. A recent survey of nearly 8,000 15- and 16-year-olds throughout the United Kingdom found that nearly all had tried alcohol, half had engaged in binge drinking, 36% had smoked cigarettes within the previous 30 days, and 42% had ever tried an illicit drug, usually marijuana (Miller & Plant, 1996). In a survey of 10% of all 12- to 15-year-old

**TABLE 21.2** Trends in Twelfth Graders' Perception of Drugs as Harmful (in percentages)

| *Do you think people risk harming themselves if they. . .* | *1978* | *1988* | *1998* |
|---|---|---|---|
| Try marijuana once or twice | 8.1 | 19.0 | 16.7 |
| Smoke marijuana occasionally | 12.4 | 31.7 | 24.4 |
| Smoke marijuana regularly | 34.9 | 77.0 | 58.5 |
| Try LSD once or twice | 42.7 | 45.7 | 76.5 |
| Try cocaine once or twice | 33.2 | 51.2 | 54.6 |
| Try MDMA[a] once or twice | — | — | 34.5 |
| Try one or two drinks of an alcoholic beverage | 3.4 | 6.2 | 8.0 |
| Have five or more drinks once or twice each weekend | 63.1 | 42.6 | 42.8 |
| Smoke one or more packs of cigarettes per day | 59.0 | 68.0 | 70.8 |

SOURCE: Adapted from the Monitoring the Future Study (Johnson et al., 1998, December 18).
a. MDMA is also known as ecstasy.

schoolchildren in Dundee, Scotland, two thirds reported having consumed an alcoholic drink and, by age 14, more than half reported having been drunk (McKeganey, Forsyth, Barnard, & Hay, 1996).

## Determinants of Child and Adolescent Drug Use

A variety of factors have been implicated in the early use of drugs. Among adolescents, specific factors include poor self-image, low religiosity, poor school performance, alienation from parents, family dysfunction, physical abuse, and parental divorce (Belcher & Shinitzky, 1998; Schydlower & Rogers, 1993). The peer group has long been recognized as a unique risk factor in adolescence, and childhood temperament is gaining acceptance as another unique factor. A moody and negative child is more likely to be criticized by his or her parents, leading to a coercive model of parenting and a greater risk of early substance abuse. Interestingly, a recent comprehensive review of substance abuse in childhood and adolescence (Belcher & Shinitzky, 1998) failed to mention media influence as an etiologic force among young people initiating drug use (Strasburger, 1998).

### *Peers*

Peer pressure may play one of the most important roles in first drug use among young teens (Jessor & Jessor, 1977) but may also be involved in drug abstinence as well (Robin & Johnson, 1996). Teens who see their friends using drugs are more likely to partake themselves; teens who believe their friends are antidrug are more likely to abstain. (Another alternative and as-yet untested hypothesis is that teens prone to drug use are more likely to search out like-minded peers.) Regardless, the media may function as a kind of "super-peer," making drug use seem like normative behavior for teenagers (Strasburger, 1997). Since teens are so invested in doing what is "normal" for their peer group, the media could represent one of the most powerful influences on them.

Peer pressure must also be placed in proper perspective:

> Teens and preteens somehow get the idea that smoking makes one sexy, athletic, cool, or macho. The tobacco industry says these ideas come from their peers. No one asks where these peers—other kids—get these ideas. Yet about the only place in our society where these silly images occur is advertising. So-called peer pressure explains little. It is merely a clever term used to shift blame from the manufacturer and advertiser to the user. Like peer pressure, "parental example" does not just spontaneously occur. Parents of today started smoking as children, and no doubt had similar silly ideas about what smoking would do for their images. (DiFranza, Richards, Paulman, Fletcher, & Jaffe, 1992, p. 3282)

### *Family*

Parents can be significant risk factors or protective factors depending on the circumstances. Abused children have been found to be at increased risk for later substance abuse (Bennett & Kemper, 1994). Similarly, a "coercive" parenting style has been shown to lead to greater substance abuse and even delinquency in adolescence (McMahon, 1994). Genetically, alcoholic parents are two to nine times more likely to produce biological children who are alcoholics (Belcher & Shinitzky, 1998). The inherited risk probably also extends to other drugs of abuse as well (Comings, 1997). At the opposite end of the spectrum, growing up in a nurturing family with good communication with parents is a significant protective factor (Resnick et al., 1997).

Latchkey children are more likely to use alcohol, tobacco, and marijuana, perhaps because they are unsupervised or perhaps because they have unrestrained access to a variety of unhealthy media (Chilcoat & Anthony, 1996; Richardson et al., 1989). The media have sometimes been labeled "the electronic parents," and if parents fail to give their children appropriate messages about drugs, the media may fill the void with unhealthy information or cues.

### *Personality*

One unusual study found that certain behavioral risk factors in 3- and 4-year-olds could predict adolescent drug use (Block, Block, & Keyes, 1988). The researchers found that lack of self-control was apparent and predictive at an early age. Absence of resilience may also be important at a young age because resiliency (the ability to overcome adversity) is also protective (Resnick et al., 1997). Likewise, positive self-esteem and self-image, good self-control, assertiveness, social competence, and academic success are all positive resilience factors. The role of media in encouraging or diminishing resiliency is completely unknown. Different children may respond to the exact same depiction completely differently (Brown & Schulze, 1990). It is possible that children who are more "media resilient" are less likely to be affected by unhealthy portrayals in the media, but only one media education study has found this to be true so far (Austin & Johnson, 1997).

## The Impact of Advertising on Children and Adolescents

An interesting and unfortunate paradox exists in American media: Advertisements for birth control products, which could prevent untold numbers of teenage pregnancies and sexually transmitted diseases, are forbidden on three of the four major national networks, yet all four networks frequently advertise products that cause disease and death in thousands of teenagers and adults annually—alcohol and tobacco (see Figures 21.4 and 21.5; Strasburger, 1997).

Tobacco and alcohol represent two hugely profitable industries that require the constant recruitment of new users. With the death of 1,200 smokers a day, and with thousands more trying to quit, the tobacco industry must recruit new smokers to remain profitable. Inevitably, these new smokers come from the ranks of children and adolescents, especially given the demographics of smoking (50% of smokers begin by age 13, 90% by age 19; U.S. Department of Health and Human Services, 1994). The alcohol industry has targeted minority groups and the young for years, particularly through promotion of sports and youth-oriented programming (Gerbner, 1990). Since 5% of drinkers consume 50% of all alcoholic beverages (Gerbner, 1990), new recruits (preferably heavy drinkers) are a must for the alcohol industry as well.

Celebrity endorsers are commonly used, and older children and teenagers may be particularly vulnerable to such ads (Atkin & Block, 1983). Few alcohol commercials in the 1990s failed to employ some combination of rock music, young attractive models, humor, or adventure. "Beach babes," frogs, lizards, and dogs are all commonly seen in beer commercials. Production values are extraordinary; costs for a single 30-second commercial may easily exceed those for an entire half-hour of regular programming. A 30-second commercial during the Super Bowl 2000 cost $2 million for national placement (Lee, 1999).

A variety of studies have explored the impact of advertising on children and adolescents. Nearly all have shown advertising to be extremely effective in increasing young people's awareness of and emotional responses to products, their recognition of certain brands, their desire to own or use the products advertised, and their recognition of the advertisements themselves. In 1975, the National Science Foundation (1977) commissioned a report on the effects of advertising on children, which concluded:

*(Text continued on p. 423)*

**Figure 21.4.** A Typical Cigarette Print Ad Emphasizing the Independence of Young Women (to Smoke)

**Figure 21.5a.** Typical Alcohol Print Ads, Usually Targeting Young Males With Messages That Combine and Confuse Drinking and Sexuality

It is clear from the available evidence that television *does* influence children. Research has demonstrated that children attend to and learn from commercials, and that advertising is at least moderately successful in creating positive attitudes toward and the desire for products advertised. (p. 179)

**Figure 21.5b.**

Although the research is not yet scientifically "beyond a reasonable doubt," *there is a preponderance of evidence that cigarette and alcohol advertising is a significant factor in adolescents' use of these two drugs* (Altman, Levine, Coeytaux, Slade, & Jaffe, 1996; Center for Substance Abuse Prevention, 1997; Evans, Farkas, Gilpin, Berry, & Pierce, 1995; Grube, 1999; Grube & Wallack, 1994; Kessler, Wilkenfeld, & Thompson, 1997; Madden & Grube, 1994; Pierce, Choi, Gilpin, Farkas, & Berry, 1998; Pollay et al., 1996; Schooler, Feighery, & Flora, 1996; U.S. Department of Health and Human Services, 1994). For alcohol, advertising may account for as much as 10 to 30% of adolescents' usage (Atkin, 1993a, 1994; Gerbner, 1990). A recent study of students' use of cigarette promotional items found that a similar figure applies to cigarettes as well: Approximately one third of adolescents' cigarette use could be predicted by their purchase or ownership of tobacco promotional gear (Pierce et al., 1998). Nevertheless, as one group of researchers (Orlandi, Lieberman, & Schinke, 1989) note,

> To reduce the argument regarding the demonstrable effects of massive advertising campaigns to the level of individual behavior is absurdly simplistic. . . . Rather, what we are dealing with is the nature of advertising itself. Pepsi Cola, for example, could not convincingly prove, through any sort of defensible scientific study, that particular children or adolescents who consume their products do so because of exposure to any or all of their ads. (p. 90)

Although there is some legitimate debate about how much of an impact such advertising has on young people and their decisions whether to use cigarettes or alcohol, advertising clearly works—or else companies would not spend millions of dollars a year on it. This leaves American society with a genuine moral, economic, and public health dilemma: Should advertising of unhealthy products be allowed when society then has to pay for the disease, disability, and death that these products cause? Tobacco companies and beer manufacturers claim that they are simply influencing "brand choice," not increasing overall demand for their products (Orlandi et al., 1989). Moreover, they claim that, since it is legal to sell their products, it should be legal to advertise them as well and that any ban represents an infringement on their First Amendment rights of commercial free speech (Gostin & Brandt, 1993; Ile & Knoll, 1990; Shiffrin, 1993). Public health advocates counter that tobacco companies and beer manufacturers are engaging in unfair and deceptive practices by specifically targeting young people, using attractive role models and youth-oriented messages in their ads, and making smoking and drinking seem like normative behavior (Atkin, 1993a, 1993b; Kilbourne, 1993; Madden & Grube, 1994; Strasburger & Donnerstein, 1999; U.S. Department of Health and Human Services, 1994). Alcohol and tobacco manufacturers are trying to get adolescents to "just say yes" to cigarettes and beer at a time when society is trying to get them to "just say no" to drugs (Kilbourne, 1993; Strasburger, 1997). As we shall see, the available data strongly support the public health viewpoint.

## Cigarettes

### *Impact of Cigarette Advertising*

Cigarette advertising appears to increase teenagers' risk of smoking by glamorizing smoking and smokers (U.S. Department of Health and Human Services, 1994). Smokers are depicted as independent, healthy, youthful, and adventurous. By contrast, the adverse consequences of smoking are never shown. The weight of the evidence is such that the surgeon general of the United States recently concluded, "Cigarette advertising appears to affect young people's perceptions of the pervasiveness, image, and function of smoking. Since misperceptions in these areas constitute psychosocial risk factors for the initiation of smoking, *cigarette advertising appears to increase young people's risk of smoking*" (U.S. Department of Health and Human Services, 1994, p. 195, italics added).

In fact, some of the industry's advertising strategies are nearly Orwellian in their sophistication. In the *Weekly Reader,* a periodical sold in approximately 80% of all U.S. elementary schools and owned, at one time, by the same company that owned tobacco conglomerate RJR Nabisco, the following contradictory themes were seen in the early 1990s: Adults in positions of authority are trying to prevent teens from smoking (appealing to teens' sense of autonomy); laws are being enforced inconsistently; most teenagers smoke; smoking is highly pleasurable and relaxing; and teens intent on smoking will do so regardless of what adults try to do about it (DeJong, 1996). An expert in adolescent psychology could not have dreamed up a more effective, "forbidden fruit" scheme to recruit new teen smokers. Other studies have also found that cigarette brands popular among teens are more likely than adult brands to be advertised in teen magazines (King, Siegel, Celebucki, & Connolly, 1998). Recently, legislation originally brought by U.S. attorneys general uncovered the fact that tobacco companies have specifically targeted teenage smokers as young as age 13 in an attempt to regain market share (Weinstein, 1998).

Perhaps as a result, nearly half of eighth graders do not believe that smoking a pack of cigarettes a day represents a health risk (Johnston, O'Malley, & Bachman, 1994). Numerous studies show that children who pay closer attention to cigarette advertisements, or who are able to recall such ads more readily, or who own promotional items are more likely to view smoking favorably and to become smokers themselves (Aitken & Eadie, 1990; Altman et al., 1996; Armstrong, de Klerk, Shean, Dunn, & Dolin, 1990; Centers for Disease Control, 1992a; Evans et al., 1995; Goldstein, Fischer, Richards, & Creten, 1987; Klitzner, Gruenewald, & Bamberger, 1991; Pierce et al., 1998; Sargent et al., 1997; Schooler et al., 1996; Vaidya, Naik, & Vaidya, 1996; Vickers, 1992; While, Kelly, Huang, & Charlton, 1996). Among teenage girls, smoking rates increased dramatically around 1967, exactly the same time when women were being targeted by such new brands as Virginia Slims (Pierce, Lee, & Gilpin, 1994). *Only a rare study can be found that tobacco advertising has no influence on children* (Smith, 1989).

Beginning in the early 1990s, some important research has more clearly delineated the impact of cigarette advertising on young people. In 1991, two studies examined the impact of the Old Joe the Camel advertising campaign. In one study, 6-year-olds were as likely to recognize Old Joe as they were the famous mouseketeer logo for the Disney Channel (see Figure 21.6; Fischer, Schwart, Richards, Goldstein, & Rojas, 1991). Even at age 3, 30% of children could still make the association between the Old Joe the Camel figure and a pack of cigarettes. In the second study, more than twice as many children, as compared with adults, reported exposure to Old Joe. Not only were they able to recognize the association with Camel cigarettes, but they found the ads to be appealing as well (DiFranza et al., 1991). Not coincidentally, in the 3 years after the introduction of the Old Joe campaign, the preference for Camel cigarettes increased from 0.5% of adolescent smokers to 32%. During the same time period, the sale of Camels to minors increased from $6 million to $476 million, representing one quarter of all Camel sales and one third of all illegal cigarette sales to minors (DiFranza et al., 1991).

Other studies have provided important evidence as well. A California study documented that the most heavily advertised brands of cigarettes—Marlboro and Camel—are the most popular among teenage smokers (Pierce et al., 1991). A similar national study by the Centers for Disease Control (CDC) found that 84% of teenagers purchase either Marlboros, Camels, or Newports—the three most highly advertised brands in the United States in 1990 (see Table 21.3; Centers for Disease Control, 1992b). In England, the most popular brands of cigarettes (Benson & Hedges, Silk Cut, Embassy, and Marlboro) are likewise the most heavily advertised (Vickers, 1992).

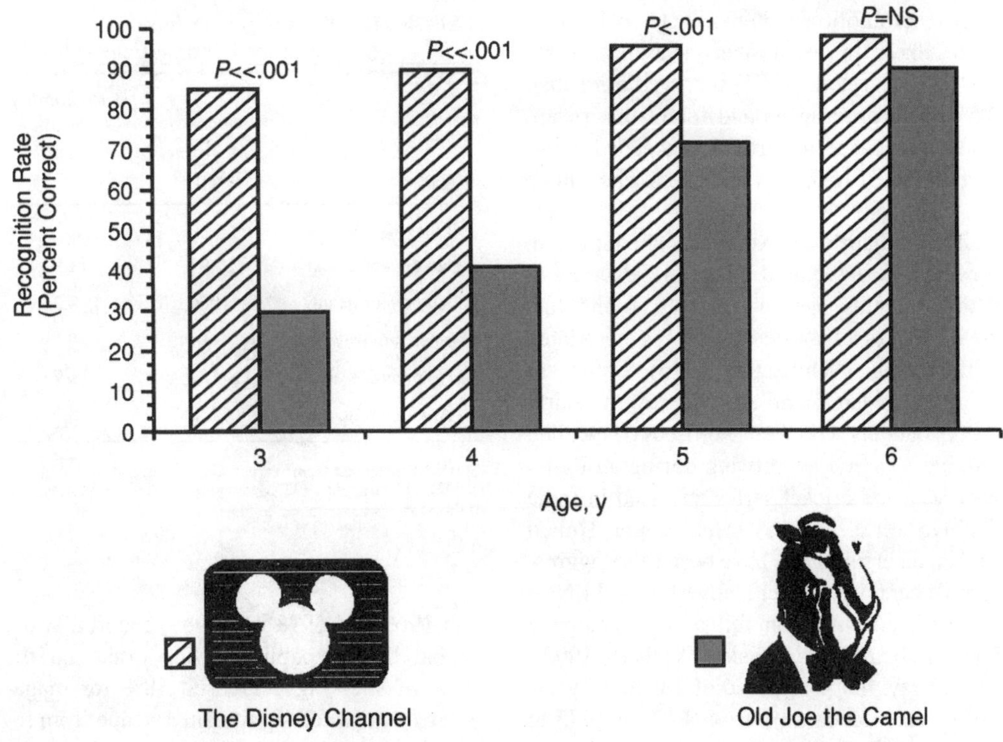


**Figure 21.6.** According to one classic study, Old Joe the Camel is as recognizable to 6-year-olds as the Disney Channel logo.
SOURCE: Copyright © American Medical Association.

**TABLE 21.3** Is Cigarette Advertising Effective?

| *Advertising in Millions* | *Adolescent Brand Preference* | *Adult Brand Preference* |
|---|---|---|
| 1. Marlboro ($75) | 1. Marlboro (60.0%) | 1. Marlboro (23.5%) |
| 2. Camel ($43) | 2. Camel (13.3%) | 2. Winston (6.7%) |
| 3. Newport ($35) | 3. Newport (12.7%) | 3. Newport (4.8%) |

SOURCE: Data from the Centers for Disease Control (1994) and Pollay et al. (1996). Copyright © American Academy of Pediatrics. Reprinted with permission.

Cross-sectional studies in the mid-1990s found that teenagers exposed to promotional items or advertising were far more likely to become smokers. A study of 571 seventh graders in San Jose, California, found that 88% of 13-year-olds reported exposure to cigarette marketing and that experimenting with smoking was 2.2 times greater among those who owned promotional items (Schooler et al., 1996). In a national sample of 1,047 adolescents ages 12 to 17, Altman et al. (1996) drew a similar conclusion. In rural New Hampshire, a survey of 1,265 sixth through twelfth graders found that students who owned promotional items were 4.1 times more likely to be smokers (Sargent et al., 1997). Evans et al. (1995) surveyed more than 3,500 California teens and found that receptivity to tobacco advertising exceeded exposure to family members and peers who smoke as a risk factor.

This is hardly an American phenomenon, however. In the United Kingdom, a survey of 1,450 students ages 11 and 12 found that awareness of cigarette advertising correlated with smoking (While et al., 1996). Similar results were also found in a survey of nearly 2,000 students who were exposed to so-called passive cigarette advertising during an India-New Zealand cricket series televised in India (Vaidya et al., 1996). Unlike the United States, other countries have been more aggressive in banning cigarette advertising. In New Zealand, consumption fell after a complete ban on cigarette advertising (Vickers, 1992). In Norway, the prevalence of 13- to 15-year-old smokers decreased from 17% in 1975 to 10% in 1990 after an advertising ban was imposed (Vickers, 1992). In fact, an analysis of factors influencing tobacco consumption in 22 countries revealed that, since 1973, advertising restrictions have resulted in lower rates of smoking (Laugesen & Meads, 1991).

Finally, a comprehensive 3-year longitudinal study of 1,752 California adolescents who never smoked found that one third of all smoking experimentation in California between 1993 and 1996 could be attributed to tobacco advertising and promotions (Pierce et al., 1998). This was the first study of its kind to use longitudinal correlational data that could yield cause-and-effect conclusions.

Several studies have documented that, as the amount of cigarette advertising in a magazine increases, the amount of coverage of health risks associated with smoking decreases dramatically (Amos, Jacobson, & White, 1991; DeJong, 1996; Kessler, 1989; Warner, Goldenhar, & McLaughlin, 1992). Recently, researchers using a logistic-regression analysis to examine 99 U.S. magazines published over a 25-year span (between 1959

**TABLE 21.4** Does Cigarette Advertising Influence Editorial Content?

| *Magazine* | *Number of Magazine-Years* | *% Probability of Coverage of Health Care Risks* |
|---|---|---|
| All magazines | | |
| No cigarette ads | 403 | 11.9 |
| Any cigarette ads | 900 | 8.3 |
| Women's magazines | | |
| No cigarette ads | 104 | 11.7 |
| Any cigarette ads | 212 | 5.0 |

SOURCE: Adapted from Warner, Goldenhar, and McLaughlin (1992). 

and 1969 and 1973 and 1986) found that the probability of publishing an article on the risks of smoking decreased 38% for magazines that derived significant revenue from tobacco companies (see Table 21.4; Warner et al., 1992). Women's magazines are particularly guilty. A study of *Cosmopolitan, Good Housekeeping, Mademoiselle, McCall's,* and *Women's Day* found that, between 1983 and 1987, not one of them published a single column or feature on the dangers of smoking (Kessler, 1989). All but *Good Housekeeping* accept cigarette advertising. This occurred during exactly the same 5-year period that lung cancer was surpassing breast cancer as the number-one killer of women (Moog, 1991).

Why is tobacco advertising so effective? Aside from the sheer amount of money spent on it, creating a density of such advertising that is difficult to counteract, cigarette advertising may act as a "super-peer" in influencing teenagers to believe that everyone smokes but them (smoking is normative behavior) and that they will instantly become more attractive to their peers if they do smoke (Strasburger, 1997). Indeed, one group of researchers (Goldman & Glantz, 1998) has found that the only two strategies that are highly effective for preventing adolescents from smoking are showing what lengths the tobacco industry will go to recruit new smokers ("industry manipulation") and sensitizing teenagers to the risk of secondhand smoke. Both strategies involve "denormalizing" smoking—in other words, counteracting the myth that smoking is normative behavior for teens.

In 1998, the U.S. attorneys general negotiated what may be a remarkable settlement with the tobacco industry, calling for the payout of more than $206 billion to the states over the next 25 years, as well as imposing severe restrictions on marketing and advertising to children (see Table 21.5). Critics point to the fact that this figure represents a mere 8% of the $2.5 trillion that the federal government will lose over the same 25 years in health care costs related to smoking (Jackson, 1998). Nevertheless, the now-substantial cigarette advertising research is hardly "moot" and will certainly have implications for alcohol advertising as well. In addition, the research may come back into play if the attorneys general settlement is overturned by a Congress that has traditionally been heavily influenced by tobacco money or a federal court decision. What may replace the concerns about advertising and promotion is increasing alarm over the depictions of tobacco use in movies, music videos, and television programs—in a sense, the new "advertising" arena for tobacco companies.

**TABLE 21.5** Some Features of the 1998 Tobacco Settlement

- Payment of $206.4 billion from the tobacco industry to the states over the next 25 years, including $1.5 billion to fund research to reduce teen smoking
- A ban on the use of cartoon characters in the advertising, promotion, or labeling of tobacco products
- A prohibition on targeting youth in advertising, promotions, or marketing
- A ban on all outdoor advertising, including billboards and signs in stadiums
- A ban on the sale of merchandise (e.g., T-shirts or backpacks) with brand-name logos
- A ban on payments to TV and movie producers for product placements

SOURCE: Adapted from *AAP News* (1999, January), p. 4.

### *Cigarettes in Television Programming, Music and Music Videos, and Movies*

Smoking seems to be making a major comeback in the movies and, to a lesser extent, on television. Before the surgeon general's landmark 1964 report on smoking, TV characters smoked nine times more frequently than in 1982 (Signorielli, 1990). By the early 1980s, only 2% of series stars smoked on TV (Breed & De Foe, 1983). However, this apparently healthy low percentage is deceptive: TV programs rarely showed characters refusing to smoke or expressing antismoking sentiments—probably so as not to offend the corporate advertisers whose parent companies also owned tobacco subsidiaries (Signorielli, 1990). The latest content analysis, in the 1990s, shows that more young and middle-aged women are now depicted as smokers and that promotions for feature films constitute a new supply of smoking scenes (Gerbner & Ozyegin, 1997). In one analysis of the 1992 fall prime-time season, 24% of the programs contained smoking content, with only 8% of those scenes involving antismoking messages. Most of the smokers were high-status "good guys" rather than unsavory characters (Hazan & Glantz, 1995). In regard to music videos, one fourth of all Music Television (MTV) videos portrayed tobacco use, with the lead performer usually the one shown as smoking (DuRant et al., 1997).

Movies are providing tobacco companies with increasing opportunities for featuring smoking. The use of passive advertising—so-called product placements—has been extremely lucrative, although studio chiefs currently deny that this practice continues. The Philip Morris Company reportedly paid $350,000 to place Lark cigarettes in the James Bond movie *License to Kill* and another

$42,500 to place Marlboros in *Superman II* (Consumer Reports, 1990).

Movies are extremely popular with teenagers, who make up 16% of the U.S. population but account for 26% of all movie admissions (Rauzi, 1998). One recent study found that, since 1960, the top-grossing films have shown movie stars lighting up at three times the rate of American adults (Hazan, Lipton, & Glantz, 1994). A separate study found that all 10 of the top-grossing films of 1996 contained tobacco use, and 17 of the 18 films in then-current distribution featured smoking (Thomas, 1996). In the most recent study of the 200 most popular movie rentals of 1996 and 1997, Roberts et al. (1999) found that tobacco appeared in 89% of the movies, consistently across all genres (see Figure 21.2). Unlike in real life, smoking rates in the movies have not changed between 1960 and 1990.

Movie smokers tend to be white, middle-class male characters, who are usually the heroes (Stockwell & Glantz, 1997). Movie depictions also tend to be very pro-smoking, with only 14% of screen time dealing with adverse health effects (Stockwell & Glantz, 1997). One group of researchers suggests that smoking in movies has always been present in children's movies, of all places. Children's G-rated movies contain a surprising amount of smoking scenes (Goldstein, Sobel, & Newman, 1999). A review of 50 G-rated animated feature films released between 1937 and 1997 by five major production companies found that more than half portrayed one or more instances of tobacco use, including all seven films released in 1996 and 1997 (see Table 21.6).

## Alcohol

### *Research on Alcohol Advertising*

Although the research on alcohol advertising is not quite as compelling as that for tobacco advertising, children and adolescents do seem to make up a uniquely vulnerable audience. Like cigarette advertisements, beer commercials are virtually custom-made to appeal to children and adolescents: images of fun-loving, sexy, successful young people having the time of their lives. Who wouldn't want to indulge (see Table 21.7; Kilbourne, 1993)? Using sexual imagery (Atkin, 1994; Kilbourne, Painton, & Ridley, 1985) or celebrity endorsers (Atkin & Block, 1983; Friedman, Termini, & Washington, 1977) increases the impact of beer and wine ads on young people.

Content analyses show that beer ads seem to suggest that drinking is an absolutely harmless activity with no major health risks associated with it (Atkin, 1993a; Atkin, DeJong, & Wallack, 1992; Atkin, Hocking, & Block, 1984; Grube, 1993; Grube & Wallack, 1994; Madden & Grube, 1994; Postman, Nystrom, Strate, & Weingartner, 1988; Strasburger, 1993; Wallack, Cassady, & Grube, 1990). More than one third of the ads show people driving or engaging in water sports while supposedly drinking (Madden & Grube, 1994).

As with cigarette smoking, drinking alcohol is portrayed as normative behavior, with no adverse consequences. But unlike cigarette advertising, beer and wine ads are frequently featured on prime-time television: Children and teenagers view 1,000 to 2,000 of them annually (Strasburger, 1997). Much of this advertising is concentrated in sports-related programming. In prime time, only 1 alcohol commercial appears every 4 hours; in sports programming, 2.4 ads appear per hour (Grube, 1995; Madden & Grube, 1994). In addition, alcohol advertisements are frequently embedded in sports programming, with banners and scoreboards featuring prominent logos and brief interruptions (e.g., "This halftime report is brought to you by . . ."), at a rate of about 3 per hour (Grube, 1995).

Such a density of advertising seems to have a considerable impact on young people. In one survey of fifth and sixth graders, nearly 60% of them could match the brand of beer being promoted with a still photograph from a commercial (Grube, 1995). Similarly, a sample of 9- and 10-year-olds could identify the

**TABLE 21.6** Tobacco or Alcohol Content of G-Rated Children's Films

| *Film* | *Tobacco Use* | *Exposure (in seconds)* | *Alcohol Use* | *Exposure (in seconds)* |
|---|---|---|---|---|
| *The Three Caballeros* | Yes | 548 | Yes | 8 |
| *101 Dalmatians* | Yes | 299 | Yes | 51 |
| *Pinocchio* | Yes | 223 | Yes | 80 |
| *James and the Giant Peach* | Yes | 206 | Yes | 38 |
| *All Dogs Go to Heaven* | Yes | 205 | Yes | 73 |
| *Alice in Wonderland* | Yes | 158 | No | — |
| *The Great Mouse Detective* | Yes | 165 | Yes | 414 |
| *The Aristocats* | Yes | 111 | Yes | 142 |
| *Beauty and the Beast* | No | — | Yes | 123 |
| *Sleeping Beauty* | No | — | Yes | 113 |

SOURCE: Adapted from Goldstein, Sobel, and Newman (1999).

**TABLE 21.7** Seven Myths That Alcohol Advertisers Want Children and Adolescents to Believe

1. *Everyone* drinks alcohol.
2. Drinking has no risks.
3. Drinking helps to solve problems.
4. Alcohol is a magic potion that can transform you.
5. Sports and alcohol go together.
6. If alcohol were truly dangerous, we wouldn't be advertising it.
7. Alcoholic beverage companies promote drinking only in moderation.

SOURCE: Adapted from Kilbourne (1991).

Budweiser frogs nearly as frequently as Bugs Bunny (see Table 21.8; Leiber, 1996). In one well-known survey of suburban Maryland children, 8- to 12-year-olds could list more brands of beer than names of American presidents (Center for Science in the Public Interest, 1988)! Rarely do young people see ads or public service announcements urging moderation (Madden & Grube, 1994). Perhaps as a result, nearly three fourths of American adults think that such advertising encourages teenagers to drink (Lipman, 1991).

Considerable research exists that the media can make children more vulnerable to experimentation with alcohol (Grube, 1995; Grube & Wallack, 1994). This survey or cross-sectional research does not yield cause-and-effect conclusions, but a few examples of such research may demonstrate the usefulness of its findings:

A series of survey studies by Atkin (Atkin & Block, 1983; Atkin et al., 1984; Atkin, Neuendorf, & McDermott, 1983) really began the investigations in this area. He found that adolescents heavily exposed to alcohol advertising are more likely to believe that drinkers possess the qualities being displayed in the advertising (e.g., being attractive or successful), have more positive beliefs about drinking, think that getting drunk is acceptable, and are more likely to drink, drink heavily, and drink and drive.

**TABLE 21.8** Are the Budweiser Frogs Effective Advertising? Commercial and Character Recall by Children 9 to 11 Years Old

| *Character* | *Slogan or Motto* | *% Recall (N = 221)* |
|---|---|---|
| Bugs Bunny | "Eh, what's up, Doc?" | 80 |
| Budweiser Frogs | "Bud-weis-er" | 73 |
| Tony the Tiger | "They're grrreat!" | 57 |
| Smokey the Bear | "Only you can prevent forest fires." | 43 |
| Mighty Morphin' Power Rangers | "It's morphin' time!" or "Power up!" | 39 |

SOURCE: Adapted from Leiber (1996). Copyright © American Academy of Pediatrics. Reprinted with permission.

Other studies have found that early adolescent drinkers are more likely to have been exposed to alcohol advertising, can identify more brands of beer, and view such ads more favorably than nondrinkers (Aitken, Eadie, Leathar, McNeill, & Scott, 1988).

A 1990 study of 468 randomly selected fifth and sixth graders found that 88% of them could identify Spuds Mackenzie with Bud Light beer. Their ability to name brands of beer and match slogans with the brands was significantly related to their exposure and attention to beer ads. The greater the exposure and attention, the greater the likelihood that the children would think that drinking is associated with fun and good times, not health risks, and the greater they expected to drink as an adult. Their attitudes about drinking were especially conditioned by watching weekend sports programming on TV (Wallack, Cassady, et al., 1990).

Children begin making decisions about alcohol at an early age, probably during the elementary school years (Austin & Knaus, 1998; Wallack, Cassady, et al., 1990). Studies document that the media can make children more vulnerable to future experimentation with alcohol because children and adolescents do not develop adult-type comprehension skills to deal with media messages until about the eighth grade (Collins, 1983). Exposure to beer commercials correlates with brand recognition and positive attitudes toward drinking (Aitken et al., 1988; Austin & Nach-Ferguson, 1995; Wallack, Cassady, et al., 1990), and children who enjoy alcohol advertisements are more likely to drink earlier or engage in binge drinking (Austin & Meili, 1994). Correlational studies indicate a small but positive (+0.15 to +0.20) effect between ad exposure and consumption (Atkin, 1993a). In addition, advertising seems particularly to affect initial drinking episodes, which, in turn, contribute to excessive drinking and abuse (Atkin, 1993a). As one expert concludes (Atkin, 1993a),

> The preponderance of the evidence indicates that alcohol advertising stimulates favorable predispositions, higher consumption, and greater problem drinking by young people. Nevertheless, the evidence does not support the interpretation that advertising exerts a powerful, uniform, direct influence; it seems that advertising is a contributing factor that increases drinking and related problems to a modest degree rather than a major determinant. (p. 535)

But no media research is perfect. Researchers cannot willfully expose children or adolescents to a barrage of alcohol ads and then watch who drinks or what brand of beer they choose in a laboratory setting any more than they can assess the effects of media violence by showing children violent movies and then giving them guns and knives to play with (Austin & Knaus, 1998). Most of the data are correlational (children who drink are more likely to have seen advertisements, for example, but heavy drinkers could conceivably choose to watch more ads).

Although there is always the possibility that adolescent drinkers search out or attend to alcohol advertising more than their abstinent peers, this seems considerably less likely (Atkin, 1990; Grube, 1993). As one advertising executive notes, "If greater advertising over time doesn't generate greater profits, there's something seriously wrong with the fellows who make up the budgets" (Samuelson, 1991, p. 40).

Furthermore, a few recent longitudinal studies *do* enable some important cause-and-effect inferences to be made. In an ongoing correlational study of 5th- and 6th-grade children, Grube and Wallack (1994) have found that those who are more aware of alcohol advertising have more positive beliefs about drinking and can recognize more brands and slogans. Their study is unique in that they discard a simple exposure model in favor of examining teens' beliefs and behaviors only when they have *processed and remembered* alcohol advertisements. In their work, the finding of positive beliefs is crucial because that is what leads to an increased intention to drink, even when other important factors such as parental and peer attitudes and drinking behaviors are controlled (Grube, 1999).

In another recent study by Austin and Knaus (1998) of 273 third, sixth, and ninth graders in two Washington State communities, exposure to advertising and promotional merchandise at a young age was predictive of drinking behavior during adolescence. And a study of more than 1,500 ninth-grade students in San Jose, California, over 18 months found that the onset of drinking alcohol correlated significantly with the increased viewing of both television and music videos (Robinson, Chen, & Killen, 1998). This may point to the impact of both alcohol advertising (television) and role modeling (music videos).

There is also a small but demonstrable effect of exposure to advertisements on actual drinking behavior, among both teenagers (Atkin & Block, 1983; Atkin et al., 1984) and college students (Kohn & Smart, 1984, 1987). Other research is less powerful but also suggestive. For example, note the following:

- Since 1960 in the United States, a dramatic increase in alcohol advertising expenditures has been accompanied by a 50% per capita increase in alcohol consumption (Jacobson & Collins, 1985).
- In Sweden, a mid-1970s ban on all beer and wine advertising resulted in a 20% per capita drop in alcohol consumption (Romelsjo, 1987).
- In perhaps the best ecological study, Saffer (1997) studied the correlation between alcohol advertising on television, radio, and billboards in the 75 top media markets in the United States and the motor vehicle fatality rate. He found that greater density of alcohol advertising significantly increased the fatality rate, particularly for older drivers, and hypothesized that a total ban on such advertising might save 5,000 to 10,000 lives per year.

### *Alcohol in Television Programming, Music and Music Videos, and Movies*

During the 1970s and early 1980s, alcohol was ubiquitous on American television. It was the most popular beverage consumed, and rarely were negative consequences of drinking shown or discussed (Breed & De Foe, 1981, 1984). Especially on soap operas, alcohol was depicted as being both an excellent social lubricant and an easy means of resolving serious personal crises (Lowery, 1980). Two initiatives tried to change this: new guidelines for the industry, written by the Hollywood Caucus of Producers, Writers, and Directors (Breed & De Foe, 1982; Caucus for Producers, Writers, and Directors, 1983), and the Harvard School of Public Health Alcohol Project in the late 1980s (Rothenberg, 1988).

The caucus suggested that its members avoid (a) gratuitous use of alcohol in programming, (b) glamorizing drinking, (c) showing drinking as a macho activity, and (d) depicting drinking with no serious consequences. The Harvard Alcohol Project worked with major networks and studios to foster the notion of the "designated driver," and this device appeared in many story lines during the next few years.

Unfortunately, several content analyses demonstrate that alcohol is a problem that simply will not go away on prime-time television and in music videos. In fact, alcohol remains the most frequently portrayed food or drink on network television (Mathios, Avery, Bisogni, & Shanahan, 1998). In addition, a new study by the American Academy of Pediatrics suggests that the "designated driver" concept may be failing as well. A survey of 16- to 19-year-olds by the American Academy of Pediatrics found that 80% think that drinking is acceptable as long as there is a designated driver. Unfortunately, nearly half think that designated drivers can still drink (Tanner, 1998)! These data seem to confirm the Monitoring the Future findings that one fourth of all students surveyed had ridden in a car with a drinking driver in 1997 (O'Malley & Johnston, 1999).

A 1986 content analysis was the first to suggest that alcohol was still extremely common on TV and in the movies despite the efforts of the Hollywood Caucus; 100% of theatrical or made-for-TV movies and more than 75% of all dramatic series contained some mention of it (Wallack, Grube, Madden, & Breed, 1990). Of the 16 most popular R-rated movies seen frequently by teenagers in the mid-1980s, *every* film contained alcohol use, with an average of 16 episodes per film (Greenberg, Brown, & Buerkel-Rothfuss, 1993). Much of the alcohol use portrayed in both media was unnecessary to the plot, and drinking was still presented as being problem-free. In addition, adolescent drinking is often treated in a humorous fashion, and teens frequently acknowledge a desire to drink as a symbol of adulthood (De Foe & Breed, 1988). Again, the impact of "normative drinking" must always be considered when adolescents are involved.

Several more content analyses have been done in the 1990s. Compared with earlier analyses, the first study found that the frequency of drinking episodes has remained relatively stable: 6 per hour in 1991 versus 10 per hour in 1984 and 5 per hour in 1976 (Grube, 1993). Prime-time drinkers are usually familiar, high-status characters, and more than 80% of the prime-time programs examined contained references to alcohol (Grube, 1993).

In the second study, Gerbner and Ozyegin (1997) found that alcohol remains the most commonly portrayed drug on American television, with one drinking scene occurring every 22 minutes, compared with one smoking scene every 57 minutes and illicit drug use every 112 minutes. On MTV, a viewer sees alcohol use every 14 minutes, compared with every 17 minutes in the movies and every 27 minutes on prime-time television. Popular movies are nearly equally rife with alcohol, with only 2 of the 40 highest-grossing titles not containing alcohol depictions.

The most recent study examining 200 popular films from 1996-1997 found that 93% of the movies contained alcohol depictions (Figure 21.2; Roberts et al., 1999). Although consequences of alcohol use were shown in 43% of the movies studied, only 14% depicted a refusal of an offer of alcohol, and only 9% contained antiuse sentiments (Roberts et al., 1999). A content analysis of music videos found that alcohol is portrayed in more than one fourth of videos on MTV and VH-1 (DuRant et al., 1997). In addition, alcohol was also associated with increased levels of sex and sexuality—again, not a healthy association for teens pondering when and with whom to begin having sex.

Finally, one study cites certain media use as a possible *cause* of early alcohol use. Robinson et al.'s longitudinal study (1998) of 1,533 California ninth graders found that increased television and music video viewing are risk factors for the onset of alcohol use among adolescents. Odds ratios for television ranged from 1.01 to 1.18, and for music videos from 1.17 to 1.47, both statistically significant.

Further studies are needed. In particular, the continued presence or absence of product placements in movies and television programming needs to be determined, as does the behavioral impact of drug-oriented Internet advertising on children and teenagers.

## Illicit Drugs in Television Programming, Music and Music Videos, and Movies

Although illicit drugs are not advertised as tobacco and alcohol are, they still make a major appearance in programming seen by children and adolescents. Here, music videos and movies are the primary culprits, the ideal venues for adolescents to be influenced. The average MTV viewer sees illicit drugs once every 40 minutes, compared with once every 100 minutes in the movies and every 112 minutes on prime-time TV (Gerbner & Ozyegin, 1997). Addiction is rare, and addicts are portrayed as being evil rather than ill (Gerbner & Ozyegin, 1997). In their recent study of popular movies and songs from 1996-1997, Roberts et al. (1999) found that illicit drugs appeared in 22% of movies and 18% of songs (Figure 21.2). Rap songs were far more likely to contain references to illicit drugs than were alternative rock or heavy metal songs. In movies depicting illicit drugs, marijuana appeared most frequently (51%), followed by cocaine (33%) and other drugs (12%).

Marijuana does seem to be making a major comeback in Hollywood movies, thanks to movies such as *There's Something About Mary, Bulworth, Jackie Brown,* and *Summer of Sam* (Gordinier, 1998). Cocaine is featured in *The Last Days of Disco,* Woody Allen's *Deconstructing Harry,* and Spike Lee's *Summer of Sam.* And heroin use is depicted quite graphically in both *Trainspotting* and *Permanent Midnight* (Ivry, 1998).

What impact these depictions have on children or adolescents is conjectural at best. Such research is difficult to accomplish, but, again, any media portrayals that seem to legitimize or normalize drug use are likely to have an impact, at least on susceptible teens. Clearly, far more research is needed in this crucial area.

## Solutions

In a decade when "Just Say No" has become a watchword for many parents and school-based drug prevention programs, unprecedented amounts of money are being spent in an effort to induce children and teenagers to "just say yes" to smoking and drinking. Half of all the tobacco industry's profits come from sales of cigarettes to people who first became addicted to nicotine as children and adolescents (DiFranza & Tye, 1990). As one group of researchers suggests, the "discussion [should] be *elevated* from the scientific and legal arenas to the domain of ethics and social responsibility" (Orlandi et al., 1989, p. 92, italics added). Clearly, advertising and programming are creating a demand for cigarettes and alcohol among children and teenagers.

Discussed below are 10 ideas that, if implemented, could very well result in significant reductions in adolescent drug use without having a negative impact on any writer's or producer's First Amendment rights.

1. *More research.* Media research is difficult, sometimes tedious, and often expensive. However, considering how significant the impact of the media is on young people, more media research is desperately needed, including adequate funding for such efforts. Specifically, more longitudinal analyses of adolescents' drug use compared with their media use are needed, as are studies of how teens process drug content in different media.
2. *Better dissemination of existing research.* A new surgeon general's report

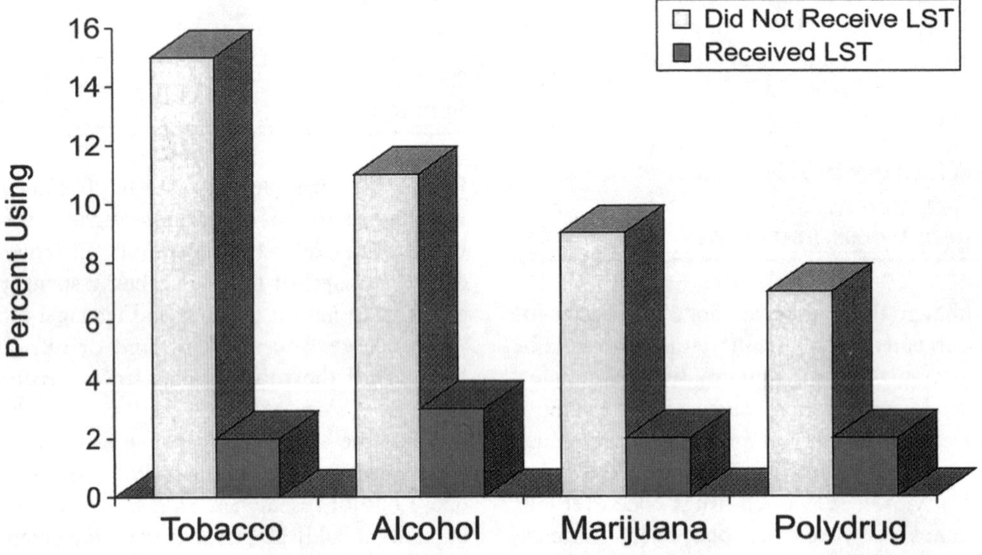


**Figure 21.7.** An LST (life skills training) approach to drug prevention has shown dramatic decreases in adolescents' use of a variety of drugs, yet has not been implemented in many communities because DARE programs already exist.

SOURCE: Copyright © Princeton Health Press.

or National Institutes of Mental Health report on television by the year 2005 would be extremely useful to researchers, health professionals, parents, and policy makers and might provide the impetus for increased funding for media research.

3. *Development of media literacy programs.* Children and teenagers must learn how to decode the subtle and not-so-subtle messages contained in television programming, advertising, movies, and music videos. Parents need to begin this process when their children are young (ages 2-3 years), but school programs may be extremely useful as well. In particular, certain drug prevention programs have been extremely effective in reducing levels of adolescents' drug use (see Figure 21.7), but such programs must go far beyond the DARE (Drug Abuse Resistance Education) approach to include media literacy, peer resistance skills, and social skills building (National Institute on Drug Abuse, 1997; Schinke & Botvin, 1999).

The United States is unique among Western nations in not requiring some form of media literacy for its students (AAP, 1999). Preliminary studies indicate that successful drug prevention may be accomplishable through this unique route (Austin & Johnson, 1997). However, increased media literacy is not a substitute for necessary changes in television and movie programming.

**Figure 21.8.** One example of a "tombstone" ad for an alcoholic beverage. Such advertising is limited to the inherent qualities of the product rather than the qualities the imbiber will "magically" acquire if he or she consumes the product.

4. *A ban on cigarette advertising in* all *media and the restriction of alcohol advertising to "tombstone ads" in all media.* American society pays a high price

**Figure 21.9a.** Two examples of dramatic counteradvertising. The questions are does such advertising work (e.g., appeal to teenagers), and can it compete with the current density of mainstream advertising and drug content on TV and in movies? While MADD clearly targets alcohol, the Office of National Drug Control Policy has yet to target either tobacco or alcohol.

for allowing tobacco and alcohol manufacturers unlimited access to children and adolescents, and the connection between advertising and consumption is significant. Any product as harmful as tobacco should have severe restrictions placed on it. Whether the recently negotiated tobacco settlement (see Table 21.5) will successfully accomplish this remains to be seen. In alcohol advertising, tombstone ads involve showing the "purity" of the product only, not all of the qualities that the purchaser will magically gain by consuming it (see Figure 21.8). Such restrictions have already been endorsed by the Federal Drug Administration, the surgeon general, the American Academy of Pediatrics, and the American Medical Association and would address the deceptive and alluring quality of current advertisements (Strasburger, 1993).

5. *More aggressive counteradvertising.* Counteradvertising can be effective, but only if it is intensive, is well planned and coordinated, and uses a variety of media (see Figure 21.9; Bauman, LaPrelle, Brown, Koch, & Padgett, 1991). To be truly effective, counteradvertising must approach both the occurrence rate and the attractiveness of regular advertising (Grube & Wallack, 1994). Some researchers speculate that the decrease in adolescent smoking in the mid- to late 1970s may be attributable to a very aggressive, pre-ban counteradvertising campaign in which one public service announcement (PSA) aired for every three to five cigarette ads (Atkin, 1993b; Brown & Walsh-Childers, 1994; Madden & Grube, 1994; Wallack, Dorfman, Jernigan, & Themba, 1993). Unfortunately, part of the agreement that the tobacco companies made in accepting a ban on smoking ads was that antismoking ads would be eliminated as well (Gerbner, 1990).

Advertisement

# ⊙TRUTH.

## THE ANTI-DRUG.

The most effective deterrent to drug use among kids **isn't the police, or prisons, or politicians.** One of the most effective deterrents to drug use among kids is their parents. Kids who learn about the risks of drugs from their parents are **36% less likely to smoke marijuana** than kids who learn nothing from them. They are 50% less likely to use inhalants. 56% less likely to use cocaine. 65% less likely to use LSD. So if you're a parent, talk to your kids about drugs. Research also shows that 74% of all fourth graders **wish their parents would talk to them about drugs.** If you don't know what to say, visit www.theantidrug.com. We can help you.

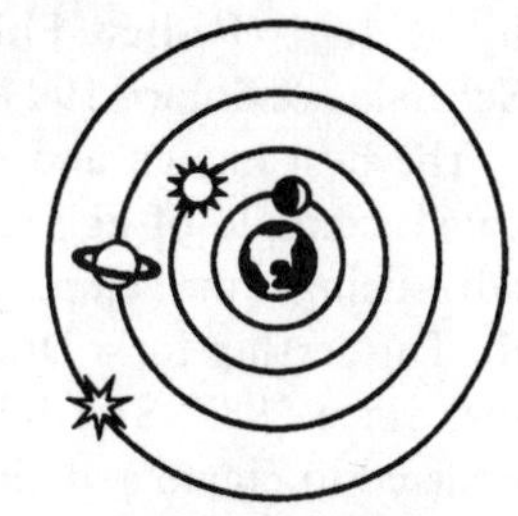

The Geocentric System

Five hundred years ago, the sun was thought to revolve around the earth. People did not know then what we know now. Truths change. We now know smoking marijuana is harmful. The younger you are, the more harmful it may be. Research has shown that people who smoke marijuana before the age of 15 were over 7 times more likely to use other drugs than people who have never smoked marijuana.

Illegal drugs are estimated to cost America over $110 billion each year in treatment, enforcement, incarceration and social damage. **But what else could you buy for $110 billion?** Well, you could build 169 new hospitals. Or 687 new universities. Or operate 366 national parks. You could hire 278,481 new high school teachers. And 400,947 more clerks at the post office. Or you could put 75,862 new buses on the road. You could send KISS on tour to every major city in America and give everyone a free ticket. This message is brought to you by the Office of National Drug Control Policy/Partnership for a Drug-Free America®

**Figure 21.9b.**

Currently, the density of public service announcements about alcohol has never remotely approached that of regular advertisements; the production values are also not comparable. Of the 685 total alcohol ads examined in one recent content analysis, only 3 contained messages about moderation and another 10 involved very brief public service announcements (e.g., "Know when to say when") (Madden & Grube, 1994). In another study of 1 week of television commercials from 1990, commercials promoting legal drugs and alcohol outnumbered network news stories and PSAs about illegal drugs by 45 to 1 (Fedler, Phillips, Raker, Schefsky, & Soluri, 1994).

The best-known and most sophisticated example of aggressive counter-advertising is the campaign mounted by the Partnership for a Drug-Free America. Since 1987, $1.1 billion has been donated to create and air 375 antidrug public service announcements (Partnership for a Drug-Free America, 1992). In a recent study of nearly 1,000 public school students ages 11 to 19, more than 80% recalled exposure to such ads, and half of the students who had tried drugs reported that the ads convinced them to decrease or stop using them (Reis, Duggan, Adger, & DeAngelis, 1992). Unfortunately, to date, not a single ad has aired dealing with either tobacco or alcohol.

6. *Use of MTV and VH-1 as excellent, specific media for targeting older children and adolescents with prosocial health messages about smoking, drinking, and drug use.*
7. *Increased sensitivity on the part of the entertainment industry to the health-related issues of smoking, drinking, and other drug use in television programming, music videos, and movies.* A few programs popular with teens, including *Beverly Hills, 90210* and after-school specials, have taken the lead in this area, but soap operas, MTV and VH-1, and movies need to follow their example. Cigarette smoking should not be used as a shortcut to dramatize the rebelliousness of a character, nor should alcohol be used to resolve crises. In addition, rock music lyrics should avoid glamorizing drinking or drug use (AAP, 1995).
8. *Reassessment of the "designated driver" campaign.* Is it working, or do teenagers misunderstand it (Tanner, 1998)? Many public health experts question whether this campaign does not give everyone else accompanying the designated driver permission to drink excessively (Wallack, Cassady, et al., 1990).
9. *Revision of the ratings systems for both television and movies.* The current television ratings are not specific enough regarding content (Strasburger & Donnerstein, 1999) and lack any descriptors to denote drug use. Several studies show that parents would prefer a more specific, content-based system (Borgman, 1996; "The Ratings Wars," 1996). The movie ratings system, originally developed by Jack Valenti in the mid-1960s, has not been revised since that time and tends to be overly skewed toward sexual content rather than violence or depictions of drug use.
10. *Campaign finance reform in Congress.* This recommendation may seem strange in a chapter about the effects of media on young people, but three major industries arguably control much of what is media-related in Congress—the National Rifle Association (NRA), the beer and wine manufacturers, and the tobacco manufacturers—and none has the best interests of the nation's children at heart. Congress can control the media, but until it is liberated from its obligations to these special inter-

est groups (Hitt, 1999), American media will remain unhealthy for young people.

## References


Aitken, P. P., & Eadie, D. R. (1990). Reinforcing effects of cigarette advertising on under-age smoking. *British Journal of Addiction, 85,* 399-412.

Aitken, P. P., Eadie, D. R., Leathar, D. S., McNeill, R. E. J., & Scott, A. C. (1988). Television advertisements for alcoholic drinks do reinforce under-age drinking. *British Journal of Addiction, 83,* 1399-1419.

Altman, D. G., Levine, D. W., Coeytaux, R., Slade, J., & Jaffe, R. (1996). Tobacco promotion and susceptibility to tobacco use among adolescents aged 12 through 17 years in a nationally representative sample. *American Journal of Public Health, 86,* 1590-1593.

American Academy of Pediatrics, Committee on Communications. (1999). Media literacy [Policy statement]. *Pediatrics, 104,* 341-343.

American Academy of Pediatrics, Committee on Substance Abuse. (1995). Alcohol use and abuse: A pediatric concern [Policy statement]. *Pediatrics, 95,* 439-442.

Amos, A., Jacobson, B., & White, P. (1991). Cigarette advertising and coverage of smoking and health in British women's magazines. *Lancet, 337,* 93-96.

Armstrong, B. K., de Klerk, N. H., Shean, R. E., Dunn, D. A., & Dolin, P. J. (1990). Influence of education and advertising on the uptake of smoking by children. *Medical Journal of Australia, 152,* 117-124.

Atkin, C. K. (1990). Effects of televised alcohol messages on teenage drinking patterns. *Journal of Adolescent Health Care, 11,* 10-24.

Atkin, C. K. (1993a). Alcohol advertising and adolescents. *Adolescent Medicine: State of the Art Reviews, 4,* 527-542.

Atkin, C. K. (1993b, Winter). On regulating broadcast alcohol advertising. *Journal of Broadcasting & Electronic Media,* pp. 107-113.

Atkin, C. K. (1994). Survey and experimental research on effects of alcohol advertising. In S. Martin (Ed.), *Mass media and the use and abuse of alcohol.* Rockville, MD: National Institute on Alcohol Abuse and Alcoholism.

Atkin, C. K., & Block, M. (1983). Effectiveness of celebrity endorsers. *Journal of Advertising Research, 23,* 57-61.

Atkin, C. K., DeJong, W., & Wallack, L. (1992). *The influence of responsible drinking TV spots and automobile commercials on young drivers.* Washington, DC: AAA Foundation for Traffic Safety.

Atkin, C. K., Hocking, J., & Block, M. (1984). Teenage drinking: Does advertising make a difference? *Journal of Communications, 28,* 71-80.

Atkin, C. K., Neuendorf, K., & McDermott, S. (1983). The role of alcohol advertising in excessive and hazardous drinking. *Journal of Drug Education, 13,* 313-325.

Austin, E. W., & Johnson, K. K. (1997). Effects of general and alcohol-specific media literacy training on children's decision making about alcohol. *Journal of Health Communication, 2,* 17-42.

Austin, E. W., & Knaus, C. (1998). *Predicting future risky behavior among those "too young" to drink as the result of advertising desirability.* Paper presented at the meeting of the Association for Education in Journalism and Mass Communication, Baltimore, MD.

Austin, E. W., & Meili, H. K. (1994). Effects of interpretations of televised alcohol portrayals on children's alcohol beliefs. *Journal of Broadcasting & Electronic Media, 38,* 417-435.

Austin, E. W., & Nach-Ferguson, B. (1995). Sources and influences of young school-age children's general and brand-specific knowledge about alcohol. *Health Communication, 4,* 545-564.

Bauman, K. E., LaPrelle, J., Brown, J. D., Koch, G. G., & Padgett, C. A. (1991). The influence of three mass media campaigns on variables related to adolescent cigarette smoking: Results of a field experiment. *American Journal of Public Health, 81,* 597-604.

Belcher, H. M. E., & Shinitzky, H. E. (1998). Substance abuse in children: Prediction, protection, and prevention. *Archives of Pediatric and Adolescent Medicine, 152,* 952-960.

Bennett, E. M., & Kemper, K. J. (1994). Is abuse during childhood a risk factor for developing substance abuse problems as an adult? *Journal of Developmental & Behavioral Pediatrics, 15,* 426-429.

Block, J., Block, J., & Keyes, S. (1988). Longitudinally foretelling drug use in adolescence: Early childhood personality and environmental precursors. *Child Development, 59,* 336-355.

Borgman, L. (1996, December 5). Proposed TV ratings lack labels that parents can use. *Albuquerque Journal,* p. B6.

Breed, W., & De Foe, J. R. (1981). The portrayal of the drinking process on prime-time television. *Journal of Communications, 31,* 58-67.

Breed, W., & De Foe, J. R. (1982). Effecting media change: The role of cooperative consultation on alcohol topics. *Journal of Communications, 32,* 88-99.

Breed, W., & De Foe, J. R. (1983). Cigarette smoking on television: 1950-1982 [Letter]. *New England Journal of Medicine, 309,* 617.

Breed, W., & De Foe, J. R. (1984). Drinking and smoking on television 1950-1982. *Journal of Public Health Policy, 31,* 257-270.

Brown, J. D., & Schulze, L. (1990). The effects of race, gender, and fandom on audience interpretations of Madonna's music videos. *Journal of Communication, 40,* 88-102.

Brown, J. D., & Walsh-Childers, K. (1994). Effects of media on personal and public health. In J. Bryant & D. Zillmann (Eds.), *Media effects: Advances in theory and research* (pp. 389-415). Hillsdale, NJ: Lawrence Erlbaum.

Caucus for Producers, Writers, and Directors. (1983). *We've done some thinking.* Santa Monica, CA: Television Academy of Arts and Sciences.

Center for Science in the Public Interest. (1988, September 4). *Kids are as aware of booze as president, survey finds* [News release]. Washington, DC: Author.

Center for Substance Abuse Prevention, Centers for Disease Control, and American Academy of Pediatrics. (1997). *MediaSharp: Analyzing tobacco and alcohol messages* [Leader's guide]. Washington, DC: Center for Substance Abuse Prevention.

Centers for Disease Control. (1992a). Accessibility of cigarettes to youths aged 12-17 years: United States, 1989. *Morbidity and Mortality Weekly Report, 41,* 485-488.

Centers for Disease Control. (1992b). Comparison of the cigarette brand preferences of adult and teenaged smokers: United States, 1989, and 10 U.S. communities, 1988 and 1990. *Morbidity and Mortality Weekly Report, 41,* 169-181.

Centers for Disease Control. (1994). Changes in the cigarette brand preferences of adolescent smokers: United States, 1989-1993. *Morbidity and Mortality Weekly Report, 43,* 577.

Chilcoat, H. D., & Anthony, J. C. (1996). Impact of parent monitoring on initiation of drug use through late childhood. *Journal of the American Academy of Child & Adolescent Psychiatry, 35,* 91-100.

Collins, W. A. (1983). Interpretation and inference in children's television viewing. In J. Bryant & D. R. Anderson (Eds.), *Children's understanding of television: Research on attention and comprehension.* New York: Academic Press.

Comerci, G. D., & Schwebel, R. (2000). Substance abuse: An overview. *Adolescent Medicine: State of the Art Reviews, 11,* 79-101.

Comings, D. E. (1997). Genetic aspects of childhood behavioral disorders. *Child Psychiatry & Human Development, 27,* 139-150.

Consumer Reports. (1990, August). Selling to children. *Consumer Reports,* pp. 518-520.

De Foe, J. R., & Breed, W. (1988). Youth and alcohol in television stories, with suggestions to the industry for alternative portrayals. *Adolescence, 23,* 533-550.

DeJong, W. (1996). When the tobacco industry controls the news: KKR, RJR Nabisco, and the Weekly Reader Corporation. *Tobacco Control, 5,* 142-148.

DiFranza, J. R., Richards, J. W., Jr., Paulman, P. M., Fletcher, C., & Jaffe, R. D. (1992). Tobacco: Promotion and smoking [Letter]. *Journal of the American Medical Association, 267,* 3282-3284.

DiFranza, J. R., Richards, J. W., Paulman, P. M., Wolf-Gillespie, N., Fletcher, C., Jaffe, R. D., & Murray, D. (1991). RJR Nabisco's cartoon camel promotes Camel cigarettes to children. *Journal of the American Medical Association, 266,* 3149-3153.

DiFranza, J. R., & Tye, J. B. (1990). Who profits from tobacco sales to children? *Journal of the American Medical Association, 263,* 2784-2787.

Doyle, R. (1996, December). Deaths due to alcohol. *Scientific American, 6,* 30-31.

DuRant, R. H., Rome, E. S., Rich, M., Allred, E., Emans, S. J., & Woods, E. R. (1997). Tobacco and alcohol use behaviors portrayed in music videos: A content analysis. *American Journal of Public Health, 87,* 1131-1135.

Evans, N., Farkas, A., Gilpin, E., Berry, C., & Pierce, J. P. (1995). Influence of tobacco marketing and exposure to smokers on adolescent susceptibility to smoking. *Journal of the National Cancer Institute, 87,* 1538-1545.

Fedler, F., Phillips, M., Raker, P., Schefsky, D., & Soluri, J. (1994). Network commercials promote legal drugs: Outnumber anti-drug PSAs 45-to-1. *Journal of Drug Education, 24,* 291-302.

Fischer, P. M., Schwart, M. P., Richards, J. W., Goldstein, A. O., & Rojas, T. H. (1991). Brand logo recognition by children aged 3 to 6 years: Mickey Mouse and Old Joe the Camel. *Journal of the American Medical Association, 266,* 3145-3153.

Friedman, H., Termini, S., & Washington, R. (1977). The effectiveness of advertisements utilizing four types of endorsers. *Journal of Advertising, 6,* 22-24.

Gerbner, G. (1990). Stories that hurt: Tobacco, alcohol, and other drugs in the mass media. In H. Resnik (Ed.), *Youth and drugs: Society's mixed messages* (OSAP Prevention Monograph No. 6, pp. 53-129). Rockville, MD: Office for Substance Abuse Prevention.

Gerbner, G., & Ozyegin, N. (1997, March 20). *Alcohol, tobacco, and illicit drugs in entertainment television, commercials, news, "reality shows," movies, and music channels* [Report from the Robert Wood Johnson Foundation]. Princeton, NJ: Robert Wood Johnson Foundation.

Goldman, L. K., & Glantz, S. A. (1998). Evaluation of antismoking advertising campaigns. *Journal of the American Medical Association, 279,* 772-777.

Goldstein, A. O., Fischer, P. M., Richards, J. W., Jr., & Creten, D. (1987). Relationship between high school student smoking and recognition of cigarette advertisements. *Journal of Pediatrics, 110,* 488-491.

Goldstein, A. O., Sobel, R. A., & Newman, G. R. (1999). Tobacco and alcohol use in G-rated children's animated films. *Journal of the American Medical Association, 281,* 1131-1136.

Gordinier, J. (1998, January 30). High anxiety. *Entertainment Weekly,* p. 18.

Gostin, L. O., & Brandt, A. M. (1993). Criteria for evaluating a ban on the advertisement of cigarettes. *Journal of the American Medical Association, 269,* 904-909.

Greenberg, B. S., Brown, J. D., & Buerkel-Rothfuss, N. (1993). *Media, sex, and the adolescent.* Cresskill, NJ: Hampton Press.

Grube, J. W. (1993). Alcohol portrayals and alcohol advertising on television. *Alcohol Health & Research World, 17,* 61-66.

Grube, J. W. (1995). Television alcohol portrayals, alcohol advertising, and alcohol expectances among children and adolescents. In S. E. Martin (Ed.), *The effects of the mass media on use and abuse of alcohol* (pp. 105-121). Bethesda, MD: National Institute on Alcohol Abuse and Alcoholism.

Grube, J. W. (1999). Alcohol advertising and alcohol consumption: A review of recent research. In *NIAA tenth special report to Congress on alcohol and health.* Bethesda, MD: National Institute on Alcohol Abuse and Alcoholism.

Grube, J., & Wallack, L. (1994). Television beer advertising and drinking knowledge, beliefs, and intentions among schoolchildren. *American Journal of Public Health, 84,* 254-259.

Hazan, A. R., & Glantz, S. A. (1995). Current trends in tobacco use on prime-time fictional television. *American Journal of Public Health, 85,* 116-117.

Hazan, A. R., Lipton, H. L., & Glantz, S. A. (1994). Popular films do not reflect current tobacco use. *American Journal of Public Health, 84,* 998-1000.

Hitt, J. (1999, July 25). Real campaign-finance reform. *New York Times Magazine,* pp. 36-37.

Ile, M. L., & Knoll, L. A. (1990). Tobacco advertising and the First Amendment. *Journal of the American Medical Association, 264,* 1593-1594.

Institute of Medicine. (1994). *Growing up tobacco free: Preventing nicotine addiction in children and youths.* Washington, DC: Author.

Ivry, B. (1998, August 28). Use of drugs is rising dramatically on the big screen. *Albuquerque Journal,* p. B4.

Jackson, D. Z. (1998, November 23). Big tobacco's chump change. *Boston Globe.*

Jacobson, M. F., & Collins, R. (1985, March 10). There's too much harm to let beer, wine ads continue. *Los Angeles Times.*

Jessor, R., & Jessor, S. L. (1977). *Problem behavior and psychological development: A longitudinal study of youth.* New York: Academic Press.

Johnston, L. D., O'Malley, P. M., & Bachman, J. G. (1994). *National survey results on drug use from the Monitoring the Future Study, 1975-1993.* Washington, DC: National Institute on Drug Abuse.

Johnston, L. D., O'Malley, P. M., & Bachman, J. G. (1998, December 18). *Monitoring the Future, 1998 data* [Press release]. Ann Arbor: University of Michigan.

Kessler, D. A., Wilkenfeld, J. P., & Thompson, L. J. (1997). The Food and Drug Administration's rule on tobacco: Blending science and law. *Pediatrics, 99,* 884-887.

Kessler, L. (1989). Women's magazines coverage of smoking related health hazards. *Journalism Quarterly, 66,* 316-323.

Kilbourne, J. (1991). *Media & Values, 54/55,* 10-12.

Kilbourne, J. (1993). Killing us softly: Gender roles in advertising. *Adolescent Medicine: State of the Art Reviews, 4,* 635-649.

Kilbourne, J. E., Painton, S., & Ridley, D. (1985). The effect of sexual embedding on responses to magazine advertisements. *Journal of Advertising, 14,* 48-56.

King, C., III, Siegel, M., Celebucki, C., & Connolly, G. N. (1998). Adolescent exposure to cigarette advertising in magazines. *Journal of the American Medical Association, 279,* 516-520.

Klitzner, M., Gruenewald, P. J., & Bamberger, E. (1991). Cigarette advertising and adolescent experimentation with smoking. *British Journal of Addiction, 86,* 287-298.

Kohn, P. M., & Smart, R. G. (1984). The impact of television advertising on alcohol consumption: An experiment. *Journal of Studies on Alcohol, 45,* 295-301.

Kohn, P. M., & Smart, R. G. (1987). Wine, women, suspiciousness, and advertising. *Journal of Studies on Alcohol, 48,* 161-166.

Laugesen, M., & Meads, C. (1991). Tobacco advertising restrictions, price, income, and tobacco consumption in OECD countries, 1960-1986. *British Journal of Addiction, 86,* 1343-1354.

Lee, W. (1999, November 5). Nothing but Net. *Entertainment Weekly,* pp. 8-9.

Leiber, L. (1996). Commercial and character slogan recall by children aged 9 to 11 years: Budweiser frogs versus Bugs Bunny. Berkeley, CA: Center on Alcohol Advertising.

Lipman, J. (1991, August 21). Alcohol firms put off public. *Wall Street Journal,* p. B1.

Lowery, S. A. (1980). Soap and booze in the afternoon: An analysis of the portrayal of alcohol use in daytime serials. *Journal of Studies on Alcohol, 41,* 829-838.

Mackay, J. (1999). International aspects of US government tobacco bills. *Journal of the American Medical Association, 281,* 1849-1850.

MacKenzie, T. D., Bartecchi, C. E., & Schrier, R. W. (1994). The human costs of tobacco use, part 2. *New England Journal of Medicine, 30,* 975-980.

Madden, P. A., & Grube, J. W. (1994). The frequency and nature of alcohol and tobacco advertising in televised sports, 1990 through 1992. *American Journal of Public Health, 84,* 297-299.

Mathios, A., Avery, R., Bisogni, C., & Shanahan, J. (1998). Alcohol portrayal on prime-time television: Manifest and latent messages. *Journal of Studies on Alcohol, 59,* 305-310.

McKeganey, N., Forsyth, A., Barnard, M., & Hay, G. (1996). Designer drinks and drunkenness amongst a sample of Scottish school-children. *British Medical Journal, 313,* 401.

McMahon, R. L. (1994). Diagnosis, assessment, and treatment of externalizing problems in children: The role of longitudinal data. *Journal of Consulting & Clinical Psychology, 62,* 901-917.

Miller, P. M., & Plant, M. (1996). Drinking, smoking, and illicit drug use among 15 and 16 year olds in the United Kingdom. *British Medical Journal, 313,* 394-397.

Moog, C. (1991). The selling of addiction to women. *Media & Values, 54/55,* 20-22.

National Institute on Drug Abuse. (1995). *Drug use among racial/ethnic minorities 1995* (NIH Publication No. 95-3888). Rockville, MD: Author.

National Institute on Drug Abuse. (1997). *Preventing drug use among children and adolescents: A research-based guide* (NIH Publication No. 97-4212). Rockville, MD: Author.

National Science Foundation. (1977). *Research on the effects of television advertising on children: A review of the literature and recommendations for future research.* Washington, DC: Author.

O'Malley, P. M., & Johnston, L. D. (1999). Drinking and driving among U.S. high school seniors, 1984-1997. *American Journal of Public Health, 89,* 678-684.

Orlandi, M. A., Lieberman, L. R., & Schinke, S. P. (1989). The effects of alcohol and tobacco advertising on adolescents. In M. A. Orlandi, L. R. Lieberman, & S. P. Schinke (Eds.), *Perspectives on adolescent drug use* (pp. 77-97). Binghamton, NY: Haworth Press.

Partnership for a Drug-Free America. (1992). *1987-1991 survey findings.* New York: Author.

Peto, R., Lopez, A. D., Boreham, J., Thun, M., & Heath, C., Jr. (1992). Mortality from tobacco in developed countries: Indirect estimation from national vital statistics. *Lancet, 339,* 1268-1278.

Pierce, J. P., Choi, W. S., Gilpin, E. A., Farkas, A. J., & Berry, C. (1998). Industry promotion of cigarettes and adolescent smoking. *Journal of the American Medical Association, 279,* 511-515.

Pierce, J. P., Gilpin, E., Burns, D. M., Whalen, E., Rosbrook, B., Shopland, D., & Johnson, M. (1991). Does tobacco advertising target young people to start smoking? *Journal of the American Medical Association, 266,* 3154-3158.

Pierce, J. P., Lee, L., & Gilpin, E. A. (1994). Smoking initiation by adolescent girls, 1944 through 1988: An association with targeted advertising. *Journal of the American Medical Association, 271,* 608-611.

Pollay, R. W., Siddarth, S., Siegel, M., Haddix, A., Merritt, R. K., Giovino, G. A., & Eriksen, M. P. (1996). The last straw? Cigarette advertising and realized market shares among youth and adults, 1979-1993. *Journal of Marketing, 50,* 1-7.

Postman, N., Nystrom, C., Strate, L., & Weingartner, C. (1988). *Myths, men, and beer: An analysis of beer commercials on broadcast television, 1987.* Washington, DC: AAA Foundation for Traffic Safety.

The ratings wars [Editorial]. (1996, December 15). *New York Times,* p. E12.

Rauzi, R. (1998, June 9). The teen factor: Today's media-savvy youths influence what others are seeing and hearing. *Los Angeles Times.*

Reis, E. C., Duggan, A. K., Adger, H., & DeAngelis, C. (1992). The impact of anti-drug advertising on youth substance abuse [Abstract]. *American Journal of Diseases of Children, 146,* 519.

Resnick, M. D., Bearman, P. S., Blum, R. W., Bauman, K. E., Harris, K. M., Jones, J., Tabor, J., Beuhring, T., Sieving, R. E., Shew, M., Ireland, M., Bearinger, L. H., & Udry, J. R. (1997). Protecting adolescents from harm: Findings from the National Longitudinal Study on Adolescent Health. *Journal of the American Medical Association, 278,* 823-832.

Richardson, J. L., Dwyer, K., McGuigan, K., Hansen, W. B., Dent, C., Johnson, C. A., Sussman, S. Y., Brannon, B., & Flay, B. (1989). Substance use among eighth grade students who take care of themselves after school. *Pediatrics, 84,* 556-566.

Roberts, D. F., Henriksen, L., & Christenson, P. G. (1999). *Substance use in popular movies and music.* Washington, DC: Office of National Drug Control Policy.

Robin, S. S., & Johnson, E. O. (1996). Attitude and peer cross pressure: Adolescent drug and alcohol use. *Journal of Drug Education, 26,* 69-99.

Robinson, T. N., Chen, H. L., & Killen, J. D. (1998). Television and music video exposure and risk of adolescent alcohol use. *Pediatrics, 102,* e54.

Romelsjo, A. (1987). Decline in alcohol-related problems in Sweden greatest among young people. *British Journal of Addiction, 82,* 1111-1124.

Rothenberg, G. (1988, August 31). TV industry plans fight against drunken driving. *New York Times.*

Saffer, H. (1997). Alcohol advertising and motor vehicle fatalities. *Review of Economics and Statistics, 79,* 431-442.

Samuelson, R. J. (1991, August 19). The end of advertising? *Newsweek,* p. 40.

Sargent, J. D., Dalton, M. A., Beach, M., Bernhardt, A., Pullin, D., & Stevens, M. (1997). Cigarette promotional items in public schools. *Archives of Pediatric & Adolescent Medicine, 151,* 1189-1196.

Schinke, S. P., & Botvin, G. J. (1999). Life skills training: A prevention program that works. *Contemporary Pediatrics, 16,* 108-117.

Schooler, C., Feighery, E., & Flora, J. A. (1996). Seventh graders' self-reported exposure to cigarette marketing and its relationship to their smoking behavior. *American Journal of Public Health, 86,* 1216-1221.

Schydlower, M., & Rogers, P. D. (Eds.). (1993). Adolescent substance abuse and addictions. *Adolescent Medicine: State of the Art Reviews, 4,* 227-477.

Shiffrin, S. H. (1993). Alcohol and cigarette advertising: A legal primer. *Adolescent Medicine: State of the Art Reviews, 4,* 623-634.

Signorielli, N. (1990). Television and health: Images and impact. In C. Atkin & L. Wallack (Eds.), *Mass communication and public health* (pp. 96-113). Newbury Park, CA: Sage.

Smith, G. (1989). The effects of tobacco advertising on children. *British Journal of Addiction, 84,* 1275-1277.

Stockwell, T. F., & Glantz, S. A. (1997). Tobacco use is increasing in popular films. *Tobacco Control, 6,* 282-284.

Strasburger, V. C. (1993). Adolescents, drugs, and the media. *Adolescent Medicine: State of the Art Reviews, 4,* 391-415.

Strasburger, V. C. (1997). "Sex, drugs, rock 'n' roll": Are the media responsible for adolescent behavior? *Adolescent Medicine: State of the Art Reviews, 8*(3), 403-414.

Strasburger, V. C. (1998). Adolescents, drugs, and the media [Letter]. *Archives of Pediatric & Adolescent Medicine, 153,* 313.

Strasburger, V. C., & Donnerstein, E. (1999). Children, adolescents, and the media: Issues and solutions. *Pediatrics, 103,* 129-139.

Tanner, L. (1998, September 30). Many teens think designated drivers still can drink [Associated Press]. *Albuquerque Journal,* p. A3.

Thomas, K. (1996, November 7). Lighting up: Tobacco has a role in most movies. *USA Today,* p. D1.

Tobacco's toll [Editorial]. (1992). *Lancet, 339,* 1267.

U.S. Department of Health and Human Services. (1994). *Preventing tobacco use among young people: Report of the surgeon general.* Washington, DC: U.S. Government Printing Office.

Vaidya, S. G., Naik, U. D., & Vaidya, J. S. (1996). Effects of sports sponsorship by tobacco companies on children's experimentation with tobacco. *British Medical Journal, 313,* 400-416.

Vickers, A. (1992). Why cigarette advertising should be banned. *British Medical Journal, 304,* 1195-1196.

Wallack, L., Cassady, D., & Grube, J. (1990). *TV beer commercials and children: Exposure, attention, beliefs, and expectations about drinking as an adult.* Washington, DC: AAA Foundation for Traffic Safety.

Wallack, L., Dorfman, L., Jernigan, D., & Themba, M. (1993). *Media advocacy and public health.* Newbury Park, CA: Sage.

Wallack, L., Grube, J. W., Madden, P. A., & Breed, W. (1990). Portrayals of alcohol on prime-time television. *Journal of Studies on Alcohol, 51,* 428-437.

Warner, K. E., Goldenhar, L. M., & McLaughlin, C. G. (1992). Cigarette advertising and magazine coverage of the hazards of smoking. *New England Journal of Medicine, 326,* 305-309.

Wechsler, H., Rigotti, N. A., Gledhill-Hoyt, J., & Lee, H. (1998). Increased levels of cigarette use among college students. *Journal of the American Medical Association, 280,* 1673-1678.

Weinstein, H. (1998, January 15). Papers: RJR went for teens. *Los Angeles Times,* p. A1.

While, D., Kelly, S., Huang, W., & Charlton, A. (1996). Cigarette advertising and onset of smoking in children: Questionnaire survey. *British Medical Journal, 313,* 398-399.

Wiencke, J. K., Thurston, S. W., Kelsey, K. T., Varkonyi, A., Wain, J. C., Mark, E. J., & Christiani, D. C. (1999). Early age at smoking initiation and tobacco carcinogen DNA damage in the lung. *Journal of the National Cancer Institute, 91,* 614-619.

CHAPTER **22**

# Television Food Advertising

## Targeting Children in a Toxic Environment

KATHERINE BATTLE HORGEN
Yale University

MOLLY CHOATE
Boston University

KELLY D. BROWNELL
Yale University

An Australian study reported that more than half of 9- to 10-year-old children believe that Ronald McDonald knows best what is good for children to eat (Food Commission, 1997). This occurs at a time when the World Health Organization (WHO, 1998) notes that rates of obesity are increasing at an alarming pace in both children and adults. Readily available, inexpensive, unhealthy foods are a major contributor to obesity (Hill & Peters, 1998). If unhealthy foods are the wares of a toxic food environment, advertising is the peddler. Given the impact of diet on health and happiness, it is unfortunate how little oversight there is of food advertising, especially considering the documented impact of advertising on attitudes and eating. This chapter will review the impact of advertising on diet and make policy recommendations for monitoring advertising practices directed at children.

### Advertising Pervasiveness

Americans spend time watching television instead of being physically active. The average adult watches 1,567 hours of television each year, about 4 hours per day for men and 4.5 hours per day for women. In 1997, the average teen watched 2 hours and 54 minutes per day, and the average child saw 3 hours and 3 minutes of television each day (Television Bureau of Advertising, 1998). Some estimates of the amount of television that children watch are even greater, averaging up to 3.6 hours per day (Avery, Mathios, Shanahan, & Bisogni, 1997). "The typical child spends more time watching television than doing anything else except sleeping and adolescents spend more time watching television each year than they do in school" (Avery et al., 1997, p. 217).

As Americans watch large amounts of television, they are also exposed to massive amounts of advertising. During the 1998 November sweeps, the major television networks averaged between 8.5 and 10.3 minutes of commercial advertising per programming hour (Consoli, 1999). Twenty-four of the top 100 advertising campaigns of the twentieth century endorsed food products (Klein & Donaton, 1999b).

Food advertising is central to the networks' budgets. The food industry invests billions of dollars to ensure that its products are well publicized. In 1997, advertisers spent $1.4 billion to promote the "food and food products" category on network TV. Advertising spending on the "restaurants and drive-ins" category followed at $1.2 billion (Television Bureau of Advertising, 1998).

Food advertising is also a major player in nationally syndicated television, with $369 million spent in 1997. Soft drinks such as Coke, Pepsi, and Kool-Aid; snacks such as potato chips, Doritos, and Cheez-Its; and confectionery goods such as Snickers, Starbursts, and Pop-Tarts ranked fourth in spending, with $235 million. Restaurants and drive-ins were fifth with $144 million. Restaurants and drive-ins also topped the list of local TV advertisers. In 1997, advertisers paid $1.3 billion to promote this segment of the food industry. This was more than double the spending of auto dealers, who took the number-two slot with $455 million. Food stores and supermarkets ranked fifth with $336 million for local ads in 1997 (Television Bureau of Advertising, 1998).

Not only is the multi-billion-dollar food advertising industry widely seen, it is also widely believed. Fifty-two percent of the adult population perceived television as the most authoritative advertising medium in a 1995 survey, followed by newspapers at only 26%. Seventy-seven percent of the public endorsed TV as the most exciting medium, 80% found it the most influential, and 40% regarded it as the most believable, followed by newspapers, magazines, and radio (Television Bureau of Advertising, 1998). The pervasive advertising on television is accepted as an exciting and influential source of information.

The typically sedentary lifestyle of many Americans is a second contributor to rising rates of obesity (Kuczmarski, Flegal, Campbell, & Johnson, 1994). The combination of easy access to unhealthy foods and the sedentary American lifestyle is a recipe for obesity.

## Targeting Children

Clearly, television advertising affects adults. Its potential influence on children is even more powerful, because children are less likely to look at media images with a critical eye (Martin, 1997). The average child sees more than 20,000 TV commercials in a year, viewing 1 hour of advertising for every 5 hours of television watched (Center for Media Education, 1998). Among ads targeted at children, food is one of the two largest categories, the other being toys (Williams, Achterberg, & Sylvester, 1993). During Saturday morning cartoons, children view an average of one food commercial every 5 minutes. An analysis of 52 hours of advertising during Saturday morning cartoons revealed that two thirds of the ads were for fats, oils, sweets, and high-sugar cereals. None of the ads were for fruits and vegetables (Kotz & Story, 1994). This level of exposure, combined with the malleability of children's beliefs, translates into a fruitful target population for advertisers. Children may not differentiate advertising and television programming as adults do (Martin, 1997; Ward, 1971), and young children do not fully understand commercial messages and their intent to sell (Kunkel & Roberts, 1991; Martin, 1997).

Advertisers began to view children as a separate advertising market in the 1960s (Kunkel & Roberts, 1991) and found the rewards were great. The *Handbook of Marketing to Children* (McNeal, 1992) strongly encourages businesses to include children in their marketing strategies, citing examples in which children were excluded from strategic planning to the industry's detriment. An estimated 40 million children ages 5 to 14 directly spend about $20 billion annually and influence the spending of another $200 billion each year (Vaeth, 1997).

The American Academy of Pediatrics (AAP) recently proposed guidelines to pediatricians and parents for monitoring children's media use. Recommendations included limiting children's media exposure, helping them develop critical viewing skills, and encouraging discussion of media content. The AAP cites the association of increased television use with obesity and decreased academic performance (Hogan et al., 1999).

### *Content of Children's Food Advertisements*

Cereal is the largest advertiser in the Saturday morning food advertisement category, and sugared cereals are the primary cereal advertised (Cotugna, 1988; Kotz & Story, 1994). Nine of every 10 food ads on Saturday morning television are for high-sugar cereals and candy bars, salty canned foods, fast food, and other "junk food" (Center for Media Education, 1998). A review of a 12-hour period of television viewing reported that food products accounted for 71% of the 225 ads during the period; 80% of those foods were judged to be low in nutritional value. The study also noted that the number of food commercials increased between 1976 and 1987 and that the ratio of high-sugar to low-sugar ads increased from 5 to 1 to 12.5 to 1 during that time (Cotugna, 1988). The situation is growing worse.

The way in which an unhealthy diet is advertised is also disturbing. An analysis of stories in 92 television food ads aimed at children found that the ads contained violence (62%), conflict (41%), achievement (24%), mood alteration (23%), trickery (20%), enablement (18%), and dependence (8%). A cluster analysis found that 64% of the ads were characterized by some combination of violence, conflict, and trickery (Rajecki et al., 1994).

Advertisements targeting children often rely on easily recognizable cartoon figures to capture children's attention. These figures take on a disturbing power in the lives of children, influencing their food purchasing choices. A 1990 study of 8-year-olds found that, when asked "Who would you like to take you out for a treat?" Ronald McDonald and Tony the Tiger were more popular than the child's father, teacher, or grandparents (Dibb, 1994). Seven of the top 10 advertising icons of the twentieth century represented the food industry, including Ronald McDonald, the Pillsbury Doughboy, and Tony the Tiger. Ronald McDonald was rated as the number-two ad icon, second only to the Marlboro Man in effectiveness and worldwide impact (Klein & Donaton, 1999a).

Leiber (1998) showed that the use of cartoon characters effectively aids product recall in children. She showed still color images of characters from TV, including the Budweiser frogs, Tony the Tiger, and Bugs Bunny, and asked 221 children ages 9 to 11 to recall the slogan associated with the characters and to identify the product the character advertised. When asked what product Tony the Tiger sells, 94% of the children said "cereal," and 81% knew that frogs sell beer. Bugs Bunny's "What's up, Doc?" slogan was the most recognized (80%), followed by the "Bud-weis-er" frogs' slogan (73%) and Tony's "They're Grrrreat!" slogan (57%; Leiber, 1998).

Children remember cartoon-related ads and toys marketed through meals specially designed for children, such as McDonald's "Happy Meal." The simplicity of the appeal makes children an important target population for advertisers, and the spending power of children leads to intense competition to capture the market.

Keebler Corporation has also recognized the financial advantage of advertising to children. Chips Deluxe® sales reached $139 million in 1997, becoming Keebler's number-one cookie. The company explained that marketing the brand to children significantly increased sales. Keebler used children's promotions such as the Chips Deluxe "Create Your Own Cookie Contest," the object of which was to "create excitement and awareness." Keebler also introduced "Dude," an animated Chips Deluxe character, in television commercials. Dude and the Keebler elves "helped make the Chips Deluxe brand relevant to children" (Keebler Corporation, 1998). Keebler's marketing communication plan that "aggressively" targeted children resulted in a 25% increase in revenue (Keebler Corporation, 1998).

McDonald's moved from the fifth to the second most frequently advertised food product between 1990 and 1992 (Food Commission, 1990, 1992). In 1997, a UK-based magazine reported that McDonald's was the most prolific advertiser in Europe (Food Commission, 1997). In 1998, McDonald's spent $486.3 million in advertising worldwide (McDonald's Corporation, 1999). About 40% of its advertising directly targets children. In 1990, the senior vice president for McDonald's Marketing testified that the average child sees a McDonald's television commercial 170 times per year, almost every other day (Bell, 1997).

Child and nutrition advocates complain that the content of children's ads lacks nutritional messages. Gussow (1973) concluded that few advertisements even hint at proper eating but, on the contrary, encourage poor eating habits. Wallack and Dorfman (1992) found that, of 20 hours of randomly selected TV over a 3-week period, none of the public service announcements (PSAs) addressed diet, even though diet is one of the three leading behavioral risk factors for poor health. In 52.5 hours of Saturday morning television, there were 10 nutrition-related PSAs, compared with 564 advertisements for food (Kotz & Story, 1994).

The increase in the prevalence of obesity parallels the increase of unhealthy food advertising on television. The greatest increases in overweight prevalence for children (ages 6-11) occurred between 1976 and 1991, and these differences were highly statistically significant. For African Americans of both sexes and all age groups, the number of children overweight at the 85th percentile increased more than 9 percentage points (Troiano, Flegal, Kuczmarski, Campbell, & Johnson, 1995). In the 1960s, researchers found that obesity in children ages 6 to 17 was directly related to the amount of time spent watching television, after controlling for numerous factors associated with obesity (Dietz, 1993; Dietz & Gortmaker, 1985).

### *Impact of Advertisements on Attitudes and Behavior*

The impact of mass marketing on children's attitudes and, more important, behavior is predictable and powerful. A study of 8- to 10-year-old children from low-income families indicated that even a single exposure to a commercial produced more favorable attitudes toward the advertised product (Gorn & Goldberg, 1977). This finding is consistent with research on how commercials for other products influence the attitudes of children. Grube and Wallack (1994) found, in a study of 10- to 13-year-olds, that awareness of TV beer advertising was related to more favorable beliefs about drinking, to greater knowledge of beer brands and slogans, and to increased intentions to drink as an adult.

A study of children ages 2 to 11 revealed that exposure to television food advertising increased caloric intake and snacking and decreased overall nutrient quality in children (Bolton, 1983). Television viewing was also strongly correlated with fourth and fifth graders having unhealthy perceptions of nutrition, controlling for gender, race, reading level, parental education level, and parental occupation (Signorielli & Staples, 1997).

In a study of 3- to 8-year-olds, the number of weekly viewing hours correlated significantly with both children's caloric intake and children's requests (and parents' purchases) of foods influenced by television (Taras, Sallis, Patterson, Nader, & Nelson, 1989). The authors of a study of 3- to 5-year-olds found that purchase-influencing attempts at the supermarket were associated with the reinforcement value of television commercials and the amount of TV to which participants were exposed. Cereal and candy, two of the most heavily advertised foods, were the most requested items (Galst & White, 1976). Likewise, a study of first graders indicated that those who viewed commercials for highly sugared foods opted for more (advertised and nonadvertised) sugary choices (Goldberg, Gorn, & Gibson, 1978).

Just as advertisements induce purchase requests and consumption, counterads for healthier foods can lead to healthier choices. In the Goldberg et al. (1978) study, children who viewed pronutritional public service announcements chose more fruits, vegetables, and other nutritious foods. A 24-minute animated program titled *Junk Food* proved most effective in reducing the number of sugary choices in that study.

A study of 3- to 6-year-olds found that participants' selection of snacks with added sugar was most reduced by exposure to advertisements for products without added sugar content and to pronutritional public service announcements accompanied by positive comments from an adult co-observer (Galst, 1980). Canadian children ages 5 to 8 chose more candy than fruit as snacks following viewing of a candy commercial, but eliminating candy commercials and exposing participants to fruit commercials or PSAs each proved effective in encouraging the selection of fruit (Gorn & Goldberg, 1982).

Although the bulk of the literature examining younger children suggests that the viewing of television commercials is associated with attitudinal and behavioral changes, a study of tenth to twelfth graders indicated that snacking did not generally occur immediately in response to commercials (Carruth, Goldberg, & Skinner, 1991). Participants reported that commercials were not associated with the initiation of snacking while watching TV. It may be that older children are not influenced by the ads to the same degree that younger children are. On the other hand, the study measured snacking during a confined period, rather than the general purchase requests examined by other studies.

Both content and quantity play an important role in marketing. In a study of 8- to 10-year-old males, participants were shown either (a) no commercials, (b) one commercial repeated three times, (c) three different commercials, (d) one commercial repeated five times, or (e) five different commercials. They were then given a choice of snack foods, including the advertised item, and were questioned about the specifics of the advertisements. The authors reported that, although recall of specifics (i.e., brand name) may be achieved with minimal exposure to TV commercials, the altering of preferences and behavior may require additional and varied exposures (Gorn & Goldberg, 1980).

These results are in contrast to Goldberg and Gorn's previous (1974) finding that, in a study of 8- to 10-year-old boys, seeing a commercial for a valued toy produced more favorable reactions to the toy and increased motivations to obtain it, but further exposure to commercials had no impact. The authors concluded that the effect of commercials on attitude and behavior is most pronounced with one exposure. When the product is highly desirable or unique, such as a valued toy, repeated exposure to advertising messages may not serve to increase motivation to obtain the product beyond the previously elevated levels. However, repeated exposure may help to *alter* preferences when products are novel, such as a new snack food, or when the outcome is similar, such as choosing between two different candy bars.

Cross-cultural studies indicate that food advertisements are associated with changing consumption patterns around the world. The author of a 1991 study of Japanese children suggested that media influence is interfering with normal eating and leading to a higher consumption of unhealthy processed food (Ishigaki, 1991). A study following an advertising ban in Quebec, leaving only U.S.-border TV stations as a source of ads, revealed that English-speaking children (those with access to the U.S. ads) were able to recognize significantly more toys available in the marketplace and reported having more children's cereals in their homes than did French-speaking participants (Goldberg, 1990). A survey of 9-year-olds in Ireland, Australia, Norway, and the United States showed that TV ads played an important role in stimulating the interests of children (Collins, Tonnessen, Barry, & Yeates, 1992).

A recent British study found that half of 828 ads analyzed were for food products, 60% of which were for breakfast cereals and confectionery/snacks (Lewis & Hill, 1998). As in the United States, Ronald McDonald is a role model abroad. As previously mentioned, just over half of Australian 9- and 10-year-olds in one study thought that Ronald McDonald knows best what is good for children to eat (Food Commission, 1997). Of 68 Japanese children from the third through sixth grade, all recognized the image of Ronald McDonald. The children claimed "they liked Ronald because he was funny, gentle, kind, and—several added—he understood children's hearts" (Watson, 1997, p. 64).

The prevalence of advertisements for unhealthy foods coupled with the pressure to be thin creates an especially difficult situation for children and adolescents. Research has indicated that television commercials promote gender stereotypes and unrealistic standards of female beauty and body shapes, thereby producing distorted body images (Lavine, Sweeney, & Wagner, 1999). The media have been blamed for creating a distorted reality that adversely affects women and contributes to eating disorders by glamorizing unhealthy behavior and propagating a false sense of homogeneity (Jasper, 1993). Theoretical frameworks such as social comparison have been used to explain the route through which the thin ideal portrayed in the media contributes to negative body image (Shaw & Waller, 1995). Between 1973 and 1991, diet food and product commercials on the three major American networks increased significantly, and the rise in eating disorders paralleled the increase in diet ads (Wiseman, Gunning, & Gray, 1993).

### *Food Advertising in Schools and Popular Culture*

Advertising has also invaded the schools. Channel One, a 10-minute news program with 2 minutes of commercials, is broadcast daily into the classroom in exchange for TVs, VCRs, and a satellite dish for the school (Consumers Union, 1996). More than 8 million middle and high school students watch the program in 12,000 schools (Mifflin, 1998). Advertisers pay $175,000 for the opportunity to target 40% of American teenagers for 30 seconds on Channel One (Coeyman, 1995).

Brand and Greenberg (1994) evaluated the effects of advertising on Channel One. In a 4-week period, 31 (69%) of the 45 commercials shown on Channel One were for food products, including gum, soft drinks, fast food, candy, and snack chips. The study also showed that advertising on Channel One affects adolescents' cognitions about advertised products, produces positive affect toward the products advertised, enhances their consumer orientations, and adds to their intentions to purchase the advertised products compared with adolescents who do not view Channel One. However, the study reported that students at schools with Channel One are no more likely than their nonviewing peers to report actual purchases of those products (Brand & Greenberg, 1994).

Richards, Wartella, Morton, and Thompson (1998) reviewed commercial marketing in schools and cited numerous examples of corporate presence. Beyond Channel One, they noted advertisements in gymnasiums, on school buses, in bathroom stalls, and even on sports teams' warm-up suits. Classroom materials sent to teachers promote using food products as learning tools, from counting Tootsie Rolls to determining which brand of tomato sauce is thicker. Students are encouraged to buy or sell products for rewards or as fund-raisers. Finally, fast food outlets and soft drink machines have become common in school cafeterias.

There has been little published scientific evaluation of the effects of in-school advertising. A rationale for allowing advertising in the schools is that children will be bombarded with marketing messages anyway, so schools may as well get something in return (e.g., money, supplies, equipment). Also, school administrators claim that, in choosing to ally themselves with certain marketing programs, they actually have more control over the content and quality of the messages delivered, thereby protecting the children. Some companies deny that the materials they give to schools are advertisements, citing their educational purposes or their need to give back to the community. Others, however, admit that reaching children and adolescents early is a valuable advantage, because children may form brand allegiances that could last a lifetime (Richards et al., 1998).

Critics argue that these advertising programs endanger the quality of education, send mixed messages, and result in the equivalent of school endorsements of unhealthy products. The schools are also modeling a sedentary behavior—watching television. Finally, it is suspected that the predominantly advertised foods on Channel One are unhealthy; children are encouraged to purchase the foods from the vending machines conveniently located in the schools and to consume the unhealthy foods as an after-school snack.

Beyond the school, popular culture has also been inundated with images of food products. Aside from television commercials, advertisers have recognized the value of product placement in movies and television shows (Williams et al., 1993). Movies targeted to children have gratuitous images of brand name fast food restaurants. Concurrently, when entering a fast food restaurant, children purchase meals with toys promoting the same movies and television shows. This placement further blurs the line between advertising and reality for children who are less adept at discriminating between the two.

## Pathway to Consumption: From the Television to the Stomach

Figure 22.1 depicts the proposed mechanism by which television advertising influences consumption. The pathway hypothesizes a two-part process in which the information is first coded and later retrieved for decision making. Analyzing the steps of the pathway also reveals directions for future research.

The process begins with advertisements. While watching television, children learn characters and slogans from the commercial breaks (Kotz & Story, 1994; Leiber, 1998). The children also learn that these triggers are associated with certain products (Leiber, 1998). Increased exposure to the ads strengthens this brand awareness.

The pathway proposes that the context in which brand knowledge is obtained influences the strength and valence of the attitude toward the product. A child's attitude toward a product that is advertised in school with a teacher present may be different from the attitude developed at home while watching tele-

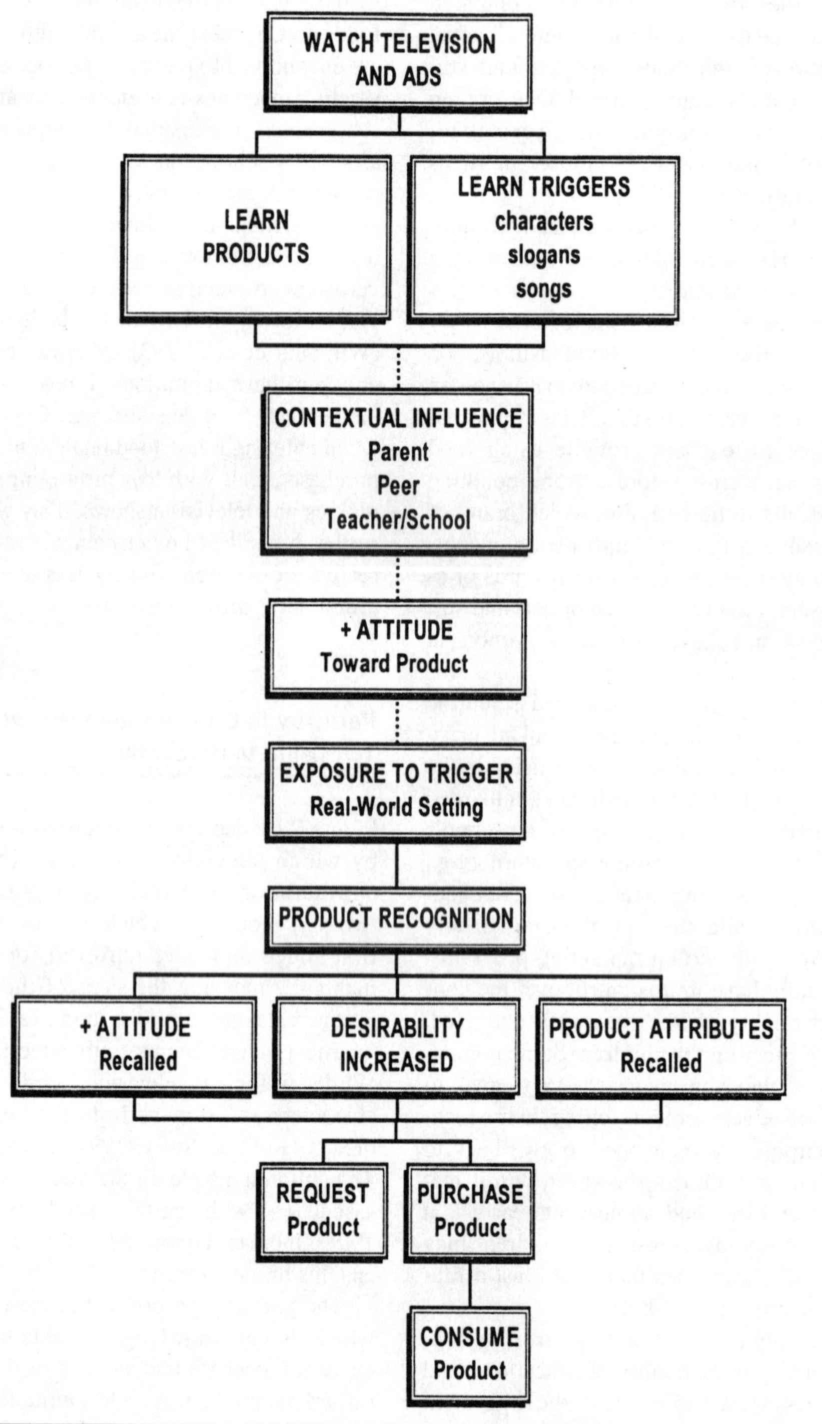


**Figure 22.1.** Pathway to Consumption From Television to Stomach

vision alone. When teachers show programs with advertisements in the classroom, students may assume the teacher's implicit endorsement of the products advertised, and the attitude may be stronger than that developed while watching alone at home. Peers and parents may also influence the attitude.

Little research has examined the role of context in a child's formation of an attitude toward a product, and none of it addresses food products. The literature suggests that parents and peers do influence adolescents' attitudes in both positive and negative ways. Meier (1991) found that siblings of smokers reported less negative attitudes to smoking. Mandelburg and Bristol (1998) found that family communication and peer influence are related to an adolescent's skepticism toward advertising. Brand and Greenberg (1994) demonstrated that products advertised in school are rated more positively. Exactly how the context affects the child's attitude toward a food product is unclear. The taste of the food may be a more powerful determinant of attitude than parent or peer influence. This is an interesting avenue for future research.

The pathway proposes that, once a child has learned the name and qualities of the product, a memory of the product will be retrieved when exposed to the triggers. Walking down the aisle of the supermarket, a child could spot the character on a cereal box. Driving down the highway, the child could see a billboard advertising the product. Upon recognizing the product, the attitude toward the product and its attributes should be recalled. This increases the product's desirability in the child's view. At this point, the child either purchases the product directly with individual funds or requests that the parent purchase the product. Once purchased, the product is eventually consumed by the child. If exercise and lifestyle patterns remain stable, this leads to an increased caloric intake, because the food products being advertised are primarily unhealthy foods, high in calories and low in nutrition. Increased calorie levels, combined with the decreased activity levels associated with watching television, lead to skyrocketing obesity.

## Environmental Intervention: The Unrealized Potential of Policy

The potent impact of children's advertising has led to a battle cry for legislation regulating the industry. An article reporting the AAP's call for a ban on food advertisements directed at children cited the exploitation of children's minds and the contribution of food ads to obesity as products of food advertising directed at children (Lipman, 1991). Similarly, the Center for Science in the Public Interest started a group called Kids Against Junk Foods to raise health consciousness among children. Kunkel and Roberts (1991) lament that, although in 1978 the Federal Trade Commission (FTC) attempted to ban ads aimed at children too young to understand their content, research findings generally are not a key factor in regulatory policy decisions.

The fight for regulation of food advertising has been compared to campaigns against the marketing of alcohol and cigarettes to youth. Williams et al. (1993) note that targeting children with food advertisements may be more dangerous than alcohol or cigarette advertising. It is possible to avoid health problems related to cigarettes and alcohol through abstinence, but it is impossible to refrain from eating. The authors plead that food advertisers strike a balance between profitable marketing principles and public health concerns.

### *Existing Regulatory Legislation and Action*

The FTC, the Food and Drug Administration (FDA), and the United States Department of Agriculture (USDA) share jurisdiction over manufacturers' claims regarding food products. Specifically, Section 5 of the FTC Act (1994) prohibits "any false advertisement" that is "misleading in a material respect," in the case of food products. The FTC, according to its statement, will find an advertisement unlawful "if it contains a representation or omission of fact that is likely to mislead consumers acting reasonably under the circumstances, and that representation or omission is material" (p. 4). Section 403(a) of the Federal Food, Drug, and Cosmetics Act (FDCA) prohibits "labeling that is false or misleading in any particular." The FTC's Enforcement Policy Statement on Food Advertising (1994) notes that, since 1954, the FTC and the FDA "have operated under a Memorandum of Understanding, under which the Commission has assumed primary responsibility for regulating food advertising, while the FDA has taken primary responsibility for food labeling" (pp. 1-2).

The FTC delineates a framework for commission action, under which it lists four general steps of investigation: (a) Identify representations made by an advertisement, (b) identify omission of material information for deceptive purposes, (c) consider the representation from the view of a consumer acting reasonably given the circumstances, and (d) in some cases, require substantiation of nutrient content or health claims through scientific evidence. If the commission has reason to believe that a violation has occurred, it may issue a temporary restraining order or a preliminary injunction, or it may serve a process on the violator. If the person, partner, or corporation violates the FTC provisions, they may, on conviction, be punished by a fine of not more than $5,000 and/or imprisonment for not more than 6 months. The penalty may increase to $10,000 and/or imprisonment of less than 1 year for repeat offenders (FTC, 1994).

The Children's Television Act of 1990 limits commercial time during children's programming to 10.5 minutes per hour on weekends and 12 minutes per hour on weekdays (Federal Communications Commission, 1999). However, the FTC lists no specific guidelines for regulating the content of advertising targeting children. This task has been assumed by several "watchdog" groups, including the Better Business Bureau's Children's Advertising Review Unit (CARU), the Center for Media Education (CME), and the Center for Science in the Public Interest (CSPI).

CARU, which reviews advertising in all media directed at children under age 12, seeks change through voluntary cooperation with the advertisers when advertising is found to be misleading, inaccurate, or inconsistent with CARU's guidelines. CARU was created by the advertisers with an advisory group of experts in education, communication, and child development, as well as industry leaders, as an alternative to having FTC regulation in the realm of children's ads. However, it can only seek voluntary cooperation from advertisers and has no legal authority over them. CARU supporters pay a fee to belong to the organization and include (as of 1998) General Mills; Kellogg Company; Frito-Lay, Inc.; Kraft Foods; Hershey Foods; Nestle USA; M&M Mars, Inc.; and Nabisco Foods (Children's Advertising Review Unit, 1999).

The Center for Media Education was founded in 1991, following the closing of Action for Children's Television (ACT), as a national nonprofit organization formed to improve the quality of children's media and influence media policy on a federal level. Through the testimony before the Federal Communications Commission (FCC) of many psychologists and through the 1992 Campaign for Kids' TV, which included advocacy, parent, and education groups, the CME helped persuade the FCC, in 1996, to require television stations to broadcast a minimum of 3 hours per week of educational programming for children (CME, 1998).

The Center for Science in the Public Interest is a grassroots health organization focused on challenging food nutrition and safety standards. Its articles on the nutritional value of popular foods such as movie popcorn and family restaurant options have garnered considerable public attention. The CSPI has called for a number of policy changes and has had a major impact on food labeling laws. Such groups can help create a climate for action at the level of the federal government.

### *Avenues for Future Intervention*

As reviewed earlier in the chapter, studies have indicated that pro-nutritional messages can counter the impact of advertisements for unhealthy foods. Perhaps sanctions similar to those passed to address tobacco advertisements could be imposed. The Fairness Doctrine Act, effective from 1968 through 1970, required that one antismoking advertisement be aired for every four pro-smoking advertisements on television and radio. In 1971, the U.S. Broadcast Advertising Ban was imposed, eliminating all cigarette advertising from television and radio (Tremblay & Tremblay, 1999).

The government could require food companies to provide money for equal airtime for healthy choices to balance the messages aimed at children. It would be difficult to completely ban advertising to children. Industries as well as individuals have free speech guarantees under the First Amendment, and an advertising ban could represent an infringement on that right. Scheraga and Calfee (1996) suggest that the 1971 advertising ban, which also ended free antismoking messages, was counterproductive because its net effect was to reduce competition in the marketplace but not to reduce smoking. Similarly, it is possible that a ban on advertising unhealthy foods to children would decrease competition while consumption patterns remain constant. Finally, it is possible that food companies, in the absence of TV advertising, might find more cost-effective means of marketing.

In 1998, as part of the $206 billion tobacco industry compromise, cigarette makers agreed to (a) make marketing changes, including a cessation of billboard advertising; (b) finance educational campaigns intended to stop young people from starting to smoke; (c) stop sponsorship of sports teams, stadiums, or events where participants are underage; and (d) pay for research intended to help smokers quit (Meier, 1999). Joe Camel, the cartoon mascot advertising smoking to children, was retired along with apparel with tobacco logos (Golway, 1998). It is reasonable to ask whether it would be beneficial to public health if similar action were taken against icons such as Ronald McDonald and Tony the Tiger and products such as Coke apparel.

The political machinery that drives the food industry is incredibly complex and much larger than the tobacco industry (Rocawich, 1994). There are at least 78 lobbying groups and trade associations organized to protect the varied interests within the food industry. If the food industry is not included as a full partner in any policy efforts, any endeavors at systemic change are likely to be unsuccessful (Sims, 1998). When the economic advantage of the industry coincides with public health benefits, changes that are mutually beneficial can be achieved. For example, Ippolito and Mathios (1991) indicate how policy affects how consumers process new information into altered behavior. Although the health effects of fiber were known from the 1970s, health advertising regulations did not allow health claims to be included in advertising messages. The advertising ban prevented widespread awareness of fiber's health benefits. In 1984, however, the FDA suspended the ban on health claims while new regulations were being determined.

Fiber cereal consumption increased significantly after the ban was lifted and producers were able to advertise the health features of the products. Adult cereals introduced after health advertising began contained significantly more fiber than cereals introduced before health advertising. Producers also decreased the sodium and fat content of the high-fiber cereals. Interestingly, the healthfulness of child cereals did not improve with the new advertising campaigns (Ippolito & Mathios, 1991). This example demonstrates the economic and public health ramifications of advertising policies. When provided with sufficient economic incentive, the food industry can market healthier foods.

The tobacco and alcohol industries provide other possible examples for interventions. One target area could be the tax deductions that businesses receive for advertising expenses. The tax code allows "reasonable advertising expenses" to be deductible business expenses (Publication 535, 1998, p. 66). The 1998 proposed tobacco bill contained an amendment to prohibit tax deductions for tobacco advertising that violated FDA regulations (Senate Records, 1998). Although the 1998 tobacco bill did not ultimately become law, such deductions could be a target for policy change (Torry, 1998). Tax deductions for advertising of unhealthy foods could be eliminated, or tax deductions might be increased for healthy foods advertised. Modifying tax deductions would give the food industry an economic incentive to advertise more healthy products and possibly provide revenue for other public health initiatives.

Less restrictive interventions targeting tax deductions or equal-time advertising are more likely to be favored by the public. A questionnaire completed by mothers of schoolchildren in the first through sixth grade indicated that parents wished that there were more direct appeals to children to be nutrition conscious (Grossbart & Crosby, 1984). In a survey of community attitudes toward public policies to control alcohol, tobacco, and high-fat food, interventions designed to protect children and youth were most strongly endorsed, followed by restrictions on advertising. However, support for regulatory controls on high-fat food was given less often than that for alcohol and tobacco, and those reporting the least personal use of high-fat foods were most in favor of control policies (Jeffrey et al., 1990). This may be due in part to the general perception that obesity is not a serious public health issue. However, recent estimates that 54% of adults in the United States are overweight (Hill & Peters, 1998) and that obesity-related health care costs exceed $99 billion annually (Wolf & Colditz, 1998) indicate otherwise.

The government has shown increasing interest in encouraging children to pursue exercise rather than watch television. In the spring of 1999, the surgeon general supported National TV Turnoff Week (originally proposed by TV-Free America, an advocacy group), noting that the current generation of children is the most sedentary in American history and voicing concern about an obesity epidemic. Although the National TV Turnoff Week has been conducted for 5 years, television networks report noticing no decrease in TV viewing during the initiative (Associated Press, 1999).

In addition to government regulation, it may also prove worthwhile to harness the interest shown by parents in counteracting promotion of unhealthy foods. Ward (1971) suggests that the family mediates the influence of television and advertising on buying behavior. In fact, a promising corollary to the Bolton (1983) study was that parental influence could have a stronger long-term effect than food advertising, suggesting a potential pathway for combating the toxic environment.

## Conclusions

Food advertising is a highly profitable segment of the marketing world, and children are easy targets. Research reveals the power of the media to influence attitudes and increase desire for products. The combination of unhealthy foods advertised and the media propagation of a thin ideal sends conflicting messages to children, which have been associated with a rise in both obesity and eating disorders.

Although organizations to monitor advertising directed at children exist, political interests make legislation and enforcement difficult. As advertising expands into the classroom, the need for regulation grows. One can only assume that the combination of unhealthy food ads with soft drink machines and fast food in school cafeterias will worsen the situation.

With the rate of obesity spiraling upward, exposing the population to earlier onset of obesity-related diseases and public health costs, action is critical. Intervention at the environmental level, where children are often unwitting targets of heavily financed persuasion, seems a promising area. If the environment remains unchanged, we cannot expect the outcome to differ.

## References

Associated Press. (1999, April 23). Kids need to turn off TV, be active, government says. *New Haven Register,* p. A7.

Avery, R., Mathios, A., Shanahan, J., & Bisogni, C. (1997). Food and nutrition messages communicated through prime-time television. *Journal of Public Policy & Marketing, 16,* 217-233.

Bell, R. (1997, June 19). Advertising. Judgment: Justice Bell's verdict, section 7 [On-line]. Available: www.mcspotlight.org/case/trial/verdict/verdict_jud2b.html

Bolton, R. N. (1983). Modeling the impact of television food advertising on children's diets. *Current Issues and Research in Advertising, 6*(1), 173-199.

Brand, J., & Greenberg, B. (1994, January). Commercials in the classroom: The impact of Channel One advertising. *Journal of Advertising Research, 34,* 18-23.

Carruth, B. R., Goldberg, D. L., & Skinner, J. D. (1991). Do parents and peers mediate the influence of television advertising on food-related purchases? *Journal of Adolescent Research, 6*(2), 253-271.

Center for Media Education. (1998). *The campaign for kids' TV: Children and television* [On-line]. Available: http://tap.epn.org/cme/ctatool/c_and_t.html

Children's Advertising Review Unit. (1999). About the Children's Advertising Review Unit. *Better Business Bureau* [On-line]. Available: www.bbb.org/advertising/caruguid.html

Coeyman, M. (1995, July 20). Follow the customer: New media ventures may help marketers target a market. *Restaurant Business, 94,* 36.

Collins, J., Tonnessen, E. S., Barry, A. M., & Yeates, H. (1992). Who's afraid of the big bad box? Children and advertising in four countries. *Educational Media International, 29*(4), 254-260.

Consoli, J. (1999, April 12). Television: Clutter climbs higher. *Mediaweek* [On-line]. Available: http://members.adweek.com/archive/adweek/mediaweek/1999/w41299/w_92.asp

Consumers Union. (1996). Selling America's kids: Commercial pressures on kids of the '90s. *Consumers Union Educational Services Department* [On-line]. Available: www.igc.org/consunion/other/sellingkids/index.htm

Cotugna, N. (1988). TV ads on Saturday morning children's programming: What's new? *Journal of Nutrition Education, 20,* 125-127.

Dibb, S. (1994, November). Advertising: Witnesses [Statement of advertising researcher, witness for defense]. Available: www.mcspotlight.org/cgi-bin/zv/people/witnesses/advertising/dibb_sue.html

Dietz, W. H. (1993). Television, obesity, and eating disorders. *Adolescent Medicine: State of the Art Reviews, 4*(3), 543-549.

Dietz, W. H., & Gortmaker, S. L. (1985). Do we fatten our children at the television set? Obesity and television viewing in children and adolescents. *Pediatrics, 75,* 807-812.

Federal Communications Commission. (1999, October 4). The Children's Television Act. Available: www.fcc.gov/Bureaus/Mass_Media/Factsheets/kidstv.txt

Federal Trade Commission. (1994, May). Enforcement policy statement on food advertising [On-line]. Available: www.ftc.gov/bcp/policystmt/ad-food.htm

Food Commission. (1990). Sweet persuasion: A diet of junk food ads. *Food Magazine, 9*(1).

Food Commission. (1992). A diet of junk food adverts: Part 2. *Food Magazine, 18*(2).

Food Commission. (1997, January-March). Advertising to children: UK the worst in Europe. *Food Magazine.*

Galst, J. P. (1980). Television food commercials and pro-nutritional public services announcements as determinants of young children's snack choices. *Child Development, 51*(3), 935-938.

Galst, J. P., & White, M. A. (1976). The unhealthy persuader: The reinforcing value of television and children's purchase-influencing attempts at the supermarket. *Child Development, 47*(4), 1089-1096.

Goldberg, M. E. (1990). A quasi-experiment assessing the effectiveness of TV advertising directed to children. *Journal of Marketing Research, 27*(4), 445-454.

Goldberg, M. E., & Gorn, G. J. (1974). Children's reactions to television advertising: An experimental approach. *Journal of Consumer Research, 1*(2), 69-75.

Goldberg, M. E., Gorn, G. J., & Gibson, W. (1978). TV messages for snack and breakfast foods: Do they influence children's preferences? *Journal of Consumer Research, 5*(2), 73-81.

Golway, T. (1998, December 12). Life in the 90's: Youth, smoking, and the tobacco settlement. *America,* p. 6.

Gorn, G. J., & Goldberg, M. E. (1977). The impact of television advertising on children from low income families. *Journal of Consumer Research, 4*(2), 86-88.

Gorn, G. J., & Goldberg, M. E. (1980). Children's responses to repetitive television commercials. *Journal of Consumer Research, 6*(4), 421-424.

Gorn, G. J., & Goldberg, M. E. (1982). Behavioral evidence of the effects of televised food messages on children. *Journal of Consumer Research, 9*(2), 200-205.

Grossbart, S. L., & Crosby, L. A. (1984). Understanding the bases of parental concern and reaction to children's food advertising. *Journal of Marketing, 48*(3), 79-92.

Grube, J. W., & Wallack, L. (1994). Television beer advertising and drinking knowledge, beliefs, and intentions among school children. *American Journal of Public Health, 84*(2), 254-259.

Gussow, J. (1973). "It even makes milk a dessert": A report on the counternutritional messages of children's television advertising. *Clinical Pediatrics, 12*(2), 68-71.

Hill, J., & Peters, J. (1998). Environmental contributions to the obesity epidemic. *Science, 280,* 1371-1374.

Hogan, M., Bar-on, M., Beard, L., Corrigan, S., Gedissman, A., Palumbo, F., Rich, M., Shifrin, D., Roberts, M., Villani, S., Holroyd, J., Sherry, N. S., & Strasburger, V. (1999). Media education. *Pediatrics, 104*(2), 341-343.

Ippolito, P., & Mathios, A. (1991). Information, advertising, and health choices: A study of the cereal market. In *Economics of Food Safety.* New York: Elsevier Science.

Ishigaki, E. H. (1991). The health and eating habits of young children in Japan. *Early Child Development & Care, 74,* 141-148.

Jasper, K. (1993). Monitoring and responding to medi messages. *Eating Disorders, 1*(2), 109-114.

Jeffrey, R. W., Forster, J. L., Schmid, T. L., McBride, C. M., Rooney, B. L., & Pirie, P. L. (1990). Community attitudes toward public policies to control alcohol, tobacco, and high-fat food. *American Journal of Preventive Medicine, 6*(1), 12-19.

Keebler Corporation. (1998). *Chips Deluxe: Everything about our best-selling cookie is magical!* [1997 annual report]. Available: www.keebler.com/annual_report/chips_deluxe.htm

Klein, D., & Donaton, S. (Eds.). (1999a). The advertising century: Top 10 advertising icons. *Advertising Age* [On-line]. Available: http://adage.com/century/ad_icons.html

Klein, D., & Donaton, S. (Eds.). (1999b). The advertising century: Top 100 advertising campaigns. *Advertising Age* [On-line]. Available: http://adage.com/century/campaigns.html

Kotz, K., & Story, M. (1994, November). Food advertisements during children's Saturday morning television programming: Are they consistent with dietary recommendations? *Journal of the American Dietetic Association, 94,* 1296-1300.

Kuczmarski, R., Flegal, K., Campbell, S., & Johnson, C. (1994). Increasing prevalence of overweight among US adults: The national health and nutrition examination surveys, 1960 to 1991. *Journal of the American Medical Association, 272,* 205-211.

Kunkel, D., & Roberts, D. (1991). Young minds and marketplace values: Issues in children's advertising. *Journal of Social Issues, 47*(1), 57-72.

Lavine, H., Sweeney, D., & Wagner, S. H. (1999). Depicting women as sex objects in television advertising: Effects on body dissatisfaction. *Personality and Social Psychology Bulletin, 25*(8), 1049-1058.

Leiber, L. (1998). Commercial and character slogan recall by children aged 9 to 11 years. *Center on Alcohol Advertising* [On-line]. Available: www.igc.org/trauma/alcohol/ads/budstudy.html

Lewis, M. K., & Hill, A. J. (1998). Food advertising on British children's television: A content analysis and experimental study with nine-year-olds. *International Journal of Obesity and Related Metabolic Disorders, 22,* 206-214.

Lipman, J. (1991, July 24). Pediatric academy prescribes ban on food ads aimed at children. *Wall Street Journal,* p. B8.

Mandelburg, T., & Bristol, T. (1998, Fall). Socialization and adolescents' skepticism toward advertising. *Journal of Advertising, 27*(3), 11-21.

Martin, M. (1997). Children's understanding of the intent of advertising: A meta-analysis. *Journal of Public Policy and Marketing, 16*(2), 205-224.

McDonald's Corporation. (1999). *Financial review: 1998 annual report* [On-line].
Available: www.mcdonalds.com/ corporate/investor/reports/ annualreport/index.html

McNeal, J. (1992). *Kids as customers: A handbook of marketing to children.* Lexington, MA: Lexington Books.

Meier, E. (1991, Summer). Tobacco truths: The impact of role models on children's attitudes toward smoking. *Health Education Quarterly, 18*(2), 173-182.

Meier, E. (1999, January). The tobacco settlement and 1999 forecasts. *Nursing Economics, 17,* 53.

Mifflin, L. (1998, December 28). Nielsen to research Channel One's audience. *New York Times,* p. C6.

Publication 535. (1998). *Business expenses* (Internal Revenue Service Catalogue No. 15065Z). Washington, DC: U.S. Department of the Treasury.

Rajecki, D. W., McTavish, D. G., Rasmussen, J. L., Schreuders, M., Byers, D. C., & Jessup, K. S. (1994). Violence, conflict, trickery, and other story themes in TV ads for food for children. *Journal of Applied Social Psychology, 24*(19), 1685-1700.

Richards, J. I., Wartella, E. A., Morton, C., & Thompson, L. (1998). The growing commercialization of schools: Issues and practices. *Annals of the American Academy of Political and Social Science, 557,* 148-163.

Rocawich, L. (1994, September). Michael Jacobson, director of the Center for Science in the Public Interest: Interview. *Progressive, 58,* 30.

Scheraga, C., & Calfee, J. (1996). The industry effects of information and regulation in the cigarette market:

1950-1965. *Journal of Public Policy & Marketing, 15,* 216-220.

Senate Records. (1998, June 15). Tobacco bill/FDA regulations and advertising tax deduction, 105th Cong., 2nd Sess., Vote No. 159. Available: www.senate.gov/7Erpc/rva/1052/1052159.htm

Shaw, J., & Waller, G. (1995). The media's impact on body image: Implications for prevention and treatment. *Eating Disorders, 3*(2), 115-123.

Signorielli, N., & Staples, J. (1997). Television and children's conception of nutrition. *Health Communication, 9*(4), 289-301.

Sims, L. (1998). *The politics of fat: Food and nutrition policy in America.* Armonk, NY: Sharpe.

Taras, H. L., Sallis, J. F., Patterson, T. L., Nader, P. R., & Nelson, J. A. (1989). Television's influence on children's diet and physical activity. *Journal of Developmental & Behavioral Pediatrics, 10*(4), 176-180.

Television Bureau of Advertising. (1998). *TV basics* [On-line]. Available: www.tvb.org/tvfacts/index. html

Torry, S. (1998, October 30). Tobacco's lobbying outlays soared in '98. *Washington Post,* p. A10.

Tremblay, C., & Tremblay, V. (1999, February 1). Reinterpreting the effect of an advertising ban on cigarette smoking. *International Journal of Advertising, 18,* 41.

Troiano, R., Flegal, K., Kuczmarski, R., Campbell, S., & Johnson, C. (1995). Overweight prevalence and trends for children and adolescents. *Archives of Pediatrics and Adolescent Medicine, 149,* 1085-1091.

Vaeth, E. (1997, October 20). Fast-food restaurants aim ad dollars at kiddie market. *Atlanta Business Chronicle.*

Wallack, L., & Dorfman, L. (1992). Health messages on television commercials. *American Journal of Health Promotion, 6*(3), 190-196.

Ward, S. (1971). Television advertising and the adolescent. *Clinical Pediatrics, 10*(8), 462-464.

Watson, J. (Ed.). (1997). *Golden arches east: McDonald's in East Asia.* Stanford, CA: Stanford University Press.

Williams, J. O., Achterberg, C., & Sylvester, G. P. (1993). Targeting marketing of food products to ethnic minority youths. In C. L. Williams & S. Y. S. Kimms (Eds.), *Prevention and treatment of childhood obesity: Annals of the New York Academy of Sciences* (Vol. 699, pp. 107-114). New York: New York Academy of Sciences.

Wiseman, C. V., Gunning, F. M., & Gray, J. J. (1993). Increasing pressure to be thin: 19 years of diet products in television commercials. *Eating Disorders, 1*(1), 52-61.

Wolf, A. M., & Colditz, G. A. (1998). Current estimates of the economic cost of obesity in the United States. *Obesity Research, 6,* 97-106.

World Health Organization. (1998). *Obesity: Preventing and managing the global epidemic* [Report by the WHO Consultation on Obesity, Geneva, June 3-5, 1997]. Geneva, Switzerland: Author.

# CHAPTER 23

# Television and Morality

LAWRENCE I. ROSENKOETTER
Oregon State University

Scientists face a seemingly unending array of public myths, one of which is that television is leading to the moral decay of our children. With the advent of each of the major electronic media, the public has been unduly alarmed. In the 1920s, the public feared that movies were ruinous in that impressionable children's habits were being shaped in an unwholesome manner. Concern with radio's negative impact on children's lives mushroomed in the 1930s. Children were spending too much time listening to the radio, and it was adversely affecting their behavior. And then there came television. The litany of possible nefarious effects grew longer, including the concern that television was undermining the character of young viewers.

Indictment after indictment of the media has been found by media researchers to be without merit. Wartella (1988) has provided an extended description of these ongoing skirmishes between the media and their critics. Hence, the dominant response of most television researchers has been to ignore or at least discount the public's concern about the relationship between television and morality (Huston & Wright, 1998).

Concern about television's influence on the morality of young viewers continues to grow. In addition to the perennial calls of alarm by the religious right, mainstream members of the media (Zoglin, 1990), government (Fineman, 1994), professional (Geiger, 1995), and citizen groups (Wildavsky, 1996) have expressed concern in growing numbers. Given the urgency of these calls, it would seem appropriate to review anew relevant research and theory to assess any role television might be playing in the development of children's values and morally relevant behaviors.

## Television as a Catalyst for Growth in Moral Reasoning

For decades, the study of moral development was at the very least dormant. The work of Lawrence Kohlberg (1984) awakened this area of inquiry and led to a burgeoning of new theory and research. According to Kohlberg's theory, individuals, including children, are actively involved in trying to make sense out of the universe in which they live. In the moral domain, this means that each child is an ethicist who invents ways of answering the question of what makes certain acts right and others wrong.

Initially, children decide that wrong acts are those that are punished. If anything is punished, it must be wrong. If something is not punished, then it must not be wrong. This earliest moral reasoning is, of course, quite flawed. It leads to problematic judgments. For example, if a thief is smart enough not to be apprehended, then there must be nothing reprehensible about the thief's behavior. Eventually, children begin to see the inadequacies of this understanding of morality and invent more adequate models of differentiating between what is morally wrong and what is morally right. Kohlberg and his collaborators have maintained that these developmental changes follow an orderly pattern of stage growth (Colby & Kohlberg, 1984; Kohlberg, Levine, & Hewer, 1984).

According to Kohlberg's view, a moral person is basically an individual who has developed advanced cognitive structures by which to differentiate between good and evil. At the highest stages, such distinctions are made on the basis of principles that can successfully delineate justice. For example, advanced moral reasoning must incorporate the principle that every human has the just claim to be treated in the same manner as every other human (the principle of equality).

The development of more advanced stages of moral reasoning requires that the individual confront situations in which his or her current moral reasoning leads to judgments that are problematic. According to Stage 1 thought, if Hitler had won World War II, then there would have been nothing immoral about Hitler's program of genocide. Stage growth stems from cognitive conflict in which the individual's mode of understanding simply does not work. Initially, individuals twist and distort circumstances in a futile attempt to make their thinking work. Gradually, they begin to sense that there are inconsistencies and internal contradictions in their current mode of understanding. Cognitive conflict then prepares the individual to abandon less mature ways of thinking and to replace them with more advanced cognitive structures.

From this perspective, television might be an important contributor to moral development. As Ryan (1976) has articulated, television is rife with situations in which moral issues are confronted. Should a TV character go out with a new man in her life when she discovers that he is married? Should a physician cooperate with a terminal cancer patient and let him take his own life? While watching television characters struggle with moral dilemmas, the viewer's moral reasoning is engaged. If the viewer's level of cognitive functioning is not able to resolve the issue, the viewer will begin to experience cognitive conflict. It is such self-perceived inadequacies that set the stage for the development of more advanced moral reasoning.

Although many commentators (Lidz, 1984; Ryan, 1976; Sutherland & Siniawsky, 1982) have documented a high incidence of moral dilemmas on television, few researchers have attempted to find associations between television viewing and the viewer's stage of moral reasoning. Rosenkoetter, Huston, and Wright (1990) examined multiple indexes of moral reasoning of kindergartners, second, and fourth graders and compared these measures to detailed television diaries provided by the children's mothers. Only at the kindergarten level was there linkage between television diet and level of moral reasoning. For these children, the more television they watched, the more likely they were to be relatively immature in how they reasoned about prohibited behaviors ("Why is it wrong to take a toy car which belongs to another child?") and about how to fairly distribute things ("Would it be fair for the teacher to give poor Billy his candy bar when the other children had to buy theirs?").

A major limitation of this study is that the families who agreed to participate were highly selected. Not only were they exceptionally well educated, but they shared a high level of concern about possible deleterious effects of television on their children. Consequently, these families regulated the viewing of their children to a high degree. This study suggests that, with sensitized and very able parents, there is probably no negative correlation between moral reasoning structures for second and fourth graders, but it leaves unanswered what associations might exist in more typical families.

Although research is clearly limited, there is no evidence to date that heavy television usage leads to more advanced moral reasoning. It may be that the moral dilemmas most often presented on television are deficient in that the major characters spend so little time sharing their reflections and ethical considerations. One genre of television that departs from the "action at the expense of reflection" style of mainstream television is the soap opera (Sutherland & Siniawsky, 1982). On programs such as *All My Children,* considerable dialogue is devoted to the characters' conflicting thoughts concerning what they should do and why. It would be interesting to compare the moral reasoning of early adolescent subjects who are captivated by one or more of the soaps with peers who are not so inclined. This would be a stronger test of the notion from cognitive-developmental theory that television's moral dilemma conflicts might facilitate stage growth.

In a recent study, Krcmar and Valkenburg (1999) examined the relationship between moral reasoning and television viewing in a much more limited manner. Subjects ranged in age from 6 to 12 and were asked to indicate how often they watched programs in the following categories: fantasy violence (*X-Men*), realistic violence (*Rescue 911*), comedies (*Home Improvement*), and child educational (*Bill Nye, the Science Guy*). They were then asked to evaluate a series of vignettes in which a victim was the object of unjustified or justified violence. The latter judgments of the subjects were probed to yield an index of moral judgment. Less mature structures were based on reasoning focused on punishment and authority, whereas more advanced reasoning emphasized an empathic orientation. The results indicated that children with heavy diets of fantasy violence and realistic violence tended to show lower scores for moral reasoning.

According to Kohlberg's theory, impaired growth in moral reasoning would follow from a paucity of challenges to one's current mode of moral reasoning. Although it could well be the case that television programs do little to challenge adults' moral reasoning, it is far less plausible that television's moral dilemmas would not be challenging to children. Nonetheless, there are indications in the Krcmar and Valkenburg (1999) and Rosenkoetter et al. (1990) studies of a link between lower levels of moral reasoning and higher levels of television viewing. This finding is not easily interpreted from the Kohlbergian perspective.

## Television as a Teacher of Moral Values

Values have been most often conceptualized as central beliefs that an individual holds that specify how one ought to or ought not to act. Values are assumed to be acquired through a socialization process in which individuals are taught important beliefs by a variety of socialization agents, such as parents. The media have typically been included as one of the socialization agents. With respect to the central issue of this chapter, we then come to the question, Does television teach or otherwise modify the moral values of youthful viewers?

As a test of this hypothesis, Meyer (1976) had small groups of 6- to 10-year-olds watch an episode of *All in the Family* in which Archie, the main character, attempts to bribe an IRS official into ignoring moonlighting income that he had not reported on his tax return. As part of an individual interview that immediately followed the viewing, subjects were asked "Is it right or wrong to cheat just a little on your income taxes?" Children who had seen the episode were then compared with children who had not seen the episode. Results indicated a significant interaction with race. Although there was no difference with Caucasian children, African American children who saw the program were more likely than those who had not seen it to agree that it was OK to cheat a little (26% vs. 15%).

More recently, McKenna and Ossoff (1998) showed 4- to 10-year-olds (divided into three age groupings) an episode of *Mighty Morphin Power Rangers* in which Rocky, one of the power rangers, was placed under a spell that led him to be irresponsible in his duty to defend his community. When subjects were individually asked "What was this episode of the *Power Rangers* about?" approximately one half of the two younger groups were able to articulate the lesson that it is important to save the town from the villains and, hence, work comes before play. As anticipated, the oldest group of subjects scored significantly higher on their understanding of this central theme.

Although in the previous two studies the moral message was central to the television program, other television programs provide moral messages that are better described as incidental. Bryant and Rockwell (1994), in a series of experiments, exposed young teenagers in small groups to 3 hours of television for 5 consecutive nights. Subjects were randomly assigned to one of the following conditions: a television program featuring (a) sexual relations between married partners, (b) sexual relations between unmarried partners, or (c) nonsexual relations between adults. Programs were chosen from such series as *Dynasty, Dallas,* and so on, and subjects were asked to rate each of the programs in order to mask the purpose of the investigation. Within the next week, subjects returned individually and were shown 14 brief vignettes selected from similar television programs. On half of the vignettes, there was a sexual indiscretion, and on the other half, there was a nonsexual crime. After viewing each vignette, subjects were asked to rate how morally bad the indiscretion or crime was.

As hypothesized, results indicated that the subjects exposed to massive programming that dwelt on nonmarital sexual relations rated the sexual indiscretions as less bad than did the subjects in either of the other viewing conditions. In sequel investigations, several individual difference variables were explored to see if they would mitigate the effect of exposure to adult soaps featuring nonmarital sex. Bryant and Rockwell (1994) found that, for teenagers with an active, critical viewing style, or with families using open styles of communication, or with families who had clear, well-defined value systems, the effect of the experimental treatment was largely eliminated.

Whereas the previous studies have focused on a particular television program or genre, Tan, Nelson, Dong, and Tan (1997) explored the self-reported viewing of tenth, eleventh, and twelfth graders for any possible association with their values. Values were operationalized with a variation of the Rokeach Value Survey (1968), which included being honest. In addition to indicating their acceptance of each of the values enumerated by Rokeach, subjects were asked to rate the extent to which their favorite television programs emphasized each of the values included in the Rokeach Value Survey, as well as the importance of each value in the achievement of their personal goals.

Although the results failed to yield an association between television-viewing measures and subjects' ratings of their own values, the researchers did find an association between the subjects' values and their perceptions of their viewings' endorsement of particular values. For example, subjects who tended to rate being honest as important tended to see the television program that they watched as highlighting the importance of honesty. Path analysis of the results indicated that even more important than the subjects' appraisal of the values emphasized by their favorite programs was the extent to which they judged a particular value to be of functional significance for their lives.

If television viewing does have an impact on the values of young viewers, then it is necessary that they be able to comprehend the programs that they are viewing. Hence, the extent to which children are able to understand television programming has been a major focus of theory and research (Collins, 1983; Dorr, 1980, 1983; Singer & Singer, 1998). Reviewers concur that children's understanding follows a developmental sequence in which the earliest gains can be seen in the child's growing understanding of the central information of the television story. Later, the child begins to infer the underlying motives of the characters, which then allows him or her to move beyond the program's explicit information and fill in some of the gaps that must be inferred.

There has been less agreement among researchers as to the typical age at which these advances occur. More recent research suggests that it perhaps occurs somewhat earlier than initially anticipated (Pingree et al., 1984). However, for purposes of understanding moral lessons that then inform moral values, there must be a third phase in which the child begins to sense that there may be a general truth that lies above and beyond the story itself. This would set the stage for a marked growth in the impact of television drama on the values of its viewers. To date, there has been virtually no research directed to such a "third phase."

## Television and the Honesty of Young Viewers

From the perspective of social learning theory, morality is best conceptualized as the avoidance of reprehensible behaviors (Liebert, 1984). A moral child is one who resists the temptations of lying, cheating, stealing, and other illicit behaviors. Such behaviors are most often learned by observing other individuals model such behaviors. Furthermore, after such behaviors have been learned and are contained in the child's behavioral repertoire, models that yield to temptation make it more likely that a young observer will likewise yield to the temptation.

Although this theory has produced an impressive body of moral development research (Bandura, 1991; Mischel & Mischel, 1976), its interface with television has been dominated by studies that demonstrate the influence of models on prosocial behaviors rather than reprehensible behaviors. With respect to the few studies that do exist, they have typically used televised modeling episodes produced by the experimenter rather than actual television programming (Stein & Bryan, 1972; Wolf & Cheyne, 1972). Such studies typically demonstrate that the observation of a model who behaves in an immoral manner does increase the probability that a youthful observer will also yield to the temptation.

Yunxiao (1998) has recently shared the results of a large-scale correlational study that he conducted in China. To assess the role of television on the ethical development of the young, the television viewing of more than 3,000 subjects ages 9 to 16 was correlated with a measure of social morality that included honesty as well as readiness to help and patriotism. Yunxiao reported that the more television subjects watched, the more likely they were to score low on the social morality measure. Unfortunately, Yunxiao did not elaborate on the magnitude of the relationship.

Television critics have been vociferous in their criticism that young people are observing television behaviors, such as premarital sex, that then encourage the observers to imitate the modeled behavior. In the terminology of social learning theory, this would be a disinhibitory effect, because the modeled behavior diminishes the observer's inhibitory tendencies. The *Los Angeles Times* (Thomas, 1995) reported that, in a nationwide poll of adolescents, 62% said that television sex influences their peers to have sexual relations at too young an age. Similarly, 66% said that shows such as *Married . . . With Children* and *The Simpsons* encourage young viewers to disrespect parents. It is unfortunate that researchers have not been able to put such concerns to a more rigorous test.

## Identification With Television Characters

The processes by which television may influence youthful viewers considered so far have been reasonably concrete. Will dramatized moral dilemmas lead children to develop more advanced moral schemas for differentiating between right and wrong? Are children able to understand and will they accept moral lessons presented on television? Do children imitate immoral behaviors they observe on television?

Some researchers, most notably Grant Noble (1983), have argued that, although the above processes may be operative, the real impact of television on children's morality is far more subtle and elusive. According to this view, television works primarily through feelings rather than cognitions, as implied by the previous perspectives. The pivotal construct for Noble's view is a hypothesized identification that develops between the viewer and television characters.

To be sure, the immediate social reality of children is their home, friends, and school. However, beyond this, their favorite television programs become an integral part of their daily life. When children regularly watch a program, they may begin to interact and respond to the program's characters as though they were real people in their immediate environment. This leads the child to an illusion of intimacy in which he or she may exchange identities with a television character or even adopt a role complementary to the television character. The phenomenon is often referred to as "para-social interaction." In either case, the consequence of such an identification is a heightened viewing experience in which the child is more likely to accept the program as real and to absorb the program into his or her personhood (Duck, 1992).

Although this view has been particularly difficult to test, it has led to a series of experiments undertaken by a variety of researchers. In the first of these studies, Meyer (1973) individually interviewed first, second, and third graders. Each subject was asked to identify his or her favorite television character, as well as a number of other questions about their viewing of television. They were then presented with a series of four hypothetical stories. In the first story, the child was asked to pretend that a fellow student across the aisle was cheating on a test. "What would you do? What would your favorite television character do? What is the right thing to do? What is the wrong thing to do? What would your parents want you to do? What would your best friend do?" This procedure was repeated for the remaining hypothetical stories, which included "Suppose you were playing with your favorite toy and a person you didn't like came up to you and took it away."

Both age and gender yielded a main effect, with boys and younger children more likely to judge violent responses as the right thing to do. But regarding the issue of identification, both boys and girls were highly likely to say that whatever they would do in these hypothetical situations is what their favorite television character would also do. Furthermore, what they and their favorite television character would do would be the right thing to do. For boys, the matrix of correlations between their choice, the choice of their favorite character, and their perception of the moral choice ranged in the area of +.60 to +.70, and with girls the correlations clustered around +.80. Meyer was cautious to note that it is unclear whether the favorite television characters were influencing the young viewers' judgment or the children were choosing television characters who represent their views.

Meyer's subjects were middle-class Caucasians, but a replication undertaken with only slight modifications studied lower-class African Americans (Donohue, 1975). Donohue also found that the older children's responses were less likely to judge violence as the "right thing to do." Contrary to Meyer,

Donohue found few differences between the genders. Again there were significant associations between what the children would do in the hypothetical situations and what they perceived their favorite television character would do. With Donohue's subjects, their friends' choice tended also to be correlated with their own choice and the perception of their favorite television character. With these children, their own choice was not related to their judgment of what their parents would do. The perceived parents' judgments, in turn, tended to coincide with the children's judgment of what the right thing to do would be.

In a sequel investigation, Donohue (1977) reasoned that institutionalized children would be especially influenced by television characters since they do not live with a family and spend large amounts of time watching television with fellow residents. To test this notion, Donohue interviewed emotionally disturbed adolescents at a state hospital. The method closely paralleled his previous work. For both genders, the strongest correlate to the subject's judgment was the subject's judgment of what his or her best friend would do. Only for females was their judgment correlated with what they thought their favorite television character would do.

Subsequently, Donohue (1978) tested a group of primarily males who were emotionally disturbed and in residence at a state mental hospital. The subjects' ages were between 6 and 10. With this group, the pattern of results closely paralleled the earlier findings. The children's own judgments were correlated with their perceptions of what their favorite television character would do and what their friends would do. There was no relationship between what they would do and either what the morally right thing to do would be or what their parents would do. Subjects did see that their parents' choice was the morally correct choice.

In the final investigation in this series, Loughlin, Donohue, and Gudykunst (1980) tested first-, second-, and third-grade Puerto Rican children who were living in a central city located in the Eastern corridor. The procedure was as indicated previously except that many of the interviews were conducted in Spanish. For both boys and girls, they perceived their choices to be very similar to the right thing to do and what their best friend would do. Only the boys' judgments were correlated with the perception of what their favorite television character would do. The girls tended to see television characters as doing what they disapproved of personally.

Noble (1983) himself has only published preliminary data that bear directly on his notion of a strong identificatory process by which television influences the morality of children. Australian children ranging in age from 8 to 11 received a battery of stories dealing with a variety of moral issues. One story, for example, raised the issue of whether it would be right to steal food for a hungry friend.

On the basis of a factor analysis, Noble identified three morality dimensions. Although the largest factor (48% of the variance) was altruism, Factor 2 (34%) and Factor 3 (18%) are directly related to the concerns of this chapter. The second factor was titled "obedience to the letter rather than the spirit of the law," and the third was obedience to authority. Likewise, the children were queried as to their favorite characters and, specifically, who they would like to be like. As hypothesized, children who would like to be like Bugs Bunny scored low on the second factor. Furthermore, those who watched Bugs a lot (as opposed to wishing to be like Bugs) responded to the stories as indicating obedience to authority. Hence, the appeal of Bugs is wish fulfillment. Children like his trickiness, which allows him to do things that they would not dare. Noble's interpretation of the data was that they are indicative of how television characters are related to the real-life morality of children.

In summary, the influence of television characters through a presumed process of emotional identification is an interesting counterpoint to other theoretical viewpoints. At present, this theory is lacking conceptual precision. If its articulations (Noble &

Freiberg, 1980) can move beyond such metaphors as "osmosis," empirical tests will become more plentiful. However, to date, the research has been highly exploratory. It is unfortunate that researchers have not been able to put such concerns to a more rigorous test.

## Television as an Agent of Culture

Gerbner and his associates (Gerbner, Gross, Jackson-Beeck, Jeffries-Fox, & Signorielli, 1978; Gross, 1977) have argued that researchers have erred in their preoccupation with exploring specific television genres, programs, or even episodes for their effect on the viewer. Rather, they suggest, a more important level of analysis follows from the realization that television represents a coherent (although not invariant) system of messages that cumulatively present the viewer with a stable worldview, including the moral sphere. This position is usually called cultivation theory (see Chapters 10 and 17).

From this perspective, the first order of business is to determine the content of this system of moral messages. Selnow examined 222 subplots of prime-time fictional television and concluded that there were four major themes: "truth wins out in the end," "hard work yields rewards," "ingenuity finds a solution," and "good wins over evil" (Selnow, 1986, p. 69). In accord with Selnow's analysis, Potter (1990) reported that the more television watched by middle and high school students, the more likely they were to agree that the messages identified by Selnow were important themes underlying television's programming.

Other analysts have likewise attempted to encapsulate the moral messages of television. Lidz (1984), for example, has concluded that television's overall message is an endorsement of a conventional, middle-class morality. More specifically, this entails "honesty, hard work, development of skill, self-improvement, performance of duty, and the trustworthiness of promises" (p. 276).

Cheung and Chan (1996), however, concluded that the central message of television is consumerism, with its emphasis on fine clothes, extravagant cars, luxurious homes and apartments, and splendid restaurants. This led them to hypothesize that extensive television viewing would be associated with the endorsement of materialistic values. They reported finding such an association with a large sample of high school students in Hong Kong.

Although cultivation theory has been a prolific contributor to television research in general, its contribution to the study of television and morality has been limited. This scarcity of empirical tests of cultivation theory and morality may stem from the difficulty of specifying the content of television's overall representation regarding right and wrong (Potter, 1990). At present, it is unclear whether this is a contentious issue or whether researchers are simply using different words to describe the same underlying themes.

A high priority for cultivation theory should be to develop a stronger methodology for determining television's moral themes. With clarification of this concern, a resurgence of tests of the cultivation model might well follow.

## Comments and Discussion

The studies reviewed here cumulatively support the conclusion that television may indeed have an impact on the morality of children. What remains unclear is how large a role television plays. Is it appropriate to view television as simply another member of the media family along with the radio and movies? Or might the role of television be dramatically greater? Perhaps its constant presence in the home may reinforce its lessons with a power unparalleled by the other media (Selnow, 1986).

If television does influence the child's morality, is its role that of a "default condition" that is operative on a small minority of children? In other words, is its influence limited to those children who are lacking the serious attention of parents, teachers, siblings, and friends who are the important socializers of morality? Is television only a force in the lives of those children whose waking hours are monopolized by it? The weight of the research cited in this chapter suggests an effect that is broader than the default notion.

Gross (1977) has suggested that there is no such thing as a television message because viewers perceive the same program in different ways. This line of reasoning would seem to suggest that the effects of *The Simpsons* and *The Cosby Show* might be interchangeable. However, might it not be that, even if there is a lack of unanimity among viewers regarding the message of an episode of *The Simpsons* or *The Cosby Show,* these two shows are still likely to have differences in their impact on young viewers? Two of the studies reviewed (McKenna & Ossoff, 1998; Meyer, 1976) support the notion that programs do have different messages that young viewers are able to understand. What is lacking is research that demonstrates that children with different television diets develop distinctive values and related behavior patterns across time.

Is it necessary for the child to have direct personal experiences to confirm television messages? Or does television influence children's morality provided that they have not had experiences that directly disconfirm television messages? This question has yet to be addressed. Given its somewhat refined nature, questions raised earlier are best dealt with first. Cultivation theory would suggest that the main influence of television is when it presents messages that represent the mainstream of the culture's beliefs.

In the earliest days of television, there was typically one television station, and its program was the only program choice available to the viewer. Today, television offers a highly varied and growing selection of programs. Is *Little House on the Prairie* really interchangeable with *Married . . . With Children*? Depending on one's choice of programming, might the impact of television be dramatically different? Researchers would do well to develop viewing measures based on a variety of conceptually similar programs. This strategy has been far more successful in establishing meaningful relationships in other areas of inquiry than research that simply relies on an index of total television viewing (Hawkins & Pingree, 1990).

At present, none of the theoretical perspectives considered appears clearly superior among the competing orientations. Hence, it seems prudent at this juncture to continue to encourage an eclecticism. Each of the perspectives considered has generated significant findings. I would favor continuing to explore hypotheses generated by each of these theories as well as maintaining an openness to other frameworks not yet introduced.

The study of television and morality has been unduly one-sided in a search for detrimental effects. Are there not programs that positively affect the moral development of young viewers? Might not *Barney* be an impetus to honesty and integrity? Has not *Mister Rogers' Neighborhood* dealt with the importance of being truthful? The research literature is virtually void of attempts to explore such programming on moral development and the processes by which young viewers might be affected. This is particularly sad in view of the fact that one of the major goals of *Sesame Street* articulated more than 30 years ago was that young children behave by rules and recognize fairness and unfairness (Fisch, Truglio, & Cole, 1999).

To be sure, there must be other factors that modify and alter the influence of television on the morality of young viewers. With respect to age, are young children more likely to be influenced than their older counterparts? Some researchers have answered "yes" because the young lack the cognitive skills and life experiences that enable older viewers to discount much of what they see on television as pure fiction (Christenson & Roberts, 1983). Furthermore, children appear to have a strong belief in the reality of anything they see displayed pictorially (Gross, 1977). Others would suggest that early adolescence is a particularly vulnerable age, for young people struggle with their values on a daily basis (Bryant & Rockwell, 1994). The critical nature of this period stems from the frail nature of the teenager's values, which seem to be in a state of constant flux. The influence of age remains an open question and most deserving of experimental scrutiny.

Will the findings of the salutary contribution of parental regulation of television viewing and the accompanying discussion about programming generalize to the moral development domain (Desmond, Singer, & Singer, 1990)? Messaris and Sarett (1981) conducted interviews with parents in a pilot investigation of parent-child dialogue prompted by television-encountered issues of morality. Parents reported that television content gives them the opportunity to provide moral instruction. For example, following a vase-breaking incident on *The Brady Bunch,* a mother told her son that "I would be very disappointed if you didn't come and tell me that you broke the favorite vase." Systematic research on such conversation needs to be encouraged.

Is television and morality an important issue? With such widespread and growing interest on the part of the public, why is there such a dearth of research publications? At best, answers to this question would be speculative. It is clear, however, that the news media are giving growing attention to issues of morality and values. Might conditions, at last, be ripe for moving the television and morality question from its present obscurity to a priority issue for researchers?

## References

Bandura, A. (1991). Social cognitive theory of moral thought and action. In W. M. Kurtines & J. L. Gewirtz (Eds.), *Handbook of moral behavior and development: Vol. 1. Theory* (pp. 45-103). Hillsdale, NJ: Lawrence Erlbaum.

Bryant, J., & Rockwell, S. C. (1994). Effects of massive exposure to sexually oriented prime-time television programming on adolescents' moral judgment. In D. Zillmann, J. Bryant, & A. Huston (Eds.), *Media, children, and the family: Social scientific, psychodynamic, and clinical perspectives* (pp. 183-195). Hillsdale, NJ: Lawrence Erlbaum.

Cheung, C., & Chan, C. (1996). Television viewing and mean world value in Hong Kong's adolescents. *Social Behavior and Personality, 24,* 351-364.

Christenson, P. G., & Roberts, D. F. (1983). The role of television in the formation of children's social attitudes. In M. J. A. Howe (Ed.), *Learning from television: Psychological and educational research* (pp. 79-99). London: Academic Press.

Colby, A., & Kohlberg, L. (1984). Invariant sequence and internal consistency in moral judgment stages. In W. M. Kurtines & J. L. Gewirtz (Eds.), *Morality, moral behavior, and moral development* (pp. 41-51). New York: John Wiley.

Collins, W. A. (1983). Interpretation and inference in children's television viewing. In J. Bryant & D. R. Anderson (Eds.), *Children's understanding of television* (pp. 125-150). New York: Academic Press.

Desmond, R. J., Singer, J. L., & Singer, D. G. (1990). Family mediation: Parental communication patterns and the influences of television on children. In J. Bryant (Ed.), *Television and the American family* (pp. 293-309). Hillsdale, NJ: Lawrence Erlbaum.

Donohue, T. R. (1975). Black children's perceptions of favorite TV characters: As models of antisocial behavior. *Journal of Broadcasting, 19,* 153-167.

Donohue, T. R. (1977). Favorite TV characters as behavioral models for the emotionally disturbed. *Journal of Broadcasting, 21,* 333-345.

Donohue, T. R. (1978). Television's impact on emotionally disturbed children's value systems. *Child Study Journal, 8,* 187-201.

Dorr, A. (1980). When I was a child, I thought as a child. In S. B. Withey & R. P. Abeles (Eds.), *Television and social behavior: Beyond violence and children* (pp. 193-230). Hillsdale, NJ: Lawrence Erlbaum.

Dorr, A. (1983). No shortcuts to judging reality. In J. Bryant & D. R. Anderson (Eds.), *Children's understanding of television* (pp. 199-220). New York: Academic Press.

Duck, J. M. (1992, September). *Heroes and heroines, real and fantastic: Children's involvement with media figures.* Paper presented at the meeting of the International Media Ecology Conference, Mainz, Germany.

Fineman, H. (1994, June 13). The politics of virtue. *Newsweek,* pp. 30-36.

Fisch, S. M., Truglio, R. T., & Cole, C. F. (1999). The impact of *Sesame Street* on preschool children: A review and synthesis of 30 years' research. *Media Psychology, 1,* 165-190.

Geiger, K. (1995, October 22). Fed up with all the TV trash? *Washington Post,* p. 22.

Gerbner, G., Gross, L., Jackson-Beeck, M., Jeffries-Fox, S., & Signorielli, N. (1978). Cultural indicators: Violence profile no. 9. *Journal of Communication, 28,* 176-207.

Gross, L. (1977). Television as a Trojan horse. *School Media Quarterly, 5,* 175-180.

Hawkins, R. P., & Pingree, S. (1990). Divergent psychological processes in constructing social reality from mass media content. In N. Signorielli & M. Morgan (Eds.), *Cultivation analysis: New directions in media effects research* (pp. 35-50). Newbury Park, CA: Sage.

Huston, A. C., & Wright, J. C. (1998). Mass media and children's development. In W. Damon, I. E. Sigel, & K. A. Renninger (Eds.), *Handbook of child psychology: Vol. 4. Child psychology in practice* (pp. 999-1058). New York: John Wiley.

Kohlberg, L. (1984). *The psychology of moral development: Vol. 2. Essays on moral development.* New York: Harper & Row.

Kohlberg, L., Levine, C., & Hewer, A. (1984). The current formulation of the theory. In L. Kohlberg (Ed.), *The psychology of moral development: The nature and validity of moral stages* (Vol. 2, pp. 212-319). Cambridge, MA: Harper & Row.

Krcmar, M., & Valkenburg, P. M. (1999). A scale to assess children's moral interpretations of justified and unjustified violence and its relationship to television viewing. *Communication Research, 26,* 608-620.

Lidz, V. (1984). Television and moral order in a secular age. In W. D. Rowland Jr. & B. Watkins (Eds.), *Interpreting television: Current research perspectives* (pp. 267-289). Beverly Hills, CA: Sage.

Liebert, R. M. (1984). What develops in moral development? In W. M. Kurtines & J. L. Gewirtz (Eds.), *Morality, moral behavior, and moral development* (pp. 177-192). New York: John Wiley.

Loughlin, M., Donohue, T. R., & Gudykunst, W. B. (1980). Puerto Rican children's perceptions of favorite television characters as behavioral models. *Journal of Broadcasting, 24,* 159-171.

McKenna, M. W., & Ossoff, E. P. (1998). Age differences in children's comprehension of a popular television program. *Child Study Journal, 28,* 53-68.

Messaris, P., & Sarett, C. (1981). On the consequences of television-related parent-child interaction. *Human Communication Research, 7,* 226-244.

Meyer, T. P. (1973). Children's perceptions of favorite television characters as behavioral models. *Educational Broadcasting Review, 7,* 25-33.

Meyer, T. P. (1976). The impact of "All in the Family" on children. *Journal of Broadcasting, 20,* 159-169.

Mischel, W., & Mischel, H. N. (1976). A cognitive social-learning approach to morality and self-regulation. In T. Likona (Ed.), *Moral development and behavior* (pp. 84-107). New York: Holt, Rinehart & Winston.

Noble, G. (1983). Social learning and everyday television. In M. J. A. Howe (Ed.), *Learning from television: Psychological and educational research* (pp. 101-124). New York: Academic Press.

Noble, G., & Freiberg, K. (1980). *Australian children's uses of television.* Unpublished manuscript, University of New England, Armidale, Australia.

Pingree, S., Hawkins, R. P., Rouner, D., Burns, J., Gikonyo, W., & Neuwirth, C. (1984). Another look at children's comprehension of television. *Communication Research, 11,* 477-496.

Potter, W. J. (1990). Adolescents' perceptions of the primary values of television programming. *Journalism Quarterly, 67,* 843-853.

Rosenkoetter, L. I., Huston, A. C., & Wright, J. C. (1990). Television and the moral judgment of the young child. *Journal of Applied Developmental Psychology, 11,* 123-137.

Ryan, K. (1976). Television as a moral educator. In R. Adler & D. Cater (Eds.), *Television as a cultural force* (pp. 111-127). New York: Praeger.

Selnow, G. W. (1986). Solving problems on prime-time television. *Journal of Communication, 36,* 63-72.

Singer, D. G., & Singer, J. L. (1998). Developing critical viewing skills and media literacy in children. *Annals of the American Academy of Political and Social Science, 557,* 164-179.

Stein, G. M., & Bryan, J. H. (1972). The effect of a television model upon rule adoption behavior of children. *Child Development, 43,* 268-273.

Sutherland, J. C., & Siniawsky, S. J. (1982). The treatment and resolution of moral violations on soap operas. *Journal of Communication, 32,* 67-74.

Tan, A., Nelson, L., Dong, Q., & Tan, G. (1997). Value acceptance in adolescent socialization: A test of a cognitive-functional theory of television effects. *Communication Monographs, 64,* 82-97.

Thomas, C. (1995, March 3). TV shapes lives of children. *St. Louis Post Dispatch,* p. 7B. (Originally published in the *Los Angeles Times*)

Wartella, E. (1988). The public context of debates about television and children. In S. Oskamp (Ed.), *Television as a social issue* (pp. 59-68). Newbury Park, CA: Sage.

Wildavsky, R. (1996, May). Why TV is so trashy. *Reader's Digest,* pp. 49-54.

Wolf, T. M., & Cheyne, J. A. (1972). Persistence of effects of live behavioral, televised behavioral, and live verbal models on resistance to deviation. *Child Development, 43,* 1429-1436.

Yunxiao, S. (1998). In U. Carlsson & C. von Feilitzen (Eds.), *Children and media violence* (pp. 215-221). Kvngalv, Sweden: Livrena Grafiska.

Zoglin, R. (1990, April 16). Home is where the venom is: Domestic life takes a drubbing in TV's anti-family sitcoms. *Time, 135,* 85.

# PART II

## Forging the Media Environment for the Future: The Media Industry and Its Technology

### Preliminary Comments From the Editors

We began this handbook by looking carefully at child viewers and their experience confronting the media as well as their reactions to this confrontation. We now shift our perspective to the other side of the box. Where does the programming come from? Why do people make programs? What goals do they have? What content do they emphasize? What technology do they use to reach children and youth? What responsibilities do they bear if they are seeking to communicate with the youth of society?

Chapter 24 by J. Cory Allen introduces us to the dynamic impulse of the electronic media industry, its economic structure. In the United States, with the development of radio in the late 1920s, the Communications Act of 1934 acknowledged that the airwaves belonged to the people, but it licensed them to commercial broadcast stations with the understanding that some public interest responsibility would be reflected in programming in order to sustain a license. When television began to spread around the world in the 1950s, most governments controlled the one or two networks, and great initial emphasis was placed (in contrast to the United States) on educational or other public informational programming. This situation has changed drastically; commercial purposes now prevail worldwide in the electronic media industry. Allen's chapter and Chapter 25 by Alison Alexander spell out in considerable detail the objectives, methods, and effectiveness of the booming commercial electronic media industry. Whereas Allen focuses more on the economic and organizational issues, Alexander reviews the type of children's programming and the content of the commercial media, including television and computer approaches.

Chapter 26 by Jerry Franklin, Larry Rifkin, and Patrice Pascual introduces us to public broadcasting in the United States and exemplifies how educational and entertaining children's programs are developed and disseminated. Chapter 27 by David Kleeman extends the child-oriented focus to an international setting. He describes the PRIX JEUNESSE, a European-based clearinghouse for children's programming from around the world.

Chapter 28, written by Peter Dirr, introduces us more extensively to the cable television system in the United States and its patterns of entertainment as well as educational programming for children. He points to the cable industry's connections to the computer nets and identifies specific program thrusts and formats that are evolving with a focus on more quality material for children. Chapter 29 by Todd Tarpley looks ahead to the newest technologies from digital television and high-definition television to personal video recorders and the Internet. He examines the relevant research on the uses of these approaches, their health and safety hazards, and constructive possibilities. This emphasis on the mixed blessings of new technology is carried even further in Chapter 30 by Ellen Wartella and Nancy Jennings, who focus on the applications of television and computer use in formal educational settings. What can be gained by school use of these new technologies? But also what risks are there of commercialization and of children being distracted from formal engagements with their teachers? They summarize available research and point to new needed research.

The chapters in Part 2 focus on the industry's use of preproduced programming. How can we take advantage of the extensive research reported in Part I and the suggestions for producers that have emerged from the studies of *Sesame Street, Mister Rogers,* and *Barney & Friends*? We close Part II with Chapter 31 by Michael Cohen, who provides a research-based but practically oriented examination of how formative research can play a role in helping writers and producers develop and evaluate educational and entertaining children's programs. We hope that industry workers in the commercial and public sectors will do much more careful planning and evaluative research for the new shows or their computer disks and Internet applications.

CHAPTER **24**

# The Economic Structure of the Commercial Electronic Children's Media Industries

J. CORY ALLEN
University of Pennsylvania

## Economic Structure

Any parent, advocate, or academic who wants to maximize the enlightening potential or curb the undesired effects of children's electronic media must first understand the economic forces and incentives that shape these industries. This chapter will analyze the economic structure of the electronic commercial media, paying special attention to the distinct economic characteristics of the children's media industries. The chapter will employ a production-centered definition of children's media in its analysis of industries, thereby focusing on media produced primarily for children ages 2 to 12.

A number of steps must be taken to encompass accurately the economics that operate in these industries. The economics of the media products must be explained, such as the costs, risks, and rewards that companies negotiate to produce goods such as movies and television programs. Equally important, however, is the economics of the media distribution systems, the companies that own the infrastructure and pay production companies for content to deliver to the audience. This chapter will identify the pertinent economic arrangements and regulations particular to each media industry, as well as three economic concepts that operate throughout all media industries: *windowing, licensing,* and *ownership.*

*Windowing,* the sale of video products through multiple media outlets, and *licensing,* the sale of characters and images to any commercial outlet, will be analyzed individually. *Ownership,* a term denoting the business reality that media companies often own the means of both production and distribution, will be discussed in a case study. Four media companies have unrivaled ownership control of the children's media industries, and the economic conditions, incentives, and implications of this development will be assessed. Once the economic framework and operations of the industries are established, the chapter will assess the success of participants in complying with industry regulations and predict economic changes in the industries that the new media technologies will catalyze.

### *Windowing*

Economically, video products demonstrate the properties of both private and public goods. Television programs are a public good because the viewers who consume them do not diminish their availability to potential viewers. A movie is also a public good in that the number of viewers does not affect its value, but it is a private good because of commercial applications imposed by the movie industry. Viewers who buy a ticket to see a movie are paying for a seat in the theater; thus, the number of seats available for sale imposes a limitation on the number of potential consumers. Nonetheless, since an unlimited number of customers can consume video products, their owners have strong incentives to sell these products to as many people and for as many prices as consumers are willing to pay. This practice of selling video products through many different channels over different points in time to maximize audiences through price discrimination is known as windowing.

Windowing has become a fundamental economic mechanism for the media industries. For example, film producers speculate how many people will pay a premium price to see their movie in a theater, how many will pay slightly less to rent it on videocassette (or more to own it), and how many will wait to watch it air on television. Windowing also influences production decisions, as economists Owen and Wildman (1992) explain: "Programs that are windowed generally have larger budgets than programs that are not windowed, and among windowed programs, budgets increase with the number of windows in which the programs are released" (p. 48). This point becomes increasingly important as large media companies acquire multiple channels of distribution. These companies can invest more money in their video products because they own outlets that guarantee the opportunity of the video products to generate additional revenue. Producers assess the competitive conditions in all potential windows for their product and often alter its content and composition to improve its chance of success in these additional markets. Lastly, windowing is especially important in the children's media industries because of audience regeneration. Children's media products have the opportunity to enjoy extended commercial success, because every newborn baby represents a potential customer completely unexposed to every children's movie, television show, or videocassette.

A window that merits separate analysis is the window of international video markets. International markets represent enormous profit centers for American media companies, in large part because of the fact that the English-language market is by far the largest in both income and population among free-market countries. U.S. companies receive 75 cents of every dollar of international television trade. More important, the "Hollywood majors" (Warner Brothers, Disney, Paramount, 20th Century Fox, Universal, Columbia, and MGM/UA), the studios that produce most of America's film and television programs, receive anywhere from 60 to 67 cents of that amount (Segrave, 1998, p. 1).

Michael Eisner, chairman and CEO of the Hollywood major Disney, provides insight into America's multimedia dominance:

> More than 200 million people a year watch a Disney film or home video; 395 million watch a Disney TV show every week; 212 million listen or dance to Disney music, records, tapes or compact discs; 270 million buy Disney-licensed merchandise in 50 countries. . . . Such figures would mean little in themselves except that they are similar to figures of other American entertainment companies, demonstrating the universal appeal of American culture. (as cited in Gardels, 1995, p. 8)

Eisner supports this belief in noting that American films make up only 10% of films produced worldwide every year, yet they garner 65% of the world's box office receipts. He does not, however, mention the economic realities that underwrite this dominance. The video markets of most countries can acquire American productions at a fraction of what it would cost for domestic productions. U.S. media companies enjoy the ability to sell their products internationally at low prices, since they have often already recouped their production costs through the U.S. windows.

### *Licensing*

Licensing is a contractual arrangement that allows copyright holders to loan out their intellectual property for another company to use. In the children's media industries, companies can license the characters and images of their media products to other companies for a fee. The fee is typically 5 to 15% of the wholesale cost of the item that uses the license. The owners of children's movies and television programs enjoy the greatest profit potential from licensing of any media industry segment or subdivision, because these two forms of media are the most popular among children. Companies seek licensing deals with children's movies because these can be marketed into big commercial events, and they pursue licensing deals with children's television programs because they entertain a child audience as frequently as every day of the week.

The toy industry has benefited the most from the character licensing of children's movies and television. In 1985, character products accounted for $8.5 billion in toy sales, and they still constitute a sizable market share of the $20 billion toy industry (Englehardt, 1987, p. 78). Other industries have also realized the rewards of character licensing. Snack food companies, fast food restaurants, and clothing manufacturers are just a few of the businesses that recognize that incorporating popular characters into their products will increase the likelihood that children will buy them. Licensing benefits both the program owners and the manufacturers in numerous ways. Manufacturers enhance the popularity of their product among children, program owners earn revenue without having to risk capital or produce the goods themselves, and both the programs and the products provide free advertising for each other. For example, Disney's *The Lion King* generated $1.5 billion in the sale of licensed products, and Disney earned hundreds of millions of dollars without incurring any risks or costs by simply contracting out the movie's characters and images (Morgan, 1998, p. 6).

This chapter will later discuss how toy companies demonstrated the profit potential of character licensing by developing their own programs based on their own toys and action figures. The lessons were not lost on the producers of children's programming—character licensing became as important a revenue stream as the income generated from television or film distribution. More important, developments in the ownership of children's media companies have combined these revenue streams. These few large companies own both the programs and the channels that distribute them; thus, advertiser, distribution, and licensing revenue flows back to the same source. Licensing has also profoundly affected the development of other children's media industries, because the characters, songs, and stories licensed from movies and television shows dominate the home video and music market. Characters from television and the movies will likely populate the new media environment as well, especially since the large children's media companies are seeking to extend their dominant presence into these markets.

### *Broadcast*

Almost 99% of the households in the United States receive broadcast television. This penetration rate is achieved in part through more than 1,200 commercial television stations broadcasting to their local communities. The broadcast signals are free—for both the viewers who watch them and the stations that transmit them. Stations broadcast television signals through the electromagnetic spectrum, a national resource that the Federal Communications Commission (FCC) manages. Congress has empowered the FCC to regulate television broadcasting by licensing the spectrum in the "public interest, convenience and necessity." Therefore, stations must obtain a license from the FCC in order to broadcast. This is a renewable 8-year contract that is given for free to stations that comply with FCC regulations. Stations that do not comply with the "public interest" obligations of the FCC can have their licenses revoked. Moreover, Congress or the FCC can amend these requirements. As such, these regulations constitute the price stations pay to broadcast. For instance, when the FCC fortified the 1990 Children's Television Act in 1997 by requiring broadcasters to air 3 hours of educational children's television per week, it imposed, in effect, a new price for broadcasters to conduct business. The self-controls section will analyze other events that forced television companies to rein in economic motives to circumvent additional regulations. (See Chapter 32 on legal issues and television.)

Broadcast television is free for viewers because they form its primary product. The business of broadcast television is to produce audiences to sell to advertisers. Companies pay money to have their products and services advertised in commercials during television programs. The price these companies pay for commercial time depends on the size and demographics of the audience that a program attracts. One ratings agency, Nielsen Media Research, monitors the viewing activities of the American population and provides the industry-accepted statistics on audience sizes and their demographic characteristics (i.e., age and gender of viewers).

The television industry uses numerous terms to analyze and sell its audiences. Programs are measured in ratings and share points. A rating point is a numerical representation of the audience size of a program, defined as a percentage of all potential viewers in the United States. A national rating point represents 1% of the national audience, or 980,000 households of the 98 million households that had televisions in 1998. A share is the percentage of people watching a show out of all the people actually watching television during the time of the show.

Advertisers price the commercial time they buy in terms of cost-per-thousand (CPMs), the price they are paying for the commercial to reach 1,000 households. Advertisers also measure the commercial time they buy in gross ratings points (GRPs). They calculate this figure as *reach* (the percentage of the households or target audience that potentially views their commercial over a certain amount of time) multiplied by *frequency* (the number of times their commercial airs over this time; Vogel, 1998, p. 159). Advertisers want to reach their target audience as efficiently as possible; therefore, they are extremely concerned with the demographics of the audiences that programs attract.

### *Sources of Broadcast Programming: Network, Syndication, and Local*

#### *Network*

Of the 1,200 commercial stations in the United States, approximately 800 are affiliated with one of the Big Four networks: ABC, NBC, CBS, or Fox. The Big Three networks (ABC, NBC, and CBS) conduct business on a network-affiliate model that has been used for decades. Fox, however, implemented a different affiliate arrangement when it formed in 1986. The Big Three supply programs to their affiliates for free, but the networks retain most of the commercial time during these programs to sell to national advertisers. Stations sell some time during network programs to local advertisers, but the main financial dividend that affiliate stations receive is an annual payment from the network known as compensation. This fee is paid to compensate stations for clearing their schedule to air network programs, thereby allowing the programs to reach a national audience. Indeed, the network programs of the Big Four are the only ones that reach a mass audience. Although cable networks and new broadcast networks such as United Paramount Network (UPN) and Warner Bros. Television Network (the WB) fragment audiences by increasing the programming options for viewers, the Big Four still attract 55% of the national viewing audience. No cable network accounts for even 5% of the viewers nationwide. As such, in 1998, advertisers paid a collective $6.6 billion to buy commercials during the prime-time shows of the Big Four (Donald, 1999, p. 6).

### *Network Program Supply Conditions*

The networks pass their programs to the affiliates free of charge, but they rarely pay full price for them in the first place. When a network reaches an agreement with a production company to place its series in the network lineup, the network pays the production company a negotiated license fee for each individual episode that it puts on the air. However, the license provides the network with the freedom to air each episode a number of times. Thus, the time-honored practice of rerunning shows is simply a method for networks to maximize their investment in each episode.

The license fee that program suppliers receive from the network generally amounts to half the production cost of each episode. Program suppliers accept this deficit arrangement because programs that receive network distribution qualify for two larger economic incentives. First, if the show becomes a hit in the United States and stays in the network's lineup for a number of years, the accumulated episodes can be syndicated and sold to stations across the country. The production company will receive a great deal of income from the cash and commercial time that stations will pay to air the show. Second, a show that achieves network status, even if it fails to become a syndicated hit, can usually be sold to international television markets.

The economic factors that dictate the supply of network programming are similar to those that operate in the production and distribution of movies. This is by no means coincidental, since the major Hollywood studios are the major suppliers of network programming. These companies have been the predominant programming providers throughout the history of network television because the FCC prevented the networks from owning the programs they aired (a rule that is no longer in effect) and because the drama and comedy formats that these studios offered found favor with audiences.

The movie companies can thrive in the deficit production scenario of network television because they have the capital to absorb insufficient license fees and even the production costs of programs that failed to make a network lineup. They can endure these losses because one hit show pays for many failures and because they have unmatched experience and support in international sales and distribution. These companies can even derive revenue from shows that failed in the United States by block booking their sales in international markets. In this practice, which, incidentally, is illegal in the United States, the companies sell their programs in packages, leaving foreign purchasers who want to buy popular American programs with little choice but to pay for failed programs as well.

### *Network Children's Television*

The indirect nature of the business of television—the fact that viewers are its products and not its purchasers—presents numerous implications. Broadcasters program to the lowest common denominator, favoring content and formats that attract the largest or most valuable audiences. Commercial concerns dictate programming decisions far more than the public interest obligations that broadcasters are licensed to represent. They serve the public interest by serving that which interests the public. Viewers have no consumer sovereignty in regard to television; they cannot vote with their dollars to influence programming decisions as they can in direct-purchase markets such as movies and home videos. Many have found this economic reality especially troubling in children's television. However, since broadcast television is a regulated industry, consumers have often taken their protests about the content or commercialism of children's television to the FCC. Some of these protests convinced Congress and the FCC to monitor, lobby, or impose new regulations on the children's television industry.

Turow (1981) traced the economic development of network children's television. Many facets of the current state of network children's television have remained unchanged since their development in the early 1960s. In this decade, the networks realized that certain advertisers, such as snack food and toy companies, only wanted to reach a child audience. The networks also discovered that a block of children's programs was a profitable use of the Saturday morning time slot, when audience sizes, especially for adults, were near their lowest. Furthermore, color TV was introduced in this decade, and production companies such as Hanna-Barbera developed limited animation techniques that provided inexpensive color cartoons to the networks.

After the landscape of Saturday morning television was set, the networks soon discovered that children's television functioned as an enormous profit center. Saturday morning television had features that let the networks make and save money. For years they set aside more commercial time per hour during Saturday morning shows than they did during their prime-time blocks. Even after they curbed this practice, they still saved on programming expenses, rerunning children's shows at a far greater frequency than prime-time fare and easily retiring the cost of the license fee that they paid for each episode. The networks did not, however, profit from licensing deals, because they did not own the programs they aired. The production companies benefited from the income provided by licensing revenues on merchandise, and the networks mainly profited from advertising. Turow (1981) concluded that, in network children's television from the 1950s through the 1970s,

> the dominant forces have clearly been the networks and their advertisers. . . . Their basic goal . . . has remained the same, namely, to bring an audience of youngsters to commercials on a cost-efficient basis. Government and public pressures have not blunted this goal. (p. 120)

Network children's television remained unchanged for much of the 1980s and 1990s, but competition in children's programming increased dramatically. Syndicated children's cartoons began airing on weekday afternoons, and the cable networks emerged offering children's programming throughout their hours of operation. Consequently, the child audience grew increasingly divided, no longer a gathering unique to Saturday morning. These developments led one network, NBC, to replace children's programs with teen-oriented sitcoms. As Fox grew into a major network, however, one of its primary goals was to establish a successful block of children's programming on both Saturday morning and weekday afternoons. The WB and UPN both imitated this focus on children's television to an extent as their networks began operating.

The major change in the business of network children's television was not a result of competition but a directive from the FCC. The FCC introduced a requirement for stations to air 3 hours of educational children's television a week. In response, all of the networks agreed to supply their affiliates with FCC-friendly educational programming—an indication that the networks also accepted this new price for doing business in children's television.

### *Syndication*

Syndicated programs are supplied to a station through a syndicator on a market-by-market basis, whereas networks supply programs to their affiliate stations on a national basis. The syndicator acts as a temporary distributor, selling the programming to stations with the goal of securing time slots in enough communities to make up a national audience that can be sold to advertisers. Syndicated programs generally consist of talk shows, game shows, reruns of popular network shows, and original programs produced for syndication. The landscape of the syndicated programming industry changed dramatically with the FCC's implementation of the Prime Time Access Rule in 1970. Intended to reclaim the hour before prime time from the networks to the local stations, the rule inadvertently created new demand conditions for syndicated television. Hundreds of independent stations entered the market, and demand for syndicated programming skyrocketed as well. Most important, the practice of barter sales became a standard form of business. In this arrangement, stations received the syndicated programming without paying any actual money; instead, they gave the syndicator an allotment of commercial time during each episode of the program. The syndicator itself could then sell the commercial time during the show to advertisers. This opportunity provided the syndicator the incentive to place the show in markets across the country to piece together a national audience so that the commercial time could be sold to valuable national advertisers.

### *Children's Syndicated Television and Program-Length Commercials*

These developments in the syndicated programming market, combined with a politically appointed, industry-friendly FCC that developed a deregulatory stance in the early 1980s, led to fundamental changes in children's television. The toy industry took advantage of these conditions, creating and licensing their own characters, making television shows and toy products about them, and earning money from the licensing fees that other manufacturers paid to capitalize on their creations. This reversed the traditional relationship between toys and television in that the toy industry no longer waited for the television industry to provide shows that could be licensed into toys. Furthermore, these programs functioned as their own commercials, portraying characters, settings, and vehicles that the company also manufactured as toys. The "program-length commercials" that the toy companies produced for themselves proved to be both a financial and popular success. In 1983, 14 such programs were on the air, and after 2 years their numbers swelled to 40, with even more toy programs in development (Englehardt, 1987, p. 78). Many advertisers supported these programs for reasons of cost-efficiency, because these shows provided access to audiences of specific demographic compositions, as opposed to Saturday morning network programs that delivered large audiences of assorted ages and both genders.

Pecora (1998) provides case studies of how far toy manufacturers entered into the business of children's television. The toy and production companies behind *He-Man,* the first major product designed as both a toy and a television show, collaborated on the production and distribution of the show and even convinced stations to carry the show every weekday afternoon. From this point on, children's television was no longer limited to the weekends. A few years later, the companies that developed *Thundercats* offered stations profit participation in either the show's distribution rights or the toys' sales. Both of these examples signify the lengths that the toy companies, program producers, and television stations would go to in order to spread the economic risks among each other and minimize the possibilities of failure.

The significance of the FCC's role—or, more appropriately, its nonrole—in the developments of these conditions cannot be understated. In 1969, ABC aired *Hot Wheels,* a cartoon based on the toy cars. Responding to complaints that this show constituted nothing more than advertisements for the toys, the FCC ruled that the show was undoubtedly a commercial for the *Hot Wheels* toys and, as such, it exceeded the permissible amount of time allowed for commercials. The commission added, "We find this pattern disturbing . . . for [it] subordinates programming in the interest of the public to programming in the interest of salability" (as cited in Englehardt, 1987, p. 75). ABC subsequently removed the show from its lineup. In 1984, the FCC removed its regulations on the amount of commercial minutes permitted during children's programs. The production of program-length commercials began, and the FCC validated their presence on the airwaves in rejecting a complaint based on the commission's 1969 *Hot Wheels* ruling (Englehardt, 1987, p. 76).

Toy-based programs remain in children's programming blocks but not in the massive quantities witnessed in the 1980s. The decrease is not the result of increased government regulations. The government did limit the amount of advertising time during children's programs to 10.5 minutes per hour on weekends and 12 minutes per hour on weekdays in the Children's Television Act of 1990. Although the repeal of regulations on advertising minutes had permitted the production of these toy-based shows, the 1990 act did not put an end to the production or programming of program-length commercials. The decrease in the number of these programs is instead due to the rise of new networks. Most of the independent stations that readily accepted weekday afternoon blocks of commercial-length programming in the 1980s have become affiliates of Fox or, more recently, the WB or UPN. Thus, the children's programs of the new networks have filled many of the time slots that syndicated programs enjoyed. Ownership interests have laid claim to many of the conditions that fostered the supply of syndicated programming, an implication that will be discussed shortly.

#### *Local*

A station can also produce or buy programming to show to its local community. Locally produced programs inflict economic risks on stations because they incur the production costs. The reward for the risk, however, is that the stations keep all of the advertising revenue the programs generate, whereas they have to share the advertising revenue they earn from network and syndicated programming. Locally produced children's programs were once a mainstay for many stations, but over time most abandoned this type of programming for network or syndicated fare that demanded less direct investment. Melody (1973) notes that many of these local shows shared a similar format, with a local personality who introduced old theatrical cartoons and pitched advertisers' products. Melody describes *Romper Room* as one local children's show that achieved widespread exposure. *Romper Room* was actually a syndicated program format produced at the local level. Local stations produced their own versions with their own "teachers," but these activities were conducted under the close supervision of Romper Room, Inc.

### ***Cable***

#### *Cable Systems*

The fundamental economic difference between broadcast and cable television is that people pay for cable. Approximately 70% of U.S. households pay for cable television service (see Chapter 28). These households are served by their local cable system, the company that installs and maintains the coaxial cable that runs through the community and into subscribers' television sets. Cable systems sell packages of cable networks to their subscribers. The cable system receives these network signals from satellites and distributes their signals through the cable to subscribers. Because cable television is not transmitted through the spectrum, and because it is a subscription service, the cable industry receives far less regulatory scrutiny from the FCC. In fact, the very infrastructure necessary for cable service generally allows cable systems to operate as natural monopolies. The local governments that permit the installation of cable generally negotiate for one cable system to provide service because they do not want multiple companies laying miles of cable throughout the community. This monopoly status provides cable systems with a great deal of economic power. There are more than 10,000 cable systems in the United States, though large companies known as multisystem operators (MSOs) own many of them. In fact, the 25 largest MSOs provide cable service to approximately 90% of the nation's subscribers (Donald, 1999, p. 8). Many MSOs own part or all of many of the cable networks they transmit.

Cable systems currently enjoy a formidable lead in the race to wire the "last mile," a competition among telecommunications industries to provide phone, Internet, and video services to American households. Nationwide, the cable of cable systems pass 95% of the American population, rivaling the penetration of telephone wires. Furthermore, the coaxial cable has far greater bandwidth than the copper wires in telephone lines, and this allows for more expansive and faster services. The coaxial cable also contains back channel capabilities that can be used for future applications of interactive television. Cable systems may therefore evolve into the sole provider of all communication applications for many households.

### *Cable Networks*

Unlike the broadcast networks, cable networks enjoy two revenue streams: advertising and subscription. Cable networks sell advertising during their programs and often give part of this time to cable systems to sell locally. The main revenue stream for networks is subscription; all cable systems pay fees to the networks that are distributed to their subscribers. Payments are made on a monthly per-subscriber basis, and the fee is arranged between the cable network and the cable system. Thus, more popular cable networks generally negotiate higher fees than the less popular ones. Furthermore, some cable networks have resorted to paying cable systems for distribution. Many new cable networks have found it necessary to initiate this reversed economic order to reach viewers because of two reasons: Some systems have the number of channels they can transmit, and other systems will only pay for networks that will encourage new customers to subscribe.

Most systems offer premium networks, such as HBO and Showtime; these networks generally do not participate in the advertising revenue stream but do charge a great deal more for subscriptions to the channel. Program supply conditions to cable networks differ in a number of ways. Cable networks cannot compete with the broadcast networks in the price they offer for license fees because of smaller audiences. In fact, reruns of network programs make up a significant portion of the programming of cable networks. Furthermore, just as many MSOs own the cable networks they distribute, many cable networks own the programming they air.

### *Children's Cable Television*

The biggest economic benefit cable networks offer to advertisers, in comparison with broadcast networks, is cost-efficient advertising. The children's cable industry has grown because children's networks provide advertisers with excellent reach into their target audiences. Nickelodeon, the first children's cable network, began as a commercial-free network. Cable systems were, nonetheless, eager to include the network in their service as a "loss leader" to encourage subscribers. The systems realized that parents would pay for cable in part because it offered a quality channel for children to watch. As Nickelodeon grew in popularity, it quickly switched to selling commercial time. Now the network regularly garners more than $200 million of the $700 million that companies spend in advanced purchase of advertising time on all networks that program for children.

Other children's networks are actively gaining national distribution over cable systems. The Cartoon Network and the Fox Family Channel entered the children's cable market in the 1990s. Fox Family Worldwide (the children's media company formed through a spin-off from parent company News Corporation and a merger with the Saban Entertainment production company) bought the Family Channel for $1.9 billion and changed it to Fox Family Channel. This price was essentially a distribution fee for the new children's cable network to gain immediate penetration into the 69 million homes that received the Family Channel. The Disney Channel differs from the other three major children's cable channels in that it began as a premium channel distributed only to subscribers who paid an additional fee. The advertising-free channel has begun migrating to the basic package that many cable systems offer in order to increase its presence in the child audience. All of these four major children's cable channels produce or otherwise own a great deal of the content they deliver. The companies therefore realize profits not just through production and distribution but also through windowing and licensing.

### *Movies*

The movie industry is an oligopoly, because a handful of companies dominate the market. In 1998, movies generated $6.9 billion in ticket sales, and 90% of this box office total went to seven movie companies (Graves, 1999, p. 5). Six of these seven were among the aforementioned Hollywood majors, who also dominate the trade of international television. This figure is not atypical; the Hollywood majors generally account for at least 80% of the box office revenues. The Hollywood majors make most of their profit in the movie industry as the distributors of films. They are the companies that finance the production of films, arrange for them to be released into theaters throughout the United States, and underwrite the advertising and promotional campaigns that accompany the release. Distributors are entitled to most of the revenue a film generates, regardless of whether the film is produced by the distributor's studio or a separate production company. Distributors receive the rental fee that theater owners pay to show a film, which typically amounts to more than half of the ticket money the theater earned from the movie. Lastly, distributors often retain the rights to distribute the film into other video markets such as home video and television.

The multiple rewards of distribution have been explained, but this business also involves a great number of risks. Most movies fail to earn back the money they cost to make. Movie companies therefore depend on a few hit films to pay for the majority of their failures. This business condition presents a tremendous barrier to entry. Competitive companies need vast sums of capital to produce a number of films in order to diversify their risks and increase the potential that a few of their films will be profitable. Moreover, the major movie distributors have long-standing working relationships with theater chains and companies. Such a track record can only be developed when a company proves it can consistently create, fund, and distribute films that people will pay to see.

#### *Children's Movies*

The market for children's movies contains additional barriers to entry because of licensing. For example, in two recent children's films, Disney's *The Lion King* (McCarthy & Warner, 1994) and Viacom's *Rugrats* (Morgan, 1998), sizable portions of each company's production costs were recovered through licensing agreements arranged with companies before the films were even released. New companies in the children's film industry will probably not enjoy licensing fees subsidizing their film to such an extent. They will not have the proven track record with companies to convince them that their licensed characters can increase the sales of their products. They would have to prove to these companies that the content, distribution, and marketing they invest in the film would appeal to the child audience and that it will provide enough free advertising to benefit the sale of licensed products. Thus, new companies that produce children's movies will have great difficulty competing with established players in terms of production quality, a major component for success since their established licensing success affords them great economic freedom to increase investments in their productions as competition dictates.

### *Home Video*

The home video market best exemplifies the potential for economic rewards in windowing a video product. Consumers spent $7 billion to see movies in a theater in 1998, but they spent more than $9 billion to rent them and $8 billion to buy them on videocassette or videodisk (Graves, 1999, p. 7). The home video industry has grown to this extent primarily because VCRs have entered 80% of U.S. households. The companies that distribute their product into the home video market have one primary pricing decision. The videocassettes can be set at a high price to sell them mainly to video rental stores, or they can be priced for less to encourage viewers to buy them. The companies that distribute children's movies and children's television programs into the home video market (and these are the two overwhelming sources of content that populate this market) do not struggle with this decision. Unlike other subdivisions of the home video market, the children's market favors one choice to an extreme: Children's videos make up an estimated 80% of the home videos sold directly to consumers (McCormick, 1996). Pecora (1998) explains that children's videos are purchased because "children are a unique market for the industry, because unlike adults, children are content to view a cassette multiple times—seldom tiring of a favorite story" (p. 125).

### *Recorded Music*

The children's music industry is essentially another licensing opportunity for children's movies and television. Pecora (1998) estimates that the music industry participants ignore the child audience because the children's market makes up less than 2% of the industry market share. Disney dominates this segment, in part because the company discovered and continued a popular and profitable formula of inserting musical numbers into its animated feature films that can then be extracted, packaged, and sold separately in tapes and compact discs.

### *Radio*

Radio has not been a popular medium with children since 1955, when the last of the nationally distributed radio programs for children left the airwaves (Schneider, 1987). The 1990s, however, have witnessed increased activity in the children's radio industry. A few companies started children's radio networks that operated for a few years, but they ultimately went off the air after they failed to gain distribution in enough markets to attract national advertising dollars. One major factor that worked against these companies was that Arbitron, the ratings agency that monitors radio audiences, does not research audiences under 12, and advertisers are very hesitant to spend money on programming without this basic sort of research. The companies that remain in the children's radio industry are primarily active in children's television and movies, and they use radio as an ancillary market. Once again, Disney is the dominant company.

Disney owns and operates the only successful children's radio network in the United States. Fox extended its presence to young listeners with its Fox Kids Countdown, a program played on 200 radio stations.

### *Ownership and the Big Four Companies in the Children's Media Industries*

The children's media industries have entered a period of economic concentration. Four companies—Disney, Time Warner, News Corporation, and Viacom—own numerous forms of production and distribution systems for children's media (Schmuckler, 1997). All of them own a major Hollywood distributor: Warner Bros. puts the "Warner" in Time Warner, News Corporation owns 20th Century Fox, and Paramount is a subsidiary of Viacom. They all have ownership interests in broadcast networks: Disney acquired ABC in 1995, and Warner Bros. and Fox both built their own networks primarily from independent stations. Viacom owns 50% of UPN and, in September 1999, initiated plans to buy CBS. They all own the major children's cable networks as well. News Corporation secured a cable outlet by forming Fox Family Channel; Viacom owns Nickelodeon; and Time Warner, besides owning one of the largest MSOs in the country, controls the Cartoon Network through its Turner subsidiary. Disney owns the Disney Channel and Toon Disney, a new channel of Disney cartoons similar in form to the Cartoon Network. In terms of program supply, Warner Bros. and Disney produce most of the programming for their broadcast blocks on Kids' WB and ABC, respectively, an ownership privilege that the FCC prevented for years through the now expired Financial Interest and Syndication Rule. Viacom produces much of Nickelodeon's lineup and may begin to do the same for CBS. The Fox networks will receive a great deal of in-house programming, because Fox Children's Network, the children's subsidiary that News Corporation spun off, merged with Saban Entertainment, a large production company in children's television. Lastly, the dominance of these four companies is international. They are all distributing their networks and programs to cable systems and satellite services reaching millions of viewers around the world, and they are also negotiating coproduction deals with television networks in several countries.

The Big Four enacted vertical and horizontal integration to guarantee that, even as the child audience fragmented, their video products would get to as many eyes as possible through as many outlets as possible. News Corporation's 1998 annual report states, "We are building an unrivaled platform but it is the performance that counts. Distribution for us is merely a means to an end—to ensure that we can market our real product—and that product is content" (p. 1). Disney's Michael Eisner gave similar justifications in explaining the company's purchase of ABC to his shareholders:

> Imagine that your livelihood depends on commuting to work on a major highway. At first, you find the tolls are within reason. Then the tolls start going up. Finally, one day the guy in the tollbooth won't raise the gate for you at any price. But, meanwhile, you watch him let other cars zip by you onto the highway. At Disney, we like to control our own destiny and concluded that the only way not to be at the mercy of these institutions ("gatekeepers") was to assure our own access if it came to that. (Walt Disney Company, 1997, p. 4)

News Corporation and Disney are both essentially stating that their real money comes from their programs and not from the media systems that distribute them. This is especially true for their children's content, since they enjoy the additional and potentially most lucrative revenue stream of product licensing. The Big Four now operate the toll roads to the child audience, and they will extract most of the profit from the programs and licensed characters that travel on them.

## Self-Controls

In his book *Children's Television,* Cy Schneider, a veteran children's advertising executive, stressed that "commercial television, even for children, is just another business," and in light of this fact he argued, "Is it fair to ask the television industry to be different from other businesses?" (Schneider, 1987, p. 5). This statement reveals a great deal about the attitude and behavior of companies in the children's media industries—economics and market competition guide their conduct until this course runs them into regulatory problems. *Self-control* is the term that describes the ability of these companies to maintain behavior in compliance with industry regulations. For instance, broadcasters failed to exercise appropriate self-control in serving the educational needs of children, as mandated by the 1990 Children's Television Act, so the FCC imposed the 3-hour rule. Companies exercised self-control more successfully in complying with the advertising standards they established in the Children's Advertising Review Unit (CARU) and in providing labeling systems for their programs. Nonetheless, both cases forced companies to negotiate their business practices with regulatory and public policy pressures.

### *CARU*

The National Advertising Division of the Council of Better Business Bureaus created CARU in 1974, during a time when the FCC had issued an unfavorable report on the state of children's television. Furthermore, the Federal Trade Commission (FTC) was considering acting on the petitions of consumer groups to limit children's advertising on television and to prohibit all types of advertising to children under 8. With these public policy pressures, industry participants realized that they needed to address these issues themselves before regulations altered business conditions. CARU established six basic principles for advertising to children, including some that reiterated FCC or FTC policies on deceptive advertising. CARU was given the authority to respond to complaints or initiate its own investigation into possible violations, yet it was not endowed with enforcement powers other than the ability to refer violators to the FCC or FTC. Nonetheless, industry compliance to the CARU guidelines has been extremely high, except in regard to its policies concerning the Internet. For the television industry, however, this compliance has prevented increased protests against advertising to children and preserved the idea that such advertising is a legitimate social and economic activity (see Chapter 19).

### *Program Labels*

The television industry agreed to design a ratings system for programs that would work in coordination with the V-chip, a device that would be installed into television sets to offer parents more power in shielding their children from programs that they considered harmful. However, the television industry designed a ratings system that addressed its own concerns about preserving advertisers instead of one that empowered and informed parents. The system provided only age recommendations for programs and not indicators of their content. Children's programs received one of two labels: "TV-Y: All children" or "TV-Y7: Aimed at older children." The television industry changed the system shortly after its debut in January 1997 in response to protest that it must contain content labels and out of fear that the FCC would design one for it. The new system provided labels such as "V" for violent content, "S" for sexual content, "L" for foul language, "D" for adult dialogue, and "FV" for the fantasy violence in children's shows. The television industry

> balked at using the word "violence" to refer to the mayhem that goes on in many children's shows . . . whether the violence is indeed of the impossible variety or whether it is quite realistic but simply performed by animated characters. (Cantor, 1998, p. 67)

The industry held firm on this distinction in children's television, asserting that otherwise the "violent" label would drive away many concerned advertisers.

## Economic Implications of New Media Technologies

New media technologies such as digital television and the Internet will undoubtedly affect the economic structure of the children's media industries. Digital cable and multicasted broadcast channels could lead to a dramatic increase in program diversity, possibly providing venues for programming that audience-maximization scheduling disfavors. The Internet presents numerous economic threats. The World Wide Web could increasingly lure children away from the television and convince companies of the benefits of e-commerce instead of television advertising. Ultimately, these technologies will converge into any and every system that transmits their digital signals, possibly resulting in a media environment in which parents and children finally enjoy complete sovereignty in their ability to select the programs of their choice, but they will most likely have to pay for this freedom.

### *Internet*

#### *Displacement of Television Viewers and Revenue*

The Internet represents an economic threat to children's television because it might steal away viewers from the child audience, thereby decreasing the advertising dollars that the cable and broadcast networks can demand. Although the Internet has only penetrated approximately 60% of the homes with children, children's media companies have many reasons to worry about the economic changes that cyberspace may bring. While the Internet offers enlightening and interactive opportunities to children, it also allows numerous commercial interests to compete for the attention and dollars of the child audience. The Internet could topple the system of economic incentives of the media industries for which the giant media companies have invested billions to control and maintain. Unlike television and movies, the Internet has minimal barriers to entry. Children's companies can develop a Web presence with financial investments far below those required for video production, and they do not face the disadvantages of traditional children's media in which the owners of the distribution systems also dominate as content providers. More important, the Web provides every website with a form of global distribution, since anyone on the Internet anywhere in the world can access most any site.

As the Internet becomes a more popular medium among children, children's companies can exploit it as a new and economical source for character creation and licensing. In fact, the toy and production companies that have been shut out of the shrinking syndication market could find new life for their collaborations on the Web, especially as the quality of video delivered from the Web gets closer to that of television. Conversely, the dominant media companies could once again employ their numerous media outlets and vast financial resources to flood the Internet with their characters and programming. This strategy might prove successful even with the number of sites and companies competing for the attention of children, given the advertising, money, and production value the major companies could devote to their websites. Thus, the new media system that offers vast educational and interactive opportunities for children could also be reduced to a commercial extension of television programs and movies.

### *E-Commerce*

Like broadcast and cable networks, Internet companies can earn money indirectly from advertisers or directly from subscription services, but they also enjoy the third revenue stream of e-commerce. The interactive medium allows customers to order products and services on-line. Internet companies have additional commercial opportunities, even for young consumers. A trade magazine speculates that, if a girl plays on "a children's web site, the site can track her interests. If she seems taken with a particular cartoon character, for instance, the site could flash an advertisement for a toy based on the character that can be bought online" (Woody, 1999, p. 72). Currently, companies have exercised self-control in selling and advertising to children on websites to the extent that legislation has been avoided. But this issue has also been overshadowed by the lack of self-control that companies displayed in complying with industry regulations concerning children's privacy rights on the Internet.

### *Privacy*

In 1997, CARU introduced guidelines for interactive electronic media that combined its existing rules of advertising to children with rules specifically addressing on-line sales and the collection of data from children. The FTC assessed the compliance with these guidelines and concluded that more than half of the children's websites violated rules on data collection. Sites were collecting information from children without parental consent, and some companies sold this data to third parties. Campbell (1999) reasoned that this low level of compliance, as compared with that of advertisers on children's television, was because "the number of companies offering Web sites to children, while including these same advertisers, appears to be much larger and diverse" (p. 744). Regardless, the lack of self-control resulted in the implementation of the Children's Online Privacy Protection Act in 1998. The law focuses on regulations for commercial websites that collect personal information from children under 13. These sites must obtain prior parental consent before collecting information, the information that they request must be limited in scope, and they must adhere to parental requests to review information collected about their child or to cease the collection and use of this information altogether.

## *Digital Television*

Digital compression technology allows broadcast stations and cable systems to deliver multiple channels in the bandwidth that one channel used to occupy, although most viewers will not own the necessary technology to experience these benefits for a number of years. These compressed channels will undoubtedly further fragment the viewing audience, possibly to such an extent that many will not attract a large enough audience to interest advertisers. Despite these uncertain economic conditions, television companies are developing networks to gain "shelf space" in the digital channel market. In the digital cable market, Fox will offer the Boyz Channel and the Girlz Channel, providing advertisers a new level of assurance as to the gender of the viewing audience. Nickelodeon and the Children's Television Workshop, the company that produces *Sesame Street,* have introduced Noggin, an educational network for children. PBS has devoted a portion of its digital spectrum allotment to a channel for children, with many of its educational programs filling the schedule. The very indication that commercial television companies, and not just public television institutions, are willing to invest in an educational network suggests that the digital television market may not impose many of the disincentives that operate against educational programming in the current television environment. Furthermore, these educational networks can provide a new window for producers of educational programs to compete for in order to earn additional revenue.

### *Convergence and Consumer Sovereignty*

As all electronic media become digital, distribution systems will eventually converge and all offer any form of digital transmission. Television sets and computers and coaxial cables and phone lines will perform similar functions since the movies, television shows, web pages, music, or phone conversations will all be transmitted as digital bits. A major consequence of this convergence is that video products will be viewed on demand and not just delivered at the discretion of networks. As digital technology empowers consumers in this manner, the media industries will be forced to adapt their economic structures. Companies that depend on advertising dollars will need to find new ways to sell viewers as commodities, but companies that produce content will still earn revenue regardless of how it is distributed. A likely economic development is that consumers will pay for this power to view on demand. Viewers will become the purchasers of programming and not its products. Such a development will provide a new form of programming selection for the children of those who can afford this power but will offer few changes in children's media for those who cannot.

## Conclusion

Technology will change the economic structure of the electronic children's media industries. These conditions could create a new, intense level of competition in these industries, which could result in the development of a wider array of programming options for children than the industries as currently structured provide. Companies will practice new economic behaviors as they begin business in these new environments, but existing economic arrangements will perpetuate as well. After all, the Internet and digital television represent new outlets for licensing, new windows for profit maximization, and new distribution systems for media companies to own. Certainly, these technologies present exciting opportunities for children. Because they will be built as commercial systems, however, it will necessitate continued collaboration among parents, advocacy groups, government regulators, and media companies to ensure that economic motives are tempered by what is best for children.

## References

Blumenthal, H., & Goodenough, O. (1998). *This business of television* (Rev. 2nd ed.). New York: Billboard Books.

Campbell, A. (1999, May). Self-regulation and the media. *Federal Communications Law Journal, 51,* 711-772.

Cantor, J. (1998, May). Ratings for program content: The role of research findings. *Annals of the American Academy of Political and Social Science, 557,* 54-70.

Chan-Olmsted, S. (1996). From *Sesame Street* to Wall Street: An analysis of market competition in commercial children's television. *Journal of Broadcasting & Electronic Media, 40,* 30-44.

Donald, W. (1999, July 8). Broadcasting and cable. *Standard & Poor's Industry Surveys, 167*(27), 1-27.

Englehardt, T. (1987). The shortcake strategy. In T. Gitlin (Ed.), *Watching television.* New York: Pantheon Press.

Gardels, N. (1995). Planetized entertainment. *New Perspectives Quarterly, 12*(4), 8-10.

Gomery, D. (1993). The centrality of media economics. *Journal of Communication, 43*(3), 190-198.

Graves, T. (1999, May 20). Movies and home entertainment. *Standard & Poor's Industry Surveys, 166*(20), 1-31.

Hamilton, J. (1998). *Channeling violence: The economic market for violent television programming.* Princeton, NJ: Princeton University Press.

Horoschak, J. (1999, April 22). Leisure products. *Standard & Poor's Industry Surveys, 167*(16), 4-19.

Katz, R. (1999, January 18). Syndie era over. *Variety,* p. 9.

Kline, S. (1993). *Out of the garden: Toys, TV, and children's culture in the age of marketing.* London: Verso.

Kunkel, D. (1998, May). Policy battles over defining children's educational television. *Annals of the American Academy of Political and Social Science, 557,* 39-54.

Leonhardt, D., & Kervin, K. (1997, June 30). Hey kid, buy this! *Business Week,* pp. 62-67.

McCarthy, M., & Warner, F. (1994, March 21). Mane attraction: Marketers, Disney put $100 million on nose of Lion King. *Brandweek, 35*(12), 1-2.

McCormick, M. (1996, December 28). News-filled year in children's media: Disney dominates audio and video. *Billboard, 108*(52), 57-59.

Melody, W. (1973). *Children's television: The economics of exploitation.* New Haven, CT: Yale University Press.

Miles, L. (1994, September 12). New kids network planned. *Mediaweek, 4*(35), 8.

Morgan, R. (1998, December 21). TV toys are making big noise. *Variety, 373,* 6.

News Corporation. (1998). *1998 annual report.* New York: Author.

Owen, B., & Wildman, S. (1992). *Video economics.* Cambridge, MA: Harvard University Press.

Pecora, N. (1998). *The business of children's entertainment.* New York: Guilford.

Picard, R. (1989). *Media economics.* Newbury Park, CA: Sage.

Schmuckler, E. (1996, February 12). Have money, will spend it. *Mediaweek, 6*(7), 20-21.

Schmuckler, E. (1997, January 27). A small world after all: The children's TV business now in the hands of only four companies. *Mediaweek, 7*(4), 30-36.

Schneider, C. (1987). *Children's television: The art, the business, and how it works.* Lincolnwood, IL: NTC Business Books.

Segrave, K. (1998). *American television abroad: Hollywood's attempt to dominate world television.* Jefferson, NC: McFarland.

Traiman, S. (1998, February 14). Kid's multimedia sees a growth spurt. *Billboard, 110*(7), 76-78.

Turow, J. (1981). *Entertainment, education, and the hard sell.* New York: Praeger.

Vogel, H. (1998). *Entertainment industry economics: A guide for financial analysis* (4th ed.). New York: Cambridge University Press.

Walt Disney Company. (1997). *1997 annual report.* Glendale, CA: Author.

Woody, T. (1999, July 19-26). See Jane shop. *Industry Standard, 2*(22), 68-82.

CHAPTER 25

# Broadcast Networks and the Children's Television Business

ALISON ALEXANDER
University of Georgia

With more than 98% of American homes having television and more than 75% of the 1,500 U.S. television stations operating as commercial entities, the broadcast business is clearly big business. Most of the commercial stations are network affiliates, which assures them a steady stream of network programs, an identified brand, and a high profile with advertisers and viewers. Yet the Big Three, ABC, CBS, and NBC, now share the airwaves with new broadcast networks. The best known of the new networks is Fox, but recent start-up networks include the WB, UPN, and PAX. Despite the increase in their numbers, networks no longer dominate the television industry. Almost half of U.S. viewing is now to cable services. Fueling these developments are the business synergies among production, distribution, cable, and broadcast business units that support media giants such as Time Warner, Walt Disney, Viacom, News Corporation, and General Electric.

Within this larger picture, children's television is a very small piece of the pie. "Children's television" refers to programs targeted primarily to children and designed to attract a majority of viewers who are children. Children's television is only a small part of the total viewing of television by children. Shows broadcast between 8:00 P.M. and 9:00 P.M. have huge children and teen audiences. A popular prime-time situation comedy may attract many more child viewers than a "children's program" does despite the fact that it is not targeted primarily to children and children are not a majority of the audience. As a result, most of the highest-rated programs for children 5 to 17 are prime-time programs.

In industry parlance, children are divided into three major age groups: 2 to 5 years old, 6

AUTHOR'S NOTE: My thanks to the many individuals who took the time to explain the intricacies of the children's television industry. Any errors or misinterpretations are mine.

to 11, and 12 to 17, although teens are frequently discussed separately from the younger age groups. Typically, when the industry talks about children's television, it is referring to the 2 to 11 age group. In focusing on the business of broadcast children's television, this chapter does not address cable television, public television, the video ancillary market, video games, or other nonbroadcast aspects of children's media environment, which are addressed in other chapters. In this chapter, the operation of broadcast network children's television is explored. The goals are (a) to identify trends in programming and exposure to children's programs; (b) to trace the structure of children's television; (c) to identify patterns of program development, production, and promotion; and (d) to identify financial patterns such as trends in profit and loss and sources of revenue.

## Analyzing Trends in Programming and Exposure for Children

Early children's shows were designed to sell TV sets by enhancing television's appeal to the entire family. Because most households in the 1950s had only one television set, programs appealing to children as well as adults were seen as a way of attracting families. By 1951, the networks' schedules included up to 27 hours of children's programs. Like much of television programming, offerings for children continued radio's tradition of action-adventure themes and a pattern of later afternoon and evening broadcasts. An early reliance on movies as a program staple was lessened in favor of half-hour live-action shows such as *The Lone Ranger, Sky King,* and *Lassie* and host/puppet shows such as *The Howdy Doody Show* and *Kukla, Frank, and Ollie.* By the mid-1950s, children's shows were shifting to afternoons. In 1954, an ABC-Disney deal brought *The Mickey Mouse Club* into childhood afternoons and nearly owned the grade-school audience. Locally produced children's shows in late afternoon were common fare, frequently involving Bozo the clown interacting with local child audiences and interspersed with showings of cartoons. By the decade's end, children's programs had completed the migration from prime time to less valuable morning, early afternoon, or Saturday morning hours.

During the 1960s, cartoons became synonymous with children's television. Reduced costs resulting from limited-action animation techniques and the clear appeal of cartoons to children transformed scheduling, and the institutionalization of the Saturday morning cartoon became complete—an unexpectedly lucrative time slot for the networks. Popular shows included *The Jetsons, Rocky & Bullwinkle,* and *Space Ghost.* The 1970s continued the Saturday animation trend with 60- or 90-minute shows that incorporated a number of segments under umbrella labels such as *The New Super Friends Hour* or *Scooby Laff-a-Lympics.* These extended shows were designed to increase audience flow across the entire morning.

The 1980s brought a revolution to broadcast, as cable and VCR penetration began to erode the network audience and international coventures began to change the production process. Cartoons remained the standard children's fare, but cable networks such as Nickelodeon that targeted children began to experiment with different types of programming for children. For the cabled home, access to children's programming increased dramatically over the 1980s.

Based on the rationale that other outlets were adequately serving the child audience and that diversity of programming for the child was greater than ever before, many of the networks were getting out of the children's television business as the 1990s began. But with the legislative requirement of the 1990 Children's Television Act as interpreted by the Federal Communications Commission (FCC) for broadcast stations, the major networks now provide their affiliates with the required 3 hours of educational/informational (E/I) programming a week. Currently, ABC's linkage with parent Disney has paid off on

Saturday morning, with a 3-hour lineup of shows from Disney-owned studios. CBS has a 3-hour lineup of shows produced by its new partner, Viacom. NBC is the only major network to target teens, with a later start and more live-action programming. The newer networks have a different strategy: They are courting the child audience, particularly in time slots other than the traditional Saturday morning. In the 1998 season, Fox and ABC vied for the highest number of young viewers in the 5- to 11-year-old range on Saturday morning. But Fox has long had a strategy to grow up with its audience, starting with a strong commitment to children's fare. Fox, like the other smaller networks, provides the required 3 hours a week of E/I programming (most of the smaller networks provide a 5-day half-hour show, with another half-hour E/I showing on Saturday). Thus, Fox not only provides the 3 hours of required children's programming a week but offers 3 hours daily of morning and afternoon entertainment programming. Other broadcast networks, such as the WB and UPN, have also made children's programming central to their business strategies. The WB relies on its ownership of cartoons, and UPN in the past has partnered with Disney.

But the biggest news of the decade is that children's viewing patterns have changed dramatically. No one can ignore the large shift over the past two decades wherein children's viewing went from 98% broadcast to 15% with the advent of cable with its targeted children's programs and networks (Petrozzello, 1998). Now only 15% of children's television viewing is to network fare; more than 77% of children's viewing is to cable, and 8% is to syndicated programs. Not only is children's viewing shifting, but it may be diminishing. Children's advertisers are concerned about an apparent drop in children's overall viewing, which has diminished by 3% in the past decade.

Because of the shift of children's attention with the boom in children's programming on cable, audience fragmentation is the key to the new media environment for children. In the United States, child-oriented fare accounts for more than 1,000 hours of airtime a week on network and cable channels (Jackson, 1999), and viewing is widely distributed across that large set of offerings. Nickelodeon garners more than 50% of child viewing, followed by the Cartoon Network at 28%. Fox totals 6% of children's viewing, with ABC, CBS, and NBC gaining less than 3% each (McClellan & Tedesco, 1999). (These 1999 figures can change dramatically with program popularity, but the overall tendency to small network and large cable channel viewership seems stable.) These are percentages of total viewing and not to be confused with ratings, which show that the networks still predominate in massing large audiences for single shows, despite a significant decrease over the decades. Saturday morning average ratings for major network children's shows ran between 1.8 and 2.2 in the four quarters of late 1997 and early 1998 (*Marketer's Guide,* 1998). This can be compared to the average 6 or 7 ratings that network Saturday morning shows received in the 1960s and 1970s. These ratings indicate that, of the slightly more than 100 million television households, about 2 million households are watching. Despite the competition that cable provides for the young viewers, few cable programs reach the audience that a network show can, except for Nickelodeon, which is the preeminent children's cable channel and averaged a 3.0 rating with children in 1998. Alternatively, the Family Channel earned a 0.1 rating. Nonetheless, the extent of cable's fare gives it lots of cumulative viewers.

For many years, industry and academic researchers have been examining children's television. Much of the industry research on children's programming is in the hands of the network research departments. Most networks' research departments work to identify appealing programs and to provide information to advertisers and affiliates about audiences. Stipp and Schiavone (1990) discussed the structure of the NBC Research Department. There are seven areas within the research department, which are listed according to size: audience research, program research, news research, affiliate research/owned stations research, marketing and sales research, social and development research, and new media research. Stipp confirmed in a personal communication that these departments remain essentially the same in structure and function in 1999. Most of these departments will, at times, conduct research relevant to children. Briefly, the audience research division looks at the size and nature of the audience. Although ratings are collected by outside audience measurement firms, the audience research area addresses methodological issues and commissions original research in specific arenas. Program research provides information on entertainment programming development. Concept tests, pilot testing, series research, scheduling research, and promotion research are within its purview. News research helps assess audience reaction to news presentation, ranging from interest and understanding to format appeal. Affiliate and owned and operated research helps individual stations improve their own ratings performance. Marketing and sales research uses program rating data to support marketing efforts but also conducts studies in areas that enhance advertiser value. Social and development research has been most involved with research on children. The department was started in 1969 to conduct a major research project on the effects of violence (Milavsky, Kessler, Stipp, & Rubens, 1982). Since the 1980s, the department has continued to monitor research on television's effects, to support self-regulation, and to monitor research on demographics, lifestyle, and attitudinal trends. New media research is designed to explore the use and impact of alternate distribution systems. The other network research departments have similar structures and functions.

Two major studies of the content of commercial television have recently concluded. Funded by the industry, the four major broadcast networks (ABC, CBS, NBC, and Fox) supported the UCLA study. *Violence on the Networks: The UCLA Reports* by the Center for Communication Policy at UCLA assessed 10 programs as raising frequent concerns about violence. Among the prime-time shows cited for glorified or excessive violence were many that are popular with child or youth viewers, including *Walker, Texas Ranger; Mantis; The X-Files; Lois and Clark;* and *Tales From the Crypt.* The UCLA study also noted that Saturday morning children's programs contained excessive violence. Supported by the National Cable Television Association, researchers at four universities conducted the National Television Violence Study (1997, 1998a, 1998b). Among their conclusions were that children's programs were worse than adult programs with regard to violence and that few children's programs show the long-term consequences of violence. Potential consequences of these portrayals are desensitization, learning aggressive behaviors, and fear of victimization.

Extensive academic research looks at television programming and children, as is seen in this volume. However, little research examines the specific linkages between individual commercial broadcast programs and their consequences. As researchers begin to demonstrate the linkage between E/I programming and child viewers, such studies should begin to enter the research arena.

## Analyzing the Industry Structure

The broadcast television business is a complex industry. For most viewers, their linkage with this industry is through their viewing of the local network affiliates in their market. Local affiliates run the shows provided by the networks. Networks profit from affiliate viewers, who cumulatively provide the national mass audience that advertisers desire. In return, the networks offer compensation (payment) to affiliates for running programs and leave some advertising space available for local sales. With the rise in the number of broadcast networks, few commercial stations remain independent (i.e., unattached to any network).

The backbone of any network is the group of stations that carry its programs: its affiliates. Traditionally, roughly 200 stations were affiliated with each of the Big Three networks of ABC, CBS, and NBC. With 200 stations, these networks cover nearly all of the U.S. homes with TV. This is crucial because this allows advertisers to reach a national audience. The newer networks have roughly 100 affiliates each.

The children's network business differs in some significant ways from other network programming. No compensation is offered for the children's programming that the major networks provide, because it is a regulatory requirement for broadcast stations. Local children's ads are also not particularly lucrative because of the relatively small audience. Costs for a Saturday morning ad in many markets may be only a few hundred dollars and, in smaller markets, could be significantly less than $100. At the local affiliate level, the program director oversees children's programming, in addition, generally, to managing all station production, community relations, and promotions. There is a long history of affiliates providing local origination children's programs. Most markets have a high school "quiz bowl." Many do local public affairs specials targeted to older children, dealing with social issues such as drugs, violence, smoking, or racism. Some provide magazine format shows that can be wide ranging in content: Some are news programs, others focus on local events, and others have an "adventure" focus. Many of these include children on air or even as writers, producers, and directors.

Networks provide the programs that fill much of the affiliate schedule: prime time, network news, soaps, sports, quiz shows, talk shows, and children's shows. Vice presidents in charge of daytime or vice presidents for children's programs manage the network scheduling of children's programming. Promotion departments, research departments, and community relations departments become involved. In the current regulatory environment, the Big Three networks are providing the required 3 hours of educational and informational programming. Their goals are to meet the regulation, to be able to point with pride to their program content, and to meet the competition within their time slot. With the increased competition from smaller networks and cable, these programmers realize that regaining large numbers is unlikely. The smaller networks provide more than the 3 hours of - required programming to their affiliates, courting the child audience, which, though fragmented, provides numbers that are satisfactory to them.

This simplified picture of local/network affiliate stations obscures larger issues of ownership. All networks own a certain number of owned and operated (O&O) stations, which form powerful station groups. Other station groups include Tribune, Gannett, Hearst-Argyle, and Cox. These groups can exert considerable pressure on the networks and act in concert in the purchase of nonnetwork syndicated fare.

## Patterns of Program Development, Production, and Promotion

### *Content Creators and Program Suppliers*

There are three basic ways in which a TV station can acquire programs: network, syndication, and local origination. As indicated previously, network programming refers to original programming funded by, produced for, and distributed by the networks. Syndication refers to TV programming sold by distribution companies to local TV stations (and cable services). Local origination refers to programs produced by local TV stations for viewers in their own communities.

The network programming process seems simple, but the work of content creators and distributors quickly becomes very complex. Some now-outdated rules shaped the original programming process. Under the financial interest and syndication rules (known as fin-syn), FCC rules limited network participation in the ownership of programs produced for them and in the subsequent syndication. Rather than buying shows outright or producing their own, networks paid license fees to production companies. After the network run, the shows were sold into syndication, with the networks barred from reaping any financial reward. Now the fin-syn rules have been abandoned, allowing networks to own their own shows and to sell them in syndication. Nonetheless, many programming practices that evolved under fin-syn remain.

The networks are now actively engaged in producing their own programs, as witnessed by the plethora of newsmagazine shows on prime time. Now it is much easier for media conglomerates to take advantage of vertical integration wherein they own both movie and television production companies as well as cable and broadcast outlets (networks and stations). Some of the major media giants include Time Warner, which owns children's entertainment firms such as Warner Brothers, Hanna-Barbera, and the WB network; Walt Disney, which owns Walt Disney Studios and Buena Vista Television as well as ABC; Viacom, which owns UPN, Paramount, Nickelodeon, and MTV, and recently merged with CBS; News Corporation, which owns Fox Animation, 20th Television, the Fox network, and multiple cable channels; and General Electric, which owns NBC as well as CNBC, MSNBC, Bravo, and AMC ("Measuring the Media Giants," 1999).

The production of children's programming is dominated by major studios, a few independents, and, increasingly, international producers and coproductions. Almost all of the major television studios are well known, although their ownership may not be. Some major studios include Columbia/TriStar owned by Sony, MCA-Universal owned by Seagram's, 20th Century Fox owned by News Corporation, Warner Brothers owned by Time Warner, Paramount owned by Viacom, and Disney. Networks may also order programs from independent producers. Note that independent means a business firm not owned by a firm that also owns a network or cable service.

Ironically, ongoing viable independents are hard to identify because, despite their number, a larger corporation quickly acquires the successful ones; the others tend to disappear. Columbia/TriStar is the single major studio not connected to a broadcast or cable distribution system. To identify the current state of this shifting mass, one must look for the names at the ends of children's programming. You will see that most are of the form "Produced by XXX (a firm you have never heard of) and XXX (a big name)." This represents the pattern of the industry: Small firms pitch ideas to networks or production companies and exchange some control over the production process in exchange for funding to produce their program content and production credit. Such a pattern of "joint venturing" is now widely recognized as an efficient organizational form for maximizing the synergy from combining the "comparative advantages" of large firms with extensive financial resources and the creativity of smaller entities with creative owners involved in operations. Increasingly, international programs and producers have gained entry into the U.S. market through these joint ventures. Nelvana, a Canadian company, is an example. It produced *Magic School Bus* and recently produced the entire Saturday morning lineup for CBS.

The barriers to program entry into the children's television market are enormous. One has only to prowl the aisles of the annual convention of the National Association of Television Program Executives (NATPE), where syndicated shows are shown to prospective buyers, to see the many creative children's program ideas out there. What factors influence which ones will make it?

Both those who purchase and those who produce children's programs operate with assumptions about the child audience that, although changing, remain important. They assume, for example, that there are gender differences in preference, with the important corollary that, although girls will watch boys' shows, boys will not watch girls' shows. They also assume that older children control the set, an assumption related to the axiom that younger children will watch "up" (in age appeal) but older children will not watch "down." Producers and purchasers also assume that children have a short attention span, that repetition is a key to education and entertainment, and that children prefer recognizable characters and stories.

Deep pockets are a necessity. Production companies retain ownership of the shows, although networks are now allowed to have some financial interest in the program. These business organizations operate on a near-term deficit-financing model, anticipating that aftermarket sales and merchandising agreements will create ultimate profitability. Networks pay a licensing fee to air the program, which is typically significantly less than the show costs to produce. The fragmentation of the current audience means less money to individual companies, so license fees, which for children's programs were once in the range of $250,000 to $500,000 per episode, have dropped significantly, to a low of $15,000 per episode (Jackson, 1999).

Networks, station groups, or individual stations want to buy from a reputable firm, someone they can trust to deliver what is promised. They would like to know that they are dealing with professionals who have been successful in similar endeavors in the past. But the children's television market is expanding with the new networks and cable services. How does it all come together in completed programs?

### *Patterns of Program Development and Production*

What is the process by which program series make it to the air? Television production is a complex business, dependent on artistic, political, and economic factors. Most series begin with a program pitch to a production company or program distributor or to a network. Pitches begin with a concept or a short narrative known as a treatment and move to a storyboard or pilot. Unlike adult series, pilots are not commonly produced. If the program is chosen for further development, the network or studio will provide development money, in return for some measure of control over content. Thirty years ago, there were probably 26 episodes produced for a weekly show, rerun once during the year. Now a 13-show contract with three to four reruns yearly is common for a weekly show. This rerun practice is possible because younger audiences do not object and change quickly.

After network programming, the largest program providers are syndicators: the companies that sell directly to TV stations and cable services. In children's television, much of the 1970s and 1980s were a story of independent stations or station groups purchasing syndicated programming. Independent stations, in order to compete in the marketplace, typically targeted audiences for sports, movies, or children's programming. Syndication companies sell two kinds of shows: off-network series (series that have appeared on networks and are being rerun by local stations) and first-run shows that are expressly produced for syndication. Off-network series are packaged so that stations pay for the right to play a certain number of episodes a specified number of times. For a children's show, the cumulation of 65 episodes allows for repeatability and makes the show salable beyond its initial run to other outlets. Programs are frequently scheduled to run daily Monday through Friday, a process called stripping. Frequently, stations purchase syndicated programming on a barter basis. In barter syndication, the producer provides the programming free or at a reduced cost but keeps some of the advertising slots in the show. The syndicator can place its own ads into the show or sell them to major advertisers. The key is market clearance. The more stations the syndicated program plays in, the larger the audience that can be offered to advertisers.

The traditional market for syndicated fare, local television, is drying up in children's programming because more and more stations are affiliated with a network. Remember that syndication accounts for only 8% of children's program viewing. Thus, some argue that syndication is a dying business. With vertical integration and network consolidation, most major networks own production studios and prefer programming from that studio or purchase a block of programming from an independent. Thus, the majority of local stations' time devoted to children's television is produced by one studio or from studios under the same ownership as the network. Independent production companies can find it hard to place their programming. *Pokemon,* the Japanese hit syndicated by Summit Media, was unable in its second year to get good placement, so it was taken out of syndication and sold to a broadcast network: the WB Kids. In essence, here is a hit children's show that could not get on television in a good time slot unless it became a network offering.

Advisory boards have become an important component of the production process. Developmental psychologists, educators, mass communication scholars, advocates, and others meet to discuss program acquisition and development. These boards offer advice on strategy and tactics within the network or production decision processes. This is discussed in detail in Chapter 33.

### *Nonprogram Content: Promotions and Public Service*

Building a successful program or lineup does not end with program completion. The process of promotion is central to encouraging child audiences to sample, or indeed to eagerly anticipate, a new program. Networks use internal program promotions as well as cross-media promotions and website tie-ins. For example, currently ABC uses TGIF (a Friday lineup of prime-time sitcoms with strong child appeal) to drive Saturday cartoon viewing. In addition, all the networks now have websites, and all the websites link to a children's programming page.

Part programming and part promotion, another popular strategy is a wraparound segment that has its own characters and interstitial material. These wraparounds include common characters, promote upcoming programs, and contain short sketches. Last season had the CBS Kidshow, ABC's One Saturday Morning, and TNBC. These are themes that link all the programs and help create branding and flow.

External promotion is an increasingly important part of the promotion process. Some marketing initiatives tie in to local businesses. Recently, CBS worked with (a) Target department stores to give away 1 million posters promoting the CBS kids block; (b) Zany Brainy, a children's store that carries the books from which the CBS shows are taken; (c) American Airlines to provide a coloring book to young fliers; and (d) Baskin Robbins to name an ice cream flavor after a character.

An often-overlooked segment of nonprogram content is the public service announcement (PSA). The Advertising Council, which is an advertising industry group designed to provide social advocacy campaigns, provides many of the PSAs that audiences see or hear. This group donates advertising space and creative talent to these campaigns, many of which are targeted to teens as well as the larger adult market. A recent publication of the Ad Council highlighted the availability for TV, radio, or print campaigns targeting children and young adults in the areas of antidiscrimination, crime prevention, fire safety, forest fire prevention, 4-H, math, and youth fitness. A major effort is now under way to address issues of school violence. Networks, however, also devote resources to their own campaigns. One of the best known is the long-running NBC campaign called "The More You Know," which for the TNBC segment features media celebrities talking about issues of interest to teens.

Educational outreach, including educational resources, Web tie-ins, and distance learning, is discussed in Chapters 28 and 29. Each of the networks offers a site for their child viewers or youth offerings. Most are interactive in some fashion, and some connect to other sites, some of which are educational in nature. Rarely can basic information such as production company, target age, educational objectives, or the E/I symbol be found. Most do include advertising.

All of this is about branding. Branding is the process whereby a product or service is seen to stand for something and to be qualitatively different from similar products or services. Branding is an outgrowth of the integrated marketing perspective that advocates the integrated use of all marketing tools to produce a brand. All networks try to create a brand for their entire service, such as NBC's Must See TV. Its Saturday morning brand is TNBC. Perhaps branding can best be understood by looking at the comments of some syndicators. Mort Marcus, president of Buena Vista Television, notes, "In this world of fragmentation, you need to be a little more consistent and you need to be branded. You need to be more of a destination, so kids can find you easier" (Schlosser, 1999, p. 28). Rick Unger, chairman of Bohbot, states, "What a network really is in the kids business is branding. The networks want to be associated with a brand or one of these networks. With a single show in syndication, it's a real crap shoot" (as cited in Schlosser, 1999, p. 28).

## Identifying Financial Patterns

Inescapably, local station revenues come chiefly from the sale of time to advertisers. Individual broadcast stations, particularly in large markets, can be very profitable, with annual profit margins in the 35 to 50% range. Yet networks have not been particularly profitable business units in recent years, as audiences erode and program costs climb. Nonetheless, media giants are gobbling up available broadcast stations, and the 1990s saw the advent of more than three additional networks. Why this seeming contradiction? The answer lies in the amortization of program costs by program content creators (major studios, independents, and international firms) and networks in the ancillary and aftermarkets. Ancillary markets include, among other things, international sales and merchandise licensing. Aftermarkets, sometimes called the back end, refer to post-first-run sales of the program.

The program costs vary widely, depending on longevity, stars, and quality. Nonetheless, children's programs are significantly less expensive to produce than prime-time programs. A dramatic series averages between \$2 and \$4 million per week, a situation comedy between \$1 and \$2 million. Children's television programs tend to average \$100,000 to \$350,000 per half-hour animated episode (Jackson, 1999). Although the profit on children's programs is smaller than on adult series, their ancillary and aftermarket potential is vast. It seems clear that part of the pitch is a potential merchandizing link and international sales. Thus, the deficit per episode (the cost per episode minus the licensing fee paid by the network) is to be made up in the ancillary and aftermarket. Concurrently with the program run, the show can be marketed internationally. Similarly, licensing and merchandising for successful children's shows can be a multibillion-dollar activity. This internationalization is helping production companies weather decreasing ratings for children's shows in the U.S. market. Henry Siegel, former president of KMG Entertainment, noted,

> The international market is where we have seen a major increase in our revenue. I'd say it has tripled over the last five years. If you can get a show that can sell products, then you've got a good business on your hands. (as cited in Schlosser, 1999, p. 28)

It is this concentration that is the key to profitability. Chan-Olmsted (1996) concluded that the children's television market is moderately concentrated and on the verge of becoming highly concentrated as major players such as Disney and Fox consolidate their activities. She notes that network-syndication ownership is a critical combination for gaining market control.

Merchandise licensing refers to an agreement that allows the right to use a name or image in exchange for a royalty fee, generally 5 to 15% of the cost of the item (Pecora, 1998). Toys, games, clothing, lunchboxes, and the many other licensed products afford the manufacturer a recognizable character with ongoing "promotion" when the program airs, increasing product visibility and demand. The entertainment industry profits from the promotion of the product and the additional source of corporate revenue. Increasingly, production companies and product manufacturers have agents to manage these contractual negotiations.

The sale of licensed products is approximately a $60 billion industry. For the toy industry, these products help to introduce some stability to a volatile marketplace. For the entertainment industry, the royalties are an important source of income. Hanna-Barbera was grossing $40 to $50 million from licensed products in the 1970s; royalty fees for Mattel totaled $10 million in 1985 (Pecora, 1998, p. 57). These agreements seem to extend the life cycle of both the toy and the program.

The toy/program tie-in can come at any time in the process. Children's films and merchandised products usually hit the market at about the same time. For television, licensed toys that can be purchased during the Christmas rush quickly follow the September premiere. Some programs evolve in popularity, and product lines emerge after that. For example, *Barney & Friends* products appeared after that show gained popularity. A few are popular toys before they become programs; *Strawberry Shortcake* and *My Little Pony* are two examples.

Despite the impact of program resale and merchandise licensing, the foundation of the children's television business is advertising. Sales for children's television ads passed the $1 billion mark in 1998, despite a trend that sees children watching less television. This can be compared to the $44.5 billion total advertising volume for television and cable together. Nationally, the children's television market is divided into two time periods. Upfront selling usually occurs in April, when advertisers make the bulk of their buys for the upcoming season, locking up the "prime" advertising real estate. What remains is bought up throughout the year on what is called the scatter market.

Whatever choices they make, advertisers buy gross ratings points (GRPs), the sum of all ratings for all programs in a schedule of buys. This is the most frequently used measure of audiences for the advertising community. Of course, these buys must be made at an appropriate CPM, which is the cost to reach 1,000 people or homes. Another frequently used measure is the Cost per Rating Point (CPP), which is the cost to deliver a single rating point. The *Marketer's Guide* (1998) reports an average CPM cost of network children's programming (cable and broadcast combined) of $5.92 in 1997-1998. This can be compared to a CPM cost in prime time of $11.93. One cable channel—Nickelodeon—controls 50% of the available children's gross ratings points (which is the same as saying that they account for 50% of all of children's viewing). Cable as a whole controls 80% of children's GRPs. However, these GRPs are very fragmented, and it is not easy to reach children efficiently.

The major advertisers on children's television are Hasbro, Mattel, Kraft, General Foods, and Kellogg, representing games/toys and cereals and approximately 36% of total children's advertising dollars. The variety of companies' spending on children's television is increasing. In 1994, toys and cereals accounted for 56% of total children's ad dollars; in 1998, that figure was only 36%. With children's programming proliferating, particularly on cable, some worry that a surplus of advertising time will be created, driving profits down. Jackson (1999) estimates that child-oriented fare accounts for more than 1,000 hours of airtime a week on network and cable channels. The number of choices creates significant audience fragmentation and gives ad buyers more alternatives for where to place their ad dollars. Whatever the outcome, children's viewing has become a very fragmented demographic, raising serious questions about how to effectively reach them.

There are self-regulatory groups within the advertising industry that strive to oversee advertising. One of these is a part of the Better

Business Bureau, the National Advertising Review Council's Children's Advertising Review Unit (CARU). Part of a comprehensive self-regulatory process of the NARC, CARU's goal is to work with the industry to ensure that advertising to children is truthful and fair. Like the larger review unit, CARU investigates complaints, recommends modifications or discontinuance of offending claims, and may refer the matter to appropriate government agencies. The major federal agency that deals with deceptive or untrue advertising is the Federal Trade Commission (FTC), which has in its time responded to numerous complaints about advertising practices to children, many filed by the former organization Action for Children's Television (ACT).

## Conclusion

Several important observations emerge from this analysis of the children's broadcast television business. First, the proliferation of content in children's programming is significantly fragmenting the child audience. Most viewing of children's programming is now to cable services. With the regulation of children's television, local stations' perception of children's television increasingly places it in the arena of public service rather than entertainment programming. The traditional Big Three are not generating major profits from their children's television over-the-air offerings; newer networks that more centrally target children are doing much better. But the real profit in children's television is in the production/distribution arena, where ancillary marketing, aftermarkets, and international coventures and distribution are a multi-billion-dollar industry. With the increasing integration of media corporations, all are sharing in these profits.

The body of television content emerging from these economic and industrial practices has been a central component of "childhood" since the 1950s. Because children are seen as a special "group" of both citizens and viewers, great concerns for the role of television in the lives of children have accompanied the development of the medium. As a result, issues surrounding children and television have often been framed as "social problems," issues of central concern to numerous groups. Large-scale academic research enterprises have been mounted to monitor, analyze, and explain relationships between television and children. Congress, regulatory agencies, advocacy groups, and the television networks have struggled continuously over research findings, public responsibility, and popular response. The regulatory decisions of the 1990s transformed children's television. We are only beginning to assess the consequences of these transformations.

## References


Chan-Olmsted, S. (1996). From *Sesame Street* to Wall Street: An analysis of market competition in commercial children's television. *Journal of Broadcasting & Electronic Media, 40* (1), 30-44.

Jackson, W. (1999, April 12). Viewer's call. *Variety,* pp. 37, 46.

*Marketer's guide to media, 1998-99* (Vol. 21). (1998). New York: ASM Communications.

McClellan, S., & Tedesco, R. (1999, March 12). Children's TV market may be played out. *Broadcasting and Cable,* pp. 20-22.

Measuring the media giants. (1999, September 9). *Atlanta Journal Constitution,* p. F-1.

Milavsky, J. R., Kessler, R. C., Stipp, H. H., & Rubens, W. S. (1982). *Television and aggression: A panel study.* New York: Academic Press.

*National Television Violence Study* (Vol. 1). (1997). Thousand Oaks, CA: Sage.

*National Television Violence Study* (Vol. 2). (1998a). Thousand Oaks, CA: Sage.

*National Television Violence Study* (Vol. 3). (1998b). Thousand Oaks, CA: Sage.

Pecora, N. (1998). *The business of children's entertainment.* New York: Guilford.

Petrozzello, D. (1998, July 27). Cable competition for kids intensifies. *Broadcasting and Cable,* pp. 27-28.

Schlosser, J. (1999, March 1). Kids syndicators get squeezed. *Broadcasting and Cable,* pp. 26, 28.

Stipp, H., & Schiavone, N. (1990). Research at a commercial television network: NBC, 1990. *Marketing Research, 2*(3), 3-10.

CHAPTER **26**

# Serving the Very Young and the Restless

## Children's Programming on Public Television

JERRY FRANKLIN
Connecticut Public Television and Radio

LARRY RIFKIN
Connecticut Public Television

PATRICE PASCUAL
Connect for Kids

In 1993, shortly after millions of young children went agog for a big purple dinosaur named Barney, a producer of a network newsmagazine called the *Barney & Friends* publicist. But he was not calling to book the preschool phenom on his show.

"I don't understand my son's fascination with *Barney*," the producer vented. He said his 5-year-old also enjoyed watching more adult fare, including New York City's local news (think "mayhem at 5 o'clock"). This educated, upper-income father was a good demographic match for PBS's investigative series *Frontline* or what was then the *MacNeil-Lehrer NewsHour.* Still, he was actually disappointed that, given a programming choice, his son would watch a show as "unsophisticated" as *Barney & Friends.*

That is a tough complaint for a public television professional to answer. It would have been better posed to one of the several child development specialists who consult to the series, since the answer really lies in how young minds see and comprehend television. Truth be told, we nonexperts could even empathize with this caller. As parents, we know the frustration when a child you love and certainly think you know embraces an idea, a music group, or a TV program whose charms escape you.

But on deeper reflection, the producer's complaint addresses something we have learned from experience: Our society's ambivalence about declaring what is good and healthy for children's development is so unsettled that we have no mandate for what our young, particularly our preschoolers, truly need from television. And our television culture is so steeped in commercialism that we have never resolved the parallel issue of what children deserve.

These are perpetual challenges to the Public Broadcasting Service (PBS) and to any noncommercial producer who tries to create programs to meet children's developmental needs. By that we simply mean that, as it entertains, TV should educate and complement what parents are trying to teach their children about getting along in the world, especially when the average child spends 3 to 4 hours a day viewing rather than doing.

So how has PBS and its 349 broadcast stations served the child audience? This chapter will look at public television's efforts to define and produce quality children's programming in the United States, with a focus on the preschool market. It is a journey from our station's perspective and will reflect our experience as coproducers of the enormously popular series *Barney & Friends.* But really, that's getting ahead of the story.

## In the Beginning, There Was Fred

To understand how public television learned to think of the child audience, you need to sit a while with that kindly man in the red sweater.

Since the 1954 launch of the series that became *Mister Rogers' Neighborhood,* ordained minister Fred Rogers has proven to be a true and constant friend to children. He has been the subject of comic parodies and tearful tributes, as if he is some relic from a time when children and the world were sweet and innocent. Nonsense, Rogers might say. (Even he can get piqued, you know.) Fred Rogers's enduring appeal is best understood by his genuine love of children and in his conviction that the path of their emotional and intellectual development is unchanging. Modern children may grow up in a world more coarse and crude than when the series began, but they still need to know that the people who leave them will return, that there is a difference between real and make-believe, that every person is special.

"Sure, the superficial stuff changes, but the essence of us remains the same," said Rogers in a 1999 phone interview. "At the root of who we all are, we long to know that we are lovable and capable of loving" (personal communication with Pascual, October 1999).

From that perspective, reinforced by his training in child development, Fred Rogers created the model for what PBS children's programming still aspires to be: a half-hour or so of quality entertainment that respects and enriches the world of the child, intellectually, emotionally, and socially.

If the process by which children learn and grow has not changed, parenting certainly has. For instance, the amount of time children spend watching TV, as documented elsewhere in this book, has grown significantly during Rogers's long series run. But his advice to parents on guiding a child's viewing has never varied: Would you want your child to emulate the characters he or she meets on TV? Do the programs that your child watches reflect your values?

After more than 40 years of working in children's television, Rogers says that when it comes to choosing TV companions for your child, "It's mighty helpful if you stick to what you believe" (personal communication with Pascual, October 1999).

Through the years, many children's advocates have tried to challenge parents and producers to consider the effects of a child's TV viewing—effects that researchers have debated and commercial networks have refuted. The idea that a child's media diet needs to be managed may win lip service when parents are polled, but ratings often tell another story. For instance, in July 1999, the *Washington Post* reported that children ages 2 to 11 made up the biggest audience for the World Wrestling Federation's *Smackdown,* a cable show featuring stylized violence performed by costumed wrestlers. The program had a published rating of TV-14, meaning even its producers agreed it should not be labeled as fully suitable for so many so young.

TV content ratings are still in their nascent phase, and it is hard to project whether they will become an effective tool for concerned parents. But no matter what technology offers, public television will join many others in arguing that children are an audience that needs protection and that, as long as the airwaves are "owned" by the citizenry, the job of protecting children does not fall solely to parents.

"We cannot put all the responsibility on the parents—more than 50% must be shouldered by the broadcaster," Rogers told an interviewer. "We're not talking about First Amendment stuff. We're talking about trying to find what is healthiest for children to see and hear, and abide by that" (personal communication with Pascual, October 1999).

## Children's Programs as a Public Service

Defining and producing what is "healthiest for children" has been an evolutionary process for public television. At key junctures, real progress was born of frustration as well as optimism.

In 1954, former broadcast network employee Fred Rogers was heading WQED/Pittsburgh, the nation's first community-owned station, when he created the live series *The Children's Corner* (in which he did not appear on camera). He did not know who was watching or how they felt about it until the puppet character Daniel Striped Tiger made the impromptu announcement that his birthday was coming up. On Daniel's "birthday," the line to join the studio audience wound four blocks from the station, Rogers recalls, which gave him an uplifting sense of community interest in the program. Rogers was able to tape the programs and share them with a few other noncommercial stations that were looking for children's programs to air.

In Milwaukee, programmer Paul Taff, who had previously produced radio specials for children, was frustrated by how little he had available to serve the children's audience and shared his complaints to the nation's 27 fledgling affiliates of educational TV. By the late 1950s, "Our allotment [of children's programs] was 45 minutes a week," recalled Taff in a 1999 phone interview. "Try building an audience with that" (personal communication with Pascual, October 1999).

Although some stations like WQED were producing local children's programs, in the absence of a PBS infrastructure, it was difficult to pool resources. To help fill the need for more and better content, National Education Television, the Ann Arbor, Michigan, station funded by the Ford Foundation, moved its operations and claimed a presence at the nation's center for broadcast operations—New York City. The station's new program manager called Taff and in effect told him to "put up or shut up" on the dearth of children's television, Taff recalls. So, in 1960, Taff moved east to head children's programming for what would become WNET and to start acquiring programs on behalf of the other community-based noncommercial stations. He would later become president of Connecticut Public Television.

One of Taff's first calls was to Fred Rogers, who had by then created and starred in a program called *Misterogers* for the Canadian Broadcasting Corporation. Taff proposed that Rogers create a quarter-hour program for public television distribution, but Rogers demurred, saying 15 minutes just was not enough time for what he wanted to do. Taff could barely afford more; he had a meager pool of money to invest in children's programs (about 30 stations contributed $5,200 per year for his acquisitions). And he faced another hurdle. When he proposed funding a new half-hour show featuring Rogers, it became clear that some programmers were unimpressed by Rogers's gentle on-air demeanor and could not see what value his program brought to children.

Taff, who believed that Rogers's "childlike, not childish" approach was perfect for the preschool viewer, sought another way to pay for the series and won a grant from Chicago's Sears Roebuck Foundation. *Mister Rogers' Neighborhood* was launched nationally in 1968; in that first year, Fred Rogers wrote and starred in 130 half-hour programs.

Once again, to measure the impact of the new series, there were no fancy audience surveys or Nielsen overnights to rely on; what Taff learned, he saw or heard from stations. When Mister Rogers visited markets for public events, "he was mobbed," Taff recalls. And although many adults still could not see Rogers's appeal, Taff said, "The adults are not the ones that judge—ask the children, that's your answer" (personal communication with Pascual, October 1999).

## The Promise of the Public Broadcasting Act

Efforts to improve commercial-free television for children coincided with the demise of live-action programs for children on commercial networks, which disappeared in an explosion of relatively cheap-to-produce cartoons with frequent interruptions for advertisements. Commercial children's series also lost broadcast slots to more marketable soap operas and game shows, and early public television enthusiasts saw both an urgent need and an exciting opportunity for a commercial-free educational service that would serve children, and indeed any American with a TV set. Even with the rise of cable and direct TV in the 1980s and 1990s, PBS still holds that distinctive commitment to quality TV for all.

Fred Rogers was one of the few producers who actually had broadcast tapes to demonstrate what children's quality programming might look like. Rogers's world looked gentle. It looked nurturing. But it also looked white and suburban. It looked unlike the lives of millions of impoverished children who rarely saw themselves on television and might never find a neighbor as welcoming as Fred Rogers.

Rogers has wondered whether that mattered to viewers, though even today he says 60% of the people who stop him on the street to talk about the series are people of color. He also took comfort in the words of Bill Isler, president of the company that produces *Mister Rogers,* who he recalls as saying, "What comes across is respect for the human being, which is color-blind" (personal communication with Pascual, October 1999).

But when television executives and child development specialists gathered to discuss what would become a public (i.e., noncommercial) broadcasting service, the difference was noted. The decline of creative children's programming on commercial networks coincided with a real willingness on the part of many Americans to try to honor and reflect the lives of minority, urban-living children, and to lift poor children out of poverty. That interest was seen in federal service programs such as Head Start, which was funded in 1965 to provide early intervention that would raise IQ scores and give disadvantaged children a brighter future. There was also a solid commitment to not treat children as a consumer target.

Such a vision inspired new producers who believed in the teaching power of television. If Head Start gave children 3 hours of culturally sensitive enrichment each day, and many other children remained unserved by nursery school and kindergarten, why not offer an hour or so of enrichment through public television? The Corporation for Public Broadcasting (CPB), as created by an act of Congress in 1967, was committed to education and to the idea that learning could be entertaining.

In New York, Joan Ganz Cooney had been thinking a lot about what educational programs might look like. After writing a 1966 report for the Carnegie Corporation on television's potential to educate preschoolers, she formed the Children's Television Workshop (CTW), along with Harvard Graduate School of Education professor Gerald Lesser and others. CTW married research on children's television and child development with new production sensibilities. Cooney, reflecting in 1995 on *Sesame Street*'s genesis, wrote,

> I wanted our new children's program to use the short segments and multiple formats that made *Laugh In* so entertaining and the most popular show on television at the time. Because I knew that children paid attention to TV, I wanted to use "commercials" to teach letters and numbers. I wanted to see a multiracial cast and both sexes on the show—no one star.

CTW was positioned to give new form to PBS's mission of providing enriching educational programming; *Sesame Street* premiered in 1969.

In contrast to *Mister Rogers,* early *Sesame Street* viewers experienced fast-paced fun, with cognitive lessons coming in short clips. The program is still rich in animated drills of early childhood lessons, as well as songs and jokes from a multicultural and multispecies cast, headed by the lovingly childlike Big Bird.

Some children's TV stalwarts had mixed reactions—mostly critiquing the series' fast pace and lack of strong narrative structure—but *Sesame Street* earned enormous goodwill for its creativity, inventiveness, and broad ambitions. It also accomplished some very significant wins for the new PBS system: The series declared that the new network was both serious and daring in serving the child audience, and a preschool audience at that. Furthermore, its cultivation of the parent as an enthusiastic coviewer made children's TV fun for grown-ups. If parents could declare that a child's program was hip, might the learning that took place actually help transform the way families looked at and used television?

To answer that question and others, CTW, and subsequently all major PBS children's series, relied on research. Wrote Cooney (1995), "Research is at the heart of what is now known as the CTW model of production—a three-way collaboration among producers and writers, experts on curriculum and child development, and researchers." In 1974, Lesser published his book *Lessons From Sesame Street,* which confirmed earlier studies that the more children viewed, the greater the series' educational impact. Children from poor and nonpoor households watched the series in equal proportions, but it was easier to measure the program's educational impact with children who had more teaching supports at home.

Popular expectations of *Sesame Street*'s impact created, it would seem, "urban myths" for educational television. In fact, in 1992, the *New York Times* reported that a spokesman for the Heritage Foundation argued against funding for CPB by saying, "*Sesame Street* is just another kids' show. No better than *Underdog* or *The Flintstones*. . . . If *Sesame Street* was so effective, why do we have such a literacy problem?" (Carter, 1992, p. A1).

Such misguided comments notwithstanding, public television programmers, ourselves included, felt we had the preschool viewer well served by *Sesame Street* and *Mister Rogers* in the 1970s and 1980s. It should be noted that CTW and some other producers used that period to develop PBS shows for underserved school-age audiences, including CTW's *Electric Company,* WGBH/Boston's likable *Zoom* (with strengths in language arts and socialization), Lancit Media's *Reading Rainbow,* and *3-2-1 Contact* (CTW's math skills series). These series served PBS's core mission of educating the young; there simply were no heady expectations of pledge revenue from grateful viewers or revenue streams from program-related sales.

## And Now a Word About Funding

But through these years, public television's financial landscape was subtly changing. The Corporation for Public Broadcasting, which receives and redistributes federal funds to PBS, its member stations, and public radio, is meant to serve as a firewall between independent program production and the politics of Congress. Outside of CPB funds, PBS directly applies for its own foundation and targeted federal grants to produce programs and initiatives. It also charges membership fees to stations—essentially licensing rights to air the programs distributed by PBS. Member stations, in turn, augment small amounts of federal funds with varying levels of state government funds, grants, viewer pledges around the programs they like most, corporate support, and other cash-generating activities such as public events. As a system, state and federal government support combined is slightly more than one third of all public television budgets.

Whereas foundations have had a major role in funding children's programs, corporate backing has a shorter history. PBS and local stations offer corporate "underwriters" on-air credits at the beginning and end of programs, but it has been a slow and trying process to bring PBS staff and local station leaders into some agreement over how to position our audiences (ethnically reflective of the United States but generally higher in income and education) and prioritize marketing without compromising our integrity and our promise to viewers to remain uninfluenced by commercial pressures.

PBS researchers long knew that corporate underwriting impressed audiences of adult decision makers. Witness Mobil Oil's sponsorship of *Masterpiece Theatre* following the 1973 oil crisis. Angry American consumers, facing gas rationing during peacetime, directed their ire at gas companies as well as oil-producing nations. The sponsorship was a goodwill effort that has proven so effective to the company that underwriting has continued, and the series is now known as *Mobil Masterpiece Theatre.* But since on-air messages could contain neither qualitative statements ("our product is best") nor a call to action ("buy this now!"), public television was simply not a vehicle through which to push sales. That made it more difficult to find the right niche for attracting corporate funding for children's programs. Although nearby parents could get the company's message, PBS has contended that children should not be the target of underwriting messages aired around children's programs.

In justification for cutting federal funds for public broadcasting in the 1980s, the Federal Communications Commission relaxed the rules on the range of messages permitted by corporate underwriters of commercial-free public TV. Qualitative statements, animation, music, and corporate tag lines began to appear.

Although corporate support was not expected to overtake the role of member donations in funding the system overall (even in 1999, PBS data show that viewers provided the largest percentage of public TV's total funding, 22%, while business contributed 14.7%), the stage had been set for increasing the pressure on the system to deliver more popular programs, hits for companies that were banking on increased sales as well as enhanced image.

Before the 1990s, preschool programs were mostly left out of this sea change. The signature series grew with the times, with *Mister Rogers* tackling sensitive subjects such as divorce and *Sesame Street* using more celebrity guests and slowing its format to allow for more story lines to develop. Our station's viewership was steady, and commercial stations were still unmotivated to serve the preschool audience in particular. Stations were able to measure adequate public support during pledge time—in the 1970s and 1980s, our own member income around children's programs was essentially flat—but expectations were not very great. We were at least secure in knowing that public television was serving a mission for America's young viewers.

## The Crisis in School Readiness

Complacency about our preschool service was challenged by strong research and the drumbeat of advocates like Peggy Charren, the founder of Action for Children's Television, who called for more attention to young viewers in particular. But perhaps the most compelling argument was made by researchers for the Carnegie Foundation for the Advancement of Teaching, who had been querying the nation's teachers on how prepared children were when entering kindergarten. The results were dismal. Not only was one child in three seen as fully unprepared to enter school successfully—because of deficits in language, socialization skills, and the like—but 42% of teachers reported that children were less ready for school than they had been just 5 years earlier.

The challenge to the nation's educational programmers was evident. The challenge to the television industry as a whole was encapsulated in the 1991 book published on the study, *Ready to Learn: A Mandate for the Nation* (Boyer, 1991). In it, educator and Carnegie president Ernest Boyer outlined five areas in which children and families could and must be better served by U.S. institutions and policy: health, community, preschool, workplace, and television. Among the recommendations in the chapter "Television as Teacher" was the establishment of a Ready to Learn cable channel (dedicated to quality preschool programming) and a $20 million investment in educational programs for preschoolers. CPB and PBS created a joint plan to attract and invest in new preschool programming.

## Enter Barney

We argued at the beginning of this chapter that public television tries to invest in programs that meet the developmental needs of the whole child. In January 1991, as the Boyer book was being published, 4-year-old Leora Rifkin picked out an early video of *Barney and the Backyard Gang* at a Connecticut video store. Why? She liked the box. But when she got it home, she had a whole-child response. She sang, she danced, and, most of all, she asked to watch the tape over, and over, and over again. To Leora, the magical dinosaur and his likable friends were a revelation. To the world of preschool programming, *Barney* would be a revolution.

Larry Rifkin, a coauthor of this chapter, came to work at Connecticut Public Television (CPTV) the following Monday. He was a *Barney* believer, even if he had seen only one video and had never met its creative team. He won the support of CPTV President Jerry Franklin, though some other staff, more attuned, as was Rifkin, to serious documentaries, viewed the tape with less enthusiasm. ("I thought Larry was nuts," said one colleague.) But knowing that CPB was committed to finding and funding new programs, and trusting that a 4-year-old was a better barometer of the video's appeal, a team quickly mobilized to contact *Barney*'s Texas producers and win their interest in pitching a *Barney* series to CPB and PBS.

The Lyons Group, a publishing business outside of Dallas, Texas, was *Barney*'s home. Far from the production hub of New York, Sheryl Leach had the idea for *Barney* literally while sitting in a Dallas traffic jam. She shared her idea with colleague Kathy Parker and began working on the project. Both women had been teachers and were working on Lyons's educational projects when their first children were born. As their children grew into toddlers, they shared a frustration about the poor quality of programs available for their children. With the help of video producer Dennis DeShazer—and with the financial backing of Lyons, which was owned by Leach's father-in-law—they figured out how to bring *Barney* to video.

The team made painstaking efforts to develop the *Barney* video series by testing it with children. They then marketed the tapes directly to preschools, trusting in the power of children's responses much as Fred Rogers did with *Children's Corner.*

What worked in the initial videos, and works today in the television series, is a thoughtful effort to model prosocial skills that all children need—such as turn taking, emotional control, and manners—with cognitive and physical skills through activity, music, and dance. Rifkin and Leach brought the TV proposal to CPB and easily won a start-up investment in the fall of 1991, with a series launch expected on April 6, 1992.

The preschool fund also awarded grants to a new series called *Lamb Chop's Play-Along,* featuring TV veteran Shari Lewis, and for new episodes of the Canadian series *Shining Time Station.* All would be funded for 13 weeks, and the new series would launch in sequence, with *Barney & Friends* coming last.

The contracts for these series demonstrated how much the world had changed since the public system first invested in *Mister Rogers' Neighborhood* and *Sesame Street. Shining Time* and *Barney and the Backyard Gang* were established productions, having been researched and developed before public television partnerships were entertained. CPB and PBS's investments would certainly help raise the production values of *Barney & Friends,* but all the groundwork had been done on the Lyons Group's dime.

Each series also had some base as a marketing "brand." *Shining Time* had an active and successful product line based on the star toy character, Thomas the Tank Engine. Shari Lewis's cast of puppets had mostly been created in her series from decades earlier. And *Barney*, even if only well-known in pockets of the country, already had six video titles and a companion plush toy.

In recognition of the early investments the producers had made in these projects, the CPB/PBS agreements included a limited plan for revenue sharing from increases in product sales after the series were launched. Again, this is a marked departure from earlier preschool productions. Fred Rogers mostly refused to create products based on his series over the years (there are hand puppets and a trolley for sale in the program's catalogue), and nonprofit CTW, which sells program-related products, has been able to report that profits are turned back into the company and production (although in 1999 it launched a for-profit cable channel, Noggin, on which older *Sesame Street* episodes and other programs appear). But in 1992, the new preschool ventures were owned by private, for-profit companies. Still, expectations for just how much interest related products would generate were unformed.

## Bringing *Barney* to a Station Near You

Public television's greatest strength, but surely its greatest challenge, is the independence of its 349 broadcast stations, which are programmed by 171 licensees. PBS is the first gatekeeper to the airwaves, evaluating program proposals, investing production funds or purchasing acquisition rights, and feeding most of the programs used by stations. Other syndication services exist, but the standards PBS exacts, particularly to make sure that children's programming is of high production quality and educational content, give PBS programs a seal of quality that programmers rely on. Still, stations are free to make their own decisions about whether a program should be used in their local market and when it should be scheduled.

That freedom is a hallmark, distinguishing the system from enormous broadcast and cable enterprises offering one-size-fits-all schedules to markets across the nation. It also makes the jobs of public television producers and publicists much, much harder.

The three series in the preschool initiative had the first advantage in gaining the attention of programmers: They would be PBS network programs as opposed to being offered through a less visible public television program syndicator. That meant that station programmers throughout the country would hear about the series in official PBS communications and its annual conference. They would see promotional feeds in which PBS programming executives announce the new shows for each season. The programs had the heightened exposure of being chosen for the first major investment in preschool programming in decades.

Still, CPTV staff—and that of any current public television producer—had to build carriage the old-fashioned way: by selling a station on a series' merits one conversation at a time. With dollars for funding the series stretched thin, money for promotion to stations and public audiences was limited. Because it had been so long since programmers had to evaluate preschool fare, there was some question about whether stations would have solid criteria for judging the series. Furthermore, *Barney & Friends* was no marquee name for public television programmers, and it was known that PBS was likely to fund just one of the series after they each had an initial 13-week debut. *Shari Lewis* and *Shining Time* were established names; a big purple dinosaur who had been created by mission-driven moms from Texas may have sounded cute, but it was not an easy sell for programmers who did not have their own children to serve as test viewers. As seen during the launch of *Teletubbies,* a British production that began airing on PBS in the late 1990s, stations know a program is working more by public response than by big jumps in viewership.

## *Barney* Out, *Barney* In

What Paul Taff knew when he launched *Mister Rogers' Neighborhood,* we sensed at *Barney*'s premiere: Young viewers were immediately attracted to the series. We had created an 800 number for viewer calls, and we, and the Lyons Group, began getting letters and calls right away from enthusiastic adults.

"I have a 1-and-a-half-year-old son who loves *Barney and Friends* almost as much as Mom and Dad!" one mother wrote. "It is comforting to see that while he is being entertained by Barney, he's also learning a lot. I'm happy to watch him imitate the children on the show and to hear his vocabulary increasing every day."

What was less clear was how well PBS, headquartered in Alexandria, Virginia, could appreciate that response. Though PBS senior executives had committed to funding one new preschool series after the initial CPB investment, by late spring, they were suggesting they might fund two. Either way, the decision would be made in advance of the June 1992 annual station meeting, which meant that a decision would be made on *Barney & Friends* only weeks into its debut.

"All three [series] generated significant responses," reported then PBS vice president of scheduling John Grant (as cited in Bedford, 1992a). *Shining Time Station* and *Lamb Chop's Play-Along* were offered extended contracts at the same time that *Barney & Friends* was becoming PBS's most-watched children's series. The decision meant that there would not be further episodes of *Barney & Friends* produced for PBS.

We learned of PBS's plans not to fund the series before the annual PBS station meeting and shared what we knew with programmers who had witnessed viewer response and were convinced of the series' potential. Press had been positive as well, with many early articles written by reporters who had seen *Barney*'s appeal—as we had hoped—through the eyes of their own children.

While we used the annual meeting to encourage unhappy programmers to lobby PBS, the strength of the protest was really borne in the grass roots, among parents. As word got out, the Lyons Group and we were deluged with calls, which we redirected to local stations or PBS.

In defense, PBS argued that funding *Barney* meant it would have to cut funds for other audiences and that offering five preschool programs (including *Mister Rogers' Neighborhood* and *Sesame Street*) seemed like excessive attention to the preschool market. Yet it was becoming clear that even Congress was willing to fund more preschool enrichment efforts, as Ernest Boyer had proposed. And the argument about misdirected resources brought this response from San Francisco's then-program director Kevin Harris: "I don't think you deal with it by not renewing a success. . . . *Barney* is now our number-one children's show. It outscores *Mister Rogers* and *Sesame Street*" (as cited in Bedford, 1992b).

By late August, PBS relented, reversing its decision to cut *Barney* and committing $1.75 million for a season of 18 programs. The reversal was unprecedented. It had been a difficult funding season for PBS on many fronts, and within the year, the director of PBS children's programs and other senior programmers would be gone.

This entire experience—being willing to gamble on a program that adults do not intuitively understand, seeing the enormous potential for public appreciation of a fresh educational program, and witnessing the willingness of PBS to reverse itself in the face of public and station response—demonstrates the strengths of public television's service to children. Television networks are, by nature, insular; being so far from the public they serve makes them risk-averse. But we find it hard to imagine any commercial network making such a turn-around. Public television's vigorous station system and the public's well-placed expectation that their voice should be heeded are powerful tools that not only can change decisions but can and should force experimentation and initiative.

## Money, Success, and Excess

It did not take long for the "*Barney* backlash" to begin. And here is where we learned not about children and their relationship to TV but about grown-ups, perception, and money.

As noted earlier, each of the producers had created a line of toys and other products related to the characters in their series, and PBS's participation in revenue sharing was approximately the same for each program. The marketing of *Barney*-related merchandise was rather traditional, but demand was not. For the holiday season of 1992, *Barney* was America's top toy.

Stations were a source of that merchandise as well, offering program-related gifts in return for viewer pledges during fund-raising drives. Although viewers can almost always buy those "thank you gifts" offered during pledge at their local store, public television has been able to sustain itself by the fact that appreciative viewers do not view their contribution as a product purchase. If they did, they would have purchased a *Barney* plush toy from Toys-R-Us for $20 instead of through their local station for $200.

*Barney*'s pledge success was nothing short of phenomenal. In March 1993, a national "*Barney* marathon" of back-to-back episodes—with live interim breaks featuring Barney and some cast members in a studio—raised more than a record-breaking $2 million.

Money became a public relations distraction. The question of why public television needed to even pay Lyons for the *Barney* series reflected concerns over whether PBS executives had struck the best deal on derivative products. But at the time that the agreement was made, PBS's doubts about *Barney*'s potential, its limited funding pool, and the significant work already done by Lyons to create the series made a greater investment imprudent, if not impossible. No one envisioned *Barney* mania, and to this day, we as originators of the arrangement feel all sides were treated, and compensated, fairly. Detractors failed to value that *Barney* gave PBS a tremendous spike in children's viewing, in parents' loyalty to public television, in membership pledges, in new underwriting dollars, and in the enthusiasm of solid producing talent who suddenly saw PBS as a viable outlet for new work.

*Barney*'s retail success was also adult driven, and it is hard to blame public TV for the ubiquity of a program-related product when parents bought it so enthusiastically. As noted in *Current* (Behrens, 1995), a newspaper covering the public television industry, the claims of how much money was being made by public television stations, and in product sales ringing up for the Lyons Group (now Lyrick Studios), were grossly inflated. Still, the message was not getting out that PBS did not have the resources to fund and produce its own wholly owned programs and that, by consequence, financial rewards had to be available to producers, not all of whom would want to form nonprofit companies. That did not, however, mean that PBS was willing to let just any potential hot property on the air. Under the leadership of former children's program director Alice Cahn, PBS used this time to develop standards for program content and quality that reflect school-readiness skills identified by the National Education Goals Panel (1991). The goals are physical/motor skills, social/emotional skills, critical thinking/problem-solving skills, language/literacy skills, cognitive skills, science study, life skills, cultural/social diversity appreciation and understanding, and music and art appreciation and performance.

The "backlash" showed us most significantly that people were still missing what made *Barney & Friends* a hit. It is not through gimmicks, as some critics charged, but through episodes that are thoughtfully planned to reflect the world and needs of a preschool viewer. Children recognize that Barney "thinks like them," said Sheryl Leach to *USA Today.* "He celebrates the child and childhood." That some adults found the series "syrupy" said a great deal about how American culture perceives childhood but little to Sheryl Leach and her producing team. "We don't really think about what the parents are going to like and dislike," she responded (as cited in Hellmich, 1992, p. 5D).

In keeping with the educational testing commitment of *Sesame Street* and *Mister Rogers,* CPTV gave a grant to researchers to evaluate *Barney & Friends.* Ten studies were conducted over a 2-year period, involving about 600 preschool and kindergarten children in cities in Arizona, California, Connecticut, Georgia, and Ohio. Results indicate that watching *Barney & Friends* can improve the cognitive and social skills of children, especially when there is follow-up immediately after the program by an adult who reinforces the program content (Singer & Singer, 1998).

## The Aftermath of a Preschool Gold Rush

We, PBS, and certainly many other stations began to get proposals, both good and bad, for the public television schedule. By the spring of 1994, an informal poll by *Current* newspaper (Bedford, 1994) showed 25 new children's programs in various stages of development—and that was just the programs that had alliances with stations or were from established producers. Seven were for the preschool market (of which five eventually made it to distribution); eight programs were for early-school-age audiences (two were made, including the animated hit *Arthur*); and 10 were for older-school-age children (from which the 1970s series *Zoom* reemerged in the 1990s).

Expectations for preschool programs, based on *Barney*'s financial success, were easily overinflated. The creation of Lancit Media's preschool series *Puzzle Place* occasioned an initial stock offering, with an expectation that the puppet-based series celebrating diversity would capture viewers and spawn product sales; however, as reported in a 1998 *Current* article (McCrummen, 1998), the series did not attract significant viewer attention or product success during fund-raising drives or in the stores.

Underwriter interest in sponsoring children's programs came alive, and *Barney & Friends* was soon sponsored by three corporate underwriters, whose messages were carefully targeted to adult viewers. Imaginative new series like *Magic School Bus* (now on Fox) were launched with underwriters from the start—in this case, Microsoft.

What was clear is that the *Barney* experience buoyed PBS by attracting creative interest and money. PBS used that interest wisely in many ways. It is fair to say, in our judgment, that *Barney & Friends* launched a revolution in children's programming, unleashing the talents of other entrepreneurial producers.

As PBS tried to evaluate the merits and funding base of many projects, it gave a green light to smart and entertaining series for older children such as *Bill Nye, the Science Guy* (now on Disney), *Kratt's Creatures* (a science and nature appreciation program), and *Wishbone* (a series featuring classic literature from the Lyons Group's parent company). And while intermittent public concerns about the violence of commercial children's television warranted research studies, PBS has been regularly praised as being "virtually free of violence."

The 1993 CPB report to Congress on school readiness, authored and edited by Jerome and Dorothy Singer, codirectors of the Yale University Family Television Research and Consultation Center, proposed many of the developments that followed. In 1994, CPB and PBS launched an outreach service called "Ready to Learn," through which 130 stations have committed to airing at least 6 hours of preschool programming per day, plus conduct training for parents and caregivers on the effective use of television. Ready to Learn was evaluated by the University of Alabama in 1999 (Bryant, 1999), which reported that parents who received the free training read 35% more often to their children, and those children were watching 40% less television than their peers. Ready to Learn is about far more than television—it also seeks to improve family literacy by requiring that stations distribute 200 books a month to low-income families. Individual series have also invested significantly in materials to help educators and parents maximize the teaching content of specific episodes.

In Connecticut, we have created our own Ready to Learn effort called "First Step." By modifying the materials provided nationally, we have renewed our station commitment to localism and educational impact; efforts to enhance the effectiveness of our children's programming are at the core of the effort. Training parents, caregivers, and preschool educators to extend the value of the program content is done through a myriad of workshops and on-site activities throughout Connecticut.

## The Challenge of New Technologies

Although PBS proudly stakes the claim that, unlike cable, we are a free, universal service, there is no doubt that cable channels have tried to claim our broader mantle of serving the child audience with educational programming, some of it even commercial-free.

PBS "is no longer the only safe haven for children's programming," said Alice Cahn, former group president of films, television, and video for CTW, in a 1999 phone interview.

> Now you find a group of parents who grew up on *Sesame Street* who say, "I do trust public television as one place. I also trust Nick Jr., Nickelodeon, Discovery Kids, and the Learning Channel. My child has CD-ROMs to play with and a library of videotapes." (personal communication with Pascual, October 1999)

The advent of cable and other in-home media sources has created a promotional challenge for PBS, says Cahn, who has launched a cable channel for CTW and is continuing *Sesame Street*'s well-established international franchise. "I don't think that public TV or perhaps even producers have done enough of a job really talking to consumers [about] why public TV children's programs are different, and the benefits and risks of on-screen entertainment" (personal communication with Pascual, October 1999).

Especially since the advent of Ready to Learn, PBS has been explicit in giving stations nine subject areas and program goals (discussed earlier) by which to judge series, even those proposed to them outside of PBS distribution.

But Cahn's thesis that a marketing and promotional challenge bedevils public TV has weight. It can be seen in the most recent study of the University of Pennsylvania's Annenberg Public Policy Center (Stanger & Gridina, 1999), which surveys the overall quality and educational content of children's programs as well as public attitudes to them. In the 1997 report, 61.1% of parents said that PBS was the best source of children's programs; in 1999, 44.3% of parents polled felt that way. At the same time, researchers found that PBS was the best source for quality, with little diminishment over the years.

PBS will never have the marketing muscle of for-profit channels, but it is trying to use its dollars more wisely. Interstitial materials and the launch of a new 24-hour PBS digital channel called PBS Kids are among top marketing strategies. Stations can distribute the new channel locally through various delivery systems, and it is available nationally through direct broadcast satellite.

On the programming front, PBS is working internally to develop new models that give local stations the option of inserting locally produced content in some children's programs; to develop more productions based on literary successes; and to test models of interactive programming for the child audience. It has also invested in an activity-rich website for children and parents, with links to all series.

## Public TV and Children: Going Forward

If one accepts our premise that children deserve universal access to quality educational programming, public TV's mission is no less vibrant in the digital future. But from our perspective, it must build future success by building on our well-established strengths.

- *Innovate.* The fact that there are many more educational choices for children now than before is a testament to the success of the TV marketplace—at least some enterprises have learned from PBS's commitment to the child viewer. But we cannot fade away. Public TV can and should continue to experiment and lead other networks in developing new types of children's programs—extending well beyond preschool viewing—with cultural breadth and sensitivity.
- *Fund. Barney & Friends'* success allowed many passionate producers to think creatively about the children's market. The public and our leaders must understand that the funding structure of public television will not allow the system to wholly own series. By all means, watch carefully to make sure that PBS executives do not begin to make profit-motivated programming choices, but if the country is unhappy with PBS hosting a commercial success, it needs to consider other ways to fund this service.
- *Avoid commercials.* PBS underwriting credits are subdued and should not be directed to the child audience—a critical distinction between them and commercial advertisements. This distinction must be honored and preserved.
- *Build community.* Continue to use Ready to Learn and PBS's school-based outreach services to promote local education and cultural enrichment. PBS stations are unique in their relationships to local communities, and that focus must be preserved, even while economies of scale for promotion and marketing are pursued.
- *Teach.* As evidenced in this book's earlier discussions of media effects, Americans simply do not accept that TV choices have a real impact on growing brains and character—at least not seriously enough to guide their children's viewing. Given our limited promotional funds, can PBS and its member stations convince adults who make

and choose programs to support television that respects children instead of trying to rush them into adulthood?

As seen in this chapter, PBS's efforts to serve children have flagged or gone astray at times. The nation's interest in defining and demanding quality children's programs has flagged much more often. But if we believe that all America's children should have the option of a universal, commercial-free preschool of the air and that older children should be able to see themselves in programs that value them more as independent and creative thinkers than as consumers, we must sustain public television.

This is a mission-based endeavor with positive results, but we should not be ashamed of seeing our future in those terms, and we should not forget from where we have come. "Everyone participating must do everything he or she can to love the viewer," says Fred Rogers. "It's very easy to make the bad or the evil attractive—most [stories] are pretty much alike. It's very difficult to make goodness attractive, and that needs to be our goal as broadcasters" (personal communication with Pascual, October 1999).

That is only possible if what we expect of children's television is more than screen deep.

## References

Bedford, K. E. (1992a, August 24). *Barney* returns to PBS, pulls pledge dollars. *Current* [On-line]. Available: www.current.org/ch/ch215b.html

Bedford, K. E. (1992b, June 8). PBS amasses biggest reserve yet for new shows. *Current* [On-line]. Available: www.current.org/ch/ch215b.html

Bedford, K. E. (1994, May 23). Surge of program projects readied for ready to learn. *Current* [On-line]. Available: www.current.org/ch/ch410.html

Behrens, S. (1995, March 6). What did *Barney* earn, and why didn't PBS get more? *Current* [On-line]. Available: www.current.org/mo504.html

Boyer, E. L. (1991). *Ready to learn: A mandate for the nation.* Princeton, NJ: Princeton University Press.

Bryant, J. (1999). *Study of children's reading use following parent training at public television workshops* [University of Alabama report, released by PBS]. Available: www.pbs.org/insidepbs/news/rtlexecsummary. html

Carter, B. (1992, April 30). Conservatives call for PBS to go private or go dark. *New York Times,* p. A1.

Cooney, J. G. (1995, May 29). David Connell's talents grew with his gifts to kids. *Current* [On-line]. Available: www.current.org/people/peop510c.html

Corporation for Public Broadcasting. (1993). *Public broadcasting: Ready to teach: How broadcasting can serve the ready-to-learn needs of America's children* (Report to the 103rd Congress and the American people). Washington, DC: Author.

De Moraes, L. (1999, July 20). UPN, getting bopped over the head for "WWF Smackdown!" *Washington Post,* p. C07.

Hellmich, N. (1992, December 2). "Barney" proves sweet kids' shows aren't extinct. *USA Today,* p. 5D.

Lesser, G. S. (1974). *Children and television: Lessons from* Sesame Street. New York: Random House.

McCrummen, S. (1998, February 16). With roots in public TV, Lancit and Truett found the market can be a beast, even in kidvid. *Current* [On-line]. Available: www.current.org/ch/ch803L1.html

National Education Goals Panel. (1991). *Goal 1 technical planning subgroup report on school readiness* [On-line]. Available: www.negp.gov/Reports/child-ea. htm

Singer, J. L., & Singer, D. G. (1998). *Barney & Friends* as entertainment and education: Evaluating the quality and effectiveness of a television series for preschool children. In J. Asamen & G. Berry (Eds.), *Research paradigms in the study of television and social behavior* (pp. 305-367). Thousand Oaks, CA: Sage.

Stanger, J. D., & Gridina, N. (1999). *Media in the home 1999: The fourth annual survey of parents and children.* Philadelphia: University of Pennsylvania, Annenberg Public Policy Center. Available: http://appcpenn.org/kidstv99/survey5.htm

CHAPTER 27

# PRIX JEUNESSE as a Force for Cultural Diversity

DAVID W. KLEEMAN
American Center for Children and Media

As media become increasingly global, their role in children's development of cultural identity is a topic of ongoing concern. Children use television as a window to their world as it expands from self to family to neighborhood, to town to country and world—but they may be unaware when flaws in that glass distort or ignore their own history or culture.

The problem is both domestic and international. Within many countries, children's television fails to represent adequately the diverse makeup of its audience. Worldwide, the flood of inexpensive programming that is designed for a global marketplace makes it difficult for an increasing number of countries to sustain their own production (Second World Summit on Television for Children, 1998). In both cases, cultures and values outside the mainstream grow up marginalized by the world's most powerful medium for entertainment, informal education, and cultural dissemination.

Two World Summits on Children and Television, as well as regional gatherings in Asia, Africa, and Latin America, have taken as their central theme the preservation and improvement of indigenous media. The United Nations' Convention on the Rights of the Child calls for children to have media experiences suited to their culture and heritage (United Nations, 1989, art. 17). In the United States, advocacy groups measure and publicize both statistical and anecdotal measures of television's diversity, as reflected both on-screen and in the ranks of entertainment industry decision makers.

Once it is acknowledged, the difficult question is how to remedy homogenization of television. Policy antidotes, whether by quota or

AUTHOR'S NOTE: This chapter, and the world of children's television, is immeasurably richer for the contributions of Ursula von Zallinger, secretary general of PRIX JEUNESSE. James Fellows, longtime adviser to PRIX JEUNESSE and founder of the American Center for Children and Media, helped to organize and develop the ideas herein and reviewed each draft.

incentive, are incomplete at best. In the United States, any such legislation would surely be struck down as unconstitutional. Worldwide, policies might create an environment in which culturally appropriate programs get produced and aired, but those policies cannot ensure quality or appeal. That is the province of producers. The people who create children's television must be skilled, motivated, and have appropriate perspective if they are to create attractive and engaging works that respond to young audiences' needs and interests.

## PRIX JEUNESSE: Personal Development, Global Perspective

For more than 35 years, the PRIX JEUNESSE Foundation[1] has been a world nexus for the creative leaders of children's television, showing how to foster high-quality programming that honors cultural diversity. The foundation produces a competition, seminars, workshops, publications, and screenings—all intentionally designed to sharpen the abilities of those responsible for children's television and to link them in a worldwide professional network.

### *Founding Concerns: Still Timely After All These Years*

PRIX JEUNESSE was founded in 1964 in response to concerns that are no less timely today: Children's programming suffered from "short transmission periods, small staffs and modest budgets" (PRIX JEUNESSE, 1989, p. 6). Bayerischer Rundfunk (Bavarian Public Broadcasting, part of ARD, the first German public broadcaster), the free state of Bavaria, and the city of Munich invited educators and other experts to "assess the achievements of TV in the area of education and at the same time provide incentive for further efforts" (PRIX JEUNESSE, 1989, p. 20). They recommended the establishment of a festival.

Zweites Deutsches Fernsehen (ZDF, the second German public broadcaster) joined the foundation in 1971 and the Bayerische Landeszentrale für neue Medien (which represents Germany's commercial channels) in 1992. The European Broadcasting Union and UNESCO are patrons of the foundation. An international advisory board ensures that its activities and services are timely, useful, and appropriate to the regions and professions being served.[2]

Remarkably, a two-person office in Munich runs the worldwide activities of the PRIX JEUNESSE Foundation. The secretary general since 1991, Ursula von Zallinger has been with the foundation since its inception. Von Zallinger is a tireless advocate and innovator in disseminating the PRIX JEUNESSE concept. She is also a living chronicle of international children's television, able to track trends and innovations (e.g., the spread of preschool magazines, inspired by *Sesame Street*) by their first appearance at the festival and their subsequent diffusion worldwide.

### *A Market of Good Ideas*

The foundation centerpiece is a biannual competition that is a petri dish for cross-cultural fertilization. The contest's prize categories have changed often over the festival's history. Currently, there are prizes for the best fiction and nonfiction programs in three age groups: up to 6, 6 to 11, and 11 to 15. There is also a prize for light entertainment, open to shows aimed at the two oldest age groups. The highest-scoring program in each of the four voting criteria—idea, realization, script, and target audience—receives a medallion. UNICEF sponsors a special prize for the program that most convincingly demonstrates how children anywhere in the world can be helped to lead a decent life and to fully develop their potential. UNESCO sponsors a special prize for the program that best promotes a better understanding of cultures. BMW offers a prize for the best program made with limited means.

Although the metal-and-glass ball awarded to the winners is highly coveted, broadcasters enter their programs and send their executives to PRIX JEUNESSE largely because the festival is a "market of good ideas." Several hundred producers and program executives from around the world gather in Munich to watch and discuss dozens of entries from more than 50 countries.

There is no entry fee, aside from the cost of copying tapes and providing script translations in the festival's four languages: English, German, French, and Spanish. In 2000, there were 214 entries from 86 telecasters in 53 countries. An international nominating committee narrowed the field to 84 finalists, to be shown at the weeklong festival. Programs that are not nominated are available throughout the festival at an on-demand "video bar."

The entries reflect enormous diversity of target audience, genre, style, subject, and, of course, cultural perspective and influence. Giving fair evaluation to programs from very different cultures, side by side, is key to the PRIX JEUNESSE competition. As such, it is the most important and the most difficult skill demanded of those who attend the festival. It is simple to dismiss a show because it "wouldn't work in my country"; it is far harder, and more productive, to ask and understand "why does it work in yours?" That curiosity and empathy is a leap away from cultural domination and toward cultural respect and exchange.

### *Try to See Things My Way*

At one level, PRIX JEUNESSE judging criteria are universal: Is the idea interesting and/or original? Is the subject well researched and developed? Are the characters well defined and their actions motivated? Is the idea translated expertly to television (e.g., art direction, camera work, editing)?

Most of the criteria, however, demand unique consideration of the culture from which the program emerges. Whether a program is appropriate for its intended age group, if it is successfully entertaining, how well it empowers children, and even whether the pace and rhythm are effective are all highly subjective questions, dependent on knowledge of (or at least empathy for) the appropriate national and media culture.

A country that extends and cherishes childhood will create very different programming than a country whose young people are expected to assume adult roles early on. A nation with rich and competitive media resources (i.e., many TV channels and high penetration of other electronic media) will probably devote more attention to the entertainment value of its programming than will a place with fewer options. Tastes, traditions, and taboos all contribute to the style and substance of a country's children's television.

### *A Jury of Peers*

Nurturing this kind of cultural reflection demands a unique and carefully designed structure for the PRIX JEUNESSE competition. In the contest's early years, prizewinners were chosen by a small select jury of producers and academics, meeting in isolation from the views of other participants. There was little opportunity to learn the particulars about why programs were produced as they were.

Since 1972, however, everyone who attends is eligible and encouraged to vote in selecting the winners, provided they attend every screening and participate in moderated discussions of the entries. Invitations to attend the festival are extended worldwide to telecasters, production companies, researchers, and other professionals involved with children and media.

The discussion groups are multilingual to further encourage cross-cultural exchange (through most of the festival's history, there were separate German, French, Spanish, and English groups). No voting takes place until all programs in a category have been discussed.

All these factors enhance the festival as a place for discovery. Because every participant has a stake in the outcome, each is actively engaged in evaluating the programs. First reactions after screening an entry are important, but final judgments follow debate about the program with people from a variety of cultures.

### *A Mouse in the House and Other Cultural Gaffes*

Violence and sex are the topics that most often reveal cultural rifts at PRIX JEUNESSE. In Scandinavia, for example, nudity and frank presentation of sexual issues are accepted with equanimity, but most violence is taboo. By contrast, violence is far more acceptable to most Asian countries than any hint of sex. These are far from the only cultural differences, however, and fascinating debates at PRIX JEUNESSE focus on far narrower points of culture:

- A 1992 Dutch program in which a boy tries to thwart his father's efforts to drive a mouse from their kitchen charmed most participants; some claimed, however, that, in their cultures, a mouse would always be seen as a sign of an unclean house.[3]
- That same year featured an exceptional, controversial film about growing up in a nomadic tribe in Niger. The film was made as part of a training workshop by Germany's ZDF. Written, directed, shot, and edited entirely by Africans, the film still had a European style and "feel." Debate at the festival centered on whether the film was true to its culture and whether it was possible to provide production training without also imparting an aesthetic different from what might grow indigenously.[4]
- Nickelodeon's *Double Dare* prompted a heated reaction, as participants from a variety of world regions labeled its messy game show stunts a scandalous waste of food (even after being told that the props were inedible imitations). Justified or not, American commercial programming has never fared well at PRIX JEUNESSE, where "efficient" programs (those that tell engaging stories with a minimum of resources) tend to be favored over shows that are highly produced. NBC's *Stuart Little* won the prize for plays and entertainment in 1966, the best showing for a U.S. commercial program until 1996, when Fox/Scholastic's *Goosebumps* came within a tenth of a point of winning its category.

The small insights one picks up at the festival may even be useful in developing programming for the global marketplace. Knowing, for example, that pigs are not acceptable characters in Islamic countries could save a sale and avert embarrassment.

Encouraging cultural expression stops short of the right to promote propaganda, however. The PRIX JEUNESSE rules prohibit "programmes that violate the principles of the General Declaration of Human Rights." In 1990, only a year after the Tienanmen Square rebellion, China Central Television provoked outrage among delegates by submitting *We Love Motherland, We Love Peace,* a short feature in which small children painted happy pictures in the middle of Tienanmen Square.

### *At PRIX JEUNESSE, Size Doesn't Matter*

The PRIX JEUNESSE festival displays on equal footing programs from countries with massive and well-funded media industries and those from places with few resources. Often, smaller broadcasters and even individual producers prove that creativity, not money, is the determining factor in producing high-quality, culturally appropriate children's television.

Each festival since 1992 has featured a program by Poland's Andrzej Maleszka.[5] His first entry was a simple outdoor game show in which German and Polish children, who did not speak each other's language, were given tasks that required them to find means of communication. More recently, Maleszka has produced comedic dramas: A boy who is sent out for milk brings home a cow; a girl wakes up able only to speak "cat"; a magic cap compels a girl to act out whatever is on television. The stories are uncomplicated and the productions unadorned with special effects. What distinguishes Maleszka's work is his world-class ability to direct young actors.

Director Berit Nesheim of Norway won prizes in 1988 and 1990 for dramas about young love, produced for Norsk Rikskringskasting.[6] Her work for television launched her career as one of her country's leading feature film directors, once nominated for an Academy Award.

Of all the champions for children's television that have emerged from PRIX JEUNESSE, however, Danmarks Radio presents a fascinating case study. The Danish public broadcaster has won international acclaim disproportionate to its size. The foundation for its success is a unique, solid, and thoughtful philosophy about television's role in children's lives.

## "Cheap and Fascinating Programs": Danmarks Radio

Denmark is in a precarious position when it comes to television. The country's unique language makes it difficult for Danish broadcasters to export or coproduce programming, except within Scandinavia. Its small population of 5.2 million people, approximately one fifth between the ages of 2 and 16 (M. Vemmer, personal communication, September 3, 1999), makes it far less expensive to acquire children's programming—especially Japanese or American animation made without cultural reference for the international market—than to produce it. An hour of acquired live action or animation costs US$3,500, whereas an hour of home-produced programming averages $12,000—ranging from $7,000 for the hosted segments between programs (the channel is noncommercial) to $120,000 for drama (M. Vemmer, personal communication, September 3, 1999).

To be certain, Denmark is hardly a developing world country. The public broadcaster's children's and youth department has an annual budget around $15 million, a considerable amount but less than the cost of some single, high-budget series in the United States. Yet Danmarks Radio continues to home produce half its programming (340 hours per year) by making what retired head of Children's and Youth Programming Mogens Vemmer calls "cheap and fascinating" programs.

The strategy pays off. Between 6:00 and 6:30 P.M. on weeknights, Danmarks Radio draws 95% of the 4- to 9-year-old audience; from 4:30 to 6.00 P.M., it attracts 50 to 65% of the 8- to 12-year-old audience, opposite three competing stations running cartoons and U.S. soaps (M. Vemmer, personal communication, September 3, 1999). These shows (and the airtime between them, which is filled with just as much care) are singularly Danish or, at times, more broadly Scandinavian. They feature the children and youth of Denmark, either in a studio setting or in familiar locations.

### *Three Unique Winners*

Three recent PRIX JEUNESSE winners from Denmark are revealing about the cultural intentions of Danmarks Radio.

In 1994, *Close Up: A Tragedy With a Happy Ending* won the prize for fiction ages 7 to 12. Although produced for an international program exchange on racism, the show was uniquely attuned to domestic issues of tensions between Turkish immigrants and Danes. Moreover, the program dealt with a perception the producers found prevalent among Danish youth, that their parents were delivering a mixed message on diversity: Be friends with children who are different, but don't bring them home.

In 1996, *Us, That's Us* won the prize for nonfiction up to age 7. The premise was simple: three small children telling jokes and riddles, posing puzzles, acting out stories, demonstrating tricks, and trying (endearingly futilely) to break Guinness world records. Fond of featuring local children on camera, the broadcaster's intent was to demonstrate that "normal" children are capable of presenting entertaining and professional-looking TV shows.

In 1998, Danmarks Radio won again, for *The Girl Behind the Veil,* in the category of nonfiction ages 12 to 17. Once more, the program was aimed at relations between Danish natives and recent immigrants. A young adult host spent time getting to know a similar-aged immigrant from Pakistan. As their relationship became more relaxed, the host was able to ask all the "naughty" (M. Vemmer, personal communication, September 3, 1999) questions about Muslim traditions that the producers knew viewers wanted to ask but couldn't. The result was to reinforce all Danes' rights to culture and religion by demystifying outwardly different traditions.

### *"A Little More Clever"*

Mogens Vemmer directed the children's and youth department at Danmarks Radio for more than 30 years. This stability and tenure confirms one of the requisites for outstanding service to children: the continuity of authority necessary to make long-term decisions and take risks, rather than swaying with short-lived trends. Danmarks Radio frequently pushes boundaries of form and content, using the trust children and parents invest in it to approach more challenging material. Topics such as death, sex, and racism are dealt with in a straightforward manner, using age-appropriate and innovative formats suited to the material. Vemmer notes,

> Danish culture allows all subjects to be dealt with. . . . As the freedom of speech has no age limit—up or down—our department has chosen . . . that this freedom must be extended to children—with explanations and illustrations understandable to the target group. (personal communication, September 3, 1999)

Asked whether his channel's programming is "educational," Vemmer replies,

> All television programs—no matter what the topic or style—should leave the viewer a little more clever, a little happier, or with a little better understanding of life. But if the viewer finds out she has been educated, the producer should be dismissed. (personal communication, September 3, 1999)

### *"Of Equal Value, Even Under Unequal Living Conditions"*

In addition to immersing children in their own Danish heritage, the channel also shows children that they are citizens of a larger world. Crews travel annually, often to developing world countries, to document children's lives and how they resemble and differ from growing up in Denmark. Vemmer cites a basic tenet of his department, to reveal that "all people are of equal value, even under unequal living conditions" (personal communication, September 3, 1999).

The Danish program *As Long As He Can Count the Cows* is something of a PRIX JEUNESSE legend. The 1986 winner of both the information category and the UNESCO prize (for the program that best promotes cross-cultural understanding), the program profiles two young boys from the Kingdom of Bhutan in the Himalayas. The older is finding it hard to keep up; he needs glasses to stay in school, a dilemma for his farming family, which has little money. Walking a fine line between documentary and docudrama, the program uses familiar issues—school, individual difficulties, a family's challenges—to reveal what life is like for a child in a very different culture.

### *Winning and Learning at PRIX JEUNESSE*

Success at PRIX JEUNESSE is important to a smaller broadcaster like Danmarks Radio, but just being there to screen and discuss programs is also vital. Vemmer describes these two very different motivations:

> To win a PRIX JEUNESSE means that you can label your activities "world's best"—and get more interest and money within your company. PRIX JEUNESSE is gold in public relations at home, but also a marvelous supermarket of friends and ideas to adopt and to make useful in your own national way. . . . After a PRIX JEUNESSE, when we sit down to watch and discuss at home, we try to find the new trends—what do children prefer in the big countries? Probably the same trend will pop up in our country—and what will be our Danish answer to that? (personal communication, September 3, 1999)

## International Contributions

PRIX JEUNESSE has been concerned with cultural diversity since its beginning in 1964. The founding members' original charter describes its purpose as being "to contribute internationally to a meaningful development and utilization of TV—in particular with regard to its effect on young people—and to improve understanding among nations and to promote the international exchange of programmes" (PRIX JEUNESSE, 1989, p. 20).

The 1970s marked the foundation's major move into supporting the cultural independence of children's television. In 1972, PRIX JEUNESSE held its first seminar outside of Germany—a program production workshop in Teheran, Iran, that drew producers from more than a dozen Asian nations. More Asian seminars followed. At the end of the decade, the foundation produced a workshop in Nairobi, Kenya, on "The Child and His Environment" to discuss the special responsibilities of African television to educate children about their land.

This trend continued through the 1980s and 1990s, to the point where nearly every year PRIX JEUNESSE produced at least one workshop or seminar in Asia, Africa, or Latin America—usually focused on production techniques for low-cost, high-quality programming. One ancillary benefit of these events is the opportunity for PRIX JEUNESSE to identify sources for program entries to the competition, as well as producers who would benefit from being invited to the festival. Most years, through the generosity of the German government, the Goethe-Institut, or others, the PRIX JEUNESSE Foundation is able to sponsor the travel of a few producers from the developing world.

### *The Busy "Off" Year*

The years between biannual festivals have never been "off" years for PRIX JEUNESSE. The foundation has traditionally organized invitational seminars or round-table meetings on specific topics that arise during the festival process but cannot be discussed in depth in the competition context. The goal is usually to develop practical services or initiatives through which PRIX JEUNESSE, often with partners in other parts of the world, can contribute to professional growth in the children's media industry. These gatherings vary in size and format, engaging leading broadcasters, researchers, educators, and experts on the particular topic in question. The discussion and outcomes are published in a "rapporteur's summary."

Topics relevant to international issues in children's television have included prejudice and understanding (1983) and children and television in a global society (1987). The concept of a world summit on television for children was first introduced at a 1993 PRIX JEUNESSE round table, when a range of organizations came together to discuss future needs and strategies for PRIX JEUNESSE and similar organizations that support the children's media industry.

### *1999: Building Regional Networks*

Through the late 1990s, in large part because of the world and regional summit movement in children's media, attention to protection of domestic children's programming steadily increased. As a result, the PRIX JEUNESSE expertise in producing workshops on how to make cost-effective, culturally rooted productions is in increasing demand. The 1999 interval year included multiple workshops in Latin America, Africa, and Asia. On each continent, the foundation is helping to develop a professional network of children's media experts through strategies specifically tailored to the region's needs.

In Asia, where few broadcasters have specific children's programming departments, professional training is most essential. Since 1976, PRIX JEUNESSE, the Asia-Pacific Broadcasting Union (ABU), the Asia-Pacific Institute for Broadcasting Development (AIBD), and the Goethe-Institut (German Cultural Institute) have held workshops in Kuala Lumpur. Many of the workshops have concentrated on magazine programs, because they can be produced inexpensively and are easy to adapt and repurpose.

Because short items are a mainstay of magazine programs, an important outgrowth of the workshops has been an "item exchange" among the ABU member broadcasters. Each produces a small number of short pieces and gives the rights to all other members in exchange for rights to their productions. The success of the item exchange has inspired the ABU to devote greater attention to children's programming, with the hope that youth producers will enjoy enhanced stature within their companies.

PRIX JEUNESSE helped introduce a connection between the ABU and the European Broadcasting Union (EBU), which invented the item exchange concept. The two unions are exchanging items on a limited basis, a first step toward establishing a world bank of short films cleared for global broadcast, each steeped in the culture of its originating country. This is an extraordinarily exciting prospect for helping children learn about countries other than their own.

In Latin America, where commercial broadcasters and state-owned channels predominate, it has been difficult to identify dedicated producers of children's programs. PRIX JEUNESSE is helping to kindle a spark that emerged from that region's independent producers. In the summer of 1999, a Latin American meeting on quality television in São Paulo, Brazil, generated the concept of a regional Center for Children and Media that would connect professionals who currently work in isolation from one another and provide a meeting point to plan coproductions or exchanges. The PRIX JEUNESSE Foundation will contribute a library of its winners to the new center, and one possibility under discussion is to launch the center with a Latin American program competition similar to the international festival.

The PRIX JEUNESSE Foundation has also supported the development of a Children's Broadcasting Foundation for Southern Africa, contributing to two initial workshops and arranging funding for a regional coproduction. This is especially auspicious in a region where production facilities and funds are extremely scarce. At the first African workshop, a participant from Ghana noted that she has access to her station's camera (singular) only 1 day a week.

### *The American Center: A PRIX JEUNESSE Offspring*

PRIX JEUNESSE has influenced organizations in other world regions as well. The American Center for Children and Media was founded as the American Children's Television Festival in 1985, a biannual competition modeled after PRIX JEUNESSE. Even as it has grown, the American Center still pays homage to PRIX JEUNESSE. Both are committed to working directly with producers and programmers—the only people who truly can improve the quality of children's media. The center also adopts the PRIX JEUNESSE tradition that participants should be active partners—not a passive audience—in every competition, seminar, or workshop.

Lastly, PRIX JEUNESSE shaped the center's position that there are common elements of excellence that transcend national or regional cultures, different children's cultures, or media environments. As Edward Palmer (1988) wrote of PRIX JEUNESSE in his book *Television and America's Children: A Crisis of Neglect,* "The search to identify underlying and unifying themes is actually facilitated by the great diversity apparent in national expressions, styles and content, and in fact it is through this diversity that they become visible" (p. 80).

## Suitcases and Pan Lids: The PRIX JEUNESSE Road Show

The programs entered in PRIX JEUNESSE represent a biannual snapshot of children's television worldwide—not ratings or sales leaders but the uniquely crafted works that reflect the pride and mind-set of a broadcaster. The foundation maintains a video library, but Ursula von Zallinger was concerned that few researchers or producers could come to Munich to exploit its resources.

The result was the introduction of a world-traveling "suitcase" of outstanding or innovative festival programs that, since 1994, has exposed thousands of people—media professionals, educators, parents, and young people—to works that challenge their assumptions about format, topic, approach, pace, style, and taboos.

The suitcase has been to cities throughout the United States, including New York, Los Angeles, Chicago, San Francisco, and Washington. It has also been to Beijing, Hong Kong, Jerusalem, Kuala Lumpur, La Paz, Manila, Mexico City, Montevideo, Montreal, Nairobi, Santiago, São Paulo, and Seoul, among others.

The suitcase is not shown because the featured programs are better than what is produced or broadcast locally; it is shown because they are different. Not every suitcase program is a winner, and some might not even qualify as excellent. Still, there is much to learn from an innovative or unusual show, even if it is a "noble failure." As has been the theme throughout this chapter, every program bears some mark of its country, culture, or media environment.

### *From Brazil's Slums to the World's Screens*

The suitcase has turned one particular program into a global hit. Wherever it is shown, audiences ask to see it for a second and third time. It is, perhaps, the ultimate example of creativity and empathy for children triumphing over low budget.

*The Boy, the Slum, and the Pan Lids,* from TV Cultura in Brazil, is only 5 minutes long. It has no dialogue or voice-over. It tells a complete story that is understandable to any viewer worldwide and manages in that short time to be exciting, mysterious, funny, and ultimately heartwarming.

Little Zeze sneaks out of his shack in one of Brazil's favelas, or slums, carrying a pan lid. His mother follows close behind, and Zeze begins running. His sister gives chase. Zeze stops at another home to steal a pan lid, sending a pile of pots clattering to the ground. A boy from that house joins the chase. Zeze and a growing group of pursuers run through the favela's narrow alleys; along the way, they knock over laundry lines, narrowly avoid collisions, and disrupt a soccer game. In the background, samba music swells to the rhythm of the chase.

Why has Zeze stolen the pan lids? That's revealed when he arrives at a stage where children are playing junkyard percussion instruments just in time to clap his "cymbals." All is forgiven, especially when Zeze offers to return the pan lids to their owners. The film closes at sunset as Zeze returns home to his mother's embrace.

*The Boy, the Slum, and the Pan Lids* was produced for an international audience as Brazil's entry to the "Open a Door" exchange (every program begins and ends at a door) run by the creators of the *Teletubbies,* England's Ragdoll Productions. It packs a dense cultural immersion into a short story. It reveals that the shacks of a favela (which are visited by few Brazilians, much less foreigners) house people who do universal things—live, love, work, play, and make music—in unique ways.

## Summary

In an era when programs such as the *Teletubbies* or the *Power Rangers* dominate public discussion of children's television globally, PRIX JEUNESSE ensures that the spotlight does not fall only on the highest-rated or most expensive programs but also on those that express television's best potential to captivate, entertain, and enlighten.

For many producers and programming executives, the festival week is an inviolable date on their calendars. It is distinct from the politicking of issue-oriented conferences or the bottom-line dispassion of program markets. PRIX JEUNESSE is a creative retreat for visual professionals, where they revitalize their critical skills, dissecting programs in a challenging environment. Given a precious week to reconnect with old colleagues and meet new ones, the festival spills over from the screening halls and meeting rooms, extending well into the night in informal gatherings.

The new century offers new opportunities for PRIX JEUNESSE. Having devoted 35 years to promoting understanding and collaboration across geographic borders, it now hopes to do the same with technological boundaries. For the 2000 competition, PRIX JEUNESSE will introduced a Web prize, open to sites related to specific children's television programs. The addition is not a hedged bet against the Internet replacing television in children's lives but is intended to encourage a healthy partnership, in which the two media supplement one another, exploiting TV's reach and the computer's active engagement.

Changes in the children's media landscape are as rapid as the clicks of a remote-wielding channel surfer. Yet PRIX JEUNESSE endures, only in part because it, too, adapts with the times. It is that which never changes that sustains the festival and the foundation—the core values of celebrating children and childhood, in all its remarkable diversity, all over the world.

## Notes

1. Information about the foundation and its activities is available at www.prixjeunesse.de.

2. International Advisory Board members include the Asia-Pacific Broadcasting Union, the American Center for Children and Media, Canada's Alliance for Children and Television, the Australian Children's Television Foundation, the Arab States Broadcasting Union, the Bertelsmann Foundation, the Commonwealth Broadcasting Association, the European Broadcasting Union, the Japan Prize, the Philippine Children's Television Foundation, UNESCO, the German UNESCO Commission, UNICEF, the University of Utrecht, and the Union de Radiodiffusion et Télévision Nationales d'Afrique.

3. *Children of Waterland: A Dormouse* won the prize for fiction up to age 7.

4. *Lele, the First Born of the Family* won the Transtel prize for the best program made with limited means.

5. *Babel Tower* won a certificate for best idea in 1992. *Jakub* and *Kitten* were highly rated finalists in 1994 and 1996, respectively. *Tele-Julia* won the PRIX JEUNESSE for fiction ages 7 to 12 in 1998.

6. *French Kiss* won a 1988 prize "without category"; *Frida* was the 1990 drama winner.

## Bibliography

Carlsson, U., & von Feilitzen, C. (1998). *Children and media violence.* Göteborg, Sweden: UNESCO.

PRIX JEUNESSE. (1994). *30 Years of PRIX JEUNESSE.* Munich, Germany: Author.

## References

Palmer, E. L. (1988). *Television and America's children: A crisis of neglect.* New York: Oxford University Press.

PRIX JEUNESSE. (1989). *PRIX JEUNESSE 1964-1989.* Munich, Germany: Author.

Second World Summit on Television for Children. (1998). *Final report.* Hertfordshire, England: Author.

United Nations. (1989). *Convention on the rights of the child* [On-line]. Available: www.unicef.org/crc/

# CHAPTER 28

# Cable Television

## Gateway to Educational Resources for Development at All Ages

PETER J. DIRR

### The Cable Industry's Commitment to Education

The cover of a brochure reads, "Few People Know There Is an American Industry That Has, Over the Past Ten Years, Donated More Than $2 Million a Week to America's Schools." Distributed widely in the Washington, D.C., area and across the United States, the brochure goes on to explain that the cable television industry in the United States is providing a wide range of educational resources and services to elementary and secondary schools, colleges and universities, and learners of all ages (Cable in the Classroom, 1999).

The cable industry's commitment to education was formalized in 1989 with the establishment of Cable in the Classroom, a nonprofit company funded entirely by the cable industry to provide educational resources and services to elementary and secondary schools in the United States. The industry's commitment to education, through Cable in the Classroom, is founded on several philosophical and pedagogical underpinnings, including free access to cable offerings; free use of quality educational programming; the absence of restrictions on how teachers can use the programs (excluding some limits on the length of use as required by copyright clearances); the ability to integrate video, text, and data resources; professional development to help teachers use the resources effectively; and encouraging responsible use of the resources. Through Cable in the Classroom, teachers (and, subsequently, students) have free access to cable television service, free educational television programming, local support from educational staff, free Internet access, unrestricted use of programs, integrated learning resources, professional development opportunities, and other educational services.

#### *Free Access to Cable Services*

Each cable company that is part of Cable in the Classroom (which includes most of the multiple system operators [MSOs], for a total of more than 8,500 local cable systems) has pledged to contact every accredited elementary and secondary school in its coverage area and offer to install and maintain basic cable television service to the school. This ongoing service (not a trial period) has been accepted by 78% of all American schools; at the end of 1999, more than 80,000 schools were receiving free basic cable service, benefiting a potential 43 million kindergarten through twelfth-grade students each year.

### *Free Educational Television Programming*

Each month, some 42 cable programming networks (e.g., CNN, Discovery, and the History Channel) provide more than 525 hours of educational programming for learners of all ages. All the programs are commercial-free. Some are created specifically for classroom use; others are reformatted from documentaries or other programs that appear in the network's regular schedule. The programs are usually broadcast outside of school hours with the intention that a teacher, parent, or school staff person will record the program for later use by a teacher and learners. All programs are copyright-cleared for at least a year, so schools are encouraged to build their own video libraries for use by teachers throughout the year. Over a period of 10 years, the cable industry has provided more than 60,000 hours of educational programming to the schools, not to mention additional programming that has been used by countless adults for their own learning. (More will be said about programming resources in the next section.)

### *Local Educational Support*

Most of the 8,500 local cable systems that are members of Cable in the Classroom have at least one staff person who serves as the education coordinator for the system. That person is in regular contact with schools, alerting teachers to upcoming programming, distributing copies of *Cable in the Classroom Magazine,* often giving workshops for teachers or bringing in others to give workshops, and generally serving as the educational spokesperson and troubleshooter for the system.

### *Free Internet Access*

As the Internet became a popular information resource in the second half of the 1990s, and as cable companies started to consider using their infrastructure to provide Internet access as well as cable television programming, the industry expanded its commitment to education by pledging to give each school passed by the system a free cable modem as the system was upgraded and Internet access was offered to the public. This High-Speed Access Project reached some 4,000 schools by the end of 1999.

### *No Restrictions on Use*

Research showed that teachers would use video resources if they could access them with no strings attached. Unlike television programming offered to the schools from other sources, Cable in the Classroom programs are totally under the teacher's control. Teachers can replay the programs whenever they wish, use them in their entirety or in parts, use them with an entire class or a single student. Typically, teachers use short segments of a program, often pausing the video to ask questions of their students, thus using television in a highly interactive and engaging way.

### *Integrated Learning Resources*

Besides providing educational television programs, the programming networks also provide vast educational resources through the World Wide Web, many of which relate directly to the broadcast programs. The immediacy of the Web allows the program providers to offer teachers and learners lesson plans, up-to-the-minute information, additional resources, and new ways to learn. Many of the resources are correlated to national and/or state academic standards. The monthly *Cable in the Classroom Magazine* (with a circulation of more than 120,000 copies per month) functions as a guide for educational programming. It lists the programs for the month by subject area, offers suggestions for integrating the programs into the curriculum, points to related websites, and allows teachers to share their success stories with one another.

### *Professional Development Opportunities*

Since its inception, Cable in the Classroom has been training teachers on how to integrate educational cable programming into the curriculum. The organization has regularly trained about 7,500 teachers per year in workshops that demonstrate strategies for teaching with technology. Following a Cable in the Classroom study (Dirr, 1997) that examined how elementary and secondary school teachers in the United States were using the World Wide Web in their teaching, Cable in the Classroom formed the Professional Development Institute to help teachers access educational resources available on the Web and integrate those resources into their classes. The training goal was raised from 7,500 teachers per year to 50,000 per year, and a series of hands-on and virtual workshops was developed to demonstrate and encourage effective and efficient uses of the educational resources available from the cable industry. The workshops emphasize the strengths of using a variety of resources to address the multimodal learning styles of today's learners. They also relate the available resources to the new academic standards that are being adopted by schools around the country.

### *Other Educational Services*

Over the years, the cable industry has joined with other educational organizations to provide additional resources to the nation's schools. Since 1994, the industry and the National PTA have developed and offered the Family and Community Critical Viewing Project. Aimed primarily at parents, the project teaches techniques for setting rules for television viewing. Even parents who are unable to attend a workshop can request a free video and workbook, 125,000 of which had been distributed by the end of 1999. The cable industry also joined with TechCorps (a national organization that provides technical assistance to schools) to create a comprehensive, on-line, self-paced Internet training tool called webTeacher that is accessible to teachers anytime, anyplace (*www.webteacher.org*). Using webTeacher, a teacher can become a proficient user of the Internet and World Wide Web for searching, e-mail, web page development, video conferencing, and distance education. In yet other joint projects, Cable in the Classroom teamed up with Home Box Office to create "30 by 30: Kid Flicks," a program to help young people understand, apply, and critically review film production techniques. It also teamed up with Court TV and the National Middle Schools Association to create "Opening the Door to Diversity," a project to help young people tolerate and appreciate diversity in today's society.

The creation of Cable in the Classroom coincided with a growing interest in education circles in the constructivist approach to education. It was a happy coincidence, because, as the constructivists were promoting student-centered, active, project-oriented learning, Cable in the Classroom was offering resources from cable programming networks that would support exactly that form of pedagogy. Teachers were shown how entire programs, or clips from the programs, could be used to support learning by individual students or groups of students. When program networks introduced lesson plans and support materials on their websites in the mid-1990s, teachers learned that they could use the additional resources to tailor their instruction to fit the varied needs and learning styles of the students in their classes.

## Educational Resources for All Ages

Through the cable industry, learners of all ages have ready access to a rich variety of educational video, text, and data resources. These resources, which support the multimodal learning styles of today's learners, can contribute to social, intellectual, and emotional development at all ages. They can be accessed on cable channels that are carried in the basic tier of programming by most cable companies and through the Internet "gateway" of the Cable in the Classroom home page (*www.ciconline.org).* What follows is only a small sampling of the available resources for learners of all ages at the close of 1999.

### *Resources for Early Childhood and Primary Grades*

*Fox Family Channel. The All New Captain Kangaroo* features readings from popular children's books, animal segments, and other activities for fun and learning. The Fox Family Channel website (*www.foxfamilychannel.com*) has parenting tips as well as suggestions for ways to use TV and the Web to talk to children about issues of interest to them.

*Noggin.* A new cable channel that combines a variety of programming from Nickelodeon and the Children's Television Workshop (CTW), Noggin aids the development of preschool children with programming such as *Allegra's Window* (problem-solving and listening skills), *Blue's Clues* (thinking, reasoning, and social skills), *Eureeka's Castle* (competition, sharing, and problem solving), *Gullah Gullah Island* (cultures and community), and *Sesame Street.* Noggin has other series for the primary school grades such as *Square One TV* (math concepts and problem solving), *3-2-1 Contact* (science and technology), *Wild Side* (animal life), *Ghostwriter* (reasoning and writing), and *The Electric Company* (reading). The Noggin website (*www.noggin.com*) provides parents with some postviewing activities and links to the CTW and Nickelodeon home pages for more materials.

*Cartoon Network.* Coproduced with the Children's Television Workshop, the Cartoon Network's *Big Bag* uses Muppet characters to encourage preschoolers to solve problems creatively while learning to cooperate.

*Nickelodeon.* Nickelodeon broadcasts a wide variety of educational programming for preschool and primary grades. *Blue's Clues* (thinking, reasoning, and social skills) and *Gullah Gullah Island* (culture and community) are appropriate for preschool and primary grade children. The Nickelodeon educational website (*www.teachers.nick.com*) provides extensive descriptions of learning activities that can be used in conjunction with the viewing of the programs.

### *Resources for Middle Grades and Junior High School*

*Nickelodeon.* Series such as *Launch Box* (the history and science of space exploration), *Mr. Wizard's World* (scientific principles and experiments), and *Charlie Brown Specials* (key moments in history) are accompanied by extensive lesson plans on the Nickelodeon website.

*Disney Channel. Amazing Animals* combines live action and animation to show characteristics of various animals. *Going Wild With Jeff Corwin* is a nature series showing animals in their native habitats. In the education section of the Disney website (*www.disneychannel.com*), teachers and parents can find activities to accompany the TV programs, as well as chat rooms and other child-rearing aids.

*Court TV.* With the National Middle School Association, Court TV has developed

*Choices and Consequences,* a video series and support materials (*www.courttv.com/choices*) to help young adolescents understand the consequences of some of the decisions they make by the actions they take.

### Resources for Adolescents, High School Students, and Adults

*CNN.* The Cable News Network's daily half-hour *Newsroom* program summarizes the top news stories. Through a daily posting on the Web (*learning.turner.com/newsroom/index.html*), learners of all ages can find additional information on each story as well as links to other sites for primary-information sources on the topics. CNN also airs weekly news summaries, *Science & Technology Week, CNN World Report,* and *Moneyweek,* as well as special programs such as the 10-part series *Millennium: A Thousand Years of History.* These are appropriate for advanced middle grade students, high school students, and interested adults.

*Ovation.* This relatively young cable channel provides visual and performing arts and humanities programming for the junior and senior high school levels. Series and programs such as *Access All Areas* (examining the making of music), *Rings of Passion: Five Emotions in the World of Art, Top Score* (behind the scenes of an opera production), and *The Immortal Emperor* are accompanied by teacher guide materials and class handouts at the Ovation website (*www.ovationtv.com*). Many of the programs are equally appropriate for middle school students, high school students, and the informal adult learner.

*C-SPAN.* For 20 years, C-SPAN has been giving the American public gavel-to-gavel coverage of the proceedings of Congress. Series specially designed for classroom use include *Washington Journal* (issues and events of Capitol Hill), *American Perspectives* (cultural and historical events), *International Programs* (views of foreign governments through coverage of their legislatures, conferences, etc.), and *Prime Time Public Affairs* (public policy programming). In recent years, the network has produced carefully designed series (e.g., *American Presidents* and *Road to the White House*) and has begun to air a wide variety of literature programming (*Book TV* airs all weekend on C-SPAN2). The C-SPAN Classroom provides support materials for motivated learners (*www.c-span.org*). This programming has great appeal to adults interested in politics, government, and literature.

*ESPN.* ESPN has seized the opportunity to use young people's interest in sports to teach the principles of math and science that are so important in some sports. *Sports Figures* uses well-known athletes to explain the math and science principles that are understandable and appealing to today's youth (*www.sportsfigures.com*) and to many adults who have long forgotten how the math and science principles underlie their favorite sports.

*A&E.* With its sister channel, the History Channel, Arts & Entertainment provides a wide variety of arts programming, which is supplemented with learning support materials at the Arts & Entertainment Classroom site (*www.aande.com*). Special programs on topics such as the *Star-Spangled Banner* and the *Underground Railroad* are accompanied by in-depth study guide material. These are also attractive resources for informal adult learners.

### Resources for Learners of All Ages

*The Weather Channel.* The Weather Channel helps students explore weather phenomena. *Look Up* (grades K-4) encourages students to observe the sky. *The Weather Classroom* (grades 4-10), with more than 200 electronic pages of experiments and instructional materials (*www.weather.com/education*), teaches the hows and whys of weather. *On the Safe Side* (grades 5-12) provides teachers with resources for teaching weather preparedness. These resources are also an excellent resource for any adult wishing to learn more about how weather works and what the current predictions are for any location in the world.

*Discovery and the Learning Channel.* Discovery's sister station, the Learning Channel, airs a weekly series, *TLC Elementary School,* designed for children in kindergarten through sixth grade. Specially edited from original Discovery documentaries, the programs provide young learners with insight to a wide variety of interesting science topics such as ants, the solar system, and the human body. Discovery organizes its daily hour-long program *Assignment Discovery* around "theme" weeks each semester (e.g., ancient Egypt, amazing planet). Discovery's comprehensive lesson plan materials, available on the Web for each program in each theme week, contain objectives correlated to the appropriate national academic standards, vocabulary words that might be new to the learner (dictionary definition, use in a sentence, spoken), links to other appropriate websites, questions to use as advanced organizers and follow-up, and classroom activities (*www.discoveryschool.com*). The Learning Channel also airs series such as *Great Books* and *Nature's Rage.* Many of these programs are appropriate for middle grades, high school, and lifelong learners.

## Research on Educational Uses of Cable and Internet Resources

Educational use of cable programming and related Internet resources presumes access to the needed technologies and motivation and preparation to use those resources. Various studies in recent years have examined those issues. It is not the intention here to provide a comprehensive review of that literature but, rather, to highlight a few of the pertinent findings.

### *Access to the Technologies*

By the mid-1990s, about three fourths of all public school buildings in the United States had cable television hook-ups (Blohm, 1997; Quality Education Data, 1996; U.S. Department of Education, 1995). At that same time, virtually all schools in the country were reporting that they had television sets and videocassette recorders (Corporation for Public Broadcasting, 1997).

By the mid-1990s, just over half of all schools had Internet access, although its speed was usually limited and it did not reach into every classroom. Internet access and connection speeds grew substantially in a short period. In 1994, 35% of all public schools and 3% of their instructional rooms (i.e., classrooms, computer labs, libraries/media rooms) had access to the Internet. By 1998, those numbers had risen to 89% of all public schools and 51% of their instructional rooms. Although there were some disparities by region of the country and poverty level of the schools, all schools experienced substantial improvement in that 4-year period (Rowand, 1999).

An even more dramatic change took place in the *type* of Internet connections. In 1994, 74% of the connected schools used dial-up connections, and only 39% had higher-speed connections using dedicated lines. By 1998, 65% of the schools were using dedicated lines, and only 22% were relying on dial-up connections (Rowand, 1999). At the same time, the number of computers in the schools had increased to the point where there were 6 students per computer and 12 students per computer with Internet access (Henry, 1998; Rowand, 1999).

In 1996, the cable industry, as part of the National Cable Television Association's High Speed Education Connection initiative, committed to provide high-speed Internet connections to all schools passed by upgraded cable systems. The impact of this initiative was just beginning to be felt in the schools at the close of the twentieth century; approximately 4,000 schools have high-speed Internet connections through their local cable companies.

### *Preparation to Use the Resources*

Technology-related staff development is neglected by most school districts. Many studies in recent years have concluded that more attention and funding should be focused on helping staff make more effective use of instructional technologies.

Early in 1999, the *Detroit News* reported on a U.S. Department of Education study that found that only one in five classroom teachers feels well prepared to integrate educational technology in the grade or subject they teach (Whitmire, 1999). The reason for this seems quite clear from other studies: No one is teaching the teachers how to use the technologies. A study conducted by the American Association of Colleges for Teacher Education, funded by the Milken Exchange on Education, found that

> most teacher-training programs fail to show their students how to incorporate technology into their classroom instruction. . . . Access to technology had increased faster than technology had been incorporated into teaching and learning. . . . Most of the institutions in the survey reported that they lacked both a plan to teach their students about technology and a way to pay for such instruction. (Basinger, 1999, p. A24)

It should be no surprise, then, that a report from the CEO Forum on Education and Technology (executives from several large computer companies and the nation's largest teachers' union) found that at least one third of all schools in the United States still lack the facilities to train future teachers to use technology effectively in the classroom (Matthews, 1999). It also should not be a surprise that most teachers have not linked the use of instructional technologies to the education reform efforts that are sweeping the nation. Although 56% of all teachers report that they have used instructional strategies aligned with new academic standards in an effort to improve the quality of instruction, only 7% report using innovative technologies specifically to support those efforts (Alexander, Heaviside, & Farris, 1998).

In the *Leader's Guide to Education Technology,* Rockman et al. (1998) note an *Education Week* study that found that 4 out of 10 teachers have had no formal training in how to use the Internet for instruction, and an additional 18% have had no more than 7 hours of training. Yet data from the U.S. Department of Education clearly show that the amount of training is directly related to how well prepared teachers feel to integrate educational technology into their lessons. Only 11% of those who have had no formal training feel well prepared, compared with 17% of those who have had 1 to 8 hours of training, and 33% of those who have had more than 8 hours of training (U.S. Department of Education, 1999).

From these and other studies, a picture emerges that many school districts are investing heavily in equipment and software but are failing to make equal investments in training their teachers to use that equipment and software. Two recent newspaper articles describe the relationship between equipment installation and teacher training in similar terms. A headline in the *Washington Post* describing advances in educational technology in Maryland read, "Study Finds More School Computers"; the subhead was "Teachers' Training Lags" (Argetsinger, 1998). Halfway across the country and a year later, the Minneapolis *Star Tribune* headline read, "Schools Wired, but Training Falls Short." The subhead went on to explain, "Report says Minnesota remains at the forefront in Internet access, but its teachers lag behind in technology instruction" (Draper, 1999).

Many teachers would welcome additional opportunities for training in effective uses of video and Internet technologies. Cable in the Classroom studies have found that two out of three teachers would welcome more opportunities for in-service workshops on technology (either hands-on or on-line; Crane, 1998; Research Communications, 1996).

### *Teacher Use of Information Technologies*

Despite the fact that relatively few teachers have been trained to use educational technologies in the classroom, many seem to intuitively understand that these technologies can be a boon to learning for some students. A 1997 study by the Corporation for Public Broadcasting found that 92% of all teachers who used television in their elementary and secondary classes felt that it helped them teach more effectively; 88% thought it enabled them to be more creative; 75% attributed increased comprehension and ability to discuss ideas to their use of television; 63% reported that it increased motivation and enthusiasm for learning; 42% felt it improved student vocabulary; and 40% noted that students prefer television over other media.

By the second half of the 1990s, 84% of all teachers used video and/or television programs in their classrooms, and, in schools with cable, three fourths of all teachers used one or more Cable in the Classroom programs (Crane, 1998; Research Communications, 1996). In the case of cable television programs (and Internet resources alike), teachers prefer to use resources that have been designed specifically for curriculum applications. They appreciate the thinking that others have done in creating user manuals and study notes. They are less comfortable with tracking down primary-source materials for which they have to do all the curriculum integration themselves.

The Cable in the Classroom studies found that the most used educational television resources were from the Public Broadcasting Service, Discovery, CNN, A&E, C-SPAN, the Learning Channel, and the Weather Channel. About half of all teachers who used video in their classrooms used three or more cable programming services.

Teachers are not just using television as a baby-sitter, as some have feared; 85% related the television programs to other assignments all or most of the time. Furthermore, teachers have specific objectives in mind when they use television: 94% use it to reinforce and expand on content that is being taught; 83% use it to respond to a variety of learning styles; 74% use it to increase student motivation to learn; and 69% use it to stimulate other learning activities (Corporation for Public Broadcasting, 1997).

A 1997 Cable in the Classroom study of how teachers use the Internet and World Wide Web (I/WWW) found that almost half of all teachers (47.8%) make some use of the I/WWW in their teaching. One quarter (23.6%) used it daily, and another 43.5% used it at least once a week. Most use was modest, amounting to less than 60 minutes per week (44.5%) to 2 hours per week (another 22.5%). About half of all Internet users (53.9%) integrated I/WWW content with other learning resources such as television programs. The most common uses are researching topics they are teaching (30.3%), accessing curriculum materials (23.0%), lesson planning (17.0%), direct instruction in the classroom (13.4%), and professional development (11.2%) (Dirr, 1997).

A 1998 study by Quality Education Data (QED) found that almost one out of three teachers (29.2%) use the Internet *daily* as a teaching aid; another 28.7% use it 2 to 4 days a week; and another 23% use it once a week. Contrary to what some might believe, the use of computer technologies and the Internet in the classroom does not diminish the use of television and video: 68% of teachers report that the introduction of computer technologies had no effect on the amount of television and video they used; 24% reported that it increased the use of TV and video; and only 8% said it decreased the use of TV and video (Corporation for Public Broadcasting, 1997).

### *Barriers to Greater Use*

Time constraints are a major barrier to teachers' use of both cable programming and the Internet/World Wide Web. Almost two out of three (65%) teachers cite the lack of time as the major barrier to their use of cable programming. Lack of adequate information in advance is second (46%). Content that does not match curriculum needs is third on the list, and inconvenient program lengths is fourth (31%) (Dirr, 1997; Faiola & Dirr, 1997).

On the Internet/World Wide Web side, budget constraints are cited as the greatest barrier, followed by lack of time to train, lack of access to phone lines, lack of equipment, lack of opportunity for training, and lack of control over materials accessed. Some of these barriers will decrease over time, especially if the Universal Service Fund (a tax initiative through which the federal government will help schools obtain Internet service) results in an improved infrastructure as it is designed to do. However, nothing on the horizon promises to improve the training available to teachers, and no one has yet tackled the problem of time constraints.

From the literature, one is left with the impression that schools are increasingly gaining access to communications and information technologies and that some teachers are attempting to integrate those technologies and the resources they can deliver into the classes they teach. However, most of the teachers are "self-taught" in these applications, and most feel conflicted by the amount of time needed to master and use the technologies. Nevertheless, they continue to apply the technologies because they sense that they are necessary modes of learning for at least some of today's students.

## How the Cable Industry Got to This Point

What we know as cable television today is a far cry from its early roots as community antenna television (CATV). In order to sell television sets in the valley community of Mahanoy City, Pennsylvania, where the signals from Philadelphia's three broadcast stations 90 miles away provided poor reception, appliance store owner John Walson put a television antenna on a large utility pole on the top of a nearby mountain and ran antenna wire down to his store. Once people saw the programming in the store, television set sales soared. With that, Walson had to provide his customers with television signals in their homes. He devised signal boosters, rented pole space from Pennsylvania Power and Light (for $1.50 per pole per year), and ran sheathed cables into the homes, giving birth to the cable television industry in June 1948. Walson eventually served 85,000 customers on his cable system, charging them $100 for installation and $2 per month for maintenance. He called his system Service Electric Company (Chiddix, 1991; Pennsylvania Cable and Telecommunications Association, n.d.; Rothman, 1996).

About the same time, on the other side of the United States in Astoria, Oregon, Ed Parsons had promised his wife that he would give her a television set as soon as TV signals became available. When KRSC-TV began broadcasting 150 air miles away in Seattle, Parsons put an antenna on top of the nearby John Jacob Astor Hotel and connected it to his home using cable wiring. When Parsons's residence became a popular site for local residents to view TV, he decided to go into business running cable to homes in town. He was soon installing 20 sites per month for $100 each (Jones & Luskin, 1996). Other cable pioneers faced with similar reception problems began to build local community antenna television systems in other parts of the country.

The first community antenna television systems served mainly rural and mountainous communities, providing one to three channels of television reception. Systems soon began to crop up in many small towns. By the late 1960s and early 1970s, technology advances, such as transistorized amplifiers, sheathed coaxial cable, and microwave ties, allowed the CATV systems to deliver 12 or more channels.

The early CATV pioneers experienced rapid success because they were providing people with a service they could not otherwise get—clear television reception in remote or mountainous areas. When companies began to try to move into more urban areas, they were met with resistance from a population that could not understand why they should pay for cable service when "television is free." That changed in the early 1970s with the start-up of new programming services. In 1972, Charles Dolan and Gerald Levin, then of Sterling Manhattan Cable, launched the nation's first pay television network, Home Box Office (HBO), to provide sporting events and uninterrupted movies to the growing television public (National Cable Television Association, 1998). In 1975, HBO became the first programming service to use a satellite to distribute programming, making its signal available to cable operators throughout the United States and greatly expanding its potential customer base. Its popularity skyrocketed. HBO saw its subscribers grow to 2 million just 3 years after the shift to satellite distribution.

Other unique programming services were soon introduced. Ted Turner launched his superstation, WTCG (later renamed WTBS) in Atlanta, in 1976. CNN, Showtime, and ESPN followed shortly. In 1979, the cable industry funded the start-up of the Cable Satellite Public Affairs Network (C-SPAN) to provide gavel-to-gavel coverage of the House of Representatives. C-SPAN, which now covers the Senate, hearings, and committee meetings as well as the House proceedings, is still fully funded by the cable industry as its gift to the American people.

Independent community antenna television systems were evolving into a new industry, the cable industry. As its infrastructure developed and expanded, the cable industry began to stimulate the imaginations of some people who saw it as a force that could change society. One such person was freelance journalist Ralph Lee Smith. He is reputed to have been the first person to use the term *information highway,* in a story written for the *Nation* in 1970. Two years later, in his 1972 book, *The Wired Nation: Cable TV, The Electronic Communications Highway,* Smith envisioned an electronic highway system that would rival the interstate highway system the United States had begun to develop under President Eisenhower. *The Wired Nation* would facilitate the exchange of ideas and information in ways not previously possible. That could transform the nation. Smith was about two decades premature in his estimates of when the nation would be wired, but many of his expectations and aspirations are now becoming a reality.

In its early years, the cable television industry was heavily regulated under the Federal Communications Act of 1934. In 1984, however, the Cable Communications Policy Act largely deregulated the industry, allowing cable companies to determine programming and set rates for cable services. That unleashed an unprecedented period of growth for the industry.

The multisystem operators (MSOs, cable companies that owned cable systems in many places) engaged in fierce competition to wire large cities with the greatest potential for subscribers. Between 1984 and 1989, it is estimated that the cable industry spent $15 billion to build new systems. The result was that, by the late 1980s, most large U.S. cities were wired for cable (Jones & Luskin, 1996).

In competing for a franchise to wire a city or town, cable companies had to negotiate with local and county governments. These negotiations often resulted in the successful cable company agreeing to provide free channels for public, educational, and government television programming (PEG channels), as well as subsidies for government, education, and community groups to support their television production efforts. That helped to spawn a loose alliance of persons who produce PEG programming, the Alliance for Community Media, which now represents almost 2,000 community media centers that operate more than 5,000 cable television channels throughout the United States (Riedel, 1999).

At the same time that the cable companies were expanding the infrastructure nationwide, program services were also expanding, resulting in what to some was a bewildering expansion of potential programming channels, a supply that often outstripped the capacity of the systems that were being built. Many of the new channels catered to very specific markets, interests, and needs, pioneering a new approach to television programming, "niche" programs.

The expansion also provided the cable operators and the programming networks an opportunity to contribute back to the communities from which they were deriving their revenues and to help future generations of American adults. The growth was seen by the cable industry and educators alike as providing opportunities to form new relationships and alliances. In 1989, several events took place that brought cable operators and cable program providers together to make sure that the educational potential of the cable technologies was, in fact, made available to educators throughout the United States.

In January 1989, entrepreneur Chris Whittle (not associated with the cable industry) announced his intention of providing a new satellite-delivered program service to schools, along with the equipment needed to receive the program and use it in classes. The program would consist of a 12-minute daily news show supported by 2 minutes of commercials, and schools were required to have their students view the program each day. The idea was criticized strongly by education groups because it introduced commercials directly into the classroom. The service was eventually banned from schools in New York and California but was adopted by some 8,000 schools elsewhere (Kamil, 1994).

Around that same time, in April 1989, CNN's Ted Turner, bolstered by the results of a pilot program he had conducted 2 years earlier with the National School Boards Association (NSBA), decided to develop a news show for high school students. Turner enlisted support from executives of three leading MSOs—Continental Cablevision, Telecommunications, Inc. (TCI), and Jones Intercable. Originally intending to incorporate "infomercials" into the news show but cognizant of the reactions educators were having to the Whittle offer, Turner changed his mind just before the press conference and announced that the program would be provided completely commercial-free.

At the press conference, the executives from Continental Cablevision, TCI, and Jones Intercable pledged to provide a free cable connection to all public secondary schools (later expanded to include all public and private elementary, middle, and high schools) passed by their cables and to provide free cable service to those schools. They also announced their intention to form Cable in the Classroom, a new nonprofit company to coordinate the industry's educational services for schools. Before long, other MSOs made similar commitments, and additional program networks were identifying programming that they could offer commercial-free, with extended copyright clearances for use by schools.

While these positive developments were taking place, the regulatory pendulum in Washington began to swing back. There was increasing pressure to re-regulate this growing industry. In 1992, the federal government responded with the Cable Television Consumer Protection and Competition Act (also known as the Cable Act of 1992). Among other things, the act codified the need for PEG channels; required cable companies to carry the signal of all the local broadcast stations in the area of the cable system; allowed broadcasters to charge cable companies for carrying their signals; allowed the FCC to regulate cable television rates; established minimum standards for customer service; prohibited local broadcasters from owning cable television systems in their broadcast areas; and prohibited exclusive franchises.

One result of renewed regulation was that it prompted some cable operators to look outside the United States for new business opportunities. Some looked to Europe, others to Latin America.

Another result of the dampened atmosphere caused by re-regulation was that it caused cable operators to form alliances with telephone companies to conduct joint research on how they might get more mileage from the existing infrastructure by blending twisted-pair telephone wires, coaxial cable, and fiber optic cables to bring richer resources into homes and businesses using the existing infrastructure as much as possible. A vision began to emerge that echoed Ralph Lee Smith's vision from two decades earlier—an information- and entertainment-rich environment served by an information superhighway. In the envisioned environment, differences between cable television, computers, and telephone would gradually disappear and be replaced by groups of information utilities that used a common standard. The convergence of the technologies began to emerge.

The regulatory environment changed again in 1996 when Congress passed the 1996 Telecommunications Act, which deregulated almost all aspects of cable television. This took place at the same time that the cable industry was beginning to feel outside competitive forces from telephone companies, satellite program distributors, and the wireless distribution industry. Companies began to realize quickly that, to be competitive, they would need more resources than most of them could muster individually. Furthermore, their services would be stronger if they were "clustered" in service areas rather than scattered in many parts of the country. That unleashed another spree of industry consolidation, with large and medium MSOs buying out smaller companies, a trend that continues today. Federal deregulation of the cable industry also unleashed an unprecedented spending spree, with all the major MSOs spending billions of dollars to upgrade their system infrastructure to accommodate the increased flow of information that was quickly evolving. Coincident with the growth of the Internet, the upgraded systems allowed cable operators to introduce Internet services as one of their products.

## Conclusion

Today, the cable industry in the United States is a robust business. The physical infrastructure of the cable companies has positioned them to be major providers of broadband services (i.e., the capacity needed to deliver the high volume of information needed for video, audio, and text resources). Most MSOs now offer 60 to 200 channels of service. The program networks (more than 175 of them at last count) are spending billions of dollars each year to create new products for the general public as well as the niche markets they serve, including education. Never before have so many homes been connected to cable (approximately 71 million) (Nielsen Media Research, 1999).

Where the consolidation of companies and convergence of technologies will lead is a topic of great debate as we begin the third millennium. Whatever the specific outcomes of the debate, it is likely that the future will see an environment more like than unlike Ralph Lee Smith's vision—one in which all persons will have easy access to vast information resources. In that environment, teachers and learners of all ages will have access to new learning resources that present and manage information in new ways.

One characteristic that sets the cable industry apart from other communication providers in the United States is that it continues to allocate a significant amount each year to provide teachers and learners with educational resources and helps them to use those resources effectively. As the brochure cited at the beginning of this chapter notes, today's cable operators and program networks provide more than $2 million per week (more than $100 million per year) in support of education. There is nothing on the horizon to suggest that this commitment will do anything but grow in the foreseeable future. Through Cable in the Classroom, teachers and learners of all ages will continue to have access to educational programming and rich ancillary materials that support a lifetime of learning.

## References

Alexander, D., Heaviside, S., & Farris, E. (1998). *Status of education reform in public elementary and sec-*

*ondary schools: Teachers' perspectives* (NCES No. 98-025). Washington, DC: National Center for Education Statistics.

Argetsinger, A. (1998, September 24). Study finds more school computers. *Washington Post,* p. M01.

Basinger, J. (1999, March 12). Colleges fail to show teachers how to use technology, report says. *Chronicle of Higher Education,* p. A24.

Blohm, C. (1997). *1997 SPA education market report.* Washington, DC: Software Publishers Association.

Cable in the Classroom. (1999). *Few people know there is an American industry that has, over the past ten years, donated more than $2 million a week to America's schools* [Brochure]. Alexandria, VA: Author.

Chiddix, J. (1991, October 29). *The evolution of cable TV: A personal perspective.* Donald W. Levenson lecture given at Pennsylvania State University, State College, PA.

Corporation for Public Broadcasting. (1997). *Summary report: Study of school uses of television and video, 1996-1997 school year.* Washington, DC: Author.

Crane, V. (1998). *Awareness and use of Cable in the Classroom programs, 1998.* Alexandria, VA: Cable in the Classroom.

Dirr, P. (1997). *The use of cable and the Internet/World Wide Web in elementary and secondary classrooms: A field study.* Alexandria, VA: Cable in the Classroom.

Draper, N. (1999, September 24). Schools wired, but training falls short. *(Minneapolis) Star Tribune.* Available: http://newslibrary.krmediastream.com/cgi-bin/search/mn

Faiola, A., & Dirr, P. (1997, July). *The use of cable and the Internet/World Wide Web in elementary and secondary classrooms: Review of literature.* Alexandria, VA: Cable in the Classroom.

Henry, T. (1998, October 22). Computers on rise in classrooms. *USA Today,* p. 10D.

Jones, G., & Luskin, B. (Eds.). (1996). *Telecommunications and multimedia encyclopedia* [CD-ROM]. Denver, CO: Jones Digital Century.

Kamil, B. (1994). *Delivering the future: Cable and education partnerships for the information age.* Alexandria, VA: Cable in the Classroom.

Matthews, J. (1999, February 22). Report: Teachers lack computer, Net training. *Washington (Post) Business,* p. F20.

National Cable Television Association. (1998). *1998 cable television year-end review.* Washington, DC: Author.

Nielsen Media Research. (1999, October). Nielsen people meter installed sample [Subscription data service]. New York: Author.

Pennsylvania Cable and Telecommunications Association. (n.d.). *The history of cable television.* Harrisburg, PA: Author.

Quality Education Data. (1996). *Technology in public schools.* Denver, CO: Author.

Quality Education Data. (1998). *Internet usage in public schools, 1998.* Denver, CO: Author.

Research Communications. (1996, September). *An assessment of the awareness and use of Cable in the Classroom services.* Dedham, MA: Author.

Riedel, B. (1999, August 2). PEG channels give public a voice. *Multichannel News.* Available: www.multichannel.com/weekly/1999/32/forum32.htm

Rockman, S., et al. (1998). *Leader's guide to education technology.* Alexandria, VA: EDvancement/National School Boards Association.

Rothman, R. (1996). Cable telecommunications: History and development. In G. Jones & B. Luskin (Eds.), *Telecommunications and multimedia encyclopedia* [CD-ROM]. Denver, CO: Jones Digital Century.

Rowand, C. (1999). *Internet access in public schools and classrooms: 1994-98* (NCES No. 1999-017). Washington, DC: National Center for Education Statistics.

Smith, R. (1972). *The wired nation: Cable TV, the electronic communications highway.* New York: Harper & Row.

U.S. Department of Education. (1995). *1995 digest of education statistics.* Washington, DC: Author.

U.S. Department of Education. (1999). *Condition of education: 1999.* Washington, DC: Author.

Whitmire, R. (1999, January 29). Teachers feel ill-prepared. *Detroit News.* Available: http:// detnews.com/ 1999/classrooms/9901/ 29/01290189.htm

CHAPTER **29**

# Children, the Internet, and Other New Technologies

TODD TARPLEY
A&E Television Networks

## An Explosion of New Technologies

***3:45 P.M.*** Johnnie arrives home from grade school. With a touch of a button, he is on-line. His computer, outfitted with a high-speed cable modem, offers instant access to the Internet.

Johnnie's own voice informs him that he has e-mail. (Last week, he chose the voice of his favorite pro wrestler, "Violent Vinnie," and the week before that the female star of the top-rated TV show *Nude Beach.*) Fifteen new e-mail messages today: nine invitations to visit porn websites, five low-interest credit card offers, and—at last!—a personal reply from the convicted serial killer Johnnie met last month in an on-line chat room.

A picture-in-picture function appears in the corner of the screen. While Johnnie was at school, his computer automatically recorded three TV shows it thinks Johnnie might like based on his past preferences: *Co-Ed Ultimate Fighting* from the Pro Wrestling Channel, an R-rated movie (*Fraternity Bloodbath*) from HBO 12, and the latest episode of *Nude Beach* in high-definition format (HDTV). After previewing each, Johnnie opts to watch them all; he'll play along with the interactive versions on-line.

Before he can settle in for another long evening of interactive entertainment, he receives an audio instant message from his friend: "Don't worry about tomorrow's homework assignment—I downloaded book reports from TermPapers.com."

Mass media have changed tremendously in the past two decades. A huge onrush of new technologies is occurring, allowing for hundreds of television channels with vastly improved picture quality; personal video recorders (PVRs) that can automatically find and record television programs based on the viewer's stated preferences or past behavior; new digital video and audio formats that improve quality and/or portability; and, most important, the Internet, with its 24-hour-a-day access to global information.

## What New Technologies Mean for Children

Will our children's futures be made better or worse by this onrush of new technology? Technological advancements almost always have both positive and negative repercussions. Although the above scenario paints a pessimistic view of new technology, the positive implications are equally powerful. Instantaneous access to an explosion of entertainment and information offers cause for optimism as well. Greater accessibility to information means that our current generation of children has the world at its fingertips. Text and documents from distant libraries are available instantaneously. Audio recordings of great speeches can instill passion in ways that textbooks may not. Classrooms in different states—or countries—can communicate instantly. Educators can share knowledge with peers via live teleconferences. Teachers can participate in live teleconferences with parents or other teachers. Materials for home-schooling parents are now easily accessible and often free. And websites created specifically for educators and special-interest groups facilitate the transfer of this information in ways that have never before been possible.

Although the effects of television and other established media on the cognitive and social development of children have been well documented, relatively little research has been conducted on the impact of new technologies. This chapter offers a brief overview of various new media technologies and discusses the available evidence or needed research addressing the role of new media in influencing the cognitive, social, behavioral, emotional, and physical development of the growing child.

## Digital Television and High-Definition Television

Standard broadcast television is transmitted "over the air" via a spectrum of radio frequencies. Digital television (DTV) is a new transmission standard that uses the existing broadcast spectrum more efficiently. This means that better image and sound quality, more channels, and additional text data (e.g., closed captioning information) can be provided in the same amount of spectrum currently used by a single channel. The Federal Communications Commission (FCC) has mandated DTV availability by all commercial broadcast TV stations by 2002 and by all noncommercial stations by 2003.

There is debate over how stations should best use the new channel space allowed by DTV. One option is to use the additional space to offer improved picture and sound quality. Others argue that the public—and station owners—is better served by offering more channels of "standard" quality television programming.

High-definition television (HDTV) is a form of DTV that offers improved picture and sound quality. It uses a wide-screen format, requires a special television set, and is of greatest interest to viewers of sports and movies. It is available now, but HDTV sets are still very expensive and there is relatively little HDTV programming currently being broadcast.

Conversely, standard definition television (SDTV) allows a single TV station to transmit several "standard-quality" programs simultaneously. Currently, television stations broadcast one program at a time. With SDTV, a station could broadcast multiple programs at once. A viewer with a digital television or converter box could then choose which of the programs to watch at any given time. In short, viewers would have more channels to choose from. This makes it possible to have children's programming, college telecourses, instructional television for classroom use, and timely local programming all at the same time. Most of these new viewing options will likely not be new original programming but existing programming being offered at multiple times. For example, a station might devote one new channel to continual airings of its local newscast and another to continual airings of its public affairs programming.

Digital technology will also affect cable and satellite television in much the same way as broadcast television. By digitally compressing the video signal, even more channels can be made available to subscribers.

Little research has been conducted on the impact of DTV on children (or adults). Potential effects are numerous. More programming options and/or better technical quality may lead to increased viewing time. Lower-income households that cannot afford cable or satellite service will have access to more viewing options. Finally, the enhanced interactivity offered by DTV may lead to an increased emphasis on "instant commerce," in which viewers are encouraged to buy products and services simply by clicking a button on their remote control, rather than having to travel to a store or mall or even pick up the telephone. Greater intrusion of commerce into television content may prove to be tempting or misleading to children.

## Personal Video Recorders

Traditional VCRs may soon be eclipsed by digital versions that operate continuously in real time. Viewers can pause and rewind any program they are watching, allowing them to create their own instant replays, take breaks whenever they choose without missing the action, and fast-forward past televised commercial breaks.

In addition, personal video recorders (PVRs) are capable of "learning" their owner's viewing preferences, then automatically recording any programs corresponding to those preferences. For example, a Tom Cruise fan's PVR will automatically record all movies featuring Tom Cruise. A Civil War buff's PVR will automatically record all programs about the Civil War.

Although PVRs are available now, little, if any, research has been conducted on their impact on children. The primary effects of the PVR will likely be more viewer control of the television schedule, less reliance on network scheduling, potentially more television viewing, and potentially less viewing of television commercials. What does this mean for children? One potential effect of less reliance on network scheduling is that parents can schedule children's viewing around particular programs rather than particular times. This could raise the quality of TV time while avoiding conflicts with family activities. The ability to bypass commercials offers greater control to parents and potentially reduces overall viewing time. Conversely, access to more programming choices could potentially lead to even more television viewing.

## Interactive Television

Interactive television has been around in one form or another since the 1970s, when an experimental system called Qube was launched in Columbus, Ohio (Davis, 1998; Krantz, 1997). One of its innovative features was the ability of viewers to influence a football game by voting on which play to relay to the quarterback (Wangberg, 1999). Interactive television gained notoriety in the early 1990s, when several cable operators launched ambitious interactive trials such as Time-Warner's much-hyped "Full Service Network" (FSN). All of these initiatives, although valuable learning experiences, ultimately failed to transform the media landscape to the extent that their supporters envisioned, primarily because they were not economically viable. Time-Warner spent more than $100 million to operate FSN during its 2-year trial but failed to generate significant revenue (Krantz, 1997). Unfortunately, consumers showed relatively little interest in paying for interactive television. The interactive trials simply cost far more to operate than they could realistically generate in revenues (Davis, 1998; Krantz, 1997).

Led primarily by the emergence of the Internet in the mid-1990s, "interactive TV" continues to percolate. About a third of broadcast and cable television networks now support interactive television in one form or another (Forrester Research, 1999). However, the most common forms are not Hollywood-esque functions like choosing the outcome of a movie but simpler, more utilitarian applications like finding out what TV program is coming up next.

The most common application will likely be interactive, on-screen program guides known as electronic program guides (EPGs; Forrester Research, 1999). EPGs are intended to replace printed TV listings or television channels that continuously scroll through the cable system's entire channel lineup. Instead of waiting several minutes to find out what is coming up on a particular channel, viewers can immediately access information about only the networks or programs they want to see. Then, by clicking on the title of the program, viewers can access even more detailed information. Electronic program guides are predicted to reach 55 million households by 2004 (Forrester Research, 1999).

Some networks and advertisers will also create interactive enhancements to their television content such as the ability to play along with a game show, access biographical information about a performer, or purchase a related product. Some of this interactive content will reside on the Internet, with viewers moving seamlessly between the two media. Microsoft's WebTV, for example, offers a picture-in-picture technology that allows television viewers to watch TV in one portion of the screen while viewing the Internet in another portion. Television programs that are "WebTV enhanced" offer on-line content that is related to the TV program, such as a quiz. Viewers who have purchased WebTV are alerted that they can click a button to view the additional content while continuing to watch the television program. By 2004, such "enhanced broadcasting" will be visible to 24 million households (Forrester Research, 1999). Simple Web browsing on TV screens will reach 13 million households.

The likely result of interactive television will be the further commercialization of television. Unlike earlier interactive trials, which were experimental and exploratory in nature, the current incarnation of interactive television is driven by economics. Since the primary goal of commercial television networks is to generate audiences to watch advertisers' messages, it is not in their economic interest to divert viewers' attention to interactive activities unless more revenue can be derived from those activities. Thus, in addition to interactive TV listings (which theoretically generate more TV viewing and hence more ad revenues), the goal of interactive enhancements will largely be to facilitate impulse purchases by television viewers, much like home-shopping channels. For example, viewers may be offered opportunities to purchase merchandise featured in or related to the program with the click of a button. This economic reality, unfortunately, means that the educational enhancements promised by early interactive experiments may not materialize to the extent envisioned. Interactive television will likely serve mainly to commercialize television to an even greater degree.

## Other Electronic Devices and New Technologies

Many other new electronic devices and technologies are entering the market with increasing speed and frequency. These include digital versatile disks (DVDs), which offer improved quality and portability over traditional videocassettes and compact discs, and new digital formats that allow users to download music and entire books from the Internet onto personal, portable devices.

The common denominator of these new technologies is greater portability, which may inevitably lead to the greater intrusion of media into daily lives. Just as the advent of the transistor led to the greater intrusion of radio into daily lives (followed in subsequent decades by portable TVs, cell phones, and gaming devices), newly emerging electronic devices and technology such as DVDs may lead to further intrusion of media.

## The Internet

In just a few short years, the Internet has redefined the media habits of children. By 2002, 21 million U.S. children ages 2 through 12 will be Internet users—about half the total U.S. population of children (Jupiter Communications, 1998). A recent survey of parents on America Online (AOL) found that children are now more likely to fight over the computer than the telephone. Nearly one third of the children reported they watch less television because of the Internet. The Kids Channel is the fourth most trafficked channel on AOL, behind only news, sports, and personal finance. Clearly, the Internet has the potential to profoundly influence children and young people.

### *Similarities to and Differences From Other Media*

The Internet combines the text-based elements of print media, the two-way communications abilities of telephones, and, often, the audiovisual aspects of television. It is thus the most "multimedia" of all media, utilizing sight, sound, and touch (i.e., via the keyboard). The Internet is less narrative than television in the sense that it is used primarily for communication, information gathering, and games rather than for passively experiencing narrative stories (Jupiter Communications, 1998). It is more interactive than most other forms of media, potentially requiring more cognitive activity. It tends to be more text-based than television or radio, requiring—perhaps even enhancing—basic literacy. It is potentially a more solitary activity than watching television: Whereas groups of people can watch television together, it is more difficult for groups to sit at a single computer terminal. Like television, it is a physically passive activity.

### *Current Research on Effects on Cognitive Development*

The Internet is perceived by many as an important educational tool for children. More than two thirds of on-line consumers feel that "it is important for children today to know how to go online and use the Internet" (America Online/Roper Starch, 1999, p. 45). Three quarters of on-line consumers believe the greatest impact of being on-line will be on education.

Many educators share this view. According to the U.S. Department of Education, more than half of all kindergarten through twelfth-grade classrooms already have Internet access (as cited in "My How We've Grown," 1999). The population of kids accessing the Internet from school will continue to grow considerably over the next few years, due in part to the integration of the Internet into the curriculum. Proposed FCC subsidies will help mitigate the financial and technological hurdles that schools face gaining on-line access; private industry is expected to donate considerable hardware, software, and bandwidth to schools (Jupiter Communications, 1998).

The Internet may, in fact, make the learning process itself more fun by providing children with the thrill of information seeking and retrieval (Tobiason, 1997). Advertising agency Saatchi and Saatchi recently published a study suggesting that the Internet can make learning exciting for young people ages 6 to 20 by providing access to "fun and forbidden" information (as cited in Kuchinskas, 1999).

On-line information retrieval often begins at "portals" or "search engine" sites such as Yahoo. These sites typically employ navigational and directory techniques based on traditional library browsing systems. Although there is no current research on the effects of search sites' structure or usage on children's cognitive development, ancillary research suggests that computer-based library browsing systems can help children overcome problems with typing, spelling, vocabulary, and Boolean logic (Borgman, Hirsh, Walter, & Gallagher, 1995).

Though the positive influence of computers on children's cognitive and social development is well documented (Clements, 1994), the appropriate amount of time spent on the computer, especially for young children, is currently debated. The American Academy of Pediatrics (AAP) now recommends that children's "screen time" (defined as time watching TV and videotapes, playing video and computer games, and surfing the Internet) be limited to no more than 1 to 2 hours a day for older children. Children under the age of 2 should have no screen time (American Academy of Pediatrics, 1999).

Despite the AAP's recommendations, Internet sites aimed at preschool-age children proliferate. The most popular include Disney.com; NickJr.com, from cable television network Nickelodeon; CTW.org, from Children's Television Workshop, the producers of *Sesame Street;* and PBS.org (with on-line areas for *Teletubbies, Barney, Mister Rogers,* and other public television programs). FoxKids.com, the website of the Fox Kids cable channel, features an icon-based language designed specifically to attract children who don't yet read ("Bits," 1999). Unlike public television, all of the above websites, including CTW.org and PBS.org, are supported by advertising; all except PBS also incorporate on-line shopping into their children's areas (PBS has an on-line store, but it is not promoted in the children's area). Many additional websites are targeted toward slightly older children; most are advertising and e-commerce supported as well.

Children's computer use is increasing. According to the Annenberg Public Policy Center, 7 of every 10 families with children now have personal computers in their homes (Annenberg Public Policy Center, 1999). Furthermore, the more electronic media children have at home, the more time they spend with them: 3.7 hours a day for children with only TVs and VCRs versus 4.8 hours a day for children with TVs, VCRs, computers, and video games. Children's free time—the hours left after eating, personal care, sleeping, or attending school—has shrunk to 25% of their daytime in 1997 from 40% in 1981 (Hofferth, 1998). This combination of increased media usage and decreased leisure time indicates that other activities—social or physical or both—are likely being eliminated.

### *Current Research on Effects on Social, Behavioral, and Emotional Development*

Computer use is not always a solitary activity and, in fact, is very much a social activity among children and teens. Eight out of 10 on-line parents with children under the age of 18 say that they sometimes go on-line while sitting with their child (America Online/Roper Starch, 1999). Younger children also prefer working with one or two partners on a computer than working alone (Rhee & Bhavnagri, 1991). The most popular on-line activity for children is e-mail, a form of social communication (America Online/Roper Starch, 1999).

Greater use of the Internet, however, has been associated with declines in communication with family members, declines in the size of a person's social circle, and increases in depression and loneliness (Kraut et al., 1998). Heavy Internet users can also exhibit symptoms of addiction similar to those of gambling or alcoholism, with similar consequences in their ability to damage personal relationships (Young, 1998). An ABCNews.com on-line survey reported that 5.7% of respondents exhibited symptoms of "Internet addiction" (Greenfield, 1999). Questions were based on a typical list used to diagnose gambling addiction and focused on whether respondents used the computer to escape their problems and felt anxiety when they could not go on-line. An additional 10% of respondents met the definition of abusers. They reported that their online time altered their moods, created negative changes in their lives, and made them neglect family obligations. Participants in the study also described feeling out of control, seduced by the hypnotic screen, and increasingly cut off from their families. A 1997 study at the University of Cincinnati found that excessive Internet users suffer from significant social stresses such as family strife or divorce (as cited in "Internet Addiction," 1999).

All of the above research was conducted among adults, and research is not unanimous on the topic of the social effects of heavy computer use. Findings of a research project on early adolescent social networks and computer use challenged the notion that adolescents who are heavy computer users experience social isolation (Orleans & Laney, 1998). Interpersonal lives and the computer activities of early adolescents reflexively amplified each other. Computer gaming was found to promote social interaction under certain conditions. E-mail communication led to interpersonal communication in the presence of preexisting peer relations.

Neither the American Psychological Association nor the American Psychiatric Association currently recognizes Internet or computer addiction as a diagnosable disorder.

The unauthoritative nature of the information available on the Internet is a concern of educators ("Will There Be," 1994). Although television programming may not always be balanced or authoritative, its level of appropriateness for children far surpasses the Internet's plethora of unfiltered content, much of it intended for adults but readily accessible to children.

A cursory analysis of the list of the 1,000 most visited websites indicates that at least 10% are adult sex sites (Media Metrix, 1999). In addition to adult content, the Web features more than 1,400 racist, anti-Semitic, and other hate sites—not to mention websites specializing in police photos and morgue shots (Taylor, 1999). A Time/CNN poll found that 44% of American teenagers have seen websites that are X-rated or have sexual content, and 25% have seen sites with information about hate groups (as cited in Okrent, 1999).

Commercial software that blocks out unwanted or adult content is available, but no blocking system is foolproof (Bjerga, 1999). Many programs, for example, automatically block access to any site in which words from a preselected list appear. But they tend to be less effective in chat rooms, in which users type in words in real time, thus outmaneuvering the software. In addition, computer-literate children can often find codes to break through filters.

Teens may be better able than younger children to distinguish authoritative from nonauthoritative content. While 83% of teens put a great deal of trust in information they receive from their parents, only 13% put a great deal of trust in information they receive from the Internet (as cited in Okrent, 1999). Although this is arguably good news, it does not speak to the possible effects of inappropriate content on younger children; it also raises disturbing questions about the 13% of teens who place a great deal of trust in information on the Internet.

Interestingly, only 17% of parents with children under age 13 express concern about on-line advertising messages aimed at their kids (Jupiter Communications, 1998). Although the FCC regulates television advertising, the Internet is not subject to such restrictions. As such, it arguably provides a new way for advertisers and broadcasters to circumvent FCC regulations. According to the Center for Media Education, some children's TV programs invite viewers to their website, where commercials and mail orders are not restricted by the FCC ("Special Report: Kids," 1999). As previously noted, websites for PBS children's programming and CTW.org are both advertiser supported.

Children may be more susceptible than adults to on-line advertising. According to online kids' site MaMaMedia, click-through rates (the ratio of visitors who click on Internet ads) are higher for kids than adults

("Special Report: Kids," 1999). A number of companies are rushing to introduce websites designed to encourage children to buy from on-line retailers of clothing, toys, and books. Several on-line shopping sites now offer credit accounts to children that are tied to a parent's credit card (Slatalla, 1999). It is estimated that children ages 5 to 18 will spend $1.3 billion on-line by 2002 (Jupiter Communications, 1998).

Regardless of the effects of the Internet, they will not likely affect all strata of society equally. Nonwhites maintain their minority status on the Internet: In 1998, only 20% of nonwhites were actively on-line, compared with 30% of whites (Cakim, 1999). Nonwhite users also have a significantly higher likelihood of accessing the Internet from academic locations or of sharing on-line access. Economic classifications also have an impact. Although half of U.S. homes now have personal computers (PCs), most are in homes with a household income of $50,000 or more (as cited in "Half of U.S.," 1999). This reinforces a decade of research on the educational use of computers in schools, indicating that computers maintain and exaggerate gender, racial, and social class inequalities (Sutton, 1991). In this sense, the Internet may play a role in widening rather than narrowing the social distance between traditional "haves" and "have-nots."

### *Current Research on Effects on Physical Health and Safety*

Parents implicitly fear the Internet because they do not want their children to reveal information to marketers, but they also fear it as a predatory environment (Jupiter Communications, 1998). Nearly 70% of parents are concerned about unsafe chat environments and unsolicited e-mail from strangers. Seventy-one percent of parents stated that they restrict their children from revealing personal information on-line. The Children's Online Privacy Act (COPPA) requires that websites obtain verifiable parental consent before collecting, using, or disclosing any personal information from children under 13. However, chat rooms on children's sites are generally accessible to anyone; the anonymity of the Internet means anyone can claim to be any age or sex. The problem is severe enough that the FBI has resorted to going undercover in chat rooms as adolescents in order to nab pedophiles. One suspect arrested in connection with soliciting sex with a minor over the Internet was a high-ranking executive of a Disney-affiliated website ("Online Executive Accused," 1999).

In addition to sexual predators, the Internet is host to sites advocating violence against others. The Time/CNN teen poll mentioned above also found that 14% of American teenagers ages 13 to 17 have seen websites that teach how to build bombs, and 12% have seen websites that show where or how to buy a gun (as cited in Okrent, 1999). Websites such as the *Terrorist's Handbook* and *Anarchist's Cookbook* have posted bomb-making information (Taylor, 1999). Congress recently passed a bill to encourage Internet service providers (ISPs) to offer filtering and to prohibit posting bomb-making instructions ("Congress Eyes Media's Part," 1999).

A militia website called the *Citizen Soldier* contains a section of links to websites of weapons suppliers, as well as military manuals that cover topics such as combat training (Berkowitz, 1999). A Ku Klux Klan chapter in Florida credits its website as the key factor in signing up new members. Many extremist sites target the young. Hate groups such as the World Church of the Creator have websites filled with simple propaganda devoted specifically to children.

Children's safety is not only affected by proviolence websites and sexual predators in chat rooms. In 1997, for example, a mother lost custody of her two young children because of her excessive Internet use ("Internet 'Addiction,'" 1997). In a similar case, police took three young children from a 24-year-old mother who they said allowed her children to wallow in filth while she surfed the Internet.

The Internet can also play a positive role in fostering children's health and safety. For example, the Internet is changing the way pediatricians and families find medical information and provide care (Izenberg & Lieberman, 1998). Pediatricians can now tap into a "virtual library" of resources, including the latest medical information. In addition to information aimed at doctors, consumers benefit directly from health-related websites such as DrKoop.com, DiscoveryHealth.com, and WebMD.com. Health and medical information sites are visited by millions of people each month (Media Metrix, 1999). Parents also increasingly use the Internet to watch their children on Web-enabled surveillance cameras at day care centers (Franklin, 1999). Cameras provide constantly updated images of day care centers to parents via the Internet, thereby placing caregivers in constant view of parents. In addition to theoretically lowering the risk of child abuse, the cameras serve as a psychological benefit for parents who are separated from their children.

## Conclusions and Directions for Future Research

New technologies, like old ones, are simply tools. The extent to which they improve or hinder the cognitive, behavioral, social, and physical aspects of children's lives is ultimately a factor of the way in which they are used.

Almost half of all parents who are on-line believe that being on-line has a more positive influence on their children than watching television does (America Online/Roper Starch, 1999). While this sentiment is encouraging, one hopes that it is reinforced by oversight and active participation in the role new technologies play in their children's lives. As with any new technology, teachers and parents must demonstrate their own capacity for learning to effectively help their children and students reap the benefits.

Research on the effects of the Internet and other new technologies is limited by the relative infancy of the technologies themselves. The Internet is still in such a formative and rapidly evolving stage of development that its very nature is still difficult to define with clarity. Long-term tracking studies have not yet been possible, and the most relevant questions for study are likely just now being formulated.

The speed at which new media technologies have developed is both encouraging and alarming, and it underscores the need for educators, parents, and researchers to stay abreast of their rapid changes. Although new technologies raise concerns about the cognitive, emotional, social, and physical welfare of children, they also open up the world to positive new ideas and possibilities. They can provide access to information and ideas from around the world, including instant communication with peers and experts. Unlocking this vast potential is ultimately the responsibility of educators, parents, and researchers alike.

## References

American Academy of Pediatrics. (1999). *Understanding the impact of media on children and teens* [Brochure]. Elk Grove Village, IL: Author.

America Online/Roper Starch. (1999). *America Online/Roper Starch cyberstudy 1998.* Vienna, VA: America Online.

Annenberg Public Policy Center. (1999). *Media in the home 1999: The fourth annual survey of parents and children.* Philadelphia: University of Pennsylvania, Annenberg Public Policy Center.

Berkowitz, H. (1999, September 14). Prepared statement of Howard Berkowitz, national chair of the Anti-Defamation League, before the Senate Committee on the Judiciary. Federal News Service.

Bits. (1999, September 27). *Media Week,* p. 78.

Bjerga, A. (1999, September 6). Kidproof, other Internet blockers for children not foolproof. Gannett News Service.

Borgman, C. L., Hirsh, S. G., Walter, V. A., & Gallagher, A. L. (1995). Children's searching behavior on browsing and keyword online catalogs: The Science Library Catalog Project. *Journal of the American Society for Information Science, 46*(9), 663-684.

Cakim, I. (1999, April 12). Analyst insight: Old racial issues in a new medium. *Industry Standard,* p. 46.

Clements, D. H. (1994). The uniqueness of the computer as a learning tool: Insights from research and practice. In J. L. Wright & D. D. Shade (Eds.), *Young children: Active learners in a technological age* (pp. 31-50). Washington, DC: NAEYC.

Congress eyes media's part in youth violence. (1999, May 17). *Cable World,* p. 8.

Davis, L. (1998). *The billionaire shell game.* New York: Doubleday.

Forrester Research. (1999). *Interactive TV cash flows* [Analyst report]. Boston: Author.

Franklin, M. (1999, August 17). Peeking in at day care via the Internet. *Dayton Daily News,* p. E4.

Greenfield, D. (1999). *Virtual addiction.* Oakland, CA: New Harbinger.

Half of U.S. homes now have PCs. (1999, June 14). *Industry Standard,* p. 102.

Hofferth, S. (1998). *Children's time.* Ann Arbor, MI: Institute for Social Research.

Internet "addiction" costs mom her kids. (1997, October 22). United Press International, Domestic News.

Internet addiction is not a way-out malady: Experts say overuse of computers can be as damaging as other obsessions. (1999, July 4). *Plain Dealer,* p. 1A.

Izenberg, N., & Lieberman, D. A. (1998). The Web, communication, trends, and children's health, part 2: The Web and the practice of pediatrics. *Clinical Pediatrics, 37*(4), 215-221.

Jupiter Communications. (1998). *Kids: Evolving revenue models for the 2-12 market* [Analyst report]. New York: Jupiter Strategic Planning Services.

Krantz, M. (1997, November). Marriage of convenience: Interactive television. *Time Digital,* features section, p. 60.

Kraut, R., Patterson, M., Lundmark, V., Kiesler, S., Mukopadhyay, T., & Scherlis, W. (1998). Internet paradox: A social technology that reduces social involvement and psychological well-being? *American Psychology, 53*(9), 1017-1031.

Kuchinskas, S. (1999, March 15). Knowledge is kool. *Media Week,* IQ section, p. 4.

Media Metrix. (1999, August). *The Web report* [On-line subscription service]. New York: Author.

My how we've grown: The net-net of an Internet year. (1999, May 3). *Industry Standard,* p. 84.

Okrent, D. (1999, May 10). Raising kids online: What can parents do? *Time,* p. 42.

Online executive accused of using Internet to solicit teen sex. (1999, September 20). Associated Press, Business News.

Orleans, M., & Laney, M. C. (1998). Early adolescent social networks and computer use. *Proceedings of the Families, Technology, & Education Conference* [October 30-November 1, 1997, Chicago].

Rhee, M. C., & Bhavnagri, N. (1991). 4 year old children's peer interactions when playing with a computer [Abstract]. ERIC No. ED342466.

Slatalla, M. (1999, August 17). Young shoppers with online accounts learn about choices and budgeting. New York Times News Service.

Special report: Kids. (1999, February 1). *Media Week,* p. 32.

Sutton, R. E. (1991). Equity and computers in the schools: A decade of research. *Review of Educational Research, 61*(4), 475-503.

Taylor, C. (1999, May 10). Cyberguide: A primer for parents on what's out there in the digital world. *Time,* p. 44.

Tobiason, K. (1997). Taking by giving: KidsConnect and your media center. *Technology Connection, 4*(6), 10-11.

Wangberg, L. (1999, June 22). Stay tuned to TV. *USA Today,* bonus section, p. 6E.

Will there be a Children's Book Week in the year 2000? (1994). *School Library Media Activities Monthly, 11*(3), 4.

Young, K. (1998). *Caught in the Net.* New York: John Wiley.

CHAPTER **30**

# Hazards and Possibilities of Commercial TV in the Schools

ELLEN WARTELLA
NANCY JENNINGS
The University of Texas at Austin

Marketing to children is a year-round activity reaching children of all ages in multiple venues: television, magazines, in-store displays, direct mail, product placements in movies and video games, and in the school. James McNeal, a leading scholar in children's consumer behavior, estimates that children between the ages of 4 and 12 spent almost $25 billion of their own money and had a direct influence on $188 billion of their parents' spending in 1998 ("Childhood's End?" 1999). According to Teenage Research Unlimited, teens spent $94 billion of their own money in 1998, an increase of $10 billion over the previous year (Goff, 1999).

This huge consumer market is important to advertisers and marketers. According to McNeal (1987), over the past several decades, marketers have realized that children spend money, influence their family's purchases, and, through their own consumer experiences as children, can become brand loyal into adulthood. It is no surprise then that the size and importance of the youth market has enticed new kinds of marketers to attend to children and youth. Now, not only are child-oriented products such as cereals, snack food, and toys marketed to youth, but so are adult-oriented products such as family travel destinations (e.g., Disney World), personal care products (children's toothpaste, makeup, etc.), designer clothes and furnishings, and consumer electronics.

The size of the youth market, the wide range of products marketed to youth, and the growth in youth marketing venues are all characteristics of today's commercialization of youth. This trend has received varying public attention over the past few decades, including attempts by the Federal Trade Commission in the 1970s to regulate television advertising to children. But perhaps the most controversial youth marketing strategy of the past decade is the growing use of public schools as advertising and marketing venues.

American business has shown an interest in reaching the captive audience of students through a variety of advertising and marketing strategies. But corporate involvement in American public schools is more than direct advertising and the development of curricular materials. This current round of business involvement in public education includes nonmarketing relationships with American public schools, including the development of public-private partnerships, outright philanthropy, and variations in corporate support for and influence on schools. For instance, corporations have realized the public relations gains from corporate philanthropy. Education-related corporate philanthropy in 1996 totaled $1.3 billion, or 20% of the $6.5 billion corporations donated to charity overall, according to Craig Smith, director of Corporate Citizen, a research group based in Seattle. A decade ago, only 5% of corporate giving went to education-related organizations (Stead, 1997, p. 41).

This entire context of corporate involvement and marketing to youth in U.S. schools will be examined in this chapter. We will look first at the history of advertising and marketing practices in schools; then we will examine various current marketing practices; and, finally, we will discuss the effects of such in-school marketing practices.

## The History of Marketing to Youth in Public Schools

It is clear that public schools provide a captive audience for marketers' messages, particularly marketers reaching a high concentration of children already age-divided. For many years before the 1990s, corporations have been interested in reaching children with product messages to sell products to children such as candy or sodas or snacks. Second, marketers have been interested in developing a consumer base for future purchases (this is the strategy behind computer companies' subsidies of in-school computers). Third, corporate involvement in schools can be used to develop a better image of the company (Molnar, 1996).

We can go back to the 1920s to find precursors of today's in-school marketing. It was in that decade that Ivory Soap sponsored school soap-carving competitions, an innovation of Edward L. Bernays, one of the country's first public relations men (Stead, 1997, p. 31). In 1929, the National Education Association published *The Report of the Committee on Propaganda in the Schools,* authored by E. C. Broome. He argued that corporate-sponsored materials should be used in the classroom only if they were deemed indispensable to the education of the students (Molnar, 1996, p. 39).

During the 1930s and the depression, American bankers tried to establish links to schools to enhance the image of banking after the depression. For instance, in 1937, the National Association of Manufacturers distributed a weekly gazette called the *Young America Magazine* to 70,000 schools. Articles included "Your Neighborhood Bank," "Building Better Americans," and "The Business of America's People in Selling." Similar messages were placed in filmstrips and audiocassettes. The purpose of the magazines was to offer "tonic that would lure children away from the troubling political tendencies of the time in which they were growing" (Ewen, 1996, p. 315). Moreover, free equipment was offered to schools by corporations (Stead, 1997). Indeed, in 1934, the Educators Progress Service of Randolph, Wisconsin, published an *Educators Guide to Free Materials* intended to aid teachers with the high turnover of information and current affairs and to offer industry a chance to participate in the exchange (Harty, 1979).

By the late 1940s and 1950s, an entire American industry sponsored a new program in the schools: Junior Achievement. The function of Junior Achievement was "to get kids interested in entrepreneurialism" (Stead, 1997, p. 31). And, according to Molnar (1996), by 1957, 9 out of 10 students saw a commercial advertisement in school each day.

Since 1979, we have seen the development of "public-private partnerships" (Molnar, 1996). An example of this is Joint Venture—a collaborative partnership of technology businesses such as Hewlett Packard and Cisco Systems; local, state, and federal governments; and schools in Silicon Valley—which is intended to increase the computer literacy of schoolchildren and to prepare them to enter the increasingly technology-oriented workforce of the region (Richards, Wartella, Morton, & Thompson, 1998). According to the National Association of Partners in Education, increases in the number of school-business partnerships have been considerable: In 1984, 17% of the nation's schools participated in such partnerships; by 1990, that number had jumped to 51% of public schools, involving 2.6 million volunteers and 29.7 million students (Molnar, 1996, p. 2). Such school partnerships can include corporations giving employees time off to serve as mentors in schools or as lecturers on special science and technology topics or donating equipment and services to the same schools (Richards et al., 1998).

By the 1980s, Whittle Communications was placing wallboards in schools. Each wallboard contained an educational message from a celebrity and product advertising (Consumers Union, 1995). In 1989, the International Organization of Consumers Unions (IOCU) issued its Code of Good Practice and Guidelines for Controlling Business-Sponsored Educational Materials used in schools (Molnar, 1996, p. 40).

## Five Basic Marketing Practices Used in Schools

The first and most obvious marketing practice is direct advertising of products to students in school buildings and school settings such as sports fields or buses. Dr Pepper is paying $3.45 million over 10 years to a school district near Dallas-Fort Worth International Airport for advertising space in gyms, stadiums, and atop two schools' roofs ("This School," 1998). School buses in Colorado Springs are emblazoned with advertising for Burger King and 7-Up (Wells, 1996). Sycamore High School in Cincinnati has a $200,000 high-tech scoreboard in its gymnasium with space for 17 advertisements on turning panels (Wolff, 1996). School newspapers and yearbooks contain advertisements for a variety of businesses (Consumers Union, 1995), and some schools are now selling advertising space on their athletes' warm-up suits (Winters, 1995).

Second, there is a long history of providing free products to children in schools, as the Ivory Soap example noted above. Today, product samples, coupons to be redeemed at local restaurants and stores, and in-school giveaways are a part of American school life. Each year, Nike provides new athletic shoes to sports teams in more than a hundred schools (Glamser, 1997). Pizza Hut provides coupons redeemable for a free personal pan pizza to students who reach their teacher's reading goals (Dodge, 1998). Each semester, Cover Concepts distributes free book covers that contain company logos among public service messages from celebrities such as Michael Jordan or Spike Lee to 31,000 schools and almost 25 million students across the country (Stead, 1997).

Third, with the privatization of school lunchrooms, there has been a growing use of fast food vendors and soft drink retailers selling food products directly in the public schools. Taco Bell sells in or delivers to 3,000 schools nationwide. Pizza Hut's products are sold in more than 4,500 schools (Jacobson, 1995). A school district in Colorado Springs signed a 10-year, $8 million contract with Coca-Cola in August 1997, with an additional $3 million guaranteed if the district sells 70,000 cases of Coke products during one of the first 3 years (White, Ruskin, Mokhiber, & Weissman, 1999). The contract calls for a yearly consumption of 1.68 million bottles of Coke products (Labi, 1999). A year into the contract, the district had consumed only 21,000 cases (White et al., 1999). To meet the consumption demands of the contract, a district administrator wrote a memo to area principals advising them to allow Coke products in the classroom and to place vending machines in easily accessible areas (Labi, 1999). Other suggestions by the district administrator included circumventing school rules that prohibit carbonated vending machines to be on during lunchtime by moving such machines "outside the meal service area" (White et al., 1999). The range of products and contracts can be expected to grow.

A fourth marketing practice, a variation on direct product sales, is the growth of school fund-raising activities by which children serve as a salesforce to generate revenue for school bands, sports groups, and technology. Students sell candy, frozen pizzas, magazine subscriptions, and gift wrap to help raise funds for school activities (Bower, 1996). Class time was interrupted in one Missouri elementary school so that the children could receive lessons on how to sell frozen pizzas as a fund-raising activity (Bower, 1996). Fund-raising has gone high-tech with Internet-based purchasing schemes where schools get a portion of on-line purchases made by family and friends. After logging on at Schoolpop.com, schools can earn money with every parent's purchase from some of the Internet's most frequented stores, including Amazon.com and eToys.com. At Electronic scrip (*escripinc. com*), parents and other Web users make donations to schools by registering their credit card numbers with the company; every time a purchase is made with the registered card, a percentage of the purchase price goes to the designated school (Wykes, 1999).

But each of these four practices is a rather overt mechanism of selling or promoting specific brands and products through the schools. More subtle forms of commercialization involve a variety of corporate involvement in schools via corporate relationships and curricular involvement. For instance, the event that seemed to epitomize the commercialization of public schools was the 1990 launch by Whittle of Channel One, a daily in-school news program that contains targeted advertisements for school-age children. Advertising was now entrenched in schools, and, in exchange, Whittle offered schools satellite dishes and television sets in order to have them provide child viewers to advertisers.

Whittle's Channel One was only a part of the growing business involvement in public schools, which took a new direction when, in 1991, at the urging of President Bush, the New American Schools Development Corporation formed to "channel business money to educational projects that corporate America considered worthy" (Molnar, 1996, p. 3). Furthermore, in 1992, Education Alternatives, Inc. (EAI) offered to contract with school districts to better manage their schools, using the same amount of money the district spent per pupil while still returning a profit to investors based on efficiency of management operations (Molnar, 1996). And that same year, Whittle Communication announced the establishment of the Edison Project, to be headed up by a former president of Yale University (Molnar, 1996). When the first Edison Project school opened in 1995, the privatization of American schools and schoolchildren was well under way.

First with Channel One and then the Edison Project, Whittle Communications serves as a model of a new sort of corporate involvement and marketing to children in America's public schools. Through the promotion of technology (coupled with advertising messages), Whittle has invaded American schools, promising media, computers, curricula, and programs that schools pressed financially cannot otherwise afford. In return, Whittle has a ready-made and captive audience of youth available for corporate relationships. Whittle is an interesting case study of contemporary youth marketing practices.

## Corporate Involvement in the Schools: The Case of Whittle Communications

The onset of Whittle Communications' Channel One at the beginning of the 1990s marked a public watershed regarding awareness of commercialization in schools. In March 1990, Whittle Communications began broadcasting its 10-minute news show to school districts across the nation and providing those districts with hardware—a satellite dish, VCRs, and television monitors to show the program to all students in a school—and all wiring and maintenance facilities. Its original goal was to reach 8,000 school districts, and, by 1992, it was accepted in 10,000. But access was not always easy. There were four major subscribing states—Michigan, Ohio, Pennsylvania, and Texas (Greenberg & Brand, 1993)—but other states, including California and New York, banned it. By 1999, Channel One was being sent to 12,000 middle and high schools, reaching a potential audience of 8 million students (Smolkin, 1999). Moreover, according to Channel One, 99% of schools that carry Channel One choose to renew at the end of their 3-year contract (Channel One, 1999).

Channel One was marketed to schools as an attempt to combat the deficiencies of American middle and high school students' cultural literacy—their knowledge of current events, political issues, geography, and so forth—with a daily student-oriented news program of 10 minutes with 2 minutes of advertising. The news itself is presented with attractive young anchors with a perspective aimed at making the news relevant to teen audiences. Although there has been some criticism of the news content by Fairness and Accuracy in Reporting (FAIR) for not focusing on breaking news, for simplifying the political reporting, and for focusing more on consumption than other economic issues, Channel One has won more than 100 educational and programming awards, including a Peabody Award for Television Journalism (Jayson, 1997, p. B9). The most obvious competitor of television news programming in the schools is CNN's *Newsroom,* which debuted in August 1989 with a 15-minute-a-day current affairs program that today is a 30-minute block of commercial-free news and features. Developed by Turner Learning, *CNN Newsroom* airs in 36,000 schools but provides no technology to the school system (Smolkin, 1999).

The original controversy surrounding the Channel One program concerned the fact that inserted into the newscast is 2 minutes of advertising for things such as jeans, running shoes, and soft drinks targeted at the captive audience of teens. By 1996, the National Education Association (NEA) created and distributed the "Preserve Classroom Integrity Pledge" (Molnar, 1996). This was only one response to the obvious commercialization of schools that became a public controversy thanks to Channel One.

Over time, concern about Channel One shifted from commercialization criticism to other criticisms, notably whether Channel One was engaging in the practice of red-lining and targeting certain economic levels and school districts. According to Morgan's 1993 study (as cited in Walsh, 1993) in which he sampled 17,000 school districts, Channel One at that time was more likely to reach urban, rather than rural, schools and had a higher representation in schools with a high proportion of African American and Latino students, compared with Anglos and Asian American students. In addition, Channel One was more likely to be shown in poorer schools with low per-student expenditures (6 of 10 schools that spend $2,600 or less per student use Channel One compared with 1 in 10 schools that spend $6,000 or more per student; Walsh, 1993).

Seemingly, Channel One's promise of technology to schools having difficulty making such purchases is a major selling point. Bill Martin, a spokesman for the National Education Association, remarked that Whittle's activities are "a contradiction of the democratic character of public schooling" (Mathews, 1994, p. B1). However, Bachen's (1998) review of research on Channel One notes that there is "only modest use of the technology for the broadcast of other educational programming and scattered efforts to use the network for the broadcast of in-school programs and announcements" (p. 137). This would suggest that the technology acquired with these contracts is not being utilized fully by the schools with Channel One.

As an extension of Channel One, Whittle Communications entered the business of school administration with the establishment of for-profit schools. With the promise of improving the country's educational system while cutting costs, Chris Whittle developed and implemented a plan to run schools like a business. Whittle initially intended to spend more than $60 million over 3 years on a new division of Whittle Communications for research and to develop a strategy for a "new American school." Following this research, Whittle would seek $2.5 to $3 billion from banks and investors, including companies with an interest in selling products to the schools. These investors would fund 200 private for-profit schools in major urban areas across the country by the fall of 1996. By the year 2010, Whittle planned to have a 1,000-school campus serving as many as 2 million students. Chris Whittle named the project after Thomas Edison as "an allusion to the revolutionary shift from candlepower to the light bulb" (as cited in Walsh, 1991).

Whittle's research team developed a strategy for the Edison Project that had an emphasis on professionalism and technology. First, Whittle planned on increasing the quality and quantity of teaching time by lengthening the school day by 60 to 90 minutes, extending the school year by an extra 6 weeks, and creating smaller classes for more one-on-one instruction. Second, Edison Project schools would have a rigorous liberal arts curriculum emphasizing reading, writing, music, art, and physical education, and the curriculum would include a character and values component. Finally, technology would become a prominent part of the educational process, with promises of a computer in every child's home and laptop computers for every teacher (Horsley, 1998).

Whittle fulfilled many of his promises regarding school structure, but on a much smaller scale than initially proposed. In 1995, Whittle opened only four schools serving 3,000 students, a far cry from the proposed initial 200 schools. By 1998, Whittle had 51 schools open, serving 24,000 students, quite a distance from the goal of 1,000 schools by the year 2010. Moreover, most of these schools were public schools that Edison runs by contract with the school district rather than start-up schools as initially intended (Lewin, 1999).

The proposed structure of the schools, however, remained intact, with mixed results. With an investment of more than $100 million, the Edison Project has been able to reduce class size, has extended the school day and the school year, and has put a computer in every student's home. Some schools report increases in parent-teacher communication through electronic mail with the addition of computers in the household, and others discovered a raised level of parental involvement in school activities. For example, parents at a school in Wichita, Kansas, gave their Edison school a fresh coat of paint before school started and have volunteered hundreds of hours tutoring students in the school (Steinberg, 1997). Moreover, Whittle reported that students in Edison schools show measurable improvements in reading and math when compared with their scores on earlier tests and with the scores of students with similar backgrounds within the same school districts (Steinberg, 1997). A later report indicated that students in Edison schools outperform students in other schools on state and national tests, with an average gain of 5 percentage points (Lewin, 1999).

Controversy has surrounded the studies of Edison school performance, with charges of odd reporting procedures and questionable practices in some schools. For instance, at a Boston school, an emergency protocol system called "Code Orange" was established for teachers to receive assistance with troubled youth in their classrooms; teachers would call "Code Orange" on an intercom system, and four or five designated adults would come to the assistance of the teacher in need. Code Orange calls could be heard in a kindergarten room two or three times a week and led to the use of therapeutic restraints on a 5-year-old child (Farber, 1998). Parental outrage led to drastic changes in the structure of the school, and, under new leadership, several changes occurred and special-needs students received the aid they required.

Several questions still remain about the Edison Project. Which of the changes in Edison schools led to the reported academic achievement? Can these results be achieved without business involvement? According to Molnar (1996), the entire school reform movement involving vouchers, charter schools, and for-profit ventures such as the Edison Project are all attempts to see if business principles can be applied to public education and are practices that further commercialize youth in schools.

## Exchanging Technology for a Captive Audience: The Case of ZapMe!

There have been other attempts to follow Chris Whittle's lead. Schools are willing to accept commercial messages in exchange for technology. Today's appeal for many marketing schemes in schools has turned high-tech with promises of computer hardware and software in exchange for the placement of a corporate logo or an advertisement in classrooms and on school buildings and buses. Various programs have been implemented, from saving Campbell's soup labels for filmstrips and projectors to shopping at participating stores to earn credits for Apple computers through the "Apples for Students" program (Molnar, 1996). One school district in Canada has accepted money from Pepsi with the understanding that computer screen savers in the lab would carry the Pepsi logo with the message "Develop a thirst for knowledge" (Jenkins, 1999). Major computer companies have donated computer equipment and advice to schools across the country; Apple Computer donated more than $8 million in equipment and advice in 1990 alone (Larson, 1991). In 1996, Sun Microsystems coordinated "Net Day" in California, where about 200 companies and 20,000 volunteers worked together to wire public schools for Internet access (Stead, 1997). According to the companies, computer contributions will create brand loyalty and generate a workforce capable of using technology. A comment from John C. Porter, director of education and university relations at IBM, reflects this joint reasoning: "It's not just our future work force—it's our future customer" (as cited in Larson, 1991, p. 12). Not only do the students represent a source of trained employees, but these young people will be the next generation of home computer owners, and a brand-loyal, educated public is a priceless commodity to computer companies around the globe.

In this tradition, a new company, ZapMe!, has been offering equipment in exchange for a captive audience. ZapMe! is a 55-employee company that provides a computer lab of 15 Compaq computers, a laser printer, a roof-mounted satellite dish for Internet connection, computer training and installation, and technical support to schools for free. As part of the contract, schools must agree to use the computers at least 4 hours a day. However, the computers come preloaded with a permanent interface known as "netspace," which features a 2-inch border around the screen where ads appear in a box in the lower left-hand corner (Bazeley, 1999). Inside the netspace border, students can connect to thousands of educational websites screened by ZapMe! as well as enter chat rooms or use message boards that are provided and monitored for inappropriate language and use by ZapMe! (Cearley, 1999). Students have their own password and e-mail address with ZapMe!—security measures ensuring that students use an alias and cannot be identified. Currently, advertising logos are limited to those companies that provide equipment such as Compaq and IBM. However, the company has recently begun to contract advertising space to other companies that are interested in the youth market. In addition to a captive audience, ZapMe! has created the ability to microtarget this audience through the use of student demographics. Each student completes a user profile, including the student's age, sex, and zip code. ZapMe! compiles this information and provides it to advertisers so that they can adjust their ads in certain school districts to accommodate for the demographics of that particular student population. Since ZapMe! began in 1998, nearly 50 schools have received the technology, and more than 10,000 schools have applied (Cearley, 1999).

Just as with Channel One, several constituencies have concerns and praise for ZapMe! Some express a concern that commercialism has gone too far by selling the demographics of the students (Cearley, 1999). Ralph Nader expresses this concern: "Schools should never help advertisers and marketers to hone their sales pitches against the young. It's borderline child abuse" (as cited in Walters, 1998, p. D3). However, ZapMe! defends its use of advertising by stating that the advertisements only appear when students click on the billboards in the lower left-hand corner (Walters, 1998) and that the brand images of the advertisers are educationally appropriate and will not include harmful products such as alcohol or tobacco products (Lynem, 1998). Moreover, Frank Vigil, chief financial officer of ZapMe!, cites two reasons for schools to use this service: (a) The Internet already has advertising, and (b) parents want their children to learn how to use the computer (Walters, 1998). Some educators agree with Vigil and see ZapMe! as an opportunity to close the gap between the haves and the have-nots. One assistant principal at a school using ZapMe! commented, "As long as the advertisers are being screened by ZapMe! then we feel pretty comfortable as long as it isn't any different from what kids are already exposed to from when they use the Internet at home" (as cited in Cearley, 1999, p. B1). Unfortunately, we do not yet have any assessments of how ZapMe! is used by students and its influence on them.

## Other Commercial Practices in Schools: Curricular Materials

Both direct advertising and marketing of consumer products in schools are readily identifiable consumer-influence practices by, perhaps, all but the youngest grade school children. By the middle elementary years, most children can identify an advertisement for a product (Wackman, Ward, & Wartella, 1977). However, more subtle marketing strategies may be beyond the awareness of even older children. In particular, corporate curricular materials can provide very subtle marketer's messages. And corporate curricular materials often appear in the classroom without the scrutiny or review of principals or boards of education. The practice of using corporate materials in classrooms is not new. It goes back decades (Richards et al., 1998), and for many years it went unquestioned. Of 45 states that responded to a survey of state departments of education in the late 1970s, 44 had no guidelines or procedures for the review of industry-sponsored materials. Several states had guidelines for the adoption of state-adopted textbooks, but most deferred review of materials to the local level of the school district leaders or classroom teachers (Harty, 1979). However, concerns arose when corporate logos began to appear in textbooks, and changes were about to occur in several states.

In the late 1970s, a review process of textbooks for racial and gender biases led to the discovery of commercialism in state-adopted textbooks, which led to changes in California's guidelines for the adoption of textbooks in the classroom. Vigilance in Public Education, a citizens action group, was conducting a review of textbooks for racial and gender biases when they found uses of corporate logos and products in primary-level mathematics textbooks. Published by Scott, Foresman, and Company, *Mathematics Around Us,* a kindergarten through eighth-grade textbook series, contained several math problems that used company names or products within the illustration. Some of the products mentioned included jelly beans, Twinkies, Tootsie Rolls, and candy corn. Lessons taught with the textbooks included subtraction using Baby Ruth candy bars, division using Cracker Jacks and Jujy Fruits, and subsets using six-packs of Coca-Cola. Pictures of companies were used as well, including companies such as McDonald's, Howard Johnson, Mobil, Texaco, Hertz, and Kentucky Fried Chicken. Moreover, companies remained uninformed of their use in this book. In response to this review process, the California State Board of Education passed guidelines in 1977 that condemned the use of state-adopted textbooks for kindergarten through eighth grade that depicted brand names, corporate logos, or selected food products of low nutritional value. These guidelines refer not only to ads but also to the "inadvertent use of brand names and/or logos in illustrations or content" (Harty, 1979, p. 109). As a result of these guidelines, the use of *Mathematics Around Us* was stopped in California during the 1979-1980 adoption cycle, when the guidelines became effective.

Although some states followed suit, others seemed indifferent to the use of these materials in their classrooms. In 1979, Louisiana adopted guidelines recommended by the Textbook and Media Advisory Council of the State Board of Elementary and Secondary Education. Two of the guidelines read,

- Textbooks should not contain materials that promote, as opposed to objectively presenting, a partisan or sectarian viewpoint.
- Textbooks should objectively present concepts of citizenship, democracy, authority, freedom of expression, and free enterprise. (Harty, 1979, p. 109)

In the 1970s, New York chose not to forbid the use of corporate-sponsored materials. In fact, New York developed a program called GIFT, Government and Industrial Films for Teaching. This program reviews, describes, copies, and disseminates corporate-sponsored films to increase their availability to teachers. New York cited the banning of these materials as censorship yet expressed concern over the scope of the materials, encouraging an expansion of topics and subject areas covered (Harty, 1979).

Despite these decisions in the 1970s, 20 years later corporate logos and products appeared in textbooks in 15 states across the country, including California, Texas, and New York. A textbook series called *Mathematics: Applications and Connections* first appeared in 1995 and was followed by a revised version in 1999, both published by McGraw-Hill and both containing pictures of corporate logos and using corporate products as examples in various mathematics problems. Examples of products used in the series include Barbie dolls, Cocoa Frosted Flakes, Sony Play Stations, Spalding basketballs, characters and sites owned by Disney and Warner Brothers, and fast food from Burger King and McDonald's. Moreover, students using the 1999 edition were asked to calculate the diameter of an Oreo cookie, and those using the 1995 edition were asked to calculate how many weeks it would take to save enough allowance money to purchase a pair of Nike shoes, with a picture of the shoes next to the question (Hays, 1999). One of the book's authors claims that the products were mentioned to make the problems more relevant to today's youth (Hays, 1999). According to another of the book's authors, no companies paid McGraw-Hill any money to have their company mentioned in the textbook (Hays, 1999). McGraw-Hill agrees and contends that permission to use logos and corporate names was sought and granted before publication. Not all companies mentioned would agree. McDonald's acknowledges its permission to appear in the textbook, but Oreo has no record of such a request from McGraw-Hill (Hays, 1999).

Although many states do not have policies on the use of corporate logos in textbooks, it seems surprising that so many states use the McGraw-Hill textbook. Texas state law allows the agency to refuse books for only three reasons: (a) refusal to correct errors, (b) failure to meet curriculum, and (c) improper binding (Davis, 1999). No mention is given to corporate logos or advertising. According to the Texas Education Agency, about one fourth of Texas districts are using the McGraw-Hill math textbook (Davis, 1999). In California, this controversy sparked a legislator to propose a state bill that prohibits commercial references in books. To much chagrin, it was discovered that such guidelines already existed in California based on the issues surrounding the *Mathematics Around Us* textbook series in the late 1970s (Hays, 1999). Doug Stone, spokesperson for the California State Board of Education, suspects that these books did not receive a thorough review before being placed and used in California schools because they were donated by the McGraw-Hill Company (Hays, 1999). Among the 37 publishers who submitted math books for consideration by the state, 20 contained commercial images and brand names in their text (Lucas, 1999). Although state legislation and policy decisions are still pending in California, the San Francisco Unified School District voted unanimously to ban the use of textbooks containing unnecessary uses of corporate logos or brand names.

Because materials usually arrive unsolicited and are not subject to curriculum review, it is difficult to determine the use of corporate-sponsored curricular materials in the classroom. But developers of these types of kits estimate that their products reach up to 2 million teachers from kindergarten through college at practically every school nationwide (Stead, 1997).

Moreover, there have been various surveys over the years that suggest that the majority of teachers use such materials. For instance, the National Education Association surveyed 1,250 teachers in 1977 about their use of corporate materials, and half of the teachers responded that they used them (Harty, 1979). Interestingly, this was fewer than Addicott (1939) discovered in 1939 when he found that 85% of elementary school teachers and administrators used advertising materials. In 1949, Netzer (1952) found that 97% of elementary school teachers in Wisconsin were using industry-sponsored materials (as cited in Harty, 1979). Finally, a 1979 survey of 1,500 teachers found that 69% had received free, unsolicited teaching materials from the industry. Of those, 45% reported using these materials. Moreover, 79% of teachers requested industry materials. The respondents in that survey gave various reasons for using industry materials: 57% said that library materials and commercial publishers did not adequately serve their needs, and half of the teachers said they sought public interest materials for balance and contrast when available. But they did have some complaints, including 30% who said there was repetitive use of brand names, and 42% said they perceived bias in the presentation (Harty, 1979, pp. 111-112).

## The Effects of Marketing Practices in Schools

In 1995, Consumers Union offered a critique of the growing corporate and marketing involvement in schools as practices that were fundamentally "perverting education," and it called for "parents and educators to unite to make schools ad-free zones" (p. 2). Consumers Union (1995) had nine major concerns about the effects of such marketing in schools:

1. Commercialization "cedes control to people outside education" (p. 32). Teachers and administrators, not corporations, should control the educational process in schools.
2. Commercialization "compromises the integrity of education" (p. 32). The purpose of education is not to create brand-loyal consumers or to help young people feel good about consumerism.
3. "Ads in school and in school materials carry the weight of an endorsement" (p. 32). They imply that schools approve of the sponsor or product.
4. "Promotional sponsored education materials blur the line between education and propaganda and lead to distorted lessons" (p. 32). Lesson plans provided by corporations often masquerade as education materials when, in fact, they promote self-interested or biased points of view.
5. "Sponsored programs and materials often bypass review processes intended to safeguard students from biased or

otherwise flawed materials" (p. 32). Corporate-sponsored materials slide in the back door and often do not receive the scrutiny of any governing board of education.

6. "The idea that teachers can serve as the gatekeepers against the biased messages often found in sponsored materials is naïve" (p. 32). Most teachers have not been educated about these materials, and most are not experts in a given topic, capable of determining the validity of materials received from corporations.
7. "In-school marketing contributes to the din of commercialism targeted at kids, and promotes materialism" (p. 33). Children are already exposed to advertising in every corner of their lives telling them to buy too many things that they cannot afford or do not need.
8. "The idea that kids aren't influenced by in-school advertising because it's everywhere reflects a naivete about the nature of advertising" (p. 33). Even adults are affected by advertising, and children are far more susceptible to its influence.
9. "The idea that school-business partnerships should have a commercial payback aspect is unethical" (p. 33). Corporations should be supporting today's youth without expecting a payback.

The reactions of school administrators and teachers regarding the effects of such marketing practices are mixed. A remark by Don Poe, athletic director of the Irving School District in Texas, typifies the attitude of school administrators reported in the press. He notes, "It's a business deal. It's good for us, and it's good for them" (as cited in Wells, 1996, p. 1B). Budgetary realities, administrators claim, force them to find creative means of meeting their obligations to students. John Stanford, superintendent of schools in Seattle, opines, "Our financial situation is forcing us to be entrepreneurial. If we were getting what we should be getting from the state legislature, we wouldn't be looking at this kind of approach" (as cited in Stead, 1997, p. 46). Peter Weigand, a Roman Catholic priest and headmaster of a private school, expressed appreciation for corporate involvement and remarked in a recent editorial, "The cynic might grouse about 'commercialism' in schools, but the educator in me suggests that our children's report cards tell a different story. Improved grades, more stimulating learning environments and new opportunities can do nothing but benefit America's students" (Weigand, 1999, p. A23).

Administrators and teachers who recognize the need for the corporate support view students as being smart enough to understand the advertising and marketing messages. Teachers seem to express an understanding that many of the curricular materials are worthwhile, and, when not, they can be easily discarded (Stead, 1997). The success of Channel One, its adoption and renewal in schools, suggests that teachers and administrators are willing to accept advertising in exchange for the technology, money, and other corporate support provided.

How do students respond to such marketing practices? Again, we find mixed reactions. "School should be an ad-free zone," says one high school senior (as cited in Glamser, 1997, p. 3A). Another queries, "Shouldn't schools be the one place we can get away from advertisement?" (as cited in Stead, 1997, p. 47). A third declares, "First the Nike cheerleaders, next thing you know, it'll be the Nike school" (as cited in Stead, 1997, p. 47). But not all students are so critical. One student says, "[Advertising in schools is] cool. I don't mind as long as [the companies] give something in return" (as cited in Glamser, 1997, p. 3A). Another adds, "I'd like to see more advertising. It's interesting to see how companies want us to see their business" (as cited in Wells, 1996, p. 1B).

Parents too are increasingly vocal about marketing practices in schools. Karen Miller, the Parent Teacher Association's legislative action director, claims that the "Three R's" have been replaced with the "Three C's": commercialism, consumerism, and classism (Davis, 1999, p. A11). However, there is evidence that, unless a particular controversy regarding a marketing practice erupts in a school district, many parents remain unaware of the extent of the commercialization of schools. For instance, Richards et al. (1998) report the results of the statewide Scripps Howard Texas Poll, which surveyed 1,000 Texas adults in June 1996 asking them how frequently they thought children were exposed to advertising at school. Forty-seven percent felt it was no more than occasionally, while 33% felt it was often or daily. Moreover, when asked if schools need more money, and where the money should come from, 28% said it should come from businesses in exchange for schools allowing them to advertise, while 44% thought it should come from increased taxes. Although there does not seem to be a groundswell of parental rejection of marketing in schools, awareness of such marketing practices may still be growing. As awareness increases, these practices may become a policy issue.

Finally, what about the students? What evidence is there of the effects of such marketing practices on them? Unfortunately, aside from opinions about such practices, the best research that has been conducted on direct influence is that concerning Channel One. This research addresses questions concerning the credibility of the newscast as a learning tool as well as the impact of the advertising contained within the broadcast. Both of these issues will be reviewed.

First, a variety of studies examining the impact of Channel One on learning outcomes suggests that modest learning from the newscast occurs and depends on how well the news content is integrated into larger plans and course content (Johnston & Brzezinski, 1992). According to Greenberg and Brand's (1993) analysis, most learning occurred for the specific news items shown on Channel One but did not generalize to other public affairs information in the short term. Upon retesting 3 months later (after using Channel One), viewers knew more about general news events than nonviewers did (Greenberg & Brand, 1993). According to Knupfer and Hayes's 1994 study, there were no significant differences in current events knowledge between various demographic subgroups of Channel One viewers, including between at-risk and not-at-risk viewers or between males and females, but there were higher test scores for high school over middle school students. Bachen (1998) concludes that the various studies of Channel One's impact on student learning range from no impact to some positive impact when teachers develop supplemental materials to extend and enhance the televised news content (p. 144).

There is some question regarding how attentively students watch Channel One. Students are more likely to attend to Channel One if a teacher attends to the program and transmits the expectation that students need to do the same (Johnston, 1995). Self-reports of paying attention to the program from a survey of 100 schools with Channel One reveal that 43% say they "usually" pay attention and 37% "occasionally" pay attention. School observations indicate that students "graze" while watching Channel One; that is, they pay attention to stories of personal interest and pay less attention to stories with lower levels of interest (Johnston, 1995).

Finally, studies also examined Channel One viewers' learning about consumption and advertised products. For instance, Channel One viewers were found to evaluate products advertised on the program more highly than their nonviewing counterparts (Brand & Greenberg, 1994). Channel One viewers expressed more consumer-oriented attitudes than nonviewers did and were more likely than nonviewers to report purchase intentions for Channel One–advertised products. However, Channel One viewers were no more likely than their nonviewing peers to report actual purchases of Channel One–advertised products (Brand & Greenberg, 1994). But as Bachen (1998) notes, we do not know whether students' consumer learning in school differs from learning about products in other contexts. In short, does the in-school setting increase or decrease the persuasiveness of advertising? Are some children more or less susceptible to in-school advertising? We really do not know.

## Summary

Marketing to youth is growing in the culture in general, and this includes American schools. Through direct sales, advertising, promotions, curricular materials, and various forms of corporate sponsorship of school activities, corporate involvement in America's public schools is increasing each year. The reasons for this are clear: Youth represent a multi-billion-dollar market for products today, they are future consumers whose brand loyalty is wanted, and they represent a market that can influence other family purchases. American schools, short on technology, money, and educational materials, look to corporate largess, whether via marketing dollars, philanthropy, or corporate partnerships, as a mechanism for sustaining schools in the face of reduced public support and growing public concerns of mediocre educational performance fostered by the 1983 governmental report *A Nation at Risk* (Molnar, 1996). Administrators and teachers seem to be able to parse the good and bad experiences they have with corporate marketing strategies. Parents and consumer advocates have been developing an awareness of the commercialization of schools in the past decade, but slowly.

The 1990 launch of Channel One and the 1995 Consumers Union report sparked public criticism about direct advertising and marketing strategies. Such recent activities, however, actually are part of a much longer history of corporate involvement in public education going back to the early decades of the twentieth century. Finally, students themselves, the subjects of such marketing techniques, have been studied far too little to clearly understand the effects, both short term and longer term, on their consumer knowledge, attitudes, and behaviors. Are children willing, gullible, and accepting of advertiser influence through the school years? Does such commercialization of youth in schools influence them to be active consumers or cynical critics of commercial practices? How does blatant corporate involvement and ongoing marketing to youth in schools affect students' attitudes toward the goals and role of public education? Are there long-term consequences for the public interest regarding the commercialization of schools? These questions are begging for research-based answers.

## References


Addicott, I. O. (1939). *A study of the nature and elementary school use of free printed matter prepared as advertising media.* Unpublished doctoral dissertation, Leland Stanford Junior University, School of Education, Stanford, CA.

Bachen, C. M. (1998). Channel One and the education of American youths. *Annals of the American Academy of Political and Social Science, 557,* 132-147.

Bazeley, M. (1999, March 21). ZapMe! school role debated: Students get computers; advertisers get a market! *Silicon Valley News* [On-line]. [Retrieved March 23, 1999]. Available: www.mercurycenter.com/svtech/news/indepth/docs/zapme032299.htm

Bower, C. (1996, September 23). Higher math: Student fund raising aids school budgets. *St. Louis Post-Dispatch,* p. 1A.

Brand, J. E., & Greenberg, B. S. (1994). Commercials in the classroom: The impact of Channel One advertising. *Journal of Advertising Research, 34*(1), 18-27.

Cearley, A. (1999, January 7). ZapMe! package has been delivered: Schools get computers, the firm gets ad time. *San Diego Union-Tribune,* p. B1.

Channel One. (1999). *Channel One network* [On-line]. [Retrieved October 13, 1999]. Available: www.primediainc.com/html2/education/ channel1.html

Childhood's end? More than ever, advertisers are targeting campaigns at children as a way to tap parental spending power. (1999). *Time International, 154,* 36.

Consumers Union. (1995). *Captive kids: Commercial pressures on kids at school.* Yonkers, NY: Consumers Union Education Services.

Davis, M. A. (1999, April 8). This space for rent: Put your product's name here. *Austin American Statesman,* p. A11.

Dodge, S. (1998, December 27). Ads adding up in local schools. *Chicago Sun Times,* p. 1.

Ewen, S. (1996). *PR! A social history of spin.* New York: Basic Books.

Farber, P. (1998). The Edison Project scores—and stumbles—in Boston. *Phi Delta Kappan, 79*(7), 506-512.

Glamser, D. (1997, January 3). This class is brought to you by ... *USA Today,* p. 3A.

Goff, L. (1999, August). Don't miss the bus! *American Demographics, 21*(8), 48.

Greenberg, B., & Brand, J. (1993). Television news and advertising in schools: The "Channel One" controversy. *Journal of Communication, 43*(1), 143-151.

Harty, S. (1979). *Hucksters in the classroom: A review of industry propaganda in schools.* Washington, DC: Center for Study of Responsive Law.

Hays, C. L. (1999, March 21). Math book salted with brand names raises new alarm. *New York Times,* pp. 1, 28.

Horsley, L. (1998, June 3). Private firm states its case for helping public schools. *Kansas City Star,* p. A1.

Jacobson, M. F. (1995, January 29). Now there's a fourth R: Retailing. *New York Times,* p. F9.

Jayson, S. (1997, January 22). Study out today details content of school TV news. *Austin American-Statesman,* pp. B1, B6, B9.

Jenkins, L. (1999, January 8). Advertisers use schools to Zap! kids. *San Diego Union-Tribune,* pp. B-3, 1, 6, 7, 8.

Johnston, J. (1995). Channel One: The dilemma of teaching and selling. *Phi Delta Kappan, 76*(6), 436-443.

Johnston, J., & Brzezinski, E. (1992). *Taking the measure of Channel One: The first year.* Ann Arbor: University of Michigan, Institute for Social Research.

Knupfer, N. N., & Hayes, P. (1994). The effects of the Channel One broadcast on students' knowledge of current events. In A. De Vaney (Ed.), *Watching Channel One: The convergence of students, technology, and private business* (pp. 42-60). Albany: State University of New York Press.

Labi, N. (1999, April 19). Classrooms for sale. *Time, 153*(15), 44-45.

Larson, J. (1991). Computers in school can be habit forming. *American Demographics, 13*(10), 12.

Lewin, T. (1999, April 7). Edison schools say students gain. *New York Times,* p. B9.

Lucas, G. (1999, June 26). Gripes grow over rampant textbook ads: Brand names grab kids' attention, publishers say. *San Francisco Chronicle,* p. A1.

Lynem, J. N. (1998, November 10). Schools' free Internet access: Built-in ads part of the deal. *San Francisco Chronicle,* p. A1.

Mathews, J. (1994, July 29). The entrepreneur's grade expectations: Whittle's mix of education and enterprise faces tests from teachers and financiers. *Washington Post,* p. B1.

McNeal, J. (1987). *Children as consumers: Insights and implications.* Lexington, MA: Lexington Books.

Molnar, A. (1996). *Giving kids the business: The commercialization of America's schools.* Boulder, CO: Westview.

Netzer, L. A. (1952). *The use of industry aids in schools.* Milwaukee: Wisconsin Manufacturers Association.

Richards, J. I., Wartella, E. A., Morton, C., & Thompson, L. (1998). The growing commercialization of schools: Issues and practices. *Annals of the American Academy of Political and Social Science, 557,* 148-163.

Smolkin, R. (1999, March 30). Tuning out Channel One: Commercials, educational value questioned. *Washington Times,* p. A4.

Stead, D. (1997, January 5). Corporations, classrooms, and commercialism: Some say business has gone too far. *New York Times,* Section 4A, pp. 30-33, 41-47.

Steinberg, J. (1997, December 17). Edison Project reports measurable progress in reading and math at its schools. *New York Times,* p. B8.

This school is brought to you by: Cola? Sneakers? (1998, March 27). *USA Today,* p. 12A.

Wackman, D., Ward, S., & Wartella, E. (1977). *How children learn to buy: The development of consumer information.* Beverly Hills, CA: Sage.

Walsh, M. (1991, May 22). Entrepreneur Whittle unveils plans to create chain of for-profit schools. *Education Week on the Web* [On-line]. [Retrieved April 23, 1999]. Available: www.edweek.org

Walsh, M. (1993, October 27). Channel One more often used in poorer schools, study finds. *Education Week on the Web* [On-line]. [Retrieved April 23, 1999]. Available: www.edweek.org

Walters, J. (1998, December 30). ZapMe! stirs up educators: Controversial program supplies cash-strapped school boards with free computers in return for running advertisements and monitoring students. *(Montreal) Gazette,* p. D3.

Weigand, P. (1999, September 1). Business is saving schools, not tainting them. *New York Times,* p. A23.

Wells, M. (1996, May 9). Ad pitches target teen consumers. *USA Today,* p. 1B.

White, A., Ruskin, G., Mokhiber, R., & Weissman, R. (1999). The cola-ized classroom. *Multinational Monitor, 20,* 16-23.

Winters, P. (1995, June 1). School bells ring for advertisers. *New York Daily News,* p. 61.

Wolff, C. (1996, December 1). Schools know the score: Advertisers providing sports equipment, money. *Cincinnati Enquirer,* p. B01.

Wykes, S. L. (1999, June 27). Schools turn to Internet. *Silicon Valley News* [On-line]. [Retrieved June 28, 1999]. Available: www.mercurycenter.com/svtech/news/

CHAPTER **31**

# The Role of Research in Educational Television

MICHAEL COHEN
Applied Research & Consulting LLC

## Context and Background

### *Media Products and Academics*

An exceptional situation occurs when highly conceptual, academic material becomes a critical component of the creation of a commercial product. Such is the case when educational television incorporates "research" into its development and programming decisions. This chapter examines the phenomenon of applied research in children's educational television. Research, by which we mean knowledge amassed and analyzed by professional psychologists and other social scientists—working either "in-house" or as external consultants—has increasingly assumed a significant role in children's programming (e.g., Pecora, 1998). This chapter will explore that role through discussions of several key areas: (a) television's curious marriage of education and entertainment; (b) the complexities of the television industry; (c) the theoretical, historical, and methodological underpinnings of research; (d) the various stages of television production at which research is used; and (e) the varieties of techniques used by professional researchers (e.g., Palmer, 1988; Palmer & Dorr, 1980). To illustrate exactly what research can offer, we shall use case examples culled from extensive experience within the children's television industry.

### *TV and the "Vast Wasteland"*

One might argue that television, since its inception as part of social life in the late 1940s, has always educated the public. After all, no prior technology had ever opened such vast vistas to so many. Never before had one been able to experience so intimately worlds so far away or to encounter people so different from oneself. In this sense, television programs—whether about lions in a distant jungle or people in a distant city—have always offered viewers a certain amount of de facto education. But commercial broadcast television did not begin life as an educational tool; it quickly developed to be a medium of pure entertainment. Television producers were not expected to create curriculum for their shows. Education was neither an explicit nor implicit goal. And during television's first decade, the novelty of its form and the content of its products were openly embraced.

This vision of television, however, as a pure and benign form of entertainment for our children vanished forever in the 1960s when Newton N. Minow, then chairman of the Federal Communications Commission (FCC), made what has become one of the most famous media statements of the twentieth century. Lamenting what he saw as television's potential harmfulness to the population in general and children specifically, Minow dubbed it "a vast wasteland" (e.g., Palmer, 1988).

Minow's remarks struck a chord deep within the American imagination, echoing hitherto unspoken but simmering fears of parents and educators. One deep interpretation of this wasteland was that television had become an intellectual desert—its identifying feature was the total absence of any useful, cognitive information and education for children. The social perception was that television risked creating an entire generation of mindless children who sat passively in front of the screen, learning nothing (e.g., Zillmann, Bryant, & Huston, 1994).

Much serious critical debate over television's role ensued. It is important to note that the prevailing voice—but by no means necessarily the only voice—articulated that television was neither "friend nor foe"; television was intrinsically neither good nor bad. For sure, television was powerful, and many believed that we should harness that power for the "forces of good." Television's enormous impact, it was believed, could be used for other than commercial interest, and, more than to simply entertain, it could be used to educate. The result was the beginning of what we now consider educational television for children—that is, television programs created with formally articulated, explicit curricular goals. The first episode in 1969 of the groundbreaking *Sesame Street* marked the symbolic beginning of this new hybrid creature: television that intentionally married entertainment and education.

### *Television's Initial Response: The "Birth" of Educational Television*

In the 1960s and 1970s, educational television flourished as shows such as *The Electric Company, Zoom,* and *3-2-1 Contact* joined the ranks, all continuing the new mission of entertaining children while helping them learn specific skills. As with school curricula, educational television's curricula functioned as a process with a beginning, middle, and end. The notion of curriculum assumes that one can take a given individual, expose him or her to a series of appropriately taught lessons over time, and produce a desired improvement (e.g., Van Eura, 1998). In this case, it was the acquisition of a set of age-appropriate skills.

During these first two decades of the genre, those skills were primarily cognitive. One extraordinary exception was *Mister Rogers' Neighborhood,* in which the emphasis was (and still is) on imagination and social and emotional development. The stated curricular goals of these early programs included the teaching of such skills as preliteracy (the alphabet), prenumeracy (numbers), basic colors, spatial orientation (distinguishing right from left, up from down), and so on. The goal was to transform Minow's desert and to "have it flower" with informative (and enjoyable) lessons for children, and result in measurable enhancement of learning skills and knowledge content. It is important to note that the majority of the "flowering" took place on public television; networks did not yet feel the necessity to produce curricular-based programming to compete in the market (e.g., Clifford, Gunter, & McAleer, 1995; Montgomery, 1989).

### *Television: The Evil Force*

With the 1980s came another profound change in America's perception of television. This change, however, was never as clearly articulated as the earlier "wasteland." Whereas Minow had bemoaned the empty-headedness of the television generation, critics in the 1980s feared its moral degeneration. No longer did television appear to be simply characterized by an absence of worthy information for children; it appeared to be actually harming them, destroying their very souls (e.g., Gunter, McAleer, & Clifford, 1991). Parents and educators began to worry that television was doing actual damage to young people, filling their minds with dangerous images of violence, sex, and immorality (e.g., Cantor, 1998; Davies, 1997). The fear was no longer simply that television might make children vacuous and promote values of base materialism; the fear was that television might make children "evil," insensitive to violence, violent themselves, and incapable of making appropriate moral and ethical decisions (e.g., Von Feilitzen & Carlsson, 1999). Television was perceived to be teaching values that were, at best, callous and disrespectful and, at worst, antisocial, antihuman, exploitative, sexist, and racist—and at the most extreme, sociopathic.

Such fears, of course, do not arise ex nihilo. The perception that television had a terrifying power to destroy young souls occurred within the context of profound changes in the American family and the economy (e.g., Washington & Andreas, 1998). Throughout the 1980s, the American landscape altered irrevocably in many key ways. The familial landscape was quickly changing: The divorce rate soared; single-parent families were increasingly common; and women began entering the workplace in record numbers. With nearly half of all marriages ending in divorce and more than half of all mothers working outside of the home, children's relationship to television was necessarily transformed. Once just a source of entertainment and skill acquisition, television was perceived, perhaps appropriately so, as having become our children's baby-sitter, caretaker, and interlocutor (e.g., Levin, 1998). Furthermore, television became more ubiquitous in the United States: Regardless of their family income, Americans owned a television.

### *Television's Response: The Second Wave*

To respond to the new anxieties over television's profound influence, the industry turned its attention to teaching values along with cognitive skills. Simply put, from its initial incarnation as a conveyer of cognitive skills, educational television moved on to become explicitly a purveyor of emotional, moral, and social values such as kindness, respect for others, and sharing. Prior to the 1980s, most Americans held to the belief that parents (and the local community—church, synagogue, etc.) were responsible for transmitting such values to their children. Moral education took place, basically, in the "home." By the 1980s, however, parents no longer felt confident undertaking this task on their own. Television had assumed too big a role in their children's lives, and it seemed too powerful in its potential for moral miseducation. New and different educational television was necessary to combat the evils of noneducational television.

Thus, the very definition of what is educational changed. Curriculum remained, but the legitimate content for curriculum broadened considerably (e.g., Valkenburg, 1995). This need for socioemotional developmentally instructive television led to the creation and acceptance of such shows as *Barney & Friends,* in which social development makes up a substantial portion of the stated curriculum. *Barney & Friends* emphasizes emotional, societal, and ethical realms while offering highly supportive but less formal lessons in reading, early numeracy, and so forth. As such, it represents another end of the continuum of shows, such as the early *Sesame Street,* in which values such as interracial harmony or respect for others were, of course, a signature component of the series but, from a curriculum perspective, were the backdrop for the transmission of cognitive skills. It is important to note the significance of the shift to a more extended definition of education. By the late 1990s, an overview of the television landscape showed that more educational television was explicitly devoted to social and emotional curricula than to cognitive learning.

### *Education and Entertainment*

Educational television, then, has responded to the increased range of children's developmental needs as the basis for its formal curriculum over its 30-year history. Its educational goals now span the cognitive and the socioemotional domains. What remains constant, however, is the challenge of providing curricular content while being entertaining and watchable. Unlike their nontelevision counterparts—the educators who create core and ancillary curricula for America's schools—producers of educational television are forced to compete with other, purely entertainment programs and, therefore, must make a greater effort to be "kid friendly." Regardless of their other functions, commercial and public television shows naturally have a primary obligation to attract and keep viewers. Obviously, this is because television is a business, and businesses must earn money to stay alive (e.g., McNeal, 1992; Pecora, 1998).

Children have to "want to watch" for an educational program to be successful. The television industry, including its special subcategory of educational television, generates revenue in basic ways. It is critical to note that commercial television understood that the preschool programming market, particularly by the late 1980s, required sound, educationally based programs. Curriculum-based programs were no longer limited to the space of public television. Public television, of course, receives individual and corporate donations, corporate sponsorships, and public fund allocations; however, it relies more and more on commercial sources of income. Network and cable television generate revenue via advertising sales, affiliation with cable providers who pay for the privilege of offering a given station, and through the licensing of products associated with individual programs. This last method acquires particular importance in the case of children's television (public or network/cable), where the marketing of dolls, games, toys, and so on in the likeness of beloved on-screen characters proves increasingly lucrative. Obviously, none of these methods works unless television programs can achieve consistently high ratings. For educational television, the quest for ratings and subsequent revenue coexists with the considerable demands of providing effective measurable pedagogical content. Accordingly, high-quality programs of this genre prove very difficult products to create. This is where research comes in.

## The Role of Research

### *The History of Research*

From the 1960s to the present, professional researchers (psychologists, educators, and market and media specialists) have played a significant part in the development of educational television, contributing to both its entertainment value and its curricular content. There was an urgent need to create highly entertaining programs that simultaneously met serious educational objectives, and research was critical to such an undertaking. Children's Television Workshop (CTW) pioneered the model of integrating research in its initial conception of *Sesame Street,* for which it is now appropriately famous. We can think of this process using an overlapping three-ringed conceptualization. The first ring represents a given show's creative content—its basic premise, characters, story line, whether it is animation or live action, and so on. The second ring represents the show's stated curriculum—whether this is a series of cognitive skills or a series of moral and social values. The third ring, which overlaps both the others, is that of research. Research evaluates both the level of appeal and the effectiveness of the integrated curriculum. Research offers educational television the critical help it needs in integrating curriculum and entertainment—it helps merge two realms that do not naturally fit together on their own. The following Venn diagram, which is the representation initially created by CTW as its model for developing *Sesame Street* specifically and educational media products in general, is an excellent visual conceptualization of the above-stated dynamic (Schneider, 1999). This model elevated research to an equal role with other disciplines and has provided the blueprint for educational media research for more than 30 years.

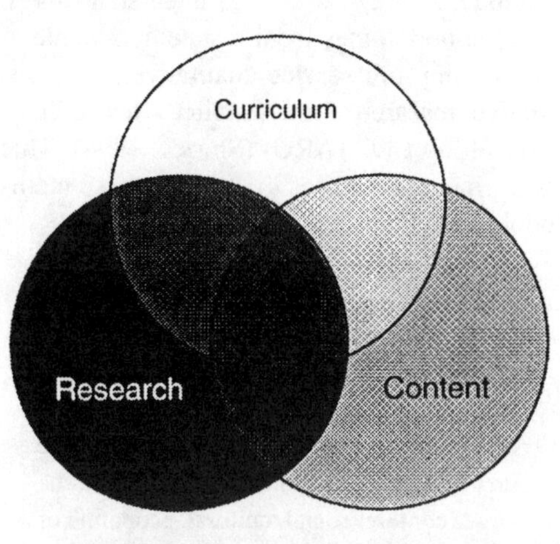


### *What Is Research?*

Before addressing its various specific functions within the industry, however, we need to define what we mean by "research." Typically, when we speak of research, we generally mean basic scientific as opposed to applied research. Basic scientific "research" refers to any investigatory activity, scientific or social scientific, that is conducted with the goal of adding to the general body of human knowledge. Applied research is conducted for the explicit purpose of solving a particular problem. Of course, the knowledge obtained from applied research endeavors may very well add to our overall understanding of the world and how it works, but, again, a good deal of applied research is not conducted with that goal as its primary motivation. Perhaps it is best to understand this differentiation with a simple example from the field of education. Psychologists will engage in basic scientific research to understand how a young child's mind begins to comprehend and develop the capacity for language and mathematics. Applied researchers (educators, psychologists, etc.) will conduct research to determine what is the best methodology for teaching literacy and math to young children. It is research conducted to solve a particular problem—in this case, how best to educate young children.

Educational television makes use of many types of applied research and, interestingly, partakes of a special subcategory of applied research known as market research. Market research is perhaps the most public form of applied research and "came into its own" in the 1950s. Market research found its roots in the field of consumer psychology, which was initially used to create and advertise new products. Market research responded to corporations' urgent need to accurately appeal to and influence the American consumer. This branch of the discipline concerned itself with testing product concepts, developing products, marketing these products, and then testing the effectiveness of marketing strategies with an emphasis on packaging and advertising campaigns. In the 1960s and 1970s, market research quickly expanded to meet the same needs for overall corporate identities, brands, and, interestingly, political candidates (e.g., Bryant & Roskos-Ewoldson, 1999).

Applied research expanded to address not only market issues but the universe of consumer markets and products as well. Researchers found they could now successfully investigate public perceptions of, and opinions about, such formal abstract entities as political candidates, government policies, corporate identities, and so forth. The result was that all and any "products" became legitimate "objects" for market research investigation. Applied research was clearly very valuable in creating products and services and in designing the most effective communications strategies to influence perceptions, attitudes, and behaviors. Specifically, within this context, individual television programs and network brands also became appropriate arenas for market research to be successfully applied.

As we can see, market research is actually a complex hybrid. Although primarily servicing corporate needs and, therefore, a "business discipline," it owes a great deal—particularly its investigative techniques—to the traditions of academic social science. Market research employs a portfolio of qualitative and quantitative research techniques. Qualitative research refers to the in-depth, open-ended questioning of individuals or small groups of respondents; quantitative research asks more restricted, closed-ended questions of a much larger number of respondents. Each method has its unique advantages.

Qualitative research—often the methodology of choice when working with children—is valuable in that it allows a researcher to delve deeply into not only what children think but why they think it and in what social contexts their ideas take shape. Qualitative techniques employed by market research include direct and indirect questioning, ethnographic interviews developed by anthropologists, and clinical observations and various projective techniques used by psychologists. Simply put, qualitative research allows us to understand what perceptions and attitudes exist in a social environment and provides an in-depth understanding of how such perceptions and attitudes develop. The most common form of qualitative research is the focus group, a now ubiquitous feature in our cultural landscape. Widely used in market research, the focus group refers to an interview and discussion with a group of children (usually a group ranging in number from 3 to 10) led by a trained researcher. The researcher has a set of questions to be answered (e.g., Is the show appealing? Do the children relate to the characters? Is the educational content comprehensible?) and focuses the interview to these ends. The researcher, however guided by these questions, is free to ask any question necessary, gently probe, use play activities, and so on in the service of obtaining the relevant data.

Quantitative research serves to tell us at what frequency these perceptions are held; in other words, it helps us come up with figures and percentages. Market research routinely makes use of the quantitative technique known as the large-scale survey, openly developed by academics—in this case, typically from the fields of sociology and social psychology. It may be best to understand these two methodologies from a statement made at an existing, full-service qualitative and quantitative research firm, Applied Research & Consulting LLC (ARC) (Shirley, 1998). This is the language it uses to describe these methodologies:

> The value of qualitative research—in terms of the depth of insight and understanding it engenders—cannot be overstated. The nature of a qualitative interview yields data that is uniquely detailed and nuanced. The process facilitates an understanding of the larger context (social, cultural, economic or institutional) in which an issue or problem exists. Because the research data are used to formulate actual strategies or solutions, it is imperative to understand the issues and problems, not in a vacuum, but in the real world in which consumers develop their attitudes toward and expectations of specific products and services, and in which they actually make decisions about selecting products and services.
>
> Quantitative research enables us to test and refine the hypotheses regarding respon-

dents' attitudes and behavior developed during the qualitative research.

Through a standard set of inductive and deductive analytical techniques (e.g., correlation/regression, ANOVA, ANCOVA, MANOVA, Chi Square, etc.), we provide statistically projectible findings that can be used by clients to develop new products and services, as well as communications, marketing and branding strategies, and to design solutions to specific business or organizational problems. Literally, quantitative analysis can identify the frequency of consumers' perceptions, attitudes, and behavior. Additionally, this research design will allow for a series of latent variable techniques (e.g., multiple regression-path analyses, principle components and factor analyses, structural modeling and multidimensional scaling), which can be used to model the often interactive effects of underlying psychographic, behavioral, motivational and attitudinal variables as a dynamic system. Moreover, if the qualitative research suggests that it is appropriate, additional research modules might be incorporated that allow for detailed decision-making analysis (e.g., conjoint analysis) or an examination of attitude structure (Q-sort, value sort). (pp. 12-13)

It was this special hybrid research product—research with a deep commitment to a fully interpreted qualitative and quantitative methodology—that allowed applied research and market research to help answer the call when the television industry initially confronted the new challenge of producing "educational" programming. Over time, meeting this challenge, which was originally an inspired response to a social need, has turned into a full-fledged federal mandate. During the 1990s, Congress passed the Children's Television Act, which ultimately required networks to provide at least 3 hours a week of programming "specifically designed to serve the educational and informational needs of children." In other words, even more creators and distributors of programs designed purely for children's entertainment now had to offer educational content as well. The television industry, over a 20-year period, thus found itself faced with a complex set of problems. A significant portion of the programming produced for children now had to integrate social and cognitive developmental learning into its shows. And it had to attend to the bottom line, continuing to succeed financially and commercially. The industry "had" to do this for two reasons: The market increasingly expected and demanded it, and now the law required it. Simply put, over a relatively short period, many television executives and producers found themselves transformed, by a variety of factors, into educators—and the role of research as a form of help had become integral to this process. Once so many television executives found themselves transformed by federal mandate into educators, the need for outside research support became even greater.

## ***Research: When Is It Used?***

Essentially, research can intervene at three main stages of educational program development: (a) the conceptual stage, (b) the formative stage, and (c) the evaluative stage.

### *The Conceptual Stage*

At the conceptual stage, before a show has even come into being, research can help to determine its potential appeal. It can test the manner in which children perceive and relate to the various characters; it can determine the effectiveness of plot narrative and of the show's setting. Research can identify whether this environment (character, story, and setting) is "ripe" as a fertile ground for an educational agenda.

*The Formative Stage*

The majority of research in children's television, though, takes place at the formative stage, when a program is being made or when it already exists and future programming is being created. At this stage, research can work to best integrate the entertainment value of the show and the curriculum; it can work to keep a successful show successful; and it can help improve a show that is flagging. At the formative stage, market researchers can help test future scripts; they can explore ways to keep plots and story lines fresh; they can help refine characters' personalities; and they can serve as educational consultants, helping to integrate the necessary curricular materials into the body of the show and to accurately define how to best incorporate the curriculum within the show to maximize pedagogical impact.

*The Evaluative Stage*

Once a show has been aired, research can accurately evaluate the effect it has had on its target audience. At this stage, research can investigate how much of a particular set of skills or information children have actually learned from exposure to the program. Researchers have identified three levels of impact: (a) the effect of educational programming on children's perceptions and attitudes toward learning and domains of knowledge; (b) specific content acquisition; and (c) how a television show has affected children's behavior, in general, away from the television.

In addition to these three stages of television development, researchers can work with producers to develop marketing and communications strategies. In this capacity, market research helps "position" television programs within their competitive set. In other words, research findings can help producers sharpen and focus attention on the show's goals, such as teaching school-readiness skills. By assessing and analyzing feedback from children and parents, researchers can help advise producers on the appropriate commercial niche to aim for when advertising and packaging their show. In sum, applied researchers, working within an academic and market research orientation, have become an integral part of the process of creating educational television shows for children and are now involved in all phases of development. Research is an essential tool in ensuring that learning goals are optimally incorporated and that curriculum-based programs actually do what they are intended to do—support children's development, affect specific knowledge acquisition, and influence their attitudes in regard to learning.

***The Work of Research***

Before moving on to the illustrative case studies, we will briefly describe what the work of research actually entails. As a rule, the research process follows a series of seven principal stages: (a) clarifying the objectives of the study; (b) creating the research study design; (c) designing the appropriate research instruments; (d) fielding the study; (e) analyzing the research data; (f) interpreting the research findings in such a way as to offer actionable and usable recommendations, advice, and consulting; and (g) a plan of action.

*Clarification of Objectives*

At the first stage, the researcher will work closely with the producers and creators. This stage requires the researcher to understand exactly what a given study needs to do. Will the study, for example, help a television show teach and communicate cognitive skills and/or emphasize social and emotional development? Will it be advising producers on how to make their show more appealing? Or will the study be designed as an impact evaluation? Is the problem identifying the appropriate content level for the right age group? Or is the problem integrating content (e.g., science, history, etc.) within an entertaining narrative?

Researchers must identify the specific problem to be solved.

### *Creation of the Study Design*

Once the objectives are clear, the next phase is the creation of the study design. The researcher must determine what questions need to be pursued and to whom those questions should be posed. At this phase, several basic criteria must be established. First, the researcher must decide on the scope of the study, that is, how wide a net to cast. Do parents, children, or both need to be interviewed, and how many? Do a variety of geographic regions need to be investigated? Next comes the choice of basic methodology: Will this be a purely qualitative study? Or is a quantitative study also in order?

Once these parameters are in place, the researcher must consider which variables will be examined. The list of key variables typically taken into account includes gender, socioeconomic status, geographic area (both region of the country and type of community, i.e., suburban, urban, or rural), race, ethnicity, and a child's age or developmental level. It should be emphasized that this last variable—the age and developmental level of the target audience—has increasingly become the most critical in educational television research. Many years ago, one could create a children's show with a target audience ranging from 2 to 12 years of age, but such a broad market is now rarely possible. The industry now creates programming aimed at increasingly restricted age ranges, with increasingly specific curriculum. We now see programming designed for preschoolers (ages 2-5), school-agers (ages 6-9), and "tweenagers" (ages 10-12).

### *Designing the Appropriate Research Instruments and Fielding the Study*

After the scope, methodology, and variables of a study have been established, the next two stages are the design and fielding of the study. At these stages, researchers decide, for example, which of the portfolio of qualitative techniques will best serve their needs. They will prepare the lists of questions for ethnographic or observational interviews (in homes or schools) or the discussion guidelines for focus group interviews (in schools or market research facilities). To field the study, they will need to know whether special materials must be sent to respondents in advance (e.g., videocassettes for examination and/or television "viewing diaries" for parents and children to record their behaviors and reactions to specific programs or general television viewing prior to the interview) and whether such materials need to be brought to the actual interviews.

Naturally, such decisions depend on the stated objectives of the study. For example, if the goal is to understand the appeal of a television show still in development, researchers might send videos of a pilot episode to children for advance viewing or bring the videos along to interviews. At a concept stage, children might be asked to look at "flat art," or storyboards, representing the show's future characters and settings. To understand the appeal of existing, popular shows, there may be no "forced" advance viewing at all. In other words, the objectives of the study always determine all subsequent research decisions—the methodology and the emphasis of the actual, final "advice." All of the above stem from the program needs.

Over the last decade, researchers have developed a portfolio of qualitative techniques to elicit information from children. These techniques are often used in combination so that no one data point is completely relied on. Children are notorious for their inability to answer direct questioning articulately, so other ways of eliciting their reactions are needed. The following is a fairly comprehensive list of the qualitative techniques used to interview children.

The classic portfolio of qualitative research techniques to use with children includes: (a) observation, (b) participant observation, (c) direct questioning, (d) indirect questioning, and (e) projective techniques.

It is assumed that the pros and cons of the research techniques of observation, participant observation, and direct questioning are obvious and intuitive to the reader. It is useful, however, to add some detailed explanation of the use of indirect and projective techniques. Taken from the material of ARC, the following is a description of the classic use of indirect and projective techniques (Tobin & Cohen, 1999):

### Portfolio of Indirect and Projective Techniques

One must not rely solely on a guideline of direct questions but, rather, employ a portfolio of research techniques to approach the subject matter at hand and to keep the children engaged in the research process.

#### *Retelling the Story*

Asking the child to retell the story is an indirect questioning technique. Direct questions requiring reflection and evaluation are generally not effective if used extensively; questions requiring the description of action are often more enjoyable and natural for children to answer, and yield rich results. It is natural for a child to retell his/her version of "What happened on that show." In retelling a story, children describe both the action and the characters in a way that makes their levels of enthusiasm and their preferences and prejudices obvious. In the same way, if information about a specific character is needed, children will respond more enthusiastically to "What did he/she do in that show?" than to "What is he/she like?"

#### *Alternative Approaches*

The structure of the research session should be fluid and flexible to allow the interviewer to follow the child's train of thought. In order to do this the interviewers must be able to think on their feet and be well informed concerning the research objectives and priorities. Having good listeners who can gently steer the children's storytelling allows them to get to the essence before the details: the salient points come naturally, and the majority of what is most important will emerge at the beginning of the research process. Timing is crucial, particularly with children under the age of eight, for whom there is rarely more than forty-five minutes of active engagement in the research process.

#### *Projective Techniques*

Children have to approach the materials in their own way. Information offered in open discussion is more valuable than that collected in the process of direct questioning. Projective questions can yield rich details by unlocking children's thinking. Projective techniques are derived from their origins in psychology. It is simply a presentation of stimuli onto which a child can "project" his/her thoughts, feelings, and opinions. The Rorschach is probably the most famous projective technique, but the use of projective techniques in applied research tends to be slightly less "pure." Simply put, the stimuli are not as opaque as in classic Rorschach but are as neutral. Perhaps the best (and seemingly most banal) example of a projective technique is the classic market research question—If X corporation were a person, what type of person would it be? Interestingly, such techniques do yield extremely important data. A good example of using projective questions to encourage further discussion of characters is by asking children to think of all of the characters that have been discussed and to select which one would be best to have around if you: had to walk by a bunch of bullies, needed help figuring out what to do after hurting a friend's feelings, were having trouble putting your new bike together, or if you just needed someone around when feeling sad. In this way, rich and valuable data on how the children view the basic nature of characters can be collected.

***Hands-on Projective Techniques***

A great projective technique for exploring children's perceptions of what they have viewed is to simply offer paper and colored pencils and ask them to "draw a picture about the show." Many children who have difficulty articulating their thoughts during group discussions "think" more fluidly while they draw and can enjoy telling you a story about their pictures. Looking for simple messages in which characters are grouped together, the activity in which they are engaged or a child's inclusion of him/herself in a drawing can yield pertinent information about children's perceptions of characters and how those characters interrelate. Additionally, the quiet drawing time can give the interviewer the opportunity to visit separately with the children.

***The Use of Manipulatives***

A simple conjoint analysis can be turned into a game for children. As an example, we use cards with illustrations of popular children's shows to stimulate discussion. The children are asked to pick their favorites. The illustrations of programs which are not of interest to the children are eliminated and then a game is played choosing favorites within pairings of the shows.

Other techniques include use of children's diaries and photo-journals before a scheduled interview or part of a longitudinal study. (pp. 13-20)

In general, researchers in children's television have increasingly relied on "semi-ethnographic" models. That is, they are conducting more and more field research in children's natural settings, at home or in school. Although focus groups in professional market research facilities are still widely used, semi-ethnographic designs often have several advantages over traditional focus group interviews. They lessen children's anxiety or stage fright, reduce the artificiality of the situation, and, potentially, may reveal more detailed information about how children react spontaneously to television within their usual peer or family groups.

*Analysis*

The fifth stage of any project is analysis. At this point, professional research skills play an especially crucial role. When the researcher meets with children to watch and discuss a television program, he or she will analyze data by interpreting the children's verbal response and their behavior while viewing, gauging their emotional reaction to the material during and after viewing the program, and interpreting their responses to projective techniques. A researcher will be watching the children closely, assessing their level of engagement with the program and determining their level of interest in and excitement about characters or story lines. Also important is whether, after the show, the children can recount what they saw or offer a number of facts learned specifically from the show.

Researchers also analyze whether children change their behavior after watching the show. How? Might they change patterns of behavior once away from the television set because of what they have seen? For example, might they demonstrate more intellectual curiosity or more interest in science?

*Interpreting the Research*

It is at the level of interpretive analysis that we encounter both the implicit challenges of market research and its close connection to the discipline of the social sciences. We confront a vast quantity of information, some obvious, some very subtle. How can we be sure that we correctly interpret the data we gather with children? When interpreting data, researchers must rely on their knowledge and experience as social scientists. Frequently, researchers are guided by anthropologist Clifford Geertz's concept of "thick description" (Geertz, 1973). Geertz reminds us that researchers, after extensive study, must finally make interpretive judgments. Often, researchers are best at making such judgments when they have multiple layers of data to work with. At a certain point, the researcher determines that these layers provide a "thick" enough base for conclusions.

#### *An Actionable Plan*

Finally, once the project has been fielded and the results analyzed, researchers must perform their role as consultants. That is, they must transform their findings into a comprehensible, strategic, and coherent "action plan" for the client, the television producer, and/or the marketer. And although the researcher is not technically part of the creative team, actionable plans may include suggestions for making a show more appealing or for better integrating educational materials into the narrative. At this stage, researchers might also recommend new marketing or communications strategies. In some cases, researchers might participate in the creation of entirely new entities such as the multihour educational environment "Ready to Learn" that research helped create for the Public Broadcasting Service in 1992 and is now commonplace in the television landscape.

## Illustrative Case Studies

Now that we have outlined the overarching process by which research involves itself with educational television, we will proceed to a series of case studies. Each of these examples represents work that illustrates a range of levels of research involvement, as well as a range of possible outcomes of such involvement. Within each case study, examples of representative methodologies will be detailed. Each case also represents proprietary research commissioned by the show's producers; more detailed findings are not available to the public.

### *CTW's Ghostwriter: A Formative Study Integrating Entertainment and Education*

The producers of the children's television program *Ghostwriter* began their work, in the early 1990s, with three ambitious goals: (a) to enhance and engender 8- to 12-year-olds' appreciation and enthusiasm for reading, writing, and literacy in general; (b) to teach specific literacy skills to children; and (c) to encourage children to be engaged in literacy behavior (e.g., reading, writing letters, etc.) away from the television program. The show's basic premise involved a group of urban children who find a mysterious friend, "Ghostwriter," who appears as a disembodied spirit who communicates only through written texts (e.g., on computer screens, on walls, etc.). By helping children decipher clues and plan strategies based on literacy skills, Ghostwriter enables them to solve mysteries that they encounter in their neighborhood.

Although research was conducted to assist the developers of *Ghostwriter* with all stages of program design, presentation, and evaluation, the present study will concentrate on the methodology and results of a video-placement study conducted to determine where and how to place the literacy moments in the program narrative (Cohen, Rosen, Hall, & Williams, 1992). To approximate the actual viewing environment, new individual episodes were provided by mail every week for 4 weeks to 135 households with second-, third-, or fourth-grade children. The children came from ethnically and economically diverse backgrounds and lived in three areas: San Francisco and Oakland, California; Hudson County and Newark, New Jersey; and Mobile, Alabama. Within 24 hours of receipt of the videos, the participating children, each of whom had viewed the pilot episode, were interviewed, at home, by a trained researcher.

The interviews began with broad, open-ended questions such as "What did you think of today's episode?" and then narrowed to more direct questions about particular narrative and literacy moments. Children were asked to talk spontaneously about the appeal, salience, and comprehensibility of the use of literacy in the shows, and researchers were able to examine the appeal and effectiveness of the narrative flow of particular literacy activities.

### *Key Finding: Literacy in the Plot Line*

Research for the study revealed that having literacy skills simply appended to the show's narrative was not an effective strategy, either for enhancing program appeal or for increasing learning. Children were uninterested in the importance of reading and writing when these skills did not form an integral part of the narrative and plot line. Specifically, research revealed that four critical factors have to be addressed for programming to increase learning, retention, and respect for literacy skills among children in this age group: Literacy activities must be explicitly required by the plot; they must have clear purposes (e.g., assisting a main character in solving a mystery); they must be connected with comprehensible concepts; and they must have high emotional stakes.

## ***Zoom: A Concept and Formative Study: Bridging Time, "Upping the Curriculum Ante," and Integrating New Technology***

In the 1970s, WGBH in Boston aired an extremely successful interactive television program for children. *Zoom* celebrated the creativity, intelligence, and imagination of its viewers and encouraged a hands-on, "minds-on" approach to all areas of learning. The show featured a consistent cast, which met in a studio "clubhouse" setting. Each episode revolved around the cast's responses to various inventive suggestions, questions, and projects sent in by viewers.

Twenty years later, WGBH decided to produce a new version of *Zoom* for a new generation of viewers. They sought research at this formative stage to determine which elements from the original show would still be successful with today's children and what new elements would be necessary to keep it fresh and relevant (Tobin & Cohen, 1997). In addition, in accordance with current requirements and trends, the program creators were also planning to incorporate more explicit educational programming, including science education segments.

Research for the study was explicitly designed to examine: (a) viewers' response to and identification with the cast, (b) viewers' interest in and response to specific activities used in the program, (c) the degree to which children were motivated to try activities at home and to contribute to the show by sending in their own ideas, (d) the effectiveness and appeal of pilot segments of explicit science education, and (e) the degree to which the program was perceived by viewers as "a comfortable place to belong" (a crucial component of the earlier program's success).

To achieve these objectives, qualitative interviews were conducted with approximately 170 children, ages 8 to 12 (with a racial balance and equal gender mix), in rural Maine and urban and suburban New York.

The children were interviewed at their schools in focus groups on two consecutive days. In addition to watching a pilot video and additional segments of the program, children participated in small-group interviews, during which they were asked to write to *Zoom* and to draw pictures of their impressions of the show.

The study revealed that the most appealing aspects of the show were those that successfully immersed the children in the content through a blending of "silly" and serious topics. Comprehension was high overall; the majority of children were able to articulate clearly what they had seen but also expressed the desire to participate more fully in the on-screen activities and to learn more about science in general. On the basis of these findings, program developers decided to incorporate e-mail correspondence and an interactive program-based website into *Zoom,* and the program continues to be highly successful.

### Sesame Street: *A Formative Study: Purely Cognitive*

An example of research focused primarily on cognitive content and pedagogical effectiveness is the following study conducted for *Sesame Street* (Gervey & Kim, 1998). This particular quantitative project was modeled on and closely resembles a classical experiment in developmental psychology. The objectives were to help *Sesame Street* enhance viewer recognition and retention of letter and number combinations, and to investigate whether variations in the grouping of letter and number segments would alter children's learning experience. Research also explored whether behavioral indications of viewing engagement (e.g., pointing at the screen, singing along, or imitating actions) acted as mediators in the learning process.

A sample of 187 ethnically diverse children was recruited from six child care centers in New York and Minnesota. The group consisted of equal numbers of boys and girls and equal numbers of children from low- and middle-income households. Each child viewed one of three variations of a single episode of *Sesame Street.* The variations involved the content and clustering of letter and number segments. Pre- and posttests were administered individually to determine changes in the children's recognition of a specific letter (D) and a specific number (14). Researchers observed the children's comments and behaviors while watching the episode.

This research provided *Sesame Street*'s producers with a quantitative-based "snapshot of learning" from exposure to a single episode of the show. Analysis of the data indicated that no correlation existed between degree of learning and observable behavior while viewing. Research findings were used to advise producers which clustering of letters and numbers was most successful in yielding the highest immediate recognition and retention for children.

### Arthur: *Formative Research: Maintaining Success, Understanding Parents and Children*

*Arthur* was already a highly successful show (with associated books, computer learning games, and merchandise) when its producers commissioned research to help identify the underlying "reasons" for the series' popularity and to inform the direction of future seasons (Tobin & Cohen, 1998).

The research design involved a month-long study with 127 public school children (grades K-2) and their parents in urban and suburban New York and in rural Northern California. The study included children who were current *Arthur* devotees, former viewers of the show, and occasional viewers, as well as the parents of all three groups. Children were interviewed in small-group discussions and observed on three separate occasions using a variety of qualitative approaches, including open discussion, direct questioning, and several different projective techniques. The first group was devoted to a discussion of the children's general viewing habits. Children were provided with two-episode videotapes of *Arthur* prior to each of the following interview sessions, during which small-group participants were asked to talk about their understanding of the episodes' plots, their responses to the different characters, and what they remembered from the show. A variety of projective techniques were used during each of these sessions.

Key program strengths identified by the research included the everyday appeal and perceived cultural diversity of the characters; the "normal" and reassuring presentation of children's anxieties and conflicts; humor; clarity of content; modeling of social skills; and the developmentally appropriate use of fantasy.

Using these findings, researchers were able to make several recommendations about how to maintain and increase *Arthur*'s success. These included maintaining the integrity of the ensemble cast, enriching the show's content through the characters' developmentally appropriate fantasy worlds, and introducing academic content via the personal interests of characters.

### *Networks and "Educational Programming Blocks": Noggin*

The final example demonstrates the role of research in the creation of an entire media environment. In 1995, research was conducted in the development of *New Kid City* (*NKC*), an interactive, multiplatform educational media service for children produced by the Children's Television Workshop, the renowned producers of *Sesame Street, The Electric Company,* and *Ghostwriter,* among many others.

CTW sought to create a new service that would present products and programming in several integrated media formats, offering subscribers a combination of a cable television "block" programming, an on-line service, software, club membership privileges, print materials, licensed products, and various promotional events, with plans ahead for movies, live shows, and theme parks. All of these services were to be united by a common educational philosophy (informed by both parents and caregivers) and a child-tested image and program design (Cohen, 1995).

The researchers' goals were to define a new educational approach by determining the current nature of children's lives; their attitudes toward different media (including books, magazines, video games, computers, etc.); their perceptions of existing branded television environments; and their perceptions and evaluations of potential key components and themes for the pilot network.

Research was conducted in three phases, over an 18-month period, and included a comprehensive qualitative and quantitative design that explored children's relationship to all media specifically and their lives in general. Findings were used to help create "pilot" concepts for such a service, and these pilot concepts were then created and tested. Simultaneously, Nickelodeon was considering launching its own full-service educational network and was engaged in research to assist them toward that end. Subsequently, CTW and Nickelodeon joined forces and launched Noggin, a cable television network and new media site dedicated exclusively to the use of quality, education-based material, initially using the library of both entities.

The issues confronting Noggin may well provide the "lens" for viewing the future of educational television. Noggin confronts the challenge of integrating education and entertainment, not only for a single program or series but for an entire television network and the expanded media world to come.

## Conclusion and Implications

Applied research is an integral component of the creation of educational, curriculum-based programming. Such programming exists, survives, and prospers in a highly competitive, market-driven environment. Applied research (consisting of market research) can also play a significant role in the success of noneducational entertainment products for children. Furthermore, curriculum-based programming has now been extended to "blocks of programming" and to entire networks. Therefore, the need to integrate legitimate educational goals with highly engaging and financially successful media products will only increase. As stated earlier, parents increasingly require it, children respond to it, and, for many, the law demands it. From an "insider's" perspective, a very interesting phenomenon has occurred: Researchers, over the past three decades, have become increasingly proficient and expert at meeting the needs of this important industry (i.e., they have become excellent providers of knowledge), and creators and producers have learned how to best use and benefit from this knowledge (i.e., how to be excellent consumers of research).

We do not believe that it is too extreme to say that this "marriage" has created a new research discipline over the last third of the twentieth century, and the application of educational television research to meeting children's needs—as technology creates unforeseen new media forms—is both exciting and limitless.

## References


Bryant, J., & Roskos-Ewoldson, D. (1999). *Media psychology.* Mahwah, NJ: Lawrence Erlbaum.

Cantor, J. (1998). *"Mommy, I'm scared!"* San Diego, CA: Harcourt Brace.

Clifford, B. K., Gunter, B., & McAleer, J. (1995). *Television and children.* Hillsdale, NJ: Lawrence Erlbaum.

Cohen, M. (1995). *Creating an educational children's network* [Report/presentation commissioned by Noggin]. New York: Noggin.

Cohen, M., Rosen, C., Hall, E., & Williams, M. (1992). *Ghostwriter: Formative research* [Report/presentation completed by Applied Research & Consulting and commissioned by the Children's Television Workshop]. New York: Children's Television Workshop.

Davies, M. M. (1997). *Fake, fact, and fantasy.* Mahwah, NJ: Lawrence Erlbaum.

Geertz, C. (1973). *The interpretation of cultures.* New York: Basic Books.

Gervey, B., & Kim, C. (1998). *Sesame Street: A formative study* [Study completed by Applied Research & Consulting and commissioned by the Children's Television Workshop]. New York: Children's Television Workshop.

Gunter, B., McAleer, J., & Clifford, B. (1991). *Children's views about television.* Aldershot, UK: Avebury.

Levin, D. E. (1998). *Remote control childhood?* Washington, DC: National Associates for the Education of Young Children.

McNeal, J. U. (1992). *Kids as customers.* New York: Lexington Books.

Montgomery, K. C. (1989). *Target: Prime time.* New York: Oxford University Press.

Palmer, E. L. (1988). *Television and America's children.* New York: Oxford University Press.

Palmer, E. L., & Dorr, A. (1980). *Children and the forces of television.* New York: Academic Press.

Pecora, N. O. (1998). *The business of children's entertainment.* New York: Guilford.

Schneider, J. (1999). *Developing educational media products: The Children's Television Workshop model* [Document]. New York: Children's Television Workshop.

Shirley, D. (1998). *ARC: A capabilities presentation* [ARC internal document]. New York: ARC.

Tobin, P., & Cohen, M. (1997). *ARC: Zoom: A formative study* [Report/presentation completed by Applied Research & Consulting and commissioned by WGBH]. Boston: WGBH.

Tobin, P., & Cohen, M. (1998). *ARC: Arthur: A formative study* [Report/presentation completed by Applied Research & Consulting and commissioned by WGBH]. Boston: WGBH.

Tobin, P., & Cohen, M. (1999). *ARC: Conducting children's research.* ARC seminar presentation given at KidPower Orlando, Paris, London, and Toronto.

Valkenburg, P. M. (1995). *The impact of television on children's imagination.* The Netherlands: Center for Child and Media Services.

Van Eura, J. (1998). *Television and child development.* Mahwah, NJ: Lawrence Erlbaum.

Von Feilitzen, C., & Carlsson, U. (1999). *Children and media.* Göteborg, Sweden: UNESCO International Clearinghouse on Children and Violence on the Screen, Nordicom, Göteborg University.

Washington, V., & Andreas, J. D. (1998). *Children 2010.* Washington, DC: Children of 2010.

Zillmann, D., Bryant, J., & Huston, A. C. (1994). *Media, children, and the family.* Hillsdale, NJ: Lawrence Erlbaum.

# PART III

## Policy Issues and Advocacy

### Preliminary Comments From the Editors

Because the electronic media enter the home and are susceptible to extensive viewing by the youngest children, concerns among parents, child advocates, and even public officials have been prominent for 40 years. Understanding children and the media therefore calls for an examination of how government agencies, industry, and new emergent advocacy groups have combined efforts to cope with the hazards so vividly outlined in Part I in the subsections Fears, Aggression, and Sexual Attitudes, and Personality, Social Attitudes, and Health. The chapters in Part III also point to ways we can foster the potential benefits of these media, as suggested in Part I in the Cognitive Functions and School-Readiness Skills section.

When we and other early workers in television research began our efforts more than 30 years ago, we felt that we were working in relative isolation. Our first goals were to establish in reasonably scientific fashion what the evidence was for positive or negative television effects. Parent advocacy groups such as Action for Children's Television took a strong role even before the great bulk of the data were in. By the early 1990s, we all began to see results in our efforts as Congress passed new legislation and as public debate about children and television entered political campaigns. Even the president of the United States referred to television and children in his State of the Union Address. We were pleased to be able to prepare a report to Congress for the Corporation for Public Broadcasting outlining the concept of a Ready to Learn line-up of preschool children's shows. This plan has been implemented by the Public Broadcasting Network (see Chapter 26).

We turn first in this part of our handbook to Chapter 32 by Dale Kunkel and Brian Wilcox on the legal and governmental approaches to children's media. These authors lay out the legislative steps and Federal Communications Commission rulings that have reshaped national policy in the last decade. They also call attention to relevant research studies that support or question government policy decisions and actions. Of special importance for our handbook is the attention they pay to the cognitive and emotional developmental levels of the children for whom policy actions are taken.

Chapter 33 by Karen Hill-Scott provides a useful overview of how the television industry responded to the federal policy actions of the 1990s. We learn not only about network and cable companies' in-house "standards and practices" responses but also about research and programming efforts that are under way.

Chapter 34 by Bradley Greenberg and Lynn Rampoldi-Hnilo uses the new age-based and content-based rating systems now applied to programming as a kind of case study. Can parents use these systems, and with what effect? Useful research in this area has already appeared, and the authors examine the strengths, limitations, and possible modifications necessary if parents are to "take back" their home leadership roles with respect to what their children watch. The issue of parent empowerment, as well as child safety and family security, is carried even further in Chapter 35 by Kathryn Montgomery, who focuses on the computer use spreading rapidly to millions of American homes. What impact on children can already be discerned from their use of the highly commercialized Internet? What safeguards against child exploitation are necessary, and what forms of advocacy must come into play to avoid the hazards of cyberspace?

In Chapter 36, Amy Jordan moves a step back from public policy and regulation to looking within the home. What can parents do to ensure their children's benign use of television and the Internet? What steps must one take within the home to control media reliance by children, and what role can industry or education play to help them along? Marjorie J. Hogan carries this emphasis on parents or other caregiving adults further in Chapter 37. She draws on research and case material to provide a series of practical guidelines to adults for how to monitor, coview, discuss, and limit children's television viewing or other media use. She goes even further in pointing out ways that parents can make their beliefs known to television stations and appropriate policy makers through advocacy groups.

Still another form of empowerment of the home viewer is through using a variety of educational resources to make media literacy and critical viewing a feature of both child and adult education. In Chapter 38, James A. Brown defines the concept of media literacy, reviews the available research literature, and outlines plans for incorporating critical analyses of one's TV viewing or computer use into the general educational curriculum.

We would like to think that the vast review of the research literature and social issues raised in this volume can yield some specific practical outcomes. Our closing Chapter 39, written by Laurie Trotta, provides a history and clearly organized categorization of advocacy efforts and groups in the field of children and the media. She leads us step by step to the present and future possibilities of child advocacy in the electronic world. Her chapter ends with an impressive outline that encompasses 33 media advocacy groups and their philosophies. If one takes the findings reported in this handbook seriously, the list may offer many readers an opportunity to move from indignation or hope toward action.

CHAPTER 32

# Children and Media Policy

DALE KUNKEL
University of California, Santa Barbara

BRIAN WILCOX
University of Nebraska

The media environment encountered by American children has changed dramatically throughout the twentieth century. At the outset, little besides print was available to supplement a child's interpersonal communication with others. Media options began to grow with the development of radio (Cantril & Allport, 1935) and motion pictures (Jowett, Jarvie, & Fuller, 1996), both of which were popularized in the early 1900s. Arguably the most profound addition was the advent of broadcast television, which generated marked changes in children's patterns of media use in the 1950s (Schramm, Lyle, & Parker, 1961). More recently, the significant increase in channel capacity brought by cable television and the interactive nature of computer networking accomplished via the Internet have created a revolution in children's access to media content, if not their actual media use habits (Roberts, Foehr, Rideout, & Brodie, 1999; Stanger & Gridina, 1999).

With the arrival of each succeeding technology, those responsible for protecting the welfare of children have demonstrated a consistent and highly acute interest in protecting youth from media harm (Wartella & Reeves, 1985). Concerns center mostly on particular types of content that may exert harmful influence on children. Yet interestingly, the policies that have emerged in response to these concerns are not grounded solely in terms of media content; rather, much of the regulatory framework in the realm of children and media policy is shaped by the nature of each medium's delivery mechanism.

## The Importance of Media Delivery Systems

For a parent or child viewer who has turned on a video screen to obtain some particular content such as a half-hour "television" program, it probably matters little whether the mechanism delivering it is a broadcast station, a cable programming service, or an Internet site. But, in fact, the delivery mechanism is a key element in determining the applicable regulatory framework.

Broadcast television encompasses stations that transmit their signal over the air, a technology that uses the publicly owned airwaves and hence requires a license granted by the Federal Communications Commission (FCC). The FCC is the independent regulatory body created by Congress in 1934 that is charged with the responsibility of administering the licensing process. Notwithstanding modest administrative fees, broadcast licenses are granted by the FCC free of charge, although not free of burden. Those accepting licenses must agree to serve the public interest, convenience, and necessity in return for receiving their license. The commission has the power to create rules and regulations that stipulate specific public interest obligations for broadcast licensees.

In contrast, cable and other nonbroadcast technologies are not bound by any obligation to serve the public interest because they do not use the broadcast airwaves to distribute their content. Consequently, cable tends to be relatively free from governmental regulation of program content. At one level, this makes little sense. If, for example, there is concern about the harmful effects of televised violence, it should not matter whether the programming is delivered by broadcast or cable television because the material's influence on a child will not vary according to how the signal reaches the screen. Yet at another level, such as the legal issues related to First Amendment protections, technological factors such as the scarcity of the broadcast media (i.e., it is a finite resource, only one user can occupy a given frequency at a time, and there are more who wish to use this resource than can be accommodated) have made differential regulation of the mass media a well-established political reality.

The debate over children's media policy has been carried out largely in the context of broadcast regulatory battles, because broadcast television has been the principal medium attracting children's attention over the last 50 years. In this chapter, we devote the bulk of our analysis to three primary areas of children's television policy that have each received significant attention over those years: (a) policies intended to protect children from adverse effects of exposure to television content, (b) policies designed to assure the adequacy of television's service to children, and (c) policies designed to protect children from unfair advertising practices. After reviewing the key developments in each of these areas, we then shift our focus to the regulatory challenges posed by new media such as the Internet. Finally, we consider the implications of the increasing trend toward media convergence for shaping policy to protect children's interests in the future.

## Protecting Children From Harmful Content

Throughout virtually the entire twentieth century, politicians and the public have expressed concern about the possible harm to children's moral development that might occur from a broad range of media, including books, comics, radio, television, and video games. No issues, however, have drawn more consistent public and political scrutiny than those of media violence and indecency, the two topics on which we focus in this section.

### *Regulation of Televised Violence*

Concern with the effects of violent programming on children dates to the earliest years of television. Congressional interest in the topic first surfaced during a 1954 hearing by the Senate Subcommittee on Juvenile Delinquency (U.S. Senate, 1956), long before any empirical evidence on the subject was available to inform policy makers. Across the subsequent decades, Congress continued to devote significant attention to television violence, albeit without ever pursuing any formal regulation until the 1990s (Cooper, 1996).

At several points over the years, social science research examining the effect of violent portrayals has played an important role in the debate about this topic. In the late 1960s, Congress directed the U.S. surgeon general to conduct a major program of research on the effects of television violence. The surgeon general's report (Surgeon General's Scientific Advisory Committee on Television and Social Behavior, 1972) drew clear connections between exposure to violence and subsequent aggressive behavior, yet it presented many caveats involving mediating variables. The complexity of the qualifications led to misunderstanding by the press and the public, with some stories even reporting that the surgeon general's report had absolved the TV industry of any responsibility for contributing to real-world violence and aggression (Cater & Strickland, 1975).

Following the release of this report, numerous congressional hearings were conducted, and the controversy they generated led to a tremendous surge in research on the effects of media violence. New hearings were held from time to time throughout the 1970s, as evidence mounted documenting the contribution of viewing violent portrayals to children's subsequent aggressive behavior. Although no formal legislation on the topic was seriously considered by Congress during this period, the hearings nonetheless generated some impact. Murray (1980) found a reduction in the amount of violence presented during prime-time network programming in the years immediately following each series of major hearings on the topic, and in 1975 the television industry adopted a self-regulatory policy known as the "family hour," which pushed programs containing violence and other sensitive material later into the evening, leaving the first hour of prime time (8:00-9:00 P.M. for most of the country) devoted solely to content judged appropriate for family viewing (Cowan, 1979). The family-hour policy proved short-lived, however, as the courts soon judged it to be unconstitutional because of strong governmental pressure exerted on the industry to take such action.

By the early 1980s, research in the area had grown so significantly that the National Institute of Mental Health (NIMH) undertook a major new review of the overall accumulated evidence (Pearl, Bouthilet, & Lazar, 1982). With a stronger base of evidence on which to draw, the NIMH report concluded much more unequivocally than had the surgeon general that viewing televised violence was causally related to children's aggressive attitudes and behaviors, as well as being a contributor to desensitization and fear. This report might have prompted stronger response from policy makers had it not been issued at exactly the time that a new regulatory philosophy was sweeping the country, that of reliance on the marketplace rather than governmental rules and regulations to ensure that the public interest was served (Fowler & Brenner, 1982). Consequently, attention to the topic of televised violence waned for several years until Senator Paul Simon decided to champion it as an important cause in the late 1980s.

Convinced by the evidence that violence portrayals led to harmful influence on many children yet uncomfortable with the prospect of any governmental censorship of program content, Simon sought an alternative path. He called on the television industry to exercise self-restraint and to show violence more responsibly; that is, to not simply reduce the amount but to avoid glamorized and sanitized violence, which research has shown to increase the risk of harmful effects. At the same time, to avoid idle promises, Simon insisted that some independent monitoring be conducted to hold the industry accountable. Simon sponsored legislation adopted by Congress in 1990 granting the industry an antitrust exemption allowing all parties to meet jointly for the purpose of discussing how to reduce violence on television. Technically speaking, the legislation required nothing of the industry; rather, it simply created the opportunity for programmers to respond to the problem, should they choose to do so, without fear of antitrust litigation, which they had often argued prohibited such action in the past.

For nearly 3 years, the industry declined to take any action in response to Senator Simon's initiative. During that same period, the level of consensus in the scientific community about the effects of televised violence began to consolidate in important ways. In the early 1990s, such organizations as the American Medical Association (1996), the American Psychological Association (1993), the Centers for Disease Control (1991), and the National Academy of Sciences (Reiss & Roth, 1993) all issued reports drawing the same strong conclusion: Viewing televised violence poses a risk of harmful effects on children. Public opinion followed right in step with these conclusions, with a strong majority holding the view that media violence is harmful to children and that there is too much violence on television (Guttman, 1994; Times Mirror Center for People and the Press, 1993; Welkos, 1995).

Sensing a shift in the political winds, in 1993-1994, the industry finally agreed to a formal response to Simon's initiative, pledging both to treat violence more responsibly in programs and to commission independent academic studies to hold them accountable for their commitment (National Television Violence Study, 1997, 1998a, 1998b; UCLA Center for Communication Policy, 1995, 1996, 1998). To the industry's surprise, these actions ultimately proved to be "too little, too late" to avoid further government intervention.

In a political context shaped by strong scientific consensus about the harms of violent portrayals, and perhaps even stronger public opinion against media violence, U.S. Representative Edward Markey began to gain support for his V-chip legislative proposal. The technology of the V-chip is relatively simple. It is an electronic filtering device that parents can use to block the reception of sensitive or potentially harmful programming they do not want their children to see, presuming that television sets are equipped with V-chip filters and that programs are categorized in some fashion that can facilitate blocking decisions.

When President Clinton endorsed the V-chip in his 1996 State of the Union Address, it was only a matter of weeks until Congress adopted Markey's legislative proposal, adding it as an amendment to the omnibus Telecommunications Act of 1996. Under the law, the television industry was given 1 year to devise its own system of categorizing programs for violence and other sensitive material (including sex and offensive language) and to then submit this system to the FCC for its approval. If the television industry failed to act, or if its system was not deemed "acceptable," then the FCC would have been required to appoint an advisory committee to design a model V-chip rating system. Oddly enough, the industry would not have been bound to actually employ the system designed by the FCC or, for that matter, any system at all. The only firm requirement in the law was that all television sets sold in the United States must be equipped with a V-chip device that would facilitate program-blocking capabilities.

Clearly, this law is strongly coercive, although technically it is true that the industry's decision to employ V-chip ratings was a voluntary one. Since the ratings are an industry-wide effort, they have been jointly designed and implemented by an ad hoc group involving three key organizations: the National Association of Broadcasters (NAB), the National Cable Television Association (NCTA), and the Motion Picture Association of America (MPAA).

Once the V-chip law had passed, the television industry faced the task of devising a system of ratings to categorize programs for potential blocking by parents. Although academic experts strongly recommended and parents strongly preferred a system of content-based ratings, the industry employed a set of age-based advisory categories for use with the V-chip blocking technology (Cantor, 1998; Gruenwald, 1997). A major controversy ensued about the adequacy of the program rating categories, and the debate was clearly influenced by the National Television Violence Study (NTVS), which, ironically, had been commissioned by the industry. NTVS research conducted at the University of Wisconsin examining children's reactions to various types of program ratings made clear that content labels (e.g., contains violent content) did not increase children's interest in programs, but age-based advisories (e.g., parental discretion advised for children under a certain age) did (Cantor & Harrison, 1997). Thus, the age-based ratings pose the risk of a boomerang effect by attracting children's attention to the very programs the rating system indicates pose some cause for concern.

This evidence, along with complaints from the child advocacy community that age-based ratings simply failed to offer adequate information for parents, led to strong criticism of the age-based ratings approach. Frequent front-page coverage was devoted to the story in most newspapers, and a congressional hearing soon served to focus the debate (U.S. Senate, 1997). Shortly thereafter, within a matter of months after first being unveiled, the industry agreed to amend the V-chip rating framework to incorporate content-specific categories that complement the age-based advisory labels (Farhi, 1997).

Passage of the V-chip legislation represents the first substantive policy adopted by the government to address the issue of media violence. It may not be the last. A recent study of the television industry's implementation of the rating system suggests that, although the age-based ratings generally reflect the content of the shows to which they are applied, the content descriptors are seriously underutilized (Kunkel et al., 1998). Most programs containing violence, for example, do not receive a "V" designation (i.e., the violence content descriptor), and this is especially true for children's programming. It is possible that the industry is reticent to label programming as violent out of fear of the economic harm that could occur from reducing the audience size (Hamilton, 1998).

Regardless of the reason underlying the pattern, this "underrating" of programs raises concern that parents may think they have filtered out all violent material by blocking programs rated with a "V" when in fact it appears that most programs containing violence do not receive the proper designation. Given that the utility of the V-chip policy is predicated on the accuracy and completeness of the rating information provided to parents, this situation potentially undermines the value of the policy. If left unaddressed, it may lead policy makers to consider further action in this area.

### *Regulating Exposure to Indecent Material*

The government has traditionally played a far more active role in the regulation of indecent material than of violence, although most of the involvement in this realm has stemmed from actions by the FCC rather than Congress. Indecency is defined by the FCC as "language or material that depicts or describes, in terms patently offensive as measured by contemporary community standards for the broadcast medium, sexual or excretory activities or organs" (Carter, Franklin, & Wright, 1999, p. 246). In other words, although indecency consists of words or pictures that are strongly offensive, not just any offensive material can qualify as indecent; to be defined as such, it is essential that the material be associated with sexual and/or excretory elements. This means, for example, that a highly graphic portrayal of violence that most people would judge as offensive could not be deemed indecent under current law.

In one of the FCC's most visible enforcement actions ever, in the 1970s, the agency took steps against a station for airing comedian George Carlin's "Filthy Words" skit, which ironically enough was a tirade against the FCC's indecency policy. In the skit, Carlin utters "the seven words you can't say on the broadcast airwaves" to a chorus of uncontrolled laughter from a live audience. When the FCC attempted to punish the station involved in airing the skit, the broadcaster appealed on First Amendment grounds, claiming that indecency restrictions were unconstitutional.

In a landmark ruling, the Supreme Court upheld the right of the FCC to prohibit indecent material during times of day when children are likely to be in the audience (*FCC v. Pacifica Foundation,* 1978). In reaching its decision, the Court had to strike a balance between (a) the First Amendment rights of broadcasters and listeners in general who wished to have access to indecent content and (b) the rights of parents who wished to protect their children from exposure to material they deemed inappropriate or potentially harmful. The Court considered the protection of children to be a compelling governmental interest. Because the FCC enforced its indecency restriction only from 6:00 A.M. to 10:00 P.M., the time when children were judged most likely to be in the audience, the policy met the Supreme Court's "least restrictive means" test and was therefore considered constitutional. Subsequent court rulings have made clear that a complete 24-hour ban on indecency, which was attempted by Congress in the early 1990s, is unconstitutional because it is not narrowly tailored and hence fails the least restrictive means test (*Action for Children's Television v. FCC,* 1991). After returning to the "safe harbor" approach, which restricts indecent material to the hours between 10:00 P.M. and 6:00 A.M., the FCC's indecency policy has consistently been judged constitutional by the courts.

Contrasting the differing fortunes of efforts to regulate indecent and violent television content, one is struck by the substantial restrictions on indecency and the more laissez faire approach to regulating violence. The contrast is particularly ironic if one bears in mind the empirical research on the effects of exposure to indecent versus violent material. As noted above, there is a substantial body of research indicating that television violence contributes significantly to the aggressive attitudes and behaviors of many children and adolescents. In contrast, there is no comparable body of data to support serious concern about any harmful effects of children's exposure to indecent content. Even though research in the area may be difficult because of ethical concerns, some researchers have applied relevant theory to argue against the expectation of any substantial effects from children's exposure to such material. Donnerstein, Wilson, and Linz (1992) assert that there is "no reason to conclude any risk of harm should be associated with [children's] exposure to broadcast indecency" (p. 116). Interestingly, this absence of empirical validation has not discouraged the courts from upholding the constitutionality of the government's restriction on indecency.

The fact that the general public finds greater offense in displays of indecency in the media than they do in depictions of violence is quite likely an important factor underlying the different approaches to policy in these two areas. Although no fundamental policy changes seem likely in either of these realms in the immediate future, it is noteworthy that scholars have begun to mine this terrain in search of new perspectives. Law professor Kevin Saunders (1996) has begun to argue that some forms of violence might be appropriately treated in the same way as indecency, while Harvard philosopher Sisella Bok (1998) has questioned why the First Amendment should prevail over other competing rights when conflict occurs. These viewpoints challenge conventional thinking grounded in the policies of the past and may ultimately yield new and unique policy perspectives for the future in a changing media environment.

## Adequacy of Television's Service to Children

Despite the fact that the media environment today offers more choices than at any point in the past, children below age 12 still average about 3 hours per day watching television; in contrast, no other single medium (e.g., books, periodicals, computers, videotapes, video games) exceeds an hour of use per day on average (Roberts et al., 1999; Stanger & Gridina, 1999). In other words, although children today have an unprecedented range of available media options, they still tend to spend more time with television than with any other type of media, much the same as their predecessors have over the past several generations. These data underscore the ongoing importance of ensuring that television delivers an adequate level of service to the child audience.

Age-related differences in children's information-processing skills govern all children's ability to make sense of any media content. Just as one would not expect all children between ages 2 and 12 to read equally well from the same book, one should not expect children across that entire age range to comprehend equally well a given television program. Younger children have been shown to perform much less well than older children in terms of understanding relations among scenes or comprehending motives and intentions of characters in typical prime-time entertainment programming (Collins, 1983; Doubleday & Droege, 1993). When children cannot comprehend the content because of its abstractness or complexity, their attention quickly diminishes (Anderson & Lorch, 1983; Rice, Huston, & Wright, 1982). In such cases, the programming would hold little if any value for child viewers. In contrast, television content that is specifically designed for children, taking into account their special needs and cognitive capabilities, can be highly effective in attracting children's attention, conveying the intended message, and accomplishing learning outcomes, as well as entertaining the child audience (Huston & Wright, 1991; Huston et al., 1992).

Broadcast stations, which operate on the publicly owned airwaves and are licensed to serve the public interest, were criticized in the early 1970s for failing to provide an adequate amount of educational programming of value to children (Hendershot, 1998; Watkins, 1988). In response, the FCC served notice that it expected the television industry to do a better job of providing educational children's programs: "Even though we are not adopting rules . . . we wish to emphasize that we do expect stations to make a meaningful effort in this area" (FCC, 1974, p. 39397).

This development is noteworthy because it established the precedent that providing service to children was an essential part of each station's public interest obligation. Yet at each key decision point in the ruling that first set this precedent, the FCC chose to eschew any formal requirements, instead relying on vague standards that called for stations to make "meaningful efforts" to provide a "reasonable amount" of educational children's programming (FCC, 1974, p. 39398). The commission hoped that this approach would accomplish the desired improvements without the need for formal regulation. In fact, there is strong consensus that the 1974 policy statement generated little response from the broadcast industry (Cole & Oettinger, 1978; FCC, 1979; Turow, 1981). The lack of any improvement in the television industry's efforts at children's programming, however, soon proved to be a moot point.

### *Deregulation of Children's Programming Policies*

In the 1980s, consistent with the prevailing trend toward governmental deregulation (Horwitz, 1989), the FCC moved in the opposite direction, adopting a policy directive that essentially relieved most stations from *any* obligation to serve the child audience (FCC, 1984a). Casting aside long-standing complaints of marketplace failure in the delivery of educational programming, the commission redefined the relevant "marketplace." That is, the FCC ruled that the needs of children could be served by a wide range of program services, including cable, satellite, videocassettes, and public television, as well as the commercial broadcast media. In determining the appropriate level of service for children, a broadcaster was allowed to take into account "the alternative program services offered to children in the relevant [community]" (FCC, 1984a, p. 1704). Thus, in most cases when alternatives were available, a broadcaster would have no responsibility to serve children under this policy. Their needs were to be met through the alternative sources available in the marketplace.

This decision to deregulate the FCC's children's programming policies led to some palpable changes in broadcast practices. Even the relatively small number of educational programs that had been provided previously on commercial television essentially disappeared from the airwaves. One study from Kansas (Kerkman, Kunkel, Huston, Wright, & Pinon, 1990) documented a significant decline in children's educational programming shortly after the FCC signaled its intention to deregulate. Another from Illinois (Wartella, Heintz, Aidman, & Mazzarella, 1990) reported that commercial broadcasters failed to provide a single educational program for children during a sample week in 1987. A third study (Waterman & Grant, 1987) produced the same finding in the much larger Los Angeles market. With the government no longer interested in broadcasters' efforts for children, educational programming clearly waned.

These developments triggered significant criticism of the FCC, with one national newsmagazine terming the situation a "national disgrace" (Waters, 1983). One of the key aspects of the criticism was the FCC's failure to consider the equity of access to nonbroadcast technologies, which typically require some form of direct payment to receive and which many families simply cannot afford. It soon became apparent that the new policy reflected a socioeconomic bias. Though children from middle- and upper-class families who could afford to pay the cost of alternative sources of children's programming (e.g., cable television, videocassette recorders and tapes) might be well served by the new policy framework, the needs of children from lower-class families were unlikely to be served at all.

To underscore this point, at a congressional hearing on children's television policy, Kunkel (1989) offered the following analogy:

> The same logic that the FCC employed in deregulating children's television could be applied, for example, in Anaheim, California to determine that public parks are no longer necessary because Disneyland is available nearby. Since children's needs for open space and recreation can be met by this alternative, the public interest would no longer require that parks be maintained. Of course, the fundamental flaw in this logic is that Disneyland charges a price for admission, a price that not all can afford. For many in the lower socio-economic strata who lack the ability to pay that price, their needs would go unserved without public parks. (p. 76)

### *Congress Approves the Children's Television Act*

Once it became clear that the FCC had abandoned any effort to regulate in this area, legislators began to pursue their own course of action. A complex and protracted political debate spanning several years ensued (Kunkel, 1991). The final product of this debate was the Children's Television Act (CTA) of 1990, a rare piece of legislation amending the Communications Act and establishing a new statutory framework for children's television policy. More specifically, the act stipulates that

> The Commission shall, in its review of any application for renewal of a television broadcast license, consider the extent to which the licensee has served the educational and informational needs of children

> through the licensee's overall programming, including programming specifically designed to serve such needs. (P.L. 101-437, Section 103)

This new law represented a landmark victory for child advocates. Yet ironically, Congress left the implementation of the law directly in the hands of the FCC, the agency that had been consistently avoiding children's television regulation throughout the past several decades. Though the CTA established a broad conceptual framework mandating that each broadcaster provide educational programming for children as part of its public interest obligation, the FCC nonetheless had to determine what programming would qualify as "educational," when it must be shown, and how much would be enough to adequately fulfill the responsibility.

As the FCC began the task of creating specific rules to implement the CTA, it was dominated by appointees of President George Bush, who shared President Ronald Reagan's ideological aversion to governmental regulation. Thus, it is hardly surprising that the FCC initially chose to allow the broadcast industry substantial discretion to determine how to fulfill the children's programming obligation when the new law was first implemented.

The FCC adopted what it called a flexible definition of educational programming, specifying it as content "that furthers the positive development of the child in any respect, including the child's cognitive/intellectual or social/emotional needs" (FCC, 1991, p. 2114). No limitations were placed on when the programming must be aired, and no guidance was provided to specify how much educational content each station was expected to provide.

The industry's initial response to the new policy framework was largely one of indifference. Rather than adding any new educational programs to fulfill the CTA's requirements, most stations simply listed on their FCC reporting forms whatever children's shows they aired as being "educational programs." Although this practice did not come to public light until several years later, many stations made frivolous claims to the FCC about the educational value of their children's shows (Center for Media Education, 1992; Kunkel & Canepa, 1994; Kunkel & Goette, 1997). Programs such as *The Flintstones* were claimed to teach important history lessons, while *The Jetsons* was said to teach about new technologies. Other shows with no apparent educational orientation, such as *Biker Mice From Mars, Teenage Mutant Ninja Turtles,* and *Yogi Bear,* were among the programs claimed by stations as fulfilling their CTA responsibilities.

Once President Clinton took office in 1993, the FCC began to pursue more active enforcement of the Children's Television Act (Hundt & Kornbluh, 1995). By 1996, the FCC adopted a much more stringent set of rules for interpreting and applying the CTA's obligations. These new rules included a minimum standard of 3 hours per week for each station's educational programming for children,[1] a more stringent definition of what content qualifies as educational, and a mandate that all educational shows be clearly labeled as such at the time they are broadcast (FCC, 1996).

Under this new policy framework, which reflects the current state of the law, educational programs must fulfill all of the following criteria: (a) The program has education as a significant purpose; (b) the educational purpose and target audience are specified in writing in the station's children's programming report, which is available for public inspection; (c) the program is regularly scheduled; (d) the program is aired between 6:00 A.M. and 11:00 P.M.; (e) the program is of substantial length (either 15 or 30 minutes); and (f) the program is identified as children's educational content at the time it is aired.

This final point is a unique development. While on the surface it may help parents to more readily identify worthwhile shows for their children to view, the requirement to publicly identify educational programs also discourages stations from making exaggerated claims of educational value, as they had done for several years before this tactic was revealed by research. Most networks have responded by applying an "E/I" on-screen logo at the start of each program that contains educational or informational content directed to children, and some television guides now include this information in their program listings. Unfortunately, shortly after the E/I labels began to appear, the more widespread use of the new V-chip ratings largely overshadowed the E/I designation. A recent survey shows that few parents understand the meaning of the E/I rating (Stanger, 1997).

### *Recent Developments in Children's Educational Programming*

The FCC's new policy framework for implementing the Children's Television Act took effect in the fall of 1997. At the time this chapter was written, two television seasons (1997-1998 and 1998-1999) had transpired under the new rules. In contrast to the years immediately following the adoption of the Children's Television Act, which saw little more than creative relabeling of existing children's shows, the FCC's clamp-down on CTA enforcement seems to have generated some meaningful improvements in children's program content.

Over recent years, researchers from the Annenberg Public Policy Center of the University of Pennsylvania have conducted an annual assessment of children's programming (Jordan, 1996, 1998; Jordan & Woodard, 1997; Woodard, 1999). These reports are based on a rigorous examination of the overall children's television environment employing scientific content analysis techniques. Each year, a broad sample of children's shows are evaluated for overall quality on criteria such as the following: (a) Does the program contain a meaningful theme or lesson? (b) Is the theme or lesson integrated throughout the program, not merely "tagged on"? (c) Does the program avoid malicious or antisocial actions? (d) Is the program enriching or beneficial for a child? In addition, programs claimed as fulfilling the CTA obligations are evaluated for their educational value on such dimensions as (a) lesson clarity, (b) lesson salience, (c) lesson involvement, and (d) lesson applicability.

The Annenberg reports identify several positive developments under the new policy framework in both the overall quality of children's programming and the educational value of those shows offered to fulfill the Children's Television Act obligations. First of all, the proportion of E/I-labeled programs that the Annenberg research identifies as "highly educational" has jumped from 29% in 1998 to 49% in 1999. In other words, roughly half of the shows aired in response to the regulatory requirements are now judged by independent observers as exemplary, a far cry from the initial pattern of exaggerated claims that *The Flintstones* or *The Jetsons* are educational.

The Annenberg data also indicate that this influx of new, highly educational programs seems to be squeezing off the air many of the shows ranked lowest in overall quality. The proportion of children's programs categorized as low on overall quality diminished from 36% in 1998 to 26% in 1999, and this shift occurred while the number of children's programs available on television increased 12% overall. Thus, not only is the overall children's television environment improving in terms of quality, but it is also growing in size.

The indication today is that children's programming in the United States is both expanding and improving, although the expansion is found primarily on cable program channels such as Nickelodeon and Disney, along with a host of other new competitors. Indeed, according to the most recent Annenberg survey (Woodard, 1999), cable networks (55%) now predominate over broadcast channels (45%) in the overall amount of children's programs provided. As noted previously, concern about the equity of access to cable television suggests that policy makers' primary focus is best directed to the delivery of broadcast service.

Yet technological changes that hover on the horizon may soon alter this priority, a topic we will consider subsequently in this chapter.

## Fairness of Television Advertising to Children

The fundamental policy concerns in the realm of television advertising to children revolve around issues of fairness. Are young children fair targets for advertisers? Is it fair to allow unrestricted advertising to children, or are some limits appropriate? Does fairness require special safeguards to constrain certain types of advertising strategies directed to children? While the answers to these questions require value judgments that can only be reached as part of the political process of constructing public policy, social science research provides an abundance of evidence to help inform those who must answer these questions.

The degree to which children are able to recognize and defend against televised commercial persuasion has been the focus of extensive research efforts since the early 1970s. Two key skills or abilities are required for a child viewer to process commercial content in mature fashion. First, the child must be able to discriminate at a perceptual level between program and commercial matter, and second, the child must be able to recognize the persuasive intent that necessarily underlies all television advertising. Without the ability to recognize persuasive intent, a young child cannot appreciate the bias inherent in commercial claims and appeals, and hence is more easily persuadable.

The evidence in this realm is reviewed at length elsewhere in this volume (see Chapter 19). In summary, there are two key conclusions that are most salient for policy makers: (a) Most children experience difficulty discriminating between programs and commercials until reaching 4 or 5 years of age; and (b) age is positively correlated with an understanding of advertising's persuasive intent, with such ability typically developing at about 7 or 8 years of age.

From a policy perspective, these findings are significant because it has often been argued that if young children are unaware of persuasive intent, then commercial practices aimed at them may be considered inherently unfair and deceptive. This principle derives from the premise that all advertising must be clearly identifiable as such to its intended audience, a concept embodied in such statutes as the Communications Act of 1934.

There are two types of regulation currently applied to television advertising shown during children's programs: (a) policies restricting the amount of time that may be devoted to commercials and (b) policies that maintain a "clear separation" between program and commercial content. When Congress adopted the Children's Television Act of 1990, establishing educational programming requirements as noted above, it also included a provision limiting the amount of commercial time during children's programming to no more than 12 minutes per hour on weekdays and 10.5 minutes per hour on weekends. This action reinstated time restrictions on advertising to children that had been deregulated by the FCC (1984b).

Interestingly, the CTA's advertising time limits were extended to cable television networks as well as broadcast stations. Although cable lacks the public interest obligations of the broadcast industry, and hence there is some question about whether the government has legitimate authority to regulate its content in such direct fashion, the industry accepted the regulation willingly. Acceding to the policy helped the cable industry in its overall relations with Congress and was relatively painless because the levels of advertising time for most children's programming found on cable were well within the new regulatory limits (Kunkel & Gantz, 1992). Compliance with the time restrictions appears generally strong; audits conducted by the FCC (1993) indicate that more than 90% of the networks and stations surveyed fall at or below the limits allowed.

The second major type of policy in the realm of advertising to children is known as the "separation principle," which holds that the public interest requires stations to maintain a clear, distinct separation between program and commercial content during children's programming. This policy was first established by the FCC in 1974 and is applied solely to broadcast stations, not cable networks. Under current law, there are three applications of the separation principle:

1. *Bumpers.* Program/commercial separation devices, known in the industry as bumpers, are required during children's programs. These devices are roughly 5-second segments shown before and after commercial breaks that say something such as "And now a word from our sponsor."
2. *Host selling.* Program characters or hosts are prohibited from promoting products during commercials embedded in or directly adjacent to their shows. For example, a Flintstones cereal commercial featuring Fred and Wilma would not be allowed to air during a break in the *Flintstones* cartoon program.
3. *Program-length commercials (PLCs).* The current definition of a PLC, which was significantly narrowed by the FCC in 1991 after an unsuccessful attempt to abandon the policy completely, prohibits "a program associated with a product in which commercials for that product are aired" (FCC, 1991, p. 2117).

The issue of program-length commercials grew controversial in the 1980s when the FCC (1984b) deregulated its prior restriction on programs with a "primary purpose" of promoting products to children (FCC, 1969, 1974), resulting in a plethora of product-driven programs targeting children (Kunkel, 1988; Pecora, 1998). Under pressure from Congress to re-regulate, yet unwilling to "jeopardize the additional revenue streams generated by product merchandising needed by many children's programs" (FCC, 1991, para. 42), the commission redefined a program-length commercial as tantamount to host selling. Because the host-selling policy had never been deregulated, this allowed the agency purportedly to reinstate a restriction on PLCs without actually limiting any existing program practices. In fact, under current law, it would be possible for a program to include unlimited product promotions within the body of the show as long as the broadcaster did not present any "traditional" commercial advertisements for related products during or adjacent to the program. In other words, current policy does little to discourage the use of full-length programs as merchandising vehicles targeting children.

Finally, it should also be noted that the advertising industry maintains self-regulatory policies established by the Children's Advertising Review Unit (CARU) of the National Council of Better Business Bureaus. These voluntary guidelines place certain limits on the advertising practices deemed appropriate for commercials that target child audiences. For example, guidelines address such areas as product presentations and claims, sales pressure, disclosures and disclaimers, and safety concerns. All of these self-regulatory policies rely on the good-faith cooperation of advertisers, because CARU provides no independent monitoring and enforcement effort.

## Future Regulatory Challenges

The three major sections of this chapter (Protecting Children From Harmful Content, Adequacy of Television's Service to Children, and Fairness of Television Advertising to Children) have all dealt with the past history of children's media policy, which is grounded largely in terms of broadcast regulation. Even though cable television diffused into a majority of American households in the 1980s, policy makers are still grappling with approaches to children and media policy that encompass a broader perspective than mere broadcast regulation. The V-chip law adopted by Congress in 1996 is arguably the first such effort, as it applies its elements equally to both broadcast and cable channels, but to date it remains the only significant policy initiative that has taken such a broad perspective.

In the future, broad approaches to policy making that encompass multiple delivery systems will be increasingly important. Broadcasting was the dominant medium in children's lives (as well as for most of society) until the 1980s, when it began to face serious competition from cable. In the 1990s, not only has cable television service grown dramatically, but other new media such as the Internet have begun to deliver entertainment, information, and even marketing messages to children. Many media soothsayers anticipate that all types of electronic communication that reach into the home—whether they originate from broadcasting, cable television, the Internet, or some other source—will likely be delivered by a single wire at some point in the not-too-distant future. This scenario underscores the importance of shifting policy makers' focus away from delivery mechanisms and directing it more toward the consideration of children's interests relative to the content in question.

Consider how such an approach might work in the area of advertising to children. Under present law, an advertiser is not allowed to employ host-selling tactics in a television commercial aired on children's programming delivered by broadcast television. In contrast, host selling technically is legal on cable networks because the policy restricting the practice applies solely to broadcasting. With websites for children now growing in popularity, many advertisers already have developed sites that feature the same popular characters involved in games and entertainment content as well as in marketing messages clearly meant to promote product sales (Montgomery & Pasnik, 1996). In other words, these websites intermingle rather than clearly separate commercial from noncommercial content. Of course, there is currently no government policy restricting such tactics on Internet sites.

An alternative approach would be for a governmental agency such as the Federal Communications Commission or the Federal Trade Commission to establish a fundamental set of policy guidelines that would apply across all media that deliver advertising directed to child audiences. One such policy might involve broad application of the "separation principle," which holds that advertisers should take steps to clearly distinguish between commercial and noncommercial content, regardless of the media delivery system involved. Another element could be to establish limits on the ratio of commercial to noncommercial content permitted across all media that specifically target children. The Children's Television Act currently sets that ratio at 17.5 to 20% of airtime (10.5/12 minutes per hour) for television, depending on whether the content is aired on weekends or weekdays. Would it be outrageous to suggest that other media venues adhere to similar limitations on their ratio of commercial to noncommercial content directed to children, or is it more appropriate for policy makers to allow unlimited marketing messages to children in one medium while significantly constraining them in another?

Obviously, these are difficult issues. It is axiomatic that communication technologies move faster than the rules and regulations that govern them, and the changing media environment certainly presents many new puzzles to be solved. Any effort to establish a broad policy framework extending beyond the reach of individual media would have to be authorized by new legislation coming from Congress. Yet there is an important counterpoint to such a proposal. The growth and international reach of new media such as the Internet raises the question of how much longer individual countries can effectively govern electronic communication at all. If content that is regulated in one country is unregulated in another region of the world, then how effective can any regulatory policies be when every home with a computer can access any point on the globe via the World Wide Web?

These are the conundrums that policy makers must face as they grapple with the future of children and media policy. The stakes are the same as they have always been: to employ the nation's resources—the media among them—for the benefit of children and to ensure the protection of the nation's youth. Newton Minow and Craig Lamay (1995) offer a thoughtful perspective:

> Officials recognize that the meaning of the public interest will change—indeed, must change—in a new communications environment in which viewers rather than programmers choose what to watch and when, and in which viewers may one day even produce and distribute programs themselves. There are few firm points of agreement on how this new communications environment should be structured or whom it should serve. . . . But everyone everywhere can agree on one precept: the public interest requires us to put our children first. (p. 14)

In an era of significant change in the media environment, there remains a single constant: the need to consider the lives of children in framing our future media policies.

## Note

1. The policy establishing that stations should provide 3 hours per week of educational/informational programming for children is a license renewal processing guideline, not a rule that requires absolute compliance. Stations that do not meet the 3-hour guideline may still qualify for license renewal, but their programming efforts will be subject to more careful scrutiny by the commission during the renewal process. In general, license renewal processing guidelines tend to accomplish the same level of compliance as a formal rule, with the primary distinction between the two being that stations may be fined for violating a rule but not a guideline.

## References


Action for Children's Television v. FCC, 932 F. 2d 1509 (D.C. Cir. 1991).

American Medical Association. (1996). *Physician's guide to media violence.* Chicago: Author.

American Psychological Association. (1993). *Violence and youth: Psychology's response.* Washington, DC: Author.

Anderson, D., & Lorch, E. (1983). Looking at television: Action or reaction? In J. Bryant & D. Anderson (Eds.), *Children's understanding of television: Research on attention and comprehension* (pp. 1-33). New York: Academic Press.

Bok, S. (1998). *Mayhem: Violence as public entertainment.* Reading, MA: Addison-Wesley.

Cantor, J. (1998). Ratings for program content: The role of research findings. *Annals of the American Academy of Political and Social Science, 557,* 54-69.

Cantor, J., & Harrison, K. (1997). Ratings and advisories for television programming. In *National Television Violence Study* (Vol. 1). Thousand Oaks, CA: Sage.

Cantril, H., & Allport, G. (1935). *The psychology of radio.* New York: Harper & Brothers.

Carter, T., Franklin, M., & Wright, J. (1999). *The First Amendment and the fifth estate: Regulation of electronic mass media* (5th ed.). New York: Foundation Press.

Cater, D., & Strickland, S. (1975). *TV violence and the child: The evolution and fate of the surgeon general's report.* New York: Russell Sage.

Center for Media Education. (1992). *A report on station compliance with the Children's Television Act.* Washington, DC: Georgetown University Law Center.

Centers for Disease Control. (1991). *Position papers from the Third National Injury Conference: Setting the national agenda for injury control in the 1990's.* Washington, DC: Department of Health and Human Services.

Cole, B., & Oettinger, M. (1978). *Reluctant regulators: The FCC and the broadcast audience.* Reading, MA: Addison-Wesley.

Collins, W. (1983). Interpretation and inference in children's television viewing. In J. Bryant & D. Anderson (Eds.), *Children's understanding of television: Research on attention and comprehension* (pp. 125-150). New York: Academic Press.

Cooper, C. (1996). *Violence on television: Congressional inquiry, public criticism, and industry response.* Lanham, MD: University Press of America.

Cowan, G. (1979). *See no evil: The backstage battle over sex and violence on television.* New York: Simon & Schuster.

Donnerstein, E., Wilson, B., & Linz, D. (1992). On the regulation of broadcast indecency to protect children. *Journal of Broadcasting and Electronic Media, 36,* 111-117.

Doubleday, C., & Droege, K. (1993). Cognitive developmental influences on children's understanding of television. In G. Berry & J. Asamen (Eds.), *Children and television: Images in a changing sociocultural world* (pp. 23-37). Newbury Park, CA: Sage.

Farhi, P. (1997, July 10). TV ratings agreement reached. *Washington Post,* pp. A1, A16.

Federal Communications Commission. (1969). In re: complaint of Topper Corporation concerning American Broadcasting Company and Mattel Inc. *Federal Communications Commission Reports, 21*(2nd series), 148-149.

Federal Communications Commission. (1974). Children's television programs: Report and policy statement. *Federal Register, 39,* 39396-39409.

Federal Communications Commission. (1979). *Television programming for children: A report of the Children's Television Task Force* (NTIS No. PB 81-108722). Washington, DC: Author.

Federal Communications Commission. (1984a). Children's television programming and advertising practices: Report and order. *Federal Register, 49,* 1704-1727.

Federal Communications Commission. (1984b). Revision of programming and commercialization policies, ascertainment requirements, and program log requirements for commercial television stations. *Federal Register, 49,* 33588-33620.

Federal Communications Commission. (1991). Policies and rules concerning children's television programming: Memorandum opinion and order. *Federal Communications Commission Record, 6,* 2111-2127.

Federal Communications Commission. (1993). Notice of inquiry: Policies and rules concerning children's television programming. *Federal Communications Commission Record, 8,* 1841-1843.

Federal Communications Commission. (1996). In the matter of policies and rules concerning children's television programming: Report and order. *Federal Communications Commission Record, 11,* 10660-10778.

Federal Communications Commission v. Pacifica Foundation, 438 U.S. 726 (1978).

Fowler, M., & Brenner, D. (1982). A marketplace approach to broadcast regulation. *Texas Law Review, 60,* 207-257.

Gruenwald, J. (1997, February 15). Critics say TV ratings system doesn't tell the whole story. *Congressional Quarterly, 55*(7), 424-425.

Guttman, M. (1994, May 9). Violence in entertainment: A kinder, gentler Hollywood. *U.S. News & World Report,* pp. 39-46.

Hamilton, J. (1998). *Channeling violence: The economic market for violent television programming.* Princeton, NJ: Princeton University Press.

Hendershot, H. (1998). *Saturday morning censors: Television regulation before the V-chip.* Durham, NC: Duke University Press.

Horwitz, R. (1989). *The irony of regulatory reform: The deregulation of American telecommunications.* New York: Oxford University Press.

Hundt, R., & Kornbluh, K. (1995). Renewing the deal between broadcasters and the public: Requiring clear rules for children's educational television. *Harvard Journal of Law and Technology, 9,* 11-23.

Huston, A., Donnerstein, E., Fairchild, H., Feshbach, N., Katz, P., Murray, J., Rubinstein, E., Wilcox, B., & Zuckerman, D. (1992). *Big world, small screen: The role of television in American society.* Lincoln: University of Nebraska Press.

Huston, A., & Wright, J. (1991). The forms of television and the child viewer. In G. Comstock (Ed.), *Public communication and behavior* (Vol. 2, pp. 103-158). New York: Academic Press.

Jordan, A. (1996). *The state of children's television: An examination of quantity, quality, and industry beliefs.* Philadelphia: University of Pennsylvania, Annenberg Public Policy Center.

Jordan, A. (1998). *The 1998 state of children's television report: Programming for children over broadcast and cable television.* Philadelphia: University of Pennsylvania, Annenberg Public Policy Center.

Jordan, A., & Woodard, E. (1997). *The 1997 state of children's television report: Programming for children over broadcast and cable television.* Philadelphia: University of Pennsylvania, Annenberg Public Policy Center.

Jowett, G., Jarvie, I., & Fuller, K. (1996). *Children and the movies: Media influence and the Payne Fund controversy.* Cambridge, UK: Cambridge University Press.

Kerkman, D., Kunkel, D., Huston, A., Wright, J., & Pinon, M. (1990). Children's television programming and the "free market" solution. *Journalism Quarterly, 67,* 147-156.

Kunkel, D. (1988). From a raised eyebrow to a turned back: The FCC and children's product-related programming. *Journal of Communication, 38*(4), 90-108.

Kunkel, D. (1989, July 12). *Testimony before the U.S. Senate Subcommittee on Communications* (Hearing No. 101-221). Washington, DC: U.S. Government Printing Office.

Kunkel, D. (1991). Crafting media policy: The genesis and implications of the Children's Television Act of 1990. *American Behavioral Scientist, 35*(2), 181-202.

Kunkel, D., & Canepa, J. (1994). Broadcasters' license renewal claims regarding children's educational programs. *Journal of Broadcasting and Electronic Media, 38,* 397-416.

Kunkel, D., Farinola, W., Cope, K., Donnerstein, E., Biely, E., & Zwarun, L. (1998). *Rating the TV ratings: An assessment of the television industry's use of the V-chip ratings.* Menlo Park, CA: Kaiser Family Foundation.

Kunkel, D., & Gantz, W. (1992). Children's television advertising in the multi-channel environment. *Journal of Communication, 42*(3), 134-152.

Kunkel, D., & Goette, U. (1997). Broadcasters' response to the Children's Television Act. *Communication Law and Policy, 2,* 289-308.

Minow, N., & Lamay, C. (1995). *Abandoned in the wasteland: Children, television, and the First Amendment.* New York: Hill and Wang.

Montgomery, K., & Pasnik, S. (1996). *Web of deception.* Washington, DC: Center for Media Education.

Murray, J. (1980). *Television and youth: 25 years of research and controversy.* Boys Town, NE: Boys Town Center for the Study of Youth Development.

*National Television Violence Study* (Vol. 1). (1997). Thousand Oaks, CA: Sage.

*National Television Violence Study* (Vol. 2). (1998a). Thousand Oaks, CA: Sage.

*National Television Violence Study* (Vol. 3). (1998b). Thousand Oaks, CA: Sage.

Pearl, D., Bouthilet, E., & Lazar, J. (Eds.). (1982). *Television and behavior: Ten years of scientific progress and implications for the eighties* (Vol. 2). Rockville, MD: National Institute of Mental Health.

Pecora, N. (1998). *The business of children's entertainment.* New York: Guilford.

Reiss, A., & Roth, J. (Eds.). (1993). *Understanding and preventing violence.* Washington, DC: National Academy Press.

Rice, M., Huston, A., & Wright, J. (1982). The forms of television: Effects on children's attention, comprehension, social behavior. In D. Pearl, E. Bouthilet, & J. Lazar (Eds.), *Television and behavior: Ten years of scientific progress and implications for the eighties* (Vol. 2, pp. 24-38). Rockville, MD: National Institute of Mental Health.

Roberts, D., Foehr, U., Rideout, V., & Brodie, M. (1999). *Kids and media @ the new millennium: A comprehensive national analysis of children's media use.* Menlo Park, CA: Kaiser Family Foundation.

Saunders, K. (1996). *Violence as obscenity: Limiting the media's First Amendment protection.* Durham, NC: Duke University Press.

Schramm, W., Lyle, J., & Parker, E. (1961). *Television in the lives of our children.* Stanford, CA: Stanford University Press.

Stanger, J. (1997). *Television in the home: The 1997 survey of parents and children.* Philadelphia: University of Pennsylvania, Annenberg Public Policy Center.

Stanger, J., & Gridina, N. (1999). *Media in the home 1999: The fourth annual survey of parents and children.* Philadelphia: University of Pennsylvania, Annenberg Public Policy Center.

Surgeon General's Scientific Advisory Committee on Television and Social Behavior. (1972). *Television and growing up: The impact of televised violence* [Report to the Surgeon General, U.S. Public Health Service]. Washington, DC: U.S. Government Printing Office.

Times Mirror Center for People and the Press. (1993). *TV violence: More objectionable in entertainment than in newscasts.* Washington, DC: Author.

Turow, J. (1981). *Entertainment, education, and the hard sell: Three decades of network children's television.* New York: Praeger.

UCLA Center for Communication Policy. (1995). *The UCLA television violence monitoring report.* Los Angeles: Author.

UCLA Center for Communication Policy. (1996). *The UCLA television violence report, 1996.* Los Angeles: Author.

UCLA Center for Communication Policy. (1998). *The UCLA television violence report, 1997.* Los Angeles: Author.

U.S. Senate, Committee on Commerce, Science, and Transportation. (1997, February 27). *Hearing on television rating system* (105th Cong., 1st Sess., Doc. No. 105157). Washington, DC: U.S. Government Printing Office.

U.S. Senate, Committee on the Judiciary. (1956, January 16). *Television and juvenile delinquency: Investigation of juvenile delinquency in the United States* (84th Cong., 2d Sess., Rep. No. 1466). Washington, DC: U.S. Government Printing Office.

Wartella, E., Heintz, K., Aidman, A., & Mazzarella, S. (1990). Television and beyond: Children's video media in one community. *Communication Research, 17,* 45-64.

Wartella, E., & Reeves, B. (1985). Historical trends in research on children and the media: 1900-1960. *Journal of Communication, 35*(2), 118-133.

Waterman, D., & Grant, A. (1987). *Narrowcasting on cable television: An economic assessment of programming and audiences.* Paper presented to the annual conference of the International Communication Association, Montreal, Canada.

Waters, H. (1983, October 17). Kidvid: A national disgrace. *Newsweek,* pp. 82-83.

Watkins, B. (1988). Improving educational and informational television for children: When the marketplace fails. *Yale Law and Policy Review, 5,* 344-381.

Welkos, R. (1995, June 14). The Times poll: Public echoes Dole view on sex, violence. *Los Angeles Times,* pp. A1, A24-A25.

Woodard, E. (1999). *The 1999 state of children's television report: Programming for children over broadcast and cable television.* Philadelphia: University of Pennsylvania, Annenberg Public Policy Center.

CHAPTER **33**

# Industry Standards and Practices

## Compliance With the Children's Television Act

KAREN HILL-SCOTT
Consultant

The past 10 years have been a time of explosive and rapid change for commercial and cable television broadcasters. The days of three networks having a semimonopoly on the viewing audience are long gone (Woodard, 1999). There are hundreds of channels and multiple technologies for receiving television signals, resulting in audience segmentation. Consumers have been diverted to alternate entertainment technologies that use on-screen formats, resulting in audience depletion. Whereas three broadcasters used to offer a children's day-part consisting of a Saturday morning block or a daily programming strip, there are now six networks and at least 15 national television channels with children's programming. Five cable networks (Cartoon Network, the Disney Channel, Fox Family Channel, Nickelodeon, and Toon Disney) are completely devoted to children's entertainment.

The proliferation of programs has caused children's advocates to register intense concerns about the quality of children's entertainment diets. While broadcasters worried about growing competition and audience shrinkage, advocates sought ways to increase the quality and educational content of broadcast programs. In 1990, the Federal Communications Commission (FCC) supported the position of the children's advocates, and broadcasters have been compelled to create or acquire educational programming. The purpose of this chapter is to describe and comment on the broadcaster compliance strategies, examine their impact on the educational quality of programming, and discuss the implications of these strategies for television in general.

### Context

Despite the plethora of programming, the power of the television medium to educate has been grossly underutilized. After decades of study, some headway has been made to reduce and mitigate violent and aggressive content, but, beyond that, most children's programs have featured endearing characters performing comedic gag strings linked into a narrative or action-adventure story line. Substantive content, not to mention edifying content, has always been secondary to pure entertainment.

In 1989, after hearings, debate, and aggressive advocacy, the FCC passed the Children's Television Act (CTA) of 1990 (FCC, 1990). This act required commercial broadcasters (those who provide consumers with television free of charge) to air programming for children that had a core educational and information purpose. Subsequently, the CTA was augmented by a collateral policy, the Children's Television Rules (the Rules) of 1996 (FCC, 1996). The Rules are known for the 3-hour broadcast requirement and for establishing reporting requirements. This chapter focuses on the strategies used by broadcasters to comply with the CTA and, more specifically, with the Rules of 1996.

These two public policies are watershed because both compel commercial broadcasters to create a new kind of television product—one that specifically benefits children. The goal of the policies was to ensure that broadcast television would deliver educational content in an entertainment format. This could be interpreted as the obligation of the broadcaster to serve the public interest in exchange for the right to use the publicly owned airwaves (Kunkel, 1998). However, in today's marketplace, where multiple outlets make it extremely competitive to draw an audience, most broadcasters perceive the policy as a regulatory burden. As Jordan (1999) reports, were it not for the rule, some broadcasters would not even offer a children's day-part.

Every broadcaster has a standards and practices department that reviews all program content for violence, bad taste, obscenity, and inappropriateness. The standards department also screens commercials for length, content, and appearance. However, with the passage of the CTA, most broadcasters decided to develop or add educational specialists to their review process to assure the public that at least 3 hours of their children's programming would be educational and informational.

## The Regulatory Requirements

The 1990 CTA requires every commercial broadcaster to air programming specifically for children that has a "core educational or informational purpose." Passage of the CTA, after a decade of FCC deregulation, was a great victory for children's advocates. Peggy Charren, founder of Action for Children's Television, announced that she could retire because, after 25 years of work, her most important goal for children had finally been achieved.

The glow of success was short-lived. Well-publicized reports on the annual FCC license filings revealed that several broadcasters were running slipshod over the requirement (Kunkel & Canepa, 1994). Children's media advocates began pushing the FCC for a minimum airtime requirement that was challenged by the networks and unacceptable to the regulators in 1990, when the CTA was passed. Though broadcasters resisted, mainly charging infringement of First Amendment rights, the FCC did rule in favor of a time requirement and other broad requirements with the 1996 Children's Television Rules (Kunkel, 1998).

The Rules are very specific on permitted broadcast hours, length of programs, scheduling and labeling of programming, and reporting requirements. The Rules do not address the issue of monitoring or evaluating content or of specifically defining attributes of an educational/informational program. The specifics of the Rules are as follows:

- Serve the educational and information needs of children under age 16
- Air children's programming a minimum of 3 hours a week between the hours of 7:00 A.M. and 10:00 P.M.
- Offer educational content in a regularly scheduled weekly program

- Ensure that the program is at least 30 minutes in length
- Direct the program toward an identified target audience
- Provide a written educational and informational objective (which can be found in the broadcaster's Children's Television Programming Report)
- List the program and educational/informational (E/I) symbol in program guides
- File a quarterly Children's Television Programming Report to the FCC (Form 398)

Neither the Rules nor the CTA actually specifies the content or format for this new media product. The CTA and the Rules permit both intellectual/cognitive and social/emotional content in educational programming. As a result, networks and creative suppliers of programming have developed several strategies to define, produce, and air programming that will meet the spirit and intent of the CTA (Jordan, 1999). Using material from firsthand interviews and an analysis of network documents, these strategies and practices can be compared and understood.

### *Method*

There are six national networks that provide close to 80% of children's E/I offerings: ABC, CBS, Fox, NBC, UPN, and the WB (Schmitt, 1999). The remainder of programming is provided by independent station groups, most of which purchase programming from preexisting libraries. This chapter focuses on the network strategies and uses information collected in semistructured interviews with the highest-level executive assigned to children's programming at each network. Supplemental interviews were conducted with programming staff, producers, and consultants. There were 12 participants, and the questions were the same for each. All were forthcoming in the interview, and each broadcaster submitted additional printed materials to document his or her development and production process. What follows in the next section is a narrative description of the interviews. The narrative includes a description of the type of programming, the target age group, the time programming is aired, the quantity of programming aired for E/I and entertainment content, and the process or strategy for complying with the CTA. Where applicable, the narrative will also identify the guidelines or criteria used by each network for meeting a good-faith standard of educational content within each broadcaster's offerings.

## Strategies for Self-Regulation and Compliance

### *Overall Findings*

The data on the networks' strategies for achieving compliance are presented for the 1998-1999 programming year. This is the most recent year for which there is some published external analysis (Schmitt, 1999) of the programming content. Changes for the 1999-2000 programming year are noted and discussed if they reflect a change in basic strategy.

Networks either acquired or developed programming for the E/I category. Fox aired two shows, one an acquisition from PBS and another show from its library. UPN acquired programming from Disney's Buena Vista Television. ABC, CBS, NBC, and the WB developed original content.

Every broadcaster that developed content used external consultants, most of them from academia, to review or validate the programs during the production process. Those consultants who were not affiliated with universities had advanced degrees and many years of experience in teaching or practice with children's learning and development. In addition, CBS has an advisory panel, Fox has an advisory committee, and NBC has a writers' symposium with outside experts as contributors.

Fox and CBS use panels on an as-needed basis, while the NBC panel meets annually. In addition to the advisory panels, this review identified 37 nonoverlapping external consultants who were involved in recurring support roles for advising and developing content. Most were established researchers from academic institutions. Two of the networks, Fox and ABC, had a key internal executive responsible for meeting E/I standards who held a doctorate in education or child development.

In 1998-1999, the six networks met the time requirement for E/I programming in very different ways. At ABC, Fox, UPN, and the WB, the E/I programming was part of a schedule that included noneducational shows. At NBC and CBS, the E/I programs were the only shows on the schedule. Fox and the WB aired programming in a daily strip plus a Saturday morning block. UPN offered a 6-day strip that did not include Saturday morning. ABC, CBS, and NBC directed programming to their target audiences in a Saturday morning block.

NBC is the only network that has a target audience of teens ages 12 to 16 and the only network that uses live-action programming. All the other networks target children ages 6 to 11 and use animated programming. Table 33.1 summarizes the amount of programming and the general strategy each network uses to meet the requirements of the CTA.

## Analysis of Network Approaches for Compliance With the CTA

### *Panels*

Three broadcasters, Fox, NBC, and CBS, have advisory panels that meet at network discretion to review programming concepts, provide feedback, and offer presentations on issues that are relevant to educational programming. The Fox advisory panel meets not only for the FCC broadcasts but for all the cable channels in the Fox Family Network.

CBS has a nine-member panel to provide general guidance and input in several areas. The panel last met in 1998 and convenes at the network's discretion. Most of the panel members are noted researchers in different areas, from multicultural issues to children's comprehension of television content. As a whole, the panel peruses the proposed new programs and helps to shape those programs selected for development. With the support and participation of a longtime consultant to CBS, the panel provided input for the network's *Handbook for Developing Educational and Informational Television Programs for Children* (Berry, 1997).

At NBC, the use of external experts and conferences with the creative community has a long history. In 1975, NBC convened the first social science advisory panel in broadcast television for a children's programming department. The panel began with very distinguished researchers who met about six times a year and advised the network on a wide range of child development issues, reviewed programming proposals, and helped define priorities for children's entertainment programming. When the CTA was passed, the network decided to develop a relationship with one consultant who was available on a continuous basis. By 1996, when the 3-hour rule was passed, the annual writers' symposium was created to specifically support E/I programming.

In contrast to the panels at CBS and Fox, the outside experts at the NBC writers' symposium change annually and fill strategic functions that directly aid or enhance the story development process. They include two practicing middle or secondary school educators, an expert on teen trends and interests, and a few experts on special interest areas (e.g., gender role development, extreme sports, teen drug and alcohol use, or teen health status). Internal participants include NBC Research and NBC Social Research, each reporting on program testing, teen feedback on NBC programs, and teen trends that have been picked up in network research. If the programming is embarking on a new series, additional experts

**TABLE 33.1** Summary of Network Offerings and Compliance Strategies (1998-1999 Season)

| *Network* | *Total Shows* | *Total Weekly Hours* | *Total Education Shows* | *Total Education Hours* | *Educational Inputs Strategy* |
|---|---|---|---|---|---|
| ABC | 8+ | 4.75 | 6+ | 3.62 | External consultants, internal standards director |
| CBS | 6 | 3.0 | 6 | 3.0 | Network consultant panel (meets occasionally), external consultant, production company consultant |
| Fox | 11 | 18.50 | 2 | 5.0 | Acquisition from PBS, internal review headed by vice president of standards and educational practices |
| NBC | 6 | 3.0 | 6 | 3.0 | External network consultant w/staff, annual writers' symposium w/outside presenters/experts |
| UPN | 4 | 12.0 | 2 | 6.0 | Acquisition from Disney (Buena Vista Television as E/I) |
| The WB | 8 | 16.50 | 1 | 3.0 | External consultant, researcher |
| TOTAL | 43 | 57.75 | 23 | 23.62 | |

related to series content are included for separate meetings with the writers. The presentations are followed by brainstorming sessions with the entire staff of writers and producers from all the shows on the NBC schedule.

### *Consultants*

Each network that is developing new content to comply with the act (ABC, NBC, the WB, and CBS) uses external consultants and/or expert panels to provide guidance and technical assistance. At ABC, there are 20 external consultants who work across the six E/I programs on the schedule. In addition, the network director of standards and practices for children's television has a Ph.D. in education. Some of ABC's shows and short-form programs, such as *Squigglevision* and *Great Minds,* are developed and produced by educators.

According to ABC, NBC, and the WB, the consultants are involved with every episode of programming. All the networks felt their consulting process was adequate. However, without analyzing the content in each script's document trail, it would be difficult to assess the extent to which the consulting process actually shapes and refines the product to meet an E/I standard. NBC and the WB expect notes and recommended changes from the external consultant within 24 and 48 hours, respectively. At ABC, the consultants attached to the programs are specifically matched to the needs of each show. For example, *Squigglevision* (formerly *Science Court*), which is developed by an educator, relies on several practicing teachers for technical assistance and input.

All the networks that use consultants report that developing E/I content is really a process in which the consultant and the creative team develop a working relationship and build trust. It is often hard to reconcile the traditions of educators with those of sitcom, comedy, and action-adventure writers.

One executive pointed out that, when he started this process 2 years ago, his expectation of how to produce the E/I programming was quite simplistic. As time passed, he became aware of what makes content educational and how hard it was for the creative staff to translate that into their long-established formats. Finding acceptable approaches to integrating the E/I essentials with the dramatic or comedy essentials is at the heart of the consulting process.

Another executive reported that the use of consultants is most effective on new shows that are specifically developed to meet the CTA rather than on existing shows where the writers are used to conceptualizing stories strictly for entertainment. Two others reported that, ultimately, the consultants provide a service that helps the quality of the story and the product. But one executive was unrepentant. Compliance was exactly that—meeting a requirement that would enable the affiliates to continue broadcasting. The executive supported the ideals of quality programming but felt that children 6 to 16 had no appetite for educational television and stated, "They know broccoli when they eat it, even if it has whipped cream on it."

### *Programming Type, Content, and Amount*

#### *ABC*

This network produces a 5-hour programming umbrella block called *Disney's One Saturday Morning.* About 75% of the total offering is E/I product, and all of the shows are human-interest comedies except for *Squigglevision,* which has fact-based science content. The ABC E/I content amounts to almost 4 hours, largely because the short-form and interstitial programs substantially add to the core offerings.

In Table 33.2, the wide variety and number of consultants is illustrated. The well-known head of an innovative all-girls middle/secondary school assists *Pepper Ann,* a show about a 12-year-old girl who is developing her abilities and self-concept. *101 Dalmatians* relies on a university-affiliated group for consulting assistance. *Doug* has three consultants, each of whom reviews selected scripts. Although ABC does not have a published set of guidelines for developing E/I content, each consultant writes up a plan for the show. ABC seems to have the most extensive and diverse approach to developing educational content.

#### *CBS*

Nelvana Productions supplies CBS with all the programming on its schedule. For approximately 2 years (1996-1998), the network consultant reviewed each show and the CBS advisory panel reviewed the proposed schedule. CBS uses its own handbook, described earlier, as a guideline for evaluating the content provided by Nelvana. As can be seen in Table 33.3, the animation schedule at CBS is mainly in the nonviolent genre, blending humor and adventure with education. One of the shows for the 1999-2000 season, *Blaster,* is based on the educational CD-ROM series.

#### *Fox Kids Network*

The Fox E/I offering *The Magic School Bus* is a highly rated acquisition originally developed for PBS. According to the Fox executive, this show is now being seen by more viewers than ever before simply because the reach of Fox is behind it. *Life With Louie,* which came from the Fox library, was the second E/I offering, and it focused on more prosocial content.

At the other extreme of programming are the highly criticized *Power Rangers* and eight other action-adventure programs with lots of destruction and mayhem. These shows air in a more favorable time slot than either of the E/I offerings. Unfortunately, *Life With Louie* and *The Magic School Bus* air immediately before the 3:00 P.M. hour when most children are not home from school. As can be seen in Table 33.4, the E/I programming represents less than a third of the network's total offering.

**TABLE 33.2** ABC and Affiliates

| *Name of Show* | *Format* | *Length (hours)* | *Category* | *Frequency* | *Strategy* |
|---|---|---|---|---|---|
| *Disney's Hercules* | Animation | .5 | | Saturday | |
| ***Disney's One Saturday Morning (Block)*** | | | | | |
| *Disney's Doug* | Animation | .5 | E/I | Saturday | 3 external consultants |
| *Disney's Recess* | Animation | .5 | E/I | Saturday | 1 external consultant |
| *Disney's Pepper Ann* | Animation | .5 | E/I | Saturday | 1 external consultant |
| *Great Minds Think for Themselves* | Animation | .0625 | E/I | Saturday | 2 external educators |
| *Manny the Uncanny* | Animation | .0625 | | Saturday | |
| *How Things Werk* | Animation | .0625 | E/I | Saturday | |
| *Boss of the World* | Animation | .0625 | E/I | Saturday | |
| *Tube Dwellers* | Animation | .0625 | | Saturday | |
| *You Rock!* | Animation | .0625 | E/I | Saturday | |
| *Nommercials* | Animation | .0625 | | Saturday | |
| *Flyndiggery Do* | Animation | .0625 | E/I | Saturday | 1 external consultant |
| *The Bugs Bunny and Tweety Show* | | .8833 | | Saturday | |
| *Schoolhouse Rock* | | .1167 | E/I | Saturday | 3 external consultants, 2 groups |
| *Disney's 101 Dalmatians: The Series* | | .5 | E/I | Saturday | 3 external consultants (as a group) |
| *The New Adventures of Winnie the Pooh* | | .5 | E/I | Saturday | 1 internal standards director |
| *Squigglevision* | | .5 | E/I | Saturday | 6 external consultants/educators |
| TOTAL | | 5.0 Hours | 3.4 (+/–) Hours | Weekly | 20 external individuals + 2 groups/entities |

NOTE: Shows listed were aired by the network for the 1998-1999 season. In 1999-2000, ABC dropped *101 Dalmatians,* added *Sabrina, the Animated Series* (E/I), and reduced *Bugs Bunny* by 30 minutes to add *Disney's Mickey Mouse Works.* It also dropped *Manny the Uncanny,* and *Nommercials* and added *Who Am I?* and *What's the Difference?* both of which are E/I, to the interstitial schedule.

The overall E/I schedule is supervised by an internal standards and practices director, who has a Ph.D. in Educational Psychology.

The Fox vice president of broadcast standards and educational practices is also a Ph.D. in education.

In the 1999-2000 programming year, Fox made changes with its E/I schedule. In addition to changing programs, Fox changed the concept of a national schedule for E/I content. Affiliates could choose when to air the E/I programming and which of three offerings they would select. For purposes of information accounting and research, decentralizing the programming choice and time slot will increase the work for researchers who are tracking affiliate compliance with the CTA.

### *NBC*

The program schedule at NBC is directed toward teens 12 to 16 years of age and is sup-

**TABLE 33.3** CBS and Affiliates

| *Name of Show* | *Format* | *Length (hours)* | *Category* | *Frequency* | *Strategy* |
|---|---|---|---|---|---|
| *Anatole* | Animation | .5 | E/I | Saturday | External consultant, expert panel |
| *Birdz* | Animation | .5 | E/I | Saturday | External consultant, expert panel |
| *Dumb Bunnies* | Animation | .5 | E/I | Saturday | External consultant, expert panel |
| *Flying Rhino* | Animation | .5 | E/I | Saturday | External consultant, expert panel |
| *Mythic Warriors* | Animation | .5 | E/I | Saturday | External consultant, expert panel |
| *Rupert* | Animation | .5 | E/I | Saturday | External consultant, expert panel |
| TOTAL | Animation | 3.0 Hours | 3.0 Hours | Weekly | External Consultant, expert Panel |

NOTE: In 1999-2000, CBS dropped *Rupert, Dumb Bunnies,* and *Birdz* and added *Blaster, Rescue O,* and *New Tales From the Crypt* to its E/I lineup.

**TABLE 33.4** Fox and Affiliates

| *Name of Show* | *Format* | *Length (hours)* | *Category* | *Frequency* | *Strategy* |
|---|---|---|---|---|---|
| *The Magic School Bus* | Animation | .5 (5) | E/I | Mon-Fri | Purchased library of former PBS show |
| *Life With Louie* | Animation | .5 (5) | E/I | Mon-Fri | In Fox library |
| *Power Playback* | Animation | .5 (5) | | Mon-Fri | |
| *Beast Wars* | Animation | .5 (5) | | Mon-Fri | |
| *Digimon: Digital Monsters* | Animation | .5 (6) | | Mon-Sat | |
| *Power Rangers Lost Galaxy* | Animation | .5 (6) | | Mon-Sat | |
| *Xyber 9: New Dawn* | Animation | .5 | | Sat | |
| *Godzilla* | Animation | .5 | | Sat | |
| *Spider Man Unlimited* | Animation | .5 | | Sat | |
| *Beast Machines* | Animation | .5 | | Sat | |
| *Big Guy and Rusty the Boy* | Animation | .5 | | Sat | |
| *Check Yourself* | Live action | .016 | PSA | | |
| TOTAL | | 18.5 Hours | 5.0 Hours | Daily Strip | Internal Standards Vice President |

NOTE: Shows listed were aired by the network for the 1998-1999 season. *Life With Louie* was retired for the 1999-2000 season and was replaced by *Sherlock Holmes* or *Under the Helmet,* both E/I acquisitions.

plied by Peter Engel Productions, a company co-owned by NBC. The schedule is called TNBC to create brand identity, and the main group of shows is composed of four sitcoms (see Table 33.5). Each is set in a different community, from an ethnically and economically diverse urban high school to a middle-class Miami household composed of a bunch

**TABLE 33.5** NBC and Affiliates

| *Name of Show* | *Format* | *Length (hours)* | *Category* | *Frequency* | *Strategy* |
|---|---|---|---|---|---|
| *Saved by the Bell* | Live action | .5 | E/I | Saturday | External consultant, symposium |
| *Saved by the Bell* | Live action | .5 | E/I | Saturday | External consultant, symposium |
| *Hang Time* | Live action | .5 | E/I | Saturday | External consultant, symposium |
| *City Guys* | Live action | .5 | E/I | Saturday | External consultant, symposium |
| *One World* | Live action | .5 | E/I | Saturday | External consultant, symposium |
| *NBA: The Inside Stuff* | Magazine | .5 | E/I | Saturday | External consultant, symposium |
| TOTAL | | 3.0 Hours | 3.0 Hours | Weekly | External consultant, symposium |

NOTE: In the 1999-2000 season, *Saved by the Bell* aired for one half-hour and *City Guys* aired different episodes for two half-hour time slots.

of foster kids and their parents. This schedule serves both the E/I and entertainment block and is developed with an external consultant closely involved in the production process.

The annual writers' symposium serves as the basis for a writer's handbook that is prepared yearly by the consultant and programming staff (Hill-Scott, 1996, 1997, 1998). It includes the development guidelines authored by the consultant and other content from the symposium. NBC also produces theme days where all four of the sitcoms focus on one subject or current issues of relevance to teens such as the value of community service or the hazards of drug use.

A sports magazine, *NBA: The Inside Stuff,* produced by the NBA, is another E/I offering on the NBC schedule. This show has its own educational consultant but very little direct interface with the children's programming department. It is part of the network's overall production package with the NBA.

### *UPN*

This network purchases programming from Disney-owned Buena Vista Television. There are no consultants or program guides because the programming is "prequalified" by the ABC process already described. UPN runs a weekly programming strip that consists of a block of syndicated *Doug* and *Recess* episodes for the E/I requirement and two entertainment-based shows to fill out the strip (see Table 33.6).

### *The WB*

The Warner Brothers network, like Disney and Fox, offers general entertainment and E/I programming. The one E/I program, *Histeria,* is produced by Warner Brothers. The WB relied on *Building Blocks: A Guide for Creating Children's Educational Television* (Trotta, 1998) for the development of *Histeria.* An educational consultant and a full-time history researcher work on the show. Because, like Fox, the WB produces one E/I show in a schedule of many entertainment products, E/I content is only 18% of its total children's program hours on the air (see Table 33.7).

## ***Compliance Documentation and Responsibility***

### *Content Compliance*

Each network transmits a quarterly report to its affiliates, which in turn is electronically

**TABLE 33.6** UPN and Affiliates

| *Name of Show* | *Format* | *Length (hours)* | *Category* | *Frequency* | *Strategy* |
|---|---|---|---|---|---|
| ***Disney's 1 Too (Block)*** | | | | | |
| *Disney's Doug* | Animation | .5 (6) | E/I | Sun-Fri | Acquisition as E/I |
| *Disney's Recess* | Animation | .5 (6) | E/I | Sun-Fri | Acquisition as E/I |
| *Sabrina, the Animated Series* | Animation | .5 (6) | | Sun-Fri | |
| *Disney's Hercules* | Animation | .5 (6) | | Sun-Fri | |
| TOTAL | Animation | 12.0 Hours | 6.0 Hours | Daily Strip | Acquisitions as E/I |

filed with the FCC. This report documents compliance with the CTA and the Rules. Although each network has an idiosyncratic approach to developing the report, the responsibility for preparing the compliance document is typically distributed among the programming, broadcast standards, and corporate legal departments. In some cases, the consultant assists with preparation of the narrative content. The responsibility for filing compliance reports usually rests with the network legal department.

The network processes for developing E/I content initiate compliance with the CTA. The airing of E/I programming demonstrates compliance, and the filing of the FCC Form 398 documents compliance with the CTA and the Rules. It takes an external analysis, however, such as the ones performed by the Annenberg Public Policy Center (Jordan, 1998; Woodard, 1999), to evaluate the extent of compliance with the law.

Generally speaking, the Annenberg evaluations of program content show that E/I programs are moderately to highly educational (Schmitt, 1999). Four shows (17%) of the offerings from the six national networks were rated very minimal in 1998-1999. They were *NBA: The Inside Stuff* (from NBC), *Anatole* (from CBS), *Dumb Bunnies* (from CBS), and *101 Dalmatians* (from ABC). Disney has dropped *101 Dalmatians* and CBS has dropped *Dumb Bunnies* from the 1999-2000 lineup, so their schedules may be stronger in the next evaluative period.

Across all broadcasters—local, syndicated, and independent stations as well as the national networks—about 20% of all the shows evaluated for the 1999 report were minimal to very minimal in educational content (Schmitt, 1999). This is a big drop from the 36% minimal reported in the previous year (Jordan, 1998). Although the total broadcast and cable offerings dwarf the network and E/I offerings, the network shows may have started a process that could ultimately improve quality overall. Every E/I show goes into a library that will be syndicated and aired again off network, on video, or on cable. From small beginnings, if E/I products can bear even a modest amount of ratings pressure, they will have more than a half-life. This is evidenced by the voluntary offerings from cable broadcasters such as Nick Jr. and Noggin (Fischer, 1999).

### *Clearances and Preemptions*

One of the big issues with compliance is not about content per se but about maintaining clearances and avoiding preemptions. The intent of the act is for children to be exposed to educational programs on a regular, consistent basis during the hours when children are most likely to see them. Early to late afternoon and Saturdays are prime viewing hours for the 6 to 11 demographic.

In contrast, local broadcasters need to earn revenues from programming they own and control, such as their local news programs that

**TABLE 33.7** The WB and Affiliates

| *Name of Show* | *Format* | *Length (hours)* | *Category* | *Frequency* | *Strategy* |
|---|---|---|---|---|---|
| *Histeria* | Animation | .5 (6) | E/I | Mon-Sat | Network/production company consultant |
| *Big Cartoonie Show* | Animation | .5 (6) | | Mon-Sat | |
| *Pokemon* | Animation | .5 (6) | | Mon-Sat | |
| *The New Batman/Superman* | Animation | .5 (6) | | Mon-Sat | |
| *Batman Beyond* | Animation | .5 (6) | | Mon-Sat | |
| *Men in Black* | Animation | .5 | | Sat | |
| *Pokemon (2)* | Animation | .5 | | Sat | |
| *Sylvester and Tweety* | Animation | .5 | | Sat | |
| TOTAL | Animation | 16.5 Hours | 3 Hours | Daily Strip | 2 External Consultants |

NOTE: In the 1999-2000 season, *Histeria* ran Monday through Friday and a new half-hour show, *Detention*, ran on Saturday.

also air in early afternoon. A win-win on clearances is one where the national broadcast schedule does not compromise the affiliates' prime revenue-generating hours. Then the FCC programming is seen in a high number of markets, which helps ratings and increases audience exposure.

The same logic applies to schedule preemptions. Certain weekend sporting events bring in premium advertising dollars, so all or part of the regular children's schedule may be preempted to carry the sporting event. Preemptions of E/I programming disrupt children's regular viewing schedule. Too many preemptions will also jeopardize a license renewal even if the broadcaster advertises that the shows have a regular second home (alternate day and time) for the target audience. Broadcasters perceive the preemption rule as a barrier to earning revenue from sports advertising.

The compliance issues around preemptions are twofold. One is if the frequency of local station preemptions is masked by network national averages. The second is if the local stations consistently provide an optimum second home for E/I programs. For educators and advocates, the ideal time is when children are watching or would expect to see their programs on television.

Advocates recently found that, even with CTA requirements for a second home, some broadcasters appear to be excessive with preemptions but use national preemption statistics to mask the local deviations from the schedule. According to an article in *Broadcasting and Cable* (McConnell, 1999), the Children's Media Center and advocate Peggy Charren are currently pressuring the FCC to require every local broadcaster to file a record on local preemptions rather than a national network average. They also want to limit the number of preemptions for individual licensees (McConnell, 1999). In the Philadelphia market, for example, an E/I program was preempted 46% of the time. The importance of the preemption issue, then, is high considering the larger context of program displacement caused by inconsistent scheduling and audience availability.

Television operates in the context of commerce; artistic creativity is second. Educating the public may not even be on the corporate radar much of the time. The content issue, even if it was settled and all programs were rated highly educational, is but one facet of getting quality programming to children. The record on schedule clearances and preemptions shows another less well-known but very important facet of accountability and compliance with the intent of the CTA.

## From Regulation to Content: A Process for Change

The CTA and the Rules are very specific about time and core purpose, but the specifics of what kind of content is appropriate for each age group were deliberately left undefined. The FCC is relying on the "good-faith judgment" of broadcasters to create eligible programming. This is why the consulting process is so important for producers, writers, *and* educators.

Producing E/I content is a very complex enterprise. In a special children's television supplement of the *Hollywood Reporter* (Fischer, 1999), one article quoted several producers involved in developing E/I content. Most echoed the comment made by Robby London of DIC Entertainment: "The ultimate challenge of these shows is to make the educational component organic to the storytelling" (as cited in Fischer, 1999, p. S-1). Laurie Trotta, former executive director of Mediascope, reported that "the process has been somewhat painful for people" (as cited in Fischer, 1999, p. S-1). Peter Engel, who produces the TNBC schedule, reports that it "adds one production day to each episode, [which] equals more money" and that he's "amazed that we still get the same amount of comedy out of a [mandated] show" (as cited in Fischer, 1999, p. S-2). Another producer, Paula Hart, who produces *Sabrina, the Teenage Witch,* does not like the extra layers of input, bureaucracy, and regulation. Overall, though, the collective sentiment was similar to the position of Toper Taylor of Nelvana Entertainment. He stated, "To be socially responsible in this age is necessary. There is definitely room for more programming that teaches through television" (as cited in Fischer, 1999, p. S-6).

### *Cultivating Awareness in the Creative Community*

Most producers of television content have a background in fields other than education or developmental psychology. As artists and business executives, their goal is to expediently obtain whatever information they need to meet FCC requirements. Seemingly simple questions such as "Why can't a 6- and 11-year-old get the same thing from my show?" have complex answers. The primary purpose of the consulting process is to communicate theoretical and research content in such a way that producers and writers are able to use it in scripts and thereby teach through television.

This is not an easy process because research is inherently heuristic and generalizations are often risky. Findings may range from ambiguous to situation-specific to conclusive. The consultant needs to be knowledgeable about child development and cognition but, most important, should be perceptive about how to translate that understanding into useful television content.

For example, the most fundamental child development precept is that how and what children learn truly varies by age, experience, and ability. An 8-year-old is not simply a diminished adult. When one takes the latter view, the tendency among television producers is to "dumb down" content rather than respond to the true developmental needs of a target audience. The consulting process can increase the respect for children's capacities where they are and address issues of importance to the age group.

Although the CTA requires broadcasters to have a target audience, it does not define who is in this audience. Advertising breakdowns are aimed at children ages 2 to 11, which encompass three distinct developmental groupings. The teen demographic is ages 12 to 20, which does not recognize the narrower groups of pre- (11-13), mid- (14-17), and older teens (18-22).

The role of the consultant is to help modulate proposed story content so that it has appeal to these wide advertising demographics but the content is specifically targeted to a logical developmental grouping. For example, in both the *Building Blocks* (Trotta, 1998) and the CBS *Handbook* (Berry, 1997), an encapsulated version of basic child development theories is presented so that the television producer can address target audience needs within the context of attaining broad entertainment appeal.

Research has also shown what features of television are most associated with learning and comprehension at different ages. Both Anderson and Collins (1988) and Van Evra (1998) provide extensive reviews of the published and unpublished literature on the relationship between television and child development. The research denudes popular myths—television is *not* a passive experience, for example—and explains how television can be produced to promote learning without eviscerating its entertainment value.

Just for the purpose of example, two frequent assertions on the problems of producing entertaining educational television are given below. Through a very brief explanation, research findings can be used to unambiguously guide television content toward the synergy of reaching and retaining an audience while promoting learning. Even though the examples are limited, they show that the consulting relationship can serve the goals of both developing educational content and bettering entertainment. Two common refrains are as follows:

*Kids only like shows that are colorful, cute, fast paced, and funny.* The form of a show can draw children to television. But content is what keeps their attention, and attention is very complicated (Anderson & Collins, 1988; Van Evra, 1998). Children turn away and engage in other activities when the television is on (Anderson & Collins, 1988). They are more likely to actually watch if the content is something they can understand (Dorr, 1986). They are more likely to stay with the show if it has formal features (recurring visual and auditory features) that signal informative components of the programming (Huston & Wright, 1994). More content is understood when the signal features appeal to a child's interests, such as animation or the use of children's voices (Campbell, Wright, & Huston, 1987).

*If it's too complicated, kids won't watch the program.* Children's attention to television is guided by their interest and ability to understand the content (Huston & Wright, 1994), not its relative simplicity or complexity. In addition, children have been conditioned to not expect much mental exercise from watching television (Salomon, 1983). If presented with a demanding cognitive effort, children will exert it, and the effort appears to produce greater comprehension (Anderson & Collins, 1988).

The research on preschool children, in particular, shows an unequivocal effect on learning content. Most recently, J. L. Singer and D. G. Singer (1998) examined the extent to which children retained the teaching content of several episodes of *Barney & Friends*. A striking finding was that the episodes that researchers had independently rated as high in cognitive content were also the ones in which children showed the most comprehension of content and usage of vocabulary from the program. A major finding from this research is that educational content is not elusive but easily codified by children and adults. Also, the study suggests that the stronger the content, the greater the retention of concepts, even in very young children.

The last two decades of research on children's viewing of television are wide ranging, covering topics from attention to personality development. Though not every area has been explored in equal depth, much of the research can be communicated to a nonacademic audience and has practical application. In contrast to the myth that research consistently denigrates television and its effects, most of the findings point to the capacities as well as vulnerabilities of children to comprehend programming and advertising. The findings point to the challenge and the opportunity for television to fulfill an educational promise.

### *Recognizing Different Traditions*

What is it that educators need to know about the development of television content? For starters, the structure of the business is very different from the academic enterprise. Broadcast television exists at the nexus of commerce and art. Advertiser revenues finance production, and if shows are not successful and popular, the revenue base for future production drops. Thus, the television equivalent of a correct answer on a test or a well-received research article is a show that is a ratings success with the right advertiser demographic.

Production schedules are compressed compared with research or teaching timetables. In most commercial television, there is no time to propose, test, analyze, and revise. A season of 26 live-action episodes may be produced in as little as 36 weeks, and that is it—the show goes on the air. Even more compressed would be a game show schedule where 1 year's production is shot in just a few weeks.

Each television format has a different pace, and the arc of different plot structures has different internal timing, which conveniently corresponds to the placement of commercials. In live action, dialogue has to match the capacity of child actors to naturalistically demonstrate complex emotions. Budgets and time constraints limit the number of settings and/or field segments within a story. Yet different settings almost always add to the ability to illustrate or apply an educational concept.

Producers in children's programming also presuppose certain axioms about what works and what does not. Jordan and Woodard (1998) identified four widely held beliefs that have contributed to resistance against the act and an unwillingness to develop an educative process to improve educational content. These were that children outgrow educational programming by the time they are 6, that older children will be interested only in social content, that educational programs are more expensive, and that boys' programming (action adventure) is better than girls' or general programming because boys control the remote and respond to advertising more than girls.

However, a year later, when Jordan interviewed programming executives and producers, she found greater support for a new dialogue (Jordan, 1999). Whereas producers were reluctant and suspicious when the rule was passed, others such as Peter Engel now said, "I'm all for the mandate—it's a wonderful arena of programming" (as cited in Fischer, 1999, p. S-2).

## Summary and Recommendations

As landmark legislation, the Children's Television Act and the Children's Television Rules seem to have created a shift toward better children's programming overall and definitely more educational/information programs on commercial networks and cable (Woodard, 1999). The review of network schedules showed a variety of approaches to developing and presenting E/I content. Using educators in the development process has definitely influenced broadcaster and producer attitudes about programming.

This chapter has indicated that process and interaction are as important as rule making if we are going to change the face of children's television. Also, when you consider the different traditions of education and television, mutual and reciprocal learning processes may be the best way to achieve fundamentally creative approaches to E/I programming.

On that note, another approach to change would be for more educators to develop careers within the television industry. Despite the small, relatively closed world of relationships and referrals in the industry, some educators have become successful producers. They include science teacher Bill Nye and Tom Snyder, the producer of *Squigglevision.* Conversely, benefits would accrue to children's programming if more writers and programming executives studied child development.

In the vein of cross-training, disseminating documents such as the CBS and NBC handbooks, the *Building Blocks* (Trotta, 1998) from Mediascope, and the reports from the Annenberg Public Policy Center (Jordan, 1999) helps bridge the differences in knowledge and traditions. The *Building Blocks* guidelines and the CBS *Handbook* both stress inputs, how producers should plan and conceptualize their shows. About half the content is on developing mission statements, goals, and objectives. The other half relates the developmental needs of the audience to the educational goals and programming approach.

The Annenberg criteria stress the merits of the core content itself. Episodes of shows are rated for clarity, integration, involvement, and applicability. In the NBC *Handbook* (Hill-Scott et al., 1999), the emphasis is not on inputs but on outputs. There are 10 criteria that define what each episode of the show must contain. There are 10 strategies that give producers the ability to determine when they have produced it.

Most importantly, D. G. Singer and J. L. Singer, (1998) point out that developing critical viewing skills among children would have the effect of raising the bar for programming. This is a bottom-up approach toward improving quality and complexity in content, as compared with the top-down impact of the Rules. However, if audiences can be maintained on the gradually improving menu of television choices, then viewer behavior will inform broadcasters to continue developing educational content. They will let the broadcasters know, without the catalyst of regulation, that the audience wants to be respected and educated as well as entertained.

## References


Anderson, D. R., & Collins, P. A. (1988, April). *The impact on children's education: Television's influence on cognitive development* (Working Paper No. 2). Washington, DC: U.S. Department of Education, Office of Educational Research and Improvement.

Berry, G. (1997). *CBS children's programs: Handbook for developing educational and informational television programs for children* [Brochure]. Los Angeles: CBS.

Campbell, T. A., Wright, J. C., & Huston, A. C. (1987). Form cues and content difficulty as determinants of children's cognitive processing of televised educational messages. *Journal of Experimental Child Psychology, 43*(3), 311-327.

Dorr, A. (1986). *Television and children: A special medium for a special audience.* Beverly Hills, CA: Sage.

Federal Communications Commission. (1990, October 18). *Children's Television Act of 1990* (Pub. L. No. 101-437). Washington, DC: U.S. Government Printing Office.

Federal Communications Commission. (1996). *Children's television rules* (Vol. 73.671). Washington, DC: U.S. Government Printing Office.

Federal Communications Commission. (1996, August 8). *Instructions for FCC 398: Children's television programming report* (FCC 98-335). Washington, DC: U.S. Government Printing Office.

Fischer, R. (1999, September 3-5). Broccoli and chocolate. *Hollywood Reporter,* pp. S-1–S-6.

Hill-Scott, K. (with Agress, E., Bauer, R., Huntington, G., Noble, Y., & Stipp, H.) (1996, January). *FCC/TNBC writers symposium.* Burbank, CA: NBC Entertainment (Proprietary).

Hill-Scott, K. (with Huntington, G., Montoya, R., McMahon, T., Noble, Y., & Stipp, H.) (1997, January). *FCC/TNBC writers symposium.* Burbank, CA: NBC Entertainment (Proprietary).

Hill-Scott, K. (with Carder-Hoffman, L., Forsyth, L., Noble, Y., Sandoval, T., & Zollo, P.) (1998, January). *FCC/TNBC writers symposium.* Burbank, CA: NBC Entertainment (Proprietary).

Hill-Scott, K. (with Kann, L., Meehan, K., Paez, M., Pinsky, D., Sherlock, B., Stipp, H., & Zandl, I.) (1999), February). *FCC/TNBC writers symposium.* Burbank, CA: NBC Entertainment (Proprietary).

Huston, A. C., & Wright, J. C. (1994). Educating children with television: The forms of the media. In D. Zillmann, J. Bryant, & A. C. Huston (Eds.), *Media, children, and the family: Social scientific, psychodynamic, and clinical perspectives* (pp. 3-18). Hillsdale, NJ: Lawrence Erlbaum.

Jordan, A. B. (with Davis, S., Fishman, J., Maxwell, K., Park, D., Schwank, L., & Wray. R.) (1998). *The 1998 state of children's television* (Report No. 23). Philadelphia: University of Pennsylvania, Annenberg Public Policy Center.

Jordan, A. B. (1999). *The three-hour rule: Insiders' reactions* (Report No. 29). Philadelphia: University of Pennsylvania, Annenberg Public Policy Center.

Jordan, A. B., & Woodard, E. H. (1998). Growing pains: Children's television in the new regulatory environment. *Annals of the American Academy of Political and Social Science, 557,* 83-95.

Kunkel, D. (1998). Policy battles over defining children's educational television. *Annals of the American Academy of Political and Social Science, 557,* 39-53.

Kunkel, D., & Canepa, J. (1994). Broadcasters' license renewal claims regarding children's educational programming. *Journal of Broadcasting and Electronic Media, 38,* 397-416.

McConnell, B. (1999, October 4). Pushing kids TV paperwork. *Broadcasting and Cable, 129,* 18.

Salomon, G. (1983). Television watching and mental effort: A social psychological view. In J. Bryant & D. Anderson (Eds.), *Children's understanding of television* (pp. 181-198). New York: Academic Press.

Schmitt, K. L. (1999). *The three-hour rule: Is it living up to expectations?* (Report No. 30). Philadelphia: University of Pennsylvania, Annenberg Public Policy Center.

Singer, D. G., & Singer, J. L. (1998). Developing critical viewing skills and media literacy in children. *Annals of the American Academy of Political and Social Science, 557,* 164-179.

Singer, J. L., & Singer, D. G. (1998). *Barney & Friends* as entertainment and education. In J. Asamen & G. Berry (Eds.), *Research paradigms, television, and social behavior* (pp. 305-367). Thousand Oaks, CA: Sage.

Trotta, L. (1998). *Building blocks: A guide for creating children's educational television* [Brochure]. Studio City, CA: Mediascope.

Van Evra, J. (1998). *Television and child development.* Hillsdale, NJ: Lawrence Erlbaum.

Woodard, E. H. (1999). *The 1999 state of children's television* (Report No. 28). Philadelphia: University of Pennsylvania, Annenberg Public Policy Center.

CHAPTER 34

# Child and Parent Responses to the Age-Based and Content-Based Television Ratings

BRADLEY S. GREENBERG
Michigan State University

LYNN RAMPOLDI-HNILO
Cheskin Research

Providing warning labels and content advisories to mass media products has long been a conundrum among congressional policy makers, parents, media industry leaders, and child activists. Although it may have begun long ago with book banning by church officials, it became explicit in the twentieth century with the labeling of motion pictures. Now a half-century after television sets became commonplace in American homes, the debate over providing viewers with advance information about some kinds of content in television shows has been actualized. In 1993, four broadcast networks—ABC, NBC, CBS, and Fox—presented the following warning in front of those shows of their choice: Due to some violent content, parental discretion advised (Mandese, 1993). Although this warning conveyed some information to assist in judging the appropriateness of program content, it was more a precaution than a revelation of the program content. Parent and child groups and political leaders marshaled their dissatisfaction (Cantor, Stutman, & Duran, 1997). After a series of congressional hearings, the 1996 Telecommunication Act included a mandate to the television industry. It had until January 1997 to create and implement its own rating system or a version would be created by the Federal Communications Commission (FCC).

To comply with the mandate, the U.S. television industry agreed to visually display information at the start of each show to inform viewers about the show's appropriateness for different age groups. Appropriateness was to be based on the show's inclusion of violent content, sexual content, and/or strong language. A two-tier rating system was developed. The first tier created a dichotomy of children's shows for children under 7 (TV-Y) and those 7 and older (TV-Y7), without any clear rationale why that age division was the chosen one. The second tier relied on the Motion Picture Association of America (MPAA) movie ratings (Stern, 1996). It focused on programming for the entire family. The labels specified that a TV show was intended for all audiences (TV-G), that parental guidance was advised (TV-PG), that the young viewer should be at least 14 (TV-14), or that the show was intended for a distinctly more mature audience (TV-MA).

This rating and labeling system came under rapid and intense criticism for lacking content-specific information (Hepburn, 1997). New negotiations between public activist groups and the new ratings oversight committee, which then consisted entirely of industry representatives, resulted in an extension of show labeling information. Content information about each show began to be added in October 1997. One label was added to the children's tier of programs to indicate fantasy violence (FV) among TV-Y7 shows, and five labels were made available for the second tier for violence (V), language (L), sex (S), adult dialogue (D), and fantasy violence (FV). This industry-modified version of the program ratings was accompanied by an agreement from the government to permit the system to be tested without further modification for some indefinite time. Two networks of note have chosen not to comply. NBC provides age-based ratings but not the content ratings, and Black Entertainment Television (BET) provides neither. In contrast, PBS opted not to adopt the original rating system but joined in using the revised system.

Implementation of this rating system has provided a rare and rich opportunity to examine the responses of parents and children while the system is still relatively new. Survey studies done early will provide a baseline for follow-up studies after the system has been in place for some period of time. Experimental studies add a component to the system as it has been implemented, with a "what if this had been done?" emphasis. This chapter brings together both those bodies of research, focusing as directly as possible on those users for whom the system was designed to provide an informational function.

In addition to the intended users of the ratings information, the research also can inform those involved with the advocacy, creation, and policing of the ratings. Much of the research tends to examine similar outcome variables, as laid out in the original proposal funded by the National Association of Broadcasters: Who is aware of and pays attention to the ratings? Who understands and is knowledgeable about the ratings? What general and specific use is made of the ratings? What misuse is made of the ratings? What attitudes exist toward them? Answers to these kinds of questions should contribute to the evolution of the system. This chapter provides an overview of the findings associated with these kinds of questions from multiple investigations.

## Parental Mediation and Responses to the Ratings System

We begin our review with parents. Although it is anticipated that older children may make more independent decisions about their television choices, a primary reason for the implementation of the ratings system was to provide additional information to parents about television programs, especially for younger children. Here, we review a portion of the literature on parental mediation of children's television behavior prior to and after the implementation of the ratings system.

As children age, parental monitoring and mediating of children's television behavior generally declines (i.e., parents mediate television more with younger children). This finding is robust and begins with parents more likely to restrict the television viewing of 3-year-olds than 5-year-olds (St. Peters, Fitch, Huston, Wright, & Eakins, 1991). Next, parents of elementary-school-age children used more positive guidance (recommendations and use of media as reward) and negative guidance (recommending against specific shows and withholding media as punishment) than parents of middle schoolers (Mohr, 1979). In a survey of seventh and tenth graders, Lin and Atkin (1989) found that television-viewing mediation was negatively related to the child's age, and these findings were replicated in a later study with fifth and tenth graders and their parents (Atkin, Greenberg, & Baldwin, 1991).

Similar concerns about parental mediation exist for such television-related technologies as cable, pay movie channels, and VCRs. Concurrent with these TV enhancements, there has been a continuing concern with how these technologies may have influenced parental mediation. Atkin, Heeter, and Baldwin (1989) investigated the degree to which parental mediation of child TV viewing (including restrictions and discussion regarding content) varied across pay, basic, and noncable households. Although they found that children with cable were exposed to more PG and R movies than those in noncable homes, in general, there were low levels of mediation and no significant differences among the three groups. Similarly, Atkin et al. (1991) found that having or not having cable played only a small role in predicting television viewing and parental mediation in their sample of fifth and tenth graders. That study also included an assessment of the impact of VCRs at the time when the VCR was considered to be the new electronic baby-sitter. VCR ownership was not related to restrictive parental mediation but was related to viewing R-rated movies. In a prior study, Lin and Atkin (1989) found that there was a significant correlation between parental mediation and rule making among children with a home VCR, and it decreased as the child grew older. Overall, the extent of parental mediation with these technologies has been low.

Although several researchers have investigated parental mediation of television (Abelman & Petty, 1989; Austin, 1993; Desmond, Singer, Singer, Calam, & Colimore, 1985) and the influences of related technologies (Atkin et al., 1989; Lindlof & Shatzer, 1990), few studies have focused on parental mediation with advisories and/or ratings. Krcmar and Cantor (1997) found that parents made negative comments about programs that contained advisories or PG-13 ratings and discouraged their children from viewing these programs. Most ratings or advisory research has focused on the influence of labels in persuading or dissuading viewers' choices directly and not as mediated by others (Bushman, 1997; Cantor & Harrison, 1996b). The ratings were created to aid parents in deciding what is appropriate for their children to watch. Now with the full-scale implementation of the ratings system, we wish to know if the information it provides is being used to inform parents' decisions about their children's viewing.

To be a useful information source for parents and others in the viewing audience, one needs consistent and accurate content criteria. Studies have shown, however, that program content and TV ratings are far from precise and too often do not match each other. Kunkel et al. (1998) reported that the age-based ratings were being applied with reasonable success, but the content advisories fell short on accuracy. More specifically, that research group reported that there was no content advisory for four out of every five depictions of violence, sex, and adult language, as they had operationalized those content components.

Content analyses also indicate inconsistent application of the ratings. Greenberg, Eastin, and Mastro (2000b) found that one of every four programs that should have had a rating identified in *TV Guide* did not have one during a 2-month sampling among eight major broadcast and cable networks. Whether no rating existed or the rating information came too late for the publication deadline is irrelevant; it was not there in advance of airtime. Moreover, 75% of the shows that did receive an age-based rating had no content descriptors. Should parents assume that the dialogue and the images in all those programs warranted no content warnings? The two most prominent content labels were the symbol D, indicating adult dialogue (38% of all content labels), and V for violence (33%); the symbol for sexual content (S) was used least. With respect to the age-based ratings, TV-PG was the most common rating (40%), followed by TV-G (28%), TV-14 (16%), TV-Y7 (9%), and TV-Y (7%). TV-MA was absent. There also were significant differences in the distribution of ratings between the broadcast and cable networks studied. Broadcast networks were more adult oriented (28% of their shows were TV-14) and cable networks oriented to more family programming (38% were TV-G).

Pursuing the accuracy question, Greenberg, Eastin, and Mastro (2000a) directly compared the ratings that appeared on the shows and the ratings as they had been published in *TV Guide.* In this follow-up study, one third of all shows that should have had ratings printed did not. Only half the shows listed in *TV Guide* matched their on-air rating. For those that did not, viewers who read *TV Guide* (or other published outlets with a similar advance deadline) were likely to think that a program had a lower age rating or less intense content than was actually shown. The published information indicated more general family-oriented programming than was actually available; 90% of the shows rated differently had a more stringent rating on-air than had been published. In a strange twist, shows intended for older audiences had more ratings information matched for age and content than did shows targeted for the youngest age groups.

Given these findings, likely unknown to the potential users of the ratings system, what then have parents been doing with this information? Here we examine parents' awareness, use, knowledge, concerns, and recommendations of the ratings system. Are the ratings helpful to parents in mediating television with their children?

To begin, a set of 9 focus groups (4-12 parents in each) and 20 whole-family interviews were conducted with Latino and Caucasian parents during late 1997 and early 1998 (Gregg, 2000; Mastro, 2000). All parents and families interviewed had a child between the ages of 6 and 10. Parents were asked to describe their awareness and use of the ratings system and give their opinions about it. They also answered questions about their parenting style, their children's knowledge of the ratings, how they dealt with their offspring regarding television, and their general concerns with television.

A primary concern among all parents was with what the ratings actually mean. Parents, especially Latina mothers, were troubled by the criteria used to rate the programs, the differences between ratings, and the accessibility of the ratings. One Latina parent responded to a question about trusting the ratings with, "I would still have to watch the program, maybe my idea of TV-Y7 is different from their [TV raters] idea of TV-Y7. Maybe I would be stricter or maybe I would be more lenient." Parents varied greatly when asked what was and was not acceptable television content for their offspring. One Caucasian parent stated, "They're not allowed to watch *The Simpsons,* because Bart is rude to his parents. Most of the shows play the parents as dumb and the kids as smart and funny." Instead of relying on the ratings system, most of these parents indicated much more active parental mediation—coviewing with their children, explaining programs, and actively permitting or forbidding individual shows. In general, these parents supported the television ratings system and what it was attempting to do but were confused about the system and considered it ineffective for themselves. Collectively, these parents suggested that the system would be more useful if the ratings (a) were displayed throughout the show, (b) were on the screen longer, (c) were verbally presented, (d) were larger in size, and (e) were displayed after each commercial break.

To provide more substantial evidence about issues raised in the focus groups and interviews, a sample of Latina and Caucasian mothers in Michigan with a child between the ages of 6 and 10 were interviewed (Greenberg, Rampoldi-Hnilo, & Mastro, 2000; Rampoldi-Hnilo & Greenberg, 2000) about 18 months after the ratings system had started. Approximately 30% of these mothers were not aware of the ratings at all. They were somewhat older and distinctly lower in average family income, and only 30% of them had more than one child. Of those aware of the ratings, they rated the clarity of the ratings below the midpoint of the scale used. These mothers considered the ratings more accurate than inaccurate, but few were strongly convinced about the accuracy. Latina mothers were most likely to let their children watch shows with these ratings: TV-G (75%), TV-PG (67%), TV-Y7 (58%), and TV-Y (42%). Caucasian mothers said they would let their children watch TV-G (78%), followed by TV-Y (69%), TV-Y7 (64%), and TV-PG (47%). Not many would allow their children to watch programs rated TV-14 or TV-MA. Thus, the shows designed and rated especially for young viewers were not judged as acceptable as TV-G shows, indicating a clear lack of understanding of those ratings by the mothers of young children.

These mothers could identify that the "V" rating indicated violence, but the other content labels fared less well among the mothers aware of the ratings system. One third did not understand the "L," 45% did not know that sexual content would be labeled, 58% believed the ratings would indicate if the show was scary, and 74% thought nudity would be identified.

Few mothers used the ratings to choose shows for themselves, only half used them to choose shows for their children, and one mother in six said they did so "every so often." Instead, their mediation consisted of (a) having bedtime rules on school nights; (b) using the VCR for alternative programming; (c) changing the channel when inappropriate content appeared; (d) discussing TV content to help their child understand; (e) coviewing with their child, especially at night; and (f) vetoing unacceptable shows.

The Kaiser Family Foundation conducted a nationwide survey in 1998 with 1,358 parents of a child between 2 and 17 years of age to determine attitudes, claimed use, perceived benefits, and their knowledge of the ratings system (Foehr, Rideout, & Miller, 2000b). Parents reported being concerned "a great deal" with the amount of sexual content (67%), violence (62%), and adult language (59%) on television. In this sample, nearly one fifth (18%) of parents were unaware of the TV ratings system. In the aware group, although 9 out of 10 thought that the ratings were a good idea, only half stated that they use the system "often" or "sometimes" in guiding their children's viewing. African American (72%) and Latino parents (73%) were less likely to be aware of the ratings system than Caucasian parents (85%), as were older parents, those with less education, and single parents. There were few ethnic differences in use and understanding of the system.

Most parents claimed to have a good working knowledge of the icons and labels used, but an independent assessment of actual knowledge did not support those claims. With the knowledge questions used in the Kaiser survey, 14% were "very well informed" and 40% were "fairly well informed," according to the investigators. The parents did somewhat better in understanding the age-based ratings than they did the content descriptors, and those who actually understood the ratings preferred the content descriptors. Large proportions of the parents, however, did not know what the ratings meant. Parents with children under 10 were not much better informed about TV-Y and TV-Y7 symbols than were parents of older children, for whom those symbols are less relevant. Parents who claimed direct exposure to information about the TV ratings system—4 in 10 of the aware parents—had a better understanding of the system. With respect to the V-chip technology itself, few parents said they would actively pursue buying a TV set equipped with the chip but will wait until their current set malfunctions. Primary advocated changes in the ratings system were for more detail and information on the shows' content, more frequent display of the symbols, and a better explanation of what the ratings mean.

In April 1999, exactly one year after its first survey, the Kaiser Family Foundation repeated it (Kaiser Family Foundation, 1999). These findings illuminate the fate of the ratings system with a parallel group of parents after another year of experience. The bottom line is that very little change occurred in that 12 months, and those changes that did occur can be characterized as lack of support for the ratings system. One fifth were still unaware that there was such a system and the same one half had "ever" used it, but 9% less than before were using it "often." Five percent less (43%) knew that the system provided both age and content information, 5% less (only 36%) knew that children's shows "like *Sesame Street* and Saturday morning cartoons" were rated, 5% less knew that prime-time dramas such as *ER* were rated, and 8% less knew that situation comedies such as *Frasier* were rated. Only one fourth knew that the ratings originated with the television industry itself.

As for knowledge of the ratings, only 10% of parents with children under 10 (down from 17%) could correctly recall any one of the specific ratings used in children's shows. Then, when asked what a TV-Y or TV-Y7 rating meant, one third of these parents responded correctly in the 1998 and 1999 studies. They did much better in correctly identifying the adult television program age ratings, except for TV-MA. But understanding of the content symbols was abysmal in both studies. Two percent were correct as to what D means, 3% for FV, 34% for S (down from 44% a year earlier), 40% for L, and 54% for V. Yet two of every three parents said it was the content-based ratings alone that provided the most useful information! If anything, the second survey provided evidence for a regression in use and understanding.

Abelman (2000) focused on profiling parents who were most likely and least likely to use the age-based ratings and to adopt the system in their decision making and home regulation of television. Findings suggest that parents who need mediation assistance the least are the ones most likely to use the ratings information in discussing TV with their children. These parents were classified as high mediators. Their primary mediation methods are working together to create and enforce rules about television, interacting frequently with their children, and using reasoning, explanation, and appeals to the child's pride and achievements as disciplinary techniques, while avoiding coercive strategies. Their children were low to moderate consumers of television, high academic achievers, and primarily female. These parents, who are characterized by strong communication practices and low external force with their child, are unlikely to use the V-chip to block TV programs because that restrictive technique would be uncharacteristic of their mediation approach.

Parents and children in greatest need of the ratings information were least likely to use the ratings, Abelman concludes. These parents create rules without consulting each other and do not offer explicit supervision or direct discipline in child rearing, particularly in monitoring television. They do not believe that television has strong impacts on their children. Their children, mostly boys, were heavy television viewers. Because this parental mediation style is relatively unfocused, in that there is not much parent-child discussion or punishment, Abelman predicts that these parents will not use the rating system.

The third profile of families was those who engaged in restrictive forms of television mediation. These parents restrict their children's consumption of objectionable content, and it was expected that they would be heavy users of the ratings, but they were not. They were found to be moderate mediators who limit the number of viewing hours and ban specific programs. These parents will likely use the ratings as a way to justify their restrictive mediation style.

In sum, this array of studies of parents indicates that parents are perplexed. Violent and sexual content and coarse language are significant concerns, these parents claim. In general, their attitude toward the ratings is supportive, indeed quite positive, but behaviors that would correspond with this attitude are largely absent. Use is quite marginal. Claims of understanding exceed actual understanding. How does one use a system that is not well understood? There also is the issue of accuracy. Many parents remain unsure of the television raters' judgments of a program's content and what age range is appropriate to view it, as compared with their own ideas of what they think their children can handle. Most are relying on their established modes of oversight, with a significant minority adding the ratings to their mediation repertoire. But those doing so may be least in need of doing so. Add the 20% of parents who admit they are still totally unaware of the ratings and the magnitude of the problem of an uninformed or disinterested public is better framed. What could have been attributed to the newness of this innovation and the need for greater familiarization seems unlikely based on the most recent Kaiser Family Foundation survey of parents.

## Youth Responses to the Ratings System

Parents are one half of the ratings system equation. Young children and adolescents also are active viewers. Many make the majority of their own viewing choices, although it is likely that some restrictions exist in terms of either total viewing time or content options. Here, we address the studies that consider how aware and attentive young viewers are to the ratings, what they understand about the ratings, and if and how they use the ratings to select or reject TV shows.

The first major study done was conducted in the spring of 1997, when only the original age-based ratings were available and had been available for less than 6 months (Greenberg, Rampoldi-Hnilo, & Hofschire, 2000). Across fourth, eighth, and tenth graders in a mid-Michigan urban center, the key results showed that attention to the ratings was low and attitudes about the system were marginally positive. These young people seldom used the ratings, their level of understanding of the ratings labels and the kinds of television programs rated were close to chance, and perceived misuse (using the ratings to choose shows they were not supposed to watch) was believed to be low. Along the age dimension, older students had more knowledge, but the younger claimed to pay more attention (although the average attention score was near the scale's midpoint), made more general use (60% more than the older groups), and perceived more misuse. Gender was not a predictor of any of their responses to the ratings system. There was equal attention, similar attitudes, and equivalent knowledge, understanding, and use between boys and girls in all the age groups. Among other predictor variables examined in the study, it was found that greater parental mediation (as identified by the youngsters), larger family sizes, and the presence of sibling influence were all contributors to increased attention, more positive attitudes, and more use, but they were not related to knowledge or understanding. Would the addition of content labels and another year make a difference? A subsequent study answered that question.

Findings were quite consistent between the two studies (Greenberg & Rampoldi-Hnilo, 2000). Students continued to report little attention, a middle-of-the-road attitude, and not much use or predicted misuse. Knowledge of what gets rated or what the age-based ratings mean did not improve. Knowledge of the content ratings was low for fantasy violence (FV) and adult dialogue (D) and highest for sexual content (i.e., they knew or could better guess that S indicated sex, and at a far higher level, than could parents in the studies reported earlier). Here, we will compare the two studies on some of the key outcome variables: knowledge, use, and misuse.

### *Knowledge*

Twelve items asked what content was identified in the ratings and which shows contained ratings. In the first study, the youth answered half of them (6.2) correctly and in the second year answered a bit more (6.9) correctly. This difference is significant ($p < .001$), but the magnitude of the change is less than one additional item correctly answered a year later. It is informative to identify what they knew and did not know:

| *Content Area* | *Percentage Correct* Year 1 | *Percentage Correct* Year 2 |
|---|---|---|
| Do the ratings tell if there is | | |
| Sex | 52 | 60 |
| Scary content | — | 33 |
| Violence | 70 | 78 |
| Bad language | 70 | 73 |
| Are there ratings for | | |
| TV shows at night | 50 | 52 |
| Soaps | 24 | 29 |
| Commercials | 76 | 78 |
| Game shows | 12 | 16 |
| Cartoons | 47 | 57 |
| Talk shows | 43 | 66 |
| News | 59 | 66 |
| TV movies | 78 | 85 |

Greater recognition that there are ratings on talk shows and on cartoons, but not the news, account for most of the change, along with moderate increases in understanding that sex and violence are described in the ratings. Because the entire set of content symbols had been in place for several months at the time of this study, the lack of larger shifts in understanding that sex, language, and violence are flagged in the ratings should be noted.

The youth also were asked to correctly match the meaning of five of the six ratings. To minimize the effect of sheer guessing, we omitted the G rating, which was near identical to its movie ratings meaning. The samples averaged 3.4 in the first study and 3.5 in the second, or no difference. Here is how they fared:

| *% Correctly Matched* | *Year 1* | *Year 2* |
|---|---|---|
| TV-Y | 52 | 58 |
| TV-Y7 | 77 | 75 |
| TV-PG | 64 | 55 |
| TV-14 | 80 | 82 |
| TV-MA | 71 | 69 |

Not surprising, they did best with symbols that contained a specific age designation (7 or 14).

Respondents in the second study were asked to match four of the five possible symbols (V, S, D, L, and FV) with appropriate definitions, omitting V.

> "Which rating means the show contains sexual content?" 73% chose S.
>
> "Which rating means the show contains bad language or swearing?" 56% chose L.
>
> "Which rating means the TV show has cartoons with violence in them?" 25% chose FV.
>
> "Which rating means the TV show has adults talking about topics that should not be heard by children?" 25% chose D.

Alternative questions might have led to more correct responses, but to the extent these questions are relatively unbiased, the symbols were not understood very well, except for sex.

### *Interpreting the Ratings*

Respondents also were asked to interpret a sample set of on-air labels. In these questions, the format was very similar to what would appear on-screen. For example, a small box framed a TV-14 symbol with labels V and D beneath it. The respondents were asked four questions about each of three boxed sets of symbols. For the TV-14, V, D label, they were asked whether the show had violence (93% correct), sex (67% correct), and swearing or bad language in it (36% correct), as well as whether the show was meant to be watched by children under 14 (85% correct). Generally, the youth answered questions better in this form than in the others we have presented. This suggests that young viewers may actually do better when presented the whole picture than when being asked to decipher the individual symbols out of context.

### *General Use of the Ratings*

This scale assessed the sample's orientation to use the ratings in choosing shows to watch or not watch. The results were mixed. In the first sample, the average (with a scale midpoint of 12.5) was 8.8, and in the second sample, it was 9.7. Although a significant increase ($p < .001$), it continues to reflect an average response between "not at all" and "not much." Nevertheless, we recognize it as an increase in self-reported general use of the ratings for program selection.

### *Specific Use of the Ratings*

Respondents reported how often they watched shows with the six different age-based ratings. The rate was no different between the two years, and the average scores of 14.4 and 14.6 were at the scale's midpoint of 15. Here are their responses:

| *Percentage Who Said Often or Very Often* | *Year 1* | *Year 2* |
|---|---|---|
| TV-Y | 31 | 37 |
| TV-Y7 | 29 | 38 |
| TV-G | 36 | 38 |
| TV-PG | 54 | 54 |
| TV-14 | 46 | 49 |
| TV-MA | 35 | 32 |

These findings are problematic. For example, in each year, about one third of the youth said that they "often" or "very often" watch TV shows with MA ratings, just about the same proportion who watch Y-, Y7-, and G-rated shows. However, an entire season of broadcast and cable television contains very few shows with an MA rating. When they respond about their frequency of viewing, they may be indicating what they would watch or what they have watched, or they may be confused by the ratings. From this study, it is not possible to sort through these alternative explanations, but it should serve as a caution in making any literal interpretation of what they (or their parents) say, in a context of incomplete understanding of the ratings system.

### *Misuse of the Ratings*

An exact comparison between the two years was not possible with this variable because of a change in response categories. However, in both seasons, the average response was essentially that the ratings were not being used for inappropriate purposes. The modal response was "never" for such purposes by "others" in elementary, middle, or high school.

Age differences on these key variables were consistent with the first study. Fourth graders claimed more use and anticipated more misuse, reported more attention, and offered more positive opinions. As for knowledge about the ratings, the grade groups did not differ in their knowledge of what gets rated, but the oldest group consistently scored highest on the other three measures of knowledge identifying the age ratings, identifying the content ratings, and interpreting the replicas of the on-air icons. The eighth graders were not far behind, and the fourth graders were the least knowledgeable. In the follow-up study, males were more knowledgeable about what was rated and could better identify the age-based ratings. The key predictors for the ratings system outcome variables were age of the respondent, television influence from siblings, independence in decision making, parental mediation, and overall television exposure.

Concurrent with the second Michigan State study, the Kaiser Family Foundation surveyed a nationally representative sample of 446 children between 10 and 17 years old (Foehr, Rideout, & Miller, 2000a). Of these young people, 80% said they were aware of the TV ratings system, and 45% of the aware group said they chose not to watch a particular show because of its rating. The ratings most likely to be a deterrent to their interest in viewing were S (44%), D (33%), TV-Y7 (28%), TV-MA (27%), and L (26%). But the largest group of children (from 44 to 70%) report that the ratings have no effect on their interest in what they choose to watch.

Four in 10 young people said their parents were using the ratings to make decisions about television viewing, a level of use that was not reflected in any of the direct studies of parents reported earlier. Almost all report no restrictions on shows with TV-Y7 or TV-PG designations, whereas from 10 to 15% report restrictions for S, V, FV, L, D, and TV-14 labels, and 21% for MA. Younger children (10-13) and girls were more likely to be dissuaded from watching a program based on its rating than were their older and male counterparts, especially if there was an S label. Younger children in this study also perceived more misuse, in this case their own. They more often reported watching a show they weren't supposed to because they were curious about it based on its rating (Foehr et al., 2000a).

Children claim a better understanding of the ratings than they actually demonstrate when tested directly on what the ratings mean. Consistent with the parent studies, they were better at correctly defining the age-based ratings than the content descriptors. Only 18% of the children could correctly identify all four age-based ratings (TV-G, TV-PG, TV-14, and TV-MA) asked about, and 25% answered none or only one of them correctly. Regarding the content descriptors, 52% could not correctly define any one of them, and only 2% could correctly identify all five of them. Even those who had received an explanation of the system and were more likely to say they understood the system "very well" demonstrated no better knowledge than those who had received no explanation (Foehr et al., 2000a).

In sum, young viewers are somewhat aware of the ratings but have little understanding of what they represent. At the time of these studies, the youth were more knowledgeable about the age-based than the content descriptors. Findings are mixed in terms of use, with some reporting very little use and others a bit more, but overall it cannot be considered substantial use. Those who were younger and female claimed greater use of the ratings, but, at least for the younger children, acquiescence to these questions (i.e., saying what they perceive they should be saying) may have been a factor.

## Related Experimental Research

Work preceding these surveys of the actual television ratings system has been largely experimental and has focused on the specific issue of potential abuse and misuse of the ratings information. The conceptual framework most often posed has been a variation of the "forbidden fruit hypothesis" (Christenson, 1992). This hypothesis proposes that the ratings may influence viewers to increase their viewing of inappropriate shows rather than refrain from viewing such programs. Thus, it posits a potential boomerang effect of the ratings on viewing behaviors whether they be movie ratings (Austin, 1980), TV warning labels (Bushman, 1997), or TV ratings systems (Krcmar & Cantor, 1997). This conception is based on the theory of psychological reactance (Brehm, 1966), which predicts that those who perceive their behavioral freedom to be threatened or restricted will be motivated to restore their freedom by engaging in the restricted behavior. Therefore, content may be more attractive to children, young people, or anyone else if parents (or other authorities) restrict or forbid viewing. An alternative conception is, of course, the "tainted fruit" possibility—being informed that a show is for older viewers or bears content that is unacceptable will be a turnoff to viewing.

Three experiments for media other than television—films with high school students, films with college undergraduates, and music albums with middle school students—produced no support for the forbidden fruit hypothesis (Austin, 1980; Bahk, 1998; Christenson, 1992). Then a series of experiments using television advisories and/or labels began. Cantor's experiments began by attaching either a parental advisory or parental violence advisory to fictitious and actual shows. Boys chose more reality-based crime shows with a parental advisory than girls did, and they chose those same shows more so overall when such an advisory was attached than when it was not. Randomly assigning different ratings to a movie did not affect the children's interpretation of the clip. The older youth better understood the advisories used (Cantor & Harrison, 1996b). In a follow-up study, Cantor, Harrison, and Nathanson (1998) had children rate their interest in fictitious TV program titles that had different ratings attached. Younger boys were more interested in programs with a parental discretion advisory than were young girls (5-9), with no differences among the older children (10-15). But the older ones were more interested in shows with more severe ratings than in those with G ratings.

Bushman and Stack (1996) tested made-for-television movies with and without labels and found that movies with labels were preferred. In a second experiment, they specifically tested whether these labels induced reactance and found that high-reactance subjects wanted to watch the TV films with labels more than the low-reactance subjects did. Finally, Bushman (1997) gave 600 subjects descriptions of six violent and six nonviolent programs that had either a warning label, an information label, or no label. Across all age groups (9-21+), there was greatest preference for the programs with the warning label, and this preference was keenest in the 9 to 11 age group.

Thus, the findings are mixed. Most have used ratings systems similar, but not identical, to that actually now in place (Hofschire, 2000). Some find support for the forbidden fruit notion that programs will be more attractive if they carry labels that are elevated, while others find evidence that "stronger" labels may deter viewing. However, the weight of the studies' evidence is that restrictive ratings attract viewers more so than not (Bushman, 1997; Bushman & Stack, 1996; Cantor & Harrison, 1996a), particularly males (Cantor & Harrison, 1996a; Chen, 1998) and older youth (Cantor & Harrison, 1996a). The tainted fruit effect has been found more with younger, female children (Cantor & Harrison, 1996a; Cantor, Harrison, & Nathanson, 1998) and when a parent-child dyad is making joint viewing decisions (Krcmar & Cantor, 1997). The field studies reviewed in this chapter indicated that the perceived normative level of misuse would be low, but higher levels were judged to be likely to occur by younger viewers, and they themselves were more likely to report doing so.

## Discussion

The field studies at Michigan State University and by the Kaiser Family Foundation certainly establish the baseline for the diffusion of the television ratings system. In fact, the follow-up studies in both settings provide a second time period for their assessment. At best, understanding, adoption, and application of the system by parents are tepid, even among those with young children. And for the youth themselves, the television ratings appear unlikely to be a serious criterion for determining what shows they choose to watch. Nevertheless, the Kaiser Family Foundation and the Center for Media Education in Washington, D.C., have begun a joint, national educational effort to better inform parents about the ratings. We shall withhold predictive judgments until that effort is complete and a further independent follow-up provides empirical results.

In the meantime, let us give our opinion as to why response has been as these studies indicate. First, if these field studies somehow would assess which parents (or children) are in greater or lesser need of such a system (Abelman, 2000), we would not be surprised that the ratings system provides a useful supplement to the in-home mediation activities of the latter. There would also not be much surprise in finding that those parents who do not provide much mediation are unlikely to use this new tool to do so. Selectivity is operative in this process. Parents who already monitor their children's television can point to the age designation or content labels as supportive of their own judgment and thereby reinforce their monitoring activities. Parents who do not find television much of a concern are unlikely to assimilate this information for any functional use. It is also worth noting that information and influence might run in the other direction; that is, many parents have suggested that they found out about the ratings from their children (Mastro, 2000). Some of the effort now aimed at educating parents in the meaning and use of these ratings might be refocused directly at their offspring. The older children are more aware of what TV has to offer in all its forms. Learning about the age and content ratings at an early age is also a likely precursor of use later in life.

Second, the credibility of the television ratings system information may be in question among many parents. This factor was clearly evident in the focus group outcomes (Gregg, 2000; Mastro, 2000) and was not well addressed in the field studies. Today, after a more extended period of ratings availability, it would be possible to determine how often parents have found themselves disagreeing with the designated rating for a show and how often they have been snake-bit by believing a show was acceptable for their child and then seeing that it was not. Or, more fairly, has the credibility of the ratings improved or faltered as they have been applied to more and more shows over a longer period of time? Has the public come to better assess the consistency or lack of consistency in ratings that are created by an unknown host of raters without hard criteria? Or do parents use different criteria that are not incorporated into the ratings system?

Third, the ratings system may be too confusing in its combining of age and content designations. The MPAA ratings for movies appear to be well understood, although the addition of an NC-17 category may have clouded even that system a bit. The television ratings have two tiers, one for children and one for all viewers, and then the content designations mean different things within different age ratings. And some age ratings do not carry content labels. One can only ponder what such a system might have looked like if fewer political interests had to be accommodated in the final version. Hofschire (2000) describes operative and planned systems in other English-speaking countries that may be simpler to understand; however, there is a dearth of research on those systems, including whether or not they are well understood. Certainly because those systems have a single rating body, the combination of ratings consistency and possibly greater ease in understanding would suggest an enhanced credibility. That in turn may lead to greater acceptance and implementation.

Finally, we pose the third-person effect as an appropriate phenomenon to consider here. The strongest expression of opinion in these studies is the need for a system that identifies what age viewer the show is appropriate for and whether it has content that may be offensive in terms of violence, sex, or language. The request for a ratings system is strong and prevalent. But who is it that needs the system to facilitate the choice of appropriate television shows? *You do. He does. She does. Their children do. But I'm OK. I know what's good and what's bad for my own children. It's all those others out there who are confused. I'm not.* Under such a rubric, the perceived imposition of this system from the outside, from very partial interests, and/or the lack of a perceived personal need may relegate the ratings to a minor personal role.

Yet we wish not to be doomsayers. We prefer some information to none and urge the ratings system to plug at least one large hole over which it has complete control to make the ratings information more consistent and reliable across shows and across networks. The raters and their staffs could network with each other (no pun intended) to arrive at a more common set of definitions for the relatively few variables with which they deal. If those definitions do not satisfy the operational criteria of social scientists, so be it. Let those definitions at least be used in common in the television industry, and make those definitions available. We can agree to disagree over them, but having them out there might go a long distance in upgrading their believability. As long as raters are prone to operate with their own brand of professional wisdom, and that wisdom differs from one network to the next, what's a parent to do but ignore the in-fighting and rely on his or her own experience and values.

## References


Abelman, R. (2000). Profiling parents who do and don't use the TV advisory ratings. In B. S. Greenberg, L. Rampoldi-Hnilo, & D. Mastro (Eds.), *The alphabet soup of television program ratings.* Cresskill, NJ: Hampton Press.

Abelman, R., & Petty, G. (1989). Child attributes as determinants of parental television-viewing mediation. *Journal of Family Issues, 10*(2), 251-266.

Atkin, D. J., Greenberg, B. S., & Baldwin, T. F. (1991). The home ecology of children's television viewing: Parental mediation and the new video environment. *Journal of Communication, 41*(3), 40-52.

Atkin, D., Heeter, C., & Baldwin, T. (1989). How presence of cable affects parental mediation of TV viewing. *Journalism Quarterly, 66*(3), 557-563.

Austin, B. A. (1980). The influence of MPAA's film-rating system on motion picture attendance: A pilot study. *Journal of Psychology, 106,* 91-99.

Austin, E. W. (1993). Exploring the effects of active parental mediation of television content. *Journal of Broadcasting & Electronic Media, 37*(2), 147-158.

Bahk, C. M. (1998). Descriptions of sexual content and ratings of movie preference. *Psychological Reports, 82,* 367-370.

Brehm, J. (1966). *A theory of psychological reactance.* New York: Academic Press.

Bushman, B. J. (1997). *Effects of warning labels on attraction to television violence in viewers of different ages.* Paper presented as part of an invited colloquium at the Telecommunication and Policy Research Conference, Alexandria, VA.

Bushman, B. J., & Stack, A. D. (1996). Forbidden fruit versus tainted fruit: Effects of warning labels on attraction to television violence. *Journal of Experimental Psychology: Applied, 2*(3), 207-226.

Cantor, J., & Harrison, K. (1996a). Ratings and advisories for television programming. In *National Television Violence Study scientific papers 1994-95* (pp. III-2–III-26). Studio City, CA: Mediascope.

Cantor, J., & Harrison, K. (1996b). Ratings and advisories for television programs. In *National Television Violence Study* (Vol. 1, pp. 361-409). Thousand Oaks, CA: Sage.

Cantor, J., Harrison, K., & Nathanson, A. (1998). Ratings and advisories for television programming. In *National Television Violence Study year 2.* Thousand Oaks, CA: Sage.

Cantor, J., Stutman, S., & Duran, V. (1997). *What parents want in a television rating system: Results of a national survey* [On-line]. Available: www.pta.org/programs/tvreport.htm

Chen, H. L. (1998). *Young adolescents' responses to television ratings and advisories.* Unpublished doctoral dissertation, Stanford University, Stanford, CA.

Christenson, P. (1992). The effect of parental advisory labels on adolescent music preferences. *Journal of Communication, 42*(1), 106-113.

Desmond, R. J., Singer, J. L., Singer, D. G., Calam, R., & Colimore, K. (1985). Family mediation, mediation patterns, and television viewing: Young children's use and grasp of the medium. *Human Communication Research, 11*(4), 461-480.

Foehr, U. G., Rideout, V., & Miller, C. (2000a). Children and the TV ratings system: A national study. In B. S. Greenberg, L. Rampoldi-Hnilo, & D. Mastro (Eds.), *The alphabet soup of television program ratings.* Cresskill, NJ: Hampton Press.

Foehr, U. G., Rideout, V., & Miller, C. (2000b). Parents and the TV ratings system: A national study. In B. S. Greenberg, L. Rampoldi-Hnilo, & D. Mastro (Eds.), *The alphabet soup of television program ratings.* Cresskill, NJ: Hampton Press.

Greenberg, B. S., Eastin, M., & Mastro, D. (2000a). Comparing the on-air ratings with the published ratings: Who to believe? In B. S. Greenberg, L. Rampoldi-Hnilo, & D. Mastro (Eds.), *The alphabet soup of television program ratings.* Cresskill, NJ: Hampton Press.

Greenberg, B. S., Eastin, M., & Mastro, D. (2000b). The ratings distribution in 1998, according to TV Guide. In B. S. Greenberg, L. Rampoldi-Hnilo, & D. Mastro

(Eds.), *The alphabet soup of television program ratings.* Cresskill, NJ: Hampton Press.

Greenberg, B. S., & Rampoldi-Hnilo, L. (2000). Young people's responses to the content-based ratings. In B. S. Greenberg, L. Rampoldi-Hnilo, & D. Mastro (Eds.), *The alphabet soup of television program ratings.* Cresskill, NJ: Hampton Press.

Greenberg, B. S., Rampoldi-Hnilo, L., & Hofschire, L. (2000). Young people's responses to the age-based ratings. In B. S. Greenberg, L. Rampoldi-Hnilo, & D. Mastro (Eds.), *The alphabet soup of television program ratings.* Cresskill, NJ: Hampton Press.

Greenberg, B. S., Rampoldi-Hnilo, L., & Mastro, D. (Eds.). (2000). *The alphabet soup of television program ratings.* Cresskill, NJ: Hampton Press.

Gregg, J. (2000). Field studies of the reactions of Caucasian parents to the new television ratings. In B. S. Greenberg, L. Rampoldi-Hnilo, & D. Mastro (Eds.), *The alphabet soup of television program ratings.* Cresskill, NJ: Hampton Press.

Hepburn, M. A. (1997). A medium's effects under scrutiny. *Social Education, 61*(5), 244-249.

Hofschire, L. (2000). Media advisories and ratings: What the experimental research tells us. In B. S. Greenberg, L. Rampoldi-Hnilo, & D. Mastro (Eds.), *The alphabet soup of television program ratings.* Cresskill, NJ: Hampton Press.

Kaiser Family Foundation. (1999). *Parents and the V-chip: A Kaiser Family Foundation survey* [On-line]. [Retrieved November 1999]. Available: www.kff.org/content/archive/1477/

Krcmar, M., & Cantor, J. (1997). The role of television advisories and ratings in parent-child discussion of television viewing choices. *Journal of Broadcasting & Electronic Media, 41,* 393-411.

Kunkel, D., Farinola, W. J. M., Cope, K., Donnerstein, E., Biely, E., & Zwarun, L. (1998). *Rating the TV ratings: An assessment of the television industry's use of V-chip ratings.* Menlo Park, CA: Kaiser Family Foundation.

Lin, C. A., & Atkin, D. J. (1989). Parental mediation and rulemaking for adolescent use of television and VCRs. *Journal of Broadcasting & Electronic Media, 33*(1), 53-67.

Lindlof, T. R., & Shatzer, M. J. (1990). VCR usage in the American family. In J. Bryant (Ed.), *Television and the American family* (pp. 89-112). Hillsdale, NJ: Lawrence Erlbaum.

Mandese, J. (1993). Marketers on TV warnings: Yawn. *Advertising Age, 64*(28), 1-3.

Mastro, D. (2000). Reactions of Hispanic parents to the new television ratings. In B. S. Greenberg, L. Rampoldi-Hnilo, & D. Mastro (Eds.), *The alphabet soup of television program ratings.* Cresskill, NJ: Hampton Press.

Mohr, P. J. (1979). Parental influence of children's viewing of evening television programs. *Journal of Broadcasting, 23*(2), 213-228.

Rampoldi-Hnilo, L., & Greenberg, B. S. (2000). A poll of Latina and Caucasian mothers with 6-10 year old children. In B. S. Greenberg, L. Rampoldi-Hnilo, & D. Mastro (Eds.), *The alphabet soup of television program ratings.* Cresskill, NJ: Hampton Press.

Stern, C. (1996). TV makes history at the White House. *Broadcasting & Cable, 126*(10), 5-8.

St. Peters, M., Fitch, M., Huston, A. C., Wright, J. C., & Eakins, D. J. (1991). Television and families: What do young children watch with their parents? *Child Development, 62,* 1409-1423.

# CHAPTER 35

# Digital Kids

## The New On-Line Children's Consumer Culture

KATHRYN C. MONTGOMERY
Center for Media Education

A child clicks an icon on her computer and is immediately transported to a richly graphic, brightly colored, interactive children's playground on the World Wide Web. Bathed in psychedelic colors of hot pink, lime green, and lemon yellow, the site's home page serenades with whimsical tunes and beckons with vibrant flashing signs. "Bug your buddies with creepy crawly e-cards made by you," says one. "Zap your friends with Wacky DigSig cards sponsored by Fruit Gushers and Fruit Roll-ups," urges another. One click on "play," another on "buzz," and the child is invited to display her own artwork on the "Kids' Gallery" or "hang out with the site's Web characters," Devin, Jessie, and Zach (*www.mamamedia.com*).

The MaMaMedia site is just one of hundreds of "destinations" created for children on the Internet. It is part of a new "children's digital media culture" that is swiftly moving into place, offering unprecedented amounts of material designed specifically for children. The growth of this new culture is being fueled by a powerful confluence of technological, demographic, and economic forces. The rapid penetration of the Internet and other digital technologies into American homes, the increase in the youth population, and a corresponding upswing in their value as a target market have all combined to create an explosion of digital products and services for children. Anticipating the convergence of digital television with on-line media, TV networks are producing children's programs in tandem with websites, as well as multiple distribution "platforms" such as CD-ROMs and video games.

With their engaging, interactive properties, the new digital media are likely to have a more profound impact on how children grow and learn, what they value, and ultimately

AUTHOR'S NOTE: I wish to thank the following people for their help in researching and writing this chapter: Jeff Chester, Gary O. Larson, Charlene Simmons, Erin Fitzgerald, Ellen O'Brien, Yalda Nikoomanesh, and Caty Borum.

who they become than any medium that has come before. "Generation Y," the nearly 60 million youth born after 1979, represents the largest generation of young people in the nation's history and the first to grow up in a world saturated with networks of information, digital devices, and the promise of perpetual connectivity (Neuborne & Kerwin, 1999). The burgeoning digital marketplace makes possible a cornucopia of content, providing a variety of experiences tailored to different interests, age groups, and tastes. The interactive features of the digital technologies hold great promise for empowering children by offering them new tools for self-expression, communication, and education. Many of the new websites for children have been received with great enthusiasm, not only by children but also by parents, teachers, and media critics. And some, like the MaMaMedia site, have received awards (Montgomery, 1999).

But powerful commercial forces are shaping this new interactive media culture. Advertising and marketing are quickly becoming a pervasive presence in the "kidspace" of the World Wide Web. The forms of advertising, marketing, and selling to children that are emerging as part of the new media depart in significant ways from the more familiar commercial advertising and promotion in children's television. The interactive media are ushering in an entirely new set of relationships, breaking down the traditional barriers between "content and commerce," and creating unprecedented intimacies between children and marketers. Because marketing to children is already a well-established, profitable industry, its imperatives are influencing the design of digital content and services for children in fundamental ways. These trends raise serious questions that will need to be addressed by researchers, policy makers, health professionals, and parents.

In this chapter, I briefly identify the roots of commercial culture in children's digital media; outline the key features of interactive marketing and advertising; discuss the implications of digital marketing on children's media; describe some of the recent efforts by consumer groups to establish safeguards for the digital era; and suggest a set of recommendations for research and policy. Because this new marketplace is evolving at such a fast pace, it is impossible to provide a definitive, exhaustive catalog of marketing, advertising, and selling practices. Therefore, I will focus on outlining the key features of the digital marketplace, discussing the major trends that are shaping it, and providing illustrations that are emblematic of its overall direction.

## The Digital Revolution

The trends in the children's digital market are part of a much larger set of developments in the digital revolution currently under way. The Internet, with its graphically rich World Wide Web, is only one component in a rapidly growing digital media infrastructure. Its emergence and growth are emblematic of the powerful role that new technologies are playing in transforming not only the media system but also the entire economy. In its short history, the Internet has undergone several critical transitions, evolving from a noncommercial, publicly funded, closed network that connected government agencies and research institutions into a privatized and increasingly commercialized global "network of networks." The expected convergence of the Internet and television into one seamless package of services using a digital set-top box (best exemplified today by WebTV) will further transform this medium. Experts predict that, within the next few years, these interactive services will become a communications, marketing, retailing, and cultural medium similar in scope to what cable TV and newspapers are today (Jupiter Communications, 1999b).

Driving the growth of the digital technologies is the promise of e-commerce, which is already expanding at a rapid rate. Although few, if any, companies on the Web have yet to make any money, the potential viability of the digital marketplace has generated major investment in the many on-line ventures. The recent spate of mergers and "strategic alliances" within the media, communications, and retail industries is intended to position these newly configured corporations to take advantage of the potentially huge profits of the digital era (Wieffering, 1999). The Internet generated approximately $300 billion in U.S. revenues in 1998, a figure approaching that of the automobile industry. Consumers spent $8 billion buying computers, books, CDs, clothing, and other items through the Internet in 1998 (Leibovich, Smart, & Dugan, 1999).

## "Digital Kids"

As "early adopters" of new media, children and youth are, in many ways, the defining users of the digital media. Even as the digital future is still unfolding, electronic media are already playing a significant role in the lives of children and teens, many of whom enjoy access to their own personal media devices. Among children ages 6 to 17, for example, 86% have access to a VCR (23% in their own rooms); 70% have a video game system at home (32% in their own rooms); 50% have a TV in their own room; 40% have their own portable cassette or CD player; and 35% have their own stereo system (Roper Starch Worldwide, 1998). Although TV remains the dominant media pastime for children (who watch an average of 17.2 hours per week, along with another 5.5 hours watching videotapes), the time spent in front of that screen is declining, while the time spent in front of the computer is going up. However, as a study by the Annenberg Public Policy Center of the University of Pennsylvania points out, "Rather than displacing television as the dominant medium, new technologies have supplemented it, resulting in an aggregate increase in electronic media penetration and use by America's youth" (Stanger & Gridina, 1999, p. 2).

Families with children represent one of the fastest-growing segments of the population using the Internet. In 1998, according to Jupiter Communications, approximately 8.6 million children and 8.4 million teenagers were on-line, figures that are expected to grow to a combined 38.5 million by 2002 (Jupiter Communications, 1999a). According to an October 1998 study from the Graphics, Visualization, and Usability Center at the Georgia Institute of Technology, 32% of 11- to 20-year-olds spend 10 to 20 hours a week on-line. Among that age group, according to self-reporting, 18.6% of this time is spent on entertainment, 17.1% on education, 16.3% on personal information, 16% on "time wasting," 11.8% on communication, 8.2% on shopping, 7.8% on work, and 4.2% on other activities (Graphics, Visualization, and Usability Center, 1998). Among children 2 to 12, the most popular on-line activities are e-mail (with 46.4% of those surveyed reporting this as a primary on-line activity), games (44%), "surfing the Web" (37.6%), and homework (30.4%) (Jupiter Communications, 1998).

Because this is "the generation that spends the most time glued to a computer monitor," explains the popular trade publication *Selling to Kids,* "online marketing is going to be more important for this group than any previous" (Stark, 1999, p. 3). Children and youth are a particularly important target for marketers because of their increased spending power, which has risen dramatically over the past several decades. This rise has been attributed to several demographic and economic trends. Not only has the number of children in the United States increased, but the divorce rate has risen, more parents work outside of the home, and more and more children are now responsible for shopping decisions that used to be strictly the domain of parents. As a consequence, children's spending power doubled between the years 1960 and 1980, and tripled in the 1990s. Children under 12 now control or influence the spending of almost $500 billion (Russakoff, 1999). In 1998, teens spent $141 billion of their own money in the retail market (Anderson, 1999).

These trends have spurred the production of a spate of new products and services designed specifically for children and teens, including a proliferation of television channels devoted exclusively to this valuable demographic group, such as Nickelodeon, Fox Kids Network, the Disney Channel, and the Cartoon Network (Mifflin, 1999). The value of children to advertisers has also spurred the creation of an infrastructure of companies studying the "youth market." As the *Washington Post* observed,

> With the number of children in America larger than at the peak of the baby boom, and their purchasing power growing faster than economists can measure it, a vast service industry of market researchers, public relations firms, newsletters and ad agencies has sprung up to lead corporate America to young hearts, minds and piggy banks. (Russakoff, 1999, p. A1)

With the emergence of new media technologies, many of these companies have been engaged in a variety of market research efforts—from focus groups to on-line surveys to less orthodox methods—to determine children's behavioral responses to new media. For example, at the Saatchi and Saatchi advertising agency, anthropologists visited children in their homes to closely observe their interaction with digital technology (Russakoff, 1999, p. A1). These experts found that children, whose "learning skills are at their peak," can easily master the new media's learning curve, which is often daunting for adults (Gruen, 1995). They also determined that the on-line world corresponds to the "four themes of childhood . . . attachment/separation, attainment of power, social interaction, and mastery/learning" ("Children Get Growing," 1995, p. 5). And, perhaps most important, they found that when children go on-line, they quickly enter the "flow state," that "highly pleasurable experience of total absorption in a challenging activity." All of these factors make on-line media a perfect vehicle for advertising to children, according to advertising executives: "There is nothing else that exists like it for advertisers to build relationships with kids" (Gruen, 1995).

Within the past several years, a host of market research firms and trend analysis companies have begun offering seminars, conferences, and trade shows with names like "Digital Kids," "Interactive Kids," and "Teen Power." They charge thousands of dollars for these events, and tens of thousands more for specialized trade publications and reports offering strategies for cashing in on the "cybertot" and on-line teen markets. For example, hundreds of eager digital "content providers" flocked to the 1999 "Digital Kids" trade show to market their services for children and teens—from new Web-based entrepreneurs such as MaMaMedia and HeadBone Interactive to established media conglomerates such as Disney and Nickelodeon (Thompson, 1999). Market research has assumed such a central role in the creation of the new digital children's culture that the process is becoming intertwined with the creation of on-line content. Some media companies have rooms in their headquarters for regular focus groups with children; others use their on-line sites to conduct market surveys with children and teens. This intense focus on research within the new media industries has produced a wealth of information, much of it proprietary, which is guiding the development of digital content and services for children.

## The Digital Marketing Paradigm

The unique features of the new media have made possible the emergence of a new paradigm for interactive marketing, which is being proselytized by a legion of new-media gurus (Godin, 1999; Peppers & Rogers, 1999). The key concepts of this paradigm have already had a powerful influence on the forms and practices of marketing on the Web and are a basic part of the design for emerging technologies such as digital television. They have also been woven into the fabric of children's on-line culture. What follows is an outline of the basic principles of digital marketing, with brief illustrations of how they are currently being put into practice, particularly in children's digital media, as well as a discussion of how they are likely to be employed in emerging new media.

### *"One to One"*

Since it was published in 1993, *The One to One Future,* by Don Peppers and Martha Rogers, has become the bible for on-line marketing, spawning an entire generation of handbooks, seminars, articles, and conferences (Peppers & Rogers, 1993). Sometimes called "relational marketing," the strategy is based on the principle of developing unique, long-term relationships with individual customers to create personalized marketing and sales appeals based on their individual preferences and behaviors. "Interactive technology," espouses Peppers (1999), "means that marketers can inexpensively engage consumers in one-to-one relationships fueled by two-way 'conversations'—conversations played out with mouse clicks on a computer, or touch-tone buttons pushed to signal an interactive voice response unit, or surveys completed at a kiosk" (p. 6). As one on-line marketing company explained it,

> This goes beyond simple transaction processing and secure payment systems: it's about building relationships with customers online—knowing each customer by name, knowing their preferences and buying patterns, observing the customers over time, and using this data to sell more effectively to them. (Perkins, 1996, p. 2)

At the heart of this system is the ongoing collection of personal information and tracking of on-line behavior. Through the data collected, the right mix of information, ads, and buying opportunities is designed in an irresistible package to "microtarget" the individual customer.

Marketers employ a variety of techniques to get to know each customer as intimately as possible. One method is the use of incentives such as games, surveys, discounts, and prizes to get individuals to supply personal information about themselves. For example, a survey can collect names, addresses, and e-mail addresses along with information about income level, attitudes, fears, and behaviors. Although a common direct marketing practice in "off-line" media, these forms of data collection can become more intrusive in on-line and other interactive media, where the response time is quick and the incentives (e.g., free e-mail, discounts, and other kinds of "instant" gratifications) can be hard to resist (Montgomery & Pasnik, 1996). Another method is the covert tracking of on-line behavior, often referred to as clickstream data. Unlike TV ratings, which generally use anonymous aggregate numbers to reveal the viewing behavior of key demographic groups, on-line usage data can track how individuals respond to and interact with advertising. A burgeoning industry has developed to provide an array of "personalization technologies" that are being integrated into the basic design of interactive marketing. For example, both Microsoft Explorer and Netscape Communicator, the two most widely used Internet browsers, allow websites and marketers to place "cookies" on users' computers, which are designed to track every move the individual makes on-line and store this information for later use (Givens, 1997).

The principle of one-to-one marketing has been employed in many commercial websites targeted at children and youth. In its 1996 report *Web of Deception* (Montgomery & Pasnik, 1996), the Center for Media Education documented a number of data-collection practices in children's websites, including games, surveys, prizes, and the use of "product spokescharacters" to elicit information. For example, one website offered "cybercash" to children, which could be redeemed for prizes. Others required "registration" to participate on the site and then used the information to send unsolicited e-mail to the child, urging a return visit. At the *Batman Forever* website, supplying personal information was presented as a test of loyalty. "Good citizens of the Web, help Commissioner Gordon with the Gotham Census," children were told (Montgomery & Pasnik, 1996, p. 8).

In response to complaints from the Center for Media Education and other consumer groups, Congress passed the Children's Online Privacy Protection Act (COPPA) in 1998, which directed the Federal Trade Commission to develop rules restricting some of these data-collection practices and requiring parental permission for collection of personal information from children under 13. (See the section "Need for Safeguards" for a fuller discussion of COPPA.) But marketers are continuing to devise other techniques for gathering personalized information and establishing ongoing relationships with children. For example, a number of children's websites now ask children to sign up for on-line "newsletters," which are sent to their e-mail addresses on a regular basis and are little more than thinly disguised advertisements for products (Center for Media Education et al., 1999).

This and other forms of Internet-based marketing do not even require knowing the real name and address of the individual, since the relationship can be established and maintained solely on-line. With the increasing innovation in technology, it has become unnecessary to ask individuals to volunteer personal information about themselves. Technological methods can be employed to develop and maintain "customer identifying data," making it possible to track customers' behavior, target them with personalized marketing messages, and marry the information from individual websites with that from other sources (Givens, 1997). Indeed, it is this ability of computer-based technologies to combine personal information from a variety of sources that makes them so potent, and threatens consumer privacy.

As more sophisticated computer interfaces are developed, the potential for more compelling and engaging forms of one-to-one marketing is growing. The next generation of digital marketing will employ human-like "interactive characters" to "build relationships based on familiarity, affection, and trust" (Hayes-Roth, 1999, p. 61). Digital television, which has already begun operating in some cities, will make possible another level of data collection and microtargeting by linking the moving image and sound of television with the interactive capabilities of the Internet (Larson, 1998).

### *Integration of Advertising and Content*

One of the most prominent features of marketing in the digital media is the blending of what has traditionally been called "content" with advertising so that there is a seamless integration of the two. The familiar 30-second television commercial is expected to become relegated to the annals of media history, a now dysfunctional form of "interruption marketing" no longer appropriate or effective in the digital age (Godin, 1999). Instead, advertising and marketing are being skillfully woven into programming or are presented as programs or "content" themselves. According to *Red Herring,* a trade publication for investors,

> What is really happening [on the Web] is what will ultimately happen on interactive television: the infomercialization of all programming. Services will deliver some content, with lots of appeals (some soft, some hard) to purchase. Requesting literature and additional information (read: volunteering for a mailing list), and actual buying, will be easily enabled. . . . This is not advertising as you and I understand it, but a more viewer-engaged, browse-and-buy genre just beginning to emerge as a form of programming unto itself. (Davis & O'Driscoll, 1995, p. 3)

This integration is a fundamental strategy in the design of children's websites. Unlike television, in cyberspace time does not restrain ad length—an ad's effectiveness is measured in part by the amount of time each child spends "in" the ad. "If you create an ad that's as much fun as the content," such as "games that kids can play that involve the products . . . then there'll be a reason for kids to click on the ads and interact with them and enjoy them," explained one executive (Roberts, 1995). With children, explained another, "Anything that is perceived as an interruption of the flow state, whether it's artwork being downloaded or an ad that is obtrusively splattered on a screen, is going to get a negative reaction" (Gruen, 1995). Consequently, the practice of disguising advertising as content may well become the norm for commercial children's sites.

Because of criticisms from consumer groups, many children's websites now put "ad bugs" or the word *advertisement* next to the "sponsored activities" and sometimes place a "bridge page" between the home website and the ad's website. But the goal of merging the identity and the experience of both the "content" and the ad is still well served. The "banner ad," the familiar flashing brand name on top of many websites, functions not just as a message from the sponsor but as a kind of gateway, beckoning one to the sponsor's own website. One click on the banner and the child is transported through a "hotlink" to another engaging playground with its own games, contests, and puzzles, the kinds of "sticky" content designed to encourage children to stay for long periods of time and to return often after the first visit.

### *"Branded Environments"*

Not only are marketing and advertising woven into many children's content areas, but the Web has spawned a new genre of sites in which the product *is* the content. In many ways, this pattern turns the concept of sponsorship and advertiser-supported programming on its head. Almost all of the major companies that advertise and market to children have created their own websites, designed as "branded environments" for children on the Web. Many are among the most popular sites visited by kids. Companies such as Hasbro, Mattel, Frito-Lay, and Lego are just a few that have created websites for children. Emblematic of this trend is Mattel's Barbie.com site. Positioning itself as a community for girls—with links to high schools and other ".orgs," the site offers a variety of on-line activities designed to appeal to girls, such as sending e-postcards, receiving newsletters, entering contests, and "voting" for their favorite Barbie. The site profiles many of the popular doll's new personas (including Soccer Barbie, Pet Lovin' Barbie, and Vintage Spring in Tokyo Barbie) as well as many of the classic styles. Following its successful Barbie Fashion Designer CD-ROM, the site also gives girls the opportunity to design their own personalized Barbie, choosing from an inventory of physical features, clothing styles, and personality traits. The personalized Barbie can then be custom-made for that child and purchased on-line for $39.95 (Thompson, 1999).

The development of "brand loyalty" among children has become axiomatic among marketers in recent years, a core strategy of the "cradle-to-grave marketing" principle. As marketing expert James U. McNeal (1992) explains, "Children begin developing brand preferences and store preferences in early childhood, even before they enter school. And not just for child-oriented products, but also for such adult-oriented things such as gasoline, radios, and soaps." This tendency is strongly rooted in the developmental needs of children, according to McNeal.

> The belonging (affiliation) need, which causes us to seek cooperative relationships, is very strong among children. . . . Also, children are looking for order in their lives. There are so many new things to encounter that some order is necessary to cope with them all. A trusting relationship in which satisfying acquisitions can always be expected helps give order to an increasingly complex life. (pp. 92-93)

"Branding" is a pervasive theme in the digital media, one that is not restricted to products but is increasingly used as a descriptive and organizing principle for all aspects of media culture. Media companies refer to themselves as brands; even public television calls itself a "brand." When speaking of strategic alliances and partnerships, companies refer to the practice as "sharing each others' brand space." At the 1999 Digital Kids conference, participants spoke proudly of "branded communities" for teens—websites built around products—invoking the slogan "Love my community, love my brand" (Digital Kids, 1999).

### *On-Line Selling/E-commerce*

A growing number of websites for children and teens feature on-line stores or links to websites that are designed to make direct sales (Thompson, 1999). A 1999 survey by market research firm NFO Interactive found that 52% of children between the ages of 5 and 17 have asked their parents to purchase an item that they have seen on the Web (Cox, 1999; Thompson, 1999). According to Jupiter Communications (1999a), "Kids and teens have become a growth sector for online shopping," which in 1999 made the important shift from "passive online advertising" to "actively targeting kids and teens for digital transactions" (p. 1). A recent Jupiter/NFO consumer survey, which queried 600 teens (13-18 years old) and kids (5-12 years old), found that 67% of on-line teens and 37% of on-line kids indicate that they have researched or bought products on-line. Jupiter forecasts that teens will account for $1.2 billion and kids will account for $100 million of the e-commerce dollars in 2002 (Jupiter Communications, 1999a).

Companies are employing a variety of strategies to facilitate on-line purchases by children, including the creation of "digital wallets," which allow parents to use a credit card to deposit a set amount of money into a child's on-line account. Websites such as IcanBuy.com *(www.icanbuy.com)* and RocketCash.com (*www.rocketcash.com*) are among the first companies to offer on-line selling to children, but others are expected to follow suit. Some are employing barter and other kinds of transactions that do not use cash or credit cards but set up substitutes for money to begin the process of getting children and their parents accustomed to making purchases on-line (Thompson, 1999). The Jupiter Communications survey showed that the biggest obstacle facing children who want to buy products on-line is their parents' refusal to let them. A number of companies are developing strategies to sweeten the notion of allowing children to spend money on-line by offering to include educational messages teaching children about financial responsibility. Some are also developing noncash forms of transaction as a first step. For example, DoughNET.com (*www.doughnet.com*) offers to let children "play with money" by investigating how the stock market works. And Beenz.com has created a form of "virtual cash" that children and adults can collect online by going to participating sites and taking part in surveys, promotions, and other marketing enterprises (Weise, 1999). With more and more schools being linked to the Internet, many of these same companies are targeting the classroom as a site for marketing and online sales to children (Manning, 1999).

Many of the websites targeted at teens encourage on-line purchases. For example, react.com (*www.react.com*) is a popular "one-stop-shopping" site for teens. Here teens can get news or information about their favorite celebrities, find out what styles are "in," play games, share their concerns, and shop. A growing number of these sites are linked to television shows, encouraging viewers to "multitask" (i.e., watch television and use the website at the same time). (Market researchers have found that children and teens are much more at ease multitasking than adults are.) For example, the *Dawson's Creek* website enables young people to interact with the main character, find out his innermost thoughts and feelings, and learn what products he purchases. This website offers an insightful glimpse into the future of interactive television, especially in the way that program content is expanded and integrated into interactive website features. By logging onto "Dawson's Desktop," a subsection of the program's site, users can click onto virtually any image on the screen, including the main character's e-mail inbox and favorite "bookmarked" websites, and link directly into an advertiser's site or on-line purchasing form (Anderson, 1999).

### *Interactive Product Placement*

Product placement, a pervasive practice in film and an increasingly common practice in television, is another central component of the digital marketing paradigm. The merging of television and the Internet will create newer and more powerful forms of product placement. "With the next generation of entertainment," explains Marc Collins-Rector, cofounder and chairman of the Digital Entertainment Network (DEN), "there'll be no differentiation between the entertainment aspects . . . and the advertising aspect of what you are watching. . . . We'll tie in the advertisements to what the characters are doing" (as cited in Frauenfelder, 1999, p. 122). The Web-based network targeted at teens was designed to become an interactive television channel. Though it went out of business in spring 2000, its combination of product placement, streaming video, chat, and instant polls has already been widely adopted by other media companies. DEN's advertising strategy was a curious blend of old and new techniques. Modeled in part on 1950s TV programs in which actors pitched products within the story line, the network also made use of cutting-edge youth marketing approaches such as "discovery marketing," which is "essentially a way to put a brand in front of someone's face yet make them think they found it on their own" (Frauenfelder, 1999, p. 122).

As digital television becomes more available, not only will products be featured as part of the story but the viewer will be given the opportunity to buy them on the spot. "Narrative strands" within a program will lead viewers to a "buying opportunity" and then return them to the story after the purchase (Digital Coast, 1999). Precursors to this planned "embedded e-commerce" can already be seen in some of the websites associated with popular television shows. For example, CBS recently began selling a bracelet on its website worn by a character in *Guiding Light,* a popular soap opera. The silver-coated replica ($29.95) was advertised during the program; promotional spots directed viewers to the CBS website (Beatty, 1999). Another website that offers similar features is AsSeenIn.com (*www.asseenin.com*), a project of successful TV producer Aaron Spelling. Here, replicas of furniture, clothing, cars, and miscellaneous products from Spelling's popular teen shows such as *Charmed* and *7th Heaven* are sold. Viewers can go to the program's website, click on a photo of the house used in the show, then click on an individual room, and then click on an item within that room. For example, clicking on a rug in the living room will immediately hotlink the customer to the retailer's website, where that exact rug can be purchased on-line (Hunt, 1999).

The techniques currently in practice on the World Wide Web are only the earliest and most embryonic representations of what is likely to become a highly sophisticated marketing and e-commerce infrastructure in the digital age. The zeal with which digital marketing is being embraced by children's advertisers and content providers alike suggests that the new digital children's culture may quickly become highly commercialized. Governed by the principles of brand loyalty, one-to-one relationships, and e-commerce, marketing and advertising in the new media are likely to become a particularly pervasive presence in children's lives.

## Promise and Peril in the Digital Marketplace

Much of the public debate over the Internet and children has been dominated by concerns about on-line access to indecent and violent material, exposure to predation, and similar harms that might befall children in cyberspace. Twice in recent years, Congress passed legislation prohibiting the distribution of indecent content to minors on the Internet. Both laws, however, have been met with constitutional challenges (Zick, 1999). To address parental concerns, the on-line industry has come forward with a series of measures to protect the safety of children on the Internet. Companies such as CyberPatrol, SurfWatch, and Net Nanny offer parents software to block out inappropriate content on the Web (Center for Media Education, 1999; Kennedy, 1996). In May 1999, the White House announced the "One Click Away" initiative, in which on-line companies have agreed to create "parents' protection pages" on all major portals, search engines, and websites. The pages are to provide access to blocking and filtering software, tools for monitoring children's activities on-line, and safety tips for both parents and children (Clinton & Gore, 1999).

However vital these issues may be, the debate over pornography, violence, and predation has in many ways diverted public attention away from other important developments in this new medium that will have a significant impact on children and youth. While there are legitimate concerns about children's access to harmful and inappropriate *adult* content on-line, it is also important to focus attention on the content and services that are being created exclusively *for* children. It is in these areas, after all, that children will be spending the vast majority of their time on-line. And it is in these areas that the full potential of the Internet—for both good and ill—will be realized.

The early trends in the development of the children's digital marketplace suggest the possibility for both promise and peril. On the one hand, children's value as a market could generate an abundant media universe, offering children a richness and diversity of experience heretofore unavailable to them. The fragmentation of the youth market into smaller, more defined demographic and interest groups also means that the new media should be better able to tailor their content to meet the needs of more children, including those who may have been underserved in the conventional media. On the other hand, the powerful influence of commercial forces at this earliest formative stage is likely to leave an indelible, long-lasting imprint on the structure and design of the entire children's digital media culture. With so much money to be made from children and teens, the imperatives of marketing and sales will likely shape the vast majority of content and services for children in the digital age.

This is not to suggest that digital media technologies will not offer children multiple opportunities for education, communication, and creativity outside of the commercial context. In fact, the World Wide Web has already made possible a flowering of educational, cultural, and civic content for children, enabling children to create their own websites and form communities across geographic boundaries (Montgomery, 1999). Although these sites are an important part of the Web, most are already being overshadowed by the much more heavily promoted commercial sites, many of them tied to popular TV shows, films, and other consumer products. The overwhelming presence of this commercial culture is reflected in the list of the most popular children's websites maintained by Web21 (*www.100hot.com/kids*). Of the top 25 sites on that list from May 1999, the only noncommercial site was the Smithsonian Institution (number 17). Dominating the list were media conglomerates (including Disney, Fox, Warner Brothers, and Nickelodeon) and toy companies (Lego, Sega, Nintendo, and Toys 'R' Us). The convergence of television and the Internet could eventually mean that the less popular noncommercial and civic services will be relegated to the hinterlands of the digital media universe. Although they may be there, few will know about them, and even fewer will find it easy to access them.

Even public television is being influenced by the new commercial imperatives of the digital media culture. Though there are rules that govern the role of corporate underwriters on public TV, no such restrictions exist in cyberspace. Although most of the websites for

PBS children's shows have been careful not to incorporate advertising or marketing, some underwriters have been able to take advantage of the fluidity of the Web experience by putting links designed to transport children to their own "branded environment" (HR: Corporation for Public Broadcasting Authorization Act of 1999). One of the most respected institutions in public television, Sesame Workshop (Children's Television Workshop), which produces *Sesame Street,* has introduced advertising into its website for preschoolers and formed a partnership with E-Toys, an online toy retailer. Though targeted to parents, the intrusion of advertising and marketing into what has traditionally been a noncommercial service raises disturbing questions about the viability of truly noncommercial children's media in the digital era (Slatalla, 1999).

There have been innovative attempts by some Web content providers to develop alternatives to the advertiser-based model. For example, JuniorNet bills itself as a kind of "gated community" for children on the Internet. For a monthly fee, the service provides an advertising-free space, offers "quality content" from such producers as Scholastic and Jim Henson Productions, and promises to protect children from questionable content by monitoring chat rooms and screening material from other sites (Flaherty, 1999). Whether noncommercial subscription services such as JuniorNet prove to be financially viable in a digital world where so much advertiser-supported content is available for free remains unclear. If such services do succeed, they could set up a new digital caste system, where only more affluent families would be able to provide their children with alternatives to a media culture saturated with sales pitches.

Concerns about advertising reach beyond the scope of media in the home as more Web-based companies are targeting the classroom as a site for marketing and on-line sales to children (Manning, 1999). Given the controversy that has surrounded Channel One's introduction of advertising into high schools, the growth of Web-based marketing to schools should be of concern to educators and to parents (Hoynes, 1997). As law professor Angela Campbell warns, "Where a Web site has two purposes—providing information and selling a product—it is easy to see that the first may be subordinated to the second" (Campbell, 1997/1998, p. 331).

## Need for Safeguards

Because this new media culture is still in its early stages, there is an opportunity—albeit a brief one—to develop safeguards for ensuring that children will be treated fairly by marketers and advertisers. Although resistance from the media industries to any regulation of "content" on the Internet or in other interactive technologies is very strong, there is a longstanding tradition in the United States of regulating advertising and marketing to children (Landesberg, Levin, Curtin, & Lev, 1998). In 1998, the Center for Media Education (CME) and other consumer, education, and child advocacy groups were able to help institute the first federal rules on children's marketing. CME's 1996 publication *Web of Deception* raised public and government awareness by documenting many of the emerging data-collection and advertising practices targeted at children on the Web (Montgomery & Pasnik, 1996). Along with Consumer Federation of America, CME petitioned the Federal Trade Commission (FTC) to develop rules to govern children's marketing on the Internet.

The FTC held a series of workshops and hearings to consider the need for more formal regulations and conducted its own analysis of marketing practices on the Web (Landesberg et al., 1998). The commission's rule-making authority had been seriously weakened by legislation in the 1970s lobbied in by media, advertising, and manufacturing interests in a successful effort to thwart regulation restricting children's advertising on television (Kunkel, 1988, 1992). As a result, the FTC asked Congress in 1998 for authorization to develop rules for the Internet. This authority was granted with passage of the Children's Online Privacy Protection Act (COPPA). The law requires that commercial websites aimed at children 13 and under must (a) give parents notice about their data-collection practices; (b) obtain verifiable parental consent before collecting information from children; and (c) provide parents with access to the collected information and the opportunity to curtail any further uses of collected information (Children's Online Privacy Protection Act, 1998). Final rules were issued in October 1999 and took effect April 21, 2000 (Children's Online Privacy Protection Rule, 1999). The debate surrounding passage of the legislation and subsequent rules also spurred on-line and advertising industries to change their present self-regulatory guidelines and to develop new ones (Quick, 1998; Teinowitz, 1997).

The new children's privacy law is only the first, small step in what must be a much broader effort to establish effective policies to curtail marketing abuses targeted at children in the digital media. A comprehensive policy agenda will need to be created if meaningful safeguards are to be put in place. The framework for this agenda must be established now, before the most abusive practices become not only firmly entrenched but also profitable and therefore very difficult to change. The new policies for the digital media system can be built, to some extent, on the existing policy framework that has governed children's television, but policy makers and researchers may need to rethink many of the existing rules (Campbell, 1997/1998). For example, children's advertising on digital television, while technically still subject to Federal Communications Commission (FCC) regulations, will not conform to analog-broadcast restrictions. Restrictions contained in the FCC 1974 Policy Statement on Children's Television, including prohibitions against sales pitches from the hosts of children's programs and the requirement for clearly defined separation between commercial material and programmatic content ("After these messages, we'll be right back"), are hopelessly out of date and inadequate in the seamless world of the Web and interactive digital television. Similarly, the Children's Television Act (CTA) of 1990 includes a provision that limits the amount of commercial time on programming for children under 13 to 10.5 minutes per hour on weekends and 12 minutes per hour on weekdays (CTA, 1990). But on a digital television children's program with links to a commercial website, that 60-minute hour suddenly becomes virtually infinite.

Because the Internet and other digital media are part of a global media system, there is also a need for safeguards that will transcend national boundaries. Consumer groups from a number of European countries have created an international forum with U.S. organizations called the Transatlantic Consumer Dialogue (TACD). TACD is working to forge a common agenda for international protections against marketing abuses targeted at children, and it recently developed a set of principles for "Children and Electronic Commerce," which was accepted by the European Commission. (See *www.TACD.org.*)

## Research Agenda

Commercialization of the digital media is taking place so quickly that there has been little opportunity for serious scholarly research on its impact. Current TV advertising safeguards are based on a substantial body of research, conducted in the 1960s and 1970s, documenting the special vulnerabilities of children to the powerful appeals of marketers (Wartella, 1984). However, research on the impact of children's advertising has declined dramatically in recent years, with most of the attention in the scholarly community focused on ensuring the effectiveness of advertising to children rather than assessing its social and behavioral impact (Wartella, 1984). A multidisciplinary research agenda is urgently needed to guide the development of digital children's media. This should include systematic studies that begin to assess the ways in which children interact with new media and the impact of new media on children's cognitive, emotional, and social development.

As part of this agenda, scholars should begin looking closely at the new forms of interactive advertising, marketing, and sales that are developing so swiftly in the digital media. As new techniques are developed, they will need to be monitored closely. Timely, independent research will need to be conducted to determine their impact. Several key issues will need to be taken into consideration when designing a research agenda in this area. Because the lines between advertising, marketing, sales, and "content" are increasingly blurred, it may be important to look at the online experience for children in more holistic terms, rather than trying to isolate "commercial messages" to measure their effects. For example, the integration of "content," interactive advertising, and direct selling is an unprecedented form of children's media, which raises serious concerns about the possibility of deception and manipulation. Researchers will also need to look at the interrelationships among different "platforms" in a child's media experience (e.g., Internet, television, "programmable objects," etc.). The emergence of an increasingly immersive media environment, made more vivid through virtual reality and human-like interfaces, may make it difficult to separate the child's so-called real-world experiences from those in the media (Calvert & Tan, 1996). Finally, it will be necessary to think beyond traditional research theories and methods and to draw on the expertise of scholars in a wide range of fields (e.g., communications, computer science, anthropology, sociology, psychology, etc.) to develop fresh approaches to the study of children and digital media.

## The Future of Digital Media: Need for Debate

Those who care about the well-being of children should join together to promote broad public debate about the future of our media system. As part of that effort, we need to expand our thinking about notions of "quality" in the media. Discussions about "safe zones" for children on the Internet have tended to frame the concept of quality around the absence of harm. If a product, program, or website contains no violence, sex, or other inappropriate material, then its very "benignness" is often labeled "quality." I suggest we begin thinking more broadly about quality, developing criteria for how the overall media culture should help prepare young people for their adult lives. Given current trends, there is little doubt that this emerging media system will play a significant role in helping children become *consumers,* and thus contributing to the growth of our economy. But in a time of declining voter participation and great cynicism about the political process, can the media also be a positive force in helping to raise the next generation to be more engaged as *citizens,* contributing to the health of our democracy?

William Damon, director of the Center on Adolescence and a professor of education at Stanford University, has suggested some key attributes that young people need to participate constructively in civil society:

> First, intellectual abilities such as reasoning skills, literacy, and the knowledge of history and economy required for making informed judgments. Second, moral traits such as dedication to honesty, justice, social responsibility, and the tolerance that makes democratic discourse possible. And finally, practical experience in community organizations, from which young people learn how to work within groups, in structured settings. (Damon, 1998, p. B4)

Although major institutions such as the family, schools, and religion will doubtlessly continue to be the primary sources of a child's civic education, the new digital media—with their powerful ability to engage children in active learning, to foster community, and to enable children to become creators and communicators instead of just passive recipients—should also play a significant role in helping to develop thoughtful, active citizens.

A key to achieving that goal will be the development of a healthy, noncommercial civic sector in the new media landscape. Although there are many promising content areas for children on the Web that could provide the basis for such an "electronic commons," there are also serious questions about whether they can be sustained over the long run and whether they can become a significant and prominent part of the new media landscape. With the growing commercialization of the Web, the viability of noncommercial civic media for children and youth is by no means guaranteed, and may very well be threatened in the new environment.

## Bibliography


Acuff, D. S. (1997). *What kids buy and why: The psychology of marketing to kids.* New York: Free Press.

Aufderheide, P. (1996). *Communications policy and the public interest.* New York: Guilford.

Barnouw, E., Cohen, R., Roberts, G., Schwartz, T., Miller, M. C., Liberman, D., Aufderheide, P., & Frank, T. (1997). *Conglomerates and the media.* New York: New Press.

Bok, S. (1998). *Mayhem: Violence as public entertainment.* Reading, MA: Addison-Wesley.

Bollier, D., & Firestone, C. M. (1997). *The networked society: How technologies are transforming markets, organizations, and social relationships.* Washington, DC: Aspen Institute.

Calvert, S. (1999). *Children's journey through the information age.* Boston: McGraw-Hill.

Cronin, M. J. (1994). *Doing business on the Internet: How the electronic highway is transforming American companies.* New York: Van Nostrand Reinhold.

Damon, W. (1995). *Greater expectations: Overcoming the culture of influence in our homes and schools.* New York: Free Press.

Davis, R., & Owen, D. (1988). *New media and American politics.* New York: Oxford University Press.

Frazier, D., Kurshan, B., & Armstrong, S. (1995). *Internet for kids.* San Francisco: Sybex.

Freedom Forum Media Studies Center. (1994, Fall). *Media studies journal: Children and television.* New York: Author.

Furger, R. (1998). *Does Jane compute? Preserving our daughters' place in the cyber revolution.* New York: Warner Books.

Hughes, R. D. (1998). *Kids online protecting your children in cyberspace.* Grand Rapids, MI: Fleming H. Revell.

Jupiter Communications. (1998, September). *Chat and instant messaging: Matching messaging technologies to diverging site applications* [On-line]. [Retrieved April 21, 1999]. Available: www.jup.com/sps/technology/briefs/9808/wt52/ wt52-01.html

Kline, S. (1993). *Out of the garden: Toys, TV, and children's culture in the age of marketing.* New York: Verso.

LaPlatne, A., & Seidner, R. (1999). *Playing for profit: How digital entertainment is making big business out of child's play.* New York: John Wiley.

Laybourne, G. (1993). The Nickelodeon experience. In G. L. Berry & J. K. Asamen (Eds.), *Children and television: Images in a changing sociocultural world.* Newbury Park, CA: Sage.

McNeal, J. U. (1999). *The kids market.* Ithaca, NY: Paramount Market.

Minow, N. N., & LaMay, C. L. (1995). *Abandoned in the wasteland: Children, television, and the First Amendment.* New York: Hill and Wang.

Negorponte, N. (1995). *Being digital.* New York: Knopf.

Roper Starch Worldwide. (1998, February 22). Kids favor Internet for homework, chatting, and surfing: As in real life, girls are greater virtual socializers [On-line]. [Retrieved June 15, 1999]. Available: www.roper.com/news/archive1998.htm

Schoolman, J. (1998, August 24). "Nag factor" plays role in what parents buy: Only 31 percent of parents are immune to their kids' whining. *Toronto Star,* p. E3.

Schneider, C. (1989). *Children's television: The art, the business, and how it works.* Lincolnwood, IL: NTC Business Books.

Schumann, D. W., & Thorson, E. (1999). *Advertising and the World Wide Web.* Mahwah, NJ: Lawrence Erlbaum.

Seiter, E. (1999). *Television and new media audiences.* New York: Oxford University Press.

Shirky, C. (1995). *Voices from the Net.* Emeryville, CA: Ziff-Davis Press.

Spigel, L. (1992). *Make room for TV: Television and the family ideal in postwar America.* Chicago: University of Chicago Press.

Transatlantic Consumer Dialogue. (1998, December 11). Comments on the Transatlantic Economic Partnership (TEP) action plan [On-line]. [Retrieved October 29, 1999]. Available: www.tacd.org/tep.html

U.S. Department of Commerce, Information Infrastructure Task Force. (1993, September 15). *The national information infrastructure: Agenda for action* [Online]. [Retrieved October 29, 1999]. Available: http://metalab.unc.edu/nii/toc.html

Zandl, I., & Leonard, R. (1992). *Targeting the trendsetting consumer: How to market your product or ser-*

*vice to influential buyers.* Homewood, IL: Business One Irwin.

Zollo, P. (1995). *Wise up to teens: Insights into marketing and advertising to teenagers.* Ithaca, NY: New Strategist.

## References

Anderson, L. (1999, June 17). Mixing teen cool with e-commerce savvy. *Industry Standard,* pp. 44-45.

Beatty, S. (1999, June 11). Latest soap-opera starlet? CBS casts a bracelet. *Wall Street Journal,* p. B1.

Calvert, S. L., & Tan, S. L. (1996). Impact of virtual reality on young adults' physiological arousal and aggressive thoughts: Interaction versus observation. In P. M. Greenfield & R. R. Cocking (Eds.), *Interacting with video.* Norwood, NJ: Ablex.

Campbell, A. (1997/1998). Ads2Kids.com: Should government regulate advertising to children on the World Wide Web? *Gonzaga Law Review, 33*(2), 312-346.

Center for Media Education. (1999). *Youth access to alcohol and tobacco Web marketing: The filtering and rating debate.* Washington, DC: Author.

Center for Media Education, Consumer Federation of America, American Academy of Child and Adolescent Psychiatry, American Academy of Pediatrics, Junkbusters Corporation, National Alliance for Nonviolent Programming, National Association of Elementary School Principals, National Consumers League, National Education Association, Privacy Times, and Public Advocacy for Kids. (1999, June 11). *Children's Online Privacy Protection Rule: Comment P994504* [Comments submitted to the Federal Trade Commission]. Washington, DC: Center for Media Education.

Children get growing online attention. (1995, November 10). *Interactive Marketing News,* pp. 4-6.

Children's Online Privacy Protection Act, S.2326, 105th Cong., 2d Sess. (1998).

Children's Online Privacy Protection Rule, 16 C.F.R. Part 312 (1999).

Children's Television Act of 1990, H.R. 1677, 101st Cong., 2d Sess., Cong. Rec. H8535 (1990).

Clinton, W., & Gore, A. (1999, May 5). *Keeping children safe on the Internet* [On-line]. [Retrieved July 20, 1999]. Available: www.whitehouse.gov/WH/Work/050599.html

Cox, B. (1999, June 9). Parents deluged with Web buy requests from kids [On-line]. [Retrieved June 11, 1999]. Available: www.internetnews.com

Damon, W. (1998, October 16). The path to a civil society goes through the university. *Chronicle of Higher Education,* p. B4.

Davis, K., & O'Driscoll, R. (1995, March). Roadmap for the Internet. *Red Herring* [On-line]. [Retrieved November 18, 1999]. Available: www.redherring.com/mag/issue19/roadmap.html

Digital Coast '99 Summit. (1999, September 8-9). Conference, Los Angeles.

Digital kids: Marketing to the postmodern kid. (1999, June 7-8). Conference, San Francisco.

Flaherty, J. (1999, March 11). Safer Web playgrounds are aimed at kids (and paying parents). *New York Times,* p. G8.

Frauenfelder, M. (1999, June). Remote possibilities. *Business 2.0,* p. 118.

Givens, B. (1997). *The privacy rights handbook.* New York: Avon Books.

Godin, S. (1999). *Permission marketing: Turning strangers into friends, and friends into customers.* New York: Simon & Schuster.

Graphics, Visualization, and Usability Center, Georgia Institute of Technology. (1998, October). *GVU's 10th WWW user survey* [On-line]. [Retrieved May 19, 1999]. Available: www.gvu.gatech.edu/user_surveys-1998-10/graphs/use/q30.htm

Gruen, E. (1995, October 25). *Defining the digital consumer IV agenda: Digital kids pre-conference seminar,* New York.

Hayes-Roth, B. (1999, September). Automating one-to-one customer care with smart interactive characters. *Web Techniques,* pp. 59-65.

Hoynes, W. (1997, May/June). News for a captive audience: The case of Channel One. *Extra!* [On-line]. [Retrieved June 20, 1999]. Available: www.fair.org/extra/9105/ch1_hoynes.html

HR: Corporation for Public Broadcasting Authorization Act of 1999, 106th Cong., 1st Sess. (1999, June 30). (Testimony of Jeffrey Chester) [On-line]. [Retrieved July 6, 1999]. Available: http://com-notes.house.gov/cchear/hearings106.nsf/768dfofaa6d9ddab852564f1004886c0/

Hunt, D. (1999, June 29). What you see is what you can get on Net: Shows test links to their viewers with on-line sales. *USA Today,* p. 3D.

Jupiter Communications. (1998, August). *Kids: Evolving revenue models for the 2-12 market* [On-line]. [Retrieved February 19, 1999]. Available: www.jup.com/sps/content/briefs/9808/cc42/cc42.html

Jupiter Communications. (1999a, June 7). Kids and teens to spend $1.3 billion online in 2002 [On-line]. [Retrieved September 20, 1999]. Available: www.jup.com/jupiter/press/releases/1999/0607. html

Jupiter Communications. (1999b, April). *Online customer service: Strategies for improving satisfaction and retention* [On-line]. [Retrieved April 21, 1999]. Available: http://jup.com/report/ocs/ocs-01.html

Kennedy, M. (1996, Summer). Information superhighway: Parental regulation—the best alternative. *University of Louisville Journal of Family Law, 35*(3), 575-593.

Kunkel, D. (1988, Autumn). From a raised eyebrow to a turned back: The FCC and children's product-related programming. *Journal of Communication, 33*(4), 90-108.

Kunkel, D. (1992, Summer). Children's television advertising in the multichannel environment. *Journal of Communication, 42*(3), 134-152.

Landesberg, M., Levin, T., Curtin, C., & Lev, O. (1998, June). *Privacy online: A report to Congress.* Washington, DC: Federal Trade Commission.

Larson, G. (1998, Fall). Changing channels: How digital television will affect the public health. *InfoActive Health,* pp. 1-8.

Leibovich, M., Smart, T., & Dugan, I. J. (1999, June 20). Internet's e-conomy gets real. *Washington Post,* p. A1.

Manning, S. (1999, September 27). Students for sale: How corporations are buying their way into America's classrooms. *Nation,* pp. 11-18.

McNeal, J. U. (1992). *Kids as customers: A handbook of marketing to children.* New York: Lexington Books.

Mifflin, L. (1999, April 19). A growth spurt is transforming TV for children. *New York Times,* p. A1.

Montgomery, K. (1999). *Children's media culture in the millennium: Mapping the digital landscape.* Manuscript submitted for publication.

Montgomery, K., & Pasnik, S. (1996). *Web of deception: Threats to children from online marketing.* Washington, DC: Center for Media Education.

Neuborne, E., & Kerwin, K. (1999, February 15). Generation Y. *Business Week,* p. 80.

Peppers, D. (1999). Foreword. In S. Godin, *Permission marketing: Turning strangers into friends, and friends into customers.* New York: Simon & Schuster.

Peppers, D., & Rogers, M. (1993). *The one to one future: Building relationships one customer at a time.* New York: Doubleday.

Peppers, D., & Rogers, M. (1999). *Enterprise one to one: Tools for competing in the interactive age.* New York: Doubleday.

Perkins, M. (1996, March). Mining the Internet gold rush. *Red Herring* [On-line]. [Retrieved November 18, 1999]. Available: www.redherring.com/mag/issue29/gold.html

Quick, R. (1998, July 22). Computer-industry group presents plan to regulate consumer privacy on-line. *Wall Street Journal,* p. B7.

Roberts, J. (1995, October 25). *Defining the digital consumer IV agenda: Digital kids pre-conference seminar,* New York.

Roper Starch Worldwide. (1998, November 24). Today's kids—especially teens—are wired to the hilt, gender gap still exists [On-line]. [Retrieved May 19, 1999]. Available: www.roper.com/news/content/news93.htm

Russakoff, D. (1999, April 19). Marketers following youth trends to the bank. *Washington Post,* p. A1.

Slatalla, M. (1999, April 22). *Sesame Street* site: Serious child's play. *New York Times,* p. E8.

Stanger, J. D., & Gridina, N. (1999). *Media in the home: The fourth annual survey of parents and children.* Philadelphia: University of Pennsylvania, Annenberg Public Policy Center.

Stark, M. (1999, March 3). Savvy Gen Y-ers: Challenge, involve them. *Selling to Kids, 4*(4), 3.

Teinowitz, I. (1997, April 21). CARU to unveil guidelines for kid-focused Web sites. *Advertising Age,* p. 8.

Thompson, B. (1999, October 24). kids.commerce: The brave new world of marketing to children. *Washington Post Magazine,* pp. 11-34.

Wartella, E. (1984, Spring). Cognitive and affective factors of TV advertising's influence on children. *Western Journal of Speech Communication, 48,* 171-183.

Weise, E. (1999, June 9). Parents pay for kids' virtual wallets. *USA Today,* p. 9D.

Wieffering, E. (1999, February 15). Consumers could pay price when Web mergers with TV: As media conglomerates consolidate power, the Internet is focusing more on selling stuff than on spreading ideas. *Star Tribune,* p. 1A.

Zick, T. (1999, April). Congress, the Internet, and the intractable pornography problem: The Child Online Protection Act of 1998. *Creighton Law Review, 32,* 1536-1555.

CHAPTER **36**

# Public Policy and Private Practice

## Government Regulations and Parental Control of Children's Television Use in the Home

AMY B. JORDAN
University of Pennsylvania

This chapter explores how information, technology, and the increasingly media-saturated home environment all serve to shape the ways in which parents direct their children's television use. It focuses on whether and how public policies and advocacy efforts designed to empower parents affect the type and frequency of oversight parents give in this realm. In reviewing research on parents' control of children's TV use, it lays out the most common mediation efforts parents employ. Finally, the chapter asks, Have the recent changes in media policies and technologies affected parents' practices within the home? Data from Annenberg Public Policy Center studies that have tracked the availability of media in the home, parents' concerns and television mediation practices, and the overall landscape of children's television are used to provide preliminary answers to this question.

### The New Regulatory Environment of Children's Television

The year 1997 brought a new look to America's television screens. New regulations governing children's educational television and a newly implemented "voluntary" ratings system created a virtual explosion of letters, numbers, and symbols in the opening moments of a program. Regulations and volun-

AUTHOR'S NOTE: The 1999 APPC survey on children and television was conducted by Jeffrey Stanger. Much of the data reported here are included in *Media in the Home 1999: The Fourth Annual Survey of Parents and Children* (Stanger & Gridina, 1999).

tary labeling practices came as polls showed parents increasingly concerned about the amount of sex and violence in the media (Hart, 1996). In addition, the general public's worries over copycat crimes and suicides inspired by the media and the escalating violence in society blamed, in part, on excessive violence in the media led to a call for action. Advocates and policy makers contend that new regulations and guidelines will empower parents to more effectively guide their children's television choices and will ultimately diminish the impact of the medium's problematic elements. Television executives, though resistant at first, have acquiesced to public pressure to head off what they fear could be more severe infringements on their First Amendment rights (Sullivan & Jordan, 1999).

### *The V-Chip*

Beginning in January 1997, all programs on broadcast and cable television (with the exception of news and sports) were required to display a "rating." (Chapter 34 presents a full discussion of the ratings system.) The ratings system is designed to work in conjunction with the "V-chip"— a computer device that has been manufactured into TV sets since July 1999. Sets with the V-chip can be programmed by parents to block out any shows that contain material that may be offensive or considered problematic. Viewers without the technology can review a program's rating by watching the opening moments of the program or referring to a printed listing, such as in *TV Guide* (although most printed listings do not contain the shows' content labels).

### *The 3-Hour Rule*

A second regulation requires commercial broadcasters to "serve the educational and informational needs of children" (FCC, 1996) by offering a minimum of 3 hours a week of educational television and identifying educational programs on the air.[1] To count toward the 3 hours, programs must air between the hours of 7:00 A.M. and 10:00 P.M., must have "education as a significant purpose," and must be specifically designed for children (FCC, 1996). Broadcasters may air somewhat less than 3 hours a week, but they must then submit to a full license review and provide evidence that they are serving the child audience in other ways. Programmers began airing 3 hours a week of educational and informational (E/I) programming beginning in the 1997-1998 season.

### *Nonregulatory Activities*

The legislative efforts of Congress (led by Representative Ed Markey, D-MA) and the Executive Office (under the leadership of President Clinton and Vice President Gore) have often been catalyzed by advocates who have demanded a more responsible media industry. Action for Children's Television's Peggy Charren argued for and gained passage of the Children's Television Act of 1990, which laid the groundwork for the 3-hour rule (Jordan & Woodard, 1997). The Center for Media Education and the Parent Teacher Association (PTA), concerned with the impact of violent television on children, also provided both pressure and expertise during the development of the ratings system. Their input ultimately led to the inclusion of the content ratings indicating violence, fantasy violence, sex, sexual innuendo, and harsh language (Cantor, 1998). It is unlikely that legislative acts such as the 3-hour rule and the Telecommunications Act of 1996 (which mandates the V-chip) would have garnered the attention and the bipartisan support they required to become law without the *insistence* and *assistance* of child advocacy groups.

The work of advocacy groups has extended beyond the passage of legislation and regulations. Parents must learn about the new information available as a result of the regulations, for example. Thus, advocacy groups such as the Center for Media Education have created outreach projects. Their V-Chip Education

Project includes "A Parent's Guide to the TV Ratings and V-Chip" and a related website (*www.vchipeducation.org;* Eisenstock, 1999). Other groups try to raise parents' awareness of the role of media in children's lives. TV-Free America sponsors an annual TV-Turnoff Week (during April). This grassroots organization provides parents, schools, and communities with an organizer's kit that encourages families to eliminate TV viewing for 1 week in order to reduce their overall television viewing and consider leisure-time alternatives (see Chapter 39).

Another important activity has involved media education (also called media literacy) projects. Media literacy curricula have been developed by media scholars (e.g., the Singers at Yale University), advocacy groups (e.g., the Center for Media Literacy), professional organizations (e.g., the American Academy of Pediatrics), and the television industry itself (e.g., the National Cable Television Association). The general premise of most of these efforts is that "teaching children to understand television can yield a more critical, intelligent audience" (Singer & Singer, 1998, p. 175) (see Chapter 38).

### *The Reasoning Behind the Activity*

The legislators, advocates, and academics who support advances in technology (V-chip and filtering devices) and increased information (ratings, advisories, E/I labels, and media literacy programs) seem to work under the assumption that parents have been largely ineffective in protecting children from the media's deleterious effects. New devices and new information, they believe, will give parents the tools they need to better guide their children's choices. Also presumed is that the natural inclination of the market and audience taste is *toward* the negative, potentially harmful entertainment and *away from* positive, enriching fare.

Such assumptions give rise to questions of whether parents want and need assistance and whether these are the resources they need to effectively control their children's media use. It is therefore important to consider how parents have traditionally influenced the choices children make about television.

## Mediating Television: What the Research Says

A review of research on parents' guidance of children's television viewing indicates that parents can and do act as mediators in the home in three distinct ways: (a) setting explicit rules (including rules about when children can and cannot watch, what children cannot watch, and how much time children can spend with a medium); (b) making recommendations (encouraging the use of media or particular media content); and (c) coviewing (monitoring children's media use by watching together). This section briefly considers the mechanisms through which parents might intervene and sets the context for an examination of one national survey's findings.

### *Explicit Rules*

Parents do believe that they wield the most influence over what their children watch. Holz (1998) found that 72% of parents say they are more influential than promotional announcements, siblings, or friends when it comes to children's viewing decisions. The majority of parents also report that they have rules regarding children's use of television. Most often, these rules are explicit. In a 1997 national survey, of those families with rules, 91.7% said they prohibited certain programs; 75.8% said they required homework and/or chores to be done before viewing; and 68.9% said they limit the number of hours children can watch (Stanger, 1997).

Explicit mediation has emerged as an important type of mediation in other studies as well (Jordan, 1990; Mohr, 1979), although it is not always clear how active parents are in creating and enforcing these rules (Dorr,

1986). In addition, parents may be inclined to falsely indicate to researchers that they have rules because this response may be seen as the socially acceptable response. In one early study, 40% of mothers reported having rules limiting viewing but only 19% of their first graders said they had such rules (Lyle & Hoffman, 1972).

Valkenburg, Krcmar, Peeters, and Marseille (1999) argue that parents who have rules about content are more likely to worry about the medium's effects on their school-age children than are those who do not. This Dutch study involving 519 parents of children between the ages of 5 and 12 suggests that parents with explicit rules (which they refer to as restrictive mediation) are more likely to have concerns about television-induced aggression and television-induced fright. They point out that "it is likely that these parents aim to minimize the negative impact of television and that for these parents restricting what their children watch is the simplest, most direct way of doing so" (p. 63).

Many of the restrictions parents have for children's viewing involve children's exposure to violent content. Krcmar and Cantor (1996) found that 70% of their sample of parents reported controlling what their children view, and close to 90% reported controlling their children's viewing when *violent* content was involved. There is, however, an apparent discrepancy between what parents say they "protect" their children from and what children actually watch. Holz's (1998) focus group discussions with children reveal that, though rules are in place, they are often not consistently enforced—a finding that may partially explain the consistently high ratings violent programs such as *WWF Wrestling, Cops,* and *Walker, Texas Ranger* receive among children ages 2 to 16 (A. C. Nielsen, 1998).

### *Viewing Recommendations*

Children indicate that their parents sometimes positively direct their viewing; that is, they make specific recommendations for programs they should watch. In one study, nearly 42% of 10- to 17-year-old children said that there are specific programs their parents encourage them to watch. Interestingly, the programs they listed were not targeted to children but were programs for a general audience or specific channels—for example, the news, *Touched by an Angel,* the Discovery Channel, and PBS (Stanger, 1997). Similarly, Mohr (1979) found that "although parents offered little guidance overall about children's evening viewing, they offered nearly twice as much positive as negative guidance about family sitcoms" (p. 220).

To make recommendations, parents need to know the content and schedule of appropriate programs. Many parents of school-age children, however, do not seem to know enough about what is on to be able to recommend specific programs. In one study, parents of preschool children could readily list enriching, educational programs for their very young children, but parents of older children had trouble naming even one "educational" program for their school-age child. Many resorted to listing a channel (e.g., Nickelodeon or Discovery) or a preschool program such as *Sesame Street* (Hart, 1996).

### *Coviewing*

Parents can monitor their children's viewing by watching programs together, a practice often referred to as coviewing. Advocates and researchers argue that parents should view programs with children to monitor their children's viewing, help them understand the medium and its content, enhance the child's learning, and diminish the effects of violent content (Ball & Bogatz, 1970; Desmond, Singer, Singer, Calam, & Colimore, 1985; Dorr, Kovaric, & Doubleday, 1989; Nathanson, 1997; Singer & Singer, 1981).

Although coviewing is encouraged, it is not clear how often it occurs. The previously mentioned Dutch study found coviewing to be more common than restrictive (explicit) guidance or instructive mediation (discussing program content; Valkenburg et al., 1999). Other researchers, however, have argued that coviewing is fairly uncommon (Dorr et al., 1989; Lin & Atkin, 1989). Lawrence and Wozniak (1989) found that families almost never watched together and that, when children watched television with another family member, it was generally with a brother or sister rather than a parent.

Consistent in the literature is the finding that, when parents and children watch television together, they are much more likely to watch adult programming than children's programming (Huston et al., 1992; Lin & Atkin, 1989). This conclusion is supported by Dorr et al. (1989), who found that "co-viewing was more common with older children whose preferences should have been more similar to those of their parents but whose needs for parental involvement were less" (p. 48). Valkenburg et al. (1999) argue that social coviewing is unrelated to the concerns about the negative impact of television; rather, "parents sit down with their child merely to watch television as family entertainment or as a means of spending time together" (p. 63).

Though many researchers have found that coviewing leads to important socializing opportunities (see Jordan, 1990; Lull, 1980; Messaris, 1986), others report that there is generally little or no dialogue around program content (Himmelweit, Oppenheim, & Vince, 1958; Mohr, 1979). Austin (1993), for example, cites a 1989 Gallup poll that showed that parents were "seven times more likely to turn the channel or forbid a program than to actually discuss the offending content" (p. 148).

The new regulations and technologies have the potential to enhance parents' current practices of restricting, encouraging, and coviewing. But do they translate into increased parental influence over children's media use? This section presents a review of recent Annenberg Public Policy Center (APPC) research on the current media environment of the home, parents' current mediation practices, and parents' awareness and understanding of the new regulations regarding one very important medium in the home: the television.

## Parents, Children, and Television: A Survey

The Annenberg Public Policy Center's research has typically taken a systemic approach to the assessment of the impact of the new television policies: a survey of parents and children (to measure their attitudes toward television and the use of television by children); an analysis of the content of children's television (to determine whether programs are being adequately labeled for age appropriateness, content, and educational value); and an assessment of insiders' perspectives on the implementation of the new rules (to obtain their impression of the challenges and opportunities for the children's television industry). (For the full report of each study, see Jordan, 1999; Schmitt, 1999; Stanger & Gridina, 1999; Woodard, 1999.) This chapter focuses on the results of the 1999 national survey of parents and children to examine whether and how new policies shape parents' mediation strategies in the new regulatory environment.

### *Parent/Child Survey Methodology*

Telephone interviews were conducted with a national random sample of parents of 2- to 17-year-olds and a random sample of their 10- to 17-year-old children in homes with televisions. The sample was drawn using random-digit dialing. Interviews were conducted with 1,269 parents and 303 of their children. The margins of error are ±2.9% for the sample of parents and ±5.7% for the sample of 10- to 17-year-olds. Interviews were conducted by Roper Starch Worldwide between April 20 and May 18, 1999.

Parent respondents were asked to focus on one particular child when answering the questions. In cases in which there was more than one child between the ages of 2 and 17 in the household, the parent was asked to focus on the child with the most recent birthday. In households in which there was a child age 10 to 17, the parent's permission was asked to interview that child. (This child may or may not have been the focus of the parent interview.)[2] Interviews lasted approximately 20 minutes for parents and 12 minutes for children.

### Findings

#### *The Availability of Media Within the Home*

The introduction of new media continues to transform the environment of America's homes with children. The 1999 APPC survey indicates that, in addition to television, nearly all homes with children 2 to 17 have a VCR (97.8%), and more than three quarters (77.4%) have cable or pay TV. Video game equipment is also prevalent, with more than two thirds (67%) of respondents reporting ownership. Nearly half (48.5%) of the surveyed families subscribed to a daily newspaper, and one third (33.3%) subscribed to one or more premium cable channels, such as HBO (see Table 36.1).

**TABLE 36.1** % Penetration of Other Media

| | |
|---|---|
| Videocassette recorders | 97.8 |
| Cable/pay TV | 77.4 |
| Computers | 68.2 |
| Video game equipment | 67.0 |
| Daily newspapers | 48.5 |
| On-line access | 41.0 |
| Premium cable | 33.3 |

Computers are now almost as common as cable television subscription, and Internet subscriptions are nearly as prevalent as newspaper ones. Nearly 7 in 10 homes with children now have a personal computer (68.2%), and more than two in five have access to the Internet (41.0%).[3]

Despite the presence of new technologies, the proportion of children with television sets in their rooms is quite high: 48.2%. Older children (12-17) are most likely to have bedroom TV sets (60.2%). Forty-six percent of elementary-school-age children (6-11) and 29.4% of preschoolers (2-5) also have bedroom TV sets.

The majority of families in this survey (87.0%) report that they own two or more working television sets. The average number of television sets reported by this sample was actually closer to three (mean = 2.75).

Considering the prevalence of multiple-set homes, it is not surprising that there has been little decrease in the average time children spend with television, even with the introduction of new media. Children ages 2 to 17 in this sample spend an average of 2.46 hours in front of the television each day, according to their parents. The average total time spent in front of screens (including television, videotapes, computers, and video games) is over 4 hours (4.35 hours/day) among the 2- to 17-year-olds in this sample. This is far more time than the amount of time children are reported spending with newspapers and magazines (0.34 hours/day), playing on the computer (0.97 hours/day), or engaged in schoolwork (1.14 hours/day) (see Table 36.2).

**TABLE 36.2** Time Spent With Media by Children, According to Parents (in hours per day)

| | |
|---|---|
| Television | 2.46 |
| Schoolwork | 1.14 |
| Computer | 0.97 |
| Videotapes | 0.78 |
| Books | 0.77 |
| Video games | 0.65 |
| Telephone | 0.55 |
| Newspapers/magazines | 0.34 |

### *Parents' Concerns About and Oversight of Television*

When parents are asked about the concerns they have regarding their children's media use, television consistently tops the list. Nearly half (43.8%) of parents say that the media influence of most concern is television (see Table 36.3). The Internet, however, has also become a source of concern for many parents. However, since this survey entered the field the week of the shootings at Columbine High School, in which the gunmen were allegedly influenced by computer games and the Internet, this finding may be an artifact of timing.

**TABLE 36.3** % Media Influence of Most Concern to Parents

| | |
|---|---|
| Television | 43.8 |
| Internet | 19.8 |
| Music | 14.1 |
| Video games | 6.0 |
| Movies | 4.6 |
| News | 4.3 |
| Magazines | 0.9 |
| Don't know | 6.6 |

Parents report being more concerned about *what* their children watch on television (70.0%) than *how much* their child watches (18.9%; the remaining were unsure or concerned equally about both). Consistent with this finding, only 23.1% of parents say that their child watches too much television.

Two thirds of parents (61.1%) report that they supervise their children's viewing a "great deal," and the same number say they have household rules about TV viewing. The majority of parents, 92.6%, also say they watch television with their children at least "once in a while." How effective is this supervision? One quarter (24.4%) of parents say their child watches inappropriate programs "sometimes" or "a great deal," while 29.6% of 10- to 17-year-olds say they watch shows their parents wouldn't approve of.

Relatively few parents (16.5%) say that there is "a lot" of good television on for their children. The 10- to 17-year-olds in this survey indicated that their parents do, however, encourage the viewing of specific programs or channels, including the news, the Discovery Channel, the Learning Channel, and PBS. These respondents also say that their parents prohibit programs, including *The Jerry Springer Show* (a talk show) and two animated adult-oriented programs, *South Park* and *The Simpsons.*

### *Parents' Awareness and Use of Information and Technologies*

Data from the 1999 APPC survey indicate that the majority of parents (72.1%) are aware of the TV ratings system and that a significant number of their 10- to 17-year-olds are aware of ratings as well. Far fewer, however, say they use the system to guide their children's viewing. Only 38.5% say they use the ratings on the screen or in printed listings on a regular basis.

At the time of the survey, television sets were only beginning to be manufactured with the V-chip device, a technology that was mandated to be included in every television set by July 1999. Nevertheless, parents voiced strong support for the inclusion of the device; 84% of parents of 2- to 17-year-olds said they "strongly" or "somewhat" favor the V-chip, and 71.9% said they would use the V-chip "often" or "once in a while" if they had one. Only about one in ten (11.1%) parents said they would never use the V-chip.

Parents in the 1999 survey were basically unaware of the policy makers' efforts surrounding educational television. Awareness of the "E/I" designation (the icon generally used to indicate educational and informational programming for children) was extremely limited; only 6.3% of parents recognized this symbol. Not surprising, a mere 2.5% said they used the symbol to guide their children's viewing.

Parents and children alike are not aware of the programs commercial broadcasters are putting forth to satisfy the 3-hour requirement. Less than half of the parents (43.5%) had heard of the show *Popular Mechanics,* the highest figure for any of the E/I programs measured (see Table 36.4). Other programs such as *Mythic Warriors* and *Histeria!*—E/I programs airing on commercial broadcast networks around the country—were nearly unknown to parents (18.8% and 14.8% awareness, respectively).

**TABLE 36.4** Parents' Awareness of Commercial Broadcasters' Educational Efforts

| *Program* | *% Awareness of Program* | *% Awareness of Educational Intent (of Those Aware of the Program)* |
|---|---|---|
| *Histeria!* | 14.8 | 42.4 |
| *Mythic Warriors* | 18.8 | 25.1 |
| *One World* | 11.2 | 33.0 |
| *Popular Mechanics* | 43.5 | 78.2 |
| *Squigglevision* | 5.7 | 46.8 |
| *Pokemon* (not E/I) | 38.0 | 27.2 |

Even those parents who had heard of the E/I programs were not likely to know that they were intended to be educational. Of those parents who had heard of *Mythic Warriors,* 25.1% knew it was educational. Similarly, of those who had heard of *Histeria!* 42.4% knew it was educational. In fact, about as many who thought that *Mythic Warriors* was educational thought that *Pokemon* was educational (27.2%).

## Empowering Parents With Information and Technology

The task of monitoring children's media use can be daunting and frustrating. Parents may have little time to supervise their children's media use. Moreover, the sheer number of media in the home can make it difficult to keep track of what children should and shouldn't be exposed to. Not only do most homes have VCRs, computers, and video game systems, but there are more shows airing on more venues. APPC's 1999 analysis of programming for children in the Philadelphia market reveals that children with access to cable television can choose from 29 different channels that air 1,324 shows (279 unique titles) specifically designed for them over the course of the week, representing a 12% increase from the previous season.

The survey results indicate that, consistent with past research, parents say they try to monitor their children's television by setting explicit rules, encouraging the viewing of particular programs, and coviewing. They say they are more concerned about the content of television than any other medium, and so they watch with their children, forbid certain programs, and suggest alternatives. Approximately a third also say that they use the ratings to make programming decisions with their children.

Despite parents' efforts and concerns, many respondents admit that their children watch programs they shouldn't. In addition, there is a low awareness of the high-quality educational programs that do exist for school-age children. Though the broadcasters have begun airing educational and informational programming, parents have yet to notice these shows or use the information provided to guide their children to more educational fare.

### *Connecting Public Policy and Private Practice*

Increasing parents' involvement in their children's television use appears to require more than improving the overall landscape of children's television. This survey, along with other APPC research on the quality of children's television, indicates several challenges to the effective use of the new technologies and information within the home environment. These include a general lack of public awareness of what's on for children; an overall low opinion of the value of the medium; and an ignorance and/or distrust of the information provided by the broadcasters.

### *Parents Are Unaware of the Diversity of Options*

Parents don't appear to know much about the quality programming available once their children reach school age. They have difficulty naming any enriching shows for older children, and they do not recognize the E/I offerings. One could argue that there are no quality offerings for children after the age of 5, but APPC's content analyses indicate that 28% of programs for elementary-school-age children and 29% of programs for preteens and teens can be considered "high quality" (Woodard, 1999). In addition, an analysis of the commercial broadcasters' educational offerings reveals that each of the network affiliates and independent channels is offering at least 3 hours' worth of educational shows, and the majority of these shows are meeting the requirements of the 3-hour rule (Schmitt, 1999).

A recent study of industry insiders' and observers' perspectives on the challenges and opportunities of the 3-hour rule found that parents are not alone in their ignorance (Jordan, 1999). One of the most striking findings of this study was the fact that, when asked to name a commercial broadcaster's educational program for children of different target ages, the "experts" struggled and often couldn't think of an E/I show unless it was a program they worked on, one that had previously aired on PBS, or one that had been canceled.

The reasons for parents' unfamiliarity with programming are not completely clear, but they may be partially rooted in the increasingly complex media environment of the home. Not only do parents need to monitor their children's television use, many also feel the need to keep tabs on children's Internet activities and computer and video game choices (Turow, 1999). What's more, the 1999 survey reveals that nearly half of all children have their own bedroom TV sets—removing much of children's viewing from the visual oversight parents may informally provide. Thus, even though parents say they set up rules and at least occasionally coview with their children, children say they can go to their rooms when they want to watch shows their parents don't want them to watch (Holz, 1998).

### *Parents Have a (Justifiably) Low Opinion of Television for Children*

Despite the large quantity and vast array of programming available to children, parents have an overall low opinion of television for children. Woodard's (1999) analysis indicates that three quarters of programs for preschoolers and more than one quarter of programs for 6- to 16-year-olds are "high quality"—programs that contain some educational value and are devoid of potentially problematic content such as violence or stereotypes. Yet parents are correct in their perception that the majority of programming for children is little more than mindless entertainment. Two thirds of programming for older children was of "low" or "moderate" quality.

Parents may also be judging the overall quality of television based on what their children watch. Nielsen ratings and the 1999 APPC survey, however, reveal that children's favorite programs are not necessarily *children's* programs. The top-rated programs from the 1998-1999 season were ABC's TGIF lineup—programs such as *Boy Meets World* and *Sabrina, the Teenage Witch* (which are designed for an older, more general audience but are popular with 2- to 12-year-olds). Also popular with children are shows such as *The Simpsons* (which often has content rating warnings of sexual innuendo and harsh language) and *Buffy, the Vampire Slayer* (which often contains heavy doses of sex and violence) (A. C. Nielsen, 1998).

*Parents May Not Trust or Understand Program Information*

Analyses of the implementation of the 3-hour rule and the program ratings for age appropriateness and content indicate that the information parents receive may not always be trustworthy. Schmitt's (1999) analysis of the educational strength of the commercial broadcasters' E/I programs reveals that, although many broadcasters have lived up to the letter of the law, there are still many shows that simply fail to convey anything educational whatsoever (even though they are touted as educational). In this study, 20% of E/I shows airing in Philadelphia were "minimally educational"—programs that could not reasonably be considered to have "education as a significant purpose." In addition, at least one study found that parents' definitions of "educational" do not necessarily match the FCC's definition either. Holz's (1998) survey of parents of 8- to 12-year-olds indicates that parents consider traditionally academic shows such as *Bill Nye, the Science Guy* as educational but perceive prosocial shows like *Saved by the Bell* as entertainment only.

The finding that parents do not recognize that broadcasters provide on-air information about E/I programming (or use it to guide their children to educational offerings) is not particularly surprising given the obtuse and idiosyncratic icons that are used to designate educational programming. NBC, for example, uses a rotating bald head with glasses (from which an E/I floats out) while ABC uses a lightbulb with a voice-over that says "illuminating programming." An inconsistent symbol system may be more confusing than revealing for parents on the lookout for educational shows.

Finally, parents may not find the ratings system to be particularly helpful as they judge the suitability of programs for their children. One problematic area is the symbol for violence in children's programming ("FV"), a rating that only 7% of parents can correctly interpret (Kaiser Family Foundation, 1998). In addition, Woodard's (1999) analysis of children's programs reveals that 75% of children's programs that contained "a lot" of violence did not carry the FV rating.

## Implications

The research described in this chapter indicates that, even though parents are concerned about the impact of media on their children, they have not yet effectively translated the new information and technologies available into greater parental supervision. To institute change at the household level, policy makers and advocates must provide more effective outreach to inform parents that the regulations do exist and can potentially be useful in the guidance of program choices. As important is conveying the information that parents have a right and responsibility to provide feedback to broadcasters who are not meeting their public interest obligations. If, for example, a parent does not believe that a program like *NBA Inside Stuff* is meeting the educational and informational needs of children, this opinion must be conveyed to the local broadcaster that airs the program, the network that provides the program, and the Federal Communications Commission that determines whether the station's license should be renewed.

It is also critical that the producers and programmers of television for children become more reliable and consistent about the information they provide. Programs containing violence should be labeled appropriately. Programs claiming to be E/I should be meeting the educational needs of the child audience.

Parents and programmers together now need to play a more active role in promoting the high-quality, enriching fare. Not only should parents educate themselves about programming appropriate for children, but they should also take the time to watch these programs with their children. Broadcasters, for their part, should devote at least as much promotional time and money to their educational shows as they do to their violence-laden, toy-based properties. Perhaps then children will find and watch programs that are beneficial rather than potentially detrimental.

Finally, research must now begin to focus on the motivations parents have for mediating children's television use. There are now enough data to support many citizens' fears that television in its worst form can be harmful to children. Yet there is also accumulated evidence that most parents use a fairly light hand in guiding their children to and away from the set. It is therefore critical to understand the social, psychological, and structural obstacles that prevent a more careful and deliberate use of the medium. Only then can we truly maximize the value of this important agent in children's lives.

## Notes

1. Cable stations such as Nickelodeon, CNN, and the Discovery Channel are not required to abide by the 3-hour rule because they are not within the broadcast spectrum.

2. The samples were weighted to the U.S. Census by race, education, and geographic region for the sample of parents, and by sex, age, and geographic region for 10- to 17-year-olds.

3. Lower-income families are significantly less likely to have a computer in the home, although 40.6% of families with incomes below $30,000 per year have a computer. These families are also less likely to subscribe to an Internet service provider. Though 41% of the overall sample had on-line access, only 14.9% of lower-income families could tap into the Internet from home.

## References

A. C. Nielsen. (1998). *Top 100 programs for children 2-12* [Special report prepared for the Annenberg Public Policy Center]. New York: Author.

Austin, E. (1993). Exploring the effects of active parental mediation of television content. *Journal of Broadcasting and Electronic Media, 37*(2), 147-158.

Ball, S., & Bogatz, G. (1970). *The first year of* Sesame Street: *An evaluation.* Princeton, NJ: Educational Testing Service.

Cantor, J. (1998). Ratings for program content: The role of research findings. *Annals of the American Academy of Political and Social Science, 557,* 54-69.

Desmond, R., Singer, J., Singer, D., Calam, R., & Colimore, K. (1985). Family mediation patterns and television viewing: Young children's grasp of the medium. *Human Communication Research, 11*(4), 461-480.

Dorr, A. (1986). *Television and children: A special medium for a special audience.* Beverly Hills, CA: Sage.

Dorr, A., Kovaric, P., & Doubleday, C. (1989). Parent-child coviewing of television. *Journal of Broadcasting and Electronic Media, 33*(1), 35-51.

Eisenstock, B. (1999). *A parent's guide to the TV ratings and V-chip.* Washington, DC: Center for Media Education.

Federal Communications Commission. (1996). *Policies and rules concerning children's television programming: Revision of programming policies for television broadcast stations* (MM Docket No. 93-48). Washington, DC: Author.

Hart, P. D. (1996). *Children/parents: Television in the home* (Survey No. 1). Philadelphia: University of Pennsylvania, Annenberg Public Policy Center.

Himmelweit, H. T., Oppenheim, A. N., & Vince, P. (1958). *Television and the child.* London: Oxford University Press.

Holz, J. (1998). *Measuring the child audience: Issues and implications for educational programming* (Survey No. 3). Philadelphia: University of Pennsylvania, Annenberg Public Policy Center.

Huston, A., Donnerstein, E., Fairchild, H., Feshbach, N., Katz, P., Murray, J., Rubinstein, E., Wilcox, B., & Zuckerman, D. (1992). *Big world, small screen: The role of television in American society.* Lincoln: University of Nebraska Press.

Jordan, A. (1990). *The role of mass media in the family system: An ethnographic approach.* Unpublished doctoral dissertation, University of Pennsylvania, Philadelphia.

Jordan, A. (1999). *The Three-Hour Rule: Insiders' perspectives* (Report No. 30). Philadelphia: University of Pennsylvania, Annenberg Public Policy Center.

Jordan, A. B., & Woodard, E. H. (1997). *The 1997 state of children's television report: Programming for children over broadcast and cable television* (Report No. 14). Philadelphia: University of Pennsylvania, Annenberg Public Policy Center.

Kaiser Family Foundation. (1998, May). *Parents, children, and the television rating system: Two Kaiser Family Foundation surveys.* Menlo Park, CA: Author.

Krcmar, M., & Cantor, J. (1996, May). *Discussing violent television: Parents, children, and TV viewing choices.* Paper presented at the annual conference of the International Communication Association, Montreal, Canada.

Lawrence, F., & Wozniak, P. (1989). Children's television viewing with family members. *Psychological Reports, 65*(2), 395-400.

Lin, C., & Atkin, D. (1989). Parental mediation and rulemaking for adolescent use of television and VCRs. *Journal of Broadcasting & Electronic Media, 33*(1), 53-67.

Lull, J. (1980). The social uses of television. *Human Communication Research, 6*(3), 197-209.

Lyle, J., & Hoffman, H. (1972). Children's use of television and other media. In E. A. Rubinstein, G. A. Comstock, & J. P. Murray (Eds.), *Television and social behavior: Vol. 4. Television in day-to-day life: Patterns of use.* Washington, DC: U.S. Government Printing Office.

Messaris, P. (1986). Parents, children, and television. In G. Gumpert & R. Cathcart (Eds.), *Inter/media: Interpersonal communication in a media world.* New York: Oxford University Press.

Mohr, P. (1979). Parental guidance of children's viewing of evening television programs. *Journal of Broadcasting, 23*(2), 213-229.

Nathanson, A. (1997, May). *The relationship between parental mediation and children's anti- and pro-social motivations.* Paper presented at the annual meeting of the International Communication Association, Montreal, Canada.

Schmitt, K. (1999). *The Three-Hour Rule: Is it living up to expectations?* (Report No. 30). Philadelphia: University of Pennsylvania, Annenberg Public Policy Center.

Singer, D., & Singer, J. (1981). *Television, imagination, and aggression: A study of preschoolers.* Hillsdale, NJ: Lawrence Erlbaum.

Singer, D., & Singer, J. (1998). Developing critical viewing skills and media literacy in children. *Annals of the American Academy of Political and Social Science, 557,* 164-179.

Stanger, J. (1997). *Television in the home: The second annual survey of parents and children in the home* (Survey Series No. 2). Philadelphia: University of Pennsylvania, Annenberg Public Policy Center.

Stanger, J., & Gridina, N. (1999). *Media in the home 1999: The fourth annual survey of parents and children* (Survey Series No. 5). Philadelphia: University of Pennsylvania, Annenberg Public Policy Center.

Sullivan, J., & Jordan, A. (1999, Autumn). Playing by the rules. *Communication Law and Policy, 4,* 483-511.

Turow, J. (1999). *The Internet and the family: The view from parents/the view from the press* (Report No. 27). Philadelphia: University of Pennsylvania, Annenberg Public Policy Center.

Valkenburg, P., Krcmar, M., Peeters, A., & Marseille, N. (1999, Winter). Developing a scale to assess three styles of television mediation: "Instructive mediation," "restrictive mediation," and "social coviewing." *Journal of Broadcasting and Electronic Media,* pp. 52-66.

Woodard, E. (1999). *The 1999 state of children's television report: Programming for children over broadcast and cable television* (Report No. 28). Philadelphia: University of Pennsylvania, Annenberg Public Policy Center.

CHAPTER **37**

# Parents and Other Adults

## Models and Monitors of Healthy Media Habits

MARJORIE J. HOGAN
Hennepin County Medical Center

## Parents' Role: Setting the Stage

### *Importance of the Parental Role*

Parents and other caregivers of children and adolescents, whether grandparents, foster parents, community elders, or other adults in a parental role, are the most important models, monitors, and mediators of appropriate media use for children and adolescents. In our rapidly evolving modern society, churches and communities no longer are able or expected to be traditional cultural teachers for youth; the homogenized picture of American culture is provided through characters, plots, and commercials on screens and other media across the land. Years ago, respected researcher George Gerbner noted that our common cultural teacher was entertainment television, "a set of cultural indicators—symbolic representations of the power relations and human values of our culture" (as cited in Huston et al., 1992, p. 21).

Media messages and images are ubiquitous and penetrate deeply into the lives of young people. In the United States, 87% of families have more than one television set per household, and 46% of homes own all four electronic media—television, VCR, video game player, and computer. In 1999, 41% of families were on-line, and 48% of children boasted a television set in their bedroom. Children 2 through 17 years of age spend an average of 4.35 hours per day in front of a screen (TV, videotape, computer, or video game). Whereas children and adolescents spend an average of 2.46 hours watching television every day, they spend an average of only 1.14 hours doing homework and 0.77 hours reading books (Stanger & Gridina, 1999).

Parents can incorporate the lessons from their own experience, values, cultural traditions, and spiritual beliefs into a unique parenting style, providing balance from the barrage of media messages encountered by children. In our diverse American society, families from vastly different cultures, countries, and circumstances struggle to make sense of our shared media as they influence their lives and their children.

In addition to being cultural teachers, parents know each individual child best. A parent understands the personality, the developmental path, and the special needs of a given child or adolescent. Children of different ages, distinctive temperaments, and diverse experience respond uniquely to media images and messages. For example, a preschool-age child who has recently lost an aging grandparent may be especially vulnerable to fears after watching a scary movie on videocassette. A child living in a neighborhood rife with real-life violence from gunfire will likely feel more frightened after seeing stories about death on the news or watching a prime-time, violent, made-for-TV movie. Young people with learning disabilities may become more distractible after any time spent watching a rapidly paced action show; homework, or any task requiring attention and organization, suffers. Many young children enjoy a rich, creative imagination; savvy parents know that such children may have heightened fears after exposure to media themes beyond their ken and control. Attuned parents provide guidance about and control over exposure to certain media offerings because they understand the strength and fragility unique to each child.

Parents are in a position to work with other partners invested in optimizing media for children and families. Many parents are integral members of PTA groups across the country and can set the agenda for these influential, local bodies. Parents and families form communities and, with collaboration and commitment, can generate neighborhood-based movements to sponsor "TV-Turnoff Weeks," alternative activities for children and adolescents, and letter-writing campaigns about good or bad media programs.

For compelling reasons, parents are in the best position to guide children in appropriate and healthy media use habits:

- Parents can be cultural teachers for children, understanding the importance of family priorities and beliefs and how media messages and images affect the family.
- Parents know and have empathy for their own children's strengths and vulnerabilities.
- Parents can partner with others (other parents, schools, and community groups) interested in optimizing media for children and in supporting media literacy in the classroom.
- Parents have the opportunity, through access and authority, to establish rules and guidance beginning in infancy and continuing through adolescence.

At Wichita State University in 1979, Philip Mohr reported that 85% of parents surveyed gave no guidance to their children about television viewing. When negative guidance was given, the genre most likely involved was an adult drama (Mohr, 1979). Mohr also found that, on Saturday mornings, 92% of parents provided no limits on television viewing, but 75% of parents established a cut-off time on school nights (Mohr, 1976). Two decades later, the Fourth Annual Annenberg Survey of Media in the Home found that 61% of parents supervised their children's television habits "a great deal," and 62% established household rules for TV viewing. Despite the rules and supervision claimed by surveyed parents, 24% reported that children watch inappropriate programs "sometimes" or "a great deal." Somewhat surprising, 93% of parents watch television with their children at least "once in a while" (Stanger & Gridina, 1999).

Parent responses to the Annenberg survey indicate persistent concern about children's television, with only 13.6% rating the quality as "very" or "mainly" positive. Those parenting older children held an even lower opinion of television offerings; a mere 10% of parents of adolescents gave television positive marks. In 1999, 44% of parents felt that public television offered the best programming for children, followed by 38% naming cable, and only 10% broadcast television. Although parents are most concerned about the influence of television on their children at all ages, as children grow older, concerns about the influence of the Internet and music lyrics increase. Consistent with findings in the past, 70% of parents surveyed expressed concern about media content, while only 19% were most concerned about the amount of time children spend with media (Stanger & Gridina, 1999). The Annenberg survey results powerfully demonstrate that parents worry about the impact of media on their children and that an investment in monitoring and improving media is a worthy quest.

### *Brief Overview of the Effects of Media on Children*

Parents and other advocates for children are becoming increasingly concerned about the potential negative impact of media. Understanding the existing research and experience regarding the effects of messages and images from various forms of media on children and adolescents reinforces the need for parental control and monitoring in the home. As Dr. Jerome Singer stated in the video program *On Television,*

> Parents have to realize that there is a stranger in your house. If you came home and you found a strange man . . . teaching your kids to punch each other, or trying to sell them all kinds of products, you'd kick him right out of the house. But here you are; you come in and the TV is on; and you don't think twice about it. (as cited in McGee, 1984)

Sometimes the impact of media exposure on young viewers is immediate and unmistakable (e.g., when a preschooler imitates violent karate moves seen on a favorite cartoon show or when children clamor for a certain sweetened cereal advertised heavily on network television). Usually, the effects of media on children and adolescents are cumulative, akin to a slowly growing stalagmite in a cave; over time, with repeated exposure to the same messages and images, attitudes and behaviors change.

Discussed in detail in other chapters in this book, several child and adolescent health and behavioral concerns may be associated with media use habits and choices (Strasburger & Donnerstein, 1999):

- Numerous studies confirm that some heavy viewers of media violence learn to behave aggressively toward others, become desensitized to and accepting of violence, and tend to view the world as a scary, hostile place. In addition, violent scenes may provide scripts for imitative behavior and may increase a viewer's appetite for violence.
- Increasing concern is being raised about the thousands of graphic, unhealthy sexual portrayals young people view yearly in the media. Only a few of these provide messages to vulnerable viewers about abstinence, safe and responsible sexual behavior, or the harmful consequences of casual sexual activity, including pregnancy and sexually transmitted diseases (Kunkel et al., 1999).
- The rates of alcohol, tobacco, and marijuana use are disturbingly high for preteens and teens across the United States. Although many factors are at play, substance use and abuse are common themes in the media, as young viewers see characters smoking and drinking in advertisements, television shows, and movies. These images normalize and glamorize substance use; this is "cool" and "sexy" (not unhealthy) behavior.
- Another example of a health risk associated with media use is the promotion and advertising of unhealthy foods (high in fat and salt, low in nutritional benefit) while telling young people that weight loss and thinness are important. Research associates heavy media use with the risk of obesity, and, clearly, hours in front of a screen means less time for physical activity.
- Young people learn from watching the world around them and from the behavior of parents, siblings, other adults, and appealing characters in the media. Myths and stereotypes about gender,

race and ethnicity, profession, and disability are commonly shown and reinforced in the media. How these issues are portrayed on the screen shapes children's beliefs about the real world, promotes schisms and differences, and defines success and influence.

With the well-founded concern about the harmful impact of media on the health of children and adolescents, the potential prosocial and educational aspects of media programs and products may be lost or ignored. Public television, although grossly underfunded, features several high-quality educational programs for children of all ages. Selected programs for children, whether on cable channels or network television, also offer options for positive entertainment and education. With parental or teacher supervision, children can explore new worlds and interests on the Internet, from pursuing hobbies to researching elusive topics to keeping current on international events. Software aimed at young girls is a burgeoning business, and, similarly, several new teen magazines have arrived on the scene for girls. Rather than emphasizing dating and dieting, this new genre celebrates the many positive facets of being female: intelligence, athleticism, and self-confidence. When negative or harmful media products and programs are recognized and their impact minimized, we will be able to appreciate the untapped benefits and joys the mass media have to offer.

## Media Education Within the Family

The ubiquitous nature of media in our children's lives, and the potential harm from exposure to media messages and images, leads parents and other caregivers to turn to media education, or media literacy, as a simple and effective approach to managing media use in the home. More than schools, communities, or government mandates, parents are in a unique and powerful position to control, limit, and shape media use habits for their children through media education.

Parents can turn to respected, experienced organizations for assistance in understanding and incorporating media education into their homes and lives. The American Academy of Pediatrics introduced its national campaign for media education, Media Matters, in 1998 and has also published a policy statement on media education in 1999 (Committee on Public Education, 1999). The campaign includes information and activities for pediatricians, other professionals, and parents. Similarly, the National Parent Teacher Association published *Taking Charge of Your TV* in 1995 (National PTA, 1995). This guidebook helps parents create a positive media environment in the home.

For families, media education is the process of becoming selective, wise, and critical media consumers. Some of the components of media education, or media literacy, include the following:

- People create (construct) media messages.
- Each form of media uses its own language and techniques.
- No two people experience media messages in the same way.
- Each media message has its own values and point of view (American Academy of Pediatrics, 1999).

Parents can teach and model these insights for children and ensure that media education permeates every aspect of life in a family. Media education is a lifelong skill that will make all of us better media consumers, whether we are enjoying a movie, reading a newspaper, listening to a political ad, or surfing the Internet. Children who are media educated should enter adolescence and adulthood with a healthy cynicism about media offerings. Is this movie worth the price of admission? Do I believe this political candidate's pledges? Why are young women's bodies being used to promote this brand of beer?

Parents can and should use every opportunity to bring media education into the family conversation:

- Sitting around the dinner table discussing a newspaper article
- Planning to watch an educational TV show about Siberian tigers as a family
- Discussing a billboard advertising alcohol while driving to a family activity
- Coviewing a popular sitcom with young teens and their friends and "talking back" to the characters about their offensive dialogue

Media education, through filtering, questioning, and analyzing media images and messages, is fun and empowering for children and adults. Media education, when incorporated into everyday life, allows children to feel "smarter than the TV," savvy about advertising, and thus better able to evaluate products and be in control of misleading messages. Media education skills are also passed on between children; for example, if your child "talks back" to the TV about violence in a cartoon, this can have a powerful influence on a young friend visiting for the afternoon. When a child cries "Aha!" upon discovering the power of deconstructing a media message and passes that skill to family and friends, the potential "impact factor" of media education is realized (Reisberg, 1997).

Basic media education principles for the family are simple and effective:

- Arrange your home to be a positive media environment.
- Establish clear, fair rules about media use for your family.
- Encourage active, critical viewing of media programs amplified by family discussions.

In addition to incorporating media education principles into the everyday life of a family, an understanding of the developmental needs and milestones of children and teens is essential to making positive media choices.

### *Infants and Children Under Age 2*

This age group should not watch TV; experts know that these very young children need positive, nurturing social time with adults and other children. They need touching, tasting, manipulating, smiling (and receiving a smile in return), and kissing! No research is available about the positive benefits of TV for infants (although some producers tout television programming and even software aimed at this group). Research and experience suggest that infants and very young children must attach securely to adults in their lives, benefit from exploring the real world around them, and need a variety of experiences, including playing with a variety of safe toys, exposure to books, physical exercise, and other multisensory, creative pastimes. Little ones require real-life experiences for brain development and for mastery of independent thinking. For these reasons, the American Academy of Pediatrics policy statement on media education (Committee on Public Education, 1999) recommends no media exposure for infants and children under the age of 2 years. (See Table 37.1.)

### *Toddlers and Preschoolers*

Parents should exercise caution with this group of children when it comes to media exposure. Toddlerhood is a developmentally fragile time when the business at hand is the emerging sense of selfhood, body integrity, separation, and individuation. Toddlers are susceptible to scary portrayals and cannot separate fantasy from reality: What they view on the screen is very real to them. Children in this age group need multisensory stimulation and a variety of activities. Encouraging imaginative play is far better for positive development than is the imitative play fostered by watching television. There can be some positive skills learned from carefully selected programming, notably on public television stations or on videotapes.

**TABLE 37.1** AAP Media Education Policy Statement Recommendations

- Pediatricians should understand health risks of media exposure.
- Pediatricians should begin incorporating questions about media use into their routine visits. Advice to parents should include the following:
  - Encourage careful selection of programs to view.
  - Coview and discuss content with children and adolescents.
  - Teach critical viewing skills.
  - Limit and focus time spent with media.
  - Be good media role models.
  - Emphasize alternative activities.
  - Create an electronic-media-free environment in children's rooms.
  - Avoid the use of media as an electronic baby-sitter.
  - Urge parents to avoid TV for children under 2.
- Pediatricians should also
  - Serve as role models for appropriate media use
  - Alert and educate parents, children, teachers, and other professionals about media-associated health risks
  - Collaborate with other professionals, including parent-teacher, school, and community groups, to promote media education
  - Continue to monitor media and advocate for increased educational and prosocial programming and messages
  - Encourage state and federal governments to explore mandating and funding universal media education programs
  - Encourage government and private institutions to increase funding available for media education research

SOURCE: Committee on Public Education (1999).

### *School-Age Children*

The work of the child in school is challenging but rewarding, including honing of language skills, thinking strategies, and study habits. Occupying too many hours with television or video games does not foster the literacy skills of reading and writing. Time spent with media steals important hours from interacting with friends, running and playing outside, and developing the skills to persevere at homework. Many elementary-school-age children still do not distinguish fantasy from reality or understand the intent of advertising. And some children have special needs (children with vivid imaginations or fearfulness or those who lack consistent, loving adult attachments), making them more susceptible to negative impacts of excessive media exposure.

### *Adolescents*

Young teens trying to answer the central question "Who am I?" encounter dubious role models and scripts for attitude and behavior on-line, in movies, through favorite song lyrics, and on television. Many teens learn misinformation about sexuality and gender roles through media. Unfortunately, they may also define desirable body shapes and facial features by images on the screen and in magazines. As teens move through adolescence into higher levels of cognitive abilities, many still cannot separate fiction from reality on the screen. Socially, adolescents need time with nurturing adults and peers. For some alienated youth, on-line companions or hours listening to music alone may take the place of real-life relationships. Although information on the Internet can greatly assist in finding information for school projects, and movies or video games can be the fulcrum for a social gathering, media should still be monitored and limited for adolescents. The weighty task of moving smoothly from childhood to adulthood is adolescence; requirements for a successful journey are good physical health, challenge and success in school, the ability to negotiate and cooperate, and the presence of supportive, available adults.

## Specific Roles Parents Play in Media-Educated Families

Keeping in mind the basic principles of media education, parents can play specific roles that work effectively within individual families. In becoming a media-educated (media-literate) family, flexibility, humor, and good communication are paramount. Media education is a process, and adults and children work together to optimize media use through the following guidelines.

### *Limit Time Spent With Media*

For many years, the American Academy of Pediatrics (AAP) has recommended that children's and adolescents' media time be limited to 1 to 2 hours of quality programming daily. Each family, according to priorities, values, and interests, must define "quality." Time spent with any form of media, high quality or not, is time away from friends and family, active pursuits, creative play and hobbies, reading, and homework.

Media-educated parents and children can discuss establishing clear and consistent rules for media use, including finishing homework before watching TV or playing video games. Some families allow more flexibility with hours on weekends or during the summer, but well-enforced, respected limits on total screen time and on the kind of programs deemed appropriate are important bases of media education. Such limits are difficult to employ for the first time with an older child or adolescent; rules are best instituted and applied consistently when children are young. Parents should explain why specific media rules are instituted: "The violence in this program doesn't teach how to solve a problem"; "the language we hear on this program is very disrespectful to others"; or "there will be no video games until your homework is completed." This respectful approach to establishing guidelines for family media use teaches children and adolescents about parents' values and limits.

Family ground rules for media should endeavor to maximize family time and optimize school performance. Individual families should determine guidelines appropriate for their home as follows:

- Establish media time limits for each family member, either on a per-day or per-week basis.
- Discuss the kinds of programs that are off limits.
- Homework and chores must be completed before TV or other media are turned on.
- Television should not be turned on before school or during mealtimes (or on school nights).
- Consider having "media-free days" once or twice each week (or "media-free weeks").
- Use a timer to help children remember when to turn off the television, computer, or video game.

The AAP as mentioned recommends no television at all for children under the age of 2 (Committee on Public Education, 1999). Infants and young toddlers are exploring their world, forming attachments to the adults and other children in their lives, and learning through multisensory input. Research tells us that reading with youngsters and providing them safe, stimulating environments to explore maximizes development. No one knows the effect that hours in front of a television screen will have on an infant or toddler; the research about early brain development is a growing field. It seems prudent to provide little ones with the active loving and learning they need, not counting on figures on a screen to supplant parents and other adults.

### *Choose Quality Programs*

Whether television shows, films in the theater or on video, or computer software, choosing quality programs and products is an essential component of media education. Families should plan their media schedule actively and wisely. If a program of interest to the family (e.g., a sporting event or a special on animals) is scheduled during the week, this show should be a planned, anticipated family event. Family media plans should reflect each family's value system, and guidelines for content should take into account ages and interests of family members. Some families may like to catch a weekly baseball game on television, while others eagerly await a nature show on public television. Another family may allot one half-hour weekly for an anticipated family comedy series. The salient concept is the "media plan."

As presented in *Screen Smarts* (DeGaetano & Bander, 1996), parents and children can discuss the reasons for choosing a particular program:

- Why do we want to see this program?
- What will we get out of the experience?
- Is this program appropriate for family members?
- Are there activities we will forgo?
- If more than one program is of interest, which will we choose?

Using a healthy diet as an analogy, as proposed in *The Smart Parent's Guide to Kids' TV* (Chen, 1994), parents decide which components of a "healthy media diet" will benefit their own children. Children and adolescents readily grasp this concept. We do not eat too many fat-laden foods because they are not good for our bodies and, similarly, too many violent or worthless programs are not conducive to healthy bodies and minds. Just as parents encourage healthy, nutrient-rich foods (although still in moderation), it is important to steer our children toward educational, positive media choices.

Leaving the TV on as "background noise" or randomly flicking through channels to find something interesting leads to complacency and unplanned TV watching. Some families check TV schedules together at the beginning of the week to make a media plan; in this way, the recommended 1- to 2-hour time limit guideline is respected (DeGaetano & Bander, 1996).

Parents concerned about choosing quality media products and programs for children are wise to consult a variety of available resources. There are excellent educational or entertaining videocassettes, cable television, or broadcast television programs available; a parent must only take the time to seek out and research these products (Singer, Singer, & Zuckerman, 1990).

- Create a collection of videotapes or borrow tapes from the local library; the public library is a rich resource for parents.
- Check websites for organizations with suggestions for educational videotapes or video games.
- Several organizations create newsletters for parents that contain suggestions for educational or entertaining products for children.

With creativity and preplanning, television and other media programs can be positive learning experiences for children and adults. Parents can use a television image as a window of opportunity for reinforcing a family belief or dispelling a stereotype. Many shows transport children to new lands and allow a wide range of experience; parents can amplify these programs with simple observations and discussions. Some simple guidelines for choosing television programs, movies, or videos for children include the following:

- Seek programs without gender, racial or ethnic, or other negative, stereotypic portrayals. Many television shows for young children have positive and useful multicultural casts and scenarios.
- Choose programs that engender discussion.
- Choose programs that are consistent with your family beliefs and priorities.
- Select a program that will teach your child something new or exciting.

*Screen Smarts* (DeGaetano & Bander, 1996) suggests qualities to look for when choosing computer software programs or video games:

- Games should require mental ability, not just a quick finger.
- Thought and problem-solving skills should be challenged.
- Ideally, skills should be applicable to real life.
- Games should enhance creativity and curiosity.
- Games with violent or sexual themes should be avoided.

As important as choosing appropriate programs and products, parents also may have to act as censors within the home, forbidding inappropriate programming. This could include the evening newscast, often featuring lurid or violent current events ("if it bleeds, it leads"); prime-time television shows; daytime "tell-all" television shows; or some music television.

More than 50% of adolescents under age 17 have attended popular R-rated movies (Strasburger & Donnerstein, 1999). Movie theaters and managers are ill equipped to check the ages of all theater patrons, and many young people slip into inappropriate movies without parental consent. Others purchase tickets to PG or PG-13 movies and attend the R-rated feature instead. Still more bothersome, many parents bring young children to R-rated movies rife with violence, graphic sexual themes, and lurid language, perhaps not realizing the potential impact on the immature viewer. Choosing appropriate media content and programming for children and teens extends to the movie theater. Firm, consistent parental rules and optimal surveillance by theater workers are important measures.

### *Be a Positive Media Role Model*

Parental roles of guiding children toward positive media choices and forbidding inappropriate media will help them to internalize the concept of choosing quality programs and products by themselves.

Children learn through imitation and reinforcement; media habits are no exception. If parents (the primary role models) hope to engender positive media habits in children, they must limit their own time in front of the screen and model preplanning and good choices in their lives. Parents who value active pursuits, love to read, enjoy time with friends and family, and tackle new hobbies with enthusiasm teach children far more powerful lessons than words ever could.

### *Arrange Your Home to Be a Positive Media Environment*

If the television sits on the dining room table and is on during dinner, if the computer is squirreled away in your daughter's bedroom, if each of your children has a personal television set in his or her bedroom, all of these media habits reinforce negative behaviors. Some simple, effective guidelines ensure a positive media environment.

- Avoid having computers or television sets in children's bedrooms; having a central, family media area encourages coviewing and discussion and limits aimless time in front of the screen.
- If at all possible, television should not be used as an "electronic baby-sitter." Although child care issues are extremely challenging for busy parents, safe, creative alternatives are preferred.
- Experts rightly believe that regular family time is important glue for today's busy families. Having the television on during mealtimes precludes a routine time for togetherness in many households; the TV should be off during meals.
- TV should not be used as "background noise." If not being accessed in a planned manner, the television should be off.

- TV and other media (computers, video games) should not be used as a reward or punishment; then, the medium assumes much greater importance in a child's worldview.
- Homework and other obligatory activities, such as chores, must be completed satisfactorily before media can be accessed.

### *Experience Media With Your Children: Encourage Media Education*

Research teaches us that coviewing, watching programs and using media products with your children, is a critical component of media education. Knowing what their children are watching allows parents to be involved in choices, to make priorities clear, and to encourage media literacy. A coviewing parent, through astute observations and questions about media messages, can make a poor program a learning experience, whereas a wonderful program watched by a child without a parent in attendance may be a wasted opportunity for learning and enjoyment.

> Co-viewing, whether with a parent, other adult, sibling or peer, provides a critical opportunity to mediate children's understanding and interpretation of the reality and morality of messages, as well as their attitudes, values and knowledge about the world in which they live and the appropriate ways to act in the world. (Eisenstock, 1994)

Coviewing can

- Influence a child's judgment about the representation of TV characters
- Help children's understanding of plots and story lines
- Mediate potentially harmful effects of aggressive and violent content (when adult disapproval is expressed and discussion of nonviolent values is advanced)

The "4 Cs" (DeGaetano & Bander, 1996), detailed below, help parents think about encouraging media-educated children:

- Critical thinking and viewing
- Communication
- Creativity
- Choices

#### *Critical Thinking and Viewing*

These are cornerstones of media education. A child who is able to analyze media messages, "talk back" to characters and images, and dissect programs is truly media literate. These skills are lifelong and will serve children well through youth and into adulthood. Examples of critical thinking and viewing include the following:

- *Discuss and dissect violent scenes in cartoons, movies, programs, and previews.* Parents coviewing such a scene can seize the opportunity to talk with a child about alternative conflict-resolution techniques, the technology used to "fake" scary or violent scenes, and adult disapproval of the violence.
- *Discuss stereotypic portrayals of female characters in situation comedies or prime-time shows.* Parents can propose alternative character traits and strengths and dispel prevalent myths about gender.
- *Discuss the portrayal of persons of color, the elderly, or disabled people on television shows.* Coviewing adults have the opportunity to point out that media misrepresent the real world and can engage children in dialogue about more realistic views of society.
- *Discuss the overemphasis on police officers, lawyers, and doctors as professionals on television.* Where is everyone else?
- *Discuss techniques used in advertisements for beer, cars, candy, or toys.*

How does the advertiser "grab" our attention? Do we get all the information we need, or is anything left out?
- *Analyze the presentation of news stories.* Why do violent news events lead the newscast? How are people involved in the news interviewed? Do we receive all the pertinent information? How do news producers grab our attention?

Helping children become critical thinkers and viewers is facilitated by thoughtful questions posed by parents (AAP, 1999; Singer et al., 1990; Work/Family Directions, 1996).

- Describe the people involved in creating the media message (writers, photographers, producers, special effects people, advertisers).
- Talk about the visual effects, sound effects, and other special techniques used in creating the media message.
- Discuss the purpose of the message. Is the purpose to urge you to buy something? To entertain you? To inform you?
- What does the child or teen viewer think about the message?
- Encourage children to notice details of programs (e.g., clothing, scenery, characteristics of people involved, time of year), sequence or plot, cause and effect, and symbolism.
- Challenge young viewers to predict the outcome of media messages, whether programs or advertisements, and to infer why characters behave the way they do.

Deconstruction, or dissection, of media is fun and instructive. (See Chapter 38.) This technique works for television programs, advertisements, movies, video games, and music lyrics—all forms of media. The only skills parents need to encourage critical thinking are communication and creativity.

### *Communication*

Family discussions about media make critical thinking the valuable exercise that it is. Encouraging children and adolescents to share their ideas in an interested, supportive manner is part of media education. Media-educated children are likely to share their insights with a friend or sibling. Once children feel comfortable with the basics of media education and critical thinking, they will incorporate their skills into everyday life, applying a critical eye to media messages and images all around (Mediascope, 1999; Singer et al., 1990).

### *Creativity*

Parents become excited about media education as they see their efforts come to fruition through the enlightenment of children. Creativity is an essential aspect of media education, making the process even more rewarding for the family. Creativity involves weaving media education skills into everyday life, suggesting new and fun ways to interact with media using the family's collective imagination to manage media in the home. The ideas for incorporating creativity into media education are limitless and include the following:

- Borrow a book from the library about a movie or program you plan to watch on television and read aloud in preparation for the event.
- Dress in costumes reflecting a movie the family plans to watch.
- Allow each family member (no matter how old) to lead a discussion after a family-watched television program or movie.
- Turn off the TV sound and make up your own family dialogue.
- Design your own commercials for a favorite product.

- Create counteradvertisements for unhealthy products such as beer or tobacco.
- Turn off a movie on videotape before the ending and have each family member predict the ending.
- Put on a family play and videotape the event.

Creativity also means pursuing nonmedia activities with gusto: taking family field trips to local zoos and museums, reading nightly from a chapter of a book, engaging in cooking adventures, and allowing time to daydream.

### *Choices*

As emphasized above, making active, positive media choices is a key part of media education. Whether browsing the Internet, renting videos at the local store, or hunkering down for a night of television, media use should be a limited, planned, and conscious activity, and only a small slice of the life of an active, creative, curious child.

### ***Understand and Use Current Ratings Systems***

For many years, the age-based Motion Picture Association of America (MPAA) ratings system has been in place for movies produced in the United States, and parents, over the years, have become familiar with the meaning behind a G-, PG-, PG-13-, R-, or NC-17-rated film. This familiarity with the ratings does not imply that parents always agree with the ratings; in fact, studies have shown that a significant percentage of parents disagree (Gentile & Walsh, 1998). Many professional organizations, as well as parents, would still prefer a content-based ratings system for all forms of media.

In 1997, the television industry, under pressure from parents, advocacy groups, and some government leaders, instituted an age-based ratings system for many television programs. This system, reminiscent of the MPAA system for movies, allows producers to voluntarily rate their own shows (Cantor, 1998; Eisenstock, 1999). See Table 37.2 for codes and explanations.

**TABLE 37.2** TV Ratings System

- TV-Y (appropriate for all children)
- TV-Y7 (directed to older children)
- FV (fantasy violence—intense violence in children's programming)
- TV-G (general audience)
- TV-PG (parental guidance suggested)
  - V (moderate violence)
  - S (some sexual situations)
  - L (infrequent coarse language)
  - D (some suggestive dialogue)
- TV-14 (parents strongly cautioned)
  - V (intense violence)
  - S (intense sexual situations)
  - L (strong coarse language)
  - D (intensely suggestive dialogue)
- TV-MA (mature audiences only)
  - V (graphic violence)
  - S (explicit sexual activity)
  - L (crude, indecent language)

SOURCE: Cantor (1998) and Eisenstock (1999).

With the advent of the highly touted V-chip, parents with this technology will be able to block certain undesirable programs in their homes. However, the rating system is far from ideal: News and sports programs are not rated; not all networks agreed to use the system; and the programs are still rated by a not-disinterested producer. Only the most intense level of content is displayed on the TV screen and determines the overall rating; content existing at lower levels is not displayed (Cantor, 1998). In addition, the rating flashes on the screen at the beginning of the program and may be missed by parents.

Studies have shown that, for some children (particularly young boys), a mature rating, whether for television or movies, increases the young viewer's incentive to watch the show or movie—the "forbidden fruit" quandary (Cantor, 1998). Ratings do not predict the appropriateness of a product or program for a particular child. These shortcomings underscore the important role parents play in mediating the media choices of children. Whether a television show or movie is rated G or higher, a parent knows the unique fears and sensitivities of a child or adolescent and should exercise the option of forbidding viewing of that program. Similarly, in some cases, a show with a prohibitive rating may be appropriate or educational at a given time and place for a given child. For example, a historical TV program on the Holocaust, the civil rights movement, or other major events, violence notwithstanding, may be a rich experience for a child coviewing with an interested parent.

Some video games and software also carry voluntary ratings for parents to use in deciding about the suitability of a product for a child. Both the Recreational Software Advisory Council and the Entertainment Software Rating Board developed ratings systems in response to legislation in 1994. However, studies have shown that only a minority of parents are aware of such ratings, even though most parents wanted products to be rated (Cesarone, 1998). Similarly, CDs and music cassette tapes may carry labels warning about explicit lyrics, once again as a cue for concerned parents. Some products also include the lyrics in narrative form. This is a mixed blessing; in the case of explicit or suggestive music lyrics, many young people are unaware of the meaning of these lyrics (or do not catch the lyrics at all)!

The National Institute on Media and the Family, a nonprofit organization in Minnesota, publishes trademarked, parent-friendly ratings called "KidScore" (National Institute on Media and the Family, 1997-2000) for children's media products on its website, including ratings for television series, movies, and video games. This system uses green (go), yellow (warning), and red (stop) symbols for parents, as well as explaining the content concerns. The National Institute on Media and the Family also publishes an annual "Video Game and Computer Game Report Card," including "The Parent Guide to Electronic Media," to assist parents in making optimal media choices for young people (Walsh, 1998).

### *Encourage Alternative Activities to Electronic Media*

Hours in front of a screen mean time is not being spent with a good book, friends, coloring materials, or an active outdoor game. Parents interested in media literacy also encourage activities unrelated to media, building strong bodies, agile minds, and lasting relationships. Research tells us that children who are regular or heavy viewers of TV tend to engage in scripted, imitative play, suggested by characters or plots in favorite programs (DeGaetano & Bander, 1996). Playing freely and creatively, making their own scenarios, characters, and plot lines is conducive to developing a rich imagination. Whether building with clay or mud, writing a story, crafting a village out of blocks, or playing dress-up, creative pursuits allow children to unlock minds and imaginations, exploring the possibilities offered in their environment. Television and other media activities are generally passive: Viewers watch make-believe characters living their scripted lives.

Parents should read to children beginning in early infancy, sharing a love of books with an assortment of characters and plots. Reading aloud fosters listening skills, an active imagination, ease with language, an introduction to symbols, and a love of books for life. Parents should also encourage children to read alone. Providing a library card or regularly adding editions to the home bookshelves enables children and adolescents to curl up with a book and be transported on endless journeys.

Engaging in exercise and sports is a healthy alternative for children, adolescents, and adults who are increasingly suffering from obesity, sedentary lifestyles, and the panoply of health problems accompanying these lifestyle risks. Running, biking, and participating in competitive sports are fun activities and essential for healthy bodies. Friendships and strong self-concepts are built and nurtured through physical pursuits.

Finally, social time with friends and family promotes emotional well-being and enhances the sense of self. Watching television often precludes conversation and interchange with others. Although video games may involve more than one player, the communication involved may be competitive and counterproductive for friendship and growth. Family rituals, including daily mealtimes together, bond the members and perpetuate identity and satisfaction. If, instead of sharing joys and experiences of everyone's day, or plans for tomorrow, or hashing out a family problem, everyone's eyes are glued to the TV at dinner, valuable relationship-building opportunities are lost.

### *Evaluate the Family's Media Use and Habits Regularly*

Keeping a media diary or log helps families to assess media education progress (Center for Media Education, 1995). How many hours is our TV on each day? Are we making wise choices in our TV use? Our computer time? What kinds of programs have we enjoyed as a family? Since thinking about media time and media planning, have we changed our priorities as a family? Are we finding plenty of other pursuits to keep us engaged and challenged?

Parents and children can evaluate family discussions. Have certain TV programs or other media programs offered opportunities for critical thinking? Have any family members had a revelation about media images and messages? Are we better, smarter, more critical viewers now? It is important for families to continually self-examine the role media literacy plays in the family's everyday life.

## Other Forms of Media: Specific Issues for Parents

### *Video Games*

Although television is the most ubiquitous of the media, other forms of electronic media commonly reside in homes across the country. An amazing 67% of families own a dedicated video system such as Nintendo or Sega, and the number of hours spent by children playing with these systems is growing (Stanger & Gridina, 1999). More than 75% of children play video games sometimes at home, and nearly 25% play every day (Cesarone, 1998). More boys than girls play video games, but the market for games aimed at young girls is burgeoning. Many concerns have been raised about the content of many of these home video games, especially violence, sexual content, and stereotypical characters. Little research exists to date directly linking the use of video games to aberrant behavior; however, many experts are concerned about the rewarding of violent behavior and the frequency of violent and sexual portrayals commonly seen in video game products.

Parents, although commonly much less facile than their young children in the operation of these games, should attempt to play the games with youngsters and use the opportunity for critical discussion about content and characters. Firm guidelines about time limits on video game play and restriction of play until homework is completed complement rules about television viewing and computer use.

### *Music*

Music videos, MTV, and rock music lyrics continue to engender much passion on both sides of the debate. The scenes in music videos and on MTV commonly contain violence (often with guns), sexual themes, or juxtapose both violence and sex (DuRant et al., 1997). Issues about explicit-lyric warning labels on CDs, raised earlier, include the lack of data about the effect of the warnings on youth and concern about the "forbidden fruit" response. Although no research to date has conclusively linked violent or sexual music lyrics to antisocial behavior, some evidence exists that a preference for heavy metal music may be a marker for troubled youth (Klein et al., 1993).

Statistics suggest that adolescents listen to many hours of music daily, often while doing homework (even over the protests of parents) or interacting with peers. Unlike other forms of media, music may provide comforting background music for teens and may act as an important definition of "who I am," allowing a teen to feel membership in a larger group.

For youth having trouble in school or socially, examining the time spent alone in a room listening to music (and not doing homework) is an essential parental role. As with television viewing, time with music may be limited to hours after homework is successfully completed and chores and other obligations are finished. Trying to enforce these rules during adolescence is challenging, especially if media education efforts have not been put into place within a family previously.

### *Computers*

More and more families are on-line, and increasing numbers of children are spending hours they used to spend in front of the TV screen with a mouse and computer screen. Many young children navigate the World Wide Web with elan and confidence and teenagers gather useful data for elusive research projects, but the perils cannot be ignored.

- Hours spent in front of the computer, again, are hours away from friends, physical activity, books, and happy daydreaming.
- Websites with explicit sexual images are a mere click away, sometimes encountered unwittingly.
- Websites sell products and advertise substances such as alcoholic beverages and cigarettes freely.
- Children's and, consequently, family privacy are not guaranteed on the Internet; children may unconsciously provide confidential information about family finances and priorities.

Blocking devices for computers are imperfect and often preclude legitimate use of the Internet. Rather than censorship, parents and media education provide the most effective, simplest means to deal with the control of the computer. Basic media education tenets should apply to computer use for children and adolescents of all ages, including limiting time spent with the computer, mandating parental supervision, encouraging discussion, and, if reasonable, keeping the computer at a central site in the family home. Parents should become as computer sophisticated as possible; children today are getting a big head start in the computer race.

Depending on interest and developmental capability, children are ready to begin computer activities at different ages. The family computer need not play a role in the life of children under 2. By age 3 or 4, manipulating the mouse and using simple child-friendly software provide a wonderful introduction to the computer. Allow children to see the rest of the family using this technology for information gathering and enjoyment. Older children require adult supervision and encouragement while playing computer games and exploring the many facets of this technology. Proper computer ethics and safety should be demonstrated and reinforced. Limiting time on-line, discussing privacy and avoidance of mature material, and other house rules must be emphasized. As children get older, parents and teachers partner to maximize use of the computer for learning, projects, and communication. Although older children and adolescents need more independence, parental rules and co-use are still vital to healthy computer habits. These young people should be encouraged to discuss their impressions of information learned, pursue new interests, and explore the technology as a rich resource for learning and communication.

Parents, by getting involved with local schools and communities, can make sure that classrooms have the appropriate technology to enhance learning. Recent statistics reveal that 27% of American classrooms have Internet access and 78% of schools have some access to the Internet (Lazarus & Lipper, 1998). In order to enter the new millennium prepared to succeed in school and career, every child and adolescent should have education about and access to computers and the Internet.

## Make Your Voice Heard: Advocacy and Activism

Parents, schools, and communities share a common goal to make media positive, educational, and prosocial for children and adolescents. These groups are natural collaborators. Some of the most effective voices for change in media have risen from grassroots campaigns, including the now defunct Action for Children's Television and the ongoing National TV-Turnoff Week, sponsored by TV-Free America based in Washington, D.C.

There are many simple collaborative efforts parents can encourage, including the following:

- Support alternative, community-based activities for children, especially after school and on weekends.
- Publicize and promote TV-Turnoff Week in neighborhoods; make this fun and inviting for families.
- Publish a simple newsletter about alternatives to TV, perhaps including some ideas for educational videotapes and good upcoming TV shows.
- Commit with other parents to not using TV as a baby-sitter in your home or play group.

Networks and local affiliates listen when many parents call with complaints (or compliments) about television shows. Using the phone or writing a letter about a stereotypic portrayal, show, or other negative message and encouraging friends and family to write can influence a local television station manager. Advertisers and sponsors of shows should also be contacted about negative programming; refusal to buy products associated with sponsors of offensive programs can also influence programming choices. The media are big, profitable businesses, and networks and sponsors depend on the support and money of the listening and viewing audience.

Many organizations across the United States are committed to media education and healthy children and teens. These groups feel strongly that parents play a key role as mediators and role models of appropriate media use for young people. Not only can these organizations be effective lobbyists and advocates on a local and national level, but they can also be a source of educational materials for parents. (See Chapter 39 for a compendium of organizations.)

## Correlation of Health and Behavior Problems With Media Use Habits

Pediatricians and parents increasingly worry about the impact of media exposure on children and adolescents. For most children, living in a loving home with consistent messages, fair discipline, and strong attachments between family members lessens the potentially harmful effects of media. However, some children may present disturbing behavior symptoms or signs of ill health; in some cases, the association between these problems and media habits is apparent.

Pediatricians and their national organization, the American Academy of Pediatrics, have long been concerned about the impact of media, especially television, on children (Committee on Public Education, 1999; Strasburger & Donnerstein, 1999). Media Matters (American Academy of Pediatrics, 1998), a national campaign for media education, offers support and education for parents and pediatricians in this important public health arena. Media Matters encourages pediatricians to become educated about media and to take a "media history" from each patient. This information about media choices and habits is discussed with families, and parallels may be drawn between this information and behavioral or health problems a child exhibits (American Academy of Pediatrics, 1998). Together, the pediatrician and parent develop a plan to introduce media education principles into the family and amend the media habits.

Specific examples of problem behaviors or health concerns include the following:

- Aggressive behavior on the playground displayed by a 6-year-old child who watches violent cartoons and videos at home
- Substance use such as early initiation of cigarette smoking in a young girl who has seen lead characters in her favorite movies smoking in a glamorous, natural way
- School problems in a 10-year-old boy who is typically on-line more than 6 hours per day
- Obesity in a young teen viewing many hours of TV daily while snacking on highly caloric and non-nutritional foods
- Trouble-making friends for a male teen who listens to hours of heavy metal music in his room every day along with playing violent video games
- Fear of going to bed in a 4-year-old who saw scary previews for a popular movie on television

Using anticipatory guidance, pediatricians can suggest media education techniques to parents of young children to prevent media problems from ever arising. If health or behavioral concerns present, as in some of the scenarios above, the pediatrician-parent team develops a plan to alter media use habits, employ media education techniques in the home, and follow the concerns closely.

## Conclusions and Recommendations

Families—parents, children, and adolescents—live in a media world. We are surrounded by media in various forms and inundated by messages and images, many of them potentially harmful to the health and well-being of young people. Positive and healthy media programs and products also exist but may be unrecognized and overwhelmed by the sheer weight of popular media.

In each individual home, parents and children should become media educated and set about creating a positive media environment. Time spent using media should be limited and alternative activities encouraged, including reading, physical activity, and creative and social pursuits. Families, depending on their unique values, interests, and needs, should carefully choose the media consumed in the home, whether television programs, movies or videotapes, music, video games, or computer programs. Parents, in addition to being positive role models, should actively coview programs with children, using this golden opportunity for discussion and deconstruction. A media-educated child—a wise, selective, critical media consumer—has learned a valuable lifelong skill.

Parents and other adult caregivers invested in the health and well-being of children and adolescents best provide role modeling, monitoring, and encouragement of media education in the home. Keenly aware of the special needs and developmental path of each child and imbued with respect and authority, parents, in partnership with other parents, schools, advocacy groups, and pediatricians, can lessen the potentially harmful impact of media on children and allow the untapped, prosocial benefits to be realized.

## References

American Academy of Pediatrics. (1998). *Media education in the practice setting.* Elk Grove Village, IL: Media Matters.

American Academy of Pediatrics. (1999). *Understanding the impact of media on children and teens.* Elk Grove Village, IL: Media Matters.

Cantor, J. (1998). *"Mommy, I'm scared!"* San Diego, CA: Harcourt Brace.

Center for Media Education. (1995). *A parent's guide to kids' TV.* Washington, DC: Author.

Cesarone, B. (1998). Video games: Research, ratings, recommendations. In *Clearinghouse on Elementary and Early Childhood Education.* Champaign: University of Illinois.

Chen, M. (1994). *The smart parent's guide to kids' TV.* San Francisco: KQED Books.

Committee on Public Education. (1999). Media education. *Pediatrics, 104,* 341-343.

DeGaetano, G., & Bander, K. (1996). *Screen smarts: A family guide to media literacy.* New York: Houghton Mifflin.

DuRant, R. H., Rich, M., Emans, S. J., Rome, E. S., Allred, E., & Woods, E. R. (1997). Violence and weapon carrying in music videos: A content analysis. *Archives of Pediatric and Adolescent Medicine, 151,* 443-448.

Eisenstock, B. A. (1994). *Empowering parents: TV literacy and the violence factor.* Paper presented at the International Conference on Violence in the Media, New York.

Eisenstock, B. A. (1999). *A parent's guide to the TV ratings and V-chip.* Washington, DC: Center for Media Education and Kaiser Family Foundation.

Gentile, D. A., & Walsh, D. A. (1998). *Parents rate the TV ratings.* Minneapolis, MN: National Institute on Media and the Family.

Huston, A. C., Donnerstein, E., Fairchild, H., Feshbach, N. D., Katz, P. A., Murray, J. P., Rubinstein, E. A., Wilcox, B. L., & Zuckerman, D. (1992). *Big world, small screen.* Lincoln: University of Nebraska Press.

Klein, J. D., Brown, J. D., Childers, K. W., Oliveri, J., Porter, C., & Dykers, C. (1993). Adolescents' risky behavior and mass media use. *Pediatrics, 92,* 24-31.

Kunkel, D., Cope, K. M., Farinola, W. J. M., Biely, E., Rollin, E., & Donnerstein, E. (1999). *Sex on TV: A biennial report to the Kaiser Family Foundation.* Santa Barbara: University of California Press.

Lazarus, W., & Lipper, L. (1998). *The parents' guide to the information superhighway.* Los Angeles: Children's Partnership, National PTA, and Urban League.

McGee, M. (Producer/writer). (1984). *On television: The violence factor.* New York: On Television.

Mediascope. (1999). *Children, the media, and drugs: A parent's guide.* Studio City, CA: Author.

Mohr, P. J. (1976). *Television, children, and parents: A report of the viewing habits, program preferences, and parental guidance of school children in the fourth through ninth grades in Sedgwick County, Kansas* [on microfiche]. Wichita, KS: Wichita State University.

Mohr, P. J. (1979). Parental guidance of children's viewing of evening television programs. *Journal of Broadcasting, 23,* 213-228.

National Institute on Media and the Family. (1997-2000). *KidScore* [On-line].
Available: www.Mediafamily. org

National PTA. (1995). *Taking charge of your TV: A guide to critical viewing for parents and children* [The Family and Community Critical Viewing Project]. Chicago: Author.

Reisberg, L. R. (1997). *The impact factor.* Elk Grove Village, IL: Media Matters, American Academy of Pediatrics.

Singer, D. G., Singer, J. L., & Zuckerman, D. M. (1990). *The parent's guide: Use TV to your child's advantage.* Reston, VA: Acropolis.

Stanger, J. D., & Gridina, N. (1999). *Media in the home 1999: The fourth annual survey of parents and children.* Philadelphia: University of Pennsylvania, Annenberg Public Policy Center.

Strasburger, V. C., & Donnerstein, E. (1999). Children, adolescents, and the media: Issues and solutions. *Pediatrics, 103,* 129-139.

Walsh, D. A. (1998). *Video and computer game report card.* Minneapolis, MN: National Institute on Media and the Family.

Work/Family Directions. (1996). *Changing channels: Preschoolers, TV, and media violence. A guide for parents and other grownups.* Boston: Work/Family Directions and Educators for Social Responsibility.

CHAPTER **38**

# Media Literacy and Critical Television Viewing in Education

JAMES A. BROWN
University of Alabama

This chapter outlines what schools and others are doing in media education, with an emphasis on teaching critical television-viewing skills. Such teaching takes the form of systematic curricula for classrooms and also stand-alone outlines and resources to help train children—as well as teachers and parents—for comprehension, critical use, and aesthetic appreciation of the media.

## Foundation Concepts

Media literacy refers to analytical, reflective understanding of print and electronic mass media, including film, their aesthetic components, institutional structures, socioeconomic contexts, and an ability to interact with media in preparing audiovisual products and in influencing media decision makers. "Critical viewing skills" is one major component of media literacy, referring to understanding of and competence with television, including its aesthetic, social, cultural, psychological, educational, economic, and regulatory aspects.

Theoretical foundations for research studying media include stimulus-response approaches, agenda setting, cultivation theory, uses and gratifications, cultural studies, critical analysis, and semiology. Researchers have explored in laboratories and field settings the results of time spent on media; exposure to violence, sex, and language; and values portrayed in media products and in advertising. They have studied not only the effects of media content but also what people do with media.

Concerns focus on the impact of the media on children's educational advancement in reading and writing skills and critical thinking. Of further concern is TV's impact on creativity, on interpersonal activity during impressionable years, and on socialization with peers and others in the wide world outside the viewing room. Television can also bring enrichment to children, including less advantaged ones, whether challenged physically, mentally, or otherwise.

## Trends in Developing Media Education for Young Viewers

### *Purposes*

What is the intent of media study? Early concern, continuing even today in some sectors, was protectionist—to inoculate children from the alleged harmful influence of media exposure by guiding them to be selective in program choices and to realize underlying determinants of media presentations and commercial advertising. More positive goals arose in regard to helping young people enrich their media experiences by learning factors behind media operations and by increasing their perception of media aesthetics and understanding so that they could make their own sense out of media products—enabling viewers to assess their values as well as weaknesses. This approach saw thoughtful media study as advancing critical thinking—similar and even contributing to more traditional education in classics, language, literature, or mathematics. A further goal was to help students appraise their own culture and that of others—including social, political, and economic aspects—through media exposure. Media study programs in the United Kingdom and Latin American countries added concern for social amelioration. Students learned how to influence media by reacting to and interacting with them and by mounting their own media programs. Another purpose was to chart how TV media portray physically disabled or otherwise disadvantaged characters in fiction and as subjects of news reports.

Hart (1998, p. 182) related major phases of media education emphasis successively developed over decades to equivalents in the U.K.'s pivotal Cox Report (commissioned by the Department of Education and Science, 1989): (a) The inoculatory and protectionist approach parallels transmitting and preserving traditional "cultural heritage"; (b) discriminating and popular arts relate to "personal growth" goals; and (c) critical, representational, semiological, and empowerment reflect "cultural analysis" characteristics.

Masterman (1985) stressed that, in media literacy, "the primary objective is not simply critical awareness and understanding, it is critical autonomy" (p. 24) to learn the process of forming personal judgments on which one can act after leaving school, when confronting media daily throughout one's lifetime.

### *Media and Youth With Disabilities*

A significant proportion of U.S. children are gifted or challenged physically, intellectually, or emotionally. Up to 8% of school-age children possess exceptional skill or talent; another 8 to 16% have exceptional disability—of whom, almost half (42%) are learning disabled (Abelman, 1995, citing several sources). Children who are intellectually gifted or learning disabled (LD) watch more television than their "nonlabeled" peers. They view more adult-oriented programming and advertising than do others; their parents have significantly fewer rules and regulations about using TV; and they are more likely to watch alone than other children. Abelman (1995) measured significantly less ability of LD children to follow narrative devices such as compressed-time editing and story lines. LD children were "very poor" at comprehending temporal sequencing in TV productions that require "attentional, organizational, and inferential activity" by the viewer. Thus, media literacy directed to youth with disabilities can help develop linguistic, cognitive, and perceptual skills by helping them to better comprehend television content and form.

Young people with disabilities are offered access to the world through TV (albeit not a substitute for experiencing the world first-hand). They can share common media experiences with nondisabled peers. Yet throughout the programming schedule, the images or role models they see of similar people with disabilities tend to be stereotypical. Their physical limitation is highlighted and used as a tool for the plot (often they are victims of manipulation or are the manipulators); characters acting as disabled are often portrayed as either uniquely courageous and inspiring or dependent and pathetic to elicit sympathy; disability is portrayed as a full-time occupation and serves to wholly identify the person; and it is the total focus of attention when that character appears. Persons with disabilities are rarely presented as individuals in their own right, with interests and experiences of most other people but with the addition of some physical or cognitive disability (Makas, 1993). Media curricula need to have viewers explore these depictions to modify narrow, inaccurate perceptions of those without disabilities as well.

Emotionally disturbed or learning disabled children watch television more than other young people, and they perceive media presentations to be more true to life and commercials to be more accurate than their counterparts do. Thus, these children can benefit from media literacy study designed for them, as demonstrated in formal research studies (Sprafkin, Gadow, & Abelman, 1992; Sprafkin, Watkins, & Gadow, 1990). Pre-, post-, and follow-up tests indicated positive development of knowledge of television conventions, characterization, and so on and less identification with aggressive characters; however, there was little change in attitude about TV in behavior regarding amount or kinds of subsequent viewing.

### *Sources of Media Education Activities*

Early on, and continuing today, isolated teachers introduced mass media topics into their classrooms, usually within the context of traditional content such as English or history or social studies. Some teachers received modest support from their school administrators, but rarely did an entire school or district introduce schoolwide systematic study of media into the curriculum (e.g., Anderson, 1980; Anderson & Meyer, 1988; Hobbs, 1998a). Schedules already crowded with curricular mandates had no time for yet another addition, so whatever media study could be introduced was typically integrated into already existing courses. Media were often considered by parents, administrators, and most faculty as ephemeral and superficial, hardly relevant to serious classroom study. Funding for necessary equipment was rare. For the same reasons, scant attention was given to contemporary mass media in schools, which sent out teachers unprepared to deal with complex socioeconomic and psychological, as well as aesthetic, aspects of media analysis. Subsequent teacher workshops for certification, accreditation, and advancement rarely included media literacy components.

Because media study in schools usually depended on the enlightened efforts of a plucky teacher or administrator, the lack of structural support limited the extent and duration of curriculum-related endeavors. Even four national projects substantially funded by the U.S. federal government (Brown, 1991) were mounted for only several years. They prepared model curricular projects for others to emulate by replicating or modifying them and then faded from the scene. The decentralized educational establishment in the 50 separate states, with more than 15,000 relatively autonomous districts and systems, left media studies development to entrepreneurial teachers or individual school principals or superintendents. This contrasted with other regions such as Western Australia, the Canadian province of Ontario, and some parts of the United Kingdom. There, media curricula in schools were mounted in province-wide centralized systems that mandated topic areas and levels of students for progressive study of media over specific spans of school years.

With schools offering only sporadic media study, especially in the United States, sustained initiatives were mounted by nonacademic organizations such as regional associations, small professional companies, churches, and public action groups. They began to offer workshops for parents and teachers to train them in understanding and procedures they could pass along to their children and students. These organizations assembled newsletters, handout sample worksheets, booklets, and audio and visual samples for media analysis. To finance their operations, they relied on foundation and corporate grants, individual donations, dues from subscribers and members, and charges for published artifacts.[1]

### *Methodologies: Kinds of Critical TV Viewing Studies*

Reviews of recent decades of television "critical viewing skills" indicate that media literacy programs of study include three general levels (see Anderson & Ploghoft, 1993, pp. 89-90):

1. Learning to produce media presentations not for potential career skills but, rather, to deconstruct how media operate and develop programs, including the "codes" of image-sound forms and formats (usually not until middle school, then high school and college courses)
2. Study of media industries and of social, economic, political, and ethical contexts to learn about forces shaping media content, including advertising economics and governmental regulation and public interest groups (offered mostly at upper secondary and college levels)
3. Critical analysis of media content, including "text" of story lines, dialogue, images, sounds, and other codes or forms of media presentation. "Meaning" of media product is found not only in the intent of the creators and distributors but in how individual viewers perceive and interpret that product (early grades, through middle and upper levels, plus college). More recent media study explores how and why people use "media"—their patterns of use, purposes, and how they interact with and interpret media depending on their individual cognitive processing. Cognition includes psychological, affective considerations; selective perception; and interpretation, making meaning of "texts."

Related to the second level above is the activist stance characteristic especially of the British and South American projects: media advocacy involving citizen consumers in media action/reaction and social change.

Studies have found that young children quickly apprehend basic codes of television visualization, partly from experience as well as from early instruction. One implication is that youngsters are not wholly gullible naifs needing urgent media training (cf. Anderson & Meyer, 1988; Anderson & Ploghoft, 1993, p. 93; Buckingham, 1992). Hobbs reported naturalistic fieldwork in northwest Kenya that confirmed that first-time viewers readily adapted to production conventions and visual "codes" when content was somewhat familiar (Hobbs, 1997, ch. 9, p. 174).[2] Teenagers have also scored highest on these aspects of deconstruction and analysis of texts compared with other levels of interpretation such as analyzing broader context and social implications (Quin & McMahon, 1993, p. 194).[3]

Meyrowitz (1998) orders slightly differently his list of three aspects of media study: media content literacy, media grammar literacy, and medium literacy. The last includes social, political, and economic environments that shape mass media institutions and operations—with questions of ownership, power, and control that determine what media present and why. The British Film Institute's primary curriculum statement organized media study expressed as broad conceptual understandings rather than as discrete objects of study or as skills or competencies—providing a theoretical frame applicable to a wide range of media integrated conceptually.

## Representative Projects and Curricula

Over decades, individual teachers, researchers, and academics as well as private organizations have explored ways to help media users develop more thoughtful interaction with media. The following section recounts patterns in those applied efforts by sketching selected projects and curricula. More details about each can be found in the references cited throughout.

### *Individual Classroom, Workshop, and Research Projects*

Individual teachers and researchers scattered in various countries early on created their own forms of media education and assessment; that led to later collaboration among kindred souls and helped spark the media literacy movement (cf. Brown, 1991; Dorr & Brannon, 1993). Noted here are some examples in the United States.

Rosemary Lee Potter, in Florida schoolrooms, sought to help young viewers think logically about TV program content, distinguish reality from fantasy, analyze content, and observe stereotypes. Aimée Dorr researched children's responses to media experience, testing their critical thinking through learning about program production and economics and through discussion and role playing (Dorr, Graves, & Phelps, 1980). Dorothy and Jerome Singer systematically studied children's attention drawn to TV's salient images and sounds; then prior guidelines and follow-up discussion prompted greater comprehension and other cognitive gains (Singer & Singer, 1983, 1994, 1998). Their curricula tested over time children's "significant gains in knowledge of how TV works" (Rapaczynski, Singer, & Singer, 1982, p. 46; Singer, Zuckerman, & Singer, 1980; Zuckerman, Singer, & Singer, 1980a, 1980b). Topics included advertising, news, stereotypes, aggression, reality versus fantasy, and production techniques. Renée Hobbs (1997, 1998a, 1998b) helped develop graduate-level media literacy training at Harvard for school district teachers.

### *Systematic Media Instruction in Schools and School Districts*

#### *United States*

A series of "critical receivership" projects in concert with schools and districts was developed by James Anderson and Milton Ploghoft (1993, pp. 91-92 for references). In 1977, they first introduced systematic media instruction to selected schools in districts with close collaboration of administrators and teachers; detailed lessons with workbooks included analysis of commercials and used entertainment to teach literary analysis.

#### *Canada*

Ontario, with one third of the nation's population, led the way in developing media literacy programs for schools. It was "the first educational jurisdiction in North America to make Media Literacy a mandatory part of the curriculum" (Pungente, n.d., p. 7). The province made media study part of the English curriculum. Ontario's Ministry of Education and the Ontario Teachers' Federation collaborated with the Association for Media Literacy (AML), which prepared a 232-page English/French *Media Literacy Resource Guide* published by the provincial government. The guide offered purposes, concepts, strategies, and models in print, photography, music, film, radio, and TV. By the late 1990s, the Atlantic provinces plus British Columbia also made media literacy part of the revised language arts curriculum (Pungente, n.d., p. 2; see also Morgan, 1998).

*United Kingdom*

The general approach is to incorporate media education into other curricular courses rather than as a separate offering. Media study typically teaches production as a step toward understanding media processes, and emphasis is put on social aspects of media impact and media involvement. In *England,* media education is included as one element within the national standards developed in the English curriculum (Kubey, 1998, pp. 58-59; see also Bazalgette, 1989; Bowker, 1991). In *Scotland,* Eddie Dick, media education officer of the Scottish Film Council, promoted media studies, developed pilot curricula and teaching resources, and compiled a database of sources and materials. The council in 1988 distributed *Media Education Curriculum Guidelines* to all primary and secondary schools. In *Wales,* local and regional educational authorities supported early projects in schools. Clwyd County's sophisticated use of traditional and contemporary theoretical perspectives, coupled with pragmatic activities—teacher training, curriculum guides, and class materials—offered a model adopted by others around the world.

*Federal Republic of Germany*

As in the United States and Canada, German schools serve separate regions with varied curricular structures and mandates, making any central coordination of media studies difficult. Each of the 16 federal states sets its own education standards. Where introduced, media education is a topic filtering through many disciplines, not as a separate subject or course. The general goal is "development of competent, autonomous, creative, and socially responsible actions in a world that is defined by media" (Tulodziecki & Schöpf, 1993, pp. 106-107).

*Germany/United States*

A unique project was the dual-country media project organized and funded by the Bertlesmann Foundation of Germany. It integrated media competence among teachers and students—including print, film, and electronic media—across the curriculum as a component of all classroom courses. The first stage began at Evangelisch Stiftisches Gymnasium high school (9-year "secondary level I" grammar school) in Gütersloh, Germany. It was replicated and expanded at Athens Academy, a kindergarten through twelfth-grade private liberal arts college-preparatory school in Athens, Georgia. Faculty and administrators reviewed the academy's entire liberal arts curriculum to fuse media literacy throughout it. The foundation's basic stance in the projects was to explore media literacy as a timely, significant challenge to traditional education and pedagogy.

Massachusetts was the site for Renée Hobbs's Billerica Experiment at Merrimack Education Center in Chelmsford. A consortium of 22 school districts provided staff development for public schools in the region. The master's degree program offered theory and analysis along with applications. Billerica schools introduced a comprehensive media literacy program for all students across the kindergarten to twelfth-grade curriculum (Hobbs, 1997, ch. 1, p. 16; Hobbs, 1998b; cf. Hart, 1998; Morgan, 1998). Media study was not offered as an independent course but, rather, was integrated into traditional subject areas, partly as a "survival strategy" to attain legitimacy for media-related study.

### Government-Related Projects

*Canada*

See "Canada" in the "Systematic Media Instruction in Schools and School Districts" section.

*Western Australia*

Government schools (K-12) devote one fourth of English syllabuses to media study. The curriculum emphasizes aesthetics and semiotics with a liberal humanist approach to popular arts (Quin, 1998, p. 107). Quin and McMahon (1993, p. 194) observed that students quickly understood textual analysis of visual codes, connotation, narrative, and characterization but needed to be informed about these elements' broader relationships to representation and ideology, and the role of media as "consciousness industries."

*United Kingdom*

In the United Kingdom, as well as in Canada, Australia, Scotland, Spain, and elsewhere, media literacy is required as part of the language arts program in grades 7 through 12 (Hobbs, 1997, ch. 1, p. 15). The United Kingdom, similar to some Latin American countries, seeks to empower media consumers as media citizens to resist industry control through corporate and political hegemony. Media study stresses "representational" and oppositional ideologies, striving to participate in both mainstream and alternate media. Critical media literacy goes beyond media content to its structures and operations, "engendering practical knowledge of how to use language for self-realization, social critique, and cultural transformation" (Knoblauch & Brannon, 1993, p. 152, cited by Brown, 1998, p. 45; cf. Lewis & Jhally, 1998).

*United States*

The U.S. Office of Education commissioned four heavily funded projects to develop media education curricula for lower elementary, upper elementary, high school, and university/adult levels (Brown, 1991). Each developed detailed modules, with teacher guides and student workbooks with applied exercises, intended to serve as models for others to emulate or modify. The first wave of these and other U.S. media literacy projects tended to be protectionist, to equip viewers to defend themselves from negative impact and questionable values disseminated through mass media. As they became more sophisticated in later decades, most projects in the United States began to offer more complex analysis of media in society, such as social and political considerations emphasized in British and Latin American media education by Masterman (1985) in the United Kingdom, Freire (1972) in Brazil, and Minkkinen (1978) for UNESCO.

In 1994, President Clinton signed into law the Goals 2000: Educate America Act, providing $400 million for state and local governments and school districts to develop standards for schools teaching content and performance in nine core subjects, including "arts," which involved media literacy at primary and secondary levels (Pungente, 1994).

By the late 1990s, some 15 states required some form of media study as part of their general curriculum for public schools (Hobbs, 1997). Prominent among them was Massachusetts's curricular revisions that included media analysis and communication skills not as a separate area but integrated into language arts, social studies, health education, and arts and science. Hobbs (1998a) pithily stated key concepts of media literacy in Massachusetts, derived by U.S. practitioners from Canadian and British educators: "that all media are constructed representations; that meaning is derived from the intersection of reader, text, and culture; and that messages have economic, political, social, and historical contexts" (p. 128). Public education in New Mexico, North Carolina, Texas, Michigan, Minnesota, Florida, and New York also offered varied forms of media literacy curricula.

### National Nongovernmental Organizations

Small "boutique" shops of persons with vision, often joined by committed volunteers, and also some larger organizations and professional companies developed conceptual bases for media education along with a wide array of booklets, handout sheets, media study kits, and audiovisual samples. They developed day-long and multiple-day workshops for clusters of teachers in metropolitan areas, for parents in major cities or school districts or affiliated with churches, and for adults generally. They promoted media literacy through print and broadcast media (e.g., magazine articles, newspaper columns, public affair talk programs). Their continued efforts sustained interest and contributed to the growing acceptance of media study as significant for today's youth and adults alike. Over the past two decades, by channeling the initiative of individual teachers searching for ideas, materials, and inspiration, they partly filled the gap in formalized teacher training in media literacy. Among them in the United States were the Parent Teacher Association, Downs Media Education Center (Stockbridge, Massachusetts, and New Mexico), Strategies for Media Literacy (San Francisco), the National Telemedia Council (Madison, Wisconsin), and the Center for Media Literacy (Los Angeles). The last, perhaps the largest producer of media literacy materials in North America, publishes original and reprinted materials, including sophisticated kits of audiovisual support and resources. It constructs strategies for teaching media literacy and conducts workshops and seminars for teachers, parents, community, and church groups. Its founder and executive director, Elizabeth Thoman, is a catalyst among regional and national organizations and actively participates in major academic and political conferences. The center publishes the quarterly *Media & Values* booklet of analysis, reviews of artifacts for teaching media literacy, and comments by leaders in the field.

Further nongovernmental support and direction for media teachers continues to be provided by regional associations and by national and international conferences, often mounted by individuals and small groups mentioned elsewhere in this review. Many hundreds of practitioners and theorists have gathered at each assembly to share their expertise, experiences, and enthusiasm to forward the work of media education. For example, Australian Teachers of Media (ATOM) developed curriculum materials, helped prepare teacher-training media programs, and communicated with regional and national administrators in education to seek their organizational and financial support. Mutual assistance groups sprang up as interest developed, such as in Canada where associations for promoting media literacy arose in half a dozen provinces. Subsequently, an umbrella organization, the Canadian Association of Media Education Organizations, was formed to promote media literacy across the country. The Jesuit Communication Project (headed by John Pungente, S. J., in Toronto, Ontario) is a catalyst for initiatives at provincial, national, and international levels; it collaborates in presenting conferences. Others such as the National Film Board of Canada and the British Film Institute (BFI) prepared media materials for teaching (Pungente, 1994). The BFI in recent years has stressed conceptual emphasis in media education, looking less to objects of study or skills or competencies and more to conceptual understanding (Buckingham, 1998, p. 39).

## Review of Media Teaching and Evaluation Concepts

### *Teaching Concepts and Applications*

Although it is challenging to put into practice, proponents of media literacy favor student-oriented inductive/heuristic learning by discovery and interactive discussion rather than teacher-focused a priori presentation of principles and data about media topics. Materials used in teaching depend on students' age and cognitional level, as well as media subjects (see examples below).

Some researchers mounted more elaborate efforts at determining outcomes, including comparing control groups with similar students who formally studied media. Some reported that young people were fairly adept at understanding the coded formats of television (cuts, fades, dissolves, etc.) with little training other than personal experience of viewing media. Other experiments reported that those without media study, adults as well as adolescents, tended to naively accept media portrayals of fictional characters and events not consistent with real-life persons, professions, and events. Similar findings turned up regarding the unquestioning reception of news coverage, with little awareness of the forces and factors behind news operations such as the economics of advertising, the role of corporate interests, and the emphasis or interpretation affected by political or other considerations.

Hobbs (1997, 1998a), in several informative articles and book chapters, provides ample information about media teaching amid uneven contexts of support. Some of the following material draws heavily from her detailed accounts.

Teachers of media analysis often adapted paradigms from British and Canadian educators. Their key concepts include the following: Media messages are constructed (this involves choices and editing); messages are representations of reality (but how valid or accurate?); messages have social, economic, political, and aesthetic purposes and contexts (financed by megacorporations through advertising to audiences attracted by program content); individuals construct meaning in media messages through interpretation (viewers interpret the content through selective perception and "negotiating" meaning); and each form and genre of communication has unique characteristics (Hobbs, 1997, chs. 1-2).

A guiding concept is to empower students to learn with media. Students' own activities can be a vehicle for learning when class content and interaction is relevant and has meaning for them. They learn through firsthand experience that they themselves can value—supported by teachers who guide, draw out, and stimulate but do not indoctrinate with a priori conclusions via lectures. Students come to analyze, assess, and communicate; those critical thinking skills have wide application. Such empowerment through media literacy has been described as the "process through which students learn to critically appropriate knowledge existing outside their immediate experience in order to broaden their understanding of themselves, the world and the possibilities for transforming the taken-for-granted assumptions about the way we live" (McLaren, cited by Hobbs, 1997, ch. 1, p. 39).

Successful media pedagogy at Marshall Middle School in Billerica, Massachusetts, included home assignments and in-class preparation through discussion prior to viewing, verbal interaction among students and teacher after viewing, and further written follow-up. Topics by different teachers included examining families portrayed on TV, analyzing broadcast news, exploring the representation of events and public figures in world history, media violence, and literary and film works.

One of the debated points of media education is whether it is appropriate to direct students, especially in elementary and even secondary schools, to reactive or proactive stances against major media industries. British and Latin American media education emphasize that as the social payoff of media analysis (e.g., Lewis & Jhally, 1998; Masterman, 1985), as Hart has noted. Others question whether social activism may diffuse or misdirect the essential purpose of becoming knowledgeable, selective, discerning media users. Some fear that individual teachers might proselytize youngsters based on their personal social-political stance, which can cause complications in local schools and districts with varied political perspectives. Although aesthetics nicely adapt to traditional curricula at most levels, larger social, economic, and political aspects of media may fit in better at advanced grades and in selected classes such as social sciences. Whether that leads to consumer activism probably depends on the participants as much as the teacher, if the classroom environment affords a proper mix of open-ended discovery and unbiased evaluation. Therefore, emphasis, especially with younger children, might be less on "activist" reforming of the medium's structures and producers' current input than on preparing media audiences by developing cognitive skills and value perceptions appropriate to translate media content toward prosocial behavior.

The British Film Institute (Bowker, 1991) promoted media education integrated across all study areas rather than a specialized course in media study. In U.K. courses at secondary level (ages 11-16), film study grew in recent decades, supplanted by television as the videotape recorder became widespread. Increased support for media education grew with a proposed national curriculum in 1988 and the Cox Report (Department of Education and Science, 1989) for English studies, which, among five major thrusts, outlined "cultural analysis," including media. This "first official recognition of the subject" (Hart, 1998, p. 26) required all primary school teachers and English departments in secondary schools to include media education as part of their courses in English and language. Reaction among teachers was mixed. In the early 1990s, efforts grew to deemphasize the contemporary "cultural analysis" model in favor of more traditional "cultural heritage" directed to English literature, but media studies continued as part of school curricula. They flourished in Scotland, supported by the Scottish Film Council and local and national education administrators. In general, however, the growth of media classroom education has not been paralleled by the growth in staff development of teachers formally trained in media studies.

Hart (1998) assembled a useful compilation of media teaching examples from classrooms. His international sampling reflects what he calls "different paradigms for Media Education or different teaching models in practice . . . [with a] diversity of educational concerns, goals, and classroom practices" (p. 3). A "Models of Media Education" analysis reported in 1993 a range of apt models for media instruction among teachers of English (Hart & Benson, 1993). Hart's (1998) case studies delineated varied methods of teaching media in classrooms around the world; data came from structured interviews of teachers and by observing their classroom practices.

### *Shortcomings in Procedures and Practices*

Hart's (1998) descriptive analyses found that teachers tended to overlook or discount the role of systems, ownership, and so forth as part of analyzing media content and processes. Teachers in the United Kingdom tended to be less informed or competent in treating topics about media processes and industry institutions—precisely where students were also least knowledgeable—than about other topics such as analyzing content, form, and audiences.

Along with effective pedagogy, those case studies reflected a pattern of shortcomings often found elsewhere (Hart, 1998, pp. 185-186). Classroom applications often lacked the following: interaction and open dialogue among students and between them and teachers; opportunity for pupils' expression of their own media experience and knowledge and for their active involvement in collaborative production of materials related to real social situations and groups; and relating media to issues of political and social power and to the structural operation of media institutions, including assessing their values and purposes.

In Northern Ireland, similar steps were taken as in England, but teachers felt underprepared and without adequate resources. Central was the study of print, and there was little focus on television. One major focus tends to be on protecting children from unquestioning absorption of advertising, but there is little about the larger media industry and socioeconomic factors in shaping media content for audiences. Another focus is on aesthetic analysis and appreciation of media content, as with literary works, rather than understanding media themselves. As in Hart's look at English classes in the United Kingdom, Northern Ireland classrooms had little equipment or other features to aid media instruction. Study was not progressively developed from year to year, leaving teachers isolated and students at the mercy of nonsequential explorations of media.

Half of U.S. high schools have some video camera and editing equipment. In many instances, low-ability students, or "alienated under-achievers" (Grahame, 1991, p. 148), typically gravitate to this area, sometimes as a last resort to keep them in school. Student media production is offered in many schools, mostly at secondary level. Its use is often pragmatic (e.g., to produce a yearbook) or to occupy less bright students. Classes are usually optional or a single stand-alone offering. Some technical-oriented media classes do not offer credit toward academic requirements. Instead, creative video work should not be ghettoed but integrated into mainstream coursework where appropriate to kindergarten through twelfth grade and beyond. Research must yet confirm whether production activity measurably contributes to reasoning, communication, or critical viewing skills.

> Students may learn the skills of group communication and teamwork, working under a deadline, creative problem-solving, oral and written communication skills—but such skills are notoriously difficult to assess using traditional methods of inquiry across large samples of students when instructional methods [and goals] vary enormously. (Hobbs, 1997, ch. 9, p. 183)

Wulfmeyer (1990) found that, among 159 social science teachers in California, the topics most apt to be used in secondary school classes were information about news media (17% of teachers), advertising (11%), propaganda (10%), analysis of bias (9%), and the power and influence of mass media (4%). Although most teachers strongly judged media studies as important for high school curricula, 40% did not treat media because of limits of time and curriculum space. Most judged that they could teach about media, but only one third of them had any college-level training in the subject (cited by Hobbs, 1997, ch. 8, p. 184). Similarly, Koziol (1989) found that language arts teachers, among 104 secondary teachers in Maryland, saw media literacy concepts as important, but curricular and time demands, along with lack of training and teaching materials, precluded such teaching; such concepts were also not among the state's specific instructional objectives. The National Council of Teachers of English found English teachers most interested in film study, especially when able to be compared with literary sources; language arts teachers often added advertising as part of media literacy study.

### *Assessing Outcomes*

Early research identified positive developments in young children's use of TV after various kinds of training in critical viewing or media literacy and developing cognitive skills related to TV use. For example, Dorr et al. (1980) studied how kindergartners applied media literacy learning to viewing TV content. Anderson and Ploghoft (1980) developed 4-year curricula in Idaho Falls for third, fifth, and sixth grades. Singer et al. (1980) analyzed elementary school children's critical thinking skills and TV production in the United States, as did Kelley, Gunter, and Buckle (1987) with secondary students in England, and Tidhar (1996) with Israeli preschoolers. Some researchers cited above sought to appraise the effectiveness of materials designed for classroom use (e.g., Anderson & Ploghoft, 1980; Dorr et al., 1980; Singer et al., 1980). Hobbs noted that further research is needed regarding teacher practices and student performance outside experimental situations.

In Western Australia, Quin and McMahon (1993) developed a measurement approach to assess the outcome performance of 1,500 15-year-old students. Questions answered in writing about media content/"text" demonstrate their skill in analyzing media sources, purpose, perspective, target audience, techniques to hold attention, and conveying mood and tone. Their responses tracked skills in comprehension in media literacy while also providing profiles of their personal behavioral habits when using media. Quin and McMahon (1993) applied some of the British Film Institute's approach, also harnessed by Hobbs and Frost (1998, p. 3): Dimensions of media analysis and media production skills were categorized and students' progress in them measured. They emphasized language, narrative, production processes, audience, and values. After viewing media content, students wrote open-ended answers to questions reflecting their competence in media analysis, including identifying genres, target audience, author's motive or intent, production techniques that attract audience attention or interest, and technical elements affecting viewer response. This reflected growth in students' awareness of production processes—the constructed nature of media messages—by which meaning is initially created through media.

Results from 16 ninth-grade teachers (in four teams, each with one or two of the six teachers who had taken a special media literacy training course)—using diverse applications of media literacy instruction—suggested which kinds of classroom practices and instruction achieved greatest demonstrable results among classes totaling more than 200 students. Students' skills in media analysis were highest when their media literacy instruction was integrated across multiple subject areas with explicit connections made with each; when materials and activities were developed by their teachers rather than applying "off the shelf" prepared modules; when both analysis and production were employed; when instruction in specific genres (news, advertising, etc.) were included; and when film and video materials were used almost daily.

Another study of 333 15-year-olds in Melbourne (Hobbs & Frost, 1998) measured the effectiveness of media training in advancing cognitive competence regarding television.

The Board of Education in Toronto, Ontario, sought to develop means to assess elementary students' ability to comprehend nonprint information and comment on it orally. Holistic criteria for scoring provided quantitative evidence useful to policy makers, administrators, teachers, and community members. The State of California uses a variety of assessment methodologies, including nonquantitative ones, to assess results of media literacy study.

In the United Kingdom, measurements of effectiveness in media training for students ages 11 to 16 noted whether they were able, orally and in writing, to recognize in nonliterary media content fact versus opinion and to identify ways to distinguish such; to identify and express opinions about elements used to inform, reassure, or persuade; to recognize techniques of presentation and judge their effectiveness; and to "select, retrieve, evaluate and combine information independently and with discrimination, from a comprehensive range of reference materials, making effective and sustained use of the information" (National Curriculum English Attainment Target 2, 1990, as cited in Hart, 1998, p. 32).

### *Teacher Training*

The focus has shifted: Following a couple of decades of grants and research for developing concepts and curricular plans, along with modules of audiovisual and print sample materials, concern has been shifting to staff development and teacher training as the apposite strategy for introducing effective media literacy programs into schools. A single specialized summer course in media literacy for teachers in 1993 grew to 12 such courses at universities across the United States the following year (Hobbs, 1997, ch. 1, p. 16).

Administrators in the State of New Mexico in 1993 began to explore teacher training in media literacy to help integrate it into high school curricula as part of the requirement for graduation. Anecdotal evidence is mixed: Many teachers use ready-made packaged media support materials (Brown, 1991) and adapt them to local circumstances and preferences. Other teachers, however, prefer to seek out and develop their own media resources and teaching plans for local classroom contexts. Thus, the central key may not be ready-made video clips, study plans, handout sheets, sample quizzes, overhead transparencies, and so on but, rather, teacher training opportunities resulting in teachers being instilled with conceptual and practical knowledge, coupled with vision and initiative, to implement sound media studies in their pedagogy. Andrew Hart (1992, p. 99) aphorized, "A teacher with resources is not necessarily a resourceful teacher" (as cited in Hobbs & Frost, 1998, p. 2).

Thus, media education for teachers should not only train them about resources and how to use sets of prepared material but should stimulate them to make their own connections between their current curricular goals and classroom practices through activities involving their students in media analysis and production. In fact, this approach itself reflects the "empowerment" focus of media literacy. As one teacher epitomized the concept, "Media literacy is learning to ask questions, to put ideas together and to discover meanings in messages by thinking for yourself" (as cited in Hobbs & Frost, 1998, p. 7).

Teachers' training in media concepts and pedagogy should be an important component, not just a course or two, in schools of education; further staff training can be out of school (in conferences, seminars, workshops, summer courses) and in school (visits by specialists, etc.).

## Future Prospects for Media Literacy Education

Factors important for developing successful programs of media literacy education can be identified by reviewing conclusions of media educators, researchers, and specialists. The following kaleidoscope of comments offers varied perspectives and emphases for drawing up evaluations and recommendations for the future.

Administrative initiative and support are needed, but, at the same time, insight and planning for media teaching must also come from the ranks. This often occurred over past decades by default, with lone teachers innovating media teaching in their classrooms while seeking information, guidance, and inspiration from far-flung colleagues through regional and national conferences, and assisted by nonacademic associations, organizations, and clearinghouses that facilitate teachers' developing local goals, procedures, and class exercises.

During the 1990s, more than 15 major conferences of scholars and educators explored media education. Hobbs (1997, ch. 10, pp. 4-17) summarized patterns of opinions among more than 500 attendees at the National Media Literacy Conference in Los Angeles in 1996. Protectionist approaches to protect viewers from their media exposure were judged by some from England as elitist and weak in understanding social science. Furthermore, that approach flies in the face of media's widespread popularity as a source of often legitimate recreation and pleasure, dooming that tactic in the classroom; at best, it develops cynical negativism rather than broad-based inquiry. Media study may be directed to artifacts of populist culture because it is relevant to students' interests and media experiences. And it helps bridge between theory and application not only in school but at home and, hopefully, later in life. Some fear implicit persuasion or indoctrination by a teacher with strongly held views, whereas others feel passive consumers must be enlightened about their potential role vis-à-vis alleged liberal media conglomerates and large sectors of the political-economic world. Many agree that media literacy per se ought not be an instrument for social change but, rather, a cognitive skill applying to broad areas of living, "promoting students' critical autonomy, described as the process of internalizing the tools of self-reflection, critical analysis and communication for one's own purposes and motives" (Hobbs, 1997, ch. 10, p. 13, paraphrasing Mendez & Reyes, 1991). Probably the ideal is to offer media education across the curriculum, rather than in an isolated class or sequence, to enrich and be enriched by other subject areas. But lest it get lost in the mix, and to expedite its place in a school, most realistic might be to incorporate media study into an established subject such as English or social studies, or as a specialist course at high school level. Quin and McMahon (1993) add that, within a single area, materials and curricula details could be more coherently structured and better able to be assessed by colleagues. Hobbs (1997) concludes that media education can be expected to expand to the broad national kindergarten through 12th-grade scene only "in communities where teachers, parents and students have a shared, common vision about their love-hate relationship with media culture" (ch. 10, p. 14), sensitive to values of respective communities, school systems, and so on.

In the meantime, alternatives to classrooms for media study include after-school programs, workshops, community organizations, churches, libraries, camps, and homes. Hobbs (1997) concludes that, because of the multiplicity of geographic jurisdictions and differing emphases and levels of education in the United States and between various countries, media literacy efforts must retain

> a high degree of tolerance and respect for diverse perspectives, methods and instructional strategies, coupled with a shared consensus that "asking critical questions about what you watch, see and read" is at the center of what it means to be media literate. (ch. 10, p. 20)

An informal reflection by Cary Bazalgette of the British Film Institute and Renée Hobbs, media educators and trainers of teachers over many years, offers a sobering consideration about the effectiveness of training media teachers: "With 100 involved in media education training, 40% will do nothing, 25% will do something moderately well, 10% will do something creatively exceptional, and 25% will do something embarrassing, dangerous, or just a plain waste of time" (Hobbs, 1997, ch. 10, pp. 15-16).

Current efforts at general education reform in the United States reflect the approach of media literacy and "critical viewing skills" education. The U.S. Congress's Office of Technology Assessment calls for "active learning and adventurous teaching" where students actively construct knowledge and understanding "through interaction with and support from other learners, teachers, information, and technologies" (cited by Bertlesmann Foundation, 1995, p. 72). For overall philosophy of classroom pedagogy, the conventional schema contrasts with the reform or nontraditional schema: The shift from conventional to reform instruction shifts modes of classroom activity away from teacher-directed to student exploration; from didactic teaching to interactive modes of instruction; from short blocks of instruction on single subjects to extended blocks of multidisciplinary work; from individual to collaborative work; from teacher as knowledge dispenser to facilitator; from like-ability groups to heterogeneous ones; and from assessment of factual knowledge and discrete skills to performance-based assessment abilities (Bertlesmann Foundation, 1995, p. 74, based on Means et al., 1993; cf. Heller & Gordon, 1994).

Media literacy can provide a process-based model linking varied courses in the arts, social studies, and science even at the elementary level of schooling.

> If media literacy is presented to [teachers] as just another add-on, there will be little hope for its adoption. If, however, media literacy is presented not just as something that meets students' needs, but something that will meet the teacher's needs to integrate disparate elements of a broad curriculum, then it stands a good chance of becoming an important part of the curriculum. (Hobbs, 1997, ch. 2, p. 41)

Resource materials crafted for classrooms and media workshops are often configured to specific contexts, so they are not always widely applicable. Furthermore, examples used in assignments and exercises become dated quickly in the fast-moving field of mass media. Most have not been tested and evaluated for effectiveness, partly because materials are modified as teachers adapt them to suit local contexts, student abilities, and teacher interests. Hobbs and Frost posited questions yet to be explored more fully: What forms of curricula and teaching practices develop what kinds of media literacy competence that best enable students to analyze media texts critically? Such findings would help in designing forms of teacher education and staff development that most contribute to teachers' understanding, attitudes, and skills as a prerequisite to offering media study to others (Hobbs & Frost, 1999, pp. 3-4).

Participants at national conferences and seminars need to acknowledge shortcomings of some media teaching and strive to establish criteria for good classroom practice (Hobbs, 1997, ch. 10, p. 2, citing Bazalgette).

Finally, Pungente (n.d.), drawing on others' explorations and from worldwide observation of media education efforts, has posited nine concrete points for sustaining and developing media education in the future:

1. Media literacy, like other innovative programs, must be a grassroots movement and teachers need to take a major initiative in lobbying for this.
2. Educational authorities must give clear support to such programs by mandating the teaching of Media Studies within the curriculum, establishing guidelines and resource books, and by making certain that curricula are developed and that materials are available.
3. Faculty of Education must hire staff capable of training future teachers in this area. There should also be academic support from tertiary institutions in the writing of curricula and in sustained consultation.
4. In-service training at the school district level must be an integral part of program implementation.
5. School districts need consultants who have expertise in media literacy and who will establish communication networks.
6. Suitable textbooks and audio-visual material which are relevant to the country/area must be available.
7. A support organization must be established for the purposes of workshops, conferences, dissemination of newsletters, and the development of curriculum units. Such a professional organization must cut across school boards and districts to involve a cross section of people interested in media literacy.
8. There must be appropriate evaluation instruments which are suitable for the unique quality of Media Studies.
9. Because media literacy [education] involves such a diversity of skills and expertise, there must be a collaboration between teachers, parents, researchers and media professionals. (p. 15)

This listing was recognized as a fitting summation by others in the field who cited it and even repeated it verbatim.

## Notes

1. Lists of these organizations are provided by Kathleen Tyner, accessible through the University of Oregon School of Education's website at *http://interact.uoregon.edu/MediaLit/FA/mltyner/resource.html.*

2. The manuscript draft of Hobbs (1997) did not use consecutive numbering throughout. Some successive chapters were paginated consecutively, but other later chapters began numbering anew. Thus, for clarity, the chapter number is added to manuscript page citations.

3. For specific details, with references to research sources, about cognitive development and age levels at which children progressively understand varied aspects of media presentations, see Part 1 of Berry & Asamen, 1993 (chapters 1 to 3, respectively, by Murray; Doubleday & Droege; and Fitch, Huston, & Wright).

## References

Abelman, R. (1995). Gifted, LD, and gifted/LD children's understanding of temporal sequencing in television. *Journal of Broadcasting and Electronic Media, 39*(3), 297-312.

Anderson, J. A. (1980). The theoretical lineage of critical viewing criteria. *Journal of Communication, 30*(3), 64-70.

Anderson, J. (1983). Television literacy and the critical viewer. In J. Bryant & D. R. Anderson (Eds.), *Children's understanding of television: Research on attention and comprehension* (pp. 297-327). New York: Academic Press.

Anderson, J. A., & Meyer, T. (1988). *Mediated communication: A social action perspective.* Newbury Park, CA: Sage.

Anderson, J. A., & Ploghoft, M. (1980). Receivership skills: The television experience. In D. Nimmo (Ed.), *Communication yearbook 4* (pp. 293-307). New Brunswick, NJ: Transaction Books.

Anderson, J. A., & Ploghoft, M. (1993). Children and media in media education. In G. L. Berry & J. K. Asamen (Eds.), *Children and television: Images in a changing sociocultural world* (pp. 89-102). Newbury Park, CA: Sage.

Bazalgette, C. (Ed.). (1989). *Primary media education: A curriculum statement.* London: British Film Institute.

Berry, G. L., & Asamen, J. K. (Eds.). (1993). *Children and television: Images in a changing sociocultural world.* Newbury Park, CA: Sage.

Bertlesmann Foundation. (Ed.). (1995). *School improvement through media in education: A German-American dialogue.* Guetersloh, Germany: Author.

Bowker, J. (Ed.). (1991). *Secondary media education: A curriculum statement.* London: British Film Institute.

Brown, J. A. (1991). *Television "critical viewing skills" education: Major media literacy projects in the United States and selected countries.* Hillsdale, NJ: Lawrence Erlbaum.

Brown, J. A. (1998). Media literacy perspectives. *Journal of Communication, 48*(1), 44-57.

Buckingham, D. (1992). *Media literacy and the regulation of children's viewing.* Paper presented at the Standards in Screen Entertainment Third International Conference, London.

Buckingham, D. (1998). Media education in the UK: Moving beyond protectionism. *Journal of Communication, 48*(1), 33-43.

Department of Education and Science. (1989). *The Cox Report: English for ages 5-16.* London: Her Majesty's Stationery Office.

Dorr, A., & Brannon, C. (1993). Media education in American schools at the end of the twentieth century. In Bertlesmann Foundation, *Media competency as a challenge to school and education: A German-North American dialogue* (pp. 71-105). Guetersloh, Germany: Bertlesmann Foundation.

Dorr, A., Graves, S. B., & Phelps, E. (1980). Television literacy for young children. *Journal of Communication, 30*(3), 71-83.

Freire, P. (1972). *Pedagogy of the oppressed.* New York: Penguin.

Grahame, J. (1991). The production process. In D. Listed (Ed.), *The media studies book: A guide for teachers.* London: Routledge.

Hart, A. (1992). Teaching with what? Making sense of media education resources. In C. Bazalgette, E. Befort, & J. Savino (Eds.), *New directions: Media education worldwide.* London: British Film Institute.

Hart, A. (Ed.). (1998). *Teaching the media: International perspectives.* Mahwah, NJ: Lawrence Erlbaum.

Hart, A., & Benson, A. (1993). *Media in the classroom.* Southampton, UK: Media Education Centre, Southampton University.

Heller, J. I., & Gordon, A. (1994). *Lifelong learning: A unique school-university collaboration is preparing students for the future.* Berkeley: University of California Press.

Hobbs, R. (1997). *Television goes to school.* Manuscript in preparation.

Hobbs, R. (1998a). Media literacy in Massachusetts. In A. Hart (Ed.), *Teaching the media: International perspectives* (pp. 127-144). Mahwah, NJ: Lawrence Erlbaum.

Hobbs, R. (1998b). The seven great debates in the literacy movement. *Journal of Communication, 48*(1), 16-32.

Hobbs, R., & Frost, R. (1998). *Instructional practices in media literacy and their impact on students' learning.* Manuscript submitted for publication. [Revised draft of article available: http://interact.uoregon.edu/MediaLit/FA/mlhobbs/instpractice.html]

Hobbs, R., & Frost, R. (1999). *The acquisition of media literacy skills among Australian adolescents.* Manuscript submitted for publication. [Abstract available: http://interact.uoregon.edu/MediaLit/FA/mlhobbs/mass.html]

Kelley, P., Gunter, B., & Buckle, L. (1987). "Reading" television in the classroom: More results from the Television Literacy Project. *Journal of Educational Television, 13*(1), 7-20.

Knoblauch, C. H., & Brannon, L. (1993). *Critical teaching and the idea of literacy.* Portsmouth, NH: Boynton/Cook-Heinemann/Reed Publishing.

Koziol, R. (1989, August 10-13). *English language arts teachers' views on mass media consumption education in Maryland high schools.* Paper presented at the annual conference of the Association for Education in Journalism and Mass Communication, Washington, DC.

Kubey, R. (1998). Obstacles to the development of media education in the United States. *Journal of Communication, 48*(1), 58-69.

Lewis, J., & Jhally, S. (1998). The struggle over media literacy. *Journal of Communication, 48*(1), 109-120.

Makas, E. (1993). Changing channels. In G. L. Berry & J. K. Asamen (Eds.), *Children and television: Im-*

*ages in a changing sociocultural world* (pp. 255-268). Newbury Park, CA: Sage.

Masterman, L. (1985). *Teaching the media.* London: Comedia.

Means, B., Blando, J., Olson, K., Middleton, T., Morocco, C. C., Remz, A. R., & Zorfass, J. (1993). *Using technology to support school reform.* Washington, DC: U.S. Department of Education, Office of Educational Research and Improvement.

Mendez, A. M., & Reyes, M. (1991). Television versus teachers: From antagonism to creativity. In C. Bazalgette, E. Befort, & J. Savino (Eds.), *New directions: Media education worldwide.* London: British Film Institute.

Meyrowitz, J. (1998). Multiple media literacies. *Journal of Communication, 48*(1), 96-108.

Minkkinen, S. (1978). *General curricular model for mass media education.* Paris: UNESCO.

Morgan, R. (1998). Media education in Ontario: Generational differences in approach. In A. Hart (Ed.), *Teaching the media: International perspectives* (pp. 145-167). Mahwah, NJ: Lawrence Erlbaum.

Pungente, J. J. (n.d.). *The second spring: Media literacy in Canada's schools* [On-line]. [Retrieved August 11, 1999]. Available: http://interact.uoregon.edu/MediaLit/JCP/articles/secondspring.html

Pungente, J. J. (1994). Live long and prosper: Media literacy in the USA. *Clipboard, 8*(2), 1.

Quin, R. (1998). Media education in Western Australia. In A. Hart (Ed.), *Teaching the media: International perspectives* (pp. 107-126). Mahwah, NJ: Lawrence Erlbaum.

Quin, R., & McMahon, B. (1993). Monitoring standards in media studies: Problems and strategies. *Australian Journal of Education, 37*(2), 182-197.

Rapaczynski, W., Singer, D. G., & Singer, J. L. (1982). Teaching television: A curriculum for young children. *Journal of Communication, 32*(2), 46-55.

Singer, D. G., & Singer, J. L. (1994). Evaluating the classroom viewing of a television series: *Degrassi Junior High.* In D. Zillmann, J. Bryant, & A. C. Huston (Eds.), *Media, children, and the family: Social scientific, psychodynamic, and clinical perspectives* (pp. 97-115). Hillsdale, NJ: Lawrence Erlbaum.

Singer, D. G., & Singer, J. L. (1998). Developing critical viewing skills and media literacy in children. *Annals of the American Academy of Political & Social Science, 557,* 164-179.

Singer, D. G., Zuckerman, D. M., & Singer, J. L. (1980). Critical TV viewing: Helping elementary school children learn about TV. *Journal of Communication, 30*(3), 84-93.

Singer, J. L., & Singer, D. G. (1983). Psychologists look at television. *American Psychologist, 38*(7), 826-834.

Sprafkin, J., Gadow, K. D., & Abelman, R. (1992). *Television and the exceptional child: A forgotten audience.* Hillsdale, NJ: Lawrence Erlbaum.

Sprafkin, J., Watkins, T., & Gadow, K. D. (1990). Efficacy of a television literacy curriculum for emotionally disturbed and learning disabled children. *Journal of Applied Developmental Psychology, 11*(2), 225-244.

Tidhar, C. E. (1996). Enhancing television literacy skills among preschool children through an intervention program in the kindergarten. *Journal of Educational Media, 22*(2), 97-111.

Tulodziecki, G., & Schöpf, K. (1993). Media education in German schools: Concepts, materials, practice, and problems summary. In Bertlesmann Foundation, *Media competency as a challenge to school and education: A German-North American dialogue* (pp. 106-110). Guetersloh, Germany: Bertlesmann Foundation.

Wulfmeyer, T. (1990, August 9-12). *Mass media instruction in high school social science classes: A survey of Southern California teachers.* Paper presented at the annual conference of the Association for Education in Journalism and Mass Communication, Minneapolis, MN.

Zuckerman, D. M., Singer, D. G., & Singer, J. L. (1980a). Children's television viewing: Racial and sex-role attitudes. *Journal of Applied Social Psychology, 10*(4), 281-294.

Zuckerman, D. M., Singer, D. G., & Singer, J. L. (1980b). Television viewing and children's reading and related classroom behavior. *Journal of Communication, 30*(1), 166-174.

CHAPTER **39**

# Children's Advocacy Groups

## A History and Analysis

LAURIE TROTTA

By the time television replaced radio as America's favorite form of electronic entertainment after World War II, the broadcast networks were already well entrenched. Many of the genres created by the radio networks—including soap operas, game shows, Westerns, news and public affairs programs, and children's shows—made the transformation to the "small screen" as well.

As the networks seized primary control of television programming, the public was left to devise its own methods for responding meaningfully to their offerings and for changing images they found troublesome. And from the earliest days television vacuum tubes sent their blue glow into America's living rooms, parents, clergy, and social and education groups have voiced concern over the influence this new force would have on children. During the nascent era of the industry, most of the concern was centered on the effects of viewing violence. Some 30 years passed before media advocates added such issues as unbridled consumerism, mediocrity of programming, and poor variety to their advocacy efforts for children.

At first, a few individuals, some journalists, and at times established institutions began working to influence the images on TV. Over time, key media advocacy groups emerged and grew to serve as articulate voices on specific issues, such as violence or stereotyping. The effects of these on shaping the values and behaviors of children were always of greatest concern. Eventually, organizations arose that focused on all issues relating to children and the media. These organizations adopted a variety of approaches, both radical and conservative, for working to change what we see on TV, but also to inform the public about its rights to influence what is broadcast over the public airwaves, and the effects of the media on viewers.

Approaches used by children's media advocates generally fall into broad categories and target different audiences. For example, a

AUTHOR'S NOTE: Nathalie J. Valdez served as research assistant on this chapter.

group of organizations exists that works directly with the creative community, using positive, industry-friendly reinforcement based on public health research to inspire change for children. Other groups use sophisticated techniques to lobby government officials, while others effectively serve teachers, parents, and community groups by providing media literacy materials.

In an effort to understand the breadth and scope of the work being conducted for children today, a total of 33 such national organizations working to promote change in entertainment for children were examined. Research was conducted by reviewing the websites and/or published materials of the key health and advocacy groups. Although variances in type, audience served, focus, budget, and size are the norm, some commonalties of approach do exist. Most of the organizations tend to weave together several of these approaches to create a mosaic of activities and initiatives that span audiences as well as methodologies.

The following methods for initiating change in children's media have been used:

1. *Some organizational use, public policy, and government:* Some organizations use government channels to effect change from within the current system on a policy level by:
   - Lobbying Congress and the Federal Communications Commission (FCC)
   - Testifying before government hearings
   - Filing FCC petitions to deny broadcast licenses or petitions of proposed rule making
   - Mobilizing the public about its rights under public interest clauses of broadcasting regulations
2. *Positive or collegial work "within" the entertainment industry:* Sponsoring informational conferences, workshops, and seminars for industry executives and creative professionals, as well as using positive reinforcement in the forms of awards and seals of approval for perceived excellence in programming. These methods help raise awareness and motivate creative professionals.
3. *Independent research:* Providing content analyses, studies, and surveys on media-related issues. The results are used to inform the public, journalists, parents, government, the creative community, and broadcasters. This approach has helped bring government scrutiny to the issues, at times instigating regulation.
4. *Technical or educational consultancies:* Some media advocacy groups offer services or referrals as consultants to the entertainment industry to provide accurate information on sensitive depictions. This process can help deter negative or harmful portrayals in early stages of a program's development.
5. *Media literacy, advocacy, and awareness:* These methods focus on publishing, training, and education to inform parents, teachers, and children of the hazards of media consumption. Several media literacy organizations also offer evaluation techniques to help parents identify and select appropriate materials.
6. *Consumer-based initiatives:* Organizing protests, letter-writing campaigns, and boycotts to exert pressure on advertisers, sponsors, and broadcasters constitute another technique. These can be effective, but have historically been used by special-interest groups to prohibit screening of individual episodes or movies, which has raised concerns about censorship from the networks and free speech advocates. Examples include protests over a single episode or a popular show dealing with a sensitive issue, such as abortion.
7. *News media campaigns:* Tactics to orchestrate campaigns in the popular press against individual programs, networks, or issues have been used to help build awareness among the general

public and advertisers, as well as to pressure broadcasters to effect change.

## Effectiveness of Children's Advocacy Efforts

How effective have advocacy efforts been in changing television? It is difficult to gauge, because much of the social change in the broadcast industry has occurred slowly, the results of a gathering of many forces and pressures over time. Government has displayed a history of voicing concern over programming issues but has taken a very precautionary approach toward regulation (the noted exceptions being those made in the 1990s, which are discussed below). Certainly, the entertainment industry, as a whole, has been slow to create better, more diverse, and nonviolent programming for children.

And yet strides have been made in the areas of public policy and public awareness and in the efforts of industry professionals to become more responsive. For example, in autumn 1999, representatives from every network, key children's production companies, and those from "new" and interactive media attended a children's television summit with representatives from the nonprofit and research communities, the National Education Association, and the Parent Teachers Association (PTA) to create quality standards for children's entertainment. (Mediascope cosponsored this event with DIC Entertainment in Burbank, California, on September 15-16.) Just 2 weeks later, a major conference sponsored by Children Now, a nonprofit working on behalf of children, drew hundreds of media and other professionals to discuss images of boys in the media.

One indicator of effectiveness could be advocates' penetration into the awareness of programmers. A poll of senior-level creative executives in children's programming was conducted by Mediascope in spring 1999. Of the programmers that responded, 40% said they believe that advocacy groups provide a valuable contribution to the children's TV industry, and 60% said they had received useful information from advocates. Fifty percent of the children's media professionals felt that advocacy groups were actually making an impact, and 70% of respondents felt that conferences and seminars were the most effective forum for advocacy groups to disseminate information. As might be expected, the majority of respondents indicated a preference for conciliatory and informational approaches to improving children's TV and eschewed the more confrontational tools that use public admonitions and government regulation.

Clearly, the advocacy movement has had an effect on building awareness of issues, motivating and inspiring industry professionals, and utilizing government processes to lobby for change. It must be noted that the underlying commerciality of the television business will—unless enormous structural changes to the system are made—most likely remain a primary consideration in the industry. However, advocates represent the public, which votes by its viewing selections, supporting quality programming for children when available. Advocates have successfully exerted government pressure in the past, and as their ranks grow, those changes will happen more quickly.

## Radio Roots: A Brief History of How TV Got to Where It Is Today

The debate over how mass electronic communications should be used—as educational tools or simply as vehicles for commercial interests—has its roots in radio as well. After World War I, radios swept the country for the first time. Along with commercial enterprises—such as Westinghouse and AT&T—educational, community, and religious groups were granted government licenses to broadcast audio signals over the public airwaves. However, these groups were soon overshadowed by the wealthier commercial stations, which could offer listeners continuous programming and slick production values. Very quickly, many of the public service stations surrendered their licenses, leaving room for mass commercialization of the medium. In return, the government ruled that commercial stations must offer airtime to serve the public interest.

In the early years of radio, direct advertising was considered unpalatable by key government and broadcasting officials. This opinion was voiced at the First Radio Conference, called by Secretary of Commerce Herbert Hoover in 1922 (Head & Sterling, 1982). National Broadcasting Company (NBC) president David Sarnoff compared the network he envisioned with the great public institutions of the day, such as libraries, and made no mention of advertising as a great profit-maker for his company (Head & Sterling, 1982). Several years later, the idea of radio sponsorship evolved, as advertising agencies took up the opportunity to fill programming voids by creating their own shows sponsored by their client companies. The 1928-1929 radio broadcast season is considered the first full-scale network advertising year, although the practice of direct advertising, wherein programming actually stopped and a commercial took its place, did not take hold until the mid-1930s (Head & Sterling, 1982).

## Television Takes Center Stage

The years 1948 to 1952 represent television's critical growth period, as the number of sets in American households rose from 250,000 to 17 million (Head & Sterling, 1982). The medium soon pushed radio aside as America's favorite source of broadcast entertainment.

The first signs of heightened controversy over violent content on TV occurred in the early 1950s, following a rise in crime and juvenile delinquency that had swept the country. *Time* and *Newsweek* published research indicating that children's fare was among the most violent on the air, and the early advocacy group National Association for Better Radio and Television (NAFBRAT) reported that "the amount of crime on children's television should dismay all parents" (as cited in Turow, 1981, p. 20). This drew attention to the need for more quality programming for children.

In 1952, Congress held the first of decades of hearings on broadcast violence, examining both radio and television as possible instigators of real-world violence. This was at a time when only 23.5% of families owned television sets and only the major urban areas of the country could receive any visual broadcasts at all (Turow, 1981). The networks argued that there was no proven link between mayhem in society and on-screen violence. Meanwhile, the National Association of Broadcasters (NAB) included a section titled "Responsibility to Children" in the first edition of its Television Code in 1952, but it offered no specific guidelines or framework to help broadcasters make responsible choices for the nation's youth (Turow, 1981).

## The Wasteland

The concept of children constituting a special audience in need of particular sensitivities was broached by the FCC in 1960, although, like the NAB Television Code, the agency issued no specific rules regarding content (Head & Sterling, 1982). One year later, then FCC Chairman Newton Minow admonished programmers at the national NAB conference for failing to create a range of informative and inspirational programs that served the public interest, coining the much-used description of the television landscape as "a vast wasteland."

That same year, a new spate of television violence hearings took place on Capitol Hill, this time led by Senator Thomas Dodd of Connecticut. These hearings were derailed when the networks again countered the reports that the action-adventure violence on TV was promoting juvenile delinquency, reasserting that no causal link actually existed between the two.

Meanwhile, in the halls of academe, University of Pennsylvania Professor George Gerbner began work in 1967 on the Media Violence Index, a more-than-30-year study of violence on TV. In 1972, the surgeon general issued a major report documenting a link between screen violence and aggressive behavior, a study that was updated a decade later.

## Action for Children's Television

In 1968, a new organization called Action for Children's Television (ACT) was formed by a group of women in the Boston area who wanted to increase the diversity of television choices available to children. ACT was to become a powerful voice for children and the media in a series of government battles that lasted through the next quarter century.

ACT first persuaded the FCC to hold hearings of proposed rule making that would govern certain aspects of children's programming. "People say the FCC was impenetrable, but in reality, we went to Washington in 1970 and were able to meet with six of the seven commissioners," said Peggy Charren, ACT's longtime president (P. Charren, personal interview, August 17, 1999). Specifically, ACT members wanted rules requiring at least 7 hours of children's programming scheduled throughout the week, not just on weekend mornings. ACT also put forth the notion that children's programs should be developed for specific age groups, each with its own developmental sensibilities.

After holding extensive hearings, the FCC rejected ACT's rule-making request. Instead, it issued a policy statement in 1974 urging broadcasters to voluntarily improve children's programming along the lines of the ACT proposals. One result was the NAB Television Code Board's adoption of special advertising rules for children's programs shortly thereafter (Head & Sterling, 1982).

Several years later, the FCC, still under pressure from ACT and other groups such as the national PTA, appointed a Children's Television Task Force to explore the extent to which broadcasters had complied with the 1974 policy statement. The task force studies found some improvement in advertising practices but little in the programming area (Head & Sterling, 1982). The FCC reexamined the issue in 1979, inviting comments on a number of possible steps that might be taken. However, before any action was taken, incoming FCC chair Mark Fowler ceased all attempts at regulation, advocating instead total deregulation for television programming, including children's.

Advocates then took the cause to Congress, and a decade later the Children's Television Act of 1990 (CTA) was passed to improve educational broadcast programming for children. Congress did so after concluding that television has a significant impact on children and that it can be used as a tool to complement traditional education, help young people learn specific skills, or help prepare for formal schooling (Trotta, 1998).

The FCC was left the task of creating the specific rules necessary to enforce the act, thus adopting the Children's TV Rules of 1996, a new set of standards designed to strengthen and implement the CTA. The guidelines outlined the number of hours television stations must air children's educational programming; sharpened the definition of educational programming; and adopted measures to improve public access to the programming. Although stations that do not comply with the rules risk losing their operating licenses, it falls to citizens and media advocates to watch the broadcasters' progress, because no government agency is monitoring the educational programming.

Peggy Charren closed ACT in 1993, and the collection of ACT's papers, tapes, and books is now housed in the Monroe C. Guttman Library at the Harvard Graduate School of Education.

## Other Fronts

At about the same time ACT was conducting its campaign before the FCC, advocates, researchers, and other concerned individuals were gathering forces on other fronts. The National Association for Better Broadcasting (NABB), a group opposed to violence in children's programming, in 1969 announced a "spectacular milestone" in broadcast consumerism (Head & Sterling, 1982). KTTV-TV in Los Angeles agreed to ban from its programming all episodes of the syndicated series *Batman, Superman,* and *Aquaman,* as well as to provide a "caution to parents" notice before airing any of 81 other series if scheduled before 8:30 P.M. (Head & Sterling, 1982). The FCC struck down this agreement, citing censorship issues; subsequently, the agency adopted a policy statement that set up guidelines for such agreements in the future.

In 1975, the National PTA adopted a resolution demanding that networks and local television stations reduce the amount of violence in programs and commercials. The following year, the American Medical Association House of Delegates characterized television violence as an "environmental hazard," while other leading medical groups, including the American Psychiatric Association and the American Academy of Pediatrics (AAP), issued statements on the risks of media violence and took steps to educate members as well as parents. More recently, the AAP garnered front-page coverage in the *New York Times* when its members agreed to urge patients to limit TV watching (Mifflin, 1999).

During the late 1970s and 1980s, a new phenomenon occurred: Court cases were initiated to explore the liability of the media in cases of real-world violence. For example, in *Zamora v. CBS et al.* (1979, as cited in UCLA Center for Communication Policy, 1995), parents of a Florida 15-year-old convicted of murdering a neighbor unsuccessfully sued all three networks for negligence for failing to prevent him from imitating television violence (UCLA Center for Communication Policy, 1995). Several other cases followed, and in 1999, parents of three students killed at a Kentucky high school filed a $130 million lawsuit against the entertainment industry, asserting that media violence had inspired the boy who shot their children.

The Reagan era's policy of deregulation in television galvanized media advocates and created a wellspring of new academic research on the subject. In 1980, the National Coalition on Television Violence was formed, and literally dozens of children's media advocacy groups soon followed. The industry also sponsored research in these areas. The National Television Violence Study (NTVS; 1996), sponsored by the National Cable Television Association, examined depictions across thousands of hours of television and reported that the types of televised violence most often portrayed on TV lead to desensitization, increased fear of being victimized, and learning aggressive attitudes and behaviors. At the same time, the UCLA Center for Communications Policy (1995) released a network-sponsored study that found that the networks were reducing violence on-screen.

Congress soon responded, passing the Telecommunications Act of 1996 that mandated V-chip screening devices for all televisions manufactured after 1999 and the creation of a rating system to identify "video programming that contains sexual, violent or other indecent material" (U.S. Senate, 1996).

Meanwhile, on Capitol Hill, the Senate Judiciary Committee, led by Senator Orrin G. Hatch, in 1998 once again examined the issue in its report *Children, Violence, and the Media,* and the NTVS (1998) revealed that 68% of all children's programming contains violence in a humorous context, considered a key factor in desensitizing children to real-world violence.

## Conclusions

The struggle between children's advocates and the entertainment industry will continue into the new millennium, and it is quickly moving to include new forms of entertainment such as the Internet, computer games, and digital media.

As the forms of media become more engaging to children, and the time spent interacting with new media is ever increasing, the efforts of advocacy groups must keep pace. Various established advocates are forming arms of their organizations to contend specifically with Internet and interactive issues. For example, the powerful advocacy group Center for Media Education (CME, see below for description) has spearheaded its Action for Children in Cyberspace initiative to ensure that digital media serve all children. Programs such as that by the Recreational Software Advisory Council (RSAC) offer ratings for Internet sites, and a host of for-profit groups have created Internet-blocking devices similar to the V-chip to help parents screen out unwanted materials from their children's computer screens.

Research is also being conducted on the amounts and nature of issues such as violence and substance use in the musical choices of young people. More research is needed before we can determine the effects of these choices on the behavior of the nation's youth.

Interactive media—specifically the "first-person shooter" computer games—are being criticized for training young people in marksmanship and for fostering the ability to methodically gun down opponents in the real world, a tragic phenomenon encountered in recent years in the nation's schools. Additional research into the effects of new media is clearly needed, for it remains unclear whether these games can be directly blamed on violence in society. The issue is exacerbated by the fact that new generations of computer games, which are forever more sophisticated and realistic, quickly outdate the research that has already been conducted in these areas (*The Social Effects of Electronic Interactive Games,* 1996). Social scientists are today beginning to formulate a research agenda that, if executed, will help us to further understand what unique effects, if any, new and interactive media have on young people and will provide the action plan for media advocates into the next millennium.

## Major Advocacy Groups and Their Philosophies

Following is a compendium of 33 media advocacy organizations working in the United States today. They are organized by the approaches and methodologies and the audiences they primarily serve, although, as mentioned above, there is great overlap in these areas. Included is a brief synopsis of each organization, its major initiatives, philosophies, and goals. The material in each instance was taken directly from the organization's website and/or published materials.

**The following nine organizations have a visible presence in Hollywood and can be considered the major groups working on a myriad of levels and with diverse audiences to effect change in entertainment for children. Audiences range from producers, writers, and directors to academicians to the general public. Methods include work in policy, outreach, direct contact with the creative community, and independent research.**

### ADVOCATES FOR YOUTH, THE MEDIA PROJECT

www.advocatesforyouth.org

Dedicated to improving the quality of life for youth by preventing risk-taking behavior. Works to create programs and promote policies that help young people make informed and responsible decisions about their sexual and reproductive health. Provides information, training, and advocacy to youth-serving organizations, policy makers, and the media in the United States and internationally. As a part of this effort, it cosponsors the Media Project in collaboration with the Kaiser Family Foundation. This project provides entertainment professionals with accurate information about sexual health issues.

#### Strategies

- HELPline at (818) 762-9668 is a free resource offering prompt research as-

sistance to TV and film writers on sexuality and reproductive health issues.
- Informational briefing series serve as a bridge between television and film professionals and the experts, including teens themselves.
- Conducts issue updates on request for creative staff and production executives.
- The Shine Awards for Sexual Health in Entertainment honor those in the entertainment industry who do an exemplary job incorporating accurate and honest portrayals of sexuality into their programming.

### AMERICAN CENTER FOR CHILDREN AND MEDIA

1400 East Touhy Avenue, Suite 260
Des Plains, IL 60018

To strengthen the capabilities, insights, and motivation of children's programming professionals; to facilitate collaboration among TV, new media, education, research, and child development experts; to evolve guidelines and standards for recognizing outstanding work; and to increase awareness of quality television and interactive media.

#### Strategies

- The Ollie Awards honor America's best children's shows; the Ollie Awards video library is available to researchers at the National Public Broadcasting Archives at the University of Maryland.
- Brings professionals together in seminars and workshops.
- Shares and provides information through consulting assistance and referral to experts.
- The center is the U.S. Council member of the World Alliance of Television for Children (WATCH), a global network of organizations supporting excellence in children's media.
- It is the coordinator of North American Advisory Committees for the international World Summit on Media for Children, held every 3 years to focus on differences in language, color, and national and cultural identities and working for the creation of a common audiovisual language that supports the rights of children.

### CENTER FOR MEDIA EDUCATION (CME)

www.cme.org

Dedicated to improving the quality of the electronic media. Fosters telecommunications policy making in the public interest through its research, advocacy, public education, and press activities. Founded in 1991 to carry on the work of Action for Children's Television, CME's primary focus is on children. The Action for Children in Cyberspace initiative was created to ensure that the new digital media serve all children.

#### Strategies

- Policy research network linking leading academics with policy professionals to develop a solid intellectual base for policy making.
- Children's media policy network that brings key stakeholders together from the child advocacy, education, consumer, and civil rights communities.
- Quarterly publication, *InfoActive Kids,* provides information on technological trends as well as a library of recent reports and a listing of key resources.
- A strategic campaign designed to reframe the public debate over the media system and its impact on children and to provide a clearinghouse for journalists.

### CHILDREN'S ACTION NETWORK (CAN)

10951 West Pico Boulevard
Los Angeles, CA 90064

Founded in 1990 by leaders in the entertainment industry to harness the power of entertainment media on behalf of children. CAN works to mobilize the Hollywood community and encourage them to reach the American public with information about the needs of children through the integration of children's issues in television programs and film. CAN serves as the entertainment industry's voice for children.

#### Strategies

Reaches out to members of the entertainment community through briefings, symposia, and conferences to inform them of the major issues affecting today's children and to encourage them to integrate children's issues in their work. Serves as a clearinghouse for information and expertise on children's issues.

- Educational briefings, an ongoing series covering topics such as health care, prenatal substance abuse, and lead poisoning; speakers for briefings include nationally recognized children's experts.
- Clipping service, in conjunction with the Writers Guild of America, West, that distributes recent news articles relating to children's issues to more than 2,000 writers, producers, and directors.
- Works with advocacy and service organizations nationwide to promote specific policies and programs that benefit children.

### CHILDREN NOW: CHILDREN AND THE MEDIA PROGRAM

www.childrennow.org

Works to improve the quality of news and entertainment media both for children and about children's issues through media literacy outreach, independent research, and public policy. Children Now is a nonpartisan, independent voice for children, working to translate the nation's commitment to children and families into action.

#### Strategies

- Media industry conferences (an annual national conference and 1-day symposia) bring media industry leaders, children's advocates, and academic experts together to help better understand the impact media have on children.
- Public opinion surveys of kids and parents.
- Independent research on television and print media.
- Newsletter containing current research on media as it pertains to children.
- Press workshops on important children's issues.
- Entertainment industry briefings that encourage constructive story lines by briefing writers and producers on issues concerning children.
- Public policy development monitors legislation and regulations affecting children's media.
- Uses communication strategies to bring children into the national conversation; newspaper and magazine features, radio and television coverage, advertising campaigns, community partnerships, and reader-friendly publications focus attention on children's needs and propose ways to meet them.
- Website disseminates information and stimulates action on behalf of children.

### HENRY J. KAISER FAMILY FOUNDATION: ENTERTAINMENT MEDIA AND PUBLIC HEALTH PROGRAM

www.kff.org

Works with entertainment professionals to help them convey health messages to the public. Builds constructive relationships with people in the industry who want to play a positive role and who understand it is possible to entertain, educate, and succeed at the same time. Core issues are reproductive health, HIV/AIDS, and health policy. Its purpose is to expand the public's access to accurate, reliable health information through the entertainment media. The program hopes to increase the number of depictions of public health issues in entertainment media; ensure that public health information in programming is accurate and balanced; monitor the amount and nature of health information in entertainment; and evaluate the impact of health messages.

#### Strategies

- Provides information to those in the entertainment media who are incorporating public health issues into their programs.
- Offers both group and one-on-one briefings on health issues to media writers and producers as a way of encouraging more story lines on these issues.
- Conducts surveys of the public.
- Works with media researchers to measure content and the impact of media depictions.
- Helps produce and evaluate public service announcements.
- Engages in partnerships with media producers to create special media campaigns.

### MEDIASCOPE
### www.mediascope.org

Works with entertainment professionals to create awareness about the effects of their work, particularly on children and adolescents. A principal objective is to encourage accurate and responsible portrayals of social and health issues in film, television, the Internet, video games, and music without compromising the creative freedom of artists. Addresses a variety of topics, including media ratings, teen sexuality, children's television, diversity, violence, substance use, and artists' rights and responsibilities. Approaches sensitive topics, such as violence, as public health issues.

#### Strategies

- Conducts pioneering research, including original studies, analyses, and bibliographies, on topics relating to social and health issues in the media.
- Provides information through its website and National Media Research Library housing 40 years of congressional testimony, scientific research, news clippings, speeches, statistics, and public opinion polls (will soon be searchable on-line).
- Mediascope Press publishes books, literature reviews, resource guides, and summaries of media studies and policies, including the National Television Violence Study and *Media Ratings: Design, Use, and Consequences.*
- Creation of voluntary guidelines that help to establish frameworks for responsible entertainment and build awareness of social issues among creative professionals working in different genres; it is preparing for a major initiative to raise awareness of ethics and social responsibility among media professionals.
- Holds workshops and seminars for entertainment professionals, often presented at film festivals and conferences; includes consultancies and referrals for writers and producers on health-related depictions to a network of leading researchers in media and children's health.
- Works collaboratively with other nonprofit and advocacy groups to mobilize

the industry and create awareness among the general public.

## PARENTS TELEVISION COUNCIL (PTC)
## www.parentstv.org

Established in 1995 to encourage positive, family-oriented television programming to the entertainment industry, PTC offers private-sector solutions to restore television to its roots as an independent and socially responsible entertainment medium. Much of PTC's success stems from motivating the public to voice its support for family-friendly programming to network executives, advertisers, public policy leaders, and the creative community in Hollywood.

### Strategies

- Organizes a group of entertainment industry leaders to serve as members of the advisory board; these individuals address issues relating to television entertainment and its impact on American families and assist in representing the interests of the PTC in Hollywood.
- Scientifically Monitoring Prime-Time Television to Assist Your Family, a program that uses analysis generated from the Media Research Center's Media Tracking System (MTS).
- Publishes special reports focusing on topics relating to the content of prime-time television, including in-depth analyses of the "family hour" and the new television ratings system.
- *Family Guide to Prime Time* profiles every sitcom and drama on ABC, CBS, Fox, NBC, UPN, and the WB; provides information on subject matter that is inappropriate for children; and offers comprehensive study of prime-time content that clearly identifies shows that promote family-friendly themes. Uses an easy "traffic light" rating system (red, yellow, and green) to signal a show's suitability for children, based on language, violence, and sexual situations as well as overall content.

## POPULATION COMMUNICATIONS INTERNATIONAL (PCI)
## www.population.org

Works creatively with the media and other organizations to motivate individuals and communities to make choices that will influence population trends, encouraging sustainable development and environmental protection. PCI works to integrate social messages into the story lines of programming, primarily soap operas, in developing countries around the globe.

### Strategies

- Provides technical assistance and training for radio and television soap operas that feature social themes, particularly in developing countries; the characters in their productions become role models for the elevation of the status of women, the use of family planning, small family size, AIDS prevention, and other related values.
- Programs encourage professionals in the entertainment industry—including soap operas, talk shows, and computer games—to recognize the positive contributions they can make to increasing public awareness of important social and public health issues.

**The following three organizations work to inform parents and educators by providing evaluations, guidelines, and other resources for navigating the media landscape. Several have devised their own film and television ratings to further as-**

**sist parents in making wise media choices.**

### COALITION FOR QUALITY CHILDREN'S MEDIA (CQCM)
### www.cqcm.org

To enhance children's viewing experiences by making quality children's media more visible and more readily available. CQCM is a national not-for-profit organization that is a voluntary collaboration between the media industry, educators, and child advocacy organizations.

Strategies

- Operates KIDS FIRST, a program that evaluates and rates videos, CD-ROMs, and television for children ages infant to 18 years, as well as conducting critical viewing workshops. Titles submitted are reviewed by volunteer jurors nationwide. KIDS FIRST is a tool for parents, teachers, children, and libraries (provides updated lists of endorsed titles and media literacy for community outreach programs). Also assists retailers by providing lists of approved titles, marketing support for in-store programs, and an established coalition of child advocacy organizations who support the KIDS FIRST program, and assists producers because approved and stickered titles are given support in the marketplace by in-store programs, publicity, and linkage with other child advocacy organizations.
- Conducts workshops at national conferences.

### DOVE FOUNDATION
### www.dove.org

A nonprofit encouraging the creation, production, and distribution of wholesome family movies and videos.

Strategies

- Awards a Dove seal to any movie or video that is rated "family-friendly" by its film review board.
- Selects certain high-quality PG-, PG-13-, and R-rated films and recommends their release in family-edited versions.
- Rallies consumer support to encourage filmmakers to produce more wholesome family-scripted movies.
- Holds Dove family film festivals throughout the United States.
- Provides young hospitalized children with educational programming through the Children's Hospital Dove Movie Channel.

### NATIONAL INSTITUTE ON MEDIA AND THE FAMILY
### www.mediaandthefamily.org

A resource for research, education, and information about the impact of the media on children and families.

Strategies

- Dr. Dave's Family Favorites picks award-winning books for preschool, early elementary, middle school, and high school readers.
- KidScore,® an innovative content-based rating system that evaluates television, movies, videos, and computer games from a family-friendly perspective.
- 1998 video and computer game report card.
- Educators' forum, a selection of curricula, research materials, and training opportunities for both child and adult educators.
- Monthly activity and quiz.
- Score card, fun, easy-to-use evaluations of your family's media habits.
- The publication *Hot Topics.*
- Media literacy tools and resources.

**A specific network of groups operating across the country is striving to build media "literacy" among parents and teachers and to educate the public on the issues surrounding media and their health effects on our nation's children. The following 19 organizations were examined; those marked by an asterisk represent coalitions.**

## ACTION ALLIANCE FOR CHILDREN (AAC)
## www.4children.org

A nonprofit information agency committed to educating and empowering people who work with and for children. AAC serves as a resource for policy makers, children's service providers and advocates, and the media. AAC provides information on current trends and public policy issues affecting children and their families. In addition, the agency facilitates dialogue among diverse community groups (child care workers, educators, parents, human service providers, advocates, media, and policy makers). AAC is committed to improving the lives of children and families and believes that sharing information is the first step toward that goal.

### Strategies

- Conducts conferences, media dialogues, workshops, and training on current child-related issues; AAC's media forums enable children's advocates and the press to discuss effective ways to disseminate information about children's issues.

## AMERICAN ACADEMY OF PEDIATRICS (AAP): MEDIA MATTERS
## www.aap.org

For more than 25 years, the AAP has addressed the impact of the media on children and adolescents. In 1997, the AAP launched Media Matters, a national campaign to make pediatricians, parents, and children more aware of the influence that media can have on children, both mentally and behaviorally, positively and negatively. A key element is to teach basic media literacy and to be more discriminating about media use. Media Matters addresses all media and covers a range of issues, including the use of tobacco, alcohol, and illicit drugs; aggression and violence; sex and sexual exploitation; nutritional issues; and self-image.

### Strategies

- Materials, training, and events.
- Sponsors regional training conferences for members on substance use in the media and works with other organizations to identify opportunities for pediatricians to participate in media education activities at the local level.
- Prepares and distributes a guide for pediatricians called *Media Education in the Practice Setting* and a booklet for parents titled *Understanding the Impact of the Media on Children and Teens.*
- Makes available a media history form made up of several questions for parents to answer to give pediatricians in the practice setting concrete information about a child's media exposure.
- The Committee on Communications is developing a policy statement on media education that focuses on the public health impact of the media and how the medical community can address such impact.
- Organizes and hosts the annual National Media Education Conference.
- Letter-writing campaign aims to prevent children from seeing potentially harmful violent or sexually explicit

content by encouraging the public to send letters to theaters and retailers in their communities asking them to provide quality family entertainment and to enforce the rating system.

### CENTER FOR CHILDREN'S MEDIA
4800 Morgan Drive
Chevy Chase, MD 20815

Provides educational, cultural, and entertaining programs for children and their families. It was established in 1989 to address the growing concern of parents, educators, children's advocates, and community leaders regarding violence, stereotyping, and cultural bias in children's film and video programs. Its mission is to broaden children's understanding of film, television, and new media.

#### Strategies

- Prepares media literacy training and production workshops.
- Holds panel discussions and festivals.

### CENTER FOR MEDIA LITERACY
www.medialit.org

To bring media literacy education to every child, school, and home in North America. The center represents a national advocacy for media literacy education.

#### Strategies

- Develops and distributes, via a printed and on-line catalog, media literacy materials to teachers, schools, parents, youth and community leaders, and others.
- Designs, develops, and conducts media literacy workshops, teacher training, seminars, and special events, and cosponsors national conferences.

### CHILDREN'S TELEVISION RESOURCE AND EDUCATION CENTER (C-TREC)*: MEDIA EDUCATION PROGRAM
444 De Haro Street, Suite 202
San Francisco, CA 94107-2347

Seeks to increase the nation's understanding of the impact of the electronic media on children. C-TREC is an educational organization dedicated to providing services and products that promote children's social development, creativity, and academic success. As a part of that commitment, C-TREC helps parents, teachers, and other professionals deal with issues related to children's television viewing.

#### Strategies

- Provides media information, analysis, and guidelines for parents, educators, and policy makers.
- Conducts "Helping Children Survive Television" presentations for thousands of parents, teachers, and health and human service professionals.
- Implements media education training programs for community leaders.
- Assists Congress and the media industry in shaping national policy regarding children and the media.
- Produces an award-winning, nationally aired radio drama series that encourages children to think critically about electronic media.
- Creates international television programming for young children.
- Provides expert commentary, analysis, and consultation for radio, television, and print media.

### GIRLS INCORPORATED: GIRLS RE-CAST TV
www.girlsinc.org

Girls Inc. is a national youth organization dedicated to helping every girl become strong, smart, and bold. For more than 50 years, it has provided vital educational programs to millions of American girls, par-

grams to millions of American girls, particularly those in high-risk, underserved areas. Today, innovative programs help girls confront subtle societal messages about their value and potential and aim to prepare them to lead successful, independent, and complete lives.

**Strategies**

- Develops research-based informal education programs that encourage girls to take risks and master physical, intellectual, and emotional challenges.
- Serves girls through their Girls Urban Initiative—delivered to girls where they already are—in schools, public housing developments, detention facilities, and other community-based organizations.
- The National Resource Center (NRC) is the organization's research, information services, and training site. Extensive research and evaluation conducted by the NRC provide the foundation for all Girls Inc. programs. The NRC also responds to requests for information on girls' issues and distributes Girls Inc. publications.
- Informs policy makers about girls' needs locally and nationally; the organization educates the media about crucial issues facing girls.

## JOIN TOGETHER
## www.jointogether.org

A project founded in 1991 by the Boston University School of Public Health, Join Together is a national resource for communities working to reduce substance abuse and gun violence.

**Strategies**

- Periodic reports, newsletters, and community action tool kits.
- Public policy panels that examine and recommend changes in public policies and practices related to substance abuse.
- Surveys that quantify and describe the community movement against substance abuse and gun violence.
- Website that serves as a resource center and "meeting place" to encourage people to join together in the fight against substance abuse and gun violence.

## JUST THINK FOUNDATION
## www.justthink.org

Stimulates critical thinking about popular media and strives to equip young people with literacy tools that will be crucial in their future. These tools include the ability to comprehend the content of media and master the technical skills to produce media messages in various forms, from broadcast public service announcements to websites.

**Strategies**

- Works with students, teachers, parents, and the entertainment industry to promote literacy for the 21st century.
- Teaches basic literacy, visual literacy, and technological literacy to encourage young people to create their own messages.

## KIDSNET
## www.kidsnet.org

The only national nonprofit computerized clearinghouse and information center devoted to children's television, radio, audio, video, and multimedia. Helps children, families, and educators intelligently access the educational opportunities available from television, radio, and multimedia sources by encouraging media literacy in children and a commitment to educational excellence in broadcasters.

### Strategies

Works with health and social service professionals, community organizations, and educators, as well as media professionals and parents, to create and disseminate educational materials for children from preschool through high school. Some of KIDSNET's outreach activities include the following:

- A monthly media guide describing programs for children, families, and educators referenced by air date, curriculum areas, grade levels, supplemental materials, related multimedia, off-air taping rights, and sources for more information.
- Media news, a quarterly resource of awards, events, legislation, regulation, technology, services, research, grants, and competitions related to children's media.
- The production and distribution of study guides to be used in conjunction with programming for children and families. Study guides are designed for various curriculum areas, including science, literature, history, social studies, and health. These are distributed to a targeted list of teachers, librarians, health workers, and social service professionals free of charge.
- Provides a unique forum for dialogue on areas of mutual interest with producers and networks representing commercial, cable, and public television.
- Offers consulting and technical assistance to children's programmers and broadcasters in education and public affairs.

## THE LION AND LAMB PROJECT
www.lionlamb.org

A national grassroots initiative providing information about the effects of violent entertainment toys and games on children's behavior. Works with parents, teachers, day care providers, social workers, psychologists, grandparents, and others—anyone interested in teaching the values of nonviolence to children.

### Strategies

- Parents action kit provides parents with information to help them better understand the effects of media violence on children's behavior. It also provides suggestions for selecting age-appropriate, nonviolent toys and games and provides tips for resolving family conflicts peacefully at home and on the playground.
- Workshops for parents and educators enable participants to learn how to transmit their own values of nonviolence to children. Titles include *Introductory Workshop: How Young Children Learn Violence, and What Parents Can Do; How to Turn Off the TV—and Turn On Your Family Life; Conflict Resolution at Home: Problem Solving Without Tears;* and *Community Solutions: Working Together to Teach Peace.*
- Violent toy trade-ins, in which children bring in violent toys and transform them into a peace sculpture as a statement of their desire for a less violent and more peaceful world.
- Peaceable play days and violent toy sales give children and parents opportunities to learn and remember all the different ways of having fun that do not center on violence as a theme.

## MEDIA EDUCATION FOUNDATION (MEF)
www.igc.org.mef

An educational organization established in 1991 devoted to media research and the production of resources to aid educators and others in fostering analytical media literacy. MEF asserts that a media literate citizenry is essential to a vibrant democracy in a diverse and complex society.

Strategies

- Produces and disseminates award-winning resources for students of media literacy, educators, parents, and community leaders.
- Conducts research on timely media issues.

## MEDIA WATCH
www.mediawatch.com

To challenge abusive stereotypes and other biased images commonly found in the media.

Strategies

Media Watch distributes educational videos, media literacy information, and newsletters to help create more informed consumers of the mass media.

## MEDIA WISE*
www.mediawise.org

Founded in 1995 through a coalition of community organizations to reduce the impact and incidence of violence in the media through public awareness, education, and community action without invading First Amendment rights. The coalition includes a broad-based group of youth-serving and other community agencies, religious and health organizations, educators, broadcasters, and young people who are committed to empowering children, youth, and adults to become discriminating media consumers.

Strategies

- Speakers bureau, an informational presentation for civic, community, parent, school, faith groups, and so on, to raise awareness of the effects of media violence and to promote media literacy and advocacy.
- Media literacy curricula, programs available for children, youth, parents, teachers, social service professionals, and others in the area of media literacy and violence prevention; includes MediaSmarts, a video-based curriculum for use in middle schools or by youth-serving agencies.
- Publications, including *Screen Smarts: A Family Guide to Media Literacy; Media Smarts 4 Young Folks: Workbook for Children Birth Through Age 8; Television and the Lives of Our Children: A Manual for Teachers and Parents; Selling Out America's Children;* and *MEDIA ALERT!*

## NATIONAL ALLIANCE FOR NON-VIOLENT PROGRAMMING (NANP)*
122 North Elm Street, Suite 300
Greensboro, NC 27401

A coalition of women's organizations committed to the reduction of entertainment violence through awareness, advocacy, and decision. NANP works to fight against violence that is glamorized and presented solely for the purpose of entertainment—that is, people being killed or injured in dramatic incidents that fail to portray physical, ethical, social, or emotional effects of the action.

Strategies

- Identifying high-risk groups and offering them alternatives to violent conflict resolution; interventions change the thought patterns of viewers exposed to violence.
- Multifaceted educational programs that organize culturally specific developmentally appropriate initiatives to address problems caused by the depiction of violence in the entertainment media.

- Creating public awareness by establishing violence as a public health issue by organizing an initiative similar to the antismoking and anti-drunk-driving campaigns.
- Community juries trained to evaluate and recommend children's television programming and videos.

### NATIONAL COALITION ON TELEVISION VIOLENCE (NCTV)*
### www.nctvv.org

A nonprofit membership organization established in 1980 to reduce the amount of gratuitous violence on television by educating the public about the harm that entertainment violence is doing to society.

#### Strategies

- Monitors the levels of violence on television (from cartoons to prime time) and in movies; sexual content and substance abuse are also measured.
- Publishes a newsletter with the results of NCTV's research and results of other researchers regarding the effects of violent entertainment; it also reports on new legislation affecting media violence.
- Disseminates information internationally through television and radio appearances, newspaper and magazine interviews, and speaking engagements.
- Organizes national protests of violent films, including *Teenage Mutant Ninja Turtles;* it has successfully organized boycotted advertisers of TV shows, including *Friday the 13th: The Series* and *Freddy's Nightmares,* causing these violent shows to be canceled.
- Gives Gandhi Awards for nonviolent prosocial films.
- Has undertaken a comprehensive survey of video games, music videos, and sports violence.
- Testifies at congressional hearings and works with other community leaders to help curb violence in U.S. society as it is linked to media violence.

### NATIONAL EDUCATIONAL MEDIA NETWORK (NEMN)
### www.nemn.org

Dedicated to recognizing and supporting excellence in educational media, ranging from general interest documentaries to material designed especially for classroom and training programs.

#### Strategies

- Apple Awards competition, a premier event in the nation honoring outstanding achievement in educational media; NEMN's catalog of award-winning productions is compiled from each year's competition and publicized to librarians and media buyers nationwide.
- An event made up of an annual Media Market and Film and Video Festival and a biennial conference; these events have made NEMN the preeminent organization linking makers, distributors, and consumers in the educational media community.

### NATIONAL PTA: FAMILY AND COMMUNITY CRITICAL VIEWING PROJECT
### www.pta.org

To partner and train together local cable television operators and local PTA leaders in the skills of critical viewing. In turn, these PTA/cable "teams" offer local workshops on media literacy and critical viewing skills to parents and teachers in their own communities. The PTA is the nation's largest volunteer child advocacy organization, with nearly 7 million members, committed to uniting the home, school, and community in promoting the education, health, and welfare of children and families. PTA leaders have been involved with the issue of violence on television in both community programs and the legislative arena since the 1970s.

Strategies

- National PTA leaders play a pivotal role in representing 5 million members at key meetings of educational groups, government organizations, the media, and other child advocacy groups.
- Provides critical viewing workshops to teach the following techniques: how to set rules for television viewing; how to stick to the set television rules; how to recognize ways in which television can be used to manipulate viewers; how to talk to children about violence on television; and how to turn what we see on television into positive and educational family discussions.
- The publication *Taking Charge of Your TV: A Guide to Critical Viewing for Parents and Children.*

### TEACHERS RESISTING UNHEALTHY ENTERTAINMENT (TRUCE)*
P.O. Box 441261
Somerville, MA 02144

A national group of educators deeply concerned about how children's entertainment and toys are affecting the play and behavior of children in the classroom.

Strategies

- Newsletter.
- Works to raise awareness about the negative effects of violent and stereotyped toys and media on children, families, schools, and society.

### TV-FREE AMERICA
www.tvfa.org

Encourages Americans to reduce, voluntarily and dramatically, the amount of television they watch in order to promote richer, healthier, and more connected lives, families, and communities.

Strategies

- More Reading, Less TV program, an 8-week program designed to encourage young students to develop a deep enjoyment for reading while simultaneously helping them to reduce the amount of television they watch.
- National TV-Turnoff Week, an annual event initiated in 1995 that encourages Americans to voluntarily turn off their TV sets for 7 days and rediscover that life can be more constructive, rewarding, healthy—even informed—with more time and less TV.

**The following two organizations work to mobilize large grassroots movements and calls to action to effect policy change in media for children. Their work encompasses a range of methods but primarily promotes public advocacy and public policy. Both conduct research as well.**

### CULTURAL ENVIRONMENT MOVEMENT (CEM)*
www.cemnet.org

A nonprofit international coalition of more than 250 organizations and 6,300 individuals founded in 1996 to work for freedom, fairness, diversity, responsibility, respect for cultural integrity, the protection of children, and democratic decision making in the media. CEM works for gender equity and general diversity in mass media employment, ownership, and representation.

### Strategies

- Builds coalitions involving media councils in the United States and abroad, including organizations and individuals committed to broadening freedom and diversity of communication.
- Opposes domination and favors abolishing concentration of ownership and censorship (both of and by the media), public or private.
- Helps organizations internationally to invest in their own cultural development.
- Works with guilds, caucuses, labor, and other groups for diversity in employment and in media content.
- Promotes media literacy, media awareness, critical viewing and reading, and other media education efforts.
- Places cultural policy issues on the social-political agenda.
- Produces and distributes the Media Violence Index, the Television Diversity Index, and other reports on media content, effects, and policy.
- Publishes the CEM *Monitor.*
- Maintains an informative website.
- Conducts on-line discussion of media and other cultural issues.

## PEOPLE FOR BETTER TV (PBTV)*
## www.bettertv.org

A grassroots coalition formed in 1998 to work toward securing public interest representation in the digital TV age.

### Strategies

- Held six community workshops across the country in the summer of 1999 to mobilize local social and religious leaders and their communities around the issue of digital TV.
- Public education and awareness regarding public interest responsibilities of local broadcasters.
- Organizing letter-writing campaign to the FCC to urge that public hearings be held and for creation of guidelines for digital TV in exchange for public use of the airwaves.

# References


Barber, B. R. (1995). *Jihad vs. McWorld.* New York: Ballantine.

Brown, L. (1971). *Television: The business behind the box.* New York: Harcourt Brace Jovanovich.

Brown, L. (1979). *Keeping your eye on television.* New York: Pilgrim Press.

DeGaetano, G., & Grossman, D. (1999). *Uncorrected proof: Stop teaching our kids to kill: A call to action against TV, movies, and video game violence.* New York: Crown.

Head, S. W., & Sterling, C. H. (1982). *Broadcasting in America: A survey of television, radio, and new technologies* (4th ed.). Boston: Houghton Mifflin.

Kotler, P., & Roberto, E. L. (1989). *Social marketing: Strategies for changing public behavior.* New York: Free Press.

Mifflin, L. (1999, August 4). Pediatrics group offers tough rules for television. *New York Times,* p. 3.

Minow, N. N., & Lamay, C. L. (1995). *Abandoned in the wasteland: Children, television, and the First Amendment.* New York: Hill and Wang.

Montgomery, K. C. (1989). *Target: Prime time.* New York: Oxford University Press.

Murray, J. P., & Salomon, G. (Eds.). (1984). *The future of children's television.* Boys Town, NE: Boys Town.

*National Television Violence Study executive summary* (Vol. 3). (1998). Thousand Oaks, CA: Sage.

*National Television Violence Study executive summary1994-1995.* (1996). Studio City, CA: Mediascope.

*The social effects of electronic interactive games: An annotated bibliography.* (1996). Studio City, CA: Mediascope.

Trotta, L. (Ed.). (1998). *Building blocks: A guide for creating children's educational television.* Studio City, CA: Mediascope.

Turow, J. (1981). *Entertainment, education, and the hard sell: Three decades of network children's television.* New York: Praeger.

UCLA Center for Communication Policy. (1995). *The UCLA television violence monitoring report.* Los Angeles: Author.

U.S. Senate. (1996). Telecommunications Act of 1996, 104th Cong., 2d Sess. Washington, DC: U.S. Government Printing Office.

U.S. Senate, Judiciary Committee. (1999, September 14). *Children, violence, and the media: A report for parents and policy makers* [On-line]. [Retrieved August 9, 1999].
Available: www.senate.gov/ 7Ejudiciary/mediavio.html

# A Final Word From the Editors

## The Future of Literacy and of Pictorial Consciousness

We introduced this handbook by calling attention to the fact that, even though written language and human reading have a 6,000-year history, really widespread popular literacy is largely a nineteenth- and twentieth-century phenomenon. The emergence of the electronic media in the twentieth century overlapped with an increase in reading and writing for great masses of children in Japan, the Soviet Union, and China, as well as many other Asian and Central European nations. Universal literacy on our planet has yet to be achieved, however. Sadly, there remain seemingly modern cultures in which male leaders continue to resist the education of women.

Learning to read fluently takes children several years of sustained motivation and effort. By contrast, listening to radio or recorded music and watching films or television provide an almost immediate impact. That direct influence may explain why the electronic media have leapfrogged over the slower-paced acquisition of literacy in attracting the attention of children and youth around the world. Once, the young Abe Lincoln, Charles Dickens, and Mary Ann Evans (George Eliot), to name but a few, found their imaginations soaring as they sat by the fire and pored over the densely written, small-print, sparsely illustrated books of the 1800s. Today, almost certainly reflecting our early exposure to film and television, we and our children prefer more lavishly illustrated books. Magazines such as *Harper's,* long known for its wordy critical essays and fiction, have moved dramatically toward shorter paragraphs and articles and more graphics and pictures. The staid *New York Times,* long resistant to the flashy, brief television news summaries or to the encapsulated journalism of *USA Today,* now presents many shorter reports and vivid, color photographs. Will we become a chiefly pictorial society, hardly reading at all, in the 21st century?

The amazing upsurge of computer usage not only by adults but also by children in just the last few years provides a challenge to such a view. Although the Internet is replete with graphics and even with the newest software such as CD-ROMs and video-moving images, reading written text and engaging in sequential information processing remains critical for effective use of computers by children. Campaign rhetoric in the United States and even the president's State of the Union Address in 2000 referred to the "Digital Divide," a recognition that not only relative economic affluence but also literacy are necessary for providing *all* children with the benefits of computer usage at home or at school. As computers become cheaper and more routinely available in most homes and schools, they will represent a countervalent force against the drift toward a purely pictorial, non-linear-thinking society that some have feared as television has taken over the world. The amazing surge in computer-based commercialism that has characterized the past few years has the potential for both economic and social exploitation of child users (see Chapter 35). At the same time, however, the very attractiveness of the cultural novelties, the games, the educational and social features of e-mail and benign chat rooms, and even product descriptions for children, are influences that can motivate improving reading skills and other basic educational competencies. Letter writing, once so central a feature of the social experience of educated children and adults across the life span, had become almost a lost art in the last half of the twentieth century. We suddenly see its modified return and attractiveness for the young with the proliferation of worldwide e-mail communication.

Not all computer experts agree with our optimistic assertion. Seymour Papert (personal communication, February 2000), one of the founders of MIT's Media Laboratory and a pioneer in computer usage for childhood education, has suggested that voice-comprehension technology is nearly perfected. Children can soon speak to a computer that will respond with still graphics and moving pictures so that reading will no longer be necessary. Only a small cadre of the elite literate will be needed to upgrade software and to design new technology. We are not ready to accept this Aldous Huxley or George Orwell pessimistic view of the human future. Here is an area for research that can start very soon in examining the impact of the "computer-television complex." One can envision that we can soon begin studies comparing (with appropriate demographic controls) children who spend several hours a day just with television, others who combine TV and computers, and others who use only computers (taking into account, of course, content variations in these media). We can see if, over a period from ages 4 or 5 to 8 or 9, we can observe differential literacy trends. Even with the great increase in home and school computer availability, there is enough variability in the timing of these developments across homes and schools that we may still be able to identify well-matched groups whom we can follow up on in the next decade.

Many of the research studies reviewed in the handbook were generated by concerns that the electronic media would severely affect the slow human gains in literacy and formal education or in logical, orderly thought. Even though the scientific data suggested that such risk might be real in a world in which only passive viewing of entertainment television prevailed, the computer society that must still spread to children all over the planet seems likely to mitigate that danger. With increased use of "home theaters" and large screens, large numbers of diversified cable channels, but also computers integrated with the television medium through "boxes" and keypads, we may be forging a new kind of consciousness. Smell transmittal is already technologically feasible, so Aldous Huxley's 1930s *Brave New World* fantasy of "smellovision" may soon be a reality. Yes, we may be more pictorial and sensory, but we may also find that we cannot be effective in this emerging electronic society unless we are also literate. Parents will have to confront their responsibility to monitor media usage by children and also to support and extend the tremendous educational potential of the visual, written, and auditory messages that come into the home. Our educators will have to build *media literacy* into their curricula not only as "add-ons" to prevent harmful influences of violent television content but also as fundamental skills in computer usage, as crucial for children as reading, writing, and arithmetic. Such media literacy, however, will be ineffective without the three "Rs." Teacher training will now require computer mastery and media literacy as well, so we can envision great changes in traditional pedagogical education and perhaps, eventually, even in classroom organization.

At the same time that we were completing the editing of this handbook, we were also finishing a study sponsored by the U.S. Department of Education regarding computer availability and usage in public libraries. We found that every one of the 98 libraries surveyed in each state of the union now had computers and that librarians were willing to help in the use of computers and software. Every library in our survey also had a preschool program, and practically all permitted borrowing videos for home use. We can take the optimistic view that books may not disappear from libraries but that libraries may also begin to play a role in training children and their parents in both reading and media literacy.

Even with the accelerating increases in accessibility of computer-based attractions for children, the most recent reports, such as that by the Kaiser Family Foundation (described in several chapters of this volume), make clear that broadcast television continues to be by far the most attractive medium for entertainment of children. The combination of federal government intervention through legislation and FCC rule making have yielded what might be called a "growth spurt" in children's television (Mifflin, 1999). The large networks and their affiliates have joined the Public Broadcasting Corporation in providing educationally slanted entertainment shows. The proliferation of cable channels has also opened new directions for child-oriented programming spearheaded by the congressional legislation; the Nickelodeon channel may have led the way, followed by the Disney Channel, the Family Channel's Boyz and Girlz Channels, the Discovery Kids' Channel, and others. The commercial success of Nickelodeon and, alas, the recognition of the vast selling power by licensing toys, games, and dolls or action figures derived from televised children's shows on both public and commercial outlets have encouraged producers to present more child-directed shows that at least have some educational and socially constructive features. The result is that there has been an increase in children's viewing of child-oriented programming and somewhat less viewing of adult-oriented shows (Mifflin, 1999).

What conclusions about writing and producing children's programming can we draw from the chapters of this handbook? A series of suggestions about the programming of entertaining children's material that can be reasonably age-specific, educational, reasonably constructive in its influence, and relatively free of those serious hazards of TV viewing for children so well brought out in Chapters 10 to 23 of this handbook can be found in *Public Broadcasting: Ready to Teach,* which we prepared as a report to Congress for the Corporation for Public Broadcasting (CPB, 1993). We believe the same principles apply to videotapes, CD-ROMs, and computer games and websites, although the research evidence for these media has yet to be accumulated. Practical suggestions along similar lines can also be found in Chapters 5 through 9 and in a number of advocacy chapters in Part 3.

## Growing Up in an Electronic Environment: Implications for Child Development and for Research

Recent research from the Stanford Institute for the Quantitative Study of Society based on self-reports of American Internet-using adults suggests that computer involvement is reflected in less time spent with family and friends, less out-of-home store shopping, and, if anything, more time being spent on work at home after regular workplace hours (Markoff, 2000). What impact will this trend, if it continues, have on children, not only through experiencing computer-focused parents but also through mimicking this adult behavior themselves and growing up either watching more television or spending more solitary time in front of the computer? The concept of home-theater rooms in which the TV is integrated with computer-driven boxes is spreading. Will we see, as the report's authors suggest, a growing "real human" social isolation among children? The "virtual" social contacts of e-mail and chat rooms may not really compensate for direct communication and play with peers. Even if organized sports like Little League or "Moms' Soccer" continue to be fostered on weekends, will there be time for just spontaneous play and "fooling around" with family members and peers?

Here is a challenge for research in the next decade. Can we generate studies that track children's attention, comprehension, and social interaction patterns in settings where both television viewing and computer activity are part of their daily experience? How early can we see some meaningful use of computers by children, and how does such experience predict later school readiness as well as general computer skills? Is it reasonable to assume that the relative "ease" of television watching will to some degree displace the time needed to master the more interactive computer skills? Will we be able to identify groups of children whose involvement with television *and* computers may be putting them at risk for social isolation? It may turn out that our human capacity for adjustment to new technologies may preclude such a possibility, but we will need careful research observation to assure us on that point.

An intermediary stop between complete engrossment of children in the TV screen and the more interactive features of e-mail or computer games may emerge as educationally oriented websites proliferate on the Internet. There are estimates that, by 2002, as many as 50% of the nearly 30 million children ages 6 to 12 will have computer access in the United States. Websites for children that include some learning materials, follow-ups on televised programming, or specific games and education sites like ePLAY are expanding and ideally may serve as "the bridge between home and school" (Cheng, 1999). Some of these websites are free to America Online subscribers; others depend on subscriptions and advertising. As early as November 1998, 50 child-oriented and to some degree educational websites were available (Sundin, 1999), but that number is growing too fast for documentation in this volume (Cheng, 1999). We can certainly recommend that parents and educators investigate PBS Online, the Children's Television Workshop Online, Nickelodeon Online, and (more for pure entertainment) the Disney Online websites, along with some mentioned above like ePLAY (Slatalla, 1999). On the positive side, in addition to educationally useful material presented in an enjoyable fashion, one can also note that most of these websites *do not* collect or distribute personal information from children. Such websites do, however, include *advertising* and promotion of products derived from their TV programming. Until our society respects children enough to subsidize such important educational outlets free of commercialism, we may have to accept advertising as a major source of revenue. Still another burden of monitoring the sites and educating children about commercialism to prevent undue exploitation will fall on parents, child care workers, and educators.

The research studies reviewed in our handbook point to significant hazards for children who watch violent content and, to a lesser extent, sexually provocative content on television. Will such content be as prevalent in the new, more differentiated cable programming now emerging? What risks may follow, especially with the high level of sexual content one can easily stumble on when "surfing" the Net? What new dangers may emerge when frequent levels of "risky" TV viewing are combined with computer game playing or the use of the Web and chat rooms by early school-age or pubescent children?

The chapters in this handbook also have pointed to many potentially constructive uses of television. One can anticipate even more effective prosocial and constructive learning possibilities when judicious TV viewing is combined with the exploration of learning materials specially prepared for the computer. How can we maximize such engagement and opportunities for children? What role can parents, educators, and producers play in enhancing the socially adaptive employment of computers by children across the spectrum?

Special problems regarding the protection of children are raised by the largely unregulated nature of the Internet and World Wide Web. How can children be protected from child abuse or unwarranted exposure to sexual or commercial exploitation in the upcoming combinations of television and computer use? There have already been a few cases of child molestation set up through initial chat-room exposure. Here, the computer's impact is even more potentially negative than the research has shown for mere exposure from television viewing because of the Internet's interactive nature. Will we need new laws, blocking procedures, and, necessarily, increasing parental or other adult caregiver education to establish suitable controls?

Beyond the risk of sexual molestation or product-purchase exploitation via chat rooms and websites, there is still a further hazard for children—*privacy* (Mitchener & Wessel, 2000). The European Union has led the way in establishing guidelines for limiting what personal data can be collected from the computer nets. These data must involve unambiguous consent or completion of a contract. They must be specifically required by law or necessary for law enforcement. Data on ethnic origins, political opinions, religious or philosophical beliefs, union membership, health, or sex life are prohibited from collection without explicit consent. We need legal specifications of children's ages of consent and protections for them lest they be lured into providing such data.

Nine Western European countries have already signed onto this accord, and pressure is being brought to bear on others and on the United States to concur in this approach. There is a great challenge for research in the next decade to examine how such privacy issues are affecting children. This issue, at best, was less critical when the focus was only the more passive nature of television viewing. Now with but the click of a mouse, millions of children may be on the brink of significant losses of privacy or legal involvement that can put the whole family in jeopardy (see Chapter 35).

For the daily follower of the latest news on cable outlet accelerated growth and website or other kinds of Internet proliferation, a handbook like ours may seem quickly outdated. We believe, to the contrary, that the research reviewed herein and the advocacy issues raised are critical in guiding us to confront the needed research and policy questions that will be emerging in the next decades. The questions raised about how children at various ages attend to and comprehend television content suggest that youngsters are active participants rather than passive absorbers of the content and structure of video materials. Will they be able to adapt to the even more active roles demanded by the combinations of TV and computers? How will the liveliness and arousal values of digital stimulation affect children's ability to learn from computerized material? Will the uses of computers lead to greater alienation (Markoff, 2000) or to more effective social networking (Weise, 2000)?

We have ample evidence of the potential hazards of unregulated television watching by children. Will the greater complexity and interaction required for computer use minimize these hazards? We think that is likely. Yet we cannot discount the possibility that websites and chat rooms may emerge that not only present children with graphic and explicit sexual content but may also teach them very specific and tempting ways to use guns, knives, or other destructive weapons. What will we need to demonstrate such possibilities by research, and what kinds of controls will be called for to avoid such risks? We believe Chapters 10 through 22 provide a full range of research approaches that can be applied to the new wave of electronic media combining television and computers. The task of compiling regular annual records of violent content on network TV programming that was possible for the Annenberg group led by George Gerbner (see Chapters 3 and 10, for example) will have to be substantially modified to provide systematic indications of such content on the vast cyberspace universe. More ingenuity may be needed to obtain from children or parents what actual content they watch or become involved with, as well as sampling the array of content available. Students of child development will be challenged to determine how children across the age spans choose and react to the great variety of Internet possibilities.

In summary, we believe that, despite some hesitations, false starts, and missed opportunities for research and policy making demonstrated in our history, industry, and advocacy chapters, a great deal has been accomplished in the half-century since television use began to spread across the world. We believe that the research, the policy questions and government and industry actions, and the advocacy efforts reviewed in this handbook can open the way for more reasoned and carefully planned approaches to scientific studies and effective interventions in the new century. Such efforts can help children to grow up effectively in a digital, "wired" world of electronic media.

## References

Cheng, K. (1999, May 3). Wee Web. *IQ*, pp. 16-20.

Corporation for Public Broadcasting. (1993). *Public broadcasting: Ready to teach: A report to the 103rd Congress and the American people. Pursuant to P.L. 102-356*. Washington, DC: Author.

Markoff, J. (2000, February 16). A newer, lonelier crowd emerges in Internet study. *New York Times*, pp. A1, A18.

Mifflin, L. (1999, April 19). A growth spurt is transforming TV for children. *New York Times*, pp. A1, A19.

Mitchener, B., & Wessel, D. (2000, February 24). Who knows what about you? *Wall Street Journal Europe Networking*, pp. 25, 31.

Slatalla, M. (1999, April 12). *Sesame Street* site: Serious child's play. *New York Times*, p. G8.

Sundin, E. (1999). The on-line kids. In C. von Feilitzen & U. Carlsson (Eds.), *Children and media image, education, participation* (pp. 355-368). Göteborg, Sweden: UNESCO International Clearinghouse on Children and Violence on the Screen.

Weise, E. (2000, February 22). A circle unbroken by surveys. *USA Today*, p. 3D.

# Index

# About the Editors and Contributors

**Dorothy G. Singer,** Ed.D., is Research Scientist in the Department of Psychology at Yale University. She is also Codirector of the Yale University Family Television Research and Consultation Center and a Fellow of Morse College. In addition, she is Research Associate at Yale Child Study Center. Formerly, Dr. Singer was the William Benton Professor of Psychology, University of Bridgeport. She is also a Fellow of the American Psychology Association.

**Jerome L. Singer,** Ph.D., received his doctorate in Clinical Psychology from the University of Pennsylvania. He is Professor of Psychology and Child Study at Yale University, where he served for many years as Director of the Graduate Program in Clinical Psychology and also as Director of Graduate Studies in Psychology. He is Codirector, with Dorothy G. Singer, of the Yale University Family Television Research and Consultation Center.

**Alison Alexander,** Ph.D., is Professor and Head of the Department of Telecommunications in the Grady College of Journalism and Mass Communication at the University of Georgia. She was editor of the *Journal of Broadcasting & Electronic Media* from 1989 to 1991. She is past president of both the Association for Communication Administration and the Eastern Communication Association. Dr. Alexander's research examines audiences and media content, with a focus on media and the family. Currently, she is examining quality children's programming by studying the Peabody archives, profiling the children's television marketplace, and studying the construction of meaning for television within the family. She is the author of more than 40 book chapters, reviews, and journal articles. Reflecting her interest in both academic and professional concerns, she is coeditor of *Media Economics: Theory and Practice* (2nd ed.) and *Taking Sides: Controversial Issues in Mass Media and Society* (5th ed.).

**J. Cory Allen** developed industry analysis skills as a paralegal specialist at the U.S. Department of Justice's Antitrust Division, Computers and Finance Section. He is currently a graduate student at the Annenberg School for Communication at the University of Pennsylvania, studying children's television and the economics of digital television.

**Joy Keiko Asamen,** Ph.D., is Professor of Psychology at Pepperdine University, Graduate School of Education and Psychology. Her research interest is in the area of the sociocultural basis of behavior, and she teaches graduate-level courses in quantitative and qualitative research methods. She has coedited two books with Dr. Gordon Berry in the area of media and social behavior, *Children and Television: Images in a Changing Sociocultural World* (1993) and *Research Paradigms, Television, and Social Behavior* (1998). She is a member of the American Psychological Association and the American Educational Research Association.

**Gordon L. Berry,** Ed.D., is Professor Emeritus of Counseling and Educational Psychology of the Graduate School of Education and Information Studies at UCLA. He was also a professor in the Communication Studies Program. His special area of research is the study of media and social behavior. His most recent book, with Joy Asamen, is *Research Paradigms, Television, and Social Behavior.* He is a member of the American Psychological Association, the Association of Black Psychologists, and the American Psychological Society.

**David S. Bickham** is a graduate student in the Division of Child Development and Family Relationships at the University of Texas at Austin. His research interests include the effects of television rating systems on the viewing preferences of children, the mechanisms through which the Internet can play a role in identity formation and transformation, and the potential uses of websites to supplement the messages of educational programs. Currently, he is involved in the analysis of nationally representative data that include children's time spent with television and the relationships between viewing specific genres of programs and various child outcomes.

**James A. Brown,** Ph.D., is Professor Emeritus at the University of Alabama. His research and teaching interests include mass media ethics, media literacy, media management, and self-regulation. He was an adviser to the Bertlesmann Foundation's media literacy curriculum project in Athens, Georgia. The London Centre for the Study of Communication and Culture commissioned his 1991 book *Television "Critical Viewing Skills" Education: Major Media Literacy Projects in the United States and Selected Countries.* In 1998, he coauthored with Ward L. Quaal the third edition of *Radio-Television-Cable Management.*

**Kelly D. Brownell,** Ph.D., is Professor of Psychology, Epidemiology, and Public Health at Yale University, where he also served as Master of Silliman College and Director of the Yale Center for Eating and Weight Disorders. His work has focused on the treatment of eating disorders and obesity, the origins of these problems, body image issues, the behavioral and health effects of weight cycling, and public policy issues with respect to nutrition and physical activity.

**Jennings Bryant** is Professor of Communication, Holder of the Reagan Chair of Broadcasting, and Director of the Institute for Communication Research at the University of Alabama. He is the author or editor of 18 books, the most recent of which are *Television and the American Family* (2nd ed.) and *Human Communication Theory and Research* (2nd ed.), and the coeditor of the scholarly journal *Media Psychology.* Bryant's research interests are in entertainment theory, media effects, the impact of advanced communications systems, and media and children.

**Brad J. Bushman,** Ph.D., is Associate Professor at Iowa State University. His research focuses on the causes and consequences of human aggression. It has been published in the top psychology journals and has been featured in in the national and international media.

**Joanne Cantor,** Ph.D., is Professor of Communication Arts at the University of Wisconsin-Madison. She has published more than 70 articles on the psychological impact of the mass media, especially the effect of media violence on children's emotions and on the factors that attract children to violent programming. Her research has been influential in the efforts to convince the television industry to provide more informative ratings for their programs. Her book *Mommy, I'm Scared* adapts the findings of her research for a general audience.

**Molly Choate,** B.A., is a first-year doctoral student in clinical psychology at Boston University. She is studying anxiety disorders in children. She graduated from Yale in 1996. After living in Ecuador for 18 months, she returned to the United States to work as a research assistant while she applied to graduate school. As a research assistant, she examined the contribution of the food industry to the toxic environment. Her interests have been focused on child psychopathology, and she has done research on conduct disorder and depression.

**Peter G. Christenson** is Professor of Communication at Lewis and Clark College. His research primarily concerns children and media, with particular emphasis in recent years on children's and adolescents' uses of and responses to popular music. Several of his recent publications include *It's Not Only Rock and Roll: Popular Music in the Lives of Adolescents* and *Substance Use in Popular Movies and Music.*

**Michael Cohen,** Ph.D., is a principal and founding member of Applied Research & Consulting LLC (ARC). Dr. Cohen has developed an international reputation as a provider of superior qualitative and quantitative studies in the fields of corporate image, product positioning, employee communications, media development, public policy, and electoral politics.

**George Comstock,** Ph.D., Stanford University, is S. I. Newhouse Professor at the School of Public Communications at Syracuse University. He was science adviser to the Surgeon General's Scientific Advisory Committee on Television and Social Behavior that issued the 1972 federal report, *Television and Growing Up: The Impact of Televised Violence,* and in 1991-1993 was chairman of the Department of Journalism and Communication, Chinese University, Hong Kong. His interests include the art and science of research synthesis, the influence of the media in the socialization of children, and the dynamics of public opinion. His recent publications include *Television: What's On, Who's Watching, and What It Means* (with Erica Scharrer) and *Television and the American Child* (with Haejung Paik).

**Roger Desmond** is Professor and Director of the School of Communication at the University of Hartford (Connecticut). He has written articles and book chapters about family mediation of television, children and advertising, media literacy, and media education. His most recent research involves parent-child computer interaction.

**Peter J. Dirr,** Ph.D., is President of the Public Service Telecommunications Corporation, a not-for-profit company that helps schools, universities, libraries, and church groups in the United States and abroad use telecommunications technologies to achieve their missions. Dr. Dirr is also the founder and Director of the Cable in the Classroom Professional Development Institute. The longest span of Dr. Dirr's professional career (16 years) was spent at the Corporation for Public Broadcasting (CPB), where he was a founding staff member and Deputy Director of the Annenberg/CPB Project.

**Ed Donnerstein,** Ph.D., Florida State University, is Professor of Communication, Director of the Center for Communication and Social Policy, and Dean of Social Sciences at the University of California, Santa Barbara. His major research interests are in mass media violence and mass media policy. He has published more than 170 scientific articles in these general areas and serves on the editorial boards of a number of academic journals in both psychology and communication.

**Barna William Donovan** is a Ph.D. candidate in the School of Communication, Information, and Library Studies at Rutgers University. He holds bachelors and masters' degrees from Loyola University of Chicago and the University of Miami, respectively. His current scholarly research interests include film studies and genre analysis, and media education and media literacy efforts. Mr. Donovan works on the impact of new technologies in the university classroom, as well as Internet dependence on college campuses, and the study of communication approaches to curbing destructive college drinking.

**Jerry Franklin** is President and Chief Executive Officer of Connecticut Public Broadcasting, Inc., managing five TV stations, four radio stations, and a for-profit production company. He has received the 21st Century Award from America's Public Television Stations, dozens of regional Emmy Awards, two George Foster Peabody Awards, and numerous other awards. He played a key role in the production of highly popular shows such as *Barney & Friends* and *Scientific American Frontiers.*

**Bradley S. Greenberg** is University Distinguished Professor in the Department of Communication and Telecommunication at Michigan State University. His research interests focus on the social effects of the mass media. Recent research, in addition to examining responses to the new age-based and content-based television ratings, includes studies of the influence of sexual content in the media, racial diversity in mass media content, and the nature of parental mediation of new media.

**Patricia Greenfield** received her Ph.D. from Harvard University and is currently Professor of Psychology at UCLA, where she is a member of the developmental psychology group. Her central theoretical and research interest is the relationship between culture and human development. She is a past recipient of the American Association for the Advancement of Science Award for Behavioral Science Research and has received teaching awards from UCLA and the American Psychological Association. A current project in Los Angeles investigates how cultural values influence relationships on multiethnic high school sports teams. She is also engaged in a cross-cultural teacher-training project called Bridging Cultures. She has edited two books with R. R. Cocking, *Interacting With Video* and *Cross-Cultural Roots of Minority Child Development.*

**Jo Groebel** is Director General of the European Institute for the Media, Dusseldorf/Paris, and Chair of the Department of Media Psychology at Utrecht University He was/is Visiting Professor at the University of California in Los Angeles (UCLA) and at the University of St. Gallen. He was/is advisor for the Dutch government, the Presidents of Germany, the United Nations, UNESCO, and several FORTUNE 500 companies. He was also head of the media monitoring missions for the European Comission and the OSCE during the DUMA and presidential elections in Russia. He is the author or editor of 20 books that were published in Europe and the United States. He worked on numerous TV and radio productions internationally and is the author of press publications including *Frankfurter Allegemeine Zeitung, DIE ZEIT,* and *Volkskrant.* In June 2000, he presented his vision on the future Digital Society during the Government Conference in Berlin with 15 Heads of State.

**Elisheva Gross** is a student in the doctoral program in Developmental Psychology at UCLA. Prior to graduate study, Gross worked extensively with several nonprofit community organizations in New Haven, Connecticut, and East Palo Alto and Los Angeles, California, to develop and produce Internet-enhanced educational programs for urban youth. In 1997, Gross cofounded and directed Plug In! a national teen forum on America Online. It was designed as both a substantive on-line community for teenage AOL members and an educational, real-life job for youth at Plugged In! a community computing center in East Palo Alto. Plug In! (now called "On the Line") has since become the largest original content area for teens on AOL and continues to employ and train a growing number of youth from low-income communities in Silicon Valley.

**Karen Hill-Scott** is a nationally recognized expert in child care and development. She has consulted on more than 1,000 episodes of television programming for public and commercial broadcasters. Several of these programs have received honors, including the Emmy, the Prism, and the Humanitas Awards, or have been recognized by children's advocates, including Action for Children's Television and the Council for Better Broadcasting. Hill-Scott's public service includes policy development, analysis, and program administration in child and family services. Hill-Scott received an Ed.D. in Learning and Development at UCLA, where she is also an Adjunct Professor in the School of Public Policy and Social Research.

**Marjorie J. Hogan,** M.D., practices pediatrics at Hennepin County Medical Center (HCMC) in Minneapolis, a large, inner-city teaching hospital affiliated with the University of Minnesota. Dr. Hogan is the Director of Pediatric Medical Education at HCMC, and a significant amount of time and energy is focused on teaching medical students and residents about the field of pediatrics, especially the care of vulnerable, underserved children and adolescents. Dr. Hogan has worked closely with the American Academy of Pediatrics for a decade, most recently as Chair of the Committee on Communications (now Committee on Public Education) and as a media spokesperson.

**Katherine Battle Horgen,** M.A., is a 5th-year doctoral student in clinical psychology at Yale University. Her research and clinical interests focus on eating disorders and obesity. She is especially interested in the application of policy to psychological problems. She has recently published works on policy approaches to the obesity epidemic, targeting the toxic environment as a major component in the increasing prevalence of obesity.

**Nina Huntemann** is a doctoral candidate in communication at the University of Massachusetts-Amherst. Her dissertation is titled *Policy and Culture in the Digital Age: How Telecommunication Reform Transformed Radio.* She has published several articles on women's use of the Internet for social change. She is also a contributing writer for *The Women's Guide to the Wired World: A User-Friendly Handbook and Resource Directory.* She codesigned a nationally award-winning website (*www.mediaed.org*) for the Media Education Foundation (MEF) and is producing a video on gender, race, and violence in video games for the MEF.

**L. Rowell Huesmann** is Professor of Psychology and Communication Studies at the University of Michigan and a Senior Research Scientist at the Institute for Social Research, where he directs the Aggression Research Program. Professor Huesmann's diverse scientific contributions have ranged from mathematical and computer models of human information processing, to multi-generation longitudinal studies of aggression and violence, to experimental studies of social behavior. His research on the psychological foundations of aggressive and antisocial behavior and books and more than 75 journal articles have attracted widespread national and international attention.

**Aletha C. Huston,** Ph.D., University of Minnesota, is the Priscilla Pond Flawn Regents Professor of Child Development at the University of Texas, Austin. She is lead author of the award-winning *Big World, Small Screen:*

*The Role of Television in American Society* and recipient of the Urie Bronfenbrenner Award from Division 7 of the American Psychological Association (1999). She was the editor of the 1991 book *Children in Poverty: Child Development and Public Policy.* A member of the MacArthur Network on development in middle childhood, she is an investigator in Project "New Hope," an experimental intervention with poor families in Milwaukee, and a member of the steering committee for the National Institute of Child Health and Human Development (NICHHD) National Study of Child Care. She is codirector of the Center for Research on the Influences of Television on Children.

**Emily A. Impett** received her M.A. in Social Psychology from the University of California, Los Angeles, where she is currently pursuing a doctorate. Her research generally focuses on issues at the interface of gender, sexuality, and close relationships. More specifically, her research examines both consensual and nonconsensual unwanted sexual experiences of men and women in intimate relationships. She is currently coauthoring several scientific papers on male violence against women and is conducting research to assess consensual participation in unwanted sex among college students in dating relationships.

**Nancy Jennings** is a doctoral candidate in the Department of Radio-Television-Film at The University of Texas at Austin. Her research interests include media effects, children's use and understanding of media, and media literacy. She has served as a Research Assistant for the National Television Violence Study, which between 1994 and 1998 monitored violence on television. Currently, she is conducting her dissertation research on children's use of media with a focus on children's use of computers both inside and outside of the school environment and how children's attitudes about computers may be influenced by parent and teacher opinions about technology.

**Amy B. Jordan,** Ph.D., University of Pennsylvania, is Senior Research Investigator at the Annenberg Public Policy Center of the University of Pennsylvania, where she directs the research on the impact of public policy on children's television. She has been the primary author of the annual State of Children's Television reports (1996, 1997, 1998) and has written and lectured extensively on the economic and regulatory forces that shape the children's television industry.

**David W. Kleeman** is Executive Director of the American Center for Children and Media, which promotes the exchange of ideas, expertise, and information as a means for building quality. The center looks worldwide for models of excellence. Kleeman is principal consultant to the international children's TV festival (PRIX JEUNESSE). He chaired the North American Advisory Board for the Second World Summit on Television for Children and is playing a similar role for the Third World Summit in 2001. The center was the U.S. partner in North America's Summit 2000 in Toronto. Kleeman advises on media projects for organizations as diverse as Fox Family Worldwide, the Harvard Center for Astrophysics, and UNICEF. He was a speaker at the White House Summit on Children's Television. Kleeman is a graduate of Harvard College.

**Robert Kraut** is Professor of Social Psychology and Human Computer Interaction at Carnegie-Mellon University. He has broad interests in the design and social impact of computing and has conducted research on office automation and employment quality, technology and home-based employment, the communication needs of collaborating scientists, the design of information technology for small-group intellectual work, and the impact of national information networks on organizations and families.

**Robert Kubey** is Director of the Center for Media Studies and Professor of Journalism and Media Studies at Rutgers University.

Trained as a developmental psychologist at the University of Chicago, Professor Kubey has been an Annenberg Scholar in Media Literacy at the University of Pennsylvania and a National Institute of Mental Health research fellow. He has edited *Media Literacy in the Information Age: Current Perspectives* (1997) and is coeditor of a series of research volumes on media education (with Renee Hobbs). Kubey also coauthored *Television and the Quality of Life: How Viewing Shapes Everyday Experience* (with Mihaly Csikszentmihalyi, 1990).

**Dale Kunkel,** Ph.D., studies children and media issues from diverse perspectives, including television effects research and assessments of media industry content and practices. He received his Ph.D. in 1984 from the Annenberg School of Communication at the University of Southern California. He was awarded a Congressional Science Fellowship from the Society for Research in Child Development in 1984-1985, during which time he served as an adviser to Congress on children and media issues. Kunkel is considered an expert on children's media policy and has delivered invited testimony at hearings before the U.S. Senate, the U.S. House of Representatives, and the Federal Communications Commission.

**Neil M. Malamuth** is Professor of Communication and of Psychology and Chair of the Communication Department at the University of California, Los Angeles. He is the recipient of the Kendall Award for Outstanding Contributions to Psychology and of the Lady Davis Fellowship. His research has focused on mass media effects, particularly sexually explicit media, and on the causes of male violence against women. He is the author of more than 100 scholarly publications and a Fellow of the American Psychological Association and the American Psychological Society.

**Marie-Louise Mares** is a Research Fellow in the Department of Communication Arts at the University of Wisconsin-Madison. Her research interests include life-span developmental changes in mass media effects.

**Lara Mayeux** is a graduate student in the Psychology Department at the University of Connecticut, where she studies mental state verbs and theory of mind in preschool-age children. She received her B.S. in Psychology from Texas Christian University in Fort Worth, with the distinction of being named the Senior Scholar in the Psychology Department. Her honors thesis investigated the impact of drug abuse on the discipline behaviors chosen by mothers in a residential drug facility.

**Dorina Miron** (M.A. in Philology, University of Bucharest, Romania; M.A. in Journalism, University of Missouri, Columbia; Ph.D. in Mass Communication, University of Alabama) is currently studying political science at the University of Alabama. Her research interests in the area of media effects are split between children's television and political communication. She coauthored two books published in Romania: *Advertising Psychology* (1995) and *The Role of Mass Media in the 1996 Presidential Election* (1999).

**Kathryn C. Montgomery,** Ph.D., is Cofounder and President of the Center for Media Education (CME), a Washington, D.C.-based nonprofit organization public interest group dedicated to ensuring that the electronic media serve the needs of children and families. Under Dr. Montgomery's leadership, CME has helped frame the national public debate on a variety of critical media issues. CME's groundbreaking studies on new and traditional media have provided essential documentation for public interest privacy initiatives.

**Michael Morgan** is Professor and Chair of the Department of Communication at the University of Massachusetts-Amherst. He has authored or coauthored more than 50 national and international scholarly articles and chapters on the effects of television on images of violence, sex roles, aging, health, science, academic achievement, political orientations, and other issues. He has directed or collaborated on international comparative research projects on media and adolescents in Argentina, China, Russia, Korea, Taiwan, and other countries. His most recent book is *Television and Its Viewers: Cultivation Theory and Research* (with James Shanahan).

**Letitia R. Naigles** is Associate Professor of Psychology at the University of Connecticut. Her major field of interest is children's language acquisition, especially across languages and varied kinds of input. She has been the recipient of a FIRST Award from the National Institutes of Health concerning children's use of syntax in verb learning and a Travel Award from the National Science Foundation enabling her to begin a project investigating early grammatical understanding with colleagues in Australia. Naigles received her B.A. in Cognitive Science from Brown University and her Ph.D. in Psychology from the University of Pennsylvania.

**Haejung Paik,** Ph.D., is currently an Assistant Professor of Communication at the University of Oklahoma and the founder of Synapteq Research, a consulting firm specializing in the development of statistical models. She received her Ph.D. in Communications from Syracuse University in 1991. Her research places special emphasis on the application of various statistical methods to the study of complex, nonlinear systems. She has coauthored books, written book chapters, and published numerous articles in both applied and research journals such as *Communications Research, Human Communication Research, Quality & Quantity, Sociological Methods & Research,* and *Artificial Intelligence Applications.*

**Patrice Pascual** is Managing Editor of Connect for Kids (*www.connectforkids.org*), a website offering news and resources for adults interested in children's and family issues. She worked in the programming, promotion, and underwriting departments at Connecticut Public Television from 1988 to 1996 and has consulted to several public television projects, including the PBS Ready to Learn Service. Pascual earned her M.A. in journalism from the University of Maryland.

**Lynn Rampoldi-Hnilo** completed the mass media doctoral program in the Department of Telecommunication at Michigan State University and recently was a guest lecturer at Stanford University. Her research had focused on the impacts of traditional mass media with adolescents and recently on how individuals self-present themselves on-line via home pages and avatars. Her interests also include the influence of multimedia information architecture and human-computer interaction on cognition, learning, and memory. Rampoldi-Hnilo is currently a research manager at an innovative market research company, Cheskin Research, in Silicon Valley.

**Larry Rifkin** is Executive Vice President of Programming at Connecticut Public Television (CPTV). During his 13-year tenure, audiences have more than doubled and CPTV programs have won 38 regional Emmy Awards, 170 Emmy nominations, 6 CINE Golden Eagle and 3 American Film Institute Awards, and recognition from the Associated Press and the Corporation for Public Broadcasting. Rifkin serves as CPTV's executive in charge of production for *Barney & Friends.*

**Donald F. Roberts** is the Thomas More Stoke Professor in the Department of Communication at Stanford University, where his research and teaching focuses on how children and youth use and respond to mass media. He frequently works with producers of children's television and children's interactive media to develop content that is simultaneously educational and entertaining. His most recent publications include *It's Not Only Rock and Roll: Popular Music in the Lives of Adolescents* and *Kids and Media at the New Millennium: A Comprehensive National Analysis of Children's Media Use.*

**Lawrence I. Rosenkoetter,** Ph.D., is Associate Professor of Research of Human Development and Family Sciences at Oregon State University. He has had a longstanding interest in the development of character. His research has explored a broad array of traits, including lying, stealing, cheating, helping, and sharing. He has also investigated the development of values and moral reasoning from a variety of theoretical perspectives. Of special interest to him has been the role television plays in the development of character. Currently, he is exploring how to mitigate the harmful effect of violent TV.

**Erica Scharrer,** Ph.D., Syracuse University, is Assistant Professor in the Department of Communication at the University of Massachusetts-Amherst. She researches patterns of media content and media influence, focusing on gender and aggression. She is the coauthor (with George Comstock) of the book *Television: What's On, Who's Watching, and What it Means* and has published in the *Handbook of Popular Culture* (in press) and *Women and Politics.* Recent studies include "Men, Muscles, and Machismo: The Relationship Between Television Violence Exposure and Aggression in the Presence of Hypermasculinity" and "From Wise to Foolish: The Changing Portrayal of the Sitcom Father."

**Nancy Signorielli,** Ph.D., University of Pennsylvania, is Professor of Communication at the University of Delaware, Newark. Her primary research area focuses on television content and how media images are related to people's conceptions of social reality (cultivation theory). In particular, her studies examine gender roles, media messages about health and nutrition, and television violence. She has written several books (including *Mass Media Images and Impact on Health,* 1993), and her research has appeared in numerous journals and edited books (including the journal *Sex Roles*).

**Stacy Smith,** Ph.D., University of California, Santa Barbara, is Assistant Professor in the Department of Communication at Michigan State University. Her research interests include the social and psychological effects of the mass media on children. In particular, she examines developmental differences in children's reactions to entertainment and news violence.

**Victor C. Strasburger,** M.D., is currently Chief of the Division of Adolescent Medicine, Professor of Pediatrics, and Professor of Family and Community Medicine at the University of New Mexico School of Medicine in Albuquerque. Dr. Strasburger has authored more than 120 articles and papers and 8 books on the subject of adolescent medicine and the effects of television on children and adolescents.

**Kaveri Subrahmanyam** is Assistant Professor in the Department of Child and Family Studies at California State University, Los Angeles. She received her Ph.D. in Developmental Psychology from UCLA. Her interest in computers and children goes back to the late 1980s when she conducted a training study investigating the effects of video game practice on spatial skills. Her research interests include the impact of children's use of computers (including games and nongame uses) and the Internet, with a special emphasis on gender issues. Her other research interests include children's reasoning and communication about physical entities such as objects and substances. She has published articles on children's computer use and their word learning.

**Todd Tarpley** is Vice President, Interactive, for A&E Television Networks. He oversees the company's seven award-winning websites, including Historychannel.com and interactive television initiatives. Previously, Mr. Tarpley served on the core project team that developed and launched The History Channel. He was a graduate research assistant at Yale University's Family Television

Research Center and served in television production capacities for programs on ABC, NBC, HBO, and Lifetime. He holds an MBA from Yale University, an M.A. in History from the University of Iowa, and a B.F.A. in Film from New York University.

**Laurie Trotta,** is an established writer and communicator of art and media issues. She is the former Executive Director of Mediascope, where she edited *More Than a Movie: Ethics in Entertainment,* a book designed to stimulate discussions of ethics and social responsibility among young filmmakers. She has produced, moderated, and participated in dozens of panel discussions on the media and social issues, including at NATPE '98 and '99, the Hawaii International Film Festival, the Taos Talking Pictures Festival, the American Film Institute Screenwriters Weekend, and the Computer Game Developers Association. She is also the author of *Building Blocks: A Guide for Creating Children's Educational Television.*

**Patti M. Valkenburg** is Professor of Child and Media Research and a Dutch Royal Academy Fellow in the Amsterdam School of Communications Research in the Netherlands. Her research interests include children's likes and dislikes in entertainment, the determinants and effects of television mediation, children's development as consumers, and the effects of media on children's moral reasoning and fright reactions. Her work has appeared in several psychology and communication journals, including *Psychological Bulletin, Developmental Review, Journal of Communication, Communication Research,* and the *Journal of Broadcasting and Electronic Media.*

**Ellen Wartella,** Dean of the College of Communication, Walter Cronkite Regents Chair in Communication at The University of Texas at Austin, serves on editorial boards of seven journals and is coauthor or editor of nine books and dozens of book chapters and articles on television's effect on children. She was Coprincipal Investigator on a multisite grant from the National Cable Television Association of the National Television Violence Study, which between 1994 and 1998 monitored violence on television. Currently, she is conducting a review of research on children and interactive media through a Markle Foundation grant. She received her Ph.D. from the University of Minnesota and completed postdoctoral study in child development at the University of Kansas and in media studies at Columbia University, New York.

**Brian Wilcox** is currently Director of the Center on Children, Families, and the Law and Professor of Psychology at the University of Nebraska-Lincoln. He has published in a number of areas related to child, youth, and family policy, including adolescent sexual behavior and risk taking, child maltreatment, and children and the media. He is currently conducting HIV/AIDS prevention research in Brazil. Wilcox is a member of the Research and Effective Programs Task Force of the National Campaign to Prevent Teen Pregnancy and is past chair of the American Psychological Association's Committee on Children, Youth, and Families.

**Emory H. Woodard,** is a Research Fellow in the Annenberg Public Policy Center of the University of Pennsylvania. His research interests include the uses and effects of children's television and new media technologies.

**John C. Wright** is Cofounder (with his wife, Aletha Huston) and Director of CRITC, the Center for Research on the Influences of Television on Children, first at the University of Kansas (1977-1996) and since 1996 at the University of Texas, Austin, where he is Senior Lecturer and Senior Research Scientist in Child Development and Family Relationships and in Radio-Television-Film. A developmental psychologist, he has studied the development of children's attention to and comprehension of television from an experimental/developmental psychology perspective. Wright and Huston's research has been supported by more than $4 million in grants from NIMH, NICHHD, the Spencer Foundation (Chicago), the Markle Foundation (New York), and the MacArthur Foundation (Chicago). Wright is currently Principal Investigator on research grants from the Hogg Foundation for Mental Health in Austin, Texas, and the William T. Grant Foundation in New York. CRITC's disseminated work in the past 23 years includes 150 articles, chapters, and presentations.

**Dolf Zillmann,** Ph.D., University of Pennsylvania, is a Fellow of the American Psychological Association and has taught at the University of Pennsylvania, Indiana University, the University of Alabama, and as a visiting professor at various European universities. He presently is Professor of Communication and Psychology and Senior Associate Dean for Graduate Studies and Research at the University of Alabama. One of his research interests is educational television.